Contemporary
Literary Criticism

Guide to Gale Literary Criticism Series

When you need to review criticism of literary works, these are the Gale series to use:

If the author's death date is:	You should turn to:

After Dec. 31, 1959
(or author is still living)

CONTEMPORARY LITERARY CRITICISM

for example: Jorge Luis Borges, Anthony Burgess,
William Faulkner, Mary Gordon,
Ernest Hemingway, Iris Murdoch

1900 through 1959

TWENTIETH-CENTURY LITERARY CRITICISM

for example: Willa Cather, F. Scott Fitzgerald,
Henry James, Mark Twain, Virginia Woolf

1800 through 1899

NINETEENTH-CENTURY LITERATURE CRITICISM

for example: Fedor Dostoevski, George Sand,
Gerard Manley Hopkins, Emily Dickinson

1400 through 1799

LITERATURE CRITICISM FROM 1400 TO 1800
(excluding Shakespeare)

for example: Anne Bradstreet, Pierre Corneille,
Daniel Defoe, Alexander Pope,
Jonathan Swift, Phillis Wheatley

SHAKESPEAREAN CRITICISM

Shakespeare's plays and poetry

Antiquity through 1399

CLASSICAL AND MEDIEVAL LITERATURE CRITICISM

for example: Dante, Homer, Plato, Sophocles, Vergil,
the Beowulf poet

(Volume 1 forthcoming)

Gale also publishes related criticism series:

CHILDREN'S LITERATURE REVIEW

This ongoing series covers authors of all eras.
Presents criticism on authors and author/illustrators
who write for the preschool to junior-high audience.

CONTEMPORARY ISSUES CRITICISM

This two-volume set presents criticism on
contemporary authors writing on current issues.
Topics covered include the social sciences,
philosophy, economics, natural science, law, and
related areas.

ISSN 0091-3421

Volume 38

Contemporary Literary Criticism

Excerpts from Criticism of the
Works of Today's Novelists, Poets,
Playwrights, Short Story Writers, Scriptwriters,
and Other Creative Writers

Daniel G. Marowski
EDITOR

Roger Matuz
Jane E. Neidhardt
Robyn V. Young
ASSOCIATE EDITORS

Gale Research Company
Book Tower
Detroit, Michigan 48226

STAFF

Daniel G. Marowski, *Editor*

Roger Matuz, Jane E. Neidhardt, Robyn V. Young, *Associate Editors*

Molly L. Norris, Sean R. Pollock, Jane C. Thacker, Debra A. Wells, *Senior Assistant Editors*

Kelly King Howes, Thomas J. Votteler, Bruce Walker, *Assistant Editors*

Jean C. Stine, *Contributing Editor*

Lizbeth A. Purdy, *Production Supervisor*
Denise Michlewicz Broderick, *Production Coordinator*
Eric Berger, *Assistant Production Coordinator*
Kathleen M. Cook, Maureen Duffy, Sheila J. Nasea, *Editorial Assistants*

Linda M. Pugliese, *Manuscript Coordinator*
Donna Craft, *Assistant Manuscript Coordinator*
Maureen A. Puhl, Rosetta Irene Simms, *Manuscript Assistants*

Victoria B. Cariappa, *Research Coordinator*
Daniel Kurt Gilbert, Maureen R. Richards,
Keith E. Schooley, Filomena Sgambati, Vincenza G. Tranchida,
Mary D. Wise, *Research Assistants*

Jeanne A. Gough, *Permissions Supervisor*
Janice M. Mach, *Permissions Coordinator, Text*
Patricia A. Seefelt, *Permissions Coordinator, Illustrations*
Susan D. Battista, *Assistant Permissions Coordinator*
Margaret A. Chamberlain, Sandra C. Davis, Kathy Grell, Josephine M. Keene,
Mary M. Matuz, *Senior Permissions Assistants*
H. Diane Cooper, Colleen M. Crane,
Mabel E. Schoening, *Permissions Assistants*
Margaret A. Carson,
Dorothy J. Fowler, Helen Hernandez, Anita Williams, *Permissions Clerks*

Frederick G. Ruffner, *Publisher*
Dedria Bryfonski, *Editorial Director*
Christine Nasso, *Director, Literature Division*
Laurie Lanzen Harris, *Senior Editor, Literary Criticism Series*
Dennis Poupard, *Managing Editor, Literary Criticism Series*

Library of Congress Catalog Card Number 76-38938
ISBN 0-8103-4412-2
ISSN 0091-3421

Computerized photocomposition by
Typographics, Incorporated
Kansas City, Missouri

Printed in the United States

Contents

Preface

Literary criticism is, by definition, "the art of evaluating or analyzing with knowledge and propriety works of literature." The complexity and variety of the themes and forms of contemporary literature make the function of the critic especially important to today's reader. It is the critic who assists the reader in identifying significant new writers, recognizing trends in critical methods, mastering new terminology, and monitoring scholarly and popular sources of critical opinion.

Until the publication of the first volume of *Contemporary Literary Criticism (CLC)* in 1973, there existed no ongoing digest of current literary opinion. *CLC,* therefore, has fulfilled an essential need.

Scope of the Work

CLC presents significant passages from published criticism of works by today's creative writers. Each volume of *CLC* includes excerpted criticism on about 50 authors who are now living or who died after December 31, 1959. Since the series began publication, almost 1,800 authors have been included. The majority of authors covered by *CLC* are living writers who continue to publish; therefore, an author frequently appears in more than one volume. There is, of course, no duplication of reprinted criticism.

Authors are selected for inclusion for a variety of reasons, among them the publication of a critically acclaimed new work, the reception of a major literary award, or the dramatization of a literary work as a movie or television screenplay. For example, the present volume includes Studs Terkel, who won a Pulitzer Prize for his nonfiction work *"The Good War": An Oral History of World War II;* Sumner Locke Elliott, whose novel *Careful, He Might Hear You* was adapted into a critically acclaimed film; and John Irving, whose novel *The Cider House Rules* received much attention from the literary world. Perhaps most importantly, authors who appear frequently on the syllabuses of high school and college literature classes are heavily represented in *CLC;* Robert Bly and J.R.R. Tolkien are examples of writers of this stature in the present volume. Attention is also given to several other groups of writers—authors of considerable public interest—about whose work criticism is often difficult to locate. These are the contributors to the well-loved but nonscholarly genres of mystery and science fiction, as well as literary and social critics whose insights are considered valuable and informative. Foreign writers and authors who represent particular ethnic groups in the United States are also featured in each volume.

Format of the Book

Altogether there are about 700 individual excerpts in each volume—with an average of about 14 excerpts per author—taken from hundreds of literary reviews, general magazines, scholarly journals, and monographs. Contemporary criticism is loosely defined as that which is relevant to the evaluation of the author under discussion; this includes criticism written at the beginning of an author's career as well as current commentary. Emphasis has been placed on expanding the sources for criticism by including an increasing number of scholarly and specialized periodicals. Students, teachers, librarians, and researchers frequently find that the generous excerpts and supplementary material provided by the editors supply them with all the information needed to write a term paper, analyze a poem, or lead a book discussion group. However, complete bibliographical citations facilitate the location of the original source as well as provide all of the information necessary for a term paper footnote or bibliography.

A *CLC* author entry consists of the following elements:

- The **author heading** cites the author's full name, followed by birth date, and death date when applicable. The portion of the name outside the parentheses denotes the form under which the author has most commonly published. If an author has written consistently under a pseudonym, the pseudonym will be listed in the author heading and the real name given on the first line of the biographical and critical introduction. Also located at the beginning of the introduction to the author entry are any important name variations under which an author has written. Uncertainty as to a birth or death date is indicated by question marks.

- A **portrait** of the author is included when available.

- A brief **biographical and critical introduction** to the author and his or her work precedes the excerpted criticism. However, *CLC* is not intended to be a definitive biographical source. Therefore, *cross-references* have been included to direct the reader to other useful sources published by the Gale Research Company: *Contemporary Authors* now includes detailed biographical and bibliographical sketches on nearly 85,000 authors; *Children's Literature Review* presents excerpted criticism on the works of authors of children's books; *Something about the Author* contains heavily illustrated biographical sketches on writers and illustrators who create books for children and young adults; *Contemporary Issues Criticism* presents excerpted commentary on the nonfiction works of authors who influence contemporary thought; *Dictionary of Literary Biography* provides original evaluations of authors important to literary history; and the new *Contemporary Authors Autobiography Series* offers autobiographical essays by prominent writers. Previous volumes of *CLC* in which the author has been featured are also listed in the introduction.

- The **excerpted criticism** represents various kinds of critical writing—a particular essay may be normative, descriptive, interpretive, textual, appreciative, comparative, or generic. It may range in form from the brief review to the scholarly monograph. Essays are selected by the editors to reflect the spectrum of opinion about a specific work or about an author's literary career in general. The excerpts are presented chronologically, adding a useful perspective to the entry. All titles by the author featured in the entry are printed in boldface type, which enables the reader to easily identify the works being discussed.

- A complete **bibliographical citation** designed to help the user find the original essay or book follows each excerpt. An asterisk (*) at the end of a citation indicates that the essay is on more than one author.

Other Features

- A list of **Authors Forthcoming in *CLC*** previews the authors to be researched for future volumes.

- An **Appendix** lists the sources from which material in the volume has been reprinted. Many other sources have also been consulted during the preparation of the volume.

- A **Cumulative Index to Authors** lists all the authors who have appeared in *Contemporary Literary Criticism, Twentieth-Century Literary Criticism, Nineteenth-Century Literature Criticism,* and *Literature Criticism from 1400 to 1800,* along with cross-references to other Gale series: *Children's Literature Review, Authors in the News, Contemporary Authors, Contemporary Authors Autobiography Series, Dictionary of Literary Biography, Something about the Author,* and *Yesterday's Authors of Books for Children.* Users will welcome this cumulated author index as a useful tool for locating an author within the various series. The index, which lists birth and death dates when available, will be particularly valuable for those authors who are identified with a certain period but whose death date causes them to be placed in another, or for those authors whose careers span two periods. For example, F. Scott Fitzgerald is found in *Twentieth-Century Literary Criticism,* yet a writer often associated with him, Ernest Hemingway, is found in *Contemporary Literary Criticism.*

- A **Cumulative Index to Critics** lists the critics and the author entries in which their essays appear.

Acknowledgments

The editors wish to thank the copyright holders of the excerpted articles included in this volume for permission to use the material and the photographers and other individuals who provided photographs for us. We are grateful to the staffs of the following libraries for making their resources available to us: Detroit Public Library and the libraries of Wayne State University, the University of Michigan, and the University of Detroit. We also wish to thank Anthony Bogucki for his assistance with copyright research.

Suggestions Are Welcome

The editors welcome the comments and suggestions of readers to expand the coverage and enhance the usefulness of the series.

Authors Forthcoming in *CLC*

Contemporary Literary Criticism, Volume 39 will be a yearbook devoted to an examination of the outstanding achievements and trends in literature during 1985. Volumes 40 and 41 will contain criticism on a number of authors not previously listed and will also feature criticism on newer works by authors included in earlier volumes.

To Be Included in Volume 40

Brian Aldiss (English novelist, short story writer, critic, and editor)—A Hugo and Nebula Award-winning science fiction author, Aldiss recently published *Helliconia Winter,* the third novel in his series about a remote planet called Helliconia.

Jorge Amado (Brazilian novelist and nonfiction writer)—Amado is recognized as one of Brazil's greatest writers, and his works have been translated into over forty languages. He is best known for his novels *The Violent Land, Gabriela, Clove and Cinnamon, Dona Flor and Her Two Husbands,* and the recently translated *Pen, Sword, Camisole.*

Ann Beattie (American novelist and short story writer)—In her fiction Beattie records the disillusionment of the "Woodstock generation" as her protagonists come to terms with middle age and a suburban, middle-class lifestyle. Her latest works include *The Burning House* and *Love Always.*

Marguerite Duras (French novelist, dramatist, short story writer, and filmmaker)—Internationally recognized for her mastery of several genres, Duras is perhaps best known for her work in film and her application of cinematic techniques to the novel. Her recent prizewinning novel, *The Lover,* has furthered her reputation as an important contemporary author.

William M. Hoffman (American dramatist and editor)—Hoffman's controversial play *As Is* has been praised for his sympathetic treatment of the tragic effects of AIDS on a homosexual couple.

Garrison Keillor (American novelist and essayist)—Host of the popular radio program "A Prairie Home Companion," Keillor gained widespread recognition and praise for his best-selling novel, *Lake Wobegon Days.*

Etheridge Knight (American poet, short story writer, and editor)—Knight published his first collection of poetry, *Poems from Prison,* while serving a sentence in the Indiana State Prison. The poems in this and subsequent volumes are rooted in oral tradition and feature common, colloquial language through which Knight conveys messages of social protest.

Tim O'Brien (American novelist)—Winner of the National Book Award for his novel *Going After Cacciato,* O'Brien focuses on the theme of nuclear annihilation and social issues of the post-World War II era in his latest work, *The Nuclear Age.*

Konstantin Paustovsky (Russian fiction and nonfiction writer)—Paustovsky's six-volume autobiography, *The Story of a Life,* received considerable attention in both the Soviet Union and the West. This work chronicles his life against a historical background that includes World War I, the Bolshevik Revolution, and the Stalin purges.

Muriel Spark (Scottish-born novelist, short story writer, poet, and nonfiction writer)—Spark is best known for her witty satires which probe themes related to morality. Her recent novels include *Loitering with Intent* and *The Only Problem.*

Kurt Vonnegut, Jr. (American novelist, short story writer, and critic)—This prolific and popular author of the novel *Slaughterhouse-Five* satirizes contemporary America and Darwinism in his recent novel, *Galápagos,* which several critics consider one of his finest works.

Diane Wakoski (American poet and critic)—In her poetry Wakoski often depicts an ongoing search for fulfillment that frequently leads to loss and betrayal. Her latest books include *The Magician's Feastletters* and *The Collected Greed: Parts 1-13.*

Reinaldo Arenas (Cuban novelist and poet)—Censored by the Cuban government for his controversial fiction and poetry and for his homosexuality, Arenas now lives and works in the United States. His recent acclaimed novel, *Farewell to the Sea,* recounts the psychic struggles of a disillusioned writer and his wife.

Ray Bradbury (American short story writer, poet, scriptwriter, novelist, dramatist, and author of children's books)—Best known for his popular and acclaimed science fiction and fantasy short stories, Bradbury recently published *Death Is a Lonely Business*, a detective story which is his first novel in twenty-three years.

Morley Callaghan (Canadian novelist, short story writer, essayist, and dramatist)—Described by Edmund Wilson as "perhaps the most unjustly neglected novelist in the English-speaking world," Callaghan has been active in literature for over sixty years. His latest novel, *Our Lady of the Snows*, like much of his work, is characterized by its journalistic prose style, ironic tone, and moralistic themes.

T.S. Eliot (American-born English poet, critic, dramatist, and essayist)—One of the most important literary figures of the twentieth century, Eliot is recognized as a major contributor to the modern age in poetry and criticism. The twentieth anniversary of Eliot's death has sparked renewed evaluation of his achievements.

Carlos Fuentes (Mexican novelist, dramatist, short story writer, essayist, and critic)—In his internationally acclaimed works, Fuentes draws upon Mexican history and legend to explore and define the identity of his homeland. Among his most recent novels are *The Old Gringo* and *Distant Relations*.

Eugène Ionesco (Rumanian-born French dramatist, essayist, scriptwriter, and novelist)—One of the most renowned exponents of the Theater of the Absurd, Ionesco employs exaggeration and black humor to explore the alienation of individuals searching for meaning in an irrational and meaningless world.

Peter Levi (English poet, novelist, travel writer, and editor)—A former Jesuit priest whose poetry often employs such Elizabethan and classical forms as the sonnet and the elegy, Levi has also written two adventure novels, *Head in the Soup* and *Grave Witness.*

Janet Lewis (American novelist, poet, short story writer, dramatist, and author of children's books)—The author of *The Wife of Martin Guerre* and other acclaimed historical novels, Lewis has also gained considerable respect for her poetry about the Ojibway and Navajo tribes of North America.

Ross Macdonald (American novelist, short story writer, essayist, and autobiographer)—A prolific and popular author of detective fiction, Macdonald is best known as the creator of sleuth Lew Archer. In his recent volume of essays, *Self-Portrait: Ceaselessly Into the Past*, Macdonald examines his long career and the geneses of his novels.

Boris Pasternak (Russian poet, novelist, short story writer, essayist, and autobiographer)—Best known in the United States for his novel *Doctor Zhivago*, Pasternak is also highly regarded for his poetry, which is often associated with the symbolist and futurist movements.

Anne Rice (American novelist and critic)—The author of the popular novel *Interview with the Vampire*, Rice has recently published *The Vampire Lestat,* the second installment of *The Vampire Chronicles.*

Nayantara Sahgal (Indian novelist, short story writer, autobiographer, and nonfiction writer)—Sahgal's writings are noted for their insightful portraits of life in contemporary India. Her recent novels, *Rich Like Us* and *Plans for Departure*, are considered important additions to her canon.

Martin Amis

1949-

English novelist, critic, short story writer, editor, scriptwriter, and nonfiction writer.

Amis has been hailed as an outstanding young novelist who satirizes the scabrous excesses of youth and contemporary society and displays an irreverent and incisive wit similar to that of his father, author Kingsley Amis. His fast-paced prose is infused with contemporary slang and foul language, and his characters are obsessed with sex, drugs, violence, and materialistic pursuits. Like such satirists as Jonathan Swift and Angus Wilson, with whom he has been compared, Amis is widely regarded as a moralist whose novels admonish against the follies of his age. Jerome Charyn concludes that ''Amis is so horrified by the world he sees in the process of formation that he feels compelled to warn us all about it.''

Amis's first novel, *The Rachel Papers* (1973), concerns the passing of adolescence and the advent of manhood. The narrator of this work, an obnoxious, self-centered English youth on the eve of his twentieth birthday, relates his misadventures in graphic and humorous detail. Most critics found this work skillfully written but were impressed, as John Mellors states, ''more with promise and felicities en route than with achievement.'' Amis's second novel, *Dead Babies* (1975), is a black comedy about a group of deviant youths who gather at a country home for a weekend of drugs and verbal and physical violence. Amis's characters reject the idealism of the 1960s in favor of the era's excesses by indulging in their wildest fantasies.

In *Success* (1978), Amis presents a less disturbing comedy of manners. *Success* centers on the relationship between two foster brothers, one privileged and one not, and their comparative degrees of social, economic, and sexual success. This novel has been interpreted as an allegorical commentary on the decline of the established order in British society. *Other People: A Mystery Story* (1981) is an ambiguous tale in which Amis relates the dual experiences of Mary Lamb, a young woman suffering from amnesia, and what may be her former self, the reprehensible Amy Hide. Mary wanders innocently into London in search of her previous life only to discover anew the complexities of contemporary society.

Amis's recent novel, *Money: A Suicide Note* (1984), has been praised as his best work. This ambitious and complicated novel contains themes of greed, excess, self-destruction, cultural depravation, sex, and love. Through satire Amis exposes the incessant debaucheries of John Self, a producer of commercials who is on the verge of directing his first major American film. Amis combines metaphor, allegory, caricature, vigorous prose, and a cast of eccentric characters in an intricately designed plot that focuses upon the surrealistic and squalid urban existence of his comic hero. Jonathan Yardley noted that Amis ''has created a central character of consummate vulgarity and irresistible charm,'' adding that Self ''emerges as one of the indisputably memorable, not to mention haunting, characters of postwar fiction.''

(See also *CLC*, Vols. 4, 9; *Contemporary Authors*, Vols. 65-68; *Contemporary Authors New Revision Series*, Vol. 8; and *Dictionary of Literary Biography*, Vol. 14.)

© Jerry Bauer

ELAINE FEINSTEIN

Second novels are difficult; following success is difficult; one thing Martin Amis ensures: *Dead Babies* offers no repetition of the joyous hilarity of *The Rachel Papers*. It is more like a declaration of war on the assumptions that made the first book possible. And it is not for the squeamish. To give what seems to me a most telling example of the games Amis now plays with language, the title rises out of a piece of invented and ambiguous slang; don't give me 'all this dead babies'. His purpose in pushing the stylishly foul-mouthed to this point is similar to his intention in throwing his privileged and corrupt adolescents into a future where the really cool can enjoy the last reaches of the technology of sex and violence, while the rest of humanity hangs about raggedly under the stanchions of some overhead bypass. This poor distorted generation, full of hatred for their parents, and terrified of any form of compassion or gallantry, is described with a total ferocity which is nevertheless frequently comic. Giles's opening dream of losing his teeth, one by one, into the mouthpiece of the telephone, echoes through the book to the point where he cannot bring himself to articulate the word 'dentist'. A sexual encounter intended to evoke *Story of O* eroticism collapses with Andy's penis caught in his zip. Nevertheless, the book is a long way from a romp. Rather as I hope for society that this is no true prophecy, I hope for Martin Amis that the nightmare of this vision will rapidly become part of his past. In the meanwhile, it is a remarkable fantasy. (p. 480)

Elaine Feinstein, "Killing Time," in New Statesman, Vol. 90, No. 2326, October 17, 1975, pp. 479-80.*

JOHN MELLORS

Everyone in Martin Amis's sad, savage and (at times) extremely funny satire [Dead Babies] 'tends to be either drunk or stoned or hungover or sick'. Living mainly on a diet of drugs, gin, strong champagne cocktails, 'para-natural Whiski' and hardly any food, the degenerates in Dead Babies are constantly retching, vomiting and ejecting burps 'like mouth farts'. But it is mental sickness from which they suffer most acutely: 'cancelled sex', 'lagging time', 'faulty memory' and 'street sadness'. Their lives are cancelled very nastily in the Mansonian mayhem at the end.

The title-phrase is used by Amis's characters to pour scorn on outmoded concepts like jealousy, faithfulness and love, and by Amis himself to describe his cast, the six 'Appleseeders' living in Appleseed Rectory in Hertfordshire and their four guests, a golden-hearted whore and a 'triad' or 'troy' of Americans. The time is the future, into which the dead babies have grown up through a period when 'sexual lassitude and disgust seemed to be everywhere among the young, and two-night stands were becoming a rarity'; but the business of the satirist, as Amis points out in a quotation from Menippus, 'is not prophecy, just as his subject is not tomorrow . . . it is today.' Yet Amis's theme is a conventional one—that relationships without affection are boring, meaningless and sterile. . . .

Martin Amis is obsessed by bodily functions and dwells with loving distaste on the digestive processes and on 'gaping vaginas, rhubarb penises and gouged behinds'. He is witty: 'A cooked breakfast? It would be like going to bed in pyjamas or reading an English novel.' His dialogue is brilliant, particularly the conversations between the blasés Appleseeds and Marvell, the earnest American. . . . The description of the obese Whitehead family packing their grotesque limbs into a small car is quite Rabelaisian. But beneath the skilfully presented shock-effects of Dead Babies, there is a sentimentally sweet and squelchy centre—a flavour I did not detect in Amis's first novel, The Rachel Papers.

John Mellors, "Raw Breakfast," in The Listener, Vol. 94, No. 2430, October 30, 1975, p. 582.*

ELIOT FREMONT-SMITH

Dead Babies reads as if it were a therapeutic exorcism of . . . leftovers, in the guise of an adolescent "Philosopher in the Bedroom." It is set "a few years hence" on an English country estate where a motley slew of misfits and grotesques gather for a weekend of pill-popping, various unpleasant and debauchy games, and talk. Endless talk. The "dead babies" are truth, compassion, and reality—things like that—and they just won't go away. One supposes it's all meant to illustrate "the end of indulgence, a sort of Gotterdammerung of the gratification culture" (as the jacket puts it)—i.e., growing up. Only it is very hard to care whether these pathetics do or don't. Amis tries to perk up the proceedings with nasty (Genet-al?) acts and

lots of brightwork wit—the tone is polished bitterness—but he seems really to be working through something for himself. Now, its . . . [a] truism that reviewers are prone to make fallacious attributions to authors' minds and motives; but in this case one does hope that Dead Babies may clear the way for the fresh, even brilliant, third novel that should be within reach of Amis's considerable gifts and abilities.

Eliot Fremont-Smith, in a review of "Dead Babies," in The Village Voice, Vol. XXI, No. 4, January 26, 1976, p. 45.

NEIL HEPBURN

Martin Amis's [Success] is structurally like a large 'X' on the arms of which his two principal characters, Gregory and Terry, slide ever downwards, in time with the measured wreck of the society that has fixed the rhythm of their desires. Gregory begins with worldly success, at the right-hand top. Terry endures at the left-hand top as much honest awareness of his failure (by the yardstick of bedded girls and spent money) as his knavish character will allow him. Events bring them slithering inexorably down their respective arms, to meet, cross and end with a bump, still on opposite sides, but with opposite fortunes: Terry is now the owner and wielder of a low kind of success, Gregory quaking in the acknowledgment that his sometime superiority not only is not compatible with the new world, but was never even real.

At the crossing-point of their two lives lies the smashed body of Ursula, Gregory's sister, successful at the second attempt in a suicide nurtured in an incestuous childhood with Gregory, and triggered by a more recent relationship with Terry. (pp. 482-83)

These developments are emblematic of the terrible (or, if you are Terry, useful) changes going on in England, where foreigners roam and brawl and reign commercially, young men sleep stoned among the rubbish bags, girls are not only ludicrously available but predatory, and everybody says 'fuck' as often as possible. It is impossible to ignore Mr Amis's use of this last device. Terry, for example, says it very often: it is the badge of his shamed origins, the index of habitual indifference to meaning. Gregory, in his Flashmanesque address to the reader, uses it infrequently, and in order to show his 'aristocratic' contempt for gentilities. And it works, as a symbolic statement of the bastardised Gresham's Law by which the spurious is driven out by the worthless.

Whether Mr Amis prefers this banausic ascendancy to the fraudulent establishment it has destroyed is not altogether clear. His own side of the X is certainly the left, or moral, hand (although the success that Success deserves is bound to lend ambivalence to his position there); but by the time Terry has forfeited authorial sympathy and a put-down Gregory been advanced for commiseration, both characters have mutinied, abandoned their roles as 'humours' in a roman à thèse, and by their outrageously animated performances in the foreground have all but obscured the panorama of manners they were intended to throw into relief. This is a pity, if it softens the ferocity of Mr Amis's assault on the apocalyptic folly of the age. But it is pure gain for the reader untainted by the urge to have his conscience flayed. For the novel is corrosively funny, and brilliantly observed. (p. 483)

Neil Hepburn, "Tonto," in The Listener, Vol. 99, No. 2555, April 13, 1978, pp. 482-83.

PAUL ABLEMAN

Martin Amis's third novel [*Success*] concerns two young men who share a London flat. Gregory is handsome, witty, elegant and derives from landed gentry. His foster-brother, Terry, is a product of the slums.... The novel spans a year in their lives and is divided into twelve sections, corresponding to the passing months.

The book is narrated alternately by Gregory and Terry. Presumably the intention, analogous to that of Durrell in the 'Alexandria Quartet', is to provide different perspectives on the same sequence of events. But for such a device to engage and hold the reader's interest, the events themselves must be interesting. Unhappily much of the action in *Success* is pedestrian and the necessity to plod through it twice becomes tedious.

Terry has a girl friend called Jan. Gregory calls her June. This is a fair sample of the level of variation of perspective. There is, however, a ponderous differentiation of diction. Gregory talks like a super-dandy out of Firbank and Terry like a super-yob. Neither of them is very convincing as a person but this drawback is somewhat mitigated by the reader's growing perception that the book is a parable about the decline of the old order in England and the new raj of the yobs. Strange things, which a critic should not reveal, happen to Terry and Gregory as the year proceeds. There are revelations....

There is not ... much erotic relief in *Success*. In dismal compensation, there is an abundance of what unenlightened folk would call bad language. (p. 23)

This schoolboy flaunting of 'rude words' is distressing, and not merely as a symptom of imaginative poverty or poor taste. The right to use such words in literature has been laboriously won over centuries. *Success* is the kind of novel that gives libertarianism a bad name. If the puritan backlash, clearly gathering strength, should succeed in once more muzzling writers, it will be this kind of self-indulgence that will be partly responsible and Mr Amis may find that the characters in his next book are only f...d up or even, admittedly no great literary loss, muckcd up.

There is a lot of sloppy writing. Gregory says of Terry: 'His teeth ... taper darkly into the metallic hecatomb of his jaws.' A hecatomb is, of course, an animal sacrifice and not a kind of mausoleum.... But such matters, albeit material, are quibbles.

Much more damning is the fact that it is hard to discern any purpose behind *Success* other than the desire to write a novel. The split narrative belts on, desperately hoping for something good to turn up. Here there is a plod through Beckettland and next a meander through Kafka country. One could, in fact, relate fragments of the novel to a whole spectrum of modern masters. But stylistic versatility doesn't necessarily generate a work of art.

And yet *Success* bristles with evidence of talent. 'When I said that pathetic thing to Gregory and stumbled down the stairs, whose face burnt the hotter with embarrassment and remorse? Mine, mine. Why? I'll tell you why. Because I have no pride, and they merely have no shame.' The build-up is adequate, if not elegant, but the final epigram is subtle and haunting.... And there is much more detail one could praise.

But alas Mr Amis distrusts his own creative imagination. There is a sub-text to this book, a surreal, lyrical novel about the eerie quality of urban life as ancient norms crumble and machines evolve like drosophilae. But Mr Amis only harvests it in moments when his guard is down. Then he remembers that he is the most with-it penman around and quickly shifts his narrative back to the plane of trendy cynicism. It is hard to escape the feeling that subconsciously Mr Amis regards *Success* as a stance rather than a novel. (pp. 23-4)

Paul Ableman, "Sub-Texts," *in* The Spectator, *Vol. 240, No. 2815, April 15, 1978, pp. 23-4.*

TOM PAULIN

[*Success*] is a constrained re-write of *Dead Babies,* that savage and brilliant satire which is set in a place of "shifting outlines and imploded vacuums ... of lagging time and false memories ... street sadness, night fatigue and cancelled sex." This consumers' hell is also the setting of *Success* which transforms London into a state of nature inhabited by the ugly, the nasty, the brutish and the short. Central to Amis's vision is a sense of deprivation which annihilates the past and makes the present moment seem an exhausted bundle of vicious, fetid and desperate energies.... The only constants in this dead secular world are "self-pity, self-disgust, and self-love"; innocence is transformed into a baby-like boiled egg, and life has a scratchy, scurfy texture that infests the rhythms of Amis's prose.

Take, for example, the "chippy" and disgruntled Terry's remarks in *Success* about the cool, "naturally stylish" Gregory:

> I want details, I want details, actual details,
> and I want them to be hurtful, damaging and
> grotesque. I nurse dreams of impotence, mon-
> orchidism and premature ejaculation. I lust for
> his repressions and blocks; I ache for his trau-
> mata.

Here, as too often elsewhere, Amis heaps up verbal triplets and refuses to write well. But in a valueless world style may be a value that he is deliberately rejecting—he prefers a hectic, spasming prose-style whose jerks and contortions resemble the death throes of an electric eel. It's this abrasive lack of coordination and the fact that the two central characters, Terry and Gregory, duplicate Quentin and Little Keith in *Dead Babies* which make *Success* a sporadically impressive but disappointing sequel. Nevertheless, Amis's sense of the way in which Terry's personality is the result of a derelict childhood represents an original revaluing of traditional notions of childhood and maturity. Terry has a murdered baby for a sister, a schizophrenic foster-sister called Ursula, and he remembers lying in bed "like a shrivelled grub", another withered baby. He is, he insists, comprehensively "fucked-up", and here Amis draws on Larkin's "This Be The Verse" in order to explore a condition of radical cynicism. His exploration isn't merely personal and neurotic—it is deeply sensitive to the mood of the late 1970s, and anyone who belongs to Amis's generation must recognise his understanding of where we are now.

This is apparent in Gregory's remark: "The world is changing; the past has gone, and from now on all is future tense." A remark which adapts these lines from Peter Porter's "A Meredithian Treatment": "The past is dead, the future dead, the now/Is here, an apotheosis of girls begins." Porter's poem critically catches the atmosphere of the 1960s, and Amis darkens that climate of liberation in order to explore what it's like to live in a cultural dead-end. Everything in this terminal world is grubby, glossy and expensive—it is like Terry looking at one of those magazines "in which girls show the insides of their vaginas and anuses to the world for money." The streets are ''like a dead newsreel reshown nightly'', and this city of consumers and transients at times resembles Eliot's ''twittering world'' of torpid commuters. It may be that Amis is attempting to take the negative way through the hell he depicts, but there is a helpless uncertainty in his treatment of it. Far from subverting or qualifying his demonic competence he tends to recommend it, and this is one of the reasons why *Success* is a comparative failure. . . . *Success* depends on the cultural associations of the word ''chippy'', which is defined as ''minding being poor, ugly and common.'' It's a term that recognises and colludes with the authority of class, and it passively submits to the condition of being an anxiety-ridden *petit bourgeois*. Here and in the description of Terry and Ursula as ''below-stairs lovers'' Amis harks back to previous class-structures (the Edwardian period, the 1950s) and this confuses the contemporaneity of a narrative which is at times reminiscent of Larkin's *Jill*. In the character of Gregory, Amis appears to be exacting a personal revenge on all the gilded fools whom he must have beaten long ago and who must therefore be scarcely worth bothering about now.

There are a few amusing moments in the story. . . . But at other times the introverted narrative lags and becomes boring. Perhaps this is because a story of two sophisticated and demented adolescents is bound to seem rankly narcissistic and eventually pointless. Like a tramp who shambles about cursing at himself, Amis's novel occupies a sort of twilight zone where neurosis only occasionally makes a statement about the essential conditions of life. This is because self-disgust is a narrowing perspective which reduces reality to the spectacle of someone squeezing spots into a steamy mirror. (pp. 74-6)

> Tom Paulin, ''Fantastic Eschatologies,'' in Encounter, *Vol. LI, No. 3, September, 1978, pp. 73-8.*

VICTORIA GLENDINNING

[In *Other People: A Mystery Story*] Martin Amis has written a modern morality. At least I think he has. A pretty, blonde young woman wakes up having lost her memory, not only of her own past but of everything. She does not even remember what shoes are for—or mouths, or clouds, or money. She has only the present, which she accepts unselectively; and like Alice in Wonderland—and Sartre—she finds that her chief problem is other people. She drifts into the company of tramps, alcoholics and criminals, 'the lost, the ruined, the broken, the effaced'. They just think she is 'simple'. Her pilgrim's progress lands her in a church hostel, then a squat, and, worst of all, a flat where classy rich drop-outs are drinking and drugging themselves to death—the seven deadly sins in person. Her lovers can remember the act and actions of love, but not love itself. And of course, she can't remember either.

She calls herself Mary Lamb—an innocent name. She thinks she is good, not bad. She hopes she is good. But she is haunted by her forgotten past—the past 'which always gets you in the end'. . . . (p. 319)

Other People ends as it begins, with an awakening—but whether into life or death I am not sure. The novel is aptly subtitled 'a mystery story'. It is quite hard to understand. The author is aware of this, and his slightly exasperated voice-over is heard at intervals, helping us along: 'I generally find I've got some explaining to do, particularly during the early stages.'

This is a very literary and word-mongering novel, and Mary's major disillusion concerns literature. She reads avidly; books

seem to take her out of her arbitrary present, even if they 'didn't quite explain how you lived with other people'. And then she realises books are not 'special': they are about the dirty present of power, boredom and desire, too. 'She felt that books were about the ideal world, where nothing was ideal but everything had ideality and the chance of moral spaciousness. And it wasn't so.'

That is a major loss of faith, for her, for an author, for anyone. This novel is full of pain, jokes and questions. It could only have been written by someone who was very highly intelligent and thoughtful. It is indeed punctuated by 'thoughts'—speculative, laconic, excellent passages about drunks, clothes, death, unrequited love, cities. It is not like anything else that I have read by Martin Amis.

As a fable, an investigation into 'how to live with other people' and the possible values of innocence and of 'good' and 'bad' it is, in its sad, funny and sidelong way, peculiarly interesting and effective. But you could be a deal less intelligent and aware than he is and be a better novelist. Intelligence and awareness may even block the passage. . . . This may be a good book but a bad novel, the work of a 'writer' rather than of a novelist. But he is never dull, and *Other People* is—and are—worth grappling with. (pp. 319-20)

> Victoria Glendinning, ''Lamb's Tale from Amis,'' in The Listener, *Vol. 105, No. 2702, March 5, 1981, pp. 319-20.*

ALAN HOLLINGHURST

One has heard a certain amount about the familiar being rendered strange by a . . . [process belonging to] so-called Martian poetry. In *Other People* Martin Amis brings back the technique to the novel from which it in part sprang—in Dickens's vivid reification—and where it perhaps more properly belongs. . . . Amis's device for isolating and poeticising the familiar is to make his protagonist an amnesiac: recovering consciousness after a critical 'event', Amy has lost her habitual associations with the ordinary and sees it as pregnant with a coded and ambiguous power. Human action appears 'ulterior, having a great and desperate purpose which firmly excluded her'—and one of the mysteries which the book unfolds is her re-initiation into adult life. The influence of Dickens is again felt in the protection of the girl in a stunned, unnatural innocence and circumstances of depravity and violence which she does not understand.

The Martian technique can turn on its user: it celebrates the phenomenal suggestiveness of things, but bring it to play on a human subject and the wit of the writer can seem to be achieved at the expense of the human subject's witlessness. This suits Amis fine—but it does give rise to certain questions about knowledge: like Virginia Woolf, Amis elides authorial free-ranging intelligence with the restricted reactions of the protagonist, and it is often hard to see where one becomes the other. Would an amnesiac think of cars as 'daredevil roadsters' or invent the elaborately overwritten descriptions of the sky, aeroplanes, the night, which recur through the book? The question is not really a censure, for it leads to a central issue of the novel: the identity and purpose of the narrator. The careful reader will soon pick up hints, and many aspects of the story have been ingeniously arranged. . . . [A] lot of the time the peculiar relation of Amy to Life seems used as a cover to produce comic or strange effects which do little to further the story, just as Amy herself shows curiously little interest in her life before she lost her memory. Of course the comedy, expectedly centred on 'the act of pain or sadness', sex, is often hilarious—especially in the character of Russ who works with Amy at a café and acts out fantasies of being molested by film-stars: 'Leave it out, Sophia . . . Aah! Raquel! Will you—Get off my—bloody—?'

Amis showed in *Success* how he can manipulate and ironise the individual and self-protecting comedies of life into a picture of experience charged with pain and fear. But in *Other People* the manipulation finally seems over-ambitious, and something appears to have gone wrong in the later part of the book: the whole thing becomes factitious, obscure, unsatisfactory. It remains more of a 'Mystery Story' than, one suspects, was intended.

Alan Hollinghurst, "Opening Eyes," in New States-man, Vol. 101, No. 2608, March 13, 1981, p. 21.*

PAUL ABLEMAN

The heroine of *Other People* is a good girl called Mary Lamb who used to be a bad girl called Amy Hide. 'Amy', of course, hides in 'Mary' as Mr Hyde hid in Dr Jekyll while another good Mary, in a nursery rhyme, had a little lamb. At the start of the book, Mary, suffering from total amnesia, flees from a hospital after, as Amy Hide, having been nearly murdered by a sadistic psychopath. But what is a sadistic psychopath doing in the world of nursery rhymes and little lambs? Demonstrating, I suspect, that Mr Amis has not really come to terms with his own creative orientation and remains determined to present himself as a cool, cynical modern who flinches at nothing.

Abroad in an utterly unknown world, like a water baby in the ocean or Alice down the rabbit hole, Mary embarks on a fabulous adventure in social climbing, mounting swiftly through the realms of winos, squatters and working folk to the heights of bourgeois bohemians. . . .

Enter the Fairy Prince, or just Mr Prince, a police officer charged, for metaphysical, one is forced to conclude, rather than official reasons, with reanimating her memory and preparing her for a new encounter with The Psychopath. Ultimately, in full possession once more of Mary Hyde's persona, in a deserted warehouse which echoes the final locations of those characteristic modern fairy tales—television crime dramas—Mary is delivered again to her destroyer who turns out to be . . . her creator, Mr Prince. . . .

Does it all work? Not really. The attempt to conflate realistic, not to say violent and sordid, incidents like rape, assault and suicide with wide-eyed fantasy sometimes results in sentimentality and this is the deadly enemy of the true fairy tale.

For all that, the book has genuine merit. For one thing, Mr Amis's prose is resourceful and, at its best, displays substantial lyricism and power of surreal imagery although it is somewhat hit-or-miss and can plunge dismally into bathos. There is, moreover, a sense of improvisation about the whole book as if the author had leaned too heavily on sometimes flagging inspiration. The last few pages, for example, generate the shoddy enigma of an author's refusal to clarify his meaning rather than the authentic one of a mystery too profound for clear expression. . . .

Still, for all its faults, *Other People: A Mystery Story* does say something about life, dreams, hallucination and, yes, the mystery of other people.

Paul Ableman, "Fairies and Violence," in The Spectator, Vol. 246, No. 7967, March 21, 1981, p. 22.

GEOFFREY STOKES

The great virtue of *Other People* is that Amis has harnessed his cleverness, turned it into a vehicle for the compassionate exploration of the world—and of the received ideas that shape it.

Not that he has entirely given up his old tricks. Former literary editor of *The New Statesman*, where he was largely responsible for fostering "Martianist" poetry, Amis has always been somewhere between shamelessly and proudly literary. . . . [It] seems clear that his title is a deliberate echo of Sartre's definition of Hell. The triangular dialogue (with the reader addressed as a passive third) and the cyclical epilogue suggest *No Exit* as well, and the narrator at one point notes that "There will have to be a hell for each of us." (p. 46)

[*Other People* ends ambiguously]—when Amis subtitled it *A Mystery Story*, he wasn't just whistlin' "Dixie"—but perfunctorily, a little as though Amis had lost the courage of his Manicheanism. And a lot as though he too had abandoned hope in the saving grace of art.

But not of artifice. For each of the ambiguous readings the last few pages allow, Amis has planted clues aplenty beforehand. Some are sly literary allusions, others subtly chiming verbal echoes. A few things are clear, though: the only way out of hell is imagination—the ownership of which is itself a kind of punishment. To imagine the twin Princes of Darkness and of Peace as real is to suffer; to discover that they are not only real but fungible, even identical, is to suffer exquisitely.

Amis, having invented it, doesn't back away from that pain, and at this moment of Western malaise, *Other People* would stand as a brave book no matter who had written it; Grand Themes are automatically suspicious. But it is particularly brave for Amis—an author securely ensconced on a comfortable level of the literary world—to break free, daring to fall on his face. Though he stumbles occasionally—the overbroad caricature of the BBC newsman would have been far more at home in an earlier book—he remains *integer vitae*. Instead of giving the finger to life, he is trying to embrace it.

It is too early to tell whether *Other People* might not be just an aberration in an otherwise predictable literary career, but it's certainly not too soon to hope it signals a permanent change. (p. 47)

Geoffrey Stokes, "Manichean's Fate," in The Village Voice, Vol. XXVI, No. 24, June 10-June 16, 1981, pp. 46-7.

EVAN HUNTER

Martin Amis's fourth novel is titled *Other People: A Mystery Story*. There are mysteries galore in its pages, but the book faces no danger of being lost in a bookshop's genre section. Mr. Amis has more "serious" matters on his mind, it would appear, and he sets about exploring them by presenting us with an amnesia victim who awakens in what seems to be a hospital and does not know who, where, or even *what* she is. Barefoot, bewildered and released onto the street by what is surely the world's most irresponsible hospital (if it *is* a hospital), she wanders out into what we later learn is London and begins to discover a strange new universe. . . .

The book details the adventures and misadventures of our heroine abroad, who takes the name of "Mary Lamb" from the snatches of the nursery rhyme she hears recited by one of a group of drunks in her first encounter with the wide, wide world of crazies at large. In succeeding chapters, she is transported from the bowels of London to its esophagus, so to speak, in stages of upward mobility that brings her ever closer to discovering her real self, the "Amy Hide" (Amis Hiding?) who may or may not have been the acquiescent victim of a would-be murderer. We never learn who this murderer was or is. He is identified throughout as "Mr. Wrong," but in an anticlimactic confrontation scene, he remains faceless, and we never quite understand whether his final embrace is intended as a kiss of death or of resuscitation. . . .

And who is this *other* person in the book, a voice that erupts interminably, sharing supposedly pithy thoughts on life and death? The very last passage would lead us to believe he is only the inept murderer coming back to do the job good and proper this time. But there are clues all along that he is none other than the godlike author himself, periodically and irritatingly intruding, commenting on action we have already seen or are about to see, and making of himself a general nuisance, as for example: "I'm forever having to cope with these rather puzzling and regrettable people. You'll be running into a few more of them too. But all under my control, of course, all under my protection and control." . . .

This other person—this sometimes smugly omniscient, sometimes sophomorically philosophical, always disembodied voice that speaks directly to the reader—is only one of the many dismaying "other people" (two words that appear like a litany on virtually every other page) in this short, bitter book. Mr. Amis would seem far too young to have acquired such a dismal view of the world. Perhaps the sun will break through in London one day.

Evan Hunter, "Mary Lamb and Mr. Wrong," in The New York Times Book Review, *July 26, 1981, p. 9.*

ERIC KORN

[In the nonfiction work *Invasion of the Space Invaders: An Addict's Guide,* Amis's obsession] (and mine), still perhaps unfamiliar to Trappists or remoter Hebrideans, is with those mesmeric machines that at the drop of a coin (usually two) proffer a screenful of bug-eyed beasts to be annihilated by buttons, vehicles to be steered by wheels or joysticks or levers, chirruping creatures to be guided through mazes; whatever the ingenuity of the programmer can devise.

The novelty and entrancement is that the challenge grows more severe as the player's skill advances. Amis gives a vivid history of the onset and course of Space-Invader Fever, the expense of spirit—and time and cash—in a waste of game.

Video-champs aren't true addicts either (nobody calls Ovett a jogging addict, or Verdi an operahead). When Amis complains that it cost him a fiver to conquer the first wave of Space Invaders, and a fiver apiece for the next nine waves, he is demanding admiration not sympathy. . . .

[This] is a fetchingly handsome book, its prose and pictures full of apt flash and wallop. Amis evokes with glum delight

the foul locales, louche habitués and impoverished jargon, the horrors of addiction: then he appraises the various games and the dodges for scoring, as if a sermon against lechery were bound up with a sex manual.

His survey is canny, passionate and splendidly partial; valuable for "Defenders", still the serious one. . . . He despises noncombatant games like "Frogger" (be kind to Amphibia) or "Donkey Kong" (be kind to Fay Wray); he praises "Missile Command" with its intricately beautiful patterns (and the thunderous finale that provokes epileptiform seizures) but absurdly travesties "Pac-Man", imagining that the gobbling monsters are the Pac-Men, which is not unlike a Student's Guide to Melville discussing a one-legged sea-captain called Moby Dick. . . .

He is properly appreciative of "Tempest", an almost abstract ballet of flickering forms and giddy perspectives. "Tempest" has nearly escaped the blast-them-from-the-galaxy format: the objective is to make geometry. This is the wave of the future, or one wave; another is ever more realistic simulation. . . .

Martin Amis feigns horror but is enjoying himself too much, in this enjoyable book, to be heeded. He doesn't perhaps grasp the deserts of eternity that videogames imply. All are potentially infinite: the reward for playing well is to play forever. Boring? But of course; boredom is the name of the game. Amis is the second best writer in English (after Amis) on bores and boredom: but English doesn't distinguish between boredom, a simple social plague, the herpes of the mind, and acedia, boredom self-imposed and self-destroying, a desperate tedium that dries lakes, flattens mountains, bleaches sunsets; behind the buzz and glitter, this is the real face of the Invader.

Eric Korn, "Space Bores," in The Sunday Times, *London, September 26, 1982, p. 33.*

IAN HAMILTON

'Dollar bills, pound notes, they're suicide notes. *Money* is a suicide note.' So says John Self, the hero of **Money: A Suicide Note,** and what he means is that money is destroying *him*. Self-destruction (along with several of its hyphenated pals: indulgence, interest, loathing) has become Self's hobby, what he does in his spare time, and what he spends his money on. But it's money's fault that this is what he spends his money on. It's money's fault that he hasn't got anything better to do with his spare time. 'The yobs are winning,' said a character in Martin Amis's **Success,** and one could almost take this as the 'burden' of his work so far. In earlier books, there have been yobs aplenty, and from the beginning Amis has scrutinised the species with some ardour. With John Self, though, he shifts the enemy to centre-stage, so that this time he can give him a real going-over.

When the book opens, Self has just arrived in New York to direct a big-money feature film, called *Good Money*. Back home in London, he has won a small reputation for his scandalous TV commercials (extolling the pleasures of junk food, tobacco, porno mags etc), and he has even collected an Italian prize for a short documentary called *Dean Street*. He is one of the new men, the uneducated media slicksters who took over in the Sixties, a practitioner and a product of junk culture. . . . Self makes lots of money but he 'pisses it away'—on rubbish food, rubbish booze and rubbish sex. He needs money very badly, but he can't control it. . . .

Although he has a spare-time problem, Self likes things that are fast. He doesn't quite know why, except that this happens to be the momentum of the moment: get rich quick, if you're not quick you're dead.... Thus, the things he is hooked on are short-term and money-based—like jumboburgers and pornography. And although Self is fat and ugly and in terrible physical condition, he's a fast talker—he can always 'gimmick' a quick deal and (by using his head) foreshorten a yob punch-up. He's 35, mid-Atlantic and of shallow parentage: his father has recently invoiced him for the cost of his upbringing. His grandfather was an inept though dedicated counterfeiter—he *made* money.

Self has an English girlfriend, Selina. She's in it for the money, too....

The big-money film deal gives Self the chance to exercise self-interest, but here there is a razor-thin separation between art and life. The movie stars he has to deal with are all freaks—money-freaks, naturally, but also ego-freaks, self-freaks. To humour them, Self must self-abase somewhat, because of money. But then, because of money, he has become quite good at this, over the years. The film's chief money-man, Fielding Goodney, is a freak also: but he's a freak of physical well-being, the kind of manufactured self that Self would pay big money for if selves could actually be bought and sold....

Self knows what he sees in Fielding: but what does Fielding see in him? It was Fielding who hired him, and it is Fielding who now supplies him with fat bundles of cash, first-class air tickets, high-tab dinners, chauffeur-driven limos, and so on. Fielding *is* money. No matter that he also seems to be going out of his way to abet Self's self-destruction—he humiliates him on the tennis court, takes him for a walk in Harlem, gets him low-grade drunk in high-grade restaurants: the point is that Fielding does these things with style, and Self, who has no style, is hypnotised....

As soon as John Self arrives in New York, he starts getting anonymous telephone calls; well, not quite anonymous: 'Just call me Frank.' Frank also says, 'I'm the guy whose life you fucked up,' and he regularly taunts Self for his drunkenness and gluttony. He berates him, too, for his attitudes to women.... Frank claims to be an aggregate of all those whom Self has treated brutishly since childhood. Somehow he knows all Self's moves—rather better than Self does, very often, since Self's memory is blurred and sometimes cancelled out by drink.... Is there a connection between Frank the Phone and the tall, red-haired lady in a veil who seems to be following him round town? If there is, Self can't ever quite muster the mental energy to work it out.

Nor does he have the wits to figure out the role of Doris Arthur, the feminist scriptwriter hired by Fielding to work on *Good Money*. At first, Self treats her just like any other chick. He makes a lunge and is frostily rebuffed. Fielding tells him that this was because she is a lesbian, and this effectively disposes of Self's interest in her. Why is it, though, that Doris Arthur's script, when it eventually arrives, seems calculated to kill off the film?... 'Someone's fucking me *around*,' cries Self. But who? And why?... All he knows is that *Good Money* has gone bad.

At moments like this, it is Self's habit to turn to the reader. He has been chatting to us from the start, with lines like 'I'd better give you the low-down on Selina—and quick' or 'Memory's a funny thing, isn't it? You don't agree? I don't agree either.' And he usually seems fairly confident that we'll be on

his side: 'I'm touched by your sympathy (and want much, much more of it. I want sympathy, even though I find it so very hard to behave sympathetically).' But then we have access to Self's inner self. We know about those quiet moments in the whore-house when he is hit by a wavelet of revulsion....

We know too about his crying jags, his entreaties that we might help him to 'make sense of things'.... Self's powerful soliloquies reveal an imaginative self rich (yes, rich) in metaphor, irony and farcical good humour—a literary self which, as the outer Self would put it, has somehow gimmicked a smart tie-up between low slang and high figurative artifice. Sometimes the tie-up comes out sounding like Holden Caulfield done over by Micky Spillane, but at its best it's not like anybody else: an urban-apocalyptic high fever somehow kept steady, helped across the road, by those old redoubtables—wit, worldly wisdom, and an eye for social detail. (p. 3)

How then might this inner Self break out into real life: is real life really worth the effort? In the novel two possible assistants are on hand. In London, there is a writer called Martin Amis. Self has met him once or twice and found him rather priggish, full of mini-sermons about moral choice. Even so, after the Doris Arthur disaster, he needs a script-doctor in a hurry, and even the puritanical M. Amis can't resist (or so it seems) the mega-bucks. Amis signs up, ingeniously rewrites the script so that each of the stars is mollified, and from time to time treats Self to his musings on the 'moral philosophy of fiction'.... But Self isn't listening. He wants his script; he wants his money....

He tries to get Amis to tell him something about *his* private life, but the novelist won't talk. The nearest the two of them get to calling a truce is when they sit down together to watch the Royal Wedding on TV. Self cries his eyes out, but when he is allowed to steal a glance at Amis, he notices that the novelist isn't looking too good, either. He sees 'a grey tear glint in those heavy eyes'. Maybe Martin is a bit like him, after all: 'If I stare into his face I can make out the areas of waste and fatigue, the moonspots and boneshadow you're bound to get if you live in the 20th century.'

There are those who do not have this wasted look. Lady Di doesn't, nor does Self's other likely helpmate, the American Martina Twain.... Martina Twain had been a fellow-student of Self's at film school, but he had always considered her out of his league: 'She's class, with a terrific education on her.' Why does she seem to be taking such an interest in him—this transatlantic, female Martin A.? She tries to get him to read books, she takes him to operas and art galleries, she offers him white wine and persuades him to cut down to two packs of cigarettes a day. Self can't make her out: after all, she's a chick, and very good-looking, and yet when he tries to introduce her into his pornographic mind-movie she doesn't seem to fit.... Sad and unwitting, Self tries to make an effort to improve himself for Martina, but the old junk life keeps tugging him back. His libido can't cope with Martina's wholesome sexual bounty. Pornography reclaims him and, thanks to Martin Amis's new script, the film world propels him to the final depths. At the end of it all, he is back in London, broke and broken.

Martin Amis is waiting for him, and even he—the cunning inventor of Self's woes—can't help feeling a bit guilty: 'I remembered Martin, here in my flat, standing over me and saying again and again in a clogged and wretched hush: "I'm so sorry. I'm so sorry."' With that said, Amis hoists himself back onto the title page and plays it cool. The subtlety of these final scenes—the teasing with notions of character, narrative and motivation—can only be done justice to by revealing the book's jigsaw of whodunnits, and I have already come too close to doing that. *Money* really needs to be read twice (at least): the first time for the sheer pleasure of encountering the grotesque and lovable John Self, for the laughs, the plot, the extraordinary urban atmospherics. The second time round (when, as Self would say, you are all laughed out) you can begin to relish the book's marvellously intricate design: the chess motif, the cosmological perspectives, the Othello murmur, the weather vein, and so on. I am already persuaded that *Money* will be thought of for years to come as one of the key books of the decade. (p. 4)

> Ian Hamilton, "Martin and Martina," in London Review of Books, *September 20 to October 3, 1984, pp. 3-4.*

ANGELA HUTH

As *Money* is written in the first person, in nearly 400 pages there is no relief from the agonies and base appetites of [the] anti-hero. Self, aptly named, is a very rich 35-year-old film director. Money is his only lifeline, though how he came to make so much is one mystery of the story: the other is why anyone should employ such an unreliable, drunken, foul-mouthed character. For Self is an alcoholic, stumbling through worlds in London and New York that make Grub Street look like Beatrix Potter. Everyone takes advantage of him, including his two-timing tormentor of a girlfriend Selina, whom he loves—though it is hard to imagine any such emotion flowering in his constantly sozzled heart.

This is a grim book: a black study of the humiliations and degradations of an alcoholic, a warning of the corruptibility of money and the emptiness of a life with no culture to fall back upon. In many ways a remarkable piece of observation, even in the hands of so good a writer as Martin Amis the repetitious activities of a drunk, sex-mad, ill-educated man become tedious. There is little cheer in such a life, and so it is in the book. But despite the dispiriting effect of Self's ways, he does extract some sympathy, and when he falls for a sad married lady there is brief hope for his salvation. He loses her, of course, in one of the moments of dark humour. There is a feeling of terrible verisimilitude about his whole bleak world.

There are some jokes, including a good family one: Self's Fiasco car must be from the same garage as Kingsley Amis's Apfelsine in *Stanley and the Women*. But there is little change of pace or colour, which instils a longing for some respite. On several occasions Self runs into Martin Amis himself: my heart quickened. Would that Amis had taken over the story for a while, releasing us from the view through Self's pathetic and unlovely eyes. But no: the author maintains the spell of gloom. He insists on his hero telling his own story. This Self does with the ruthless determination of any drunk, and like any drunk he goes on too long. He shows an extraordinary talent for unhappiness: it scintillates on every page until the sort-of-happy ending.

> Angela Huth, "Stateside Scenes," in The Listener, *Vol. 112, No. 2877, September 27, 1984, p. 32.**

A. N. WILSON

Ever since Chaucer wrote *The Canterbury Tales*, authors have been appearing in their own work, so we don't have to suppose that Martin Amis's appearance in [*Money*] is simply a fashionable attempt to embody the fads of post-structuralist critics. When Chaucer comes into *The Canterbury Tales*, we all busily start pencilling IRONY in the margin without having the *hang* of his jokes. He was writing for an audience of—what?—at most a hundred people at the court of Richard II. A similar flavour is given off by *Money,* only I should conjecture that the audience of real initiates is much smaller. I just about 'clicked' at the more obvious literary allusions—the Ashbery Hotel, the Nigerian novelist Fenton Akimbo, the fast food known as Seckburger. But a good half of the jokes were lost on me, since Amis's humour, like Chaucer's, is designed to shut you out rather than draw you in.

Yet Chaucer is still around, and the impenetrable in-joke (witness the popularity of *Private Eye*) is no real barrier between an author and his public. I thoroughly enjoyed *Money,* even though I don't think I understood it. There are moments where it seems unedited (for instance, there are at least two extended eulogies on the delights of the 'handjob', i.e. masturbation). And there are passages where the self-parody is so perky ('Defiantly, I squelched the book shut') that it could win a *NS* competition. The prose is never descriptive of the thing it describes; rather, in a high old romantic manner, of the author's mood.

Style was the man for the young Amis and this book contains his best exercises yet in the prose equivalent of butting.... But *Money* is struggling towards something much more heavy and complicated than a sort of sub-Chandlerian linguistic joke. If one says it is meant to be a comment on capitalism in decline, the nature of contemporary society etc etc, one doesn't mean to be insulting.

I could have done with it being about 150 pages shorter, not because I didn't admire the verbal jokes, but because I never got interested in any of the characters. I don't think Martin Amis did either. 'When I get through with you, sunshine, there'll be nothing left but a hank of hair and teeth' is a sentence repeated once too often in the book. It could be the author speaking to the emanations of his own fancy. They lack substance somehow. They mark the end of the young Amis, because here he's 'gone about as far as he can go'. Something different next. For, as John Self observes, 'I've got to stop being young. Why? It's killing me, being young is fucking killing me.' (pp. 30-1)

> A. N. Wilson, "Young Scumbag," in The Spectator, *Vol. 253, No. 8154, October 20, 1984, pp. 29-31.*

JOHN GROSS

Everything [in *Money*] turns on detail—on the intricate web of allusions that Mr. Amis spins, the boldness and energy of his language, the stealth with which he stalks his prey. New York and London as they appear in his pages are recognizable versions of the real thing, but he enjoys improving on nature, heightening the color here, substituting a comic invention there. The makes of cars his characters own, for instance. Fielding Goodney glides through Manhattan in a long sleek Autocrat; Self's Fiasco needs a major overhaul (poor Self); somebody else runs around London in a little black Iago—and not by chance, either, since references to *Othello* bubble up throughout the novel.

Above all Mr. Amis has endowed Self (realistically or not) with a witty and insinuating narrative voice. Much of the wit is brisk and slangy, but it can also luxuriate into virtuoso extended metaphors. "My head is a city," Self laments, and he proceeds to explain how various pains have taken up residence in various parts of his face: "A gum-and-bone ache has launched a cooperative on my upper west side. Across the park, neuralgia has rented a duplex in my fashionable east seventies. Downtown, my chin throbs with lofts of jaw-loss. As for my brain, my hundreds, it's Harlem up there, expanding in the summer fires. It boils and swells. One day soon it is going to burst."

Like many recent novels, but more lightly and deftly than most, *Money* also calls frequent attention to its status as a work of fiction. Although Self hardly ever reads a book, he gradually becomes intrigued by a writer who lives in his part of London, an unnervingly polite character called Martin Amis. He arranges for Amis to revise the script of the movie on which he is working, and from that point on the writer—the fictional writer—threatens to usurp the novel—the real novel. It is like the Escher drawing of a hand drawing itself.

A nagging question remains—is it worth expending all this art and ingenuity on a character as trivial as Self? He has his representative significance, no doubt; he could serve as an Awful Warning in a homily on the consumer society or the Me Generation; but do we really need nearly 400 pages of him?

Not if we regard *Money* as a conventional novel, a more or less realistic slice of life; and if we do, it is easy enough to see the ways in which Self simply doesn't hang together as a character. He is far too eloquent and well-informed to be as brutish as we are asked to believe, and far too fastidious in his responses. But in practice this kind of inconsistency doesn't seem to me to matter very much since he has only one foot in the real world anyway. He is also a walking bundle of appetites, naked Ego (with a strong dash of Id), Self by name and self by nature—as much a creature of fantasy, in some respects, as Gargantua or Ubu Roi.

The comedy and horror of the untrammeled self make a more powerful theme in Mr. Amis's hands than the theme of money. But if the wider social message of his novel doesn't go very deep, *Money* remains a highly original and often dazzling piece of work.

> *John Gross, in a review of "Money: A Suicide Note,"*
> in The New York Times, *March 15, 1985, p. C25.*

JONATHAN YARDLEY

[In *Money*] Martin Amis has written a big brave book. It is amply endowed with flaws, as most big brave books are, but they are entirely overshadowed by the breadth of its ambition and accomplishment. It takes great risks, it boils with energy, it gives offense, it even manages—this in an age when nothing any longer seems unexpected or surprising—to shock. And for all of that it is so unremittingly, savagely hilarious that reading it is quite literally an exhausting experience, from which one emerges simultaneously gasping for air and pleading for more.

Money is not a book for everyone, though it is rather difficult to say with any confidence who are the ones that will like it and who are those that will not. Most certainly it is, in the word of the English friend who alerted me to it, "scabrous": "dealing with," as Webster has it, "or characterized by suggestive, indecent or scandalous themes," not to mention "unpleasant, repulsive or reprehensible in some way." From first page to last it is one long drinking bout, interrupted only briefly by a period of relative sobriety; it contains incessant sexual activity, much of it onanistic; it has a generous supply of sordid language that would not pass muster in polite society; and it has an unkind word for just about every race, creed or nationality known to exist.

Scabrousness on such an overwhelming level ordinarily would offend me, as I have come to believe in recent years that it exists in most contemporary fiction principally to call attention to itself and to the person who is writing it. But it is impossible to imagine *Money* without it. That is because Amis has done something entirely remarkable: he has created a central character of consummate vulgarity and irresistible charm, and he has insinuated himself into this character so completely that the voice with which he speaks is that man's and that man's alone. In *Money* we listen not to Martin Amis speaking through John Self, but to John Self speaking through Martin Amis. We go a long way back—perhaps all the way to the Compson children in *The Sound and the Fury*—to find a novelist so utterly possessed by his narrator; the result, as they say in the macho world John Self inhabits, is awesome. . . .

The greedy man as unwitting 20th-century victim may be the central business of *Money,* but an awful lot of other stuff is going on as well. There is a mysterious telephone caller who may be Self's conscience and may be his manipulator: Who knows? There's the surprising—and to my taste neither obtrusive nor gratuitous—introduction of a character named Martin Amis, a young British novelist who lives in Self's neighborhood and eventually gets involved with the movie. There's an extraordinarily vivid depiction of contemporary Manhattan: "Heat, money, sex and fever—this is it, this is New York, this is first class, this is the sharp end." There's show biz. . . . And through it all is a sense of dread: "I have a sharp sense of my life being in the balance. I may never look back, or I may never recover. I tell you, I am terrified. . . ."

In fact, there is so much in this novel that a review can only begin to suggest it. Its principal shortcoming, if anything, is that ultimately there is too much; the book is too long and, like John Self, is in constant danger of spinning out of control. But this may well be the madness in Amis' method. If there is excess here, then there is also excess in John Self and excess in the 20th century he so pornographically and flamboyantly mirrors. This is his novel, all right—call it "John Self: His Own Book," if you will—and in it he emerges as one of the indisputably memorable, not to mention haunting, characters of postwar fiction. He is an outrage in every word and action, yet it is impossible not to love him. His greed is deplorable, yet his innocence redeems him. He dreams, he yearns, he desires; so, alas, do we all.

> *Jonathan Yardley, "The Comic Madness of Martin Amis," in* Book World—The Washington Post, *March 24, 1985, p. 3.*

Jacques Audiberti

1899-1965

French dramatist, poet, novelist, journalist, and essayist.

Audiberti's work is characterized by a passionate, flamboyant use of language and a strong sense of the melodramatic and absurd. His novels are complicated and often obscure, his poetry is both formal and extravagant, and his plays combine absurdist farce with surreal melodrama. Commenting on the "verbal delirium" of Audiberti's poetic style, Kenneth Cornell noted: "Elements of the swift and torrential burst which give so much of Audiberti's verse an epic tone and which impede to some degree ready comprehension find their way into everything he writes." Maintaining that humankind has wandered disastrously from its natural state, Audiberti developed two obsessive themes: the conflict between Christianity and paganism, and the existence of an inextricable primitive force in every person.

Audiberti was born and raised in Antibes, a Mediterranean city that figures symbolically in much of his work. When he was twenty-five he moved to Paris, where he lived until his death. Beginning his career as a journalist, Audiberti soon turned to poetry, novels, and eventually the theater. He first received significant critical attention with the publication of *Race des hommes* (1937), a volume of poetry displaying the abundance of imagery and lyric outburst characteristic of all of his collections, including *Des tonnes de semence* (1941), *Toujours* (1943), and *Vive guitare* (1946). Audiberti's novels have received less attention than either his poetry or his plays but are similarly distinguished by philosophical concerns and by "the rugged beauty of his poetic language," as Constantin Toloudis noted. Referring to Audiberti's first novel, *Abraxas* (1938), Toloudis declared: "The religious symbolism, the allegorical character of the voyage, the tone and texture of the language in the tale recounting the adventures of the intrepid hero . . . , amount to an eloquent, almost exhaustive exposé on the lore of Audibertian themes and devices." Audiberti's other novels include *Carnage* (1942), *La nâ* (1944), *Cent jours* (1950), and *Les jardins et les fleuves* (1954).

Audiberti began writing for the theater relatively late in his career. The emphasis on language and the dramatic verbal flow in his plays have led critics to laud the vitality and originality of his work as well as fault it for unchecked loquacity and extravagance. As Leonard Cabell Pronko noted, "the danger is that vigor, imagination, lyricism, and rhetoric may take over." As with his poetry and novels, Audiberti's plays explore complex philosophical and religious concerns. Many of his dramas reveal his preference for the disordered, natural paganism of antiquity over the structured, often perverted Christian myth of the twentieth century. In *Quoat-Quoat* (1946), a satire of nineteenth-century melodrama, a spy is absurdly condemned to death, then released from his sentence by the Captain, who holds tenuous control over a ship which is, like the world, at the mercy of primitive forces. The spy, however, defies his ordered fate by committing suicide; only in death is he master of his own destiny. Realizing that he too has lost control of his Godlike destiny, the Captain raises his arm and destroys the ship, presumably returning the world to nothingness.

The violence of paganism similarly proves victorious over Christianity in *Opéra parlé* (1956), a drama in which a young goddess is forced to marry an evil baron who represents Christianity's vindictive aspects, and a previous lover revenges his loss by embracing evil and attacking Christian outposts. Evil is often central to Audiberti's works, as is the conflict between the soul and the flesh. For Audiberti, evil arises from the repression of such natural drives as sex and aggression. In *La fête noire* (1945), a young man's sexual frustration gives birth to a beast which roams the countryside raping and killing young women; the killing of a goat believed to be the beast fails to eliminate the violence. Through this play Audiberti implies that the beast is in every man and woman and that the violence of the past reasserts itself interminably. *Le mal court* (1947), Audiberti's most successful play, is a conventional fairy tale about a princess's decision to turn to evil after observing the ruthlessness of society. Like many of Audiberti's protagonists, she is able to transcend society's atrocities and rise to a more divine state only through intentional indulgence in and awareness of evil.

(See also *Contemporary Authors,* Vols. 25-28, rev. ed. [obituary].)

KENNETH CORNELL

The current polemic on the question of obscurity in verse . . . continues a debate which has consistently occupied critics since Baudelaire, Verlaine, Rimbaud, and Mallarmé set new examples for lyric utterance. Scarcely any modern French poet of note has been spared the charge of obscurity, but it would seem that despite critical admonition, clarity in the traditional sense of the word has been almost entirely exiled from the poetic realm. (p. 100)

In the majority, obscure poets, like many modern painters, seem intent on distilling what to them is the essential meaning of their theme. It is, moreover, upon inner rather than sensory vision that such meaning depends. Into this broad class, that of poetry obtained by removing the extraneous, one can fit the compositions of Eluard, Reverdy, Apollinaire, and, for the most part, those of the Surrealists.

Present-day French poetry does offer, however, another type of obscurity, one which stems from superabundance, from a kind of verbal delirium. . . . [In] contemporary French letters the most extraordinary example of this plethora of images, of this chaotic expansion of ideas, comes from the pen of a journalist, poet, novelist, and dramatist named Jacques Audiberti.

Although he is now nearing his fiftieth year, Audiberti has only recently become known as a poet. In October, 1933, he explained to readers of the *Nouvelle Revue Française* that when he was about fifteen years old he had written verse concerning landscapes and impressions, but had abandoned that literary form until about 1930. . . . In this same article of 1933, he announced his poetic credo in a few sentences which aid in understanding his subsequent production. He states that for him poetry is a technique of pride, of pride in man's being both the child and the parent of God. . . . His personal talent, he feels, could accomplish blank verse only with difficulty; he composes most easily in Alexandrines and prefers to impose on himself the most severe phonetic and technical constraints. The purpose of his poetry is to sing the destiny and grandeur of man and to convey the tortured gayety of existence. Apparently Audiberti's poetic world is of epic proportions, nor is this belied by the titles, the matter, and the tone of most of his poems. The lyric resurgence which took place in his being about 1930 produced a long poem, not usually given in his bibliography, which was based on the life of Napoleon and entitled "**L'Empire et la Trappe.**" This poem, which produced on Marcel Fombeure the impression of an unchecked torrent of words, was not immediately followed by new composition in verse. In truth it was not until 1936 when Gallimard published *Race des hommes* that Audiberti's poetry came seriously to the attention of the public.

The volume astonished rather than pleased the critics. Again what struck those who read his poetry were the wild, untrammeled flow of words and images, the vast vocabulary, and the epic sonority of many of the lines. These might have been accounted qualities had not their excess approached Orphic madness and the strange combinations of words suggested an incoherence alien to French literary discipline. . . . Audiberti's extravagance appeared to demand explanation and it was immediately offered, according to the precepts of Taine, by reference to an environment in which impulsive Italian and Southern French blood scorned moderation, Audiberti's native Antibes. A few short poems of which the settings are the Mediterranean region supported this theory in a very literal fashion, but the poet's landscapes just as often were Parisian, pseudo-historical (past, present, and future are all telescoped for Audiberti), or in an imaginary realm.

It is an easy matter to damn the author of *Race des hommes* as so in love with words that coherence and meaning are lost. In a later poem "**Stèle aux mots,**" and in a long essay of 1942, "**La Nouvelle Origine,**" he confesses his infatuation with words, not only for their connotation but for their sound. Poetically this is not really vicious, for Audiberti's abundance of vocabulary, his combinations of strictly classical terms with technical, rare, exotic, or popular words, offer the element of surprise, that element which Apollinaire once called the mainspring of the modern poetic spirit. . . . Audiberti's poems, especially those which are long, contain a great diversity of tone, the serious passage suddenly offers a little oasis of comical, ironic, or erotic development and then returns to more sober tonality. This is certainly contrary to the idea of literary form as the expression of unity, yet it is perhaps more true to life and is not without savor. The mind which . . . endows a bridge or a subway with such strong sexual symbolism avoids boredom. The curious manner in which the idea is no sooner expressed than it is borne forth in many directions, the recurrence of the theme seemingly engulfed in the flood, the dual notes of revolt and ecstasy, and especially the visionary strength of the lines make their author appear as having reached one of the extremes of possible poetic originality.

Audiberti's poetic themes are generally difficult ones because they represent combinations of ideas. In "**Palinodie,**" from the mouth of a conquering tyrant comes the sentiment of pity struggling out of brutality, pride, and passion, in "**La Vallée**" praise of the written word is transformed into a bitter cry against existence, and in those poems which have as titles the name of some celebrated historical personage the conflict of emotions takes on the character of the paradoxical. Such themes, as Mr. [T. S.] Eliot suggests, are likely to beget obscurity, and in Audiberti's case the cause is equally the desire of expressing things in a new way. . . . [As] Maurice Chapelan has wisely written, Audiberti's manner admits of only one school, *Audibertisme,* which can be composed of only one member, at once the master and the terrific disciple.

There has been no sign of evolution either in Audiberti's subjects or in his style. The poetic volumes which followed *Race des hommes,* bearing the titles *Des Tonnes de Semence, Toujours,* and *Vive Guitare,* all demonstrate the thematic vastness which appears the poet's natural atmosphere. At times it would seem that he is intent on accomplishing a mission, once proposed by Lautréamont, of remaking the Romantic poem. A long, lyric meditation on the ocean and shorter pieces on Solomon, Semiramis, and Catherine the Great express passion, power, and destiny but omit sentimentality and tenderness. Perhaps an even more temerarious project, that of modernizing Baudelaiare, was the inspiration of "**A la créole.**" Each of the volumes, and notably *Vive Guitare,* contains a few short lyrics usually written in lines of seven or eight syllables which naturally lack the amplitude, sonority, and complication of the long poems. These brief songs, however, do not appear as the author's proper realm; rather are his thought and respiration attuned to the full and impressive Alexandrine. In expressing the intense, the cruel, and the vast, Audiberti finds his true measure.

Elements of the swift and torrential burst which give so much of Audiberti's verse an epic tone and which impede to some degree ready comprehension find their way into everything he writes. . . . [His] novels and especially his plays are filled with lyric outbursts. Although the development of the intrigue is more hindered than helped by this poetic complement, its presence aids in giving a mysterious meaning to reality. The story of Zouizoui, told in the novel *Septième,* and that of Satto, related in *Abraxas,* transcend the narrow limits of a story, thanks to the addition of poetic imagery. In the former, envious desire for a neighboring apartment dominates a woman's life and it is to the author's credit that the apartment gradually assumes living stature capable of harming and healing; in the latter work the travels of a young Italian from Ravenna become a poetic odyssey. One of Audiberti's most curious novels called *La Nâ* has, as one finds the title indicates, mountain snow for its subject and often reaches an epic tone.

Audiberti's vocabulary is unpredictable; so too are the actions of his characters. In recent years a part of his activity has been the writing of plays and in this form he has shown the intention of making the stage more poetic. As successively *Le Mal Court, Les Femmes du bœuf,* and *La Fête noire* have been produced, the journalistic press has labeled them as incomprehensible. Their reaction is understandable, for in Audiberti's plays immediate realities are quickly swirled by a torrent of words into the realm of cosmic revolt, universal passion, and gigantic evil.... Philippe Soupault, the staunch advocate of complete literary liberty, has taken his defense, reminding detractors that our twentieth century is an age in which the inconceivable is likely to be the product of the immediate future. He praises *La Fête noire* as a splendid example of a new type of play which has been liberated from the shackles imposed by the naturalists, by the "Théâtre libre," and by the psychological dramatists.

In Audiberti, despite his difficulty and excess, one has the creator of a sort of magic.... Illogical and strange as is his succession of images, out of them emerges that picture he has set himself to paint, existence at once tortured and comic, man with coexistent grandiose, petty, cruel, and tender sentiments, and his relationships with an extremely complicated modern world. (pp. 100-04)

> *Kenneth Cornell, "Audiberti and Obscurity," in* Yale French Studies, *Vol. 2, No. 2, 1949, pp. 100-04.*

PIERRE MÉLÈSE

The idea of an avant garde is an essentially fluid one, and can only be determined in connection with the present. The reason for this is that, in art as in literature, there have always been artists desirous of side-stepping tradition or conformity and of expressing their ideas in new forms. Each generation of artists attempts to create a brand new style, in that it proclaims, more or less clearly, that a particular mode of expression ... is exhausted and a new fashion is required to interpret a new attitude towards life. (p. 1)

In rejecting the conformity of "bourgeois" plays and dramas, the interplay and subleties of the so-called psychological theater and the polemics of the philosophic theater, this new theater had to be a breakaway theater, both in subject matter and in form. In denouncing the stupidity and irreality of ideologies, the authors of the new school—if one can speak of a school—ignore theatrical rules and bring to bear new techniques (scene shifts more in keeping with the movies than the theater, use of visual and audiophonic equipment, rejection of the box set), and bring into focus a new form of dramatic language by means of chaotic and brutal lyricism or by a language purposely neutral and of everyday speech.... [One result is the tendency

toward] works brought into being by poetic imagination, by the word that creates or sustains the idea.... (pp. 1-2)

[In this] group, Jacques Audiberti is one of the most significant playwrights. In a dozen or so plays he has liberated the theater of all contingencies: it is the extravagant subject matter, the uncommon situations, the effervescent and frequently irrational eloquence, the spirit of satire and of parody that make up the originality of this author, for whom poetry once again has a right to the theater.

For Audiberti, the theater is, above all, speech: the characters only enter the stage to rave. However, freed from formal logic, the most essential instincts find their expression through a clashing of phrases and metaphors by virtue of which the idea is recreated: one speaks, and the word brings forth the thought.... Audiberti's style is a verbal inebriation, an accumulation of raw words, of carnal comparisons, of assonances, a series of images, uncontrollable metaphors of obvious irrationalism, the most unexpected union of words. Audiberti invents a rhythm and diction which is in agreement with an irresistible stage movement. This is why his theater is as much an actor's theater as an author's theater: he needs interpreters ready to join in his game.... It is especially with [*L'Effet Glapion* and *Le Mal court*] that he has touched a public that has been enchanted by the unreal and fantastic character of his plays, by his ever-changing invention, his verbal virtuosity and his sense of theatrical effect, due at times to ludicrous and uncommon stage-setting.

In these theatrical adventures, in the comicity of farce as well as in melodrama, Audiberti tries to project familiar events in an unreal setting. (pp. 2-3)

> *Pierre Mélèse, "The Avant Garde Theater in France," in* The Theater Annual, *Vol. XVIII, 1961, pp. 1-16.*

JACQUES GUICHARNAUD with JUNE BECKELMAN

[As in the plays of Michel de Ghelderode, a] combination of farce and melodramatic horror, blended with outbursts of poetic language, is also at the basis of most of Audiberti's plays. But Audiberti added parody and an accumulation of surprises, thus creating a very special type of adventure-comedy. His effects are sometimes facile: the intrusions of typed characters like the volcanic and revolutionary Mexican woman in *Quoat-Quoat* or disguised characters like La Bequilleuse in *les Naturels du Bordelais,* who is successively a dealer in aphrodisiacs, a fashionable poet, and a police assistant; behavior contrary to the situation or station of the characters, like the Prime Minister's arrogance toward his king in *le Mal court,* the Princess's strip tease in front of the Cardinal in the same play, or the puny son's unexpected success with thirty women in *les Femmes du Boeuf.* But he uses his comic and even farcical elements, borrowed from various traditions, as pretexts for verbal embellishments and displays. Where Ghelderode always pushes in the same direction, Audiberti freely breaks loose. He draws his comedy from the Boulevard, from farce, from melodrama—imaginative fireworks and a burlesque poetry whose boldness goes beyond parody and irony, and reintroduces anxiety, mystery, horror. The scene in *Quoat-Quoat* in which the hero tells his secret to the captain's daughter, the scene in *le Mal court* in which the Princess describes her own body, the transformation of the characters into crickets in *les Naturels* are so many quasi-surrealistic or terrifying extensions of situations otherwise parodic and simple.

The objective of the parodies and an unrestrained, often delirious poetry is to disclose a monstrous reality behind the jesting or the absurdity of the adventures. Audiberti's drama is built on the relations between a surface life, represented by the plot and its absurd reversals, and deeply hidden primitive forces. The surface life is like a repercussion, a reflection which in itself can be treated lightly. The god Quoat-Quoat, the Evil that spreads, the earthly and mythical forces of *l'Ampélour,* the natural forces of *les Femmes du Boeuf* or *Pucelle,* the sensual appetites of *la Logeuse* are all representations of forces that are perhaps hidden but always present and controlling.

Audiberti's originality lies in the play between the language describing the monsters and ambiguous scenic effects. The language creates a state of belief in the supernatural, in its incarnation. And at just the right moment, the spectacle presents a tableau, not of the incarnated supernatural, but of a coalition of concrete phenomena, all characteristic of the monster, and implying that the monster is really within man. The character-poets, as well as Audiberti the poet, are creatures almost equal to God or the Devil, but they are limited. They create belief, they create the effects, but they do not succeed in giving individual and permanent flesh to the forces they have evoked. What remains of their works are but corpses and myths. Unfortunately Audiberti popularized the theme of the creative imagination to such an extent in his last play *l'Effet Glapion* that it lost all its disturbing magic.

Doubtless a good example of *poésie de théâtre,* Audiberti's works are sometimes too complacent with regard to themselves. What constitutes their charm contributes also to their weakness. Although the onslaught of images, springing out of the familiar, and the variations of the variations on a central theme create the plays' poetic atmosphere and give them their savour, they also attract more attention than they should and somehow make the mask opaque instead of contributing to its transparency. (pp. 160-61)

> Jacques Guicharnaud with June Beckelman, *"Poetry and Discovery,"* in their Modern French Theatre: From Giraudoux to Beckett, *Yale University Press, 1961, pp. 155-77.*

LEONARD CABELL PRONKO

[Audiberti's world] is poised dramatically between good and evil. Here, however, evil is seen not as the work of the devil, but as the result of the whims of some malevolent deity, or of man's constant frustration in his human condition. It is a world of creatures tormented by love and a vague metaphysical yearning that goes beyond love, but which cannot be satisfied.

Good, on the other hand, is usually expressed in terms of that which is natural. Audiberti is fond of mountains and forests, trees and lakes, peasants and provincials, all that which is part of, or has remained closest to, nature. But man must sooner or later awaken to the realization that he is now separated from his natural realm and dwells outside the Eden that was once his.... All men, the dramatist suggests more than once, are more or less God, and if they but knew how, might tap the supernatural that surrounds them. The world we enter here is a magic one in which wonderful transformations, strange metamorphoses, and frightening creations are possible. It is very unlike the world we usually inhabit, and completely dissimilar to that one we see in the drama of the so-called realists, for Audiberti attempts to give a new kind of realism to the theater— or rather a very old kind of realism: the realism of the theater

which is, of course, nonrealism, for the theater is not reality. It is what the author calls an "accepted delirium," an "authorized oasis of lies." Upon this oasis, working with themes rather than clear-cut ideas . . . , Audiberti builds his amusing, frightening, disconcerting, and not infrequently thought-provoking plays. The danger is that vigor, imagination, lyricism, and rhetoric may take over. On occasion they lead the dramatist to embroider at length upon inessentials, to create superfluous characters or scenes for the pure joy of invention. His too full-blooded creative imagination is perhaps responsible for certain *longueurs* and for the diffuseness of some of his later plays (like *Les Naturels du Bordelais*). Audiberti, like the other avant-garde writers, knows no rules, and although he is generally faithful to such basic tenets of dramatic writing as plot and character, he restricts himself to no genre, and claims that his inspiration has come more from opera than from drama. This can be seen in the lyricism of his works, in the musicality of his dialogue (where interior rhymes are not infrequent), and in his use of song or verse. Indeed, *La Hobereaute* was first published under the title *Opéra parlé* (*Spoken Opera*), and was followed by an opera libretto, *Altanima.*

Audiberti is least successful in plays with a modern setting, for the period pieces are more richly suggestive and possess that poetic aura that only time can give, and which helps us suspend our disbelief, thereby rendering more acceptable the stage magic we witness. *L'Effet Glapion* (*The Glapion Effect,* 1959), admittedly a "vaudeville," borders on the trivial, while the cruel *Les Naturels du Bordelais* (*The Bordelais Natives,* 1953), modern murder mystery of a sadistic Don Juan, falls apart as the puzzling characters are metamorphosed into crickets, hoping thus to escape the pain of being men; but here there is none of that almost tragic inevitability which we feel in *Rhinoceros,* and the metamorphosis seems more a fantastic intrusion than a realistic conclusion. *La Logeuse* (*The Boardinghouse Keeper,* 1954?), is saved by its energetic creation of the title character, Madame Cirqué, mature, strong-willed, intense, mettlesome, animal, yearning to be dominated by a man's will, but apparently condemned to remain unsatisfied. Every male who comes within range, falls under her charm, and finally grovelling at the feet of this modern-day Circe, assumes the role of wife or mistress. (pp. 180-82)

Audiberti's earliest long plays, *Quoat-Quoat* (1946) and *Le Mal court* (*Evil is Abroad,* 1947), are among his most appealing, for despite their bitterness, they are well larded with humor, and possess a unity and a tidiness rarely found in this author. *Quoat-Quoat* is to some extent a satire of 19th century melodrama. In an atmosphere somewhat reminiscent of *H.M.S. Pinafore,* the youthful Amédée sets off on a dangerous governmental mission to Mexico. Before long he has fallen in love with the captain's daughter (against the governmental restrictions controlling the actions of secret agents), has stepped outside time for a moment to live his future exploits, and is arrested by the captain for his infringement of the ruling, and condemned to death. The action is incongruous and nightmarish, and we are convinced by the generally farcical treatment of the play that all will end well. Indeed, at the last moment, a mysterious woman passenger reveals that Amédée is not the real secret agent but a decoy, and he is therefore pardoned. But Amédée refuses to live, believing that he must face his own death, because to survive now would be to become someone else; and he runs up on deck before the firing squad. The play does not end here. The good but grim captain, we begin to suspect, is someone more than the captain of a ship—he is perhaps God himself, and his ship a grotesque representation of life's voyage. As the curtain falls, the good Lord raises his hand to annihilate ship and all, returning the universe to primeval emptiness.

Quoat-Quoat combines fantasy and farce with serious issues like death, identity, good, and evil. It is a distant relative of *Godot,* amusing, suggestive, ambiguous, although less so than Beckett's masterpiece.

Le Mal court . . . is Audiberti's greatest commercial success. During three rapid acts, in a glittering conventional 18th century atmosphere, the author recounts the awakening of innocence to an awareness of evil. Princess Alarica, about to cross the border of Occident, whose king she is to marry the following day, learns that for political reasons the King has cancelled his marriage contract. . . . Her trusted governess, she further learns, is a spy for the government of Occident. Antigone-like, she cries out bitterly, "People are tricking everywhere! . . . The world is ignoble." As the play ends, the Princess has learned her lesson and adapts herself to the world, becoming hard and ruthless in order to cope with life and with her role as ruler of the miserable kingdom of Courtelande.

The plays that follow, *La Fête noire* (1948, *Black Feast,* originally published as *La Bête noire, The Black Beast*), and *La Pucelle* (1950, *The Maid*), are already blemished by that diffuseness which is Audiberti's greatest flaw. But they are vigorous, intense, earthy pieces in which the Audibertian preoccupations with good and evil, metamorphosis and identity, reality and illusion, are exposed in a colorful avalanche of words.

La Pucelle is a highly original treatment of the Joan of Arc story, dealing not with the oft-described battles, victories, and trial, but with the identity of Joan as she discovers her role as heroine. At the same time that the tomboyish Joannine leaves home for war, she leaves behind her colorless double Jeannette who marries the boy next door. As the play closes, ten years later, an itinerant theater is presenting a play based upon the events of Joan's life. But their principal actress has defected to a neighboring troupe, and Jeannette is pressed into the role of Jeanne. As she is "burned" at the stake, a strong wind catches fire to her dress, and the peasant Jeannette, like her heroic double Joannine, is burned to death. The theater, we are told, is like a Mass which re-enacts what actually happened and thereby gives it a new reality. Lest we be puzzled by this interplay of identities and realities, the Duchess, herself (like us) a part of life's mystery, warns us that "it isn't the world's business to furnish us answers, but enigmas." Clarity and explanations are not part of life, nor are they part of Audiberti's theater. Only the vitality and mystery of life persist.

In *La Fête noire* the frustrated desire of the strangely attractive but mysteriously unlovable Félicien gives birth to a horrible monster that ravages the countryside, violating and killing young women. Men and the Church (amusingly satirized in the person of Monseigneur Morvellon) join to destroy the beast, but none can face the truth that the beast is a part of man himself, and they kill a goat thinking they have thereby annihilated evil. Félicien, renowned throughout the civilized world for his studies of the monster, is finally destroyed by the monster itself, in the shape of the jealous and angered Lou Desterrat who finds his niece in Félicien's arms, and shoots the couple.

La Fête noire is a difficult play, and its obscurity cannot be ascribed only to the richness with which the characters express themselves. The author fails to make clear the precise origin of his monster, and even leads one to assume that Félicien

himself is the beast, while later he allows the pretty young Alice, perhaps more lucid than the others, to assert that all women are the monster. Félicien's error, at any rate, seems to have been that he idolized women, making them something inhumanly perfect and desirable, whereas they are real beings that must be accepted as they are. . . . The disappointed idealist become monster and nihilist is a familiar figure here, reappearing in the godlike captain of *Quoat-Quoat,* the embittered Princess of *Le Mal court,* the sadistic Don Juan of *Les Naturels du Bordelais,* and the renegade Christian, Lotvy, in *La Hobereaute.* All these characters betray a metaphysical preoccupation, an effort to discover a meaning behind apparent meaninglessness.

Audiberti has stated that, while theater may be both reflection and diversion, it is the former that interests him particularly—which is not to say that his theater is not diverting. But the reflection here, as elsewhere in the avant-garde theater, remains germinal, it is not developed logically, but is expressed thematically with variations and *fioriture.* . . . (pp. 183-86)

La Hobereaute (1956?; the title refers to a kind of small falcon, *The Hobby*) is one of Audiberti's most ambitious and richly suggestive works, in which the struggle between good and evil is depicted in terms of the conflict between nature and the Church. In a highly flavored Middle Ages (9th century Burgundy), the dying druidic religion, the cult of the oak and the mistletoe, makes a desperate attack on the new religion. La Hobereaute, a spirit of nature who flies through the air and slips to the bottom of the lake where she sees enthroned "the silence of motionless, dazzling truth," is ordered by the druid priest to marry the hideous and criminal Baron Massacre, rather than the upright, noble, and sensitive warrior Lotvy, whom she loves. Such an unjust marriage, between utter natural purity and absolute corruption, can only bring discredit to the church that sanctions it. Lotvy swears eternal war on such a religion, and turns to burning convents and violating nuns. When he comes to the monastery near the Baron's chateau, where he hopes to fight his enemy and win La Hobereaute for himself, he is captured by the Baron and bound to a tree. There he is killed by one of his own followers who believes he has gone over to the nobles' faction. La Hobereaute, embracing him, is strangled by the jealous Massacre, who then kills himself. Amidst the litter of corpses wanders the spirit of Aldine, Lotvy's sister and La Hobereaute's serving woman, who has drowned herself.

The familiar theme of the obsession with love or desire which renders monstrous, personified by Massacre, is here contrasted to the more idealized love of Lotvy and La Hobereaute. Lotvy, Kemp suggests, may be understood to represent Roman wisdom, a lay wisdom—perhaps wiser than that restrictive sagacity of the Church. (pp. 186-87)

The precise meaning of *La Hobereaute* is not always clear, but in its total impact it surely suggests that man, torn between good and evil (Lotvy), persecuted in his natural feelings by a malevolent deity or some unjust earthly rule (Massacre, the Church), can now find happiness and unity (union with the nature goddess) only through death. Bound to the tree (the tree of life, the cross of man's suffering), Lotvy can at last be united with La Hobereaute, for death has released the sprite and returned her to her former supernatural condition. She is, in fact, the spirit of the universe, nature personified, and man is her child. (pp. 187-88)

Audiberti's humanism and pantheism reach full flower in this play that, in many ways, embodies the virtues and defects of his theater: a vigor that gives dramatic accent, but sometimes distracts; an inventiveness that enriches, colors, and amuses, but not infrequently diffuses; and an ambiguity that is both suggestive and obscuring.

In Audiberti's world we are far indeed from the "corpsed" universe of Beckett in which "there is no more nature." If evil and anguish persist, at least Babel lies some distance down the plain, and we have almost reached the doors of Eden. (p. 188)

> Leonard Cabell Pronko, *"From Babel to Eden,"* in his Avant-Garde: The Experimental Theater in France, *University of California Press, 1962, pp. 154-96.**

GEORGE WELLWARTH

One of the marks of a great critic is his ability to grasp the significance of a particular work of art. To understand the meaning of a work is sufficiently difficult in itself; but to be able to place a work of art into its historical perspective upon first seeing it is a gift granted to few. The fact that he was totally unable to understand the work makes Yeats's remark about Jarry's *Ubu roi* all the more impressive. . . . Yeats had the critical perceptiveness to see that his play changed the whole course of creative thought in the theatre. "After us," he wrote, "the Savage God!" More than twenty years later Antonin Artaud was to prove the truth of Yeats's prophecy; and more than twenty years after Artaud wrote *Le Théâtre et son Double* Jacques Audiberti was to write a series of plays with the Savage God—the malignant power of the cosmos—as protagonist.

Awareness of and protest against the power of the Savage God is a characteristic of all current avant-garde drama. A sense of the twisted malignity of the universe hovers over all the plays of Ionesco, Beckett, Genet, and Adamov, but only in certain of the plays of Jacques Audiberti does this presence attain the stature of an invisible protagonist permeating the work.

Jacques Audiberti does not belong wholeheartedly to the avant-garde school of drama, and his plays look a little strange in the company of Ionesco, Genet, et al. With most avant-garde dramas, as soon as the curtain rises there is an instant assault on form and language which shocks the audience and forces it out of the conventional dramatic frame of reference. Audiberti does not operate in this way. His plays look superficially like perfectly ordinary plays in an unusual or exotic setting. All of these plays, however, have some peculiar, even fantastic, twist in the story that renders them unintelligible as ordinary melodrama. The whole secret of understanding Audiberti's drama—and, indeed, most avant-garde drama—is not to expect to understand the plot as such. . . . In the avant-garde drama . . . the plot is either a seemingly haphazard conglomeration of illogically connected incidents or a perfectly ordinary story with one or two unexpected insertions which suddenly make it unintelligible in the context of ordinary dramatic conventions. The point of all this is that in the avant-garde drama the plot is unimportant per se. The avant-gardist never tries to tell a story. Instead, he uses incidents to illustrate a theme. . . . Beckett is not writing about the activities of two aimless vagrants in *Waiting for Godot:* their aimless meanderings are illustrative of the pointlessness and hopelessness of human existance. Precisely *what* Vladimir and Estragon do is not important at all. . . . What is important is that the incidents serve to clarify some general theme. In the avant-garde drama, plot is relegated to a position of literally no importance whatsoever; only the theme matters. It is necessary, therefore, when studying the avant-

garde drama to *disregard* the actual incidents of the play and apprehend instead the general theme of the author. Then one can observe how the incidents of the play, which may at first have seemed to be willfully meaningless, serve to illustrate the theme.

The two principal themes that Audiberti derives from Antonin Artaud are (i) the conflict between paganism and Christianity and (ii) the presence of a primordial spirit of evil in human affairs.

In Audiberti's eyes, as in Artaud's, paganism represents a purer state of mind than Christianity. Paganism was the first religion. It was a result of man's spontaneous, unsophisticated, unreasoned reaction to the powers of Nature. It was therefore far more real than the artificial, civilized, reasoned religion that Christianity represents. Paganism was a natural, instinctive reaction; Christianity is merely a patchwork of afterthoughts laid over the reality of human nature, which it stifles for the sake of social convenience. Anything that takes the human being away from his inborn reality is evil; and since in Audiberti's eyes the human being is evil to begin with, it follows that all artificial religions represent greater gradations of evil. The simplicity of instinctive human nature represents the best of all possible worlds in a universe where all possible worlds are bad.

Audiberti's second point—the pervading presence of evil in all human affairs—is usually expressed through his obsession with the idea of the controlling power of sex. He feels that in his sexual activities the human being comes closest to being an animal. With this emphasis on sex Audiberti pares all men down to one common level and gets rid of the artificial social distinctions that serve to differentiate people from each other in the traditional drama. . . . There is another, less obvious, reason for the emphasis Audiberti places on sex and that is the assumption that the act of intercourse merges us with Nature and therefore brings us nearer to the primordial evil. This view leads him to a sort of Manichean dichotomy between flesh and spirit with the flesh always conquering and leading inevitably to disaster.

The conflict between paganism and Christianity, which runs through all of Audiberti's plays, is treated overtly only in *Quoat-Quoat* (1946) and *Opéra parlé* (*Spoken Opera,* published 1956). In *Quoat-Quoat,* for example, Audiberti is talking about the latent power in the primeval myths that formed the human character far back in prehistoric times, long before the advent of the skin-deep, artificially superimposed pseudomyths by which we live now. (pp. 73-6)

The important point in [the] apparently extremely confused plot is that Audiberti undoubtedly wishes us to believe that as the curtain falls the captain destroys his ship and everyone on it with the stone of the ancient god Quoat-Quoat. This does not mean that Audiberti literally believes in the existence of a childish black magic, but rather that he feels that the modern world represented by the ship, with its weblike overlay of arbitrary legal minutiae, is still basically at the mercy of the turbulent atavistic forces that originally molded the human spirit. To both Artaud and Audiberti the true expression of human nature is the phenomenon of the Malay native running amok, slashing without regard through the gradually woven net of "civilized" conventions. Only Amédée in a sense escapes. Although he too dies, he dies by his own choice, by making an existential decision and declining any longer to be bound up and batted back and forth by directions that do not concern him as a separate individual. Amédée is the rebel-hero of whom Camus speaks. He finds his death—and, paradoxically, his freedom at the same time—by taking his stand and saying thus far will he permit himself to be driven and no furthur. (pp. 76-7)

In *Opéra parlé* Audiberti again writes of his belief in the latent power of paganism. Here he describes the eclipse of paganism by Christianity as being a voluntary and temporary one. Set in the ninth century, A.D. the play tells of the cutting of a straight highway through the depths of a forest in eastern France. This straight road symbolizes the ascendancy of Christianity, with its mute promise of a definite destination at the end, over the mysterious tangled forest of druidic paganism. It is the triumph of the ordered over the arcane, of the highway over the labyrinth. The builder of the highway has under his care a young girl who had been entrusted to him by the Grand Master of the Pagan order. As the play opens, the Grand Master appears again and takes "a stone both visible and invisible" from between the girl's eyes. . . . This act deprives her of her powers as a pagan goddess. She is now no longer free to merge with the woods and the waters and to communicate with the animals, for she must marry a Christian and subjugate herself and all that she represents to him. The holy oracles have spoken. . . . But the Church of Christ will fall in its turn as well and then the pagan gods will come back from their eclipse. Meanwhile the young goddess must marry a Christian. She obeys and marries Baron Massacre, who embodies the bloody, vengeful, unnatural aspects of Christianity; but the pagan spirit cannot be entirely subjugated. While the girl loses her powers and becomes the wife of the baron, her real lover, a previously exemplary military officer, turns his back on Christianity in disgust at this unjust and incongruous union and becomes a sort of Robin Hoodlike outlaw specializing in the destruction and plunder of churches and monasteries. At the end all three protagonists are killed, as befits the conventions of the tragic melodrama that Auberti uses as his framework for this story on the theme of the immortality of the pagan spirit. (pp. 77-8)

[Audiberti's] point is that the essence of paganism is freedom from arbitrary, socially initiated coercion and that it is therefore closer to the Nature from which man originally sprang and from which he derives his true being. Paganism is not good in itself: it is merely *natural* and therefore inevitable. There is no absolute good in Audiberti's cosmos—only absolute evil and the comparative good that is to be found in not attempting to act against one's nature. In so far as men drift away from their origins, they become progressively more evil. This is the basis of the series of plays Audiberti has written about the problem of evil in society.

His first play of this type, and probably his best-known play, is *Le Mal court* (*The Evil Runs,* 1947). As usual, the plot is unimportant in itself, serving only to illustrate the theme, which is that of the omnipresence and inexorable force of evil. Audiberti uses a conventional fairy-tale plot: beautiful young princess, daughter of an impoverished king, goes to marry rich young king; wicked cardinal intervenes and prevents marriage for political reasons; beautiful young princess heartbroken, etc., etc. Audiberti carries his classic fairy-tale formula only up to a point: the rich young king does not throw the wicked cardinal into an oubliette so that he can marry the beautiful young princess at the end. Instead, the princess, Alarica, finds as the play proceeds that she is, and always has been, ringed around with evil and deceit. Her illusions about the goodness of life and the decency and trustworthiness of people drop from her

one by one in a series of painful shocks. . . . There is absolutely nobody she can trust. Everyone is self-seeking, corruptible, and dishonest because everyone is living and ordering his existence within the context of an artificial and corrupt society. As the series of shocks she is obliged to undergo bludgeon her into an awareness of the true nature of the world, Alarica realizes that she must make her compromise with it if she is to survive as something other than a pawn. She determines to fight evil with evil—to let "the evil run." She deposes her amiable, bumbling old father, disregarding his pleas for filial respect, and resolves to rule with complete ruthlessness. If everything is evil, then the most evil wins.

If evil in *Le Mal court* takes the form of personal deceit, in *La Fête noire, La Logeuse,* and *Les Naturels du Bordelais* Audiberti links it with sex. Sex is for Audiberti a manifestation of elemental Nature. As such it is evil in itself, but evil also arises from its repression, from its transformation in society to something artificial and therefore perverted. This state of affairs brings about a paradox: evil is implicit in repression and perversion, and evil also comes when the long repressed force of sex inevitably breaks out with cyclonic savagery. (pp. 78-80)

Audiberti's most explicit statement of this theme and at the same time far and away his best play is *La Fête noire* (*The Black Feast,* 1948), which is also the most successful and faithful dramatization of the theories of Antonin Artaud. *La Fête noire* takes place in a wild and mountainous region of southern France, where Felicien, the hero of the piece, is the local doctor. Felicien's one desire is to win the love of a woman. But this is precisely the one thing that always eludes him. As the unnatural repression builds up in him, Felicien becomes a sort of perverted superman figure, a symbol of the masculine drive, the motor force behind men's actions, hemmed in by the restrictions imposed on its free outpouring by the laws of civilized society. Audiberti sees Felicien as Superman Bound—and bound so effectively that his ineluctable force can emerge only in a horribly twisted form, maliciously revenging itself on the culture that has fettered it. Felicien's pent-up fury escapes from him and, like an angry genie at last released from his bottle, takes the form of an evil beast that roams the country literally ripping open any woman it meets. At first this ecstatic and elemental fury spends itself on the women who have rejected Felicien, but gradually it eludes his control and becomes an independent scourge to punish all women for their disavowal of sex. This Jack the Ripper-like scourge is not to be taken literally, of course: it is the embodiment of Artaud's "plague," the instinctive force that the drama should express.

The second act of the play is a semifarcical parable about the killing of the beast. The whole countryside is up in arms as a result of the outrages committed, and Felicien is appointed leader of the hunt. The "beast" is cornered in a small square in front of a mountain-side shrine. . . . The "beast" is driven on and turns out to be only a broken-down old goat. The goat is then ceremoniously killed with much blowing of trumpets and sprinkling of holy water, and the only person who recognizes the "beast" for what it is and has the courage to say so is driven off by the soldiers. Just as the bells are beginning to toll in celebration of the death of the "beast," word comes that another girl has been ripped apart in a neighboring village, but nobody takes any notice of this: the "beast" has been officially killed; therefore, any further evidence of its presence is to be ignored.

Audiberti's parable here concerns the gradual suppression by the Church of the natural human sex drives. Through its ritual and liturgy the Church has tried to stifle the natural human impulses and mold the human spirit to an artificial ideal. But this molding process has inevitably been as unsuccessful as the killing of the "beast" in the play. The continual repetition of the forms and rituals, as well as the living repression of Nature in the celibacy of the clergy, has had the effect of numbing the senses of the arbiters of civilized behavior.... (pp. 80-1)

At the end of the play Audiberti changes the atmosphere of his parable from farce to irony. Felicien has become world-famous as the slayer of the beast.... Felicien has grown rich by selling relics of the beast: he is just about to dispose of the beast's eleven thousandth tooth. In short, the beast has become a sort of religious cult.... But the beast has in fact now become real and out of its creator's control: at the end it destroys Felicien himself.

La Fête noire is important in the history of the modern avant-garde drama because it is the most perfect realization of Artaud's theories. Not only does Audiberti use the "plague" (in the form of the destructive beast) as his binding theme, but he also follows Artaud's specifications for involving the spectators in the vortex of emotion. Just before the "beast" is led in to be killed, Audiberti has the following stage direction:

> Brouhaha. The ground shakes under the audience's seats. Green leaves fly through the auditorium. At the back of the stage a hairy, sallow face floats by. It will be quite easy to bring about this rapid apparition.

Here Audiberti directly follows Artaud's suggestions for encircling the audience and involving it in the action.... (pp. 81-2)

It is extremely difficult to form any judgment of Audiberti's work. Some of his plays exemplify more perfectly than any others the theories of the twentieth-century avant-garde drama. However, Audiberti is primarily a poet, and he frequently goes off into lyric flights that are for their own sake rather than for the play's. As a playwright he is distinctly out of his element. His plays are written as if he had carefully read Artaud and had deliberately followed his method in constructing them. They are like textbook examples of the avant-garde drama—lifeless, dry, dispassionate, carefully dovetailed, and laboriously planed. Yet despite his lucid approach, Audiberti is difficult to understand, perhaps more difficult than any other avant-garde dramatist.... Audiberti's obscurity is caused not by his meaning being implied, but by its being abstruse. Like most poets whose minds work easiest in the channels of symbolist verse, Audiberti is essentially a mystic; and mysticism on the stage is hopelessly out of place. The essence of stage writing is clarity, while the essence of mystical writing is its arcane quality. The apparent obscurity of Ionesco, Beckett, and Genet can instantly be made clear by good stage production: the obscurity of mysticism cannot. (pp. 83-4)

George Wellwarth, "Jacques Audiberti: The Drama of the Savage God," in his The Theater of Protest and Paradox: Developments in the Avant-Garde Drama, *New York University Press, 1964, pp. 73-84.*

ALFRED CISMARU

Nineteen-sixty-six marked the twentieth anniversary of Jacques Audiberti's debut in the theater. His *Quoat-Quoat* (1946) enjoyed a *succès de scandale* as great an accomplishment a playwright can hope for since it invariably establishes his reputation. Audiberti's fame has increased ever since, strengthened by one intriguing play after another....

The playwright's position in the development of French contemporary drama, while well established, defies categorization. His comic vision is neither "corpsed" as it is with Ionesco or with Beckett, nor is it imbued with any measurable or distinct hope. But while, according to him, evil is permanent and Eden has been irremediably lost, man is still left with the memory of his former grandeur, of the time when he shared with God some of His divine qualities without yet being a despicable subordinate. This was the epoch of the animal, the fiery, fierce master of Nature whose independence had been nullified once he had allowed himself to be metamorphosed into a human, thus constituting a servile race of beings much like domesticated wolves lured by an artificial safety and enticed into abandoning their boundless freedom in order to become pitiable, chained creatures destined for permanent bondage. (p. 122)

[Audiberti's] early career as a journalist for some twenty years, as author of six books of poetry and sixteen novels, did not fully reveal the intense thinker and the *aficionado* of metaphysics that he showed himself to be in 1946 when his *Quoat-Quoat* was first produced. Having written nineteen other plays since, his theater now finds spectators all over the world.... His reputation is, then, even more established than that of most avant-garde playwrights with whom he shares a devout disrespect for tradition, rules and plot. The wide critical acclaim deluged over him has perhaps been summarized by the renowned literary historian Jean de Beer who declared that "in a few years, Audiberti's works will be in even the most elementary textbooks for the study of the French language." Such praise need not be construed as exaggeration in spite of the dramatist's style which is unashamedly sensual, replete with verbal gymnastics and often frustratingly opaque.... Professors and students are obviously willing to make the extra effort if the text is that of an unquestionable talent.

In the present analysis my concern is not, however, directed towards Audiberti's language. It is rather aimed at a discussion of some of his most representative plays in the light of his perception of man's condition which incorporates both an awareness of the present terrestrial hell and the sweet, worthless memory of a virile, free past, however lost, however elusive now. Situated at the border between myth and reality, these plays point to man's impossible though inflexible position of fallen angels who can neither fully accept nor even partially reject their *status quo* except by means of violence, a delirious pursuit of poetic parodies, monstrous transformations and death.

Quoat-Quoat furnishes a case in point. The hero, Amédée, is sent to Mexico on a seemingly dangerous spying mission. Traveling on a boat to his destination, Amédée ignores his superior's directives concerning discretion and anonymity and falls in love with the Captain's daughter. He is arrested by the Captain and is subsequently condemned to death; but a female passenger reveals that Amédée, is not a secret agent but only a decoy. The hero is pardoned and he could go free; only the assumed role has "stuck," he can no longer be himself, and he chooses to run up on the deck before the unaware firing squad. The ship's Captain, who is perhaps God, defied in his arrangement of a subordinate's existence, decides to destroy the entire vessel (which stands perhaps for life's journey), thus returning the world to its primeval emptiness.

The alternation of farcical treatment with the serious discussion of grave issues such as existence, death, good and evil, makes for an amusingly ambiguous play whose obscurity is difficult to pierce. Amédée, who had agreed to work for the state, lost both his identity and freedom. Much like the animal become man, in spite of the intense recollection of his first self, he can no longer play his former, natural role even when he has a chance to: for once lured into joining another society, another order, another race, there is an unsolvable dichotomy between the new, alien (although progressively more familiar) environment and the memory of a freedom that is all the more regretted since it is now eternally gone. This impulse can only be resolved through death, and Amédée's search for annihilation, understood from this point of view, is poignant. . . . [The captain-god] does not understand . . . that in seeking his own death Amédée had done more than delude his master: he had also mitigated his suffering with the realization that he could choose the time and manner of putting it to an end. The hero's affirmation of his own absoluteness puzzled even divine authority, and the Captain's decision to dissolve the entire ship, including himself, contains perhaps the fantastic suggestion that God, angered not only by man's disobedience but also by man's ability to compete and reaffirm his freedom in one last gesture, realizes the impossibility of a solution that would remain outside of violent, personal and universal extinction. Audiberti's conception of the struggle between man and God could, then, be reduced to a simple combat between the lured and the lurer, with no winners possible and with the end result viewed as an ironic and pathetic draw. (pp. 123-24)

[*Le Mal court*] is another example of Audiberti's predilection for similar themes. Here the main character is the Princess Alarica, a disappointed young girl who allows herself to be seduced. Tricked, Alarica has no recourse but to forget her powerfully pure and indomitable past and become as oppressive as everyone else by indulging with gusto in all types of ruthless activities as ruler of her kingdom of Courtelande.

The play is filled with an atmosphere of chastity and lust, ranging all the way from the naive innocence of the Princess to her later strip tease provocation of a Cardinal and her final conviction that, since *le mal court,* one can only bow to it with all the reverence that an almighty sovereign deserves. . . . The role assigned to her precludes any change, any return to a more blissful, purer past. But the memory of her former independence from evil acts as a consoling springboard from which the opposite extreme, freedom from the good, is viewed as a worthy and attainable replacement. . . . At the end of the play we deduce that, when that stage will be reached, she will turn on herself to perform the ultimate gesture of personal affirmation: suicide. Thus, Alarica's solution is not unlike Amédée's and the Captain's personal and deliberate dissolution.

A re-orchestration of a somewhat analogous theme occurs in *Les Femmes du Boeuf* (1948), Audiberti's most admired one-act piece. Here the author examines the possibility of survival of a human returned to the animal state, and while the farcical elements surpass normal credibility, the verbal embellishments and the imaginative fireworks make our acceptance of the quasi-surrealistic main character perfectly plausible and unreserved. Ox, a rich butcher, shelters no less than thirty women in his home. . . . But the Ox is lonely nevertheless: his weight of 290 lbs. is such that it assures death to one daring enough to approach him. . . . His offspring, through an ironic twist of fate, is the very opposite of his father. He is effeminate, gentle, he likes contemplation and poetry and, unable to stand his father's gigantic force, he flees to the mountains where he lives as a shepherd. Only the Ox's women have taken a fancy to him,

and while the butcher tosses all alone, at night, in his immense bed, his women go to visit the son.

Behind the jesting comicality of events is hidden the author's concern for man's inability to return successfully to his former, more worthy state of complete animality. The Ox, a freak in human terms, has been endowed by Nature with considerable strength and virility. This not only makes him different but it also keeps him apart from the *others* whom, as a human being, he needs as much as does anyone else. An animal in body, a man in spirit, he is condemned to see all of his possessions . . . pass on to a frail and not-too-witty son whose weakness of body and mind provide the very sources of his success. . . . [The] coarse, oversized butcher can hardly be metamorphosed into the brittle poet he would like to be, and when in his final speech he speaks of the one Amazon he will be able to embrace, we are not surprised that he calls her Death, and that the play actually ends with this word. According to Audiberti we have regressed so that there is no place in our human world for the brute strength and sheer corporeality of our happier ancestors. (pp. 124-26)

Audiberti's extreme pessimism, repugnant as it might be, is a constant in his drama. It appears again in *La Fête noire* (1948), a much discussed and obscure full-length play. The hero, Félicien, is a mysteriously attractive man whom, however, no one loves. His frustrated desires have seemingly given birth to a horrible monster that now ravages the region, raping and killing young women. At one point we are even led to believe that the monster is Félicien himself. But the authorities which pursue the killer manage to catch a goat and destroy it, thus thinking that they have eliminated Evil itself. Unaware that perhaps the monster is in man himself, the town's vigilance is relaxed, and the monster can continue, more or less freely, his destructive activities. Félicien himself is threatened by the beast, who later takes on the appearance of Lou Desterrat, the uncle of Alice who gives herself to the hero out of fear of the monster and thinking that the end of the world has come. Jealous and enraged at the sight of his niece in Félicien's arms, Desterrat kills both lovers and the curtain falls, appropriately enough, on many more unanswered questions than the play had begun with. For example, are we to think that there was more than one monster in *La Fête noire*? Indeed that the title pointed to an entire world of beasts engaged in some black, nightmarish feast? Or that all women are the monster, as Alice affirms at one point? Or that the monster is in the organized part of our society, in the authorities which kill the goat? These and many other enigmas are expressly left without explanation, for Audiberti does not think that the role of the artist is to furnish answers, especially since life itself is empty of solutions and replete with puzzling, unsolvable riddles.

But in addition to the vitality and mystery of life which persist in the play, we can also perceive, on close examination, the resemblance which exists between Félicien, the disappointed idealist-monster, and the uncompromising Amédée of *Quoat-Quoat,* the embittered Princess of *Le Mal court* and Le Beouf of *Les Femmes du boeuf.* All four characters betray a metaphysical preoccupation which leads to an extreme effort to find a practicable middle ground between their unchangeable position in life as human beings beset by human problems, and their former, unchained state of beings close to nature and free from the pettiness, prejudices and prevarications that humanity all too often incorporates. (pp. 126-27)

In *La Fête noire* . . . the presence of at least one other monster, Lou Desterrat, would seem to indicate that once the animal has had a taste of humanity, even when he turns monster again, as Félicien does, he cannot hope to be spared by other monsters whose experience with mankind has been more limited. This is also and especially pointed out in the final stage directions which specify that, after the murder, Lou Desterrat "turns, grabs hold of his knife and assumes a defensive position." Does he fear the authorities, or a stronger, less human monster than he is? Or are they and it one and the same? No matter, for Audiberti's fantastically involved suggestions and implications have already awakened and intrigued the spectator's mind to the point where he questions the degree and validity of his own humanity, lest he too be part monster, part human, insecure in his most inner self and doomed like the heroes and heroines he faces. (p. 127)

[In *La Logeuse* (1954)] we meet the female counterpart of the Ox. She is Madame Cirqué, a strong, spirited animal whose greatest desire, that of being possessed and dominated by a man, is destined to frustration just as much as the desire of possession of her predecessor. All men who approach her become shy, weak and effeminate, and end up groveling at the feet of this energetic super-female who, deep inside, is as lonely and insecure as was the Ox. Her need to play her proper, human role as mistress or wife can never be realized because it is always the men to whom she attaches herself that assume the part. But in spite of their futility, her repetitive efforts are pursued throughout the long drama, and as a matter of fact the play ends with still another attempt at a liaison which, however, we suspect, will abort like all the others. The only difference is that, as she shows a room to a new tenant-lover, the threatening noise of fireman's sirens is heard in the distance, and the smell of gas looms in the entire house. Her final remark, "I always get along fine with men," partially muddled by the sirens, points to a bitter and ironic admission of defeat. But as in the Ox's case, her impending death (she makes no move to escape from the imminent danger), is also her liberation.

Audiberti's disturbing conclusions reappear in one of his most noted plays, *La Hobereaute* (1958). The title refers to a small falcon, the hobby, pictured as the spirit of nature, or as Nature herself, and personified in a beautiful, unchained member of the dying Druid religion. The action depicts, in general terms, the struggle between good as represented by Nature in La Hobereaute, and evil as incarnated in the Church. La Hobereaute, the innocent, last vestal of her creed, is ordered by the Druid High Priest to marry Baron Massacre, a powerful member of the new Roman Church. Massacre is described as an evil, hideous criminal, and he contrasts pointedly with the blameless and fair heroine. Moreover, the latter is in love with Lotvy, a courageous and romantic warrior who now must swear an eternal war on the religion that sanctions such a preposterous marriage. . . . Finally captured by Massacre, he is bound to a tree and put to death; whereupon La Hobereaute embraces the dying Lotvy and is herself killed by the Baron who then commits suicide. (p. 128)

The incongruous mixture of comicality and tragedy notwithstanding, *La Hobereaute*'s immense and scandalous success was due not only to Audiberti's unusual images and violent language, but also to the fact that the play synthesizes the author's metaphysical preoccupations more than any of his past dramas. Under the cloak of the familiar theme of man's obsession with love and desire, Audiberti's picture of the ideal animal, Lotvy, turned human and dying, seemingly, as the victim of an all powerful Church, points most efficiently to the futility and inevitability of the combat between the lurer

and the lured. Lotvy, the pure brute whose pure instincts are denied by a malevolent deity, can only find satisfaction in acts of destruction characteristic of the human he had to become: he wages war, burns and rapes (and these are viewed as essentially human actions no animal is ever guilty of) because these are his only means for fighting his rival, Baron Massacre, and for attaining unity with La Hobereaute. Having been lured into loving her even after she married the Baron, even after she herself abandoned her freedom to become human, he is condemned to lose both his former innocence and animalistic dignity. But with all the turpitude and violence of his human role, he still guards within him the memory of a loftier and more exalted past. Unable though to return to it as he is incapable of forgetting his love, he can only seek escape in death, and it is for this reason that he carried his sword to the very castle inhabited by Massacre, unafraid and with full knowledge of the odds involved. Lotvy's crucifixion must then be performed by the Church itself, the least monstrous and most humane body on the face of the earth. Only its power is compromised and diminished by the fact that the time and place are chosen by the victim whose suicidal attempt at regaining his independence raises him, to the elevated heights he used to occupy before the metamorphosis. La Hobereaute herself, who had lost her affinity with and source in Nature, that is to say in the Eden of the animal kingdom, when she agreed to the human marriage with Massacre, must also resort to seeking death in a way that is not dissimilar to that of her lover. Finally, Massacre's own suicide can be viewed as the result of the realization that the grandeur of his two victims was at its highest when they ceased to exist, and if his was ever to equal theirs, he too had to terminate his participation in the human existence and regain, through death, a freer, purer state all too hastily and unwittingly abandoned. (p. 129)

[Audiberti's] personages are humans who try, vainly but valiantly, to return to a more innocent, animalistic state. As such there is little wonder that they often sink into scatophagous activity. But the scandal initially caused by some of the plays has always made way to a critical appreciation of the highest esteem. This appreciation is not only esthetic and does not merely originate in the author's engaging and immobilizing style. It is also and above all an approval of a theater which, however unorthodox, reflects the equally disturbing preoccupations of most contemporary dramatists who try to come to terms with the contradictions and tribulations of our times. But whereas the more recent avant-garde playwrights decreed humanity dead, and the universe a huge, "corpsed" absurdity, Audiberti's work shines with the memory of Eden. His drama is, perhaps, a more valid experiment than one which turns within irremediable nothingness: he looks back, to be sure, but this is a novel direction in a world increasingly ashamed and forgetful of its past and concerned only with the emptiness of the present. (p. 130)

Alfred Cismaru, "Audiberti's Quest for Eden," in Renascence, *Vol. XIX, No. 3, Spring, 1967, pp. 122-30.*

W. F. SOHLICH

Audiberti has created a popular theater by popularizing themes of cultural discontent. The protagonists of his most significant plays, *Quoat-Quoat, Le Mal court, La Fête noire,* and *Opéra parlé,* are haunted by the memory of a remote past when man could give free play to his instincts and live attuned to the cyclical rhythms of the cosmos. Their nightmare is born of the frustrations which the severe restraints of modern civilization impose on them for the sake of "higher" ideals. They are pathetic puppets who are manipulated by politicians or unknown powers and usually prefer death to the life of contemptible underlings. *Quoat-Quoat* takes place on a steamer at sea bound for Mexico. . . . In a series of mis-adventures and incongruous reversals [the hero Amédée] discovers that he is a mere pawn in the game of international intrigue. . . . Alarica, the heroine of *Le Mal court,* is the innocent princess of the imaginary country Courtelande which is what one would call today an underdeveloped country. She is supposed to marry King Parfait of the wealthy Occident. The marriage plans, however, are merely a political subterfuge by which the Occident hopes to force Spain into an alliance. Alarica is being used, like Amédée; but she learns from the vicious ways of the Occident, dethrones her senile father and promises to make her country a formidable adversary of the corrupt Occident. In *La Fête noire* Audiberti condenses historical moments—the rustic primitive, the Christian, and the era of scientific positivism—into a 19th century setting. Félicien, an apparently shy country doctor, is a puppet who is caught between his role as an enlightened scientist who has freed, or so it seems, a remote mountain community from the scourge of a ravaging monster and his own savage instincts. When he realizes that the monster dwells within him and that neither religious purification rites nor scientific progress can exorcise it, he commits suicide. In *Opéra parlé* historical chronology is contracted to an essential moment of ninth century Burgundy, marking the ascendancy of Christianity over Celtic paganism. (pp. 286-87)

Audiberti's plays are structured to convey the emotional stresses of modern life, not to revive the myth of the noble savage. The Aztec culture lives only in the mind of Amédée, Courtelande survives by adopting Western ways, the rustic life of the peasants in *La Fête noire* remains as alien to Félicien as his scientific pursuits, and Celtic paganism is a thing of the past. The dramatic use of primitive cultures simply helps stage the nightmare of characters who experience the pathetic cleavage between the desire to communicate with what is savagely free in them and the rigorously defined social roles to which a sovereign political and civil authority condemns them.

The duress which the protagonists suffer and, ultimately, the violent response they give to the politics of repression, are best illustrated by their pursuit of erotic love. (pp. 287-88)

The plays, however, lack the conviction that even rites consecrated to Satan could reawaken man from the nightmare of modern life. The failure of erotic love, the certainty that the primitive paradise is forever lost, and the overwhelming presence of the accumulated dead weight of a cultural tradition that has uprooted man from nature and alienated him from that part of his personality which dimly recalls his ancient freedom, combine to situate this theater in the mainstream of the absurdist drama.

As a playwright, however, Audiberti is not as innovative as Beckett, Ionesco, or Genet. He prefers a neo-classical form—*La Fête noire, Le Mal court,* and *Opéra parlé* are three act plays, *Quoat-Quoat* a one acter—and although he frequently employs stunning visual and gestural effects, he relies primarily on dialogue to convey meaning. The abstractness of the themes of his major plays attests to his indifference to formal problems and the bird's eye view which he has of the human comedy to his personal removal from what he calls the nightmare of modern life. He does not invent but rather popularizes themes of cultural malaise which unmistakably reveal the influence of

Nietzsche and Freud, Georges Bataille and Antonin Artaud, and even Michelet. As a result, his drama appears slightly contrived. Yet the extraordinary power of his language, the sense of freedom and passion which it discloses while naming the horror of history and the futility of life, compensate more than adequately for the conventionality of the themes. Scathing parody of administrative jargon, earthy popular speech and slang, sensitive lyrical passages and breath-taking incantations combine to create a dense, almost opaque, style that has been matched only by such virtuosi as Rabelais, Hugo and Céline. Audiberti, like no other modern French playwright, has rediscovered an almost childlike joy in the act of creation. He approaches writing as pure play, as Huizinga understands it, as ". . . a free activity standing quite consciously outside 'ordinary' life as being 'not serious', but at the same time absorbing the player intensely and utterly." Audiberti associates the free activity of play with an ecstatic state produced by speaking and conceives of the act of literary production as a deliberate break with history, or what Huizinga calls ordinary life. . . . (pp. 290-91)

The hope which language holds out for Audiberti can neither be entirely explained by his occult belief in the incantatory power of words, nor can the authenticity of this hope be entirely refuted by allegations of mystification. A detached scepticism toward facile solutions of the difficulty of living and an almost blind drive to realize the potentialities for living collide to create a verbal phantasmagoria with restlessly shifting and clashing phantasms which are tenuously related to each other by the anxiety and the joy which give birth to them. In play Audiberti transcends the zones of diabolical control. As a virtuoso of the word he conquers his freedom in that intermediate zone of make-believe between a hostile world, which his characters refuse, and the primitive paradise, which they only know as longing. The inflation of language, however, also tends to abolish language itself. The total sensorial impact of his theater acts on the configuration of speeches, metaphors, and images like a vortex which blurs formal distinctions. . . . But words have a history. They are not innocent; they denote and connote something. The spoken word, however, especially when it is part of a rhythmic sequence, can become an adequate equivalent of cosmic forces, which surge and subside, never cease to be and yet devour their own substances in the eternal spectacle of birth and death. The spoken word is not a thing like the written word. It does not persist as a sign in space. It has material qualities and dies like any biological organism. Its form of temporality is duration. Each spoken word pertains to an immediate past and projects simultaneously into an immediate future as part of a tonal sequence. Thus in speaking the speaker always experiences the uniqueness of his here and now; he is always in the unfolding texture of duration.

That is the triumph of the player over the playwright. While his drama attests to the tragic dissociation of inner aspirations and reality, of social and private speech, Audiberti the manipulator and mystic of the word experiences joy and presence in the conquest of that reality by a constantly renewed act of self-creation. This verbal victory, however, is Pyrrhic since it is won at the expense of dramatic content. Even the plays discussed here suffer somewhat from an overly abstract and indifferent formulation of dramatic tension and character relations. The frequent recourse to historically remote settings also suggests that the playwright has difficulties in creating a contemporary theater with a contemporary setting. His early plays are good because the playwright is still concerned with the necessities of his medium. But *Cœur à cuir* (1956) and *Le*

Soldat Dioclès (1956) are significantly radio plays—a theater of pure sound—and *Les Patients,* which sets to the music of Marcel Mirouze the theme of the permanence of war and the refusal of the owner of a curiosity shop to get involved, is a *poème à voix.* When Audiberti returns to the stage with contemporary settings in 1962, with *Pomme, Pomme, Pomme* . . . and *La Brigitta,* . . . his increasing detachment from the human situation through an esthetic of gratuity has become only too apparent. Dadou, the Adam figure in *Pomme, Pomme, Pomme,* is a play-actor. As long as he writes songs exclusively for the joy of singing he obtains a measure of happiness. In *La Brigitta* a motor scooter serves as a means of liberation from the nightmare. (pp. 296-97)

W. F. Sohlich, *"The Theater of Jacques Audiberti: The Player and the Playwright,"* in Revue des langues vivantes, *Vol. XLIII, No. 3, 1977, pp. 286-97.*

WENDY SCOTT

Is it a voice from the grave we hear echoing through the lines of Jacques Audiberti's most oft produced play, *La Hobereaute,* or is it simply that, to the delight of his admirers and the despair of his detractors, this prolific writer has refused to lie down and die? . . . [Those] hostile critics who predicted the instant demise of a playwright at least one of whose plays had been produced almost every year in Paris since 1946 have been proved wrong. The battle between enthusiastic admirers and bewildered critics, which characterised the 1950's and 60's, seems now to have died down and the reviewers have returned to those earlier, familiar descriptions of Audiberti as innovator, manipulator of words, latter-day Victor Hugo. (p. 125)

Anything which Audiberti has discovered beyond his mortal existence is unlikely to have appalled him as much as did conditions in his life-time. He spent over thirty-five years writing esoteric verse, long, turgid novels, semi-autobiographical stories, diverse essays and plays which range from vaudeville to poetic avant-garde. Yet the common objective of all his works was to portray a universe which was a profoundly personal one, but which was immense in its implications. Human life, according to Audiberti, and he shares this obsession with Artaud, was composed of 'le mal', in the sense both of evil and of suffering. There are two classes of individual in Audiberti's world, the torturers and their victims. Torturers for him were people like soldiers, policemen, doctors and scientists, all of whom try to impose their will on their weaker fellow men. Sex and violence were two important aspects of human behaviour through which suffering could be caused. . . .

Escape through death is no answer to the evils of the world as seen by Audiberti. But [*La Hobereaute* suggests] . . . an alternative, possible means of escape and that would be through pursuit of a pure and simple innocence, such as that experienced by the Pagans of old. Audiberti saw the pre-Christian era as a time of perfect communion with nature, before man became 'civilised'. Elsewhere, Audiberti had already demonstrated his further affinity with Artaud in a marked preference for paganism and a horror of things modern. . . . In *La Hobereaute,* whose plot had already been developed in *Carnage,* a novel of 1942, we witness the confrontation between a primitive water-sprite, the hobby bird of the title, and all the aspects of modern civilisation, including Christianity, which are gradually impinging on the tangled, pagan forests and are symbolised by a new federal road. The fairy creature, whose physical passion

is in perfect communion with the elements of air, earth and water embodies purity and innocence.

As with all characters in Audiberti's works, her innocence does not remain intact for long. Maître Parfait, the only remaining pagan priest in this Christian ninth century, realises he has to submit to the inevitable accession of Christianity, so agrees to marry his goddess of Nature to a wicked and corrupt Christian. He hopes that by making her become flesh he will get his revenge on the Catholic Church. . . . He forces her to marry the mean and disgusting baron Massacre and to foresake her love for the gentle, romantic Lotvy. So 'la hobereaute' is a little like the water-sprite in Giraudoux' *Ondine* who also marries a human being whom she fails to change, but it is a far cry from the stupidity and ignorance of Giraudoux' Hans to Audiberti's evil Massacre. (p. 126)

It is not religious faith as such which Audiberti is attacking through this play, indeed there is a kind of spiritual communion between the heroine and Lotvy after death at the end, but it is rather the iniquities of any organised religion. The baron Massacre represents the vindictive aspects of Christianity and the sugary lies of politics and all human relations. He pretends to repent of all his notorious murders and rapes, yet continues to behave promiscuously and violently after his marriage to 'la hobereaute'. She sinks into a deep melancholy and the effect on the young Lotvy, who loves and has lost her, is even more striking. So disillusioned is he with the Christian Church, for all it has done to the woman he loves, that he throws himself desperately into the service of evil and becomes more brutal and vulgar than Massacre himself. . . .

Lotvy's conscious debasement of himself, in order to be on the same level as the woman he loves and to share the misery of the world, has its equivalent in many of the main characters of Jacques Audiberti's plays. There is the suggestion that, given the existence of human weakness, it is essential for man to indulge in the iniquities of the flesh before he is ready to escape into a divine state. Even the baron Massacre becomes infuriated by 'la hobereaute's acceptance of his crude ways, by what he calls her 'lack of Christianity'. He cannot even provoke her by pawing her maid before her very eyes, and this makes him feel even more guilty. . . . (p. 127)

All of Audiberti's principal characters follow a similar career: they begin as privileged and enchanted beings, living in a kind of religious trance with exceptional senses or knowledge: they debase themselves to enter the world of ordinary men, they indulge in sex and every kind of human weakness and sin; and, finally, there is sometimes a promise that they will transcend the world again and return to their former, mysterious and heavenly realm. The most obvious case of this need to traverse evil in order to arrive at true purity is probably Alarica in *Le Mal court.* The title of this play . . . signifies not only that evil is running riot, but also the implied wish that it should be as short-lived as possible.

This play too, like the majority of Audiberti's plays, has a historical setting with fictitious names but main events which imitate fact. This is one of several plays which suggest that Audiberti was influenced to some extent by Ghelderode's theatre, with its gloomy historical settings peopled by malformed human beings, often on crutches. . . . But the historical allusion is by the way. As the Cardinal says in the play: 'le passé a moins d'importance que l'avenir', and Alarica is a most modern dramatic creation. When the curtain first goes up, she appears the typical, listless adolescent. But she soon belies this traditional realism through her unusual language and her increasingly extraordinary behaviour. Never was there a purer nor more innocent soul than hers at the beginning of the play. Yet, even then, she realises something, as if in a child's nightmare, of the horrible bestiality of man. . . . Alarica follows the same path as that taken before her by Artaud's Beatrice in *Les Cenci,* at first appalled and later attracted by absolute evil. Images of man versus beast, black versus white, abound. The very struggle between Good and Evil, which is waged in the background of all Audiberti's writings, is here actually fought out in concrete form on the stage. And Evil wins.

Instead of trying to suppress the wild beast which is sexual passion, Alarica wants it to run free; instead of abhorring male eroticism, she welcomes a man into her bed at the first opportunity. In an amazing incantation, she describes and exposes her body to her entire retinue. . . . [Only] after everyone is profoundly shocked by this behaviour, so unseemly for a queen, does she suddenly feel cold and ashamed. . . . Finally, she achieves what she wants, which, as she tells the spy at the beginning of Act III, is 'que la réalité vienne', that she cease to live her former, false life. She is now unutterably cruel to her dear old father and she debases herself for a cheap love.

Alarica, then, like Lotvy and 'la hobereaute', has chosen to embrace the evils of human behaviour with welcoming arms. She has decided not to try to ignore, nor to try to reform, nor like Aldine to try to escape from the hell on earth, but rather to outdo and outshock the sinners around her. One can only speculate as to how far Jacques Audiberti, while decrying the unacceptable acts of his fellow human beings, developed his theory of the need to experience the world of flesh before achieving transcendence as a form of excuse for the indiscretions he committed in his own life-time.

What *can* be established is that he arouses our sympathy for characters whose weaknesses often border on perversity. Félicien in **La Fête noire** is a Provençal Jack the Ripper, yet Audiberti depicts him as a lonely individual, searching for love. The black beast is separate from Félicien; it is the exterior and concrete image of his repressed sexual passion and that it should come into being at all is the fault of the many women who have refused his advances. Two peasant girls, Alice and Mathilde, represent the two different faces of Woman, the romantic and the sexual, and Félicien is unable to communicate with either. He repels Alice with his vulgar and presumptuous talk of sex and humiliates Mathilde by over-idealising Woman and thereby making her feel ashamed of her physical instincts. All attempts at love fail, according to Audiberti, because of the inescapable paradox that a man's love for woman, however idealistic, is always accompanied by base desire. The Beast, as this play illustrates, is in every one of us and outlives any individual man. . . . (pp. 127-28)

If there are visions of a world without God and without morals throughout Audiberti's writings, there are also frequent references to the Christian religion and much evidence of an underlying need in the writer of a belief in God. The proximity of death in 1965, as we can tell from his final diary **Dimanche m'attend,** made the need more urgent. It increased his love of his fellow men and his desire that Christ should return and free men from the evil and suffering in the world. But this firm return to Christianity is foreshadowed by some images in the plays. In **Le Cavaliseul,** for example, Mirtus goes off in search of Christ and hopes to go beyond Man or God. It is Mirtus' father, though, who comes closest to this ideal state through a vague dream, a distant, poetic vision of a pool of water with the scent of 'la cendre et le rosier'. There is a suggestion of a possible escape from the bonds of flesh and of discovery of a spiritual love and peace, wherein the artificial barriers between different religions melt away.

The transcendent, heavenly state described by Mirtus' father seems to represent a nearness to God. Although Audiberti experienced such peace occasionally in the contemplation of nature or in the appreciation of literature, and at the end of his life in visiting churches, only his most privileged heroes manage to transcend the evil of the world and it may be that this was only possible beyond death. (p. 129)

Wendy Scott, "'Afin que de l'enfer je sorte': Jacques Audiberti Revisited," in Modern Languages, *Vol. LXI, No. 3, September, 1980, pp. 125-30.*

CONSTANTIN TOLOUDIS

Audiberti never felt the need to publish his confessions in the manner of Rousseau or Stendhal. For all his obsessions with profound ethical and theological questions, he managed to keep his intimate self away from window dressing sensationalism inherent in the genre that appealed to his illustrious predecessors. What he did feel compelled to assert as part of his calling is the function of chronicling events of his real life in the course of an ever transforming, dynamic narrative movement, conferring mythical status and glamour of a literary nature to the most banal, most platitudinous and dull of all texts: The autobiographical anecdote. (p. 42)

[To the extent] that the author's writings are accountable in terms of conscious, intentional projects, one can clearly distinguish a category of texts in which Audiberti's predominant concern is autobiographical in nature, or of a nature that he would consider *à clé.* Sometimes the narrative is almost entirely without a plot: **Cent jours** and **Dimanche m'attend** are written as diaries. The former chronicles a well marked period of the author's life: July 3 to October 18, 1948, the period during which Audiberti interrupts his life in the capital to spend a hundred days in his native Antibes. The title of the book is explained explicitly as a reference to Napoleon's return from Elba in 1815. However, there is little in the corresponding events that can be even remotely considered convincing as a reasonable analogy. The latter is also presented as a diary but it offers no definite information on chronology. Neither is it limited to covering any specific period. It includes reminiscences from the author's early childhood as well as scenes from his very recent stay in the clinic, in Issy-les-Moulineaux, during the illness from which, the following year, he was to succumb. There is no plot, no chronological order in the narration. Audiberti reminisces about the main events of his life and about the people who influenced his career as a writer. . . . (p. 42-3)

More or less in the same category are **Urujac, La Nâ, . . . Monorail.** Unlike **Cent jours** and **Dimanche m'attend,** these books attempt to maintain a distance between author and narrator. In a thin disguise of fiction, the identity of the narrator is not directly linked with Audiberti, but even to the uninitiated reader, the anecdotal fabric of the narrative is a transposition of real episodes and an account of real experiences from the author's life.

Urujac is based on a series of events that took place during Audiberti's trip to the mountainous region of Auvergne. The narration involves a rudiment of a plot and a somewhat more elaborate thematic development in connection with the reality of the man of Urujac, the reality of prehistoric man which is sought in this remote mountain village. In a constant shifting between myth, magic and dream involving a group of researchers on a scientific expedition, Audiberti uses the fictional situation as a pretext for a meditation on a primitive state of the human species, very close to nature, having the purity of its forces.

In *La Nâ*, the narrator is introduced at first as a writer living in Paris. The narration is in the first person and the anecdotal content here also consists of autobiographical notations. One day, a heavy sculpture of a head carved in stone was sent to the narrator's hotel room, left on the floor, without an explanation. The mysterious object soon became an irritant. The permanence of its presence became a constant reminder of all his little anxieties, his fears, his failings and his fatigue. And he could see no hope for relief until he decided to take a trip to the mountains. Predictably, this departure is experienced as an attempt at an escape toward some sort of spiritual liberation and renewal. But the attempt does not succeed. . . . The memory of the stonehead persists, his "inner demons" keep reemerging, even when he reaches Antibes, on a visit to his birthplace. . . . There is very little plot as such. Moreover, the few anecdotal sections of the book are haunted by digressions. The first person narration keeps returning to a meditative mood, intermittently becoming reflective, analyzing the narrator's involvement in the writing process. (pp. 43-4)

As for *Monorail,* instead of an anonymous narrator who stays outside of the tale he weaves, acting mostly as a privileged "witness," Audiberti invents a character who becomes the protagonist and thus an object of analysis and observation. Thus the narrative unfolds in the third person, consisting of an emotional self-analysis, while recounting the key events of his life: his childhood and early youth in Antibes, his difficult beginnings in Paris, his first timid encounters with women, his "love life" and his sad wreck of a marriage. In analyzing the protagonist of *Monorail,* Audiberti shows how lucid he can be in analyzing his own weaknesses, his own handicaps: his extreme sensitivity, his timidity, his inability to free himself from the clutches of authority exercised by others. Here again, there is no plot. Only a series of "chronicles" and "digressions." *Monorail,* like *Urujac* . . . and *La Nâ,* is only slightly fictionalized autobiography. (pp. 44-5)

It is in Audiberti's nonautobiographical novels that we find his best. . . . [When] the shift of emphasis away from the limited perspective of the author's subjective, intimate world of individual consciousness is unambiguously adhered to, the narrative reaches its ultimate amplitude, its exemplary performance. The novels in this instance are of a more "finished" quality. The reader is introduced to representational axes of time and space on a much bigger scale. The decor is enriched through description of travel and changing landscape, often in far away, exotic lands in a foreign country or in mere fantasy land. The anecdote explodes as it strives to go beyond the provinces of the real and the possible, to deal with dream, with the occult or with the supernatural.

Themes and arguments are stated in fiction that the narrative institutes by following two major strategies, more or less consistently. One strategy consists in building a story, with a significant degree of complexity, around a small incident or problem / situation involving either one individual or a couple. The other strategy involves the conception of a grand design, develops into allegorical system, engages collectivities, assumes the proportions and the movement of an epic and results

in a text which articulates a message of wider philosophical implications.

Novels composed by the first strategy, which most often have as principal setting the city of Paris, include [*Carnage, Le Maître de Milan, Les Jardins et les Fleuves*]. . . . (pp. 45-6)

In *Carnage,* the setting at first is the Jura region, the "land of lakes and precious stones" and "spectacle makers." The text of the third person narrative is divided into segments intended as more or less distinct tableaux. In a succession of episodes unfolds the drama of Carnage, a man "full of violence," moved by wild, primitive forces, and of Médie, alert and intelligent, but tender and innocent . . . having grown up like a naiad, by the lake, in almost wild freedom. In her late twenties, she dreams above all of a blissful fulfillment of her femininity. Then the eldest of the Gomais brothers, Carnage, enters slowly into her life. . . . Médie is presented at first as a strangely primitive creature, wild but gentle, symbol of natural purity and vulnerability. But her marriage to Carnage transforms her. In the second half of the novel, the setting is a working class neighborhood, in the eleventh Arrondissement, in Paris, where the couple takes up residence and runs a laundry. Médie gradually turns into a shrewish matron. In his native environment, Carnage was the incarnation of cruel, savage animal forces. . . . But marriage "civilizes" him, turns him into a moneyed, bourgeois businessman. *Carnage* is one of Audiberti's most impressive accomplishments, owing principally to the rugged beauty of his poetic language.

In *Le Maître de Milan,* the pivotal involves again a couple and an unfortunate, sad love story. The "Master of Milan" is Genio Stragglioffon, governor of Lombardy, active, intelligent, accomplished, powerful. He is fifty-two, firm-muscled, well-dressed, married—but hardly in love with Bianca, his wife of twenty years. . . . One day he met Franca. Dressed shabbily, she had a wretched appearance and was "neither pretty nor beautiful." She also had an infirmity: she was dumb. But she was eighteen and desirable; the very first moment he saw her, behind the closet door, in a tiny utility room, at the end of an aisle in the governor's palace, he was overcome by the urge to possess her. Conveniently, the young girl showed no fear, and seemed rather eager. There was no contest, no resistance. A consciously shared complicity in an act of otherwise plain, uncomplicated lust—only the encounter was to become the beginning of an affair. Franca lived under the supervision of Mathilde Bracciapelli, her aunt. . . . Though pathologically sensitive to the dangers consequent to her niece's exposure to male company, she suspects nothing of the sordid affair in which the threat becomes so real with the man involved being her employer. And this is precisely what disturbs Genio. As his uneasiness grows so does his determination to find a way of informing the unsuspecting aunt of the nature of his relationship with the niece. . . . Mathilde will learn his secret simply by reading a novel, *Omerta,* written by him to meet the special needs arisen in the circumstance. . . . According to plan, it was arranged so that the book fell into Mathilde's hands which—also according to plan—she then read and understood. To no one's surprise, Genio eventually has had to part with Franca. Life had a lot more in store for him however. His political fortunes already show signs of an upswing: he is about to become the next Minister of the Interior. (pp. 46-8)

[*Les Jardins et les fleuves*] also deals with a man's obsession. . . . The core anecdote around which the novel is built has for its ingredients a set of unusual circumstances that end up haunting the relations between a father and his illegitimate daughter. Jean-Désiré Lazerme, an actor and director/producer of an itinerant theater company, is the protagonist. Armène Béchart was the fruit of a brief involvement with Chatain Béchart, wife of a compulsive swindler, during one of the latter's entanglements with the law. Béchart never suspected his wife's indiscretions but Armène, well before reaching her teens, knows that Jeandé is her natural father. One day while on a tour in Algeria, Jeandé receives a visit from his daughter and before long, circumstances conspire to make it impossible for him to prevent his underaged daughter from following the theater company to Saudi Arabia. In a society of strict rules of moral conduct, Jeandé will soon be forced to consent to a marriage ceremony in the French Consulate, in order to legitimize the girl's cohabitation with him in a country where he had not dared disclose that she was a bastard. This way, the girl, frequently stricken by fits of nervous hypertension, complicated by asthma and hay fever, would have the comfort of his tender care and his constant supervision. And this is how Jeandé arrived at the alarming realization that his destiny had an unmistakable resemblance to that of Molière. By his own assessment, his feelings for his daughter grow in a way that appears less and less simple.

In France he continues to be disturbed, anxiously searching for a way out, when he discovers that his marriage is not legally in order. When at that point he succeeds in persuading Armène to marry one of her suitors (who happened to be a rich Chilean), and leave the country, Jeandé is inexplicably thrown into the despair of a deep, hurting loneliness. In retrospect, memories of intimate moments he spent with her are developing into bewitching, tyrannizing desires. How will the inferno of this ambivalent passion end? Will it kill him? Will he fulfil his destiny by dying of it, on the stage, like Molière? . . . The delicate, tender treatment of incest in this book constitutes a telling statement about the capacity of love of the great performers in the theatrical world, of geniuses like Molière, Chaplin, or Jouvet to whom the novel is dedicated. (pp. 49-50)

Novels composed by the second Audibertian strategy tend to take hold on a wider geographical setting. Audiberti's ideas on religion and theology find their most eloquent and most rigorous expression in these novels. . . . It is also by this approach to narrative fiction that he makes his most convincing statement as a man of letters: He confirms his fatalistic attachment to poetic language as an end in itself while at the same time displaying his most emphatic anticlassical bias by stressing expansiveness over reduction, movement and continuous permutation over fixity and static design, in any pretext of mediation or representation through language.

The basic trends of Audiberti's narrative style are manifest most prominently in his very first, most truly seminal and by far richest and most ambitious novel, *Abraxas*. As an author's first, it is exemplary in every respect. A third person narrative, it integrates conventional spatio-temporal axes chosen for the effect of didactic abstraction, with a rhythm and tone that promote an overall effect of epic movement. The action is set in Italy, Spain and Portugal, in the fifteenth century. Both space and time are evoked expressly to stress the transitional character of a certain period in history. The person lies between the Middle Ages and the modern era, which is about to be inaugurated into the Renaissance. It is a world which is also about to "explode" and expand westward by exploration and discovery of new lands. The central character is Satto Caracasio. At thirty-six, a recognized portrait painter of prelates, he is burning with a mysterious desire for spiritual uplift and renewal. His best chance at it comes when he obtains from the archbishop of Ravenna the privilege of escorting the ashes of Saint Apollon to the village of Hertombreros, in far away Galicia. The religious symbolism, the allegorical character of the voyage, the tone and texture of the language in the tale recounting the adventures of the intrepid hero from Ravenna, amount to an eloquent, almost exhaustive exposé on the lore of Audibertian themes and devices: the plethora of anecdotal motifs, the changing of narrative angles of approach, the digressive descriptions, the long periods, the poetic imagery, and that familiar Audibertian idiolect here adjusted for the dicta of ceremonial characters in ritualistic, epigrammatic or incantatory statements of scholars and clerics, Catholic princes and Jewish wisemen, slick monks and thieving gypsy tribal chieftains, now ominously grave, now humorous or burlesque.

In the end of his adventure, at the peak of success, having grown in wisdom and power, proclaimed Admiral of Portugal, Satto feels nevertheless an exile, a prisoner. Though he is "cut off from Ravenna, his mother," the time has come for him to return. . . . The voyage will come to an end, with the yearning for *nostos* finally undermining the will to move on and to "conquer." *Abraxas* may or may not be "one of the most beautiful books of our times," as Michel Giroud suggested in 1973. It certainly is much less esoteric than its title suggests. Other than prefiguring the basics in Audibertian thought and stylistic inventions, it underlines most effectively the epic character of the author's literary enterprise, definitely in the area of the novel, if not in everything he wrote. . . . (pp. 51-2)

Constantin Toloudis, in his Jacques Audiberti, *Twayne Publishers, 1980, 154 p.*

Thomas (Louis) Berger

1924-

American novelist, editor, short story writer, and dramatist.

In his fiction Berger focuses through satire on characters who attempt to survive life's comic absurdities, paradoxes, and myths. Berger's work defies categorization, evidencing his ability to write fiction in a number of different styles and genres. He parodies the Western in *Little Big Man* (1964), futuristic fiction in *Regiment of Women* (1973), detective fiction in *Who Is Teddy Villanova?* (1977), medieval romance in *Arthur Rex* (1978), and utopian fiction in *Nowhere* (1985). Berger has stated that his intention for writing in different styles is "to celebrate [a genre], to identify and applaud its glories." He has also written several novels that comment on the human condition from a contemporary, middle-class American perspective. Among the distinguishing features of Berger's novels are his black humor and his interest in themes related to language. This latter concern, according to Brooks Landon, "unifies [Berger's] . . . apparently unalike novels into one of the most sustained and systematic investigations of language in American literature."

Berger's first two novels, *Crazy in Berlin* (1958) and *Reinhart in Love* (1962), and two later works, *Vital Parts* (1970) and *Reinhart's Women* (1981), detail the life of Carlo Reinhart from World War II through the late 1970s. Reinhart is depicted through much of the series as a failure in personal relationships and business ventures who is susceptible to the unscrupulous manipulations of others. Despite Reinhart's absurdly comic and emotionally painful experiences, he maintains hope. In *Crazy in Berlin,* Reinhart is introduced as an idealistic young soldier who is dismayed by the horrors he witnessed in World War II and by the corruption he observes in postwar Europe. The other novels relate Reinhart's attempts to establish his identity amidst the social changes in postwar American society. *Reinhart's Women* details the middle-aged protagonist's difficulties with women and the success and greater self-esteem he gains through his mastery of the culinary arts. Critical reception to these works has varied, but Guy Davenport views the series as "the definitive comic portrait of our time."

Many critics consider *Little Big Man* to be Berger's finest novel. In this work he parodies the Western through the picaresque adventures of Jack Crabb, who observes the local color of the frontier from the perspectives of both the Indian and the white man. Berger demythologizes frontier life and mocks the heroic-epical stance of many Westerns to investigate the elements which contributed to misunderstanding and cruelty between the two cultures. In his parody of the detective genre, *Who Is Teddy Villanova?,* Berger focuses on Russel Wren, a part-time dramatist and "hard-boiled" private investigator who attempts to track down an international villain. Wren also appears in *Nowhere,* in which he travels to a utopian society named Saint Sebastian. In detailing the social and cultural values of Saint Sebastian, Berger satirizes such topics as nationalism, literature, and American social values. Berger parodies literature and myth and investigates such moral themes as evil, love, and truth in *Arthur Rex,* his retelling of the legends of King Arthur.

Language and its effect on individuals is a prominent theme of *Neighbors* (1980) and *The Feud* (1983), two of Berger's

© Jerry Bauer

most critically acclaimed works. In these novels, Berger's protagonists are victimized by linguistic confusion and differing interpretations of reality. *Neighbors* is a Kafkaesque tale in which Berger creates a surrealistic atmosphere and uses black humor to satirize contemporary American social values. In this work, the banal life of a respectable suburbanite is upset by a series of alternately sinister, friendly, and threatening visits from his new neighbors. Michael Malone considers *Neighbors* a "flawlessly crafted morality play, constructed out of the most subtle minutiae of perception and expression." In *The Feud,* two communities become engaged in harrassment and counter-harrassment following the misinterpretation of a casual remark. As in *Neighbors,* themes related to language are developed within a comic context. Two of Berger's novels, *Little Big Man* and *Neighbors,* have been adapted for film.

(See also *CLC,* Vols. 3, 5, 8, 11, 18; *Contemporary Authors,* Vols. 1-4, rev. ed.; *Contemporary Authors New Revision Series,* Vol. 5; *Dictionary of Literary Biography,* Vol. 2; and *Dictionary of Literary Biography Yearbook: 1980.*)

ALAN CHEUSE

With the publication of his 11th novel [*Reinhart's Women*], the prodigiously talented Thomas Berger turns his mordantly comic Reinhart trilogy—*Crazy in Berlin* (1958), *Reinhart in Love* (1962), and *Vital Parts* (1970)—into a world-class series. . . .

The new novel presents Reinhart at 54, serenely sailing into late middle-age. Having divorced Gen a decade before, he now keeps house for dutiful [daughter] Winona, who has dieted her way to become a svelte and highly paid fashion model and her father's sole support. (Meanwhile, [son] Blaine has become a miserly stockbroker with a skitterish wife and two rude children.) That Winona's sexual proclivities run to women is only the first surprise that turns grandfather Reinhart's new life into a comedy of the commonplace.

The mood here is less biting than in the earlier books as Reinhart achieves a "hearty Elizabethan" happiness moving back and forth in a daily round full of devoted daughters, lovers, friends, and neighbors. Berger devotees will notice the evolution, too, of the Reinhart style from a heavily complicated syntax that relied as much upon wit as drama to a plainer, more demonstrative prose.

> *Alan Cheuse, in a review of "Reinhart's Women,"*
> in Saturday Review, *Vol. 8, No. 9, September, 1981,*
> *p. 60.*

BENJAMIN DeMOTT

The words "ennobling" and "masterpiece" occur in [promotional ads for *Reinhart's Women*], and the author is identified as "our greatest living comic novelist." It's the kind of language that also surfaces regularly in literary journalism and in the conversation of excessively serious-minded readers, and the resulting hunt for *profundum*—the "greatest" has to be profound, no?—stimulates a ton of Ph.D. theses. And once the hunt begins, the likelihood of the living writer ever becoming a life-enhancing resource for the folk inevitably declines.

That's a pity, because the Reinhart series deserves to become such a resource. . . .

When first met, in *Crazy in Berlin* (1958), the hero of Berger's Reinhart series was a foot soldier in the Army of Occupation, controlling his weight (200 lbs. plus) and attempting without success to comprehend various middle European historical and political mysteries. *Reinhart in Love* (1962) picked up this hero at his return to civilian life in miserable Ohio, introducing his mindless parents and ghastly bride (Genevieve), and showing him failing at a seedy job (real estate sales) and a creepy higher education on the G.I. Bill. In *Vital Parts* (1970) Reinhart, aged 40, put on poundage but otherwise remained a loser. Enraged by his son Blaine, one of several lemons produced by the assembly-line radicalism of the 60's, saddened by his overweight daughter Winona, nicknamed Baby Whale, nauseated by the ghastly Genevieve, he took refuge from home and family in a fledgling cryonics enterprise. Certain signs hint, at the end of *Reinhart's Women,* the new volume at hand, that the hero may have managed, at 54, to put his downside behind him, but don't bet on it. For most of this book's length Reinhart's chief occupations are keeping house for daughter Winona, who supports him (the former Baby Whale has dieted down into lucrative fashion modeling), caring for his drunken daughter-in-law Mercer (wife of Blaine, the lemon radical, who's now

a Tory stockbroker), and fighting off physical attacks launched by two hateful grandsons and the divorced but pertinacious (and still ghastly) Genevieve.

It's not merely the hero's down-and-outness, of course, that makes him stand forth as representative of the under-represented. It's his peculiar combination of innocence, ignorance, appetite, crudity, moral confusion and readiness to mix it up—before or after options disappear—with the enemy. Reinhart in *Vital Parts* sneaking into a bedchamber to slice off his snotty radical son's dirty locks while the boy sleeps—this is the fellow I prize. Or Reinhart (again in *Vital Parts*) setting up an appointment with the prostitute Gloria and explaining seriously, as to a credit manager, why she should accept a check. . . . Or Reinhart in *Reinhart in Love,* called on to rouse his macho monster of a father-in-law, who's asleep in the living room, and discharging the duty with a carefully screened, satisfyingly powerful, openhanded shot to the back of the man's head.

Violence? You better believe it. There's nothing in the Reinhart series to match the carnage in *Little Big Man* (1964), Berger's report on the rearing of Jack Crabbe by Native American Cheyennes. And *Little Big Man* has to be ranked as this author's best single book—a unified, hard-driving tale that opens with the destruction of a wagon train by an Indian band looking for a pot of coffee, ends with mad General Custer at his Last Stand firing his "Bulldog Pistols [in a] classic stance," and, in between, seldom dwindles into tranquillity.

But Little Big Man is remote from the ocean of contemporary life, whereas Reinhart is up to his curled lip in same. *Reinhart's Women* opens with the discovery, by the unemployed hero, that the woman he is wooing is involved in a lesbian connection with his daughter Winona. The balance of the story is about Reinhart's ascent, aided by his daughter's girlfriend, who's a food company executive, to jobs as a supermarket demo chef and as a TV morning-show kitchen act. (Reinhart has improved the hours of middle life by becoming a good cook.) The best scenes are those recording the hero's attempts to cope with the beastly grandsons and various supermarket and morning show apparatchiks. But from start to finish, we're in an America thoroughly recognizable to anyone who climbs down from gift Arabian horses long enough to run his own traffic lights.

Arby's and K-Marts and McDonald's America, that is—mall and condo and underground-garage America wherein the only intimations of salvation come when, out to lunch with Reinhart at a place called Winston's, you're served (amazing!) a passable lamb stew. Berger knows this world to the insides of its disposable placemats. . . . He knows about Jack, the over-the-hill movie star who tours "Song of Norway" in Nowhere Cities and dies unattended in the men's room of a heart attack, and about Edie, the extra tall gal who works in a bowling alley and buys slippers of synthetic fur that resemble big bear claws and are called Abominable Snow Shoes.

Most important, he knows that, speaking unsentimentally, forbearance and fierce realism are all that many inhabitants of this world can muster in the line of survival technique. In a culture of junk schools, phoney work, cash nexus "relationships," and unreasonable ambitions, what exactly can a grandfather in good health say to a 6-year-old grandson who's trying to kill him with a cuestick except that the lad should wait a while till he's tougher? "There's a thing you should know about being nasty," Reinhart says calmly, while fending off the attacking child, "You should be big enough or smart enough to get away with it without being treated even more nastily in return. Otherwise you're a fool.'' (pp. 9, 28)

Possibly the simple secret of Reinhart's value is just this: The fellow has hunkered down here in the U.S. of A. He's stuck it. He is a man of no standing growing up stunted, naturally, blowing it in a thousand helpless ways, dreaming on into late middle age of the coup that will turn him overnight into a Somebody, knowing it's not in the cards, knowing (in totally unsystematic fashion) that They, The Managers, have more or less stolen his humanity, yet working hard to avoid being needlessly cruel to anyone. The messy disorder of the books he inhabits, the looseness of their composition, the flatness—these become, finally and mysteriously, emblems of parts of his own nature.

Yet often in their cheerfully harsh pages you catch a faint echo of voices you can hardly believe are audible anywhere on earth: crazy-marvelous voices out of our precious past, unpressed militiamen, sauced-up Green Mountaineers, Yankees building up fury at the massacre of their hope on a village green, daring to tell themselves that failing to fight the exploiter and oppressor means betraying their history. What is it but cowardice to go on eating this muck? Sealing off that sound in a library carrel, in exchange for the tinsel of Comic Greatness, strikes me as some kind of ultimate ripoff. (pp. 28-9)

> *Benjamin DeMott, "Further Adventures of a Loser,"*
> *in* The New York Times Book Review, *September*
> *27, 1981, pp. 9, 28-9.*

PEARL K. BELL

In one of the strangest literary careers in recent memory, Berger has set himself the task of mastering many different genres—Western, private eye, hardboiled crime documentary, Arthurian legend, science fiction (with a message about sex roles), and, in the recent *Neighbors* [1980], Kafkaesque fable about motiveless harassment and victimization. Yet that witty and mordant voice is clearly heard in only four of the eleven novels Berger has published over the past twenty-two years.

This group stands outside his experimental forays into various genres, and deals with an engaging creature named Carlo Reinhart, the protagonist of Berger's first novel, *Crazy in Berlin* (1958). He is a huge, intellectually eager but unfinished G.I. racketing around the American Zone just after the end of the war, and he turns up again at irregular intervals in *Reinhart in Love, Vital Parts,* and now *Reinhart's Women.* That first novel was an ambitious mixture of high moral earnestness and knockabout farce, in which the callow twenty-one-year-old Reinhart, at once guilty and brashly assertive about his German ancestry, forces himself to think honestly, for the first time in his life, about his unexamined prejudices toward the Jews, his ambiguous feelings about the Germans, and the sober lessons of the war. Unlike his fellow-soldiers, most of whom are high-rolling entrepreneurs in the black market, Reinhart wants to hear out the ordinary Germans he meets, and he thus becomes the recipient of some bizarre confessions that may or may not be true.

But on another level of *Crazy in Berlin,* beyond the obsessive monologues about Jewishness and Germanness, Reinhart's escapades displayed Berger's exuberant talent for ridiculing the military. Though anticipating the mood of *Catch-22,* Berger's novel was much more demanding in language and ideas, which

probably explains why Heller's novel, published three years later, caught the tide of success that Berger missed.

In *Reinhart in Love* (1962), he is mustered out of the Army and comes home to Ohio, where he is constantly entangled in the extravagant lunacies of postwar America. . . . Reinhart no longer gives much thought to the burning issues of political and personal morality that had absorbed him in Berlin; daily life has proved too much for him.

It became brilliantly clear in the next volume, *Vital Parts* (1970), that Berger is a master of satirical farce, instinctively drawn to the mad, the ludicrous, the grotesque. For some perverse reason he has given himself the room farce demands only in this wonderfully funny novel, which converts the world of Reinhart into gleeful caricature which never lapses into cruelty. (pp. 74-5)

Though the Berger of *Vital Parts,* with its ingenious absurdities and slapstick vitality, might be thought to bear some resemblance to horsemen of the apocalypse like Vonnegut and Pynchon, his sensibility is crucially different. He came closest to their mood in *Crazy in Berlin,* set as it was in a time and place not yet recovered from the insanities of war, but not even there did Berger indulge in the doom-haunted cackling of the absurdists, and in the later Reinhart novels he was too deeply engaged with the comic fate of one good man to reduce him to a prophetic symbol of the cataclysm before us. In any case Berger is too quirky and too much of a loner to join any modish chorus. Indeed, in the past decade he has removed himself so reclusively from the literary hurly-burly that, according to one account, his publisher has never met him.

Paradoxically, the tone of *Vital Parts,* even at its most antic, is genial—not a quality one associates with a recluse. But this geniality has led to a bewildering slackness in *Reinhart's Women* [1981]. The farcical episodes have become strained and unfunny, which is perhaps inevitable in a novel whose principal, indeed obsessive, subject is the joy of cooking. And not just boiling and buttering, as Julia Child once characterized the main activity in American kitchens, but the intricate art of French high cuisine. . . .

[Nothing] that happens in the course of *Reinhart's Women* engages Thomas Berger's imagination very deeply—except for the preparation and consumption of all manner of glorious food. Unlike that other zealous celebrant of cooking in fiction, Günter Grass, who was equally generous with recipes and kitchen hints in *The Flounder,* Berger has not bothered to relate his culinary enthusiasm to some loftier and less perishable theme. Food in a novel, however expertly described, offers little food for thought.

In this last book, Berger seems to have closed in upon himself. None of the genre novels has been a parody, and Berger claims to be celebrating each form he turns to, but there is a self-conscious sterility to most of these displays of literary virtuosity. Only the Western, *Little Big Man,* breathed an air of its own unbeholden to the cast-iron mold of formula. Yet *Vital Parts,* loose and free, crackles with exuberant vitality as Berger skewers the malice and greed that threaten his good-natured and feckless hero on every side. It is hard to know what to make of Berger's idiosyncratic body of work, but one thing is clear: the Reinhart lode has been exhausted. Perhaps Berger, and Updike, should listen to Harry Angstrom's complaint about the movies: "D'you ever get the feeling everything these days is sequels? . . . Like people are running out of ideas." (p. 75)

> *Pearl K. Bell, "Sequels," in* Commentary, *Vol. 72,*
> *No. 4, October, 1981, pp. 72-5.**

JONATHAN BAUMBACH

Thomas Berger is hardly an unknown novelist, though he is not one of our literary heroes either. Berger's work has been too intelligent and abrasive, I suspect, to seduce a large middlebrow audience from its less demanding distractions. *Reinhart's Women* is the author's eleventh novel and fourth in the series concerning that oversized, now aging, innocent, Carlo Reinhart. All of the novels are virtuoso performances, studded with dazzling prose turns. The brilliance of the language is a distancing factor, one that seems to antagonize readers that use fiction as a secondary form of drug abuse. Although original, Berger is not conspicuously innovative. He is mostly indifferent to matters of form, and has been virtually ignored by the most outspoken admirers of the new. Berger is too entertaining a story teller to be taken for avant garde, yet he uses language with as much surprise and originality as the best stylists among his contemporaries.

Unlike his other novels, which reimagine various classic genres, the Reinhart series deals directly (obliquely and directly) with the contemporary world. *Crazy in Berlin* (1958), *Reinhart in Love* (1962), *Vital Parts* (1970) and *Reinhart's Women* encompass thirty-five years in the decline and fall of Western civilization, starting with the implications of the holocaust and concluding (for the moment) with the present—"the most boring era in the history of the race." A moral rage informs these books that is as harsh and uncompromising as anything in our literature.

In Berger's fictional world, haunted by paradox, almost every expectation is defeated by the following awareness. Characters change radically while remaining in some profound way the same. Reinhart's daughter, Winona, who seems placid and acquiescent in her relationship to her father, is a tyrant to her lovers. His son, Blaine, once a sloganeering anti-war hippie (*Vital Parts*), emerges in *Reinhart's Women* as a prudish mean-spirited businessman. It is as if the landscape Reinhart wanders through—a symbolic landscape that misleadingly resembles our own—were an extension of the hero's dream. Reinhart is a quixotic knight, a saintly failure, in a decadent, shape-shifting world in which "the truth is always the reverse of appearance." As with the fiction of Flannery O'Connor, a writer with whom Berger shares certain concerns, satiric elements transform themselves into nightmare.

The surprise of Berger's language parallels the metaphoric exaggeration of his narratives. In a Dickensian passage in *Reinhart in Love,* the contents of a medicine cabinet savages the quixotic hero. . . . A man out of touch with himself is vulnerable to the perils of the inanimate. Perpetually disillusioned, Reinhart is perpetually susceptible to new illusions, which is to say he is engaged romantically in a world primed to disappoint him. He is a loser but mostly because the grail he has pursued—the American Dream—was unworthy of his quest.

The major reversal in *Reinhart's Women* is in the character of Reinhart himself. After a succession of failures detailed in the first three books of the series, Reinhart emerges at fifty-four uncharacteristically at ease with himself. . . . It is his mastery in the kitchen that has given the former bumbler and lifelong failure a new found sense of self. . . . This Reinhart is not the incompetent of the earlier books; he has become master of a craft, has found his art form.

Reinhart may be all right, but the world is as disappointing and perverse as ever. . . . The self-made chef and inadvertent patriarch is equal to most of the surprises Berger has in store

for him. *Reinhart's Women,* allowing for the irony that informs all of Berger's work, comes close to being a success story. Reinhart, the novel's standard bearer, is a figure of impressive competence in an otherwise corrupt and shoddy world.

Following the nightmare vision of *Neighbors, Reinhart's Women* is itself a kind of paradox. It is a novel in which innate decency triumphs at least in part over malice, in which utopia is envisioned as a community of chefs. Having centered himself (like the Cheyenne in *Little Big Man*), Reinhart has become aware of the feelings of others and so is capable of genuine kindness. One sees it most notably in his relationship to his oblivious daughter-in-law, Mercer, and in his relationship with his painfully shy neighbor, Edie Mulhouse. One also sees it in his surprisingly graceful treatment of the horrendous Genevieve and Blaine. It is a triumph of Berger's extravagant prose that Reinhart's humanity—nothing harder to make interesting in fiction than kindness—is as much a pleasure to witness as the horror show surrounding it.

Thomas Berger is one of our true originals. . . . Berger is one of our liveliest prose writers, a tale teller of unobtrusive though nevertheless savage moral concern. There are brilliances in all of the eleven novels, though not all, given the difficulty of tour de force over the long run, are fully sustained. The first half of that flawed masterpiece, *Neighbors,* is worth, I say with Bergerlike hyperbole, the entire canon of most of our recent literary reputations. There is no Berger novel . . . that I hesitate to recommend, none that will not offer some pleasure to those interested in the possibilities of the prose sentence or the range of invention of a highly charged imagination. *Reinhart's Women* is Thomas Berger's most graceful and modest book, a paean to kindness and artistry, a work of quiet dazzle.

> *Jonathan Baumbach, in a review of "Reinhart's Women," in* The American Book Review, *Vol. 4, No. 3, March-April, 1982, p. 16.*

ANNE TYLER

[*The Feud*] focuses upon the startling speed with which events can develop into something more than themselves. At one point in the novel, a small-town police chief arrests a boy for scaring people with a pistol. It's only a starter pistol, though, as another man argues, and it's probably not even loaded. As if to demonstrate otherwise, the police chief takes a gun from his desk drawer. The other man protests: What he's pulled out is a .22 automatic. It's not the starter pistol at all.

"I never said it was," the police chief replies. "I am just showing you what kinda weapons I've took away from kids. . . . Now the slug from one of these can travel a mile or more and kill or maim. Or suppose it was to hit the head of an engineer of an express train going to the city: he'd fall down on the controls, and the train'd keep going when it got to the terminal downtown and plow right into the building and kill everybody on board and a whole lot of innocent strangers who just happened to be there at the time."

That paragraph—proceeding from empty starter pistol to mass mayhem in the blink of an eye—is a sort of miniature of the novel as a whole. The plot of *The Feud* is a gigantic sprawl of disasters triggered by the smallest of events: a discussion as to whether a customer in a hardware store should get rid of his unlit cigar before examining a can of paint remover. The customer is Dolf Beeler, a factory foreman from the little town of Hornbeck. The hardware store, in neighboring Millville, belongs to Bud Bullard. Hornbeck and Millville are within walking distance of each other, but by the time the two men's quarrel is in full swing, it seems perfectly logical that a Hornbeck boy who's tangled with the law in Millville believes that the Millville police need extradition papers to arrest him.

Feuds abound, of course, in fiction; some Hatfield or McCoy is always fascinating some writer, from Shakespeare on down. What makes Thomas Berger's version so fresh is the innocent bewilderment of most of the people involved. Neither Dolf nor Bud enters the feud by intention; neither man takes pleasure in prolonging it. It somehow just happens—set off in the first place by a third party, a marvelously drawn crank named Reverton who walks around with a pistol meant for his imaginary enemies and who spends his spare time in the library researching "the extraction of gold from seawater, Asiatic techniques for training the will, magnetism, and the Pope's secret plan to introduce into the non-Catholic areas of the world an army of secret agents whose mission it was to poison the public reservoirs."

Equally well drawn is Eva Bullard, a busty 14-year-old Juliet who ruins her elopement with 17-year-old Tony Beeler when she eats his share of jelly doughnuts. Tony has been pining for Eva for months, but it takes only an evening to see she's not yet old enough to have any personality. (pp. 1, 24)

The humor in *The Feud* is the kind that arrives in a rush; it doesn't feel set up. This is remarkable when you consider the extremeness of some of the events—Tony's smashing a lemon meringue pie in a policeman's face, Reverton's Three Stooges-style fight with a couple he's caught "corpulating" in a body shop, the endless complications caused by the fact that the two towns' police chiefs are also feuding. There's a temptation to read the best bits aloud to everyone within hearing—which would be a mistake because, like all truly funny moments, these are part of the very fiber of the story.

The novel is set during the late 1930's, a time when a six-bit haircut is a scandal and an order of Coke and potato chips costs 10 cents. Reading of the two little towns, you imagine the road between them to be the gentle, winding, untrafficked road of fairy tales. . . . When Harvey Yelton, Hornbeck's none too ethical chief of police, slides out of his car, he holds on to his holstered pistol so it doesn't catch on the steering wheel—an act that somehow defangs him; it makes him seem homely, intimate, almost lovable.

Perhaps because of that homeliness of tone, *The Feud* is a warmer book by far than Thomas Berger's others. The earlier comedies—*Regiment of Women,* for instance, and The Reinhart Series—were so acidic that we weren't sure we wanted to laugh. And *Neighbors,* perhaps his most effective novel till now, was more rigid in its design, more obviously calculated. *The Feud* has no such faults. When Thomas Berger pokes fun at his characters here, he does it fondly, with inspired perception. When he describes an event, it seems the event is taking place almost of its own volition; it fairly tumbles out. As a result, *The Feud* is both endearing and surprising—a comic masterpiece. (p. 24)

> Anne Tyler, *"Home Folks at One Another's Throats,"* in The New York Times Book Review, *May 8, 1983,* pp. 1, 24.

GARRETT EPPS

Who knows what evil lurks in the hearts of men? Thomas Berger knows. And like the Shadow, Berger transforms the terrible news into dark and haunting laughter.

In his 12 novels, Berger has exploited (and exploded) the Western novel (*Little Big Man*), the whodunit (*Who Is Teddy Villanova?*) and the Arthurian romance (*Arthur Rex*). But in books like *Sneaky People, Neighbors* and *The Feud,* he returns to the bland anonymity of small-town America, a past and present never-never land of shady lanes, white frame houses and little boys playing ball.

Not that he finds anything soothing in these familiar scenes. Only Nathanael West has come close to Berger's vision of terror, chaos and depravity under the surface of "normal" American life. (p. 3)

On an ordinary October day, Dolf Beeler [in *The Feud*], "a good husband and a nice man," goes from his home in Hornbeck into the neighboring town of Millville to buy paint remover. Dolf makes a false step while choosing between a pint and a quart, and suddenly finds himself staring into a pistol wielded by a man he had thought to be a Protestant clergyman. "You went to buy paint remover and you had a gun pulled on you?" Dolf thinks in amazement. But pistols aren't the worst of it; before long, the minunderstanding over turpentine has plunged the Beelers of Hornbeck and Bullards of Millville into a fiery landscape of shotguns, car bombs, arson, attempted robbery, mental collapse, coronary thrombosis, suicide, sodomy, resisting arrest and assault with custard pies.

The two sides in this battle are not hillbillies in wool hats, but solid citizens of an idealized 1930s landscape that looks a lot like rural Pennsylvania. They are not fighting about money, sex, land or even principle; in fact, nobody is quite sure what the whole thing is about. But it's war nonetheless. "We got our pride at stake here," explains Reverton Kirby, a stalwart of the Bullard faction. "They get away with that, and the next thing you know they'll be riding us down like dogs and violating our women and all." (pp. 3, 14)

I marked my copy of *The Feud* with a star wherever its blend of irony, parody and slapstick made me laugh out loud; some pages look like a map of the Milky Way. My favorite moment comes when Bernice, having seduced Harvey Yelton, confronts him with the news that she is pregnant: "I don't have to remind you of what you'n'me did the other day," she says.

Somewhat surprised, Yelton replies, "That was just *yesterday*. . . . Everybody in the world but you, I guess, would know you can't get pregnant one day after inter-what-do-they-call-it. Now, anybody but me might get real mad about that. . . . And if he was carrying a gun, he might shoot you with it."

In presenting this pageant of ignorance, rage and deceit, Berger is harsh but never cruel. In all their variety, his novels have consistently presented a serious view of humanity as a race utterly spoiled by something that looks a lot like Original Sin. This merciless vision frees Berger somehow to love even his least prepossessing creations.

Certainly one would need to read widely to find a figure less prepossessing than Reverton Kirby, a skinny runt with a pistol in his waistband and a chip on his shoulder, eternally on the prowl against the faceless enemies he imagines creeping up behind him. . . .

In the Beelers, Kirby finds what he has long wanted—a tribe of enemies who are numerous, confused and unarmed. Somehow, by the book's close, he has found his own brand of heroism and peace—and the reader has seen him as a soul capable of loving and inspiring love. Berger is all the more powerful as a novelist because he can make us care about Reverton without dropping his detached, ironic pose.

"Why, down in the coal country," Reverton tells his cousin Bud, "they got mines that been burning real quiet since the Year One. All of a sudden smoke and fire shoots out of the cracks in the ground, and boils the water in the ponds, and the ladies do their wash there."

Something much like that happens in *The Feud;* Thomas Berger taps into the fire down below, and turns it into something cleansing and safe. That he makes it look easy only adds to the achievement. (p. 14)

> *Garrett Epps, "Thomas Berger's Comedy of Errors," in* Book World—The Washington Post, *May 15, 1983, pp. 3, 14.*

JACK BEATTY

Thomas Berger has written thirteen novels, but *The Feud* is the first I have read. It won't be the last. Mr. Berger possesses the defining gift of a major novelist: he creates a unique fictional world that has the same moral dynamics as our world while being flavorsomely idiosyncratic in style, tone, and point of view. Reading him is like looking in a funhouse mirror—it's both comic and creepy. Those clowns in there are possibilities of you.

The first sentence of *The Feud* testifies to Mr. Berger's peculiar genius. It seems straightforwardly denotative, yet it prefigures much that is to come, it establishes mood, and it provides an image for the novel's whole art and action.

> One Saturday morning in the middle of October, Dolf Beeler, a burly, beer-bellied foreman at the plant in Millville, but who lived in the neighboring town of Hornbeck, came over to Bud's Hardware in Millville to buy paint remover and steel wool for the purpose of stripping a supposedly solid-walnut dresser to the wood that underlay the many coats of varnish.

Berger works as fast as fear; by page two Dolf is arguing with Bud's son, Junior, over whether his cigar is apt to ignite the flammable paint remover. In what we later recognize as yet another image for this novel of misperceptions, the cigar is unlit, the danger it represents therefore purely notional. Dolf is explaining this to Bud when Bud's cousin, Reverton, a man who claims to be a railroad cop but isn't, pulls a gun on Dolf and forces him to apologize to Junior. The gun is a harmless starter's pistol, but Dolf doesn't know this. Humiliated, he swears revenge; and so begins the feud between the Beelers and the Bullards.

What follows is a macabre comedy of bad manners in which appearances are disastrously deceptive.... [Premises] breed paranoid conclusions. *The Feud* is set in the late 1930s, but its moral atmosphere belongs to the cold war....

All the characters are dangerously prone to treat their feelings like facts. They are ruled by psychological phantasms that, like the feud itself, have only tenuous ties to reality.

Reality is represented here as pretty grim stuff, full of heart attacks and nervous breakdowns, abused children and hints of illegitimacy, sudden violence and constant indignity. One of the characters has a dream of which the author revealingly says that it "gave you the second chance reality rarely allows."

The feud, then, is a form of dream, a layer of varnish covering the hard wood underneath. Remove it and the characters are left with the bleak finality hinted at in this glimpse of Dolf at the mill: "Dolf had come here after dropping out of high school, and he had never worked anywhere else." Its rhythm inflects that sentence with poignance. Thomas Berger is an exquisitely subtle artist who can conjure character and emotion from the slightest verbal means. Take this final example. An old janitor comes to sweep up the town jail; not finding the sheriff there, he informs his replacement: "He genly leaves a word for me." That "genly" is not only good comic dialect but also potently suggestive of that man's social fate. It is the literary equivalent of the inspired brushstroke by which a great painter captures the essence of human soul.

> *Jack Beatty, "A Comedy of Bad Manners," in* The New Republic, *Vol. 188, No. 20, May 23, 1983, p. 39.*

MICHAEL GORRA

The feud [from which the title of Berger's novel is derived] is a construct in words, not a series of actions, and in Berger's world the two have no set relation to each other. The novel's most memorable passages are rhetorical ones, descriptions of what might happen rather than of what has happened. In consequence, *The Feud* has an emptiness at the place where its central action should be. It has instead a series of subplots and minor motives, which the characters imagine are related to and controlled by the feud, so that the ordinary accidents of their lives seem part of a huge and rapidly spreading chaos. In *Sneaky People,* Berger examined the turmoil that lay beneath the surface of life. *The Feud*'s concern is with the need to invent that turmoil, which can alone provide an explanation for lives that may not otherwise have one.... By the end of *The Feud,* causality is an exploded balloon. Little wonder, then, that its characters seize the chance to make their lives intelligible, however farfetched the explanation.

Berger's target isn't small-town life but realism's assumption that life makes sense. His characters believe it does because they see their world as an embodiment of the clichés of popular fiction—what else is a feud?—which Berger's deliberately clumsy language mimics.... Berger's prose is an imitation realism, a comic-book realism, whose conventions he attacks in the same way he has, in his other books, taken on those of westerns, science fiction and heroic romance. Like all parodists, he loves the predictable; his art depends on his ability to capture the essence of highly stylized forms, whose inadequacies he both exposes and regrets. The bitter twist of Berger's comedy is its suggestion that truth and intelligence have their costs, that life in a comic book is more attractive than life in the world.

The Feud, like other works that are comic on a grand scale, isn't particularly funny on the page-by-page level—and I think deliberately so. Laughter relies on a sense of causality, which Berger wants to avoid. The novel is consequently slower and less uproarious than some of his other books—his best novel, *Neighbors,* in particular. Yet one is impressed by Berger's willingness to risk that slowness in pursuit of a world of nonsense, and impressed as well by the craftsmanship so evident on every page. This novel about the failure of causality has, paradoxically, no loose ends. Everything its characters say and do is recalled in some fashion before the end, including Harvey Yelton's threat to ban Halloween in Hornbeck.

For twenty-five years Thomas Berger has used comedy as the basis for an assault on convention. *The Feud* isn't his strongest novel, but the value of his work is so unquestionable that any more pointed cavils seem irrelevant. (pp. 742-43)

> Michael Gorra, "Comic-Book Quarrel," in The Nation, *Vol. 236, No. 23, June 11, 1983, pp. 741-43.*

W. RIGGAN

Thomas Berger's fiction frequently seems like so much bird-hunting with a howitzer: he hits the target, but what's left is not of much use. . . . [In] *The Feud,* as in *Sneaky People* (1975), he takes aim at the venal vicissitudes of small-town America in some slightly hazy, more innocent era when a quarter still got a kid into a movie *and* bought a soda and a candy bar, when wives stayed home all day, blacks shuffled around to the back door and young folks were easily identifiable as good or bad eggs.

Sneaky People may well be a send-up of fiction by such authors as Updike and Cheever (like Updike's Bech, the protagonist sells cars) and offers a nice, neat exercise in multiple narrative viewpoint and low-comic plotting. *The Feud* does little to expand on that modest accomplishment, however, and seems largely a rehash, with similarly dim yokels pursuing similarly mundane goals and getting into similarly petty scrapes with each other and the law. Here the dominant stylistic traits are dialectal dialogue and narrated monologue. . . . That's part of the fun in *The Feud,* of course, but sophisticated irony and deft manipulation of language are asked to sustain an entire novel based on the silly but deadly little spat between Dolf's family in Hornbeck and the Bullards of nearby Millville. The unfortunate result is literary overkill. Berger needs to stalk bigger game or use smaller-bore weapons.

> W. Riggan, in a review of "The Feud," in World Literature Today, *Vol. 58, No. 2, Spring, 1984, p. 276.*

CHRISTOPHER LEHMANN-HAUPT

Vitality is the missing ingredient in Thomas Berger's *Nowhere*. . . .

Certainly, one can't fault *Nowhere* for its lack of inventiveness. Russel Wren, the shabby private eye who first appeared in Mr. Berger's *Who Is Teddy Villanova?* (1977), is warned by phone one day that his office is about to blow up. When it does, after Wren has barely escaped, he is whisked off by unidentifiable forces to investigate the perpetrators, a terrorist group from the little known and nearly invisible European country of St. Sebastian, where a fat sybarite named Sebastian XXIII is King, where blond people are considered inferior to all others, where the children are brought up on old American films, where rudeness is punishable by death and where the Ministry of Clams (sic) settles all matters not in the jurisdiction of the Ministry of Hoaxes, the Ministry of Disaffection, the Ministry of Allergies or the Ministry of Irony. . . .

Nor can one complain that Mr. Berger's story isn't amusing and wittily written, although examples that can be taken out of context are difficult to find. Still, the reader knows at once that there are certain limitations to utopian novels, no matter how cockeyed or absurd the utopia in question may be. Everything will depend on the author's ability to ring variations on the familiar linear situation of the traveler in a strange land encountering one peculiar thing after another.

From its outset then, Mr. Berger's novel manages to convey the work in store for the reader more effectively than it does the fun that will result from the work. And indeed, the whimsy of it all soon grows forced and tedious. Though *Nowhere* struggles bravely to poke fun at every excess of the contemporary world from the cold war to racial prejudice, it wears itself out in the process and ends up being part of the problem instead of the solution.

> Christopher Lehmann-Haupt, in a review of "Nowhere," in The New York Times, *April 29, 1985, p. C18.*

FREDERICK BUSCH

Nowhere continues the shabby career of the hero of *Who Is Teddy Villanova?,* a playwright named Russel Wren who can't finish his second act. In *Villanova,* he was a silly gumshoe. In *Nowhere,* he is a joke about private eyes, a dreamer and an innocent abroad whose adventures provide Mr. Berger with occasions for commentary on Wren's America as much as on Saint Sebastian, the Ruritanian Nowhere to which Wren is transported. . . .

Wren promptly encounters the nation's quaint, pederastic ways. The monarch, Rupert, is a benevolent despot who entertains Wren while explaining that Freud was really named Froelich and was discovered because Rupert's great-grandfather recognized "their common keenness for collecting classical antiquities and Jewish jokes."

The chauvinism of Saint Sebastian is a running funny note in the novel, and a slap at any nation's excessive pride. . . . The silly inwardness of Sebastiani culture is reminiscent of that of the Nova Zembia of Nabokov's *Pale Fire,* although the passion and passionate wordplay of that novel are not Mr. Berger's aim. He is after wicked puncturings of pride and pomp. . . .

Thus, Saint Sebastian's scholars edit their national encyclopedia in the knowledge "that we are absolutely inconsequential and that what we do has no value whatever." . . .

The novel, then, is about subversion of what Mr. Berger seems to think are prevailing follies. Wren calls himself "a subversive element." A Sebastiani replies, "In all the world, only an American would boast of that." Mr. Berger would write a novel boasting of that.

In his note to his 1967 novel, *Killing Time,* Mr. Berger wrote that "A work of fiction is a construction of language and otherwise a lie." The author of the Reinhart series and of the wonderful *Sneaky People* has not given us his most exquisite language or his most breathtaking premise; yet one does accept parts of the novel as truthful—and funny—commentary. So one does allow the novel, in the words of *Little Big Man,* "a lien on our credulity."

> Frederick Busch, "Sebastiani Terror," in The New York Times Book Review, *May 5, 1985, p. 17.*

BRUCE ALLEN

[*Nowhere*] is an unlucky combination of intemperate farce and dystopian vision. . . . Its hero, Russel Wren (who has appeared previously in Berger's work), failed playwright and sometime private eye, rendered homeless when terrorists bomb his Manhattan apartment building, is whisked off by mysterious means to the remote country of Saint Sebastian, "an appalling little principality" somewhere near Germany and Czechoslovakia. It's a perversely self-satisfied "microcosm of Europe" ruled by an upside-down ethos (original thought is discouraged; the citizens spend their days at the movies; "Blonds," downtrodden inferiors, organize an underground liberation movement) that excites Wren's contemptuous ire. . . . There are good random gags, but you hate yourself for laughing at this petulant, satirical petit point. Berger at his best—for example, in his wonderful last novel, *The Feud*—is a delicious comic writer; at his worst, he's a crank. *Nowhere* is the crankiest Berger yet.

> *Bruce Allen, in a review of "Nowhere," in* Saturday Review, *Vol. 11, No. 3, May-June, 1985, p. 71.*

DAVID W. MADDEN

[The] dustjacket proudly proclaims that *Nowhere* is a spoof of the "classic spy thriller"; however, a closer look reveals that Berger is working some far more interesting literary ground. Less a version of a John LeCarre thriller, *Nowhere* stands as a 1980s version of *Gulliver's Travels* in its manipulations of utopian conventions. In writing a utopian fiction Berger is not emulating Edward Bellamy, who in *Looking Backwards,* creates a technologically desirable alternative reality; instead, his aim is to explore the possibilities, however extravagant and exaggerated, of human nature. The first significant convention of a utopian fantasy is the journey motif, an odyssey that is either imaginary or extraordinary. In this case the means of travel is quite credible—a jet—though the circumstances of Wren's departure are hazy and unlikely (he awakens to find himself aboard a plane that is landing, and without money, identification, or even a passport).

A second important convention of utopian fiction involves the incredible existence of an unknown land or country. Although Wren does not encounter flying islands or territories where humans and beasts have inexplicably reversed roles as Gulliver does, the detective is baffled to learn of the existence of this heretofore unknown state which is bordered by the two more equally obscure countries of Gezieferland and Swaitna. Additionally confusing is the fact that the place has a seemingly illustrious history that has somehow placed it at the center of European politics and art (Botticelli's "Birth of Venus" was modelled by a former Saint Sebastian queen, and other works of art are actually forgeries of the originals that are housed in the current prince's castle).

But most important of the utopian conventions is the creation of an imaginary society, a society that, though it may seem preposterous, does possess a certain integrity and coherence of its own. Life in Saint Sebastian is not only different but paradoxical; as soon as one point is settled, its opposite also holds true. Such paradox ultimately leads Wren to the conclusion, "As with so many of the phenomena I had encountered in this country, what had seemed utterly preposterous at the outset had a milligram or two of reason in it when more closely examined, but rarely if ever enough to bring it even into the

neighborhood of the desirable." Wren's decision is finally Gulliver's—he must return to his own, however distressing that return may be.

With *Nowhere* Berger confims once again why he is one of America's most original novelists. He has the remarkable ability of consistently exploring new fictional possibilities even while returning to familiar characters such as Carlo Reinhart and Russel Wren.

At the same time Berger manages to develop ever more fully certain consistent themes: the radical disjunction between appearance and reality, the relationship between crime and the criminal, the banality and absurdity of modern life, the comedy of human manners, and the innate tendency to seek and identify scapegoats. The words of some characters from Bacon's utopian *New Atlantis* could well apply to Berger's performance here, "for indeed we were astonished to hear so strange things so probably told." (pp. 16, 23)

> *David W. Madden, in a review of "Nowhere," in* San Francisco Review of Books, *Summer, 1985, pp. 16, 23.*

JOHN SLADEK

Berger seems to belong to that generation of "artisan" novelists—Anthony Burgess and Kingsley Amis spring to mind immediately, but it's hard to think of American examples (except for Norman Mailer)—who see themselves as craftsmen plying their honest trade. They approach each new genre novel as though it were just a different style or size of shoe—cowboy boot, space boot, gumshoe—to be hammered out on the usual last. I have great sympathy with this down-to-earth view. One of the reasons I've always liked Thomas Berger novels is that I like to see a good formula, well-wielded by a guild master.

I like [*Nowhere*], for example, a lot, even though I know it doesn't really work. It has the necessary ingredients of a good comic novel, it has the right outline, there are many moments of wonderful farce, yet it never quite comes together into a finished product.

The title invites comparison with Butler's *Erewhon*, and there are some similarities. In either novel, the protagonist finds himself inexplicably in a strange land where all the rules are different. Both Berger and Butler ridicule our conventions by reduction, exaggeration or inversion. . . .

[Berger's] protagonist, the private eye Russel Wren (first seen in *Who Is Teddy Villanova?*) is kidnaped in New York by a CIA-like group and sent as a spy to San Sebastian, and the fun begins.

Only it doesn't. Once the novel leaves New York behind, it also seems to leave behind Berger's usual fine sense of the ridiculous, so that he is reduced to raising a laugh by any possible means.

There is the O. Henry device of using a pompous locution for comic effect: within a few pages, we meet persons of swarthy hue, and also of tender years, a palm gets crossed with coin of the realm, things are done by reason of, by people who proceed to do them, and so on. . . .

Berger has better luck creating comic characters. My own favorite is Clyde McCoy, an American journalist stranded in San Sebastian since 1945, a born survivor and a self-made super-drunk. Another wonderful soul is the cable clerk, a man who likes to converse in the cliches of Boston Blackie films (starring Chester Morris), and I don't mean maybe! . . .

Whenever the novel gets away from American culture for a page, however, things get dull. Berger's observation of a New York cop holding back a crowd, on the other hand, gleams with his best wit. . . .

Unfortunately, Berger is so much better at dealing with the reality of American and especially New York culture, that the big-city beginning of the book comes in an easy first—and San Sebastian, nowhere.

> *John Sladek, "Thomas Berger's Spy Spoof," in* Book
> World—The Washington Post, *July 7, 1985, p. 9.*

Roy (Alton) Blount, Jr.

1941-

(Has also written under pseudonyms of Noah Sanders and C. R. Ways) American essayist, nonfiction writer, journalist, and poet.

Blount's humorous essays often center on aspects of American life not usually treated by other writers, as evidenced by such titles as "Why There Will Never Be a Great Bowling Novel," "Hymn to Ham," and "Song against Broccoli." His first book, *About Three Bricks Shy of a Load* (1974), won praise for its amusing yet affectionate recounting of a season Blount spent with the Pittsburgh Steelers football team. The book focuses on the players' personalities and their attitudes toward the game. Blount drew heavily on his Georgia background in *Crackers* (1980), a collection of satirical essays chronicling the years of Jimmy Carter's presidency. Much of the book is a witty appraisal of the significance of this period for Southerners. *One Fell Soup; or, I'm Just a Bug on the Windshield of Life* (1982), *What Men Don't Tell Women* (1984), and *Not Exactly What I Had in Mind* (1985) include essays, reviews, poems, and other short pieces originally published in various magazines. Reviewers of these books lauded Blount for his quirky humor and his ability to recognize the hilarious hidden in the ordinary. Cathleen Schine notes: "One can say of many humorists, 'Nothing is sacred to him.' For Roy Blount, nothing is mundane."

(See also *Contemporary Authors*, Vols. 53-56 and *Contemporary Authors New Revision Series*, Vol. 10.)

© *Thomas Victor 1986*

MIKE THARP

Mr. Blount, author of *About Three Bricks Shy of a Load,* spent [the 1973] season with the [Pittsburgh] Steelers "in a professional capacity somewhere between a tick and a consultant," according to the book's jacket. Whatever his perspective, it allowed him the mobility to become what basketball players call "a floater and a fringer"; gliding in and out of conversations, incidents, activities, storing them all away until he could recollect their emotional overflow in tranquility.

Earlier this year, Mr. Blount published in The New Yorker a poem on the difficult grace of the entrechat leap in ballet. He applies the same whimsical insight to such topics as Mean Joe Greene . . . , the professional athlete's body . . . , or Pittsburgh itself. . . .

Mr. Blount focuses more on the personalities of the team than on the games themselves. (The book's title comes from one Steeler's sideline evaluation of the team's psychological makeup.) The author's use of language reflects his appreciation of nuance and sound in the voices he listened to from July to January.

> Mike Tharp, *"The Boys of Autumn: Three Versions,"* in The Wall Street Journal, *November 8, 1974, p. 10.**

ROBERT W. CREAMER

[*About Three Bricks Shy of a Load*] is a terrific book. It's another look at pro football, but don't be put off. I have never read anything else on pro football, fiction or nonfiction, as good as this, nothing that explains so well the paradox of the brutality and subtlety of this repelling and fascinating game, nothing that brings alive so brilliantly the people whose lives are enmeshed in it: the players, the coaches, the owners, the flunkies, the hangers-on. Several writers have lived closely with professional teams, as Blount did with the Pittsburgh Steelers, but none of them, not even George Plimpton, is as bright and as sensitive, as tough and talented as Blount. He is an exceptionally gifted writer, and his book is, in a very real way, a work of art.

> Robert W. Creamer, *"The Games People Watch,"* in The New York Times Book Review, *December 1, 1974, p. 90.**

MICHAEL SRAGOW

Imagine Willie Nelson singing with a Spike Jones back-up band, or Dan Jenkins mating with Flannery O'Connor. That'll give you some idea of the pop zest and folk wisdom, the deep-dish country humor and acute sensibility, and, most of all, the sheer satiric *chutzpah* that Roy Blount Jr. has put into *Crackers: This Whole Many-Angled Thing of Jimmy, More Carters, Ominous Little Animals, Sad Singing Women, My Daddy and Me.* It's the most uproarious collection of loosely connected essays since Bruce Jay Friedman's *Lonely Guy's Book of Life.* It's also a warm and penetrating portrayal of what it means to be a native Georgian—or, for that matter, an American—in the age of Jimmy Carter. (p. 39)

When Blount wrote *About Three Bricks Shy of a Load: A Highly Irregular Lowdown on the Year the Pittsburgh Steelers were Super but Missed the Bowl,* he described the agonies and ecstasies of pro ball as well as Peter Gent did in *North Dallas Forty,* but he also gave his readers a taste of the social-ethnic spices that make up the hearty steel-town stew. He conveyed how the Steelers became special heroes (and sometimes villains) to people like steelworkers—how football, like hockey, could work as a steam valve for an entire city. Similarly, in *Crackers,* instead of becoming one more peanut parodist, Roy Blount really gets down and chews over the roots of the Carter administration. Like Mark Twain, he pits the sagacity and saltiness of the cracker barrel against the smooth, evasive rhetoric of the soapbox.

Blount has an original slant on his subject: he's both a Georgian (transplanted to Massachusetts) and a presidential "sympathizer." He acknowledges that Carter has shilly-shallied for too long—that he's become a middle-of-the-dirt-road pol. But to Blount the dirt that clings to Carter—his vestigial country flavor—has the potential to save him. Unlike most post-Woodstein pundits, Blount doesn't want a white-knight administration. He prefers honest-to-God characters—blacks or rednecks—who could show the world that our common American stock still has some native wit, heart, and color.... Incompetence bothers Blount less than inhumanity. (pp. 39-40)

Blount takes on not only prefabricated politics, but also the entire polyester quality of modern American life. A typical Blount declaration: "What we need is to back off from devices and emphasize good shit and common life. A lot of people would be embarrassed to say that. But, hell, I don't care, I'm from Georgia." Because Blount's southerners have been kept down in national status for so long, they've also stayed down-to-earth. Blount intersperses his drawling commentaries (on everything from the media to "**Heterosexism and Dancing**") with verbal snapshots of earthy, fictional Carter relatives.... Critics might argue that he indulges a southern penchant for the grotesque. Blount would probably reply, with Flannery O'Connor, that southern writers can so aptly render "the grotesque" because they can still recognize what it is. (p. 40)

> *Michael Sragow, in a review of "Crackers," in The New Republic, Vol. 183, No. 13, September 27, 1980, pp. 39-40.*

HARRY CREWS

[*Crackers*] is an exceptional book in nearly every way. It may be the best book you'll read this year; certainly it will be the funniest. The book is "about" nearly everything and everybody in the country. There is no index to it, presumably because it would take about 20 years to make one, despite the fact that, as things go in this age of bloat, there are only 291 pages. But what pages! ... Roy Blount Jr., as all good free-lance journalists should, apparently has been everywhere, talked to everybody, read everybody, kept notes, and now subjects it all

to his own biases and prejudices and notions of the rightness of things.

Understand, in Blount's world a man is a Good Ol' Boy you'd hang out with and trust, or he is a sorry, spineless, egg-sucker you wouldn't take to a dogfight. Blount admires Crackers, and Crackers are people who know where they are from and who are proud of it, who take things personally, who resist every effort to standardize them, who are always ready to defend what is rightfully theirs and who are subject to slap you if you insult them. Defined in such a way, Crackers conceivably could come from New York or California or anywhere. But Blount knows *Georgia* best, being from just outside Atlanta, so he turns to that state to find a yardstick by which to measure all things Cracker.

The yardstick is Jimmy Carter. He chooses Jimmy Carter for precisely the reason that he lacks everything Blount admires. "Jimmy ran on all the things he wasn't. He wasn't a racist, an elitist, a sexist, a Washingtonian, a dimwit, a liar, a lawyer, a warmonger, a peacenik, a big spender, a Republican, an authoritarian, an ideologue, a paranoid, or a crook. He had found one last creditable ism: isn'tism. People in Georgia had said of him, 'Well, there's not a whole lot *to* him.' Jimmy turned that into a forte."

The president comes in for some mean licks in this book. He is measured in every possible way and in every possible way he comes up short. Blount recounts a long hilarious visit with Brother Billy down in Plains, and he finds he much prefers Billy over Jimmy. Billy's way of talking, his looks, his every action lets you at least know dead solid certain who he is. Even Jerry Jeff Walker, who wrote the very fine song "Mr. Bojangles" and who has to be the craziest man ever to pick up a guitar, comes off looking a whole lot better than our president. But by the end of the book Blount makes it clear how he will vote....

In many ways, Blount's performance in *Crackers* is a triumph over subject, proving—if it needed proving again—that there are no dull subjects, only dull writers. Anyone who read his first book, *About Three Bricks Shy of a Load,* or who caught any of his work in *The New Yorker, Esquire* and other publications knows that wherever he looks he finds something funny....

Crackers is the funniest book I've read in a decade, and I know, too, that I could not ask for a more knowledgeable, well-written commentary on our times.

> *Harry Crews, "Laughing through Georgia," in Book World—The Washington Post, September 28, 1980, p. 3.*

GENE LYONS

[*Crackers*] is a shamelessly patched together series of magazine articles, little more than a sustained hooraw written to get even with prigs who don't understand the South. Styling himself a "Crackro-American," Blount has built the whole book around one basic joke: Southerners who seem dumb are really full of sly wisdom. "This may confound your stereotype of Georgians," he tells the reader early on, "but I don't own any firearms." A bit later he accounts for Brother Billy Carter's nasty edge: "He may resent something. He may resent that people tend to assume that a man from South Georgia is quaint, for one thing." In the interest of having some fun with readers who do assume that, Blount has invented an utterly contrived style: "*What?* NAW. That ain't no way to write a damn sentence! That's the limpest damn piddliest damn saddest-looking most clogged and whiney damn hitching-around piss-and-corruption-covered damn sentence I ever saw."

Now *those* sentences are the literary equivalent of an opossum playing dead. And against the background of today's South they illustrate how the self-consciously Southern writer's problem of voice has become particularly acute. The sons of Savings and Loan presidents in Atlanta suburbs, which Blount happens to be, don't talk like that any more than the sons of Savings and Loan presidents in suburban New Jersey talk like John Travolta in *Saturday Night Fever.* . . .

To his credit, Blount avoids mention of the famous "New South," as well as of Kirkpatrick Sale's silly-sinister "Sunbelt." The best pieces in the book concern Brother Billy, captured more or less in the raw in his pre-Libyan days. The odd career of Jimmy and the rest of his kin purportedly ties the collection together, but there are too few laughs, too little substance and too many stories like **"I May Have Sung With Jerry Jeff."** This is merely a tale about forty-eight drunken hours spent in the company of Jerry Jeff Walker, a country-rock singer born and raised in upstate New York but metamorphosed into a Professional Texan. Blount's attempts to justify such material on a thematic basis are simply ludicrous. "I'll admit, I'm glad Jerry Jeff isn't in the White House," Blount appends to the piece, out of nowhere. **"Whiskey and Blood,"** ostensibly about country music, consists mainly of Blount's own lyrics, pages and pages of them. . . . Blount has his moments of wit, but they are a magazine writer's moments at best and do not justify the price of a hardback book. (p. 617)

> Gene Lyons, "Voices of Nothingness," in The Nation, *Vol. 231, No. 19, December 6, 1980, pp. 616-19.*

A. J. ANDERSON

When a book is called *One Fell Soup,* and subtitled *I'm just a bug on the windshield of life,* you can be pretty sure that it's whimsical as all get out. Blount, who boasts of having written for several dozen periodicals, here dumps before us a very large tray of mixed *patisseries*—short stories, articles, reviews, poems, you name it—which have appeared in some of those periodicals. Considered singly in their diverse sources, they may well have had some momentary appeal; but en masse, they resemble nothing so much as an assortment of immiscible ingredients. Indeed, his ceaselessly wild and wooly puns and japeries begin after a while to cloy. It's simply too much jabberwocky to take straight.

> A. J. Anderson, in a review of "One Fell Soup: or, I'm Just a Bug on the Windshield of Life," in Library Journal, *Vol. 107, No. 16, September 15, 1982, p. 1755.*

CATHLEEN SCHINE

Crackers, Blount's last book, was an easygoing, disbelieving, Georgian drawl on Jimmy Carter and the good old South. *One Fell Soup,* on the other hand, is a pleasantly random gathering. Blount seems able to write about almost anything, and for almost anyone. . . . He has had a regular column, he tells us, "somewhere, off and on, since I was fifteen. . . . Sometimes in conversation with family and friends, or even just out in the woods nude, glowing eerily, late at night alone, I will refer to myself as 'this column.'" After so much practice, he writes

with conversational ease—or seems to, anyway. Surely these pieces were written lying down, a typewriter propped comfortably on Blount's stomach?

In the introduction, Blount says that the book was almost called "*The Book of Love.* Answering the question, raised by the Monotones in 1958, 'I wonder wonder wonder . . . m'ba-doo-oo *who,* who wrote the Book of Love?'" Other disturbing questions discussed in *One Fell Soup:* **"Why There Will Never Be a Great Bowling Novel," "Is the Pope Capitalized?"** and which came first, the chicken or the egg . . . ? (p. 539)

There are some dead spots in *One Fell Soup*—a too-lyrical description of ballooning, a predictable jab at economics jargon—but most of the book saunters by, humming merrily. Blount investigates the homeliest phenomena with such burning thoroughness that the pieces become implicit parodies of every solemn, semischolarly academic or journalistic inquiry.

In the best section of the book, "Love and Other Indelicacies," Blount takes on the naughty and the sensuous by being a little naughty and sensuous himself. In **"So This Is Male Sexuality,"** he recoils from Shere Hite's approach to writing about sex: "I like to read about food, but I don't want to read a lot of 'I like to chew a bite of peas three or four times and then just let it rest on the very back part of my tongue where it arches up a little and . . .'" There is a learned and gentle essay on testicles, **"The Family Jewels,"** which considers these curious objects in their various historical and cultural contexts. Roy Cohn is invoked. So is Mother Teresa. "Incidentally," Blount notes, "*orchid* is Greek for 'testicle,' which may account for the pride with which girls used to wear them on prom dresses."

Blount's reports from the odd corners of human existence are more than funny—they are illuminating. One really *understands* testicles after reading **"The Family Jewels,"** and one is grateful. But one is also grateful for the jokes. Blount parodies sex studies in **"The Orgasm: A Reappraisal"** ("The orgasm is not really ideal for everyone"). He parodies gossip columns in **"Whose Who"** and advice columns in **"Wired Into Now"** ("Q. If I knew famous people, would they like me?"). He jabs at journalistic forms and "topics" with the enthusiasm of a child poking a rotten tree trunk with a stick, then sits, grinning, watching all the funny little facts crawl out. One can say of many humorists, "Nothing is sacred to him." For Roy Blount, nothing is mundane. (p. 540)

> Cathleen Schine, "Baseball, Socks, Sex and Laughs," in The Nation, *Vol. 235, No. 17, November 20, 1982, pp. 539-40.*

LARRY L. KING

Roy Blount Jr. frets because the MacArthur Foundation has started handing out grants of $30,000 per year and up, tax free, to a number of Americans it has deemed to be geniuses.

What upsets Blount is that those of us who do *not* receive genius grants are automatically branded non-geniuses. He fears critics will start their reviews of his books, "Blount, though no genius . . ." Or, even worse, the foundation folk may get to futzing around with their computers and call him up to say, "Listen, we worked out a generalized assessment for everybody in the country as to how much of a genius each is, and you have to send Robert Penn Warren thirty-five dollars a month." . . .

He is offended, too, because one of the grants went to a fellow who wrote a book about panda bears. Blount believes that is not genius material, not a subject heavy enouth to qualify. Blount himself writes only on Big Themes—as in *One Fell Soup.* It is about pigs, chickens, lentil soup, the singing-impaired, cricket-wrestling, bowling, Ronald Reagan, genius grants and other heavy stuff. . . .

Though temporarily unable to send Roy Blount $30,000, it gives me great pleasure to here officially designate him a semigenius at the very least. I have been reading his stuff for years and he seldom fails to break me up. He is Andy Rooney with a Georgia accent, only funnier. . . .

My favorites in [*One Fell Soup*] include Blount's famed food songs (including such hits as **"Hymn to Ham," "Song to Pie"** and the unforgettable smash, **"Song Against Broccoli"**) and poems to include **"Reagan, Begin and God."**

It is only fair to warn that certain pucker-brows who wear stuffing in their shirts will not much enjoy perusing The World According to Blount. They will find him less than Serious while eschewing such vital subjects as the Trilateral Commission or whatever it is and death and Fellini movies. A pox on 'em. Roy Blount does, too, write about serious subjects. Sometimes. Like his piece called **"The Wages of Fun,"** which is about casual bedroom calisthenics and how a boy can't hardly fall deep in love for one night anymore without risks to his health. . . . About the low level of Education: there was this student who, assigned to write something in the third person, began "When I entered the room, Mack and Irene were there." . . . Economics is treated by Dr. Blount: inflation is when President Jackson on your $20 bill begins to look like King Farouk; recession occurs when Jackson begins to look like Elisha Cook Jr.

One Fell Soup may not be Blount at his best on every page— it's a bit spotty here and there—but it is fun and chuckles enough that if you have not made his acquaintance in the past I doubt you will regret meeting him in these pages. He is, as even *The New York Times* admits, "an amusing Georgian." That's more than you can say for Jimmy, Ham, and Jody.

> Larry L. King, *"The Ingenious Comedy of Roy Blount Jr.,"* in Book World—The Washington Post, *January 23, 1983, p. 3.*

ANATOLE BROYARD

After his highly praised *Crackers* and *One Fell Soup,* we can feel [Mr. Blount's] ironic detachment sliding toward desperation in *What Men Don't Tell Women.* Some of the book is still very good, for Mr. Blount has a sharp eye and a fine ear. He just needs a good heart-to-heart talk with himself, a review of his situation. He's like a man whose tennis court ought to have its lines refreshed.

Though there's nothing here as wildly inspired as the piece in *Crackers* on country blues, Mr. Blount is pretty good on sportswriters. The opening of this piece, **"Women in the Locker Room!"** is wonderful, as he proposes Walt Whitman as the ideal sportswriter for our times. . . .

At the opera, Mr. Blount finds himself thinking what a perfect Othello Franco Harris, the Steeler's running back, would make. He tries to imagine how an opera singer, after expostulating in song, in robust Italian with a full orchestra for support, can go home and enjoy an ordinary quarrel with his wife.

Here and there, one finds pleasant touches like "nonobjective phone conversations," or people who say to writers "I *saw* your book," as if this were the same as having read it. To call oneself a writer, Mr. Blount says, "sounds like something you would assert, falsely, in a singles bar." Elvis Presley in his coffin looked like Katy Jurado. "Faustian jobs" are where the money is. "When something is classic, you can never think of an example of how it's done."

But an interminable article about comparative salaries is bloated and stale. Nor is Mr. Blount fresh or funny about computers, semiotics and structuralism, the making of lists, the truth about history, dogs and cats, feminism, Santa Claus, Watergate, cheerleaders, daylight-saving time, the Reagan Adminstration, or New Year's Eve. As his ideal sportswriter might say, he strikes out in *What Men Don't Tell Women* more than Dave Kingman does. Even the title is forced, for this is merely a random collection of pieces.

In an interesting passage on telling jokes, Mr. Blount talks about the "double edged poignance" of certain kinds of humor. He describes the sadness implicit in the final inadequacy of wit, the fact that the relief it affords is only temporary and partial. We laugh at our futile attempt to joke away our disillusion and indignation. At its best, Mr. Blount's book is rather like that.

> Anatole Broyard, *"Wit's Temporary Relief,"* in The New York Times, *April 28, 1984, p. 14.*

DAN GREENBURG

It was going to take a lot to get me to laugh. I had been working steadily for two weeks on my 1040 form. . . .

Into this setting Roy Blount's book [*What Men Don't Tell Women*] arrived, promising drollery. I was in no mood for drollery. I was in the mood for tedium and pain, but I dipped into it anyway. Through clenched teeth a chuckle escaped. And then another. I will tell you three things that made me chuckle, but they'll be out of context so you might not think they're funny. First thing:

"What do we speak of when we speak of 'literature'? Before we can begin to 'answer' that question, we must ask another question: 'What do we speak of when we speak of "What"?'"

Second thing:

"I like compost. . . . But not very mulch!"

Third thing:

"You need to be in a dynamic mood to turn over a new leaf, unless it is a tiny leaf—like, 'Okay! From this day forward I will never again clip my fingernails except over a receptacle of some kind!'" . . .

[The] sections of Mr. Blount's book that I think he does best [are] those that deal with the war between men and women, a topic that has been of particular interest to me in recent years. I should point out here that, his title notwithstanding, Mr. Blount's book of humorous essays is only half about what men don't tell women. The other half deals with such diverse subjects as Daylight Savings Time, Elvis, Southern hospitality, hats, opera, television commercials, sweating, computers, sportswriting, list making, cheerleading, salaries, cat books, what to do on New Year's Eve, how to visit the sick and what it is that authors do.

Mind you, I'm not complaining. Almost all of the above are awfully funny. But the parts I like best are the shorter sections on contemporary male-female relations that appear between the aforementioned essays like layers of meat between decks of a gigantic club sandwich. These sections are called "Blue Yodel 1," "Blue Yodel 2," etc., "in tribute to Jimmie Rodgers, the Singing Brakeman, who made an art of the pained moaning sound." They are written in the voices of various confused men with names like Wes and Linc and Jubal, and they are as fresh and darkly amusing as anything I have read on the subject. For example, a man named Marv says:

"I talked to April's psychiatrist. He explained that she felt overpowered by me because I was so objective. I should lose my temper, he said. I talked to April about it. She said he was right. So the next time she cried, I yelled and flung my arms and jumped up and down and got incoherent. It did me a lot of good. You know what she said? 'I thought I could at *least* count on you to be objective.'" . . .

Another man named Cooper speaks of the inadvisability of telling your woman that you've been faithful to her:

"Or maybe you say you are faithful and here's how they go: They get rigid. Get struck to the core. And they say, 'Who is she?' Right? And you say—you're astounded. You say: 'No, I didn't say anthing about *in*fidelity. I said *fi*delity. Fih. Fih.' That's a bad thing about that word. You feel silly saying 'Fih.' And they say, 'Is she pretty?'"

So anyway, there I was, chuckling away at old Blount and not putting the requisite measure of pain into my 1040 form. I had a marvelous time. I hope the I.R.S. doesn't hold that against me.

Dan Greenburg, "On Southerners, Salaries and 'Fih'," in The New York Times Book Review, *May 13, 1984, p. 12.*

KENNETH TURAN

Roy Blount Jr. has his priorities on straight. Let other humorists cope with balances of trade and Star Wars weaponry. This bluegrass Quixote tilts against those nagging but less publicized problems most in need of his kind of attention. Book titles, for instance. Blount had planned to call this merry collection [**What Men Don't Tell Women**] *Clean Sheets* or, alternatively, *Or, My Mind Is All Made Up (But You Can Hop On In.)* But

he decided that **What Men Don't Tell Women** had a longer shelf life, even if the contents have little to do with the dust jacket. . . .

As any reader of his previous collections knows, Blount, . . . is no gladhander; he understands life too well to greet it with a ready smile. He knows about those listless afternoons when "before long it is nearly time to relax and look back over the events of the day; and there haven't been any yet." (p. 72)

[Few] things sit well with the author. He feels strongly that "scrambled eggs should never be assembled in vat-sized proportions." He is not happy with the way the sick are visited (it is wrong to say, "My sister had *both* of hers taken out *with no anesthetic*," or to speculate, "Your trouble is too many cola drinks. Probably been going on for years. So that a kind of fine brown sediment . . ."). He distrusts hat manufacturers ("One Size Fits All adjustable hats don't fit all") and the *oeuvre* of Francis Ford Coppola, who "created an idiosyncratic, overextended Hollywood studio, to be sure, but it produced some extraordinarily underextended movies—as if Napoleon had marched his armies into Russia in order to seize the 'Style' section of *Pravda*."

Still, if Blount is in the tradition of the great curmudgeons like H. L. Mencken and W. C. Fields, he refuses to yield to despair. There are, he believes, a few contemporary items worth preserving. He likes the way sportswriting resembles country music. "It is sometimes very good, and sometimes when it is really bad it is even better." Or the way a dog acts when caught on the couch: "He leaps as if scalded and exclaims: 'I'm off! I'm off the couch now! Oh Lord! I wasn't . . . I was just . . . I was guarding it!'" (pp. 72, J14)

And what is there worth preserving about Roy Blount? Just about everything. The author of such delights as **Crackers** and **One Fell Soup, or I'm Just a Bug on the Windshield of Life** . . . delights with every comic essay, from his sly insights to his deadpan palaver to the surprises that lurk in the tail end of his folk-elegant lines: "There comes a time in life when it is unseemly to awaken late in the afternoon of January 1 on someone's snooker table, naked save for a tiny conical hat (whose elastic strap has ridden up to just under your nose), shriveled tuxedo pants, and a crust of onion dip and confetti." At one point Blount confesses, "Syntax is my bread and butter," and just this once he is not kidding. (p. J14)

Kenneth Turan, "Curmudgeon," in Time, *Vol. 123, No. 23, June 4, 1984, pp. 72, J14.*

Robert (Elwood) Bly

1926-

American poet, critic, essayist, translator, and editor.

One of the most prominent and influential figures in contemporary American poetry, Bly writes visionary and imagistic verse distinguished by its unadorned language and generally subdued tone. His poems are pervaded by the landscape and atmosphere of rural Minnesota, where he has lived most of his life, and are focused on the immediate, emotional concerns of daily life. Bly is often associated with "deep image" poetry, a loosely defined movement whose adherents include James Wright, Donald Hall, and Louis Simpson. These writers look to the unconscious for inspiration, as does Bly, who uses the term "leaping" to define the associative process by which images combine to create a poem. Bly's use of imagery reflects the influence of such surrealist writers as Federico García Lorca and Pablo Neruda, and he has frequently translated the work of these and other international poets. Primarily to provide a showcase for these authors, Bly founded a magazine and press, *The Fifties,* which is still in existence as *The Eighties.* During the 1960s Bly was active in protests against the Vietnam War, and his political and social convictions are prominent in the poetry he wrote during that period. Although still convinced that the poet must attend to public concerns as well as the private, interior world, Bly has directed his recent work toward a more personal exploration of natural, spiritual, and familial matters.

Bly's first volume, *Silence in the Snowy Fields* (1962), established him as an important voice in American poetry. The serene, haiku-like poems in this book evoke the pastoral settings of the Midwest and espouse the virtues of solitude and self-awareness. His second volume, *The Light Around the Body* (1967), which won the National Book Award, is noted for its overtly political content, centering on Bly's reactions to the horrors of the Vietnam War. These poems typify his attempt to merge the personal and the public, an effort, as he explains in his essay written during the same period, "Leaping Up into Political Poetry," necessitated by the hate and injustice rampant in the world. Before donating his National Book Award prize money to an antidraft organization, Bly delivered an acceptance speech attacking the American role in Vietnam and chastising the literary world for its silence on the issue. Howard Nelson observed that *The Light Around the Body* is "an angry, uneven, powerful book, and clearly with it Bly made a major contribution to the growth of an American poetry which is truly political and truly poetry."

Political concerns are again present in Bly's next major work, *Sleepers Joining Hands* (1973), but they are fused with the quiet tone and pastoral imagery of his first book. One of the subjects explored in *Sleepers Joining Hands* is the division within each individual of male and female consciousness, an area of considerable importance to Bly. In an essay included in this volume, "I Came Out of the Mother Naked," Bly advocates a return to the virtues of the "Mother" culture which, in opposition to the currently dominant patriarchal system of rationality and aggression, stresses a sensuous, spiritual awareness of self and nature. Though some critics faulted *Sleepers Joining Hands* for flatness and pretension—most notably Eliot

Weinberger, who renounced Bly's talent and importance as a poet in his review—others praised the book and asserted the continuing validity of Bly's work.

This Body Is Made of Camphor and Gopherwood (1977), a book of prose poems written in a visionary style, lays the groundwork for *This Tree Will Be Here for a Thousand Years* (1979), in which Bly again attempts to bridge the gap between the conscious and unconscious. In his introduction to this volume, Bly claims that his intention is "to achieve a poem where the inner and outer merge without a seam." With its emphasis on nature, solitude, and quiet contemplation, *This Tree Will Be Here for a Thousand Years* represents a return to the concerns first developed in *Silence in the Snowy Fields.* The inward-looking, personal quality of these poems is even more strongly present in *The Man in the Black Coat Turns* (1981). Many of the poems in this volume examine the dynamics of father-son relationships and male grief, focusing particularly on Bly's feelings about his own father and sons. Bly has also produced several prose works, including *Leaping Poetry: An Idea and Translation* (1975) and *Talking All Morning* (1980). The latter is composed primarily of interviews but also includes a number of poems and essays.

(See also *CLC*, Vols. 1, 2, 5, 10, 15; *Contemporary Authors,* Vols. 5-8, rev. ed.; and *Dictionary of Literary Biography,* Vol. 5.)

DONALD WESLING

Talking All Morning is a highly persuasive cultural statement whose leading idea is that the American commonwealth wishes to suppress ecstasy and concentration, which are the performal sources of poetry. "We've destroyed our whole culture with this slurp television," Bly says at one point; and at another, the final words of the book, admitting his own implication in the perplexity:

> The problem is, how does poetry maintain itself as a vivid, highly colored, living thing? It's possible that originality comes when the man or woman disobeys the collective. The cause of tameness is fear . . . It is a fear that we will lose the love of the collective. I have felt it intensely. What the collective offers is not even love, that is what is so horrible, but a kind of absence of loneliness.

That will suggest the tone of the whole book: moral, prophetic, eloquently self-suspicious. Other ideas in the book, considered and embroidered in nearly all the interviews and essays and poems, may be phrased as imperatives: Live with more depth; bring the female aspects of the personality into full equality with the male aspects; write a poetry which is, like that of the Russians, personal and political at once, cutting both ways; earn every line with two hours of solitude; every poem through its images a true graph of the intermittence of the mind's life; for the health of the art, poets should attack other poets with friendly criticism. When he goes on the attack himself, Bly condemns English poetry, particularly that of the eighteenth century; the later Robert Lowell, who seems as if he has been "at parties too often"; recent forms of primitivism, recent translations; what he calls "barn-door poetry" and "poetry of the Okefenokee"; John Ashbery ("an utterly academic poet"). Against these he would set ancient Chinese poetry and Basho who hoped to get into poetry "the flavor of the inner mind"; Kabir; Wordsworth and Whitman; Lawrence, Rilke, Lorca, Pasternak, Kinnell, Hall. For Bly, all the useful poets are the ones who explore inwardness.

The interviews in this book are full of daring assertions and analogies, and striking phrases arrived at in the process of talk; they reflect too the struggle of definition, of thinking, and are especially appealing when Bly doubles back to question himself, as in his sentence: "I love the oral quality of primitive poetry, but how can a university be oral?" . . . Bly may be often wrong, but in my view his thinking is more consistently productive than any other commentator on recent American culture and poetry. . . . In its crazy wisdom [*Talking All Morning*] is totally unified, the product of an organic sensibility.

In turning now to Bly's book of poems [*This Tree Will Be Here For a Thousand Years*], which I find less strong than his book of talk, I want to focus on the subject of prosody and poetic form which is the remarkable absence in Bly's poetics. Why does Bly emphasize the image above every other element in the poem? Why does he insist on the image as the essential of poetry? Apparently he does so because the image achieves its effect only by denying its essence *as a word*. It functions by making us aware of something other than it is. The image cannot be mapped as a device because it does not coincide with syllable, word, phrase, sentence, or any other type of equivalence or form of grammar. It is resistant to scrutiny, and

Bly wants it that way. He wants details of the world in his poetics, not details of language. His is a magnificent poetics of essence and effect, but must remain incomplete until it adds consideration of the formal means.

In Bly's poetry, there is little play with words, with linebreaking, with the pleasures of sounds in words, nothing grand or dense. The poems spring their images on the reader in end-stopped lines, usually an image to a line, sometimes arriving at a plateau of plain declaration for contrast. There was no compelling rhythmic or musical reason to keep writing lined verse, given Bly's wish to bring the dream-image to the foreground of his poems, and to translate and promote the image-freighted poetry of Trakl, Lorca, and Neruda. Accordingly, Bly's turn to the prose poem is a natural development from his premises, because the requirements of rhythm and sound in the prose poem are not so obtrusive, and the poet may more immediately start calling up images and rapidly associating them.

There are four prose poems among the forty-four short poems in *This Tree Will Be Here For A Thousand Years,* Bly's first book primarily in lines after his prose poem books of the 1970s, *The Morning Glory* (1975) and *This Body is Made of Camphor and Gopherwood* (1977). I can find no difference between the lined poems in *This Tree* and the lined poems written before Bly's prose poems; his work makes no marked technical advances, largely, I imagine, because he is concerned with spiritual advances. Yet for readers the spiritual can only be made valid through and by means of choices prosodic, lexical, and syntactic. Where Bly plainly intends his poem as a testimony and vehicle of ecstatic transport, the reader may find it, while faultless, rather unmusical and bland. (pp. 147-50)

> Donald Wesling, "The Recent Work of Donald Hall and Robert Bly," in Michigan Quarterly Review, Vol. XX, No. 2, Spring, 1981, pp. 144-54.*

GREGORY ORR

[*The essay from which this excerpt is taken was originally published in* Poetry East, *Spring-Summer 1981.*]

In a time when poets seemed content simply to quietly or emphatically write their poems and keep on with business, Robert Bly was determined to think and write seriously about how important poetry is. We see this determination throughout *The Fifties* and *The Sixties* and in an important essay called **"A Wrong Turning in American Poetry"** which first appeared in *Choice*.

A good deal has been said about Bly's translations, and it's obvious that his efforts in this field brought about a revitalizing of American poetry. But the same could be said about W. S. Merwin and many others who were actively translating at this time, and yet the impact of other translators was not as strong. Why? Because Bly didn't simply translate, he championed the poets and the ideas about poetry that their work embodied. When he translated Rilke, Neruda, Vallejo, Garcia Lorca, Trakl, and (much later) Tranströmer, he did his best to speak about their notions of poetry.

When, in conjunction with his translating, Bly affirmed what he called "the image" (and which has since acquired the critical label, "deep image"), he was attempting to reunite American poetry with the mainstream developments of Romantic poetry as it had evolved on the European mainland: a poetry structured by symbolic imagination and making *extensive* (Neruda, surrealism) or *intensive* (Rilke, Tranströmer) use of symbols. If we seek a literary definition of symbol, we might well turn to Pound's definition of "the 'Image'" as "that which presents an intellectual and emotional complex in an instant of time.... It is the presentation of such a 'complex' instantaneously which gives that sense of sudden liberation; that sense of freedom from time limits and space limits; that sense of sudden growth, which we experience in the presence of the greatest works of art." (from "A Retrospect") (p. 149)

This notion of image which Bly repopularized is that of the crystallized intelligence of the unconscious mind, and as such it incorporates into poetic theory useful contributions from the dream theories of the depth psychologies of Freud and Jung. What Bly's talk of "the image" accomplished was a naïve and necessary affirmation of the symbolic imagination that structures lyric poetry.

If traditional symbolist theory sees the role of the image as the embodied lyric epiphany (either that moment in time that transcends time, or that which fuses and reconciles a poem's opposing forces), then another role for the image is probably at work in the politicised, anarchic intensity of surrealism from which one major aspect of Bly's own poetry is derived. In surrealism, we have a bubbling cauldron of images rather than a crystal.

Bly's essays, in the historical context of American poetry in the mid-fifties, represented the most intense public thinking about poetry's human importance that was taking place in English. The response to those essays, then and now, varied greatly: to many young poets, they were inspirational; to many of his peers, they were provocative; to many of his elders, exasperating and impertinent. Bly kept (and keeps) the pot of American poetics boiling. His pot is a stew: a bewildering richness of ideas and opinions—many of them contradictory, many of them seeming to be only half thought out. His intelligence is usually a moral one, occasionally a moralistic one.

I have mentioned the role of the image and the affirmation of symbolic intelligence as two lasting contributions from the early essays of Bly, but I think any attempt to locate and trace the continuity of his ideas and themes might be wrong-headed. Bly's ideas appear to arrive full-blown from the unconscious and seldom seem the product of discursive thought.... Bly is in large part a teacher-guru of the Way of Poetry—someone to whom ideas about poetry and poetry's role in culture and politics are as important as poems themselves. He has this in common with Gary Snyder, though their styles of presentation differ. If both of them are occasionally obscured by (and resented for) the largeness of their respective followings, we must never forget that their ideas are of utmost importance to poets and people who care about poetry.

Robert Bly has, in his time, changed American poetry: opened up new directions it might move in, inspired some poets to explore those directions, others to react strongly against such prospects. His role, stature, and style seem to me equivalent to that of Ezra Pound in the early decades of this century. (pp. 150-52)

> Gregory Orr, "The Need for Poetics: Some Thoughts on Robert Bly," in On Solitude and Silence: Writings on Robert Bly, *edited by Richard Jones and Kate Daniels, Beacon Press, 1981, pp. 146-52.*

BILL ZAVATSKY

[*The essay from which this excerpt is taken was originally published in* Poetry East, *Spring-Summer 1981.*]

In his own poetry, his many translations, in his magazines, anthologies, essays and interviews, and in his public talks and readings, Robert Bly has given more to American poetry in the last two decades than any other writer who comes to mind. Beyond his considerable literary influence, the issues to which he has addressed himself—the unconscious, the masculine and the feminine, our relationship to animals and growing things, our search for a spiritual center, war—place him beside those very few of his contemporaries who have persisted in affirming the union of the poetic and the moral in our time....

Bly's concern has even led him to encourage criticism of his work, something I can remember no poet ever doing publicly, and ... I have taken him up on that invitation. (p. 127)

"In the last sixty years, a wonderful new poem has appeared. It is the object poem, or thing poem," Bly wrote in *News of the Universe.* Why no mention of Imagism, still warm in the grave as a movement by 1920 but powerfully influential in American poetry far beyond its heyday? An important part of the Imagist project seems to have been the reconstitution of the object. All those tiny poems about an oriental fan or billowing waves or faces in a subway station—Imagism was a miniaturist's art and the emphasis was on close-ups of objects. It's surprising that Bly can praise Rilke's many poems about things and forget the many that William Carlos Williams wrote.... It was Williams who unfurled the banner which read "No ideas but in things." It's essential to read Rilke, but it's also important not to bypass huge pieces of our own history, and [Bly] is often running off to Europe at the expense of the lessons to be learned at home. Finally we must struggle on our own ground. (pp. 127-28)

But I want to talk a little more about Imagism. Let's say that Imagism was an act of father-consciousness—the violent stripping-away of the "feminized" rhetoric and idealized subject matter of the Victorian period. (p. 128)

In rescuing the object from the ornamental excrescences of Victorianism, Imagism also whittled away most of the traditional subject matter—much of it novelistic—of poetry.... Even narrative was sacrificed so that the object could be seen more clearly. Once the demolition and removal operations had been performed, poets like Pound wanted to begin building long poems again. The modernists had a new set of tools at their disposal: free verse, permission to use the rhythms of ordinary speech, the image, and—perhaps most important of all—the technique of collage juxtaposition. Using it in *The Waste Land,* Eliot jumped the reader from past glory to present despair in the space of two lines. But Eliot finally abandoned the technique, maybe seeing before Pound that it was a blind alley, suitable for ironic effects but trapped in the fragmentary—basically a poetry *of* despair, of the impossibility of making connections between things. "A bundle of broken mirrors," Pound called *The Cantos,* and his harsh self-judgement seems just. (pp. 128-29)

[Bly] has said that "the prose poem appears whenever poetry gets too abstract. The prose poem helps bring the poet back to the physical world" (*Talking All Morning*). I agree, but see the prose poem as the beginning (or return) of something larger. I believe that the hunger which created the prose poem and which has deepened our appetite for it in the last ten or fifteen years is the hunger for story. (pp. 129-30)

[The] prose poem began as a kind of vestigial organ which has been growing larger and larger over the past hundred years, sprouting eyes and limbs; it has been crawling and staggering towards the lost half of what poetry used to do: tell stories. It has unconsciously been constructing a back door to poetry and teaching itself how to open that door. Puzzled because it is a creature of the unconscious, it doesn't even half know where it's been going. But by now it is apparent that the prose poem is another means by which narrative, however surrealist-oriented at the moment, is re-entering the poem.

"The narrative poem has disappeared," Bly said in *Talking All Morning*. "This doesn't mean that nobody can tell stories anymore, but it means that the narrative is not really useful now for describing what has been found out." Or does the loss of narrative represent a loss of wholeness on our part? Has our poetry been, in fact, short of an expressive organ it cannot do without?

Let's assume that my comments about the prose poem are correct, and that there is a hunger today on the part of many poets for story-telling. We can't leave the reader out of this, either; maybe one reason most people don't read poetry is that the poems are too difficult to follow, too confusing. Maybe most poets don't really *care* whether anyone feels or understands their work. (pp. 130-31)

If my hunch about the connection between narrative and the feminine has any merit, more feeling ought to be coming back into poems and more characters will appear in them as poets begin to tell stories again. We will have a poetry that will leave readers touched rather than feeling stupid, charged with energy about the possibilities of poetry rather than feeling they ought to get a Ph.D. to understand the allusions. (p. 131)

One of the meanings of the title of Bly's 1973 book, *Sleepers Joining Hands*—the book which contains **"I Came Out of the Mother Naked,"** his major statement on mother culture—is that the relationship-making aspect of the feminine would *like* to make connections but is still unconscious to them, "asleep." The image suggests two, or perhaps endless ranks of "sleepers" (those devoted to the exploration of the unconscious hence committed to the development of the feminine) closing ranks in a manner which could be either affectionate, militant, or both.

But for all his discussion of the feminine, we have nothing in Bly's work that resembles a real woman, and only lately, in the prose portrait of his father in *Growing Up in Minnesota,* have we had anything like the portrait of an actual man. . . . There are a couple of charming poems in which one or more of Bly's children appear, and those poems count, but I am here talking of work in which some kind of interaction is depicted, and that happens most fully on the adult level.

The model of the feminine that Bly puts forth in the mother essay is basically that of the Good Mother/Bad Mother—the fecund, loving, nurturing mother and her opposite dark side, the Teeth Mother who devours her young. For all its usefulness, this model is an abstraction, an idealization that needs to be grounded in flesh-and-blood women to come alive. Bly's goddess is a nature goddess; the poet was raised a farm boy and still lives in the country, so this shouldn't strike anyone as strange. (p. 132)

In attacking "confessional poetry" Bly equates "confessional" with "autobiographical." (As for "confessional," a useless term, couldn't we substitute the phrase "personal crisis poetry"?) Does it need to be said that not all autobiographical writing is crisis material? Or, from the opposite angle, that it need be goofy or trivial?

Bly takes the "confessionals" to task for lack of specificity in their work, but the figures of the human he puts forward in his own poetry (few as they are) are just as vague, just as idealized. Why should our images of nature be detailed and those of the human be blurry?

[Bly's] idea that Berryman, Plath, Sexton, and others were killed by the kind of poetry they wrote doesn't make sense. They wrote out of crisis situations in their lives—the wound preceded expression of it, and to think otherwise is to substitute cause for effect. (Bly himself has said that the writing of poetry often begins in the hope of healing a psychic wound.) If these writers had written a different kind of poetry, would they have lived? I think, instead, that had their lives been happier, they would have written another kind of poetry.

Perhaps because these writers faced their dark side, writing out of what Jung called the "shadow," we want to turn away from them. It's never pleasant to glimpse what is broken or incomplete in our being, or even in the lives of others. In a 1976 article [Bly] praised the classical moderns for the amount of "shadow work" they did, and maybe it is true that as the shadow emerges, we can begin to move along the path of spiritual regeneration. Certainly Jung believed that we had to face what was negative in us before we could begin to heal the damage. That so many writers from the "Brahmin" class of American letters faced the darkness and were swallowed up by it at the same time that their social class was losing its long-held grip on our society hardly seems a coincidence. (pp. 136-37)

And so, when in one of the interviews in *Talking All Morning* [Bly] claims that the richness of the "interior animal life" which he sees in Lorca "cannot be expressed with images . . . of curbs and broken bottles and the objects with which Williams hoped to express it," I see him pushing away a realization of the shadow (and again favoring the European over the local, as if nothing of spiritual importance could happen here). American shadow is going to look different from Spanish shadow. Williams saw it reflected everywhere, in trash, in broken chips of glass, in the bums, even in the dog-droppings of the Rutherford and Passaic streets—the sense of inadequacy, of failure, the holes in our being. Williams doesn't turn away from this ugliness; rather, he embraces it. (p. 138)

Bly can praise the Eskimo shaman who "takes on illnesses, visits other worlds, reminds each person he or she meets of the night side," but these activities also describe, at least to some extent, the poets of personal crisis. If nothing else, let's distinguish them from other poets whose work, as [Bly] says, is "concentrated on the human," poets like Williams, Reznikoff, and Ignatow, who don't point towards self-destruction.

Perhaps [Bly's] "problem" is that he doesn't want to face the shocks of the human in his own work—that is where his own shadow-area may lie. His rural upbringing makes it easier and natural for him to emphasize the land and animal life over people. The surrealist poetry he has advocated, written, and translated, and whose influence he has brought into American poetry has moved us closer to the unconscious, to the feminine, and has been of incalculable value. I don't mean to disparage his love for trees and animals. But a surrealist poetry isn't well-equipped to deal with everyday experience, particularly the poetry of relationship. Surrealism is an ecstatic mode, and a poetry written out of moments of ecstasy leaves much of life untouched. Maybe there are disadvantages to leaping around. . . . (pp. 138-39)

Rather than one kind of poetry—"leaping poetry"—being suitable for all that happens, I am suggesting that at least several kinds of poetry are necessary to capture the variety of human experience, and none of them is "better" than the other.

In *News of the Universe* [Bly] writes: "This book asks one question over and over: how much consciousness is the poet willing to grant to trees or hills or living creatures not a part of his own species?" Is this really "the" question? What about granting consciousness to other people? We have so many poems with things and trees and rivers and hawks in them, but so few that really bring us what it is like to experience another human being. A poet like Robinson Jeffers loved the land and the wildlife while exhibiting a consummate contempt for people. Does Bly think that we will automatically grant respect and affection to women and to people of color if we grant them to trees and animals? I think that leap is a much more difficult one, and in our poetry we ought to be teaching ourselves how to make it. (p. 139)

> Bill Zavatsky, *"Talking Back: A Response to Robert Bly," in* On Solitude and Silence: Writings on Robert Bly, *edited by Richard Jones and Kate Daniels, Beacon Press, 1981, pp. 127-39.*

J. MARTONE

The wildness of Bly's imagination and his passionate commitment to poetry make . . . [*Talking All Morning*] one of the most important—certainly the most provocative—commentaries on the relationship of poetry to life to come along in quite a while. The collection gives us both a comprehensive review of Bly's career as a poet and abundant discussion of politics and poetry, the varieties of surrealism, translation, Jungian psychology and the deep image.

Bly's concern with inwardness informs this book from beginning to end, and the importance he attaches to the contemplative way is an important response to the heyday of the poetry workshop (of which he is deeply suspicious) and what might be called corporate poetry. "My advice to anyone if he wants to write," Bly tells us, "is to go and live by himself for two years and not talk to anyone." Bly's insistence that the poet be thrown back upon internal, imaginative resources goes hand in hand with his attack on craft-centered American poetics. For Bly, an overemphasis on technique in poetry results—as American technology characteristically does—in a substitution of facility for consciousness. At its worst, a poetry obsessed with technique not only loses touch with the passions but finally replaces thoughtfulness with organizational strategies. Recorded in 1972, Bly's rejection of craft as the basis of poetry is the most radical argument in this collection, and it is all the more powerful in light of much of today's poetry.

Bly's frequent use of a Jungian language and his discussions of the Great Mother will no doubt make many readers uncomfortable, but the intensity of his vision is hard to resist.

> *J. Martone, in a review of "Talking All Morning," in* World Literature Today, *Vol. 55, No. 4, Autumn, 1981, p. 680.*

DONALD WESLING

Robert Bly's previous book, *This Tree Will Be Here For A Thousand Years,* a far slighter work than his new one [*The Man in the Black Coat Turns*], was the occasion for a memorably brutal attack on the poet, his work and his many admirers by Eliot Weinberger [see *CLC,* Vol. 15]. . . . "A windbag, a sentimentalist, a slob in the language," Weinberger called Bly. And again: "Not since Disney put gloves on a mouse has nature been so human. . . . A festival of the pathetic fallacy . . . wistful and cloying . . . this utterly safe, cozily irrelevant poet." This flinty account, unusual in America reviewing for its being entirely negative, showed Bly as the Robert Frost of his generation, pushing a faint Modernism further than any poet ought on sheer charm of public presence.

In the interests of polemic, Weinberger neglected Bly's work as translator, editor and critic; and in his remarks on Romanticism, on the relation of poetry to politics, on the relation of American poets to audiences, he committed a number of oversimplifications of his own. But no matter, for the attack without mitigation is what keeps the review current. Bly himself has been a fierce reviewer. . . . Since, in his critical prose, Bly has urged young writers to take out after established ones, he wouldn't want his own work to be exempt.

This is pertinent to the new book, because the last (and best) poem has inscribed in it an image of the reviewing relationship. Bly describes going on his knees, peering into a culvert, seeing sky and lake out the far end of the tunnel. . . . **"Kneeling Down To Look Into A Culvert"** divides its speaker into two persons and times, the ordinary, present-day self and the water-serpent, which must return to be ritually murdered by its more highly evolved . . . heirs. By degrees the second self comes to dominate the poem. It seems to me a successful poem in the rather rare genre of archetypal memory, original because it shows the perspective of the parent who will be replaced. By analogy, the reviewer is to the text as the child is to the father—an executioner.

Conceivably the reviewer is also a collaborator. Who knows whether Bly reads Weinberger, and who cares? Nonetheless, there are changes in both style and subject matter in *The Man In The Black Coat Turns.* Weinberger had laughed at Bly's obsession with the theme of the Great Mother, and the new book, more as a completion than as a radical change, meditates on the theme of male grief, the relation of a man to the father he will replace and to the son who will replace him. (The book is dedicated to the poet's son.) Weinberger had condemned Bly's inaccurate or unsequential imagery, his inability to conceive the line as a unit of musical measure, his tone of "numbing sincerity"—and the new book does make improvements under all these headings.

Until recently (he has started talking about "grounding the poem in sound"), Bly spent a lot of energy refusing to talk about tone and poetic technique, insisting that the function of writing was to lead to something beyond, to "inwardness." In his practice, this limited the range of his experiment to the production and association of images—images which (for him) succeeded precisely where they refused their existence as words. To some of his readers, if not to him, this neglect of the medium of language still seems a real impediment to his development as a writer. This is acutely so for those of us who admire Bly's Quaker-like or Oriental quietness, his ability to leap from the homely to the scholarly, his gentle defamiliarizing of ordinary objects, his sense of family and his new book's inquiry into male grief and the dilemmas of a failing patriarchy.

Bly's work thus raises the question, which cannot be answered here, of whether a poem can morally individuate its experience without a style that makes language new. Of the twenty-four poems in this collection, I would say three are among the very best Bly has ever done. These are the one . . . [mentioned] earlier and two prose poems, **"A Bouquet of Ten Roses"** and **"Finding An Old Ant Mansion."** Three or four others are admirable work, and the remaining eighteen poems are subject to Weinberger's strictures or those that follow herewith.

For all Bly's attempts to wean readers from the unecstatic usual, his own poems are to quite a high degree predictable. Every poem in this book is written in the present tense, making for a plenitude of *this-this-this* immediacy but reducing the chances for reflective memory of the past and imaginative projection into the future. Many poems use the "we" of general humanity, with Bly obliging us to feel with everyone else: "We walk, the glass / mountain opens, we fall in." But what if one of us doesn't fall in? As in any book of Bly's poems, you can expect undistinguished phrasings such as "torn to pieces," "clamber out of sleep," "the walnut of my brain," and habitual lists—the names of colors, states of the union and months of the year. Those familiar cues of Bly's favorite inwardness, "black," "dark" and their cognates, are here—by my count, there are twenty-five occurrences of "dark" in this book. One poem, **"Eleven O'Clock at Night,"** is cliché from start to finish. At least three others vault to the opposite difficulty of runaway, unconnected imagery.

Plainly, here, the coherence of the imagery must be a special test of merit, since little else interests this poet. The brief poem **"A Sacrifice in the Orchard"** moves from the man with the Roman nose on the roof to thousands of moles crossing the lawn, to grief-stricken parents, to a blue raft, to goats, to men in the branches who are apples, and so on. Illogical leaping imagery can be magnificent, and Bly manages it in the water-serpent poem and others. But unintended nonsense is always a mistake.

Some of these poems do grow by rereadings, which discover hidden connections between images. . . . Bly is an attractive character, winning, gentle, opinionated, uneven, incapable of masterpieces but hitting on some good small things because the work is less limited than his ideas of what it should be.

Perhaps the best way to regard Bly is as a preacher or wisdom-writer. This book shows wisdom in its attempt to take up the great untouched subjects of fatherhood and replacement. The wisdom is rarely delivered in complete poems, but the parts are often fine enough. . . . Oddly, Bly's prose poems in this set seem to be more thoughtful and coherent than the ones set up in lines. Stranger still . . . , Robert Bly is consistently wilder and wiser about human experience in his interviews, published last year as **Talking All Morning** . . . , than he is in any of his poems. (pp. 447-48)

> *Donald Wesling, "The Wisdom-Writer," in* The Nation, *Vol. 233, No. 14, October 31, 1981, pp. 447-48.*

PETER STITT

Robert Bly's new book, **The Man in the Black Coat Turns,** is the most somber he has written, though it is far from being either morbid or depressed. As usual with him, the surfaces of these poems crackle with energy, liveliness; we are attracted most by the crazy progression of the images. . . . The conflict in Robert Bly's work has always been between aloneness and community. He began with solitude, in the magnificently introspective poems of **Silence in the Snowy Fields.** Since then he has been very much a public poet—an antiwar activist, a

performer on many campuses, the author of political verse. But in this book he returns to the world inside.

Mr. Bly has often complained that American poetry in general is too literal, too obvious. His own technique is based on the work of the surrealists and expressionists and embodies to an unusual degree Freud's early model of the conscious and unconscious levels of the mind. Mr. Bly's method is free association; the imagination is allowed to discover whatever images it deems appropriate to the poem, no matter the logical, literal demands of consciousness. (p. 15)

It is the images that carry meaning in a Bly poem, and because the images are arrived at spontaneously rather than logically, there is always a danger that the reader will not be able to follow the twists and turns of the poet's thought. Thus some of the poems here seem fragmented. But when the method works—which is most of the time—a surprising truth is reached. In this book, what is most surprising is a disjunction between the surfaces of the poems and their dark interiors. The speaker appears to desire the sense of closeness derived from family life, but in the pattern of his images he clearly longs for separation and solitude. These lines are typical:

> the son stops calling home.
> The mother puts down her roll-
>   ing pin and makes no more
>   bread.
> And the wife looks at her hus-
>   band one night at a party, and
>   loves him no more . . .

Mr. Bly's radical attempt to incorporate free association into American poetry makes him one of our few truly original contemporary poets. **The Man in the Black Coat Turns** is easily his richest, most complex book. (p. 37)

> *Peter Stitt, "Dark Volumes," in* The New York Times Book Review, *February 14, 1982, pp. 15, 37.**

LEE BARTLETT

Rather than being simply another poetry anthology . . . , **News of the Universe** is both a celebration and an argument: a celebration in the sense of Bly's obvious joy at the possibility of a poetry of "expanded consciousness," an argument in the sense of establishing an other-than-modernist line as the major movement in 20th century poetry. In his journal *The Fifties* (later *The Sixties* and *The Seventies*), Bly has established a fruitful editorial strategy; in the *Leaping Poetry* issue, for example, he writes a series of short essays all centering on the notion of association, then follows each essay with a number of poems which serve as object lessons. His method in **News of the Universe** is the same, though here greatly expanded from the earlier volumes, as he gives us eight essays and over 150 poems and parts of poems, most of which do not appear in the standard anthologies.

Bly sees Descarte's formulation, "I think, therefore I am," as the bulwark of the "Old Position," solidifying an earlier Augustinian view of nature as evil. Because man thinks, he therefore possesses a certain nobility which sets him apart from his environment. For poets like Lessing, Pope, and Arnold, nature became the Other, something either to be feared or to be disdained, with civilization held out as the path to salvation. Romanticism was, of course, a rebellion against this trend, but Bly finds little use in the English Romantics who (save Blake) remained "primarily in the realm of feeling"; even Keats, Bly suggests, found it necessary in a poem like "Ode to a Nightingale" to return to the comfort of human society at the last moment, unable to sustain himself in a "twofold consciousness." Rather, Bly turns to Nerval, Hölderlin, and Novalis as examples of poets who were willing to accept the "dark side" of nature in their praise of the unconscious—night, sexuality, woman—over against Wordsworthian idealization.

Bly continues by suggesting that we reconsider what "modern poetry" is. There is, he admits, a genuine tradition of modern poetry sourced in Corbiere and La Forgue, and continuing through Eliot, Pound, Cummings, and Auden, and its essence is irony. The major tradition, however, is for Bly the Novalis—Hölderlin—Goethe line, a line whose mood "is not ironic but swift association." Where Eliot accepts with resignation that the mermaids will not sing to him, poets of the primary tradition (Rilke, Jeffers, Lorca, Lawrence, and, later, Rexroth, Roethke, Everson, and Snyder) will not, as they refuse to recognize a gap between human consciousness and the consciousness of nature. (pp. 66-7)

Bly's earlier essay on the Great Mother, **"The Teeth-Mother Naked at Last,"** drives an anthropologist friend of mine to distraction with what he says are its half-truths and misinterpretations. With *News of the Universe*, Bly opens himself to the same charges. Occasionally, he gets his facts a little muddled and sometimes his interpretations are certainly superficial. . . . Yet, where many critics all too often seem to have the words without the music, Bly may be confusing the lyrics a bit, but he certainly has the melody. And it is lovely. (pp. 67-8)

> Lee Bartlett, in a review of "News of the Universe: Poems of Twofold Consciousness," in Western American Literature, *Vol. XVII, No. 1, Spring, 1982, pp. 66-8.*

CHARLES MOLESWORTH

[*The Man in the Black Coat Turns*] has three untitled sections, each with a loose stylistic unity. The first section includes poems that will be familiar to readers of *The Light Around the Body* (1967) and Bly's eight other previous volumes. Thematically the section deals with blocked energies and institutional failure ("the Empire / dying in its provincial cities"), but there are also hope and "days that pass in / undivided tenderness." An elegy for Pablo Neruda is included as well, perhaps Bly's most touching, scrupulous poem. Throughout, Bly tries to release the numinous qualities of everyday things, and to bring into everyday consciousness the Jungian perspectives of oneiric space and time.

The second section is comprised of six prose poems, and the longest and best of these is **"Finding an Old Ant Mansion."** Here Bly's spiritual allegorizing is starkest and most forceful, as he literally domesticates a natural object, a "wood-chunk," and in the process focusses his associative search for a "complete soul home." . . . The prose poems are to my mind Bly's best work, because his ear is resistant to fixed measures and he works more comfortably with a prose rhythm that relies on an alternation of intensity and relaxation of stress and watchfulness. Many poets turn slack in the prose poem, becoming indulgent in their use of imagery and too precious in their cadences. But Bly, having absorbed such French models as Ponge, finds in this genre just the right mixture of play and contemplative energy. In a sense we can see Bly at work in his prose poems; he has less need to hide the secret springs of his thought and feeling, and so puts us closer to the heart of his enterprise.

The third section of this book contains a dozen poems, all demanding and different from what have come to be Bly's distinctive lyric forms. These will take some getting used to even for Bly's partisan readers, but they show us he is genuinely a poet of growth. His whole project and ethic are founded on the principle of growth, on breaking through convention and repression to reinvigorate the joys of transformation and discovery. He has lived up to his own demands in this regard.

But a few of the poems in this section are for me unsuccessful, most clearly **"A Sacrifice in the Orchard"** and **"What the Fox Agreed to Do."** These rely on images too exclusively, or make too great a demand on their own centering thrusts by excessive "leaping." Imagistic density and associative leaping are central elements of structure in Bly's work, of course, but if used too drastically or too purely, they harm the overall effect. This is only another application of the aesthetic truism that any stylistic feature cannot in itself sustain a well-made artifact.

The best poems of the third section, however, are challenging because they extend the variety of Bly's structures. Here the best examples are **"Four Ways of Knowledge," "Crazy Carlson's Meadow,"** and **"Words Rising."** These poems are distinctive, but they share some features, specifically a concern with plotting the mind's curves and submersions on its way to self-awareness. Still far from being a discursive poet, Bly has turned from the sheer enactment of imagistic condensation and expansion (which sometimes made his poems too willful, too driven, despite his claims of spontaneity), to a subtle examination of the intersections of waking and archaic consciousness. These examinations require differing structures, so the pace of the poem's unfolding varies more frequently. There is more abstract language than Bly formerly allowed . . . , and more reliance on setting a scene. Certain themes persist and are carried over from the first two sections, especially the need to confront and accept the father, but there is a feeling of improvisation, of true searching, despite a more formalized sense of structure. (pp. 282-84)

> Charles Molesworth, in a review of "The Man in the Black Coat Turns," in Western American Literature, *Vol. XVII, No. 3, Fall, 1982, pp. 282-84.*

WAYNE DODD

[*The essay from which the following excerpt is taken was written in 1982.*]

Go back now twenty years later and you will still find it, lying silently in ditches beside the road, drifting noiselessly in with the snow at nightfall, standing dry and bristly in a field of weeds: *the spirit of the American prairie.* For that's what Bly discovered for us in *Silence in the Snowy Fields*: the spirit of the American (prairie) landscape. Nowhere a trace, not one blurring linger, of language or perception from another culture or geography (all influences of Spanish, Chinese, Latin American—and other—poets not withstanding). Just the American land, breathing into and through Bly. And us. I would even go so far as to say, if pressed, that however much else Bly may have contributed to the ferment of American letters, this has been perhaps his most important contribution—aside from the rich offering of the poems themselves. Once we had experienced *Silence in the Snowy Fields*, the body of America was never again the same to us—never again "merely" there, never again *external* to our own locus of spirit, no longer obedient to even the most carefully translated commands from "English" poetry. Since *Silence,* a developing generation of new young poets has been able to take for granted the subtle and important knowledge of our geographical lives these poems provide. (p. 223)

[It] is *consciousness* these poems are concerned with, consciousness of the world of solitude, of darkness, of isolation, of silence: the other world—sleep, the hidden or unseen, *the rest of it.* That's what the silence is filled with, what it frees us for: the other half, the realm of dark knowledge, night. The fields and rural buildings here open out into this large dimension of (our) being. "We are all asleep in the outward man," Bly quotes Boehme, as an epigraph for the book, then goes on to offer poems which, taken all together, call to us, *Wake up! Wake up!* in (and through) the inward man. This is the persistent urge one feels in *Silence in the Snowy Fields:* the urge to spiritual perception. We sense the need to discover the other-dimensionality of being. "There is unknown dust that is near us," the poem **"Surprised By Evening"** begins, "Waves breaking on shores just over the hill, / Trees full of birds that we have never seen, / Nets drawn down with dark fish." . . . *Everything,* we sense, is fraught with incommensurably greater meaning. In a substantial number of these poems we have the overwhelming sense that somehow we have suddenly broken through a thin covering into a purely subjective landscape. And yet *it* is the one that seems more real; indeed, in those moments we believe that it is *the* real. . . . [In] a poem such as **"Return to Solitude"** there is the implication that entire histories go on in a kind of subjective isolation, a place of solitude:

> What shall we find when we return?
> Friends changed, houses moved,
> Trees perhaps, with new leaves.

There is an urgency about the moments and events in these poems. Everything is darkly radiant with something which, Bly manages to suggest, we need urgently to know. (pp. 223-25)

But of course the physical details, in Bly, are the essential ingredients, for they are the windows we see through, they are the doors we fall through, the vessels we find ourselves in. . . . The poems continually plunge inside: ourselves, the landscape, the face of the American prairie. The spiritual content, we feel, does not exist as some detached or detachable "significance"; it is the content of *this* body (or bodies): *these* places, *these* moments, *these* people. And if one should have a sudden epiphany, a plunge to an unconsciousness knowing of the gestalt of wholeness in a moment, it will likely be while driving toward the Lac Qui Parle River, through small towns with porches built right on the ground. Or while walking in a corn field. Or among odorous weeds. Authentic language, Bly says elsewhere, arises out of a depth, "coming up from . . . every source." And what Bly offers, in the images and language of these poems, is not an excess of originality, but an ecstasy of appropriateness and recognition.

A successful poem, it seems to me, can profitably be talked of as if it were a living thing, through and in whose body we find beauty, density, grace, *further* life. All bodies are different of course, as all persons, all poems, all experiences. But even the most limited glimpse of a person's physical presence, the merest hint, can bring the whole of it rushing into our consciousness. . . . In *Silence in the Snowy Fields* the *whole* Bly is reaching for is that insistent sense of spiritual reality which the *family* of poems must identify. And we know what the

family, individual in their bodies, will look like: clear-eyed, blond haired, physically alive to the dark winters inside them. . . . Poem after poem in this remarkable book successfully enlarges a bare-bones narrative, exemplumlike in its simplicity, with an incomparably greater sense of existence, a complex presence of life. We come to be aware, as Bly is aware, of the abiding presence of a hidden order, the sacred masked by the ordinary. (pp. 225-27)

Wayne Dodd, "Back to the Snowy Fields," in Robert Bly: "When Sleepers Awake," *edited by Joyce Peseroff, The University of Michigan Press, 1984, pp. 223-31.*

BROWN MILLER

[Robert Bly's *The Man in the Black Coat Turns*] is a clear case of an established, important poet larded by his own theories and specialties of style, turning them into fetishes. He seems to be writing poems to fit his theories, to prove them valid. The poems mean little but have the facade of Bly's earlier, better poems. He is now self-consciously trying to be the poet we expect him to be. The results are mannered and self-indulgent, not much more than words on the page that resemble poems from a distance. I say these things mournfully; I say them with respect for Bly's past achievements intact. Though his importance as a poet and thinker has been exaggerated, I do value some of his work. Unfortunately, Bly's reputation is so formidable it can cause a reviewer in *The New York Times Book Review* to call this collection Bly's "richest, most complex book" [see excerpt above by Peter Stitt], an absurd statement from my viewpoint. I can find no poem as a whole, and only a few isolated lines that engage, compel, or even mildly interest. Boring images and flat reporting are presented with mock significance, with attempted resonance. (p. 22)

Brown Miller, "Searching for Poetry: Real vs. Fake," in San Francisco Review of Books, *July-August, 1983, pp. 22-3.***

HOWARD NELSON

If one thinks of [*This Tree Will Be Here for a Thousand Years*], as Bly suggested, as a sort of annex to [*Silence in the Snowy Fields*], it seems a paler, lighter sequel to a strikingly original book. Actually, if we wish to see it in relation to Bly's other work, *Tree* is interesting more for some of its differences from *Snowy Fields* than its resemblances, and for the signs it contains of developments that were still to come. First and most significant is the way in which death appears in these poems. Death was evoked repeatedly in *Snowy Fields*, but except in **"At the Funeral of Great-Aunt Mary"** it was more or less impersonal. . . . In the poems collected in *Tree* we . . . see death becoming more literal and more personal. Bly turns toward his own death, and the deaths of people near him. This turning would be crucial in bringing him into a new phase in his poetry.

Thoughts of death arise in many of the poems in *Tree.* In **"Writing Again"** Bly gives an impressionistic description of writing "of moral things," and then ends abruptly with these lines: "Well that is how I have spent this day. / And what good will it do me in the grave?" . . . [Similarly, in] **"Prayer Service in an English Church"** the sight of an hallucinatory "ghostly knot" in a page of the psalm book, the priest's call for the savior to come again, and the singing of old people standing nearby, combine to create a reverie which leads to a sudden and piercing vision of "the last day . . . / the whispers we will make from the darkening pillow . . ." (pp. 188-90)

To thoughts and premonitions of death another element is added. Bly's growing consciousness of death does not derive solely from the fact that he himself is growing older. The death of his brother [previously written about in **"Christmas Eve Service at Midnight at St. Michael's"** in *The Morning Glory*] must have had a strong effect on him, and it becomes evident in two poems in *Tree* that the advancing age of his parents has affected him as well. In **"Driving My Parents Home at Christmas"** he observes his mother and father as they sit with him in the car, and says, "their frailty hesitates on the edge of a mountainside." He is struck not only by the frailty but also the distance of old age. . . . When the poet watches them go into their house and "disappear," it is clear that he is very much aware that they will soon disappear through a different door.

A four-line poem called **"Late Moon"** expresses the awareness of death in connection with a parent more obliquely. Like many of Bly's tiny poems, it describes a glimpse of hidden knowledge or feeling, the moment held within a spare configuration of images. The poet observes the waning moon, "half of it dark now, in the west that eats it away," casting its light over his father's farm. The juxtaposition contains a dimly-lit awareness that the father will die; the phrase "eats it away" suggests that he may already be afflicted. (pp. 190-91)

Like **"Driving My Parents Home at Christmas,"** **"Late Moon"** contains a doorway. In **"Late Moon,"** however, the poet does not watch someone going through the door but rather has an unexpected encounter there: "As I turn to go in, I see my shadow reach for the latch." The suddenly appearing image of the shadow will jump out at the reader aware of Bly's study of Jung and his use of the shadow in **"Sleepers Joining Hands."** But of course the shadow's association with death is at least as old in the psyche as its association with a hidden part of the personality, elaborated upon by Jung. Both of these associations are at work in the poem. As a son realizes, with new depth and immediacy, that his father will die, his sense of his own mortality deepens as well: it is elders, and parents especially, who stand between us and death. At the same time the son will likely feel a closeness to his father he had not known before, and in that opening of feeling he encounters a part of himself which had been hidden to him.

The turning described in **"Late Moon"** can be taken to stand for Bly's turning toward the new phase I've mentioned. In this tiny poem mortality and the father loom together within the poet's consciousness, and bring him to a door. The shadow he meets there is not only the shadow of death but the shadow of his relationship with his father. After twenty years of celebration of the feminine, it was this relationship that would become the focus of his next book, published in 1981, *The Man in the Black Coat Turns.* Thinking of the resonant landscapes of *Snowy Fields* and the more acute consciousness of mortality in poems scattered throughout *Tree*, we can make a generalization: if it was Mother Nature that helped Bly on his journey toward the feminine, the Mother, it was Father Time that brought him to the father.

But when Bly wrote about the feminine and the Mother, it was psychic forces he was dealing with. He was finding ways of talking about kinds of consciousness; individualized, flesh and blood women were even scarcer in his work than men. But in

Black Coat it is not just *the Father* but *his father* that he focuses on. . . . Bly's attention in his poetry has been weak in "the middle ground"—the ground of ordinary human lives and fundamental human relationships. He had been a poet of fields, lakes, and trees, and of what they can draw forth from the man among them in solitude. He had been a poet of the political, historical, and psychic life of his country; of the soul's journey; of animals, ordinary objects, and the body. But he had not, before he was about fifty years old, dealt much with the ground of human relationship. In *Black Coat* he makes a concerted effort to do so. He still reaches out beyond the personal and the particular: *Black Coat* is in large part an extended meditation on the masculine soul, on wounds that are not only his or his father's but are shared by many men; it is the irrepressible nature of Bly's mind to do so. But at the center of this meditation stands the distinct and memorable figure of the poet's own father.

Before examining this figure, however, there are some other aspects of *Black Coat* that should be commented on. The first is its mood and emotional weight. The book contains just twenty-four poems, but it has the feel of a substantial, major collection. This is due not to the fact that many of the poems are somewhat longer than had been usual for Bly, but to their seriousness and emotional density. In tone *Black Coat* is Bly's most somber book since *The Light*. A sober and reflective mood prevails, and except in few cases, the kinetic and dazzling effects of Bly's more excitable style, and the ecstasies which sometimes seem aggressive, have been avoided. . . . [Ecstasy] and grief make up one of the principal dialectics at work throughout Bly's poetry; as he wrote in **"Wanting to Experience All Things,"** in *The Light,* "The heart leaps / Almost up to the sky! But laments / And filaments pull us back into the darkness." In *Black Coat* it is the downward motion of the spirit that Bly is dealing with, and honoring. The gravity is not that of anguish and moral outrage, as during a Vietnam War, but of a quiet, steady awareness that human lives and ties are so easily and often broken. (pp. 192-94)

If Bly is not "leaping" in terms of emotion in *Black Coat*, the same can be said for his use of association. There are poems here—**"Kennedy's Inauguration," "What the Fox Agreed to Do," "A Sacrifice in the Orchard"**—written in Bly's wilder surrealistic, leaping style, but leaping does not seem the right term for the poems that are most characteristic of *Black Coat*. There are striking disjunctures in the flow of thought, but there is also the contemplative tone and at times a discursive manner that make the shifts feel more like juxtapositions than leaps. In such poems as **"The Prodigal Son," "The Grief of Men," "Fifty Males Sitting Together,"** and **"Crazy Carlson's Meadow,"** distinct sets of images are poised against one another, and the meaning of the poems lies largely in the interplay among them. These poems are configurations of parts that form a unity, but not the sort of unity that yields readily to paraphrase. In them, Bly achieves a remarkable richness of idea and emotion.

At the same time that Bly has calmed and darkened his tone, and added tension to his associative style, he has also started to work more deliberately with the formal aspect of the poem than he had in any of his previous books. The middle section of *Black Coat* is made up of prose poems, but many of the other poems have been shaped with obvious care into regular stanzas. The stanzas are of Bly's own devising, roughly syllabic; he still does not acquiesce to forms handed down by tradition. (pp. 194-95)

One other aspect should be noted: *Black Coat* is considerably allusive. There are important biblical references, and figures such as Heraclitus, Pythagoras, and Descartes, Osiris and Odin, make brief but significant appearances. Bly's allusiveness is not nearly as extreme as Eliot's or Pound's, but it springs from a common desire: to recover the past and make it useful. The source most in evidence in *Black Coat* is the fairy tale. Bly entered the study of fairy tales through Jung, beginning in the early 1970s, and it has been a major phase of his activities since. (pp. 195-96)

Having made these general comments about *Black Coat*, we can turn again to the subject of the father. Bly's father had appeared fleetingly in Bly's earlier work.... [The early references provide us] with the knowledge that some fundamental estrangement has afflicted the relationship between Bly and his father. (pp. 196-97)

[There is one particular] antecedent to the *Black Coat* portrait [of Bly's father] ... which is of special importance—which is in fact an invaluable companion piece to this book and to Bly's poetry in general. In 1976 the University of Minnesota Press published a collection of autobiographical essays called *Growing Up In Minnesota: Ten Writers Remember Their Childhoods.* Bly's contribution was **"Being a Lutheran Boy-God in Minnesota,"** a piece which can stand among the best of his writing. It celebrates the life on the farms of an earlier day, praising the farm culture especially for the respect it accorded physical work—the loss of which Bly sees as a key breakdown in modern culture.... Woven through the essay are two character sketches: Bly's description of himself, which includes discussion of the psychological type he refers to as "the boy-god"; and a portrait of his father, who emerges not as a god but as a decidedly heroic figure, the carrier of noble and adult values.

"Being a Lutheran Boy-God in Minnesota" does not merely supplement *Black Coat*; it complements it. The essay is joyous where the poems are somber and meditative, and this contrast is especially noticeable in their portrayals of the father. In the essay the father comes across as a man of great strength and integrity—in short, of wholeness. In the poems, while he is still heroic, we hear also of his "invisible limp," his isolation, and some of the pain and distance that are part of the relationship between father and son. (pp. 197-98)

[In the essay Bly] says simply, "To be able to respect your father is such a beautiful thing!" That respect remains when Bly comes to write the poems in *Black Coat*. But in them there is also a considerable amount of pain that clearly goes a long way back in the relationship. It is the pain of distance and of a longing for reconciliation. The key poems for this theme are **"My Father's Wedding"** and **"The Prodigal Son."** (pp. 199-200)

Bly is describing in [**"My Father's Wedding"**] the situation of "the strong male" whose strength involves stoic loneliness. He regards such a man with compassion and respect, and not only because the person described is his own father. But the father-son relationship is central to the poem, and he expresses what it is like to be the son of such a man.... **"My Father's Wedding"** is emotionally complex, but one does not smooth over the complexity or pain of the poem in saying that, ultimately, it is a love poem.

The same can be said of **"The Prodigal Son,"** another poem which deals directly with separation from the father and the longing for reconciliation. This poem is an outstanding example

of [Bly's associative method] ..., in which the disjunctures of thought feel more like juxtapositions than leaps. The title refers us immediately to the well-known parable of Jesus (Luke 15:11-32), but Bly adds to this basic reference other elements which complicate and personalize the poem's meditation on fathers and sons. (pp. 202-04)

In **"My Father's Wedding"** and **"The Prodigal Son"** Bly writes as a son. In **"For My Son Noah, Ten Years Old,"** he writes as a father, though his own father is in a way present there too, in the imagery of wood in the opening stanza: "The lumber pile does not grow younger, nor the two-by-fours lose their darkness, but the old tree goes on, the barn stands without help so many years." In other poems his contemplation of the male soul is not linked explicitly to his own father-son relationships. In his earlier poetry Bly had described the male soul (e.g., **"A Man Writes to a Part of Himself"**) or the masculine principle (e.g., **"The Busy Man Speaks"**) damaged by being cut off from the feminine. Now he describes something else: a loss of feeling is still involved, but now it is feeling wedded to conviction, purpose, intensity, and sacrifice. (p. 208)

The loss of intense, active feeling which is also a loss of purpose and direction is one of several griefs drawn together in **"The Grief of Men,"** a poem in which the poet's father appears again and which is one of Bly's most moving meditations on "the masculine condition." (p. 210)

The poem gives ... a complex intellectual and emotional definition of the abstraction Bly uses for his title. The grief that it defines includes fatigue, failure, loneliness, and responsibility. The poem's total definition is greater, and more moving, than the sum of its individual parts. It creates from several thoughts one thought. (p. 212)

Black Coat contains what is certainly one of the finest "object poems" Bly has written: **"Finding an Old Ant Mansion."** As an object poem, a prose poem, and a poem containing animals, it is in the line of *The Morning Glory*. But it occurs within the first of Bly's books which focuses strongly on human relationships, and it is the awareness of family ties, sacrifices, labor, and gifts extending across human generations that emerges most strongly from the observation of a natural object here.

The poet awakens, alone, on "the first morning in the North," from a dream which transformed the rubbing of the sleeping bag on his ear into a rattlesnake biting him.... [The] self-absorption and anxiety of the dream break up as he awakens. They are replaced by physical pleasure as he goes out and walks in the chill, cloudy morning. His feet feel the earth beneath them—"And how good the unevenness of the pasture feels under tennis shoes! The earth gives little rolls and humps ahead of us ..."—and once again the body's sensations rouse the mind and imagination.... The poet comes upon a chunk of wood lying on the ground. He examines it briefly, notices that it has been partly hollowed out, though the wood itself is still solid, not rotted, "only a bit eaten by the acids that lie in pastures." When he carries it back to the house and puts it on his desk, he sees clearly that it was once the home of a colony of ants.

In the passage where Bly describes the interior of the "ant mansion" we see the logic of association working marvelously. Ideas and feelings enter quickly and smoothly. As the color of the wood is compared to that of workman's benches and eating tables, the ideas of labor and nourishment appear; that the tables are old ones seen in Norwegian farmhouses introduces the idea of ancestry as well. Brief references to caves, barns, cows and mangers, dusk and fall, add to the fabric of associations: the long past, the sturdiness of wood, animal warmth and sacred energies linked with it, and the falling darkness of time, all come quietly into the poem. Then we get a more elaborate comparison: "A little light comes in from the sides, as when a woman at forty suddenly sees what her mother's silences as she washed clothes meant, and which are the windows in the side of her life she has not yet opened...." This brings in the motifs of work and generations again, but also thoughts of lives passed in anonymity and the sacrifices and feelings that secretly connect one generation to another. All of these associations will be significant as the poem unfolds, and the beauty of the passage is that it introduces what will be the poem's major themes without our being aware of it. The images and their associations brush against one another here and subtly prepare the mind for what is to follow.

After describing the physical details and the mood of the mansion, Bly pictures the life that went on inside it, when "the ant legions labored" and "the polished threshold [was] passed by thousands of pintaillike feet." The passage is richly alive and lyrical, and Bly allows his imagining a generous range. At one point he speaks of the ants "with their electricity for all the day packed into their solid-state joints and carapaces"; elsewhere he speaks of the ceilings of the "balconies" as being "low and lanterned with the bullheat of their love." The ants are "almsgivers," and "the infant ants awaken to old father-worked halls, uncle-loved boards." Ordinarily no one objects when an insect is thought of as a sort of tiny, organic machine, but comparisons to human beings are likely to arouse not only objections but indignation. Hayden Carruth, in [his review of *Tree* (see *CLC*, Vol. 15)] ..., was prompted by some of Bly's statements about the consciousness that may exist in the natural world to remind us that "distance and difference are what makes us conscious, not fuzzy homologies." ... The lines on ants just quoted are colorful and impulsive, yet they are not to be explained merely as the product of a fit of warmheartedness, or light-headedness. The interesting thing is that Bly is serious in his admiring fascination for ants, which is actually far from the fanciful anthropomorphism it may sometimes appear to be. Does it mean anything to use the word "love" in connection with ants? ...

In a poem in *The Morning Glory* in which ants also appear, **"In the Courtyard of the Isleta Mission,"** Bly suggested that it is possible, and desirable, "to put ourselves in the hands of the ants." This is a risky statement, no doubt ill-advised since it is almost certain to be interpreted as a dismissal of intellect, moral choice, and individuality, in favor of pure instinct. (pp. 219-22)

When Bly says that we should "put ourselves in the hands of the ants," or when he speaks of "the bullheat of their love," running underneath his words is a sense of life lived at one with itself and yet also on behalf of something greater than the life of the individual ant or human being. (p. 222)

At the end of the paragraph that describes the ants' love, Bly says of "the sane wood" of the mansion that it was "given shape by Osiris' love." The love of a god which is expressed in the green life of the earth and the death and rebirth of the seasons encompasses the creatures that live and work in the darkness inside wood as well as those who live and work in the light of fire, electricity, and human consciousness.

But the poem does not end with Osiris' love. The motif of human ties and relationships suggested earlier in the poem takes

root, and it flowers throughout the next long paragraph. Bly says of the mansion he has described as a physical object and as a vessel of life, "Now it seems to be a completed soul home. These balconies are good places for souls to sit, in the half-dark." ... He thinks of placing the mansion on an altar, as the object of a small ceremony to honor ancestors; he wants to invite the souls of the dead to take lodging in this object that both the ants and his imagination have lived in.... (pp. 223-24)

Then Bly takes a final step in his meditation, returning to the ants and the motif of anonymous labor. The key correspondence between ants and men is stated directly: "What the ants have worked out is a place for our destiny, for we too labor, and no one sees our labor." And here the poet's father appears once more: "My father's work who sees? It is in a pasture somewhere not yet found by a walker." "And the life of faithfulness goes by like a river / with no one noticing it." When Bly spoke of the "father-worked halls [and] uncle-loved boards" of the mansion, the ideas of work, love, and generations came together, and indeed they circle close to one another throughout the poem. Work, carried out with some consciousness of the benefit of others, can be a form of love. Likewise, love is a form of work. Together they make up a force that keeps the human colony alive. This force is what the poem envisions and celebrates. In general, such work and love attract little attention, as the poem says, but here they are found in a pasture and well praised. (p. 226)

What is it that human beings labor on, comparable to the mansion or hill to which ants devote their labor? In **"Finding an Old Ant Mansion,"** with its concentration on ties extending across generations, it is a family, but by extension also the life of the race itself, the sprawling, elaborately evolving hill parents, ancestors, and the family of man as a whole have created and maintain. In another poem, however, Bly focuses on a particular aspect of the life of that vast hill: language. Fittingly, he dedicates the poem, **"Words Rising,"** to an elder poet, Richard Eberhart. Here he compares human beings not to ants, but to bees: "We are bees then; language is the honey." Because it nourishes human consciousness and the human spirit, language is crucial to the unique life of our hive. (p. 227)

The poem evokes light, sounds, movement, and smells, but it says that it is not only through the power of imagery that language links us with the past. It does so even more immediately through the sensuousness of words themselves. It is the sound of words that carries the unconscious memory of the old life: "the sound of words / carries what we do not." ... The poem makes an astounding assertion—one that is beautiful partly because it is so extreme. In it Bly imagines language alive with all the life from which it sprang, and so challenges us to learn to speak and understand it. (p. 228)

In one way **"Words Rising"** is one of the less personal poems in *Black Coat*, but in another way it is personal.... While his poetry is not as devoid of sound as it is sometimes made out to be, it has been the spirit that has been foremost for Bly, and language has been, until recently, something of an unpraised servant.... In **"Words Rising,"** while he does not use the pronoun "I" after the first stanza, Bly acknowledges that for him the spirit has lived through language, and that as a poet he has lived through his vocation in language. Bly's emphasis has been on the way psychic energy moves in poetry, and silence and solitude remain important to him, but it is language that connects the poet to the world.

"Finding an Old Ant Mansion" and **"Words Rising"** are both joyful poems; in them affirmations are made with only a few nods to the grief that is so important an element in **Black Coat** as a whole. I do not mean to withdraw emphasis from that element by ending with them; it is crucial to the overall tone and thought of the book. **Black Coat** is an affirmative book, but its affirmation rises both from the desire for healing and reconciliation (like all of Bly's books) with a father, with the flow of life greater than one's own life—and from an awareness that there are griefs which do not heal. . . . (p. 230)

In **Black Coat** we . . . see Bly making a book that is not a miscellaneous collection. The unity here is thematic. In this book he extends his meditation on the theme that has been central to him since some of his earliest poems, such as **"Where We Must Look for Help," "A Man Writes to a Part of Himself,"** and **"The Fire of Despair Has Been Our Saviour"**: the dual recognition that we are broken, isolated creatures, and that in our fragmentation lies the purpose of our lives. Before **Black Coat,** Bly had focused on the fragmentation *within* man, and on our need to reestablish our relationship with the nonhuman world. Here he enlarges his vision of fragmentation and healing: it took him a long time to bring human bonds and community into his poetry, but in **Black Coat** he has done so in an impressive and moving way. **Black Coat** significantly enriches both his vision and the body of his work. (p. 231)

> *Howard Nelson, in his* Robert Bly: An Introduction to the Poetry, *Columbia University Press, 1984, 261 p.*

Octavia E(stelle) Butler

1947-

American novelist and essayist.

Best known as the author of the Patternist series of science fiction novels, which involves a society whose inhabitants have developed telepathic powers over several centuries, Butler explores themes which have been given only cursory treatment in the genre, including sexual identity and racial conflict. Butler's heroines are black women who are powerful both mentally and physically. While they exemplify the traditional sexual roles of nurturer, healer, and conciliator, these women are also courageous, independent, and ambitious. They enhance their influence through alliances with or opposition to powerful males.

Four of Butler's six novels revolve around the Patternists, a group of mentally superior beings who are telepathically connected to one another. These beings are the descendants of Doro, a four thousand-year-old Nubian male who has selectively bred with humans throughout time with the intention of establishing a race of superhumans. He prolongs his life by killing others, including his family members, and inhabiting their bodies. The origin of the Patternists is outlined in *Wild Seed* (1980), which begins in seventeenth-century Africa and spans more than two centuries. The novel recounts Doro's uneasy alliance with Anyanwu, an earth-mother figure whose extraordinary powers he covets. Their relationship progresses from power struggles and tests of will to mutual need and dependency. Doro's tyranny ends when one of his children, the heroine of *Mind of My Mind* (1977), destroys him and unites the Patternists with care and compassion. *Patternmaster* (1976) and *Survivor* (1978) are also part of the Patternist series. The first book, set in the future, concerns two brothers vying for their dying father's legacy. However, the pivotal character in the novel is Amber, one of Butler's most heroic women, whose unconventional relationship with one of the brothers is often interpreted in feminist contexts. In *Survivor*, set on an alien planet, Butler examines human attitudes toward racial and ethnic differences and their effects on two alien cultures. Alanna, the human protagonist, triumphs over racial prejudice and enslavement by teaching her alien captors tolerance and respect for individuality.

Kindred (1979) departs from the Patternist series yet shares its focus on male/female relationships and racial matters. The protagonist, Dana, is a contemporary writer who is telepathically transported to a pre-Civil War plantation. She is a victim both of the slave-owning ancestor who summons her when he is in danger and of the slave-holding age in which she is trapped for increasing periods. *Clay's Ark* (1984) reflects Butler's interest in the psychological traits of men and women in a story of a space virus that threatens the earth's population with disease and genetic mutation.

(See also *Contemporary Authors*, Vols. 73-76; *Contemporary Authors New Revision Series*, Vol. 12; and *Dictionary of Literary Biography*, Vol. 33.)

―――――――

KIRKUS REVIEWS

[*Patternmaster*] is fine, old-fashioned sf about a distant future in which the earth is ruled by Patternists whose psi powers let them control the "mutes" who have no mental voices and do battle with the Clayarks. . . . A brief passage two thirds through the book offers a throwaway explanation of how this state of affairs came to be, but the how and why are less important here than the compelling conflict between Teray and his brother Coransee, both of whom seek to become Patternmaster—the ruler of this strange world. [*Patternmaster* is escape] fiction in the best Patterned tradition.

> A review of "Patternmaster," in Kirkus Reviews, Vol. XLIV, No. 10, May 15, 1976, p. 612.

PUBLISHERS WEEKLY

After centuries of mutations and conflagrations, Earth's survivors have settled down into a neatly stratified system of détente [in *Patternmaster*]. The Patternists are the elite rulers, linked to one another in a vast mental chain of telepathy and empathy. . . . The reigning Patternmaster is growing old, and his two sons are in hot competition for his job. Teray, the younger, just out of school and still naive, falls into his older brother's superior pattern and seems doomed to extinction until he meets a sexy outsider-Patternist woman who can augment his powers when she "links" with him. The author carefully spells out the ground rules of her unique world, and the ensuing story of love, chase and combat is consistently attention-holding.

> A review of "Patternmaster," in Publishers Weekly, Vol. 209, No. 24, June 14, 1976, p. 104.

KIRKUS REVIEWS

[*Mind of My Mind* is the] first chapter in a history that Butler has already taken up at a much later stage in *Patternmaster* (1976). *Mind of My Mind* begins with Doro, a ruthless mutant as old as the pyramids who has spent the last 4,000 years trying to breed a race in his own image. The culminating experiment is his daughter Mary. . . . Despite some ragged moments, Butler is clearly on to a promising vein—something like Zenna Henderson's "People" stories without their saccharine silliness. There's a lot of intrinsic energy in the Pattern idea, and one wants to see where this erratic, gifted storyteller will pick it up next.

> A review of "Mind of My Mind," in Kirkus Reviews, Vol. XLV, No. 8, April 15, 1977, p. 453.

MICHAEL S. CROSS

[*Mind of My Mind*] is a diverting novel about a mutant race emerging from humanity. . . . The novel is concerned with their construction of a telepathic "pattern" that permits them to build their own society. Butler has created some believable characters and placed them in a believable landscape. While neither the ideas nor the plot is new, the novel is readable and entertaining.

> *Michael S. Cross, in a review of "Mind of My Mind," in* Library Journal, *Vol. 102, No. 14, August, 1977, p. 1682.*

BILL CRIDER

The title character [of *Survivor*] is Alanna Verrick, a wild human adopted by Missionaries and carried to a distant planet occupied by warring tribes: the Gharkohn and the Tehkohn. The Missionaries are devoted to spreading the sacred God-image of humankind; they find the hair-covered humanoid Kohn repulsive, and naturally they choose to side with the wrong tribe, considering both more animal than human. (p. 110)

The story is well told in alternating sections which reveal the past (first-person narratives by Alanna and Diut, her Tehkohn mate) and present (third-person narratives). The Kohn culture is well developed, too, and is built around their peculiar colorations. They can change color at will in order to blend with any background, though emotion causes involuntary change, and one's true color determines his station in life. A Hao (leader) must be blue, for example.

The Missionaries and their hypocrisy are perhaps too easy a target, and some of Butler's ironies seem too obvious. The Tehkohn are much more sympathetic than the humans, except for Alanna. She survives, both physically and in the reader's memory. (pp. 110-11)

> *Bill Crider, in a review of "Survivor," in* Best Sellers, *Vol. 38, No. 4, July, 1978, pp. 110-11.*

JOANNA RUSS

Octavia Butler's *Kindred* is more polished than her earlier work but still has the author's stubborn, idiosyncratic gift for realism. Butler makes new and eloquent use of a familiar science-fiction idea, protecting one's own past, to express the tangled interdependency of black and white in the United States: the black heroine's great-great-grandfather is a white man who can, half voluntarily, call her back into his time to help him in emergencies; Dana, drawn wholly involuntarily, must save him to preserve her own ancestry, at least until the conception of her great-grandmother—and Rufus is a Southern slave-owner, confused, spoiled, a rapist with a remarkable gift for self-destruction. *Kindred* is a family chronicle set in a small space; the limitations let Butler concentrate on the human relations and the surprising-but-logical interplay of past and present.... Although characterizations in the past are detailed ... Dana's present-day marriage is sketchy and her aunt and uncle, who disapprove of her white husband, are talked about, not shown. Past events may simply have crowded out the present or Butler may mean to indicate that Dana's present-day difficulties in being black are nothing to her past ones—she gets shut of the appalling Rufus only, finally, by killing him. *Kindred* is exciting and fast-moving and the past occurs without a break in style—a technique that makes it more real—even down to characters' speech (Butler describes their accents but wisely doesn't attempt to reproduce them). The end is crossed-fingers hopeful with some chance of sanity "now that the boy is dead" though Dana has assured her own birth at a price: her left arm, lost at "the exact spot Rufus's finger had grasped it." (pp. 96-7)

> *Joanna Russ, in a review of "Kindred," in* The Magazine of Fantasy and Science Fiction, *Vol. 58, No. 2, February, 1980, pp. 96-7.*

ELIZABETH A. LYNN

Wild Seed is Butler's fifth novel, the prequel to *Mind of My Mind, Patternmaster* and *Survivor,* the other books in her *Patternist* series.... *Wild Seed* begins in Africa in 1690 and ends in the New World just before the Civil War. Its thematic core explores the question of what it means to be human, expressed through the experiences and emotions of Doro, a 4,000-year-old mutant whose sense of brotherhood in the human race has been changed and largely obliterated by his powers, and Anyanwu, a younger but also specially gifted immortal.

Immortality, shape-changing, psychic powers, the passing of one mind into many bodies: these are not new ideas to the science fiction canon, and the theme of what it means to be human has fascinated sf writers since Mary Shelley wrote *Frankenstein.* Doro's existence is obsessively dedicated to breeding a line of people with various psychic gifts, and for his people he is God. Anyanwu is forced to join the gene pool, to pass on her abilities of healing, shape-changing and great physical strength to Doro's people. But Anyanwu is an intelligent, resolute and powerful woman, and her dedication to those of her own genetic line equals Doro's: again and again she tests, thwarts and escapes his control, forcing him to confront his own weaknesses and to adjust his plans to her choices and to her moral concerns.

Butler's prose is spare and sure, and even in moments of great tension she never loses control over her pacing or over her sense of story. Her writing is staccato rather than lyrical. Her use of history as a backdrop to the struggles of her immortal protagonists provides a texture of realism that an imagined future, no matter how plausible, would have difficulty achieving; the novel is often grim, but it is never casually brutal.

> *Elizabeth A. Lynn, "Vampires, Aliens and Dodos," in* Book World—The Washington Post, *September 28, 1980, p. 7.**

TOM EASTON

Wild Seed is a tale of conflict and resolution stretching across a century and a half, from 1690 to 1840. It is warm, involving, sympathetic. And I am recommending it ... as a potential Nebula winner. It's that good. Immortality is a difficult theme to handle effectively, for long life must have its effects on personality, effects too few writers seem able to sense. An immortal must, Butler says, acquire either Anyanwu's wisdom and sympathy or Doro's coldness, callousness, canniness of survival. They are opposites in many ways, but elements of both are necessary for a truly successful immortal, and their blending might well occur as Butler paints it.... Butler's story, for all that it is fiction, rings true as only the best stories can.

> *Tom Easton, in a review of "Wild Seed," in* Analog Science Fiction/Science Fact, *Vol. CI, No. 1, January 5, 1981, p. 168.*

FRANCES SMITH FOSTER

The mythology that Octavia Butler creates in her first three books, *Patternmaster* (1976), *Mind of My Mind* (1977), and

Survivor (1978), has elements of familiarity. She writes about a future society wherein a network of telepaths control the Earth and occasionally get out of control themselves. She writes of colonists who settle on an alien planet and battle hostile, furry creatures. She writes of strange, micro-organisms brought to Earth by astronauts that threaten the existence of human civilization. She writes of genetic evolution and selective breeding. Like most contemporary women authors, she writes of women in nontraditional roles. (p. 37)

[Reviewers] consider her a speculative fiction writer who is adequate, potentially outstanding, but at present neither particularly innovative nor interesting. However, Octavia Butler is not just another woman science fiction writer. Her major characters are black women, and through her characters and through the structure of her imagined social order, Butler consciously explores the impact of race and sex upon future society.

Ironically, many speculative fiction scholars have been lamenting the neglect of those very areas with which Butler has been dealing. Marilyn Hacker, for example, has declared it a "serious drawback" that speculative fiction has devoted so little attention to "the vast area of human experience" which includes "family structures, child-rearing, and child-bearing, sexual relations—and relations between sexes (*not*, as some men would have it, the same topic at all)." Ursula Le Guin is one who has decried the fact that "in general, American sf has assumed a permanent hierarchy of superiors and inferiors, with rich, ambitious, aggressive males at the top, then a great gap, and then at the bottom the poor, the uneducated, the faceless masses, and all the women." And Pamela Sargent has mentioned, what most of us know, that "the number of black sf writers can be counted on the fingers on one hand." Since Octavia Butler is a black woman who writes speculative fiction which is primarily concerned with social relationships, where rulers include women and nonwhites, the neglect of her work is startling.

Octavia Butler consciously chose to introduce the *isms* of race and sex into the genre and obviously did not set out to write "fine, old fashioned sf." . . . A brief summary of her mythos and an analysis of her female characters will show the significant changes that Octavia Butler is making.

She posits a society of mentally superior persons created by the selective breeding of those with special sensitivities, mentally linked to each other in a hierarchical pattern. Our space exploration will cause a cataclysmic event which compels these persons to manifest themselves and to take a more direct role in governing human society in order to insure its survival. The humans of ordinary abilities, with the consensus of this ruling class, will try to preserve the "American way of life." The story goes like this: one day not too long from now, our first starship will return to Earth. Contaminated by a space virus, our heretofore disciplined and loyal astronauts will evade their quarantine, return to their communities, and spread a disease which will eventually kill one-half of the world's population and mutate the children of any afflicted who survive. It is characteristic of Clayark disease, as it will be called, that those infected will be compelled to spread their contagion; thus, "Clayarks" will become the common enemy of every healthy human being on Earth.

At this time, the Patternists, persons whose psychic proclivities had been developed secretly through several centuries of breeding, will reveal themselves. Doro . . . had bred these people

partially to insure himself a continuous resource for his own revitalization and partially to satisfy his intellectual curiosity. Individually, these telepaths have influenced people for years, but it was not until the mid-twentieth century that their appetites for power and their mutual antagonisms were controlled enough to allow them to organize. A Patternist society developed when Doro's daughter, Mary, during her transition from latent to active telepath, created a mental connection between herself and the most advanced actives. Mary, as the nucleus, became their ruler, for not only was she the strongest, but through the pattern, Mary was able to neutralize the inherent hostilities of actives, to discern satisfying outlets for their special skills, and to relieve the suffering of latent telepaths by facilitating their transition and thus ridding society of much of its violence and crime. (pp. 37-9)

The Clayark crisis will not only cause the Patternists to reveal themselves but will necessitate their dividing Earth into sectors protected and ruled by Housemasters. This will create new governing units, new loyalties, and new cultures, for so insidious will be the Clayark micro-organism that the survivors of sectors decimated by Clayarks will not be admitted into other Households, but will become wild humans who spend their lives hunting and being hunted. The new elite will be determined not by color, sex, or national origin, but by extrasensory powers. . . .

[The] Missionaries of Humanity [a group of loyal mutes allowed by the Patternists to search for a planet on which to continue their race] will find a "second earth," but it is inhabited by Kohn, furry creatures of various hues from rare blue to most common yellow. The Kohn have a humanlike form, but because their fur, color, and culture are different, the Missionaries will consider them primitive, inferior, and tractable. This ethnocentricity will allow one of the tribes, the Garkohn, to enslave the Missionaries as easily and unobtrusively as the Patternists had, thus giving a clue that it is not entirely their lack of extrasensory abilities as much as their limited concept of humanity that jeopardizes the survival of most of the human race. These colonists will receive another chance to continue Earth's culture when Alanna, a wild child saved from execution and adopted by a Missionary couple who dared defy custom, liberates the colonists from the Garkohn. (p. 39)

The story line is interesting but not provocative. Having no particular technological ideology and inventing no special devices, presenting a hierarchical society with no extraordinary personality developments, Octavia Butler does seem a mite old-fashioned. But her story has striking differences from other literature of the genre, and it is because of her particular mythos that she can assiduously develop the implications of these differences without sacrificing the pleasure of her tales. First, the elite in Butler's new world includes women. White males are proportionately represented in the lower classes not because they are male, but because as a sex they possess no unusual quantity of special gifts and a usual quantity of foibles. And, most significantly, Butler's major characters are black women. (p. 40)

One of Butler's major concerns is the possibility of a society in which males and females "are honestly considered equal." This idea is developed by her manipulation of three major characters; however, it is important that she also creates several secondary female characters who are not identified by race. The reader can then assume that these characters are not necessarily black and therefore generalize about the position of all women in future society even as the levels of racial integration that Butler assumes are recognized.

In *Patternmaster,* Jansee, the lead wife of Patternmaster Rayal, is an excellent example of Butler's use of minor female characters to suggest the ambiance within which the major characters exist. Jansee is the only sibling that Rayal did not kill during his struggle to gain the Pattern. Jansee, the "strongest sister," had chosen not to compete with him, not through fear, but through a strong reverence for life. She chose instead to be Rayal's conscience. As such she risks his wrath continually, steadfastly lecturing Rayal about his duties to his subjects and goading him into critical analyses of power. (pp. 40-1)

Another example of a minor character who gives insight into the possible roles of women is Gehl in *Survivor.* Gehl is a Garkohn huntress with whom Alanna, the protagonist, has exchanged language lessons and friendship. Like so many of the Butler women, Gehl is ambitious but realistic. "I'm going to challenge the Third Hunter," she tells Alanna. "I can beat him. I know I can. . . . Natahk (the First Hunter) . . . says my ambition will kill me. He knows that if I beat the Third Hunter, I will take on the Second." But Gehl has no intention of sacrificing her life in pursuit of ultimate power. She does not, for example, plan to challenge Natahk, for, as she says, "I only challenge where there is a chance for me to win." . . . Gehl does become Second Hunter in the tribe and the mistress of Natahk, thus forming a union with power. (p. 41)

Among the ideas garnered from secondary characters is the possibility that society will eventually allow open access to jobs and positions of authority; that while some women will be defeated by their ambitions and jealousies, many will exhibit an unusual resistance to self-destructive power quests; and that one way women will compensate for their physical limitations is by forming liaisons with persons of power. While such alliances may be sexual, Butler makes it clear that these women, powerful and purposeful in their own right, need not rely upon eroticism to gain their ends.

A brief analysis of the evolution of her three major women characters facilitates further understanding of Butler's speculations on the future. The first book, *Patternmaster,* gives us Amber as a significant and complex individual who functions as a symbol, a catalyst, and a mentor. The plot, however, centers around the struggle between an older brother, Coransee, and his younger brother, Teray, for the inheritance of the Pattern. Amber discerns in Teray a power to heal as well as to kill, and in teaching him to develop his humane tendencies, she teaches him the skills he needs to ultimately defeat his brother.

In *Mind of My Mind,* Mary gradually emerges as the protagonist; however, a central issue in this work concerns the effect of extraordinary mental powers upon individuals and their social relationships. Mary is the most developed of Doro's several children who people this book. She comes into her own when she overthrows her father; but Doro, his experiment, and his use of power are as much a focus of this work as Mary, who defines the limits of and represents an alternative to Doro's power.

It is not until the third novel, *Survivor,* that Butler presents a heroine. From beginning to end, *Survivor* is Alanna's story. Unlike Mary and Amber, Alanna has no extrasensory powers. Alanna . . . is an archetype, the kind of human who can survive in the future. Her attempts to overcome her weaknesses, to know and protect that which is vital, and to accept necessary

changes inform our sensibilities concerning the potential of ordinary human beings and constitute the plot.

Each of these women is black. This is given as a fact, and it does, at times, affect their attitudes and influence their social situations; however, racial conflict or even racial tension is not the primary focus of the novels. Butler explains that she feels no particular need to champion black women, but that she writes from her own experience and sensitivities. . . . [She] affirms her place in Afro-American literary history without excluding her work from a larger context. Butler is theorizing upon the same questions that Ursula Le Guin, for example, has raised: "What about the cultural and the racial Other?" Like Butler, Le Guin affirms the inextricability of humankind. . . . Butler explores the future implications of racism and sexism by focusing upon relationships between powerful persons who are various kinds of Other.

In *Patternmaster,* Amber . . . is not only a healer of special skill, but also "a terrifyingly efficient killer." . . . (pp. 41-2)

When Amber chooses to become Teray's mentor, she is choosing to join her power with his. She chooses further to become his lover, and finally, without consulting him, she conceives their child. But she will not marry him. . . .

Not only does Butler introduce a rarity in science fiction, a major character who is an independent and competent woman, but she makes this woman bisexual. (p. 43)

The relationship between Amber and Teray shows how males and females may relate to each other in the future, but it is secondary to the inevitable confrontation between Teray and Coransee. Amber has taught Teray to use his killing powers and to discover his healing strength as well. She, as mentor, made him ready for the confrontation, and she, as lover, becomes the catalyst for the fight. Teray decides he can help Amber, free her from Coransee, only by winning the Pattern. The central conflict of the novel, the rivalry between the brothers, is symbolized by their attitudes toward this woman: Coransee desires to subjugate her and to benefit from her skills through ownership. Teray wants her to be free and hopes she will freely work with him.

In *Patternmaster,* the major woman character complements the male hero. Teray has defeated Coransee, Amber nurses his wounds. "You saved me," he tells her. "Healed you," she corrects. . . . Teray has won the Pattern and Amber agrees to set up her House in Forsythe to be near him. Together they represent a good power. . . . [In *Mind of My Mind*] Mary is the mother of the Pattern and thus has preceded Amber by many years. Perhaps it is for this reason that race is a more obvious concern. Amber, though consistently described as black, attributes no particular significance to her ancestry. Mary, on the other hand, must reconcile a number of racial issues in order to establish the First Family.

Although the question of power is central to *Mind of My Mind,* and once again we have a serious confrontation between conflicting manifestations of that power, the resolution of basic questions concerning race is vital to the overall theme. (pp. 43-4)

The best summary of Butler's speculations on race can be seen through the relationship of Duit, the gigantic Hao, and Alanna, our archetypal human, biological child of an Asian woman and an African man, foster child of the European-Americans, Jules and Neila Verrick. Alanna tries to explain her marriage to her Missionary-of-Humanity foster parents and to gain their blessing for the union: "'I'm a wild human,' said Alanna quietly. 'That's what I've always been. . . . I haven't lost myself. Not to anyone. . . . In time, I'll also be a Tehkohn judge. I want to be. And I'm Duit's wife and your daughter'." . . . The Verricks cannot accept this. Alanna's relationship with the furry blue alien is beyond their tolerance. With tears in her eyes, Alanna accepts their limitations and says, "For a while, I was your daughter. Thank you for that anyway." . . . The Verricks represent those for whom racism may prove to be inextricable. For them the future is uncertain. We leave them following their cartload of possessions, searching for a place where they may live as they have historically. Alanna, able to reconcile the reality of her heritage with the demands of the present, survives.

The Earth people's failure to be humane is contrasted to the behavior of the Kohn at the naming ceremony of Alanna and Duit's daughter, Tien. Tien is a thickly furred, deep-green little girl who to the Kohn is "strangely shaded" and has "wrong hands and feet." But in their ritual, they accept her, saying, "We are an ancient people. The Kohn empire was the handiwork of our ancestors. . . . We are a new people. . . . In each child we welcome, we are reborn." . . . (pp. 47-8)

For the feminist critic, Octavia Butler may present problems. Her female characters are undeniably strong and independent; but whether, as Joanna Russ insists is crucial, "the assumptions underlying the entire narrative are feminist," is uncertain, for "who wins and who loses" is less clear than that a compromise has been made which unifies the best of each woman and man. For Afro-American literary critics, Butler can present problems as well, for their attention has been focused upon the assumptions and depictions about the black experience of the past and the present; yet the implications of Butler's vision should be a significant challenge. For the science fiction critics, Butler's work offers numerous areas of inquiry, but there should exist no doubt that in her contribution this writer has already given us "something really first rate." (p. 48)

> *Frances Smith Foster, "Octavia Butler's Black Female Fiction," in* Extrapolation, *Vol. 23, No. 1, Spring, 1982, pp. 37-49.*

BEVERLY FRIEND

[Dana, the] heroine of *Kindred*, is . . . at the mercy of an outside force. An unpublished writer, she is working at a mind-stultifying job with a temporary employment firm when she meets and marries co-worker and fellow author, Kevin. They are just setting up housekeeping in a new residence when Dana is suddenly pulled back to the year 1815 to save a little boy, Rufus Weylin, from drowning. But this tale goes far beyond a mere recitation of twentieth-century woman facing nineteenth-century life, for while Kevin and Rufus are white, Dana is black. Even more important, Rufus, son of a tyrannical plantation owner and his hysterical, ill-natured wife, is also one of Dana's ancestors; and he has a link with her so powerful that it calls her back from the present to save him from intense moments of danger throughout his entire lifetime. Thus, a contemporary black woman comes to experience the life of a slave on a Maryland plantation, although she does return to the twentieth century sporadically and briefly throughout the novel at those moments of absolute terror when the belief in her own imminent death triggers an involuntary return. (p. 51)

All in all, she makes six trips into the past, called each time by Rufus's near encounter with death. Each return Dana makes to the present is triggered by the possibility of her own death. Once she returns during a hideous beating; another time she causes the return by desperately slitting her own wrists. Each visit to the plantation accounts for from a few minutes to several days in Dana's own time, but comprises months to years of the past. Thus, she follows Rufus from childhood to adulthood while she scarcely ages herself. Throughout, she feels a moral responsibility for Rufus: "Someday, he would be the slaveholder, responsible in his own right for what happened to the people who lived in those half-hidden cabins. The boy was literally growing up as I watched—growing up because I watched and because I helped to keep him safe." Dana goes on to question her role as the guardian for Rufus: "A black to watch over him in a society that considered blacks subhuman, a woman to watch over him in a society that considered women perennial children."

Dana's role in this society, as subhuman and perennial child, is reinforced in the third trip when Kevin, who has been embracing Dana, unwittingly transfers with her. In Rufus's world, they cannot admit to being man and wife and are forced to enact the role of master and slave. And Dana fears the corruptive potential of such a civilization, even on her husband, if he should be stranded there. . . . (pp. 53-4)

How does Dana keep it from marking her? She doesn't. It marks her, although she manages to hang onto her sanity through continual reexamination of her situation. . . .

But living does not always look better. Dana's third trip ends with her being beaten so badly that she suddenly returns to the present without Kevin. When she next visits the plantation (on the fourth trip), eight days have elapsed for her, and five years have gone by for Kevin. He has left the plantation, gone north, and Dana must now send for him and await his return. At one point, when the waiting becomes unbearable and she discovers that Rufus has never mailed her letters to Kevin, she attempts to run away. She is caught. Nothing in her twentieth-century education or experience had prepared her to succeed. . . . (p. 54)

Perhaps the twentieth century does not help her because she does not utilize it effectively. Dana . . . [is] able to carry material into the past. In fact, she has a bag tied to her, ready to go the moment she is transported. And what is in the bag? All the things she needs and misses from civilization: toothbrush, soap, comb, brush, knife, aspirin, Excedrin, sleeping pills, antiseptic, pen, paper and pencil, and spare clothing. Prior to one of the trips she also packs a history of slavery and maps of Maryland, but this outrages Rufus, who demands that she burn them.

And so Dana works and survives as a slave, learning all the skills necessary to survive as a house worker, but not showing sufficient stamina to succeed as a field hand. Her twentieth-century ability to read antagonizes Rufus's father, who fears education for his slaves, and causes danger to herself and others when she teaches the slave children to read. Her knowledge of history is no help and only stands her in good stead by preventing her from killing Rufus until he has raped her black great-grandmother, assuring the inception of Dana's family tree.

Finally, when Dana does act, there are repercussions. She murders Rufus (who well deserves it), but justice does not then triumph. His death causes the end of life on that plantation, and the slaves are then sold off. Dana does not get away unscathed, either, losing an arm in her final wrench from past to present. (pp. 54-5)

No one would intellectually argue against the proposition that life is better today for both men and women, but few realize what . . . [this novel has] didactically presented: that contemporary woman is not educated to survive, that she is as helpless, perhaps even more helpless, than her predecessors. Just as Philip Wylie pointed out in *The Disappearance,* a world of men might be strife-ridden, but it would go on; a world of women would grind to a halt, sans transportation (no pilots, bus drivers, train engineers), sans full grocery shelves (no farmers or truckers), sans adequate health care (no ambulance drivers, paramedics, few doctors). Men understand how the world is run; women do not. Victims then, victims now. (p. 55)

> *Beverly Friend, "Time Travel as a Feminist Didactic in Works by Phyllis Eisenstein, Marlys Millhiser, and Octavia Butler," in* Extrapolation, *Vol. 23, No. 1, Spring, 1982, pp. 50-5.**

JOHN R. PFEIFFER

In *Kindred* (1979), and *Wild Seed* (1980), a prequel connected with *Patternmaster* (1976) and *Mind of My Mind* (1977), Octavia Butler produced two novels of such special excellence that critical appreciation of them will take several years to assemble. To miss them will be to miss unique novels in modern fiction. . . . [In *Wild Seed*] she has re-evoked the pre-European African tribal voice to present characters who will live through the nightmare centuries of the slave trade. In *Kindred* she excavates the ordeal . . . of slavery in America before the Civil War. Nevertheless, and therefore more remarkably, these are the novels of character that critics so much want to find in science fiction—and which remain so rare. Finally, they are love stories that are mythic, bizarre, exotic and heroic and full of doom and transcendence. With them Butler has at once made her best work inimitable and set a standard she herself cannot always be expected to meet.

Clay's Ark tells of Asa Elias Doyle ("Eli"), only survivor of an expedition returning from Proxima Centauri in about 2020 who carries an exobiological "disease" that can transform humans into physically stronger, healthier, smarter people that are, however, no longer human. Children of disease survivors are a beautiful but radically mutated bioform. With his first "victims" Eli begins an enclave of brutal but empathic supermen who try to live in hiding, hoping to protect humanity from their disease. . . . But human men will inevitably discover the enclave and the disease will run its course upon the Earth.

The similarity of *Ark*'s premise to that of *Andromeda Strain* is, we may be grateful, superficial. It has much more affinity with the stunning Australian film, *Road Warrior.* . . . Zenna Henderson's "People" narratives also come to mind: Henderson's shy supermen are sentimentally wholesome while Butler's are complex and any analysis of them edifying. But Butler's own *Wild Seed* and *Kindred* are a better measure of her talent, and *Clay's Ark* doesn't meet their standard, although it adopts the principal points of departure of *Seed* and *Kindred,*

which include the history of slavery and racism, the deep psychic structure of female and male persons, and finally the possibility of a love relationship between them. In its present state the psychobiology of male and female humans is distinct: One is predatory, voracious, and inseminating; the other is fastidious, sequestering and nourishing. These personalities are both ancient and modern.

But *Ark* is simply too short. It is barely long enough to relate the incidents of the story. It doesn't return often enough to character to satisfy our interest in [the characters]. . . . The male "lovers" of the women of *Wild Seed* and *Kindred* cannot love. Perhaps Eli of *Ark* can. But the brevity of the novel conveniently permits Butler to avoid showing how he might. Nevertheless, Butler's craft is now so strong that even one of her works of intermission is a delicious confection. Read *Clay's Ark.* It will be among the best things published this year.

> *John R. Pfeiffer, "Latest Butler a Delicious Confection," in* Fantasy Review, *Vol. 7, No. 6, July, 1984, p. 44.*

ALGIS BUDRYS

Reading [*Clay's Ark*] . . . turns out to be a pleasant surprise. The title does prove to be empty of meaning, but I have the feeling that's not Butler's fault; it hardly sounds like an author's title. *Clay's Ark* . . . is the name of the interstellar spaceship that comes back to Earth with a plague aboard; the story has nothing to do with anything ark-like nor with the spaceship per se. We never even see it, or its landing in the southwestern U.S. The story follows the surviving crewman, and then other people he infects over a period of years. (p. 34)

In any event, the story works. What the crewman infects Earth with is an alien symbiote that transforms the metabolism of humans and causes them to have children of superior physical and mental powers in an alien shape. The nature of the infection is such that its victims cannot effectively prevent themselves from having children and can barely hold down the pace at which they will infect others.

The race of *homo sapiens* is doomed; what has been brought back from the stars is the end of human history. (pp. 34-5)

That's what it's about, and Butler creates this tale with verve, originality, and an apparent gift for the circumstantial detail circumstantially told. This latter attribute may instead be a present inability to write in more than one tone of voice, but in any event she never strains for a pitch she's not up to. While rather far from ever reaching a resolution of any kind, this book is an effective piece of work in what might be called the "slice of death" school of SF writing. And there is the possibility a sequel is coming. (p. 35)

> *Algis Budrys, in a review of "Clay's Ark," in* The Magazine of Fantasy and Science Fiction, *Vol. 67, No. 2, August, 1984, pp. 34-5.*

Hortense Calisher

1911-

American novelist, short story writer, and autobiographer.

In her novels and short fiction Calisher explores the complexities of human experience with analytical precision and poetic imagery. She established her reputation as a gifted prose stylist early in her career, and she has been especially praised for her short stories. Virgilia Peterson attributes Calisher's success to her "brilliant manipulation of language, her endlessly apt observation of character and behavior, and the sudden illuminating generalities with which she is not afraid to sprinkle her texts."

Calisher's first book, *In the Absence of Angels* (1951), includes semiautobiographical stories and other pieces which are dark in tone and reflect her interest in the human psyche. *False Entry* (1961), her first novel, is about a man whose retentive memory and position as an encyclopedist allow him to intrude into the lives of others through his knowledge of their pasts. *Textures of Life* (1963) explores family associations through the relationships between a young, bohemian newlywed couple and their relatives. In *The New Yorkers* (1969), a companion novel to *False Entry*, Calisher portrays the life of a young woman who had murdered her mother upon discovering her with a lover. After many years of protection and denial by her relatives, the woman is able to admit her crime. These novels, in addition to the short fiction collected in *Tale for the Mirror: A Novella and Other Stories* (1962) and *The Railway Police and The Last Trolley Ride* (1966), solidified Calisher's reputation as a writer with a clear sense of human character.

In her later works Calisher has continued to examine the anxieties of people. The novel *Mysteries of Motion* (1983) departs from her characteristic contemporary urban settings to examine a diverse group of people selected to inhabit a space colony in a near-future society. Their mission, to preserve humanity from a polluted and overpopulated earth, is thwarted by sabotage and mechanical failure. The group, unable to safely reach their destination, are left to orbit the earth forever. Critics consider *Mysteries of Motion* to be Calisher's most ambitious work. Calisher returned to the contemporary urban settings of her earlier work in the collection *Saratoga, Hot* (1985). Calisher calls these stories "little novels," for "they seem to try for more than the short moments of a life. They try for the life."

(See also *CLC*, Vols. 2, 4, 8; *Contemporary Authors*, Vols. 1-4, rev. ed.; *Contemporary Authors New Revision Series*, Vol. 1; and *Dictionary of Literary Biography*, Vol. 2.)

GERTRUDE BUCKMAN

It is always gratifying to make the acquaintance of a writer of intelligence and feeling; it is these qualities which most clearly mark the work of Hortense Calisher, whose stories in the last few years have made their quiet, cogent bids for our attention. Miss Calisher is an eminently sober writer; without affectations or flashiness, without recourse (with the one exception, perhaps, of **"In Greenwich There Are Many Gravelled Walks"**) to immediate dramatic circumstances, she regards the human situation, the relation of one to one, of one to the destroying "everybody," with exactitude, compassion and restraint.

All these stories [in ***In the Absence of Angels***] are essentially sad, or rather, sorrowful, for most of her characters suffer from their difference, their isolation, their concern with those terrible needs of the human being which for most of us seem destined never to be fulfilled. This might seem maudlin if Miss Calisher had in her any extravagance, either of matter or method; it might prove thoroughly depressing, if her clarity of vision at close hand did not have its more important extensions, permitting her to hold, with calmness and maturity, to the "long view" which adumbrates the possibility, at least (even if only by inescapable, ironically necessary contrast), of a more satisfactory existence.

It is a pity that this long view does not take in lighter-hearted areas. Miss Calisher seems quite undisposed toward humor, except of a rather grim sort, as in **"Heartburn,"** a kind of allegorical fantasy of a tormenting inhabitant of a person's body which can only be expelled by being passed on to another who has expressed disbelief in its existence. This is not, of course, an amusing story—Miss Calisher's intention is never to entertain—it simply expresses her recurrent theme in slightly different terms. The difference, however, is not unwelcome; it lends an air of sprightliness to a collection which suffers somewhat from almost doggedly explicit seriousness. . . .

Miss Calisher's explicitness is the result of a virtue; she is a thoughtful and conscientious writer, and her choice of words pleases and rouses admiration for its precision, honesty and taste. Her use of language lies somewhere between science and inspiration. But she disdains short cuts, she will not make those concessions to the imagination, those delightful leaps of language or idea which might provide the relief of laughter to modify our plight even in a world which is giving us all such a hard time, the world in which, "in the absence of angels and arbiters from a world of light, men and women must take their place."

Gertrude Buckman, "Unfulfilled Yearnings," in The New York Times Book Review, *November 18, 1951, p. 46.*

CHARLES LEE

[Miss Calisher's] gifts are many. Her stories [in *In the Absence of Angels*] are fresh in their material as well as in their special slants of revelation. She attains that miraculous "solidity of specification," to borrow a phrase of Henry James, that achieves substance for her settings, aliveness for her characters, and convincing interpenetrations of both with the temper of the times. She deals equally successfully with the aged and the young, with the ordinary and the psychopathic, with male and female. She catches the compulsive talk of drunk and extrovert with the same skill that she explores the meditations of a mistress. She has the eye of an artist, the ear of a playwright, the balance of a judge, the mind of a psychologist, and the heart of a saint. Miss Calisher strikes one as a person who can never be fooled.

In varying ways her stories deal with people in love, out of love, searching for love, or incapable of love. They deal with the humanity of an obscure teacher, the insecurity of an "assimilated" Jew, the heartlessness of egotism, the terrible mob-imposed conformities of a department-store employee, the hungers of the young, the tragedies of the old. They range from the disintegrations of uranium to the deadlier disorders (since they are the real detonators of destruction) of hate, tribalism, and prejudice. And yet, though full of terror and torment, they are neither without compassion nor, more important, without hope. *In the Absence of Angels* Miss Calisher seems willing to pin her badly bruised faith on the virtuous potentialities of man. (p. 37)

Charles Lee, "People and Love," in The Saturday Review of Literature, *Vol. XXXIV, No. 48, December 1, 1951, pp. 37, 43.*

ALICE S. MORRIS

False Entry is, in essence, the self-analysis of a man in his forties, an eminent encyclopedist, successful enough, liked enough, but *dégagé*. He is "an eternal listener at the orchestrations of others," a man bitterly familiar with the "evening agony of non-life." The one woman he has found with whom he might share a responsible love, he sees as a danger, threatening the invasion of his secret self. Alert to this perversity, he realizes he must bring his buried "scrap of truth" to light, and into focus, as it has never been, with the truth of ordinary reality.

He sets out, then, to chronicle his life with unsparing honesty, traveling the impartial stream of memory where, the psychologists tell us, all secrets may be come upon, dredged up, their implications intact. There is a poetic justice in his doing so, for the uses to which he has put a prodigious memory are among the clues to his own truth.

Son of a London dressmaker and a profitless father already ignobly dead, the chronicler, by an accident of chance, made his entry into life—false entry No. 1—in the house of his mother's most loyal clients. Old Mrs. Goodman, Sir Joseph, Lady Rachel and the Goya-eyed children, with their pointed red leather birthday slippers sent by an uncle in Gibraltar, compose a household suffused in a fragrant sense of the past, a present of "easy slipper" generosity and grace. As his mother's pinbearer, he becomes one of the family's "benevolences"—included in its games, enfolded in its embraces and confidences; yet, unalterably and intolerably, not of it. "On those days (at the Goodmans') I was like a statue warmed down from its niche into living for a day, and at night, when I was returned to my corner . . . a fantasy of life remained behind my brow."

In the Alabama town of Tuscana, where his mother emigrates when he is 10, this fantasy remains to shape him, fostering his need to assume false colors, to be secret, to enter the lives of others forearmed with more knowledge of them—by hearsay, gossip and memory—than he will ever let them have of him. This *folie de grandeur* underlies all his acts. It draws him to Miss Pridden, curator of Tuscana's mansion-museum, who permits him private entrance, the freedom of the library. . . . It leads him to substitute "Pierre Goodman" for George Higby on the petition by which his mother meant to change his name to that of her new husband—a subterfuge that has a tragic effect.

When he graduates from a college in the North, this underlying drive for singular distinction takes him back to Tuscana to deliver "eyewitness" testimony against the local Ku Klux Klan—though his testimony is based on highly dubious evidence. As a result of this action, his stepfather, an innocent victim, loses his life and, indirectly, his mother hers. Now, under equally specious credentials, he has entered the Goodmanesque household of the Mannix's—and discovered the woman he loves.

As Pierre Goodman unfolds his palimpsestic history, healing gusts of the present more and more invade and freshen his hermetic self-enclosure. One more journey is called for: he revisits the Goodmans in London, there to find that time and change do, indeed, happen to us all. In possession, now, of his own scrap of truth, he is ready to align it with the bravery and mystery of the ordinary. He says to old Sir Joseph: "I am George Higby"—the rejected name of the man he sees at last as his true spiritual father.

This brave and major book, with many of its scenes drawn to the measure of a masterpiece, fulfills and amplifies a prerogative of the novel: to throw new light on life, and provide a vicarious experience of human living, profound, enchanting and revelatory. (pp. 4, 38)

Alice S. Morris, "Sealed within a Secret Self," in The New York Times Book Review, *October 29, 1961, pp. 4, 38.*

JEAN MARTIN

[*False Entry*] will be much admired by the *cognoscente*. It carries forward the Jamesian tradition of rococo writing filigreed over hair-splitting thought, so that the breaking of a promise becomes equivalent to the shattering of a mountain. In Calisher the art lies in all that she puts into a sentence. From a glittering vocabulary she chooses words that bejewel the tiara of sentence structure: "I see truth," she says, "as an old, hobbled unicorn limping through the forests of allegation and denial, pausing here and there to try to warm itself at some sun-foil of proof that shines for a moment through the trees. . . ." With Calisher, life lies underneath the sentence and the art decorates the top. (p. 411)

Calisher's exquisite art . . . [calls for a reader] whose pride in his understanding of the writing craft makes up a large part of his pleasure in reading. Those more simple readers who are out for a story will here miss the point. That the moral crises involved in the story are very small potatoes is unimportant; the telling is all.

False Entry is the recounting of the interior drama of a man who makes false entry into people's present lives by abusing information about their past which he has gleaned obliquely and illicitly and which he retains by virtue of a labyrinthine memory. By this peculiar form of intellectual dishonesty he violates his own integrity of self; and of this inner, intense drama Calisher's telling is acidulous, incisive, intricate and fiendishly intelligent. (p. 412)

Jean Martin, "Ways of Telling It," in The Nation, Vol. 193, No. 17, November 18, 1961, pp. 411-12.*

GRANVILLE HICKS

Miss Calisher is particularly sensitive to the pathos that is involved in the process of growing older. One of the best of the stories [in *Tale for the Mirror*] is "**The Scream on Fifty-seventh Street**," the story of a woman who is living alone in a city apartment after losing her husband and selling their place in the suburbs. The effect on Mrs. Hazlitt of the scream, her dismay at the absence of any response, her futile efforts to solve the mystery—all these are rendered with great precision. But the point of the story is not the impersonality and indifference of the city but the aloneness of Mrs. Hazlitt. . . .

Miss Calisher sometimes joins humor to pathos. There is a funny story, "**The Rehabilitation of Ginevra Leake**," about an uncommonly unattractive girl from a good Southern family. Astonishingly, Ginny finds fulfillment in the Communist Party. . . . This is material for farce, and Miss Calisher does not neglect her opportunities, but we are not allowed to forget how sad Ginny's situation is.

Even so light-hearted a story as "**Mrs. Fay Dines on Zebra**" has an edge of sadness, a touch of nostalgia, and nostalgia is frequent in other stories. In "**The Night Club in the Woods**" the narrator and her husband, just married and on their honeymoon in Bermuda, meet Mrs. Hawthorn, a flamboyant, rich, middle-aged woman, who refers vaguely to her husband, Harry, the Senator. Later, visiting her home in Connecticut, they realize that she is still living in her days of youthful glamour. . . . At the end the narrator says that she has told the story of the visit to Hawthornton many times but now she knows how it should be told, for "it is no longer Mrs. Hawthorn's story. It is ours." . . .

When her characters long for either the glory and glamour or the simplicity and calm of the past, Miss Calisher understands that they are really longing for their lost youth. Yet she herself is not immune to nostalgia, as such stories as "**Time, Gentle-**

men!" and "**May-ry**" show. The narrator speaks, affectionately and humorously, of her father as a survivor from the Victorian era, as a man who refuses to be tyrannized over by time, as someone she wishes she could emulate.

Part of the pathos of life, Miss Calisher sees, grows out of its complexity. In the title story John Garner, a mediocre lawyer in his thirties, lives with his wife and four children in an old house up the Hudson and commutes to the office in the city where he is employed. Into his rundown but sedate neighborhood moves Dr. Bhatta, "with his entourage of two faded Western lady secretaries, a number of indeterminately transient guests, and a faintly rotten, saffron breeze of curry." John finds Bhatta a puzzling man, a combination of charlatan and sage, of philanthropist and racketeer. . . . [After several] bewildering contacts with Bhatta, John is so disturbed that he cannot sleep, and he tells himself his tale for the mirror—the tale of the simple life he might have led. . . .

Miss Calisher's is not a great talent, but it is a fine one. She has her own feeling about life and her own admirable ways of expressing it. . . . Within her range she is beautifully precise, and her way with language is exciting. I have read stories that moved me more deeply than Miss Calisher's, but I have seldom read any that gave me more satisfaction.

Granville Hicks, "The Quiet Desperation," in Saturday Review, Vol. XLV, No. 43, October 27, 1962, p. 22.

GLORIA LEVITAS

Miss Calisher, over the decade since the publication of her first collection of short stories, has made some small changes in her approach; she is beginning to develop a sharp, yet compassionate, irony which stands in fine contrast to the sometimes self-conscious earnestness of a few of her tales.

Her skillful imagery and precise use of language have grown even more refined. And her ability to illuminate the interchangeability of the weird and the commonplace may one day become her most valuable literary asset.

Yet, the overall impression of [*Tale for the Mirror*] is that Miss Calisher has settled rather more comfortably and somewhat less excitingly into the mold which she set for herself ten years back. Then, as now, her concern was with the "knell of sadness for something that had been, that had never quite been, that now had almost ceased to be." And this singular concern often involves her in a melancholy sentimentalism that blurs the acuity of her vision by reducing all of life's problems to the lack of communication between human beings.

Loneliness—and the inability of people to live in the present because of it—is her theme. . . .

In the title novella, *Tale for the Mirror,* Miss Calisher has crystallized more formally than usual her concern for the driven people who cast solitary shadows across her chiaroscuro landscape. In the story an Indian neurologist sets up his practice in a conventional suburb. He is a purveyor of dreams—a seeming fraud—who houses the sick and insane and offers them, in return for their money, the illusion of involvement with the world. With this illusion, this "tale for the mirror," man is able to fortify himself against night terrors and pretend to an omnipotence he does not have. Yet Bhatta, the neurologist, has no convincing tale for *his* mirror. His fraud is practiced on himself; he is as much victim as con man, and like the others, he too is a seeker in the night. . . .

If Hortense Calisher's intimate vignettes seem strangely static in a world mad with motion, if they never wander beyond their intensely personal framework, if she has glued together the crumbling pieces of the world of her maturity with the illusion of hope, she has at the same time created some of the most discomfortingly vivid writing of this decade. And in all she writes, no matter how despairing, there is a strange human dignity that cannot be realized without pain; nor can it be easily forgotten.

> Gloria Levitas, "Solitary Shadows of Driven Souls," in Books, November 4, 1962, p. 13.

FELICIA LAMPORT

Textures of Life deals essentially with relationships, exploring many of their nuances with considerable skill. It opens at "the chilliest damned wedding lunch" any of the guests can remember, with the chill emanating from Elizabeth and David, the young bohemian bride and groom. The couple has submitted to this conventional celebration for the sake of Elisabeth's mother, Margot. . . .

The relationship between mother and daughter develops throughout the novel, sometimes in labyrinthine exegeses, sometimes in fine flashes of insight. Elizabeth, whose great book-bag is "her reticule, purse and home," is scornful of her mother's involvement with the "nice things" that spell security to Margot and pretentious clutter to her daughter. These two, with their attitudes as separate as parallel lines, are nevertheless entangled through the compulsion each feels in the presence of the other to act out the other's image of herself.

At the start, Margot, intimidated by her daughter's sullen confidence and disdain, wishes fiercely that Elizabeth will be made in time to "see what life is" to understand and perhaps even share her mother's point of view. But when time, and the birth and illness of Elizabeth's baby bring this wish close to fulfillment, leaving her daughter worn and reduced, no longer bohemian, no longer a determined and confident sculptor, Margot finds herself wishing that she could "see Elizabeth her old, savagely untidy self, slopping about in her old wolf-colors, instead of this thin, pinched non-slattern, so sallowly clean." For David and Elizabeth themselves, the change in their lives is not tragedy but development. . . .

Miss Calisher's style is so full of grace at its best, and her imagery so fresh and imaginative, that her few, but still too frequent, lapses into obscurity or preciosity are disproportionately obtrusive. When Elizabeth looks at her baby "so softly respiring," there is a temptation to speculate that if the baby— and the other characters—would give up respiring and start breathing, *Textures of Life* would be a good deal more alive.

> Felicia Lamport, "Miss Calisher's Super-Intense Art," in Books, April 28, 1963, p. 4.

NANCY HALE

[*Textures of Life* is] an extraordinarily moving and satisfying novel which is in part a voyage of exploration into how youth lives today, in part a probing of the meaning of the terrible antagonisms between a mother and daughter, and over all a new evaluating of the intimate relation between rejection of material things and domination by them.

Are Liz and David really different from yesterday's young people? More heartless, or more highminded? It is a likely theme, and in the course of an exciting story told by a writer with an acute eye and ear, a dozen questions pop out in a reader's mind to surprise him: Are the young really evading responsibility, after all? Will life itself succeed any better in disciplining them than their parents could? How about their insistence on being free of things: can they keep it up after a child, strangely afflicted, is born to them? Do they become any more tolerant of the old parental imperfections? Any more objective about themselves? Does life ever grant them a realer apprehension of what it means to be an artist?

The characters in *Textures of Life* live these questions through. Their story, which is primarily Liz's story, is rendered with a depth of perception which at once compels the reader's confidence. This, he feels, is the way these people must have been. In fact, such is Miss Calisher's acuteness, and precision of style, that it comes as a shock when, in the midst of dialogue with Jewish-American cadences, British locutions like "in a muddle" and "chivied" appear, to be followed by "We've only to sit still" and "Whatever are you doing there?" in the mouths of Americans of Italian and German descent. . . .

In a novel of experience, like *Textures of Life*, there seem no limits to the submerged territory a gifted writer can map. In telling an absorbing and important story about compelling characters, Miss Calisher has mapped such territory. Perhaps not the least of her gifts is that she knows how to give the reader his own insights, instead of keeping them all within her book.

> Nancy Hale, "After the Wedding, Brr-r-r," in The New York Times Book Review, May 12, 1963, p. 5.

DAVID BOROFF

Miss Calisher can be "placed" in two ways: as a *New Yorker* writer . . . , and—without even the faintest pejorative intent— as a woman writer deriving from the tradition of Edith Wharton and Willa Cather. In the *New Yorker* manner, she offers the small tilt of awareness rather than the explosive revelation, vignettes of grace under pressure rather than existentialist travail. As a woman writer, she is concerned with those junctures of experience in which the amenities of our civilization are threatened, and with the sad, shabby, sometimes ennobling ways in which the patchwork of human relationships is somehow maintained. It is easy to say, therefore, what Miss Calisher is not. She is no hipster goddess, no cheerleader for sexual epiphanies, no architect of new novel forms designed to end the novel. She writes in a humanistic tradition, which seems spacious enough for her needs and which she has significantly enriched. The intensity of her commitment is also reflected in her prose. She is an immaculate stylist, a precisionist of the utmost rigor, and an arresting phrase-maker. If the compass of her writing is fairly narrow, there is an admirable consistency about her work.

Extreme Magic consists of a novella—the title story—and eight short stories that have appeared during the past decade. . . . One or two are little more than extended anecdotes, like the opening story, which is a spoof on the study of phonetics. But the modesty of Miss Calisher's unassertive tone can be misleading. In **"Two Colonials,"** for example, there is a wonderfully muscular vindication of common sense and good will. The story concerns a little Midwestern college which used to turn out teachers and social workers and now offers courses in

Kierkegaard and guided missiles. The villainess in this gentle academic pesthole is a faculty wife, Portia-Lou Mabie, who "had a talent for endorsing the worthiest convictions in a way that made their very holders wish immediately to disavow them." An academic from England, Alastair Pines, falls into her formidably Anglophile clutches, but he is not nearly English enough for her tastes. When he refers to a colleague as a "short round sort of chap. Little Jew with a beret," Mrs. Mabie indicts him as an anti-Semite. But it turns out that Pines and Weil, the refugee Jewish professor, are natural allies, while Mrs. Mabie, in her squeamish revulsion against the word Jew, is the authentic bigot. (pp. 36-7)

The novella, *Extreme Magic,* is artistically less tidy than the short stories. It concerns a man who, after the tragic death of his own family, is reclaimed by the torments he witnesses in the lives of a local innkeeper and his wife. Nevertheless, even in her weaker efforts Hortense Calisher can, in a phrase, get at some buried nerve of experience. And at her best she sounds rich and complex chords that reverberate lastingly in the mind. (p. 37)

> David Boroff, "The Saving Remnants of Grace," in Saturday Review, *Vol. XLVII, No. 18, May 2, 1964, pp. 36-7.*

EVE AUCHINCLOSS

[*Extreme Magic*] is a collection remarkable for uneven achievement. The sensibility is extremely feminine—in the faintly pejorative sense—and the talent diaphanous, but two stories, anyway, are limpid and moving. Others are depressingly glib and secondhand—surely the possibilities of the struggle with a foreign language, the refugee professor stranded on a mid-American campus, the disintegration of a suburban marriage, the ghastly middle-aged woman afloat in Europe, etc. have been exhausted by now. The writing is sometimes skilfully evocative, the nuances suggestive, the imagery just; but then there are ornaments (many of them) as trashy as "the river gave a little shantung wrinkle." . . . People write like that when they are afraid of running out of gas; it happens too often in this collection. But there are two stories, **"The Rabbi's Daughter"** and **"The Gulf Between,"** that are harmoniously true and moving—even substantial—because they rise from authentic experience: in this case cultivated, haute-bourgeois, upper-West-Side Jewish life, a little down on its uppers. Miss Calisher has a real sense of a past; . . . she can show where things come from; what people really are; how they feel; how they affect one another; why what happens happens. Each of these stories covers no more than twenty-four hours, but in each, individuals, a family, a culture are realized with almost abashing intimacy.

After stories of such quiet purity, the novella *Extreme Magic*— a mixed-up effort to construct a plausible armature for an *omnium gatherum* of fancy and fanciful details—is incomprehensible. The protagonist is a small-town husband who has lost his family in a fire—potentially interesting: but what does she make of it? After a spell in a plush sanatorium, he turns up as a cultivated, queerish antique dealer in Dutchess County. Characters make emphatic appearances, then disappear for good after a few pages; others come, go, come back, go—but why? Finally a pair to whom one had hitherto paid only routine attention involve the antique dealer in a charnel-house finale and the ambulance wails out of the night to carry away another toppled mind. The story is full of solemn nods toward symbols

that never give up their mysteries; the writing is forced and pretentiously Jamesian. It is sad that the author of stories as civilized and scrupulous as the best in this book should allow herself such posturings. (p. 17)

> Eve Auchincloss, "Good Housekeeping," in The New York Review of Books, *Vol. II, No. 10, June 25, 1964, pp. 17-18.**

SANDRA SCHMIDT

Hortense Calisher's style is smooth and stately. It turns sentences like figures in a minuet, with matted polish, subdued flair. When Miss Calisher tells a story, there is a fascinating interplay between action and reflection: characters are apt to go off into extended cerebration only to have a good swift motivating kick from behind. . . .

Journey from Ellipsia is about an upstanding, intelligent oval. Oversimply, it is a science-fiction story. The oval, from a far, teardrop-shaped planet where everything has rounded itself into the form of a perfect ellipse, has come to earth to—horrid thought—change. He intends to trade shapes and places with an envoy from earth, for a purpose that will apparently emerge as the story progresses.

The ellipsoid's progress, as it flits and fumbles through a world that has variety and mutability, gender and appendages, is a masterful and joyful look at earth and humanity from the outside. For one thing, the ellipsoid—whose only name, Eli, is casually dubbed in for him by a human character—is a delightful person. He is a naïf and rushes toward new experience at a whirlwind rate. But he is also wise and while he experiences he learns.

For another thing, Miss Calisher avoids the kindergarten sweetness-and-light and high-school hysteria that characterize so many published paeans to life, as well as the heavy-handed symbolism and fraught analogy of so many others.

And both she and Eli have senses of humor as well as visual and auditory senses. . . .

But these things aren't enough. I am as eager to suspend disbelief as anybody, when it comes to anything even vaguely resembling science-fiction—if there is a reasonably sturdy hook to suspend it from. The intricacies of style of this book seem completely unjustified by the story. In the end, the plot fritters itself away, the characters who have been so carefully and fully molded dissolve, and the interesting themes that peppered the first part of the book—like the well-organized international conspiracy of women against men—evaporate into thin air. Even Eli, whose hindsight remarks throughout the book have led the reader to expect more, disappears on a puff of wind.

> Sandra Schmidt, "Oval's Progress," in The Christian Science Monitor, *November 11, 1965, p. 11.*

R. V. CASSILL

Among the talents that have thrived particularly in this decade, I can think of none that has moved forward so serenely and surely as Hortense Calisher's. Each of the books she has published since 1961—[*The Railway Police and The Last Trolley Ride*] is the sixth—has shown her perfectly sure of herself and of the direction her art was to take. The note she sounded was never strident. Sometimes it may have seemed too muted, refined, and almost lost in the complications of her prose. Now in at least one of the two novelettes here published—*The Railway Police*—she has made a well-nigh perfect synthesis of symbol, language, narrative and theme. It opens a view on concentric mysteries which approaches the limits of intelligibility without incurring obscurity.

The narrator and chief character is a woman who suffers from hereditary baldness. She is also a person of charm, wit and well-shaped character, whose respect for her womanly role has always led her to hide this baldness with an artful variety of wigs. She is modestly wealthy. Her avocation is social work—avocation, because her real task is to discover and accept her womanliness, a reality represented for her by the gradually resolved riddle of her hairless head.

She denies this primary condition of her existence, not merely by wearing wigs but by aborting the child who might have carried the ambiguous sign into another generation. These denials do not prevent her from searching with cunning, imagination and sophisticated meditation for the means of affirming what she truly is.

In a central episode, both comic and terrifying, she attempts an actual marriage with a balding gentleman whose anthropological and artistic tastes imply he will accept her ultimate unveiling with joy. Alas, when she brings her smooth skull in contact with his lips during a passage of love in the dark, he shudders—"not in ecstasy." (p. 4)

Miss Calisher's choice of baldness as a central symbol of the female nature may appear idiosyncratic and even frivolous. Providentially, the novelette contains a specific caveat against such misinterpretation: "It's entirely possible to be both honest and frivolous, a role that men deny exists, of course, since only women are perfect for it." There are, in fact, a multitude of such directional signals in the seamless texture of her narrative. The author has thought of everything—as the creators of such small masterpieces must—and by those transformations, in which observation and reflection become imagination, has brought a tide of truth flowing through the confined channel of her symbols. (pp. 4-5)

The Last Trolley Ride also shows off Miss Calisher's skill in catching the nostalgia of pastoral reminiscence and ornamenting its movement with colored streamers of words. Here vignette opens on vignette as the story strays back and forth from the present to the 1920's and 1890's in small towns in upstate New York. The history of two marriages is played out in fragments against a dramatic spread of landscape. Somewhat disappointingly, the import of these marriages is never clearly disentangled from the charms of the picturesque background. This fuzzier one of the two novelettes is a pure pleasure to read, but it stops short of the revelation that climaxes pleasure in a full esthetic experience. (p. 5)

> *R. V. Cassill, "Feminine and Masculine," in The New York Times Book Review, May 22, 1966, pp. 4-5.*

VIRGILIA PETERSON

At a time when mystery, not to say mystification, has gone out of fashion and there is a general conviction that all codes are about to be cracked, Hortense Calisher goes on stubbornly writing novels and stories that are wrapped in a mystery inside an enigma. Like a mineral spring, her imagination keeps bubbling up with hot and sometimes sulphurous narratives that both attract and repel. Her work attracts because of her brilliant

manipulation of language, her endlessly apt observation of character and behavior, and the sudden illuminating generalities with which she is not afraid to sprinkle her texts, despite the current vogue for writers of fiction to keep their thoughts to themselves. Yet this very virtuosity ends [in *The Railway Police and The Last Trolley Ride*] by repelling the reader who needs to know, and cannot discover, what deeply matters to Miss Calisher and what she really means to say. Perhaps she is merely too clever to get it across. Or perhaps her one love is the word itself. (p. 66)

[What] in fact, is *The Railway Police* about? Surely, Miss Calisher has long since shown herself to be too devious to say anything as simple as that we all want to be accepted and loved for what we are. If on the other hand she is speaking of the burden of private shame, surely she is not suggesting that, like her lady social worker, we should all uncover it and pay the consequences? It seems unlikely that anyone as devoted to mystification as Miss Calisher should write a story against it, as indeed it also seems peculiarly ironic and interesting that this writer, who happens to have herself a wild and unforgettable abundance of hair, should have conceived of its absence as her symbol for private pain.

Nothing written by the same hand could be more different than the second story in this volume, the novelette called *The Last Trolley Ride*. At first glance, there seems to be no mystery whatever. Certainly there is none in the title. A last trolley ride, a most meaningful trolley ride to the chief characters in the tale, actually does take place. The trolley itself, serving as a kind of *deus ex machina*, determines the fate of the two gawkily inarticulate and touchingly innocent couples . . . whose hesitancies and confusions are wildly reminiscent of some of Shakespeare's lesser comedies. What happens to them is recounted some thirty years later by one of the men involved, with a desire to clarify and perhaps even to edify the grandchildren of both. There is real sweetness in this story, but occasionally, too, alas, an archness heretofore undetectable in any of Miss Calisher's work, even through a magnifying glass. Whether or not the denizens of small New York canal towns were as wholesomely free of corruption (except for a bit of gossip, snobbery, and shrewd dealing) in those far-off pre-super-highway, pre-assembly-line days as Miss Calisher paints them, she certainly makes you see it all through the misted lens of nostalgia. Moving back and forth in perspective with a technical proficiency that was conspicuous for its absence in the work of Grandma Moses, she all the same brings Grandma's simplicities to mind, and with them their concomitant catch in the throat.

Yet *The Last Trolley Ride* is not without its mystifications, too. Both young men, for instance, happen to be called Jim (though this arbitrary little confusion is in part dispelled by the fact that one Jim refers to the other as "mate"). Both wanted wives, both had their eye on the rather neglected fringe-of-the-town sisters, of whom Lottie, older and much plumper, could do nothing else but make ambrosial fritters, while Emily, the younger, was for all practical purposes at least the prize. You learn, of course, which man gets which girl (or vice versa), but you never do quite find out, even during the last ride of the Batavia-Sand Spring Interurban (an early folly of the local millionaire's), which girl which man wanted. Still, some thirty years later, just before the story is being set down, you are not sure, with the women gone by then and the two men now close enough to tell one another the truth, whether one Jim really did lay down his life, as it were, in willing sacrifice for the other.

But what does the clever, the sophisticated, the exacerbatedly aware Hortense Calisher mean by this idyll of hers? Is she saying, as she pulls up her ample sleeve: "You expected a snake and look—it's a nice white rabbit!" Or does the rabbit only look like a rabbit because of her conjuror's art? It is not impossible, knowing the rest of her work, that with this long, prettily written, and unarguably appealing story, *The Last Trolley Ride,* she has pulled out her neatest trick so far, and left us without a clue as to how or why she did it. (pp. 66-7)

> *Virgilia Peterson, in a review of "The Railway Police and The Last Trolley Ride," in* The Reporter, *Vol. 35, No. 8, November 17, 1966, pp. 66-7.*

ANATOLE BROYARD

On Keeping Women is the kind of novel that leaves no velleity unturned. It is an anthology of all the impulses, ideas and reflections about love and marriage than might conceivably occur to a modern woman. Here is an image that occurred to me while I was reading it: In the days when men and women danced together, it was a common thing to see a woman who was far superior to her partner and who reacted to the disparity by introducing into her movements all sorts of little accelerations, embellishments and flourishes while the man labored flat-footedly through a box step. In trying to keep up with Miss Calisher, I felt like that man.

Lexie, the heroine, has four children, and the intricate way in which these five people continually interpret one another makes it seem as though they are gifted with extrasensory perception and I am not. I have a hell of a time following them. This particular dance floor also has those stroboscopic lights that make me, at least, rather dizzy....

I rather like a rich, even an overripe prose—or, at least, I like it better than the currently fashionable deadpan or phenomenological style. Writers such as Saul Bellow, John Updike—and, of course, Hortense Calisher—always give you something to chew on, a bag of freshly buttered popcorn while you watch the movie. To go even further, I don't think you can do justice to a complex character without using a complex sentence once in a while. There is a sensuous—even a sensual—pleasure in the rise and fall of a sentence.

All too often, though, Miss Calisher's rhetoric seems to me to mire her characters as well as the movement of her book. Take this passage about a party: "The whole noble, fretful stream of human gossip that goes scalding along the glory-road, parroting the normal or murdering by proxy, or only sweet-talking with youth—sugar which'll drown in the morning—or seeing dog-blind." A passage like this one *competes* with the progression of the novel instead of encouraging it....

On Keeping Women opens with Lexie lying naked, after a wild party next door, on a lawn on the banks of a river. She has been left there by a former lover who is defeated this time by too much drink and too much reflection, and she is determined to stay where she is until the commuter buses roll past on the road. She wants to make a statement, so to speak, naked to her enemies. I have everything and nothing to hide; something to that effect. Through sheer technical virtuosity, Miss Calisher sustains Lexie there, naked on that grassy bank, for 325 pages, even until her stilted husband returns from Spain, where he has been hospitalized with hepatitis. The two of them, facing busloads of neighbors, hand-in-hand, clothed only in an ambiguous desire for a better life, make quite a picture.

> *Anatole Broyard, "Family Situations," in* The New York Times Book Review, *October 23, 1977, p. 14.**

JONATHAN PENNER

As the story of Lexie (surname: none given) unravels [in *On Keeping Women*] browsers will be disappointed who—seduced by the title, aroused by the opening tableau—expect a romance of savory sex. So will those hoping for a tale of women's liberation, though the title seems to hint at that too. The principal subject of this novel is simply the showing—in Lexie, her husband Ray, their four children—of various states of wretchedness, various combinations of hysteria, bitterness, boredom, disgust, despair....

What fills this novel is not action but talking and thinking, most of it lamentation. Domestic misery is a given, a circumambient medium in which Lexie and her tribe drown protractedly, with drowning people's strenuous repetition of futile gesture. It is therefore odd that one begins so soon to wonder, and finishes the novel without ever being made to feel, where and by what these people are being so painfully pinched.

The Hell of this family is never shown us during its construction. It results from no one's villainy. Nor does simple error, of heart or of mind, ruin these lives. In fact, human acts (except for the implausible rush of them at the end) have little consequence or meaning.

One sees the pain of these characters less in pity than in bewilderment. What has happened, or is happening before our eyes, to make them so unhappy so often? One nearly squints, trying to make it out. But the feeling remains that one has forgotten to put on one's glasses; it's like watching tennis being played vigorously without any ball.

This lack of intelligibility comes down to the paragraph, the sentence. Things, even the simplest things, tend to be put obliquely: no "He cried," but "Tears haggled for his face." Lexie's "thoughts often elide, or express themselves truncatedly in her own code." And so it is whether we are in Lexie's mind or not—so much seems to be put together with missing parts. Inevitably, the parts that remain become overladen....

Such language ... steals the life from characters. They are made to speak and think, not as people may, but in extended passages of what is inescapably written discourse....

This will be called a novel "about" language, currently a stylish interpretation, though superficial—a bit like a bird's being "about" bone and feather. Again and again, the author plainly invites such a reading.

> *Jonathan Penner, "One Foot in the Quicksand," in* Book World—The Washington Post, *November 6, 1977, p. E8.*

RICHARD EDER

[*Mysteries of Motion*], set in a near future, is not precisely science-fiction, despite technical detail about the workings of space travel. The ill-conceived, ill-used shuttle Courier, with its human cargo—a philosophic publisher, a diplomat, an Iranian exile, a black woman journalist, an industrialist, a German refugee poet and an Irish-American medic—is a symbol of our vagrant and overheated civilization.

Mysteries of Motion is an ambitious book. The sicknesses of our time crisscross and converge both in the space project—a

Utopian venture quietly and fatally undermined by the military establishment—and in its characters, whose biographies occupy most of it. . . .

The original concept of the mission, advanced by Gilpin, the publisher, is that a representative sample of humanity, including misfits and the infirm, should be sent out in the 100-passenger Courier to settle in a space station. If humanity is to try to escape a deteriorating world and reconstitute itself elsewhere, Gilpin argues, it must go in a full and variegated version and not as elite specimens.

The military and space bureaucracy resist this humane notion, but Gilpin's political influence prevails; or seems to. In fact, the authorities manage to switch all but a half-dozen of Gilpin's choices and put their own Right Stuff types on board instead. Furthermore, in the grand tradition of Washington fiddle—tanks that break down, guns that jam and cases of whiskey transported at taxpayer expense—the Courier's specifications are skimped and its payload disastrously increased. And the government men are only second-class Right Stuff; and only one of them survives.

This bare-bones story is not simple to winkle out. Calisher has a great deal on her mind, and the reverberations that she sets going, the subtexts and allusions, accumulate in such profusion as to turn the story into a cavern of echoes. Even the simplest actions are hinged and come apart in the middle to let digressions through; it is, to a troublesome extent, narration by rumor.

If the space trip provides the book's central image—civilization is in an uncertain, dwindling orbit distorted by greed and lack of vision—its substance is in the lives of the half-dozen passengers chosen according to Gilpin's vision. Each contains some share of the virtue and shortsightedness of contemporary history.

Gilpin himself is the liberal imagination: reforming, powered by inherited wealth and privilege, and all but literally impotent. Mulenberg is a multinationals tycoon, a man of burning but limited vision. Veronica is a prodigy from Barbados: tall, beautiful, a brilliant writer and untamed spirit. Mole is shining and betrayed youth, the rebellious son of a space-agency overload who smuggles himself aboard the shuttle just because he senses that his father has doomed it. Lievering is Europe's displaced person, a German Jew on a verge between poetry and nervous breakdown. Wert is a decent and dedicated diplomat who embraces the complexity and horror of the Iranian tragedy and brings his wife, a torture victim of the shah, along on the trip. . . .

Wert, a humane bureaucrat, is the most interesting character in the book. He is also the only one who seems to possess a life revealed rather than imposed by the author. The others, all larger than life, lack it. They are epigones, free and powerful as archangels: and, like archangels, created for the sake of their celestial missions. They win some and lose some—it is not always easy to tell which—but they do not alter, or lose their laundry.

Mysteries of Motion, written in a mannered prose that becomes a fidgety form of lethargy, is a novel of ideas and prophecy. The ideas are good, and the prophecy may be; but the novel, instead of advancing them, entraps them.

> *Richard Eder, in a review of "Mysteries of Motion,"*
> *in* Los Angeles Times Book Review, *October 9,*
> *1983, p. 1.*

JOYCE CAROL OATES

[*Mysteries of Motion,* a] massive, densely plotted novel of the not-very-distant future is Miss Calisher's most unexpected work of fiction and, surely, as ambitious as anything we are likely to see published this season. No summary of the interwoven plots, no discussion of the novel's many ideas, can suggest the quality of this unusual work, which is at once a defiantly risky species of science fiction and a thoroughly realistic psychological novel—traditional in its fidelity to the analysis of human personality under stress. Suspenseful as the novel becomes, especially as its frightening conclusion approaches, it is primarily a meditation upon the nature of heroism and self-sacrifice in the service of an ideal. (p. 7)

Mysteries of Motion is remarkable in its scrupulous attention to the details, both technological and psychological, of space flight: the sensations of liftoff and an attempted docking; the malaise of nongravity . . . ; the finicky attention to food, drink, hot water, comfort; the commingled wonder, apprehension, excitement, boredom; the necessary claustrophobic focusing upon one's fellow travelers. Space travel begins to seem not at all visionary but merely practical, inevitable. Earth as the humanists would know it is finished. Gilpin wonders, as we do, ''why even ordinary citizens still relegated so much of what was happening in the world to science fiction. They themselves were fiction, to the scientists.''

As the fated Citizen Courier approaches its destination—as the novel confronts its series of surprising climaxes—Miss Calisher's prose becomes increasingly economic, urgent, surrealistic. Only one passenger goes mad, but all share in the hallucinatory nature of their predicament. As the novel ends, a mechanical failure prevents the spaceship's landing. It orbits the space habitat, its passengers awaiting rescue, futilely or not they cannot know. . . . Terror and optimism alternate. Gilpin's logbook is addressed to us in increasingly incoherent language (''broken time, broken language, broken lives always fusing—breaking the mold?''). Long after the journey has ended for the reader, the Citizen Courier's eloquent voices linger in the mind, haunting and prophetic. . . .

''Are we the country behind you, or the one before?'' Gilpin asks rhetorically at the end of the novel and (perhaps) the end of his life. These voyagers set out in search of an ideal, a new civilization. And the fact that they find it difficult, as we all no doubt would, to abandon their earthly concerns, does not in Miss Calisher's mind diminish the heroism of their attempt.

Mysteries of Motion is as demanding a novel as Miss Calisher's *False Entry* and *The New Yorkers,* but its rewards are well worth the effort. (p. 26)

> *Joyce Carol Oates, ''The Citizen Courier in Outer*
> *Space,'' in* The New York Times Book Review, *No-*
> *vember 6, 1983, pp. 7, 26.*

BRUCE ALLEN

Hortense Calisher's fiction has intrigued and baffled readers and critics alike since her first stories began appearing more than 30 years ago. . . .

The difficulties inherent in her work are magnified, not just by Calisher's interest in formal philosophy and the new sciences (such as psychotherapy and astrophysics), but also by the mandarin style which bespeaks her allegiance to the example of Henry James. Her prose is, at times, either sonorously rich or else terse, crabbed, and urgent. Her sentences are confusingly, densely packed.

All these qualities and emphases are formidably present in *Mysteries of Motion,* Calisher's ninth and most ambitious novel. It takes the form of a "logbook" kept by Tom Gilpin, who's a passenger on the first American space shuttle for civilians, the Citizen Courier, en route to "the first public habitat in space," known as "Island US."

The time is the 1990s. The main narrative—a small, sturdy heart pulsing inside this book's oversize body—concerns the Courier's troubled voyage and moves suspensefully toward resolving the mysteries that gradually trouble its travelers: the identity of the unseen other passengers; the nature of the payload that threatens to deflect the vehicle off course; their suspicion that the spacecraft is piloted but by remote control and that NASA may have known that the mission would fail.

But the major space is taken up by extended flashback accounts of the lives of the inhabitants of Cabin Six. Tom Gilpin, our narrator, is a wealthy journalist, whose editorial urgings have forced the government to democratize the Courier's passenger list. People from all levels and walks of life are on board. . . .

The novel's complicated structure presents these people's interrelationships as examples of "the movements we make toward one another's mystery." Backward and forward we're tossed in and out of both first-person and omniscient narration, as we listen to Gilpin imagining what's going on in their minds. . . .

Calisher's characters live for us because there's a weight of *relatedness,* an impression of depth and extent about them; we willingly follow as she explores them in all their aspects, even with her slow, meditative pace and the frustrating thickets of her heavily stylized prose. . . .

In the climactic pages, the inhabitants of Cabin Six learn that they have become "the outside people" to those left behind on earth. I mustn't reveal what has happened to them—and what yet may happen. But I will give a clue: It seems to me *Mysteries of Motion* is saying that the Citizen Courier's hopeful flight toward the territory ahead is emblematic of our needs as individuals to go outside and beyond what we are, to transcend. The spacecraft is burdened by that "payload" it must, yet cannot, jettison; so are we all weighted down by responsibilities and relationships that continually exert their claims on us just when we think we've broken free of them. Thus is "motion," itself, inevitably a "mystery."

That may be a needlessly reductive way to approach a rich, troublesome novel, whose intricacies and challenges readers should explore for themselves.

Bruce Allen, "More than an Adventure, This Ambitious Novel Deserves Attention," in The Christian Science Monitor, *January 18, 1984, p. 22.*

ROSELLEN BROWN

Shall we take seriously the distinction Hortense Calisher makes between short stories and the "little novels" that constitute *Saratoga, Hot?* What does a novel—even a novel *manque*—have or want that a story doesn't aspire to or leaves open or unexamined? And—the first question, perhaps—does it matter?

If it does, it is only because the author herself is proposing an ambitiousness of a different, larger order. Her own epigraph to this book invites us to hold certain expectations of size and form: "Some short works are close to the novel in spirit. They seem to try for more than the short moments of a life. They try for the life." ("Some people," she is further quoted on the book's jacket as saying, "don't fall into absolute moments but into little conditions.") The proposal is intriguing: we ready ourselves for a new angle of approach, an obliqueness; for multiple points of view, perhaps, and for blank spots in the narrative that will be like certain elliptical paintings that throw what content they do possess into sharp relief.

But the stories in *Saratoga, Hot,* do not seem to fit her own description, and Miss Calisher does herself a disservice by creating these expectations. It is a thoroughly worthy collection of stories (some are more successful than others), but only a few imply more offstage life than many a good tale would. . . .

"The Library" may come closer to Miss Calisher's ideal—it is the tantalizing recollection of a man who is called on to identify the body of a remarkable woman he has shared over the years with two friends. But here the question arises whether, in the search for the perfect scale for these lives, the mininovel is not really an excuse for the absence of thorough characterization. For one thing, the teller of the story is more observer than actor; we glimpse the woman he—they—loved only through snatches of repartee. The compression of these shared histories is at times dizzying. . . .

On the other hand, the scene in the morgue is present, whole, rendered: the young woman who shows the bodies asks each viewer, with touchingly calculated spontaneity, about an object of his or her clothing, a pin, a hat—something so petty and *live* it reduces one next of kin to grateful tears. But the tangle of relationships at the center of the piece, however intriguing, is a little too intricate for its size and slightly out of focus. . . .

Such stories as **"Sound Track,"** about a cocaine-sniffing actor and his ex-child-star-pop-queen wife, and **"Real Impudence,"** which throws together a Greenwich Village minister, a hairdresser to rock stars and his avid-to-marry mother, attempt to use Miss Calisher's wired language and her ironic tolerance for the absurd to mock the world of pop culture. Some of the writing here is precise and witty. . . . But the characters at the heart of these stories are tinny, and their speech turns out to be a weird amalgam of British and Yiddish whose aberrant rhythm must be meant to sound like showbiz. The majestic movement of Henry James's style was likened once to that of an elephant laboring to pick up a pea. It is a distortion of Miss Calisher's best feature as a writer—her emotionally capacious and heavily wrought prose style—that puts these lighter stories on the brink of that danger.

"Saratoga, Hot," the long title story, is the only one that might rewardingly be called a little novel because of all it implies of life outside its frame. Subtle and clotted to the point of obscurity, it is still a suggestive, lively, entertaining and promising mix of earnest characters. These include Tot, a young man; Nola, the woman he first crippled in an accident and then married; and a large cast of denizens of Saratoga Springs, N.Y., some sinister, some straight, all devoted to horses—to owning them, riding them, betting on them, dabbling in petty and not so petty crime. Horses, women, money, chance—"a better pursuit than happiness"—make us long for a large book in which these characters and forces can deepen and play against the color of the half-innocent, half-corrupt landscape of the race track.

Hortense Calisher ought to have more faith in the short story—it has served her well over the years, as she has served it beautifully herself, offering what she has called, in a celebrated description, "an apocalypse in a very small cup." The cup in *Saratoga, Hot* is neither larger nor newly shaped, but it is more than half full, which matters more.

Rosellen Brown, in a review of "Saratoga, Hot," in The New York Times Book Review, *May 26, 1985, p. 10.*

SUSAN ISAACS

If Hortense Calisher's *Saratoga, Hot* has any appeal, it is to the intellect, not to the heart. The seven short stories and one novella in this collection are filled with word play, self-conscious imagery, and a number of isolated, emotionally deadened characters, who seem more personifications of anomie than human beings.

The selections are billed on the book jacket as "little novels." At the beginning Calisher writes: "Some short works are close to the novel in spirit. They seem to try for more than the short moments of a life. They try for the life."

The only life in these works is the life of the mind. Calisher, who has published nine novels, numerous short stories and novellas and her autobiography, is certainly an accomplished writer, but *Saratoga, Hot* is far from her best effort. The stories are flat, although now and then they are observant, clever, or inventive. In "The Sound Track," record industry moguls do not merely abuse the language, they attack it; their English is as cheap as their spirit and as unstructured as their intellect. . . .

Often, however, the author's style is "literary," but that alone adds nothing to the richness of a piece. In fact, it's a minus because it's so calculating it distances the reader from the essence of a story: character, setting, meaning, plot. It is merely language for language's sake. . . .

"The Passenger" [relates] the musings of a writer as she travels by train to New York. The narrator recalls other train rides she's taken and in the course of reminiscence reveals herself. All this is a little murky; it's difficult to figure out whether the narrator, passing through life on the metaphoric train, is trying to reach out to her fellow passengers, or whether an overnight train trip is so satisfying for the writer—the perpetual observer—because it is brief, enabling her to avoid entangling alliances.

The reader feels remarkably little frustration at the lack of clarity in "The Passenger" because he doesn't care about the characters. The same is true in "Gargantua"; its inhabitants are concepts—not particularly intriguing ones—not people. . . .

Two pieces in this collection, "The Tenth Child" and the novella-length "Saratoga, Hot," are broader in scope and more successful. The former is a satire of family life and living on Park Avenue. The latter is an examination of a husband and wife—she, a crippled artist, and he, a poor relation of the horsey set—and their relationship to a larger social milieu, the racing season at Saratoga. These characters still do not touch the reader very much, but at least they are somewhat animated, and part of a larger world.

Saratoga, Hot's appeal, then, is for the technician. Occasionally the writing is sprightly or incisive, but it has all the humanity and emotional resonance of a well-constructed double-crostic. For some readers that may be sufficient. For this reader, it is not.

Susan Isaacs, "Exercises in Style," in Book World— The Washington Post, *June 9, 1985, p. 8.*

BRUCE ALLEN

[*Saratoga, Hot*] is a rich and challenging collection of eight longish stories that claim to be "close to the novel in spirit. . . . They try for the life." There's indeed an abundance of life in these packed, occasionally turgid tales, and an impressive variety of subjects and personalities. . . . (p. 76)

The two standout stories dramatize the plights of observers for whom observation isn't enough: "The Passenger" is a woman writer engulfed by the lives of people she meets while traveling by Amtrak train; and the brilliant "Survival Techniques"—perhaps her very finest story—brings a Manhattan retiree into mysterious intimacy with the "street people" who seem to threaten, mock, then finally clarify his own precarious existence.

Calisher's stories are densely written and dance to their own inner music. She pursues narrative and psychological leads wherever they take her, and is sometimes guilty of leaving the reader behind. But her best, absorbingly dramatic and filled with real rhetorical splendor, are seductively readable and impossible to forget. (pp. 76-7)

Bruce Allen, in a review of "Saratoga, Hot," in Saturday Review, *Vol. 11, No. 4, July-August, 1985, pp. 76-7.*

Truman Capote

1924-1984

(Born Truman Streckfus Persons) American novelist, nonfiction writer, short story writer, essayist, dramatist, scriptwriter, and memoirist.

While accomplished in a variety of genres, Capote achieved his greatest acclaim with his nonfiction novel *In Cold Blood* (1965). This work, which recounts the murder of a Kansas family in 1959, is characteristic of Capote's fiction in that the main characters exist outside the bounds of conventional society. Many of Capote's protagonists are social deviants, ranging from the slightly eccentric to homosexuals, transvestites, alcoholics, and prostitutes. Although Capote experimented with several different styles, critics often divide his work into two general categories: the more somber, grotesque pieces have been referred to as "dark" or "nocturnal" and the colorfully humorous works have been called "light" or "daylit." Observing the marked range of Capote's work, Mark Schorer noted: "His is, in fact, a various prose, equally at ease—to name the extremes—in situations of dark and frightful nightmare, and of extravagant comedy."

Like many of the characters he depicted, Capote led an unconventional lifestyle. When he was young his parents divorced, and he spent much of his childhood in the South being shuffled from one set of relatives to another. To combat his loneliness and sense of displacement, he developed a flamboyant personality which played a significant role in establishing his celebrity status as an adult. Renowned for his cunning wit and penchant for gossip, Capote became a popular guest on television talk shows and was the frequent focus of feature articles. He befriended many members of the social elite and was as well known for his eccentric, sometimes scandalous behavior as he was for his writings.

© Thomas Victor 1986

Capote began writing at an early age and became a celebrity with his first novel, *Other Voices, Other Rooms* (1948), a work noted as much for the dust jacket's sensual portrait of the young author as for its literary content. The notoriety caused by the suggestive photograph helped the book become a best-seller and anticipated the role publicity would play in Capote's subsequent work. Set in the South, the novel centers on a young man's search for his father and his loss of innocence as he passes into manhood. The work displays many elements of the grotesque: the boy is introduced to the violence of murder and rape, he witnesses a homosexual encounter, and at a carnival he shares a ride with a female midget who makes sexual advances. Each of these sinister scenes is distorted beyond reality, resulting in a surreal, nightmarish quality. Capote's first collection of short stories, *A Tree of Night and Other Stories* (1949), shares the dark tone that marks *Other Voices, Other Rooms,* yet some of the stories are lighter and more humorous, prefiguring the mood of much of Capote's work published in the 1950s.

The novel *The Grass Harp* (1951) focuses on an orphan whose eccentric relatives add much humor to the story. Exemplifying Capote's "light" tone, the plot includes such elements as an attempt by the boy's relatives to escape reality by living in a tree. The heroine of *Breakfast at Tiffany's* (1958) is also ec-

centric. Possessing wit and charm, she is an enigma who profoundly affects the people around her. This novel was adapted for film. Capote began writing nonfiction in the 1950s as well. *Local Color* (1950) is a collection of pieces recounting his impressions and experiences while in Europe, and *The Muses Are Heard* (1956) contains essays written while traveling in Russia with a touring company of *Porgy and Bess*.

From his nonfiction Capote developed the idea of creating a nonfiction novel, a work that would make use of fictional techniques to present fact. In 1959 he chose as his topic the murder of Herbert W. Clutter and his family and spent the next six years gathering data. The resulting work, *In Cold Blood,* contains four sections which juxtapose the wholesome qualities of the midwestern family with the twisted psyches of the two murderers. Advance publicity and multimedia promotion led to high sales and a lucrative film contract, yet critical reaction to the book was mixed. While some questioned the artistic validity of a novel dealing solely with fact, others applauded Capote's narrative skill at developing irony and creating suspense.

Capote published little after *In Cold Blood*. *The Dogs Bark* (1973) collects previously published nonfiction pieces, and *Music for Chameleons* (1980) contains assorted prose works written after 1975. The work to which Capote devoted his final years, *Answered Prayers,* was unfinished at the time of his death. Excerpts from this intimate account of high society appeared in *Esquire* magazine and generated controversy over its unflattering portraits of celebrity figures with whom Capote had socialized.

Critical assessment of Capote's career is highly divided, both in terms of individual works and his overall contribution to literature. In an early review Paul Levine described Capote as a "definitely minor figure in contemporary literature whose reputation has been built less on a facility of style than on an excellent advertising campaign." Ihab Hassan, however, claimed that "whatever the faults of Capote may be, it is certain that his work possesses more range and energy than his detractors allow." Although sometimes faulted for precocious, fanciful plots and for overwriting, Capote is widely praised for his storytelling abilities and the quality of his prose.

(See also *CLC,* Vols. 1, 3, 8, 13, 19, 34; *Contemporary Authors,* Vols. 5-8, rev. ed., Vol. 113 [obituary]; *Contemporary Authors New Revision Series,* Vol. 18; *Dictionary of Literary Biography,* Vol. 2; and *Dictionary of Literary Biography Yearbook: 1980, 1984.*)

GEORGE GARRETT

[Truman Capote's *In Cold Blood*] is, flatly and without question, his biggest, boldest, most serious, most difficult and best written work. Which is saying a great deal. In many ways it is his most vital and interesting work, and certainly it is the most ambitious and risky. It is more, then, than a good book by a good writer. It is more than a demonstration of growth, power, and promise for the future. It is a frank bid for greatness. A great many of our serious writers would and indeed *have* settled for a good deal less than what Capote has already done and earned for himself—a long season of honorable and sustained creativity blessed with the fortunate comforts of recognition and an assured place as a good writer. Capote deserves great praise for doing this book. His action is exemplary.

Starting with a frankly brutal and sordid subject, one which could just as easily have languished in the pages of *True Detective* and *Police Action,* he has brought together his gifts and powers, already demonstrated separately, as a storyteller and as a reporter, to tell "A True Account of a Multiple Murder and Its Consequences." Using his gifts for a controlled and charged language and a beautiful style to advantage, he has arranged the telling, the sequence of related events, in such a way that the reader is compelled to share the whole urgent experience. Building around a conventional, four-part classical structure, he manages to keep suspense at a very high level throughout. The first three sections race along, breathlessly yet easily, moving back and forth between murderers and victims and, later, the hunters and the hunted, without strain, always allowing for great freedom of time and space, for the metaphorically relevant digression, the superb use of the tricky flashback, permitting profoundly realized and dimensional characterization, and, not least, a cumulative, haunting evocation of place. In the final section, with the killers at last caught, devoted to their trial and punishment, we see the work of a virtuoso. For at this point the *original* suspense has been dissipated and the conclusion is obligatory. As Capote's artful arrangement of the story proves, he could easily have avoided

this challenge had he wished to. For there is no such thing as inevitability in the structure of a story. It is the sign of a real storyteller that he makes his arrangement *seem* inevitable. Capote not only performs this magic trick, but also he manages to reach his own chosen and obligatory conclusion without a weakening of either intensity or interest. I can think of very few writers, living or dead, who could have done this.

These qualities and others in *In Cold Blood* may seem even more remarkable to readers who have followed Capote's earlier work. He has always been known as a distinguished stylist and as an imaginative storyteller, but he has not previously shown a great deal of interest in the possibilities of innovative arrangement. He has not been a technical experimenter. . . . And though he has created a rich gallery of interesting and memorable characters in his fiction, he has never until now displayed such ability to handle a large number of characters, all of whose lives and fortunes are intricately and subtly inter-related, and to treat them with depth and understanding. There are true moments of unveiling, of startling revelation. Before this he had seemed content to offer a kind of fan dance, showing only glimpses and then chiefly by the allusive method of signs, clues, hints and symbols. Here the chief characters are stripped. If what is exposed is yet another veiled mystery, that is itself a profound revelation. It is exactly the kind of thing he seemed to be sidestepping in his other work. And, no getting around it, *In Cold Blood* is fundamentally a blood and guts story. Truman Capote's previous accomplishments have a great many virtues, and they have been acknowledged and praised; but nobody has ever accused him of being a blood and guts writer.

The fact is that he has been most frequently and conveniently labelled as a writer of romances, of the school of Poe and Hawthorne, a fabulist. (pp. 3-4)

[No] matter how different superficially *In Cold Blood* may seem to be from Capote's earlier work, both fiction and non-fiction, it is rooted in that work. It exists as part of the context of all his work. (p. 4)

The marked difference between his fiction and *In Cold Blood* ironically works to make the relationship between them more evident. In his three novels and his short stories, whether written in his "nocturnal" or "daylight" manner (as critics have seen fit to classify his work), Capote has, indeed, written a certain kind of romance or fable. For all their truth and decorative detail, both *Other Voices, Other Rooms* and *The Grass Harp* take place in a never-never land, a kind of no-man's land deliberately isolated from at least the world of "realistic" fiction, and even if the New York of *Breakfast At Tiffany's* is a real place, the central character, the marvelous Miss Holly Golightly, is as extraordinary and magical as, say, Bellow's Henderson in *Henderson, The Rain King.* Moreover, she, unlike Henderson, is seen at one remove, filtered through the consciousness of a writer-narrator. One of the characteristics of the story which does not depend on apparent surface credibility or verisimilitude, whether it is fable pure and simple or romance, is that it has always been pre-eminently a *moral* tale, from Aesop until now. This is inevitable, since attention is by rhetorical consent and agreement diverted from what happened to what is being said. Classical and medieval rhetoricians, too, often ignored at present, dealt with this kind of writing in all its possible forms in great detail. It was recognized as more directly *allegorical,* in the widest and deepest sense of that word, than work with what we might think of as realistic surface. On the simplest level this merely means that though foxes, jackasses and lions don't really talk to each other, what they have to say to each other in a fable and what they do may have truth and meaning. In a romance like *Other Voices, Other Rooms* it means that nightmarish, grotesque and surrealistic things may happen and be meaningful, that Joel Knox, Zoo, Randolph, Jesus Fever, Miss Wisteria and all the others may suffer wounds, but the wounds are not real. Collin Fenwick, Dolly, Catherine, Judge Cool and the others in *The Grass Harp* are more obviously involved in a social world. The world comes up against them where they sit, happy outcasts in a tree house; but again their triumphs and their suffering are seen at the little distance of romance. The effect is, by definition, allegorical and moral. Holly Golightly seems to be vaguely conscious of her own allegorical function when she defines it: "Good? Honest is more what I mean. Not low-type honest— I'd rob a grave, I'd steal two-bits off a dead man's eyes if I thought it would contribute to the day's enjoyment—but unto-thyself-type honest. . . ." So, while apparently asserting a position beyond ordinary *morals,* she defines as honestly her own morality, her own clear sense of good and evil.

Even though each of these works is quite different, all have the outlines of a fairly clear, consistent, and conventional moral framework. Conventional in the literary sense. Which is to say unconventional only if measured against what are, again conventionally, thought to be the basic accepted standards of American middleclass morality. In each of the books it is the outsiders and the outcasts who are, by virtue of their disengagement from worldly values, the examples of goodness. Those who seem to get along well in the "real" world, that is the world of practical affairs, are exposed as either deceitful or self-deceived. (pp. 4-6)

From the first, then, we shiver for the Clutters, fearing their fate, because they are such natural victims. . . . Each of the Clutters, in the terms of [Capote's] fiction, manages to include all the "bad" characteristics. In fiction, of course, neither the inverted morality nor the signs and symbols thereof are new. These are working conventions, bordering on pure cliché in modern fiction. Certainly in romance and even in more "realistic" fiction these conventions are accepted. Perfectly (ironically) *respectable.* But here we are up against a real and different problem. The Clutters were real people, not symbols of anything, and their murder was a matter of brutal fact. At least at the outset, then, the effect is ambiguous. We find ourselves asking, no doubt as the author intended, is Capote still following the Old Law or will his work be a new dispensation? (pp. 6-7)

When we get to the killers we begin to get answers. They come on as clearly labelled as the pilgrims in the Prologue to *The Canterbury Tales.* Both are hurt because of accidents; both are tattooed; but there is a difference. Dick Hickock's tattoos are crude, cheap, conventional. Perry Smith's are "more elaborate—not the self-inflicted work of an amateur but epics of the art contrived by Honolulu and Yokohama masters." (p. 7)

Perry Smith is perfectly, patly, and in almost every detail a spooky embodiment of Capote's earlier fiction. He has all the right characteristics: a rich and childish imagination, his dreams including one marvelous recurring dream which is mystical in beauty and implication, his physical deformity, his sensitivity, even his background. (p. 8)

It is probably the amazing fact that a real human being could accidentally have all the characteristics of his typical fictional protagonists which permitted Capote to give us through his study of Perry Smith a fascinating look at the curious workings

of a murderer's *psyche.* By the same token, however, for or maybe because of all his natural sympathy and compassion for Perry Smith, Capote clearly sets him in sharp contrast to the other killer, Hickock. Hickock is intelligent, but not nearly so interesting. The result is that he receives fairly short shrift in comparison to Smith. And much about him is given pejoratively. He likes to run over stray dogs; he pursues little girls; he asserts his dubious masculinity by making love in the presence of Perry, etc. All these things, by the way, must come to us through *Perry,* but in context are treated like facts. There is, of course, a real and neat narrative value to be derived from this contrast of the two. Since we never really know Hickock the way we do Smith and since we are never invited to squander much sympathy on him, he can serve beautifully as a conventional "heavy." It is quite necessary to engage as much of the reader's sympathy as possible for Perry. So there has to be a foil, a sacrificial victim served up to ease the reader's reluctant conscience and to appease, like patent medicine, the reader's taste for conventional morality. In the making of fiction this method is honorable and traditional, and it works well here. So well that we are thoroughly engaged in the pathos of Perry Smith, and his final words from the gallows are deeply moving, come close to real tragic utterance, leave Perry at the end as a kind of inverted, mid-century Billy Budd. But when one realizes *how* this has been achieved, by the trick of fiction, that author and reader have conspired to make Hickock expendable, catharsis is dissipated by ambiguous feelings.

Again the problem is that we are dealing with a real murder and a real hanging. The author goes to great pains to emphasize the *reality* of the story. (And for an epigraph he has invoked Villon's *"Ballade des pendus,"* which is for *all* the hanged.) That we do not get the same kind of involvement with Hickock as we do with Smith is a failure in this book. A wise failure, though. Perhaps even a shrewd one. For the whole truth and nothing but the truth of this event, even if it were possible to articulate, would not likely be acceptable to the general audience. Better half a loaf. . . . Except that in one sense the trick of heaping the burden of evil on the head of Hickock is what is sometimes called cheating.

There are so many superbly realized things, large and small, in this book that one can be easily diverted and almost distracted from other flaws. Almost, but not quite. The two chief and central actions of the book are the murder and the hanging. Although we are given plenty of the painful details of both actions, neither scene is presented as directly as other scenes. In each case, a little differently, Capote has chosen to shy away from the heart of these scenes, to "write around" them.

There is good narrative justification for holding back on the naked brutality of the murder scene until late. What happened is essential to the suspense of the story in Capote's arrangement, and so we do not really know and do not see the event happen until the killers have been caught and confess. Meanwhile, in the interim, something else happens. By then we have been led into deep involvement with the killers. The account of the murder, though horrifying, is by then curiously remote and comes too late to damage the other rhetorical purpose. By putting the account of the murder exactly in the language of the confessions, gaining the virtues of documentation of course, Capote gains another more subtle effect. That language simply cannot compete with the author's. Possibly there is the horror of understatement by comparison, but the effect is to soften the event of the murder. It can be reasonably argued that Capote gives his reader a gracious plenty of detail from which to shape a completely *imagined* scene and that this, another time-honored device of fiction, is often much more powerful than a headon and direct encounter with the scene. Nevertheless there is a very real and nagging question as to whether or not the author wanted to give us that scene fully. Had he ever done so, early or late, he could probably never again have engaged the reader's sympathy for Perry Smith. And had he chosen to do so he would have risked appealing to and arousing some very deep, atavistic human feelings that are more powerful than poetic. And had he done so he might also have weakened the satirical effect of the fear and corruption which beset the little town. Still, it might have been more honest.

In a somewhat more subtle and complex way, Capote has managed to "write around" the hanging. The most shocking elements of a hanging occur not at the hanging itself but in a nightmare of Perry's. But that is not precisely the problem. It is not a question of gruesome or explicit details. One of the most memorable hangings in fiction is Faulkner's disposal of Popeye in *Sanctuary* in a very few lines. In this case it is a question of the right details, of something being missing. Within the exclusive context of the book it is very hard to say what may be missing, just that as a scene this does not somehow measure up to many other less important scenes. The *Life* magazine article and interview, however, has come along with a kind of an answer. He was there. His own personal involvement and the scene he witnessed are described, and significant details are given which do not appear in the book. They are powerful and deeply moving things which had to be sacrificed, evidently, because of the author's decision to keep himself out of the story.

That decision was his and his alone to make, but it is a fair subject for consideration. In telling the story with a novelistic arrangement and the seeming objectivity of the novelist, Capote has had to exclude, except by implication, his own story, the entire story of his engagement and involvement. It is simply not in the book. But we know through the widespread publicity if no other way that he was very much involved. And not just reporting. He was witness to important parts of the story, and it is precisely his involvement and nobody else's which has shaped the whole story and its arrangement. (pp. 8-10)

[While] this deliberate suppression of self does give the narrative a fairly straight line and a great deal of strength, it also appears to be the cause of certain weaknesses. Some sign of final commitment is missing. Of course the author is already there, carefully arranging the order and sequence of events, moving his characters on and off stage etc. If the truth about the "consequences" is really his concern, why doesn't he really appear? Curiously enough, the weakest parts of the book are precisely where the author had the most firsthand knowledge, the most direct encounter with the experience. *And he himself was very much part of the experience of many of the characters*. His presence, his actions, his questions must have affected them, just as, now, the finished book is bound to have an effect on them too. If he has removed himself from the experience, we are entitled to ask what else he may have chosen to remove or suppress. A reporter need not necessarily deal with this question. A valid witness cannot ignore it and be really believed.

There is something missing, then, in this story which Capote says is what he really thinks about America. Of course, there is nothing new or shocking or even unfashionable in what he appears to think. We have been told by all kinds of people, some of them good men and many of them not artists at all,

that unless we do something (nobody quite knows what) about all that's "desperate, savage, violent" we are going to suffer the consequences and they will be very bad. Capote's tale, as it stands, reflects this profound concern with accuracy. Somehow, though, the Clutters were not representative abstractions, and neither were Dick and Perry. They did not live or die to prove any point or to illustrate what anyone may or may not think about "America." In spite of the local dismay and shock, the brutal and terrible death of the Clutters proves nothing about the nature of God or the universe one way or the other. The deaths of Dick Hickock and Perry Smith tell us nothing about justice. With enormous skill, skill and art beyond the means and reach of most of his rivals and contemporaries, Capote has managed to give some pattern and meaning to a brutal, stupid, pointless, senseless murder and some of its consequences. He has been able to arouse compassion and to evoke pity and terror. In all fairness, nobody is really treated like an abstraction. But somehow, in some almost indefinable way, the romancer has overcome the reporter and the final effect is one of "nocturnal" romance. Which, of course, is a false rendering. (pp. 10-12)

In Cold Blood is a work of art, the work of an artist. There is much truth in it, though whether or not it is "true" is at least debatable. Whether or not it turns out to be a classic, it is an important and provocative book, one which is bound to generate the kind of deep interest, intense discussion, re-reading and scrutiny which only a very few really excellent books deserve to enjoy. (p. 12)

> *George Garrett, "Crime and Punishment in Kansas: Truman Capote's 'In Cold Blood'," in* The Hollins Critic, *Vol. III, No. 1, February, 1966, pp. 1-12.*

ROBERT LANGBAUM

No one at this late date has to be told that [*In Cold Blood,* the] spectacularly best-selling account of the murder of the Clutter family in Holcomb, Kansas, on November 14, 1959, makes good reading, that it is not only the sort of thriller you "can't put down" but the sort that the most sophisticated people can thrill to. The question I want to take up arises from Mr. Capote's claim, made in an inconspicuous note at the end, that this, his "ninth published book, represents the culmination of his long-standing desire to make a contribution toward the establishment of a serious new literary form: the Nonfiction Novel." (pp. 570, 572)

Most reviewers extolled the book, but pooh-poohed the idea of a nonfiction novel as too patently absurd to be worth discussing. I would like to give the claim serious consideration, because the tie between journalism and the novel is an old and perplexing one, going back to Defoe. As Ortega y Gasset has observed, the novel is the only literary form that does not want to look like a literary form—that wants to look like a bundle of letters, a journal, an autobiography, like life itself. We know how many novels are really autobiographies or accounts of true crimes—but disguised, with perhaps some loss from the disguise. Why not, therefore, substantiate the novel's claim to truthfulness by being truthful? (p. 572)

Mr. Capote wanted primarily, I believe, to call attention to the artfulness of his book. For many people think, when they hear a book is "true," that the facts wrote it and that anyone given the same facts would come up with the same book. He wanted also to tell us that the book is no digression from his career as a fiction writer, but a "culmination"—that all his experience writing stories went into it. By taking him at his word and comparing his book to a novel, we can both appreciate his achievement and see its limits. For its best effects are novelistic and it falls short just where it is not novelistic enough.

Mr. Capote tells a mainly chronological narrative with himself as omniscient and invisible author. He might have enhanced the reportorial quality and given us a more intricate novelistic structure had he made us aware of his evidence, of how he came to know the facts. Instead the book itself, without the *Times* interview [in which Capote described his five years of research], requires the same confidence we give a novelist before we can get on with the story. Mr. Capote gains the advantages of any writer who uses a historical or allegedly historical subject—public significance, and an effect of fatefulness that comes of our knowing in advance how the story must come out. Mr. Capote achieves a hallucinated fatefulness through repeated references to the black Chevrolet that carries the murderers inexorably to their victims—although the murderers start hundreds of miles from their victims and with no apparent connection to them. There is the same hallucinated fatefulness in the return of the murderers from Mexico to Las Vegas, where they are arrested just after they have withdrawn from the post office the boots that match the footprints found in the Clutter house.

De Quincey long ago pointed out, in discussing *Macbeth,* that the writer turns crime stories into high literature by throwing "the interest on the murderer: our sympathy must be with *him*," our "sympathy of comprehension," not "approbation." Mr. Capote manages to do this, with really reprehensible murderers; but he also writes a detective story, in which our interest is in seeing the criminals caught. In the same way, he writes a tragedy of fate; but he also writes a suspense story, by deliberately withholding information—we do not learn until midway in the book how the criminals so much as know of the existence of their victims. It is because Mr. Capote has combined literary levels and captured all possible audiences that his book is selling so well. (pp. 572-74)

[Mr. Capote's point in this work is that the Clutters] were like you and me, the sort to whom the inconceivable does not happen. That is why Mr. Clutter, when he was awakened that night, spoke gently to the murderers, led them to the rest of his family and allowed them to tie him up and tape his mouth—because, conceiving only rational motivation, he assumed they were only after money. When Perry Smith cut his throat, he screamed out beneath the tape his supernatural surprise. His son, daughter and wife experienced nightmare come true as, after his murder, they waited bound and taped to be shot one by one. But until that point, the Clutters were not equipped to conceive of—*evil,* we are tempted to say; for the parallel with Dostoevski suggests itself when we deal with gratuitous crime. But Mr. Capote is, by implication at least, more nihilistic than Dostoevski. For what the Clutters could not conceive of was sheer screwiness.

The case is like that of Oswald, when we thought there must be an organization behind him because nothing so catastrophic as President Kennedy's assassination could have occurred for no reason at all. Because of the human need to rationalize experience, the citizens of Holcomb, Kansas, assumed the murderers must have come from their own limited circle, must have been connected to the victims. The chief detective, Dewey, when he finally got confessions from Smith and Hickock, felt disappointment; for "the confessions . . . failed to satisfy his sense of meaningful design. The crime was a psychological

accident, virtually an impersonal act; the victims might as well have been killed by lightning."

That, at least potentially, is Mr. Capote's vision of American life—an apparently placid surface shot through by sporadic eruptions of violence. To show the Clutter case as not unique, he describes other multiple murders, all zany, all with an aura of sexuality about them. The sexual aura would seem to be *de rigueur* for murder stories nowadays; and it is not crimes of passion that interest us, but rather murder as a substitute for sexual expression, as stemming from sexual and emotional deficiency. Mr. Capote depicts his murderers, with exquisite precision, as deformed and stunted. (pp. 575-76)

[Yet, the] criminals are not insane in any simple technical sense, or there would have been no story worth telling. Mr. Capote, supported by the ambiguous psychiatric evidence, artistically blurs the distinction between sanity and insanity, as it is blurred in so many criminals of literature—in a motiveless malignity like that of Iago, or in Raskolnikov. As against the criminals of nineteenth-century literature, who had more positive qualities than the rest of us, more energy and moral complexity, the frantic gestures of Mr. Capote's criminals point only to the void at their center. Does this make them different from us, or have they hit the zero we all approach?

This is a question Mr. Capote has not resolved—the question of how seriously we are to take the shallow lives of his respectable people, the sort of life represented by the Clutter daughter, leader of the 4-H Club and champion baker of cherry pies. Mr. Capote no doubt wanted to admire these good people so much at the center of American life. But they did not really interest him, and they come out therefore rather like soap-opera characters. His depiction of them is not, like his depiction of the criminals, penetrated by his intelligence. He fails, in other words, to fill out his vision of American life, because he fails to be sufficiently ironical—if for the sake of journalistic impartiality, then journalism has here interfered with comprehensiveness.

Another such failure of irony is in the fact that the psychiatrist's report at the trial is given as entirely adequate to the case, whereas in any good novel, there ought to be an ironic disparity between such an analysis and the living mystery of the characters. Perry Smith is finally enigmatic. Yet Mr. Capote announces without reservation that the report confirms Perry's own analysis of his motives—an analysis showing only that Perry was intelligent enough to have picked up on the socio-psychological point of view. (pp. 576-77)

In Mr. Capote's short story, **"The Headless Hawk,"** the hero recalls his childhood attraction to carnival freaks and realizes "that about those whom he'd loved there was always a little something wrong, broken." It is that sensibility in the author that makes the characterization of Perry the triumph of this book. For Perry is irresistibly attractive, with his talent for music and drawing, his fine feeling for words, his gentleness—he prevented Dick from raping the Clutter daughter and made the Clutters comfortable as he could after he tied them up. Yet he is not sentimentalized; for the gentleness makes the murderousness all the zanier. We are never allowed to forget that he is a child-man, a freak.

Mr. Capote said in the *Times* interview that he wanted to achieve with nonfiction "the poetic altitude fiction is capable of reaching." He achieves such altitude in the characterization of Bonnie—the one Clutter who is "broken"—as a ghost. In life, she was always cold and she feared her children would remember her "as a kind of ghost." After her death, the detective's wife saw her in a dream, crying, "To be murdered. No. No. There's nothing worse. Nothing worse than that. Nothing." Real speech is made to yield that much poetry because it has been prepared for by a carefully arranged pattern of imagery. Mr. Capote works like those *avant-garde* moviemakers who turn real-life shots into art in the cutting room.

The highest altitude is reached in Perry's dream in the death house. All his life Perry had dreamed of a snake that would fall upon him out of a diamond-laden but foul-smelling jungle tree, and of a towering yellow, a sunlike, parrot that would wing him to paradise. Once in the death house he woke up shouting, "The bird is Jesus." And then, in this climactic dream, he sees himself in his favorite guise as the entertainer Perry O'Parsons, tap-dancing up a short flight of gold-painted prop steps. But when he takes his bow at the top, the strange audience, mostly men and Negroes, do not applaud. . . . [In the dream], through a powerfully ironic comprehension of the whole of Perry's psychic life, Mr. Capote has achieved a genuinely literary moment. (pp. 578-79)

And yet the penetration . . . is at odds with the flatness of the other characters. The insight into Perry does not contribute to any general vision; and the book rather loses literary magic and turns into journalism after the hallucinated events leading up to the murder and the capture of the criminals. Here, as in his symbolist fiction, Mr. Capote fails to understand all the implications of the imagery he sets in motion (his best stories are the sentimental comedies, like **"House of Flowers"** and **Breakfast at Tiffany's,** which stick frankly to the surface). This limitation makes him a lightweight, although a sophisticated craftsman, a "pro" in the best sense of the word. The implications of **In Cold Blood** are so frightening that more rigor would undoubtedly have made the book less entertaining. As it stands, **In Cold Blood** is first-rate entertainment that at moments gives illusory promise of being something more than that. (pp. 579-80)

Robert Langbaum, "Capote's Nonfiction Novel," in
The American Scholar, Vol. 35, No. 3, Summer,
1966, pp. 570, 572-580.

CYNTHIA OZICK

[*The essay from which the following excerpt is taken was originally published in* The New Republic, *January 27, 1973.*]

Time at length becomes justice. A useful if obscure-sounding literary aphorism, just this moment invented. What it signifies is merely this: if a writer lives long enough, he may himself eventually put behind him the work that brought him early fame, and which the world ought to have put aside in the first place.

I remember reading somewhere not long ago a comment by Truman Capote on his first novel: it was written, he said, by somebody else.

Cruel time fleshes out this interesting, only seemingly banal, remark: who is this tiny-fingered flaccid man, with molasses eyes and eunuch's voice, looking like an old caricature of Aeolus, the puff-cheeked little god of wind? We see him now and then on television talk shows, wearing a hayseed hat, curling his fine feet, his tongue on his lip like a soft fly, genially telling dog stories. Or we read about the vast celebrity parties he is master of, to which whole populations of the famous come, in majestic array of might and mind. (p. 80)

[Were] these non-qualities implicit in that long-ago Somebody Else—that boy whose portrait on the back cover of **Other Voices, Other Rooms** became even more celebrated than the prose inside? Who can forget that boy?—languid but sovereign, lolling in the turn of a curved sofa in bow tie and tattersall vest, with tender mouth and such strange elf-cold eyes. Like everyone else whose youth we have memorized and who has had the bad luck to turn up on television afterward, he was bound to fatten up going toward fifty. . . . (p. 81)

On the face of it he was bound to become Somebody Else, in short: not only distant physically from the Dorian Gray of the memorable photograph, and not simply psychologically distant according to the chasm between twenty-three and forty-eight, and not merely (though this chiefly) distant from the sort of redolent prose craft that carried **Other Voices, Other Rooms** to its swift reputation. An even more radical distancing appears to intervene.

It's not only ourselves growing old that makes us into Somebody Else: it's the smell of the times too, the invisible but palpable force called *Zeitgeist*, which is something different from growth, and more capricious. Books change because we change, but no internal reasons, however inexorable, are enough to account for a book's turning to dust twenty-four years afterward. **Other Voices, Other Rooms** is now only dust—glass dust, a heap of glitter, but dust all the same.

Robert Gottlieb, editor-in-chief of Knopf, some time ago in *Publishers Weekly* took shrewd notice of how the life expectancy of books is affected: Solzhenitsyn, he said, can write as he does, and succeed at it, because in Russia they do not yet know that the nineteenth century is dead.

A century, even a quarter of a century, dies around a book; and then the book lies there, a shaming thing because it shows how much worse we once were to have liked it; and something else too: it demonstrates exactly how the world seems to shake off what it does not need, old books, old notions of aesthetics, old mind-forms, our own included. The world to the eager eye is a tree constantly pruning itself, and writers are the first to be lopped off. All this means something different from saying merely that a book has dated. All sorts of masterpieces are dated, in every imaginable detail, and yet survive with all their powers. **Other Voices, Other Rooms** is of course dated, and in crucial ways: it would be enough to mention that its Southern family has two black retainers, an old man and his granddaughter, and that when he dies the old man is buried under a tree on the family property, the way one would bury a well-loved dog, and that the granddaughter, having gone north for a new life, is gang-raped on the way, and comes back to the white family's kitchen for love and safety. . . . In Harlem now, and in Washington, Watts, Detroit, Newark, and New Rochelle, they are dancing on the grave of this poetry. It was intolerable poetry then too, poetry of the proud, noble, but defective primitive, but went not so much unnoticed as disbelieved; and disbelief is no failing in an aesthetic confection. Even then no one thought Jesus Fever, the old man, and Zoo, the kitchen servant, any more real than the figures on a wedding cake; such figures are, however vulgar, useful to signify outright the fundamental nature of the enterprise. Dated matter in a novel (these signals of locale and wont) disposes of itself—gets eaten up, like the little sugar pair, who are not meant to outlive the afternoon. Dated matter in a novel is not meant to outlive the *Zeitgeist*, which can last a long time, often much longer than its actual components, digesting everything at hand.

But *Other Voices, Other Rooms* is not a dead and empty book because Zoo is, in today's understanding, the progenitrix of black militancy, or because the times that appeared to welcome its particular sensibility are now lost. Indeed, the reason "dated matter" has so little effect on *Other Voices, Other Rooms* is that it is a timeless book, as every autonomous act of craft is intended to be. A jug, after all, is a jug, whether bought last week at the five-and-dime or unearthed at Knossos: its meaning is self-contained—it has a shape, handles, a lip to pour. And *Other Voices, Other Rooms* has a meaning that is similarly self-contained: Subjectivity, images aflash on a single mind, a moment fashioned with no reference to society, a thing aside from judgment. One can judge it as well made or not well made; but one cannot judge it as one judges a deed.

And this is why it is not really possible to turn to the *Zeitgeist* to account for *Other Voices, Other Rooms*' present emptiness. (pp. 81-3)

Other Voices, Other Rooms is the novel of someone who wanted, with a fixed and single-minded and burning will, to write a novel. The vision of *Other Voices, Other Rooms* is the vision of capital-A Art—essence freed from existence. . . .

[This novel] belongs not to the hard thing we mean when we say "life," but rather to transcendence, incantation, beatification, grotesquerie, epiphany, rhapsody and rapture—all those tongues that lick the self: a self conceived of as sanctified (whether by muses or devils or gods) and superhuman. When life—the furious web of society, manners, institutions, ideas, tribal histories, and the thicket of history-of-ideas itself—when life is not the subject of fiction, then magic is. Not fable, invention, metaphor, the varied stuff of literature—but *magic*. And magic is a narcissistic exercise, whether the magic is deemed to be contained within language or within psychology: in either case the nub is autonomous inwardness.

The [American] *Zeitgeist* is just now open to all this. Yet *Other Voices, Other Rooms*—a slim, easy, lyrical book—can no longer be read. Dead and empty. (pp. 84-5)

Something needs to be explained. It is not that the novel was written . . . by Somebody Else; after twenty years all novels are. It is not that the mood of the era is now against Poetry and Transfiguration; the opposite is true. Above all, it is not that *Other Voices, Other Rooms* is dead and empty only now; it always was.

What needs to be explained is the whole notion of the relation of *Zeitgeist* to fiction. In fact there is none, yet there is no fallacy more universally swallowed. For what must be understood about an era's moods is this: often they are sham or nostalgia or mimicry, and they do not always tell the truth about the human condition; more often than not the *Zeitgeist* is a lie, even about its own data. If, as Gottlieb persuades us, Solzhenitsyn comes to us with all the mechanism of the Tolstoyan novel intact, and yet comes to us as a living literary force, it is not because the nineteenth century is not yet dead in the Russian mind, although that may be perfectly true. It is because, whatever its mechanics, the idea of the novel is attached to life, to the life of deeds, which are susceptible of both judgment and interpretation; and the novel of Deed is itself a deed to be judged and interpreted. But the novel that is fragrant with narcissism, that claims essence sans existence, that either will not get its shoes drekky or else elevates drek to cultishness—the novel, in short, of the aesthetic will—*that* novel cannot survive its cult.

Further: one would dare to say that the survival of the novel as a form depends on this distinction beween the narcissistic novel and the novel of Deed.

On the surface it would seem that Capote's progress, over a distance of seventeen years, from *Other Voices, Other Rooms* to *In Cold Blood*—from the prose-poetry of transfiguration to the more direct and plain, though still extremely artful, prose of his narrative journalism—is a movement from the narcissistic novel to the novel of Deed; Capote himself never once appears in the pages of his crime story. But there is no forward movement, it is all only a seeming; both the novel and the "nonfiction novel" are purely aesthetic shapes. In *Other Voices, Other Rooms* it is the ecstasy of language that drives the book; in *In Cold Blood* it is something journalists call "objectivity," but it is more immaculate than that. "My files would almost fill a whole small room up to the ceiling," Capote told an interviewer; for years he had intertwined his mind and his days with a pair of murderers—to get, he said, their point of view. He had intertwined his life; he was himself a character who impinged, in visit after visit, on the criminals; and yet, with aesthetic immaculateness, he left himself out. Essence without existence; to achieve the alp of truth without the risk of the footing. But finally and at bottom he must be taken at his word that *In Cold Blood* has the blood of a novel. He cannot have that *and* the journalist's excuse for leaving himself out of it—in the end the "nonfiction novel" must be called to account like any novel. And no novel has ever appeared, on its face, to be more the novel of Deed than this narrative of two killers—despite which it remains judgment-free, because it exempts itself from its own terms. Chekhov in "Ward No. 6," one of the most intelligent short novels ever written, understood how the man who deals with the fate of the imprisoned begins to partake of the nature of the imprisoned; this is the great moral hint, the profound unholy question, that lurks in *In Cold Blood*. But it is evaded, in the name of objectivity, of journalistic distance, all those things that the novel has no use for. In the end *In Cold Blood* is, like *Other Voices, Other Rooms,* only another design, the pattern of a hot desire to make a form; one more aesthetic manipulation. It cannot go out of itself—one part of it leads only to another part. Like *Other Voices, Other Rooms,* it is well made, but it has excised its chief predicament, the relation of the mind of the observer to the mind of the observed, and therefore it cannot be judged, it escapes interpretation because it flees its own essential deed. Such "objectivity" is as narcissistic as the grossest "subjectivity": it will not expose itself to an accounting.

Despite every appearance, every modification of style, Capote is at the root *not* Somebody Else. The beautiful reclining boy on the jacket of *Other Voices, Other Rooms* and the middle-aged television celebrity who tells dog stories are one, more so than either would imagine; nothing in Capote as writer has changed. If the world has changed, it has not touched Capote's single and persistent tone. Joel Knox in the last sentence of *Other Voices, Other Rooms* looks back "at the boy he had left behind." False prophecy. Nothing has been left behind—only, perhaps, the younger writer's habit of the decorated phrase. What continues in Capote, and continues in force, is the idea that life is style, and that shape and mood are what matter in and out of fiction. That is the famous lie on which aesthetics feeds the centuries. Life is not style, but what we do: Deed. And so is literature. Otherwise Attic jugs would be our only mentors. (pp. 86-9)

Cynthia Ozick, "Truman Capote Reconsidered," in her Art & Ardor, *Alfred A. Knopf, 1983, pp. 80-9.*

ALFRED KAZIN

What interested me most about *In Cold Blood* . . . was that though it *was* journalism and soon gave away all its secrets, it had the ingenuity of fiction and it was fiction except for its ambition to be documentary. *In Cold Blood* brought to focus for me the problem of "fact writing" and its "treatment." There is a lot of "treatment" behind the vast amount of social fact that we get in a time of perpetual crisis. These books dramatize and add to the crisis, and we turn to them because they give a theme to the pervasive social anxiety, the concrete human instance that makes "literature."

In Cold Blood is an extremely stylized book that has a palpable design on our emotions. It works on us as a merely factual account never had to. It is so shapely and its revelations are so well timed that it becomes a "novel" in the form of fact. . . . What makes *In Cold Blood* formally a work of record rather than of invention? Because formally, at least, it is a documentary; based on six years of research and six thousand pages of notes, it retains this research in the text. (p. 210)

Why, then, did Capote honor himself by calling the book in any sense a "novel"? . . . Capote wanted his "truthful account" to become "a work of art," and he knew he could accomplish this, quite apart from the literary expertness behind the book, through a certain intimacy between himself and "his" characters. (pp. 210-11)

Fiction as the most intensely selective creation of mood, tone, atmosphere, has always been Capote's natural aim as a writer. In *In Cold Blood* he practices this as a union of Art and Sympathy. . . . Capote's "truthful account" is sympathetic to everyone, transparent in its affections to a degree—abstractly loving to Nancy Clutter, that all-American girl; respectfully amazed by Mr. Clutter, the prototype of what Middle America would like to be; helplessly sorry for Mrs. Clutter, a victim of the "square" morality directed at her without her knowing it. None of these people Capote knew—but he thought he did. Capote became extremely involved with the murderers, Perry Smith and Dick Hickock. . . . (pp. 211-12)

This fascinated sympathy with characters whom Capote visited sixty times in jail, whom he interviewed within an inch of their lives, up to the scaffold, is one of many powerful emotions on Capote's part that keeps the book "true" even when it most becomes a "novel." (p. 212)

[The] book itself goes back to the strains behind all Capote's work: a home and family destroyed within a context of hidden corruption, alienation and loneliness. Reading *In Cold Blood* one remembers the gypsy children left hungry and homeless in *The Grass Harp*, the orphans in *A Tree of Night, The Thanksgiving Visitor* and *A Christmas Memory*, the wild gropings of Holly Golightly in *Breakfast at Tiffany's* toward the "pastures of the sky." One remembers Capote himself in his personal pieces and stories in *Local Color* searching for a home in New Orleans, Brooklyn, Hollywood, Haiti, Paris, Tangier and Spain—then returning to Brooklyn again in "A House on the Heights." (pp. 212-13)

The victims in *In Cold Blood* were originally the Clutters, but by the time the crime is traced to the killers and they are imprisoned, all seem equally victims. . . . Capote's more urgent relationship is of course with "Perry and Dick." Almost to the end one feels that they might have been saved and their souls repaired.

This felt interest in "Perry and Dick" as persons whom Capote knew makes the book too personal for fiction but establishes it as a casebook for our time. The background of the tale is entirely one of damaged persons who wreak worse damage on others, but the surface couldn't be more banal. (pp. 213-14)

Terror can break out anywhere. The world is beyond reason but the imagination of fact, the particular detail, alone establishes credibility. It all happened, and it happened only this way. The emotion pervading the book is our helpless fascinated horror. . . . The Clutters are stabbed, shot, strangled, between mawkish first-name American "friendliness" and bouncy identification with one another's weaknesses. (p. 214)

The fascination of Capote's book, the seeming truthfulness of it all, is that it brings us close, very close, to the victims, to the murderers, to the crime itself, as psychic evidence. Killing becomes the primal scene of our "feelings" that with all the timing of a clever novelist and all the emphatic detail brought in from thousands of interview hours by a prodigious listener, Capote presents to us as a case study of "truth" we can hold, study, understand. (p. 215)

Capote had always been rather a specialist in internal mood, tone, "feeling"; now an action, the most terrible, was the center around which everything in his "truthful account" moved. He was ahead of his usual literary self, and the artfulness of the book is that it gets everyone to realize, possess and dominate this murder as a case of the seemingly psychological malignity behind so many crimes in our day. The book aims to give us this mental control over the frightening example of what is most uncontrolled in human nature.

Technically, this is accomplished by the four-part structure that takes us from the apparently pointless murder of four people to the hanging of the killers in the corner of a warehouse. The book is designed as a suspense story—why did Perry and Dick ever seek out the Clutters at all?—to which the author alone holds the answer. This comes only in Part III, when the book is more than half over. Each of the four sections is divided into cinematically visual scenes. . . . Each of these scenes is a focusing, movie fashion, designed to put us visually as close as possible now to the Clutters, now to Perry and Dick, until the unexplained juncture between them is explained in Part III. Until then, we are shifted to many different times and places in which we see Perry and Dick suspended, as it were, in a world without meaning, for we are not yet up to the explanation that Capote has reserved in order to keep up novelistic interest. Yet this explanation—in jail a pal had put the future killers on to the Clutters and the supposed wealth in the house—is actually, when it comes, meant to anchor the book all the more firmly in the world of "fact"—of the public world expressed as documented conflict between symbolic individuals. It was the unbelievable squareness of the Clutters as a family that aroused and fascinated the murderers. The book opens on Kansas as home and family, ends on Alvin Dewey at the family graveside. . . . The circle of illusory stability (which we have *seen* destroyed) has closed in on itself again. (pp. 215-17)

[The] point made is that there is no "sense" to the crime. This is what relieves the liberal imagination of responsibility and keeps it as spectator. (p. 219)

Alfred Kazin, "The Imagination of Fact: Capote to Mailer," in his Bright Book of Life: American Novelists and Storytellers from Hemingway to Mailer, *Little, Brown and Company, 1973, pp. 207-41.**

JOSEPHINE HENDIN

There are writers who hate people, who thrive on the rage that bristles in every American city. They are the few who say what so many seem to feel in silence: anger is the only irresistible emotion. They know the crowd craves blood because they crave it themselves to feel thoroughly alive. What they appeal to is whatever makes the crowd roar at the car about to crash at the races, the man about to jump from the roof. Such writers want to seem respectable—they intellectualize their gripes, sexualize their fear, politicize their rage. Some angries even come masked as victims who fear colossal social or political malice, and dread someone else's fury. But what really torments them is their own addiction to cruelty. What they fear is what they would like to do. Yesterday's paranoiacs are today's closet murderers. (p. 87)

[There are also] writers who are into hate, but out of love with it, who use various devices to reduce their anger. Donald Barthelme and Truman Capote are depression-freaks whose anger is muted to pessimism and discontent. Their rage takes the form of despair over the possibilities for life. (p. 89)

The most chilling thing in *In Cold Blood* is Truman Capote's contempt for the Clutters, who were murdered by Perry Smith and Dick Hickock. It is living in cold blood, not merely murdering in it, that fascinates Capote and shapes his description of the Clutters into something less than kind. (p. 90)

Against the Clutters' stark emptiness, Capote places his complex, intensely sympathetic portrait of Perry, a half-breed drifter, a loser raised in orphanages where he was often beaten, where, at the age of seven he first dreamed a dream so rich in symbolic connections, so baroque in its imagery, so beautifully violent that it could not help but appeal to an author whose books had hitherto been so lush. After being battered by a nun for wetting his bed, Perry dreamed that "the parrot appeared, arrived while he slept, a bird taller than Jesus, yellow like a sunflower, a warrior-angel who blinded the nuns with his beak, fed upon their eyes, slaughtered them as they pleaded for mercy, then so gently lifted him, enfolded him, winged him away to paradise." The "holy spirit" for Perry was violent revenge, a child's dream of a force great enough to overwhelm the forces that overwhelmed him. This spirit of vindication came to Perry Smith in reality, in the form of the writer who would have so much compassion for him, who would immortalize his suffering and his act as he faced Herb Clutter, knife in hand.

"Who is lonelier, the hawk or the worm?" Capote raised that question in *Other Voices, Other Rooms,* and it must have obsessed him throughout *In Cold Blood* as he turned the encounter between Smith and Clutter into a collision between two emotionally dead men—the "hawk" and the "worm" who are equally locked in their own isolation. The one murdering, the other dying, they are only Capote's most dramatic symbols for human "interaction."

Capote sees everyone trapped between one kind of death and another. Even the FBI man hunting the Clutters' killers is really investigating himself. As he watches a bonfire of the Clutters' effects, he asks, "How was it possible that such effort, such plain virtue could overnight be reduced to this—smoke thinning as it rose and was received by the big, annihilating sky?" Between the "annihilating sky" and the "scraping tumbleweed" lies Capote's vision of the American soul living, dying, and murdering in cold blood. Capote's despair over the ruined Perry Smith is the index of his distance from the Clutters. But his insistence that cold hate and cold life are the American

experiences is probably his wish more than his fear. Is it better to deep-freeze fury than to feel it, or even see it?

"Only connect!" wrote Forster. But for Barthelme and Capote, the only valid connection is to the evil, anger, or death they see at the center of every human being. . . . In the fiction of both Barthelme and Capote, knowing or caring about people is invariably the experience of evil and suffering. Barthelme's aestheticism and Capote's journalistic "realism" serve as devices for distancing both the writer and the reader from the violent core of their work. What grips Capote in the world is finally what justifies the depression, the quiet frustration that runs through all his serious novels. Reality is where Capote's fantasies happen.

The Dogs Bark, Capote's recent collection of portraits, interviews, and travel memoirs, underlines what makes the world irresistible to him. Places are, for Capote, most vivid as stage sets for the perpetual combats in his mind. (pp. 90-1)

Capote infuses his own violence into the quietest, emptiest places; he brings it to his portraits and interviews with public persons, particularly with those men who have been among the greatest symbols of virility. Humphrey Bogart is neatly struck down for his stupidity in less than two pages. . . . Having nailed Bogart for having the moral sharpness of a meat cleaver, Capote gets Marlon Brando for his confusion. Interviewing Brando in Kyoto during the filming of *Sayonara,* he makes him seem ridiculous for his pursuit of philosophy, his professed ambivalence over his success, his perpetual appearance of discontent. Noting—as any interviewer would—the gap between the piles of books on Zen and the lacquered trays heaped with food brought into Brando's opulent hotel room, Capote reduces most of what Brando says to merely the pretension of a "boy on the candy pile." During the Bogart sketch and the Brando interview, the adroit, mannered ad hominem attack so absorbs Capote's energies that he will not even acknowledge that the enormous success of these men was rooted in precisely what he mocks them for. (p. 91)

People are no longer repelled by a fiction whose aggression is so clear cut, so much the point. This is less because the angries provide a catharsis than because they recreate in an overt drama the fury that inheres in everyone—not just muttering loonies on the street. . . . Capote and Barthelme—sophisticated, Olympian—. . . [tap] the anger of the cosmopolite who regards the world as so intrinsically disappointing that he "knows" it deserves no more than the poisonous aphorism, the clever put-down.

Debunking is now the American pastime, the obsession that marks our attempt to cut the past down to the paucity of the present. George Washington was an expense-account fraud! Kennedy only a hollow man! This war against the dead, however true any of its specific attacks, signals the degree to which many of us live sophisticates have become snipers, addicted to the cheap shot at whoever is too unstained for current taste. And this in turn is the mark of our preoccupation with our own impotence and power, the nonsexual yin and yang of our time. (p. 93)

*Josephine Hendin, "Angries: S-M as a Literary Style," in Harper's Magazine, Vol. 248, No. 1485, February, 1974, pp. 87-93.**

RICHARD GRAY

In 1967 a distinguished group of writers and commentators met at a small liberal arts college in Georgia to discuss one particular question: the state of Southern literature. What, they asked themselves and each other, had happened to the regional tradition since the great period of the ''renaissance'' between the wars? What would happen to it in the future? The excellence of Southern writing during this period was . . . partly the result of a specific historical occasion, a complex series of social and cultural pressures that had eased it into birth. Could this excellence survive its occasion; and could the qualities of imagination recognized as distinctively Southern still remain viable long after the circumstances that had given them prominence had passed away? (p. 257)

I do not intend to summarize the conclusions of that meeting in Georgia here. . . . Rather, my purpose in mentioning it at all is simply to illustrate what is perhaps a fairly obvious point: that this, the problem of survival—by which I mean, of course, survival through the agency of genuine, creative development—is a major one for Southern literature now. For the writers born after the great generation that emerged in the twenties and thirties have been placed in a peculiarly disagreeable situation. They have been born too late, really, to benefit from the stimulus of crisis . . . ; but they have been born, equally, too early not to be oppressed by the example of those, the writers before them, who were able to enjoy what they have missed. They are without the large, new perspectives available to men writing at a moment of transition, and, what is perhaps worse, the perspectives they *do* enjoy have been overused, most of them, already. . . . Southern writing, to put it briefly, is in the same danger that any body of writing is after a period of immense achievement. It is in danger of going stale, and it does not necessarily help matters that (as that gathering in Georgia indicates) some Southern writers are themselves aware of this.

What particular forms do these dangers assume? . . . In a way, there are almost as many answers to that as there are people writing in the South. But one broad danger, one trap into which many tend to fall is illustrated well, I think, by two authors who enjoy perhaps the most colorful reputations in recent American letters. I mean by this the dramatist Tennessee Williams, who was born in the border state of Missouri, and Truman Capote, from Louisiana. The trap is, essentially, one of style: the writer takes the familiar characters, situations, and themes and then weaves them into a baroque conceit possessing neither original substance nor extrinsic value. The world so imagined hardly exists—or, at least, hardly deserves consideration—on any other level than the decorative: it offers us a group of charming grotesques, preserved in amber. What is Southern about it, really, is not a certain quality of perception, a sense of engagement between past and present, the public and the private, myth and history: but a turn of phrase or personality, a use of the bizarre and sensational for their own sake, which has the net effect of creating distance. For regionalism is substituted a form of local color, and a very precious and slightly decadent form at that, in which the gap between drama and audience seems deliberately widened so that the latter can revel without compunction in a contemporary ''Gothick'' fantasy. (pp. 257-58)

[Capote] began, as he has explained on more than one occasion, as a prose purist, a stylist *par excellence*. Every sentence he wrote was an elaborate concoction, with the sort of purity of line and grace of cadence that is perhaps the inevitable product of an aesthetic never seriously violated by life. The inspiration was purely literary, an inbred one; and much of its literariness

stemmed from the fact that Capote seemed to know all of the more important Southern writers intimately—know them so well, in fact, that he could reproduce them with only the ornate, facile beauty of his own phrasing added on. Reading his earlier fiction, consequently, is rather like reading a clever pastiche: the enjoyment lies in the element of recognition involved as much as anything else, in discovering the familiar and known beneath the altered surface. Here, as an illustration of what I mean, is a passage from his first novel, *Other Voices, Other Rooms*.

> Noon City is not much to look at. There is only one street, and on it are located . . . a combination barbershop-beautyparlor that is run by a one-armed man and his wife; and a curious, indefinable establishment known as R. V. Lacey's Princely Place . . . across the road . . . stand two . . . structures: a jail, and a tall queer tottering ginger-colored house. The jail has not housed a white criminal in over four years, . . . the Sheriff being a lazy no-good, prone to take his ease with a bottle. . . . As to the freakish old house, no one has lived there for God knows how long, and it is said that once three exquisite sisters were raped and murdered here . . . by a fiendish Yankee bandit who rode on a silver-grey horse . . . ; when told by antiquated ladies claiming . . . acquaintance with the beautiful victims, it is a tale of Gothic splendor. The windows of the house are cracked and shattered, hollow as eyeless sockets; . . . the . . . walls are ragged with torn, weather-faded posters that flutter in the wind.

Most of the influences behind this passage are obvious enough, I think, and scarcely need to be mentioned here. It begins with a cunning imitation of Carson McCullers's prose, flat, dry, a little unnerving; moves on into the world of lazy backwoods whites that interested Caldwell so much; and then concludes with a series of macabre, Grand Guignol touches that recall in turn Eudora Welty, Poe, and Faulkner. What is perhaps less obvious on first reading, however, is how self-conscious, even narcissistic, Capote manages to remain throughout all this; he is acutely aware of the fact that he is parodying his masters—the people whose visions appear, appropriately diminished, in his sentences—and he seems to want us, his readers, to share in his awareness. So that, it may be, is one reason why he refers to ''a tale of Gothic splendor'' toward the end of the description. The phrase does, of course, have an immediate application—to the stories told by the old ladies about the ''fiendish Yankee bandit.'' But coming when it does it seems to have a much wider relevance than that, to stretch out, in effect, and bring the entire portrait of Noon City within its scope. It, the city, is we feel being ''placed'' more than anything else is—identified with a context in which books can refer only to other books and for which, therefore, no forms of life are available except those aleady filtered through another imagination. And as if to confirm this impression, in the very next sentence following this one Capote uses two figures that could almost be described as emblems, or identifying signs, of the Southern Gothic mode: the windows staring out at the newcomer like eyeless sockets (compare the opening moments of *The Fall of the House of Usher*), and the posters fluttering like an abandoned banner in the wind (compare the closing pages of *Sartoris*). The magic circle is, as it were, closed by these further touches, the reduction of the landscape, to a twilight kingdom of remembered fictions, quite complete.

What has happened to Capote since the appearance of *Other Voices, Other Rooms* is, I think, just as interesting as this—and, in its own way, just as commonplace. He has tried a number of different genres and styles, some of them Southern, some not, and all without apparent conviction or originality: macabre fantasy in *A Tree of Night* has been followed by pastoral comedy in *The Grass Harp,* picaresque adventure in *Breakfast at Tiffany's* by straightforward reportage in *In Cold Blood.* Every one of these, needless to say, is well enough done on the level of technical competence. But not one of them carries any sense of genuine engagement; more important, not one of them helps Capote to solve his major problem of achieving a synthesis between myth and event. *In Cold Blood* . . . is a perfect illustration of this since all it does, essentially, is reverse the terms of Capote's predicament. Pure fantasy, the legendary kingdom of *Other Voices, Other Rooms,* is replaced in this book by the cult of the fact; and the ornate style, by one of scrupulous meanness. As a result of these changes events are now seen through an eye that most resembles that of the camera, without values, beliefs, or allegiances. They are separated off from the human context, in which connections are made and meanings arrived at, and presented as if they possessed some significance of their own—*possessed* significance rather than *assumed* it from the ideas brought to, and the legends drawn from, them. History may have become Capote's subject here, perhaps, but it is history recorded as a series of arbitrary occasions, lacking the determining force of myth; and as such it is not likely to convince the reader that the book represents much of an advance on its predecessors. Certainly it will not encourage him to place it in the same category as those works—such as "Ode to the Confederate Dead," say, or *World Enough and Time*—for which fact and legend, event and interpretation, seem equally indispensable. (pp. 260-62)

> *Richard Gray, "Aftermath: Southern Literature Since World War II," in his* The Literature of Memory: Modern Writers of the American South, *The Johns Hopkins University Press, 1977, pp. 257-305.**

ANNA SHAPIRO

Like Truman Capote's earlier *A Christmas Memory* and *The Thanksgiving Visitor, One Christmas* is a childhood memoir the length of a short story, packaged, after magazine publication, as a book. It covers some of the same territory as the earlier volumes, too. . . .

[The focus of *One Christmas*] is on 6-year-old Buddy, as Mr. Capote was then called, as he journeys from Alabama to New Orleans to be reunited with a father who's a stranger to him. . . .

The story is almost a parody, a thumbnail sketch of the circumstances (a revered mother, an estranged father) that make for emotional problems, centered, with wine-darkened, memory-dimming hysteria, on Christmas. That, with the disingenuously gooey message that a distant, frightening parent can nevertheless be loved, make it the cynical Christmas card it is.

> *Anna Shapiro, in a review of "One Christmas," in* The New York Times Book Review, *November 13, 1983, p. 19.*

J. F. DESMOND

Pathos has always been Capote's strong suit as a writer, especially childhood pathos. What more apt subject than the first visit of a small boy to his estranged father's house in New Orleans at Christmastime? [In *One Christmas,* the] trip becomes an initiation into disillusionment. . . . [The child's] revenge for having his illusions shattered is to manipulate his father into buying him an expensive present.

What saves this slight tale from becoming treacle is Capote's irony in the delicate interplay of childhood sensibility and recollective vision. Looking back years later, the adult Buddy sees his father's own desperate attempt to love him, unrequited until too late. Much is subtly suggested here, but one also notices how much more Capote could have done with it. (pp. 422-23)

> *J. F. Desmond, in a review of "One Christmas," in* World Literature Today, *Vol. 58, No. 3, Summer, 1984, pp. 422-23.*

Alejo Carpentier (y Valmont)

1904-1980

Cuban novelist, poet, journalist, editor, musicologist, essayist, and critic.

Carpentier is considered a significant and influential figure in Latin American fiction. A writer of varied interests and learning, he infuses his novels and short stories with references to music, history, politics, science, art, mythology, and other subjects. His novels are usually complex and detailed, particularly when describing the lush settings and exotic cultures of Latin America. While some critics have faulted Carpentier for excessive display of scholarship, others consider this density a vital part of his craft. Emir Rodriguez Monegal stated: "Obsessed by the temporal limitations placed on human experience, Carpentier employs American nature as a luxuriant, chaotic backcloth, the colourful history of the New World as a pretext, to explore through the medium of a remarkably erudite imagination the multi-dimensional experience of American man."

Carpentier was born in Havana to parents of French and Russian descent. After he was briefly jailed in 1927 for signing a manifesto against the Cuban dictator Gerardo Machado y Morales, Carpentier sought voluntary exile in Paris. There he encountered the work of such French surrealist writers as André Breton and Louis Aragon. Although he considered his own attempts at surrealism unsuccessful, the movement provided an alternative to the realistic "nativismo" style then popular in Latin American fiction. Carpentier returned to Cuba in 1939 and worked as a writer and producer of radio shows and as a professor of music. He spent most of the 1940s and 1950s living in Europe, the United States, and South America. When the Cuban revolution led by Fidel Castro occurred in 1959, Carpentier returned to his own country. At the time of his death he was serving as Cuban cultural attaché to France.

Carpentier began his first novel, *¡Écue-yamba-ó!* (1933), in 1927 when he was in jail. This work combines politics and folklore in a depiction of the struggles of black Cubans. Though considered his least effective novel, *¡Écue-yamba-ó!* initiates the fascination with history and myth present in all of Carpentier's work. His second novel, *El reino de este mundo* (1949; *The Kingdom of This World*), set in eighteenth-century Haiti, is the story of a rebellion led by a slave against the tyrannical leader of Haiti, Henri Christophe, who is himself a former slave. In his influential essay "De lo real-maravilloso americana," included at the beginning of this book, Carpentier describes his theory of the quality in Latin American literature which depicts a reality infused with magic and myth, reflecting the rich and varied culture of the region.

Though not widely read in the United States, Carpentier's next work, *Los pasos perdidos* (1953; *The Lost Steps*), was critically acclaimed in Europe. The novel is structured as the journal of a disillusioned musicologist who, bored by his life among intellectuals and artists in New York City, travels up the Orinoco River in South America to research and collect the musical instruments of primitive tribes. During his journey he encounters a number of cultures, each representing a different epoch of history, culminating in an Eden-like world in which natural instincts and forces take precedence over the intellect. The

novel is structurally complex and contains meticulously detailed settings and references to many disciplines and fields of thought. In his introduction to the English translation of the book, J. B. Priestley calls it "a masterpiece, an inspired idea most wonderfully transformed into an enduring novel."

El siglo de las luces (1962; *Explosion in a Cathedral*) was also highly praised. This novel is a historical epic which follows the lives of three characters as they take part in an early nineteenth-century Caribbean uprising headed by Victor Hugues, the representative of the French revolution in the Antilles and the founder of Guadeloupe. Like Carpentier's other novels, *Explosion in a Cathedral* explores the cyclical nature of history and time. Although the novel has many political themes, it evidences Carpentier's reluctance to align himself with any specific ideology. His participation in Fidel Castro's administration affirms his support of the Cuban revolution, but most critics find in his work the conviction that no government is ideal or permanent and that every revolution is destined to be followed by another.

In *El acoso* (1956), Carpentier relied extensively on his knowledge of music. This novel is carefully constructed around Beethoven's *Eroica* symphony, which the protagonist, a revolutionary activist who has taken refuge in an orchestra hall, listens to as he recalls his past. *El recurso del metodo* (1974; *Reasons of State*) is a satirical account of an incompetent dictator of a fictional Latin American country who spends most of his time in Paris and is eventually deposed by a revolution. In an ironic ending, the exiled dictator is appointed foreign ambassador to the country he formerly ruled. Carpentier's last novel, *El arpa y la sombra* (1979), centers on Christopher Columbus's discovery of the New World and portrays the impact of the mythological and natural lushness of Latin America on the European sensibility.

The short stories in *Guerra del tiempo* (1958; *The War of Time*) echo the concerns of Carpentier's novels, with particular emphasis on illusion and the distortion of time. He also published a volume of poetry and several collections of essays on literature, as well as books on music and architecture.

(See also *CLC*, Vols. 8, 11; *Contemporary Authors*, Vols. 65-68, Vols. 97-100 [obituary]; and *Contemporary Authors New Revision Series*, Vol. 11.)

SELDEN RODMAN

After reading this erudite yet absorbing adventure story [*The Lost Steps*] . . . , one can readily understand why it has won a high award in France and has had, as its publishers say, a great critical success in Spanish-speaking countries as well. A story by and about an intellectual is not likely to be well received in America. Not only in politics but even in the sciences a man with a deeply cultural background who tries consciously to relate his work and his personality to the historical trend of culture is suspect among us. Henry James and T. S. Eliot are still suspect. And despite my awareness of this national limitation—if it is a limitation—I find myself becoming not a little suspicious, too, when I find the protagonist of an adventure story discussing his sexual prowess in terms of the Greeks and the Israelites, invoking Descartes in a dugout canoe, and quoting medieval Latin poems in the jungle.

This is completely unfair to the author, of course. His novel is about an intellectual, a composer and musicologist, who escapes the hothouse atmosphere of intellectual New York (and his tiresome wife, an actress) on the pretext of searching for rare primitive wind-instruments among the aborigines of the upper Orinoco tributaries. Taking with him his mistress, a lightweight surrealist given to quoting Rimbaud and invoking the signs of the zodiac, he finds that she doesn't wear well in a frontier hotel besieged by revolutionists, and begins to fade physically in a tropical cyclone and amid the earthy preoccupations of the savages.

When she conveniently develops malaria and is beaten up by a wholly natural and womanly *mestizo* to whom she makes improper advances, the hero ships her back to civilization, finds himself in the arms of the *mestizo*, and begins to write deathless music on a dwindling supply of paper. When the paper gives out, his anxiety returns—though his fears will hardly be shared by the experienced novel reader, who knows that his disappearance has been widely publicized, that it is only a question of time before a rescue plane appears to whisk him to New York. Soon finding that it was a horrible mistake, that neither his wife nor mistress has what he wanted, and that his inspiration was left behind him too, he returns to the Orinoco, only to find that the trails to the hidden village have been obliterated and that his love . . . has long since married.

This is unfair, too. The plot is suspensefully unfolded. The dialogue and the descriptions are brilliantly poetic. The parable of the loss of elemental capacities and virtues in modern, urban life bears constant retelling. . . . Still —.

Well, it doesn't quite come off. Perhaps it is because the hero is so very, very much the intellectual that it is difficult, despite the breathlessness with which the three women abandon themselves to him, to be convinced that he is also a man. You can't believe he is a true artist, either—he surrenders his art too easily. He feeds not on life but on self-pity. As for the minor figures, their characterization is much too pat and perfunctory. All in all, it's a book full of riches—stylistic, sensory, visual—but as a novel it's just a little cheap.

> Selden Rodman, *"Journey into the Night,"* in The New York Times Book Review, *October 14, 1956, p. 5.*

WILLIAM PFAFF

The rejection of modern urban civilization, the return to the primitive—this is a hackneyed and dangerous subject for a novelist. And Mr. Carpentier, who writes of a journey from New York City to a South American forest [in *The Lost Steps*], does not completely escape the dangers of the subject. It is not that he is cheap or superficial in what he says about the character of life in a contemporary city or about the values of a primitive society. His comments are mature and his conclusion is an honorable one. But theme and conclusion are conventional and provide little in the way of evaluation of either society that is novel. What matters in this book is the journey. It is an extraordinary trip, provoking a kind of intellectual excitement I have found in only a handful of novels. If Mr. Carpentier says very little about modern life and values that has not been said before, and as well, he does say things about the physical world, about travel and time, about the growth of culture, that are breathtaking. . . .

[*The Lost Steps* is] a triumph, a rare and fine book, full of extraordinary insight, written with a kind of intellectual validity, versatility and maturity that are very rare in the books that make up a year of American publishing.

The hero of *The Lost Steps* is a New York musician (born in Latin America) who writes motion picture scores. He is offered a commission to travel into the uplands of a South American country to collect some primitive musical instruments for a museum. (p. 211)

So the trip begins, first to a Latin city where a revolution breaks out, then to the river that is the route to the interior. And the journey, which is described with personal knowledge (Mr. Carpentier has made a similar trip up the Orinoco in Venezuela), becomes quite strikingly far more than a physical adventure. It is a journey into time.

In the Latin city (Havana?) the travelers have met the Romantic Age. They have gone back a hundred years. Then, as they approach the forest, they go still further into the past as civilization recedes. They stop at an oil camp, at a river village, at an Indian settlement (and by this time the mistress has quit, unable to live without the cushion of civilization; the hero finds the classic peasant woman, feminine and intuitive, with no nonsense about astrology or St.-Germain-des-Prés). Finally the party reaches the heart of the forest. They have passed through Romanticism, through the Middle Ages of peasantry and festivals, to the Land of the Horse, the age of the Spanish conquest, to the Land of the Dog, finally to the land that was before history began—where there are found "the plants that have fled from man since the beginning . . . the rebel plants, those which refused to serve him as food, which crossed rivers, scaled mountains, leaped the deserts for thousands and thousands of years to hide here . . . the diabolical vegetation that surrounded the Garden of Eden before the Fall." (pp. 211-12)

It is an intellectual novel, and a highly disciplined one. It is not primarily *story* (as is, say, *The Cypresses Believe in God,* a Spanish novel of comparable stature); it resembles the work of Malraux or Koestler in being adventure which has its primary meaning at the moral and intellectual levels. And unlike most American novelists, Mr. Carpentier has the kind of control that enables him to write of matters that veer very close to sentimentality without becoming sentimental or evasive. There is a vigorous and important element of cynicism in what the narrator has to say about his own weakness and perverseness. He writes, too, with justness; while he has contempt for falseness, he is not arrogant.

But most remarkable is the time theme. Mr. Carpentier's knowledge of music and of history and anthropology, at the service of a first-rate artistic talent and a highly original mind, make the book a brilliant and enviable accomplishment. (pp. 212-13)

> *William Pfaff, "The Intellectual Excitement of a Journey into Time," in* Commonweal, *Vol. LXV, No. 8, November 23, 1956, pp. 211-13.*

DOROTHY VAN GHENT

I do not think that a novel with such qualities of magnificence as Carpentier's **The Lost Steps** owes very much that is important to habits of mind associated with a particular culture; at least I can find nothing singularly Spanish-American in its attitudes and special poetry, although a great part of the setting is South American. Its grandeur of conception, the splendor of its imagery, the powerful sweep of its energy are qualities of an individual greatness of mind. It is a mind deeply cultivated in the European tradition, immensely learned, profoundly passionate. . . . Carpentier's energy is gigantic and pellmell, sweeping colossi on top of each other with ruthless, contemptuous daring. It is Balzac to whom he is closest. Because of the anthropological character of a good deal of the materials of **The Lost Steps,** I think particularly of Balzac's "Le Peau de Chagrin," where, at the beginning of the story, a vision is invoked of the succession of the epochs of human life and culture, out of the chaotic dusts of a museum. Carpentier's narrative also starts in a museum, from which his protagonist then descends physically through successive cultural epochs, back to pre-history (not by any science-fiction marvels, but by a journey up the Orinoco to stone-age tribes). In both the sense of spiritual responsibility is tremendous, though Balzac arranges this by magical terrorization and Carpentier by the realism of despair.

In general pattern, the book can be simplified to an "escape" from the contemporary urban wasteland, and the discovery of a truly human way of life, using man's capacities in coherent and fruitful adjustment with his environment, under stone-age conditions. But this simplification to an "escape" pattern distorts and obscures a special problem with which the book deals, that of the artist (the main character is a composer), whose link with his own time is inexorable and cannot be "escaped" unless he ceases to be an artist, that is, ceases to be himself. It also distorts and obscures the very dense, complex emotional import of the book, which lies in the wrought textures of the scenes, and in the extraordinarily concrete vision of the cultural ages of man, given as the actual physical experience of a twentieth-century traveler.

The narrative begins in a metropolis which one assumes to be New York though it is not named; it is all the great modern cities of the world piled on top of one another, and though its places are as familiar as Rockefeller Center and the Museum of Modern Art, they exist in an atmosphere of gigantism and crowdedness whose impact is overwhelmingly claustral, mad, frivolous, sterile, and dangerous. Through a number of domestic and professional pressures, the narrator finds himself forced into acceptance of a job with the Museum of Organography which involves a trip to South America in search of certain primitive archetypal musical instruments. The trip is complicated by the presence of his mistress—a bohemian Belladonna, lady of situations—who, as they cover the steps of receding time back into the Middle Ages, back to the year One, and still further back to the Homeric age and the stone age, guilelessly carries with her in her person the twentieth-century wasteland; but she is finished off fairly early in the narrative by her own anachronism, in "a perfect revenge of the authentic on the synthetic." The temporal strangeness—a sense of the living jungles of time surrounding the thin human enterprise—begins during their initial stay in a South American capital, an efficient modern city of civilized luxury; despite the presence everywhere of electrical power and machinery, and the swiftness with which the most progressive techniques and procedures have caught on, stranger things occasionally happen than the break-down of the sewage system during the spring rains. . . . At junctures like this, the invariable explanation is "It's the Worm!" "Nobody had ever seen the Worm. But the Worm existed, carrying on its arts of confusion, turning up when least expected to confound the most tried and trusted experience." A minor revolution breaks out, with serious shooting in the streets, and the musicologist and his mistress are confined with other foreigners to their hotel for several days. Exasperation becomes panicky when the telephones are cut off. " 'It's the Worm,' said the manager, echoing the joke that had become the explanation of the catastrophic goings-on. 'It's the Worm.' " . . . The living presence of the Worm establishes the mediaeval magnitude—the realm of Jung's dragon, of autonomous demonic powers—at the beginning of the recession into time. (pp. 275-77)

The dust-jacket states that the upper reaches of the Orinoco and the Gran Sabana, traveled by Mr. Carpentier, supply [the] setting. It is a landscape of marvel, of a great and terrifying beauty. . . .

I have spent so much time on this book because of what seems to me its altogether unusual achievement, but I cannot give any adequate suggestion of its intellectual depth, subtlety, and passion, or of its narrative power. (p. 278)

> *Dorothy Van Ghent, "The Race, the Moment, and the Milieu," in* The Yale Review, *Vol. XLVI, No. 2, December, 1956, pp. 274-88.**

MILDRED ADAMS

[The theme of **The Kingdom of This World**] is the power of the powerless. It is laid in that spectacular period at the turn of the eighteenth century when French rule in the island [of Haiti] was crumbling and native rule was seized by the slave Henri Christophe who, building a black state and a fortress that still survives, attempted "to ignore Voodoo, molding with whiplash a caste of Catholic gentlemen" in the white pattern.

In form a novella, the book is in substance a handful of heady moments woven together by literary craftsmanship of a high order. Its author, in a preface written for the Spanish edition (published in Mexico in 1949), claims that his story is founded on a most careful documentation of people, places, chronology and events. Few readers who are swept along by its vivid mixture of horror, violence and humor will stop to check. Such are its author's fictional skills that the world he paints becomes by that process the world which is believable and believed. If, behind that creative miracle, there lies a corresponding actual world, or what he calls in that same Spanish preface "the marvelous real," one can only admire his zest for history.

The literary profile of Haiti which Mr. Carpentier presents does not differ in important detail from that which was painted in the Nineteen Twenties by Blair Niles or William Seabrook. What distinguishes this new interpretation is the modern and very different attitude displayed toward what lives behind that profile. Where earlier authors wrote as compassionate Anglo-Saxons, describing the alien violence of a black rebellion, Mr. Carpentier, born in Cuba, writes as a Caribbean describing the people and habits of another island. Sociological values dear to the Nineteen Twenties have for him neither validity nor relevance. Pity does not enter his book, nor middle-class morality, either of the bed or of the counting house, nor judgments based on a non-Haitian code.

The hero of this book is the slave Macandal who, having lost his right arm and physical prowess to the rollers of a sugar mill, increases his hold over his people by enlisting the powers of magic, and comes close to destroying his white masters through a creeping death found in a yellow mold. All the play of terror, delight in imagination, primitive panoply of distortion and pretense that was derived from Africa and is native in Haiti, surges forward to immortalize him. In comparison, Henri Christophe appears dwarfed and blundering, a carbon copy of a white tyrant forcing his way up in terms that the French taught him, terms which in the end not only betray him but render him grotesque and absurd. The lesson is implicit. (pp. 4, 20)

> Mildred Adams, "From Magic, Power," in The New York Times Book Review, May 19, 1957, pp. 4, 20.

MARTIN PRICE

[*The Kingdom of This World*] is less what one expects a novel to be than it is a symbolist prose poem. Set in Haiti, it follows the revolutions of power through the lifetime of a slave, Ti Noel, who lives beneath the notice of his rulers and conquerors until, in his moment, he rules too. The book moves from the splendid surfaces of greatness and apparent stability to the darkness, of jungle and passionate myth, which surrounds and inevitably surmounts them. . . . Mr. Carpentier gives us a series of brilliant scenes, almost suffocatingly dense in their imagery (although the prose matrix is cool and precise), elaborated with baroque ornateness and frivolity. In studied oppositions of character and event, in ironic appreciation of each doomed elegance or barbaric grandeur, the author establishes his mastery.

But Alejo Carpentier is . . . so knowing and studied a writer, so obsessed on the one hand with the bulge and glisten, the curve and thrust, of human energies, and so devastatingly aloof from the trumperies of the rational orderers, that his book becomes an unpleasantly overwrought performance, an exercise in Flaubertian exorcism without an Emma to anatomize. One can see a kind of Polybian cyclic view of the forms of power in this pageant of kingdoms, tyrannies, and revolutions; but the finicky sensuousness of the description and the calculated dissonances of images have some of the tawdry refinement of Victorian diabolism and the remoteness of Tiffany glass. This hectic splendor becomes, in its way, a denial of all one can mean by "this world," and the book leaves one with an impression less of baroque exuberance than the kind of mannerist tension which endows a Madonna with a disembodied grace that has a curious voluptuousness. (pp. 155-56)

> Martin Price, "In the Fielding Country," in The Yale Review, Vol. XLVII, No. 1, September, 1957, pp. 143-56.*

KATHLEEN NOTT

Alejo Carpentier's *Explosion in a Cathedral* is a remarkable and enjoyable *tour de force,* and his re-creation of a Caribbean world at the time of the French Revolution and its naval wars, is even gripping. But his imaginary characters—his family of rich Havana orphans—seem to me to be conventional-fictional and hence to belong nowhere particular in time or space. One of them, Esteban, holds the story together by his involvement with Victor Hugues, the terrorist, who became Commissar in Guadeloupe and organised privateering to finance the local Revolution. Victor, who is biographical, is much more all there and illogically real: life *is* not only stranger than fiction, but often better at it.

Esteban's chief function seems to be to show you what Carpentier thinks about essential disillusion after the blissful dawn and the inevitable degeneration of idealism. This is often a good, even exciting, adventure story but since the author is not primarily interested in people, the moral and psychological significance is at about the level of a kind of "black" Boy's Own Paper—a clean wind of piracy plus some rather less hygienic sex (all very virile and modern). What really interests Carpentier is Things, an "existentialist" taste common in Spanish-American poetry. Beginning with the warehouse in Havana (salt fish, wine, ginger, red and green parasols, feathers) objects crowd every page, and there are marvellous descriptions and catalogues of kinds of trees, kinds of noises made by different kinds of rain, and kinds of crustacea or plankton. Wonderfully done but becoming at last an almost "absurd" inventory of nature. (pp. 89-90)

> Kathleen Nott, in a review of "Explosion in a Cathedral," in Encounter, Vol. XX, No. 5, May, 1963, pp. 89-90.

EMIR RODRIGUEZ MONEGAL

[Educated] in France, cosmopolitan in his culture and an expert musicologist, Carpentier is the very type of the Latin American intellectual whose roots lie in the Old World. Nevertheless, his work is profoundly "American." Obsessed by the temporal limitations placed on human experience, Carpentier employs American nature as a luxuriant, chaotic backcloth, the colourful history of the New World as a pretext, to explore through the medium of a remarkably erudite imagination the multi-dimensional experience of American man. What, in his first important book, *The Kingdom of this World* (1949)—a lively, somewhat Borges-like evocation of the history and mythology of Haiti—appeared no more than a rather decorative game, became in *The Lost Steps* (1953 . . .) explicit allegory. The hero of this book, a musicologist, undertakes a voyage backwards through time; a voyage that takes him back simultaneously into pre-history and into the depths of the South American forest, the living green matrix of the continent. . . .

What saves this tale from the over-obviousness of allegory is its lucidity. In the heart of the jungle, the musicologist realises that he is doomed, that he must go back to New York: he lacks the materials to annotate a new musical composition he is working on. This awareness (somehow autobiographical) touches a delicate point in the relationship between Latin American intellectuals and Latin American realities. . . .

[Carpentier's] next novel, *El Acoso* (*The Chase,* 1956)—a somewhat artificial reconstruction of a Cuban revolutionary attempt in the epoch of Machado—was by contrast a severe disappointment, a mere exercise in narrative virtuosity. But it was followed (in 1962) by what is probably Carpentier's masterpiece, *Explosion in a Cathedral* [1963] . . . , a highly intelligent neo-romantic literary construction, reminiscent in its scope of the great novels of Victor Hugo. In his latest novel, Carpentier achieves a remarkable and disquieting evocation of Caribbean history in the epoch of the French Revolution, on the eve of the Wars of Independence in Latin America. Begun in 1956 but not published till six years later (after the Cuban revolution), the novel can be read to-day as an exciting historical melodrama, full of insights into the revolutionary mind, or as a striking study in historical parallels. The fate of the protagonist, an idealist who starts his career as a revolutionary and ends it as a slave-owner and dictator, is extremely significant. Carpentier handles this remote, yet very topical, even explosive material with remarkable assurance.

A novelist of considerable stylistic ambition, a subtle observer, gifted with a rich verbal sensuality, Carpentier manages to avoid the facile tendentiousness of his predecessors in the *genre,* pursuing a private investigation into the nature of time—its unreality, its reversibility, its cyclical character—which has many points of contact with the literary speculations of Borges. In a book of short stories, *Guerra del Tiempo* (*The War of Time,* 1958), Carpentier has made explicit his own metaphysical concern with time, giving another clue to some of the most controversial implications of his great novel. To-day he lives in Cuba and has an important official post. But he has refused (like so many of the best Cuban writers) to follow the line of socialist realism. In or out of Cuba he goes on building up, scene by scene, his America of the imagination. (p. 106)

> *Emir Rodriguez Monegal, ''A Genre Renewed: Alejo Carpentier,'' in Encounter, Vol. XXV, No. 3, September, 1965, pp. 104, 106.*

J. B. PRIESTLEY

I have always been very cautious indeed about using terms like *masterpiece* and *genius.* Scatter such terms carelessly and you debase the coinage of criticism. Greet every goodish book with a shout, then you are simply out of breath when a great book comes along. Taking not one country but the whole world, we can say there are only a very few masterpieces and literary men of genius in any generation. These are very rare birds indeed. And now, having made this point, I will state very deliberately that in my opinion *The Lost Steps* is a work of genius, a genuine masterpiece.

If anybody wants my advice about how best he or she can fully appreciate this masterpiece, then here it is. Read it first, perhaps quite quickly, to discover what happens. Then, after not too long an interval, settle down with it to savour and suck the marrow of it. And there are two good reasons why this is the best method. First, *The Lost Steps* is an unusually rich narrative, a plum pudding among the various desserts of prose fiction. Secondly—and this is even more important—it is a novel designed to be read, enjoyed, understood, on several different levels, just like that marvellous old Spanish masterpiece *Don Quixote,* which has layer after layer of irony and, when properly read, *is always wiser than you are.*

The Lost Steps is a superb example of what I like to call . . . *Symbolic Action.* We read and hear a lot about symbolism in fiction these days. . . . But all too often we find so-called symbols stuck into a narrative like plums into a cake. This is not what I mean by *Symbolic Action,* which demands that every setting, every important event, everything that happens if it has any significance at all, have symbolic depth and value. Such work can be read (or seen and heard in performance), enjoyed, understood, on more than one level. . . . True symbolism relates our outer world to our inner world; the symbol itself rises from depths we cannot penetrate; and though symbolic work offers us one level of meaning below another there always appears to be a final level that can never be properly explored, being just beyond the reach of consciousness. And we can find all this in *The Lost Steps.*

On the first level here we are offered a fascinating story of adventure and travel. We are told how a musician, leading an empty life doing film work he despises, accepts a commission to find some very rare primitive musical instruments in the Amazonian jungle; and how he does find them among remote Indians, with whom he lives quite happily by the side of a simple but rich-natured woman he can truly love; and how he is ''rescued'' and returned to a civilization he comes to dislike more and more, and then, eagerly returning to his jungle Eden, how he discovers he cannot find his way back and that the woman he loves now belongs to another man. This would be a magnificent piece of story-telling even if it had no significance in depth. Let me offer as an example of Carpentier's unusual skill in narrative what is, after all, only a minor episode. On their way to the jungle, the musician and his mistress spend some days in a large hotel in the capital city of the country. There some kind of revolution suddenly arrives with a hail of bullets. Now this is a fairly familiar situation in stories of Central or South America. . . . But has anybody ever done it better than Alejo Carpentier does here in about fifteen pages? The monstrous tragic-farce of such a sudden eruption of violence; the suggestion of the brittle insecurity of our urban society, in which, when we discover we cannot switch on electricity or turn on water, we feel entirely helpless: it is all here in those fifteen pages.

In this place I feel I must digress from the novel's various levels of meaning and significance to say something about its narrative *richness,* mentioned earlier. Carpentier combines a sharp observation of detail, a poetic eye for strange or visionary effects, and great eloquence. In the fiction he wrote before *The Lost Steps* . . . I felt that the mixture was too rich for the subjects, rather like that almost black and sticky fruit cake which Canada exports, too rich for teatime. But in this novel he has a big bold theme, a large-boned narrative, that can stand up to his opulent treatment of it. No doubt now and again, when the story halts and he rains images on us, we may feel he is indulging himself—a common fault of eager and generous writers—and may long for less opulence and splendour. . . . But in the main he succeeds triumphantly in *putting us there,* where his narrator is, while at the same time suggesting various heightened and enriched states of mind. For all its mass of realistic detail—and wherever Carpentier actually went he certainly kept his eyes open and his mind receptive—this is essentially a *poetic* novel. And if it had not been, he could never have succeeded in making it so deeply symbolic, could never have appealed to us on these different levels, to which I must now return.

Clearly we have here a journey in space, from Broadway to mysterious reaches of the Orinoco or the Amazon, but what is far more important, we have also a journey in time. This is a point he makes most eloquently over and over again. . . . Carpentier's musician-narrator, trying to find the very primitive instruments, first sailing up the great river and then going, still by water though along narrowing channels, deeper and deeper into the jungle, travels back and back in time, not merely observing but *living with* older and older human societies. And because he began with nothing but his disgust and despair in a huge modern city, with its meaningless hordes spending all day doing what they don't want to do and then killing the rest of their time with idiotic amusements, the further the narrator goes back, the earlier the society he lives with, the more satisfying and rewarding his life is. So it is when he is living with the simple woman he loves, at last outside our civilization, in a clearing on the very edge of the unknown, that as a composer he is moved, after years of sterility, to begin creating an ambitious and deeply serious work.

It may well be objected that a man who never wants to see one of our cities again, who is happy at last because he has done with our civilization, should not be eagerly scoring a work that demands a large orchestra, a trained choir, and a concert management. This of course has always been the weakness, the rather absurd side, of thinkers and artists who ask us to turn our backs on civilization. . . . Of course Carpentier is well aware of this inconsistency. (He is exceptionally well aware of most things, writing out of an unusual experience in many fields, from cultural history to remote travel, a good memory and a rich imagination.) But then he is not offering us sociological polemics but a poetic symbolic novel. And here he is not only taking a journey back in time, he is also exploring man's inner world.

So we arrive at the deepest level, half-hidden in the dusk of the mind. . . . It is the world over which Jung's Collective Unconscious, our psychic inheritance, presides. There may be found the Jungian archetypes, such as the Anima, created out of man's age-old experience of woman, and lit with magic because it rises out of the magical depths of his unconscious. The musician does not passionately prefer his jungle companion, Rosario, to his wife, Ruth, or to his New York mistress, Mouche, simply because she has none of their affectations, because she is at once truthful and serviceable, modest yet ardent. These qualities are important, but there is something else: he has been able to project upon her figure of uncomplicated womanhood the magical image of the Anima, so opening to him the depths of his unconscious, bringing nourishment to the soul. When he knows he has lost her, he is once again the victim of that old *malaise,* that continual but mysterious sense of frustration, which haunts our civilization.

He finds that "something else" too in the whole way of living remote in the jungle, where men are existing close to Nature, dependent on a few simple skills, and where, because there is no iron barrier between consciousness and the unconscious, with the numinous in its depths, a primitive pattern of living is deeply satisfying because it seems to him to have in all its daily tasks almost a ritualistic, a liturgical, quality and depth. . . . And all this is at the opposite extreme from the frustrated and sterile existence of the musician when we first meet him, spending his days in the city among the tapes and film apparatus of the studios, writing and recording music for idiotic advertisements, and only seeing his wife, starring in a Broadway long-run hit, on Sunday mornings; an existence to which he has to return after his "rescue," itself only a huge false publicity stunt. Such an existence produces a constant feeling of *malaise,* of dissatisfaction and mysterious frustration, just because it erects a barrier between consciousness and the unconscious, shuts off the inner world, the magic, the numinous, and so seems sterile and meaningless. (pp. 5-10)

For a considerable time now—at least a hundred years—the most lasting and significant fiction has, in the final analysis, taken our society itself as its chief character. And here *The Lost Steps* joins a notable and enduring company of novels. Carpentier's musician, who finds his own deepest creative feeling in the remote jungle, is not only Man going back through the ages, he is also you and I. He is ourselves discovered in our inner worlds, where our present civilization is so woefully, perhaps desperately, inadequate. Carpentier is not imploring us to live the simple life somewhere. In this tale of a search and how it ended, so magnificent and memorable in its descriptive power, so rich in its poetic symbolism, he is both enchanting us and making us face a piercing and profound criticism of our modern society. It is for this reason that some people, wishing to remain complacent, uneasily and hurriedly dismiss this book. . . . I am not going to pretend that [Carpentier] has achieved absolute perfection in this work: for example, there is to my mind a certain loss of freshness and force, a suggestion of huddling and hurrying to make an end, in almost all the sections that follow his "rescue". But reading it again has only confirmed my original conviction that here we have a masterpiece, an inspired idea most wonderfully transformed into an enduring novel. (p. 11)

> *J. B. Priestley, in an introduction to* The Lost Steps *by Alejo Carpentier, translated by Harriet de Onís, 1967. Reprint by Avon Books, 1979, pp. 5-11.*

HENRY TUBE

Che Guevara's favourite novelist, we are told, was Alejo Carpentier. The choice—if we discount mere courtesy in one who was an honorary Cuban citizen towards Cuba's greatest living writer—seems at first thought surprising. Carpentier is a highly cultivated and self-conscious writer. His grand canvases, crowded with events, richly baroque in detail, are controlled at every point by their author's fastidious learning and tone of faintly mocking detachment, so that he often seems the nearest heir to Thomas Mann. True, his favourite theme is disturbance and revolution, whether personal or collective, but his standpoint is scarcely that one associates with a committed revolutionary, since the invariable outcome of revolution in his work is the state of corruption and stagnation which originally caused it.

Of the three novels published in [England], *The Kingdom of This World* (1949) is the earliest and smallest. It tells the story of the slave rising in Haiti during the French Revolution. There are certain key characters in the book . . . , but these characters do not dominate the action in the ordinary manner; rather they come and go, disappearing into passages of natural description, scenes of bloodshed, Voodoo, or the building of Henri Christophe's fortress above the palace of Sans Souci. The impression given is of a world made up of multitudinous and constantly changing elements, whose human inhabitants obey in their successive frenzies of construction and destruction the same natural laws as the rest of creation.

The Lost Steps (1953) is an ambitious extension of this idea, set in modern times. . . . The book gives full scope to Carpentier's powers. Every Latin American writer must have wanted to find the opportunity and the words to convey the staggering physical reality of his continent; many have tried to express the meeting of the Old World with the New. Few have succeeded in doing both inside the covers of one book, let alone, as Carpentier has done in *The Lost Steps,* fictionalising one of the central dilemmas of our time, the conflict between man as part of a natural order and man as part of his own order.

In *Explosion in a Cathedral* (1962), Carpentier returns to the Caribbean during the period of the French Revolution. The novel is written round a real-life character, Victor Hugues, who governed Guadeloupe at the behest of Robespierre and Cayenne at the behest of Bonaparte, but in manner it has advanced beyond *The Lost Steps* to an enormously matured version of *The Kingdom of This World*. That is to say, where the central character in *The Lost Steps* consciously submitted himself to the power of the past, to the primitive geography of the Andes, as a man might allow himself to dream in the knowledge that he can wake up whenever he wishes to, the characters of *Explosion in a Cathedral* are again dominated by events. (pp. 47-8)

[Victor Hugues's] personal odyssey from trader to dictator, from pre-revolutionary idealist to post-revolutionary pragmatist, is magnificently charted, but the book's greatness lies in its breadth and movement. The natural life of sea, islands, fish, insects coalesces with the seething affairs of human beings at a particularly riotous period of historical change to make an endless pattern of revolution and consolidation, order and disorder. . . .

[The stories in *The War of Time*] are as it were the watercolours which complement the novels' oil-paintings. **"The Road to Santiago"** chronicles the fortunes of a Spanish drummer-boy who contracts plague in Flanders and vows to make a pilgrimage to the shrine of St James when he recovers. His religious fervour ebbs and flows with worldly blandishments. In **"Right of Sanctuary,"** a Minister in an overthrown South American government takes sanctuary in the embassy of another state and ends by becoming that state's ambassador to the man who overthrew him. In **"Journey Back to the Source,"** time is reversed and a demolished mansion slowly re-acquires its bricks and its dead owner, who turns gradually into a child. In **"Like The Night,"** the narrator says goodbye to his sweetheart and sets off for Troy, but Troy becomes the New World, the Old World and finally again Troy. In **"The Wise Men,"** five different Noahs in five Arks built at the command of five different gods float together on the Flood and disperse as it goes down.

Although a reader new to Carpentier would be best recommended to begin with the novels, these stories are all quintessentially his in theme and treatment. Here in miniature we find

the absurdity of human ideals, the inevitability of change which those ideals, in spite of their absurdity, help to bring about, and above all the passionate expression of what Carpentier has called the 'marvellous reality' of life. The more one thinks about it, the more one sees how close Che Guevara was to being at the center of Carpentier's whirlpool. (p. 48)

Henry Tube, "Stirring Times," in The Spectator, Vol. 224, No. 7385, January 10, 1970, pp. 47-8.

DAVID GALLAGHER

The sophisticated mind and compulsively idiosyncratic prose style of Alejo Carpentier have won his novels, both in the original and in translation, a wide circle of admirers, and there is no doubt that he is one of the half-dozen or so most impressive novelists in Latin America. . . . [His] novels deploy an essentially European view of tropical America. In all his novels tropical nature is displayed with wide-eyed wonder, so much so that a younger Cuban writer, Edmundo Desnoes, has felt Carpentier to be trading too facilely in exoticism. . . .

Carpentier is a great deal more, however, than a latter-day Chateaubriand. There is a richly dense texture to his prose that few writers could equal. It responds to a program outlined in his book *Tientos y Diferencias* in an essay called **"Problematica de la Actual Novela Latinoamericana."** Unlike the European writer who need only *mention* a pine tree, say, for his reader to know exactly what he means, the Latin-American writer, according to Carpentier, must *show* and *demonstrate* his landscapes.

No doubt the assumptions behind this program would earn Edmundo Desnoes's disapproval, and perhaps betray the fact that Carpentier's intended market is indeed not necessarily a Caribbean one. For why, one might say, should Graham Greene be exempted from demonstrating snow to the Cubans if they have to demonstrate their ceibas?

Carpentier extracts from his exotic settings a number of distinguishable ideas about the human condition.

In his novel *El Siglo de las Luces* (1962—literally "The Age of Enlightenment," published in English as *Explosion in the Cathedral*), Carpentier explored the effects of the French Revolution on the Caribbean islands. The novel offered a synchronic view of history: in times of revolution, it seemed to be claiming, men believe in historical change; they become involved in historical events, carry out reforms.

In the end the reforms are ineffectual or even revoked; nothing really changes at all. Only the archetypal, eternally repeated experiences of man, such as birth, copulation and death really count.

In *War of Time,* a collection of stories, there is a similarly synchronic tale, **"Like the Night,"** in which the emotions are described of a young man sailing off to war. Imperceptibly the narrative shifts from Agamemnon's fleet setting out to conquer Troy, to a Spanish fleet bound for the Indies, to a French fleet bound for the Caribbean in the 18th century, to the embarkation of American troops for Europe during World War II.

Whatever the detail and time of the situation, there are archetypal situations that never change. The anguish of the Mother that her Son might be Killed; the Parting with the Fiancée; the Loading of Provisions onto the Ship; the belief that Victory will Destroy Evil forever and that War will bring Glory and Medals; and the disillusioned discovery that War is Caused by

Economic Factors and anyway Solves Nothing. (Carpentier is liberal in his use of capital letters.)

Most of these stories extract archetypes from particular situations in similar manner. There is one, however, **"Journey Back to the Source,"** that marks an interesting departure for Carpentier. Latching on to the now venerable tradition of Latin American literature of often gratuitous fantasy, he describes the life of a man backwards, from death to birth. When this man and his wife go to church to be married, they "regain their freedom." One day, a party is given to celebrate the hero's minority, and "one morning, when he was reading a licentious book, [he] suddenly felt a desire to play with the lead soldiers lying asleep in their wooden boxes."

This pleasantly self-indulgent story is a worthy exponent of the inventive, thoughtful writing of a very fine novelist. . . .

David Gallagher, "Archetypal Situations," in The New York Times Book Review, *July 5, 1970, p. 20.*

ANTHONY WEST

With a new collection of short stories, *War of Time* . . . , Alejo Carpentier does a great deal to justify the pronouncement of Dame Edith Sitwell, quoted on the dust jacket, that he is "most certainly one of the greatest writers alive at this time." . . . [The] evident superiority that justifies [her] words lies in the depth of his penetration of the meanings for individuals of the broad spectrum of cultural experiences that constitutes the Latinity—if it may be so called—of Latin America. He is a major contributor both to that entity's understanding of itself and to the outside world's awareness of it. His novel *The Lost Steps* . . . is the best account of the impact of the South American environment on the Latin sensibility that has so far been written. It describes that sense of being drowned in unconquerable space and overwhelmed by the obduracy of an utterly unaccommodating terrain which crushed and smothered Simón Bolívar's spirit by revealing to him the futility of the ambition, to which his Latin heritage had committed him, to create another European order in South America. Unlike Bolívar, Carpentier's hero did not find his revelation lethal but derived from it a heightened awareness of the character of the Latin-American destiny, which is not to be a second anything—European or American—but to be something new, peculiar to that place. It is a book that has been read and understood by all too few North Americans. . . .

Of the five stories that make up [*War of Time*], all are fine examples of Carpentier's beautifully controlled and considered manner, but only one deals with his major theme. **"The Highroad of Saint James"** is an extraordinarily successful attempt to compress the reality of the initial Latin experience of the New World into a fifty-four-page anecdote about a Spanish soldier who twice sets out for Santiago de Compostela in fulfillment of a vow and on both occasions gets sidetracked into embarking for New Spain. In a series of marvellously precise metaphors Carpentier conveys the tragedy of the early forms of colonialism—the Old World intentions wholly unrelated to the New World realities, and, above all, the overwhelming sensuous experience for the only partly liberated medieval mind of this abundance of the undreamed of, the unregulated, and the unforbidden. It is all told in the simple story of a man who is doomed to long for Europe as it is not when he is in America, and for an America that is a European dream when he is in Europe.

The other stories in the collection do not come up to **"The Highroad of Saint James,"** either in their intensity or in their richness of content, but they are extremely well written and enjoyable. (p. 188)

Anthony West, "Conquistador," in The New Yorker, *Vol. XLVI, No. 41, November 28, 1970, pp. 188-89.*

RAYMOND D. SOUZA

Carpentier's first novel [*¡Écue-Yamba-Ó!* (1933)] contains elements that he would expand, refine, and use as the basis of his major works. *¡Écue-Yamba-Ó!* reveals his interest in the documentation of his novels, a technique that he would combine with an appraisal of an individual's subjective way of viewing the reality of his personal existence. Carpentier's novels present an interpenetration of the subjective and objective, of the temporal and the eternal, of man as an individual and man as a member of the species. He accomplishes this coordination by the skillful use of archetypal patterns and structural devices. *¡Écue-Yamba-Ó!* marks the beginning of Carpentier's novelistic efforts to capture the marvellous elements of Latin-American reality. (p. 30)

[*¡Écue-Yamba-Ó!*] covers the complete life of a single protagonist, Menegildo, a Negro. The novel is divided into three major parts that separate Menegildo's life into three distinct phases. In the first, we view his birth and childhood and the beginning of his movements out of this stage. The second section presents Menegildo's experience as an adolescent with its attendant awakening of powerful emotions and ends when he departs to live in the city. In the third part of the novel, Menegildo becomes an adult and a member of a ñáñigo sect. The individual cycle of existence closes with Menegildo's death, but life goes on in the presence of his son who will bear his name.

¡Écue-Yamba-Ó! is only partially successful. The contents of the novel indicate that the author did extensive research before writing. It contains, for example, a lengthy glossary and even has photographs to introduce the reader to the realm of the ñáñigo sects. Although these elements contribute to the novel's authenticity, they give it a documentary quality that appeals purely to the reader's intellect rather than his emotions. We observe ritual, for example, but we do not experience it and, therefore, gain no emotional appreciation of what it means to its participants. . . . In *¡Écue-Yamba-Ó!*, rational observation fails to capture the irrational realities of the ñáñigo world. (p. 33)

The major thrust of Carpentier's career has been toward making the unbelievable believable. In his view, Latin-American reality is so contradictory and awe inspiring that real events seem bigger than life. He has stated, "For me the American continent is the most extraordinary world of the century, because of its all-embracing cultural scope. Our view of it must be ecumenic." He has attempted to convey these convictions by painstakingly researching his novels and by developing a rich and flowing language. The writing of *¡Écue-Yamba-Ó!* marks the beginning of the movement toward this goal, and it was an experience that would serve Carpentier well in the composition of future novels. (p. 34)

El reino de este mundo [1949] takes place in Hispaniola and relates different phases of the Haitian Wars of Independence. The novel is divided into four main sections, and each chronicles an important stage of the independence movement. (p. 35)

The first part narrates the exploits of Mackandal, a Negro rebel who led an early slave uprising that used the poisoning of livestock and people as a major tactic. Terror gripped those in power as the island became filled with the stench of death, but Mackandal was finally captured and executed in 1758. The second part deals with the outbreak of a rebellion led by Bouckman in 1791. Bouckman suffered the same fate as Mackandal, but the organized Negro forces prevailed and defeated the French in 1803. The third division deals with Henri Christophe, the hero who became a tyrant. . . . The final part occurs during the period of the government of the mulatto Boyer (1820-1843), a time of reunification after the collapse of Christophe's government. During Boyer's rule, many of the old abuses are still perpetuated, and there is a definite need for a renewed struggle against tyranny. Ti Noel, a slave who witnessed and at times participated in many of the events in the other sections, is faced with the problem of deciding whether he should use the knowledge he has acquired during the course of many years to answer the needs of his people. (pp. 35-6)

El reino de este mundo is greatly superior to Carpentier's first novel, and the reader is more apt to find himself involved in this work than in *¡Écue-Yamba-Ó!* The language is more authentic, and one feels a movement on the part of the author toward a recognition of the subjective dimensions of his characters. However, the reader senses that Carpentier's emphasis on the verisimilar aspects of this novel caused him to eschew imaginative narration to some extent. The result is that we have an outline of what might have been a major novel. The characters are not well developed; they are really caricatures. There is a multitude of historical events that are only briefly covered in the novel, and this combination of great breadth with little depth precludes the development one would like to see. *El reino de este mundo* does represent a considerably expanded view of Latin-American reality, when contrasted with *¡Écue-Yamba-Ó!*, and this new undertaking must have presented a number of technical difficulties to its author. (p. 38)

In his first two novels, Carpentier deals mainly with characters who do not share his cultural or social background. The appearance of *Los pasos perdidos* in 1953 marks a change in this procedure, for the main protagonist in this novel is a man who shares Carpentier's cultural formation. This would also be true of his portrayal of Esteban in *El siglo de las luces* (1962). Esteban is depicted as an intellectual who questions and sees the flaws in all schemes. Both of these novels evidence an all-encompassing view of mankind. In this respect, they could have been more abstract and removed from the reader than his first two novels. Such is not the case, however, for Carpentier solved the difficulties of presenting an interpenetration of the subjective and objective by allowing his protagonists to be more intimate reflections of a reality he personally knows. This does not mean that his later novels are intimate writings, for Carpentier always maintains a fairly objective stance, but they do reflect more comprehension and understanding of the inner motivations of their characters. Carpentier is a detached writer, and one does not find in his novels the type of examination of the dark recesses of the human soul that a Carlos Fuentes or Ernesto Sábato demonstrates. The novels of Fuentes and Sábato tend to overwhelm the reader with their stark intimacy, as their characters pursue the answers to moral dilemmas. Carpentier's approach is calmer, more detached and ideological, and he is at his best when he is portraying men whose intellectualism or personality keeps them somewhat removed from their own passions. This ability was not used to the best advantage in the first two novels. In fact, it was a decided liability, for he

achieved detachment when passionate commitment was required. Fortunately, this distance, which proved to be a weakness in Carpentier's first two novels, became a distinct strength in *Los pasos perdidos* and *El siglo de las luces.*

Los pasos perdidos is Carpentier's most personal book. The novel is presented in the form of a diary, and this first-person narration helps to create a greater sense of intimacy than one is accustomed to finding in Carpentier's works. It should be pointed out, however, that the novel is a narration controlled by the intellect, told by a man whose emotions are subordinate to his thoughts. Carpentier demonstrates a complete command of the language, and the novel is a fully developed, mature work. In *Los pasos perdidos,* he found a way to capture the temporal dimensions of Latin-American reality. (pp. 38-9)

Los pasos perdidos allows its reader to consider different types of disorder and formlessness. In its presentation of the contemporary world, we view a civilization that has lost its possibilities and seems on the verge of dissolution. Human existence has become petrified into sets of hollow patterns devoid of vitality, and one senses that all forms will soon crumble into dust. In his journey into the past, the protagonist encounters a reality that is in the process of forming, where vital forces have not yet imposed order on existence. It is a realm of pure potentiality bursting with chaotic energy. The novel moves from a chaos generated by the destructive forces of dissolution to the chaos that precedes the creation of new forms. It should be pointed out that the protagonist's ordeal, as he moves between these two domains, is the main concern of the novel. His voyage and quest occupy center stage in *Los pasos perdidos.* The processes of chaos and the transition from form to formlessness, however, would become major considerations in Carpentier's next novel, *El siglo de las luces* (1962).

The protagonist-narrator in *Los pasos perdidos* is a product of the modern world, a civilized man who has been trained to think and ponder to the extent that his intellectualism almost paralyzes any ability to act. He is swept up into a great adventure more by the forces of circumstance than by the efforts of his own will. In contrast, the main character in *El siglo de las luces,* Victor Hugues, is a man of action who subordinates philosophical and intellectual considerations to deeds. He is a man of great vigor and will, who greatly influences all those who come in contact with him. In many respects, he is the exact opposite of the protagonist in *Los pasos perdidos.* Despite these essential differences, they do hold one thing in common. They both attempt to overcome the limitations of the present, hoping to bring into being a better and more complete existence. Indeed, this is a quality common to most of the main characters in Carpentier's novels. They are motivated by the desire and conviction that the creation of a better world is within man's grasp, and Carpentier's novels constitute an examination of the many roads taken to realize this goal.

At times this nostalgia and longing for a "Lost Paradise" leads Carpentier's characters into major undertakings. In *El siglo de las luces,* Carpentier examines the revolutionary process as a means to attain this end. The characters in this novel participate in a mass movement, attempting to realize their goals in contrast to the highly individual search conducted by the protagonist in *Los pasos perdidos.* Carpentier returns in *El siglo de las luces* to the collective approach utilized in *El reino de este mundo* but with much greater success. He avoids the fragmentary structure of his second novel by narrating the personal destinies of three main characters during the entire course of *El siglo de las luces.* Their lives span the temporal limits of the work, and this gives it great cohesiveness despite the broad historical context covered.

El siglo de las luces deals with the arrival and spread of the French Revolution throughout the Antilles between 1790 and 1809. The novel is anchored in historical events, and its most important figure, Victor Hugues, actually existed. Carpentier first learned of Victor and his role in history during a forced stop in Guadalupe, an island that Victor governed during a part of the French Revolution. Carpentier found in this remarkable man who had been neglected by history the perfect vehicle for the development and expression of his most consuming concerns. . . . The unusual but forgotten Victor must have appeared to be an excellent example of the marvellous reality of the New World, which could seemingly swallow and hide in the records of its past such an imposing figure. He exemplifies the incongruities of Latin-American reality and human existence and serves as the embodiment of a collective movement in Carpentier's novel. (pp. 44-6)

Some critics feel that Carpentier evidences in his novels an ambivalent attitude toward revolution. [Luis] Harss points out that "revolutions, in Carpentier's books, are always short-term failures but, as he goes to great pains to assure us, harbingers of greater things to come." Reaction within revolutionary Cuba to *El siglo de las luces* was, as one might suspect, mixed. . . . A thorough study of *El siglo de las luces* will produce contradictory evidences in favor of and opposing revolution. Actually, it is doubtful that Carpentier had any intention of espousing a moral or utilitarian view of revolution. The presence of contradictory positions toward revolution in the novel is due to the interpenetration of subjective and objective views.

From an individual's subjective outlook, a particular revolution is either good or bad. Seen from a historical perspective, a revolution is simply an agent of change, one of many patterns within a cyclic evolutionary process. One finds in Carpentier's works the conviction that there is a progression of meaning and order in history, and he conveys this by the way he organizes his novels. The impression that existence is chaotic and without meaning emanates from the individual's subjective view with its temporal limits. Within a historical context, chaos is often presented as a stage in the process of dissolution, a process which simultaneously signals the death of one order and the birth of another. Carpentier tends to emphasize the objective by avoiding as much as possible the personal aspects of his characters. We all have ideas and attitudes that do not belong to us as individuals but to the age we live in. They originate in the world that is exterior to us and form part of the collective experience of our times. It is this part of the individual that Carpentier stresses in his works.

Carpentier's career marks the international acceptance of the Cuban novel. He is the most consistently successful Cuban novelist, and his work has won him an enviable international reputation. His achievements have given the Cuban novel a degree of prestige as never before, and in many respects he helped prepare the way for novelists such as Cabrera Infante, Lezama Lima, and Severo Sarduy, by establishing a record and tradition of excellence. (pp. 50-1)

Carpentier shows in his novels a dedicated sense of discipline and rigorous intellectual control. They are thoroughly researched and minutely planned before they are written, and his books rely greatly on the presentation of visual reality. This results in the creation of well-structured works deftly directed and controlled by the author, but it also reduces their spon-

taneity. Although Carpentier is interested in the process of dissolution and the role of disorder and chaos in human existence, these concerns are largely treated thematically and never become technically incorporated into his novels. It should be noted that he has been much more experimental in some of his short stories. . . . Until the appearance of *El siglo de las luces,* however, his novels have tended to be more innovative thematically than technically.

If one wished to single out the most outstanding faction of Carpentier's art, careful consideration would have to be given to his style. His language is elegant, polished, and a testimony of his knowledge. He is a consummate craftsman and the very essence of his work is reflected in his style. . . . [His language] charms and inspires as it flows on, bringing into the world of reality the marvellous and incredible. It beguiles us into accepting a realm in which the particular illustrates the general, and permanent values are discovered in the midst of disorder and chaos. For Carpentier there is much comfort in regarding the tribulations of human existence from the long view of extended time. It is a lofty perspective that few can achieve let alone convey, and the skill with which it is presented in Carpentier's novels testifies to the unifying forces operating in his work. Carpentier searches for the absolute without falling into the trap of offering absolute certainties, for he is aware that human existence will always be tempered by limitations. His is a dispassionate voice in a time of extremes, and in his search for permanence Carpentier has created novels that will be with us for a long time. (pp. 51-2)

Raymond D. Souza, "Alejo Carpentier's Timeless History," in his Major Cuban Novelists: Innovation and Tradition, *University of Missouri Press, 1976, pp. 30-52.*

GORDON BROTHERSTON

Of the three or four main characters in Alejo Carpentier's novel *Explosion in a Cathedral,* Esteban is the one chosen to guide us through a world especially dear to his author: the 'theological archipelago of the Caribbean', as it is called, the luminous heart of America to which both author and character, as Cubans, belong. In the brig *L'Ami du peuple* with her two attendant ships, Esteban escapes to the ocean on an American 'odyssey', from the port of Pointe à Pitre in Guadeloupe, where his former friend Victor Hugues, a champion of the French Revolution, is establishing his historical reputation as 'the Robespierre of the Isles'. (p. 47)

The elements of what Esteban sees [in this world] are universal, like those of any vision. But their setting and configuration are specific to Esteban's native America, to his 'Hesperides without names': his experience could not have been had by anyone anywhere. In case we have overlooked this, Carpentier reminds us later on that the beaches trodden by Esteban only then, 'three centuries after the Discovery', were beginning to have deposited on them their first pieces of polished glass: 'glass invented in Europe and strange to America'. By means of details like these, Carpentier suggests that the wonder of the American world is something unique, continental and for itself. So that Esteban's epiphany would seem to serve him principally as knowledge of a special condition. In a gesture of great boldness Carpentier would seem ideally to be distinguishing an American culture, manifest in a dazzling variety of forms traceable to the very beginning of Creation. (pp. 49-50)

Ideas such as these recur throughout Carpentier's mature writing and are important to the interpretation of this and of his two previous novels *The Kingdom of this World* (*El reino de este mundo*, 1949) and *The Lost Steps* (*Los pasos perdidos*, 1953). The first of these further resembles *Explosion in a Cathedral* in charting the progress of a revolution which despite European promptings assumed its own 'native' form: the uprising of the one-armed black slave Macandal (1767) which preceded Henri Christophe's successful seizure of power and the emergence of Haiti as the first Latin American state to win independence from Europe. In the prologue to *The Kingdom of this World*, Carpentier explained how he had come to write it, after an unplanned visit to Haiti in 1943. What he experienced there first converted him to his American religion: Henri Christophe's fortress La Ferrière ('a work without architectural antecedents, heralded solely by Piranesi's *Imaginary prisons*'), the dance and music of the Voodoo cult, and so on, all in intimate harmony with the strange and luxuriant flora and fauna of the place. Here, he claimed, was a spectacle of such wonder and marvel that any attempt, like his own, to describe it historically and realistically could not but produce a kind of magic. This enthusiasm was matched with strictures on the 'surrealist' writers of Europe and those Latin American writers who failed to see their own amazing surroundings properly because of their subservience to the literary fashions of Europe.

Now for Carpentier it mattered to draw distinctions of this kind, since confessedly he had himself been guilty of the sins he now condemned. As with Asturias, a Parisian education during the inter-war period (1928-39) alerted him to his own glamour as a Latin American writer, and reinforced a 'French connection' he already had via his paternal ancestry. And like Asturias's, his first published work benefits from it, his 'Afro-Cuban' novel *Ecue-yamba-O* (1933) having an exoticism akin to that of the *Legends of Guatemala*. This first novel was in fact an odd mixture of primitivism and camp collage, visible in other works of the period. . . . The main character in *Ecue-yamba-O*, Menegildo, scarcely exists in his own right; he appears rather as a caricature of a black America which is oppressed and at the same time exotic. As a token of his change of heart in Haiti, Carpentier vigorously disowned this early work when he became the champion of America's magic reality in all its fullness. And in the narratives of his second period, more than one character is shown to be reprehensible precisely for having sold America short, for being insensitive to its true wealth. (pp. 50-1)

With its bold title, *The Kingdom of this World* succeeded in presenting American reality not as a marketable commodity but as something for itself, and announced a serious concern with origins which runs through Carpentier's subsequent writing. Yet it should be said that his censure of the European surrealists, as 'vapid necrophiliacs' 'writhing in sterile dilemma', has something decidedly bad-tempered about it. After all, both Breton, during his visit to Haiti, and Benjamin Péret (whom Carpentier knew) with his translations of Maya literature, had taken the profoundest interest in ancestral America, as indeed had Antonin Artaud during his time in Mexico. And it is not clear that their sense of 'le merveilleux', as hyperawareness of the natural world . . . differs all that much from 'lo maravilloso' as defined by Carpentier. More seriously, for all its brilliance *The Kingdom of this World* by no means vindicates the intimate connections between natural setting and social behaviour which is made so much of in the prologue. Partly for this reason no doubt we find residues of his earlier paternalism towards indigenous and ingenuous America. Ti

Noel, the black slave who witnesses Macandal's rising and execution, is better treated than Menegildo (of the disowned *Ecue-yamba-O*). But Ti Noel is not equal to the grander ambitions of the novel, and the sophistication and racial attitudes attributed to him, as Carpentier's narrative voice, are often improbable or simply insulting.

In his next novel, *The Lost Steps*, Carpentier ranged through the time and space of America more boldly and comprehensively than in any of his other works. We move from a twentieth-century English-speaking metropolis (which could be New York), through the colonial quarters of a city in Latin America (like Caracas, where he lived in the 1950s), to the stone-age life of an Indian tribe in the depths of the South American jungle (he travelled up the Orinoco while in Venezuela). These three settings are linked solely by the presence of the first-person protagonist, a professional musicologist doing field work. The 'meaning' of his journey, in larger terms, is made explicit in various ways: the presentation of each setting as a cultural moment of American history; the allotting of a special role to the woman he knows best at each stage, his actress wife, his intellectual French mistress Mouche and his stone-age lover Rosario. The novel ends by appearing to ask: 'May we retrace lost cultural steps and find our true selves?' For the moment, more important than the answer in principle is the particular route which Carpentier has mapped.

We find the thesis of *The Lost Steps*, evident enough in the novel, even more conveniently set out in Carpentier's essay **"On the marvellous reality of America"** (1962; **"De lo real-maravilloso americano"**), which grew out of the prologue to *The Kingdom of this World*. He now turns to his continent only after engagement with such recognizably distinct world cultures as the Chinese and Islam, and thus contrives to suggest that what is true for them is true for it. In these circumstances the novel should reflect the integrity, 'lo distinto' as Carpentier puts it, of American reality in the most thorough-going fashion. In his barely-known world, his 'Hesperides without names', the novelist should indeed 'name the things' of his creation: 'just as Adam put names to the animals and plants in the Bible, so should our fiction writers baptize all that surrounds them'. He should embark on a 'journey to the seed', no less, in evolutionary terms, and retrace, as Carpentier's novel endeavours to, the 'lost steps' whereby 'style is affirmed through history'.

Such notions recall the more extreme forms of nineteenth-century evolutionary thought, in particular the kind of comprehensive 'history of Creation' (*Schöpfungsgeschichte*) elaborated by Haeckel, with his dictum 'embryology recapitulates ontology'. And in taking his argument to such lengths Carpentier does not avoid a certain philosophical awkwardness. In *The Lost Steps*, the novel of his thesis, apart from such difficulties as the fact that the hero is not an aboriginal or ancestral American, the course of the steps he takes is forever balked by the paradox of the observing consciousness (which had troubled evolutionists). The action of the hero is divorced from Carpentier's essay-like meditations, of which there are plenty, on the meaning of our backward progress in time: the narrative is either slack or simply dramatic. In contrast to Esteban who finds his way back to the first luxuriance of Creation as a lonely bather (with intuitions of having once been a fish), a 'human step', and then is again himself, the musicologist either vanishes entirely or barges his way back, set too firmly in himself for anything like the fine transitions of Esteban's exploration. . . . He appears as a kind of intellectual conquistador who fails to become part of what he records, a dilemma admitted at the close of the novel perhaps, but hardly reckoned with in the main narrative.

The musicologist does not vindicate Carpentier's continental philosophy, so much as he exposes its limitations. Through him, no effective continuity can be forged, in Carpentier's own terms, between the natural and the social world. He remains an observer or an intruder, someone on or from the outside, which is where Carpentier himself must be standing when he says in the prologue to *The Kingdom of this World:*

> And by virtue of the virginity of the landscape;
> of the formation, ontology and magic presence
> of the Indian and the negro; of the Revelation
> which their recent discovery entailed; and of
> the fertile racial mixture it propitiated, America
> is far from having exhausted its wealth of my-
> thologies, What is the whole history of America
> but a chronicle of 'marvellous reality' (*'lo real-
> maravilloso'*)?

Only someone essentially uninvolved in this reality could generalize about it in this fashion, equating Indian with Negro, and both, as objects of discovery, with innocent natural landscapes. In the last instance, if the musicologist represents a culture, it would be that of the Spanish conquistador. His glamour is that of the jungle adventurer, ravishing his innocent Rosario (who doesn't even have an Indian name), intolerant of the insubstantiality of his enlightened French mistress Mouche, and discontent with the modern, rootless, English-speaking existence led by his wife. As with the characters in **"Journey to the Seed"** (**"Viaje a la semilla"**, completed 1944, an earlier 'evolutionist' story which also moves backwards through time to a 'primary condition'), the Discovery is all-important, for before it, we are told, nothing really existed. It is as if without the very intrusion which Carpentier re-enacts in *The Lost Steps,* America would have remained unseen and uncharted, in a perpetually virginal genesis, with no true life or ontology of its own. Carpentier has censured the Americanism of novels previous to his own, from Güiraldes and Rivera to Ciro Alegría, for being too exotic, and for the falsity of what he calls their social nativism. If *The Lost Steps* differs from these precedents it is principally because of its scope and its erudition (in every sense of that word).

Carpentier's great achievement, *Explosion in a Cathedral,* carries forward but crucially modifies the enterprise of the two previous novels we have been discussing. The pages which recount Esteban's vision are among the most felicitous he has written, outstanding yet not obtrusive in the novel as a whole. In this work he succeeded in using his proclivities as a writer entirely to his advantage, in a way he had not done before.

First, he condenses his evolutionist philosophy into a single crucial moment. The American genesis glimpsed in *The Kingdom of this World* and so elaborately pursued in *The Lost Steps,* is confined to the Caribbean shore, a Revelation for itself. In this smaller but teeming arena he may approach the most elemental forms, the most virgin origins. Details are observed exactly, even microscopically, and have the clean-cut quality of an engraving by Dürer. . . . The luxury of creation witnessed by Esteban can be credibly both primeval and 'baroque', and correlate natural and cultural form. (pp. 51-5)

Second, and more important for the novel as a whole, Carpentier works out an unprecedently rich relationship with Esteban, who is the only character who appears more or less consistently throughout the narrative. He is manipulated of course, but delicately and not at the cost either of his autonomy or of the acceptability of the 'ideas' Carpentier wants to put across, the 'philosophy' he elsewhere crams down his reader's throat. Rather, in this novel, he helps us to perceive them as something less than axiomatic and universally valid, but nonetheless inspired. Through Esteban he found a way of indulging intimate enthusiasms without being bound, as he was in *The Lost Steps,* to his American creed, with all its flaws, begged questions, convenient hiatus and covert prejudices.

Above all, Esteban is a solitary. Like Joyce's Stephen Daedalus, whose name he shares, he is ostensibly embarked on an odyssey, the voyage of Homer's epic. But his discoveries are not public. At best, as we have suggested, his American dream is opposed to the historical society activated by Hugues, from which he grows increasingly estranged and alienated. But the vision which sustains it is private, unshared and unproductive of any conceivable morality. In his 'unpeopled ocean' he is simply and ironically the 'owner' of it all. However, in a second Revelation granted to him when he goes back aboard the brig, his atavism is given a firm social shape which exists in oblique and amusing relationship with his momentary yearnings to reacquire gills and a tail as a true denizen of the Caribbean sea. (p. 56)

It would of course be a gross mis-reading of *Explosion in a Cathedral* to attribute Esteban's brand of Caribbean atavism directly to his author, even if we suspect he would not find it unattractive. For, as if to prevent this confusion, Carpentier sometimes brings Esteban dangerously close to a political and literary caricature. . . . Esteban's very propensities as a dreamer, as the visionary to whom the deepest truths are revealed, are subtly made contingent on the kind of character he is. . . . Through Esteban's musings we learn that anyone really anxious to enter the paradise of America, to be truly part of 'so inaccessible' and unspoilt a Creation, and to make it his permanent home, must revert to being a fish.

This comes almost as a sophisticated joke at the expense of the writer who loses himself in the solitudes of America, so relinquishing his 'proper' place in the order of things. We discover an effective distinction between America's 'wealth of mythologies' and the real world. . . . As a would-be fish, transported by the joy of his 'ineffable vision', Esteban bears the same relationship to Carpentier as René, the solitary dreamer in the American wilds, bore to Chateaubriand. Indeed, when at the end of the novel Esteban is returned, somewhat peremptorily, to his initial asthmatic condition and to suffering from a quasi-incestuous love for Sofia, he becomes the devotee of René, 'without parents, without friends, more a solitary than ever' . . . . By showing Esteban up as a lonely dreamer, whose Americanism amounted to a luxury, Carpentier offered a fine criticism of his own earlier writing. And behind the various postures of his character he effectively establishes a surer and less vulnerable position of his own. (pp. 57-8)

As a literary artifact which plays on Carpentier's great range of professional ingenuity, this novel resists many of the criticisms which have been levelled at him more generally: that he views his supposed homeland in the spirit of a Spanish conquistador, or of a French Romantic; that he relishes Latin America for its anachronism, its underdevelopment. Indeed, just because of the trouble that other Latin American writers have taken to attack as well as to praise him, he has in practice been paid the rarest honour: that of being considered a continental point of reference. (p. 59)

Gordon Brotherston, ''The Genesis of America: Alejo Carpentier,'' in his The Emergence of the Latin American Novel, *Cambridge University Press, 1977, pp. 45-59.*

RONALD SCHWARTZ

Considered by most critics the single most productive Latin American writer, Alejo Carpentier has contributed a steady stream of fiction from the early 1930s up to the present moment, irrespective of the various ''booms'' or highlights taking place in South America and elsewhere over the past twenty years. Carpentier, with a very fine international reputation as a novelist, remains one of those Latin American writers who is consistently translated into English. *Explosion in a Cathedral*, his major novel and the third to be translated into English, is written in the frame of a traditional realist novel. (p. 1)

Explosion in a Cathedral is not considered one of the novels of the ''boom'' in Latin American literature, but it certainly is a forerunner and best exemplifies Carpentier's cosmopolite background and his baroque prose. *Explosion* is a burst of creative energy containing some of Carpentier's best narrative prose.... *Explosion* contains a profusion of sights, sounds, brilliant atmosphere and a plot filled with adventure, violence, intrigue, love affairs, and confusion—the confusion of revolutions, French and Spanish. We witness history in the making, the illusion of democracy, freedom, the roots of colonialism implanted in the Caribbean, the disillusions of false idealizing, the cyclical patterns of history emerging to envelop the elliptically fictional inventions of Carpentier, leading his protagonists from their freedom to their eventual destruction. The breakdown of the century of Enlightenment with the coming of the French Revolution is related to us through the adventures of a single family left orphaned by the death of a Cuban merchant. They are Carlos and Sofía, brother and sister, and their cousin Esteban.

Seven long chapters divide a sequence of forty-seven sections that record revolutionary tumult and worse in a wide variety of settings in Europe (Paris, Bayonne, Madrid) and America, culminating in the rising against the French in Madrid on May 2, 1808. We are introduced to the image of the guillotine, its ''diagonal blade gleaming'' being transported by ship from Europe to the New World, a silent but lethal protagonist observed by the narrator Esteban (or Carpentier): an image that sets the scene for the bloodshed to follow. At the novel's inception a Cuban merchant has just died, leaving his son and daughter and a nephew to fend for themselves. The abrupt removal of parental authority is the signal for a new life for the children; they explore the house, play practical jokes, and fall under the influence of the mysterious Victor Hugues, who introduces them to ''fashionable'' ideas of emancipation and freemasonry. (pp. 3-4)

In Carlos and Sofía's home hangs a huge painting by an unknown Neopolitan master who confounded all the laws of plastic art by representing the apocalyptic immobilization of a catastrophe. It was called ''Explosion in a Cathedral,'' this vision of a great colonnade shattering into fragments in mid-air, pausing a moment as its lines broke, floating so as to fall better, before it dashed its tons of stone on to the terrified people underneath. It is this recurring image in the painting that prophesies the revolution that is forever in Carlos, Sofía and Esteban's consciousness as the novel moves toward its cataclysmic conclusion. Sofía is convent-educated; since her father's

death she has become a mother to Esteban and head of their household and later mistress of Victor Hugues, who seduces her on a sea voyage they take to Haiti after Sofía's house and world crumble before her very eyes in Cuba. When Victor Hugues first meets the orphaned children they are innocents, naïve to any concerns outside of their own home. When Esteban, an asthmatic, falls violently ill, Dr. Ogé, under Victor's influence, is sought out. The children must ride from their home into the harbor, into a world of mulattos and *mulatas de tal,* a world so strange to them that they see it as a vision of hell, unlike anything they ever experienced. Sofía's sexual and intellectual enlightenment proceed in concert to those of her brother and cousin under the tutelage of Victor Hugues, who himself represents the new tide of the Age of Enlightenment, bringing rebellious ideas and revolution with him into their Cuban homeland. When revolutionary uprisings take place Sofía and Carlos remain in Cuba while Esteban follows Victor to Europe and the revolution. Hugues, an admirer of Robespierre, is sent to Guadeloupe to take over the island and to convey there the first guillotine. Esteban accompanies him as his secretary, witnesses the degeneration of this idealist—who defends his ideals by bloodshed but once his ideals fall, feels nothing but cynicism. Nevertheless, the revolutionary ideology had taken hold of all three. (pp. 4-5)

The novel traces Carlos, Sofía, and Esteban's movements from Cuba to other Caribbean ports and to Europe, as well as their intellectual enrichment and eventual disillusionment with the ''age of science.'' When they arrive in Haiti they find Port-au-Prince in the throes of bloody revolution. Although they are witnessing the birth of a new humanity, it is essentially Esteban who is Carpentier's *porte-parole*, who witnesses the European enlightenment, becomes a revolutionary, and finally diminishes, loses all his individuality, and is swallowed by the events over which he has little control. The major strength of the novel lies in Esteban's ruminations, his critical propensities, and his disillusionment, which is narrated fully among all the ''events'' of this panoramic novel. But it is not easy to trace a single character's thought patterns because of Carpentier's somewhat baroque style. This style, however, enriches the flow of the narrative with a profusion of events, characters, and places, allowing Carpentier the full scope of his frequent magnificent prose passages. (pp. 5-6)

Carpentier's historical perspective adds much to his recreation of events and atmosphere—for example, his rendition of the siege of Guadeloupe. He even captures the very odor of the victories in the Caribbean: ''Victory, that was good. But better than that, tonight there would be fresh hams, studded with cloves of garlic.'' ... Carpentier is a vigorous writer, masculine, vibrant. It is incongruous that his chief protagonist, the intellectual Esteban, is not stronger, more virile. However, Victor, Carlos, and Esteban are all literary creations of the author's own cosmos and represent particular facets of character. (pp. 6-7)

If one were to characterize Carpentier's writing, it is the ambitious scope of his narrative that sustains his readers in almost all of his novels and especially in *Explosion in a Cathedral*. Carpentier obviously gives great attention to his choice of words, whatever the subject or thematic matter of his prose.... It is obvious that Carpentier writes from his own experiences and with an authentic artist's perspective. It is the nuggets of descriptions of experiences he himself has lived that charge this historical novel (the story line of which is deceptively simple) with its attractiveness. For when Esteban's great adventure is over and he decides to return to Cuba the novel collapses into a stream of sequential events. (pp. 7-8)

[Carpentier] has fused novelistic technique with the vital experience of Latin America. *Explosion in a Cathedral* is a passionate work, vibrant with exotic images, colorful, full of the grandeur and sweep of a traditional eighteenth-century historical novel but narrated with a contemporary awareness. *Explosion* is a long, rich, episodic novel about the roots of colonialism in the Caribbean and contains the sights, smells, and sounds of Latin America, shows Cubans in search of their own mythic roots in the Caribbean. It is an intelligent work containing a unique stylistic device—quotations from Goya's etchings, which in the novel's final scene are utilized to brilliant effect, when Esteban and Sofía die in the street fight against Napoleon's troops and almost appear to enter one of Goya's most famous canvasses. (pp. 10-11)

Victor Hugues gives *Explosion* its strictly historical dimension, but the novel is mainly a chronicle of family fortunes artistically conceived by Carpentier in cosmic time. Just as a variety of his artistic or literary perceptions can be crammed into a single sentence as evidence of his baroque style, so can great historical experiences. He reduces the Spanish Revolution to a total of four lines and the individual tragedy of Esteban and Sofía to a mere detail in a great and rather simple pattern. Yet because of the wealth of embellishment, the over-use of pictorial effects that clutter the scenes, causing a somewhat dense texture, *Explosion* is a hard novel to penetrate despite the simple conclusions. The novel is one that appeals more to the mind than to the emotions, and the reader's involvement is minimal.

As fiction, *Explosion* is among the last of historical novels ever to come out of Latin America. Many choose to read into it a critique of the Cuban Revolution of 1959. Other critics, like Luis Harss, believe the descendants of Esteban and Sofía or their nameless doubles are alive in Cuba today, once more arraigned before the tribunal of history, perhaps waiting to be sacrificed again. Preferring to sidestep these political innuendos, I choose to view the "image" of Carpentier's fictional premise as his rendition of history expressed through his fictional or semifictional personages and not to believe that the author is an apologist for any particular political ideology. It is Carpentier's fictional way of dealing with history that gives his narrative [what John S. Brushwood has called] a "magical" quality. Carpentier's magic for me resides in his talent as a writer. (pp. 11-12)

Carpentier's novel deserves to be read, with its author's flair for developing character and description in a historical setting as well as his fertile imagination. But baroque stylists sometimes exceed their limitations. Carpentier's latest translated novel, *Reasons of State* (1976), did not fare very well with American critics precisely because of its tedium, its pages and pages of lists of objects and sensations that do not advance the cause of narrative or character, and its poor mixture of politics and comedy.

Although Carpentier's later novels do contain much tiresome philosophy, *Explosion* represents the almost perfect marriage of history and fiction. It has drive, a sweeping panorama, depth, perception, and artistry; its enduring symbolic title has cinematic references—for the "explosion" is the Spanish Revolution caught in a "freeze" frame. Carpentier suggests a static portrait. It will take the "unfreezing" or a greater war effort to liberate the western hemisphere from its French oppressors. For Latin America is a marvellous setting, a literary miracle on which Carpentier has built his career. The concept of the "marvellous" is part of the mythical image of America, and Carpentier proselytizes for belief in the reality of the marvellous, a cultural reality in spite of a real or "objective" reality. Carpentier's idea—that the reality of the marvellous is the guiding romanticized mythical image of America—gives *Explosion* its strength, its primitive character, its notion of triumph, its goodness. For Carpentier writes with a French sensibility and a dense baroque style tempered by innocence. He is a modern-day Chauteaubriand, a master stylist, a giant among contemporary Latin American novelists. (p. 13)

Ronald Schwartz, "Carpentier: Cuban Cosmopolite, Baroque Stylist," in his Nomads, Exiles, & Emigres: The Rebirth of the Latin American Narrative, 1960-80, *The Scarecrow Press, Inc., 1980, pp. 1-13.*

James (P.) Carroll

1943-

American novelist, poet, nonfiction writer, and dramatist.

An ex-Roman Catholic priest, Carroll has gained popular and critical attention for his novels, which examine moral, religious, and social issues and their effects on individuals. Many of his characters are Irish Catholics who attempt to reconcile their personal aspirations with social and religious demands. While he was a priest, Carroll wrote several books on spiritual matters, concentrating on the importance of prayer and hope. Carroll left the priesthood in 1974 to devote his time to writing.

Carroll's first works to draw critical response were the verse collections *Forbidden Disappointments* (1974), a volume about personal experiences and his struggle to maintain his religious faith, and *The Winter Name of God* (1975), in which he recounts his journeys in the Christian Holy Lands where he renewed his faith. Carroll's first novel, *Madonna Red* (1976), focuses on religious issues within the context of an espionage thriller. *Mortal Friends* (1978), his next novel, centers on an Irish rebel who immigrates to the United States and becomes involved in political and criminal intrigue in Boston during the mid-twentieth century. Carroll combines fictional characters with such historical personages as Boston Mayor James Michael Curley and several members of the Kennedy family. Betrayal, revenge, and redemption are themes examined in this work. In *Fault Lines* (1980) and *Family Trade* (1982), Carroll focuses on moral issues. The former centers on two men and a woman involved in a love triangle, while the latter revolves around the dilemma of a man involved in international espionage.

Prince of Peace (1984), regarded as Carroll's most ambitious novel, is set during the Vietnam War era and traces the lives of two childhood friends who become Roman Catholic priests and fall in love with the same woman. Carroll examines the effects of the war, love, and social and religious issues on the two priests. He also correlates the conflicts that arise between the idealistic young clergymen and the church hierarchy to the larger social conflict in the United States at this time between many young people and figures of authority.

(See also *Contemporary Authors,* Vols. 81-84.)

FRANCIS SULLIVAN

It is an amiable poetry, James Carroll's small book [*Forbidden Disappointments*], partly because the language of it is uniformly simple and self-giving, partly because the vision of each poem is like a recovered boyishness with the motes and beams of adult ignorance and wickedness stuck in its eye. Perhaps that's the best way to describe the style and themes of the book: boyhood and its innocent expectations recovered by the same boy later, after he has been stroked by what men and women do, so that he can find out who he is, the grown man.

© Nancy Crampton

"**Dear Pop**" says it best: how the mature man curls up in the eye of the boy and sees what he once saw of God, of states in life, of noncontradiction, of fatherhood, physical and spiritual, but it is the matured mind that sees with the eye of boyhood now....

When James Carroll succeeds with his "eye of boy/mind of man" approach to the experience of religion, family, priesthood, sex, war, the poems become lovable—no other word for it—and, since they are confessional, mainly, the poet becomes lovable. When he fails, as I think he does in "**The Captive Speaking**," in parts of "**Dear Pop**" and in youthful references to God and his father and mother, the poems become as uneasy as adolescents on display. Perhaps, also, a very youthful gaze cannot grasp full magnitudes of either terror or ecstasy. Precise gods and precise demons, the creations of one's own experience, not of another's instruction, stretch a poet's sensibility enormously, and require of him or her a complex response, one that will avoid obliteration for the poet without obliterating the god or the demon. (p. 365)

His poetry is really lovable when his maturity sees reality through a boy's eye, or when he wears his refugee face. His poetry is emotionally awkward when he sees with boyish mind. But, whichever way it is with him, here, in this book, once again, is a poet climbing out of the pews, the boxes, the pulpits, the manuals, the rules, in order to stand where a human being can be fashioned and can then fashion human beings. (p. 366)

Francis Sullivan, in a review of "Forbidden Disappointments," in America, *Vol. 132, No. 18, May 10, 1975, pp. 365-66.*

PUBLISHERS WEEKLY

In this literate and agonizingly honest personal testament [*The Winter Name of God*] Father Carroll, a poet as well as a Catholic priest, doubtless speaks for many Americans in these disturbed times. In 1973 he found himself losing his faith in God. Hoping to resolve his doubts he journeyed to the Holy Land. . . . In the Holy Land he wasn't impressed by the cheap marketable mementos of the passion of Jesus. But the longer he remained in the Holy Land, the more deeply he understood the meaning of "Abba" (father) and of his own heritage. For the genuinely religious-minded, his account of his recovery of faith will prove a vital reading experience.

A review of "The Winter Name of God," in Publishers Weekly, *Vol. 207, No. 70, May 19, 1975, p. 173.*

GERARD REEDY

The Winter Name of God, a prose "summer's chronicle," and *Forbidden Disappointments,* a collection of twenty-three poems, complement one another. The poems especially help to underscore the heart of the chronicle, James Carroll's interpretation to himself, through memory, of his family. The point of re-entry, and of previous departure, is religious faith. "How is your God my God?," Carroll asks in a poem, **"Dear Pop."** The prose chronicle develops a richly personal concept of God as *Abba* in such a way that Carroll's renewed faith renews the meaning of his parents' "embraces," a focal image in both books.

The time of *Winter Name* is post-Vietnam. Its author, at the time of writing a Paulist priest, has grown war-weary from anti-war activism. "It had something to do with God. . . . None of the rest of my life would hold if I could not sustain a sense of his nearness." In the summer of 1973, Carroll retreats to a monastery "halfway between Bethlehem and Jerusalem," there to think, go over his life, and read the Scripture, especially the gospel of John. "I was alone and confused and desperate for a word that would explain me to myself." The word becomes *Abba.* Through it, Carroll understands again Jesus' relation to his Father, and his own relation to his mother and father. The key to Carroll's broad use of *Abba* involves both a clinging to and a letting go. In his own life, this means that painful differences in theology and politics—his father is an Air Force General—do not empty his cry of *Abba* but strengthen it. (pp. 217-18)

Carroll interrupts his narrative with his thoughts on a number of topics like the revolt at Masada, midrash, Catholic attitudes towards the body and the "world," male chauvinism, and suicide. Some of these are integrated in his personal search for faith and understanding, some are not. Having assumed the ethos of the searcher and doubter, Carroll occasionally strikes the false note of preachiness. I find the sermons on "flesh" and the "world," for example, full of clichés. On the other hand, Carroll does partly integrate his critical remarks about male chauvinism with his central concept of *Abba*; he notes that of course we must include the feminine, e.g., our mothers,

in any adequate notion of "fatherhood." The point was obvious to me—but only after Carroll made it. *Winter Name* frequently talks of suicide and occasionally of its author's fear of starting his day. In regard to his own dark moments, Carroll is finally ironic: "Where has been the real desolation in my life?" He redeems any elements of over-dramatization in his chronicle with final, ingenuous self-effacement. (p. 218)

The language of *Winter Name* tends to evoke rather than explicate meanings, especially in the core passages about fatherhood. . . . His style of writing, in general, is not exemplary. He uses "is" endlessly. He frequently resorts to sentences composed of subjects only; he emphasizes by using italics where the trained eye and ear expect greater syntactical adroitness. . . . Even Carroll's poems now and then speak in this breathless prose, symbolic of exploding emotions that he leaves, coyly or lazily, undeveloped.

Although Carroll includes a few tight, controlled poems in *Forbidden Disappointments,* much of the volume is talky, overly reliant on *meaningful,* stock phrases and situations, and imagistically destitute. The first four poems seem especially flat. . . . Too many of these poems simply blurt out experiences in miniphrases without the semblance of ironic control. It will not do simply to state that one has stayed up late, smoking cigarettes and worrying. How differently, more honestly, and more precisely has Carroll worried about the war and God than you or I? Part of the limited success of *Winter Name* is owing to the image of *Abba,* developed over many pages; this image transforms the author's anxiety and hope into an object of contemplation and makes criticism of content beside the point. The poems often lack such transformation; surely this may occur also through complex rhythm and syntax, but here Carroll is especially weak.

The title comes from the last two words of one of the best poems, **"Someone in the Review Board."** The four-line stanzas of this poem discipline Carroll's emotion and thought, as does the dominant, skillfully developed image of the "soft middle," the charge against the speaker by someone on the review board for ordination. The new, Frostian image of the last stanza partly achieves its success because the previous stanza has ended definitely, syntactically and thematically, in a Eucharistic reference: "Does that mean I am tough around / the edges like, say earth? Or, before breaking, bread?" The controlled form mirrors the frank acceptance of the potential destruction of self and others in a priesthood. In Carroll's hand this *topos* remains "forbidden"—and thus interesting—but certainly not disappointing. Other poems also delight. Four poems (**"Crows," "Cobbler," "Rain Dance,"** and **"The Window of His Room"**) consist of visual perceptions, well-drawn, with a political or theological punch. In **"Mom in Your Boots,"** Carroll finds a fresh image and builds it into a frightening question about the closeness of tragedy to our innocent family joys.

As in *Winter Name,* the best writing depends on apparently autobiographical incidents, although not all the autobiographical poems merit equal attention. The last poem, **"Pentagon: A Memory,"** is the most successful of the longer poems given; it happily avoids the cuteness of **"The Captive Speaking"** and the wordiness of **"Dear Pop"** (a poem which still holds some brightly conceived passages). (pp. 218-19)

There are many sudden beauties in *Forbidden Disappointments.* One finds far more good parts of poems than sustained structures. . . . James Carroll exhibits the bursts of power and fresh perception that poems cannot live without. The present volume too often lacks the complementary virtues: sustained discipline of thought and form, ironic rejection of stock situations, and attention to certain generally accepted rules of good writing. (p. 219)

> *Gerard Reedy, in a review of "The Winter Name of God" and "Forbidden Disappointments," in* Commonweal, *Vol. CIII, No. 7, March 26, 1976, pp. 217-19.*

PETER S. PRESCOTT

The Day of the Jackal has whelped many cubs, of which [*Madonna Red*] is neither the last nor the worst. This time around the politician marked for assassination is Sir Alisdair Ferris-Cogan, British ambassador to the United States and a Roman Catholic. The IRA thinks Ferris-Cogan a traitor and has sent its best gunperson, a lovely woman with the code name of Juneau, to shoot him in the Washington cathedral just as he is awarded the papal Order of Gregory the Great. British intelligence gets wind of the plot, but in best "Jackal" fashion offers its man as bait.... The situation is muddled by the Britishers' inability to imagine that the assassin might be a woman and by a renegade nun who proves impenitent when taxed by her cardinal and a priest for celebrating Mass....

Because plausibility is a virtue little esteemed by writers of romances it may be captious to complain about the implausibility of this one, but I'll complain anyway—if only because the incredible part of this story is entirely unnecessary, a gratuitous trick that requires a lot of tedious preparation. The foundation for this trick is laid early in the book and in such a self-conscious manner that no reader with an IQ above 79 can possible fail to catch it, can fail to regret the great dull stretches that this device imposes on the remainder of the story. James Carroll has worked himself into a situation where one of his characters is entirely unbelievable. That's a particular pity becuase he has, in the rest of his narrative, been at pains to lend body and credibility to the suspense: the cardinal and the priest, for instance, are drawn with care and the talk about Catholic dilemmas, while hardly subtle, shows an informed intelligence at work.

> *Peter S. Prescott, in a review of "Madonna Red," in* Newsweek, *Vol. LXXXVII, No. 25, June 21, 1976, p. 84.*

NEWGATE CALLENDAR

On one level, [*Madonna Red*] is a suspense story about an Irish activist loose in Washington, out to get the British ambassador. Carroll, however, has much more than that in mind. *Madonna Red* is a very up-to-date book about the problems of Catholicism in the modern world; about the role of women in the church; about the obligations of priesthood and the doctrine of unfaltering obedience to the bishop.

Carroll has created believable people. He avoids being goody-goody on the one hand, anticlerical on the other. His portrait of a conservative, well-meaning bishop rings true. His priest, an ex-commando (Vietnam hero with all the trimmings), is faced with problems that he alone has to surmount. The wife of the ambassador, a non-Catholic, worries about the Catholic education her little girl is receiving.

But under all this is sheer menace. A skilled killer is on the prowl, and Carroll works things up to a terrific climax. He is

a skillful writer who knows every trick of the genre. Indeed, at the beginning of the book there is as neat a piece of misdirection as one is going to come across in any crime novel anywhere. Congratulations on a job well done.

> *Newgate Callendar, in a review of "Madonna Red," in* The New York Times Book Review, *July 11, 1976, p. 34.*

PEGGY MURPHY

From the outset [of *Madonna Red*], the reader is involved in a fast-moving plot. At first, Sr. Delores seems an extraneous part of the action, but she is more than just another appointment on the cardinal's calendar. If nothing else, she underscores the fact that women are demanding they be heard especially by those who seem unable to take them seriously.

Many readers will probably see through Juneau's cover early in the book; for others, she will be unveiled only at the end. Either way, the suspense never lets up. The author's rambling descriptions can often seem tedious, yet it is his meticulous attention to detail that gives life to each character and that makes each scene as familiar as one's own living room.

Madonna Red can and should be read as a thriller, but much will be lost if the reader fails to notice what it has to say about the church, faith and politics. The issue in the end is not really women. It is life as lived by those who are courageous or fatalistic enough to do what they must.

> *Peggy Murphy, in a review of "Madonna Red," in* America, *Vol. 135, No. 3, August 7, 1976, p. 61.*

WEBSTER SCHOTT

Mortal Friends extends from the first fires of the Irish Rebellion in the 1920's to a few months before the assassination of John Kennedy, who appears and speaks in the novel along with his tough Irish family, worldly Harvard friends and clan's boozy chaplain, Richard Cardinal Cushing.

It's a novel about real and imagined happenings. It's fashionable and knowing, if not downright hip. Designed to follow the cycle of a human lifetime—that of its protagonist, Colman Brady—it's written in strong and occasionally eloquent language, and develops plots as complex and interrelated as the roots of human behavior itself. *Mortal Friends* is a serious work of fiction intended for a wide audience. It informs, entertains, and does so without abandoning intellectual standards. James Carroll has observed life carefully, and thought about what he saw.

Colman Brady dominates *Mortal Friends* the way a beautiful, damaged piece of sculpture might dominate a park. He appears on the first page as a 22-year-old farmer awakening his orphaned younger brother and sister to play Druids and help him greet the dawn of his wedding day in Four Mile Waters. He closes the novel nearly 45 years later, as an industrialist frontman for the Boston Mafia, walking away from the loss of his only son, determined that the half-Irish, half-Sicilian grandson by his side somehow must move forward in manhood free of the violence, exclusion and possessive love that have stripped him of nearly everything he values.

Expelled from his dead parents' farm by the British, Brady learns killing in the service of the Irish rebels, especially the folk-general Michael Collins. When Eamon De Valera double-crosses Collins and sets up his assassination, Brady's wife, brother and sister are murdered by one of De Valera's renegade gangs. Brady settles the score. He tracks down and kills each man in cold blood. Then he flees to America with his infant son, Michael Collins, named in honor of the brooding Irish hero.

In Boston, Brady learns what power can do. He goes to work as dump foreman, insurance agent and Democratic club treasurer for Mayor James Michael Curley. At home it's lace curtains and Irish Catholicism. At work it's manipulation, deals, influence and bargaining for more of everything, as Boston boils with the Sacco-Vanzetti trial, bootlegging, the Depression and an alliance of Italians and Irish.

Mayor Curley is the dark underside of Edwin O'Connor's blarney-tongued, roguish Skeffington-Curley in *The Last Hurrah*. Mr. Carroll shows us an engaging crook and demagogue who undercuts or destroys his supporters, depending on where the advantage lies. Brady becomes the partner of Gennaro Anselmo, the North End Mafia chief whose pardon he sponsored on Curley's behalf. Brady also becomes bonded to Anselmo for life, indebted to him for favors and wealth that buy concessions and appointments all the way from the White House to the Vatican.

Curley and Anselmo illustrate two of Mr. Carroll's ideas that shape characters and determine events in *Mortal Friends*:

One is that historical characters should be seen whole in fiction. . . . John Kennedy is all too human, Joseph Kennedy proudly buys public officials, Pope John XXIII sounds naïve, Franklin D. Roosevelt appears cruel, and Samuel Eliot Morison is long-winded. . . . The other idea derives from Irish mythology, with its associations of defeat and betrayal. Each of the five sections making up *Mortal Friends* ends in a defeat hinging on a betrayal. . . .

The pleasure of *Mortal Friends* is its fullness. . . .

The story of Brady's love affair with the suicidal wife of a proper Bostonian is a novel within the novel. Brady and Anselmo sitting on a waterfront bench plotting a crime in Sicily is a complete short story. Mr. Carroll's dialogues are America overheard. He knows what men and women do and think about in private. He knows church politics in Rome, and can graph the paramilitary arrangements of the underworld.

Too often, Mr. Carroll's characters speak in the same voice. Too often, chance turns the direction of the novel. And Mr. Carroll has almost no sense of humor. But these are flaws, not holes, in *Mortal Friends*. Before this novel, James Carroll was a Paulist priest, a church philosopher and a sometime playwright at the Berkshire Theater Festival in Stockbridge. Now he is a novelist of consequence and beyond making it.

> *Webster Schott, "Defeat and Betrayal, Irish-Style," in* The New York Times Book Review, *April 30, 1978, p. 15.*

LEON LINDSAY

Instead of building [*Mortal Friends*] around a real-life central character like Boston's Mayor Curley . . . , James Carroll skillfully creates a fictional hero who operates on the fringes of reality—first as a close aide to Curley and later as the "legitimate" business straw for the local underworld boss. . . .

Through Brady's fortunes—more ill than good in the long run—Mr. Carroll views the many levels of Irish society in Boston; the underworld ascendancy of the Sicilian mafiosi in the North End; and the cool ability of the Protestant Yankees to retain their power even while seeming to lose it.

Although there is the basic glorification of Irishness one might expect, Mr. Carroll does not neglect the unattractive aspects of the Hibernian character and mores. He is especially rough on some of the more famous of Boston's Irish. Carroll's Curley is the good-bad pol whom we have met in other—no doubt accurate—portrayals. His ruthless framing of his confidant Brady dashes the younger man's political aspirations and sends him into the arms of the mob leader—and ultimate tragedy.

Roman Catholic officialdom—in Rome as well as Boston—is shown as more hypocritical than holy. The treatment of real people like Cardinal Richard Cushing and the Kennedys (Joe Sr., Jack, and Robert) comes close to defaming the dead while avoiding libel of the living.

Occasionally it seems that the author has taken on too much. Mr. Carroll sometimes lapses into melodrama or cliché. The contrivance necessary to maneuver events to keep fiction from running afoul of reality—always a problem in this kind of novel—is too obvious at times. The use of coincidence as the author begins to unwind this tragic story toward a somewhat hopeful end is a bit disappointing.

But *Mortal Friends* is a success. It is skillfully plotted, written with polish and occasional brilliance, highly entertaining, and thoroughly Irish.

> *Leon Lindsay, "A Long Way from Tipperary," in* The Christian Science Monitor, *May 18, 1978, p. 18.*

THE NEW YORKER

[*Mortal Friends* is a] large, ambitious, and nearly unreadable novel about an Irishman, the Irish Rebellion of the nineteen-twenties, and the Boston (Irish-Italian) Mafia, in which the flawed but larger-than-life hero is swept through a stormy life from Tipperary to Boston's North End, City Hall, *and* Beacon Hill. . . . Mr. Carroll builds his plot on the theme of betrayal that runs through Irish history and literature, but he loads onto it too many stories and subplots, and he does not have an ear for the spoken word or an eye for artistic proportions. To get to the story, the reader must wade through streams of consciousness, schoolboyish poeticizing, and professional lectures. There is a television special lurking inside of all this.

> *A review of "Mortal Friends," in* The New Yorker, *Vol. LIV, No. 14, May 22, 1978, p. 138.*

JOSEPH PARISI

Following the tested recipes of Haley, Doctorow and Puzo, with a pinch of Capote, James Carroll's ambitious family saga [*Mortal Friends*] traces three generations of the Colman Brady clan over four decades—from Tipperary to Southie, Beacon Hill, and all around Bean Town. Along the way, a number of historical personalities put in special appearances. . . . With the several strands of Brady biography, the novel thus intertwines episodes from the Irish Rebellion and ensuing Civil War, the Sacco and Vanzetti case, vendettas of the Irish-Italian Mafia, Boston politics in the '30s, Senate subcommittees of the '50s, and Vatican II, among many other things.

While most of this material is ingeniously deployed, and Carroll's interpretations are just cynical enough to be probable, the historical notes often seem potted, creating a lecture-hall lull in the midst of the action. The extensive technical details—on guerrilla tactics, stock manipulation, sail-boating, Boston geography—albeit usually germane to the story, also seem self-indulgent displays of the author's expertise.

That said, I hasten to add that Carroll conveys far more than local color through his skillful mix of fiction and fact. In focusing on Colman Brady and his family, he highlights the character and shifting fortunes of the Irish on the old sod and in the new land. Above all, though, Carroll seeks to show the moral dilemmas that even the well-meaning man faces when doing the "right thing" leads to unexpected and finally uncontrollable evil. (p. 18)

For all the convolutions of plot, the wealth of information and large cast of characters, the novel usually moves at a fair clip, particularly during the second half. But the detailed description of Brady's motives and gradual moral degradation notwithstanding, the man himself remains, in the last analysis, unsatisfying. (Nor is he helped by a familiar supporting cast of social and psychological clichés.) Directly or implicitly through the saga, Carroll suggests his protagonist's lacks are the inevitable result of an incapacity to love truly, the corruption of power and a malignant destiny that is the peculiar curse of the Irish. Perhaps, but for these themes to have worked fully, Colman Brady should have been a more convincing character. As it stands, *Mortal Friends* is less than the sum of its parts. (p. 19)

> *Joseph Parisi, "Pluck of the Irish," in* The New Leader, *Vol. LXI, No. 15, July 17, 1978, pp. 18-19.*

BEN YAGODA

Mortal Friends spanned three generations; *Fault Lines* spans two days. And where the earlier book, a story of the rise of a Boston Irish dynasty, had scores of characters, this one has but three.... (p. 85)

In a more focused book than *Mortal Friends,* where grandness of plot and scale cannot be relied upon to hold the reader's interest, stylistic assurance and insight into character must take its place. Carroll displays neither. His prose does not sing, and—aside, perhaps, from David's need for Eddie—we get no sense of the presumably highly charged relations among the three principals, upon which the book depends. Instead of *showing,* Carroll *tells,* with flat lines like "Cheney's feelings about Eddie were chaotic" and "He was completely focused on her."

The one successful element in *Fault Lines* is the portrait of Eddie's young son, Bren. Indeed, Carroll is eloquent in depicting the intense and often contradictory states of mind and action the boy is made of—loneliness, fantasy, prevarication, resentment, gentle manipulation, and above all, the need for love. When it comes to adults, however, *Fault Lines* disappoints. James Carroll does better with a cast of thousands; in his case, less is less. (p. 86)

> *Ben Yagoda, in a review of "Fault Lines," in* Saturday Review, *Vol. 7, No. 14, October, 1980, pp. 85-6.*

STANLEY ELLIN

In *Fault Lines,* James Carroll presents us with three people who are the points of a triangle bound to implode. The mover and shaker of this trio is Cheney McCoy, celebrated and talented star of stage and screen, who involves himself so intensely in his stage roles that he comes to live them offstage. Considering that the role he's currently rehearsing is that of Richard III, some of whose less lovable traits Cheney already shares, it's clear that those treading on his self-declared prerogatives are going to face retribution sooner or later.

The two marked for it are David Dolan, an antiwar activist who had taken refuge in Sweden during the Vietnam War and who has now secretly returned to the United States; and Eddie McCoy, Cheney's wife (from whom he's separated) and also the widow of David's brother Brendan. Hostage to everyone's fortune is little Bren, Eddie's child by her first husband, but so adored by Cheney that he formally adopted the boy and, despite his separation from Eddie, now feels he has a powerful claim on him. Inevitably, all wind up together on an isolated Maine island where a lifetime of accounts must be settled for each one.

This material could trip up many an author, but Mr. Carroll deals with it masterfully. The characters are shown in depth, are always plausible and, even in Cheney's case, sympathetic. And while the climax—actually a dual climax—is a shade contrived, I found the story gripping from start to finish.

> *Stanley Ellin, "Enviable Heroes," in* The New York Times Book Review, *December 14, 1980, p. 10.*

EUGENE KENNEDY

[In *Fault Lines*] James Carroll has written a miniature in which the lines that connect the lives of the main characters are drawn together so tautly that they almost shatter the small frame of the narrative. Having filled a vast and airy canvas with the colorful characters of *Mortal Friends,* Carroll has chosen a more restricted and more demanding background for this very Catholic exploration of our sinful condition and our varied attempts at redemption and salvation. This is a catholic novel in the richest sense of that phrase because it addresses itself to profoundly human issues, to conscience and responsibility, to the fact so many would like to ignore, that everything in our relationships with each other makes a difference, that at close quarters with each other there is no vague refuge beyond moral referent "in which nobody else is hurt." This is a book about people who, like most of us, are capable of big mistakes and who, even in pursuit of forgiveness or in the act of attempting to heal those who are hurt, sometimes make things worse instead of better.

James Carroll also treats a subject which will clearly be a main preoccupation of the generation that turns forty during this decade.... Many are attempting to pick up their lives again and to make them whole by a return to what appear to be more conventional styles of life. Spouses want to love each other truly, they want marriage to work even after they have been through ones that haven't; they want things hooked up again into a circuit of meaning that has suddenly become urgently important once more.

Hooking things up, of course, is the business of religion and the themes of its perennial task undergird Carroll's work. His characters represent the bright, wounded generation that lost itself in the evil cloud of the Vietnam war, in the years when assassinations and upheavals of every sort gave an apocalyptic cast to modern life, in the days when, perversely enough, liberation seemed at hand. (pp. 216-17)

The book centers on . . . four characters and how the lines of their lives are finally winched together on an island off Maine with a dramatic intensity that almost overwhelms the theological issues that are the core of Carroll's and so many serious writers' concern.

All of this is managed with considerable narrative skill and counterpoint, as in the contrasts between McCoy in *Richard III* and in real life. The boy Bren seems to be the least successful of these engaging characterizations; his head contains far more careful observation and reflection on life than is likely even in the most precocious six-year-old. This does not destroy him, however, as the centerpiece of everyone's concern. He is perceived by and means something quite different for his mother, his uncle, and his stepfather, all of whom are so caught up in salvaging their pasts that they cannot see him very clearly for himself.

Carroll's story explores broken lives, wrong judgments, the cruel harshness of too easy love, and the moral pressure that invades the universe when we recognize the marks we leave on each other every day. All this is evoked, with remarkable effect, on a small stage surrounded by forces of nature, forest, and tides that threaten to move in and retake it at any moment.

The questions that arise transcend those about the individual fates of the leading characters. It is no small achievement to cause a reader to inspect the ragged edges of these lives to discover meanings that may not be immediately apparent, and to survey one's own for a more accurate sense of true moral courage. It is a book about the faults that are, for all of us, the crooked lines spoken of by Claudel, through which we make our way toward unlikely and unexpected redemption. (pp. 217-18)

> *Eugene Kennedy, "The Bright, Wounded Generation," in* Commonweal, *Vol. CVIII, No. 7, April 10, 1981, pp. 216-18.*

CHRISTOPHER LEHMANN-HAUPT

There comes a point in James Carroll's absorbing new novel, *Family Trade,* when Jake McKay, the young protagonist, is offered the following moral equation to consider: Jake's family trade, which is international espionage, may well have caused him psychological injury. But what does that count when weighed against the world's avoidance of nuclear catastrophe?

That may well be what was bought with all the lying and withholding of love that went on in his lifetime: a couple of baby steps away from the abyss of Armageddon. Can Jake grasp the huge significance of that? Well—sniff, sniff—he guesses that maybe after all he can.

Now, James Carroll, himself the son of an American intelligence officer, may well be trying to tell us something significant here. Judging from Jake's somewhat irritating self-absorption, Mr. Carroll may be shaking a finger at the generations of Americans who have gotten disillusioned by all the cold war huggermugger of the 1960's and 70's.

On the other hand, maybe he's taking a neutral stand on the issues of national defense and espionage. . . . Maybe what Mr. Carroll means to say is that all of us who were children in the 1940's were wounded by the war; and our challenge remains to overcome those wounds.

One thing is certain though. As he did in his previous novels, *Madonna Red, Mortal Friends* and *Fault Lines,* Mr. Carroll builds his plot with big bright alphabet-blocks of moral confrontation. Anyone not engaged by what has come to be known as old-fashioned value-conflicts framed in an old-fashioned novelistic form might just as well stay away from *Family Trade.*

Myself, I was sufficiently caught up by the story to fret about some of its technical problems. I kind of enjoyed the early scenes where Jake, as a first-year student at Georgetown University in 1960, puts to route single-handedly the obnoxious tradition of freshman hazing. These serve to establish Jake's potential for leadership, and thus the letdown of his later failure.

I found both entertaining and frightening the long flashback to the collapse of Berlin in 1945. The episode in which Jake's father and his companions blow up the airplane in which Hitler might have escaped is a wonderful World War II fantasy. The scenes of Russian atrocities are terrifying and serve their purpose with hellish effectiveness. All in all, Mr. Carroll is a storyteller of growing power, and in *Family Trade* he has bitten off his biggest drama yet and made of it a surpassing banquet.

But I wonder about his having switched away from Jake's point of view to tell the flashback of the fall of Berlin from an omniscient perspective. Obviously, Jake couldn't have experienced it directly, because he was only months old and lying in a crib in London at the time. Just as obviously, he can't be told what happened by an eyewitness to Berlin's collapse, because that would weaken the effect on him of the revelations in the novel's final section.

The problem seems to be that learning what actually happened in Berlin puts us readers at too much of an advantage over Jake. Knowing what we do about his parents' generation's heroism makes Jake's ignorance seem all the more a weakness in him and heightens his apparent callowness and self-absorption. This is what throws the novel's moral balance out of whack and makes us wonder if Mr. Carroll isn't trying to teach us some lesson in patriotism instead of casting light on a tragic dilemma.

But then again, maybe the problem isn't that simple. . . . Maybe one just can't frame the problem of national survival quite so conventionally anymore.

> *Christopher Lehmann-Haupt, in a review of "Family Trade," in* The New York Times, *June 10, 1982, p. C22.*

PAUL GRAY

Family Trade closely follows the iron-curtained rule of its genre. Those who like their espionage fast paced and complicated will not be disappointed. Big issues are at stake here; the struggle between East and West may hang in the balance. Winston Churchill and Allen Dulles appear in walk-on roles. An ordinary man is suddenly entangled in a web of deceptions, risking his life for reasons he does not understand. But Author James Carroll . . . makes these familiar conventions seem fresh and even plausible. His characters are not puppets of the plot. They grow and change. They struggle with divided loyalties, knowing that their secret activities on behalf of some grand design force them to lie to their loved ones, betray them if necessary.

In 1960 a Georgetown University freshman named Jake McKay spots his father, "one of the most powerful men on the quiet side of Washington," at an art museum. But who is that beautiful blond woman on his arm, and who is that equally attractive girl with her? Jake hears his father exchange endearments with them in German, a language he did not think the elder McKay knew. Stunned by what he assumes is a scene of infidelity, Jake confides in his Uncle Giles, his mother's brother and a cultural attaché with the British embassy. In a matter of days, Giles defects to Moscow. Jake's father, after a period of debriefing by his CIA superiors, suffers a stroke. Jake, already physically crippled since infancy by the explosion of a V-2 rocket that hit his parents' house in London, now comes down with a debilitating case of moral paralysis. His family is in tatters, and the two men he loved most are beyond his question: "How can I be on the team when nobody tells me what we're playing?"

A flashback to 1945 begins to unravel the tangles. John McKay Sr. and Giles Patterson lead a joint U.S.-British commando raid into the heart of Berlin. Their ostensible purpose is to destroy the airplane that is ready to lift Hitler from the burning city. Their real job is to keep German nuclear research out of the hands of the invading Soviets. Since the resistance group that they must work with is made up largely of Communists, this part of the mission proves tricky. The resistance leader helps them; they, in turn, evacuate his wife and baby daughter to the West.

Having jumped backward, the author suddenly leaps ahead. It is now 1980, and Jake is an English professor in Boston, still maimed by the events of two decades earlier. . . . On cue, Magda Dettke, the infant from Berlin, appears in his office. Her mother, the woman Jake had seen in the museum 20 years ago, is dead. Magda now works for British intelligence, and she has startling news. Giles wants to redefect, but he will do so only if his nephew helps him cross from East to West Berlin. Jake realizes that his visitor and he are still children, possessed by the "ghosts of his father and her mother." Somehow they are both fated to complete "our parents' business."

Of course Jake goes with Magda to Berlin and finds himself in far greater peril than he had imagined. But his rite of passage is not only the literal trek from East back to West but the psychological journey toward true maturity. Experiencing the sense of danger that his father must have felt so often during his exploits, Jake comes face to face with the enemy. . . . It is time, he decides, to enter the free world.

Such moments adroitly balance the exotic and the familiar; an adventure that will shake Moscow and Washington also leads to a personal discovery, and both results seem equally important. In his fourth novel, Carroll again reveals the commercial instincts that made his *Mortal Friends* (1978) a bestseller. In addition, this book reveals a serious novelist behind the popular entertainer. Like Graham Greene and John le Carré, Carroll brings global strife and problems home to hearts and minds, their points of origin.

Paul Gray, "Our Parents' Business," in Time, *Vol. 119, No. 25, June 21, 1982, p. 76.*

ALAN CHEUSE

James Carroll in recent years produced two long "mainstream" novels, *Mortal Friends* and *Fault Lines*. In these books he attempted with some success to give us nothing less than, in the former, the character of the city of Boston and, in the latter, a view of love and art and family ties in post-Vietnam War America. *Family Trade*, his new book, shows him struggling courageously, with mixed results, to combine his taste for spy fiction with the desire to create more serious contemporary types. (pp. 14, 23)

The prose as well as the psychology of [the opening section of *Family Trade*] is far from compelling . . . ; there are too many flaccid passages given over to Jake's teen-age crises and not enough attention to the pace of the book. Not until the middle of the novel, in the section entitled "London/Berlin 1945," do we get a smartly composed set piece that shows us what Daddy did during the war—and what Mr. Carroll can do with the spy genre when he puts his mind to it. If the third and final section—set in Boston and Berlin in 1980—were as tightly written and well paced, the reader might care a great deal more when Jake, having become a mediocre English teacher with an unresolved past, finally undergoes what Mr. Carroll calls "the great passage rite he should have accomplished years ago." By playing spy for a day, the handicapped Georgetown graduate comes "to learn what he was made of" and redeems the memory of his by now long-dead C.I.A. father. But *Family Trade* itself lacks a similar resolution. Is it a thriller? Is it "mainstream"? Mr. Carroll's emphasis on Jake's emotional crises makes it tilt now one way, now the other, and the result is not entirely satisfying. (pp. 23-4)

Alan Cheuse, "Spies and Lovers and Action," in The New York Times Book Review, *July 11, 1982, pp. 14, 23-4.*

JONATHAN YARDLEY

This exceedingly long novel [*Prince of Peace*] is so packed with good intentions that it practically begs to be liked, but this hope is defeated by the ineptitude of the book's construction. James Carroll is clearly a writer of deep convictions on any number of important matters; in *Prince of Peace,* though, he has not found a satisfactory way to translate those convictions into interesting fiction. Instead he has written a gassy, didactic novel that only intermittently engages the reader's emotions and from the outset strains the reader's credulity past the snapping point.

The narrator of the novel is Frank Durkin, a New Yorker who has joined an English Benedictine monastery and is now at a "contemplative outpost" in Israel. Though Durkin is occasionally a participant in what takes place, *Prince of Peace* is not his story but that of Michael Maguire, who "was the most famous priest in America for a time; the priest against Vietnam" and until a few years ago was Durkin's closest friend. The novel describes, in the most elaborate detail, Maguire's most private thoughts, emotions and actions during periods when he and Durkin were thousands of miles apart. The reader apparently is expected to believe that Durkin is privy to all this information; but the reader, being no fool, does not.

Thus *Prince of Peace* seesaws erratically between the occasional plausible periods when Durkin is witness to and/or participant in the action, and the far more frequent implausible ones when he simply disappears, unannounced, into the mask of omniscient author. The effect, for even the most tolerant reader, is jarring; just when you've been lulled into forgetting that Durkin exists, suddenly he pops back into the narrative to offer a ponderous aside, of which the novel has all too many, or to resume his own role in the proceedings.

This role, such as it is, is that of the betrayed. Within only a few pages we learn that a decade ago Durkin, then a university professor, had lost his wife to the defrocked priest Maguire, with whom she had been having an affair for years. Now his young daughter, Molly, has come to Jerusalem to tell him that Maguire is dead at 50 of a heart attack and to entreat him, at her mother's request, to come back to New York for the funeral. His bitterness is still great but he agrees to do so, out of respect for the past they shared and out of lingering love for both Maguire and Carolyn, the woman they both married.

His journey to the funeral becomes, of course, a journey into the past. The story begins in Inwood, a small working-class neighborhood at the northernmost tip of Manhattan, where Maguire and Durkin grew up under the rigorous discipline of the neighborhood priests. From there Durkin goes to New York University and Greenwich Village, where he learns skepticism, and Maguire goes to Korea, where he commits an act of heroism that results in his capture by the Chinese. After three years as a prisoner of war, much of that time spent in solitary confinement, he emerges with a powerful commitment to the faith that helped him survive the camp. When he and Durkin meet again in New York, his friend recognizes that he is a rare man. . . .

His passage to that point occupies the bulk—and bulk, alas, is the word for it—of the novel. Maguire decides to join the priesthood, attends Catholic University (characteristically, Durkin pauses in mid-narrative to provide an extensive history of that institution, complete with theological commentary), serves his apprenticeship at a New York parish and finally is ordained by Cardinal Spellman, who eventually becomes a considerable figure in the novel. He is posted to a relief operation in Vietnam. . . . It takes several years and a second tour of duty in Vietnam, but in the end Maguire becomes an antiwar activist in the Berrigan mold, and his life takes various dramatic, or melodramatic, turns.

What we seem to have in the life of Michael Maguire is a metaphor for the history of postwar American Catholicism. When he enters the church it is under the inflexible hand of Spellman, who represents both the church's commitment to rigid theological orthodoxy and its longing to establish itself in the American secular firmament. But when the church attempts to silence his protests against the war, he realizes that he is expected to cut his conscience to fit its design; his rebellion against church authority mirrors that of the priests and laymen who, in the '60s and '70s, sought to get out from under the iron hand of Rome and exercise a degree of independence.

The metaphor is all well and good, but it is not enough to sustain a novel that staggers along under the burdens of an unconvincing narrative device, a hackneyed plot and a paucity of genuinely interesting characters. James Carroll is an intelligent writer who is capable of expressing himself with considerable passion, but in *Prince of Peace* he simply has not given the reader much to care about. Strong feelings aren't enough; fiction also needs real people.

> Jonathan Yardley, "Clerical Errors," in Book World
> —The Washington Post, *October 14, 1984, p. 3.*

WEBSTER SCHOTT

[*Prince of Peace*] has a lot going for it—hot topic, flashy writing, forbidden sex and the impression that important things are being said about God in politics.

James Carroll . . . tells three stories here. One concerns the "glorification" of a charismatic American priest who ignites the anti-Vietnam War movement of the 1960's. The second story is about the transformation of the United States Roman Catholic Church from an ethnic spiritual monolith to a politically ambitious corporation run by autocratic and cynical executives. The third story is about disloyalty.

The stories are nearly irresistible. They illustrate and complement one another, and by telling them Mr. Carroll may make everyone mad except those who think God gave up on organized religion some time ago.

Mr. Carroll's hero is a real hero. Michael Maguire comes home from the Korean War bemedaled and celebrated for sustaining himself for 33 months in a Chinese P.O.W. camp by memorizing the New Testament and doing 1,500 push-ups every day. . . .

It's Michael Maguire's plight throughout *Prince of Peace* to believe he must "do something that makes the world better" while his church's hierarchy must do everything to enhance its temporal power.

As a deacon in a ghetto church Michael meets the woman he will love the rest of his life. . . . He also has his first collision with Francis Cardinal Spellman, "Spelly" to irreverent insiders. Spellman and Robert Moses collude to tear down the parish school for an access ramp to the Lincoln Tunnel.

But it's the apocalypse of Vietnam that sets Father Michael Maguire, coordinator of Catholic Relief there, into open rebellion against Spellman and the hierarchy and eventually makes Maguire a fugitive from the law for destroying draft registration records.

With a plot so complicated that it defies summary, Mr. Carroll lays out a fictional scenario in which the ruling Ngo family—President Diem, his brother Archbishop Thuc—attempt to eradicate Buddhism and turn Vietnam into a Catholic oligarchy. In the novel, monks are murdered in their temples. Buddhists—"prisoners of error," Spellman calls them—receive Catholic Relief rice only after baptism. In an insane war against Communism—Spellman and the State Department take the President Diem's bait—the United States Army is destroying an entire culture while counting the bodies of burned children as fallen enemies. Michael sees it all. Mr. Carroll's Vietnam writing is the finest in the novel. . . .

I like *Prince of Peace* best as fictionalized social history because it connects recent events into a coherent and credible statement of what has divided American Catholicism, with intellectuals and zealous young clergy on one side, with much of the church's power structure on the other side and with a passionate struggle between the two over social morality. It's a front-page story at least once a week.

Mr. Carroll's novel seems less successful as a psychological study of a priest and his friends caught in this struggle as the novel circles and explores the darker themes of pride and betrayal. When the author reaches inside his characters he finds confusion. Michael, who strangely uses four-letter words all the time, is a patsy to the church hierarchy for the first half of the novel, and it seems improbable that entering an adulterous relationship would turn him into a lion. Yet the characters do act with conviction, however unearned; Michael and Durkin, the narrator, who returns from a monastery to preside over Michael's funeral, never tire of talking about what their motives might be. They think too much and surely would benefit from several months in therapy.

Prince of Peace reaches for John Gardner's kind of moral fiction. It's a fascinating tale that shows how difficult it is, even for a novelist of James Carroll's considerable gifts, to create characters out of ideas about right and wrong.

Webster Schott, *"Maguire the Mettlesome Priest,"* in The New York Times Book Review, *November 4, 1984, p. 44.*

WILLIAM O'ROURKE

For novelists there has always been the Ripley's-Believe-It-or-Not problem: truth has shown itself over and over to be stranger than fiction: more vivid, alas, more, imaginative.... When recent history is used, the fictional device employed is the *roman à clef,* where foolhardy authors dare libel laws and serve up "thinly veiled" characters lifted from life. In some cases, *romans à clef,* key novels, are attempts at serious literature; the ringside seat books are potboilers, generational sagas, Leon Uris-like fare. James Carroll's new novel, his fifth, *Prince of Peace,* falls somewhere in between the two types, half historical soap opera, half *roman à clef.*

The narrative method Carroll has chosen may have been the easiest, but it leaves the novel with a plodding structure and a repetitive way of telling the story: which is, roughly, the tale of the 1960s Catholic anti-war resistance, as lived by the war-hero, priest, and movement celebrity, Michael Maguire, told, with some mixed emotions, by his adoring boyhood chum, Frank Durkin. The novel reads as an informal biography composed by a friend, but a friend, unfortunately, who is not a likable chronicler. Durkin accurately describes himself as "a two-bit professor at a second-rate college, a sometime contributor to small-circulation journals," a fellow who hopes to write a novel one of these days, and who is, apparently, something of an unexamined sexist, a classic homophobe, a licentious prude, and, most injurious to the book, not a very good writer.

Carroll may have wanted to portray just such a person, but he certainly risks censure (and a flawed book) when he makes such a creature his novel's narrator. We are treated throughout to such gems of reflection and dead stick prose from Durkin as, "I was filled with regret, but also stern acknowledgment that opaque hardening is the only law that heartbreak knows;" and "Jesus was the ultimate Mister Goodbar."

The hybrid mentioned earlier, part soap opera history, part *roman à clef,* though a taxing form, can be handled dexterously. E. L. Doctorow's *The Book of Daniel,* which uses the Rosenberg case, is an example; but Doctorow kept the central figures of his story intact and distorted the peripheral figures, while Carroll does just the opposite. His peripheral characters are true to life, but the central figures are distorted. His priest-resister, Michael Maguire (whose last name may be a dig at Cardinal Spellman's chancellor, Archbishop Maguire, who had a hand in giving Daniel Berrigan the bum's rush out of the country in 1965) is a Frankenstein creature: the torso of Philip Berrigan, the head of Dan, arms and legs, ecumenically, of William Sloane Coffin and Daniel Ellsberg, and the fingers of anyone's guess. For those familiar with the actual history and personalities of that period of Catholic resistance, *Prince of Peace* is an affront. Carroll can rightly claim that few know that history intimately anyway—and that his book is a novel

and should be judged as such; but it is as a novel that *Prince of Peace* falters most: what is verified history is at least informatively retold; what Carroll invents is hackneyed and too easy.

The soap opera gravity of Carroll's re-imagining of events and participants pulls all action and characters into the most predictable of orbits, rather than the weird and eccentric orbits of actual life. Popular fiction demands rather simple conflicts, but Carroll's model seems to be more an episode of *Dallas,* rather than, say, *Gone with the Wind.* Father Maguire and the narrator form a not-so-classic triangle: they are in love (and both eventually marry) the same woman, an ex-nun from a wealthy family. Maguire performs the original marriage ceremony in some sort of sacred and profane version of a *ménage à trois* (overall, the sex in the novel is written in a romantic style where breasts seem always to be described as "flaring"). (pp. 694-95)

The novel doesn't improve much when we're away from domestic wars and onto the battlefield. Maguire's heroics in Korea, as depicted, are right out of a *G.I. Joe* comic book.... (p. 695)

There is a serious and important subject buried in the center of Carroll's novel; and, because of it, *Prince of Peace* is more disheartening than bad. At the novel's core is the history of the Vietnam war, told from a Catholic perspective, though one quite chauvinist; "given its peculiarly Catholic Origins we should have" felt responsible for Vietnam, the narrator keeps reiterating. Where Vietnam is concerned, though, there is plenty of blame to go round. Most of this is done through you-are-there conventions, since Carroll makes young Father Maguire, newly-ordained, the right-hand man of ... Father O'Shea, who is the right-hand man of Spellman while the Cardinal tours and wheels and deals in Vietnam. That material is the most affecting, since it reads, more or less, like straight history, not the chopped-up and rearranged story of the Berrigans and the East Coast Conspiracy to Save Lives.

Prince of Peace is slated to become a best seller ..., but I'd be surprised if it actually becomes one.... [It] will not be the many narrative flaws, wooden characters, and lack of eloquence that would prevent *Prince of Peace* from becoming a best seller; more likely, it will be its one principal virtue: too much depressing and painful history about the Vietnam war, served up too plainly—and, in that case alone, all too true. (pp. 695-96)

William O'Rourke, *"Hybrid but Hackneyed,"* in Commonweal, *Vol. CXI, No. 22, December 14, 1984, pp. 694-96.*

SAM BASS WARNER, JR.

Today Americans float in a sea of institutional manipulation. The big powers: the governments, the campaign teams, the business corporations, the unions, the lobbies, the academies, the insurance companies, and the churches compete with each other for power and control while citizens make their way in little social groups, bobbing about on waves of public relations and media blather.... In such a society expressions of benevolence decay into fantasies of benign missions, and fears of evil decay into nightmares of Communist menace and warfare. James Carroll's latest novel, *Prince of Peace,* describes such a world, our American world, through the story of a war hero turned priest, turned peace activist, turned renegade priest.

After World War II, after the parents and grandparents of immigration, a generation of young American Catholics graduated from the seminaries and schools and entered the service of their church. They were fired with the hope that they could lead their church in a campaign to reform America and the world. Like many Americans before them they set out with the ignorant fantasy of a benign mission. *Prince of Peace* describes how this youth and good will, the only worthwhile treasure the nation ever possessed, was attacked by powerful political and church leaders and how a generation of young American Catholics learned of their, and our, true circumstance.

James Carroll is a popular novelist who tells his story in the classic style, through the adventures of a few closely linked characters. . . . The narrator is a child-man, Frank Durkin, the lifelong and dependent friend of the hero, Father Michael Maguire. Durkin is a common modern type, a man who has made his way out of a working class neighborhood as a good student. He becomes a professor of English at New York University, but neither the tradition of literature nor experiments in sexual liberation enable him to find a solid identity. Plausibly enough he continues his dependency upon his schooldays' pal, Michael Maguire.

The core of the novel is built around the lonely hero, Michael Maguire, and his loss of innocence and faith. . . . The Viet Nam passages, Michael's bit by bit discovery of the forces surrounding him, and his subsequent attempts to struggle against them, represent some of the best writing in the book.

This novel carries two meanings for me. First, as a non-Catholic it takes me through my experiences of the war years and the peace movement from the point of view of people I had only read about, or seen at a distance, the peace-activist priests. As a former Paulist priest, James Carroll was one of them.

Second, *Prince of Peace* informs my present sense of frustration and isolation. The good will of America has been destroyed, and a generation of hopeful young people have been beaten down. No final amnesty has been proclaimed. The novel suggests the cause of that defeat and the reason for our present helplessness: it is a failure of community, the locking of Americans into narrow social boxes. At the beginning of the novel, Durkin and Maguire revisit their old Manhattan neighborhood. The scene is a church breakfast, a testimonial for the local returning war hero. Maguire's shame and embarrassment about Viet Nam, and the uncomprehending remarks of the parishioners, announce the book's repeated theme: the broken bonds of human understanding.

The novel ends with the ecumenical scene of human solidarity we Americans love to read about and to watch on film. Fr. Maguire is dead, and as a renegade priest he has been refused burial by the Roman Catholic Church. The funeral is held, instead, at the Episcopal Cathedral of St. John the Divine. The vast church fills with representatives of the peace movement. . . .

But this is an event set in the 1960s; you cannot credibly invent such a scene for 1985. No group would gather to confront today's America, whether it be its bombs, its poisons, its secret police, its poverty, the destruction of its citizens. Carroll's novel tells why.

> *Sam Bass Warner, Jr., in a review of "Prince of Peace," in* Boston Review, *Vol. X. No. I, February, 1985, p. 22.*

John Pepper Clark

1935-

Nigerian poet, dramatist, critic, autobiographer, and scriptwriter.

Along with Wole Soyinka, Clark is one of Nigeria's foremost anglophone dramatists and poets. He writes in English in order to reach the widest possible audience in a country where many different languages are spoken. However, African images, themes, settings, and speech patterns are central to Clark's writing. Having been raised in the Niger delta and educated in English literature at Ibadan University, Clark describes himself as "that fashionable cultural phenomenon they call 'mulatto'— not in flesh but in mind!" Critics note a wide range of influences in Clark's work, from ancient and modern Western sources to the myths and legends of Clark's people, the Ijaw.

Clark's first two plays, *Song of a Goat* (1961) and *The Masquerade* (1965), contain elements of classical Greek and Shakespearean drama, the poetic plays of T.S. Eliot, and the folk literature of the Ijaw people, which, according to Clark, has much in common with classical drama. In the first play, a barren woman consults with a masseur and conceives a child by her husband's brother. Unable to accept this situation, both the husband and his brother commit suicide. The child, grown to manhood and oblivious of the circumstances of his birth, is the tragic hero of *The Masquerade*. He travels to a strange village and becomes engaged to a beautiful, strong-willed girl. When the young man's background is revealed, the girl's father forbids her to marry, but she refuses to abide by his decision. In the violent denouement, all die. Both plays are written in verse and share a relentless aura of doom; neighbors function as a chorus, commenting on the tragic happenings. *Song of a Goat*, *The Masquerade*, and *The Raft* (1966) were first published in the volume *Three Plays* (1964). *The Raft* concerns the misadventures of four men on a raft who attempt to bring logs downstream to be sold. Critics generally view the play as an exploration of the human condition or as a character study. It has also been interpreted as an allegory of the political division of Nigeria and as a critique of society based on economic determinism.

Ozidi (1966), Clark's first full-length play, was adapted from an Ijaw saga, the performance of which traditionally took seven days and involved mime, music, and dance. Clark retains many of these elements in his version and also uses masks and drums for the first time in his work. *Ozidi* is a revenge drama which, like Clark's earlier plays, involves a family curse and a series of violent actions. Clark also satirizes political corruption in this work.

A Reed in the Tide (1965) was Clark's first volume of poetry to be published internationally. Besides new poems, the volume also includes many pieces from Clark's first poetry collection, *Poems* (1962), which was published in Nigeria, and some from *America, Their America* (1964), a prose and poetry impression of the United States based on Clark's year in a post-graduate fellowship at Princeton University. Most of the poems are "occasional verse," inspired by something in the poet's immediate surroundings. Such poems as "Agbor Dancer," "Fulani Cattle," and "Girl Bathing" are based on Nigerian scenes;

others based on Clark's trip to the United States reveal his impression of the country as harsh and unfeeling. Two of Clark's most famous poems, "Ibadan" and "Night Rain," simply describe the Nigerian landscape. Many of his poems, however, go beyond concrete description to take on symbolic value. For example, in "Agbor Dancer," Clark reflects on how he as a writer has moved away from his native culture in his art, in contrast to the dancer. Folk beliefs dominate many of Clark's poems, including "Abiku" and "The Imprisonment of Obatala."

Stylistically, Clark's early verse reflects his study of English poetry, with Gerard Manley Hopkins being the most obvious influence; one of Clark's poems is entitled "Variations on Hopkins." Like Hopkins, Clark uses complicated metrical patterns and rich, sensuous language. Critics note that Clark begins to move away from this style in the later poems of *A Reed in the Tide*. They applaud this simpler style and contend that his most beautiful and effective lines are those filled with nature imagery. *Casualties: Poems 1966-1968* (1970) is almost journalistic in its concentration on the Nigerian-Biafran conflict, during which Clark supported the Nigerian government. Because of the detailed and intimate knowledge of the war that Clark imparts to the poems, the volume is heavily annotated. The role of the artist during war, an emotional issue of the civil war in which many writers actually fought, is also an underlying theme. Clark contends that an artist is valuable both as a healer and as a reporter of war.

Besides his poetry and drama, Clark has also written literary criticism. He has published *The Example of Shakespeare: Critical Essays on African Literature* (1970) and *The Philosophical Anarchism of William Godwin* (1977) and has contributed to such prestigious literary journals as *Black Orpheus* and *Présence Africaine*. He is a professor of English at Lagos University and a founding member of The Society of Nigerian Authors.

(See also *Contemporary Authors,* Vols. 65-68 and *Contemporary Authors New Revision Series,* Vol. 16.)

———————

ANTHONY ASTRACHAN

John Pepper Clark is in an unusual position for any playwright, much less a young playwright in a young country: his plays must be reviewed as literature by critics who have not seen them performed. This is the condition in which one often writes about Sophocles, Shakespeare, Racine. Fortunately, Clark can stand the comparison. At his weakest, he is more competent than many dramatists more widely known outside Africa; at his strongest, he is magnificent. His *Three Plays* can compete as equals on the stage of world literature without losing a cowrie's worth of their African qualities.

Lest the gods of tragedy deem the drawing of such praise *hubris,* let us ward off nemesis with a close, even a carping look. My doubts and disturbances, where they arise, do not detract from my opinion that Clark is a first-rate dramatist; great quality produces great expectations, and expectations should be examined.

Song of a Goat . . . and *The Masquerade* are a related pair of tragedies that make one look to the *Oedipus* plays for analogy. The language and feeling of both are so rich in action that the reader is compelled to stage them in the theatre of his interior vision, and not having seen them becomes less of a handicap. The third play, *The Raft,* is not strictly speaking a tragedy and is less brilliant than the others, but as we shall see, it has something in common with them.

Song of a Goat tells of the fisherman, Zifa, who has become impotent after the birth of his first child. He and his wife Ebiere ask a masseur for help, but the masseur can neither cure nor remove the curse and suggests that Zifa make over Ebiere to his brother, Tonye. All three reject the notion, but the idea has been planted, and eventually Tonye and Ebiere make love but without ceremony. When discovered, Tonye hangs himself before Zifa can kill him, and Zifa drowns himself. Clark lists neighbours as chorus in this tragedy, but to me half the function of chorus is exercised by Orukorere, Zifa's half-possessed aunt. (pp. 21-2)

The language evokes the pity and terror which are the prime aims of tragedy, and the dramatic construction has an aura of doom. . . . Orukorere evokes the terror of the offense that is still to come, in her half-crazed nightmare:

> I must find him, the leopard
> That will devour my goat, I must
> Find him. . . .
>
> (p. 22)

These and other lines are so rich in myth that again and again they bring to mind the Oedipus plays. And this speech of Orukorere's hints at a development by unveilling, a tragedy of revelation that is the keynote and the vehicle of action in *Oedipus Tyrannos.* Yet this is what in fact is missing in *Song of a Goat.* There is no development, no suspense, nothing like the change of Oedipus from saviour of Thebes to ruler to investigator to prosecutor to transgressor and victim. There is no change, growth or degeneration in Tonye and Ebiere to bring them to sin, nor are we sure their coming together is a sin. . . . If Clark means that adultery without ceremony is a sin, he does not make it clear.

And indeed the basis of the tragedy is not clear. Is Zifa's impotence after he has fathered one child punishment for an offense? An offense of Zifa's and one by his father are hinted, but never given enough emphasis to bear the burden of tragedy. Perhaps impotence is an offense in itself in a society where fertility is all; the sexual and agricultural imagery strengthens this suspicion. But there is no action on Zifa's part that brings him low. He even fails in his attempt to kill his offending brother—and it seems to me to ask too much of the reader or spectator to think that Tonye's suicide is caused by Zifa's pursuit of him. Tonye kills himself because he has offended his brother or dishonoured his family, not because—at least not only because—he is afraid of Zifa's wrath. Zifa's tragedy is a tragedy without cause. Tonye and Ebiere too, though they have done something, have had their act predicated from the beginning in Zifa's impotence so that they too seem victims of external forces.

The Masquerade is not only a sequel to *Song,* but a tradedy of the same kind, a tragedy without *hubris.* A young man, Tufa, has won the heart of Titi, a girl who has previously refused all suitors. There is some mystery about Tufa. In mid-play it is revealed that Tufa is the offspring of the accurst union of Tonye and Ebiere (who is now said to have died giving birth to him, though in *Song* she is merely said to have miscarried), and Diribi, Titi's father, drives him forth. When Titi follows him, Diribi pursues and kills her. Tufa goes off to kill himself, and Diribi, spiritually emasculated by his vengeance, is left to punishment in Forcados.

Pity and terror are again present in language and plot, the more so in the contrast between the lyrical love passage between Tufa and Titi in the first scene and the grim destruction of the last. There is more suspense, more development in the dramatic construction—the revelation does not come at the beginning and the characters react more strongly when it does come. Titi, for instance, rejects the idea that marrying Tufa necessarily means pollution. . . . But Titi also rejects the chance to elope with Tufa, which might mean eluding the curse, because she wants to finish her bridal pageant. By insisting on the fulfilment of one custom, she lays herself open to the nemesis of another. This strengthens the myth qualities of the play.

So, perhaps, does the curse pursuing the family of Zifa, but again the curse is not brought down by action on the part of the tragic hero-victim. Diribi implies that Tufa trangressed by concealing his birth—the masquerade of the title. But how can it be a masquerade when Tufa does not know the circumstances of his birth until they are revealed in the market place? The curse on the house of Laius is renewed by a fresh act in each generation, witting (Antigone's burial of her brother) or unwitting (Oedipus's slaying of Laius and marriage with Jocasta). Similarly with the curse on the house of Atreus. But the curse on the house of Zifa depends on no act. It is an external force whose victims are helpless against it. . . . (pp. 22-3)

The Raft, too, is a play of victims, though it is no tragedy. It is the story of four men on a timber raft drifting down the Niger. They get caught in a whirlpool and rig a sail so a storm will blow them out, but the raft breaks up and Oloto is carried off on the part with the sail. There three survivors drift until a steamboat comes up; Ogrope, trying to swim to the boat to ask a rescue, is beaten off by its crew and caught in its stern-wheel. Kengide and Ibobo drift on toward Burutu but become lost in the fog while trying to make a landfall by night. There is no why and wherefore—only the showing of four fairly well differentiated characters falling victim in different ways to a hostile environment. There is no apparent connection between a character and his particular misfortune.

The language is not so rich as in the other two plays; there are fewer metaphors, and the strengths lie in the evocation of life on the river and of Ijaw proverbs and customs rather than in the virtue of the words themselves. *The Raft* lacks the qualities of myth that make the other plays so intense.

One might say that the characters have too little action and the raft too much. When I read the play I thought it would be difficult to stage. . . . Clever staging cannot make great theatre out of a piece that has too little dramatic action. (pp. 23-4)

Still, producing all three plays at once on the interior stage, I am excited by the pity and terror of the two tragedies, by the vividness of their language and their myth-like qualities. I am more quietly pleased by the apparent accuracy of the dialogue and the unveiling of character in *The Raft.* I am also depressed by the fact that in all three plays, the protagonists are victims of punishment without cause, or punishment beyond their deserts, whether from society, gods or nature. . . .

I can imagine someone saying, "Well, this is the way of Ijaw tragedy, and you cannot expect it to be like Greek tragedy." I would not be satisfied. Greek tragedy set the canons for world tragedy, and if Clark is good enough to be mentioned in the same breath with Sophocles, he owes us and himself a better strophe. The novels of Achebe and the plays of Soyinka show that individuals can assert themselves against society and environment and gods, in the most traditional cultures of Africa. I wonder if the things I find missing in Clark's plays are entirely deliberate omissions, left out in accordance with the dictates of a philosophy, a world view or a culture. These plays are all quite short. If Clark had to write a three-hour play as rich and intense as these, he might be forced to a degree of plot development and character assertion that he has not yet achieved.

Despite these dissatisfactions, John Pepper Clark has already achieved a great deal. . . . Despite *and* because of Aristotle's canons of tragedy, Clark's plays are good plays, and if his best work is still to be written, Nigerian drama has a truly exciting future on which to raise the curtain. (p. 24)

> Anthony Astrachan, *"Like Goats to the Slaughter: Three Plays, by John Pepper Clark," in* Black Orpheus, *No. 16, October, 1964, pp. 21-4.*

MARTIN ESSLIN

I must, at the very outset, disclaim any special knowledge of the social and cultural background from which [Wole Soyinka's *Five Plays* and J.P. Clark's *Three Plays*] spring. That, indeed, I presume, must have been the reason I was to review them in these pages—to provide, for once, the corrective of a change of perspective, as it were; of focus, of view point to submit them, like organisms in a laboratory, to a survival test *in vacuo* by seeing how they appear to someone who in the course of his professional work has to read an endless succession of plays from totally different backgrounds, and who will therefore, almost automatically, apply to them the same general yardstick; who will judge them not as African but as plays pure and simple.

Having said this, I am bound to add that I think such a test hardly possible. It may be so with poetry, which deals with the basic human emotions on a purely individual plane: affection, loneliness, joy, sorrow and the skills with which they are expressed might be truly universal. But drama deals with the basic human emotions and predicaments in a social context, both in the interaction of several characters on the stage, and in the even more important interaction between the stage and the audience. The basic human emotions are still involved, but they are expressed through social conventions which may be totally different from one society to another. (p. 33)

This is not to say that universal, or almost universal, drama is wholly impossible. There may, after all, be social conventions that are shared by very large sections of humanity, if not by all mankind. The prohibition of incest, for example, is one of these; hence Sophocles' *King Oedipus* comes as near to universal drama as can be imagined. Its subject matter is universal; and this allows the supreme craftmanship of the play's construction and the greatness of its poetic expression to have an equal appeal to all epochs and all nationalities. In other words: in order to reach truly universal acceptance a play must fulfill both conditions—it must have a subject matter that is accessible to the maximum number of different societies; and it must be an example of supreme craftmanship in construction and language. (p. 34)

These considerations should make it easier to understand why the work even of major dramatists, past and present, is less easily acclimatised in different social environments than the work of poets or even novelists.

But, it might be argued, the work of the two playwrights we are here discussing, Wole Soyinka and J. P. Clark, should be largely exempt from these considerations; for, after all, *they* are writing in English. Far from being an advantage, in my opinion, this is a further handicap. Not that these two playwrights are in any way at a disadvantage in using the English language. On the contrary: both are real masters of all its nuances and are, indeed, very considerable artists in English. Here again the problem arises from the nature of drama itself. These plays are by Africans about Africans in an African social context. And they are, largely, about Africans who, in reality, speak their own African languages. It is here that the problem lies. We are here presented with African peasants, African fishermen, African labourers expressing themselves in impeccable English. Of course in reality they speak their own languages equally impeccably and the playwrights have merely *translated* what they would have said in those languages into the equivalent English. Precisely! Which is to say that these original plays labour under the universal handicap of all translated drama. And anyone who, as I have to almost daily, has to deal with the problems of plays in translation will know what an enormous handicap that represents! How should a French peasant in a play by, let us say, Pagnol, speak in English? If one translates him into an equivalent rustic dialect—from Provencal into, say, West country—the character will be completely changed. . . . But if you translate the French peasant dialect into standard English, the peasant will cease to be a peasant altogether. In other words: realism in translations of this kind is quite impossible. Realistic plays in non-Standard idioms are *untranslatable*. Only highly stylised *poetic drama* has a chance in translation. And that surely is the reason why J. P. Clark writes entirely in a highly stylised free verse. . . . The question arises however: would it not have been more effective and easier for J. P. Clark to deal with his subject matter in realistic, vernacular, prose terms? To me this certainly is true of his play **The Raft** which deals with the plight of four Nigerian lumbermen helplessly drifting to perdition downstream. This is tragedy, but it is realistic tragedy; much here depends on the differentiation between the townsman and the peasant, the old man and the younger generation. The free verse submerges rather than emphasises these differentiations, it also detracts from the purely technical side of the tragedy, the men's various attempts to salvage their craft. To deal with such a subject in verse would only be justified if the situation could be raised up to the level of an eternal poetic symbol. Thus the very fact that verse is used constitutes a programme of tremendous ambitiousness; and I don't think that this particular play can live up to such a high ambition. It is therefore literally crushed under the load of its poetic objective. As a realistic play in realistic prose it would have been most gripping. But for such prose in the mouths of African working men there is no equivalent in English. These are the horns of the dilemma on which a playwright like J. P. Clark can be impaled.

I am, in my own mind, not quite clear as to the reasons that prompt African playwrights to use English in preference to their own rich and highly poetic languages. Is it that they themselves are more at home in English? In that case there might be very strong arguments for their concentrating on a realistic treatment of the life of English-speaking Africans. . . . Or is it that African playwrights use English because they want a larger, more universal audience? . . . Or is it that, English being the language of the educated classes in Africa—or at least in ex-British Africa—and education spreading ever wider, English will become the lingua franca of educated Africans in those countries regardless of national borders? If that is so, the playwrights concerned are faced with the task of evolving a new, truly African brand of English which will eventually be able to embody the emotions, customs and daily life of the people concerned as efficiently and beautifully as West Indian English expresses the characters of the people who use it in daily life as well as in literature. I, personally, don't know which of these assumptions is true. I merely throw them out as possible starting points for debate in a situation which clearly is in need of some very thorough discussion of a number of basic issues.

Having listed the handicaps and dilemmas inherent in J. P. Clark's and Wole Soyinka's work, I should like to emphasise that I have done so merely to highlight the magnitude of their achievement. Despite the limitation that, for a European reader, the social context of their subject matter is often difficult to savour in its full emotional implications and impacts, and despite their use of English, the limitation that restricts them to stylised poetic, or at best semi-poetic, treatment of that subject matter, they have in a considerable number of cases succeeded in moving and uplifting a reader who is a hardened professional not easily moved or uplifted by plays he reads and (as a professional producer) re-enacts and re-produces in his mind's eye.

Of John Pepper Clark's **Three Plays** it was **The Masquerade** which came nearest to achieving this effect on me. . . . The central issue of the play, whether it is indeed a sacrilege for a young girl to get married to the son of a mother who died in childbirth after having committed adultery, is difficult to grasp for an outsider. But the atmosphere of relentless doom is so strong, the father, Diribi, acts with such utter conviction, that I for one, was carried along. Indeed the high degree of stylization which springs from the author's need to relate his tale in a timeless free verse tends to obliterate the local colour to such an extent that the European reader is constantly reminded of similar doom-laden wedding incidents among simple people in Spanish, French or German literature or, for that matter, in the equally stark and relentless world of Scottish Ballads. (pp. 34-6)

Clark's language is remarkable for what I can only describe as highly sophisticated simplicity. This is how one of the priests relates the heroine's last struggle with her father, who found her playing marbles, with her baby brother on her lap:

> . . . . With a bound
> She was running, kneeling, presenting the baby
> As a shield although clutching it back
> From harm and all this in one motion—
> Do forgive my running nose.

How subtle the description of the conflicting motives that drive the girl to use the baby as a shield and to protect it at the same time! And how brilliant the insertion of the physical effect of having to relate this terrible incident to the speaker. The translation of emotion into its physical expression is of the very essence of drama. How enviable, for any European, is the African playwright's ability to refer to any aspects of the physical side of the human condition without shame or self-consciousness. In a European play, the line about the running nose, would have been hopelessly sentimentalised into something like

> Forgive me, grief has overcome me quite . . .

or

> Tears, bitter tears prevent my going on. . . .

clichés that drown the immediacy of physical sensation in empty phrasemaking. (p. 36)

[In **Song of a Goat** and **The Masquerade** Clark has] attempted something in the nature of a cycle of plays on the working out of a family curse, no less than a Nigerian *Oresteia*. It is an ambitious undertaking. And it nearly succeeds. Not completely though. For, unaware of this intention at first reading it, I found **Song of a Goat** not quite convincing. The motivation of the tragedy, which is simply the husband's inability to engender a child, is far too simple and unoriginal to support the weight of full-scale tragedy across the generations. Moreover, the wife's seduction of the husband's younger brother, is also, at least for my admittedly quite differently conditioned feelings, far too clumsily straightforward. Instead of primeval tragedy (of which the second part of the diptych undoubtedly has the atmosphere) we are, in this crucial first part merely left with a rather predictable incident from the pages of any popular newspaper. But here too the stark timeless and almost placeless simplicity of the language invests the trivial event with the dignity of near-tragedy.

I have already pointed out why the very timelessness and placelessness of J. P. Clark's language seems to me to militate against his own intentions in the third play in the volume **The Raft**. The four men on the raft could only be individualised and fully motivated by being treated far more realistically. Left as stylized and generalized figures their actions seem unnecessarily arbitrary. But here too, a very ambitious objective—the raft as an image of human life and man's dependence on his fellowmen and sheer chance—is very boldly and imaginatively pursued. (p. 37)

I have, at the beginning of these remarks, expressed some fundamental considerations which, in my eyes, make the endeavour to create an English-language African drama, a difficult and problematical enterprise. But—*if* the social conditions exist which will make such an enterprise possible, if an African English-speaking culture is indeed emerging, then Wole Soyinka and J. P. Clark will have every right to be regarded as two of the pioneers who in the field of drama achieved the first decisive breakthrough. (p. 39)

Martin Esslin, "Two African Playwrights," in Black Orpheus, *No. 19, March, 1966, pp. 33-9.**

JOHN POVEY

J. P. Clark is among the best of contemporary African poets, for his work has both a technical and emotional range, more extensive than that measured by his contemporaries. If he lacks the rigorous technical precision and intellectual structure of Christopher Okigbo, he avoids the attendant coldness and detachment of such poetry as he exposes his intimate and unexpectedly tender vision.

Clark is a poet who exists between two worlds and two cultures. I realize nowadays how carefully one must hedge about such a hackneyed truism with equivocal qualifications but the critical commonplace must still be allowed a rough general truth. As an African poet he draws his verse out of his environment, which is the traditional and contemporary life of Nigeria. As an English language poet he derives his style from the multiple influences which fashion the diction and imagery of contemporary poetry. He uses the English, which he handles with such fluent skill, to seek a necessary synthesis, an English language poetry that is localized yet not parochial, simultaneously uniquely national, yet inherently universal. The titles of many of his best poems indicate his natural attachment to the African scene, its landscape and its heritage. . . . But for the outsider, Clark's international audience, the apparent mystery of these titles can be readily resolved from a footnote and the experience which Clark conveys is invariably a human one. Clark begins with the African scene, charges it with his style forged out of the discipline of English poetry and then leads the reader to his personal, even intimate, revelation. As Clark himself has explained in his introduction to *A Reed in the Tide* . . . : 'As our epigraph goes, a man has two hands. In other words, he comes of a mother, and he comes of a father, each of a different family with a separate set-up. As the offshoot of such a union, a man not only fuses elements of both sides but he also constitutes a new independent whole.' It is this 'new independent whole' that we must seek in Clark's work if he is to be other than merely derivative. His achievement of this synthesis is the mark of his quality. . . . (pp. 36-79)

From the English side the two most obvious influences which impinge upon Clark's style are the ubiquitous forms of T. S. Eliot and G. M. Hopkins. It is possible to find other echoes. . . . But these are passing moments. The more significant derivative elements are those which become absorbed within the truly personal style.

It would be possible to see the styles of Hopkins and Eliot as the extremes of twentieth century English poetic attitudes. Hopkins' lush, rhetorical excess, charged with sensuous force in both sound and vision, is almost the antithesis of Eliot's verse; dry, acid, with its occasional sharply flippant comedy standing amongst the powerfully repetitive logic of his spiritual diagnosis made in words as precise as cold. Hopkins as a poet celebrates his own passion; Eliot confronts his world with sardonic detachment.

The influence of Eliot is probably more common in Clark's work though it is less simply demonstrable in that its nature is less ostentatious and so more readily absorbed into inconspicuousness. It is most clearly seen in Clark's poetic plays. Eliot had demonstrated that a poetic rhythm could be devised for the stage from the effects of Anglo-Saxon verse. . . . The stressed lines of *Murder in the Cathedral* and *Family Reunion* are the initial steps in forging a new language for the theatre. The same technique so successfully employed, particularly in Clark's first two dramas *Song of a Goat* and *Masquerade,* derives from Eliot's stage experiments.

In Clark's poetry the influence is also present though less obvious. **"Ivbie"** owes much of its language and structure to Eliot's *Waste Land*. It is indicative of the recognition of a more individual style that when Clark reprints **"Ivbie"** in *A Reed in the Tide* he eliminates the most obviously derivative sections and republishes only the latter, most African and original sections. In this poem there are the same apparently haphazard sequences which mirror the muddled and dissonant range of experience. There is the characteristic emphasis derived from the studied repetition typical of the opening lines:

> It is not late now in the day
> Late late altogether late,
> Turning our doubled backs upon fate . . .

Common in Eliot too is the arbitrary but emphatic line division that becomes almost a mannerism in Clark's dramatic speeches.

> In the irresolution
> Of one unguarded moment
> Thereby hangs a tale . . .
>
> (pp. 38-9)

The influence of Hopkins is more obvious but perhaps this may partly be because he is less easily assimilated. His unique stressed, sprung-rhythm form is immediately recognizable. This obviousness may also derive from one's feeling that Hopkins' style is, in fact, much closer to Clark's own natural voice, for what may sometimes appear like Hopkins may rather be a fresh verbalizing of Clark's own inherently sensuous poetic vision. On several occasions Clark openly admits that he is playing with a style, contriving a pastiche, and yet the results are more poetically serious than that word would generally make us expect. **"Variations On Hopkins"** has as its opening couplet:

> Ama are you gall bitter pent
> Have paltry pittance spent.
>
> (pp. 39-40)

This tiresome academic exercise is not undertaken to suggest any plagiarism of course; it is to establish the significant presence of the influence of the English literary tradition upon the style of Clark, to set him—that 'one hand' of him—into the wider tradition. The language he is using has been shaped by a series of influential writers yet he must take this language, absorb and incorporate it with all its 'foreign' limitations into a style with which he seeks to describe the African experience that constitutes his 'other hand'.

It is here that an outsider such as myself has to admit limitations. The choice of English for this poetry is dangerous because it sets up the expectation of a too ready and total comprehension. How can an English critic evaluate this other African part? I can recognize that the setting and occasionally the attitudes and assumptions will seem 'foreign' to me. Clark is undoubtedly right when he poses the inevitable question. 'How can one speak of or detect vernacular rhythms, influences and sources present or imagined in works by African creative writers in English and French, unless one is versed in the vernacular of a particular author?' . . . This is unchallengable, yet it is also a counsel of perfection that would lead a reader to despair, for it would imply that the only valid criticism of Clark could come from someone fluent in Ijaw. . . . There is, for all the limitations in one's specific, and in this case African, knowledge an area where critical observation can be delimited. The starting point for this assertion is the fact of the choice of the English language which, no matter how modified by African usages remains a language available to the tools of English literary criticism if those devices are handled with modesty and good sense. Clark himself has observed of his language choice, '. . . language—which for me, a Nigerian, is English, a language that no longer is the copyright of any one people or nation'. . . . It is necessary to admit frankly that I am incapable of detailing, or even demonstrably perceiving, the effect of Ijaw epic oral poetry upon Clark's writing. This would be an important task and perhaps some Ijaw critic could indicate the association of this contemporary poetry with an older vernacular tradition. . . . Yet one can still point to another synthesis more obvious than the linguistic one and one much more apparent to the outside reader. This is the application of the English language style to the description of the African scene.

Clark records with joy and warmth the African landscape. Rarely is his writing simply descriptive. It is apparently so in **"Ibadan"** perhaps because its almost haiku-like brevity permits minimal speculation. The economy here better exposes the sudden visual impact which is the mark of the successful poetic image.

> Ibadan,
>   running splash of rust
> and gold . . . flung and scattered
> among seven hills like broken
> china in the sun.

Those who have flown from Lagos to Ibadan will recall that as the plane descends the corrugated iron roofs of the houses catch the sun suddenly and brightly and Pepper Clark's image precisely captures that scene. There are many points in this poem worthy of mention but enough to point out the subtle rhetoric achieved by the line division and the balanced colour antithesis of gold and rust, to see how competent a piece it is. In **"Girl Bathing"** the description and the response are more openly sensual. The scene is archetypal in literature. One recalls the moment when witnessing the girl wading thigh deep into the sea Stephen Dedalus makes the supreme dedication of his aesthetic soul. It is interesting that there is only one specifically 'African' word in this lyric—'cassava' in her basket. Yet there is in this poem such warm intensity that it appears that the dazzle of the scene becomes part of the vision of the woman and Clark's halting separation of phrases becomes a measure of his passing witness. 'And as she ducks / Under, with deft fingers plucks / Loose her hair . . .' When after the

description he rhetorically celebrates her beauty 'O girl . . . so ripe with joy', he records his own equal and generous response. **"Girl Bathing"** is a simple example of the way in which Clark moves from description, which is by its nature static, into intimate involvement. (pp. 40-1)

[The] significance of child memory is common in Clark's work and is the basis for his most tender and sensitive poems. His poem **"For Granny, From Hospital"**, is a childhood memory intimate in a way that seems entirely unsentimental. It describes one of those moments when a gesture, casual in itself, becomes a supreme illumination. He recalls the time 'fifteen floods ago', when suddenly his grandmother, unaccountably 'strained me to breast'. He speculates about this sudden moment of intimacy in lines that surge with a poetic intensity, the long insistent stress of the lines matching the emotion as he concludes:

> Or was it wonder at those footless stars
> Who in their long translucent fall
> Make shallow silten floors
> Beyond the pale of muddy waters
> Appear more plumbless than the skies?

His vision here, both delicate and impassioned, incorporates sky, water, land, in a harmony which creates an inevitable unposing sympathy between human beings and their landscape in a natural manner that has been unobtainable in Western literature since the Romantics.

A longer poem, **"Night Rain"**, which has often been quoted by Gerald Moore as one of the most effective of Clark's poems shows a similar type of memory—a memory suddenly illuminating across years, across the gulf imposed by adult experience. He begins when he is woken up from sleep by pounding rain and then, within the structure of the poem, there is a transition in time, a sudden shift from present to memory, and the poet sees himself back as a child, watching the rain dripping through the thatch of the African hut. As he describes his mother moving her bins of corn out of the way of the leaks he uses a sudden vivid and very African image. He talks of the water slopping across the floor 'like ants filing out of wood'. The image is effective in creating an exact picture of the encroaching water puddle and yet it does this through the use of an association that is only familiar to us through the illumination of this poem. The concluding lines, like several of Clark's better poems, assert the possibility of unity; of an emotional stasis. The dangerous owls and bats cannot fly so the rain brings a kind of safety. . . . Land, sea, the rain-filled sky are made harmonious in the poet's vision. (pp. 43-4)

Clark's new volume [*A Reed in the Tide*] included from his earlier Mbari collection largely those poems which were already best known through the anthologies. The greater part of the rest were taken from the poetic interludes in Clark's autobiographical record of this abortive scholarship year at Princeton, *America Their America*. This is a sharp, sometimes perceptive but generally ungenerous book. The disgruntled mood that must have very understandably possessed Clark as he came up against the patronizing restrictions of his Princeton scholarship is not restrained and invades the poetry of this period in his life. The poems are not improvements upon the sensitive involvement of, say, **"Agbor Dancer"** or **"Abiku"**. Yet this is not evidence of a diminution in Clark's obvious and genuine literary talent. America, even had it not been the source and occasion for so much personal irritation to Clark himself, is not kind to the visting poet. The impact of its staggering excess invites an attitudinizing which reflects only the inevitable shock at its vehement materialism, its violent self-assertion. The temptation to capture this surface grossness in sharply satirical lines is apparently irresistible, and causes a particular, false, kind of cleverness. The tone hollowness is exposed more obviously in the facile attack of the poem's lines than in the American social fabric so scathingly displayed. After all American urbanization is a more subtle and complex thing than the lines which record the first shock of the poet-tourist's arrival can indicate. Lines like these are just as slick and superficial as the gadget culture they seek so scathingly to denounce.

> A dime
> > in the slot,
> And anything
> > from coke to coffee
> Spews down your throat,
> > from crackers to candy . . .

The rhythm of these lines takes on that same cheap syncopation as the matching sound of the juke box which would in reality accompany this scene. (pp. 45-6)

Clark can show moments of concern for 'my brothers in the wild America', but it is a mood that would require involvement and that is not a noticeable reaction in this series of poems. The merciless impact of the American scene enforces a kind of shocked repulsion which allows only a posturing both in deed and in poetry.

Clark comes closer to his authentic voice in three poems he wrote while living down in New Jersey: **"Three Moods of Princeton"**. Here he was not merely the passing spectator he had been in New York, so perhaps time allowed a contemplation more contemplative than the tourist glimpses of **"Times Square"**. Yet it is interesting to see that even here the 'three moods' are the three moods of the landscape and not the moods of Clark and the moods are those rather obvious pathetic reactions to the decline of autumn and winter's death. The picture created is, in the final analysis, only descriptive while Clark's better poetry—as all valid verse—must move beyond the visual to establish the underlying intellectual and emotional awareness that engages the poet's awareness. Suggestively enough Clark deliberately describes the Princeton scenes in the images of Africa, linking the two continents with his careful metaphor.

> The elm trees, still
> Shaven bald and gaunt,
> In the brief buba
> They wear after snow
> Are a band of alufa
> Deployed down the neighbourhood.

The last poem is this collection entitled, **"The Leader"** begins:

> They have felled him to the ground
> Who announced home from abroad,

There is an ironic way in which the lines are true of Clark as he wrestled with America in his verse. Yet the observations one was able to insist upon in relation to his earlier poems are still critically valid. The poetic conception is still sharp, the gradually forged new style becomes more flexible, there is still an intimacy and awareness in his vision. At the moment the sad distress of Nigeria's turmoil must be dampening the ready hope that celebrated the African scene in the earlier poems, yet one has a specific confidence that the later work of Clark will carry out the achievement of his earlier verse into a more profound maturity, which will not only be a technical but also a perceptual advance. (pp. 46-7)

John Povey, "The Poetry of J. P. Clark: 'Two Hands a Man Has'," in African Literature Today, *No. 1, 1968, pp. 36-47.*

CHARLES R. LARSON

Ozidi seems to me the finest achievement of a somewhat erratic literary career. . . . Indeed, one wonders how Clark attained such excellence so early (his only previous drama hinting at such powers was *Song of a Goat,* which has its flaws). No matter: *Ozidi* is as fine a play as we are likely to receive from West Africa for a very long time.

In a prefatory note, Clark says that *Ozidi* "is based on the Ijaw (southern Niger delta region) saga of Ozidi, told in seven days to dance, music and mime. . . ." Drawing on his own Ijaw heritage, Clark has skillfully reconstructed this traditional tale of crime and vengeance. Ozidi is born after his father, Ozidi the elder, was murdered by his own tribesmen in an act of defiance against their king, the father's idiot brother. Grown to manhood, Ozidi avenges his father by killing the murderers, but he carries his desire for revenge too far and accidentally kills his own grandmother, the repository of the family traditions and power. He is punished by Engarando, the Smallpox King, and left on an island to die in tragic isolation from all humanity. Such is the skeletal plot of the drama, which I confess suggests little of its many strengths.

For his form, Clark has returned to the Greeks and the Elizabethans, weaving one of the longest dramas (which may be its only weakness) yet to come from modern Africa. . . . However, this is not intended as a criticism of Clark's achievement, for in its length and variety of scenes the story assumes the dimensions of an epic saga, as Clark himself has called it in his prefatory note. (pp. 55-6)

Ozidi, then, is epical both in its dimensions, which encompass family dynasties and Ijaw national myths, fusing the dead with the living, and in the basic theme of quest or revenge around which the dramatic structure turns. The scene in which Ozidi goes berserk in his rage for revenge and accidentally kills his grandmother is a powerful piece of drama. Clark has retained all of the pomp and spectacle of the Ijaw seven-day cycle, which Clark himself has said bears a strong relationship to Elizabethan dramatic form. . . . Blood and guts; grotesquery and violence; fighting, dancing, music, and chanting—all highly Africanized with songs in Clark's own vernacular language—abound in this electrifying saga of Ozidi the avenger. The printed dialogue cries out for actual performance, and Clark rarely allows the pace to slacken.

Ozidi the younger is a brilliant creation, especially in the painful earlier scenes in which he is being tutored by his witch-like grandmother, Oreame, in the arts of courage and bravery. . . . In many scenes Clark has used Ozidi's naiveté so simply, so beautifully, that he becomes the kind of character an actor would wait a lifetime to play. . . .

Oreame in many ways becomes as important a character as Ozidi, repository that she is of all the mystical values of the family's strength. Again and again, it is she who spurs Ozidi on to avenge the death of her son, Ozidi the elder. In her cold-bloodedness she is a kind of African Lady Macbeth. And she is so real a character that one is led to recall that African writers have created few important female characters in their literature. No longer can this be said to be true. Oreame becomes demoniacally possessed with Ozidi, striving as did Medea or

Clytemnestra to set aright the wrongs she believes have cursed the family household far too long. Together, these two characters unify the play and give ample proof of dramatic maturity of John Pepper Clark. (p. 56)

Charles R. Larson, "Nigerian Drama Comes of Age," in Africa Report, Vol. 13, No. 5, May, 1968, pp. 55-7.*

JOHN FERGUSON

[*Song of a Goat*] is a powerful play. The debt to Greek drama is large, but the result is in no sense imitative or derivative. The theme of the curse suggests the curses on the house of Laius or Atreus, and their working out in *Oedipus* or *Agamemnon*. Greek plays often begin or end with a divine figure, and the masseur here serves that purpose. . . . Orukorere plays the part of Cassandra in *Agamemnon,* though the comparison with Tiresias in *Oedipus* has also been drawn. The neighbours form the chorus, but Clark does not attempt to link his movements with song and dance sequences; there might be scope here. The movements are taut, and the characters economical in number and conception. Like Greek drama, the play is religious in tone. Some of the devices and approaches of the Greek playwrights are used with great skill; for example the concept of the Messenger's Speech is beautifully adapted to describe Zifa's self-immolation in the sea. Aristotle claimed that the most moving constituents of tragedy are *peripeteia* (when a course of action designed to serve one end lends to diametrically opposite results), and *anagnorisis* or recognition. It would be hard to find a better *peripeteia* than Ebiere's attempt to remove the curse of sterility through her relations with Tonye, an attempt which leads to the death of Zifa, Tonye, and (through miscarriage) the child she has conceived. There are two moments of recognition—perhaps even three. The first is Zifa's recognition of the truth about Ebiere and Tonye. The second is Zifa's recognition of the truth about himself. The third is perhaps Orukorere's recognition that the destruction of the goat had come not, as she had feared, through a leopard (from outside, openly), but through a snake (from inside, secretly). The numinous close reminds us of the end of Oedipus in *Oedipus at Colonus,* and the closing words "Come away, tomorrow is a heavier day" are Greek in mood.

The play is poetic drama, and must be judged as poetry as well as on its dramatic merits. The verse is free; the basic line is unusually short for so sustained a piece of writing. The effect is, so to speak, to bring the play nearer to lyric and further from epic. This has its dangers. On the one hand there is the danger of overwriting, and Clark has not altogether avoided this. Lines like

> Or sports him no spoors?

are hard to stomach even from Orukorere, and the animal symbolism seems overpainted—goat and leopard and snake, fish and bird and chick. . . . On the other hand the inevitably prosaic lines like. . . .

> And I'm sure my son is no goat.

become more bathetic than they need. There is by compensation much of great beauty. (pp. 14-15)

I have stressed the comparison with Greek tragedy; it is a tribute to the work that the comparison can be made. But it is not Greek tragedy; it can stand on its own two feet as Ijaw tragedy.

Song of a Goat is in many ways the most remarkable play to emerge from Nigeria. Clark's other plays need not delay us so long. *The Masquerade* is a companion piece to *Song of a Goat;* it is a not unworthy companion, but inevitably its impact is less powerful. Here the curse has passed to a new generation. (pp. 15-16)

The Masquerade has both qualities and defects from which *Song of a Goat* is free. The verse-writing is more certain but less memorable; there is less climax and less anticlimax. The finest writing is in the love-talk of the first act, which recalls some of Christopher Fry's more mellifluous passages. Its lightness contrasts well with the sombre gravity of the final scene. The handling of plot is untidier, less taut, less controlled, though one critic has argued that there is more suspense and more development in the dramatic construction. But the play's great merit is the character of Titi's father Diribi (and, though less strikingly, of her mother Umuko). The characters of *Song of a Goat* are elements in a plot, but Diribi lives. If *Song of a Goat* was Clark's *Oedipus*, *The Masquerade* is his *Antigone*, and it turns out to be the tragedy of Creon-Diribi. The ending is majestic. . . .

The third play *The Raft* is very different. Four lumbermen, Olotu, Kengide, Ogro and Ibobo, are taking a raft down the Niger. The raft drifts from its moorings, out of control. The four are cut off from all except one another, and left to face hunger and danger together. (p. 16)

In many ways this is a very good play, and it is excellent to see Clark striking out in a fresh vein. This is a fresh variation of the theme of a limited number of people shut up together; Fry's *A Sleep of Prisoners* comes to mind. Clark's originality lies in conceiving a setting in which he can combine the element of restriction, confinement and limit with the element of unlimited openness. This means that he can work together the character-conflicts of the limited situation with the ageless theme of the quest, in this case for landfall, and the end of the play, with Ibobo and Kengide calling in the fog, and answered by steamer sirens and shouts of fear, is masterly.

Not that there is nothing to criticize. The language is good, easier and firmer, less overdrawn. Similes and metaphors are fewer and less fantastic; the comparison of the untravelled Kengide to a wall-gecko remains in the mind. The play is marked for its judiciously direct descriptive writing. . . . But though the language is good, the themes are not always relevant, and the long conversations between Ibobo and Kengide as they coast down to Burutu seems used by the author to air his views on a miscellany of subjects, including women, homosexuality, politics, economics, colonialism and many other incidentals. They are well presented—there is a delightful description of three types of women, the log, the placid stream and the tossing wave—but the author's personality obtrudes upon his characters. Furthermore, the closed-room theme demands a sharp differentiation of character. (Sartre's *Huis Clos* is a good example.) Clark is more interested in words and ideas than people, and the differences, though real, need exaggeration for effective drama. Finally the play is exceedingly difficult to produce. The first episode is and must be largely in darkness, and in general, by definition of the situation, too little happens, and the more dramatic moments are not easy to stage convincingly. This is clear in reading; it was clearer still in performance. (pp. 17-18)

John Ferguson, "Nigerian Drama in English," in Modern Drama, Vol. XI, No. 1, May, 1968, pp. 10-26.*

PAUL THEROUX

[*The essay from which this excerpt is taken originally appeared in* Black Orpheus.]

Affected language and precious syntax work to John Clark's advantage in his plays. The tense atmosphere of *Song of a Goat* and *The Raft* profits by the convolutions of language, lends a brittle quality to the movement. But language can be an irritant and, where the whole edifice of a play stands up because of the brittleness, the tiny structure of a poem is not enough to support it. (pp. 120-21)

As long as poets continue to write good poems using traditional forms it is foolish to say that the metrical rhyming poems is out-moded. One of the great *villanelles* of all time was written by Dylan Thomas ('Do not go Gentle into that Good Night') and some of Robert Frost's best poems are fractured sonnets. Clark cannot be criticised for using the forms—he must be criticised for misusing the forms or for not meeting the demands of the forms he appears to be attempting.

T.S. Eliot, writing on Pound, says, 'In *Ripostes* and in *Lustra* there are many short poems of a slighter build . . . equally moving, but in which the "feeling" or "mood" is more interesting than the writing. (In the perfect poem both are equally interesting as one thing and not as two.)' It is the writing that intrudes in the early poems of Clark. If the writing does not openly irritate, it distracts. (p. 121)

Clark's best poems either crush us or lift us up with simple words, as in **"Streamside Exchange"**:

Child: River bird, river bird,
         Sitting all day along
         On hook over grass,
         River bird, river bird,
         Sing to me a song
         Of all that pass
         And say,
         Will mother come back today?

Bird: You cannot know
         And should not bother;
         Tide and market come and go
         And so has your mother.

The poem asks a simple question with simple words; the reply is a crushing statement of the loneliness that men must bear. Also the rhyme is not intrusive. It is a quiet poem but leaves us with a mood that cannot be shaken off.

Despite the many exclamation marks that Clark uses in his poems, he still seems to be a writer of extremely quiet poems. The effects are heightened by the simplicity and quietness and, as in **"Streamside Exchange"**, there is often great intensity in the writing. Usually, Clark is content to set a scene, make a picture or describe a drama without acting in it or having a 'dramatic movement'. It is a brilliant stroke to have the 'bird' end the poem above; the child may or may not be silent, but his further questions must be our own. The dramatic action takes place after the poem has ended; the reader is responsible for the drama. In setting the scene well Clark has given us all the ingredients of the drama without telling us what we should think, how we should act our part. It must be difficult for a writer of dramas to leave off so early; it may also be the reason for his failure in other poems where, by trying to create dramatic action, he loses control and founders in his own language. (pp. 122-23)

In the often-anthologised **"Ibadan"** the scene is set delicately:

Ibadan,
      running splash of rust
and gold—flung and scattered
among seven hills like broken
china in the sun.

Poets compare cities to women (Paris, the raped whore; New York, the long-legged neon blonde, and so forth). Clark's poem on Ibadan presents an image that is both vivid and new. Ibadan flashes before us. I have never seen Ibadan, but when I read this poem a city materialised before me, a city of dazzling light, of both randomness and order. The sun stands out in the poem and dominates as it must in that city. The poem is interesting as one distinct visual experience, the mood and the writing fused.

I think John Clark's best poem is **"Night Rain"**. There is a natural rhythm in **"Night Rain"** which the subject demands. . . . Not only does the subject, rain, demand rhythm, it also gets it in the best possible way. There is no metrical pattern in **"Night Rain"**, yet there is metre; there is no regular rhythm, yet there is the rhythm of rain, irregular as the rain's rhythms are. . . . The images of the sleeper conscious of the rain and waiting, of the rain joining with the sea-water to rise and purify are deftly handled. . . . Read in its entirety this poem sets a mood that lulls with a peacefulness and acceptance that is very rarely matched in modern poems. The rain that soothes also makes people move, that washes clean also washes things away. It is a prayerful poem but cannot be called a strictly religious poem; it is peaceful but not monotonous. It is difficult to place this poem in correct thematic relation to Clark's other poems. It can be said, however, that the most successful poems in *Poems 1962* are the ones in which the narrator is unmoving, observing the patterns that exist in nature and in man's nature. Clark writes on many themes, not all of them consistent with the efforts in his best poems. Fulani cattle bother him because they appear inscrutable; but in describing the exterior of the cattle he has given us enough information to lead us to the place where conjecture must begin.

There is a thin line between Clark's good poems and his bad ones. The poor poems are obscured by the use of pyrotechnic and imprecise language. The good poems are illuminated by simple and direct language. Ambiguity exists in both kinds, although it is hard to take in the poor poems. If Clark has a 'general theme' it has escaped me. This is not a weakness in Clark. It shows him to be a far more curious and hungry individual than one might suppose. There is something to be said for the poet giving in to every impulse and indulgence in his poems, but it must be admitted that neither randomness alone nor symmetry alone makes art out of the substance of the poet's impulse. (pp. 123-25)

Paul Theroux, "Six Poets: Dennis Brutus, Lenrie Peters, Okogbule Nwanodi, George Awoonor-Williams, John Pepper Clark, Christopher Okigbo," in Introduction to African Literature: An Anthology of Critical Writing from "Black Orpheus," *edited by Ulli Beier, Northwestern University Press, 1970, pp. 110-31.**

ADRIAN A. ROSCOE

Colonialism, with its mischievous effects on the psyche of the educated African, tended to generate writing that looked away from the continent towards the home of the ruling power. . . .

Local description was rare, couched in the diction of an alien tradition, and unevocative of an authentic sense of place and time. In the French states negritude in the thirties directed the artist's attention to his own people and traditions; but the verse which emerged was often stylistically polemical rather than concretely descriptive of the landscape. One cannot scream loud and long at the white world and still spare much effort for the private contemplation of one's own environment. Hence, there was a need in West Africa ... to *celebrate anew* a landscape which poets had largely forgotten. The situation is now being remedied. From the pens of the anglophone poets a more personal style of poetry is emerging, which, free of slogans and flag-waving, directs our attention towards the details of physical Africa and the natural phenomena that inform it. Indeed, in J. P. Clark's work it seems that this, rather than an Africanised style of language, is his particular answer to the problem of authenticity. Take, for example, his slight poem "**Streamside Exchange**", a simple dialogue, in a rural African setting, between a child and a bird ... or again, his poem "**Night Rain**".... The poems are examples of young talent soaring on trembling pinions. Clark has no settled style yet, and the second piece especially has a whiff of undergraduate days about it, giving an impression of good material inadequately controlled and organised. More to our purpose, however, is the direction in which the poet's imagination is turned. The setting of the first poem, undoubtedly taken from Clark's own Ijawland in the Niger Delta; the carefully pictured details of the second—the rain, the sleep mats, the wooden bowls and earthenware, diligent mother moving items about the floor, the owl and bat wet and forlorn on the iroko tree—these all indicate the poet's sensual and imaginative harmony with the rural life of Africa. But this in itself is not so significant as the more crucial fact that the poet's attention *is in fact* turned towards that life, a life which he has shared and is prepared to regard as worthy of his art. Despite the poet's university education there are no signs of cultural neurosis here. Clark is not a poet *déraciné*, and when he chooses a subject for his verse he evidently does not feel the pull of an alien landscape at his back.... His work stands, too, at the opposite pole from the rant of negritude's more extreme outbursts.... Clark evidently feels no compulsion to write in this vein. As certain poems show, he is sensitive to Africa's pains, but by and large he enjoys inner peace and contentment, enjoys celebrating the harmony which he feels between himself and his African environment.

Clark's engagement with the local scene stems directly from his professed interests. He sees himself as a private poet anxious to communicate with an audience. Hence his concern for 'nature and actuality', which, he believes, 'provides the personal link between each poet and his audience'. His poetic rendering of familiar aspects of the African scene—"**Fulani Cattle**", "**Agbor Dancer**", "**Tide Wash**", "**For Granny**" and the "**Water Maid**" are examples additional to those already quoted—are, in his words, 'attempts to realise natural concrete subjects ... for the reader in a personal memorable way ... in the unconscious hope of adding some fresh dimension to life'. Let us, finally, examine Clark's short poem "**The Year's First Rain**", a piece mimetic of the first mighty encounter between parched Earth and the opening storm of the rainy season and aptly rendered as a cosmic sexual union.... This is a well-organised piece, and the gradual filling out of the lines in mimesis of the storm's development is skilfully done. More important for our discussion, however, the poem aptly illustrates how an African poet as 'liberated' as Clark can work with a local theme and yet do so in a style which echoes the metropolitan tradition. We have noticed Osadebay's reliance

on British poetic diction and heard Okara imitating the voice of Dylan Thomas. The pull of the British tradition remains strong, for Clark here is obviously feeling the influence of Hopkins, a poet whose deliberately rude handling of language for special effect might be expected to appeal to a young free spirit like Clark. (pp. 36-9)

Clark's artistic directions seem to be settled—he is eager to celebrate the details of the African landscape; but he still acknowledges European masters and enjoys imitating them. Unlike Okara, he does not seem concerned about developing a distinctly African poetic idiom. (p. 39)

• • • • •

[*Song of a Goat*] does not succeed, or rather it partially succeeds as poetry but not as drama. There might be various reasons for this; but one suspects that the basic truth of the matter is simply that Clark, in 1961, was a young writer with a fair command of verse but no sense of theatre: his skill in verse he had cultivated over a number of years, but in the dramatic crafts he had served no apprenticeship. Thus he was able to bring to the play's theme, setting, and structure, all the critical taste of the Honours School of English, but none of the life-giving sense of real theatre.

Perhaps, too, Greek tragedy is deceptively simple. Its thin contours require a heavy clothing of pity and terror for it to succeed artistically; there is, after all, little else to hold the imagination in a form where richness of colour and variety of scene and *personae* are all severely pruned. *Song of a Goat* possesses this same thinness of texture, without the complementary charge of pity and terror—except that Clark finally stumbles across a certain amount of both qualities when Zifa and Tonye commit suicide. But pity for those who suffer unnecessary death is a universal emotion which arises spontaneously. Here it is not felt to rise from an artistically prepared situation within the play, for we have not really felt much sympathy with any of the three protagonists before they are destroyed at the denouement. The chorus, too, is unsatisfactory; it is simply a crowd of busybodies, who help neither to carry the play's values—whatever these might be—nor to focus attention on the hero's decline; and the whole movement of the action fails to demonstrate that inexorability of fate, that relentless turning of the slowly grinding mills of god that so fascinates in Greek tragedy.

The play's merits lie rather in its poetic qualities, though even these are an indication of why the play as a whole fails; for they are those qualities that evoke a sense of place and atmosphere rather than the movements of a soul; qualities which describe an outer, rather than an inner, landscape. This is hardly surprising when we recall Clark's professed concern for 'nature and actuality' and his 'attempts to realize natural concrete subjects ... in a personal memorable way'. It is significant, then, that *Song of a Goat* is strong in descriptive pieces. Its landscape is at once recognisably different from the Yorubaland scenes of Ladipo, Ijimere, or Tutuola. The sense of darkness that goes with high equatorial forest gives way to the more open ground found among the creeks of the Niger Delta, where the Ijaw live. (p. 201)

The view of the sands, with its boats and baskets scattered about, the view of the ancestral hall blown down in the market place—these have the making of fine insets, though they stand amidst verse whose halting movement suggests a need for more discipline and control; verse which suffers from obvious infelicities while displaying, at times, signs of developing power.

There are some fine passages, too, near the beginning of the play, where a conversation about the impotency problem is carried on in a continuously oblique vein between Zifa and the Masseur. Significantly, the verse here gains its vitality from basing itself on typical African modes of expression. The oblique style is itself a common feature of Ijaw conversation about delicate subjects; also the Masseur describes Ebiere's impatience with Zifa's impotence in imagery culled directly from the African environment—the storehouse which Ladipo and Ijimere drew on so successfully. . . . (pp. 202-03)

And yet, unfortunately, Clark's poetic talent works erratically. Alongside lines as mature as the following . . . :

> Do not, my people, venture overmuch
> Else in unravelling the knot, you
> Entangle yourselves. It is enough
> You know now that each day we live
> Hints at why we cried out at birth.

we find lines of astonishing ineptness, which introduce either absurd notions or grave disruptions of tone: 'Say', cries Oru-korere, 'has / Lightning struck him down that walked / Into the storm, his head covered with basin?' (pp. 203-04)

The Masquerade is evidently meant to share an organic link with *Song of a Goat.* . . . Tufa is the son of Tonye, who 'stole' the wife of Zifa, his brother. The connection, however, is of little importance, since it is not woven artistically into the fabric of the play. Despite this deliberate suggestion of continuity (perhaps Clark in these first three plays has the idea of a trilogy in mind), the events of *The Masquerade* do not grow naturally out of those in *Song of a Goat*. The reference to Tufa's origins is important in so far as it gives him a bad family background. This in turn sets up one of the themes of the play (albeit a theme not pursued very far), which is the conflict between traditional and modern attitudes, especially over a subject like marriage. Diribi is a traditionalist; Titi his daugher a modernist. . . . But, curiously enough, this information about Tufa—that he had 'real' parents and a 'real' blot on his pedigree—while conveniently getting some dramatic conflict started, virtually destroys what seems to be offered as a basic idea in the play, namely *that Tufa has magical origins*, that he is not, in fact, a real human at all. The dramatist cannot have it both ways; he tries, but fails.

The faults of *Song of a Goat* are repeated in this second play. Essentially, *The Masquerade* is not very dramatic, though, again, it contains some good descriptive verse. The embryo of good drama is here, but it is doomed to a still-birth. The mystery surrounding Tufa might have been exploited much more skilfully. It is hinted at, even in the opening scene when the villagers see an upturned moon and prophesy disaster 'down the whole delta'. With the ground thus prepared, and despite the spoiling effects of Diribi's revelation about Tufa, we are built up, in a rather flat kind of way, for a revelation of earth-shaking proportions. But we are disappointed. The denouement leaves us coldly unimpressed, a little angry at the villagers' cruel treatment of a stranger, but not really sympathetic to the stranger himself. If the mystery surrounding Tufa is inadequately exploited, so, too, is the fundamental conflict between Titi and the traditionalists.

With such chances missed, the play lacks life. That vigorous interplay of opposing forces which generates good drama is missing. Neither is there a sufficient charge of mystery to excite the audience into an active, reaching-out curiosity about the nature of the main *persona*. The play fails to engage us closely;

it seldom shocks and rarely stirs our sympathy. The hero is dull; the heroine, for all her modernism, is little better; the minor figures are scarcely worthy of mention. Perhaps in plays as short as this, in-depth portraits are hard to do; but Clark succeeds much better in *The Raft*, where he is faced with precisely the same restrictions.

The dialogue, on the whole, is modelled in shallow relief. There is little variety in tone and vocabulary firmly to distinguish one speaker from another. Doubtless Clark would argue that all his Delta people share the same stock of phrases and images; that they are, in a sense, linguistically homogeneous. But to succeed at this shallow modelling, where a slight shift of tone, a slight change in the turn of a familiar phrase, and a slight disordering of a standard sentence pattern, can give the lie to character, change the meaning of a whole situation, or subtly force the reader to modify an established view—to succeed in this exercise demands the prodigious skill of a Pope, a Racine, or a Jane Austen.

The Masquerade is designed around a tragic diagram, and one notes again Clark's concern for something close to classical unities: there is a concentration of scene; the *personae* are few; it is a *Drama of one night*. What is more important, however, is that the play advances the local-rootedness of Clark's work. The plot, for example, is based on a legend widely known along the West Coast of Africa. It centres on the magical suitor who suddenly appears in the market-place and lures away a local maiden—usually a girl who has defied convention in some way and delayed marriage. Perhaps she has refused the man who is her father's choice; perhaps, like Titi, she is a modernist who has her own strong views about love and marriage. The suitor in the legend turns out to be made up of false parts; his beauty is all spurious. He is a sort of *ignis fatuus*, a will-o'-the-wisp who leads girls astray as a punishment for their independence, for their rebellion against accepted social convention. (pp. 204-06)

The Ijaw setting is, once more, beautifully evoked. The play is decorated with vivid images of the Delta creeks, of boats, tides, fishing, and the sea—all that fills the lives of the Ijaw people. When Clark's figures speak, they express themselves naturally in images and allusions that arise from their background. . . . With its images of tide, stream, and blood, the verse is attractive in its home-rootedness; it successfully calls up the environment whence it springs. And yet, isn't there a vague sense of contrivance about it? Doesn't it all seem too self-conscious? It is the dramatic poet's task, having decided on his idiom, to make the verse pour from these people in a wholly natural, free-flowing way. Yet it does not. The metaphors seem to have been forced into the verse pattern with spanner and wrench. One can almost hear Clark saying: 'now Diribi has to speak, let's be sure he's given all the right images and allusions'.

More successful are the insets we get from time to time, where a straightforward description of a reported scene is offered—a description that does not involve the unburdening of the speaker's heart and mind; one that could be taken out of the tapestry of the play and offered as a separate poem, complete in itself. The first meeting between Titi and Tufa is a case in point. It comes as a picture provided by a witness. . . . The description is richly vivid and the scene was obviously created when the poet's imagination was on the boil. It is an example of the external painting that Clark does so well.

But the inherent faults of *The Masquerade* as drama are not fully compensated by an achievement of this sort. Surface glitter in dramatic verse can never make up for the absence of life below or within. It is not until Clark's third play, *The Raft,* that this kind of inner life is arrived at.

Take a log raft, place four men aboard, free it from its moorings, and float it off at night down the labyrinthine creeks of the Niger, and you have the formula for what is by far Clark's most successful piece of dramatic writing. (pp. 206-08)

[Clark's choice of setting in *The Raft*] is a masterly one, for this basic situation contains both naked simplicity and endless complexity. This commonplace situation vibrates with a meaning that reaches far and wide, into problems that are individual, national, continental, and humanly universal. Even the separate items in the formula can clearly have a dual significance. The rivers and creeks *are* the rivers and creeks of this part of Nigeria. The tides encountered on them *are* the real tides that flow in from the Atlantic, bringing ships and sometimes fog. Yet the reader feels there is more here; and this is precisely what Clark wants him to feel so that the underlying ideas of the play can be appreciated. Hence one senses that the waters of life and the river of life are being alluded to; and, having reached this far, the imagination soon begins to conjure other meanings—the idea of water as a spiritual cleansing agent, for instance, its use in ritual, and so on; meanings which arise naturally in an African context. Indeed, the practice of expelling evil by water-borne means is still known in this area of Nigeria. Then there is the powerful suggestiveness of the tides, with their ebbing hints of death and their flowing associations with birth, new growth, and optimism. The raft is a real workaday raft; but also, on a political level, the ship of state, and, for the individual, the vessel of life of which each of us is skipper. The situation, then, is fraught with suggestiveness, and Clark exploits it to the utmost. Loading his play with as much meaning as it can bear, without its sinking into sheer confusion, he can make subtle allusion to the human condition in all its aspects, be they private, national, racial, or universal. Although the focus is essentially on Nigeria's own situation, the debates set going in the play effortlessly assume a wider significance.

The play, then, invites, and withstands, close scrutiny. It is a play that puzzles, that leaves questions unanswered. It has a moral ambiguity which is at once honest and consciously modern. The fearful questions of the four characters—'Who are we?' 'Where are we from?' 'Where are we going?'—have echoes all round the modern world. The play does not pretend to provide answers.

The predicament of the four men on the raft—Oluto, Kengide, Ogro, and Ibobo—drifting helplessly in the night, is meant to be taken as the predicament of the Nigerian nation as a whole as it looks for directions, searches for a teleology while floating about in the dangerous waters of the modern world. The raft is adrift, its moorings gone. Who or what cut it loose? Will anyone tell the four men where they are? Can anyone tell them where they are going? Without stars or moon to guide them (where Clark presumably means the certainties of the old order), they are lost.... When Ogro says he can see trees on the bank drifting past, Kengide insists, rather obviously, but with a special charge of meaning, 'Don't be an idiot; it's we / Who are doing the drifting.' The symbolic nature of their predicament is now increasingly pressed home. (pp. 208-09)

When a bowl is placed in the water to determine the direction of the tide, it is found to be spinning. The raft, it seems, is in the arms of Osikoboro, a great whirlpool said to lie at the confluence of all the creeks. Again, this situation is, on one level, real enough, and yet symbolic too; for the whirlpool is often appealed to as an image for West Africa's predicament in the modern world. (p. 210)

However, the whirlpool hazard is safely negotiated, and now the stagnation of a becalmed situation becomes the subject of complaint.... Soon, in an obvious and rather prophetic reference to the divisive forces at work in the ship of state, the raft breaks in half after a sail has been hoisted to help move the vessel out of its becalmed state. Olotu is now on one section of the craft and his three companions on the other. Ogro wants to swim to Olotu and save him; but Kengide discourages him and Olotu is swept out of sight to his doom. The scene ends with a restatement of their basic plight: 'We are all adrift / And lost, Ogrope, we are all adrift and lost.'

The raft floats helplessly on, until a big steamer passes. Ogro confidently swims to it for help; but he is beaten back into the water and drowns. Clearly this is a foreign vessel, a representation of the outside world, and the West in particular. The point of the incident is clear. Ogro, his friends, and their broken raft are not wanted by the crew of the passing ship; they receive no help in their calamitous situation. They are alone. They are powerless. Their situation, to use a happy phrase of Clark's that occurs here and as the title of his book of verse, is that of 'a reed in the tide', moving at the mercy of forces beyond its control. There seems to be no hope. Even when, near the end of the play, the raft approaches Burutu, its destination, a brief eruption of hope is smothered by a blanket of fog. The two survivors can see nothing; they are drifting helplessly past Burutu towards the open sea. (pp. 210-11)

There is something approaching great art about the close of this play: two men, holding hands, shouting hopelessly in the night. They have no control over their situation; they drift on to an unknown fate.... A fact stressed at the close is the aloneness of Ibobo and Kengide now, an aloneness which stands outs starkly as a modern feature against a traditional African background of family and tribal togetherness. The modern predicament is heavily underscored by this final emphasis. (p. 211)

The play, then, concentrates on a central predicament that is richly allusive. In addition, however, Clark achieves a more convincing characterisation here than he did in his first two plays. His figures now have a life of their own; they are more strongly individualised and their differing attitudes make for dramatic colour and conflict. Kengide is a man who knows the modern world and its ways—or thinks he does. He wears his moral outlook (a mixture of materialism, selfishness, and tough realism) like armour to protect him from the blows of a cruel world. (p. 212)

Ibobo is more a traditional man, rather ignorant of the modern world. He holds a traditional view of marriage, is naïve in his attitude to officialdom, too ready to believe he will be treated with justice and honesty. He knows nothing of such strange practices as homosexuality, respects the dead, and chides Kengide for not doing so. Unlike Kengide, he is not soured by life, but retains a delightful innocence of mind and soul. Kengide calls him 'the boy from the bush full of taboos'; but he wins our respect more readily than his companion, who, for all his wordly wisdom, has a good deal of cowardice and selfishness in him. When the two men are left alone at the close, however, it looks as though we are meant to feel that neither of them—neither Kengide the modernist nor Ibobo the traditionalist—has the answer to the nation's problem as it drifts helplessly on the reef-strewn waters of the modern world. In the final clinging together, it is Kengide who is the more afraid of being left alone, of being deserted by tradition. But there is no neat resolution to the play because there can be no neat resolution to the situation the author is exploring.

Song of a Goat was published in 1961. When we turn to *Ozidi,* published in 1966, we can detect a critical change that has taken place since Clark's career began. This is no Graeco-African play, but a work that is solidly African. A prefatory note informs us that 'the play is based on the Ijaw saga of Ozidi, told in seven days to dance, music and mime', and this at once suggests that [if], in *Song of a Goat,* Clark was uncertain of the direction in which his art should move, he has now, five years later, made up his mind. He has decided that to write successful neo-African drama, his work must sink a taproot into his own indigenous culture; *Ozidi* represents a deliberate and wholesale 'return to roots'. We should notice also that his material is drawn directly from one of Africa's ancient, and yet still flourishing, species of pre-drama; for *Ozidi,* in its oral form, as Clark's note announces, is an elaborate specimen of the 'drama-suported narrative'. . . . (pp. 212-13)

The differences between *Song of a Goat* and *Ozidi* are numerous and basic. The first was spare in outline, displaying all the economy necessary for a successful imitation of classical practice. . . . *Ozidi* is *not* in the classical tradition. . . . This is crowded drama, teeming alike with characters, scenes, and events. It calls for an orchestra consisting of master drummer, side drums and a horn blower; and, in the manner of Yoruba theatre, almost every scene is alive with singing and dancing. There is, too, a great deal of processing, solemn ritual, magic rites, mime, and horrific stage spectacle in an enormous amalgam of those dramatic phenomena that Africa has kept alive for centuries. If the characters in *Song of a Goat* are seen at one crucial moment in their lives, the central figures of *Ozidi* grow from youth to old age before our eyes: the hero indeed is not born until after the play has begun and, thereafter, we watch him develop from childhood to adolescence and manhood, and then fall to his doom. A static, marble-cold Greek quality is replaced by a frantic sweep of hot gory action, epic in its proportions and African in its abundance. (pp. 213-14)

[*Ozidi*'s] opening scene, with its invoking of the sea spirits, its offering of libation, and its procession to the stream; with its use of a narrator-cum-leading actor, and its involvement of the audience in the ceremonies, not only partakes of indigenous practice, but, by this very fact, gains that exciting tingle and anticipation of live theatre which Clark's first two plays so patently lacked. It is as though this play had been written with the aim of a live village performance in mind, and *Song of a Goat* for perusal as a text in the library. The dancing, ritual, and singing set a pattern which is continued throughout the play. Indeed, the work ends with a dance led by the narrator, who, though still dressed as Ozidi, recalls his initial function by now casting away the dramatic illusion. . . .

The play describes the murder of the first Ozidi, the birth and rise of his son as an avenger, and the son's decline into a condition of loneliness and humiliation. It exhibits, therefore, the simple rise and fall of the tragic diagram. Richer dramatically than *Song of a Goat*, *Ozidi* also represents a successful poetic endeavour, even if one still has a sense of perusing fine material that is often insufficiently controlled and organised. The play's proximity to indigenous modes is stylistic as well as thematic; hence it is not surprising to find that the imagery once more rises consistently out of the natural environment of

Clark's people. 'The rains / May soak my skin', blubbers the demented Temugedege, pushed rapidly from the throne of Orua, 'but I am not salt, and / In the sun I like to bask as a crocodile / On the river bank.' (p. 216)

Such usage is well enough for it gives the play an African flavour. But Clark has more artistic considerations in mind. Not only must his imagery be drawn from the Ijaw locale; it must also be so woven into the texture of the play as to poetically carry its themes and reflect its movement. Hence we find rain, river, tide, and flood—those basic elements of the Ijaw scene—providing an artistically appropriate background to a play dealing with the rise and fall of a young hero and his enemies. For instance, the villains of Orua, those who savagely slew the first Ozidi and set their hearts on slaying the second, forever use hunting imagery, which both reflects their daily lives and vivifies their role in the play. (p. 217)

The rise of the second Ozidi, and his return to Orua, the scene of his father's slaughter, are frequently rendered in harvest imagery that suggests growth and ripeness. Indeed, by means of this type of imagery Clark, in Act III, skilfully crystallises the main events of the play. . . . Readers who detect what seems to be an echo of Elizabethan poetic language here (the verse of *A Winter's Tale* readily springs to mind) may feel that Clark's writing is affected or imitative; but the point to be seized is that Clark's fellow tribesmen do talk in this way. They bring to the English language a ready-developed sense of poetry, for the common currency of language in West Africa, as we have seen in our examination of the proverb, is highly metaphorical and pictorial. There is no gulf between the nature of Clark's stage language and the language used on the highways and byways of Nigeria, a truth which should light a beacon of hope for those who have despaired of a future for English poetic drama. (pp. 217-18)

But the importance of *Ozidi* for our study lies in the testimony which it offers to Clark's wholehearted espousal of the dramatic heritage of his own people. Although written in English, in theme, style, idiom, and inspiration, *Ozidi* is, quite simply, African. (p. 218)

> Adrian A. Roscoe, "West African Prose" and "Drama," *in his* Mother Is Gold: A Study in West African Literature, *Cambridge at the University Press, 1971, pp. 71-131, 176-248.**

OKPURE O. OBUKE

The similarity between Soyinka and Clark as poets, it is . . . assumed, lies in their common rejection of Negritude and the lack of ideological content in their poetry. On the other hand, the differences in their poetry, it is argued, are traceable to the degree of their imitation of Western models: thus, Soyinka, being "more intellectual, sophisticated and complex, is more Westernized," while Clark, reputed to be "more simple, down-to-earth in his imagery, more visual and descriptive and less complex, is therefore more African."

It seems to me that there is no more facile way of looking at the works of two "serious" African poets than to employ the above arguments and conclusions; they are examples of the frequent oversimplification and over-generalization of some critics of African literature. Furthermore, a "prescriptive" criticism that compares one African poet with another on the basis of who is "more African" and who is "less African" is likely to have a negative influence on African writers, because such a criticism would seek to circumscribe writers to arbitrary notions of what is African poetry and what is not. (p. 216)

[The] difference in the poetry of Wole Soyinka and J. P. Clark is not so much in the subject matter and themes, but in their *treatment* of similar themes. Clark's poetry lacks the thematic unity of Okigbo's and the obscurity of Soyinka's, but like these poets, he experiments with a new form of "synthesis" of an alien medium and local color. In 1967 Clark had complained that "Nigerians did not know as much about their oral traditions as they did about European mythologies"; his poetry therefore draws heavily on his Ijo background but at the same time shows a genuine interest in style—often preferring simple idioms and unobtrusive metrics. On the other hand, Soyinka achieves a more personal idiom, obscurity and "deliberate weightiness" and greater complexity in the organization of his poems, often moving from personal experiences to metaphysical reflections about the world. Like J. P. Clark, he draws heavily on traditional mythologies and idioms which he re-creates to show their relevance to the modern world. His obscurity often arises partly from the personal nature of his poetry and partly from his attempt to achieve "inexplicable multi-dimensional symbolism."

A comparison of the subject matter of the poetry of Clark and Soyinka shows how very close together these two poets are thematically. J. P. Clark has published three major volumes of poetry: *Poems* (1962), *A Reed in the Tide* (1965) and *Casualties* (1970). *A Reed in the Tide* may be divided into two parts; the first contains nineteen poems, including the two segments from **"Ivbie."** The second contains sixteen new poems, probably written during Clark's visit to America. Thematically some of these poems, such as **"Emergency Commission," "His Excellency the Masquerader"** and **"Child Asleep,"** together with **"The Leader"** and an earlier poem, **"Hands over Head,"** belong to what is usually regarded as the "political" poems concerned with power struggle and resultant upheaval.

Casualties is divided into two parts: part one has twenty-eight poems entitled "Casualties," while part two has eleven poems entitled "Incidental Songs for Several Persons." There is hardly any unity of theme in part one, and the only unity in part two is the fact that all the poems are "Songs" for the poet's friends and acquaintances. As in his earlier collections, Clark covers a wide range of subjects, but often the events in the poems are the poet's personal experiences and reflections about people he knew. His concern with the political upheavals in Nigeria during the "crisis" seems to have determined the choice of the title, *Casualties*. (pp. 216-17)

[While some of the poems in Soyinka's *Idanre and Other Poems*] have near-parallels in subject matter and are as concerned with the re-creation of local traditions as is Clark's poetry, Soyinka's audience is not a local but rather a universal one, and the poet frequently moves from personal experience to equally personal abstractions and metaphysical reflections. Even when the two poets write on an identical subject or a nearly identical one, they do not merely duplicate one another; rather, their similar poems help to underline their differences.

The two poems entitled **"Abiku"** are an example of this "similar dissimilarity" of the two poets. Both poets make use of the widespread African belief about the child who is born and dies, one called an *abiku* among the Yorubas and an *ogbanje* among the Ibos. Soyinka is not content merely to describe this phenomenon; he conveys the universal weaknesses of man in relation to an implacable fate. He is concerned with the whole

question of life and death; and in *Idanre and Other Poems* "Abiku" falls within the heading "Of Birth and Death." That the poet is here definitely interested in the metaphysical question of life and death is clearly borne out if we read the other seven poems within the same grouping. (p. 217)

Whereas Soyinka takes an altogether darker and more sinister view of the nature of the *abiku*, . . . Clark's poem identifies the *abiku* with the human group, and his poem is an appeal to the *abiku* to abandon its wanderings and return to this human society. There is a plea to the *abiku* not to continue to "bestride the threshold" but to "step in and stay for good," or alternatively, to stay away altogether, out on the baobab tree. The baobab signifies the fertility tree under whose shade women who want children sit, occasionally when the child is expected to be conceived. . . .

This unusual child, the *abiku*, is a spirit child "fated to a cycle of early death and rebirth to the same mother." . . . Clark's poem emphasizes the tragedy of the mother caught in this cycle of birth-death of an *abiku* child, hence the general mood of quietness and tenderness of the poem and the strong plea to the *abiku* to stay, so that the mother may at last have some rest and happiness. . . .

In Soyinka's poem, on the other hand, the poet speaks with the lonely voice of the spirit child. He is represented as a creature of a different order of beings, too removed from humanity for rituals and pleas to be of any value, and seems to mock the futile attempts of man to control an inexplicable fate. . . . Soyinka in this poem therefore uses the *abiku* myth to reflect on a more universal concept of rebirth and the mystery of life and death.

Clark uses more concrete images that are familiar and homely. These include reference to the "leaking thatch," "floods brim the banks," "bats and owls tear in at night through eaves," "bamboo walls being ready tinder for fire at harmattan" and the "knife scars" on the *abiku*. On the other hand, Soyinka's images are highly symbolic and metaphorical. The whole concept of the *abiku* is a mystery, just as the concept of life and death is a mystery; the *abiku* therefore takes refuge in riddles: "I am the squirrel teeth, cracked in the middle of the palm."

Such a difference in the treatment of a similar theme in the poetry of Clark and Soyinka could also be seen in the poems **"Night Rain"** by Clark and **"I Think It Rains"** by Soyinka. The subject matter of the two poems is not exactly the same but is close enough for another interesting comparison of how the two poets handle similar subjects. In "I Think It Rains" Wole Soyinka seems to be more concerned with personal reflections on various moods of the mind than with actual descriptions of a particular incident of rain. The whole poem is built up in a series of metaphors, and the poet establishes a close link between rain and "these closures on the mind" which will be loosened if it rains. (p. 218)

Clark's **"Night Rain,"** on the other hand, describes a typical heavy downpour at night that is common in the Niger delta. The poet gives the whole experience concreteness through visual images. The poet wakes up sometime in the dead of the night ("what time of night it is, I do not know") and hears the "insistent drumming and droning of rains upon their roof-thatch and shed." The rest of the poem tells us what he observes and hears, what the mother does, the effect of the night rain on him and his family. As in the earlier poem, the language is simple, the images are familiar and concrete and help create a graphic picture of the whole experience. While Soyinka seeks to establish a more intellectual and metaphysical link with the physical phenomenon, Clark seeks to concretize his experience and externalize it in visual imagery. (p. 219)

Clark's **"Night Rain"** actually belongs to a group of his early poems (which should be read for any detailed analysis of Clark's poetry). Many of these poems deal with his experience in his homeland, Ijo—especially his childhood experiences. There are frequent references to "childhood cries and 'noise of babel'," and often, for consolation, the poet finds security in the "dark peace of the womb" or in maternal care. . . . The poem **"For Granny (from Hospital)"** belongs to this group.

"For Granny (from Hospital)" also shares other characteristics with poems like **"Obatala," "Two Seedings," "New Year"** and **"Tide Wash";** in addition to describing personal experiences or incidents or re-creating traditional mythologies, it contains "images of cosmic chaos" and also images of physical and spiritual loss and separation. In **"For Granny (from Hospital)"** Clark records the reminiscences of a childhood experience. Lying on a sickbed in hospital, the poet recalls an experience which took place "fifteen floods today," fifteen years ago, when his grandmother took him away from his home and when they were in a canoe on the River Niger, his grandmother suddenly "strained him to [her] breast." She hugged him with the alarm and fear characteristic of one who is terrified. In this poem Clark casts his mind back to that incident, wonders why she did it and guesses at possible reasons: was it a sudden recognition of the loud note of quarrels among the poet's father's many wives conjured up by the "raucous voice" of the flood tumbling into the river? Or was it a reaction of fear caused by the reflection of the "footless stars" on the "muddy waters" that reminded the grandmother of something, possibly the poet's insecure home? The poet does not provide definite answers to these questions but rather succeeds through a combination of images to create an atmosphere of fear, insecurity, uncertainty and the sense of personal loss. The earlier images of the poem—the dark night, the raucous voice of rain tumbling down banks of shaky reeds—lead to the final images of the "footless stars" that "appear more plumbless than the skies" and establish a pervading atmosphere of fear throughout the poem. (pp. 219-20)

The interplay of memory and imagination forms an essential element of **"Cry of Birth."** The poet recalls the peculiar anguished cry of a child at birth and imagines his own and hears it in his imagination. The poet then proceeds to reflect on the phenomenon of the cry at birth, which is universal. He seeks an answer to the why of that phenomenon of a child entering this world with a cry, a sort of protest. . . .

The movement from a personal experience to a more philosophical and universal reflection, though not very typical of Clark's work, exists in a number of his poems. In such poems he comes quite near this quality of Soyinka's verse, although his images remain more concrete. In the first version of **"Fulani Cattle"** there is a "philosophical tag" at the end: "vouchsafe to me, / As true the long knife must prevail / The patience of even your tail." In the Moore and Beier anthology Clark replaces "vouchsafe" with "reveal," but the "philosophical tag" more or less still lingers on.

More often, however, the outstanding characteristic of Clark's poetry is the descriptive element, the ability to lend concreteness to his experience through simple visual images and well-chosen simple words. The short poem **"Ibadan"** is an example of Clark's economy of words in presenting an aerial view of Ibadan. The poem suggests the impressions of one looking at the old city from some form of elevation, and the immediate impression is one of planlessness. The poet describes the old rusty roofs interspersed with bright shining roofs, and tall modern buildings juxtaposed with shabby huts. The juxtaposition of the modern and the old, the rich and the poor in a sprawling, unplanned town is at once captured by the images of "running splash of rust and gold—flung and scattered." . . .

Clark's interest in African mythology is evident in many of his poems. . . . The poem **"The Imprisonment of Obatala"** is a further example of Clark's successful attempt to re-create traditional mythologies and represents a mixture of the legend of Obatala the Creator and all-powerful God and the poet's impressions. . . . (p. 220)

Clark's poem is not anthropologically accurate in its use of all the details of the original Yoruba myth, but it nevertheless is authentic in its own way of adapting the original myth to re-create a new poetic myth. . . . The poem emerges as a new creation embodying a more universal meaning. It may be seen as a "universal ritual drama of wrong, wrath and reparation" symbolically enacted in the drama and developed through a series of evocative and visual images. . . .

Clark and Soyinka belong to the same generation of Nigerian poets. They have much in common in the subject matter of their poetry as well as in the resources that form the content of that poetry. Both are experimentalists of a new form of literature in some ways characteristic of their literary age in Nigeria. There is, however, a discernible difference in their attitudes to their subjects as well as in their styles. Any serious study of these poet-playwrights has to take into account their wealth of publications in drama and poetry; therefore an oversimplified and generalized categorization of their works fails to do them justice. (p. 222)

> *Okpure O. Obuke, "The Poetry of Wole Soyinka and J. P. Clark: A Comparative Analysis," in* World Literature Today, *Vol. 52, No. 2, Spring, 1978, pp. 216-23.**

THOMAS R. KNIPP

The dominant themes of West African poetry, fiction, drama, biography, and history can be examined from the perspective of two inter-connected mythic patterns, one historical and the other psychological. The historical myth is one of the important ingredients of modern African intellectual life—a created *usable* past. It is a countermyth to the white Western myth of the savage continent enlightened by Europe, in the name of which (under the cover of which) Europe penetrated, conquered, and parcelled out the continent. (p. 124)

The second myth is psychological—a pattern with variations of the personal experience of the Westernized African. The pattern is that of a cyclical journey. The young African moves away from his roots and his culture in a process that takes him from the village or mission school through the regional or urban secondary school to the national university and then abroad to complete his education, his alienation, and, by this time, his disillusionment. From the vantage point of Europe or America, he begins to see or seek his own Africanness and the richness of his heritage. He then begins the long, not always successful, journey back. There are many variations, but Senghor's exile and Okigbo's prodigal—and a hundred poetic personae and statements in between—conform to and derive their meaning from this cyclical pattern.

Poems, Clark's first collection, was published in 1962 in Ibadan by Mbari Publications.... [It is] a very "young" book, containing forty poems Clark wrote in his twenties, seventeen of which were later included in *A Reed in the Tide.* Generally speaking, these are the "African" poems—the poems that grow out of the myths discussed above.... The remaining poems might be seen as belonging to two groups or modes: the poems of the suffering young man and homage to Hopkins.

The hostile criticism of Clark usually focuses on these poems, not entirely without reason. In these modes Clark is often "precious" in three ways: first he is very bright, more concerned with articulating his verbal dexterity than his feelings.... Secondly he is capable of poetry of no overt Africanness. This lack of the specifically African is aesthetically neutral, but dangerous. The young Clark's verse, free of the African touchstone, can quickly turn bombast, as it does in **"Cry of Birth,"** where he laments "poor castaways to this darkling shore." ... Thirdly he assumes the precious posture of existential despair—or is it romantic agony? (pp. 125-26)

Young poets pay the price for learning in print, and yet some of Clark's early, seemingly discarded poems work—within limits. The tone of these poems is personal, even intimate, and the mode is dramatic. (p. 126)

The strongest single influence on the prosody of the young Clark was clearly Gerard Manley Hopkins.... [The] critics have not treated this discipleship kindly. In some cases their harshness is justified. Poems like **"Variations on Hopkins"** and **"Of Faith"** do not really work; they seem merely exercises in technique, dextrous, wordy, vacuous. Although **"Horoscope"** is a good poem, it is true that the Hopkins influence works best in poems that are purely descriptive and that focus on Africa—the Ibadan poems, **"Girl Bathing,"** and **"The Return of the Fishermen,"** for instance. The happy effects of the few good non-African poems show Clark's poetic sensibility functioning outside the mythopoeic patterns which are the focus of this paper. The sad truth, however, is that most of the non-African poems don't work. Either Clark assumes exaggerated postures of thwarted passion or existential *angst* or he uses Hopkins' prosody to flex his aesthetic muscles. It seems that Africa—that is, Clark's own Africanness—gives his work focus, control, taste, and judgement and gives his devotion to Hopkins a needed specificity and purpose. (p. 127)

Each West African poet develops his own stance, mood, and perspective in giving poetic expression to his own experience of Westernization, that is, to the psychological myth of the cyclical journey. Senghor writes as an exile, David Diop as a rebel, Gabriel Okara as a lonely African, Awoonor and Okigbo as prodigals. I speak, of course, of a mood or attitude which pre-dominates but is not necessarily ubiquitous. No label is readily available for Clark's characteristic mood, but the poet himself suggests the attitude almost insistently. The longest poem in the first volume is **"Ivbie,"** two sections of which are reprinted in the exact centre of *A Reed in the Tide.* In the glossary to *Poems* Clark defines *ivbie* as a "hands-over-head signal and cry by women at time of great loss or wrong for which there can be no remedy or justice." In their nostalgia, their sense of loss, their pain, their accumulated fatalism, Clark's African poems are *ivbie*.... (pp. 127-28)

The poem **"Ivbie"** is in six sections; it is, in fact, a group of six short meditative poems on the theme of the European dom-

ination of Africa. The pervasive tone is regret, coupled with a sense that it is too late for remedy and, especially in section six, an atavistic longing to return to the primitive. (p. 128)

A Reed in the Tide was first published in 1965, only three years after the Mbari publication [of *Poems*]. It was during those intervening years that Clark made his eventual trip to the United States. Seemingly, this trip was important in the development of the poet. It extended the pattern of personal experience on which the psychological myth of the prodigal is predicated. Thus it enabled the poet to clarify his perspective and find his voice. It provided the specific occasion for ten of the new poems in the last half of the volume and might well have been crucial in the process by which the poet selected the poems for republication and by which he designed or structured the collection. What Clark did was discard most of the private, non-African poems while including rearranging those with specifically African subject matter.

Although critics have differed on the merits of the volume, they have tended to treat it as one of the major collections in West African poetry. The practice of most critics has been to praise or blame individual poems.... What both the artist—by selection, inclusion, and collection design—and the critic—by approbationary comments—seem to be acknowledging is the expression in *A Reed in the Tide* of Clark's consciously African role and voice. The role is mythic, the discovery of the poet's African self within the context of Africa's defined history. The tone is *ivbie:* lament for the remembered but unreachable past in the African poems, an outsider's recoil from the oppressive and sterile in the American poems.

The first fifteen poems in *A Reed in the Tide* are on specifically African subjects, the first two being domestic recollections of childhood. They are all reprinted from the Mbari collection. Exactly in the middle of the volume are two sections of **"Ivbie."** These are followed by the American poems, most of which also appear in *America, Their America,* a context which should not be ignored because it illuminates considerably. Here is the double mythic structure, a collection which begins with memories of childhood, granny, and mother and ends with a meditation on Marilyn Monroe and which, in the process, develops and explores the helpless tones of *ivbie.* Included among these tones is the aggrieved concern in the prefatory personal note over the dilemma of "that fashionable cultural phenomenon they call 'mulatto.'" The dilemma of the cultural mulatto—the one who has moved out psychologically in the mythic pattern and must grope his way back to the wellsprings of his being—continues to torment Clark through the decade. (pp. 129-31)

"For Granny (from Hospital)" is a strong poem, richly suggestive. The recollection of a simple intense act—his grandmother's embrace—leads to speculation about both domestic and cosmic issues over which the poet has no control and which he must endure.... With only a little straining, the reader can view the grandmother as a symbol of an Africa unable to prevent the child's long journey to loneliness, but a morally and historically rich and nurturing Africa nonetheless. Nostalgia and helplessness infuse the poem.

"Night Rain" is told in the present tense. The poet as a boy (the persona) awakens to a night-time rainstorm and listens to his mother move the family's possessions away from any possible rain damage. Reassured and reassuring his sleeping brothers, he settles again "to our sleep of the innocent and free." ... This is a very specific kind of sleep, that of the innocent and free. Such a sleep is possible only at a certain point in cultural time, that is, before the start of the mythic journey when the mother—his mother, Mother Africa—can still protect him and link him securely to nature. The mother and her capacity to act are the keys to the poem.

The collection begins with these domestic recollections and strong maternal images. It moves through encounters with the African past (legend) and through poems of description to that crucial moment and poem **"Streamside Exchange"** when the persona loses his mother. In some of the poems the poet sends out strong attitudinal signals—laments of alienation. After the **"Ivbie"** section, the poet is hurled to the farthest reaches of his journey, the farthest outward experience of America.

"The Imprisonment of Obatala," one of the most celebrated of Clark's poems, is one of the least successful, not, as Dathorne suggests, because of its "misuse of legend," but because it is too obscure in statement, image, and progression. In trying to reformulate the myth of Obatala and appreciate Suzanne Wenger's batik at the same time, it tries to weave far too complex a texture. Even Clark's notes to the poem don't help. **"Abiku,"** on the other hand, is a fine poem based on Yoruba legend. Here the *abiku,* the spirit child repeatedly born to die, is fused to vivid images of village life and to a strong people. . . . (pp. 131-32)

If Clark portrays Africa's strength in maternal images and its complex richness in the reworking of legend, he projects its beauty, with mild eroticism, in poetic descriptions of women. **"Agbor Dancer"** is a widely praised poem, one of those which reflects what Adrian Roscoe calls "the poet's sensual (sensuous) and imaginative harmony with the rural life of Africa" [see excerpt above]. It does this, as do **"Night Rain," "Fulani Cattle,"** and others, by recording an observed African experience or phenomenon followed by a personal response—a form of structural development characteristic of Clark. (p. 132)

"Girl Bathing" is a good, again mildly erotic, poem in which the development in sprung lines of a single image—that of a lusciously ripe African girl wading—forcefully carries the sense of an Africa which is clean, natural, and beautiful. Eroticism of a kind is also present in **"The Year's First Rain,"** which depicts the onset of the rainy season in copulative imagery of great energy. Much of this energy is derived from the rapid, intricately rhymed lines—in other words, from Hopkins. . . . If the slangy and the archaic do not quite work in the rump/ trump rhyme, the verbs do; and so do the slight syntactical inversion of "all the while waiting" and the heaviness of the participle "burdened." Clark learned well from Hopkins. To the extent that this mastery bespeaks a "borrowed tradition," it measures the distance Clark has travelled on the psychological journey; but it does not indict the poem or the poet.

Too much praised, slight **"Ibadan",** also a product of the poet's love of Hopkins, makes the point most clearly; the prosody is *learned,* not borrowed, but the vision is lovingly indigenous. The same can be said for **"Ibadan Dawn,"** which has not fared well with the critics. . . . I would argue that [it] is good poetry. Behind Hopkins' sprung rhythm and paratactic statements is a specific image . . .—a rooted African image— that releases energetic, emotional, tumbled language, which the poet makes all the more effective through a restatement of almost Wordsworthian simplicity and clarity in lines 13-14.

> Morning comes breathing flowers, warm and light
> Of limb, to charm earth from vice of night. . . .

Thus it can be argued that Hopkins's presence in Clark's early poetic life has mythic significance, but it is aesthetically neutral rather than malign. If it leads him to the pompous and bathetic, as Theroux suggests [see excerpt above], in some of the discarded personal poems, it enables him in the African poems to use simple language in focused yet complex and energetic ways. (pp. 133-34)

The volume concludes with Clark's American poems. Among these are three short lyrics which Clark calls **"Three Moods of Princeton,"** and which he claims in *America, Their America* he offered as bouquets, only to have them received as brickbats. The first was written in the autumn, the latter two in the winter. Although they are slight and charming, they do seem to contain a kind of psychological progression. The first is a simple description of autumn, a novel experience for the poet. "The leaves so golden, shower in the wind." The second Africanizes the experience of winter through metaphor, as does Okara's "The Snowflakes Sail Gently Down." The bare, snow-covered elms are depicted as wearing a *buba* and having the appearance of a group of Fulani peddlars. The third poem personalizes winter. In fact, it is *about* the poet, referring to his "bed / of bile." And as a manifestation of *ivbie,* is asks the ultimate question of the atomic age:

> And say,
> Nurse, when shall the corpse lie?
> There, ding, dong, ding—
> When all the world is a mushroom pie. . . .

"Two Views of Marilyn Monroe," "Times Square," and **"Cave Call"** are, very possibly, the best of Clark's American poems. The first consists of two short lyrics, elegiac in mood, projecting a sense of loss. Clark says they "express my silent gnawing hunger." The third is a fine, imaginative rendering of a subway ride. The images of the crowd and the train are effective. . . . One is tempted to read this poem as a parable of the African's journey. The persona plunges into darkness, is swept into a marvellous contrivance of technology described as a "beast . . . tugging me blind," and finally emerges sick and reeling, into the afternoon, grateful for having survived the experience.

"Times Square," to which Clark's critics do not pay a great deal of attention, is the best of these. Again, the images are strong—images of day, night, the market at night, and human figures at night. They are sad images of soiled, used people and objects. The sterile facelessness of the day gives way to the abandoned melancholy of the night. . . . Although the poem and its images are not aggressive or ideological, they do call to mind Senghor's "New York." But Clark's mood has none of the optimism of Négritude. It is, rather, the melancholy mood of a sensibility diminished by its encounter with technology. "Ivbie." (pp. 135-37)

There is a finality about *A Reed in the Tide,* and a sadness, as there is in *America, Their America,* which ends with the author forcibly ejected from America and hoping (without hope) to see his American friends again.

This latter is a bad book in many ways. (It illustrates the unfortunate side of talented Africans' easy access to print.) It is predictable, conventional, sophomoric, and reveals the complete failure of Clark's ear to catch the rhythm and pattern of American speech. But Clark is an intelligent and talented man, and the book does have its moments. Many of the poems in the second half of *A Reed in the Tide* appear in it. The book and the experience it records provide a context within which poems like **"Home from Hiroshima"** and **"Cuba Confrontation"** . . . exhibit greater energy and sharpness. Thin as some of them are when standing alone, they prove most effective in context as the distilled observations of a sardonic outsider determined not to be impressed by America and not to be fooled. One wishes there were more poetic reflections on American political adventurism from the man who offers the following as an epitaph for Washington D.C.

> A morgue
> a museum
> Whose keepers
> play at kings,
>
> (pp. 137-38)

There are some fine poems in the collection [*Casualties*] and its occasion—the Biafran War—is an event of world significance. In one sense, *Casualties* is the lyric expression of the narrative of the war. But the overriding interest in the collection is the partially stated but carefully managed narrative of the author's activities during and attitudes toward the war. There are thirty-nine poems in the collection, more or less chronologically arranged, divided into two sections. The first twenty eight, written during the war (the subtitle of the book is *Poems 1966/68*), touch on national events from the first coup through the emergence of Ironsi to the final triumph of Gowon. They also describe personal experiences including meetings with Okigbo and Clark's reaction to his death.

The poems and the accompanying eight pages of notes constitute not just an autobiographical narrative but an *apologia* for a man whose conduct and comments during the war angered his fellow Nigerian artists. . . . The narrative point on which Clark insists is stated in the preface to the notes as follows: "The pity is that I have had no part at any time in the drama still unfolding." What he is acknowledging and seems to be regretting (if the word "pity" is to be taken seriously, as I think it should be) is that while Achebe and Okara were supporting the clan and grieving for suffering humanity, while Okigbo was dying, while Soyinka was enduring solitary confinement in a Northern prison, Clark was withdrawing to the edges of both conflict and ideology. The poetic consequence of this withdrawal is that Clark assumes in his poems the ironic role of passionate bystander and internal outsider. (pp. 138-39)

In one sense, the war repatriates the poet; it brings his prosody and imagery back from Hopkins to Ijaw fable. (p. 139)

To the degree that the collection is not an *apologia* but a statement of the real human issues of war, **"The Flood"** and **"The Casualties"** are the key poems on which both its meanings and its quality rest. The first . . . personalizes the psychological casualties of war, the second the social casualties; and they both reveal one of the most serious casualties, the

destruction of the historical myth through loss of hope and love. (p. 140)

Of all the important West African poets, Clark is the one who seemed early in his poetic career the least caught up in the psychological and historical myths which provide the framework for a characteristically African perception of reality; or, at least, he seemed most capable of functioning poetically outside of them. But the various early poses of the suffering young man have dropped away; they were, in fact, all but edited out of the second volume [*A Reed in the Tide*]. What remains—or rather, what emerges—from the twenty-year period between the mid-fifties and the mid-seventies is a pattern of intellectual movement coupled with a kind of emotional stasis. Clark's poems really do complete the circle of the myth of the journey. The early African poems present haunting maternal images—granny's convulsive hug, the protective mother of **"Night Rain,"** the suffering mother of **"Abiku,"** the needed mother of **"Streamside Exchange."** The nostalgia of these early poems suggests the psychological distance the poet has already travelled from the African hearth, a hearth projected in images of strength and love, implicit in which is the whole historical myth—the whole usable past.

These poems are followed (in editorial arrangement, not necessarily in time of composition, which is the mythopoeic point) by the poems of flight and America, where Clark the outsider observes ironically the sterile technological world he cannot accept or control. Here the red nailed "talons" of the Western woman in **"Boeing Crossing,"** America's winter snow, automats, store mannequins, skyscrapers, and subway all project a sterile world which, in political poems like **"Home from Hiroshima,"** is revealed as menacingly, destructively mad. Clark's return journey brings him not to an Africa that restores the soul with strength from the past and promise of the future, but to a country sunk in corruption and falling into war. In *Casualties* the poet insists that none of this is his doing; he is powerless.

The journey from his granny's arms and his mother's house to the funeral pile, the "crash of columns and / collapse of rafters,"—from **"Night Rain"** to **"Night Song"**—and to the brutal police beating at Warri is a movement out and back, but in all of it the poetic tone and stance are of powerlessness. The "lead tethered scribe" and the passionate by-stander of the war cannot act constructively. Watching the war, he cannot prevent the destruction of myth—the meaning and hope of Africa itself. He can only cry out, or ululate, *ivbie*. (pp. 142-43)

Thomas R. Knipp, "'Ivbie': The Developing Moods of John Pepper Clark's Poetry," in Journal of Commonwealth Literature, *Vol. XVII, No. 1, 1982, pp. 123-44.*

Leonard (Norman) Cohen

1934-

Canadian poet, novelist, dramatist, and songwriter.

Cohen is often regarded as a "black romantic" because the love and beauty he writes about in his poetry and fiction is accompanied by a sense of loss and suffering. In his early verse he established the sensual and surreal imagery that remain dominant in his later work. Cohen explored Judaism, Christianity, and mythology through conventional lyric poetry in his first two collections, *Let Us Compare Mythologies* (1956) and *The Spice-Box of Earth* (1961). A number of these poems include elements of vivid and exaggerated violence, thus creating a nightmarish quality. In *Flowers for Hitler* (1964), Cohen discusses politics, science, and philosophy, yet there is no central theme to these poems. What emerges instead is the anguish and guilt of an introspective poet.

Cohen began writing fiction in the early 1960s, using the rich imagery and ornamental language that he had developed in his verse. His first novel, *The Favourite Game* (1963), centers on a writer from a wealthy Jewish family and has many autobiographical elements. The narrative follows the protagonist from childhood to adulthood and records his struggle to understand his art and his life. *Beautiful Losers* (1966) reflects on the relationship between the protagonist, "I," and his recently deceased wife, as well as his association with "F," who had been the lover of both "I" and his wife. Set against the main plot is the story of the mysterious Indian saint, Catherine Tekakwitha.

Cohen began to gain popularity as a songwriter and performer during the mid-1960s and has recorded such albums as *Songs from a Room* (1969), *Songs of Love and Hate* (1971), and *Death of a Ladies' Man* (1977). Cohen published less poetry during these years, and critics were generally disappointed in the collections *Parasites of Heaven* (1967) and *The Energy of Slaves* (1972). The poems in the latter volume, which are apologetic in content, yield "little resemblance to the Leonard Cohen who excited and rewarded readers years ago," according to James Healey. In *Book of Mercy* (1984), Cohen returns to spiritual themes in poems modeled after traditional Hebrew prayers for forgiveness.

(See also *CLC*, Vol. 3; *Contemporary Authors*, Vols. 21-24, rev. ed.; and *Contemporary Authors New Revision Series*, Vol. 14.)

MILTON WILSON

For the last hundred and fifty years or so, poets have spent a good deal of their time looking for a tale worth telling and for a landscape of meaningful objects to set it in. The poems they wrote were often about the search itself. The bag of good tales was no longer open before them, as it had been in Chaucer's or Shakespeare's time; and, although the unweeded garden, the perilous seas, the dark oak forest and the enchanted cave might still display their store of tempting images, these images

had lost their credentials and new ones had to be acquired from associationism, neo-Platonism, anthropology, psychology or poetic tradition. . . . But the archetypal poetic myth still awaits explication, and one wonders if the best we can hope to find is an archetypal alphabet, out of which languages are born and die, subject as much to the whims of history as to poetic necessity. Perhaps Prometheus, Endymion and the Wandering Jew, the tree, the stone and the rose, aren't "necessarily" so. The key to all the mythologies may lead to nothing but comparative mythology. But this is at least something, and, as McCaslin says in Faulkner's "The Bear," the poet has to talk "about something."

Leonard Cohen quotes this passage to introduce his first book of poems, *Let Us Compare Mythologies*. Whether he regards his title as a comprehensive index to the book as a whole, I don't know. It applies obviously to a couple of poems near the beginning, where what the dust-jacket calls "the relation of Gentile and Jew" is treated explicitly. But the comparative mythology does not stop there. A poem like **"Rites"** suggests mythologies within mythology, the rites of youth against the rites of age, and in **"Rededication"** (which follows it) the cyclic myth of nature prevails with difficulty and the rededicated soul hopes that his "disturbing spring" will lead to "no October." (pp. 282-83)

[In Mr. Cohen's book, demon] mistresses and sacrificial pyres loom up in tenements and on streetcorners. But the point is not that the dying myths are really alive, but that they are only just alive. The book is a swan-song, and it begins with an elegy. Satan in Westmount is a pretty feeble Satan. The lover (in **"Song of Patience"**), his throat marked by his demon mistress (who uses a needle and thread instead of her teeth), doesn't really need to carry a stake in his pocket. A little patience will finally dispose of her and her handiwork. Yet the lover thinks of her decay with mixed feeling. He is sad to see one of "history's beacons" dissolve into the sea; but he will also rip the embroidery from his throat with some relief. . . . Nevertheless, swan-song though it may be, as *Let Us Compare Mythologies* draws to a close, visions and prophecies fill the air. There is a long **"Exodus"** and then, in the last poem, the promised land suddenly turns up in everybody's myth at once. (p. 283)

Mr. Cohen knows how to turn a phrase, his poems at their best have a clean, uncluttered line, and he writes "about something." Not that he always evades the dangers of his own methods and materials. He can fall into the contemporary mythologizer's chief pitfall: that of taking the alphabet for the language, of attributing more power to his images than the context he provides can justify; instead of working for them, he may let them work for him. When sun and gold, blood and stone, flower and bird are thus tapped for an automatic flow of unearned power, they sometimes refuse to cooperate. . . . Although at certain moments Love may seem the key to all the mythologies, Mr. Cohen has not given it a convincing image or an articulate voice. Perhaps the comparative mythology of his modern Egypt is not yet adequate for his Exodus, much less his Promised Land. Like some other Canadian poets, he is engaged in the struggle to turn what is given to modern man into a myth that is not just academic nostalgia or archetypal primitivism. He is unlikely to give up or turn to neo-classicism, and if he ever really writes his Exodus it should be a tale worth reading. (pp. 283-84)

> *Milton Wilson, in a review of "Let Us Compare Mythologies," in* The Canadian Forum, *Vol. XXXVI, No. 434, March, 1957, pp. 282-84.*

NORTHROP FRYE

[The poems in *Let Us Compare Mythologies*] are of very unequal merit, but the book as a whole is a remarkable production. The erotic poems follow the usual convention of stacking up thighs like a Rockette chorus line, and for them Mr. Cohen's own phrase, "obligations, the formalities of passion," is comment enough. But it is an excess of energy rather than a deficiency of it that is his main technical obstacle. Sometimes moods and images get tangled up with each other and fail to come through to the reader, or allusions to books or paintings distract the attention and muffle the climax, as in **"Jingle."** In short, this book has the normal characteristics of a good first volume.

To come to his positive qualities, his chief interest, as indicated in his title, is mythopoeic. The mythologies are Jewish, Christian, and Hellenistic. The Christian myth is seen as an extension of the Jewish one, its central hanged god in the tradition of the martyred Jew . . . , and Hellenism is the alien society which Christianity has come to terms with and Judaism has not. The mythical patterns of the Bible provide some of the paradigms of his imagery. . . . Other mythical figures, such as the *femme*

fatale at the centre of **"Letter,"** **"Story,"** and **"Song of Patience,"** and the dying god of **"Elegy,"** are of white-goddess and golden-bough provenance. Mr. Cohen's outstanding poetic quality, so far, is a gift for macabre ballad reminding one of Auden, but thoroughly original, in which the chronicles of tabloids are celebrated in the limpid rhythms of folksong. The grisly **"Halloween Poem,"** with its muttering prose glosses, is perhaps the most striking of these, but there is also a fine mythopoeic **"Ballad"** beginning "My lady was found mutilated," which starts with a loose free verse idiom and at the end suddenly concentrates into quatrains. The song beginning "My lover Peterson" is simpler but equally effective, and so is another disturbing news item called **"Warning."** In **"Lovers"** he achieves the improbable feat of making a fine dry sardonic ballad out of the theme of a pogrom. No other Canadian poet known to me is doing anything like this, and I hope to see more of it—from Mr. Cohen, that is. (p. 309)

> *Northrop Frye, in a review of "Let Us Compare Mythologies," in* University of Toronto Quarterly, *Vol. XXXVI, No. 3, April, 1957, pp. 308-09.*

E. W. MANDEL

Leonard Cohen may be discovered reading . . . the Old Testament or more probably the Sabbath service to which his *The Spice-Box of Earth* is a kind of gloss. In one of the . . . [illustrations] we find an appropriate rabbi, the figure in which Cohen appears throughout his handsome book. He is rabbi as dancer, as holy man (an incarnate Baal Shem Tov), as lover (especially in **"Credo"**), as God's opponent in the fierce, personal way of **"Absurd Prayer"**, and as God's exponent in priestly satire. The role enables Cohen to produce some inspired pieces of what might be called synagoguery, exuberant faking of religious sentiment for the sake of exoticism. But since Cohen's rabbi is meant to be something of a charlatan, not to say a wounded teacher in a "silent, looney bin", no one need complain that the boisterousness is merely put on. In fact, more than once Hebraism mingles gaily with Hellenism as Cohen throws a mantle of Marvellian wit over his prayer shawl (notably in **"The Priest Says Goodbye"**), and along with the carpe-diem poems there are some wildly ironic versions of poetry's celebration of its own immortality. The best, I think, is the hilarious **"Cuckold's Song,"** but some will undoubtedly prefer the rollicking dance with Layton in **"Four Penny"** or the "sun-flower" tribute to the Van Goghs in **"Good Brothers."** Ranging as it does through Montreal taverns, fairy tales, and Greek myth as well as Hebrew lore, *The Spice-Box of Earth* is richly diverse in subject and tone, but nonetheless it is not a random collection of lyrics. It is unified, powerfully, by recurrent patterns and an informing theme. Cohen's intensely personal and sensual approach, in fact, is dictated by a precise scheme, the pattern of which is delineated in the symbolism of his title, the Sabbath poems, and the totally serious and accomplished prose-poem, **"Lines from My Grandfather's Journal,"** which concludes the book. In these, Cohen points to the source, if that is not too cool a word, of his vision: the "Separation" service, the Cabbalistic psalms, and the Song of Songs imagery of the Sabbath ceremonies. Like the Sabbath songs, the spice-box image provides a commentary on Cohen's remark in the **"Journal"**: "I played with the idea that I was the Messiah." Here, as in the Safed chants which inspire the poems, symbolism, a bringing-together, images the atonement or the coming of the predicted Messiah who will unite dismembered Israel. In the light of such Messianic thought, Cohen's images and *dramatis personae* stand out with something more than the quaint local colouring of ghetto and synagogue. The recurrent fathers and sons, masters and slaves, lovers and victims of Cohen's book reveal themselves finally as forms of one of the oldest metaphors of poetry, the wedding of heaven and earth. It is this metaphor which accounts for the sense of urgency and crisis in Cohen's poetry and equally for the extraordinary joy which bursts out in spite of his awareness of "the smell of burning cities." For it is a metaphor which can transform handkerchiefs into burning clouds, lawns into green prayer shawls, houses into silver flags, and broken, tormented bodies into jewelled spice-boxes. (pp. 140-41)

> *E. W. Mandel, in a review of "The Spice-Box of Earth," in* The Canadian Forum, *Vol. XLI, No. 487, September, 1961, pp. 140-41.*

DAVID BROMIGE

[*The Spice-Box of Earth*] contains some fifty poems on various aspects of sexual love. One of the most successful of them is called simply **"For Anne"**. . . . [In it there is] none of the delight in language for its euphonic sake alone which enhances and mars the companion pieces; there is only a clear, rueful statement of a widely-felt truth. But so clear is the statement that it gives rise to doubts concerning the authenticity of the other poems. The poet declares that he is not in the habit of appreciating the greenness of his own fields—a common failing. Yet most of the book consists of the expression of such appreciation. Here may be a clue to the impression of artificiality one gathers from *The Spice-Box of Earth.* One suspects that at times the ornateness of the language obscures a paucity—not of feeling—but of communicative maturity. The emotion is there, but the emotive thought has not crystallised; it lies dispersed in abstract nouns and adjectives.

A poet, if he wishes to keep his poems alive, must watch closely for those words whose meanings have decayed, and drive them away from his work. These are words like "heart", ruined by bad poets and successful song-writers; like "lovely" and "splendid", destroyed by advertising media. Leonard Cohen is obviously aware of the obsolescence of "heart", for it can be no accident that it does not appear once. But other ruined words—"beauty", "golden", and "glory", for example—frequently recur. And when a poet as perceptive as Leonard Cohen uses these words and others of like ambiguity, there are grounds for belief in his partial lack of creating consciousness. But only partial.

For in every poem that repeats the hard simplicity of **"For Anne"** he is successful. In poems of the other, luscious mode, he is less often so. (p. 87)

There are poets, passionate men by definition, who can never communicate—in their poetry—sexual passion. I do not believe Leonard Cohen is among them. **"Beneath my Hands"**, **"Celebration"**, and **"The Priest Says Goodbye"**, speak of his possibilities. But for these to become actual, he will probably have to write less about love, and think about it longer.

Cohen's poetic nerve cannot, in the end, be completely hidden by the flesh of words. His fine perception is apparent in **"Before the Story"**, **"As the Mist Leaves no Scar"**, and **"Summer Haiku."** . . . Above all, he brings the impression of good health to his poetry. The afflictions mentioned here are curable, and once Cohen has freed his sensibility from what West called "the thick glove of words" he will be able to sing as few of his contemporaries can. (p. 88)

> *David Bromige, "The Lean and the Luscious," in* Canadian Literature, *No. 10, Autumn, 1961, pp. 87-8.*

DANIEL STERN

In his first novel, **The Favorite Game** . . . , the young Canadian poet Leonard Cohen has created a kind of interior-picaresque novel, extraordinarily rich in language, sensibility and humor. As in the traditional picaresque tale, his hero is a rogue, though an essentially good-natured one. . . .

[It] is clear from the first page that we are in the hands of a genuine poet. The method is oblique, lyrical, and condensed. The childhood flirtations, the death of a father never really understood, the whining and self-pity of the mother, the oceanic emotions of adolescence—all are sharply etched with original imagery and wit. It is pleasant proof that conventionality of material need never dictate conventional treatment.

Mr. Cohen traces his poet from childhood to young manhood in a series of short, quickly shifting scenes. Breavman and his personal Sancho Panza, Krantz, treat every phenomenon around them to bright and sympathetic dissection. As Jewish boys from the "fancy" section of Westmount in Montreal, they have brushes with the surrounding French Canadian *goyim*, from which they emerge bruised but amused. . . . Other incidents follow, principally sexual, but never without pointed observation. The vignettes grow more serious in tone as Breavman's "sentimental education" continues. He and Krantz take divergent roads, Breavman's to school in New York, where he meets Shell. She is his one genuine romance, his Connecticut Yankee—the *shiksa* who seems to be the destiny of so many Jewish *picaros* in contemporary fiction. However, she is not his final destination. The journey of discovery has not yet run its course.

In spite of the gift for narration and character delineation revealed in these pages, the total effect is, finally, somewhat insubstantial. Mr. Cohen has told his personal story in a succession of loose, brilliant sketches, often vague in their direction. Perhaps next time he will weave a tale that will more firmly bear the weight of his undoubted talents.

> *Daniel Stern, "Picaros in Montreal," in* Saturday Review, *Vol. XLVI, No. 40, October 5, 1963, p. 42.*

A. W. PURDY

When Leonard Cohen published **Let Us Compare Mythologies** . . . , his book was of such merit as to invite comparison with [Earle] Birney's *David* and Irving Layton's first book, published in 1945. Now, a little more than eight years later, he has a fairly substantial body of work behind him: two more books of poetry and a first novel. An assessment of his work is long overdue, and with the publication of *Flowers for Hitler*, 1964, it becomes possible to take a look at the contemporary writer in relation to the past.

Cohen's first two books of poetry were, I think, absolutely conventional in metre and form. They gained distinction from other people's poems through a heavy sensuality, sometimes almost cloying, integral in nearly everything he wrote. As the title of his first book [*Let Us Compare Mythologies*] implies, comparative mythology, coeval social habit and mores were also included. Most avant-garde work south of the border seemed to have escaped his attention; or if it didn't, then he paid little heed. And English poetry in this day and age apparently has nothing to teach anyone.

For the last few years in this country there has been strong emphasis placed on such things as mythology and "archetypal myths", and whether it was Humpty-Dumpty who fell first or Adam. All of which seems rather a literary game to anyone who has to live in the world of now, go to work on a streetcar, say, and eat jam sandwiches for lunch in a quiet factory-corner away from the machines.

But Cohen makes use of the Bible and fairy tales in his myths, suburban neighbours, his own grandparents, Jewish popular customs, almost anything that will make a poem. Insecurity is a prime factor, and much of his work conveys a strong feeling that the world as presently constituted is liable to fly apart any moment. . . . (pp. 7-8)

As well, Cohen writes about sex; not the adolescent fumbling with a girl's bra-strap behind the closet door type either. Cohen's is a knowledgeable sex which explores the gamey musky-smelling post-coital bedroom world. No clinical nonsense either. Nor pregnancies. Romance rules supreme, and one measure of his success is that both Cohen's first two books sold out fairly quickly. But they are also good poems.

You could say that many of them expound the philosophy of meaninglessness very convincingly: i.e., they have an initial concrete incident or feeling, which is expressed so well that its magic drives any question of such things as meaning right out of your head. Take this passage:

> My lover Peterson
> He named me Goldenmouth
> I changed him to a bird
> And he migrated south
>
> (pp. 8-9)

It's rather Sitwellish. "The King of China's Daughter", or something like that. In other words it's an attitude and way of writing a good craftsman can easily employ, though perhaps not quite at will. You adopt, for a poem's purposes, a particular way of thinking or feeling, then write the poem. And if you believe this suspension of personal identity and belief is possible and desirable, then the poet is in large degree an actor who plays many parts; but an actor so skilful you can't always tell the difference between acting and fakery. For instance, "My lover Peterson". What does it mean? Nothing. But it's magic.

Think of all the young poets who burst suddenly on the not-so-astonished world. Rimbaud, Chatterton, even the young Dylan Thomas. Is Cohen at the age of 30 one of these? I think not. Though very definitely one could compare poems in this first book with the youthful Yeatsian romanticism of "I will arise and go now to Innisfree". . . .

But Cohen has other facets too. In one of them he creates his mythology from the Auschwitz furnaces, imbuing it with a peculiar and grotesquely modern sensitivity. . . . (p. 9)

I am aware of something common to much modern verse in Cohen. Not just disillusion and gamey decadence, but the present fact that all good things in life are done and past. A longing for what was, the sense of inadequacy in what is. One would think the ten-year-old yearned for his mother's breast, the adolescent for puberty, the stripling for renewed puppy love, and the only common denominator we all have is return to the womb fixations. The "fall" in other words. Once we were happy, now we are not. Rather ridiculous. Also completely ruinous for any possible present content.

Well, what does the reader want from a poem? Rather, what do I think he wants? Primarily, I suppose, to be entertained. And that involves tuning in on some emotion or feeling or discovery that is larger and more permanent than he is. Some flashing insight that adds a new perspective to living. Values also. And that is a great deal. Most of the time it's asking far too much.

Will you find any of these things in Cohen? Realities shoved from the periphery of your mind to forefront by the author. Not copy-book maxims, just real things and feelings.

Perhaps in Cohen's world the things he writes about exist, but only rarely do they touch on my personal existence. I admire the poems tremendously; they are the work of a master craftsman, who must simply be living in another time dimension than my own. I admire many of them as works of art I don't believe in. (p. 10)

With *The Spice-Box of Earth*, 1961, Cohen brought to near perfection the techniques and rhythms of his first book. The "tone" seems a mixture of the Old Testament and, probably, other Jewish religious writings.

But I think this "tone" is important. Cohen rarely over-states or exaggerates. His emphasis is secured by under-emphasis, never finding it necessary to raise his voice. There is always a casual offhand prosody, which lends even his rewrite job on the Bible the authority of someone present on the scene, and probably making notes behind his fig leaf. (p. 11)

The Favourite Game, a novel, appeared in 1963. As first novels go (and most of them don't stay around long), it was a decided success. This one tells the story of Laurence Breavman, Montreal poet, child voyeur, adolescent in a world without fixed values. (p. 12)

In any formal sense the novel has no plot. Time passes, of course. Breavman becomes older, his experiment with being alive more complicated. He is passed like a basketball from girl friend to girl friend (euphemisms for bedmates), arrives finally at his Great Love, and predictably forsakes her in the end. For permanence in anything is anathema to our boy. Remember please, he is a writer.

If the above seems to indicate I disliked Cohen's novel, then appearances are misleading. I read it first last year, and again for the purposes of this review. Without a plot, without any "message" or insight into what it's like to be an ordinary human being and not Laurence Breavman, the book held me interested, if not spellbound, on both readings. The reason: reality seeps through somehow, with convincing detail and dialogue.

What Cohen's poetry lacks is found here in large measure. *The Favourite Game* is rich in humour, zest for living, the sort of febrile intensity a moth who lives less than 24 hours might have; also, the continual sense of Breavman watching himself watching himself, which is, I think, a characteristic of most writers. From every corner of the room, ceiling and floor, Breavman watches himself, because he wants to write it all down later. He wants to say what it was like to be uniquely himself, and yet to be Everyman as well. (pp. 12-13)

Cohen has, in this book, developed the technique which will enable him to write other and better novels. This one is not a failure, but is badly flawed in that it seems to tail off at the end without saying anything very convincingly. Not that I mean a moral should be pointed or a tale adorned. But no one will care very much that Breavman will never return to his Great Love. He becomes suddenly rather a cardboard figure. He was created in the author's mind, and in some important way seems to be there still, not working very hard at getting out and being Laurence Breavman.

But *The Favourite Game* is an interesting novel, up to this point. What it says about being alive is its own parable, never stated explicitly. Much of the dialogue sounds like tape-recorder stuff. On this evidence, it can hardly be doubted that Cohen is a novelist possessing much more than mere "promise". . . .

[With *Flowers for Hitler*] Leonard Cohen recognizes the necessity to get away from his sensuous unrealistic parables and flesh fantasies. Cohen does change.

But the change has puzzled me somewhat. I've asked everyone I know who's interested in poetry what they think of *Flowers for Hitler,* and why. Some shared my own small puzzlements. The answers I got boiled down to equal approval and dislike. None thought the book outstanding, and some thought it pretty undistinguished. (p. 13)

[The book has several] themes. But none come through as overriding strengths that make the book a consistent whole, as Cohen undoubtedly wished. Not that they should necessarily; for life is a pot-pourri, a grab bag of seemingly unrelated things. But lacking thematic consistency, the poems do not accurately portray reality either. They seem playful exercises, poems for the sake of poems. Hitler and the communal guilt ploy seem to me like the talk of a good conversationalist who had to say something, whether it was real or not.

Here's what Cohen says of his poems on the cover: "This book moves me from the world of the golden-boy poet into the dungpile of the front-line writer. I didn't plan it this way. I loved the tender notices *Spice-Box* got but they embarrassed me a little. *Hitler* won't get the same hospitality from the papers. My sounds are too new, therefore people will say: this is derivative, this is slight, his power has failed. Well, I say there has never been a book like this, prose or poetry, written in Canada. All I ask is that you put it in the hands of my generation and it will be recognized."

Let's assume that the claims Cohen makes for his new book are sincere, dubious as that may seem. The bit about the "golden-boy poet" and "dungpile of the front-line writer" I choose to ignore, for it seems gratuitous ego and sales come-on. But are Cohen's sounds new? (By sounds I take it he means his idioms, tone, and contemporary speech rhythms.) In other words, has Cohen effected a revolution in prosody, written something so startling that time is required before his innovations are recognized? Has he done that?

No.

I agree there has never been a book like *Flowers for Hitler* published in Canada. Cohen is an individual poet, possessing his own strong merit and equally indubitable weaknesses. But even so there are traces of other people's influence. Laurence Hope's *Indian Love Lyrics,* surprisingly enough. Some of the Elizabethans. Donne's "Sweetest love I do not go"—cf. *The Favourite Game.* Waller's "On a Girdle". Swinburne with arthritis. Dowson's "Cynara" even.

But I'm not very fond of that favourite game. Cohen has come swimming out of all such traces of other poets, emerges as himself. And re. the dust jacket blurb, I don't want to fall into the trap of treating an author's ad agency gabblings as important. Only poems are. And pretentiousness aside, there are a few things in *Hitler* which I value:

> I once believed a single line
> in a Chinese poem could change
> forever how blossoms fell
> and that the moon itself climbed on
> the grief of concise weeping men
> to journey over cups of wine

Of course that is the "old" Cohen. Here is the guilty "new" Cohen:

> I do not know if the world has lied
> I have lied
> I do not know if the world has conspired against love
> I have conspired against love
> The atmosphere of torture is no comfort
> I have tortured
> Even without the mushroom cloud
> still I would have hated

And so on. He ends the poem: "I wait / for each one of you to confess." Well, he's gonna have to wait a long time. Liars, torturers and conspirators don't confess by reason of such poems as this one. And the life Cohen portrays in his poems has to be unreal by my personal standards.

Sure, I've done all the things he says he's done. But I'm not personally preoccupied with guilt, and I think few people are or should be. Life being lived now, and personal change more important than morbid preoccupation with past imperfections, I feel no particular urge to confess anything; though in a sense I suppose I have, in the first sentence of this paragraph. What then IS important in poetry and life?

Well, much of the time being alive at all has puzzled me. What am I going to do with my awareness, the mixed curse and blessing of sentience? Yes, live—it includes things I haven't even thought of yet. It also includes the various dictionary emotions, including a negligible amount of guilt. What then is important?

Perhaps to take a new and searching look at people, re-defining what they are as against what they were previously thought to be. Man himself is the unknown animal. We know more about nuclear physics, crop rotation and fertilizers than we do about our own nature and potentialities. As well, we might look for a new road on which mankind can travel. The one he's on now appears to be heading straight for The Bomb. Science, politics, philosophy and something like religion are all mixed in with the new poetry.

Those are grandiose things of course. Has Cohen discovered any new roads, or should I expect him to discover them? That question too is theatric, perhaps ill-considered. Well then, is he living now, asking the questions we all ask ourselves, making discoveries about himself, explaining the scope and nature of what a human being might be? Sometimes he is.

But I'm no longer puzzled about Cohen. He has changed, veered at a sharp angle from his previous work, struck off in another direction entirely. For the "now" poet is an exploding self, whom critics cannot predict, nor can the poet himself. Where he is going he does not know exactly, and where he has been he can only remember imperfectly. He inhabits language as well as the world, infuses words with something of his own questioning stance, his own black depression and joyous life.

One can only guess where Cohen is going now. But when I see the human confusion and uncertainty of his [*Flowers for Hitler*] . . . , I have hope it may be terra incognita where he is going. With a ballpoint pen. And may survive there and map the territory. (pp. 14-16)

> *A. W. Purdy, "Leonard Cohen: A Personal Look," in* Canadian Literature, *No. 23, Winter, 1965, pp. 7-16.*

MILTON WILSON

It's useful to think of *Flowers for Hitler* as the author auditioning himself for all the parts in an unwritten play. Useful because it underlines the process of self-recovery and self-discovery that is at the centre of these poems. In a jacket-note Cohen says that these poems won't appeal to the reviewers who praised his previous (second) collection, *The Spice Box of Earth* (1961). But I suspect that anyone who really liked the latter in all its range of style and substance (that is, not just its lusher surfaces and sounds) will like *Flowers for Hitler* even better. From the new perspective what looks wrong with the earlier work is a kind of premature coming to terms with himself. In *Flowers for Hitler* Cohen isn't so much shifting his ground; he's trying to unjell himself before it's too late. He's taking a more searching and uncompromising look at the poetic substance that he exists on, at all the things that he can remember, imagine, absorb, separate, excrete, transmute, forget. By an untalented poet such a book would be a bore. But Cohen is potentially the most important writer that Canadian poetry has produced since 1950—not merely the most talented, but also, I would guess, the most professionally committed to making the most of his talent. What we get in a great deal of *Flowers for Hitler* is the retuning of a virtuoso instrument, elaborate mnemonic devices, a series of techniques for the extraction of selves, a disciplined fulfilling of irrational tasks, a combination of derangement and restoration within the poetic process. I am sure that for Cohen this is (among other things) the necessary means to poetic survival. But for the reader who is convinced of the fineness of the instrument, *Flowers for Hitler* can be an exciting book in its own right. (p. 353)

> *Milton Wilson, in a review of "Flowers for Hitler," in* University of Toronto Quarterly, *Vol. XXXIV, No. 4, July, 1965, pp. 352-53.*

LAWRENCE M. BENSKY

[In *Beautiful Losers,* our] scholar is squirming right where we left him in the last book about an agonized man who couldn't finish a task he felt compelled to continue. Our scholar, this time as other times, has lots of troubles, foremost among them an inability to reconcile his expanded, desperate historical consciousness about his subject (a saintly Indian virgin who died a martyr, with the help of the Jesuits, in 17th-century French Canada) and an inverted preoccupation with his own body, which eliminates too seldom and ejaculates too often. (p. 30)

[Our scholar] has enough trouble to fill Montreal. His wife, who was carrying on a viscous exploratory cabal with his best friend, has killed herself. His best friend (who writes the second part of the book in the form of a letter from beyond the grave) is a French separatist politician, homosexual lover of our scholar since boyhood, and long-winded expostulator of irrelevant pseudo-philosophical truisms about life. Particularly our scholar's life.

If our scholar could get to the truth about his Indian girl, then he could reconcile his inability to understand his dead wife, Edith, a descendant of the same Indian tribe as the saintly princess, as art would have it, his dead friend, F. (whose part of the book tells us what happened to the Indian girl, which our scholar never gets around to doing), and perhaps he could even defecate his way into a wider reconciliation. (pp. 30-1)

Constipated, masturbated, fantasy-sated, our hero promises the experienced reader of anguished monologues another ride through another hell. . . .

When he gets back on the track, it usually isn't for long, as in section 41: "Catherine Tekakwitha was baptized on the eighteenth of April (the month of Bright Leaves) in the year 1676. Please come back to me Edith. Kiss me, darling. I love you, Edith. Come back to life. I can't be alone any more. I think I have wrinkles and bad breath. Edith!"

All this gets him is a long letter from his friend, F.

F. is writing from the hospital where he's about to die of an obscure disease, the result of sexual excesses. He's still active enough to whip out a letter of more than a hundred pages to our scholar, all done while the other hand is under the skirt of his nurse. F., unlike his friend, is an activist. He's for an independent French Canada . . . ; he's for sexual liberty (which in this case *is* synonymous with license), and he's for helping out his friend. In fact, he bequeathes his tree house to his friend, and at the book's end the scholar, now even older, is still trying to lure little boys up a tree to take their clothes off.

The book is done an injustice by such a summary; Mr. Cohen . . . is not writing a "story" as such, though he sometimes seems to think he is. What he's done is more of a pastiche of the bodily functions than a created "story." If only he and his messy gang would stop jabbering about cosmic issues and leave us to our enjoyment of the rest!

Mr. Cohen is much too intelligent to keep up the game very long; what he relishes, one concludes from their quality, are the bursts of expository eloquence which erupt on occasion, but too infrequently. The rest of the time we're learning about Cosmic Issues through the excretory and sex habits of a dead Indian girl; an old scholar; and a boring French-Canadian politician. (p. 31)

> *Lawrence M. Bensky, "What Happened to Tekakwitha," in* The New York Times Book Review, *May 8, 1966, pp. 30-1.*

GEORGE BOWERING

Nobody who is interested in Canadian books can be unaware of the Leonard Cohen boom. . . . Leonard Cohen could become the Jewish Kahlil Gibran. That's the danger when a poet has as much myth hung on himself as in his poetry.

Cohen is good enough and smart enough to proceed despite the photographs and magazine articles. He is, after all (or before all), a serious writer with a vision of himself that is more enduring than kodak. His work as a whole shows that. The newest book, *Parasites of Heaven,* is his least important, but in it one may find his greatest strengths as surely as his most obvious tricks and shortcuts.

I think that the reason for any confusion and blurring lies in the kind of thing Cohen is trying to do. He is [an] ultimate lyric man. That means that he shows any range of his discoveries, mundane to metaphysical, always through his consciousness of singular self. In that way he is the epitome of Western man, formed by post-Hellenic European modes of perception and thinking. The difficulty comes in confusing the discovery through self with the apprehension of identity, that awful put-on. (p. 71)

Some people don't realize the problem the poet has here, or how he is facing it. . . . A reviewer in Toronto complained that the first person singular appears too often in Cohen's book. But that is not a valid objection concerning lyric poetry, whether Shakespeare's sonnets or Cohen's songs. One might as well object that there is too much of the past in an epic. The first person *is* singular—each is—and hence worth singing of. The 23rd Psalm is written that way, but it is surely as universal as any poem may be.

In fact it is when Cohen is too much aware of the gallery outside the self that the poetry goes sour. The poetry goes sour often enough in this book to give the impression that we hold here a gathering of loose ends and leftovers to pad out the core of really good poetry written since *Flowers for Hitler*. Cohen leftovers, especially for fans, are of course more palatable than some large meals served up by other Canadian poets. I list some of the faults I see/hear:

Terrible adolescent effects and/or clichés. (pp. 71-2)

Dependence on similes for making startling images. The simile is the easiest way to write, being a reason-oriented and self-indulgent practice more than a responsive one. This trick is probably one reason why kids of all ages pick up on Cohen's poetry so easily.

Letting the will spin off surreal images, rather than finding surreal images by putting the will to sleep. . . .

Cutting prose lines into sandwiches with recurrent sentences to make the semblance of lyric order. . . .

Mock-profundity. . . .

Using the tricks of rhetoric (politician's repeated syntax, e.g.) rather than the magic of the cantor.

BUT. There are some poems here that will always be among Cohen's best, and thus will be around for a long time. One of these is **"Two went to sleep."** . . . It is composed beautifully (by) for the voice of incantation—literal sense ends and the spirits of the age are liberated by its images. . . .

Cohen is usually at his best when he plays with the main old magic-calling form, the ballad. In the ballad he is impelled by his self's dance to a measure, not his intellect's groping with the looser forms where the content, i.e. the whole verbal experience, has not proven to be that interesting to the second person, i.e. the reader. This is also why Cohen's guitar songs are good—they accept help from authentic muses, and don't give his intellect time to show off its own creations.

Keep looking at that belly-button, Leonard Cohen. It got angel dust in it. (p. 72)

> *George Bowering, "Inside Leonard Cohen," in Canadian Literature, No. 33, Summer, 1967, pp. 71-2.*

HUGH MacCALLUM

[In *Parasites of Heaven*] Leonard Cohen continues to experiment with modern idioms to produce effects of incantation. The range of the collection is narrow. None of the poems has a title, but many could have been simply called "song." Their manner is relaxed, informal, almost negligent, and there is often an air of improvisation. Frequently the source of a poem appears to be in a rhythm or cadence, and a number contain some kind of refrain. . . . Many poems employ strong ballad rhythms, or rhythms that are liturgical or recall children's verse, and most give the impression that they were written to be sung or chanted. . . . (pp. 361-62)

Cohen is at times a kind of intellectual's folk-singer, and no doubt this effect is increased when he recites to the accompaniment of music. . . . Highly mannered and stylized, this is the sort of poetry in which verbal gesture is of central importance and everything else remains in soft focus. Situations are indistinct, for the poet is not talking about events but about a style of living. . . . Imagery tends to be flamboyant and a trifle esoteric, flouting conservative order by its extravagance. . . . The tone hints at a paradox—glibness, it suggests, is a sign of sincerity, a guarantee that the speaker has enough sensibility to elude the pitfalls of logical respectability. More important, perhaps, is the way much of this poetry seems to represent a kind of graceful clowning in the face of a chaotic world. But it would be a mistake to seek a high degree of unity in the volume. These poems were written over a period of nearly a decade, and they appear to represent, not a phase of the poet's work, but a particular type of poetry which has been for him of limited but continuing concern. There are prose poems scattered throughout the collection, and their crisper, harder manner reminds one that Cohen has other powers at his command. (p. 362)

> *Hugh MacCallum, in a review of "Parasites of Heaven," in University of Toronto Quarterly, Vol. XXXVI, No. 4, July, 1967, pp. 361-62.*

ELI MANDEL

How do you approach a book like Leonard Cohen's *Death of a Lady's Man*? It already possesses its own dubious reputation, having been withdrawn once from publication to undergo drastic revision, having appeared in tantalizing glimpses in interviews about the poet's contest with his muse, having manifested itself as an album by a rock producer notorious for his wall-of-sound method and his guns.

Nothing is or could be innocent in the funereal world of Cohen's newest book. All contrived. All part of the longest continuing performance by a writer whose major task appears to be not simply deciding how long he can maintain public interest and by what new means, but defining the latest role in the long history of the deaths and resurrections of Leonard Cohen. (pp. 51-2)

Death of a Lady's Man is a massive book of poems and journal entries, wildly energetic, threatening to fly apart in any one of the thousand directions to which it is attracted, a witty, moving, despairing book, lyrical, dramatic, musical, endlessly entertaining, often boring, even terribly self-indulgent—further revelations of a mind and personality that will continue to baffle our best critics and to entrance and offend an audience he cultivates and seduces. . . .

The book is organized around themes of betrayal and Cohen's favourite game of masochistic revelation and sexual self-pity, a strong source of his attractiveness.... In fact, in much of its rhythm and range, *Death of a Lady's Man* calls to mind *Beautiful Losers* with its scatological imagination, its mixture of pop culture, apocalyptic yearning, religiosity, and a kind of insane contemporary sociology. Like the earlier book, too, it offers some political mythologizing, though it shows none of the urgency Cohen felt in his earlier attempt to visualize Canada as a possible metaphor of cultural, social, and aesthetic revolution born out of the sexuality of the Montréal French-English-Jewish underground.

The major devices of the book are the journal entry and the poem in draft form, each allowing for the method of replay, drafts appearing in several different versions alongside commentaries and critical analyses, journal entries drawn from three or four apparently continuing series plus occasional notebook sources.... The whole apparatus of the notebook collection locates the work in the modernist tradition of the poem in process and the forged documentary, an ironic comment on Cohen's subject of dedicated aestheticism and sexual honesty, the ostensible theme of the work.

At its best, *Death of a Lady's Man* employs the prose-poem for those incantations and repetitive compulsive prayers Cohen handles with almost magical luminosity: **"The Plan,"** for example, playing brilliantly with the theme of good intentions; or **"The Rose,"** offering a genuinely visionary passage on manifestations of one of the great metaphors of poetry.

The book provides, too, flashes of the lyric powers that have always been so attractive a part of Cohen's work, albeit in the fragmentary fashion accounted for by the "journal-istic" mode. There are lyrics as lovely and assured as **"Now I Come Before You,"** surely worthy of Blake and Smart, if only for a moment.... (p. 52)

But whatever successes in the book, it's difficult to avoid the feeling that there's something finally slack at the centre. Cohen's method is without doubt surrealistic, what Robert Bly recently called "leaping poetry." ... It's enough to take you by the heart and shake you as if you were in a great windstorm or encountering for the first time one of those huge ships of imagination that Fellini or Rilke saw. Or, to use Bly's example, it's as if the poet suddenly leapt from one brain to another, or as if he has shifted or flown from one world to another, as in the time of inspiration when he rode on dragons.

Cohen is capable of those great leaps of imagination; that is why he remains one of our best, most loved poets.... But too often in *Death of a Lady's Man,* he is content to substitute tonal modulation for the structural change that is poetry, letting his marvellously ironic voice carry the poem toward the leaping only language will allow, and which once having heard in his words we yearn for again. That I suppose, for a poet like Leonard Cohen, is a kind of death. (pp. 52-3)

> Eli Mandel, "Leonard Cohen's Brilliant Con Game," in Saturday Night, *Vol. 93, No. 9, November, 1978, pp. 51-3.*

TOM MARSHALL

Death of a Lady's Man is a kind of notebook consisting of prose poems, loosely constructed free verse, ballads and lyrics; most of it is concerned with the difficulties of the marriage relationship. It is a better book, I think, than Leonard Cohen's previous return to print, *The Energy of Slaves,* but it is also well below the standard set by his most successful prose and lyrics of the past. There is simply too much self-indulgent surrealism, too much of what has the effect of (not very interesting) automatic writing, too much repetition of idea and effect. The book would certainly have benefitted from some pruning. I suspect that anyone other than the most confirmed Cohen addict and vicarious participant in the Cohen legend (of whom, however, there are probably still a good many) will enjoy parts of it while finding the whole just a little tiresome. Certainly that has been my experience.

> Tom Marshall, "Self-Indulgent Cohen," in The Canadian Forum, *Vol. LVIII, No. 686, January-February, 1979, p. 33.*

JOSEPH KERTES

Many great poets have renounced secular life for religious faith. John Donne is a notable example and T. S. Eliot another. George Herbert went so far as to burn his secular verse and to leave behind one of the most laconic and beautiful theologies in literature. In the 50 prayers that comprise Leonard Cohen's *Book of Mercy,* his first volume in six years, there is evident a similar pattern. While the renunciation of a state of "sinfulness" may be an unusual development, readers of Cohen's work should not be entirely surprised by it. Though he has occasionally been accused of self-indulgence and egocentricity, much of Cohen's writing suggests an ethic based on selflessness and on a denunciation of differences among people and nations. As early as *The Spice Box of Earth* (1961), the poet was asking us to consider the evil inherent in our nature and, in *Flowers for Hitler* (1964), enjoining us to assume responsibility for our darker side.

Book of Mercy carries these themes one step further. Cohen condemns himself for giving in to his own worst excesses: "I pace the corridor between my teeth and my bladder, angry, murderous, comforted by the smell of my sweat." And he offers himself to the deity of mercy....

Whether or not we associate the creator in this passage with the one who presides over the Judeo-Christian world does not seem to concern Cohen a great deal. Though there are distinct similarities, and though the poet often addresses the creator as "the Lord" and "God," he seems more concerned with locating and meditating on a source or embodiment of mercy than with adding his voice to those of the biblical prophets. In fact, he describes himself in the 22nd prayer as "the monkey struggling with the black tefillin straps" (used for prayer). The volume, therefore, is principally a quiet one—less caustic than any Cohen has written. In the 11th prayer, the poet sits in meditation and requests solitude.... (p. 21)

The job of the poet, as Cohen sees it, is to attempt to comprehend the nature of mercy and thereby to lead humanity toward harmony. The poet's blessing is that he has been "permitted ... to suffer carefully." His curse is that it is virtually impossible to grasp the character of perfection: "Who can tell of your glory," the poet asks in the 10th prayer, and "who dares expound the interior life of god?" He must reconstruct the "word" and learn to spell the "Name" because the divinity of *Book of Mercy* represents the "king of absolute unity" and each person is but a "portion" of that unity: it is "the Name that unifies demand."

The poet, then, cannot create the world anew, as Cohen realizes. . . . He can merely invoke the creator to inspire him toward a proper representation of the world that is free of individual prejudice. . . . (pp. 21-2)

Whether or not this volume signals an end to Cohen's "secular" life, *Book of Mercy* will stand as one of the most honest and courageous attempts in Canadian writing to grapple with ultimate truth. (p. 22)

> *Joseph Kertes, "Born Again," in* Books in Canada, *Vol. 13, No. 6, June-July, 1984, pp. 21-2.*

TONY COSIER

[This] collection of prose psalms [*Book of Mercy*] comes across as a private book between a lonely man and his God. Not that Leonard Cohen is working entirely outside of a tradition. He takes both tone and phrasing from traditional psalms. His idiom is Jewish: he lets his dialogue with God come down to "a Jew's business."

Cohen is in great need of mercy. He calls himself ashamed, nervous, weak. He dances with a broken knee. His forehead is in danger of caving in against itself. His heart has given birth to an ape. . . .

Cohen works through his agonies doggedly. He calls on God to "crush my swollen smallness, infiltrate my shame." He cuts himself off from his earlier works, his earlier philosophical stances. He cuts himself from what seems worst in his cultural heritage, the "black Hebrew gibberish of pruned grapevines," and "the revolt that calls itself Israel." He works toward what seems best in that tradition: open thought, respect for the family, frailty before God. He tries to "end the day in mercy that I wasted in despair." (p. 200)

For all his literary trappings, Cohen is not a prophet at heart. He looks neither God nor humanity directly in the eye. At one point, he even expresses doubt that God exists. And this doubt is an integral part of his stance. . . . He centres his continuing dialogue almost entirely upon pronouns—he and I and you—and shifts these constantly, so that Cohen is sometimes he, sometimes I, occasionally even you, while God is sometimes he, sometimes you, and the reader is always guessing.

Cohen's heart is, as he puts it in his final statement, "a rage of directions." He sees his life as a wall of filth, yet he moves toward a pinprick of light. If he is sincere in that attempt, the *Book of Mercy* shows him to be something more than that man "uninhabited by a soul" that he tells us he is afraid he may be. (pp. 200-01)

> *Tony Cosier, in a review of "Book of Mercy," in* CM: Canadian Materials for Schools and Libraries, *Vol. XII, No. 5, September, 1984, pp. 200-01.*

Guy (Mattison) Davenport (Jr.)

1927-

American short story writer, critic, translator, essayist, non-fiction writer, poet, editor, illustrator, and librettist.

Davenport is a scholar and translator of classical literature whose fiction, poetry, and criticism are influenced by the modernist movement, particularly the works of Ezra Pound. Like Pound, Davenport infuses his writings with historical, literary, and mythic allusions, seeking to reveal the perpetuity of human history by relating the archaic and the modern within the context of new literary forms and techniques.

In his experimental fiction, Davenport often places historical personages outside the eras in which they actually lived in order to draw connections between the past and present. He employs techniques associated with collage, particularly parataxis, to rearrange and correlate ideas and events and to broaden their implications. Davenport calls his stories "assemblages of history and necessary fictions." His first collection, *Tatlin!* (1974), is generally considered his finest volume of fiction. Critics especially praised the stories "Robot," which concerns the discovery of prehistoric paintings in the caves of Lascaux, France, and "The Dawn in Erewhon," in which Davenport examines utopian ideals from the perspective of Dutch philosopher Adriaan von Hovendaal, a man of great physical and intellectual power. Curtis Johnson stated: "By tapping an immense erudition and by combining traditional and avant-garde techniques and forms to write about actual persons and events, [Davenport] has created a vast flowing poetry celebrating the mind of man."

Davenport's other short story collections include *Da Vinci's Bicycle* (1979), *Eclogues* (1981), and *Apples and Pears* (1984). Flight and photography are recurring motifs in *Da Vinci's Bicycle*. Ezra Pound, Franz Kafka, Ludwig Wittgenstein, Richard Nixon, and photographer Jacques-Henri Lartigue are among the people who appear in this collection. *Eclogues* and *Apples and Pears* were not as well received as Davenport's earlier fiction. Several stories in these volumes are based on Charles Fourier's utopian theories which promote sexuality as a liberating force for society.

The Geography of the Imagination (1981) contains essays on a variety of topics, including history, art, and literature. In his essays Davenport blends scholarly studies with imaginative probings in a witty, accessible style. Some critics expressed uneasiness with the influence of Pound and with Davenport's laudatory assessment of such poets as Louis Zukofsky and Charles Olson. However, many agreed that the essays are consistently learned and stimulating. George Steiner concluded: "The fact is that Guy Davenport is among the very few truly original, truly autonomous voices now audible in American letters."

(See also *CLC*, Vols. 6, 14 and *Contemporary Authors*, Vols. 33-36, rev. ed.)

GEORGE KEARNS

Stories, Guy Davenport calls them, so they are stories. Yet none of our usual senses for "story" suggests the combination of audacious invention, sentence-by-sentence surprise, playfulness and archaic wonder of the world Davenport began mapping out in *Tatlin!* and continues to explore in *Da Vinci's Bicycle*. We may take story, says the OED, as an aphetic of history, and then recall that before history became social science, or even a "continuous methodical record," it was a "knowing by inquiry, an account of one's inquiries." Davenport inquires widely, among familiar things seen or positioned freshly: Nixon in China; Stein in Paris; Mussolini's posturing rhetoric; the prehistoric paintings at Lascaux and Altamira; Picasso's *Guernica;* and among things half-forgotten or likely to lie outside our field of vision: Balbinus, poet and briefest of emperors, speaking to us from a jug; the liberated and liberating imagination of Charles Fourier; Robert Walser, Swiss writer who spent twenty-seven years of self-imposed exile in mental hospitals; the anthropologist Marcel Griaule listening to the harmonies of Dogon cosmology; or Joseph Nicéphore Niepce making, in 1816, the earliest known photographic plate ("Geese walking back and forth across the barnyard erased themselves during the long exposure."). The results of his investigations invite us to participate in plotting connections among points on a multi-dimensional mapping, while Davenport fashions them into a stylish world of pleasure, offering nothing less than the possibility of paradise regained. It is not often, now that I am grown up, that I take such primitive delight in stories.

We may begin arbitrarily at any point on this map, this unpredictable Möbius strip, this time-warp where Herakleitos intersects with Niels Bohr and reminds us (*Tatlin!*) that *the same road goes both up and down* and *the beginning of a circle is also its end*. Begin with a minor "character," the photographer Jacques-Henri Lartigue, who pops up ("**Au Tombeau de Charles Fourier**") surrounded by Dogon myths, but not too far from Wilbur Wright, Gertrude Stein, Beckett talking to Guy Davenport in a Paris café, Henry James observing Blériot descend from the first cross-channel flight (although what James saw "he did not bother to say")—and Da Vinci's bicycle. (p. 449)

Lartigue's pictures, images from and for a terrestrial paradise, include many of what he called the "magic adventure" of flying: kites, gliders, primitive flying machines—as well as bicycles. The Wright brothers came from a bicycle shop, making the imaginative leap that Leonardo missed, intent as he was on birds, and we are now in several worlds at once, returning to that first bicycle of 1493, crudely sketched by the master's ten-year-old protégé and buried from sight until our own time. Lines reach out, suggesting complex codes beyond chronology, structures that shift and glimmer, get charmed by passing gods ("Persephone stood at all the angles of time"), making us wonder at times if we have seen what we think we have seen. Lartigue went on taking pictures over a long lifetime, but did not show them publicly until 1963, a solitary persistence of vision unconcerned with the rewards and demands of civilization (in Fourier's damning sense of the word). That persistence, too, would appeal to Davenport, whose characters, he says, are "pioneers of the spirit" and have the "instinct to forage."

Davenport himself is prime forager among them, crafting glorious *bricolage* out of their provisions for the life of the spirit, communicating, with the help of dizzying parataxis and continuous subversion of our expectations, the sheer verve of his and their pragmatic intelligence. . . . Davenport's foragers have all intuited at least a portion of a holistic universe to which familiar categories—mind/matter, myth/history, fact/fiction, sanity/madness—are no longer a helpful guide, a universe whose irreducible particularity forms a complexity forever resistant to system and generalization. . . . The foragers are shaped into a phalanx against all who believe that "the gods are indifferent to gravity. . . . Those who go to the inhuman to place their hopes upon its alien rhythms, its bitter familiarity with nothing, its constant retreat from all that we can love," making them "hostages to vastation" (Balbinus in "**C. Musonius Rufus**"). (p. 450)

Fourier, in whom discourse was never *happier,* saw Eden as "a thousand documents and traditions attesting to the existence of a happiness vanished and lost, but which may stimulate *les modernes* to seek/rediscover (*rechercher*) another social order" (*Théorie de l'unité universelle*). Davenport's characters—modern or ancient, they are all contemporaries—holding fragments of these documents and traditions, meet in unexpected combinations within his paragraphs and sentences. . . . Within these stories, we need not wait for the new social order, a new discovery, or some distant system to be perfected. "Nature loves to hide," says Herakleitos in *Tatlin!* "The most beautiful

order in the world is still a random gathering of things insignificant in themselves." (p. 451)

Fourier called the evil Civilization, erected on bayonets and famine, false industry, the world *à rebours,* a hell of suppressed desires, almost lifeless: "The parades of the civilized are insipid with monotony. In Harmony they are infinitely varied." Writing with an assurance that Harmony will arrive, he oscillates in impatience and immediate imagination between the future and present tenses. Davenport is less sure that Harmony will come with time, although the escape hatch of language seems always within reach. Civilization's tragic rumblings are in the background. Nero's Rome, which shackles the philosopher C. Musonius Rufus to a chain gang. British justice, which executes one John Charles Tapner, whose grave is honored by Victor Hugo, himself in exile from the civilization of Louis Napoleon. Stalinism, crushing the false Soviet dawn in the mind of the artist-engineer Tatlin, crushing it so well that you will not find Tatlin's name in the index of the Great Soviet Encyclopedia, although in an article explaining the errors of Constructivism he is remembered as the designer of practical uniforms for workers. . . . Kafka weeps at the end of "**The Aeroplanes at Brescia**," not knowing why; but we know why: man's newly realized dream of flight is about to be co-opted by Civilization.

Central among Davenport's stories, his masterpiece I suppose, is the astonishing and erotic novella, "**The Dawn in Erewhon**" (*Tatlin!*), where his themes and many of his characters converge, as Adriaan van Hovendaal and companions of both sexes achieve a miniature up-to-date phalanstery of "amorous innovations" in the midst of the twentieth century. While Davenport's stories may be read separately, they offer their fullest pleasures when allowed to modify each other, as within a single field. Our pleasure is to watch characters appear, find themselves transformed and developed, take on different meanings as different minds pass through them. He will find, if he is lucky, a critic-anthropologist as sensitive as a Lévi-Strauss, but inevitably there will be duller explainers, term papers, panel discussions, dissertations. (p. 452)

Now is the time to read Davenport, before we are obliged to restore from criticism the innocence of his *ordre dispersé* (Fourier's cherished method of composition); now, for (Gertrude Stein on painting) "when everybody knows it is good the adventure is over." Adventures these stories are, in which the trinity of *delectet, moveat,* and *docet* move together in harmony. "But let us desist," as Robert Walser says, about to meet his fate on "**A Field of Snow on a Slope of the Rosenberg**," "lest quite by accident we be so unlucky as to put these things in order." (p. 454)

George Kearns, "Guy Davenport in Harmony," in The Hudson Review, *Vol. XXXIII, No. 3, Autumn, 1980, pp. 449-52, 454.*

WILLIAM C. WATTERSON

Oscar Wilde once complained about the provincialism of certain Bostonians in terms that still apply to the educated of America: "They take their learning too sadly; culture with them is an achievement rather than an atmosphere." It is especially refreshing, therefore, when a polymath such as Guy Davenport plays freely over a broad range of topics, as he does in [*The Geography of the Imagination,* a] collection of 40 pieces published in various journals over the past 10 years. Rich in wit and insight, these essays on history, literature and art eschew the systematic rigor of academic discourse in favor of a critical idiom that is bold and exploratory. Whether book review, biographical sketch, personal reminiscence, or lively commentary on the work of a writer or painter, each effort aims to invigorate, not embalm. Davenport occasionally steps on some of the clay feet that plod down the polished floors of academe, but he sees the critic's task as reaching for new horizons in evaluating the current state of our culture.

His observation that "a geography of the imagination would extend from the shores of the Mediterranean all the way to Iowa" articulates the principle informing Davenport's most important discussions. For this classicist and translator of Archilochus, Heraclitus and Sappho, a full awareness of the cultural "moment" can come only from a historical erudition coupled with a lively dance of the mind. History actually confers "meaning," it does not merely refine our understanding of a work of art.

Like Northrop Frye, Davenport traces metamorphoses by positing a core of archetypes that recur in different genres, narratives, symbols, ideograms and images. When Eudora Welty in "Delta Wedding" or Edgar Allan Poe in "The Fall of the House of Usher" self-consciously rewrite the Orpheus myth, for instance, they are recasting the essential truths of humanity in a context that is familiar to them and not simply polishing old statues.

At times Davenport seems to be a cultural anthropologist who will use any evidence available to illuminate a civilization or to shed light on a work of art. With his mentor, Hugh Kenner, to whom this book is dedicated, he fights against the exclusivism of intellectual categories sanctioned by the university. He reminds us that "cultus," the dwelling of a god, gives us our word "culture." And culture at its richest is made up of created things that must be approached with sensitivity, curiosity and a tough-mindedness, for they contain a mystery transcending the reductionistic impulse of much formal academic inquiry.

What Davenport means by a "geography of the imagination" is a map of inherited terrain with boundaries that every serious artist must expand. Moreover, since this cartography has a temporal as well as a spatial dimension, its *terra incognita* is virtually infinite; hence he must scrutinize the history of culture not with Spengler's perspective of linear exhaustion, nor with Vico's belief in cycles, but with an eye to the continuous dialectic between the primal and civilizing instincts of man. Davenport's central image amounts to the pastoral wilderness within, where the archetypes are mediated in acts of creation and contemplation. Pablo Picasso and Pavel Tchelitchew are thus seen, somewhat romantically perhaps, as great artists whose personal energies and supreme historical consciousness have allowed them to achieve a radical innocence.

The wide variety of fare Davenport offers will irritate the stodgy and delight the sophisticated. Natural sciences at Harvard in the 19th century and its influence on the modern poetic idiom (Davenport has written an engaging book on Louis Agassiz), the history of table manners, translating Homer, hobbitry, images of the American Indian, Picasso's debt to the cave painting of the Dordogne, James Joyce's use of Mithraic symbolism, Poe's taste in interior decoration, Mayan birdlore and Charles Olson's "The Kingfishers," the originality of Ralph Meatyard as man and artist, and Daedalian impulses in modern poetry and painting—all of these are discussed. So are more standard topics, including Ezra Pound's use of mythology and land-scape, Joyce's debt to Homer and William Carlos Williams' city poetry. The critic revels throughout in the ironic and the arcane, and is at his best decoding Joyce or Pound or Louis Zukofsky. "Iconography is that sublime and most painstaking of humanistic disciplines," he tells us in his essay on Tchelitchew, and there are plenty of labyrinths in modern art that require the Theseus-like ingenuity of a Davenport....

Few of what he calls the "professariat" would dispute his observations on Walt Whitman, Poe, Herman Melville, or Wallace Stevens, but his paeans to Olson and Zukofsky may strike some as hyperbolic. (p. 16)

Favoring, as he does, the eclectic sensibility of high art (he notes, in an essay entitled **"Cummings"** that "one of the things utterly forgotten about poets is that they come in hierarchies and orders"), Davenport nonetheless waxes critical of those whom the academic world has lionized. He does not much care for "self-expression" as a substitute for profundity in poetry, and he dismisses Robert Lowell as a grand bourgeois, a stylish wordsmith who coats his confessions with a thin glaze of rhetoric. What Davenport values is not so much a particular voice in a particular time as a disembodied voice synthesizing everything it knows about history and art. The elusive density of Pound's *Cantos*, their linguistic subtlety and their cognizance of world history, for example, interest him more than Lowell's Puritan guilt, religious conventions and diction, and Yankee slang of maritime origin.

Davenport's witty style is quite in keeping with his view of civilization as nurturing *jeux d'esprit*. Quotations from classical Greek, Latin, French, Italian, and German are embedded in the author's own racy and sometimes colloquial prose. At the same time, there is a striving after the epigrammatic in Davenport's skillful use of generalizations, metaphors and puns....

Davenport's learning is immense, his ideas original and his delivery polished and easy. In his impassioned discourse, in his enlightened love of comparison, in his intellectual passion for art we glimpse the 18th century's firm sense of values. Oscar Wilde would see Guy Davenport's free play of mind as a triumph. (p. 17)

> William C. Watterson, "A Mapping of the Mind," in The New Leader, Vol. LXIV, No. 13, June 29, 1981, pp. 16-17.

HUGH KENNER

Guy Davenport is grateful for "having been taught how to find things": all that he has ever done, he's willing to hazard. He learned it during a whole childhood of looking in fields [as described in the essay **"Finding"** in *The Geography of the Imagination*].

> Every Sunday afternoon of my childhood, once the tediousness of Sunday school and the appalling boredom of church were over with, corrosions of the spirit easily salved by the roast beef, macaroni pie, and peach cobbler that followed them, my father loaded us all into the Essex, later the Packard, and headed out to look for Indian arrows....

The eye that found the Indian arrowheads on Sunday afternoons in South Carolina is by now the most astute eye in America. What can it not find! 2,000 trimly ordered words defile to brings news of what is findable in a single picture so familiar we have never learned to see it, Grant Wood's *American Gothic*. (p. 66)

[Davenport's] prose is as packed with information as the picture, which contains "trees, seven of them, as along the porch of Solomon's temple," "a bamboo sunscreen—out of China by way of Sears Roebuck—that rolls up like a sail," and sash windows "European in origin, their glass panes from Venetian technology as perfected by the English."

The farmer's eyeglasses even, which Phidias would have thought a miracle, are fetched from deeps of history. "The first portrait of a person wearing specs is of Cardinal Ugone de Provenza, in a fresco of 1352 by Tommaso Barisino di Modena," and "the center for lens grinding from which eyeglasses diffused to the rest of civilization was the same part of Holland from which the style of the painting itself derives." This is precisely relevant. Grant Wood once thought he would be a Post-Impressionist; discovering "this Netherlandish tradition of painting middle-class folk with honor and precision" was what sent him back to Iowa from Montparnasse.

American history is a story of bringing and of leaving behind: fateful choices. What was brought has imprinted the New World with strange traces of prior origins. On an old road through the Santa Ynez Mountains in California, certain rock surfaces are scored with ruts spaced exactly as were the wheels of Roman chariots. The stagecoaches that marked them were built to Spanish measurements, and the wheels of Spanish coaches had been spaced to fit the ruts of Roman roads in Spain. Such transfer of patterns is wholly automatic; no one involved need know that it is happening. (pp. 66-7)

Every glimpse in America includes artifacts bearing such tales. Most of us, though, resemble most of the time certain people who used to tag along on the Davenport family's Sunday expeditions: people "who would not have noticed the splendidest of tomahawks if they had stepped on it, who could not tell a worked stone from a shard of flint or quartz."

Likewise there are people who draw pay for being art historians and do not think to inquire into the credentials of a pose that displays man and wife side by side. . . .

Has so much ever been found in what we tend to dismiss as a pointlessly elaborate caricature? And are these findings embarrassed by the information that Grant Wood was thinking not of husband and wife but of father and spinster daughter, prowling males held at bay with that pitchfork? Can a picture know far more than its painter meant, or knew? Certainly, as he spreads out his trove of arrowheads for our inspection, Davenport is apt to incur the suspicion that time past did not deposit them in the fields where he gathered them, that they dropped there rather through holes in his own pockets. Is it perhaps the knowingness of a Kentucky professor that Davenport generously attributes to Grant Wood? We have extraordinary difficulty believing that poets or painters really know very much. This implies that the only way to signal the possession of knowledge is to deliver a lecture.

In Poe's "To Helen" we encounter a "perfumed sea," and have two options. We can dismiss "perfumed" as a typical bit of adjectival silliness. Or we can remember, with Davenport, "that classical ships never left sight of land, and could smell orchards on shore," moreover "that perfumed oil was an extensive industry in classical times and that ships laden with it would smell better than your shipload of sheep." And as for the pertinence of classical times, "those Nicaean barks

of yore" in Poe's verse get their adjective from "the city of Nice, where a major shipworks was: Mark Antony's fleet was built there."

Yes, yes, but did Poe really know all that? He knew enough, certainly, to make the ships "Nicaean" and to mean something by it. Beyond that nothing is provable, unless someone can show us a letter of Poe's remarking on the odors that wafted to Mediterranean ships from Provençal orchards. The skill of locating such documents and the strategy of citing them make up what is called scholarship. When the document is lacking, literary explication can appeal only to plausibility. Poe wrote "To Helen" when he was still a boy, and we don't know at all what lore floated through schoolrooms then. Davenport's Poe can scarcely be read by Americans, who have systematically forgotten everything he thought they knew. (p. 67)

There's no getting around the way Davenport's poets and painters, as we get to know them, come to resemble Guy Davenport: a special case, no doubt, of something he draws our attention to, "Ernst Mach's disturbing and fruitful analysis of science as a psychological history of scientists. . . . The theory of relativity is in the genius of its conception and in the style of its expression as much a projection of the uniquely individuated mind of Einstein as *Jerusalem* is of Blake's." If that's true of science, and it probably is, then a century's effort to deliver the study of literature from mere accidents of personality by rendering it "scientific" lies inert now, dissolving in ironies. Around its corroding wreck Post-Structuralism, Interpretation's current craze, dances a rite of barbaric despair. . . .

It's pleasanter to linger with Davenport, a sweet mind and a fructive. Certainly he can't be convicted of not having a theory, though it is not a theory of reading but a theory of history. It is very likely untrue, but it got his book written. It says, I was happier at ten than I am at fifty-four, and a like pattern is discernible in America. As the fields where we sought those arrowheads are now under an immense lake, so oblivion has engulfed American consciousness, and artists vainly array particulars hardly anyone can command the knack to read. Hence these pages, in which I take pleasure in my own bright arrays, culled in homage from Poe and Pound and Grant Wood and Whitman and Joyce and Zukofsky and Eudora Welty and as many other sly but masterful spirits as I've had occasion to pay attention to.

It may very well be the import of our age, that literature is not the text, does not contain its meanings, is merely what happens in some mind in the presence of a text. If so, then the choice of another mind to spend time with is crucial to your well-being. The mind that conceived *The Geography of the Imagination,* and executed its elegant meaty sentences, is one I'll commend. (p. 68)

Hugh Kenner, "A Geography of the Imagination,"
in Harper's, *Vol. 263, No. 1575, August, 1981, pp.*
*66-8.**

HILTON KRAMER

As a mode of literary discourse, criticism—when it is not simply opinion-mongering—tends to be shaped by the objects in which it takes the most intense and protracted interest. An ideal sympathy is established between the critic and the habits of vision to be found in the kind of poem or painting or other art work that most urgently engages his attention, and this sympathy—amounting at times to a passion—determines the very style of the critic's discourse. It also, of course, determines the limits of the critic's vision.

In the case of Guy Davenport, whose critical writings have now been collected in *The Geography of the Imagination,* the principal shaping spirit is emphatically that of Ezra Pound. Not only is Pound's poetry upheld as the fulcrum of the modernist achievement and his prose esteemed as the fount of all critical wisdom, but in other respects, too—above all, in his fundamental outlook on modern civilization—Pound is embraced as a man to be admired and a mind to be emulated. . . .

Now it takes a lot of talent and a lot of learning for a writer to live up to the standards of such a formidable model, and it should therefore be said straightaway that Mr. Davenport, whatever his deficiencies may be and notwithstanding the smaller scale of his accomplishment, acquits himself remarkably well in meeting those standards. He certainly brings the requisite learning, discipline, sensibility and versatility to his many literary endeavors and is not to be confused with the multitude of cranks and ignoramuses who have somehow found in *The Cantos* a warrant for their own misguided effusions. (p. 7)

Far from finding the sheer range of Pound's linguistic, historical and esthetic interests in any way daunting, [Davenport] has addressed himself to a similar variety of challenges with an impressive energy and application.

Thus, among the many subjects discussed in *The Geography of the Imagination* are the writings of Homer, Walt Whitman, Edgar Allan Poe, Louis Agassiz, John Ruskin, Marianne Moore, Wallace Stevens, Osip Mandelstam, Gertrude Stein, James Joyce, Louis Zukofsky, Charles Olson, Eudora Welty, and Pound of course, as well as the paintings of Pavel Tchelitchew, the photographs of Ralph Eugene Meatyard, and the music of Charles Ives. Much attention is given, too, to prehistoric art and to the scholarship that has focused on primitive and prehistoric culture. Mr. Davenport is an exceptionally able reader of difficult modern texts and is often wonderfully alert to the sort of unlikely connections that illuminate a whole literary landscape. Who but Guy Davenport would describe Ruskin's "Fors Clavigera" as "kind of Victorian prose *Cantos,*" and then make a case that proves it to our satisfaction?

This impassioned discipleship to Pound clearly brings many advantages to a mind as responsive and well-stocked as Mr. Davenport's, but I am afraid it also accounts for some of his less appealing articles of belief. He appears to share with the master an implacable hostility to modern society and a corollary myopia in the realm of politics. (It is entirely characteristic of this point of view that Pound's place of confinement in Italy at the end of World War II is casually described as "the concentration camp at Pisa.") Sharing Pound's radical estheticism, Mr. Davenport follows his lead in despising virtually everything about the modern world except its artistic accomplishments.

This, to say the least, places a certain restriction on the range of Mr. Davenport's sympathies, and it is well to be aware of it in attempting to come to terms with his work. Reading Mr. Davenport's essays—and his stories, too, for they naturally derive from the same order of vision—I am reminded of a passage in Edward Shils's new book *Tradition.* "Modern culture," writes Mr. Shils, "is in some respects a titanic and deliberate effort to undo by technology, rationality, and governmental policy the givenness of what came down from the past." This is precisely what writers of the Poundian persuasion find intolerable in modern culture, and against which their

every argument, allusion and creative endeavor is marshalled. That this "titanic and deliberate effort" may have brought certain benefits to mankind is never for a moment considered a serious possibility, for it is a proposition that ill accords with a purely esthetic view of experience.

What is yearned for as an alternative to the debacle of modernity (as it is thus thought to be) is the ethos of "the ancient cultures," which are alleged to have possessed "critical tools for analyzing reality" superior to ours. . . . What is to be valued in the 20th century is not so much what it has initiated as what it has rediscovered—most especially the "renaissance of the archaic" that has been pioneered by certain artists, writers and scholars. It therefore follows that the figures to be admired, above all others in our time, are "the artists who were performing the great feat of awakening an archaic sense of the world." (I am quoting from the essay called **"The Symbol of the Archaic,"** which is Mr. Davenport's fullest statement on this subject.) These figures, not surprisingly, are precisely the writers and artists—in one of his Pound essays, Mr. Davenport describes them as "the whole Tribe of Daedalus"—to whose work he devotes the bulk of *The Geography of the Imagination.*

Mr. Davenport is, to be sure, duly modest about what this exertion on behalf of the archaic has brought us. . . . Yet he harbors no doubts about the ideal we should set for ourselves. "The nearest model for a world totally alive was the archaic era of our own culture, pre-Aristotelian Greece and Rome," which is much to be preferred, one gathers, to the world in which "the railroad tracks went down and the factories up" and "our sciences began to explain the mechanics of everything and the nature of nothing."

Exactly how this yearning for the archaic comports with the complexities of the art he most admires and most frequently writes about is a matter not easily explained, and in fact Mr. Davenport never does attempt to explain it. "The essence of daedalian art"—which is to say, the modernist art he most esteems—"is," Mr. Davenport observes in **"The House That Jack Built,"** "that it conceals what it most wishes to show: first, because it charges word, image and sense to the fullest, fusing matter and manner; and secondly, to allow meaning to be searched out." Which suggests what in fact seems to be the case: that this whole romance of the archaic is an elaborately constructed preserve for exercising the ruminative powers of the literary mind, and bears little, if any, relation to the actualities of life in those coveted "ancient cultures." In this respect, certainly, Mr. Davenport remains completely faithful to the spirit of *The Cantos,* in which history is constantly being manipulated to serve the purposes of image, ideology and myth. (pp. 7, 21)

About certain poets who elected to write under the strict authority of the Poundian imperative—Louis Zukofsky, for example, and Charles Olson—Mr. Davenport is often wonderfully illuminating. But he writes always as a sectarian critic, overrating the achievements of the faithful and as censorious as any philistine in condemning those who depart from the true path. Robert Lowell, insufficiently attentive to the appeals of the archaic perhaps, is thus described as "a thoughtful, serious, melancholy academic poet" whose work belongs to "a broody school of professor-poets whose quiet, meticulous verse is perhaps the lineal and long-winded descendant of the cross-stitch sampler." Mr. Davenport is anything but a critic for all seasons.

As a writer of short stories he is, in a way, even more of a sectarian than he is as a critic. In his first book of fiction,

Tatlin! . . . , Mr. Davenport created a mode of fiction that, despite its obvious debt to Pound, was highly original—stories constructed along the lines of a pictorial collage that are part historical fable, part learned essay, part lyric idyll. Densely written, studded with esoteric allusions, an unfamiliar vocabulary and quotations from many languages, and often obscure in the actions they depict, these stories definitely qualified as a species of "daedalian art," carefully concealing meanings that have to be painstakingly "searched out." Yet at least one of the stories in that first book—**"Robot,"** an absorbing account of the discovery of the Lascaux caves—was something of a masterpiece.

Alas, none of the stories that Mr. Davenport has given us since that time is either as absorbing or as fully realized. In the concluding essay of *The Geography of the Imagination,* he provides us with a very detailed account of what he was up to in *Tatlin!* but none of the stories in *Eclogues,* his new collection of fiction, proves to be nearly as interesting as his explanation of his method and his intention—which, roughly summarized, is that he employs the techniques of collage for the purpose (you guessed it!) of awakening us to the splendors of the archaic.

As its title suggests, the fiction in *Eclogues* is yet another parcel of learned and obscure idylls. Whether these stories are set in antiquity or in the modern world, however, what occurs in them is often difficult to follow—until, that is, the inevitable cast of young, willing, beautifully endowed male characters in the "modern" stories begin to peel off their jeans or some other item of "vestiary sensuality" as a prelude to a sexual frolic.

The sexual *parti pris* that governs the evocation of the archaic in this fiction is anything but obscure. In the story called **"The Death of Picasso,"** a middle-aged male scholar sequesters himself on a European island in the company of a young man, entrusted to his care, who has had a history of sexual delinquency. After various vicissitudes, none of them interesting, the young man offers himself to the older man, and the latter is moved to declare his love. . . .

And where does Picasso come into this? His death is reported on the radio in the course of the story's development, but that event merely announces the theme. What we are invited to believe is that the erotic glow of this tale somehow embodies the essence of the ancient Mediterranean culture—that "ancient ambiance"—so often alluded to in Picasso's neoclassic art. . . .

What is not to be doubted is that Mr. Davenport's stories will prove to be a boon to literary academics looking for new examples of "daedalian art" to explicate. What a labor of research awaits them! And what a comedy it is to find that the destination that awaits us at the end of this long descent into the archaic is—the seminar room! (p. 21)

Hilton Kramer, "After the Archaic," in The New York Times Book Review, *September 6, 1981, pp. 7, 21.*

ELLEN WILSON

[The essays collected in *The Geography of the Imagination* show that Davenport] brings to the task an awesomely well-stocked mind, and a clean, vigorously declarative style which, no matter how involved the subject or abstruse the information he teases out of it, enlightens rather than obscures.

These are valuable gifts, and it is difficult at first to see why he does not better succeed in his undertaking, or rather, why his success does not better please. In essay after essay—on Poe or Pound, on Eudora Welty or Walt Whitman—Davenport serves up a feast of influences, inferences, and allusions, most of them interesting and often even relevant. He catches O. Henry adapting the Persephone myth in "The Church with the Overshot Wheel"; he bounces *The Adventures of Pinocchio* off Ovid's *Metamorphoses.* As a literary anecdotist he excels Donald Hall, earning bonus points for focusing, here as elsewhere, on the illuminating detail or the evocative setting. . . .

But Guy Davenport's virtues, literary and intellectual, do not produce essays consistently or even generally satisfying. The reason has something to do with the painstakingly crafted mediocrity of many of the writers he chooses to explicate. To tell the truth, Davenport is most interesting when he writes on incidental topics, or on authors too universally approved to leave much of an opening for errors of taste or judgment. In other cases, the disjunction between the subtlety of his discussion and the insignificance of his subject becomes exasperating and almost painful. (p. 1358)

At first the sheer multiplicity of things Davenport finds to say about favorites of his like Louis Zukofsky or Charles Olson or Jonathan Williams overwhelms the reader and silences doubt. His appreciation is so genuine, and he works with such energy and intelligence and confidence in the value of what he is doing. But then he slips by letting fall a quote or two, and the spell is broken. (p. 1359)

And there is the puzzle: that this lover of words cunningly arranged, and interested observer of whatever may be put into words, should reveal such inexplicable preferences. Perhaps his very delight in complexity—his ingenious cataloguing of literary strata of significance whole Grand Canyons deep—blinds him to the unlovely obscurities of his favorites. His capacious enjoyment of the arcane, the unobvious, and the enigmatical weakens him as a critic, since his interest in an author appears to be indexed to the degree of difficulty he has in puzzling out the meaning. But without embracing the opposite extreme of shallowness and predictability, I can't help thinking that the excessive and even wanton obscurity of Olson et al. restricts their potential audience to those who read poetry like a Rubik cube.

The Geography of the Imagination is a rich and often provoking cultural atlas, which includes portions of the literary landscape better left *terra incognita.* It is an impressive demonstration of Guy Davenport's powers, analytic and empathetic—but also regrettable confirmation of the old saw that there's no accounting for tastes. (pp. 1359-60)

Ellen Wilson, "Rubik Cubes," in National Review, *Vol. XXXIII, No. 22, November 13, 1981, pp. 1358-60.*

GEORGE STEINER

To "review" Davenport seems a crass intrusion. But in terms of the bleak condition of our current fantasies this intrusion may be justified. The fact is that Guy Davenport is among the very few truly original, truly autonomous voices now audible in American letters. Name Guy Davenport and William Gass. There are not many others to set beside Borges, Raymond Queneau, and Calvino. Adult dreams are as hard to come by just now as Davenport's more arcane imprints.

A Davenport sentence or short paragraph (the fragment, the aphorism, as in the early Greek poets and pre-Socratic thinkers, is Davenport's core) is instantaneously recognizable. . . . There would be no harm in simply using the remainder of this review to make a mosaic and montage of quotes. (p. 196)

Guy Davenport is faithful to Ezra Pound's injunction that prose ought to be at least as well crafted as verse. He is a master of subtle pace. Seemingly short sentences and fragmentary phrases open, via unexpected commas, into sequences as opulent as Japanese paper blossoms dropped in clear water. Davenport's gait has the spare, funny lyricism of the music of Erik Satie. I say this with reference to the grammar. (Note the deft, whimsical uses, sometimes reminiscent of Gertrude Stein's, of the historical present.) The vocabulary, especially in recent texts, is a different matter. It is baroque, precious, crazily inventive. I take my examples from **"On Some Lines of Virgil,"** a long montage story in *Eclogues* and, incidentally, one of the most hilarious, tenderly risqué accounts of sexual awakening in all modern literature. The reader must be ready for such finds as "gressorial," "tump," "grig," "nuchal," "daddled." He will find Davenport to be a virtuoso of opaque yet immediately suggestive verbs: "to jaunce," "to shirre cingles," or "to snoove," which rings precisely like something out of the dream dictionary of Shakespeare's Bottom.

This coruscating idiom is, of course, a part of Professor Davenport's ecstatic bookishness. He breathes open and hidden quotations, allusions, bibiliographic references, mandarin puns. (p. 199)

Such bookishness, such investment in the zany, esoteric lusts of learning, puts Davenport in a definite tradition. Coleridge, supremely of this breed, spoke of "library-cormorants," of men whose nerves are set to twanging by a footnote. Burton's *The Anatomy of Melancholy* often foreshadows Davenport's mosaic of allusions. They include Nabokov—witness the mad fun of his notes and index to Pushkin's *Eugene Onegin*—and Borges, haunter of the Universal Library. And here again Pound is essential to Davenport's perspective. There are numerous ways in which his parables and prose collages are a counterpart to, a garland woven around, the omnium-gatherum of Pound's *Cantos*. Indeed, Pound and Davenport seem to represent a cultural omnivorousness, an attempt at making a complete inventory of the world's aesthetic-poetic loot, which is radically American.

Guy Davenport is equally American in a seemingly antithetical commitment to the informalities of the wild, to the innocence of untutored space. The campfire at nightfall, the sodden slog through the Maine woods and along a Vermont trail, the dive into the quarry pool in the slow heat of the Indiana or Kentucky summer—these are talismanic to Davenport. He rivals, he echoes Thoreau and Mark Twain in the knowing sensuality of his immersions in the American Arcadia. He sings the light rust on the Virginia hills, the dark pools of the Poconos. Shelter him for the wet night in an old mill up White Mountains way and Davenport hugs his luck: "Packrats in little white pants, and spiders, and lizards, no doubt, I said, and we will make friends with them all." (**"Fifty-seven Views of Fujiyama."**)

It is Davenport's genius to bring together a Byzantine high literacy and a profoundly American at-homeness on the earth. This interplay gives his whole work its offbeat freshness, its irreverent piety. . . . The cardinal terms in Davenport are continuity and unison, the cross-weave of time and of space, of experience and of innocence, made possible by montage and collage. The bison painted in the prehistoric caves at Lascaux unconsciously rhyme with Goya's etchings of bulls and Picasso's "Guernica." All times, things, forms intertwine in arabesques of manifold oneness. Ovid tells of men turning into animals, Darwin of animals turning into men. Science and poetry must spring from the same music of mind, from the same intimation of harmony, or they are nothing. Art is simply a way of seeing precisely. . . . (pp. 199-200)

It follows that there are really no differences, in tactics or panache, between Davenport's "fictions" and the literary essays now assembled for the first time [in *The Geography of the Imagination*]. The same angular elegance, erudition, and fun are manifest in both. Professor Davenport threads garland of praise and acute definition around Charles Olson, Louis Zukofsky, Marianne Moore, and Eudora Welty (this last essay being one of the finest analyses available of Miss Welty's guarded but compassionate art). The several essays on Pound are a celebration. (pp. 200-01)

Professor Davenport is illuminating on the Wittgenstein-Gertrude Stein language games and on their enactment in William Carlos Williams: "When he quotes, early in *Paterson*, a sign saying that dogs are not allowed in a park except on leashes, he wants to catch us in the Steinian-Wittgensteinian moment of seeing that, yes, the sign has a kind of purpose, but as dogs can't read, the sign exists in a sleep of reason." The covert reference to Goya is almost Davenport's signature. If this order of criticism has a fault, it is only that of generosity.

But this largesse and lightness of touch can betray Davenport. It will not do to say that Ezra Pound was driven mad by "the simple fact that the United States issues no money at all but borrows money issued by a private bank." He adds, "The hideous and obscene taxes which we pay our government are actually interest on this perpetual loan, ineradicable and unpayable." . . . Davenport's phrasing leads one to suppose that he either sympathizes with or agrees with (or both) Pound's lunatic economics. It is this "Sisyphean economic insanity," argues Davenport, that explains Pound's views on the international fiscal conspiracies of the Jews. "Such was the geometry of his vision." As it happens, it was a vision that led to some of the more nauseating anti-Semitic and anti-American diatribes in the literature of hysteria and propaganda. Undoubtedly, the issue is a tangled one as far as Pound's personal actions and mental dispositions go. But Davenport's sprightly elegance defuses altogether what should be, to him, as to other "classic imaginations," a key question. Ezra Pound and the German philosopher Martin Heidegger are very probably the two great masters of humanism in our time. This is to say that they have spoken out with more authority, with more lyric energy than any other twentieth-century poets or thinkers against the ecological devastation, the vulgarization of personal style, the blind greed that characterize our mass-consumption polity. It is in Pound's *Cantos* and in Heidegger's metaphysical and anthropological writings that we find the great restatement of classical and Confucian ideals of civic comeliness, of humane at-homeness on what is left to us of our begrimed planet. Yet in the lives and pronouncements of both men there are significant involvements with totalitarian, Fascist inhumanity. What are the underlying connections? What is it that makes high literacy so vulnerable to the siren calls of barbarism? Davenport prefers to pass.

This is true also of a second compelling domain. The world of Davenport's *ficciones* and reflections is one of homoeroticism. **"The Death of Picasso"** is among the few masterpieces of homosexual sensibility after Proust. But when it comes to perceiving articulately the pressures of this eros on the very nerve centers of modern art, thought, and social consciousness, Davenport evades. It is this evasion which reduces his vignette of Wittgenstein, in this gathering of essays, and many of the Wittgenstein allusions and presences throughout his works to trivia.

These are not, I think, random lapses. Pound's aesthetics, Pound's repertoire of what matters in the health of art and of man's social condition lie at the core of Davenport's enterprise. His hermetic wit, the sharp disingenuousness of his questionings of human discourse and gesture look to Wittgenstein, just as directly as so much in archaic Greek lyric poetry looks to the riddles and metaphors of the pre-Socratics. Guy Davenport's unreadiness to come to grips with the tragic substance of either Pound or Wittgenstein, with the larger implications of their positions, suggests a central reticence. Davenport seems to shield both himself and his readers from the full, perhaps anarchic deployment of his own strengths. A certain preciousness, a courtly scruple interposes between Professor Davenport and his daemon.

Already, however, anyone who cares for order and for grace in the exposed life of American letters is abundantly in Davenport's debt. He is, as the dour British locution has it, "not everyone's cup of tea." But to a growing number he will, I am confident, be nectar. (pp. 201-02, 204)

> *George Steiner, "Rare Bird," in* The New Yorker, *Vol. LVII, No. 41, November 30, 1981, pp. 196, 199-202, 204.*

PUBLISHERS WEEKLY

It takes a lot of energy and endurance to read the long title story in this new collection [*Apples and Pears*]. . . . Davenport . . . has a rather opaque style; here he writes in English, but weaves in so much Dutch and French that the monolinguist may feel inadequate to the task of understanding his prose. The most successful story [in *Apples and Pears*], "**Fifty-Seven Views of Fujiyama**," follows several travelers as they track courses in Vermont and Greece that parallel the journey of Basho, the Japanese poet. In "**The Chair**," Kafka accompanies the Rebbe from Belz on his daily walk and notices that the Rebbe's words are received with such respect by his entourage that the effect is ridiculous rather than profound. Davenport, with his unique perceptions, experimental style and pedantic allusions, is not easily accessible, but the persevering reader will unearth many treasures. (pp. 32-3)

> *A review of "Apples and Pears: And Other Stories," in* Publishers Weekly, *Vol. 226, No. 16, October 19, 1984, pp. 32-3.*

SAM TANENHAUS

At his best, Guy Davenport writes essays that conjure up a lush arcadia roamed by such mythological titans as Pindar, Einstein, and Disney. In his fiction, also about culture heroes, the magic falters. Davenport is a bona fide polymath, steeped in languages, the arts, and science: sometimes he crystallizes diverse ingredients into vivid Cubist portraits, full of arresting planes; but often, snared in his own learning, he muddles his collages with showy erudition and promiscuous name-dropping. A random page of his new collection, *Apples and Pears*

and Other Stories, turns up Seurat, Braque, Proust, César Franck, Picasso, Sartre, Richard Wright, and Epicurus.

A minor culture hero, the French sculptor Henri Gaudier-Brzeska, killed in World War I, narrates "**The Bowman of Shu**," a sequence of paragraphs forced into a lame surrealist construct. It begins promisingly, as Corporal Gaudier (he appended "Brzeska," after his Polish mistress), eye-deep in his foxhole, whittles the beautiful out of the horrific, paring a rifle stock into a "woman with her arms as interlocked rounded triangles over her head." But this image is soon crushed in a fusillade of pretentious reminiscences ("the godlike poet Brooke and the catatonically serious Middleton Murray, and the devout, Tancred, Flint, FitzGerald," etc.) and gnomic utterances ("Out of the new, a past"; "Love, hope, tremble, live"). Purporting to link Gaudier's fate with that of Modernism, this clutter deadens both.

Davenport's fussy prose betrays him in "**Fifty-Seven Views of Fujiyama**," alternating accounts of mountain journeys, each paralleling the travels of the 17th century haikuist Basho. Davenport manages Basho's stylized, diction well enough—"I wept to see it, and knelt before its presence, very happy and very sad"—but stumbles with the contemporary couple tramping through New Hampshire. . . . The story means, I think, to propose a universal language of wonder, bridging chasms of time and place; but instead of bending the flexible rhythms of speech into an authentic style, Davenport makes his travelers mouthpieces for a sort of aesthetic Esperanto, sapping them of identity and flattening the various landscapes into a single drab tract.

He fares better with the built-in artifice of "**The Chair**," a parable about doctrinal piety as a burlesque of true devotion. . . .

Davenport's device [in "**Apples and Pears**"] is a diary, subdivided into fragments, often titled. . . . The diarist is Adriaan van Hovendaal, randy scholar of Charles Fourier and a holdover from *Tatlin!*, Davenport's first volume of fiction. In "**Apples and Pears**," Adriaan resumes his copulations with a new protégé, an opulently endowed painter named Sander. They are joined by Sander's sister, Grietje, then by Jan, Hans, Saartje, Bruno, Kaatje, and others, distinguishable only by name, in activities that would be salacious did Adriaan not report them in a stupefying pastiche of *Ulysses*. . . . Not even the author's original illustrations—meticulous panels of men in bulging briefs, men bulging without briefs and, oddly, briefs bulging without men—stimulate the benumbed reader to any tumescence of his own. . . .

What's strangest about this lunacy is its deliberate execution. Instead of building on the wonderful essays in *The Geography of the Imagination*, Davenport has mysteriously recycled his weakest material. *Apples and Pears*, 10 years in the ripening, is described on the dust jacket as a "novel-length work of fiction," an absurd phrase which possibly masks a warning: the next decade may yield yet another harvest of dubious fruit.

> *Sam Tanenhaus, "Briefs Encounter," in* The Village Voice, *Vol. XXIX, No. 51, December 18, 1984, p. 72.*

BOB HALLIDAY

The art of allusion, of adding layers of meaning and context to a fictional world through a system of references and quotations, has been near the center of all of Davenport's fiction to date, and *Apples and Pears,* his fourth and most recent story collection, is no exception. Once again, unusual demands are made on the reader's knowledge of literary history, philosophy, art and language, especially as they relate to the modernist eruptions which took place during the early part of this century.

Davenport makes a gesture of acknowledgement to Pound with the first story, **"The Bowmen of Shu,"** which takes its title from one of the translations in Pound's *Cathay* collection. In it, using the detached, impressionistic paragraphs which have become a feature of his fictional style, Davenport projects a collage of irreconcilable experiences which gave rise to stylistic radicalism among the artists of the World War I period. While focusing on the Vorticist sculptor Henri Gaudier-Brzeska, killed in the trenches in June 1915, the story evokes the discovery of a primitivist esthetic powerful enough to wrench beauty from the seemingly inexpressible ugliness European civilization had brought upon itself. Through this new art, atrocities arising from social conventions can be ripped aside to reveal the spontaneous beauty of natural energies underneath. *"It will not look like you,"* Gaudier-Brzeska tells the subject of his *Hieratic Bust of Ezra Pound*. "It will look like your energy." . . .

Nature is more directly the subject of **"Fifty-Seven Views of Fujiyama,"** the second and most purely lyrical of the stories. Alternate paragraphs follow the 17th-century haiku poet Basho as he sells his house and sets out with his neighbor Kawai Sogoro on his famous journey on the narrow road to the north. Davenport clearly feels affection for this poet who "would have [traveled] light enough except for gifts my friends loaded me with at parting, and my own unessential one thing and another which I cannot throw away because my heart is silly," and suffuses his descriptions of landscapes in pre-Westernized Japan with a sense of wonder.

Counterpointed against the account of Basho's journey are narratives of similar expeditions into the countryside taken by travelers in later centuries. A contemporary young American couple sets off on the Vermont Trail, which passes through a long-abandoned orchard. Davenport's narrator reflects this wilderness in musical prose. . . .

Wonder at the landscape has a place in this narrative, too, but in a more ambiguous and troubling way. The couple gets lost, the narrator seems to hallucinate an old mill while seeking shelter from a rainstorm, and his girlfriend sprains an ankle as they make their way through an uncharted swamp.

Other travelers make brief appearances, including a naturalist who provides paleontological data on plant distribution and an anonymous visitor trying to recall a forgotten Spanish word for the aged Ezra Pound. All of these strands are woven together by repeated reminders that all travel is really through time. . . . The individual narratives fuse into a single situation: that of the artistically sensitive personality in an encounter with nature.

"The Chair," briefer and more conventional than the other stories in the new collection, follows Franz Kafka as he watches the Rebbe of Belz taking his evening walk at Marienbad. As the Rebbe makes his pronouncements, Kafka experiences a personal revelation. "O the goodness of the Master of the Universe," says the Rebbe, "to have created apples and pears. . . . [The Rebbe's] chair held aloft by its bearer, Dr. Kafka notices, has now defined what art is as distinct from nature, for its pattern of flowers and leaves looks tawdry and artificial and seriously out of place against the green and rustling leaves of the apple and pear trees."

This equation of apples and pears with the superiority of nature over artifice is the bridge to **"Apples and Pears"** itself, the longest and for this reader the weakest piece of fiction that Davenport has produced so far. Like much of his earlier writing, this novel is written directly under the influence of Charles Fourier's utopian social theories, which center on the concept that suppression of human desire is the great source of evil in human social systems.

"Apples and Pears" takes the form of a series of notebooks written by the Dutch philosopher Adriaan Floris van Hovendaal, who is involved in a group attempt to put Fourier's theories into practice. The notebook entries are interspersed with letters, reminiscences and other forms of narrative by the various characters participating in or observing the experiment. Readers of the earlier long Davenport story, **"The Dawn in Erewhon,"** will recognize some of them a decade or so further into their lives and will also meet some new ones. . . .

It would take more space than is available here to begin to catalogue the varieties of nonsense Davenport contrives for these characters in the name of Fourierian utopianism, but what we have here is certainly not Brook Farm. The problem seems to be that he views human desire to be primarily sexual desire, and tailors his characters accordingly.

Since the viewpoint is obsessively male homosexual, all of the men are handsome, muscular and admirably endowed by nature to inhabit the cheerful porno scenario Davenport devises for them. The females are beautiful enough to be functional. Those who are creative, like Adriaan and Sander, are understood to be highly gifted. The chief activity of this little community, aside from the production of masterpieces, is masturbation, male primarily, which is practiced in full view of the reader so relentlessly that even those who share Davenport's apparent delectation in all of this will be stupefied.

The style Davenport chooses for transmitting this vision is often distressingly cute, full of blushes, wrinkled noses and kisses on the corner of the mouth, repetitive to the point of fetishism on the subject of male parts and undergarments. These faults are shared by Davenport's illustrations for the story, which are sentimental and shallowly pretty despite references to de Stijl and other artistic styles. The narrative is heavily peppered with Dutch, most of which will be intelligible to readers with a knowledge of German, and overlaid with allusions to such other visions of a better future as Samuel Butler's machineless Erewhon and the noble society which was expected to follow the French Revolution, represented here by references to the months of the Napoleonic calendar.

The untenability of this sexual never-never land is obvious in the fact that no even remotely credible character ever turns up to shatter all the onanistic fantasy. No truly adult sexual emotion is ever recorded. No policeman ever turns up to check into all the kiddie sex.

The overall effect is of *The 100 Days of Sodom* gone sappy. While Sade's monsters are always ready to incinerate a spouse or throw a coprophagous banquet in demonstration of some wildly overextended philosophical point, Davenport's beautiful and sexually inexhaustible creatures miss no opportunity to shed their jeans and *onderbroeken* and have another go at it in the name of poor, dead Fourier. As with Sade, one would like to dismiss the whole thing as satire, but it possesses too much of the sincerity of cherished personal fantasy to permit such an interpretation.

"Apples and Pears" is disappointing not because of its sexual views, which are infantile and harmless, but because it represents a failure of imagination. Despite its erudite and multicultural armor of allusions to imagined earthly paradises where innocence and sin regain their true meanings, the work fails to reveal the least trace of real humanity or substantial emotion amid all the coupling and creating it chronicles. The eccentric Fourier, to whom Davenport dedicates the entire volume, surely had other things in mind.

> Bob Halliday, *"Guy Davenport's Terrestrial Paradise," in* Book World—The Washington Post, *January 20, 1985, p. 8.*

JEROME KLINKOWITZ

Guy Davenport's fiction is enriched by a stimulating blend of history and imagination, and *Apples and Pears and Other Stories* adds healthy amounts of philosophy and sexuality which have been developing in his earlier collections. Each of them, from *Tatlin!* (1974) and *DaVinci's Bicycle* (1979) through *Eclogues* (1981) and this newest book, ends with a much longer work, often approaching novella length. These concluding pieces are good signals of Davenport's methods and goals, and looking back through them shows how *Apples and Pears* emerges as his major work to date.

The first two books are characterized by such "necessary fictions" as Kafka brushing shoulders with Wittgenstein at an air show.... Such contrivances are needed, Davenport believes, because a person is nothing more than he or she knows; by bringing imagination to bear on history, the human record is both enlarged and made more completely our own. (p. 216)

Philosophy faces Davenport's test in **"The Dawn in Erewhon,"** the 130-page novella which ends *Tatlin!* Here he makes his first tentative moves toward fleshing out a utopian ideal in the shared sexuality of Adriaan von Hovendaal and his friends Bruno and Kaatje. Sex itself, with a Fourier-like philosophy quietly implicit, runs a happy riot among the French children in **"On Some Lines of Virgil"** which closes *Eclogues*. In *Apples and Pears* Davenport brings it all together: the necessary fiction of Gaudier-Brzeska pondering Modernism from the trenches opposite the western front and Kafka mimicking the self-taken Rebbe of Belz, the enrichment of a present-day camping trip with the travel journals of a classic haiku poet, and most impressively a four-piece collection within the collection, **"Apples and Pears."**

This latest fiction set in the world of a contemporary Fourierist philosopher draws on all of Davenport's characteristics and makes for his strongest work. Philosophy, sex, and history are not allowed a moment's domination over each other, but instead fuse in a convincing imaginative vision.... The theme of apples and pears runs through the collection, often providing a context for Davenport's deeper thoughts on art and experience. At the end of **"The Chair,"** when the Rebbe pauses to inspect an orchard, Kafka notes that his chair, when held aloft by its bearer, "has now defined what art is as distinct from nature, for its pattern of flowers and leaves looks tawdry and artificial and seriously out of place against the green and rustling leaves of apple and pear trees." *Apples and Pears* constantly holds art up to nature, just as Adriaan's philosophy is always given the test of action. As he and his friends establish an ideal communal household of love and culture, so Davenport creates a fictive world in which the activities of making art and love combine in a natural philosophy for which belief need rarely be suspended.

Guy Davenport's world is one of nature and intelligence in ideal balance.... Adriaan's belief that for utopia to exist a complementarity must be restored between nature and artifice, Erewhonian time receding to a pre-machine age so that Fourier's Harmony may begin.

That Harmony is based on the attractions of desire, and **"Apples and Pears"** gives desire free rein. Through the novella's four sections characters undress, share each other's beds and clothes, and make love in all combinations of sex and age. "Poetry in the Harmony will be a system of analogies and correspondences noted by children and gifted adults," Adriaan notes, and as author Guy Davenport reifies this aesthetic with sex. His characters paint, write poems and philosophy, and love each other's bodies all in the same spirit of unfettered creativity. (pp. 216-17)

Throughout **"Apples and Pears"** Davenport struggles to locate what he calls, here and also in the title of his collected essays, "the geography of the imagination." For Adriaan it is an attempt to create "the Ohio of Fourier's vision," while for Davenport it is to test the limits of a philosophical ideal by actually writing out all the possibilities. If prose can contain them, then the vision is sound, just as Fourier believed that there must be some design answerable by "the natural attractions immutably built into our being." In *Apples and Pears and Other Stories* Davenport, to his great credit as a writer, follows these desire to their ultimate fruition in fictive event. (p. 218)

> Jerome Klinkowitz, in a review of "Apples and Pears and Other Stories," in The Review of Contemporary Fiction, *Vol. 6, No. 1, Spring, 1986, pp. 216-18.*

Samuel R(ay) Delany (Jr.)

1942-

American novelist, short story writer, critic, memoirist, and editor.

Delany is regarded as one of the most inventive writers in the science fiction genre. He is often associated with authors who gained prominence in the New Wave science fiction movement of the 1960s, including Thomas Disch, J. G. Ballard, and Roger Zelazny. Like these writers, Delany places less emphasis on the physical sciences and technology and more on the social and psychological aspects of his created worlds and characters, thus expanding the traditional scope of science fiction to include aspects of mainstream literature. Delany evokes his complex societies through poetic language replete with symbolism, imagery, and metaphor. Although each of his created worlds is unique, his books share several concerns, among them language and myth and their influence upon perception, the difficulties of communication, and the act of creation. Many critics and readers find Delany's narratives confusing because of their nonlinear storylines, shifting characters, and distortion of time. Despite varied critical response to his works, Delany has acquired a strong cult following.

A number of Delany's novels are structured as quests and allude to myths and archetypes, combining elements of ancient tales with modern rationalism. *The Jewels of Aptor* (1962), Delany's first novel, initiates his thematic vision and his intention to draw on literary tradition in union with allusion and stylistic experimentation. In *Babel-17* (1966), Delany explores the complex interplay of language, thought, and culture in his tale of two civilizations at war. *The Einstein Intersection* (1967) and *Nova* (1968), two of his most mythically suggestive works, include elements of the Holy Grail legend and the myths of Orpheus and Prometheus. *Dhalgren* (1975) is widely considered Delany's most demanding creation. The novel elicited critical controversy because it lacks a point of reference for the reader; it has no beginning or ending, nor a definite sense of time or place. Even its protagonist has no identity other than "The Kid," whose quest is to discover his true name and background. In *Triton* (1976), Delany depicts a utopian society where every type of social relationship and sexual identity is acceptable. Delany's recent novel, *Stars in My Pocket Like Grains of Sand* (1984), was praised by Tom Easton as "a magnificently intricate work of the imagination, an awesomely ambitious extrapolation of the human condition." In this volume, the first of what he calls a "diptych," Delany devises new language interpretations intended to circumvent sexism in conventional English.

In addition to his novels, Delany has written short stories collected in *Driftglass* (1971) and *Tales of Nevèrÿon* (1979), and several critical works, including *The Jewel-Hinged Jaw* (1977) and *The American Shore* (1978). Delany has won the Nebula Award four times: in 1966 for *Babel-17*, in 1967 for *The Einstein Intersection* and the short story "Aye, and Gomorrah," and in 1969 for another short story, "Time Considered as a Helix of Precious Stones," for which he also received a Hugo Award.

(See also *CLC*, Vols. 8, 14; *Contemporary Authors,* Vols. 81-84; and *Dictionary of Literary Biography,* Vols. 8, 33.)

Courtesy of Henry Morrison Inc.

DOUGLAS BARBOUR

From the beginning, Delany has been noticed and praised as an important new talent in science fiction. *Babel-17* and *The Einstein Intersection* won Nebula Awards, as has some of his shorter fiction; one story, **"Time Considered as a Helix of Semi-Precious Stones"**, won both the Nebula and Hugo Awards. . . . As Judith Merril points out, Delany "is in a unique position in sf today: everybody loves him. The 'solid core', the casual readers, the literary dippers-in, the 'new-thing' crowd—Delany is all things to all readers". I believe Delany has earned such accolades.

Delany is not only a gifted writer, he is one of the most articulate theorists of sf to have emerged from the ranks of its writers. As the author of a number of important critical essays and an editor of the short-lived speculative quarterly, *Quark,* he has done much to open up critical discussion of sf as a genre, forcefully arguing its great potential as art.

Although his short stories reveal the same concern with craft as do his novels, and deal with the same basic themes, the novels provide the best guide to his development as a writer. I deal with them under four headings: the quest pattern; his use of the figures of the artist and the criminal; cultural invention; and style and structure, a large section dealing with his use of literary and mythological allusions, his continual concern to develop a poetic prose in which image and metaphor are of primary importance, and his slowly maturing vision of the novel as ''a monumental metaphor''. Although Delany's early novels can be discussed under these headings, they are neither as complex nor as sophisticated as his later ones. Because *Empire Star* represents a sudden leap forward in terms of his handling of his diverse materials, it and the novels after it require a more thorough discussion than the earlier work. Furthermore, it can be argued that *Nova* represents the culmination of all the experiments with form and style that begin in *Empire Star,* although the concern with style is present in his work from the beginning. (pp. 106-07)

One reason Delany is such a fine sf writer is that, like Le Guin and Russ, he puts his characters in concrete cultural situations, in which they can be seen to act quite naturally. For his future human civilizations he invents a multitude of cultural possibilities. These depend on whether his outlook in a particular novel tends toward utopia or dystopia, whether he attempts to show progress or regress. Unlike Le Guin he does not posit a single future history stretching over a number of novels. In his early novels, he tends to use fairly ordinary methods to suggest the kinds of culture his characters represent; in the later galactic novels, he tends to use manners and *mores* to show up cultural differences, and to present a number of different cultures within a single system, usually galaxy-wide; this presentation of a whole scale of cultures within a single civilization is hinted at in *Empire Star* and presented in some depth in *Babel-17* and *Nova.* (p. 108)

The huge galactic civilization of *Empire Star* contains every kind of culture, from simplex to the most multiplex, on its many planets. Throughout, the speech patterns of the various characters reveal their cultural levels.... Since *Empire Star* is really concerned with demonstrating that a fiction is a world created out of language, it seems only proper that in it the indications of cultural difference should be language more than actions.

In *Babel-17,* Delany explores the relationship between language and culture, or, more specifically, between language and *Weltanschauung,* more comprehensively than previously. As in *Empire Star,* the forms of speech of the people in the military, Transport, Customs, or the pirate society of Jebel's Tarik, imply various differences in outlook in those subcultures. The linguistic theme is carried much further, however, in the detailed examination of the implications of a ''new'' language such as Babel-17. In his presentation of Rydra's analysis of Babel-17, and in her discussion of translation problems with the totally alien Ciribians ..., Delany extrapolates in the ''soft'' science of linguistics, using as his speculative base the Sapin-Whorf hypothesis of linguistic relativity.

In *Babel-17,* Delany also presents a galactic civilization in detail for the first time, rather than just implying its existence as he does in the previous two novels. He also returns to a kind of social analysis within the fiction not seen since *The Fall of the Towers.* Working within the basic outline of sf's ''future history'', Delany creates many original variations on its ideas. *Babel-17* differs from most earlier novels not only in its linguistic speculations but in its implicit assumption that cultural shifts and differences are revealed more in ''software'' and social behaviour than in technological changes. This assumption pushes Delany's later novels speculatively further than

most hard-science sf, which tends to assume that no matter how much the world or universe may change in terms of scientific or technological advances, peoples' behaviour will remain the same. Sf writers have only recently begun to imagine that people might very well radically change the manner of their lives in new and different circumstances. The visions of change can be unpleasant ..., but Delany tends to project such large overall civilizations that, although the worst possible kinds of living conditions can be found within their borders, the general outlook is hopeful in its range and openness to alternative possibilities. He presents some startling, yet suggestively probable, new ways of life, without obtrusive moralising. They are possible, therefore worth exploring.

Delany assumes, in both *Babel-17* and *Nova,* that in the future technology will be humanised somehow, bringing to an end man's alienation from his work and thus from his world. This assumption, which gives both books an aura of humane speculation missing in much science fiction, is fully worked out in *Nova,* but it is present in *Babel-17* in the single area of Transport, at least. Much of the cultural interest of the novel focuses on the difference between Transport and Customs. Transport is the name for starship personnel, who live apart on every world in their own sector, while Customs is everything else, most specifically all planet-based business, and its members lead more ordinary lives than Transport people do. (pp. 110-12)

Although the presentation of Transport is perhaps the most interesting cultural speculation in *Babel-17,* Delany creates representatives of other cultural possibilities within his projected future. The rigid military establishment, still very like the military of today, the somewhat superficial ''society'' of the higher-ups in the War Yards, shown at their worst/best during the dinner party held for Rydra and her crew ..., the ''pirate'' society of Jebel's Tarik, with its spartan readiness to fight and its almost medieval dining customs and entertainments, including an official jester ..., where a desire for culture and a high cruelty mix spontaneously, and the criminal and prison sub-culture of the Alliance implied in Butcher's memories of his recent past life ..., fill in a picture of a huge and varied society, like any large human society but ''different'' too.

The Einstein Intersection represents a completely ''different'' situation. As the non-humans of that novel unsuccessfully attempt to live through the alien, to them, culture patterns of man, the whole problem of their insuperable differences from us is reflected in the chaos of their social and cultural behaviour. Change is the only constant in their world, as the ever-increasing pace of the narrative implies. There can be no cultural constants in such a situation, ... though the people have to realise this before the knowledge can be put to use. While they try to live by the myths of man, they cannot create a viable culture of their own.... [But] their more profound hope is to recognise that they do not have to live out the old myths at all, that the ''difference'' they seek to hide or dissemble is the key to their cultural and racial salvation. Therefore, Lobey's eventual acceptance of his difference, and his pattern-breaking recognition that he does not have to repeat the myths associated with him, are the proper responses to the situation.... Using a variety of fictional techniques to render this insight in concrete language, Delany achieves his most multiplex novel thus far.

Nova is even larger and more multiplex. One, perhaps even minor, aspect of its richness of invention is the full presentation of completely humanized technology that has resulted in a totally new and galaxy-wide culture. (pp. 112-14)

Delany invents a technology full of hope for the human condition in *Nova*. Positing the end of the worker's alienation from his work, which Marx exposed in *Das Kapital,* he postulates the concomitant end of man's alienation from the universe around him by showing that anyone who serves as a cyborg stud on board a starship, an opportunity open to all, communes with the cosmos itself. Yet *Nova* is not a utopian fiction. . . . Fully aware of the political and ethical vagaries of man, Delany knows that technological changes cannot alter man in any *absolute* way. *Nova*'s galactic civilisation is better than ours, on the whole, but it is not absolutely good. Men can now choose their work, and even enjoy it, but there are still rich and poor, even if only relatively poor. The political/economic system is a modified form of capitalism, in which certain groups, or cartels, have achieved economic and political power over vast numbers of people, if only in an abstract manner. In this civilization, as usual, individuals, even the most powerful, still suffer the personal pains of love and hate.

The invention of a technological breakthrough which fundamentally changes man's relationship to his work is only one aspect of Delany's cultural speculation in *Nova*. He creates a galaxy split into three sectors: the oldest, Draco, ruled from Earth and conservative; the newest, the Outer Colonies, a mining area mostly, with analogues to the "third world" of contemporary politics, has been settled by the poorer classes; while the third, Pleiades Federation, settled by a kind of middle class breaking out from the confines of Draco, which was opened up by governments and large corporations, like the Reds. The people from these different sectors reflect their backgrounds in their actions, speech and total behaviour. Lorq deliberately picks his crew to represent all three sectors, and, as they interact and converse, a complete picture of their differences emerges. As in *Empire Star,* Delany makes good use of speech patterns to represent cultural differences. (pp. 114-15)

The civilization of the three sectors is so diverse and extensive, Delany must use important details to imply whole areas of experience. For example, education in this plug-dominated universe is obviously different from what we have today. Only a few glimpses of "education" are given, but they add up to an impressive vision. . . . Most "education" is . . . democratic . . . , providing entries into all possible ways of life in the galaxy. (pp. 115-16)

I have not even begun to indicate the range and variety of ways in which Delany fills in a large cultural mosaic in . . . [*Nova*], but I believe he has created one of the most fully realized pictures of an interstellar society, within the confines of one novel anyway, in all sf. Yet he does not stop at that. All this background is subjected to the philosophical speculations of various characters in the novel. Thus the use of the Tarot, combined with Katin's explanation of why it has become important in the post-Ashton Clark universe, reveals the spiritual roots and sophistication of *Nova*'s invented civilization. There is also an historical analysis, placing that civilization's beginnings in the twentieth century, with the major exception of the invention of the philosophical backing for plugs in the twenty-third. . . .

The continuing argument about the basic "lack of cultural solidity" in *Nova*'s universe is central to one of the themes of the novel. Lorq first hears about it, when, with Prince and Ruby Red, he listens in on his parents' garden party conversation as a young child . . . , but the problem is brought up in relation to various characters throughout the novel. Katin is obsessed with it because, as a novelist-in-the-making, he is aware of the importance of social analysis in the Novel. The refrain, "we live in an age where economic, political, and technological change have shattered all cultural traditions" . . . , is counterpointed against concrete presentations of cultural activities throughout the novel until it culminates in Katin's realization, near the end, that it is mistaken. (p. 116)

Delany's entirely decorous, fictional analysis within the narrative of the culture he has invented for *Nova,* breaks new analytical ground in contemporary sf. (p. 117)

Samuel R. Delany's work reveals that . . . he is by far the most self-conscious practitioner of his art. His own term "multiplex" probably best describes his work (attitudes, ideas, themes, craftsmanship, all their inter-relations, as well as his relation, as artist, to them all). A poet . . . , Delany is one of the finest wordsmiths in sf, a true "maker". His great perseverance in continually developing his craft and never resting on his past achievements is revealed in the steady growth of artistry and multiplexity that can be traced through his first seven novels. His study of fictional craft has led him to the conclusion that fictions are "models of reality" whose relation to "the real world" is ambiguous and oblique, and totally unlike that of an historical report or newspaper article. As a result of this realization, he has become one of sf's most important experimenters, discovering, in the novels since *Empire Star,* new and exciting ways to use the forms of fiction in the creation of fictions. (pp. 119-20)

> *Douglas Barbour, "Cultural Invention and Metaphor in the Novels of Samuel R. Delany," in* Foundation, *Nos. 7 & 8, March, 1975, pp. 105-21.*

PETER S. ALTERMAN

Within the last few years, there have been additions to the anthology of science-fiction definitions which are not rooted in archetypes, themes, or emotional responses, but in the way language is used in science fiction. Whether or not they are universally applicable, these recent linguistic definitions do help shed light on one of the field's most enigmatic and controversial writers, Samuel R. Delany. A stylistic analysis of Delany's fiction does assist the reader in understanding the larger fictive concerns at work in his novels. (p. 25)

Delany's literary style is a combination of subtly derived linguistic techniques coupled with a disturbing liberation of certain structural elements. Within Delany's novels, time, logic, and point of view are cut loose from traditional literary positions, and function relativistically. Yet these free elements are rigidly controlled by the rules of a relativistic universe, thereby fulfilling Delany's comment . . . [in the appendix to *Triton* (1976)] that technical possibility actualizes metaphor in science fiction.

In *Dhalgren* (1975), after Kid has made his first run with the Scorpions against Emboriky's, he retreats to the Reverend Tayler's for a meal and meets Ernest Newboy. There he corrects the galleys for his collection of poems, *Brass Orchids*. Lanya meets him and they realize that for him one day has passed, but for the rest of Bellona, five days have passed. . . . The issue of the linearity of time in Delany's novels is clearly shown here. In Bellona, time is not a constant.

In the relativistic universe, time is indeed not a constant, but is related to the velocity and frame of reference of the observer. This is dramatized in *Dhalgren,* and although it is a physical reality of the universe we all inhabit, we persist in viewing time as a universal and linear norm.

The uses of time in Delany's novels, here and more notably in *Empire Star* (1966), violate certain conventions of prose fiction. What seems to be a fantastic use of time is in fact a realistic use of time, because time is psychologically a function of the state of the observer and physically a function of the velocity of the observer. In more traditional fiction, the use of psychological time is well understood. But when Delany applies relativistic physical laws to time, the psychological metaphor of variable time becomes confusing, because the metaphor has been transformed into fact.

Empire Star presents much the same kind of tortured time. Comet Jo, the first "hero" of the novel, travels through a universe which is bent back on itself in a cycloid motion. Everything has already happened. He meets the same people, including himself, at various times of their lives. On one level, this is a nice manipulation of technique, showing the development of the hero's awareness of historicity and his part in it. But then Delany turns the technique on its head by showing the reader that time is, indeed, twisted in the universe. The center of the galaxy, Empire Star, gathers in time and space through a warp, bends it, and returns it in different sequence. This further confuses the reader, who has been expecting a proper linear end to the story. In fact, time and space are warped around gravity wells. And *Empire Star* is designed to be read as a sequence of perceptions of the same story. . . . The properties of physical space are here used to serve the aesthetic and formal needs of the novel. (pp. 25-6)

[In his book *Structural Fabulation*, Robert Scholes] points out that the modern novelist's response is to accept the impossibility of recording the real, and to create a system based upon subjectivity. This position is interestingly much like Delany's position, for he not only accepts narrative subjectivity, but he applies to the subjective presence of, say, time, a physical concept which supports his unique use of time. In this manner, what Delany is doing by insisting upon a subjective or eccentric temporal mode is both satisfying the need of the modern novel to emphasize the impossibility of rendering the world outside, and at the same time presenting a close and scientifically acceptable vision of the world.

In a like manner, Delany deals creatively with the question of point of view, which is another shifting element. In *Empire Star,* the narrator is ostensibly a crystallized and objective point. Yet throughout the novel, we learn more and more about the point of view (not as a character, but as a force in the novel). Jewel, the narrative device, eventually unfolds enough of the plot for us to understand that the ordering of the elements is left to us. There is no attempt made to explicate or order the sequence of actions for the reader. The first reading is from the point of view of Comet Jo, learning his way from youth to maturity to an understanding of the nature of his task in life. This position leads to a second reading, of the nature of the society of the Lll, and the story of their freedom and bondage, with Jo playing a minor role. Then a third sequential reading, from the point of view of the Jewel itself, is suggested.

In each of these readings, more of the substance of the novel is revealed, and each uses a different point of view. Yet there is only one novel. The answer to this paradox is that at the end of the novel, the reader is challenged to read multi-levelly (multiplexially), with an eye on the growth of the narrator, protagonist, and universe. . . . (pp. 26-7)

A second example of the fluidity of the narrator is in *Dhalgren*. Kid clearly is responsible for writing the journal, and therein perhaps the novel, but there are many Kids. There is Kidd, the confused immigrant, Kid the Poet, who also may be Ernest Newboy, Kid the Scorpion leader, and finally, the Michael Henry. Which Kid is the narrator of *Dhalgren*? They all are, for as Kid ventures farther and farther into the maze of Bellona, he changes. And as he changes, the novel he writes changes. In order to understand the nature of the narrator, one must then not attempt to discover a static character, but to apprehend both a personality and the way that personality changes. Perhaps this is a major confusing element of the novel, for we read the novel through Kid's eyes, but those eyes are not the same throughout the novel.

The metaphor of a person's changing as he grows is literalized and exaggerated. But Delany has also accepted an implicit requirement of that act—his novel changes as its narrator changes. In the absence of many traditional science fiction motifs, this one stylistic element—the concretizing of a metaphor—gives *Dhalgren* the unmistakable flavor of science fiction.

A third area where Delany's fiction is unexpectedly fluid is in his use of logic. (p. 27)

Delany's non-linear, non-rational logic is predictably built upon a mathematical model: Gödel's Law. . . . The resultant universe is one in which traditional rational explication takes second place. It is a universe of experience and emotion. It is a world where the protagonist may not know what is going on, but will be able to act on the experience of something's happening.

This is, in fact, what Lobey does [in *The Einstein Intersection* (1967)]. He reacts with no intellectual understanding of what he is doing. Furthermore the chapter epigraphs are all related to the chapters they present, sometimes by clear logical links, but more often by non-linear relationships, which exemplify the creative link between the artist's rational experience and his non-rational translation of that experience into his art. Taken together with the text of the novel, the epigraphs form an example of the novel's concept of the relationship between experience and art. Delany seems to be trying to manipulate the textures of experiences, not the meanings of those experiences, in order to elicit emotional responses from the reader and from his protagonist. . . . Delany . . . [asserts] that his fiction is designed to elicit a range of ordered responses from the reader, generated by sequences of key orders, images, or patterns. The rational and logical form of traditional prose . . . attempts to create a pattern of purely logical, intellectual responses to a closely reasoned argument, what the novel would consider an "Einsteinian" response. *The Einstein Intersection* manipulates experiences to produce the desired sequence of emotional reponses from Lobey and from the reader.

The same sequence of choreographed patterns is called for in *Dhalgren* when, for example, the giant red sun rises over Bellona. There is no rational explanation presented for it. Nor is there any causal link with it in the text of the novel. Yet the wonder it creates is a response to the wonder Kid and the reader feel at the marvelous mating of Kid, Lanya, and Danny for the first time. . . . Yet the major effect of the giant sun cannot be apprehended by looking for logical connectives, although they are present. We must read it as a symbolic response to the experience of coming awake in a new world of wonder, of making love, and being loved, for the first time.

While this concern with patterns of response may seem to be a retreat into the philosophy of communication, it is central to

Delany's style—a style which baffles many readers. Once again, Delany has taken a normally static element, logic, and wrenched it into a new, fluid role. At the same time, he has founded his actions in legitimate theoretical bases. In so doing, he has reconciled the ideological problem of the modern novelist, identified by Scholes—that of the limitations of realism—with a theory of science fiction as a stylistic construct reconciling the various forms of experience within a relativistic and formal universe.

Each of the three areas broken free by Delany—time, point of view, and logic—is broken on the authority of some valid, or potentially valid, physical law or thesis. In turn, the freedom these elements lend to Delany's novels requires close attention from the reader, lest he become confused by looking for the traditional prose forms.

Close attention is just what Delany gives to his fiction, most obviously to the very sentences out of which the novels grow. In the essay **"Thickening the Plot,"** Delany sets about to define the creative process in concrete terms. In this essay, he stresses the photographic accuracy of his imaginings, the completeness with which he visualizes his subject, and describes how he forces visual precision into his language. He also notes that the very process of converting the vision into language changes the scene being described, so that the final product is a surreal translation, a partnership between the rich word and the richer vision, the translation of the vision affecting the vision itself. This methodology implies a rigid adherence to the concrete, the sensual, the "realistic" world on one hand, and to the mythic, metaphoric elements of language on the other. Here again Delany confronts the opposing moments of force, the photographic "real" and the untrustworthy "subjective."

The practical effect of striving for the precise evocation of experience gives a unique flavor to that experience. Delany's novels display an intense sense of being in touch with the physical world. In fact, the effort of accurately rendering the physical drives Delany to confront the limits of perceived experience, the point at which language breaks down under the intensity of his gaze, and forces him toward a new use of language.

For example, the presence of multiplicity and simultaneity in Delany's mental images of reality demands that he jam multiplicity into the essentially linear and sequential form of English prose. (pp. 27-9)

The handling of simultaneous material in a necessarily linear form is a good indication of the kind of word-by-word craftsmanship in Delany's prose. In resolving the problem of rendering a "fantastic" or science-fictional sequence realistically, he visualizes the subject matter completely, rather than retreating from it into vague cubist shapes or highly mannered prose. And remarkably, by striving to describe the seams of reality, he breaks through "reality" to describe the perceiving mind as much as the perceived experience. The parenthetical statement is a good example, for it is both a pause in the exposition and a gloss on the transcribed experience without. Together, reality, observer, and language form a collage of meaning. It is like his concretizing of metaphor. The vaguely *like* becomes the solid *is*. Precision is what these two techniques share.

Delany's theoretical concern with the uses of prose appears frequently in his fiction, almost as if the work was a test-bed for linguistic theory. He considers the totality of the story, plot, character, language, etc. to be a *textus*, or web of meaning, within which the text proper resides. The manner in which

textus translates into text he alludes to with the term metonymy, the concept of language as connotative rather than denotative. . . . It is therefore not unusual to find images of myths, meanings, and memories, as well as convoluted symbolism in Delany's fiction. His concept of language and literature implies this rich depth of layering. . . . That each major group of metonymic meanings has an analogue in the surface of the story is proof enough of that. What Delany does with this technique is to make the reader feel the weight of meaning and symbol around the text, i.e., invoke a *textus* for the story. This enriches the story, and charges the linear tale with alternative meanings, possibilities, and significance. It is another way of transcending the limitations of realism, of working in the subjective mind of the reader.

In other places, Delany's insistence on the perception of language as a burdened element is more baldly stated, or worked into the tale. . . . (p. 30)

The image of the text as a web of meaning itself is present in the body of Delany's fiction, especially in *Babel-17* [1966], which in this light can be read as an animated recitation on the nature of the relationship between language and meaning:

> She rose slowly, and the web caught her around the chest. Some sort of infirmary. She looked down at the—not "webbing", but rather a three particle vowel differential, each particle of which defined one stress of the three-way tie, so that the weakest points in the mesh were identified when the total sound of the differential reached its lowest point. By breaking the threads at these points, she realized, the whole web would unravel. Had she failed at it, and not named it in this new language, it would have been more than secure enough to hold her. The transition from "memorized" to "known" had taken place while she had been. . . .

In this example, Rydra Wong has just learned how to think in the highly artificial language of Babel-17, which forces her to think, perceive, and react in an extremely precise and rapid way. The web is an image of the effects of language on the mind and of the mind as shaper of reality. This scene becomes symbolic of the inter-relationship of mind, language, and reality, a web like the triple-stressed web Rydra lies in, analyzes, and breaks.

The experience of the work of art transcends the language used to construct it, because of, not in spite of, the nature of Delany's use of words. The technique Delany uses is to move beyond the literal, not by a retreat from concrete reality, but by approaching the literal closely, so closely that the mind of the narrator/artist shows through. Delany's prose style is an amalgam of elements: the precise visual rendering of images coupled with a conscious use of metonymy to create a language of experience.

Complementing Delany's theoretical concern with the function of his prose is an equally obvious concern with structural issues, such as the definition of the novel in *Nova* [1968], the relationship between theoretical criticism and creative writing in *Dhalgren,* and, of course, the question of point of view in *Empire Star*. . . . Whereas Delany's idea of language is accretive and inclusive, his idea of literary forms is much more rigid and formal. (p. 31)

Many of Delany's novels . . . are characterized by a conscious discussion of the formal nature and function of literature and the relationship between experience and art. In every case, art is able to organize experience, bringing pattern and order to chaos. This issue manifests itself in Delany's use of language: the order of realism rests uneasily on the chaotic subjectivism of the perceiving narrator. These two stylistic elements identify a central concern of his fiction: his prose attempts to render the texture of the chaotic universe by actualizing literary metaphors with scientific theory, and the larger construct of his prose attempts to organize that chaos into intelligible, translatable forms.

For Delany, the process of artistic creation is an attempt to derive order from the chaos of experience. More precisely, it is an attempt to reconcile the contrary demands of the subjective perspective of the artist, who must admit to experiencing life from a biased point of view—the structural requirements of formal literary patterns, which can wrench meaning and order from randomness, and the restrictions inherent in language as a medium of transmitting vision. In Delany's prose, neither the subjective nor the objective—neither the chaos of the individual mind's perceiving, nor the artifice of literary device, is given primacy. Just as metaphor is solidified by fact, experience is ordered by the effect of art upon the raw material of the mind, which is able to translate the chaotic elements of life accurately into words. Delany's later novels, especially, are arenas in which life and language confront one another and come together to form a dialectic of literature. Delany's science fiction includes and capitalizes on the tension between scientific theory and linguistic potential. (pp. 33-4)

> *Peter S. Alterman, "The Surreal Translations of Samuel R. Delany," in* Science-Fiction Studies, *Vol. 4, No. 11, March, 1977, pp. 25-34.*

HOWARD WALDROP

Some writers in the [sf] genre have been accused of not having all the lights on in their marquees. Samuel R. Delany, on the other hand, is charged with having so many lights on in his that what is spelled out there is sometimes lost in the brilliance and glare.

Delany, who surfaced in the '60s, is the award-winning author of brilliant shorts ("Aye, and Gomorrah," "Driftglass") and novels (*The Einstein Intersection, Babel-17*) and of the long self-indulgent critical failure, *Dhalgren.*

His latest, *Distant Stars* . . . is in that most inappropriate of packages, the heavily illustrated trade paperback. . . .

For his money the reader gets six stories (including the Hugo and Nebula-winning **"Time Considered as a Helix of Semi-Precious Stones"**), the short novel *Empire Star,* something Bantam calls "a fascinating new essay" (which is only an introduction) and, HAL help us, "the first computer-enhanced artwork created for a science fiction book." . . .

Delany is a wordsmith, a craftsman who creates images that are by turns shocking and full of wonder. His best works make their own pictures. He certainly doesn't need this kind of package, or this kind of hype from his publisher.

The stories range from award-winner to throwaway (though the worst that can be said of his stories, like **"We in Some Strange Power's Employ, Move on a Rigorous Line,"** included here, is that they don't *work*). A couple of pieces of major

Delany, an okay story, some trivialities and lots of Quaker Puffed Air between the words.

> *Howard Waldrop, in a review of "Distant Stars," in* Book World—The Washington Post, *August 30, 1981, p. 6.*

PETER STAMPFEL

For years, I've been turning non-science fiction readers onto the field by lending them a copy of Delany's classic out-of-print short story collection, *Driftglass*. It usually makes a convert, but not always; some people lack taste, or a sense of wonder. Three of the *Driftglass* stories are reprinted here [in *Distant Stars*], so I had a chance to read them again. That was nice, but . . . I would rather have seen all new material, and the other stories don't quite reach the standard set by *Driftglass*. . . .

Two of the stories, **"Corona"** and **"Time Considered as a Helix of Semi-Precious Stones,"** concern themselves in part with popular music of the future. **"Corona"** typifies Delany's writing, combining an epic compassion with utter nastiness, juxtaposing suicides and saviors. Great science fiction like Delany's understands and relates the breadth and depth of human possibility.

Gotta sense of wonder? Wanna hot read? C'mere, kid.

> *Peter Stampfel, in a review of "Distant Stars," in* VLS, *No. 1, October, 1981, p. 8.*

JEANNE MURRAY WALKER

Twelve years after its publication, Samuel Delany's *Nova* seems prescient. Like many science fiction novels, *Nova* articulates the need for and the difficulty of exchange between individuals and among groups. Specifically, in *Nova* Delany portrays a race for fuel, the scarcest and most valuable commodity, which finally pivots the whole world into economic chaos. Inverting the quest motif used in romances since the Middle Ages to portray Christian social unity, Delany portrays an economic quest which instead kills the ruler, wreaks havoc in the social system, and upsets the economic fate of nations. Since Delany defines the most important kind of social exchange as economic, questing is inevitably a search for the most valuable economic commodity, fuel. *Nova* shows that such a quest can benefit a whole group, as it did in medieval romances. But ironically it destroys another group. This irony arises from Delany's change in the definition of "the land." What romances used to portray as "the kingdom" or "the land," Delany portrays as fragmented into divisions, into competing geopolitical entities. Rifts between these entities caused by competing economic alliances and interests cannot be healed but can only be deepened by individual quests, which, like society, are defined in economic terms. (p. 221)

If science fiction portrays society with particular and unique focus, as its critics claim, and if society can be defined as exchanges among individuals, then it cannot be surprising that *Nova* is a fiction which focuses on an aspect of the exchange among men. By structuring *Nova* as an ironic quest, as a search for an economic grail, the success of which further divides the land, Delany portrays the inability of economic exchange ever to cure divisions and re-unite groups.

What energizes *Nova*'s social commentary is its structural resemblance to medieval quest romances. Delany calls attention to the quest form of the novel through the character Katin, who, Delany pretends, wrote the fiction of *Nova.* Katin dictates notes for the novel into his tape recorder, notes which are interspersed with the action of *Nova* throughout. In one of the most telling of these, Katin directs his young, vagabond gypsy friend, the musician Mouse, to think about the grail. He recites the history of the romance, from Chretion de Troyes to Charles Williams, observing that authors usually die before completing their romances. Katin, who is a novelist in the modern self-conscious mode, presumably escapes this fate by purposely ending his novel in mid-sentence so that it will remain unfinished at his death. With this elaborately reflexive gesture, Delany suggests that he wishes *Nova* to be read in the grail romance tradition.

Although the form of grail romances varies, it is possible to generalize their elements. The story is set in a land ruled by an aged or ailing ruler whose illness or infirmity mysteriously imprisons the waters of the land. The hero enters the dry, infertile land, questing for the holy chalice, a quest which he has undertaken because he has particular powers of virtue. While he experiences mistaken identity, wandering, confusion, and fear, the land and its people continue to be afflicted. But eventually the hero performs an action or asks a question which magically restores the king to health, frees the waters, and causes the land to flourish. The precise task to be performed by the hero and the exact effect on the king differ. But in all forms of the medieval romance, individuals achieve virtue by contemplating something beyond themselves. Their virtue is recognizable, questing is rewarded by finding the object, the ruler is capable of being cured by the quester's discovery, and the land can be re-united.

The magic reversal in the medieval quest structure results in unity among members of the social group defined as "the land." (pp. 222-23)

Although Delany uses the quest form to structure *Nova,* he postulates a different system of social coherence than the one postulated by medieval grail quests. *Nova* assumes a social system based on the exchange of material commodities. The system of exchange in *Nova* is very like capitalism, where individuals struggle in free competition with one another for ownership of material goods. In a world where fuel, rather than the chalice, has become the most valued object to search for, every characteristic of the grail quest must be permuted. The quester must be egocentric and defiant rather than pure and unworldly wise. The ruler must be incurable. The land must remain hopelessly divided. Only the *form* of the quest remains. The meaning of the form is entrusted to artists who are portrayed in the novel as unable to dictate or change the social structure. Therefore, the form of the quest in *Nova* has become ironic.

Delany had a choice, of course, about how to structure the fiction of *Nova.* His decision to use the inverted quest motif implies that he wanted to contrast the ideal form of social exchange with one which operates in society at present. The contrast implicit in *Nova*'s structure itself carries meaning. By referring to the idealized quest and its eucatastrophic ending, Delany not only emphasizes the failure of his hero's quest; he implies the possibility of a better social system. Yet Delany does not leave the contrast implicit. The two artists within *Nova,* the novelist Katin and the musician, Mouse, comment on the structure and meaning of the novel. And the point they make repeatedly is that no real social alternative exists. It may be possible to imagine better social forms in art, forms like

the grail quest, but those are aesthetic constructs or structures of past history. They are not models for possible action. We are all trapped in a pattern of social exchange which divides us from one another. The only thing that can free us is action and that only temporarily.

It remains to see precisely how, in *Nova,* Delany works out the grail quest form. The major elements are the desired object, the land, the quester, and the ruler. *Nova* sets these out in a mutated and nuanced relationship to one another, a relationship made more subtle by the comments of the artists within the novel. The element most essential and most sought after in *Nova* is the fuel which Delany calls "illyrion." It is illyrion which stokes the fires at the moon's core, making its surface habitable. It is illyrion which creates energy to fuel ships that fly from one galaxy to another, connecting races and uniting cultures. Mined under the sea, manufactured with great difficulty in factories, illyrion is the key to economic power—and therefore to political power.

Delany makes it clear that if it is used properly, fuel could unite men and stabilize society. (p. 224)

But "the land" in *Nova* is divided because people compete for fuel rather than sharing it. Delany presents "the land" as three separate galaxywide powers whose separate economic interests, histories, and identities roughly parallel those of the communist bloc, the capitalistic nations, and the Third World countries. There is Draco with its power center, the Earth; the Plieades, which were populated later; and the Outer Colonies, whose political identity is just beginning to emerge from the other two. The primary division among societies in *Nova* is caused by the competing interests of wealthy, entrenched nations and ascending, enterprising nations. They both take what they can from a third group of nations. Siphoning off the planet's natural resource, illyrion, they use it in an economic war against one another. Eventually, fuel becomes the most valuable economic commodity, the lever by which one group can pivot another into economic and social disaster. (p. 225)

Delany painstakingly explores the reason why fuel's potential to unite "the land" is not realized by telling the story of Lorq von Ray, the hero quester of *Nova.* The grandson of a space pirate who settled on the Plieades and began destroying the economic empire of Draco, Lorq is locked in combat with Draco's most powerful family, the Reds. The elder von Ray, we are told, blew up "any emissary from some Draco monopoly trying to extend itself into new territory" on the Plieades. . . . Most crucial for the plot of *Nova,* he smashed the ships of the Red family. The hostility which grew up between the pirate von Ray and the capitalistic Reds during that generation is aggravated by the desperate struggle for illyrion in the year 3162. Lorq's father foresees that the Outer Colonies, where the richest illyrion mines exist, eventually will dominate not only Draco and the Reds but also the Plieades and his own family unless some way can be found to "lower the price of Illyrion by half." In order to do this, Lorq must find a new source of illyrion. . . . He accepts the challenge. Ultimately he gets a spaceship, collects a crew, and drives the ship into a nova—a burned-out sun filled with illyrion. He collects seven tons of the scarce element, dumps it on the world market, destroys Draco's economy, and insures (temporarily) the economic superiority of the Plieades. (pp. 225-26)

As Lorq completes his quest he realizes that by perpetuating disunity among political groups, by ruining Draco, he has bought his own personal freedom. By *choice,* he has "struck down one third of the cosmos to raise up another and let one more go staggering.'' . . . Such a choice, whether made as a private individual or as a representative of a political group, must inevitably involve moral responsibility, he reasons. Even though Lorq claims, ''I feel no sin in me,'' he concludes, ''Then it must be that I am free and evil.'' . . . This conclusion bursts in upon him with both intense euphoria and intense guilt.

In truth, Lorq's quest, like his grandfather's, like any quest in a system which is primarily economic, is driven by a ''selfish, mercenary, egocentered vision.'' . . . As challenger of the ruling power, he makes his own rules. Near the end of the novel, Lorq defines his quest—the plot of the novel, the conflict between his family and the Reds—as a game. In this game, he admits that he makes his own rules and that the object he wins is meaningless; winning is the point. . . . Unlike the medieval quester whose quest succeeded because of his selflessness and his conformity to the external demands of Christianity, Lorq's quest succeeds because of his egocentricism and his lack of obligation to any social conventions.

No wonder such a quest is unable to unite ''the land.'' To be sure, illyrion has some characteristics of the grail. Its tight bonding suggests a metaphor for social unity, and its function as fuel implies its usefulness in implementing stable and enduring social bonds. But the ideal which inspires Delany's quester reverses the medieval ideal which made the quester subservient to the meaning implicit in the grail. *Nova*'s grail is treated by Lorq as nothing more or less than a material commodity. The world of *Nova* is the first upset by too little, then by too much illyrion. In either case it is a world where groups are out of alignment, off balance, where some suffer while others prosper, where the object of exchange is used to divide rather than to unite.

Lorq's choice to quest within an exchange system which can never produce a unified society leads him to understand his plight as an individual within such a system. What follows is alienation and, ultimately, death. When Lorq comprehends the magnitude of his personal responsibility for questing in such a world, he is blinded. . . . By conquering Prince Red and gathering his great burden of illyrion, Lorq discovers that human action cannot be measured merely in terms of existing social systems. He comprehends the meaning of good and evil—that is, he comprehends the fact that he could not avoid exercising choice, and yet his choice to save a social group could never have united the land. Understanding, he returns to his childhood home to await death. (pp. 227-28)

Delany depicts a world in which the shocks and crises in society are ultimately the fault of the ruler's conservatism; the latter's desire to keep things as they were turns out to be a desire to keep things to himself. Aristocracy in *Nova* is static, self-perpetuating, and oppressive. When Prince Red refuses to participate in exchange, his refusal cannot be reversed. Although the main action of the novel takes place against a backdrop of constant chatter about how social change has ''shattered all cultural tradition'' . . . , the failure of tradition is not the problem, as Delany shows. . . . Tradition is implicit, even in the novel's virtuoso re-use of the grail form. People do exchange, because they must. They have no choice but to trade in cultural forms as well as in useful objects. The real task, given the failure of kinship exchange, as Lorq's father insists, is to discover what is the single most valuable commodity, and to insure that your group has enough of it to maintain power. He defines exchange as, at base, economic. Economic exchange cannot replace the kinship exchange which could potentially heal the

rift between the Plieades and Draco. But Delany depicts an aristocracy so conservative and isolated that it turns aside all attempts at exchange.

It is reasonable to condemn the quester in *Nova* for his furious, egocentric, rule-breaking existentialism and for his lack of concern for Draco and the Outer Colonies. But such a judgment must take into consideration the fact that his choice has not only been limited by the system of economic exchange but also defined by the ruler's prior refusal to exchange with anyone, to keep the social rules. . . . If Lorq has chosen evil, he has done so under circumstances when it was not easy to do anything else. (pp. 229-30)

The inverted quest form which Delany uses in *Nova* introduces permutations into every aspect of the form, and therefore the book is saturated with irony. This irony is appropriate since Delany is depicting a world where hoarding or maliciously flooding the market are essential means of satisfying one's own need. Economic exchange reverses the fundamental pattern set up in kinship exchange where granting someone else his desire is the best way of satisfying oneself. Delany investigates in the plot of *Nova* one alternative to what Ursula Le Guin depicts in *Left Hand of Darkness*. In Le Guin's novel, exchanges between individuals keep society seething with change. But balances, however precarious, are struck by kinship exchanges. An even more important contrast is set up in *Nova* between economic exchange and the Christian social ideal which the quest form originally embodied. In order to see how Delany interprets this implicit contrast, we must turn to *Nova*'s artists, Katin and Mouse.

Katin and Mouse personify opposite elements within the book: the conservative, traditional form of the grail quest and the futuristic, apocalyptic events of the story. These opposite tendencies are embodied also in the ruler, Prince, and the quester, Lorq. But there they are assigned definite moral values. In the figures of Katin and Mouse, we are able to gaze at these alternatives in morally neutral form. They confirm that any ideal of absolute social unity is artificial and unattainable in a social system of economic exchange. Katin's writing is a *comment* on social action, and Mouse's music is an *alternative* to social action. But neither artist steps in to do what the quester fails to do. (p. 230)

Katin's shrewd analogy between the physical, the psychological, and the social suggests the levels on which exchange of illyrion, the grail, operates in the novel. Like particles of matter, social systems and psychological systems can be knocked off balance. *Nova* is the story of all three. A sun goes nova; Lorq's ''perception of the world outside''—his social role—grows inconsistent ''with the knowledge of the world within''; and he causes a deep shock to ''shift and run through the empire.'' . . . In a society like that of *Nova*, Katin suggests that these kinds of imbalances are related and inevitable. (p. 231)

Mouse, with his lack of tradition, typifies the modern man who cannot even imagine social unity. Because of his rootlessness and his eagerness for the future, fear is Mouse's dominant emotion. . . . Like Lorq, Mouse is obsessed not only with the present but also with the future. He is the only one of Lorq's crew who has no interest in the ancient customs of his gypsy ancestors. And although he has been educated, he fails to make connections between various facts he has memorized. So sparse is Mouse's knowledge and so informal is his sense of the world that Katin groans, ''Oh for the rebirth of an educational system where understanding is an essential part of knowledge.'' . . . Thus, through this lack of form and pattern, Mouse is able to generate intense meaning in the present. Yet, unlike the meaning Lorq is driven to create, which alters history and victimizes a third of the population, Mouse's art harms no one. On the contrary, Katin claims that it is precisely Mouse's art, without form, which draws on no tradition, that can reveal to the people around him true ''social significance.'' . . . Social significance exists apart from patterns. It lies in individual human action.

Neither of the fictional artists in *Nova* provides the solution to the problem of questing in a society whose primary exchanges are economic. Although Katin escapes being blinded by the nova as Lorq was blinded, his exemption from Lorq's fate does not imply that his art can heal the differences between societies or make them understand that their individual well-beings lie in their unity. Delany never considers books as objects of exchange. They reify and distill human action in retrospect. They posit interconnections. They hypothesize patterns of history. But the novel form is portrayed as already obsolete. It is Mouse's musical images which move and threaten and instruct people in *Nova.* Yet the price of their social effectiveness is that they isolate their listeners from one another and disappear almost as soon as Mouse summons them.

Through Delany's portraits of Katin and Prince, we discover the strengths and limitations of pattern; through the portraits of Mouse and Lorq we discover the strengths and limitations of action. By ordering the action of *Nova* in the quest pattern, but assuming a value system quite different than that assumed by medieval romance writers, Delany shows that neither pattern nor action operate as they once did. Both fail. The land can never be united as long as the grail is a material object and the system of exchange is economic. Yet individuals must continue to quest. Through their quests they find meaning for themselves, though they may damn others. Understanding this and bearing the guilt which arises from such understanding is the only true heroism in *Nova.* (pp. 232-33)

> *Jeanne Murray Walker, ''Reciprocity and Exchange in Samuel Delany's 'Nova','' in* Extrapolation, *Vol. 23, No. 3, Fall, 1982, pp. 221-34.*

GREGORY RENAULT

Published as pornography rather than science fiction [*The Tides of Lust*] could be easily overlooked as a temporary aberration by an otherwise excellent science fiction writer, or even viewed as simply a pot-boiler dashed off to finance the author's wanderings. . . . However, against an immediate inclination to dismiss the work as mere pornography, *The Tides of Lust* should be read as a significant attempt by Delany to explore further the artistic possibilities of contemporary mass culture. His most recent ventures into comics and adult fantasy represent an expansion of the thematic concerns of his more numerous and well-known science fiction works; in *The Tides of Lust* Delany utilizes yet another mass culture formula—pornography—as a vehicle for the development of speculative fiction. (pp. 116-17)

At its most immediate, the novel seems to be a chaos of sexual episodes, a survey of sexual possibilities: hetero- and homosexual couples and foursomes, children and adults, whites and blacks in various combinations, necrophilia, incest, rape, sadism, masochism complete with leathers, sexual use of excrement and urine, and a sacrilegious orgy are described within 173 pages—a spectacle both attractive and disgusting. A minor theme at this level is the American stereotype of the black male's sexual potency (ironically, given Delany's recent outspoken concern with sexual politics, there are no black *women* in the novel), a theme satirized through exaggerated caricature in name and description. (p. 118)

But under the apparently chaotic, erotic satire lurks a greater order and deeper theme. *The Tides of Lust* is an elegantly ordered exploration of chaos, the immediate sensuality of which is mediated by ''icily instructive'' intellectual form. In its own terms, the novel is truly speculative, moving beyond formal constraints of the genre to explore the larger concerns of knowledge and creativity. A consideration of the formal organization (structure) of the work, the symbolic character figures, and finally the Faust theme should provide us with the proper attention/intention for this speculative novel.

Like Freud's conscious, rational analyses of the psyche's unconscious urges, Delany's treatment of somatic sensuality is in turn highly intellectual and formal. This is first of all seen in the internal organization of the novel, whose structure is the abstract embodiment of the theme. The primary narrative is ordered by almost classical unities of space and time, portraying events which occur during a twenty-four hour stopover of the seventy-five foot *Scorpion* in a small southern port. However, this apparent homogeneity is belied by a series of secondary narratives.

Of utmost importance for this and subsequent stages of the argument is Delany's comment from a critical article, contemporary with *The Tides of Lust,* noting that ''Everything in a science fiction novel should be mentioned at least twice (in at least two different contexts)''. This is a central principle of the novel's organization. Though nominally linear and realistic, the narrative is systematically broken up by numerous ''detours'' which occur throughout the text, formally set off from the narrative proper by various labels. These secondary narratives, or asides, are all grouped in pairs, a formal repetition which provides structural unity. There are five groups.

(1) ''*The Scorpion*'s log'' appears in the first and last chapters, beginning and ending the framework of secondary narratives. The first entry provides the autobiography of the main character known as the Captain, and features those interpretative pointers to the reader mentioned above. The second entry (final aside) is a comment to the reader about the book itself.

(2) Next follow two pairs, each member of which alternates chapters with a member from the other pair. Chapters two and four feature ''Bull's Tale'' and ''Sambo's Tale'' respectively, both of which take the form of autobiographical stories of incest. The racial-sexual theme . . . is present in the color symmetry: Bull is white, Sambo black.

(3) The third pair, from chapters three and five, are surreal inserts similar to the ''music'' and ''choreography'' of Pynchon's *Gravity's Rainbow.* These are descriptions of male homosexual couplings, labeled as cartoons. . . . Here the racial theme is continued: in each episode one participant is white and one black.

(4) The novel's theme is explicitly stated in the two addresses, ''Proctor's Address'' and ''Catherine from the Altar,'' which appear in adjacent (rather than staggered) chapters five and six. These two ''comments'' frame the dramatic climax, the simultaneous events of an orgy in St. Mark's (mentioned, but not described), and Robby's psychedelic experience in Proctor's loft. Following each address, a subplot rejoins the main plot with the death of the character involved in that subplot. . . .

(5) Finally, the segment "Bull, Returned" in chapter six (the second-from-last) balances off the previously mentioned "Bull's Tale" in the second chapter. But unlike the latter segment, this one features male homosexual content similar to the two cartoons, except that in this encounter both partners are white (as in the original "Bull's Tale"). (pp. 118-19)

Even as it unifies the apparent chaos of the sexual episodes, this structure allows Delany to transcend the usual restrictive limits of theme in fiction, to speculate. Traditionally, author, work, and reader are seen as radically separate, discrete moments of the total cultural process of literary production and consumption. Here, in the "log" sections and the two addresses especially, Delany dissolves these distinctions, speaking to the reader directly, via the characters, or by parable, intentionally emphasizing the ambiguity of creator and created, of reader and what is read. . . . Proctor's address says (twice, of course) of Catherine that "She has spied on the devil. But so have you." . . . At this point, reader complicity has been raised, and the narrative emphasis shifts from Proctor addressing the characters (his audience) to Delany addressing the reader (*his* audience): we too, have spied on the devil by vicarious participation in the questionable acts in the book, merely by reading it. The name of Bull's hangout, The Hall of Mirrors, is . . . a wicked reminder of how much of the reader is reflected within—as the representative character Peggy-Ann finds out to her discomfort. . . . As Proctor says in another reflexive remark, "There are more of us than most of you think. Correction: there are more of us than most people who will read this will think." . . . This blunt assertion of pervasive deviance occurs in statements which collapse fictive and social audience, character and reader (and, by implication the respective forms of figurative and literal discourse); the substantive point is made via a formal one as well, a unified "truth" which, Proctor-Delany asserts, makes the book dangerous. (p. 120)

The central motif of the book is the Faust theme. Quotes pertaining to Faust head each chapter, and the text is full of references to Faust, magic and illusion. The "pretentious" quality that Delany refers to in the "Author's Dedication" must in part refer to the audacious use of pornography to develop this theme. As we have seen, the immediate, sensuous level of the text is rife with polymorphous sexuality; consideration of the structure and character figures at the formal level takes us from the totally perverse to the totally unjust, from voyeurism to complicity/revulsion. The issue that then emerges is that of forbidden knowledge—and we begin to see the suitability of pornography for the investigation of this theme after all.

In his address Proctor tells us that man has devised three systems for "effecting the oblivion necessary for sanity: the bourgeois preoccupation with work; the religious, moral, ethical, religious matrix; and the erotic life." He further says: "The artist is perhaps the only one free to indulge in all three, religious, erotic, and ergonic, simply to fulfill his calling. He reports to the practitioners of each what is going on within the circles of the others." . . . This statement on the primacy of artistic practice for human meaning takes us to the deepest level of the text. Delany's "Dedication" notes that "these pages bear the most circumscribed reverence for sanity"—circumscribed because the roundabout route he takes us through is one of sexual, moral and religious chaos, one of *in*sanity. The testing of our sexual sensibilities explores limits in one area, while the debasing of religious-ethical values in the subplots . . . tests them in another. This part of the theme of *The*

Tides of Lust, then, involves the negation of the self-sufficiency of those "sanity systems" pointed out by Proctor. If Proctor's comment can perhaps be seen as a direct indication of the thematic thrust of the book (implied authorial intent), then the following quote from Peggy-Ann locates the intended reader reaction. She says, during the period of remorse she suffers following sex at The Hall of Mirrors, that "'Sometimes I think considering the world in classically theological structures is a waste of . . .' She looked around the room. 'I shouldn't say things like that here. It's meaningless.'" . . . From the perspective of Proctor's comment, we can see that the "inappropriate" quality of the setting applies not merely to the bar Peggy-Ann is in at that point in the story, but (because of the bar's symbolic function) to the whole novel, itself an example of how the artistic work is capable of transcending the limits of the other partial realms of experience.

Proctor is the appropriate mouthpiece for this messianic message: described as scientist, artist (painter, poet, novelist, musician), and libertine all in one, who better personifies man's quest for knowledge and creativity? . . . This symbolic creator informs us of the order which emerges from the initial chaos resulting from Delany's idol-testing. . . . That is, Proctor-Delany-Faust reflexively tells us (reader-as-vicarious character) that the importance of the book (any work, but especially this one) lies in its aesthetic form, not in instruction or entertainment. This statement [is] effective at this point only because Delany has first sucked us in with entertaining porn and then used the same medium to distance us. . . . Art's beauty (and, by implication, the importance of this book) thus lies not in immediate titillation, nor in a "message" about excess, rape, or injustice, but in the self-reflective symmetry of the text—a symmetry demonstrated in the two preceding sections, a symmetry itself the subject of the theme it conveys.

The Tides of Lust is a celebration of confusion, of the possibilities for new growth within chaos. Blurring of distinctions is both a technique and theme within the book: characters blur into one another . . . , author and reader merge in the work. . . . [The] comments blur the distinction between the creators in the work and the creator *of* the work. . . . Here the blurring of creator and created, intention and effect, adds to the moral confusion, the blurring of good and bad. . . . (pp. 122-24)

Delany's emphasis on aesthetic form further explores this paradox in the realm of knowledge—the artifice behind meaning which allows truth to emerge from lies (fictions), reality from illusions, sanity and order from chaos. . . . This [idea of] the artist as liar, together with the reference to the artist as criminal in the quote from "Proctor's Address" . . . , encompasses a moral and epistemological paradox clearly showing that the chaos, the blending here celebrated is not done without principle; rather, all are ordered by (are realms of activity subordinate to) the dimension of aesthetic form. How appropriate, then, the Faust motif: art, concerned with "effects"—illusion—is truly magic in its ability to let chaos cohere in that symmetry which begets sanity.

Fiction's illusive aspect, the truth of its visions, is repeatedly emphasized. . . . It seems that Delany is also aware that, however paramount the principle of aesthetic form, it also partakes of the same contradictions it orders, that its fragility is one with its strength.

Thus the *telos* of Delany's preoccupation with aesthetic form. Just as the formal structures within the book bring order out of apparently chaotic pornographic episodes, so the theme of the importance of aesthetic form makes intelligible the negation of "sanity systems" developed through that structure. *The Tides of Lust* portrays the beginning of "an age of moral chaos such as is only hinted at in the tale of the expulsion from the garden" . . .—a problem which is then abstractly handled through the text's internal organization (the formal symmetry); this structuring then provides both the model of and the vehicle for the substantive thematic argument that aesthetic form can in turn provide a road to sanity via the self-conscious fashioning of meaningful illusion.

Like those German Idealist philosophers or the supremely confident crusaders of the avant-garde, who saw in art's creative syntheses the answer to fragmented experience, Delany locates the possibility for a resolution of scientific, moral, and sexual chaos in the transcendent communicative superiority of aesthetic form. As he notes in *The Jewel-Hinged Jaw*, "The relation of art to the world *is* the aesthetic field of a given culture." . . . Given the vision of art-in-the-world presented in *The Tides of Lust*, well might the characters remark (again, twice) on the possibility of a "new age" in the final pages of the novel . . .—though this blending of altered artistic practice with social change may be another "pretentious" aspect of the book, its least satisfactory one. Nevertheless, Delany's speculative pornographic venture shows the concern with the politics of microsocial situations, sexual relations, and (above all) discourse which have come to the fore in his most recent work. By his transformation of pornographic formula literature Delany is, as it were, "speculating with a hammer," attempting a creative reformation of our contemporary cultural practice— surely an experiment as worthy of serious consideration as his other, better/known offerings. (pp. 124-26)

Gregory Renault, "Speculative Porn: Aesthetic Form in Samuel R. Delany's 'The Tides of Lust'," in Extrapolation, *Vol. 24, No. 2, Summer, 1983, pp. 116-29.*

MICHAEL R. COLLINGS

Delany's sub-sub-title to *Neveryona, Some Informal Remarks Toward a Modular Calculus, Part Four*, indicates that this novel is in some sense part of a larger structure, Part Three being the Appendix to the earlier *Tales of Neveryon*. . . . Characters from the earlier book recur in the novel, although some of them fleetingly, since *Neveryona* concentrates on the adventures of Pryn, a girl from the mountains of Ellamon, as she journeys to the fabled city of Kolhari and beyond, meeting with strangeness everywhere and struggling to interpret the signs and symbols which surround her.

In many respects, *Neveryona* fits comfortably into Delany's canon. Kolhari, for instance, shares elements of *Dhalgren*'s Bellona—it is a mysterious city, full of bridges and shadows, somehow insubstantial, more of a construct than a thing. Characters are recognizably products of Delany's imagination, frequently naked, with glittering chains on wrists or ankles, with dirty fingernails or bare feet.

Neveryona is not merely derivative, but represents a new manifestation of Delany's continuing concern for language and the magic of fiction, whereby words become symbols for other, larger things. . . . *Neveryona* seems weighted with the same sense of mysterious function, weighted with symbolic meaning yet defying simple classification as a tool or a map. Delany's language defines his concern for language as subject, just as the events of the novel define concerns for penetrating origins

and beginnings, for constructing myths which make reality more meaningful.

The mythic and the real overlap in the novel. The narrative voice, for example, displaces the reader from the tale. The objective tone brackets the narrative, with the narrator occasionally breaking in to remind the reader that the tale is from long ago. The narrator self-consciously creates a system of signs by which to create his magic . . . frequently denying that he will tell the tale that he is in fact telling. And the apparatus which concludes the book—the interchange of letters concerning the Culhar fragment—further implies a layering of reality and myth that becomes increasingly difficult to define.

"To write for others . . . it seems one *must* be a spy—or a teller of tales," Pryn discovers. Delany is both. *Neveryona* is a stirring fable of adventure and education, of heroic action and even more heroic normality in a world where survival itself is constantly threatened. . . . Yet beyond the fable, there lies the report of the spy—of one who has observed the actions of humans in crisis and sent a report—appropriately in code, in the signs and symbols of language.

A first reading points to similarities between this and other Delany's works; but *Neveryona* requires careful re-reading (ideally in tandem with *Tales of Neveryon*) and thoughtful stripping away of layers of texture. It becomes more meaningful as one works through the indeterminacy of its episodes to see meaning in surface meaninglessness, and intelligibility in mazes of symbols. (pp. 31-2)

Michael R. Collings, in a review of "Neveryona; or, The Tale of Signs and Cities," in Science Fiction & Fantasy Book Review, *No. 16, July-August, 1983, pp. 31-2.*

DARRELL SCHWEITZER

[*Neveryona*], Delany's second foray into imaginary world fantasy is, I regret to say, another disaster. I think he's finished as a novelist. Here's why: There are parts of books that the author regards as best. He may be very fond of his ability to describe bizarre scenes or the way he handles dream sequences or the way he molds his characters to present differing philosophical viewpoints, or whatever. There is a great temptation particularly when one is established, to write a "good parts version," which contains these things the author particularly likes to the exclusion of all else. This phenomenon is called self-indulgence. We all struggle with it. But Delany has lost the battle long ago, or else he never realized he had a problem. . . .

Neveryona is four hundred pages of muddy lectures. *Everybody* explains things at vast length to everybody else. Curiously, they all speak in the same voice. Curiously also, after twenty pages of chatter, sometimes you're left wondering what they were all trying to say.

The book has no virtues as fiction, aside from an occasional striking image or vivid scene. The chatter excludes any humanity from the characters. You don't believe them for an instant. . . .

But it is senseless to try to criticize this in terms of *story*. It seems to me that Delany has lost interest in writing fiction altogether, and is turning out tracts and essays. Unfortunately, *Neveryona* isn't even very good as an essay. Its predecessor, *Tales of Neveryon,* was at least interesting as a commentary on the fantasy field. *Neveryona* just gets lost in its own verbiage. A more disciplined writer might have made a novel out of some of the material, but as is there's just nothing there. The grammar isn't even very good. . . .

The parallels between Delany's career and Heinlein's are disturbingly close. A brilliant writer lost totally in a sheer lack of novelistic discipline. Only where it took Heinlein thirty years to come unglued, Delany did it in less than ten. He is now writing his own equivalents of *I Will Fear No Evil*, etc. Of course Heinlein has partially redeemed himself with *Friday*. Maybe Delany will yet. He needs desperately to be forced to write a novel less than 200 pages long, in which less than half the total text is dialogue. But alas, he is established as marketable commodity now, and the time at which some editor might have saved him is probably past. We can still hope, but in the meantime (to steal a good line from Doug Fratz) I must, out of the deepest respect, consider his career to have ended in 1969 with the publication of *Driftglass*.

> *Darrell Schweitzer, in a review of "Neveryona," in* Science Fiction Review, *Vol. 12, No. 3, August, 1983, p. 46.*

SANDRA Y. GOVAN

Typically, sf is not the genre scholars and critics of Afro-American literature turn toward to see the way that black fictionalists shape a vision of black experience and character. Our critical stance has presupposed that an Afro-American author is either creating a space for him- or herself somewhere within the Afro-American literary tradition—whether one calls that tradition "protest," "nationalistic," "Neo-hoodoo," or "the literature of black affirmation"—or is jumping into the "mainstream" to play the "I-am-an-American-writer-who-happens-to-be-black" shell game with both the black and the white critical establishment. By focusing on writers who have lent themselves, conveniently, to our presuppositions and who have obliged us by creating works we review and judge according to expected patterns, we have developed a critical astigmatism which prevents us from clearly seeing black writers who work outside our established norms. This serious limitation has, until recently, prohibited us from recognizing the achievements of so gifted a writer as Samuel R. Delany, merely because he works in a popular form. Having repeatedly received both Nebula and Hugo awards (the two most coveted prizes in science fiction), Samuel "Chip" Delany is one of the field's preeminent authors. He is also a writer who, while working in a genre long dominated by whites, brings to his speculative worlds a black presence and a subtle black perspective. (p. 43)

Delany, in his fiction, is not enamored of the technical or "hard" sciences—physics, astronomy, thermodynamics, computers. His forte is the adult novel utilizing the "soft" sciences—biology, psychology, anthropology, linguistic theory. Technological gadgetry, specialized computers, or, in *Nova,* "sockets" attached to people to "plug" them into machinery are simply facets of the setting and not the prime cause for the story. One is drawn into Delany's stories because they have a complexity; an acute consciousness of language, structure, and form; a dextrous ability to weave together mythology and anthropology, linguistic theory and cultural history, gestalt psychology and sociology as well as philosophy, structuralism, and the adventure story. Frequently the hero of a Delany adventure is likely to be a violent artist who produces both beauty and death. What is ultimately appealing about Delany's work

is that it is stimulating, even if one cannot entirely peel back all the intricate, sometimes enigmatic layers of meaning. Delany challenges his audience. His work is studded with epigraphs, allusions, and symbols which force a reader to stretch to make connections. *The Einstein Intersection,* for example, offers epigraphs from a Pepsi slogan . . . to John Ruskin to Emily Dickinson in order to cue us to his protagonist's development on his quest.

Delany has a clearly articulated concern for what he terms "aesthetic discipline—that which makes most accessible all the substance of a given work." Because of that obvious concern, most of the critical attention his work receives focuses on the aesthetic apparatus he uses to frame his fiction. For instance, critics examining *The Einstein Intersection* look immediately to its mythic elements. An alien from a group inhabiting Earth after humankind has vanished, Lo Lobey, the novel's protagonist, is half-man and half-animal in appearance. For critics, Lobey is Pan; he is Theseus; he is Orpheus. He is also a latter-day Ringo Starr, the Beatle who did not sing. . . . That alien Lobey has adopted, in part, the appearance of a black man—"brown face with spun brass for hair"—is unremarkable.

In *Babel-17* what impresses critics most is Delany's handling of language and linguistic theories. *Babel-17*, we're told, is about communication, verbal and nonverbal; it makes use of the Whorf-Sapir hypothesis, which suggests that "language shapes perception drastically and completely." Rydra Wong, poet and heroine, must break an enemy code, Babel-17, undecipherable to military cryptographers. The code, however, is a language by itself, one that obliterates "I"—the self—as a basic referent, one that forges linguistic traps and dangerous patterns of action, capitalizing on typical gestalt psychology. Delany's knowledge of linguistics and semiotics is everywhere apparent in the novel, as are the connections to structuralism and French symbolism (Rimbaud, the French symbolist, in a direct allusion becomes "the Rimbaud," Rydra Wong's spaceship). . . . Obviously, communication via language, symbol, or sign is the central element of *Babel-17*. Yet most discussions of the text wholly ignore Delany's subtle stress on ethnicity. Rydra Wong is an Asian woman. The one man she relies on when she is distressed by her own formidable powers of perception is an African man, Dr. Markus T'mwarba, her psychotherapist.

In *Nova,* a black man moves from the role of strong support to that of hero proper; but again, most of the critical response to the novel concentrates on Delany's wedding of form to theme: space opera to the mythic quests for power, for art, for meaning, for free will. *Nova* follows the adventures of Captain Lorq Von Ray and his adversaries, Prince and Ruby Red, through the galaxy to an exploding star, a nova, to bring back the rare element Illyrion. . . . The son of a Senegalese mother and a Norwegian father, Lorq Von Ray is a black man and hero clearly at the center of this novel.

Samuel Delany's vision of future and possible worlds is a vision in which race, however subtly manifested, is as emblematically significant as any of the other concerns his work treats. If in *Nova*'s Lorq, Delany has rendered one of his most commanding signs denoting the significance of black folk in his speculative future, in his other works black people are viable too. His black characters may be heroic, or they may merely assist the protagonist. What most matters is that, in science fiction worlds in which very few blacks have appeared, they are *there*. (pp. 44-5)

Delany has described his future worlds as places "where things have changed. In most of my futures the racial situation has changed and changed for the better. As a young writer I thought it very important to keep an image of such a possibility before people. I don't ever remember subscribing to the idea that 'being black doesn't matter.' I wanted to write about worlds where being black mattered in different ways from the way it matters now." In *The Einstein Intersection* and *Babel-17* Delany clearly succeeds in articulating a difference. In *Nova*, valiant as Lorq is, the sexual mythology attached to black man/white woman is sufficient to show us that being black in the distant future still matters to some in a way not so different from our present. However, that Lorq is able to pit his strength and will successfully against the Reds, rather than be lynched by them, says something different about the cycle of violence and oppression blacks of the future may endure.

Delany's recent novels *Dhalgren* and *Triton* are vastly different from either the stories in *Driftglass* (1971) or Delany's previous novels. *Dhalgren* (1975) is probably his most controversial novel; certainly it is his most challenging. Its setting is not distant stars but Earth and a contemporary city embodying urban decay. (pp. 46-7)

There is no question that *Dhalgren* is saturated with fragmented versions of Delany's own experiences. It is his retelling, through the persona of an amnesic schizophrenic artist dubbed the Kid, of his excursions through those socio-psychological barriers mentioned earlier—only this time with the violence unrestrained. For the bulk of the novel, the Kid resides in violence-torn Bellona, a wounded "autumnal city" existing in some undefined, undisclosed physical parentheses at the outer edge of the normal world. Bellona (named after the Roman goddess of war) has suffered some unmentioned cataclysmic holocaust. Most of its population has departed, yet it is not a closed city; wanderers from cities like Seattle, Washington, and Euclid, Ohio, drift in and out. . . . No economic, social, physical, or temporal laws apply in Bellona. Days and years are ironically designated by the Bellona *Times*, the whimsical town newspaper; it might declare 1995 the year in one issue and 1776 the year in the next. A gigantic orange sun may rise and set in the space of an hour, or twin moons may rise unaccountably. Most of the city operates on a quasi-communal model, drawn from Delany's intimate knowledge of commune and extended family life.

Kid, the psychologically wounded poet-protagonist, is a distorted reflection of Delany. Like Delany, he has been a wanderer, and he keeps a writer's journal. Like Delany, he uses poetry to distill meanings, composing *Brass Orchids* in the midst of Bellona's confusion and becoming a celebrated Wunderkind. . . . Like Delany, the Kid participates in various kinds of sexual activity, all sanctioned by the social mores of the city and by its communal structure. (The novel's sexual explicitness disturbs many critics.) And, like Delany, the Kid has been a patient in a mental hospital. Both have suffered from hallucinations, disorientation, general nervous breakdown; Kid still loses huge blocks of time, measured in days and weeks, not merely hours. Unlike Delany, though, the Kid's parentage is half-Indian, half-white; he is not black, but he becomes the leader of a group/gang called the scorpions, most of whose membership, male and female, is black.

Race as an issue is unavoidable and unmistakable in *Dhalgren*. Three-fourths of the scorpions are black. Bellona is still, after the holocaust, bifurcated by race. There are fewer goods and supplies in the city's black sections than in its white neighborhoods, and there are snipers who shoot blacks from the tops of deserted buildings and arsonists who burn black neighborhoods. There is also the Reverend Amy Tayler, a black evangelical minister who directs her church's Evening Aid Program for the hungry, and who preaches vehemently about the moral state of Bellona. . . . Finally, there is George Harrison—rapist (according to the Bellona *Times*), hero, macho sex symbol to white women and white homosexual men alike. Obscene posters of George, displaying his genitals, abound in Bellona; his vaunted sexuality is mythic. His exploits are so famous they mask the real man. George Harrison is so much larger than life that, when a second moon inexplicably rises over Bellona, the inhabitants name it George, and after their fear subsides, they go on about their business having further mythologized his prowess.

In Delany's 1976 novel *Triton*, race and sex are entirely different concerns from those of *Dhalgren* or those of present-day America, yet more than a vestige of classic racism and sexual chauvinism is ingrained in the psyche of the chief protagonist, Bron Helstrom. *Triton* is about many things: communication, human sexuality, and bigotry among them. Bron is a narrow-minded, isolated man, so self-serving that he is incapable of reaching outside himself to love another or even understand another despite his best intentions. He abuses Miriamne, a black woman with roots in Earth's Kenya, ostensibly because her sexual preference is not his. He hates Sam Jones because Sam is handsome, expansive, and friendly to everyone, even Bron. Bron thinks of Sam as an average "type," only to discover to his great annoyance that "good looking, friendly, intelligent," oppressed-by-the-system Sam, "doing his bit as some overworked salesman/consultant," is actually "the head of the Political Liaison Department between the Outer Satellite Diplomatic Corps and Outer Satellite Intelligence; and had all the privileges (and training) of both." This news shocks Bron, but what rocks him is the discovery that black Sam, before coming to Triton, had been a "sallow-faced, blond, blue-eyed waitress . . . with a penchant for other sallow-faced, blond, blue-eyed waitresses who . . . were all just gaga over the six-foot-plus Wallunda and Katanga emigrants who had absolutely infested the neighborhood." . . . Complete sex change is a possibility in the outer worlds, and before the novel's end Bron makes one. However, the physical change cannot change a psychologically distorted personality, and Bron remains an alienated loner unable to make meaningful human contact. One of Delany's major white characters, he is, in the author's words, the "epitome of the unsavory WASP."

Delany's variety of black and mixed-blood characters represents his method of grappling with his own position as a black American writer. In a "multiplex" configuration that includes the metaphorical, the allegorical, the figurative (the use of the Ull in *Empire Star* is an allegorical reminder of the cycle of oppression, guilt, and responsibility that slavery begets), Delany parades black characters across the spectrum of his speculative fiction not simply to attest to black survival in the future, but to punctuate his social criticism of our present. While he does not dwell on a "black experience" as we would encounter it in familiar mainstream Afro-American literature, Delany does give us memorable black characters, and his science-fiction novels affirm the diversity and vitality of black life. Obviously, in some of the novels, Delany utilizes existing negative racial mythologies about blacks, but, in all his works, he twists the commonplace images and stereotypes to his own ends, creating a far richer and clearly pluralistic future, while at the same time ever so carefully structuring a pointed commentary on the present. . . . Other science-fiction writers may have tried to omit or obliterate black folk in their versions of the future, but in Samuel Delany's speculative world a black consciousness *is,* and black folk *are,* an insistent presence. (pp. 47-8)

Sandra Y. Govan, "The Insistent Presence of Black Folk in the Novels of Samuel R. Delany," in Black American Literature Forum, *Vol. 18, No. 2, Summer, 1984, pp. 43-8.*

SOMTOW SUCHARITKUL

Perhaps the most exciting event in science fiction this month is the publication of Samuel R. Delany's new novel *Stars in My Pocket Like Grains of Sand.* . . . It is the first half of what the author calls a "diptych," but it stands well on its own, both as a story of complex human relationships and as a tour-de-force of novelistic structure.

Delany has not written a science fiction novel for almost 10 years. He first rose to prominence with such novels as *Babel-17* and *Nova,* works that superimposed, upon the old cliche-prone space opera plots, dazzling new linguistic techniques. His gargantuan *Dhalgren,* over a thousand pages of recursive, dense writing, was a kind of Rubicon for him, and was the most vehemently debated science fiction novel of the mid-'70s. Traditionalists condemned the novel's apparent lack of plot and what they perceived as murky self-indulgence. His next novel, *Triton,* was an uneasy compromise between the new Delany and the old; there followed a series of works of literary criticism, heavily influenced by semiotics and infiltrated with jargon, sometimes undigested. Then came a fantasy series set in the universe of Neveryon, which took the trappings of sword-and-sorcery and lampooned them with such lofty humor that few saw the jokes.

But the novel in hand marks a return to science fiction . . . to the galaxy-busting universes with which Delany first made his name. The tightly controlled plotting is back. What's new is that he has distilled his decade of experimentation and critical soul-searching and finally made it all work. This is an astonishing new Delany, more richly textured, smoother, more colorful than ever before—and without the lumps of pretension that have disfigured other work of the past few years. This is one of Delany's finest novels, and as such must be considered one of the finest in science fiction.

Stars in My Pocket Like Grains of Sand is constructed as a series of set-pieces, and set-pieces within set-pieces. In the prologue we meet Rat Korga, a man reduced to zombie-like servitude by means of "radical anxiety termination," a sort of super-lobotomy that rids one forever of psychological problems—and much else besides. . . .

The long central portion of the book chronicles roughly a day in the life of Marq Dyeth, an urbane citizen of the galaxy who inhabits an astonishingly complex universe. He is an industrial diplomat, and as such must deal constantly with planets with wildly differing societies and mores. There is a galactic information war going on, one of whose weapons is the destruction by massive cultural pollution of pristine planets. In Marq's overculture of humans and aliens, all sentient beings are known as "she" and all sex objects as "he"; and by this tiny shift in language Delany renders insecure all the reader's notions about how a culture should behave. To this world comes Rat Korga. He and Marq fall in love—and their relationship literally sunders the fabric of galactic civilization.

That Delany actually brings off so hyperbolic a plot is astonishing. But more than that: there are enough novel images and weird concepts for a dozen books here, and they come at you relentlessly. Despite its length, this is not a flabby book. It is terse and muscular and explosive, and its author more in control than ever before. It is Delany's first true masterpiece.

Somtow Sucharitkul, "Samuel R. Delany: The Universe as Metaphor," in Book World—The Washington Post, *January 27, 1985, p. 11.*

GERALD JONAS

Even for a writer of such consistently high ambition and achievement as Samuel R. Delany, [*Stars in My Pocket Like Grains of Sand*] represents a major step forward. It is a work of adult science fiction. Anyone who considers such a description inherently oxymoronic has only to open the book and start reading. But a word of caution: read slowly. This is not the science fiction of *Star Wars,* or even of *Dune,* which may be enjoyed—indeed, may be most enjoyable—when consumed at a breathless rate that hurries past any infelicities of plot or phrasing. Mr. Delany's fiction demands—and rewards—the kind of close reading that one ungrudgingly brings to *serious* novelists. His characters live complex emotional lives in complex societies. To unpack the layers of meaning in seemingly offhand remarks or exchanges of social pleasantries, the reader must be alert to small shifts in emphasis, repeated phrases or gestures that assume new significance in new contexts, patterns of behavior that only become apparent when the author supplies a crucial piece of information at just the proper moment.

What makes *Stars in My Pocket Like Grains of Sand* especially challenging—and satisfying—is that the complex society in which the characters move is one of the author's own imagining: a universe of the far future, which contains more than 6,000 inhabited worlds and a marvelously rich blend of cultures. The inhabitants of these worlds—both human and alien—relate to one another in ways that, however bizarre they may seem at first, are eventually seen to turn on such recognizable emotional fulcrums as love, loss and longing.

Mr. Delany is well aware of the demands his novel makes on the reader—especially the reader who is unfamiliar with the science fiction technique of revealing the nature of an imagined society through the words and actions of characters so thoroughly at home in the society that they never stop to contemplate the rules that govern their own behavior. In past novels, such as *Dhalgren* (1975), Mr. Delany showed himself capable of stylistic experimentation to convey an otherworldly ambiance. Here his goal is clarity—without sacrificing the complex vision that lies at the core of his work. . . .

Stars in My Pocket Like Grains of Sand is the first half of what Mr. Delany calls a diptych of novels. . . . But while this book ends without answering all the questions it raises, it does not feel "incomplete." Sentence by sentence, phrase by phrase, it invites the reader to collaborate in the process of creation, in a way that few novels do. The reader who accepts this invitation has an extraordinarily satisfying experience in store for him/her.

Gerald Jonas, "Sex with the Six-Legged Strangers," in The New York Times Book Review, *February 10, 1985, p. 15.*

Michel del Castillo

1933-

Spanish-born French novelist, memoirist, and short story writer.

Del Castillo is best known for his autobiographical novel *Tanguy: Histoire d'un enfant d'aujourd'hui* (1957; *Child of Our Time*), a powerful account of the suffering he endured as a child during World War II. Because of his mother's outspoken pro-Republican beliefs, she and del Castillo were forced to flee their homeland toward the end of the Spanish Civil War. They made their way to France, and once there sought sanctuary with del Castillo's conservative, bourgeois father. However, he rejected them and turned the pair over to authorities for arrest and internment in a camp in southern France. Del Castillo soon became separated from his mother and was eventually sent to a Nazi concentration camp. He survived this experience but encountered further cruelty at a Spanish reformatory, where he stayed until he escaped to Paris in 1949. Critics hailed the sensitivity and restraint with which del Castillo presented his story, noting especially the absence of hatred and anger toward his parents and persecutors. As Jerrold Lanes commented, del Castillo "has no complaint, although his life has been one of incessant suffering; no demands, although he has had nothing, and no expectations because he has seen everything."

Although del Castillo has remained in France since 1949, many of his works continue to draw upon Spain for inspiration and setting. The background for *Le colleur d'affiches* (1958; *The Disinherited*), for example, is the Spanish Civil War. In this novel del Castillo examines the disillusionment of a young boy from the slums of Madrid who initially embraces communist ideology only to discover that violence and corruption exist in communism as well as in fascism. The novels *Le manège espagnol* (1960; *Through the Hoop*) and *Gerardo Laïn* (1967; *The Seminarian*) are set in contemporary Spain. The first book is a satire about a student who claims to have seen Christ and is ridiculed by the religious community, and the second novel centers on two orphaned seminary students suffering from loneliness who begin a homosexual relationship. Throughout these works del Castillo elicits a strong sense of pathos for his protagonists.

Del Castillo's recent works are less directly influenced by his past. *Le silence des pierres* (1975) presents a contrast between two sisters: Isabelle, a hypochondriac whose psychosomatic illness devolves into insanity, and Patricia, who yearns for personal fulfillment yet remains with her sister until she too begins to lose her sanity. *La nuit du décret* (1981) is a psychological detective novel in which the lives of an inspector and a man with a mysterious, perhaps criminal past become inextricably linked. *La glorie de Dina* (1985) concerns a man who publishes a book about his mother's scandalous life in Paris during the 1930s.

(See also *Contemporary Authors,* Vol. 109.)

© Jerry Bauer

WILLIAM DUNLEA

The alias Michel del Castillo has chosen for his autobiographical novel [*Child of Our Time*] is "Tanguy." This "child of our time" was born twenty-five years ago in Madrid, of a French father and Spanish mother, three years before the civil war. His father, a feckless bourgeois opportunist, deserted them at its outset and returned to France; his mother, a journalist and indefatigable *ism*-ist gave her all for the Republican cause, until there was no Republic. . . .

[Tanguy and his mother] escape to France, where they are vouchsafed some assistance by the father, but following a bitter wrangle he denounces his wife to the authorities. Accordingly she and Tanguy are interned in a camp for political exiles in the Midi. . . .

France has been half-occupied by the Germans two years when Tanguy's mother is finally able to avail herself of a chance to slip back into Spain with a party en route to join the Free French. Even without the separation the child can understand none of this; he clings to her promise that she has arranged to get him out a week later. Before the week, and upon his ninth birthday, the house where he is waiting is raided because it is sheltering Jews. He is arrested with them and they are led into sealed boxcars bound for a German concentration camp. . . .

Tanguy's tragedy is that he is a boy who was never a child; an exile who never had a home; a déclassé without a background. A victim of war to be sure, but an orphan of love also. His obsession to find his parents is symbolic, for the yoke of their indifference has worn him so deeply that only by confronting them can he possibly become a person. Quest unifies life, and love, the X factor in all lives, is the quest most compulsive; but hope is its pivot. . . .

Child of Our Time is the kind of novel destined to be devoured by its theme. This is a magnum theme that taps all the portentous questions of this epoch. As fiction it would communicate symptoms, as fact it bears a stigma. While it is as fictional narrative that it scores its impact, it is as fact alone that it reads into one's consciousness.

Far from "artless," however, is the telling. Michel del Castillo is an instinctive craftsman expressing in lucid French what he experienced resolutely in Spanish. His narrative, wiry and piercing, yields momentum only toward the end. One is violently moved—much the more since Castillo is disarmingly without vindictiveness—yet it is in that incomparably less personal way that we are moved by a story which we acknowledge to be true.

For we are too frequently and uneasily conscious that this is after all a novel, autobiographic or not. And even as its horrors are being related in relays one may catch himself in such pious evasions as "there but for the grace of God," "the sins of the fathers, etc." Through purging self the author presses home the nexus of our common guilt. But this guilt is congenital as well as acquired, and only the reader who perceives that the author is, therefore, one of *us* will have a proper sense of participation in these events.

> William Dunlea, "Portentous Themes of a Troubled Epoch," in Commonweal, Vol. LXIX, No. 3, October 17, 1958, p. 77.

ANTHONY WEST

[*Child of Our Time*] is an account of the childhood and adolescence of its author, Michel del Castillo, lightly disguised as fiction (the author calls himself Tanguy in the book). This information, in conjunction with the pretentiousness of the title, sounds like bad news, and it may prepare the reader for one of those familiar exercises in self-regard in which the author, announcing that he is, in the words of the popular song, a wile wile chile, complains that life is not kind and his parents are not loving enough. Del Castillo has legitimate ground for complaint, but his book is not of that sort at all. It is, on the contrary, one of those rare books that are genuinely courageous and noble. It penetrates all pretenses; it penetrates effortlessly, and with a terrible innocence, to those recesses of experience that lie far beyond the scope of the aesthetic and that have some claim to be termed part of man's knowledge of reality. It has been said that Michel del Castillo begins where Anne Frank leaves off, but this is imprecise. Del Castillo was born in August, 1933, and, a refugee from the Nationalist uprising in Spain, was put in his first concentration camp, in France, at the age of seven, before he had lost a child's simplicity and directness. . . . Anne Frank was older and more mature. She had already entered the world of concepts that is the home of the aesthetic falsification of the nature of reality. There already existed in her mind an ideal life in which people were not driven into hiding and in which they did not live in fear of a mysterious, immanent evil. She conceived this ideal as the normal, and regarded the reality with which she was faced as a break with normality; like those hiding with her, she saw herself involved in something improbable, almost unreal, that belonged to the world of the conceptual. Del Castillo had never had the experience of happiness and decency from which such an ideal might be constructed. The terrible, merely implied end of the girl's diary is the knocking at the door that means discovery and the end of hope—the hidden group come out into the ordinary street of their daily bread, under the familiar sky, to face the realization of their worst fears as the facts of existence. Del Castillo cannot continue the story from that point because he was never on the side of the door on which it was possible to hope. (p. 172)

[Years later del Castillo's mother reappeared in his life and] wanted him to hate the class to which his father belonged, and to hate a whole army of others in social and political categories whom she felt to be responsible for the evils of the modern world. Sorrowfully, he recognized in this the spirit that had turned him from a human being into a thing in a category—a Communist child—and had put him into the camps and the reformatory. The love of mankind and of life itself that he had learned in the darkest corners of the world excluded hatred; he could only pity those whose dreadful inner poverty and inability to love allowed them to surrender to this false emotion. He had come to realize that hate is not a true feeling but an expression of fear of what is hated, and that surrender to fear is what makes cruelty and injustice. His mother, by making hating her enemies her life's work, had emptied her heart. In the void, there was nothing left for her son or for anyone else. (pp. 174-75)

> Anthony West, "Young Man Beyond Anger," in The New Yorker, Vol. XXXIV, No. 37, November 1, 1958, pp. 172-77.*

JERROLD LANES

What a summary [of *Child of Our Time*] cannot suggest is the tone of the writing and the quality of del Castillo's sensibility. He has no complaint, although his life has been one of incessant suffering; no demands, although he has had nothing, and no expectations because he has seen everything. The brutality of Tanguy's situation has stripped him down to the core of his nature, without any of the trappings and pretense; yet it is this unrelieved horror, we find, that has preserved his innocence. . . .

But in spite of itself, *Child of Our Time* is a terrible indictment, for as the excellent title of the translation insists, del Castillo's life cannot be dismissed as merely the product of freakish coincidences. The locale typifies something widespread and the individuals express a whole society—composed, perhaps, largely of the well-intentioned, but too ineffectual to prevent del Castillo's tragedy and others like it, not to say to repair them. The refusal of the author to express a condemnation he has every right to pronounce, and the extraordinary poignancy of his voice, make our failure still harder to bear. We cannot live down the impact of this innocence and simplicity; but can we live up to it, either? (p. 23)

> Jerrold Lanes, "The Incomparable Proof of Man's Triumphant Spirit," in Saturday Review, Vol. XLI, No. 51, December 20, 1958, pp. 22-3.*

RICHARD WRIGHT

From Dostoevsky's *The Possessed* to Arthur Koestler's *Darkness at Noon,* a Niagara of serious fiction has depicted man's outliving the mythological symbols of Christendom and his agonized groping for some new faith. In no area of contemporary life has this dilemma assumed so intense a form as in the reality of the rise and meaning of world Communism. Hitherto this dramatic Communist reality has been almost exclusively treated in the literature produced by bourgeois philosophical novelists who repeatedly posed the question of Communism in terms of: If there is a God, then Communism is an aberration, a sin, a spawn of intellectual pride; but, if there is no God, then Communism is the logical consequence of a Godless universe; anything is possible; man becomes God; the floodgates to criminality are open; etc., etc.

Yet I, an ex-Communist who spent ten years under Party discipline, never met a single functioning Communist whose actions were informed by such absurd and abstract notions. (p. 21)

It was, then, with a sense of relief that I turned the gripping pages of Michel del Castillo's second novel, *The Disinherited,* which tells the story of the making of a Communist in terms of how I saw and lived that process. I do not exclude other processes; perhaps Dostoevsky's and Koestler's mentally tormented heroes really do exist, but they surely would (and this applies as much to Marx as to Lenin and Stalin) have had no human raw material to organize and catapult into tragic action if the conditions of poverty and degradation, as so graphically depicted by Castillo, had not thrown up hordes of violently exasperated men eager to embrace any philosophy that even hinted at redemption or liberation.

How is it that so many of the portraits of Communists presented to us have been pale-visaged high-brows thrashing about in the throes of metaphysics—high-brows whose presence or absence would not have mattered much, as history has so amply demonstrated? Hundreds of thousands of intellectual Communists, as Khrushchev has testified, have been slain for jay-walking in the path of the revolution and that revolution has roared relentlessly on. . . . Why did not the Communist or ex-Communist intellectuals recount the experience of those voiceless ones instead of extolling and celebrating the state of their own tired and frayed nerves?

In *The Disinherited,* Castillo has done this. Olny, his hero (if such calloused and determined men can be imagined in that genre), embittered and hard, simple in action but confoundingly complex in reaction, springing out of a quarantined slum on the outskirts of Madrid just prior to Franco's onslaught on Spanish freedom, is a truly terrifying man whose existence calls into account our responsibility, for our society produces Olnys with the same skilled efficiency that River Rouge produces Fords. Not even Gorky ever drew such pictures of human brutality and suffering. Beneath the Spanish Church and State, today as then, is a subworld where there is more death than bread, where curses have superseded caresses, where murder is a casual joke, where sadism is entertainment, where prostitution is almost respectable, where all human joy has been put on deposit in the cathedrals to be withdrawn in a life beyond the grave. And with what terse power Castillo delineates the volatile, sodden, drunken, and dreamy denizens of this slum! (pp. 21-2)

Castillo, artist that he is, reaches no hard conclusions in his dramatic recital of degradation, sacrifice, and death; instead, he concentrates with white-hot heat on showing his chief char-

acters becoming entangled in a web of insoluble contradictions. The brooding Santiago, impelled, like so many before him, toward Communism out of Christian love, finds himself a traitor lurching between the exploiters and the exploited and is slain by his Communist comrades; led by Santiago into the Party and freed of poverty and hunger, Olny is frozen with horror at the tragic price he pays, a symbolical and biological emasculation. Carlos, a dry, arrogant, crippled intellectual, discovers that he can't fight Franco's dictatorship and approve proletarian dictatorship at the same time, and he reaches that point of despair that makes him give his life for a revolution in which he no longer believes; Loto, the fifteen-year-old boy who swears continually to keep up his courage and prefers to die in battle than live in a slum; a kindhearted and weary priest who, about to die before a Communist firing squad, stands bewildered at complexities of life never hinted at in the Scriptures—all these brave and trembling men slide down the grim Greek route to defeat, without glimpsing why they are fighting or what they are dying for, shipwrecked upon the shoals of their own illusions, yet somehow managing to cling until the end to their dream of a world of peace for all mankind.

Out of this welter of negation, the sheer fierceness of despair tints the horizon of feeling with the afterglow of hope. Only the proud and bitter Spanish women—Olny's mother and wife (Consuelo and Marianita) emerge with some tattered dignity in Castillo's laconic narrative, but theirs is a dignity born more of biological functioning than of clear-eyed hope.

Castillo restates the Communist drama in a manner that reminds us that its strength is in each hungry body, in each outraged sense of human dignity, in each alienated personality, in each thwarted dream of comradeship and love, a challenging reality that is not all new and that predates the appearance of proletarian political parties. Anti-Communist, anti-Fascist, Castillo writes with blazing fury about men thrown into conflict by forces in themselves they but dimly perceive. His is a new voice whose accent is on the wordless words of the heart. (p. 22)

Richard Wright, "Ill-Paid Were the Players of the Communist Drama," in Saturday Review, *Vol. XLIII, No. 16, April 16, 1960, pp. 21-2.**

VIRGILIA PETERSON

The story of *The Disinherited* takes place just before and during the Civil War in Spain. The author, Michel del Castillo, was himself only three years old when this war, engaged in by Communists and Fascists at the expense of the people (as all wars are fought), erupted. But from his own earliest memories and from eyewitness report, he has re-created the atmosphere with a blood-curdling, brutal exactitude. . . .

The Disinherited is neither a pro- nor an anti-Communist book. In his preface, the author states that it was never his intention "to write a political book." Yet the whole pith, the very heart of it, is political, not only because it describes war, but because implicit from the start is its concern for the seeming impossibility of securing peace and the right of the unequal as well as of the equal to a place in the sun.

Strictly speaking, this is not a novel at all, since the disenchanted men and women who people it are archetypes rather than individuals and their fate hangs far less on what they do than on what position they occupy in the shaken and trembling social structure in which they were born. Delicate or gross, burning or blank, their faces are not so much unique as they are different aspects of the general face of man. In other words, it is not as a work of art, but as an exhortation that this book is to be read.

Virgilia Peterson, "A Tragic Novel of Spain's Civil War," in New York Herald Tribune Book Review, April 17, 1960, p. 5.

DANIEL M. FRIEDENBERG

The late Spanish writer Arturo Barea once commented that the Spanish novel of our times seems unreal to readers in other Western countries because of the harsh domination of misery and hunger. When to this almost overwhelming obsession for merely enough food and warmth to keep alive is added the horror of civil war and social chaos, we encounter a subject matter that stands outside our experience. The world of Michel del Castillo is inhabited by people who have been forced into a mold that breeds either saints or monsters.

The principal failure of *The Disinherited,* as seen by a sympathetic outsider, flows from its distorted view of the Spanish Civil War. According to Michel del Castillo, the split in Spain was between Communists and Fascists. This is a historical lie. The Reds were an unimportant minority in the Popular Front and for most of the Civil War. It was only the cowardice of Léon Blum, Neville Chamberlain and Roosevelt—who jointly feared that aid to Loyalist Spain would lead to general war—that pushed the Spanish Reds into a position of power. Stalin alone was willing to supply ammunition and planes to the Loyalists, and the local Communists increasingly insisted that he who pipes the tune should call the dance.

A historical distortion should not affect the value of a novel. But the inner meaning of *The Disinherited* rests on the premise that the only political choice is between Communism, a logical but tyrannic doctrine, and some species of Fascism. Since the latter is inconceivable to Michel del Castillo, the only *true* alternative to Communism has to be Christianity, though one devoid of priests. The author reasons as follows: The world without God is absurd, dominated by cruelty and hunger; the world should not be absurd: therefore, *either* Communism is true since it makes sense, gives a pattern to the seeming absurdity of events, *or* there is a God.

The need for faith, in its intense Spanish form, seems to have led Michel del Castillo to accept both Communism and Christ, somewhat like old Tolstoy at Yasnaya Polyana. The commissars and the priests are rejected, but both are striving for truth, one human and the other divine. Writing from the bitter experience of concentration camps and sadistic reformatory schools, the author emotionally washes his hands of all cruelty but clings to the hope of some kind of redemptive doctrine: "There are two kinds of men: those capable of dipping their hands in their brothers' blood to make history, and those who quietly wiped away the tears of the wounded to write the history of God. You had to choose between vengeance, humanly justified, and absurd, transcendent love." I have an uneasy feeling that Michel del Castillo may resolve his tension by emulating the career of his spiritual 19th-Century predecessor, Mariano José de Lara, the torn Spanish journalist who committed suicide at the age of 28. (p. 27)

Daniel M. Friedenberg, "A Casualty from Spain," in The New Republic, Vol. 142, No. 24, June 13, 1960, pp. 26-7.

EMILE CAPOUYA

[*Child of Our Time*] was a powerful book, telling us what we all know and never know well enough about this blessed era of ours. Moreover, it suggested that Mr. del Castillo was a writer of talent. Now he is thirty years old and the author of some half-dozen books, and this last one is thoroughly bad.

The English title, *Through the Hoop,* is an attempt to catch the spirit of the original *Le Manège espagnol,* which can be taken as a pun, meaning both "the Spanish school of horsemanship" and "Spanish trickery." For the author intended a satire on that present-day Spain that is still on horseback, his theory being that there must be plenty of material for satire in the Peninsular Museum of Social Anomalies. But the author has been poorly served by his literary sources. In this book the marriage of French wit and Spanish grotesque has produced an abortion.

Some people smile at the very mention of Ireland, others giggle at all references to Spain. Such audiences are too easily pleased. It is a mistake for a writer to address them, since they cannot goad him into art. I happen to agree with the author's conviction that the Franco regime and the Spanish church are first-class calamities, but a plague is not necessarily funny. I also feel sceptical about the likelihood of the Holy Spirit's descending on a slender-witted student, but that is not in itself a grand joke either. For those things to be funny the author must make them so. He has not done so. With his methods, he could not.

The first section of the book carries an epigraph from Stendhal, and it appears to me that Mr. del Castillo often imitates the great novelist's staccato style, his delineation of character by *pronunciamento,* his delight in paradox. These habits sometimes make a bore of the great novelist; but Stendhal never confuses matters by attempting Spanish slap-stick as well. Nowhere in his works do we find two rival gossips and talebearers pulling each other's hair because of professional jealousy, nor a long succession of characters with significant names. Mr. del Castillo has two priests named, approximately, Father Smiles and Father Choleric. . . .

I have not stated yet that the story is mostly about the martyrdom of the young student mentioned earlier, who goes forth to preach Christ crucified, and is starved, stoned, and finally shot. Even the author concedes that this last is not funny at all. But the admission comes too late; the novel was a botch long since.

Emile Capouya, "The Windmill Gambit," in Saturday Review, Vol. XLVI, No. 9, March 2, 1963, p. 40.

PIERRE COURTINES

For the past ten years, Del Castillo has been living in Paris, and it is significant that, although he writes in French, [*Through the Hoop*] is wholly Spanish in feeling.

His subject is contemporary Spain: its politicians, clergy, military men, socially ambitious and grasping middle class. Each character depicted seems to be shown wallowing, as it were, in the mire of self-interest. And into such a complex pattern of self-interestedness, the author has inserted a student whose strange aberration is that he sincerely believes Christ has visited him. (p. 342)

Linked to . . . [the] central unifying theme, the novel again and again reiterates the subtheme, ordinary boredom, which motivates many of its characters. This *taedium vitae* impels many "désoeuvrés," among men, women and clergy alike, to seize upon any bit of gossip, which they enlarge, exaggerate and distort in an effort to give themselves importance or, at any rate, embellish the dull monotony of their daily lives. The author writes with humor and sympathy. If he is more than a bit harsh on members of the clergy, it is because he stresses their human weaknesses, which, in turn, reflect some dominant characteristics of the Iberian Peninsula—so clearly individual and so easily criticized by the unwary or unsympathetic onlooker. Michel Del Castillo knows the weaknesses of the country of his origin, and he does not pull his punches.

This novel is altogether one of striking power and will add to the reputation of its author, who is already known as a "spokesman for the generation cradled in the concentration camps of Germany." His opinion of contemporary Spain should be listened to with attention, as should the questions he raises through the intermediary of a simple, childlike hero, whose mysticism and genuine fervor have all the attributes of the true faith. (pp. 342-43)

> *Pierre Courtines, in a review of "Through the Hoop,"* in America, *Vol. 108, No. 10, March 9, 1963, pp. 342-43.*

ANTHONY WEST

[*Through the Hoop*] is an entertaining and lively-minded satire that marks the transformation of Michel del Castillo, the author of *Child of Our Time,* from an amateur into a professional writer. In his first book he described an experience so strange and so terrible—he was a child who survived imprisonment in a concentration camp—that his mode of expression was of much less importance than his mere ability to make the statement. The book had its value simply as testimony. It was natural to suppose that the effort of making such a disturbing communication would exhaust the talent, and del Castillo's somewhat obviously manufactured second novel, *The Disinherited,* aroused more good will than enthusiasm. It seemed that he had had his say. *Through the Hoop,* however, is a satirical novel in the light manner of Anatole France's *The Amethyst Ring,* and it is filled with good things. It crosses country full of perils, having as its subject the consequences for a group of people living in a small Spanish town of a young man's nervous breakdown and collapse into religious mania. If del Castillo were simply to make an anticlerical joke of all this, the book would be inexcusable, but his handling of his theme, difficult though it is, is almost faultless. The clouding of the young man's mind and its painful clearing after the crisis of his confrontation with the stern essence of things are described with a maturity of comprehension and with a delicacy that are quite remarkable; what del Castillo has successfully shown is the agony of a mind that is facing a religious test but that has been immersed in religion without understanding it. . . . The organization of the book owes a lot to Anatole France, a better writer than many people nowadays think, but the stylistic model del Castillo has taken is laconic and dry, with many direct approaches from author to reader, including footnotes commenting on the action. It suits del Castillo well and his Spanish material even better. The strength of the writing, however, is a matter of attitude; though del Castillo is intellectually French, he is in love with Spain. The warmth of feeling that underlies even his harshest criticisms makes *Through the Hoop* a thoroughly satisfying novel. (pp. 170, 173)

> *Anthony West, "Ordeal by Fire," in* The New Yorker, *Vol. XXXIX, No. 10, April 27, 1963, pp. 168-70, 173.* *

EDMUND FULLER

[*The Seminarian* is] a story of isolation in community, of discipline and its collapse, of faith and its wavering, of love and its aberration. The setting is a seminary near Baeza, in the highlands of southern Spain. The narrator and title figure is Gerardo Lain, approaching 18. An orphan, he knows no home or family beyond this religious community. He is the prize-winning student and a principal soloist in the choir.

His realization of a crisis within himself begins with the death of a fellow-student, someone he had scarcely known. Yet the sight of the dead youth in his coffin, the solemnities of the requiem mass, the funeral sermon, the loud outcries of the bereaved mother, combine to arouse in Gerardo an onslaught of haunting doubts that shake his faith. In this instability and loneliness he first becomes aware of an attraction between himself and another fellow-student, also a member of the choir, Juan Alvear.

Juan is Gerardo's opposite in many respects, physically far more robust and athletic, a poor student who must struggle to pass, and one not likely to suffer spiritual crises. . . .

Juan is also an orphan. Having no homes, the two students remain together at the seminary throughout the summer vacation. Their relationship moves swiftly into homosexual passion—recognized during the summer, and reaching its physical expression after the beginning of the new academic year. Given the elements of Gerardo's nature, a violent denouement is inevitable. Unfortunately, it is so constantly forecast that the suspense is altogether a matter of when the catastrophe will occur and precisely what form it will take.

This extreme simplicity of dramatic line is both the merit and the defect of this short novel. It is beautifully written. . . . Yet it disappointed this reader. . . .

If loneliness and lack of affection within the seminary discipline are themes, they are hung too much upon this specially vulnerable figure [Gerardo]. The homosexual element obscures and confuses the problems of religious vocation and discipline. Gerardo thinks the physical love of Juan has delivered him from the morbid preoccupation with his fellow student's death—"because death doesn't have any special meaning for me now. I'm trying to imagine life, instead." If del Castillo is suggesting that the context of the seminary is what makes the reach for life impossible to Gerardo, the point is not convincing. The net result is a story that does not get beyond a classic neurotic case history.

> *Edmund Fuller, "Of Faith and Its Wavering," in* The New York Times Book Review, *March 1, 1970, p. 50.*

SARA BLACKBURN

There is surely nothing objectionable about a novel that wants to show how deprivation, discipline, and a total denial of sexuality combine to drive a young man mad. But [in *The Seminarian*] the author's fascination with charting the progress of his hero's repressed sexuality, and the manner in which he does so, is so doggedly predictable at every point that my response to it vacillated continually between exasperation and amusement as the tale plodded irrevocably toward its inevitable (shocking) conclusion.... Whatever publishing decision prompted the novel's appearance in this country was, at best, unwise; readers who encounter its previously highly praised author for the first time in *The Seminarian* will go out of their way not to read him again.

Sara Blackburn, "Around the Bend," in Book World—The Washington Post, *March 15, 1970, p. 10.*

ROBERT J. CLEMENTS

The Seminarian draws on Castillo's two years in a Jesuit school at Ubeda in the south of Spain. It is the first-person diary of seventeen-year-old Gerardo Laïn, who is preparing for the priesthood in a seminary at Baeza, and traces the course of his infatuation with Juan Alvear, a fellow-orphan from Seville. This is the plot; more compelling is its theme of loneliness, the craving for companionship and affection.

Despite the austere beauty of masses, Holy Week processions, and other ceremonies, the seminary is pervaded with a peculiarly Spanish asceticism.... In their sermons, several of which are reproduced, and in the confessional, the fathers display the most rigid orthodoxy, creating what Gerardo calls an oppressive atmosphere of lying and hypocrisy. The boys take "discipline" (self-flagellation) in the morning, and Gerardo wears a tight chain around his waist. Clerical suspicion is ever-present: boys with visitors must leave doors open; priests are not allowed to visit boys at night; Gerardo is chided for his "sensuous walk" and for keeping his hands in his pockets.

In Baroque Spain mystical poets sublimated their sexual drives by assuming the identity of "spouses of Christ." Gerardo admits to a "mystical bent," and as love grows, at first indefinable, between the two orphans, Gerardo assumes the invert role. He is the "prima donna" of the choir, the only one whose voice can reach the highest notes of the *"benedicta tu"* in the *Ave Maria*. His imagination is excited by the image of Christ's naked body. The building up to the homosexual act is delicately handled, yet it all culminates in a tragedy that is unconvincing in its timing even though not in its motivation.

The retention of his faith is a constant struggle for Gerardo. While there are moments when he feels grace as a "fine rain" on his soul, his doubts are unremitting, particularly after a fellow-student dies. Gerardo cannot accept all the talk about Resurrection. When his masters try to reassure him by recalling Jesus's faith, Gerardo objects that Jesus had no grounds for doubt, since "He had talked with the Father." But even this shows that Gerardo's doubts exist within a framework of belief: after his first sin he feels doomed, and hysterically beseeches Satan to "pull me down in the abyss."

The priests, who face the same loneliness and the same temptations, seem, for the most part, to have put Satan behind them. The most important and lifelike of these is Father Nordel, who watches the growing bond between Gerardo and Juan and tries to break it up.

We put down the book depressed by the medieval quality of life in the seminary. Del Castillo's point is that there is something very wrong with this antiquated education and its overemphasis on morality. (pp. 30-1)

Robert J. Clements, in a review of "The Seminarian," in Saturday Review, *Vol. LIII, No. 22, May 30, 1970, pp. 30-1.*

GITA MAY

[*Le Silence des pierres* is] a novel of subtle and fleeting moods and of unspoken thoughts and emotions....

The picturesque setting is an old house surrounded by a spacious garden. The hotels and beaches of Biarritz are not far, however, with their inevitable throngs of tourists and vacationers. But within the big house sounds are muffled and the windows are shuttered against the bright sunlight. The reason for this is that in the master bedroom a young woman, Isabelle Etcheveyen, languishes, victim of an illness which is obviously psychosomatic in nature. Isabelle's self-absorption and progressive physical and mental disintegration are the background for the central theme of the novel, which is the story of her elder sister, Patricia, beautiful and yearning for life and its pleasures, yet fiercely protective of the ailing and demanding Isabelle, who is slowly sinking into insanity. (p. 809)

The author deftly uses dialogue as a means to reveal the inner preoccupations of his characters. Description is resorted to sparingly but tellingly. The dramatic focus, however, continues to be on Patricia's intense loyalty to her clan. Images, sounds, and scents acquire symbolic meaning in this appealing story of familial devotion and covert rebellion within the placid framework of provincial life. The other members of the family occupying the big house are sketched in quick touches combining pathos and humor.... Dominating ... [the] motley cast of characters is the strong-willed yet tormented Patricia, her fine, regular features and haughty reserve concealing her inner anguish and frustration.

Also vividly evoked is the steady invasion of the quiet, lovely countryside by modern technology in the form of *routes nationales* and sleek but impersonal new dwellings. Less visible but equally portentous clashes between the traditional ways and values and the constant encroachments of urban, mechanized civilization are repeatedly alluded to throughout the novel. The author's principal concern is obviously the theme of illusion and reality, the ideal versus the real. The highminded, chivalrous Patricia can be considered as an allegory of the pride and insularity of provincial, tradition-bound France. But her self-sacrifice—her final decision to stay in the big house and take care of her mad sister—is at best, as she herself clearly realizes, a quixotic gesture. She is under no delusion regarding her gallant, futile efforts to resist accepting things as they are; yet she is determined to pursue her single-handed battle against the relentless forces of change and "progress." (pp. 809-10)

Gita May, in a review of "Le silence de pierres," in The French Review, *Vol. L, No. 5, April, 1977, pp. 809-10.*

M. RUMEAU-SMITH

[The protagonist of *La nuit du décret*], Santiago Laredo, a young police inspector in southern Spain, is surprised when he receives a transfer to Huesca. At first he is happy at the prospect of moving to a more healthful climate, but this joy soon turns into misgivings, then into real anxiety as, little by little, he learns of his future boss at Huesca, Avelino Pared. Pared is an old man portrayed at great length to Laredo and to the reader by various people who have known him at some point in their lives. Chapter after chapter, these stories add to the uncomfortable anticipation of the meeting of two men who have never seen each other before but feel strangely attracted to each other's personality....

Fifty years of Spanish history, from prewar times to the death of Franco, are intermingled with images of Pared: against that background Pared appears as a cruel demon symbolizing Spain under Franco. Gathering information about Pared becomes an obsession with Laredo and changes his personality. . . . Laredo finally meets Pared: a frail old man, sick, quiet and utterly harmless in appearance. But gradually Laredo is led to understand that Pared has investigated him thoroughly and knows his life story as well as Laredo knows Pared's and that his appointment to Huesca has been long planned. Planned also by Pared is his own death: he will die by the hand of Laredo.

La nuit du décret is an impressive piece of fiction, one in which suspense, deep psychological insight, metaphysics and politics all blend to create the powerful, terrifying puzzle of two human lives. The themes of death, guilt and revenge are major threads of the novel, which is written in a passionless, pitiless, accurate style. Partially a detective novel, partially a novel about detectives, the book is in fact a reflection on human destiny and on the meaning of life and death. In its depth and richness it is reminiscent of a novel by Dostoevsky.

> *M. Rumeau-Smith, in a review of "La nuit du dé-cret," in* World Literature Today, *Vol. 56, No. 4, Autumn, 1982, p. 653.*

ALLEN THIHER

Winner of the Prix Renaudot in 1981, Michel del Castillo has begun to acquire a reputation in France in recent years. In *La gloire de Dina* he offers a Proustian demonstration of the impossibility of seizing the essence of another person. . . . The narrator is the son of the fabulous Dina. He lives with her during part of her period of glory until, during World War II, she abandons him. . . . In the fifties the narrator encounters his mother again, though she is now a caricature of the beauty who captivated high society during the thirties. The narrator's writing is thus motivated by a quest for time past. It is also motivated by the narrator's discovery that another of Dina's sons has published a novel about her as well. In this rivalry with an unknown half-brother, the writer seeks to free himself from the past and perhaps lay claim to an identity.

Beyond Proust, the novel's attempt to reconstruct the truth of a past life looks back to the romantics. Del Castillo uses constant romantic hyperbole to inflate every description and to invest events with singular importance. The Sicily of the narrator's childhood is a land of primitive passion, and the Paris and France of his adulthood is a place of extraordinary inner turmoil. This hyperbole is also part of *rétro* sensibility, or perhaps the most marking aspect of a renewed romantic world view. . . .

The resurgence of romanticism in no way means that del Castillo does not have very contemporary ambitions. In the character of Dina he wants to portray a certain historical exemplariness. She is a woman who was caught between two generations: unable to accept the social code that ruled woman's fate in the early twentieth century in Sicily, she was born too early to profit from the equality that contemporary France offers women. Hence it would appear that the narrator exonerates her for being a capricious, role-playing woman, a self-deceiving victim of history, incapable of being either mother or vamp.

> *Allen Thiher, in a review of "La gloire de Dina," in* World Literature Today, *Vol. 59, No. 3, Summer, 1985, p. 393.*

Christopher (Ferdinand) Durang

1949-

American dramatist and lyricist.

Durang is regarded as one of the leading comic dramatists in contemporary American theater. In his plays Durang satirizes such topics as literature, cinema, parochial education, psychiatry, and family life. He draws humor by extending recognizably mundane situations to comically absurd extremes. Black humor, parody, and slapstick are standard devices in his plays. Durang concedes that some critics and playgoers are bound to be offended by his irreverence, yet he intends not to affront but to continue to interpret "the nature and purpose of the universe."

Durang began his literary career while a graduate student at the Yale University Drama School; almost all of his plays were originally produced at the Yale Repertory Theatre or in off-Broadway playhouses. He first drew significant attention with *The Idiots Karamazov* (1974), a play which he wrote with Albert Innaurato. In this play the dramatists lampoon classic works of fiction and satirize the pretensions of literature by mixing literary allusions and slapstick humor. *A History of American Film* (1976) was Durang's first play to be staged on Broadway. In this chronicle of film Durang parodies American movies to reveal how stereotypical characters and actions have influenced American culture. *Sister Mary Ignatius Explains It All for You* (1979), for which Durang won an Obie Award, is his best-known work. In this controversial play, Durang satirizes education in Catholic schools by focusing on a tyrannical, hypocritical nun who inspires fear in her students and ends up shooting four of them—a homosexual, an unwed mother, a rape victim who has had two abortions, and an alcoholic—to maintain order in her classroom. In *Beyond Therapy* (1981), Durang satirizes psychiatry. In this play a lonely man and woman meet through personal ads, but their relationship is hindered by their psychiatrists.

Durang's recent plays include *Baby with the Bathwater* (1983) and *The Marriage of Bette and Boo* (1973; revised, 1985). The former offers a farcical view of child-raising, while the latter is a black comedy about a young man whose father is an alcoholic and whose mother is emotionally and physically drained from having suffered several stillbirths. The mixed critical reactions to these plays reflect the general response to Durang's work. Most critics applaud his outrageous satires, but others contend that the humor is often sophomoric and fault his plays for lacking discipline. However, it is generally agreed that *The Marriage of Bette and Boo* is his most unified work. According to Ron Cohen, "[Durang, who] often seems to run out of play before running out of gag variations on his one-joke themes, here propels us with grand economy and clarity."

(See also *CLC*, Vol. 27 and *Contemporary Authors*, Vol. 105.)

© Jerry Bauer

Though *Baby With the Bathwater* . . . runs a mere 80 minutes, broken by an intermission, it seems to take much longer than that in its savagely gleeful contemplation of the insanities of parenthood.

In a string of farcical scenes, we watch the idiotic nursing and rearing of a child until, full-grown and a survivor somehow, he becomes a father himself and makes a start at trying to avoid the mistakes of his own upbringing, during which he was mistakenly raised as a girl named Daisy until, at 15, it dawned on him that he was a male. . . .

The "Child" does not appear until near the end when, after several hundred curtly dismissed visits to an analyst whom we hear but do not see and whom the youth . . . addresses from the forestage, "Daisy," who by now has taken to calling himself Alexander Nevsky because of his liking for the Prokofiev film score, decides to quit college after 13 years of trying to complete the first sentence of an essay on *Gulliver's Travels*, and settle down with the young woman he has impregnated after more than 1,000 affairs with members of both sexes.

This last sentence can only give you the barest glimpse into the fecundity of Durang's comic imagination.

At the very start, when John suggests that Helen sing the infant a lullaby, she opens up with "There's No Business Like Show

DOUGLAS WATT

[Durang] continues to write like a fiendishly clever undergrad with some fresh slants but an inability to make them coalesce into a fully sustained evening of theater.

Business,'' and a bit later on nanny tries to soothe the child by reading an excerpt from *Mommie Dearest*. The jokes and non sequiturs, some hits and some misses, fly thick and fast, but the only thread that comes near binding the scenes together is Durang's ferociously merry and completely unsentimental outlook.

That's a lot, but it's not quite enough to make for a full evening's entertainment, at least at this stage in the author's career. . . .

Durang's outrageously satiric view of society should never be checked, just better organized and less trendy than it is sometimes inclined to be. Like ''Daisy,'' it's time he left the campus.

> *Douglas Watt, ''A Savagely Comic-Strip View of Society,'' in* Daily News, *New York, November 9, 1983. Reprinted in* New York Theatre Critics' Reviews, *Vol. XLIV, No. 18, Week of December 12, 1983, p. 78.*

CLIVE BARNES

Christopher Durang is in love with madness. His plays have a craziness to them, but also a bitterness. You laugh with an aftertaste of bile. He is a purveyor of what might be called black farces.

His latest play, *Baby With the Bathwater*, . . . is a typical example of his dangerous wit and anarchic sense of humor. Nothing is sacred to Durang—certainly not motherhood.

Here, in *Baby With the Bathwater*, the farce seems full of flying babies through flying windows.

Helen and John are just an ordinary couple—and we meet them billing and cooing, and soon squawking—over their first-born child. It might be a boy, it might be a girl. They are too polite to enquire. . . .

Providentially a Nanny appears on the scene—and a very curious Nanny she is. Sadistic, mean and commanding, her first actions are to frighten the baby, send [Helen] out to buy paper and pencil to start on a career as a novelist—to be soon abandoned—and quickly seduce the husband.

Of course, Durang's plays are almost impossible to describe because they depend partly upon his fantastications of idiom and language which pour out like a stream of unconsciousness, and also the sheer bizarre nature of his mind.

He challenges us to think the unthinkable and laugh at it. A little nervously.

For example, Helen and John's domestic bliss, they are three in a bed with Nanny, is interrupted by a young woman who arrives with a German shepherd, which is unseen but very heard.

She is distraught because she has lost her baby. Her apartment was devoid of furniture. She left the baby on the floor, went out, and the German shepherd—who loves meat—ate the baby.

Now she absconds with Helen and John's baby, they chase her, she is killed by a passing bus, the baby escapes because the wheels miss him/her, and John resourcefully kicks the dog under a truck.

Funny? In practice, in performance, in Durang, yes, it is. Hilariously funny. It is also sick. And the funniness and the sickness of the piece emerge because the characters and even the incidents are scarcely more than a slight off-beat away from what passes as normal.

> *Clive Barnes, ''Like Durang? You'll Love 'Bathwater','' in* New York Post, *November 9, 1983. Reprinted in* New York Theatre Critics' Reviews, *Vol. XLIV, No. 18, Week of December 12, 1983, p. 80.*

FRANK RICH

''I just don't want to make the child insane, that's all,'' says the mother, Helen, to her husband, John, as they contemplate their newborn baby in its shiny wicker bassinett. Given that these parents inhabit Christopher Durang's new comedy, . . . *Baby With the Bathwater*, need I tell you that they soon drive their child absolutely bonkers? . . .

Helen, John and Nanny are secular versions of Mr. Durang's Sister Mary Ignatius: they're adults who sadistically chew up their young, then spit the remains onto a psychiatrist's couch. And, a few bright lines notwithstanding, we can't ignore that Act I of *Baby With the Bathwater* is a strained variation on past Durang riffs. We're so inured by now to this writer's angry view of parental authority figures that at intermission we feel like shaking him and shouting: ''Enough already! Move on!''

Which is exactly, to our amazement, what he does. If Act I of *Baby* is a string of *Mommie Dearest* gags in which Mr. Durang's feelings of victimization are more pronounced than the freshness of his comic invention, the second gives us a different, more provocative range of feelings and far funnier lines in the bargain. The explanation for this is simple: the writer finally lets us see his play's victim, rather than just his tormentors.

That victim at first seems a typical Durang sick joke. Baby, we learn, spent his entire childhood as an inert lump—a condition his mother attributes to a lack of ''joi de vivre.'' He would awaken only to attempt suicide by running in front of a moving bus, and his gender was indeterminate. Though his parents named him Daisy (as in the song containing the lyric ''half-crazy''), the child would also assume names ranging from Ponchita Pierce to Charles Kurault. When we meet the college-age Baby, he is played by a man . . . wearing a dress.

But if Mr. Durang hasn't abandoned his hyperbolic style in defining his protagonist, Daisy proves a fuller creation than the outrageous facts suggest. Watching the character undergo therapy, we feel the pain that leads him to have more than 1,700 sexual partners, that makes it impossible for him to find an identity or a name. We also feel, as the unseen doctor says, that Daisy can't blame his parents forever—and, after several hundred sessions, Daisy actually does start to overcome his childhood.

Perhaps more revealingly, the therapist also breaks through his patient's writing block. For 10 years Daisy has been trying to complete a freshman English composition that begins with an incomplete sentence: ''*Gulliver's Travels* is a biting, bitter work that—.'' When Daisy at last becomes able to complete that sentence, Mr. Durang achieves an equivalent breakthrough. A playwright who shares Swift's bleak view of humanity, he conquers bitterness and finds a way to turn rage into comedy that is redemptive as well as funny. By the time Daisy has moved beyond therapy Mr. Durang has moved well beyond his last play, *Beyond Therapy*. The somewhat hopeful ending of *Baby* is earned, not contrived.

This isn't to say that more work can't be done. If Daisy is the first Durang hero who works through his rage to become an adult—instead of just joking the anger away or pulling out a gun—he could bear further examination still. The author's compulsive gag-making might also be in tighter control. Only Mr. Durang could hit comic targets as varied as the Spence School, *The Brothers Karamazov*, CBS network executives, James Taylor, The New York Post, Ascap royalty policies, Sylvia Plath, *A Doll's Life* and Cliff's Notes. Some of the punchlines are indeed priceless, but not all of them are germane....

Baby With the Bathwater is a big but not final step toward the definitive Durang play....

> *Frank Rich, " 'Baby', New Durang Comedy," in* The New York Times, *November 9, 1983, p. C21.*

JOHN SIMON

Christopher Durang is such a funny fellow that his plays cannot help being funny; now, if they could only help being so un-disciplined. In *Baby With the Bathwater,* however, even his humor is slow getting started: The first act skitters by mostly on titters. The second act has more substantial laughs, though seldom up to Durang's best, and the happyish ending seems meretricious. The first act is about bringing up Daisy, a baby of indeterminate gender, whose dad, John, is an unemployed alcoholic, and whose mother, Helen, would prefer to such mortal children as Daisy immortal brainchildren such as *Princess Daisy* or *Scruples*. (p. 67)

But though inept or demented guardians are favorite targets for Durang, young parents and babies do not fit comfortably into his sphere of interest. It is only when the talented but suicidal girl-boy Daisy begins to grow up, and the problems with parents, teachers, and psychiatrists become a two-way street or bottleneck, that the author begins to warm to his existential gridlock. Even so, the scattershot humor tends to wander through the play like an amusing amnesiac oblivious of character and situation. Thus lengthy jokes about ASCAP are quite funny, but hardly relevant. And isn't it too bad that in Daisy's confession to his/her therapist, "My parents aren't really evil, and maybe my plan to hire a hitperson to kill them is going too far," the irrelevant linguistic jab ("hitperson") should be sharper than the germane psychological joke?

Free-floating satire and rampant absurdism are all very well, but even the wildest play must let its characters grow in wild-ness and match up mouths with jokes, rather than let the latter come indiscriminately from any lips, indeed any Durang play. It's funny to have Helen write Cliff's Notes for *The Thorn Birds*, but when an actual school is brought onstage, it's not so much anti- as pseudointellectual—Daisy's essay that is prac-tically a suicide note is given an A by the headmistress for successfully blending the styles of Donald Barthelme and *Ses-ame Street*.... Theatrically, it may be all right to throw out the baby with the bathwater, but only if one did not first, in the writing, throw out the baby and keep the placenta. (pp. 67-8)

> *John Simon, "Brotherhood Weak," in* New York Magazine, *Vol. 16, No. 46, November 21, 1983, pp. 65-8.**

ELLIOT SIRKIN

[There are] signs of interesting new life in the theater, and a great deal of the credit belongs to the new Off Broadway that has sprung up along Theater Row, a grisly block on West 42nd Street that you wouldn't want to walk down after midnight, but where you can see work that is, if nothing else, high-spirited and novel.... [Two new plays are] at least interest-ing—*Baby With the Bathwater* by Christopher Durang and *Isn't It Romantic* by Wendy Wasserstein. Despite their defects, the plays *feel* new; there is nothing moldy or genteel about either of them.

Written by authors still in their 30s, both present a series of hard-driving skits, most of which conclude with some kind of punch line or shock—a new dramatic shape that probably issues from the playwrights' childhood apprenticeships in front of the TV screen. This gives *Isn't It Romantic* and *Baby With the Bathwater* a compelling stop-and-go movement. Unfortunately, in both works the prevailing emotional atmosphere is one of injured self-regard and subliminally rationalized prejudice.

The playwrights have the energetic satiric bent of good college humorists, and are unmistakably present-day New Yorkers, as witness their dialogue, with its facetious mockery, its spurts of hysteria and its quotes from old show tunes. (p. 202)

Christopher Durang's [plays] could not be termed in any way conversational, unless you count as conversation the mono-logues unhinged and sometimes brilliant people deliver on the subway. *Baby With the Bathwater* . . . doubles the aggressive venom of its predecessor, *Sister Mary Ignatius Explains It All for You,* but it also has a lively, rough vitality. Basically, it is a brutal, knockabout portrait of the traumas endured from birth by a typical suburban boy; he is unseen by the audience until the last act, when he appears in his analyst's office wearing a dress. It's a striking moment, and Durang's explosions of un-disciplined gall have a great deal of verve. But . . . *Baby With the Bathwater* is finally not much more than a bitter private preoccupation presented as the essence of unprejudiced truth.... Durang seems stuck on a female creature who might best be described as the Mad Gorgon. She has her deranged charms, but she can't entertain us forever.

The real surprise of *Sister Mary Ignatius Explains It All for You* was its popularity. Why should a short play that took the standard Tom Lehrer swipes at Catholic education have been such a great success—and with people who didn't know the first thing about parochial schools? The answer may be that it was not Sister Mary the ideologue who held the author and his audience in such a state of rapt horror, but Sister Mary, the female tyrant. If the complacently irrational Sister Mary didn't remind you of your sadistic camp counselor, then perhaps she was your crazy math teacher who penalized for erasures or your mother on the warpath, the unpredictable and rampaging Bad Mom so beloved of psychiatry.

For a writer of Durang's intelligence, the weaknesses of Cath-olic dogma could never have been much of a challenge. The damage caused by early exposure to an overbearing woman is his real subject and in *Baby With the Bathwater,* his dread of viragoes is everywhere. There is a copy of *Mommie Dearest* read from as a bedtime story, a lascivious nanny, a pompous busybody and a belligerent school principal who yells orders at her male secretary.... The smirking, oblique pleasure that Christopher Durang seems to take in allowing his Valkyrie trio to dominate the action and terrorize everyone in sight makes it hard not to conclude that he is, at heart, a writer who divides humanity into the humiliators and the humiliated.

What Durang doesn't seem to realize is that, in reality, his bossy, erratic women are pitiful and confused neurotics, often as victimized as their charges, and that their quest for dominance often has an element of genuine concern. Without the *outré* comedies of Tennessee Williams, the very existence of a writer like Durang would be impossible, but when Williams created an overwhelming woman, he didn't create a psychopathic fiend—at least not always. In *The Glass Menagerie,* desperate, designing Amanda Wingfield drives her children to flight or withdrawal because she wants a better life for them that obviously will never be. Challenged, she moans, in complete sincerity, "So my devotion to my children has made me a witch."

But Durang's witches are *just* witches. He seems to believe that if only someone would chloroform these murderous shrews, we would all grow up happy, free and whole. It's us against them, and perhaps the most dramatic aspect of his renegade Catholicism is that he seems to be the only person on earth who thinks the Catholic Church is run by women.

At the end of *Isn't It Romantic,* the heroine, wearing a man's hat, dances around her apartment in what looks like an old Judy Garland routine. The point? Apparently her waif days are over, and now she will star in her own life. At the end of *Baby With the Bathwater,* the hag-ridden hero gives up his dress and has a child by a dear, shy wife. The point? Apparently he has exorcised the Mad Gorgon. Yet neither image is convincing: Wasserstein's cattiness and Durang's paranoid belligerence can't be canceled out so easily. Both plays reflect life with an uppity contempt that could trivialize and sour just about any subject, though to their credit these two playwrights never stoop to diaphragm jokes, like Tom Stoppard who, alas, does. (pp. 202-04)

> *Elliot Sirkin, in a review of "Baby with the Bathwater," in* The Nation, *Vol. 238, No. 6, February 18, 1984, pp. 202-04.*

CLIVE BARNES

Christopher Durang, playwright, actor, man about town, humorist around ideas, returning native, strikes me as the kind of person who might well giggle uncontrollably at funerals. Especially his own. For he has a funnybone where other people keep a skeleton.

His new play, *The Marriage of Bette and Boo,* . . . is the anatomy of a marriage, seen through the bland, sightless eyes of a son.

The father was a drunk, the mother rendered an emotional cripple largely by her tragic succession of stillborn children, the grandparents were certifiably nutty, the family background stained with the oppression of the Roman Catholic Church, and the son himself is primarily absorbed in a scholarly enquiry into the novels of Thomas Hardy. Just plain folks!

The play, of course, is a farce.

Durang, in the person of the narrator-son, played, incidentally, by himself, explains at the outset the purpose of his dramatic exercise.

"If one looks hard enough," he tells us, "one can generally see the order that lies beneath the surface." So this is meant to be an anarchic leap beneath the level of what he terms "ordinary reality."

Yet in a sense his reality, which while frenetic, funny, and church-bizarre, is ordinary indeed. It does have a logic, a disturbing order which stems from inevitability.

Durang exaggerates. . . . But the framework of Durang's story seems palpably possible.

If this is a comedy it is a comedy with teeth, a farce with dentures, a burlesque complete with bridgework and enough fancy dentistry to make an orthodontist cheer. (p. 268)

Durang has the ability of making the real absurd and the absurd real. It is all done by mirrors.

We are not going to identify actually with Durang's crazy family—such families do not visit theaters except for surgery—but all of its members have the ability to strike odd chords of recognition.

Moments of absurdity—a drunk trying to vacuum up spilt gravy, a priest immitating sizzling bacon or a percolator—have a kind of nightmarishly possible impossibility.

And some [of] the phrases wrap up immortal kernels of fortune-cookie truth. Imagine a woman saying: "I think I am going deaf." And then, without a beat, adding: "God, I hope so!"

And Durang's put-upon hero—his portrait of the young man as an artist—trying to distance his family, and at the same time to understand Thomas Hardy and predestination, has a manic credibility. He is so much a creature of his own times and circumstances he could have been invented by his own psychiatrist. (pp. 268-69)

Durang as his own hero looks distantly befuddled, and has just the right air of the play happening to someone else, someone actually not quite so smart, who is living just off center-stage.

He is funny but pained, and it is this pain that on occasion gives the play a vicious touch of a reality not simply beyond therapy, but beyond a joke. Durang not merely shows a nerve in this play, at times he practically bares it, and the nerve is evidently his own. (p. 269)

> *Clive Barnes, "Marriage to End All Marriages," in* New York Post, *May 17, 1985. Reprinted in* New York Theatre Critics' Reviews, *Vol. XLVI, No. 8, Week of May 20, 1985, pp. 268-69.*

FRANK RICH

Christopher Durang's comedy, *The Marriage of Bette and Boo,* is so speedy and chipper that it could almost be mistaken for a Bob Fosse musical. . . .

Yet here is what happens in this new family play by the author of *Sister Mary Ignatius Explains It All for You:* A woman gives birth to four successive stillborn babies, each of whom is unceremoniously dumped on to the hospital floor by the obstetrician. There are onstage deaths by stroke and by cancer. One character is an alcoholic, another a psychotic, another senile. And heaven help those who seek solace from the neighborhood priest. As Father Donnally . . . explains, he is powerless to do anything except "mumble platitudes" to the "stupid people" who come to him with "insoluble problems."

How can one reconcile the tragic goings-on in *Bette and Boo* with its buoyant style? For Mr. Durang, that's no problem—

it's an esthetic and moral calling. Once more he is demonstrating his special knack for wrapping life's horrors in the primary colors of absurdist comedy. In Mr. Durang's world, there is no explanation for misery: Even if one sifts through "the endless details of everyday life" hoping to "order reality," nothing will make sense. In *Bette and Boo,* as in his previous *Baby With the Bathwater,* the playwright lays out the loony facts of a boy's grotesque childhood, hoping the utter comic insanity of it all will somehow ease the pain.

What remains unclear this time is whether Mr. Durang is easing the pain or merely papering it over. *Bette and Boo* . . . is sporadically funny and has been conceived with a structural inventiveness new to the writer's work: As the story progresses, its chronology pointedly becomes more scrambled and its connections with any literal reality increasingly sever. But at the same time, Mr. Durang's jokemaking is becoming more mannered and repetitive—an automatic, almost compulsive reflex. *Bette and Boo* has a strangely airless atmosphere, and it says little the author hasn't said with greater wit and emotional ferocity before.

In a sense, this play is Mr. Durang's version of *The Glass Menagerie*—with the playwright himself cast in the role of the narrator-son, here named Matt. The tale begins with the marriage of Matt's parents . . . and ends over two decades later with the family's dissolution. By then, Matt is making his way in the world and has begun to accept the lessons of his upbringing. "I don't believe that God punishes people for specific things," says Mr. Durang at evening's end. "He punishes people in general for no reason." . . .

[The] author performs his downstage monologues with an ingratiating air. But his cherubic smile fades in the affecting episodes that impale Matt at the end of each act. Forced to participate in horrifying parental scenes—rather than merely to joke about them—Mr. Durang, both as playwright and actor, ceases to be an entertainer and becomes a crippled boy, shivering in the shadows. It says a lot about the increasingly visible limitations of the author's style that these two brief spells of real darkness are more biting than all the terribly bright dark comedy that is the dazzlement of *Bette and Boo.*

> Frank Rich, "Stage: 'Bette and Boo' by Durang at the Public," in The New York Times, *Section III, May 17, 1985, p. 3.*

LINDA WINER

Christopher Durang has been the wicked and wonderful kid cartoonist of the modern theater for a while. Now he is one of its masters.

The Marriage of Bette and Boo . . . is wicked, wonderful and cartoony. Yet, where earlier Durang (especially his controversial *Sister Mary Ignatius Explains It All for You*) used his demented hilarity with a one-sided glee, *Bette and Boo* is both demented and compassionate.

And wise, hysterical and incredibly sad. Like *Sister Mary,* this one suggests Durang's own exorcism of the Catholic Church. . . . Like *Baby With the Bathwater,* the new macabre comedy is irreverent about motherhood. Yet *Boo* also is a crazy gem of a family saga—as if *A Long Day's Journey* were told in comic strips. Through two lean but dense, unhurried hours, a generation unfolds.

Of course, "folds" is far too calm an image for Durang, whose humor comes bent into violent and silly shapes. His characters babble self-obsessions and hurtle agonies in 33 scenes of simple, deadpan sentences. . . .

There is not a false note or extra word, while Durang manages to ask, "Why did God make people stupid?," "How could God punish people for no reason?," and "Do people never change?" Durang does. He gets better.

> Linda Winer, "Durang's Wise, Wicked Family Saga," in USA Today, *May 17, 1985.*

RON COHEN

The Marriage of Bette and Boo may well be Christopher Durang's milestone "cri de coeur." The absurdist playwright, who in past works often seems to run out of play before running out of gag variations on his one-joke themes, here propels us with grand economy and clarity through the ill-starred union of a man who can't stop drinking and a woman who can't stop trying to have babies, even though a mismatching of blood types produces all but one stillborn. And as is familiar in a Durang play, a cloud of Catholic guilt hangs over their lives.

To be sure, Durang's version of a "cri de coeur" is hardly a long wail of anguish. His people are cartoons, the 33 scenes are short and sketch-like, and the pain for the most part is obscured by both giggles and deeply funny nonsequiturs. Still, the characters, as brightly cartoony as they are, are drawn with such consistency and purpose that they take on their own level of reality. And by the time we reach the end of the story, with the playwright quietly questioning the immutable patterns of the lives of Bette and Boo, the play is surprisingly moving. The presence of Durang onstage—as narrator and the only child of Bette and Boo to survive the battle of RH factors—reinforces the impression of life observed through a comically askew vision. (pp. 269-70)

That Durang is able to pull jokes out of some of the darkest elements of everyday life is nothing new. That he is able to touch our feelings at the same time is a remarkable new dimension in his work. (p. 270)

> Ron Cohen, in a review of "The Marriage of Bette and Boo," in Women's Wear Daily, *May 20, 1985. Reprinted in* New York Theatre Critics' Reviews, *Vol. XLVI, No. 8, Week of May 20, 1985, pp. 269-70.*

JOHN SIMON

Christopher Durang's latest *The Marriage of Bette and Boo,* is more recycling than writing. Here, again, the quasi-autobiographical boy-hero growing up absurd, as in *Baby With the Bathwater;* the despairing view of heterosexual relations, as in *Beyond Therapy;* the riotous but rabid anti-Catholicism of *Sister Mary Ignatius.* Yet less mordant, merry, poignant, for all the attempt to impose a more thought-out structure, with artfully scrambled chronology and cannily incremental repetition. Its sprinkling of felicities notwithstanding, the play left me lukewarm. Absurdist theater may provoke chills and fever, hot flashes and cold sweat, but never, never tepidity.

The Brennans, Bette's folks, and the Hudlockes, Boo's, are upper-middle-class families upended by their various demons; so Bette, who wants nothing but babies, and Boo, who wants nothing so much as his bottle (the other kind), will end up on their emotional uppers. (p. 83)

Bette is so average, it hurts. After Matt, she produces only stillborn babies, yet believes in the power of prayer to overcome an Rh negative. Her spiritual adviser, Father Donnally, is the last to believe in such miracles; and, indeed, a surly doctor . . . keeps delivering her of dead infants he tosses on the ground like rotten fruit. (This running gag does not evolve sufficiently to justify its blackness.) As for Matt, Bette and Boo's growing boy, he acts both as narrator and as his parents' crutch, whipping boy, and internecine weapon. He becomes a Thomas Hardy scholar, and lopsided parallels with the tragic denizens of Wessex sprout all over like Hardy perennials.

There are smart one-liners, speeches, even entire funny scenes— notably a retreat where Father Donnally, who couldn't keep a Philemon and Baucis together, counsels on marriage. But it's all overlong and strains to be funny and aching at once, yet often misfires so that the humor becomes painful and the ache risible. ''Meaning well is not enough. On some level, Attila the Hun may have meant well.'' ''Don't try to change anybody; if you don't like them, be mean to them if you want.'' Not unfunny, but lacking the little extra bite or final honing. Such unviable epigrams keep dropping like those stillborn babies. (p. 84)

John Simon, ''The Public Goes Private,'' in New York *Magazine, Vol. 18, No. 22, June 3, 1985, pp. 83-4.**

Sumner Locke Elliott
1917-

Australian novelist, dramatist, and scriptwriter.

Elliott writes well-developed novels that are concerned with human relationships, particularly as they reveal repressed emotions and desires. His first and best-known novel, *Careful, He Might Hear You* (1963), is told largely from the point of view of an orphaned boy whose aunts are fighting for his custody. The novel was recently adapted for film.

Elliott's other novels have diverse themes and plots. *Edens Lost* (1969), a domestic tale of family secrets and guilt, was described by Joyce Carol Oates as "a peculiar mixture of old-fashioned wonderment over the interlocking fates of human beings and oblique, sketchy, sardonic flashes of life as lived, or half-lived, by quite modern and rootless people." *The Man Who Got Away* (1972) concerns a man who uses self-hypnosis to travel backwards through his life in order to analyze the important events that helped shape his personality. *Going* (1975) is a futuristic antiutopian novel in which the aged female protagonist tries to escape enforced euthanasia but eventually concludes that death is preferable to life in the new world. *About Tilly Beamis* (1984) chronicles the lives of the two personas of a divided psyche.

Elliott has written two plays, *Buy Me Blue Ribbons* (1951) and *John Murray Anderson's Almanac* (1953), that were produced on Broadway. He has also authored more than thirty television plays and has adapted the work of other writers for that medium.

(See also *Contemporary Authors,* Vols. 5-8, rev. ed. and *Contemporary Authors New Revision Series,* Vol. 2.)

© Jerry Bauer

RICHARD WATTS, JR.

It is no doubt of keen personal interest to the young actor-producer named Jay Robinson that a comedy has been written that is said to parallel his own career in the theater. But Sumner Locke Elliott's *Buy Me Blue Ribbons,* which Mr. Robinson produced and acted in . . . , certainly isn't helped as entertainment for outsiders by the fact that it happens to deal with his case history. Indeed, it gives the play, which is pretty bad to start with, the additional handicap of being embarrassing.

The basic situation of *Buy Me Blue Ribbons* offers, I will concede, the possibility of an entertaining comedy about show business. It tells how a rich young man, with a lot of temperament and ambition to be an actor, is persuaded to back a romantic drama in which he is to play the lead. When it develops that the part is beyond him, he is forced by the leading actress and the manager to leave the cast, which causes him to have tantrums. It has been pointed out in the advance publicity that this has something or other to do with Mr. Robinson's actual life in art.

But, even if the embarrassment resulting from the personal identification and the uncomfortable feeling that you are watching a performer psychoanalyze himself were absent, Mr. Elliott's comedy still wouldn't have been entertaining. Despite the opportunities for affectionate mocking of the idiosyncrasies of play production, *Buy Me Blue Ribbons* is strangely lugubrious going, offering the always stupefying sight of actors trying gamely to be funny but being thrown by their material.

There are all sorts of references to famous people in the theater and lines that are intended to be witty, ironic and knowing about the curious business of putting on a play, but somehow none of them works out. There are two or three passably funny remarks and observations, but the fun is only too rarely forthcoming. *Buy Me Blue Ribbons* has a reasonably tedious first act, after which things change just a bit. They get worse.

> Richard Watts, Jr., "A Dim Comedy about the Theater," in New York Post, *October 18, 1951. Reprinted in* New York Theatre Critics' Review, *Vol. XII, No. 21, October 22-October 28, 1951, p. 206.*

FELICIA LAMPORT

In the midst of the current spate of anti-novels, this amusing and touching aunty-novel comes as rather a refreshing change. *Careful, He Might Hear You,* set in Australia, deals with a six-year-old boy and his four maternal aunts, all of whom are directly or peripherally engaged in a battle for his custody.

The child's gay, somewhat unconventional mother, Sinden, has died at his birth after feyly christening him P. S. ("for that's what he'll be—a postscript to my ridiculous life"). She has left him to the joint custody of her former lover and her asthmatic sister, Lila. . . .

Since the former lover is a publisher in New York, remote from the child in time, space and interest, P. S. has been brought up by Lila and her husband, with occasional visits to and from his other Australia-based aunts, Vera and Agnes. As the book opens, his fourth aunt, Vanessa, who has lived since childhood with a rich cousin in London and luxury, is about to return to Australia with the intention of taking over P. S.'s guardianship herself. The struggle that follows is successively amusing, disturbing and horrifying, as the child, drawn both physically and emotionally from one aunt to another, tries to keep his balance intact and his loyalties flying while playing the role of shuttlecock in an increasingly grim and active game.

Mr. Elliott's characters seem, at first glance, to be drawn from a bush-wacky version of George S. Kaufman's notebooks. . . .

Gradually, Mr. Elliott broadens and deepens his characters until, strangely, they become appealing for what seemed to be their faults and are damned by their apparent virtues. . . .

Mr. Elliott has, for the most part, been remarkably successful in telling his story largely from the child's point of view without making the reader feel cramped within the limits of a six-year-old mind. It is only when he strays into the cute (as when the P. and O. boat becomes "the piano boat," or when P. S. overhears the phrase "gold digger" and applies it to his prospector father) that a feeling of confinement is likely to set in. Mr. Elliott also achieves the difficult feat of drawing the reader from amusement to involvement.

Novels about nice children often move on slow, sticky feet, but Mr. Elliott's pace and wit manage to infuse a brisk tang into the air of his formicary.

> *Felicia Lamport, "Shuttlecock in a Grim Game," in Book Week—The Sunday Herald Tribune, October 20, 1963, p. 4.*

SAM HYNES

[*Careful, He Might Hear You*] belongs to a number of special categories: it is set in Australia; it is narrated largely from a child's point of view, and it is focused on a climactic courtroom scene. All of these categories pose their own special problems: it is hard to make "Down Under" interesting, at least to a non-Australian; it is hard to get enough meaning into a child's observations, without making the child an unbelievable monster, or a tiny replica of Henry James; and it is hard, after so many courtroom novels and films, to make a trial scene freshly dramatic. Mr. Elliott stumbles slightly at each of these hurdles. He never quite falls, but his progress is uncertain enough to make his novel a little clumsy, and a little dull. (p. 46)

His publisher describes Mr. Elliott as a writer of television plays. It is interesting to note, in the light of this experience, that he has not written a dramatic novel—that is to say, the book does not divide into strong scenes built on dialogue and gesture. Instead, it treats the action in rapid fragments, swinging backward and forward in time, cutting and panning, hurrying the characters along toward their destinies. The result is

an effect of blur—the effect a moving camera gives—and of haste rather than pace.

Mr. Elliott is obviously an able professional writer. His prose is graceful and assured, his dialogue reads like possible speech, and he has a trustworthy (if not too inventive) eye for detail. But if these gifts were enough to make a good novelist, we would have a lot more of them than we have. What is missing from *Careful, He Might Hear You* is the novelistic properties of form and pace. A man who can write this well *ought* to be a good novelist. Mr. Elliott, in his first novel, isn't one yet. (p. 47)

> *Sam Hynes, "Discords Down Under," in The New York Times Book Review, October 20, 1963, pp. 46-7.*

HUGH McGOVERN

The plot [of *Careful, He Might Hear You*] is simple enough. Two sisters struggle for possession of the child of a third sister who is dead. The trouble is in the telling of the story. My feeling is that if author Sumner Locke Elliott had told it in the classic curved line, progressing from the beginning to the middle to the end, he would have better achieved what he set out to do—to wit, tell a tale of terror and suspense. As it is, his narrative follows at random so many diverting bypaths, so many twists and turns in time . . . , that suspense is frittered away and terror is never realized.

A further difficulty, at least to a male reader, is that this is strictly a story about women and, it seems, for women. The focus is entirely on the two sisters, Lila and Vanessa. The child, "P. S.", and other male characters in the story scarcely exist. As a consequence, the two contending sisters act in a female vacuum, and the motives of their behavior are unclear. (p. 609)

Lila is no foil for Vanessa; nor, for that matter, is anyone else. In the end it is Vanessa who defeats Vanessa. Somehow, even this doesn't tie up all the loose ends lying around. What really drove Vanessa? Whom does P. S. really love? Why does sister Vere drink, and why is the fourth sister, Agnes, a religious nut? Who knows? (p. 610)

> *Hugh McGovern, in a review of "Careful, He Might Hear You," in America, Vol. 109, No. 19, November 9, 1963, pp. 609-10.**

WILLIAM BARRETT

The family dissension in *Careful, He Might Hear You* by Sumner Locke Elliott . . . is no more than a squabble of aunts over the guardianship of an orphaned nephew, yet it . . . provides a deep and touching picture of the intricate hostilities of those who ought to be, but are not, nearest and dearest. For a first novel . . . the grasp of the fictional medium is astonishing. The style is graceful and supple; Mr. Elliott's ear for dialogue is impeccable, and he skillfully shifts perspectives from character to character without the least hitch or strain to the smooth pace of his narrative. . . .

The characterization throughout is rich and sure, as the story moves back and forth from the devious imagination of the child to the troubled or self-deceived minds of the adults. Some of the aunts, like Vere and Agnes, are charming grotesques, but all are thoroughly human. Mr. Elliott writes with compassion for all of them, even the cold Vanessa, so that once we are sure she is not going to have the boy, we find her more to be pitied than hated.

William Barrett, in a review of "Careful He Might Hear You," in The Atlantic Monthly, Vol. 213, No. 1, January, 1964, p. 118.

GEORGE OPPENHEIMER

Reading [*Some Doves and Pythons*] by Sumner Locke Elliott . . . is somewhat like attending a cocktail party of strangers. The guests are for the most part celebrities—denizens of the literary, stage, screen, and TV worlds. For a few minutes they seem aloof. Then, after a short period of self-consciousness (which also exists initially in the author's style), they start to unbend, and you find yourself in the company of greatly entertaining people. They aren't the sort with whom you would care to become deeply involved, although while you are reading you cannot help yourself. Mr. Elliott has the power of drawing you into their problems, their intrigues, their neuroses, especially those of Tabitha Wane, representative of literary and theatrical artists. . . .

Some Doves and Pythons is a novel rich in characterization and in its polished and wickedly satirical style. . . .

The climax comes at a party when, for once, Tabitha's stage management falters. Abruptly the pawns refuse to be moved as she has planned, and the Queen is about to be taken. Mr. Elliott's delineation of Tabitha is such that, even while we know that she fully deserves everything that is coming to her, we still feel for her.

For those who know the fiercely competitive climate of the talent-agency business, *Some Doves and Pythons* is compulsive reading. For others who delight in humor tinged with venom, prose dipped in acid, and a tale that Jane Austen might well have enjoyed, once she got over her initial shock, the novel provides excellent diversion.

George Oppenheimer, "A Party of Strangers," in Saturday Review, Vol. XLIX, No. 10, March 5, 1966, p. 46.

GLENDY CULLIGAN

[*Some Doves and Pythons*] must be described as a regional novel. The region is exurbia, and the birds of a feather who flock there are migratory from New York, which is why the doves of the title are not paired with hawks as at the Pentagon, but with some elegantly attired snakes-in-the-grass.

Elliott's heroine, Tabitha Wane, is a successful agent, numbering among her clients a mixed bag of novelists, song writers, playwrights and producers, who assemble at her expensively simple country house over a weekend crucial to their respective careers and submit themselves to her devious manipulations. . . .

Moving force of her houseparty and her agency, Tabitha is also the spine of a novel which, despite its large supporting cast, really amounts to an extended character study of a true-deceiver. Tabitha's genius for deception of herself and others constitutes her strength and weakness. Without it she would be discouraged by the mediocrity of some of her clients and the treachery of others. On the other hand, without it she would be able to see them for what they are, and thus presumably be able to rid herself of their insupportable weight. . . .

So sharply detailed are [Elliott's] observations of this aggressive female . . . that personnel of publishing and related trades are likely to look around them for a real-life model. Aside from its in-group interest as a possible *roman a clef*, the novel has some general entertainment value but suffers from the author's vacillation toward his principal character. At times she antagonizes him into harsh caricature; at others, cons him into presenting her as a figure of pathos, complete with memories of traumatic rejection in childhood. Unfortunately, intrusion of empathy violates the ground rules for satire, which requires a consistently cold eye to be cast on its subject matter.

Glendy Culligan, "Crossbred," in Book Week—The Sunday Herald Tribune, March 6, 1966, p. 16.

JOHN LEONARD

There's a vision in one of De Quincey's opium dreams of old women who sit knitting, knitting eternity away. The old women are suddenly understood to be knitting themselves. They consist of their stitches.

Faced with a novel as excellent as *Edens Lost,* the reviewer resorts to analogy because, having rummaged through your box of adjectives, you find most of them broken or misshapen. "Lyric," "dark," "compelling," "shattering"—like old keys used too often in the wrong locks, on the wrong books, they have lost their power to inform. . . . And so—although *Edens Lost* is lyric, dark, compelling, etc. with the quality of a complete experience, surprising and convincing—it seems simpler to say that Mr. Elliott is a master weaver. He sits down at his loom and makes brilliant figures, absorbing patterns. Too late you realize that *you* are the fabric; that the design consists of your own nervestrings; that your implication is irrevocable.

Time: before World War II. Place: Australia. Mood: at first, gothic. Angus Weekes, 17-year-old orphan, leaves Sydney for a resort hotel in the Blue Mountains, to visit the extraordinary St. James family. The St. Jameses are everything that Sydney was not—unpredictable, witty, attractive, a kind of Brideshead without Catholicism. Angus is enchanted, and falls in love with the mother, Eve St. James. . . .

St. James, a retired judge who holds family court, absorbs all Eve's energy. One daughter, Bea, is hostile. Another, Stephanie, flirts with death. The son, Tip, ignores his fiancée. The games the family plays come to seem ritual substitutes for love. Eve is revealed, through Angus's eyes, as a frightening creature.

Effective, so far. But we suspect Angus, who is sensitive without being terribly intelligent. We are meant to suspect him. The next two sections of the book . . . demonstrate just how much Angus didn't understand. The final truth is horrifying. Not tricky horrifying not grotesquely horrifying, but psychologically horrifying because it's so undeniably right, so unflinchingly observed, so desolating. Having all been victims, we all learn how to be executioners. . . .

Mr. Elliott does several things dazzlingly well, and they are the important things. He writes with grace. His range and imaginative grasp are enormous. He can suggest sex without turning it into an autopsy or an atrocity. While most novelists today are so locked up in themselves that their books are claustrophobic, he enters the minds of one young man and two very different women and transfixes us with what he finds there. He makes us *know.*

The key to all this is the family, which of course we are in the process of abolishing. . . . But just as the abolition of God left us with the personal responsibility for all the things we used to blame on Him, the abolition of the family will leave us with the terrifying responsibility for who and what we individually are. . . .

Certainly this is one of the finest novels of the year, and it's been a while since I read a work of fiction as troubling and as satisfying at the same time.

> John Leonard, "All About Eve," in The New York Times, *September 9, 1969, p. L45.*

GUY DAVENPORT

[*Edens Lost,* a] competently executed domestic melodrama from Down Under, has little to recommend it beyond the obvious virtues of any novel. It delineates the manners and tribulations of a family at the time of the Second World War. Mr. Elliott has a Jamesian grasp of the tenuous devotion of the Australians to the English amenities, and he draws his characters with the gentle hand of the Edwardian novelist, so that there is a nostalgia inherent in both his substance and style.

The Eden of the title is a summer resort in the Blue Mountains west of Sydney, and it is plural because it is a different paradise to each of Mr. Elliott's characters. . . . The matriarch of this establishment is Eve St. James, whose husband, Heath St. James, is a ruined and guilt-ridden judge who has retired from the bench after hanging an innocent man.

So placid a beginning ought to lead up to disclosures and catastrophes. . . . Mr. Elliott is satisfied to show us a very tame skeleton in the closet and to trace the growth and disillusionment of the St. Jameses and their friends. (pp. 56-7)

This is the kind of British family novel that is written best by Colin Spencer and Angus Wilson, and even by the long-winded Doris Lessing, who shares with Mr. Elliott a total lack of humor. Mr. Elliott is primarily interested in relationships, especially those masked by civility or the guile which passes for civility among sophisticated people. Thus, the Eden of the St. James children and the waifs they have taken in is an illusion. In their grown-up years it is not they who suffer for the dispelling of the illusion, but Mrs. St. James, who had suffered enough before to keep the illusion whole.

Mr. Elliott, as readers of his earlier books will remember, writes with a fine sensitivity for the subtlest nuances of feeling in his characters; yet, once we have read so convincing a novel, we begin to question the amount of evidence offered us. There is no reason why realistic fiction must tell us so much to achieve so little. The sole advantage of such length, and such copious detail in a novel this slight is the elbow-room it gives the author to weave several plots together.

Novel readers, I suppose, are an idle lot, and will thank Mr. Elliott for helping them pass the time, but the critic might ask with justice if the story is worth quite so much scenery, weather, and snail-paced narration. *De gustibus.* But I have a suspicion that his talent might be more effective in the short story. (p. 57)

> Guy Davenport, "A Tame Skeleton in the Closet, Illusion in the Parlor," in The New York Times Book Review, *September 28, 1969, pp. 56-7.*

ROBERT F. JONES

Back in the days before gay liberation put some figurative hair on homosexuality's chest, it was the fashion among gentle old queens to write gentle old novels explaining how they got that way. These aching apologias were not pornographic in the explicit, contemporary manner. They were schoolgirl romances with all-male casts. . . . Above all, they were "sensitive."

In [*The Man Who Got Away*], Sumner Locke Elliott has written either a limp extension to those tales of yesteryear or else the finest parody of them ever attempted. The man who got away is George Wood, an unappreciated (naturally) dramatist and public television director . . . who one fine summer's afternoon simply ups and disappears from his lavish Long Island estate. Through the course of 33 sensitively written prologue pages, we are introduced to his frigid second wife, Ruth; his crude but loyal associates, one of them a dumpy hysteric named Charlotte Custis and the other a mincing fruit nee Aaron Burger but now called Andre Bouclez; and his light-of-love-gone-dim, a burnt-out case of Hollywood beefcake named Archie Hurst. . . .

Suffice it to say that all of the women in George Wood's life are utter bitches (except for his first wife, oddly named Ron, who dies tragically); that his male friends and/or lovers are properly drunken, suicidal and poetically inclined; that George is "hurt" again and again by a cruel, unfeeling world that denies him the peculiar but beautiful fulfillment he meekly desires, but that he finally succeeds in returning to that grotesque realm of baby talk—"poon" and "goo-goo"—where the failure in human communication begins, and where Elliott suggests it ends.

I would like to think that this book is a parody. The sensitivity of Elliott's unmanned hero merely translates into self-pity. The author's seemingly casuistic concern with words and scenes for their own effect becomes a kind of literary onanism. It is precisely these failings that the best of today's writers are trying to correct. Gay or otherwise, we have had enough of the limp wrist in 20th-century writing. Let's hope Sumner Locke Elliott was telling it is no more.

> Robert F. Jones, "The Course of True Love Never Did Run Smooth," in Book World—The Washington Post, *September 10, 1972, p. 4.*

SARA BLACKBURN

[In *The Man Who Got Away,* a] man disappears—from his wife, his friends, his job. He's been playing around with self-hypnosis and memory, and one day he physically disappears, it's not important how, and finds himself moving backwards into his life, reliving it from the present going back, but watching himself with all the perceptions he had before he began dewinding. Faceless when we meet him as a middle-aged New York professional, George Wood gradually takes on character and dimension as he moves back through his life. . . .

Sumner Locke Elliott has written a kind of Freudian suspense novel that is also a love story about a man's longing and desire for his own life. To somehow understand that life—the urgency he feels to impress others, his talent for being liked, but "empty, having missed the boat, the bus, the point"—George finally reels back to infancy; and Mr. Elliott, treading where few novelists would dare, manages this with a startling authenticity that brings to mind Robert Lindner's recording of his patient's infantile recollections under hypnoanalysis in his "Rebel Without a Cause."

The reconstruction of George's life is always right in texture too: We're set faithfully into changing era and season by what people are wearing, exactly how it smelled that day on the island, how the adult voices sound as they filter in from the front porch into the summer bedroom. And the structure of the book works so well that by the time it is over, an eerie and absolute connection extends from one end of its hero's life to the other, not simply a device that shocks and moves us into understanding, but a series of careful links, each well-made in itself, that expand a life until it is turned, dazzlingly, inside out.

Mr. Elliott's novel is far from perfect: It is too long by perhaps 60 pages in its center and tends to sag from that weight toward the end, just before its most powerful section. And it takes a bit too long to get started, with George's office assistants, who mourn his disappearance, rather grotesquely satirized. But in a time when fiction is reflecting the new lifelessness, the new powerlessness, or whatever it is that makes so many current novels so drained of vitality, it's a great pleasure to read Sumner Locke Elliott.

Sara Blackburn, "Four Novels: Dewinding, Competing, Indulging, and Breaking Free," in The New York Times Book Review, *October 15, 1972, p. 2.**

CHRISTOPHER LEHMANN-HAUPT

[What Sumner Locke Elliott] does well in **The Man Who Got Away** is just about everything it takes to write a first-rate novel: he sketches interesting characters with a minimum of strokes; he poses curious puzzles that keep telescoping into more curious puzzles; he writes in prose that flows like warm honey. And, best of all, he begins his story with a puzzle so peculiarly and pleasantly shocking that nothing more would have been needed to keep us reading at least a third of the book.

The moment George Wood disappears into thin air one morning while shaving in front of his bathroom mirror, we willingly suspend our disbelief. And by the time we discover that George is traveling backwards through the crucial scenes of his life . . . , we are too caught up with his problems to suspect Mr. Elliott of simply using a gimmick.

But a gimmick is all it finally turns out to be, or so it seems at the end, when George, about to disappear into the beginning of his life, realizes too late (too soon?) that he loves the wife he left behind (ahead?). For by this point the mysteries of the plot have boiled down to such pure soap opera (who is George's real mother?) and the psychic hocus-pocus has become so irrelevant to whatever slight meaning the story still retains, that one is forced to conclude that instead of resorting to the more hackneyed but no less significant device of, say, having George recall his past on a psychoanalyst's couch, Mr. Elliott has simply found a flashier way to tell an ordinary story backwards. Certainly, what Mr. Elliott does he does well, but . . . what he does well was perhaps not worth doing.

Christopher Lehmann-Haupt, "Well Done! But Worth Doing?" in The New York Times, *October 18, 1972, p. 45.**

ANATOLE BROYARD

I can't understand why writers are always grinding out novels of the future when that future almost invariably turns out to be boring and unconvincing. It is usually the same future, too,

that the last such novel described, as if there were only one version. In 1995 or 2000, or whenever it is, we find that life has been depersonalized. Instead of multiplying the possibilities of individual expression, the advance of technology has "paradoxically" reduced them. . . .

The novel of the future is usually pessimistic. But why? Why shouldn't things improve? It is no less likely than the other way around. Why not depict a society made up of successful psychoanalysands? Or happy psychotics, snug in the bosom of an insane world? At least they would be more fun than the familiar cast of robots, or lobots as they ought to be called.

When I try to think of futuristic novels that made the trip worthwhile, only Aldous Huxley's *Brave New World* and Walker Percy's *Love in the Ruins* come to mind. Neither is a great work of art, but at least they are provocative and give you something to think about—which is more than I can say for *Going,* by Sumner Locke Elliott. Here we are, in 1995 again regimented in the name of rationality, the atmosphere scrubbed so clean that it hurts our eyes, major crimes, disease and poverty practically conquered.

And here are the same old corroded ironies. If we want to eliminate crime, we have to do away with desire. To abolish unhappiness, we have to surrender its opposite. We are condemned to eat tasteless muffins, wear paper clothes, live in goldfish bowls. Our instinctive unruliness can be controlled only by a fascist state.

The novel opens on the day of Tessa's "going." She is 65 and euthanasia is the form of Medicare that has been voted for her generation. Voted by whom? Why? How were they persuaded? We don't know: all we know is that Tessa's gotta go. She has a few last words for the judge, though, before they drag her off, and this is the substance of the novel. Tessa tells us about "the old ways," which now, suddenly, seem heartbreakingly beautiful as the gas hisses into the death chamber.

Tessa's husband couldn't bear to figure in a futuristic novel and committed suicide. She "felt his death inside her as though she had swallowed a cold raw fish whole." . . .

Some of Mr. Elliott's imagery set me thinking. A man named Harry Platt sends Tessa's daughter Joan "away on a rollercoaster of hilarity." At the suggestion that she might encourage this same Harry, Tessa's other daughter, Barbara, shudders "as though a tarantula had walked between her breasts." Put these together with that whole raw fish and I think you can make a case for eliminating all figures of speech from this particular writer's style. I see no reason why certain authors should not simply face up to the fact that they haven't got the knack. Like Captain McWhirr in Conrad's *Typhoon,* I feel like asking what's the sense of talking in images. What good does it do?

Anatole Broyard, "A Cold Raw Fish Whole," in The New York Times, *February 5, 1975, p. 35.*

THOMAS LeCLAIR

Sumner Locke Elliott's **Going** is an engaging—and therefore ultimately unsuccessful—anti-Utopia written largely in the language of nostalgia. The year is 1990. Love and Patriotism rule the new U.S.A. The air is clean, but meals and minds are mush. Niceness prevails, even when the euthanasia bus collects citizens on their 65th birthday. Tess Bracken, an aristocratic lady who has lost two daughters and a husband to the age of goodness, isn't ready to board the bus when the novel opens. She escapes for the afternoon from her "Ladiesaid" overseer.... Her last-day tour of the present and past memories completed, Tess decides the world's not worth her staying on. At the end she runs toward the bus: going, going, gone.

Mrs. Bracken is a nice old lady, and her memories of a Jamesian life managed in mid-century America are pleasant, but I don't care if she gets on the bus or not because Elliott trivializes the issue. When the euthanasia bus rolls down the block, serious questions about social power and individual freedom seem unavoidable, but Elliott insists on the superficial terms of past *noblesse oblige* versus current vulgarity. He's more interested in demonstrating the attractiveness of a Town and Country life and decrying the power of Tess's tradesman son-in-law than in showing how euthanasia became the new Social Security or rendering its horror.

Tess's life—her attachment to her father, her sexual and social awakening, her relations with a persistent suitor—has a low-key interest and charm in its own right, but Elliott overplays the significance of this life by placing it in a contrived jeopardy. If the 1990's are going to be the twilight of civilization, more than nobility, graciousness and sitdown breakfasts will be lost.

Like Tess's husband, Elliott has "old-fashioned manners" and is "deeply sincere." His prose is that of an excessively civilized uncle describing his stamp collection: fussy, decorous and predictable. Uneasy with present/future vulgarity, Elliott is good at evoking the "richness" of a paneled past with gauzy nouns and polite verbs. This is harmless enough and sometimes entertaining, but when Elliott presumes to offer sentiment and cliché as cultural criticism even the simple pleasures of anachronism are spoiled.

> *Thomas LeClair, "Police Deals, an Anti-Utopia, Some Old Hollywood,"* in The New York Times Book Review, *February 9, 1975, p. 6.**

ANNE TYLER

Sumner Locke Elliott has always been especially good at showing us the outsider's view of the inside, whether it's the child's hazy glimpse of the grown-ups' world in *Careful, He Might Hear You,* or the orphan boy's yearning toward the insular family of *Edens Lost.*

In *Water Under the Bridge,* . . . "outside" is a large swath of the population of Sydney, Australia. "Inside" is the Mazzinis, a family so newly rich, so arrogant and socially elevated, that there is a continual hushed, delighted ripple of gossip surrounding them.

We first meet the Mazzinis at their extravagant lawn party in 1932. . . . They're one of those families that are utterly doomed, tracked down by tragedy till every new horror is just something else to count on your fingers. The parents are shot by a midnight intruder; a daughter's fiancé dies in a plane crash; another daughter goes through a series of wretched marriages and scandalous divorces; and the son, after years of trying, finally succeeds in killing himself off in a car accident.

But what makes the story so absorbing is not this string of disasters, but the lives of those outsiders watching—the guests at that 1932 party, who forever afterward meet and engage in different ways and part to meet again. We see them last in 1973, and they are still, at least indirectly, gazing upon their own faded snapshots of the Mazzini family. Some have had their whole histories altered by this fixation; yet it's they, and not the Mazzinis, who draw us onward through the book. In *Water Under the Bridge,* Sumner Locke Elliott has shown himself, once again, to be a master at celebrating the voices of ordinary people—rich, tangential, infinitely varied, murmuring around the edges of life's small and large catastrophes.

> *Anne Tyler, in a review of "Water under the Bridge,"* in The New York Times Book Review, *August 28, 1977, p. 7.*

JIM PASCALE

[*Water under the Bridge* is a] well-paced story [that] must be considered an historical novel, with whatever pejorative overtones the phrase carries. One wouldn't guess by the title that the characters are not stereotypes, but neither are they consistently portrayed as engaging and credible. . . .

[There are] too many characters to deal with in this short book. So some of them are gotten rid of—all tragically of course—and the narrative breezes lightly along. . . . It is almost as if the author senses a weakening illness entering the plot, momentarily dispenses with the sick members and infected scenes, and promptly introduces others until all have perished. In the end one is left with little to contemplate. And, as might be expected, in a number of important meetings and partings between lovers, one of them is forced to say, "Oh well, water under the bridge."

> *Jim Pascale, in a review of "Water under the Bridge,"* in Best Sellers, *Vol. 37, No. 8, November, 1977, p. 228.*

THE NEW YORKER

"'One time they put me in the tank with a real live shark,' Aunt Flora said, looking at Mrs. Binns hungrily" are the opening words of this strange novel [*Signs of Life*]. The main character, however, is not Aunt Flora or Mrs. Binns but Aunt Flora's sister, Virginia, who recalls scenes from her long life as she lies dying, senile and unloved, while her relatives await the end. Around 1912, Virginia's young soul was scalded and toughened when her dizzy mother ran off with a married man and left Virginia and Flora, aged twelve and ten, in the care of their well-to-do grandmother. . . . By the time Virginia sets out for New York to catch a husband, she has acquired an abiding distrust of all the females in her family—a self-fulfilling prejudice that comes back to haunt her in the form of her own embittered daughter. . . . Mr. Elliott organizes the old woman's flashbacks with care and economy—when episodes overlap, there is always a good reason—and his dark sense of humor, evident in the opening lines, sparkles throughout.

> *A review of "Signs of Life,"* in The New Yorker, *Vol. LVII, No. 13, May 18, 1981, p. 169.*

CHRISTOPHER SCHEMERING

Welcome to the world of Sumner Locke Elliott, and what a provocative world it is. Here the characters caress one another with wit and cruelty in such a civilized fashion that the reader doesn't know whether to be amused or horrified. Elliott is a popular novelist with dash and sophistication and, although his situations and conflicts are familiar, his insights are plentiful and his settings—pre-World War I society life, silent-picture

Hollywood, the New York party circuit during Prohibition—are marvelously evocative.

The central heroine of [*Signs of Life*], which traces the romantic history of four generations of American women, is Virginia, a woman of great charm and beauty who was born at the turn of the century. Now the once-vital Virginia is dying, and it comes as no surprise when Flora, her sarcastic sister, muses, "That is unlike her." As the narrative floats back and forth between the present and past, Virginia—not amused—reviews her life, defining herself in terms of those whom she has loved. . . .

Although this comedy of manners pretends to be about the eternal male-female dilemma, it's really a delicate essay on familial affections: the pettiness, ambivalence, the shaking-of-the-head non-communication between mothers and daughters. Virginia's brilliant grandmother, expedient mother and loveless daughter provoke one another in such surprising and complex ways it's impossible to point a guilty finger at any of them. Elliott is simultaneously ruthless and compassionate with his characters and thus is able to strike a tantalizing, if precarious, balance between sentiment and satire. This is a book to . . . be absorbed slowly, and savored.

> *Christopher Schemering, in a review of "Signs of Life," in* Book World—The Washington Post, *June 7, 1981, p. 6.*

RICHARD FREEDMAN

When is a soap opera not a soap opera? When it's written with the alertness and distinction of Sumner Locke Elliott's *Signs of Life,* which—like Maupassant's *A Woman's Life*—austerely but compassionately traces the cradle-to-grave experiences of its heroine.

Virginia Green's life is slowly ebbing away as she lies in bed and recalls manifold loves and betrayals. . . .

Mr. Elliott suggests in this novel that to love and be loved is to live, but also to betray and be betrayed. . . .

Virginia herself betrays her best friend by marrying her friend's fiancé. She has two children, both disappointments: Charley, a bisexual who marries a ghastly wife and drinks too much, and Mary, a pedantic plodder whose one love was her alcoholic music teacher. In her last years, Virginia finds herself in Mary's cold care, so lonely that she dials Weather in order to have a voice to confide in.

But this is to make *Signs of Life* sound more depressing than it is. Mr. Elliott delightfully evokes the innocent vulgarity of the 1920's, and his mordant wit prevents the tone from ever becoming lachrymose. Most remarkably, he is able to see life from a woman's point of view and—to this reader, at least—render it accurately and convincingly. (p. 14)

> *Richard Freedman, "Valley Forge to Broadway," in* The New York Times Book Review, *June 7, 1981, pp. 14, 29.**

KIRKUS REVIEWS

As in *Signs of Life* (1981), [in *About Tilly Beamis*] Elliott tightropes precariously through a roiling, date-hopping tale of passions—balancing his somewhat overdrawn characters between adventurous psycho-philosophical speculation and solid, plain-Jane storytelling. In 1978, Edward Patterson (old-family, profile like a Roman coin) is astounded at the sight of long-dead Tilly Beamis, whom he once was to marry. Meanwhile, back in 1976, Tanya Van Zandt is also on Tilly's trail—reading Tilly's memoir/diary in Sydney, Australia. . . . In the 1976 time-frame Tanya visits the crumbling (but still brassy) ex-Miss Australia who brought Tilly to America; she travels to a dismal outpost to confront Jack, the failed actor to whom Tilly gave her heart and trust. . . . Tanya uncovers how Jack's rejection drove the pregnant Tilly to the brink of suicide—at which point Tilly "felt the presence of her other self . . . confident, pragmatic, hard as agate, and angry, wonderfully angry," the self which had spoken to her years ago in the guise of her doll "Tanya." Are Tilly and Tanya one and the same, then? So it seems—as the narrative fills in Tilly's last years: in 1950s New York she settled for the "dense purity" of Edward; but a hint of incest sent her traveling westward, to death (?)—while Tanya lived on, pragmatically marrying a shockingly ugly "Frog Prince." And it is back in New York in 1978 that Tanya, scoured to emptiness, suffers the lack of Tilly—and her lost heart. Elliott's themes twirl upon implausibilities; though Tilly and Tanya are believable separately, their split and reunion is not. Still, this is an inventive, occasionally even mesmerizing venture into the chimeras of a conflicted, divided psyche: clinically unconvincing but with a measure of metaphorical impact.

> *A review of "About Tilly Beamis," in* Kirkus Reviews, *Vol. LII, No. 3, February 1, 1984, p. 98.*

PUBLISHERS WEEKLY

[*About Tilly Beamis* is a] very strange story about Australian Tilly Beamis, whose sweet, generous nature is a foil for Tanya, her strong, manipulative inner self. Modern readers will interpret this as a tale of schizophrenia, but the author chooses to portray Tanya's eventual takeover of Tilly in a mysterious, spiritual cast. The novel opens in 1978, with Tanya leaving New York for Australia, where she hopes to research Tilly's past and so understand her own cool, independent nature. So begins Tilly's story back in the 1950s, her love for womanizer Jack Quist, her abortion and her intention to marry proper, boring Edward Patterson. Here Tanya, disgusted with Tilly's complacency, conveniently snuffs out Tilly's life (a supposed bus accident) and so emerges full force. The story then swings from Tilly to Tanya in a manner both clever and occasionally predictable. The plot has some interesting twists, though the writing is marred by perplexing transitions and a melodramatic tone. (pp. 72-3)

> *A review of "About Tilly Beamis," in* Publishers Weekly, *Vol. 225, No. 7, February 17, 1984, pp. 72-3.*

Nicolas Freeling

1927-

(Has also written under pseudonym of F. R. E. Nicolas) English novelist, short story writer, and nonfiction writer.

Freeling's novels of crime and suspense are acclaimed for intelligent writing, well-developed characters, and vividly detailed settings. Like French detective novelist Georges Simenon, with whom he is frequently compared, Freeling investigates crime psychologically, exploring the motive as much as the method behind the crime. He also takes a sociological approach to criminal behavior, looking at its impact on society as well as on the individual. Action in Freeling's work is deemphasized: storylines depend upon relationships between characters and insights into human nature, and they are advanced in large part through internal monologues and stream-of-consciousness techniques. This aspect of Freeling's fiction has generated mixed reactions: as Robert Taubman observed in a review of *Criminal Conversation* (1965), Freeling "writes certain scenes so well that one wishes he knew where to stop before disappearing out of the genre altogether." However, many cite Freeling's ability to go beyond the standard limitations of detective fiction as the source of his success, and Hester Makeig considers him "far and away the best thriller writer in his field."

Freeling's best-known character, introduced in his first novel, *Love in Amsterdam* (1961), is Inspector Piet Van der Valk, a Dutch detective who employs unconventional methods and is gruffly compassionate in his tolerance for human weakness. John R. Coyne, Jr. described him as "a cranky, gentle, bumbling, brilliant, nonconformist student of human behavior," and Tom Sharpe considers him "one of the most interesting fictional sleuths to appear in the Sixties." After producing a series of well-received novels about this character, Freeling killed off his hero in *A Long Silence* (1972). Following the demise of the popular inspector, Freeling introduced another recurring character, French detective Henri Castang, in *A Dressing of Diamond* (1974). Reflective and compassionate, Castang shares many of Van der Valk's qualities, including the compulsive need to explore beneath the surface of the criminal and the crime. The Dutch setting of the Van der Valk series is replaced in the works featuring Castang by a small provincial town, but the sense of place still figures prominently. Freeling has also used Van der Valk's widow, Arlette, as the protagonist for several books, the first of which was *The Widow* (1979).

Although most of his books are parts of various detective series, Freeling has also written novels that have no predominant crime theme and others with no serial character. Among the former novels are *This Is the Castle* (1968), and among the latter are *Valparaiso* (1964), published under the pseudonym of F. R. E. Nicolas, and *The Dresden Green* (1966). In addition, Freeling has written *Kitchen Book* (1970) and *Cook Book* (1972), both based on his early career as a professional cook in restaurants throughout Europe. Freeling received England's Crime Writers Award and France's Grand Prix de Roman Policier for *Gun before Butter* (1963) and the Mystery Writers of America Edgar Allan Poe Award for *The King of the Rainy Country* (1966).

(See also *Contemporary Authors*, Vols. 49-52 and *Contemporary Authors New Revision Series*, Vols. 1, 17.)

Photograph by Al Morrison

ANTHONY BOUCHER

Freeling is the only major crime writer who can, for all his individuality, be classed with Simenon. The unorthodox patient hunch-playing Van der Valk is a policeman who Maigret would understand (far better than his somewhat tried superiors); and such a sensitive relationship between killer and detective as this book portrays can be compared only to Simenon at his best. The feel, the ambience of Freeling is as Dutch as Simenon's is French. The present case [in *Question of Loyalty*, published in Great Britain as *Gun before Butter*] involves Van der Valk with a corpse which has at first no identity and then too many identities, and with the serious border racket of butter-running; it is a first-rate story of crime and detection, and even more impressive as a subtly powerful novel of people and society. *Question of Loyalty* is one of the finest crime novels of this already distinguished year.

Anthony Boucher, in a review of "Question of Loyalty," in The New York Times Book Review, *October 11, 1964, p. 47.*

ROBERT TAUBMAN

Nicolas Freeling writes the quietest and most interesting kind of crime novel. *Criminal Conversation* is so nicely set in Amsterdam that one may suspect the influence of Dutch painting. It has the hard stuff too: blackmail, murder, some of the best families dubiously involved, and the fashionable faceless detective. Like Simenon, he writes certain scenes so well that one wishes he knew where to stop before disappearing out of the genre altogether. It ends in a lot of hep psychology, with the criminal neurologist penning a confession in Humbert Humbertese and working his way out of the implication that he's a criminal at all. (p. 127)

> *Robert Taubman, "Portrait of a Baby," in* New Statesman, *Vol. LXX, No. 1793, July 23, 1965, pp. 126-27.**

HESTER MAKEIG

The writing [in *Criminal Conversation*] is so intelligent, and the complicated characters so clearly drawn, with all their little eccentricities, that there is no need to say more. For my money, Nicolas Freeling is far and away the best thriller writer in his field. . . .

> *Hester Makeig, "It's a Crime," in* The Spectator, *Vol. 215, No. 7156, August 20, 1965, p. 241.**

IAN HAMILTON

In *The Dresden Green,* Nicolas Freeling lets us know once more that he is surely doing crime literature a big favour, heaping such erudition on a maligned genre. Not just erudition; this new novel offers an up-to-standard supply of bleak internationalist wisdom as well as the usual flourish of scarred, aphoristic insights into what makes people love and hate the way they do. There is throughout an unremitting effort to impress and it all but buries the slight mystery of what to do with a big symbolic diamond. Though neither profound nor especially original, Freeling *is* an intelligent crime writer—interesting to see what he does when he no longer feels the need to prove it.

> *Ian Hamilton, "Frolics," in* New Statesman, *Vol. 72, No. 1848, August 12, 1966, p. 235.**

THE NEW YORKER

[*The Dresden Green* is a] new thriller by the creator of Inspector Van der Valk, in which that interesting man does not appear. His absence is a disaster. Van der Valk's engaging personality and his dark, humanistic brooding would seem to be essential to Mr. Freeling. Here, without that central energizing force, Mr. Freeling's intelligence, his inventiveness, and his polish all fail him. . . .

> *A review of "The Dresden Green," in* The New Yorker, *Vol. XLIII, No. 42, December 9, 1967, p. 248.*

ALLEN J. HUBIN

Nicolas Freeling, whose books I've greatly admired, has lost me with his latest, *This Is the Castle*. . . . Perhaps the difficulty is that Mr. Freeling has very nearly abandoned the mystery format and has produced a novel of almost total inaction. His not very interesting protagonist is a troubled and insecure popular novelist. . . . We are shown, in strokes both broad and unobtrusive, a picture of some 24 hours in his life and that of his family. . . . What Mr. Freeling has to say about crime here is presented so subtly as to be nearly invisible.

> *Allen J. Hubin, in a review of "This Is the Castle," in* The New York Times Book Review, *January 12, 1969, p. 43.*

STUART HOOD

[Nicolas Freeling] is an author who knows very precisely how to give melodrama a sufficient veneer of psychological probability to make it acceptable to a reader who generally finds whodunnits the most boring of all categories of literature. . . . His *Because of the Cats* or *The King of the Rainy Country* were better [than *Tsing-Boum!*] but, for my money, he is still streets ahead of Simenon. (p. 619)

> *Stuart Hood, "Post-Freudian, Pre-Freudian," in* The Listener, *Vol. 81, No. 2092, May 1, 1969, pp. 618-19.**

DAVID HARE

Nicolas Freeling's work indicates the way the intelligent detective novel is moving, for better, for worse. He is what you could call a self-confessed master of the genre, in the sense that he writes the kind of jumpy, assertive prose and develops the kind of intermittent, significant plots which win Golden Daggers, Silver Truncheons and the rest of the fancy weaponry the trade brandishes at its favourite sons. Fair enough. He deals increasingly with the same areas of life as the average modern novel, and in the same vocabulary. His world-weary detective Van der Valk is as *déraciné* as the next man, and would snuggle comfortably into the arms of a book by Sartre. He belongs to that lost strain of men who've sauntered for fifty years through European literature.

Well there was a time, and so on, when you could tell a detective novel from any other kind. They had a different shelf at the public library. But Freeling's latest book [*Over the High Side*] blurs the distinction still further, as the author high-humouredly pushes his story aside to make sure it doesn't intrude on his ironic view of a Dutchman in Ireland. As you can imagine, the treatment is resolutely unvulgar.

> *David Hare, in a review of "Over the High Side," in* The Spectator, *Vol. 226, No. 7453, May 1, 1971, p. 600.*

JOHN R. COYNE, JR.

The Lovely Ladies is Nicolas Freeling's twelfth novel, and his best. There's the customary picture of everyday life in Holland, where most of his works are set . . .; the descriptions of food . . .; the realistic characterization of women and the common-sensical treatment of sex. But best of all is Inspector Van der Valk of the Amsterdam police force, a cranky, gentle, bumbling, brilliant, non-conformist student of human behavior whose primary concern is why rather than how crimes are committed. Van der Valk cares little for the standards of behavior imposed on him by a rigidly conformist Dutch society, and the pleasure in reading a Freeling novel comes largely from the often-comic contrast between artificial social demands and the personal code of conduct and point of view of a man who makes his own judgments. Van der Valk doesn't always live up to his code. But he tries. (p. 938)

John R. Coyne, Jr., *"The Last Individualists,"* in National Review, Vol. XXIII, No. 33, August 24, 1971, pp. 937-38.*

ANATOLE BROYARD

[In *Auprès de Ma Blonde*] I found very little stimulus or sensation, and the structuring was of a sort that strikes me as more likely to frustrate one's hunger than to satisfy it. . . .

So here we have Inspector Van der Valk, who has been favorably compared with Maigret, Lew Archer and Nero Wolfe. Temporarily promoted to the position of commissaire in The Hague, he is no longer on active police duty, and we realize immediately that he is going to take on a case in a private capacity. He does. He is visited by a young man who works as a clerk in a jewelry and antiques shop. This fellow has a presentiment that all is not right in the shop, and, to protect himself from possible involvement, goes to Van der Valk.

Van der Valk becomes intrigued and, in pursuing the young man's suspicions, gets himself killed, right in the middle of the book. He falls . . . , shot in the back by his informant, Richard. . . .

Not only is it impossible to believe that this weakling could have screwed up his courage to such a point: It is also utterly illogical. To kill a famous policeman before he even has a case against you—a very minor case at that—is an action that no reasonably experienced mystery reader can possibly accept. It just doesn't figure. What is far worse is the fact that one of the most famous detectives in contemporary suspense fiction is killed by a nobody.

The disproportion is joltingly absurd: It leaves us all off balance, filled with disgust at such a frivolous turn of fate. If Mr. Freeling is tired of Van der Valk, or of suspense novels, why can't he simply put the inspector-commissaire out to pasture in that little cottage in the Vosges he's been so looking forward to? Why reward his years of honorable service with such an insulting and meaningless death?

And that's not all. When Van der Valk is killed, a windy narrator—some acquaintance or another of the inspector's—tells the rest of the story, in which the dead man's wife, Arlette, is the protagonist. Apart from the superfluousness of his long and boring introduction of himself—which brings an already slow narrative to a funeral march—he himself is unnecessary. Why not let Arlette tell her own story?. . .

How the heels are brought to heel is as unconvincing as everything else. Even now, I don't know what their racket was, what they killed Van der Valk to protect. As far as I can tell, the book's principal crime is against the reader—and the people who praised its predecessors. If you want to be thorough, you might add the English language, too, to the list of its victims.

Anatole Broyard, *"A Crime against the Reader?"* in The New York Times, *July 19, 1972, p. 35.*

TIMOTHY FOOTE

Few enterprises launched in the hopeful '60s have been as successful as a square, spare gumshoe called Inspector Van der Valk. The humane Amsterdam police detective was the creation of Nicholas Freeling. . . . Since then Van der Valk has been probing characters, savoring cookery and solving crimes (mainly murder in high or low degree) around Holland and neighboring countries. Van der Valk books have attracted a steadily growing international audience and collected a handful of top mystery-writing prizes. More than that, Freeling goes beyond the formulas of suspense to offer a complex picture of postwar Europe, uneasy with its new prosperity and haunted by past fears. In American thrillers, only Ross Macdonald's use of the surf and drug culture of California has similar resonance. Like Macdonald, Freeling writes so well that readers may feel he should devote himself to straight fiction or—considering the state of the contemporary novel—be grateful that he does not. . . .

As with Simenon's Inspector Maigret, exposure to Van der Valk is likely to prove infectious. Even when the story seems to unwind in slow motion, Van der Valk's reflective concern for the role of character in crime makes the trip worthwhile.

Timothy Foote, *"Once More with Freeling,"* in Time, Vol. 100, No. 5, July 31, 1972, p. 59.

NEWGATE CALLENDAR

As mysteries go, there is no great mystery in Nicolas Freeling's *Auprès de Ma Blonde*. . . . Early on, the criminal(s) and crime(s) are made clear, and the only question is how retribution is going to be made. But Freeling can always be depended upon for something different, something that puts his books into a special class, and he does not disappoint in *Auprès de Ma Blonde*. Indeed, there is a stunning surprise here, involving his popular Inspector (now Commissaris) Van der Valk of Amsterdam.

The book is more than a detective story. Freeling always has concentrated on character and ambience, and *Auprès de Ma Blonde* ends up a study of a woman's character. Purists might find the last part of the book just a shade too pat, with everything falling into place too easily. No matter. Freeling is one of the masters of the genre. He has taken a situation built around shady doings in the jewelry business and created a plot that for the most part runs in tangents and oblique lines, and he nevertheless simply roots the reader in his chair. The air of civilized urbanity that runs through the book is to most detective novels what Henry James is to Zane Grey.

Newgate Callendar, in a review of *"Auprès de ma Blonde,"* in The New York Times Book Review, August 6, 1972, p. 24.

O. L. BAILEY

That singular Dutch policeman, Inspector Van der Valk, is now ten years old! In 1962 his creator, Nicholas Freeling, introduced him in the superb and beguiling adventure, *Love in Amsterdam,* and it wasn't long before the most diehard of Inspector Maigret fans were willing to let Van der Valk share at least some of the honors. From the beginning, Van der Valk, like Maigret, displayed a concern for the role that character plays in crime, and he pursued unorthodox solutions. *Criminal Conversation,* one of Freeling's best, had Van der Valk stalking a virtually uncatchable killer through an intriguing psychological game of nerves.

While the tenth in the Van der Valk series may not be Freeling's best, *Auprès de Ma Blonde* . . . is destined to be the most memorable: It is Van der Valk's swan song. . . .

A seemingly minor incident sets him off on a personal investigation that becomes—yes, he is killed in the middle of it—his last case. . . .

Freeling fans will inevitably speculate as to whether [Van der Valk's wife] Arlette will carry on the series. Whatever. Few detective novels pay as much attention to the milieu in which the detective plies his trade. Freeling has given us a picture of a part of postwar Europe that puts his work in a class by itself. If this is your introduction to Van der Valk, *Auprès de Ma Blonde* will make you want to read the previous nine; and if you are an old friend, you will want to reread them. (p. 61)

> O. L. Bailey, "On the Docket," in Saturday Review, Vol. LV, No. 34, August 26, 1972, pp. 61-2.*

THE NEW YORKER

The end of Inspector Van der Valk. That's right, Mr. Freeling kills him off—has him assassinated—on page 8 [of *Auprès de Ma Blonde*]. . . . This is a most unsatisfactory book, and not only because of the death of its hero. It never recovers structurally from that murder, there is far more palaver than action. Mr. Freeling's tendency to put on literary airs has never been more apparent, and the resolution, when it finally comes, is largely lacking in impact.

> A review of "Auprès de ma Blonde," in The New Yorker, Vol. XLVIII, No. 28, September 2, 1972, p. 72.

NEWGATE CALLENDAR

Having killed off his Amsterdam police detective, Van der Valk, Nicolas Freeling takes us to Paris in *A Dressing of Diamond*. . . . Alas, the book is a bore. Perhaps Freeling was more interested in trying to characterize his lady magistrate, his French cops, and so on, than in creating a real mystery. In *A Dressing of Diamond,* the characters talk, talk, talk, until the reader could scream. The talk is not that interesting. The characters themselves are not that interesting. The book has something to do with a kidnapping, but it is completely lacking in tension, and it takes a real effort to get through it.

> Newgate Callendar, in a review of "A Dressing of Diamond," in The New York Times Book Review, June 30, 1974, p. 33.

TIMOTHY FOOTE

Two years ago, Nicolas Freeling committed a rare and shocking crime which might be described as protagonisticide. In *Auprès de Ma Blonde,* with no advance warning, he killed off his own central character, a laconic Amsterdam detective named Van der Valk, through whose human but gritty sensibility the author had previously filtered a dozen of the best psychological suspense novels written in Europe since the war. . . .

Faithful Freeling readers who, since *Love in Amsterdam* (1963), have stoutly prized Van der Valk even above Simenon's Inspector Maigret, ground their teeth and waited. Now comes *A Dressing of Diamond*. . . .

The book is full of Freeling's virtues. There are secondary characters so swiftly and seductively sketched that they threaten to run off into novels all their own. Still, most Freeling fans may wonder if much is gained by introducing [Henri Castang], the new hero. *A Dressing of Diamond* is likely to send them

figuratively off to Strasbourg to stone the author's house and shout, "Bring back Van der Valk!" The judgment may be a scrap premature. Freeling is not quite the chameleon poet of crime he thought he was, but he remains a writer worth waiting for.

> Timothy Foote, "Crime as Punishment," in Time, Vol. 104, No. 5, July 29, 1974, p. 65.

TOM SHARPE

Nicholas Freeling's *What Are the Bugles Blowing For?* [published in the United States as *The Bugles Blowing*] suffers from faults. . . . [He] has created a new detective, Henri Castang, who works in a French provincial town. There is a crime and a criminal. The hope begins to dawn that Mr Freeling has finally given up his ambition to be a literary giant and is going to play the detective story straight. But then comes a barrage of tiresome assertions on matters sociological, political, bureaucratical and legal—and suddenly we are returning yet again to the palace of Art. Of course, no writer wants to have to turn out formula books and a good writer least of all—and Mr Freeling *is* a good writer. But novelists ignore their limitations at their peril: in trying to write a significant novel within the framework of the detective story Mr Freeling has thrown out the baby with the bathwater.

> Tom Sharpe, "Happy Hooker," in New Statesman, Vol. 90, No. 2323, September 26, 1975, p. 382.*

NEWGATE CALLENDAR

There are two schools of thought about Nicolas Freeling's detective stories: they are brilliant, subtle, unconventional, sensitive or they are wordy, slow-moving, boring, pretentious. *The Bugles Blowing* . . . is not going to change the minds of anybody in the respective camps. It starts with a murder in Paris, and it has Henri Castang as a Maigret-like French cop. But most of the book is an attempt to create a strange character; and a lot of it is, or at least seems to be, deliberately obfuscatory. For a long time it is hard to see what Freeling has in mind. The Freeling approach thus remains a constant. Some will call this book philosophic and subtle. Others—this reader alas, among them—will consider it a waste of time.

> Newgate Callendar, in a review of "The Bugles Blowing," in The New York Times Book Review, February 22, 1976, p. 38.

JEAN M. WHITE

[*Sabine* is] the third in the new Freeling series with Henri Castang, a French provincial policeman. Castang is an original in his own way. But I still long for Van der Valk, who over a decade of mysteries grew sadder, wiser, perhaps a bit wearier but no less compassionate and tolerant of human frailties. . . .

But I suppose that we should give Castang a chance. . . .

Castang is at his best in trying to surface with the truth in the undercurrents of human relationships, and Freeling's characters are brilliantly drawn. . . . But Castang is too enamoured of his own ruminations, and the middle of the story begins to sag, overburdened with his lengthy interrogations of suspects. It isn't that Freeling neglects detection, for he has a firm hand with plotting. And he is a very good writer, indeed, who rewards with a right turn of phrase and a stroke of insight. But, unlike Van der Valk, Castang can be a bore at times.

Jean M. White, in a review of ''Auprès de ma Blonde'' and ''Sabine,'' in Book World—The Washington Post, February 19, 1978, p. E6.

JANE S. BAKERMAN

When Van der Valk was killed, I was angry at Nicolas Freeling.... When Henri Castang appeared as Freeling's new creation in *A Dressing of Diamond,* I read the book, of course, but resisted any real interest in that proposed series. But recently, I worked my way down ... to the second Castang book, *The Bugles Blowing,* and I'm hooked again....

With all the details, including the identity of the murderer, revealed at the outset, *The Bugles Blowing* is not a standard ''blood in the streets'' detective story; Freeling novels generally aren't. It begins bloodily enough, with the triple murder of a portrait painter, his subject, and her daughter, killed by the woman's husband when he surprises the victims in the midst of an orgy. The simple outline of the case allows for the most rampant sensationalism, but Freeling avoids that easy appeal. Instead, the story focuses on the personality and background of the killer, the investigation of the crime during a blistering French summer, and the final verdict....

As in the earlier works, Freeling shows us [Castang and his wife, Vera,] a believable couple who are independent, competent people.... The author moves in and out of their home with skill and frequency so that the reader remains absorbed and interested in their lives as well as in the investigation, but Freeling never so violates their privacy that they become mere figures on a page; they remain startlingly real beings. The Castangs' characterizations are adroit and clear—but master that he is, Freeling has left lots more to be told, so the book is both satisfying and intriguing.

Jane S. Bakerman, in a review of ''The Bugles Blowing,'' in The Armchair Detective, Vol. 11, No. 2, April, 1978, p. 122.

DAVID LEHMAN

Wolfnight is the sixth in a series featuring Henri Castang, a provincial French police *commissaire* whose terse and deliberate exterior belies a complex sensibility and a streaming consciousness. As the book's center of gravity, Castang is no less compelling a figure for seeming at times to be a hybrid creation: he wears Maigret's raincoat, he has Philip Marlowe's way with words . . . , and he seems destined to inhabit Graham Greene's world, where conscience is king.

With his studied realism, Freeling insists on the difference between ''real cops'' and those of fiction, ''where a tricky twist has to be thought up every ten pages to keep one excited.'' The atmosphere of *Wolfnight* as one character wittily observes, works to ''dedramatize the melo'' or ''unmelodize the drama'' in the name of the author's high moral seriousness. The result is a superior police procedural that never fails to ''keep one excited'' while it relentlessly makes its pungent points about political corruption and the dark side of the French national character. Freeling's fans will not be disappointed.

The plot, each tricky twist of the way, discloses itself indirectly—in dialogue, itself clipped and oblique, and in the protagonist's thought processes....

Freeling's idiosyncratic style makes demands on his readers but rewards them with wit and humor and with an unusual depth of feeling.

David Lehman, in a review of ''Wolfnight,'' in Book World—The Washington Post, July 4, 1982, p. 9.

JANE S. BAKERMAN

To the dismay of hosts of his fans, Nicolas Freeling killed off his initial hero, Piet Van der Valk, in *Auprès de ma Blonde* (1972; English title: *A Long Silence*). Some of his readers, upon hearing that news—and before reading the book—lapsed into dismay.... Most Freeling buffs, however, had the good sense to abandon fretfulness and replace it with respect for [his wife] Arlette's developing character and with eager anticipation of her further appearances. To their gratification, there have, so far, been two of those later appearances. In addition to becoming the protagonist of the second half of *Auprès de ma Blonde,* Arlette has been featured as the hero of *The Widow* (1979) and of *Arlette* (1981), both fine, thoughtful (though admittedly discursive) novels.

Arlette Van der Valk Davidson is, in fact, one of Nicolas Freeling's most fully rounded, convincing creations. Her pursuit of her first husband's killer in *Blonde* was an extremely effective introduction to her new prominence, and the two later novels which feature Arlette herself are equally strong. In each of the books, Arlette copes with three difficult situations: her own changing role in both her personal and professional lives; her attempts to solve a crime or crimes; and the struggle of every contemporary human being to come to grips with a rapidly changing, evidently (in Freeling's view) deteriorating world.

Arlette's efforts to understand her city, her world, and her times offer Freeling wide scope for social commentary, a fact which would surprise no careful reader of the male-dominated novels. By making his female hero a symbol of search on the philosophical as well as the narrative level, Freeling continues a well-established practice and gives it a new slant. Arlette and her creator don't bother much with political posturing, but they do offer a refreshing, moving, beautifully crafted examination of evil from a female point of view. Not many male detective fiction writers practicing today could bring that off. Freeling can; Freeling does. (pp. 348-49)

Jane S. Bakerman, '''Arlette': Nicolas Freeling's Candle against the Dark,'' in The Armchair Detective, Vol. 16, No. 4, Winter, 1983, pp. 348-53.

BOOKS AND BOOKMEN

From time to time recently I have been concerned that the tendrils of Freeling's highly personal style were coiling themselves inhibitingly round his novels' moving parts. I am delighted to announce that the danger is past and that in *The Back of the North Wind* everything is in perfect working order. The approach is as distinctly idiosyncratic as ever: this blend of direct explication, internal monologues, sharp often comic observation, serious debate and sudden devastating action has a taste as peculiar to Freeling as, say, that strange heat-tremor of distorted psychology is to Highsmitih. Perhaps it's something to do with being a foreigner in France. Perhaps in the end Anglo-Saxon self-consciousness is eroded and you can start taking the risk of being thought serious. For, make no mistake about it, Freeling's books are extremely serious. He writes novels in which crimes are tracked to their causes and the policemen are as concerned with their own motives as those of the criminals they pursue.

The policemen in question here are Divisional Commissaire Richard of the *Police Judiciare* and Commissaire Castang, his homicide expert. Old fans will know them well, but not perfectly well. Unlike many series characters they do not stand still: their function is not to make life easier for their creator but to give him the chance to stay with his creation as it grows and perhaps ultimately decays. . . .

[*The Back of the North Wind*] is a thoughtful book, disturbing at times, and at times moving and exciting too. Mr Freeling probably does not need to be told how good he is, but it never did anyone any harm. He is very good indeed, firmly established in that premier division of crime novelists (no more than half a dozen, quick and dead) for whom the generic term is inadequate. He is, simply, a novelist, and it's about time he was taken very seriously indeed.

A review of "The Back of the North Wind," in Books and Bookmen, *No. 335, August, 1983, p. 30.*

REGINALD HILL

No Part in your Death is really three novellas loosely linked in theme to provide the strength which a one-piece plot usually gives a thriller. It is well to realize this from the outset, otherwise you may spend too much time during Part Two anticipating that the narrative of Part One is to be resumed, or at least referred to in consequential terms. There are links of various kinds, certainly, the most obvious and most important being the involvement of Henri Castang, *Commissaire* of the *Police Judiciaire*. But there are no retrospective whodunit revelations.

Castang is becoming so introspectively obsessed with the problem of violence that, as I read, I began to have fears that Mr Freeling was preparing him for the Reichenbach fall in the wake of his famous Dutch predecessor, Van de Valk. . . . I am happy to say I was wrong here.

The present novel takes us to Munich in the first section and to Dorset in the third, while the second is set in Castang's own police district in Vosges. In each section there is a violent death and in each case Castang feels himself personally involved, at times almost to the point of responsibility. . . . But the book is more than just a meander through the mental processes of a cop with a conscience. The geographical spread and the variety of motive and situation which breed the crimes are of the essence too. . . .

The novel is written in that nervous, oblique, bitty style which is Mr Freeling's trademark, nine tenths internalized impressionistic monologue—either the characters' or the narrator's own—and one tenth straight objective description. His later books have moved further and further from the formal narrative line which the great story-tellers tread. At the moment all the proper pleasures of crime fiction are still there—mystery, action, excitement, detection—but in odd proportions and strangely stressed. If Mr Freeling travels much further in this direction, we may be faced with the genre's first Samuel Beckett! It is a prospect at once daunting and exciting, and for those interested in crime writing for more than quick thrills or petty puzzles, *No Part in your Death* is not to be missed.

Reginald Hill, in a review of "No Part in Your Death," in Books and Bookmen, *No. 345, June, 1984, p. 29.*

Mavis Gallant

1922-

Canadian-born short story writer, novelist, and dramatist.

Considered an important contemporary fiction writer, Gallant is particularly praised for her finely crafted short stories, many of which have been published in *The New Yorker*. A Canadian who has lived most of her adult life in France, Gallant often depicts the plight of people who, whether by circumstance or choice, find themselves detached from what is familiar to them and who face an indifferent world. Gallant's ability to vividly evoke surroundings and their effect on individuals is a central aspect of her work. In a review of *Home Truths* (1981), Joan Harcourt notes that Gallant's stories are "marked by acute observation, a stunning ear for the exact word, both in dialogue and description, and a sophisticated, cool wit."

Gallant was born in Montreal. After her father's death early in her childhood, she was shuttled between numerous schools in Canada and the United States before settling in Paris. The short stories in her first book, *The Other Paris* (1956), explore the theme of dislocation, particularly as experienced by Americans in Europe. Similarly, her novel *Green Water, Green Sky* (1960) concerns the destructive relationship of an American mother and daughter who live abroad. The sense of exile and despair developed in Gallant's early work continues with the eight stories and novella collected in *My Heart Is Broken* (1964) and the novel *A Fairly Good Time* (1970). The latter is the story of a Canadian woman living in Paris who is troubled by her isolation and her memories after the collapse of her marriage to a French journalist. For *The Peignitz Junction* (1974) Gallant shifted her focus to Germany. James Brockway praised the book as conveying "with remarkable success a sense of the amorphousness, the mess, of life." Expatriation is again the given condition of the characters' lives in *From the Fifteenth District* (1974), another collection of short stories and a novella. These pieces take place in Europe around the time of World War II.

In *Home Truths* Gallant focuses on the essence of Canadian identity as it is developed and expressed both at home and in Europe. The stories in this collection are divided into three sections: "At Home," "Canadians Abroad," and "Linnet Muir." The "Linnet Muir" sequence includes stories which closely parallel the events of Gallant's own life. Linnet Muir is an intelligent, independent young woman who goes to Montreal with little money and few prospects yet is determined to succeed. Like Gallant, Linnet becomes a newspaper reporter, but she grows to realize that her position in the professional world is tenuous, and the men she works with are unwilling to accept her as an equal. *Home Truths* was widely praised for its skillful, unflinching portrayal of characters adrift in confusing, uprooted lives. Maureen Howard observed, "Gallant has made it her business to look back. In the hard act of knowing her origins, she has written powerful stories."

Gallant has also written a play, *What Is to Be Done?* (1984), about the experiences of two young Montreal women who are communist sympathizers during World War II. The play, which examines the idealism of the protagonists, is lauded for its compelling depiction of the period.

© Jerry Bauer

(See also *CLC*, Vols. 7, 18 and *Contemporary Authors*, Vols. 69-72.)

PHYLLIS GROSSKURTH

Mavis Gallant has been an expatriate in Paris for thirty years, and in her introduction to *Home Truths: Selected Canadian Stories* she expresses an expatriate's unease, defiance, and conviction about her decision to write outside her own country. Clearly she is still fighting a battle with the Canada she left many years ago. Whether or not that country has long since vanished is irrelevant, for it has continued to furnish the world of her imagination. Her defiance finds expression in the hurt she feels in discovering that the word is sometimes spelled "expatriot." She knows that whatever she writes will be in the language that shaped her sensibility, though the Canada of her youth imposed restraints from which she could free herself only by geographic separation.

Wherever she is, she writes out of her roots. . . . Her Montréal is a state of mind, an emotion recalled, an apprenticeship for life. It is a world in which people learn the subtle skills of hurting, and the restraint necessary to prevent the hurt from showing. In **"Thank You for the Lovely Tea,"** Ruth, a boarder at one of those sham-Gothic private schools, and two of her chums are taken out for tea by the woman who hopes to marry her father. Ruth remarks casually to her friends: " 'My father and Mrs. Holland drove all the way to California in this car,' reducing the trip (undertaken with many doubts, with fear, with a feeling that hotel clerks were looking through and through her) to a simple, unimportant outing involving two elderly people, long past love." The tea party ends with dismal finality, and the two friends invited to share the treat are not speaking.

Parents and children manage a tense co-existence. Irmgard in **"Jorinda and Jorindel"** manages to survive nicely by aping her parents' smug dismissal of those who don't conform to their rules; but parents who have been careless about their lives needn't think they can make any demands on feelings. "You're only my father. That's all you are," says the grim Rhoda, whose father has reached the limits of geographic and emotional distance in **"The Prodigal Parent."** . . .

The Linnet Muir stories, almost all of which originally appeared in *The New Yorker,* are told in the first person. Linnet recalls herself as a child who was always in the way, a girl who was too young to work, a reporter who managed to get a job only because the men were away at war. She is the camera's eye who returns to Québec from New York: "the only changes were from prosperous to shabby, from painted to unpainted, from smiling to dour. I was entering a poorer and a curiously empty country, where the faces of the people gave nothing away."

The faces give nothing away, but Linnet nonetheless understands the office pecking order, which is based on who is given a linen towel; she understands the irritation her presence causes her godmother, who has designs on her father; and she understands the myths that sustain French Catholics and English remittance men. Years later, she learns that there were some things she had not understood, and these were the most interesting of all—that Dr. Chauchard wrote poetry, and that the exotic Mrs. Erskine had opened her fur cape and without coyness lain down on the railroad tracks with her current young man. "There is a raffish kind of nerve to her, the only nerve that matters."

Mrs. Erskine is a relatively minor character, yet she gains such a hold on the imagination that one wants to know all about her raffish past and her ambiguous future. Gallant's characters have a compelling reality; they cannot be tied down to any particular setting. We know that most of them are going to move on to somewhere else. Theirs are marginal lives existing in a permanent state of transition.

In this sense it is odd that the stories in this collection have been tagged as Canadian. Gallant's particular power as a writer is the sureness with which she catches the ephemeral; it is a wry vision, a blend of the sad and the tragi-comic. She is a born writer who happens to have been born in Canada, and her gift has been able to develop as it has only because she could look back in anger, love, and nostalgia.

Phyllis Grosskurth, "Close to Home," in Saturday
Night, *Vol. 96, No. 10, November, 1981, p. 68.*

MARK ABLEY

[*Home Truths*] has an uncommon beauty; it will probably be the finest collection of stories published this year in Canada, or anywhere else. It also has an uncommon poignancy. Mavis Gallant left Montreal more than 30 years ago, and *Home Truths* bears repeated witness to the efforts made by this solitary, distant writer to come to terms with her own past and her own country. (p. 74)

A few of these 16 stories are reprinted from earlier collections. Most of them, however, have never before appeared in book form, including the sequence of six stories about Linnet Muir, a girl with a powerful resemblance to the young Mavis Gallant. These tales are, among other things, an evocation of Montreal in the days when Quebec nationalism was all but limited to the Roman Catholic Church, and when no "normal" anglophone would dream of learning French. The city is prosperous and secure, yet alive with tension below its graceful surface. It almost becomes a character in the eyes of this precocious, alert, strangely innocent girl who is avid for experience and hungry for understanding.

Such a hunger has never left Gallant, who constantly exposes our motives and failings with precision. Her work displays a remarkable continuity; the first story in this book, **"Thank You for the Lovely Tea,"** was written when she was only 18, yet its shrewd analysis of ignorance and self-deception is entirely characteristic of the mature artist. (pp. 74, 76)

Sharp comments about [Canada] turn up throughout the fiction, as well as in the introduction; Gallant does not hold a grudge against her nationality, but she spares it little love. Having spent much of her adolescence in New York and much of her adulthood in France, she has needed to define an identity and to ponder habits of mind which most of us take for granted. Her simplest conclusion is that to be Canadian is absolutely "respectable"—absolutely worthy of respect. Yet one remembers Linnet Muir's reactions on returning from the clamor of New York to the grey streets of wartime Montreal: "People who do not display what they feel have practical advantages. They can go away to be killed as if they didn't mind; they can see their sons off to war without a blink. Their upbringing is intended for a crisis. . . . But it is murder in everyday life— truly murder." No wonder Mavis Gallant lives in Paris.

It is a sign of the richness of her work that several memorable stories have been omitted from *Home Truths*. A fairly good novelist, Gallant is virtually unrivalled at the art of short fiction where her true peer is the great Russian writer Anton Chekhov. They share an ability to press a lifetime into a few resonant pages as well as a desire to show the dark side of comedy and the humor that lurks behind despair. Most of all, they share the capacity to make sympathy an objective, unsentimental attitude. Gallant can write with curiosity and perceptiveness about the kind of people who would never read a word of her work—a rarer achievement than it might sound. She is famous for not forgiving and not forgetting; her unkindness is usually focused on women and men who have grown complacent, never reflecting on their experience, no longer caring about their world. With such people she is merciless, yet with others, especially children bruised by neglect, she is patient and even kind. In the end, perhaps, understanding can be a means of forgiveness. One hopes so, because Mavis Gallant understands us terribly well. (pp. 76, 78)

Mark Abley, "Home Is Where Complacency Is," in
Maclean's Magazine, *Vol. 94, No. 45, November 9,
1981, pp. 74, 76, 78.*

MARK CZARNECKI

What is to be Done? is the first play by Mavis Gallant. . . . It is also the title of Lenin's classic work proposing that a Communist party guide the proletarian revolution. A copy of this tract becomes a treasured possession for Jenny . . . and Molly . . . , two young Communist sympathizers living in Montreal during the Second World War. Ironically, the object of their worship is in Russian, and the impossibility of cultural translation in the broadest sense spurs slow disillusionment and a gradual acceptance of more private concerns; in Jenny's words, "Society doesn't need cleansing—it should just be a bit more curious." . . .

[Jenny and Molly spin] on a whirling carrousel of party indoctrination sessions, intimate chats and welcoming parades for the heroes of Stalingrad, who turn out to be disguised apparatchiks from the Soviet Embassy. Jenny is the quintessential earnest virgin, barricading herself against life behind impossible ideals until VE-Day brings sexual initiation, a modicum of reality and a monumental hangover. Molly is a yearning war bride ("born faithful") who finally realizes that a woman's role in the revolution is to fold the parachutes after the men have landed in the cornfields. . . .

What is to be Done? is ambitious, invigorating and blessed with a quirky rhythm which continually employs indirection to find direction out. Its generous servings of language are especially appreciated, but at three hours the play is far too long, and much of the second act is redundant. However . . . , *What is to be Done?* still presents . . . an accomplished theatre debut.

> *Mark Czarnecki, "Daughters of Revolution," in* Maclean's Magazine, Vol. 95, No. 47, November 22, 1982, p. 78.

RONALD HATCH

Home Truths, Mavis Gallant's new collection of short stories, is a welcome addition to her growing number of collections. In some ways this volume is an innovation for her, since, as the subtitle "Selected Canadian Stories" indicates, the collection centres on the concerns of Canada and Canadians. Such a volume would have been unthinkable only a few years ago when the majority of her readers were American. . . . Since Gallant has always made it clear that she is a Canadian, she finds herself at a loss to explain her sudden lionization [in Canada], and has remarked ironically: "Thirty years of career elsewhere were needed first." . . .

Although most readers will be delighted that the set of Linnet Muir stories has finally been collected [in *Home Truths*], a number of reservations have been expressed about singling out Gallant's "Canadian" stories for a special volume. The question has been raised if this is not a little artificial, an injustice to someone who has always been recognized as among the finer international writers. Yet Gallant has already devoted a volume of stories to the post-war German situation, and if she can write about Germany then why not about Canada? (p. 125)

Gallant herself is decidedly uneasy with the narrow limits that have sometimes been placed on what constitutes Canadian art, and finds herself puzzled that people should be in doubt about their nationality. As to what makes a Canadian, she comments that "the first years of schooling are indelible" in creating one's national base, and that "a deeper culture is contained in memory." Certainly one of Gallant's main concerns in fiction over the years has been the portrayal of children gaining social attitudes and the part that memory plays in the creation of the present.

Many of the stories contained in *Home Truths* are about children who are deprived of their own deepest personality, of their core, and the sorts of manoeuvres that their bodies and minds make to regain their lost centre. The story "Saturday," Gallant comments, is about language, in that the main character, Gérard, has been deprived by his parents of his first language when, as French Canadians, they decided to leave behind the Roman Catholic Church to find freedom from darkest tyranny. Since the Church was tied to language (indeed, most things in Quebec are tied to language) it was necessary for them to make a complete break by speaking English. The irony is that the decision achieves anything but freedom for Gérard, who is spiritually hobbled without his own language—forced to speak English badly, and unable to feel his way back into French. The rest of the family have not really escaped the old patterns either: Gérard's mother, freedom-loving in theory, becomes another version of the self-sacrificing French-Canadian mother, with her abhorrence of sexuality; the daughters have happily married English Protestant husbands, but are going about their business of raising large families in the old style. Indeed, one of Gallant's points is that most people do not mind the restrictions of security. Satisfyingly comfortable, such roles provide tremendous security. The story depicts how each member of the family is trapped in his own particular labyrinth, with the exception of the youngest child, who appears to be altogether unusual in his single-minded pursuit of his own life. Having kept French for his personal, almost private language, Paul speaks spontaneously, thereby inhabiting a different world from the socially constructed people around him. The story ends in a blinding moment of illumination when Paul achieves a fragment of genuine communication with his father, choosing a French phrase which daringly echoes the words of God. A particular delight of these stories about Quebec is the way Gallant freely uses French phrases from time to time without feeling the need for a translation.

Although these stories are within the realist tradition, Gallant supplements realism with so many other techniques that one rarely finds a story that feels wholly realist. **"Jorinda and Jorindel,"** for example is about a young girl of eight, and her experiences at a summer cottage not far from Montreal. Nothing could be more familiar. But in fact the story begins late at night with a lonely woman shouting across the lake that she has finally learned to dance, a shout that wakens young Irmgard from a dream of a witch, a dream that will haunt the story to its end, and which will never be quite resolved. Gallant uses a virtually surreal frame "to place" the quite normal experience of children discovering that three is one too many. All summer long, Irmgard has played with Freddie, a French-Canadian boy, until Bradley arrives on the scene from New York and Irmgard discards Freddie for what she takes to be Bradley's superior virtues. But what I have called the "surreal frame" also intrudes at crucial moments, so that neither child remains simply himself. Freddie has some of the qualities of an intuitive *naif,* and Bradley—with a sty in his eye, a poison ivy rash, and tennis elbow—is well on his way to developing all of the odious qualities of a self-serving individualist. (pp. 126-27)

The story is also evidence of Gallant's keen eye for comedy, especially class absurdities. She includes a superior English housekeeper who actually interviews Irmgard's mother, and who refuses to do a scrap of work when she discovers the country house is a humble Canadian cottage, and rented at that. As the title indicates, the story also contains fairy tale overtones, for Irmgard's dream is the Brothers Grimm story of Jorinda and Jorindel, where a witch catches the child who ventures too close to the castle. Irmgard is herself not sure who is the victim—Freddie, Bradley, or herself. When she tries to tell her parents, they reply adamantly: "No dreams at breakfast," a reply that cheers them up immensely, for as Gallant remarks, they are as delighted as children by rules. Ending with a witty allusion to *Alice in Wonderland*, the story becomes a combination of dream, fairy tale and literary reference, thereby constructing a child's world that is both socially realistic as well as possessing all the darker psychological elements of mystery and terror. Ordinary seeming acts assume the power and cruelty of mythic design.

Although many writers have explored the ways in which Canada's puritanical past influenced children (one thinks immediately of Hugh MacLennan, Robertson Davies, and Margaret Laurence), Gallant is surely one of the more brilliant writers to show the dialectic which exists between the individual and this puritanism. Whereas many writers have simply criticized Canada's dour Scottish inheritance, Gallant seems far more aware that the social code is in large part maintained by the individual's need to sustain his sense of reality. Instead of attacking an abstraction, therefore, Gallant delights in portraying the various possible reactions to what has been called Canada's "curse." . . . Interestingly enough, Gallant has prefixed to her Introduction to the volume as a whole a quotation from Boris Pasternak: "Only personal independence matters." . . . Gallant is only too aware of how difficult it is to escape from the reified sense of social reality into true freedom—if such a thing can be said to exist.

Indeed, one might even say that the concluding stories, those based on the character of Linnet Muir, are Gallant's most recent and subtle attempt to define and to *create* personal freedom, for it has become clear in her latest fiction that the very act of writing, of creation, is one of the ways to allow the imagination to develop freely with as few restrictions as possible. It is even possible to use Michel Butor's idea of fictional narrative as "research" in connection with these stories, for there is an ongoing sense of discovery that accompanies the narrative line. In other words, the emphasis is not so much on the well made plot as on the process of revelation made possible by the kind of circling narration that Gallant employs. For many readers, probably, this aspect of the stories may well be lost; the historical accounts of old Montreal are so graphically drawn that one is tempted to sit back and enjoy the evocation of a *genius loci* that has now practically vanished. For example, Gallant's account of a Remittance Man is a particularly trenchant sociological analysis of a breed of Englishman that virtually disappeared with WW II—the black sheep sent abroad by his father to become the darling or the dismay of the colonies.

These Montreal stories also bear a certain resemblance to Margaret Laurence's *A Bird in the House* in that they are told by an older woman looking back over her earlier years. Like Vanessa MacLeod, Linnet Muir is very much a rebel, determined to live her own life from her own perceptions, to stand on her own feet. When she returns from New York to Montreal at the age of 18, she firmly believes that once the war is over a new world will be ushered in, a world where Truth with a capital T will reign. She has been reading Freud and Lenin, and believes these codes will unlock a new age. A new kind of character for Gallant, Linnet is a young woman with tremendous self-confidence and daring, who in her personal life believes it is time for the revolution to begin. When she applies for an office job with a Government department, she demands a position with the men and not the "coolies." Part of the

interest is in watching how this young girl meets the challenge of the male establishment head-on, and then learns to her surprise that men create limits for themselves only slightly larger than women's. By jumping the fence to the men's side, she has only landed in another kind of compromise: there is no new truth, no new freedom, only different kinds of slavery. And so, as the stories progress, Linnet and the reader both discover that her revolutionary behaviour is as much a kind of *reaction* to the given sense of reality as the pusillanimous acceptance by the men and women around her.

Far more terrifying still is the knowledge that it is impossible to live forever in the space between zero and one—the undefined space before maturity. Eventually decisions must be taken that locate the individual firmly in the social world whether she likes it or not. And here is where Gallant's skill as a writer reveals itself, for she nowhere attempts to describe a solution; instead she allows the meaning to emerge from between the spaces of the narrative, leaving each reader to come to his own understanding of what Christopher Isherwood used to call a "dynamic portrait," one that changes the closer one looks. Indeed, the very balance of Gallant's prose style makes this apparent. In the closing sentence of **"In Youth is Pleasure"** Linnet says: ". . . time had been on my side, faithfully, and unless you died you were always bound to escape." In binding one to escape, we have a sentence that denies what it seems to be advancing—the very ambiguity that is central to Gallant's depiction of the real, which every individual both creates even as he is created by it. For Gallant, the problem is to bring this crucial relationship, which usually remains buried beneath and within perception, to the surface so that in critical moments the fissure between the individual and his world can be experienced. In this way, freedom itself may be achieved—if only for brief moments. For all their mimetic verisimilitude and seeming simplicity, then, the Montreal stories constitute a major challenge to the reader, a challenge that one could term, with some small hesitation, ontological. (pp. 127-29)

Ronald Hatch, in a review of "Home Truths: Selected Canadian Stories," in The Canadian Fiction Magazine, *No. 43, 1982, pp. 125-29.*

RICHARD PLANT

Written by Mavis Gallant, this group of scenes [*What Is to Be Done?*] from the wartime experiences of two Montreal women—Jenny, 18, unmarried; Molly, 20, married with an unwanted child and a husband overseas—cannot be described as dramatic. Closer to a collection of prose fiction vignettes—the kind that quietly reveal glimpses of life or human character—*What Is to Be Done?* lacks the intense unity and dynamic force that the conflict between evolving characters provides for traditional realistic drama. What seems meant to hold these vignettes together is their chronological arrangement and a persistent irony that undercuts their air of nostalgia.

In essence we experience a collection of ironic insights about war and peace, justice, fascism, Marxism, and the new world expected to evolve after 1945. More specifically as it relates to Molly and Jenny—or to women in general—we see a world of social injustices that need to be righted. The effect of the play is of life passing by, a bit zanily and slowly, repeatedly introducing the question, "What is to be done?" You may go to sleep in the theatre, but if you are awake to the proliferation of little insights, the play will foster the darkly humorous answer: "It won't happen again. It won't happen again." (pp. 15, 17)

Richard Plant, in a review of "What Is to Be Done?" in Books in Canada, *Vol. 13, No. 4, April, 1984, pp. 15, 17.*

BOYD NEIL

Mavis Gallant's first play, *What Is To Be Done?,* has a lot in common with her recent tiny, perfect stories in *The New Yorker.* Whether Gallant is thrusting at the bureaucratic pretences of Mitterand's government in *The New Yorker,* or in this play, gently reminding us of the heady political idealism that, like pimples, seems to descend indiscriminately on many people under the age of 21, she does it with the bitter humour of someone who has been there, who at one time shared that political naïveté.

Indeed, *What Is To Be Done?* tastes of autobiography, at least in the central character of Jenny. Jenny is a 19-year-old journalist-in-the-making, who spends World War II dreaming of the defeat of Fascism and plotting ways to move from the Department of Appraisements and Averages at a Montreal newspaper to the editorial department and a career in Strategic Journalism. (Gallant, too, fought an uphill battle in wartime Montreal to be accepted as a journalist before her escape to Paris in the early 50s.)

But more important than autobiographical detail is Gallant's success in telling us a little about wartime Montreal and the psychology of political belief, and in telling us a lot about the Jennys of the world who only want to be "useful", and those, like Jenny's friend, Molly, who look at the world with a vague sense of despair. She manages it without the traditional stuff of drama: conflict, emotional peaks, showdowns. Instead, she uses the tools of the novelist and short-story writer—imagery, heightened language, and narrative texture—and focuses them on the psychology of individual character.

By writing a play as she would a short story, with plenty of room left for ingenious settings (a Second Front rally complete with phony Red Army generals) and stage business (a faulty toaster that blares French war news), Gallant succeeds where some other novelists and short-story writers turned dramatists fail (not, of course, Chekhov). She has made a play that works as well on stage as it does on the page.

Boyd Neil, in a review of "What Is to Be Done?" in Quill and Quire, *Vol. 50, No. 6, June, 1984, p. 32.*

MAUREEN HOWARD

[Mavis Gallant] is a very good writer indeed; so accomplished as a social critic of her country and of the European cities where she has chosen to live (Paris has been her home in recent years) that many of us who have admired her stories in The New Yorker over the years may not have given full credit to her range or to the strongly imagined shape of her work, the best of which is in this new selection [*Home Truths*]. . . . Can-

ada is not a setting, a backdrop; it is an adversary, a constraint, a comfort, the home that is almost understandable, if not understanding. It is at once deadly real and haunting, phantasmagoric: the Canadian presence varies from story to story.

In "**Jorinda and Jorindel**," which sweeps together the fragmented myths of a summer and the commentary of a clever little girl into a fairy tale, Irmgard, who is not quite 8 years old, observes of her cousin: "Bradley is not required to think of answers; he is American, and that does. But in Canada you have to keep saying what you are." It is exactly this kind of pressure that operates to good advantage in all the stories. (p. 1)

In *Home Truths* most of Mrs. Gallant's Canadians are either bound by convention or wasted by efforts to transcend a culture they perceive as imitative, provincial and second-rate. The struggle to wrench a personal identity out of a skewed national identity can lead her to create grotesques and buffoons: matrons, Red Queens, who wear pearl earrings like the Duchess of Kent's. . . . Bertie Knox, clerk and mimic, can do any Canadian accent, but during World War II he keeps a photograph of himself over his desk "in full kilt, Highlight Light Infantry, 1917: he had gone 'home,' to a completely unknown Old Country, and joined up there." . . .

With few exceptions, these stories are set in the late 1930's and 40's. Mrs. Gallant has a sharp sense of history. Incidents are carefully dated—Prohibition, Depression, treaties, the entrance of Canada into "Hitler's war." She writes of a Canada that was and makes good use of her Red Queens and clownish clerks to set up cultural pretensions and longings. She's funny and perceptive on houses, on dress—the customs of a country in which you could almost never be right.

Quick as she is with telling details—flat nasal accents, ugly reddish-brown streets—Mrs. Gallant never patronizes her country. There is no complicit wink at the reader, no easy put-down—the mere reference to shopping mall, beer brand, K Mart, the smart visual that asks for the conditioned response in too many American stories of recent years. Her Canadians are as particular and complex as Eudora Welty's Moodys and MacLains. When she uses types—the cold godmother, the remittance man—it is to redefine an attitude, correct a memory. . . .

In "**Varieties of Exile**," the disreputable or younger son sent out from England—the remittance man—is played off against the real refugees who flood into Montreal. These "Belgians, French, Catholic German, Socialist German, Jewish German, Czech" come to Linnet Muir, she admits, "straight out of the twilit Socialist-literary landscape of my reading and my desires." The story is about Linnet's willful idea that people must behave according to the script in her head. The refugees are romantic. The remittance man she meets on a commuter train is not. Looking back, she can date her discovery that life does not adhere to literary models, nor can she peg people, get them all down. The refugees are busily assimilating, even taking out Canadian passports. The remittance man—vaguely intellectual, a woolly socialist—she has written off. But he appears heroically in casualty lists as "Maj. Francis Cairns, dead of wounds in Italy." . . .

Mrs. Gallant has a remarkable sense of place. Her snowy streets and stark row houses are as carefully drawn as Elizabeth Bowen's English cities in wartime. Her men and women do not live their exacting stories in a void. Where you are is as important as what you are. It's more than atmosphere—whether you find Paris, Geneva, the south of France liberating, therefore possible, or whether you live thinly in those cities as an outsider, but know that going home will never do. She is as sure of her Montreal as Joyce was of his Dublin—that it is the place from which the stories flow.

She has written well about France and Germany, though there is more dependence on reportage and a tendency to be anecdotal when she cuts free of her Canadians. *The Pegnitz Junction* was an arresting novel that strained for invention trying to get at the roots of Nazi culture and ended up mannered. *A Fairly Good Time*, about a young Canadian woman finding her way through a French marriage, was poised, a lively novel of manners, but it did not have the urgency—Mrs. Gallant's voice, with the distinct Canadian burr, claiming that this story must be told—found in the best of *Home Truths*.

Here she is most likely to astonish when she buys her own wisdom and refuses to be orderly and neat, so that we hardly notice the plot within plot, or that the untidy asides, further reflections (she is always so bright) will not give a single or good answer. Many of these stories are quests—a search for answers that turn out to be conflicting or partial. (p. 26)

In **"Bonaventure"** a musical prodigy is terrified of nature. Staying in Switzerland with the widow of a famous composer, a keeper of the flame, he is plagued by insects, plants, bird song. Water from a natural spring seems to him bilious, diseased. It is all too mysterious, too random. He does not want to learn the names of trees, or mountains. His parents have been overly explicit about the accident of his conception, which he has come to see as an unnatural act: "They kept feeding him answers when he hadn't asked for anything." Their love, the widow's primordial strength are abhorrent to him, and he makes a dash for civilization and its easier discontents. What pursues the prodigy is "the possibility of lapsed genius" and the possibility that he is sickly, ordinary like his father, a mild Canadian. The truth, which he runs from, seeps through in this story like a dark hereditary stain.

The same fears come to Linnet Muir, but there the dangerous debts to a moody, disconsolate mother and an attractive, bohemian father are acknowledged in a calm retrospective voice, though never completely set aside: "I began to ration my writing, for fear I would dream through life as my father had done. I was afraid I had inherited a poisoned gene from him, a vocation without a gift. He had spent his own short time like a priest in charge of a relic, forever expecting the blessed blood to liquefy." Mrs. Gallant cuts deep. It is not merely what you are that is problematic, there is also the terrifying proposal of what you may never be.

I have one quibble with *Home Truths* as a collection: aside from the amazing **"Jorinda and Jorindel,"** the opening pieces in "At Home" do not give the reader the full promise of what is to come. I recommend **"In the Tunnel"** and **"The Ice Wagon Going Down the Street"** from the next section, "Canadians Abroad," as particularly good examples of her success with more ambitious tales. I don't think this indicates that Montreal is better seen from Paris, but the ideas of exile and return, reclaiming and remembering do seem to up the ante in Mrs. Gallant's fiction. The Linnet Muir stories, written from the mid- to late 70's, are wonderful, actually full of a young woman's wonder at the past. They bear a thematic resemblance to Mary McCarthy's *Memories of a Catholic Girlhood* . . . in the search through family legends, hearsay, lies for a story that will approximate some version of the truth.

Like Miss McCarthy, Linnet Muir attempts, reasonably and unsentimentally, to discover what really happened, who people *were:* but that line of inquiry yields to and finally nourishes richer material—the more difficult stories that reveal herself. . . . Mrs. Gallant's reconstruction of Linnet's return home in the war years is closely informed by exact events, by place and authentic emotions, as good stories always are.

Linnet is 18 and already knows too much, then sets herself to finding out a good deal more. She has raced ahead and is engaged to be married. In **"Between Zero and One,"** we find her working in a wartime office among statisticians and engineers, faking a job she does not understand. "I spoke to Mr. Tracy: What occupied the space between Zero and One? It must be something arbitrary, not in the natural order of numbers. If One was solid ground, why not begin with One? Before One there was what? Thin air?" Mr. Tracy says, "Don't worry your head." Going back to that time, Linnet associates it with her belief that limits are different for women and men and with the terror that lay before her in a headstrong marriage, the warnings she did not heed. Many years later she can only repeat the same questions without answers: "How do you stand if you stand upon Zero? What will the passage be like between Zero and One? And what will happen at One? Yes, what will happen?" That "yes" still looks forward bravely, even if life does not prove out.

A Canadian friend of mine remembers going to a stadium to welcome the young Queen Elizabeth and her new husband—30,000 little boys yelling and waving the Union Jack. Canada has changed dramatically, irrevocably. Mavis Gallant has made it her business to look back. In the hard act of knowing her origins, she has written powerful stories. Her home truths tell us what we can (and cannot) do with what we have been assigned. (pp. 26-7)

> Maureen Howard, *"When the Identity Is the Crisis,"* in The New York Times Book Review, *May 5, 1985, pp. 1, 26-7.*

ANNE TYLER

No one knows the importance of location better than Mavis Gallant, who has made it her lifelong business to chart the ways in which mere geography can affect a character's very soul. Herself a Canadian now permanently transplanted to France, she is also sensitive to the results of *dis*location. Never is she more skillful, more warily alert, than when she is describing the feelings of foreigners—even if they're just very slightly foreign: French Canadians among English Canadians, or a woman among men, or a child among grown-ups. (pp. 40-1)

[*Home Truths*] is divided into three parts. The six stories in the part called "At Home" are set in Canada, but in several different versions of Canada. In **"Thank You for the Lovely Tea,"** it's a country almost more English than England—a place where Queen Victoria's birthday is still celebrated some 30 years after her death, and where any outward show of emotion is condemned as "American." In **"Saturday,"** which is a wonderfully rich, tumbling, seemingly uncontrolled story about a large French-Canadian family, it is a country split cleanly in half; the father cannot tell his five sons-in-law apart because they are all English Canadian, and therefore "interchangeable, like postage stamps of the Queen's profile." . . .

The four stories in the section called "Canadians Abroad" concern people so out of place that they seem at times to be dreaming their surroundings. The tone here is often disjointed and abrupt—intentionally, one assumes. A musician edgily perched in a disquieting Swiss household is haunted by his mother's bitter, histrionic voice. A young girl alone in France falls into the clutches of an unpleasant acquaintance from home and cannot seem to free herself but drifts along, in a sleep-walker's daze. . . .

The final section, "Linnet Muir," contains six stories about a young Canadian woman living in Montreal during the Second World War. Because she is New York-educated—and a bit left-wing to boot—Linnet is something of an outsider in her own country, and as pieces of her past emerge it becomes plain that she's been an outsider of one sort or another all her life. This is easily the strongest section in the book—a moving, oddly sweet group of stories given sparkle by their thorny heroine. (p. 41)

As befits a writer with a strong sense of place, Mavis Gallant can color in an atmosphere for us with just a few well-chosen words. [A] doctor's old-fashioned office with its sentimental pictures; the musician's dank lodgings in Switzerland; the desolate landscape of northern Canada as seen through the eyes of an English war bride—they are more than visible to us. They convey a feeling: they draw us in, or weigh down our spirits, or comfort us, or chill us, as the case may be.

Place is not all, of course: she has a keen grasp of character, too, and will often pause in the midst of a story to sum a person up in one succinct paragraph—his life as seen from outside, with a dispassionate, telescopic remoteness. Or she will muse on people at leisure, rightfully trusting her readers to be as fascinated as she. . . . (pp. 41-2)

Or a single remark may demonstrate the whole man, as when a father—divorced and many times remarried—apologizes to his small daughter for falling asleep during a performance of *Peter Pan*. "I'm sorry, I should not have slept in your company," he says. "It was impolite." The apology is unnecessary (as it turns out, his daughter was sulking only because the actors had English accents instead of Canadian), but it is splendidly revealing in its courtliness, its solemnity and easy charm. All at once, we know exactly how this man must have dealt with his wives.

The paradox in these stories is that while they give a satisfying sense of fullness, they imply too a great wealth of other material left unsaid. Like the most interesting of real people, they seem to keep holding just a little something back for the next visit. Let us all hope for many more visits from Mavis Gallant. (p. 42)

> Anne Tyler, "Come to Canada," in The New Republic, *Vol. 192, No. 19, May 13, 1985, pp. 40-2.*

LINDA LEITH

[Partly] as a result of her research into the Dreyfus case of 1890s Paris, Gallant has in recent years concentrated her attention to an unusual extent on the city and its inhabitants. Indeed, between 1979 and 1983, she wrote about practically nothing else; the stories in *Overhead in a Balloon* all date from this period. They are all about Parisians of such various descriptions that they are truly "stories of Paris."

The collection opens with **"Speck's Idea"**, which . . . is one of Gallant's finest stories. It has been brushed by Gallant's interest in Dreyfus and French antisemitism. Sandor Speck is an art dealer whose wife has recently left him (she screamed

"Fascist!" at him from the departing taxi) and whose business is suffering through what looks like an irreversible economic downturn in the Paris of the late 1970s. Inspired by the desperate need for a cultural renaissance, Speck gets the idea for a redemptive retrospective of the work of Hubert Cruche, an all-but-forgotten French painter. In the process of putting the show together, Speck comes up against French antisemitism and right-wing politics, which barely give him pause, and against the artist's eccentric and mischievous widow, Lydia. A businessman who believes that "the commerce of art is without bias" and for whom nothing political has ever seemed to be "above the level of a low-grade comic strip," Speck zealously persists with his plans for the show even after he discovers that Cruche was anti-American during the war—in short, a Fascist. By the end of the story, Speck has finally gotten the matchless Lydia to agree to the show and is seeing himself "at the centre of a shadeless drawing, hero of a sort of cartoon strip." The connection between ostensibly apolitical commerce and the new right has been illuminated.

Between 1980 and 1982 most of the stories Gallant published were squibs she has referred to as the "marginalia" to her work on Dreyfus. These topical, often fragmentary, and quirkily surprising satires on French life and letters are represented in this new collection by **"The Assembly"** and by three more developed stories about a *littérateur* called Henri Grippes. These fictions seemed such a radical departure from the kinds of stories Gallant was known for that they baffled some readers when they first appeared in *The New Yorker*. In them Gallant puts herself in the shoes of a variety of odd and unsavoury characters and plays with authorship and authority quite zanily. There's something of the cartoonist about Gallant in these squibs—or as much as there can be in a purely literary artist—and it seems appropriate that the title of one of them (it happens to be one that isn't reprinted in *Overhead in a Balloon*) is **"La Vie Parisienne,"** which was the name of a comic strip popular in Paris during the 1890s. Gallant may have gone off on a tangent from the comments about comics in **"Speck's Idea,"** but those comments are typical of her incongruous approach to writing political fiction. The result has been that she has extended her range: Gallant works within a larger circle now. The striking similarities—in characterization, in tone, and in context—between the squibs and the rather less crazily comic fictions (like **"Larry"** and **"Luc and his Father"**) reprinted in this collection suggest that the squibs are not to be seen simply as an aberration.

In the fall of 1983, Gallant published a series of linked stories that span the adult lives of three Parisians over a period of more than 40 years. Edouard marries the Jewish-born Hungarian actress Magdalena in Nazi-occupied Paris so that he can get her to relative safety in the free zone. He meets his second wife, Juliette, shortly afterwards; she is 18 and he is with the Free French in England. They are unable to marry (Magdalena is a Catholic convert and for years refuses to grant Edouard a divorce) until Juliette is too old to have children. The four very short stories that describe the course of the two true loves of Edouard's life are told quietly and with perfect grace. Though they are less obviously political than much of her work and though they seem poignant rather than comic, even these love stories reveal Gallant's always acute awareness of historical context and her inimitable sense of irony. (p. 37)

Here, too, Gallant has slipped in a reference to comics: a publisher of comic books has taken over the apartment Magdalena lived in when Edouard first knew her. It's enough to make the title of the collection seem punningly suggestive of a balloon over a cartoon character's head. But the balloon in the title story is the kind that sways silently between the clouds and the Burgundy Canal, and it's associated with the woebegone protagonist's need for salvation, or at least for a friend. The title story is a weighty tale of betrayal, but Gallant's playfulness ensures that it, like the other stories in this volume, will seem lighter than air. There's much more to this collection than mere levity, but there's levity too, and there's nothing mere about it. (p. 38)

Linda Leith, "La vie Parisienne," in The Canadian Forum, *Vol. LXV, No. 753, November, 1985, pp. 37-8.*

James Galvin

1951-

American poet and editor.

Much of the imagery in Galvin's two collections of poetry, *Imaginary Timber* (1980) and *God's Mistress* (1984), is based on the landscape of the West and Southwest. Nature and its relation to humanity are among Galvin's predominant concerns; vivid descriptions and bold, loosely connected images characterize his poetry. According to Thomas Swiss, "the logic that compels and organizes the lines is dreamlike," and he also notes the influence of the Spanish surrealist poets on Galvin's work.

(See also *Contemporary Authors*, Vol. 108.)

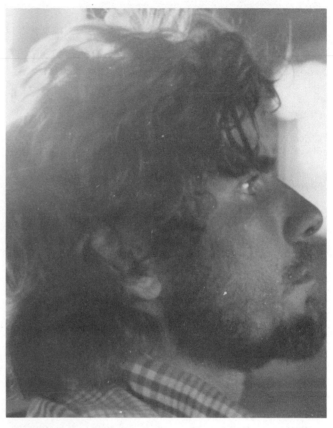

Courtesy of James Galvin

PUBLISHERS WEEKLY

James Galvin's debut collection [*Imaginary Timber*] is undeniably interesting and irritatingly inessential. He has a way of continually throwing the reader off balance with tropes that are somewhat wide of the mark. . . . This unbalancing act is reinforced by shifts from clean, straightforward American vernacular into series of . . . peculiarly skewed images, which only rarely hang together. Some of Galvin's verses and prose poems are set in his native Southwest and feature mothers and fathers who seem more word than flesh. These poems can be admired but not loved, and in the last analysis their artificiality becomes exasperating.

> *A review of "Imaginary Timber," in* Publishers Weekly, *Vol. 218, No. 10, September 5, 1980, p. 66.*

MARGARET GIBSON

[In *Imaginary Timber*, Galvin's] subject is distance from the world, from the past and prairie life, from childhood, family, his lover, the self. The problem the poems pose is that people vanish into themselves, into death; objects vanish in the distance. How shall we then connect, believe, close distances? In love with the problem, Galvin says he does not know "the smallest necessities / Joining hands to complete the world," and that we "take root in the sound of our own breaking." The idiom throughout is familiarly fashionable these days: an isolated authority is instructing us in the mystery of randomness, speaking with an elegant seizure of subjective sadness and abstracted passion—perhaps because, in these poems, the mind "Like Columbus on the edge of the world / feels the grip of all it cannot grasp." But without that grasp, poems—and our lives—begin to sound derivative.

> *Margaret Gibson, in a review of "Imaginary Timber," in* Library Journal, *Vol. 105, No. 19, November 1, 1980, p. 2331.*

RICHARD HORNSEY

[James Galvin's perspective in *Imaginary Timber* is] fresh and . . . [his] work seldom leaves the impression of having been forced onto the page in order to conform to a preconceived structure.

Quite aware that death is the only certainty, James Galvin focuses his intelligence and poetic imagination upon the significance of life. Unlike those who have been saved through religious faith and have retreated into the country of "imaginary timber" he wishes to face and try to understand the flux which characterizes the natural world. But it is not the world of surfaces and superficial reality which concerns him most. The rural settings of his poems and the recurring images of snow, sky, mountains, rain and trees allow him to probe the deeper meanings underlying their existence. . . . [To be] aware one must be able to imagine as well as feel and it is this positive, vital use of imagination to which the title of the book refers rather than to the negative one associated with escape and blind faith—the kind of imagination necessary for the making of metaphors which are the true indicators of how well we understand the union between the inner and the outer natural world. (p. 105)

Galvin strives for . . . arresting, economical imagery constantly surprising the reader with his original perceptions. . . . [He is] a writer who is confident in his language and mature in his vision. The aim is to show, through poetic form, how "mystery joins things together" and it is in the awareness of this union that the significance of our lives can be affirmed. (p. 106)

Richard Hornsey, "Theme and Variations," in The Ontario Review, No. 15, Fall-Winter, 1981-82, pp. 101-12.*

THOMAS SWISS

James Galvin's poems [in *Imaginary Timber*] are evocative: composed on a rationale wholly their own, the logic that compels and organizes the lines is dreamlike. Galvin's precursors are the Spanish surrealists, and he directly acknowledges his debt in poems like **"Notes for the First Line of a Spanish Poem,"** and the homages **"Lemon Ode (For Neruda)"** and **"Ode to the Brown Paper Bag."** The latter poem takes as an epigraph a line from Cesar Vallejo: "Mystery joins things together." . . .

Galvin's method is prelogical: he allows mystery to join things without inquiring into the nature of that mystery. Instead, he focuses on bringing to light—naming—those things which he sees linked. The poems offer very few explicit connections. It's an interesting approach and, for the most part, a successful one, especially when the speaker of the poem is able to convince the reader to risk a leap of perception, a leap of faith. . . . (p. 347)

In his preface to *Los Versos del Capitan*, Neruda wrote, "in many ways, I think that all books should be anonymous." The success of Galvin's poems depends on the reader's willingness to trust the speaker, to accept the voice finally—and this is Neruda's point—*as our own* speaking. In **"Lines about the Recent Past,"** what surprises and delights the reader is Galvin's ability to discover a range of images and ideas that register an equivalent emotional response.

Many of the poems are set in the West and Southwest. In **"Sadness,"** Galvin uses his powerful technical gifts to integrate the abstract quality of sadness with the physical qualities of the landscape. By the end of the poem, the whole scene has been remarkably and artfully transformed. . . . (pp. 347-48)

Other poems are filled with lessons and lists, parodies and adages and some serious aphorisms that resonate more than they explain. Many of his lines touch us with their sense and simplicity: **"Everyone Knows Whom the Saved Envy"** is the title of one poem in which he also writes, "It isn't such a bad thing / to live in one world forever." In other poems he reminds us that "everything is its own reward" and "everyone died because everyone does."

Perhaps the strongest poems of all are those which concern the death of the speaker's mother and the handful of love poems in the third section of the book. His themes are traditional: loss, loneliness, anxiety. Yet the poems are not joyless or without affirmative revelation. In **"That Falling We Fall,"** a poem about death, the reader strongly senses Galvin's fundamental rhythmical sense, his ability to move us with music *and* meaning. After describing the "descant pleasantries of terror," the funeral which "leaves us standing with flowers," he writes:

> Joy, no joy; the dead,
> Their arms raised like violin bows
> About to begin, begin to sway slowly together.

My mother was friendly, they will like her.
They will comfort her.
They will tell her this
Will never happen again,

This will never happen again.

Like many of the poems in *Imaginary Timber,* **"That Falling We Fall"** is haunting in its clarity and vision, its human instruction. (pp. 348-49)

Thomas Swiss, "Moving from Station to Station," in Southwest Review, Vol. 67, No. 3, Summer, 1982, pp. 345-49.*

PUBLISHERS WEEKLY

Galvin's voice is strong, concise and muscular in [*God's Mistress*] . . . , largely set in the Mountain States. "Where I live," he writes, "distance is the primal fact. . . ." Humans are cast on a backdrop of rugged mountains, forests and streams, and we see varying relationships of people with nature. The poet recalls his childhood when he hunted for grouse in spruce woods. Elsewhere, he fears for the safety of a forest during a drought. At times the physical world is evoked not only in its own right but as a reflection of human moods and emotions. Galvin writes in short sentences and phrases, combining metaphor and lyricism with colloquial speech. Skillfully crafted, these poems reveal the poet's long and thoughtful relationship with the natural world.

A review of "God's Mistress," in Publishers Weekly, Vol. 225, No. 21, May 25, 1984, p. 56.

JOSEPH A. LIPARI

[*God's Mistress*] captures the look and feel of the contemporary rural American West. Building a home, ranching, fishing—all come to life in exact observations and powerful commentary. The portraits of people here are even more vivid than the landscapes. In **"Almost Noon,"** for instance, the poet examines a photo of his dead mother: "There are smaller, darker shadows gathered in your ears. / They are planning an invasion." With a simplicity and reticence that is almost Chinese, Galvin suggests correspondences between the human and the natural, but most often he presents the world as it is—resilient to our need for meanings.

Joseph A. Lipari, in a review of "God's Mistress," in Library Journal, Vol. 109, No. 12, July, 1984, p. 1330.

KENNETH FUNSTEN

[James Galvin in *God's Mistress*] suffers from . . . [a] loose quality. Integrity of language is sacrificed to the power of the emotion. It's more American advertising.

Galvin's product is the fast-disappearing landscape of the American West, and his powers of description are strong. He writes of the futile mating of nature with nature: "Like huge somnambulating farmers, / Dust-devils work the fallow ground." His **"High Plains Rag"** personifies prairie grass. His voice is like the lonely coyote's yowl. In fact, everything he writes harbors a tone of lament, of the poetic elegy.

Kenneth Funsten, in a review of "God's Mistress," in Los Angeles Times Book Review, *September 23, 1984, p. 10.*

RICHARD TILLINGHAST

[In *God's Mistress*] Galvin's style is characterized by the strikingly direct statement, often at the beginning or toward the end of a poem, the literary equivalent of the preemptive strike: "There is another kind of sleep, / We are talking in it now," or "What happens is nothing happens," or "I'll tell you what the soul is made of: / More dust." The rhetorical force of these statements derives from their boldness, and they are a challenge to the reader's understanding. But in the subtle give-and-take of reading, a writer who challenges in this way runs the risk of being rebuffed with "So what? or "I don't believe you." The first line of **"The Importance of Green"** has the rhetorical suddenness I have mentioned—"Small towns are for knowing who's poor"—but the plain sense of the line is at best a half-truth.

Still, this is an attractive book with some memorable poems in it, such as the three-page **"What Holds Them Apart."** The poem has a Western spaciousness and a sense of human aloneness in the natural scheme of things that has traditionally been the gift of poets like Robinson Jeffers, William Everson, Gary Snyder and Richard Hugo. (p. 362)

James Galvin has a voice and a world, perhaps the two most difficult things to achieve in poetry. His world is the West that exists not on film or in the ski-lodge condos of Vail and Aspen, but in the lives of those who live and work in the outback, who, as Galvin puts it, "haven't heard the West is over." His laconic, understated voice can be heard in [such poems as

"Whistle"] . . . . An imagination is at work here, an imagination that can describe a mine shaft as "one man's monument to hard luck, an obelisk of air pointing straight down" and a house as "a flower made of timber." Why then, does a writer with such strengths allow himself to write in the following "neo-surrealist" period style?

> down where you can imagine the in-
>   comparable
> piety of the schoolbus,
> the wherewithal of bees,
>
> down where you can be a drawer full
>   of dust
> as night comes on under full sail,
>
> and the smooth rain,
> in its beautiful armor,
> stands by forever. . . .

Anyone who has spent a semester in the Brand-X Poetry Writers' Workshop could have written those lines in his sleep. It's a pastiche of Mark Strand and W. S. Merwin and a dozen others at their most facile. "Smooth rain" and "beautiful armor" are too bland to think about. The same could be said of the anaphoric stanza structure ("down . . . down . . . ") and the formulaic "heightening" kicked into operation by the word "forever." James Galvin at his best (and that best is very, very good) would set those lines up on a fence post, like an old tin can, with the Grand Tetons as a backdrop, and shoot them full of holes. (pp. 362-63)

Richard Tillinghast, "Blunt Instruments," in The Nation, *Vol. 239, No. 11, October 13, 1984, pp. 361-63.**

Albert Goldbarth

1948-

American poet and editor.

Goldbarth's verse is distinguished by its discursive form and linguistic vitality. His concerns range from matters of historical and scientific importance to the personal and commonplace. Goldbarth describes himself as favoring "the extended poem that includes narrative, or has scope enough to play with large bodies of time, or that finds room for dialogue or quoted source materials, that can build up litany or weave motifs in and out with the huge sweep a suite has." His work often combines the explication of complex ideas with wit and verbal play. Although Goldbarth has been faulted for overloading his poems with detailed descriptions and information, most critics praise his work for its energy and intelligence.

A prolific poet, Goldbarth has generated a significant amount of critical response throughout his career. His first three major volumes—*Coprolites* (1973), *Opticks: A Poem in Seven Sections* (1974), and *Jan. 31* (1974)—contain long poems written in a style that is both playful and serious, conversational and erudite. This approach to poetry characterizes most of Goldbarth's subsequent work. In a review of *Opticks,* Dave Smith faulted Goldbarth's poetry for immaturity, self-consciousness, and an overabundance of words and images, yet he also praised Goldbarth's ambition, noting: "Even the worst of his poems demonstrate his marvelous equipment, his intelligence, his straining for vision."

Comings Back: A Sequence of Poems (1976) demonstrates Goldbarth's penchant for juxtaposing disparate objects, facts, and conceits. Robert Cording noted that this technique is characteristic of Goldbarth's works: "Goldbarth's poems depend almost entirely on two conditions: the accumulation of random ideas which, at some point, suddenly 'click' into a pattern; and the shift in tone which usually accompanies that 'click' (from a light, playful, undercutting voice . . . to a more serious, charged voice)." In *Different Fleshes* (1979), Goldbarth explores the possibilities of the prose poem. A book-length work in verse, this volume contrasts the past with the present and life in Texas with life in Paris. Goldbarth connects the various elements through the story of Vander Clyde, a Texas-born female impersonator who worked in Paris during the 1920s and 1930s. *Original Light: New & Selected Poems 1973-1983* (1983), which is thematically organized into three sections, has further established Goldbarth as a poet of ambitious scope.

(See also *CLC,* Vol. 5; *Contemporary Authors,* Vols. 53-56; and *Contemporary Authors New Revision Series,* Vol. 6.)

VICTOR CONTOSKI

Comings Back discusses returns. It begins with a quotation from A. A. Milne: Christopher Robin begging Pooh not to forget him. Thus the reader is thrown back to the associations of his childhood, and the first coming back is his own. *Comings* back—not *goings* back—suggests an interesting perspective in

which everything is seen from the original place, the original time. Goldbarth speaks of the poet as a maker of lists, and in effect the entire book is a list of various comings back, often in surprising contexts. **"Wire,"** for example, juxtaposes the barbs in barbed wire and the stars. Whenever the poet mentions one, the other keeps coming back. (pp. 419-20)

The poet discovers relationships between the most unlikely objects. Hence a high degree of intellectual excitement pervades his poetry. In a sense he rediscovers the laws of physics, not only the various relationships of matter to matter but the moral implications of those relationships. In **"Clock Invention,"** sections on the invention of the sandwich and sections on clocks alternate so that the poem itself becomes a kind of sandwich. So many things have been made into clocks (magnifying lenses, pinheads) that we come to see them everywhere. The poet even presents his small intestine as a timepiece, and as he does we suddenly see the connection between clocks and sandwiches. The poem, a love poem with a traditional love theme, *carpe diem,* gathers force as words vibrate with accrued meanings; *we* (poet and reader, poet and lover), *meat* (roast beef, the flesh of our bodies), and light (time and knowledge).

We will set up
a side of roast beef, with a kitchen-knife in

like Excalibur, on a pedestal.
For our sundial. For the blade's shadow,
for the light on the meat.

In a world of such relationships even accidental disorders make their own sense. In **"The Errors"** broken glass reflects the rainbow, *rabbi* is misprinted as *rabbit*, and Columbus discovers a whole new world as he sets out for *the undies*. Time and again the poet shows us surprising connections between the physical world and the imagination, the sensual and the spiritual. . . .

He gives the impression of not being able to write fast enough to keep up with the flow of his thoughts. Hence a conversational style. Several poems take the form of letters. Rimes, when they occur, lie so imbedded in natural speech that at times the reader may miss them altogether. But no matter. Goldbarth is less interested in "Art" than in ideas, in intellectual excitement. The book makes its impression as a whole in which all parts are closely and unexpectedly related. (pp. 420-21)

> Victor Contoski, *"Late Returns,"* in Prairie Schooner,
> *Vol. 51, No. 4, Winter, 1977-78, pp. 419-21.*

MARY KINZIE

[Albert Goldbarth's assumption in *Comings Back* is] that our dislocated musings are the repositories of significant inner logic, that the gaps between our thoughts are where true sense is to be found, and that our jumbled nightmares, faithfully presented in all their jumble, embody ultimate meaning. From the kindliest perspective, one might say the ultimate meaning was simply that we *are* jumbled and dream-driven creatures. From a perspective less kind, which the certain smugness of Goldbarth's coterie attitude may invite, ultimate meaning may be a much more limited matter of the poet feeling matey and singularly veracious with a number of the sensitive, disaffected cronies to whom he addresses a quantity of verse epistles. . . . In a poem that begins "Dear Liz: A dream. For which I offer / No exegesis", an old Scot appears, "his arms, / from the wheeling, were terraced; his tongue / revolved in his brogue like a gerbil." "And in that moment," writes Goldbarth, whatever it was, "I knew, Liz, how / it would turn out okay for people / like us." In the long **"Letter to Tony: Suitable for Presentation as a Gift"**, Goldbarth writes to console his friend for the break with Sharon and throws around a great deal of Egyptian lore because together he, Sharon, and Tony had seen the scarab at an Egyptian exhibit. Leaping brusquely "Over the winking penis of Thoth", Goldbarth lands on the emblem for this looping, tasteless coprolith—the dung beetle. To cheer Tony up, he elaborates the various ways in which the sun rises like "A ball of shit", and jauntily calls what results, "This art: these smear gifts renewed at every birth."

Goldbarth's poems of pure whimsy drag along in frantic repetitions, as in **"The Pocket Song,"** which is about the eating of, and transformation of the entire world into, peanut butter and tuna fish, the former repeated nine times, the latter an equal number of times with an additional treat in "tuna meat" and "tuna snow", and a duet between both in "foaming peanut butter / fish, gray tuna." The quotation that introduces the book, intended perhaps to assuage the frantic, hip, overwritten "hard truths" that make up the volume, is from the prose of A. A. Milne, "Pooh, *promise* you won't forget about me, ever." There's something unclean about Goldbarth's careening back and forth from *Winnie-the-Pooh* or his deliberately darling "peanut butter banks" to the "vulva-pink corsage / of tuna

fish" on a girl's shoulder; just as there is something ridiculous about his attempt to romanticize "the sugary give of a nipple" into the heavy-handed final lines of **"Sugar Rises"**: "The strength / is *in* the smallness, in / bearing the sweetness no matter what the cost." (pp. 33-4)

> Mary Kinzie, *"How Could Fools Get Tired!"* in
> Poetry, *Vol. CXXXII, No. 1, April, 1978, pp. 31-52.**

LORRIE GOLDENSOHN

A long book, stuffed with dreams, anecdotes, personal letters, jokes, and quotations from newspapers, books, and magazines, Albert Goldbarth's *Comings Back*—its cover decorated by a snake swallowing its tail, and presenting its body as an emblematic, unbroken circle—prominently bears as its subtitle: *A sequence of poems.* Thereby putting us on notice that *Comings Back* is intended to be taken seriously as a book in bulk, with plenty of cross-reference and continuity to stitch each poem to its fellow. (p. 137)

Whether Goldbarth is dealing with events from his waking life, or treating events from dream or history, there is always the same cascade of nouns and proper nouns, the same open throttle on images, the same busy pumping of clauses, and the same migratory levels of diction, from elevated to lowdown with gong-like regularity. But while this load of particulars can give excitement to the contents of poems, making them seem amiably thick with notions and ideas, in too many cases the effect is mechanical and heavy-handed. All the poems feel the same in touch and tone, their bonhomie forced. Lacking emphasis, and uninterested in any form of restraint, Goldbarth's intelligence is too much in love with its own bustle.

Little good is done in this situation by plugging in the long poem called **"Letter to Tony,"** and subtitled "suitable for presentation as a gift," which seems to vary the emotional range of the book by adding a prolonged bout of hysteria. The poem selects shit as its central metaphor for art and love, using a bit of Joseph Campbell, and a misquotation from Yeats among its justifying sub-texts: "for (sic) / love has pitched its palace (sic) / in the place of excrement." . . . (pp. 137-38)

But none of this really validates the obsessive content of the poem, which quotes a lot more, and deals very summarily with friend Tony, the dedicatee, and Tony's desertion by his lover. The connections are always either minimal or obvious. Finally, the emotion ostensibly cooked up for Tony seems specious. (p. 138)

While other poems, and even parts of this one, have many of the virtues of good conversation, with interesting tidbits about the world, still the bits tend to curdle in the poems, as fact-dropping becomes a variant species of name-dropping. Goldbarth has a habit of stopping short, or of driving too easily past his conclusions. He says:

> . . . Isn't
> this the art we wanted all along, this cathartic
> implying of knowledge . . . Though in the long run we
>   expect
> it will enhance, and not assuage,
> most questions.

And: "We learn to live / with our errors and call them our beauty."

This pat doctrine makes me restive, as I wait for less implying and more of that enhancing. While grateful to Goldbarth for not leaning too heavily on surrealist juxtapositions, . . . I want a less fervid dedication to insouciance; not so many strung-out perceptions and a less compulsive concern with the drippings and danglings of the body's parts: "the sexual loneliness / seeps through my mattress, and hangs gray semen / stalactites into the dark below my bed."

Explicit as they are, these details are not confessional manners. There is an interesting gap between the specificity of the names spelled out—Elmwood Park, Salt Lake City, Syl, Tony, Ellen (all the nicknames denoting extreme intimacy), the myopic examination of normally quite private details—and the near-total silence imposed on the larger-scale details of relation. Curiously in line with Goldbarth's other omissions of development, his poems actually concentrate fairly little on anything personally revealing, even if the surface is ostentatiously studded with the apparently intimate. The result of the surface, finally, is a sophisticated form of hiding; of poem as peek-a-boo. (pp. 139-40)

> Lorrie Goldensohn, "Loading the Rifts," in Parnassus: Poetry in Review, *Vol. 7, No. 2, Spring-Summer, 1979, pp. 124-40.*

MICHAEL KING

[Albert Goldbarth] doesn't give a damn for narrative continuity, or rather distrusts it, as a scam we all use to convince ourselves that experience is not in fact uneven, discontinuous, disjunct. A novel is seldom well-equipped to pursue that insistent disconnection in events; even the most experimental prose asserts its linearity in time. But in Goldbarth's best work the poems cartwheel and leapfrog over time and defy it, so that the sense of coherence, of wholeness, derives from layers of related meaning held in simultaneous relation.

This layering of time is not entirely new in modern poetry, of course. Goldbarth has referred to Ezra Pound's dictum, "All ages are contemporaneous" as precedent, and Pound's own poetry sustains the theory within which chronology is subordinated to logopoeia. Goldbarth has none of Pound's ideological tenacity or didacticism, or his desperate attempt to deny Time entire: "Time, time is the evil." Goldbarth's attitude, on the contrary, is nostalgic, but undeceived about poetry's powers of defiance. . . .

Different Fleshes is a work partly about the distance linking the past and present, more particularly about choices made which separate one sort of future from another. It is hardly as abstract as all that; the poem stretches from Round Rock, Texas in 1878, through Paris in the 'twenties, back to central Texas (Austin) a hundred years later. Its central figure is one Vander Clyde, born in 1897 in Round Rock, who later traveled to Paris and became a world-famous female impersonator and acrobat, under the name "Barbette." Barbette's heyday was in the 'twenties at the Cirque Medrano, amidst the many other literary and artistic exiles of the time, many of whom make appearances in the poem. . . .

The poem's chronicle of Vander Clyde/Barbette reaches back to the Texas past of Sam Bass (d. 1878), notorious Texas outlaw, and forward to contemporary gay bars, in Austin where Goldbarth now lives. As visitors to that exotic country might guess, the connection is not so preposterous as it might seem. Sam Bass, who was shot and killed near Round Rock, was known to have robbed banks while dressed as a woman. And

Barbette, eventually injured in a stage fall, returned to Austin in the 'thirties, thus completing the circle. . . .

Readers of Goldbarth's earlier work . . . will recognize the characteristic connection made between the exotic and the quotidian, in a cyclic rhythm. Structurally the poem moves between three distinct temporal and cultural eras: Vander Clyde/ Sam Bass / Round Rock at the turn of the century; Barbette / the Expatriates / Paris in the 'twenties; and the poet, writing, in Austin in 1978. Vander Clyde's transformation into Barbette threads the poems together, and gives it its central theme of metamorphosis; but several of the most effective passages are the poet's personal meditations which interrupt the narrative and heighten its emotional power. . . .

The enlivening connection unifying this wide range of material is the metamorphic impulse Goldbarth finds within each element of it. Vander Clyde's leap from Round Rock to Paris, from country fieldhand to dazzling acrobat (what Cocteau called "this unforgettable lie!") is seen most importantly as a leap of imagination. Barbette's stage illusion was only a minor art, but it shows its kinship with the swirl of artistic and literary experimentation going on about her, much of it produced by more famous expatriates: Hemingway, Joyce, Pound, Stein, Picasso, Chagall. The urge to exile also connects all these illustrious names with that of Barbette; beyond that, Goldbarth is pursuing an aesthetic connection which is not so much historical as psychological: "This was astronomy: how every skin/ like a moon/has a dark side." Often those invisible topographies have their comic aspects. Out of a photograph of Brassai, Goldbarth conjures up Torgues, the Human Gorilla, who also performed at the Cirque. Sometimes the joke is an entertaining sleight-of-hand, not unlike Barbette's illusions; Goldbarth cuts from the last words of Sam Bass—"'the world is bobbing around me!'"—to Monet painting *The Banks of the Seine*: "Everything : watermovement waterface. [. . .] in the bobbing of daylight."

It's a nice touch, since both events happened to occur in 1878, but the poem is less interested in the superficial echoes of impressionism than in their emotional implications. Even as the water of the Seine will not hold still for the brush of Monet—"Go to paint it x, by the time your brush maneuvers / no matter how quick / it's x prime"—so the poet's material keeps shifting under his attention. The ruling body of ***Different Fleshes*** is the moon, circle of changes, although the poem is not quite a Spenserian lament over mutability. Indeed, the poet evokes wry sympathy for the most unlikely mutations, the grey world of transvestism, at a gay bar called "Austin Country." . . .

The empathy in these passages—the "Austin Country" episode follows related material about the "Gender Clinic" in Houston—is neither trendy nor artificial; Goldbarth simply cannot deny a kinship between these Others, represented for him by Barbette, and those of his own generation who now seem to wander in other directions, still seeking to "fill up themselves." He addresses his friends, some by name, as "My dear born-in-my-year," and discovers a tragi-comic catalogue of wounds, injuries, old scars of failed attempts at metamorphosis. . . .

Amidst all these natural and unnatural disasters, the poem stands as an attempt at metamorphosis that will succeed, that will sustain itself as a work of intellectual and historical imagination. One by one, the expatriate writers pass through the Parisian scenes, and Goldbarth even imagines a meeting between

Barbette and Hemingway (who reported on the Cirque in the course of his work as a journalist), as a representative movement of the acrobatic leap of imagination that underlies any act of creation: "Or maybe they did trade a look, a moment only, in recognition. The same itch on two such different fleshes." The poem is a mask as elaborate and artificial as the extravagant cosmetics of Barbette, and each of these writers was engaged in constructing a mask which would, by covering his everyday skin, reveal a richer and more profound, because created, body. (p. 5)

The various worlds of history and art come together in a final invocation to the moon, goddess of metamorphosis who presides over the making of the poem, and to whom the poet prays to succor both his friends and literary predecessors. If there be transformations, let the new forms be magical, let them delight the lives of his friends as her transformation did Barbette, who speaks only one line: "'I felt I had found it, my city, my Paris.'" . . .

The retelling of **Different Fleshes** makes it sound perhaps more somberly philosophical than it is. . . . [The book has] characteristic Goldbarth flavor: musing, self-mocking yet fundamentally serious, sensual, one metaphorical idea leaping or tailing into another, long contemplative passages brought short by comic rhetorical questions, and sudden bursts of arcane knowledge borrowed or invented from an obscure text. It is a style he has been developing throughout his earlier books, all of which exhibit a concise lyrical imagination while persistently developing thematic ideas into longer forms. In book after book, most notably **Opticks, Jan. 31,** and **Comings Back,** he has flirted with sequential form and implicitly the "narrative continuity" which continually eludes him. **Different Fleshes** comes closest to recounting a historical narrative, but in each of these works he takes as much pleasure in pursuing a sheer wealth of suggestive tangents and backwaters in the material, merely because they are there. He has discovered them, and he makes the reader delight also in his discoveries. . . . (p. 6)

Michael King, "'Different Fleshes': The Poetry of Albert Goldbarth," in The American Poetry Review, *Vol. 9, No. 2, March-April, 1980, pp. 5-6.*

JOHN ADDIEGO

A roller coaster music is generated in the three poems in [**Who Gathered and Whispered Behind Me**], a montage of voices and images pitching crazily through a range of chronological, historical and biblical frames that keep to one thematic trace: family love in its largest sense, the personal cosmos, which is immortal.

It sounds risky. It is; ambitious, often dangerously self-conscious and expansive, the approach (now, almost a Goldbarth trademark) is fused into a remarkably effective synthesis, especially in the first, longest and central poem, **"The Window Is An Almanach,"** a complex elegy for the poet's grandmother, Rose Seligman.

"The Window Is An Almanach" will likely elicit comparisons, for good and bad reasons, with another elegiac piece by another important Jewish-American poet, Allen Ginsberg. But if comparisons are sought (and Goldbarth's multi-media, polyphonic style invites comparison), the more appropriate parallel artist would be the one Goldbarth borrows from in the poem: Marc Chagall.

Chagall's anti-intellectual, whimsical, dream-centered visions have a similar montage effect as the overlapping series of voices, quotes and points of view in Goldbarth's poem. The Russian-born painter, printmaker and designer frequently borrowed a Yiddish joke, historical event or folktale as partial source material in his work, which was often described as simplistic, disconnected and/or irksomely fascinating by his critics. Goldbarth dedicates twelve stanzas to Chagall in this poem (paralleling the number of stained glass windows designed by the Russian artist at the Hadassah-Hebrew University Medical Centre in Jerusalem). He quotes him frequently, and describes a young Chagall's discoveries his first year in Paris (1910) in a careful and heart-centered style:

> Light.
>
> he thinks, is retrieval: it sees and remembers, and
> the lamplustre patterns Vitebsk on his peeling
> Paris garret's walls—here in the paints and crusts
> of a wind-whistled room, he can open light's tight
> lovers-hug and warm himself by the sparks it never
> let go.

For Chagall, the light in Paris conjures home, much in the way the thick, Yiddish voice of Goldbarth's deceased grandmother conjures his poetry, his mixed comic/serious tone. . . . (pp. 136-37)

Using the grandmother voice in intermittent passages, Goldbarth enlarges her thematic messages about Light and Dark, particularly her renditions of tales from a thirteenth-century book of esoteric Jewish mysticism (*Sefer-ha-Zohar*, the Book of Splendor or Radiance). The *Zohar* is quoted and paraphrased by Goldbarth, to the effect of augmenting a continuous mystical concern throughout the poem which connects historical, biblical and spiritual allusions to a recurring childhood recollection of the light appearing under the door of his dying grandmother's room. . . .

Here, a comparison with Ginsberg's "Kaddish" is justifiable, another poem of contorted love and final praise, which ends with the dying mother's spiritual advice to the poet: ". . . the key is in the bars, in the / sunlight in the window."

Although a type of 'Light-as-vehicle-for Immortality' theme is shared in both poems, the parallel is essentially slight, and relies too heavily on placing Content as a separate entity, independent of Form in poetry. Ginsberg's confessional outpouring, his self-and-family-deprecating approach, is in direct contrast to the humility, ranginess and optimism in Goldbarth's work. (p. 138)

What gathers behind Goldbarth's composition is a collection of the sources of his work: his grandmother's story-telling style and spirit, the ancient parables and traditional concerns of his people, the vision and words of a father-artist figure. A thematic message of immortality engendered by the light passing through our receptive, translucent beings comes to life in the rich mixture of the poem's presentation. Goldbarth is the fleet master-chef-poet of a generation in sensory overload, offering a transcendental soul-food of language and vision to our sterile, spiritless fare.

This new book of poetry is convincing evidence of Goldbarth's importance, not as a pioneer in style so much as a vessel for a times and a people. His use of montage and found-poem techniques (quotes leap from a text on near death experiences to another on Color and Optics, the Book of Zohar, the words of Chagall and other artists) is uniquely powerful and appropriate. . . . The variety of tones, allusions, voices and points of view are remarkably connected. (pp. 138-39)

Who Gathered And Whispered Behind Me bespeaks Goldbarth's compassion and acrobatic imagination, his ability to combine disparate narrative styles and sources into one vision which is humane, humorous, complex and illuminating. (p. 140)

> *John Addiego, in a review of "Who Gathered and Whispered Behind Me," in* Northwest Review, *Vol. XX, No. 1, 1982, pp. 136-40.*

CHARLEY SHIVELY

Different Fleshes plays a wide panoply of macho he-men in Texas and Paris against an extraordinary drag queen, Barbette, nee Vander Clyde. Ernest Hemingway, perhaps the leader of the pack, is paired against the transvestite acrobat: "The same itch on two such different fleshes." What this itch might be is not entirely clear; it's evidently not sexual, since Barbette is never given the slightest tint of sexuality. Perhaps the "itch" is the demands of manhood, the he-man requirement so unsparingly enforced upon young boys. . . .

Albert Goldbarth uses Barbette as a foil, and to do so he must make him/her utterly unique, singular. . . . To cast Barbette as an extremity, Goldbarth must eradicate clues of other faggots in Paris. His main source is Sylvia Beach's *Shakespeare and Company*. In *Different Fleshes* Goldbarth lists most of the straight men included in Beach's index—but few of the queers. . . . Likewise among the lesbians. . . . Cocteau has to be mentioned, since the heart of *Different Fleshes* is quotation from him, but the citation is curious: "the not-so-innocent fun . . . once called Toulouse-Lautrec . . . and, later called that poet/artist/homosexual man's man/film director/novelist/bonvivant: Cocteau." The term "a gentleman's man" is common in Grade B British films, but what is a "homosexual man's man"?

Barbette was interesting to Cocteau in part because Vander Clyde demonstrated that sex/gender distinctions are all jokes/illusions/roles. Goldbarth cannot give up his polarities, contrasts, copulations; even queers have to be understood as crossovers, inverts. . . .

The strict polarity between man/woman—a binary way of thought—also accompanies a split between Black and white. Goldbarth often calls Black people "darkies" in *Different Fleshes*—presumably speaking in Texan dialect, but such racist usage is neither cute nor amusing and does not echo Barbette at all. . . .

Authors, of course, have their licenses to invent, but not without being accountable. One convincing leit-motif of *Different Fleshes* is the lavender gloves, which Sam Bass a tough outlaw wore to rob the Round Rock bank in 1878; Vander Clyde found them playing as a boy and wore them doing his act; they are reproduced from a drawing by Toulouse-Lautrec for the cover and elsewhere in the book. These gloves help hold the book together, but other inventions are less convincing. . . .

While *Different Fleshes* has its weaknesses, I enjoyed reading it; there is a pace, drama, movement and organization which make it more than a hodgepodge. The form will be familiar to readers of H. D. (*Helen in Egypt*), Pound, Williams, Olson, Dorn and others. The particular strength of Goldbarth is his unremitting quest for surfaces, appearances. Skin without pretentious interior dialogue. Even his uses of Joyce, Hemingway, Beach, Fitzgerald, Monet and others never goes into their cre-

ations or personalities: they are artistic celebrities; they shine in some Parnassian glow, spotlighted for all time as immortal, names worth dropping, anecdotes worth copying. These are not people so much as geological strata, shelves to look at, scenes to peep into, and then pass on. Thus Goldbarth is at his most profound, his very best and most deeply illuminating in describing Barbette's cosmetics:

> By its light, we're drawn to the table of blue, chartreuse, slut's red, the delicate tinge of the clam's hinge, the pearl of the clamshell's secret mantle, wimple black, a cat's-arch of comet, glint off gendarme buttons, oranges, fecal smears, a bride's ephemeral white, ink, cobalt, eggshell, fox's-tail, indigo, ember, pigeon, sourdough, strawberry, moss and veal, lime.

Near the end, Goldbarth acknowledges his greatest weakness: "It's been a long poem, and many people have spoken in it, and many about Barbette, but Barbette hasn't spoken." Denying voice to the queer is no accident; it is a part of the tight world Barbette was trying to escape. . . . [Goldbarth's] failure to give more voice to Barbette is a crime—both literary and moral. If Barbette is still alive, perhaps she/he can take revenge and scratch Goldbarth's eyes out. . . .

> *Charley Shively, in a review of "Different Fleshes: A Novel/Poem," in* The American Book Review, *Vol. 4, No. 3, March-April, 1982, p. 11.*

ROBERT CORDING

[Albert Goldbarth] has that rare gift of seeing metaphor in almost any event, of discovering a poem in the most unlikely places. And, while it may be true that . . . Goldbarth's poems at times can appear as if they've been generated more from verbal dexterity than a need to be written, it might be asked: of what writer isn't this true? And, isn't the real test whether or not the poems, even the slighter ones, are informed by a generosity of imagination in touch with our human condition? After reading *Original Light: New and Selected Poems 1973-1983* . . . , it's clear that Goldbarth's poems are, as Richard Hugo put it, "always, always, human," and it's their humanness which gives them their peculiar force.

It would be too easy—and too damaging—merely to praise Goldbarth for his inventiveness, his seemingly effortless handling of a number of styles and voices. For his poems almost always involve serious concerns—the distance between what we want and have; the way memory, though it records all that is lost, has the power to cut across time and thus unify; the way symbols are made from accidental ordinary events; the way families stretch their understanding of themselves over generational time; the way historical events mirror themselves over and over. I'm not claiming that these are *new* ideas, or that the poems are good because they embody these ideas. Rather my point is that Goldbarth's poems, often dazzling in the Donne-like way they yoke disparate conceits, and almost always fearlessly playful in their approach, can mask the reasons for their being written. It's too easy to forget that for all of Goldbarth's bravura, the poems' punch lies in the way they affect us: over and over they tenderly remind us of the conditions of our humanness.

Original Light is organized thematically rather than chronologically. . . . Although the poems, as Goldbarth's note admits, weren't originally "written with this kind of ordering in mind," they not only don't suffer from it, but actually take on added dimension—the force of their focused concerns. This is especially true of section one ("**Distances**") and two ("**A Sanguinary**") where the poems read like well planned books. (The third and final section, "**Chronologues**," seems grouped, at least to me, for stylistic reasons).

As an introduction to these three sections, and to Goldbarth himself, a fine longer poem, "**The Importance of Artists' Biographies**," is placed by itself as the book's initial offering. This poem, like so many others, juxtaposes a series of seemingly disparate events. I'll name just a few, in hopes of simulating the texture of the poem: a corner of a Michelangelo painting over which Durer once painted a spider; a court lady who, looking at another "real" spider, wonders what it must have been like to see the spider Adamically, before all our information about spiders; the "real" spider in the speaker's study which becomes the word "spider" in the poem; the light waves which bring the spider both to the speaker's eyes and to the farthest stars; the relation of science fiction writing to the speed of light. Goldbarth's concern here is central to the book: though there are enormous distances in our lives—between the word on the page, the real object it signifies, and its conceptualization in the reader's mind; between a "life and a credible fiction of a life"; between objects in space or between intimate lovers—these distances may not, ultimately, be crushing. In Goldbarth's metaphor, if all light returns because the universe curves, then too, perhaps all that we imagine forms a kind of galactic gallery where nothing we've seen "can be lost." The rest of *Original Light* goes on to examine this strange paradox of familiarity and strangeness, of the way the world, our personal and familiar lives, and history all involve strange conjunctions of closeness and distance; and how it's only our repeated, error-prone imaginative attempts that yield some understanding. (pp. 91-2)

Goldbarth's poems depend almost entirely on two conditions: the accumulation of random ideas which, at some point, suddenly "click" into a pattern; and the shift in tone which usually accompanies that "click" (from a light, playful, undercutting voice . . . to a more serious and charged voice . . .). In fact, Goldbarth's mastery lies in the way he's learned to wield his pyrotechnics so that his sentiments have all the force of sentimentality, but without its affectation.

Of course, while Goldbarth's style of writing,—in which the poet is always in the poem, letting you know, playfully, that you're reading a poem,—protects the writer from sentimentality, it also risks the accusation of being a game played for the sake of cleverness. And when Goldbarth's poems fail, they do so because they remain, too largely, abstract exercises which have failed to sufficiently humanize themselves. For me, it's always the attention to details, their patient accumulation, which convince that the poem is not written for the sole purpose of drawing attention to its cleverness or its teaching of a moral lesson. (p. 93)

While I believe the thematic arrangement of *Original Light* adds strength and coherence to the book, I wish there had been some way of denoting the chronology of composition as well. I kept thinking I'd read a number of these poems in magazines recently—"**M = L/T**," "**Worlds**," "**Diagrams**," "**Distances**," "**A Theory of Wind**," "**Praise/Complaint**"—to name a few. And, if these were the "new" poems, then they suggest that Goldbarth's work has broken new territory, and has achieved that special combination of playfulness and seriousness which underlies all of his work in more profound ways than ever

before. Whatever, *Original Light* contains ten years of work which both deserves careful attention, and which will repay that attention tenfold. (p. 95)

Robert Cording, in a review of "Original Light: New and Selected Poems 1973-1983," in Carolina Quarterly, *Vol. XXXVI, No. 2, Winter, 1984, pp. 91-5.*

DIANE WAKOSKI

A selected poems by a poet not yet forty, barely thirty-five years old at publication, seems strange to me, even in this fast age of technology. Such a collection invites a retrospective view of the poet's career, as well as a comparison with other poets who are the history of any century. Thus, I approached [*Original Light: New and Selected Poems, 1973-1983*] with skepticism and doubt. And after reading it now several times over, I still feel that it is in no way the proper time in the life of Albert Goldbarth for him to have a selected poems. He is not an original. Yet. Though he is witty, intelligent, a fine craftsman, and even a very very good poet. On the other hand, this book does what a very good first book should do, or what a carefully savored second or third book, when well-edited, should do: it gives us the mind and imagination and, to the present, the scope of a new poet, one whose work is worth careful attention and study. . . .

Goldbarth's best poetry evolves a study of being, using ideas from physics and philosophy about time, distance, motion and light. In the poem from which the title is derived, "**The Importance of Artists' Biographies**" he states,

> to see, to really see,
> this creature as itself: a black-backed
> stalk-eyed sac-bellied pinch-jawed scuttler on too
> many too bristled legs. . . .

In many ways, this is the theme of the book: what seeing really is and what really seeing is. He explores light as the source of everything and like many philosophers looks for the original light, the source of everything in paradox and the paradoxes of physics. There are a number of wonderful poems in the book, particularly in the first section, titled "**Distances**," that will delight and beguile any intelligent reader. My own favorite, "**Still Lives**," indulges in imagistic description which leads to revelation after revelation of vision. . . .

I also particularly liked "**There is a Legend about a Piano That Somehow Got Flushed into the Sewers of Chicago**" which leads the reader through all of Goldbarth's imaginings on the subject of light, pianos, time and spatial history. Anyone who stays up late or eats donuts will find "**All-Nite Donuts**" irresistible ("But all of our zeroes are here/made sweet.") and if you've ever taught English you will find "**The Errors**" full of familiar desperation somehow made compassionately acceptable ("An adult does have control of the lives of young people to a certain extinct."). And "**M = L/T**" in which we see the brocade gown of a statue of the virgin eaten by moths whose wings and cocoons repeat the ruby and blue of the garment, as well as "**Distances**" with its eighth grade physics both blend the BOK (bits o knowledge) that Goldbarth stuffs his poems with and his continuing meditation about the sources of life and being.

The book is divided into three sections, and to me they are of diminishing interest. One sees the genius and brilliance of Goldbarth's mind, bringing technical knowledge together with philosophical understanding and human caring in the first section. This is continued somewhat in the second section, "**A**

Sanguinary," but these poems are all much more self-consciously about the process of being a writer, and even fine writing on the subject as found in **"The Form and Function of the Novel"** and the long exploration in **"A Sanguinary,"** start to lose me as a reader. I feel that I am being preached at, told about poetry rather than experiencing it wholly and sensuously, as I do in the first section of the book.

The third section brings me to a subject that I'd like to write a book about, one that angers me, and only because I respect Goldbarth's talent so much, and love his "real" poems so much, will I indulge myself slightly in this tirade. It is against the poems, and especially the KIND of poems found in this third section, **"Chronologues"**. They are, for the most part, dramatic monologues spoken in the voice of either actual historical persons, or persons who fit properly into historical reality. Voices from a Salem witch trial, a German archeologist and scholar of the eighteenth century, a late fourteenth century alchemist, etc. Most of the poems concern terrible human situations such as the witch trials, the Dresden bombing, or natural catastrophes.

What is my tirade? Certainly not against dramatic monologues or poems written out of historic sources per se. But rather, it is against a whole kind of poetry which I will choose to call "academic" because it is written, not out of a poet's personal experiences and miseries (or joys) but rather from a kind of armchair voyeurism which unlike speculative fiction or other immense acts of imagination, seems to me to allow the poet to take on a kind of moral omniscience, a moral smugness, and an authoritative air about things which are not his business. . . .

It is not the history, *or* the act of the imagination I am decrying. Goldbarth is among the best in doing his research and even in imagining what his characters might have said in these situations. It is the dishonesty and ultimately the lack of authenticity one has in writing about battles that are not one's own, as if they were. . . . Imagining others' holocausts always seems like, not only an act of presumption, but also an unnecessary reality. When I reach the third section of Goldbarth's book, I say, "Doesn't he have anything interesting or important in his own life to write about?" . . .

I believe in the tradition of Whitman, where the poet sings of himself and tries to understand and even bridge huge gaps through that singing. But the *Song of Myself* is 180 degrees away from [Henry Wadsworth Longfellow's] *The Song of Hiawatha*. It was simply dishonest (and, in my opinion, a bit stupid) of Longfellow to think he could present himself as understanding/identifying with American Indians. It was an excuse to indulge in preaching, do-gooding, and moralizing which looks pretentious and dishonest and wrong to us today. I would suggest that Whitman is a better model for today's poets than Longfellow. I would argue that Goldbarth has some of that Whitmanian magnificence when he honestly indulges in his real ego, his big sense of himself, and not when he tries to disguise it through historical voices or even in self-conscious discussions of writing poetry. If I could take the prerogatives of an older poet, one who has not yet had a selected poems, and has said that she will not until she is at least fifty, I would say, Sing, Sing, Sing, Albert, using your "original light," your ability "to see, to really see," which is enormous. *Original Light* is a book which leaves me with the feeling that I have found a new poet who has not yet sung an original song, but who might well if he doesn't let the dust of MFA programs bury him in **"Chronologues,"** if he allows himself to move

the distances which he already makes me feel are being suggested in his best poems.

Diane Wakoski, "The Life of Albert Goldbarth?" in
The American Book Review, *Vol. 6, No. 4, May-June, 1984, p. 8.*

MICHAEL SIMMS

Flip through any literary magazine published in the last ten years and you are bound to come across at least one poem by Albert Goldbarth. Scan the poetry shelves of any respectable bookstore in America and you will see at least one of his (by the last count) seventeen books. Despite this buccolingual persistence, Goldbarth never seems to repeat himself. Like Heraclitus, he knows you can never step into the same river twice. His personae include adolescent lovers, masochistic slaves, aphoristic fabulists, philosophical plumbers, and semi-literate students. He fashions metaphors from the deductions of historians, theologians, and physicists, integrating their arguments into poems which remain, somehow, intensely personal and concrete. His voice changes so quickly that sometimes it's hard to tell whether we are listening to a green-haired punker or the white-haired Lao-tzu. Goldbarth's poems are ambitious, unpredictable, profound, and funny.

When he was asked recently how many poems he had published in magazines, Goldbarth replied that counting the number of publications is "dangerous for a poet"; then he joked that he had far more acceptance slips than he had poems. An unfriendly critic might agree that some of his uncollected poems would have been better left in his notebooks. Collecting the poems for *Original Light* has given him an opportunity to bring together a sampling of successful pieces that represent the range of subjects and styles he has embraced over the last ten years and an opportunity to wrest a unity from that potential chaos by carefully selecting and ordering those poems. The book is made up of three long sections arranged thematically, as well as a prefatory poem, **"The Importance of Artists' Biographies,"** which introduces the recurrent themes of the book: our conceptions of time and distance, the self-consciousness of the artist, the "wise-ass jokes" that history plays. (pp. 344-45)

One of the best poems in this collection is **"The Errors,"** a four-part improvisation on a series of solecisms (*When your sad the whole world seams wrong*) adapted from the writing of students at Central YMCA Community College in Chicago. From these accidental gifts, Goldbarth embarks on a meditation about the mistakes that have determined the course of people's lives. A foreign student arrives by "errplane" to be robbed and raped on a bus. A pregnant woman takes thalidomide on her doctor's orders. A magazine editor prints Goldbarth's "rabbi" as "rabbit." Columbus dies thinking he has discovered a route to Cathay. A student writes that Columbus opened up a whole new world "when he set sail for the undies." Goldbarth uses these instances and others to argue that the errors in our language describe our random painful lives more accurately than anything we mean to say.

Goldbarth is ambitious. A typical poem might start with a domestic image, state its significance, move to a similar image drawn from astronomy, bring up, in passing, considerations of biology and history, then return to the domestic scene. Though none of his poems are as predictable as my outline makes them seem, there is a certain predictability about the way his subjects open up, attempting to find metaphysical significance in commonplace images. For this reason, I am relieved to find short, restrained poems such as **"Wings"** and **"And"** in this collection because they break away from the free-wheeling argumentative formulas that form the strategy of many of the poems. Paradoxically, the inclusion of the less ambitious poems emphasizes the ambition of the book as a whole; the smaller poems tend to make the voice more accessible, the texture less dense, the themes more apparent, and the style more varied.

Goldbarth offers his readers many gifts. Like the paintings of Jackson Pollack, Goldbarth's poems sometimes seem like great chunks of the universe, torn free and floating, not limited by the borders of art. What other contemporary poet could get away with having ale and cheddar wedges with Wordsworth, Lamb, and Coleridge, the latter asking "Who is this / *Nonsequitur* in our otherwise Smooth Grouping?"? Goldbarth has an endearing empathy for immigrants, prostitutes, visionaries, and victims, and he is forgiving of the foolishness and cruelty of the prophets and losers he describes with bizarre conceits. . . . His poems move through take, double-take, retake. His ability to see and to see again encourages us to observe the world more closely and to take courage from the small happenings of our profoundly ordinary lives. (pp. 345-46)

Michael Simms, "The Same River Twice," in Southwest Review, *Vol. 69, No. 3, Summer, 1984, pp. 344-46.*

WILLIAM LOGAN

Goldbarth's huge outpouring [represented in ***Original Light: New and Selected Poems 1973-1983***] is of course suspect in a time that legislates spareness. His imagination teems with Aristotelian possibility, however, and he clearly hates to let any opportunities go to waste. . . . The mechanistic metaphor distinguishes Goldbarth's work—he is as infatuated with science as a fourteen-year-old just introduced to physics. Few poets, perhaps unfortunately, find science quite as necessary as Goldbarth does, and of those who do I think none retains quite his innocent awe in the face of it:

> Up in a corner, a spider's spinning this
> real web that enters your world
> as a word, "web," on a page, "this" page, then
> light through a window
> lifts the spider as light lifts everything

seeable and brings it, at the same speed
it was just now brought to my eyes,
to the stars.

It is as if to say, "Gee, Pop, the light takes this image, see, and then, and then. . . ." And then, in this poem at least, come science fiction, quasar travel, planet hops. The poem must also juggle—admittedly, it is a long poem—two early Greek artists, an anecdote about Dürer, a short biography of Michelangelo, various spiders, a lover both real and imagined, the nature of time, a print by Saul Steinberg, and an asterisk. Goldbarth doesn't exploit topics so much as list them.

Goldbarth's hodgepodge organization demands too many facts and not enough flesh. His poetry is almost entirely directed toward the satisfaction of ideas (I can imagine his dog-eared *Britannica,* his tattered textbooks), but those ideas are rarely quickened—they are webs or skeletons or chandeliers whose structure can be admired or applauded, but which have little further significance. He cannot fuse the image and the information, the subject and design, and so his poems at times depend on violent juxtaposition: a Norse voyage to Vinland in 1120 and the lover leaving the poet at 11:20. When the violence works, as it does, oddly enough, in that example (the poem ends speaking of endings, and of the flat earth—"Back then they didn't have / watches to stop and so their world did"), he creates something wholly individual. Unfortunately, it doesn't always work—a longish poem about St. Augustine and pianos ends with the Saint at a urinal, "tinkling" like a piano.

None of Goldbarth's poems seems much different from any other. Each maintains a uniform voice, a uniform depth, a straight line on the oscilloscope. Even in the poems deriving from his childhood or from his father's death, the symbols are coldly manipulated. This is not a failure to feel but a failure to transmit feeling. His best poems are perhaps his dramatic monologues, when he stops being Albert Goldbarth for a moment. His cynicism is more compelling than his innocence, and the romantic effusions to which he is often susceptible seem only a nod toward a current dogma the poet acquiesces to but does not believe in. His poems are strongest when they are most resolute in their oddity. Their fierce science is proof against any easy accommodation with charm. (pp. 104-05)

William Logan, in a review of "Original Light: New and Selected Poems 1973-1983," in Poetry, *Vol. CXLV, No. 2, November, 1984, pp. 103-05.*

Richard (A.) Grayson

1951-

American short story writer.

Grayson's short fiction is characterized by his unconventional humor and imaginative, offbeat observations. In his stories Grayson examines a diverse range of topics, including popular culture, history, family relationships, and the art of writing. Although he experiments with narrative point of view and incorporates puns and gags into many of his pieces, Grayson has also written traditional, loosely autobiographical stories about growing up in a Jewish-American family in New York City.

Grayson's first collection of stories, *Disjointed Fictions* (1978), was described by Hank Malone as incorporating "a lot of Talmudic wisdom showing-up in the wise-crack format of the Marx Bros." and reflects Grayson's skillful use of parody and satire. The title story of his second book, *With Hitler in New York and Other Stories* (1979), portrays Hitler as a normal, even likable person, with only a hint of the darker side of his personality. "But In a Thousand Other Worlds," also from this volume, presents the story itself as the protagonist. Having been rejected by publishers, the story is hospitalized and its condition is diagnosed as unpublishable. The canine hero of the principal story in *Lincoln's Doctor's Dog and Other Stories* (1982) becomes a renowned lecturer and eventually a state governor. Grayson described this story as an attempt to blend topics of recent best-sellers, among them diseases, animals, and historical biographies. Another story noted for its outrageous situation is "Oh Khrushchev, My Khrushchev," included in the collection *I Brake for Delmore Schwartz* (1983). This piece features a man who is hopelessly in love with the late Soviet leader.

(See also *Contemporary Authors*, Vols. 85-88 and *Contemporary Authors New Revision Series*, Vol. 14.)

Photograph by Nguyen Van Cao. Courtesy of Richard Grayson

George William Fisher, in a review of "Disjointed Fictions," in Long Island Poetry Collective Newsletter, *October, 1978.*

GEORGE WILLIAM FISHER

So what's a person who mostly reads poetry and non-fiction doing with a book of stories? Fact is that lots of modern fiction is innovative, defiant of form, and often less self-conscious, more daring than most poetry we read. We see an evolving open form, assimilating poetic advances and rapidly transcending category. Read aloud, it even *sounds* great. In [Grayson's] *Disjointed Fictions,* things fall into place or seem to or maybe not. Richard Grayson is frequently witty, nearly always irreverent; we catch him in the midst of talking to himself, trying to put it all together, commenting on the process of writing, managing to skirt self-indulgence as he steps in and out of his stories. He tries for scope and simultaneity with mixed results, though; his connections are often tenuous, the parts sometimes refuse to link. Maybe it's intended; the book's title implies as much. Grayson is most effective when he works in direct forms. . . .

HANK MALONE

Disjointed Fictions is a funny, very readable, collection of "short fictions" written by one Richard Grayson. . . . Mr. Grayson's premise appears to be that since he cannot write a piece of sustained fiction, like a novel, that he will write a book-length manuscript, building it, piece by piece, with clever fictions, ramblings, and fragments. . . .

These literary morsels and tid-bits suggest a very fine talent, capable of much larger work; so the premise of an inability to sustain a longer fiction is, I think, clearly contrived for the purposes of doing this kind of thing; just jogging along in print, writing one's heart out in a wide ranging variety of styles and fictions, relating nearly everything and everyone (especially celebrities) to himself in some very intriguing ways. It is a wildly narcissistic narrative, on the surface; very bright, wise, very "Jewish," very "New York," and often very funny, if you enjoy "put-on" and a subtle kind of surrealism that bursts occasionally in all kinds of ironically-wise ways.

Disjointed Fictions is full of fun for a literate reader (comix readers beware), with lots of puns and pot-shots at everyone and everything. And yet, it is a strangely haunting work as well. Grayson's sense of logic is both convoluted and precise, and with this book I have discovered another fine American talent whose future work should be more than a light entertainment. Grayson is both a philosopher and a class-clown, and in *Disjointed Fictions* there is a lot of Talmudic wisdom showing-up in the wise-crack format of the Marx Bros.

> Hank Malone, in a review of *"Disjointed Fictions,"* in Smudge Review, *Winter, 1978.*

SUSAN LLOYD McGARRY

Reading Grayson is often like watching a clown on the high wire. In using "I" as a character, he walks the tightrope of pretending to be someone else. He teeters, he stumbles and finally he falls down towards the real Richard Grayson, only to be stopped, just in time, by the safety net he has already rigged. . . . He sketches the gestures of despair too grandly; it becomes funny by its extreme and by the fact of being written down. The honesty of this "I" is another illusion. In most of his stories, he creates a fiction and then exposes it as fiction, claiming to speak in his own voice, but that voice is another pretense, another fiction. Do two fictions imply a reality? as two negatives imply a positive? Are two fictions a double fiction?

The baring of the soul becomes a literary device. (pp. 88-9)

The character "I" starts to be a kind of icon. Grayson can say "I" and not worry about consistency of character. The exterior becomes caricature. Thus, he can concentrate on the internal world, the subjective reality. . . .

Many of Grayson's stories deal with famous people or at least mention them. Or sometimes popular songs or current television programs. All of this adds a taste of authenticity; we know they exist; they remind us of reality. In a way, the famous are more real than us; Grayson calls a story about the well-known, **"Real People."** . . .

He sometimes invokes the famous as one might invoke the gods. Often, in Grayson's stories, we perceive famous people in the same way that the audiences of Ancient Greece would perceive the protagonists of the classic plays. They already knew the story and the characters from myths; the dramatist had to provide the internal sense for the actions. So, today, each public personage has certain traits that are their coat-of-arms to the world. Everyone knows them but without intimacy. Grayson's "I", as well, is more a personality than he has one.

Most of his stories deal with identity, sex, or sexual confusion, or confusion about identity. . . .

His logic is that of a dream. [Consider **"Talking to A Stranger"**:]

> Zelda's mother tells her: Don't you realize that every third time you see him you end up crying? Zelda tells me this. We decide that neither of us wants our relationship to continue the way it's been going.
>
> We make a decision. We will skip every other date. . . .

How great it would be if we could skip every other date and that way skip all the problems. His humor is a different kind of cover-up. He points to the truth while denying it. (p. 89)

Many of his stories deal with problems. Actually they concern problems; they don't deal with them. One of these problems is isolation. Families live in separate mental compartments. People rarely understand each other for isolation is the other side of the importance of the individual in Grayson's work. His characters don't *fail* to understand or share; they are too involved in their mental landscape to try. Grayson's cure for isolation is to find an equivalent of the self. . . . (pp. 89-90)

But Grayson's stories often have the most depth when his characters are unlike him, at least superficially. Perhaps the distance from himself allows him to concentrate more fully on the internal. I am sometimes astounded by his ability to speak in a woman's voice, as in . . . **"Kirchbachstrasse 121, 2800 Bremen."** . . .

The delicateness . . . surprises after the hectic pace of so many of his stories.

He often writes about writing, but as a kind of bad habit which you and he are indulging. . . .

But it is to dreams that Grayson looks. Most of his stories deal in dreams. Dream, a form without an obvious rational framework, instead an underlying emotional structure that makes sense someplace past the rational part of one's brain.

His stories exist in fragments without much plot like the pieces of an ancient vase at an archaeological dig. The designs of Pan and his troupe don't make sense until you imagine the vase around which they were dancing.

By Grayson's definition of the profession, we are the psychiatrists of his stories, although we run the risk of becoming too emotionally involved with the patient. . . . (p. 90)

Dreams, mirrors, reflections, memories, dominate his work. . . . He is always seeing *through* something, prisming reality. His characters are always watching, observing, thinking, looking, but not acting. They are passive, as if the drama of their lives was really a television program. In **"Go Not to Lethe Celebrates Its 27th Anniversary: A Soap Opera Journal Special,"** Grayson tells the story of his life as if it were a soap opera with the main character being Richard Grayson as acted by Grayson Richards. Television is almost another form of dream to Grayson, although it often seems more like nightmare. . . . (pp. 90-1)

He engages the reader actively in his stories. If not through questions then through direct address. . . . His idiosyncratic plots also make the reader work. Often there is no plot per se but rather an imposed structure such as questions and answers or a listing of the events that take place in a period of time. . . .

Most of Grayson deals with modern times: in short, family, isolation, confusion, sex.

The cover of his excellent book, *Disjointed Fictions,* suggests all of Grayson to me: a hand with two fingers crossed and out of joint. The fragments out of kilter but the whole still there, and all very human. Animal, vegetable or mineral, I wish Grayson more readers.

If you liked this you will probably like Richard Grayson's stories; if you didn't like this you will probably like them anyway. (p. 91)

> Susan Lloyd McGarry, *"Twenty-Seven Statements I Could Make about Richard Grayson,"* in Aspect, *Nos. 72 & 73, 1979, pp. 88-92.*

PAGE EDWARDS

Most of [the stories in **With Hitler in New York and Other Stories**], like prose photographs by a *paparazzo,* push the modern fiction fad of using news items, the famous, the historical, the ridiculous—not always to humorous effect. . . . Little more than cleverly linked scenes, these pieces are quick, conscious attempts to dazzle—lists of characters, interviews, jokes, adolescent memories are juxtaposed randomly. The tone throughout is that of an innovative (and talented) comedian on an off night. Grayson is willing to take fictional risks, but most often the stories deflate at the end.

> *Page Edwards, in a review of "With Hitler in New York and Other Stories," in* Library Journal, *Vol. 104, No. 11, June 1, 1979, p. 1276.*

STUART SCHOFFMAN

How to get a bead on Richard Grayson . . .? Yes, his fiction is experimental, which is to say it displays only selective respect for literary conventions. . . . Genre aside, however, Grayson often resembles an astigmatic photographer who, searching desperately for the focus, twists his lens this way and that, finding a good setting only at random moments.

A telling detour en route to the stories. . . . On [the front flap of **With Hitler in New York and Other Stories**], Grayson playfully confers responsibility for Jewish-American culture (which includes Woody Allen, Philip Roth, Al Jolson and "a certain kind of vulgarity typified by the town of Woodmere, Long Island") upon the bomb-wielding anarchist who assassinated Czar Alexander II in 1881, thus provoking the wave of anti-Semitism that swept millions of Jews to America. . . .

We thus anticipate a satirist but encounter instead a coy but compulsive autobiographer with a parlorful of predictable Jewish relatives, all the way up to Great-Grandma Chaikah who watches Dinah Shore. Grayson sketches his kin with the customary mix of scorn and love, but to make them as fascinating to us as they apparently are to him, he needs to work harder. And it is not enough to portray the young artist as soap-opera protagonist, as the author does in many stories. Alexander's anarchist may have made Richard Grayson inevitable, but he did not make him special.

What is special, though, is Grayson's gift for dreaming up outrageous premises. In the title story, a frolicsome Fuehrer lands at Kennedy on a cut-rate Laker flight, sips an egg cream, pushes his American girlfriend into a swimming pool. "'You're a sadist, you know that?' Ellen says to Hitler."

Or consider **"Chief Justice Burger, Teen Idol"**:

> COMING NEXT MONTH. . .
> EVERYTHING YOU EVER WANTED TO
> KNOW ABOUT WARREN BURGER! . . .

[Next] comes a piece in which Abraham Lincoln is "a big klutz" who hates to shave and complains that he's sick of flapjacks. After reading a lame spoof of those bisexual-albino-seeks-same personal classifieds, we begin to suspect that Grayson is shaking funny ingredients together like dice; by the odds, good numbers will sometimes come up. . . .

The most affecting piece in the collection is a wry and self-knowing one entitled **"But in a Thousand Other Worlds,"** in which the main character is the story itself. Rejected by the New Yorker, then the Atlantic, the story is rushed to Coney Island Hospital, where its condition is diagnosed as hopelessly unpublishable. . . .

We are hardly surprised to . . . discover that Grayson's stories "have appeared in more than 125 literary magazines over the past seven years." Conservatively assuming one story per magazine, that comes to an average of a story every three weeks. If the author could just slow down, his talent might seem far less of a blur.

> *Stuart Schoffman, "A Parade of Jewish Relatives," in* Los Angeles Times Book Review, *July 17, 1979, p. 6.*

ETHEL SHAPIRO SARRETT

How would the Jewish residents of Brooklyn react if Hitler came to visit them today? This is the premise of the title story of . . . [**With Hitler in New York and Other Stories**]. . . . Richard Grayson has the wild sense of humor of a "Saturday Night Live" regular. Some may find his gags offensive; others will be laughing all the way to the analyst's couch.

In the title story, the narrator picks up a German chap named Hitler at Kennedy Airport and brings him back to Brooklyn to the general apathy of everyone concerned. . . . Hitler gets stoned over the Belt Parkway, translates a Yiddish song on the Brighton Beach boardwalk, and comforts the narrator when his grandfather dies. What is the reader to make of this? Is Grayson saying that the post-Holocaust generation is so jaded in 1979 that they would not care very much if another Hitler appeared? Or is he, since his Hitler is not a Nazi leader but a Bremen college student and brewery worker, trying to rid Jewish-Americans of their irrational (if understandable) antipathy to things and persons German? Grayson seems to want to have it both ways.

In a section titled "Family," Grayson gives us portraits of normal Jewish life—with a lot of *mishigass* thrown in. . . .

But there is poignancy here as well. In **"Wednesday Night at Our House,"** Grayson employs a question-and-answer format to schematize the dreary, immobilized lives of a Brooklyn family of five, each member too weak to help the others.

Grayson takes risks. Sometimes his jokes fall flat. But more often than not, the reader is dazzled by the swift, witty goings-on.

> *Ethel Shapiro Sarrett, "Saturday Night Hitler," in* Newsday, *September 9, 1979.*

PUBLISHERS WEEKLY

These 22 brief, sometimes forced, sometimes playful stories [in **Lincoln's Doctor's Dog and Other Stories**] . . . are not for everyone. Grayson is not successful in all of his experiments and the uneven quality of this collection will disappoint some. However, this writer of stories is not afraid to take risks, not a bad quality, and he can be very funny indeed. Try **"Here at Cubist College,"** an entertaining spoof of the academic world, or the amusing title story in which Sparky, Lincoln's doctor's dog, becomes a successful politician and lecturer. In quite another vein, **"I, Eliza Custis"** tells the story of Washington's granddaughter, and in other tales Grayson writes of the '60s and '70s and being young in New York. Grayson has many voices, plays many roles in this collection, but he seems to be a versatile, interesting experimenter with promise for the future.

A review of "Lincoln's Doctor's Dog and Other Stories," in Publishers Weekly, *Vol. 221, No. 15, April 9, 1982, p. 42.*

NICHOLAS J. LOPRETE, JR.

Despite my initial reservations regarding this volume when it reached me, I must confess I like Richard Grayson and his work. . . .

[The twenty-two fictions in *Lincoln's Doctor's Dog and Other Stories*] display a versatility which commands attention. And they are very much in the American grain—that vein of autobiography which has been a constant from the beginning of our literary history down to the confessional mode of the recent past. The title-tale, which is certainly captivating, pretends to be the biography of Lincoln's doctor's puppy who grows up to be elected to a state governorship and achieves fame as a lecturer. Grayson can parody human excess and human frailty, parent-child relationships, and recreate a 1960's scene with poignancy. There is even a dazzling memoir of George Washington's granddaughter. And in **"Diarrhea of a Writer,"** Grayson exposes that pride and pain which are the nutrients of a writer's growth. The questions he had wanted to ask Saul Bellow . . . all fade when the Nobel Laureate tells Grayson, "I'll look for you."

Richard Grayson has been found, at least by this reader, and found-out, too. From the evidence he is serious and comic, charming, given to outrageous puns, and a sharp-eyed observer of and participant in Life's absurdities.

Nicholas J. Loprete, Jr., in a review of "Lincoln's Doctor's Dog & Other Stories," in Best Sellers, *Vol. 42, No. 2, May, 1982, p. 47.*

SMALL PRESS REVIEW

Lincoln's Doctor's Dog & Other Stories is a collection of 22 fictions by Richard Grayson, all funny, all playful and all engaged in the shift from persona to person, from voice to voice that characterizes the wit of experimental fiction. Grayson achieves some startling effects in **"A Sense of Porpoise"** in which a porpoise replaces a boy's dead father. The situation produces the pun, but also some fine speculations on the relationship of child to parent. **"Why Van Johnson Believes in ESP"** has the character of both parody and the play that is at the heart of new narrative technique. The complications of narrative voice become even greater, often funnier, sometimes more frightening in the autobiographical stories about growing up in New York in the late 60s and early 70s. (pp. 8-9)

A review of "Lincoln's Doctor's Dog & Other Stories," in Small Press Review, *Vol. 14, No. 9, September, 1982, pp. 8-9.*

IVAN GOLD

[The title *I Brake for Delmore Schwartz*] may have had life as a bumper sticker before it was placed on this collection of 15 short stories, all previously published in little magazines. . . . The stories generally revolve around a chap named Richard Grayson. This character . . . is a writer from Brooklyn, uneasy in his Jewishness and very concerned with the esthetics and mechanics of turning things into fiction, and fictions into things. . . .

Mr. Grayson's stories are full of insanity, nutty therapists, cancerous relatives, broken homes, fiction workshops, youthful theatricals at Catskill bungalow colonies and the morbid wizardry of telephone-answering machines. Writing at less than the top of [his form, the writer appears as a sensibility] . . . in search of a story, [a grab bag] . . . of meaningful memory, acute perceptions and mordant social comment, which . . . [he does not seem to be] able to sift through and transform into art. Yet now and again for Mr. Grayson the shticks become inspired, as in a two-page meditation on the letter "Y" (**"Y/Me"**) in the present volume and in the story **"Inside Barbara Walters"** in *Disjointed Fictions* (1981).

The histories of some of Mr. Grayson's other characters, like that of Saul in **"That's Saul, Folks,"** are artfully telescoped and given equal valence with the history of the times. That is to say, where were *you*, reader, when the lights went out for the city of New York? In **"Is This Useful? Is This Boring?"** fictional beings named Joyce Carol Oates and Donald Barthelme square off over the issue of the fragment as a viable literary form, but then they patch up their differences. The title story threatens for a while to turn into a well-made story about two friends involved with the same woman, and both fearful, in the computer age, of continuing to lead the hand-to-mouth artistic life, but it pulls back just in time. If one is not blessed with a gift for extended narrative (a problem Mr. Grayson faces squarely in **"How Not To Write a Novel"** in *Lincoln's Doctor's Dog and Other Stories,* 1982), then why not go for the sprint? And in a 24-page pamphlet, *Eating at Arby's* (1982), Mr. Grayson mastered, or invented, a style equidistant between Hemingway's short stories and Dick and Jane, a feat probably useful and, at that length, far from boring.

In **"Nice Weather, Aren't We?"** in the present collection, the grandfather of the character Richard Grayson has been leafing through an anthology of Jewish stories put together by a famous writer named "Ballow." "He looked at me conspiratorially. 'Personally,' he said, 'I prefer your little antidotes.'" Others may, too. (p. 29)

Ivan Gold, "Uneasy in Brooklyn," in The New York Times Book Review, *August 14, 1983, pp. 12, 29.**

ROBIN HEMLEY

Here is an imaginative and engaging writer who breaks all the conventions of contemporary fiction with a certain devilish relish. Grayson gets away with everything your Writing Teachers told you not to do [in *I Brake for Delmore Schwartz*]. His stories are self-conscious, fragmentary, and biggest sin of them all, usually plotless. But we forgive Richard Grayson all his sins, mostly because he is so imaginative and clever, and he has such a strong, compelling voice. Totally unafraid to take risks, Grayson tells stories from the points of view of a man in love with Nikita Khrushchev, a man obsessed with the fact that he looks like Delmore Schwartz, and even from the perspective of the cold that killed our ninth President, William Henry Harrison. Personification. Another writing sin.

At various points in his narratives, Grayson dares you to read on: "You really want to read this?" he asks at the beginning of **"Nice Weather, Aren't We?"** "You don't have to, just to humor me. It's all right. I know I'm a nice guy, I don't have to prove anything to you . . ." With a beginning like this, my first reaction is, "You're right. I don't have to read this," and I almost put down the story as my nagging little Writing Teachers would have me do. But Writing Teachers are a little like your conscience; they're meant to be ignored. And Grayson's voice helps you ignore them. When I started this story, I thought it would be my least favorite, but now I think it's one of his best. He keeps setting you up in this story, telling you he only writes true stories, that everything he says is true, and then destroying each one of his illusions. And each time he does it, you masochistically want him to go on manipulating you. He manipulates you with such a flair and with such whimsical details that you can't hold it against the guy. . . . (pp. 123-24)

Yes, Grayson's concerns are metafictional, but he's not just another Coover, Barth, or Donald Barthelme. Though Grayson isn't quite as polished as these writers, he's got something else over them. He's not simply concerned with breaking stylistic conventions and letting things like character fall by the wayside. Grayson's stories, however wild, are humane. And the first person functions as a well-rounded, independent character in Grayson's work, often taking on a confessional attitude.

The titles in this collection are often as whimsical as the stories they describe: **"Oh Khrushchev, My Khrushchev," "Slightly Higher in Canada," "Y/Me," "That's Saul, Folks."** Still, as much as I am engaged by Richard Grayson's writing, I feel a bit like someone reporting on an underachieving genius. Sometimes his rule-breaking doesn't work, and his stories are a little *too* spare, fragmented, and self-indulgent. At these times I'd like to go up to Mr. Grayson, shake him by the shoulders, and say, "Get serious, stop having so much fun. Now let's see what you can *really* do." . . . (p. 124)

One thing's for certain, though. Grayson always hits the mark as far as voice is concerned. Few contemporary American writers have such a compelling, intriguing voice, totally believable and unabashedly contrived at the same time. (pp. 124-25)

> *Robin Hemley, in a review of "I Brake for Delmore Schwartz," in* Another Chicago Magazine, *No. 15, 1984, pp. 123-25.*

JAIMY GORDON

Eating at Arby's and *Disjointed Fictions* clamor for laughs before one ever opens the covers. True, *I Brake for Delmore Schwartz* is a dignified volume, except for the title and the enclosed red bumper sticker that spells it out in large letters. But the flamingo-pink cover of *Eating at Arby's* announces that Richard Grayson ran for Town council lately in Davie, Florida, with a campaign promise to give horses the vote; and the back of *Disjointed Fictions* reports that he was once a candidate for the Democratic Vice-Presidential nomination. Both books offer columns of testimonials on Grayson's work. . . . [The] critics are, on the whole, somewhat puzzled by Grayson. . . . They invoke Steve Martin, "Saturday Night Live," and the muse of stand-up comedy to explain Grayson, though a certain uneasiness lingers between the blurbs: If this is "Saturday Night Live," can it be literature? . . .

This willingness to be a public clown—or, more accurately, to present the appearance of a wistful nobody scribbling away in private who occasionally bursts out as a farcical publicist, exposing himself before the world—continues unabated inside Grayson's prolific but never prolix fictions. The several strains of his humor occur in more or less varied combinations according to the story, and I much prefer those loosely segmented

chains of association in the first person (happily, two thirds of the stories in both *Disjointed Fictions* and *I Brake for Delmore Schwartz* fall into this category), where all his mannerisms exist side by side, to his more symmetrical and abstract pieces; for, in the absence of first person, Grayson's prose loses much of its charm and is shown to be a rather blunt and inelastic tool. Grayson is not a graceful stylist, and as soon as the expression of a personality (or the illusion of this) disappears from them, his inventions and satires move on leaden feet. This is particularly true of *Eating at Arby's,* whose conceptual plan may sound comic, but which, as literary experience—that is, as something to read—is all but insufferable. Manny and Zelda speak the same stiff, uncontracted idiom with which Dick and Jane stupefied us in second grade. . . . [This] little book has two virtues, of a sort: it does not take a subtle intellect to feel the point of its satire, so that Grayson's contempt, which almost any dolt can share, is ultimately reassuring; and it is all over in twenty-four pages.

The variegated texture of the first-person narratives that most engage his admirers and baffle his critics is challenging to describe, since it is through juxtaposition that these deliberately unshapely tales achieve their effects. There is a strain of soap-operatic exhibitionism in Grayson; sown through *I Brake for Delmore Schwartz* are revelations of an embarrassingly personal nature, often maudlin, often clearly untrue. . . . A commonplace Jewish East Coast extended family, divided between New York and Miami and subject to cancer and bar mitzvahs, is put to use in many of Grayson's stories, variously as the basis for anecdotes that would not go over badly on the borscht circuit . . . or for highly suspect pathos. In one story in *I Brake for Delmore Schwartz,* the narrator's sister has drowned; in another, leukemia has snatched her away; in *Disjointed Fictions* (**"Escape from the Planet of the Humanoids"**), a sister is still tirelessly dying; the reader is instructed to "Feel this:"

> The pain of frustration that a man feels when he is trying to write a sentence about how a character feels at his sister's funeral and can only come up with this fragment: *Better her than me. . . .*

The thread of the pathetic family saga intertwines with another highly characteristic one that I will call the lament of the shlemiel in the creative writing workshop. He's no longer in it, of course, but it has left its mark. This narrator worries about the quality of his fictions, checking them against mumble-mouthed platitudes of the craft; and these are travestied evenhandedly whether they arise from the post-modernist school or the Famous Writers' School. . . . [The] voice disintegrates into a muddle of pomposity and self-pity: as a writer who misrepresents people as characters and otherwise can "get away with murder," the narrator is "a pretty powerful person"; well, no, he says, actually he writes out of a neurotic need for attention; in fact, he writes to get revenge on some Italian kids who once called him "Irving"; then the narrator changes his mind . . . —maybe he didn't learn anything in college after all. So much for the tenets of the experimentalists. . . .

This is the Grayson manner in endless variations: alternate strains of impudent posturing that breaks down in self-parody, equally disingenuous confessions of the writer's ineptitude; and, withal, punchlines and puns that he will labor for many paragraphs to set up, like, "I never promised you a prose artist," and, "Fiction's no stranger than Ruth." All these parts are suffused with the appealing confessional anxiety of a small-time writer scrabbling against odds and without much concern for his dignity to get a little renown for himself. (p. 21)

It seems worth noting that Grayson perceives his readership, so far, more clearly than his readership perceives him. There is a sound precedent for that loose-jointedness of his fictions that so confounds his critics, a venerable one that reaches back far beyond the mimetic and novelistic bias that is in fact a middle-class parvenue in the world of letters. It is the satiric tradition of Erasmus and Rabelais, of Diderot, of Swift and Sterne and Peacock, and one may find in this tradition, as in Grayson, the shape of a miscellany founded on loose associations of ideas, frequently with humble apologies from the author; idiosyncratic asides, digressions, and non sequiturs; catalogues and inventories; structures of information borrowed from extra-literary domains of the language; dialogues, patterns of query and response, and other instances of the unexpected, the undignified, the fitful, the intellectually pretentious breaking down into parody. But the brevity of Grayson's fictions is his own design, based on a just though severe estimate of the attention span of a literary peer group he understands all too well. . . . The narrator of *I Brake for Delmore Schwartz* walks the streets of New York, Citicard in hand—the same streets trod by Isaac Bashevis Singer and by the shade of the departed Schwartz—asking himself if it wouldn't be smarter to take a course in computers for a guaranteed fourteen grand a year, than to perist in this thankless manner of living.

Perhaps the persistent confusion about where to place Grayson in the contemporary literary scheme is owing to the imperfect self-knowledge of that public of which Richard Grayson is the jester. We—and I mean you and I—live in a strange literary economy where most writers between the ages of twenty-five and forty accept the lot of the sort-of-published, the semi-solvent, the great unread, against the backdrop of an age of media super-celebrities; so that we are unable to escape the evidence of our under-appreciation though fully aware of the ludicrousness of its contrary. Richard Grayson constructs a literary persona out of just this predicament. He is a satirist and parodist so timely that his brothers and sisters may not yet discern themselves in his mirror. Certainly our hapless group that writes and studies writing and cogitates about writing but cannot know its audience deserves its own comedian, if it can learn—as Richard Grayson has—to laugh at itself. (pp. 21-2)

Jaimy Gordon, "From Our House to Bathos," in The American Book Review, *Vol. 7, No. 1, November-December, 1984, pp. 21-2.**

Peter Handke

1942-

Austrian dramatist, novelist, memoirist, scriptwriter, short story writer, essayist, and poet.

The recipient of the 1973 Georg Büchner Prize, Handke is regarded as a major German-language writer and an important contributor to the international postmodern movement in literature. His best-known play, *Kaspar* (1968), is considered a masterpiece of post-World War II German literature. Influenced by the philosopher Ludwig Wittgenstein, Handke focuses in his works on the relationship between language and reality. One of the major themes of his early drama is the inability of language to convey reality. This is illustrated in what Handke calls his *Sprechstücke,* or "speak-ins," which lack plot, characterization, and dramatic structure. Instead of dialogue, the actors engage in cliché-ridden, fragmented monologues designed to make the audience aware of how language can distort reality and impede true expression. As Handke turned increasingly from drama to fiction during the 1970s, his focus also shifted from an emphasis on the problems of language to an exploration of its potential.

Early in his career, Handke gained a reputation as Europe's *enfant terrible* when he challenged members of *Gruppe 47,* which included some of Germany's most established authors, on their use of dramatic and fictional conventions. In his first *Sprechstücke, Publikumsbeschimpfung* (1966; *Offending the Audience),* which became a great success in Germany, Handke uses minimalist techniques similar to those employed by Samuel Beckett. This play consists of four speakers who inform the audience that there will not be a dramatic performance. The speakers alternately compliment, insult, and mock the audience, culminating in a crescendo of abuse directed toward both the audience and the conventions of theater. Stanley Kauffmann stated: "The power of [*Offending the Audience*] is in its calm, ruthless progression. . . . The effect is like an acid bath to eat away the corrosions of cultural torpor, to reveal the mind-pattern that produced them."

In *Kaspar,* his first full-length play, Handke is concerned with the role of language in defining an individual's social identity. The play was inspired by the true story of a teenage boy who was found wandering the streets of Nuremberg in 1828. The boy had been isolated and had little knowledge of language. While this story has been reworked several times by significant German writers, Handke's version is an abstract parable about the implicit value of language. Kaspar is tutored by four off-stage voices who attempt to condition him to the rules and values of society. Handke portrays Kaspar, and humankind in general, as trapped between the necessity of language as a means for expression and the ways in which language is used to restrict and distort individual identity.

Handke considers *Der Ritt über den Bodensee* (1970; *The Ride Across Lake Constance*) to be the culmination of his previous dramatic works. In this play he denies any mimetic relationship between the drama onstage and real life. For example, the actors use their actual names onstage, rather than assuming fictitious identities, and the props simply represent props on a stage. Through repeated use of non sequiturs and alogical se-

© Jerry Bauer

quences, Handke confuses expected correlations between language, objects, and action.

Handke's first two novels, *Die Hornissen* (1966; *The Hornets*) and *Der Hausierer* (1967; *The Peddler*), like his *Sprechstücke,* investigate the connections between language, reality, and perception. His third novel, *Die Angst des Tormanns beim Elfmeter* (1970; *The Goalie's Anxiety at the Penalty Kick*), was his first work of fiction to draw significant attention. This book involves a former soccer player who leaves his job as a construction worker under the assumption that he has been fired and murders a woman for no apparent reason. *Die Stunde der wahren Empfindung* (1975; *A Moment of True Feeling*) centers on an Austrian press attaché residing in Paris whose mundane life is suddenly upset by a series of crises involving his wife, daughter, and mistress. *Die linkshändige Frau: Erzählung* (1976; *The Left-Handed Woman*) concerns a thirty-year-old woman who suddenly becomes adamant about ending her marriage and beginning life on her own. These three works focus on the subjective consciousness of the protagonists and explore themes related to language. Handke creates a surreal atmosphere in which the characters attempt to understand their inexplicable actions and establish self-identity. These novels have generally been well received, and several critics have compared them to works by Franz Kafka and Alain Robbe-Grillet.

Handke has also written several nonfiction works. *Wunschloses Unglück* (1972; *A Sorrow Beyond Dreams*) is a memoir he wrote during the months following his mother's suicide. In addition to recalling events in her life, Handke also addresses the dilemma of balancing factual details with fictional technique in order to give literary and universal significance to his mother's life while preserving her dignity as an individual. *Das Gewicht der Welt* (1977; *The Weight of the World*) is a journal of observations and anecdotes that Handke kept from 1975 to 1977. The brief entries in this journal offer a minimalist portrait of Handke's personal life and his artistic ideals.

Slow Homecoming (1985) consists of three novellas that were originally published separately in German: *Langsame Heimkehr* (1979), *Die Lehre der Sainte-Victoire* (1980), and *Kindergeschichte* (1981). The first section of the English translation, "The Long Way Around," details the odyssey of a European man, self-exiled in Alaska, who journeys across the United States on his way home. This story has been interpreted as a metaphor of Handke's artistic development from a maverick suspicious of literary conventions to an established artist concerned with reconstructing form and meaning. The second section, "The Lesson of Mont Sainte-Victoire," is both an essay concerning the conception of the first piece and a meditation on art using Paul Cézanne as a model. The final section, "Child Story," presents a realistic account of a divorce and the father's difficulties in raising his daughter by himself. Although this last piece adheres to literary conventions, critics note that Handke continues to seek structures capable of revitalizing literature and effectively communicating his ideas. June Schlueter suggests that "Handke's interests now lie less in the limitations of language than in its possibilities."

(See also *CLC*, Vols. 5, 8, 10, 15 and *Contemporary Authors*, Vols. 77-80.)

STANLEY KAUFFMANN

[In *Kaspar and Other Plays*, a] fascinating and distinctive theatrical talent from abroad makes its American debut on paper.... [His] full-length play *Kaspar* is published here with two short plays [*Offending the Audience* and *Self-Accusation*], and they reveal that Handke has his own clear voice and vision.

His plays are difficult to describe: there are no stories and no characters in the usual sense. The lines (in translation) mesh like gears, and the cumulation is not only progressive in the usual way, it is also a tensile structure of contradictions. The *whole* is all.

The two short pieces are called *Sprechstücke*, which is translated as "speak-ins." The first, *Offending the Audience*, calls for four speakers who have no roles, only a good deal of material which they are asked to divide among themselves equally. They bid us welcome, then proceed to tell us what to expect in the piece and what not to expect; they anatomize patterns and formulas in theater-going and theater conventions, they anatomize the audience's delegation of responsibility to safe, aloof representatives, they tell us our tiny secrets so convincingly that they can command us to blink or to swallow, or not to blink or swallow, having broken down our resistance and privacy by being us. Then the speakers proceed to offend us, as a means of fiercest communication: excoriating us from

every angle—political, sexual, social, ethical, hypochondriacal. One by one they cut off our escape hatches, our solace that the epithets don't apply to us; sooner or later some epithets come along that do apply to any one of us. After a crescendo of abuse, the speakers again quietly bid us welcome, the curtains close, and roaring applause is piped in through loud speakers.

The power of the piece is in its calm, ruthless progression, its arrogance and its humility. (The excoriation ends with the term "fellow-humans.") The effect is like an acid bath to eat away the corrosions of cultural torpor, to reveal the mind-patterns that produced them.... (p. 19)

The second *Sprechstück*, called *Self-Accusation*, is for two speakers, male and female, and is a kind of middle ground between the first piece, in which speakers deal with the audience, and the third, in which speakers deal with another figure on stage. Here the speakers' subject is themselves, an "I" composed of both of them, male and female, who proceeds from the sentence "I came into the world" through the acquisition of awareness, physical abilities, moral education and remission, habits, self-doubts, to the conclusion:

> I am not what I was. I was not what I should
> have been. I did not become what I should have
> become. I did not keep what I should have kept.
>
> I went to the theater. I heard this piece. I spoke
> his piece. I wrote this piece.

Kaspar, the major play in the book, is based on the idea—not the story—of Kaspar Hauser.... Kaspar was a boy of sixteen who suddenly appeared in the streets of Nuremberg one day in 1828, without a word of any language and with no name.... There is no reference to the story in Handke's play, no historical setting; the idea is used only as a metaphor of delayed "birth."

Most of the play is printed in double columns: one column for Kaspar's actions and words, the second for the (simultaneous) words of the "prompters"—at least three speakers who are never seen and whose voices, says Handke, may be pre-recorded. Those voices relate to Kaspar as teacher, chorus, censor, mocker, torturer—creating a largeness in which he is invisibly contained. Kaspar arrives with only one sentence in his mouth, which he repeats frequently: "I want to be a person like somebody else was once." Through the course of sixty-five brief sections, the prompters educate him in speech and cognitions, deliver him from the womb of relative wordlessness into the world of words, and their consequences.... There is also an intermission during which Handke suggests that fragments of speeches by presidents and popes and by writers and poets at official functions should be piped over loudspeakers into the lobby and even out into the street. He supplies a possible text.

This last suggests Ionesco, but it is the only section that does suggest him: Handke does not generally work with a mosaic of banalities to depict horror. Artaud, too, might seem nearby because of the attacks on traditional theater and the air of torment that hangs over these works; but Handke renounces neither literature nor psychology, nor the culture that contains them: he is working *through* that culture as through a cavern or a tunnel. It is Beckett, I think, who has been strongly influential on Handke, but not *Waiting for Godot*—with which *Kaspar* has been compared abroad: rather two novels, *The Unnamable* and *How It Is*. In those two books Beckett moved from volubility to painful broken gasps; Handke reverses that order, but the theme is similar: there is no way to be conscious without being conscious of the agonies of consciousness.

Handke's dramatic technique seems to me less related to *Godot* than to *Play,* interwoven and polyphonic in verbal structure, rather than serially progressive. All three of the plays in Handke's book present marvelous opportunities for directors and actors who have eyes and ears and imagination and courage. . . . (pp. 19, 30-1)

There will be more to be said of Handke as these plays are produced and as more work of his is translated. Meanwhile, the good news is that we have a new dramatist of genuine significance, who's very much a product of his age but who has found his own way to reach the bright burning point at which existence begins; to see how terrible and precious that point is; and who has the gift to put his vision in theatrical modes that cry out for performance. (p. 31)

> *Stanley Kauffmann, in a review of "Kaspar and Other Plays," in* The New Republic, *Vol. 162, No. 9, February 28, 1970, pp. 19, 30-31.*

FRANK CONROY

The Goalie's Anxiety at the Penalty Kick is, for the most part, straight descriptive prose. There is no narrator, no direct intrusion of the author's voice to distract the reader from the flow of events. The personal language of Handke the playwright is supplanted by the impersonal language of Handke the novelist.

"When Joseph Bloch, a construction worker who had once been a well-known soccer goalie, reported for work that morning, he was told that he was fired." The overt form of *The Goalie's Anxiety at the Penalty Kick* is a detailed, almost meticulous account of Bloch's experiences during the following week or so.

In simple prose, which appears at first to be exclusively concerned with facts, Handke creates a central character whose banality arouses our curiosity. "In the evening he left the hotel and got drunk." We are told no more because it's just that simple. He eats grapes and spits out the skins. He goes to the movies with childlike seriousness. We wonder why Handke watches him so carefully. (p. 5)

It is at precisely the moment one begins to wonder if the author is on a private trip and if the book will be no more than another esthetic manifesto. . . . It is at just that moment that Handke introduces a totally surprising development (not to be given away here) which alters not only our stance towards Bloch but our expectations of the book itself, which we suddenly realize is about more than its hero.

Bloch is crazy and becomes crazier. His disintegration parallels certain suspenseful elements in the plot, and the book can be read as a thriller. Beyond that, it is an ambitious tour de force in which Handke deals with the interrelationships of man, external reality and time.

Bloch understands little about his situation, which pricks the reader to the exhilarating task of figuring it out for himself. Behind Bloch is reality, the impersonal power contained in the flow of events. It is not the banal events themselves he fears but the inescapable relentlessness of their arrival, one after another, in the stream of time. Handke's achievement is that he contains a theme of such abstractness in a naturalistic novel. The symbolic final paragraph, in which 28 words bear as much

weight as they might in the most closely worked modern poetry, sums up the book so brilliantly one is tempted to think Handke had the image first and went backwards to write a book capable of supporting it. Not that it makes much difference.

Handke is an artist of rare talent and serious intent. Except for the use of surprise—as stunningly successful in this book as in his plays—*The Goalie's Anxiety at the Penalty Kick* employs fresh techniques which enlarge our sense of his special intelligence. (pp. 5, 22)

> *Frank Conroy, in a review of "The Goalie's Anxiety at the Penalty Kick," in* The New York Times Book Review, *May 21, 1972, pp. 5, 22.*

RICHARD LOCKE

Peter Handke's novel [*The Goalie's Anxiety at the Penalty Kick*] is first cousin to Robbe-Grillet's *The Voyeur*—it, too, details the psychotic disorientation of a murderer and spends a deliberately agonizing amount of time tonelessly describing his obsessive, depersonalized perceptions of reality. But *The Goalie's Anxiety at the Penalty Kick* has none of the elegant, tantalizing bordello gamesmanship of Robbe-Grillet's recent books. Peter Handke is a very clever, cold, unrelenting fellow. No French games for him. Throughout his novel—as in all his work—one feels the gray scholastic influence of such word-philosophers as Kant and Wittgenstein and of the Jesuit seminarians and law professors whom he had known as a student in Austria.

For Mr. Handke's subject is always the relationship of language and reality. He regards language as a kind of plastic coating we cover the world with—a rigid, distorting but comforting smooth and solid substance that keeps everything and everybody in his place: epistemologically, socially, psychologically. All of Mr. Handke's works are attempts to cut into this plastic coating and peel it away in long, purposely boring, repetitive strips of words—until the audience or reader is made intensely, unbearably conscious of the fundamentally arbitrary connections between words and things, until the linguistic mucilage that holds the world and our minds together crumbles and we discover that what we thought was a plastic coating is in fact the only substance, the only order, there is.

What is impressive about *The Goalie's Anxiety at the Penalty Kick* is that these abstract thoughts are conveyed through an apparently simple, realistic story and style. The novel follows a few days in the life of a one-time professional soccer goalie who thinks he's been fired from a construction job, murders a girl he's picked up and then hides out in a small border town awaiting the police. But this description of the book as a thriller doesn't capture the deliberately exasperating experience of reading it. Mr. Handke puts us so close to the surface of his hero's mind that we never get any relief: there's no past time or familiar psychology or stylistic charm or author's intrusion to fill in any depth or give any color. We are reading a facsimile of the mental processes of a man in whom the conventional, "normal," "natural" epistemological mechanisms have broken down. . . .

At the very end of the novel Mr. Handke supplies us with a perfect symbolic description of the book itself: "If you looked at the goal-keeper [throughout a soccer game, instead of looking at the runners] it seemed as if you had to look cross-eyed. It was like seeing somebody walk toward a door and instead of looking at the man you looked at the doorknob. It made your head hurt, and you couldn't breathe properly any more."

This is exactly the hero's state of mind and it is the reader's too as he goes through the book. This is hardly a pleasant experience, nor is it meant to be other than a disquieting, vivid lesson about language, about reality. Unlike such comparable American avant-garde writers as Joseph McElroy or John Ashbery, Peter Handke is nearly without an emotion beside esthetic and philosophical curiosity. He is brilliant, ingenious and uncongenial—a bit like cod liver oil: unpleasant but presumably good for you.

> Richard Locke, "A Literary Troublemaker," in The New York Times, *June 8, 1972, p. 45.*

CLIVE BARNES

The more I see and read of Peter Handke the more and more ready I am to accept the common European view that he is one of the most important young playwrights of our time. This was reinforced by seeing [*Kaspar*]. . . .

This is in no sense a play in the ordinary, or even the extraordinary, sense. There is always the lingering suspicion that Handke might be playing a very elaborate practical joke on the audience. Indeed to appreciate the play at all—especially the beginning—requires a certain act of faith on the part of the audience. And yet just as, say, it is very evident that Jackson Pollock was not merely scribbling haphazardly on canvas, or that Merce Cunningham is only joking when he means to be, so it is with Handke. The man is an original artist. . . .

The play appears to be about two things. First, how a human being can adapt to a hostile environment. And, second, how we become what we speak—how language has a life and power of its own quite distinct from the things its words, as it were, symbolize.

Mr. Handke himself calls his play "speech torture," and that, people should be warned, is a pretty apt description of certain aspects of it. For the first 10 minutes or so—perhaps longer—Kaspar, who collapses onto the stage like a disarticulated puppet, says nothing but one sentence. The sentence is: "I want to be a person like somebody once was." He repeats this with dozens of nuances and varieties of expression. But it is still less than stimulating.

However at times, not often perhaps, boredom can be a legitimate means of artistic expression—it can make a point that nothing else can. And slowly Mr. Handke's play is revealed to us. Kaspar spurred by mysterious figures, called the Prompters, eventually acquires control over himself and mind.

After the intermission . . . the Prompters become surrogate Kaspars, looking like Kaspar, dressed like Kaspar, and presumably representing the mature Kaspar's past. But the mature Kaspar is not all that mature. He ponders on pain and violence, and also on the poetry and inner motivations of language. It is a strange, chaotic play that never quite entertains, but still stimulates and provokes. . . .

This rewarding . . . production will appeal most to those specifically interested in the future rather than the past of the theater. It is aggressively avant-garde, and "No, No, Nanette" it isn't. Yet it does have its own special excitements.

> Clive Barnes, "Handke's 'Kaspar' Is Staged in Brooklyn," in The New York Times, *February 16, 1973, p. 26.*

MARTIN GOTTFRIED

[*Kaspar*] is remarkable drama. But Handke is intellectual rather than artistic, intellectual in a particularly German way and, ironically, typical of the postwar German writers whom he lambasted when first scrambling to notoriety and success several years ago.

But unlike his early works (*Offending the Audience, My Foot My Tutor*), *Kaspar* is accessible, direct and pointed. Though early on it also uses fragmentary language as an attack on conventional reasoning, the play goes on to show what Handke had really been driving at—the fiction of orderliness that he feels has been used to give a bad name to a more natural chaos. In short, the author is an intellectual primitivist. (pp. 309-10)

Handke has thrown [Kaspar] to the modern social scientists to demonstrate that civilizing is really a conditioning process; our ordering of human life an enslavement to rote procedures of thought; our sense of logic and reason a series of preconditioned responses. . . .

Handke's condemnation of thinking patterns and reflex logic; his hatred for scientific thought conditioning; his disrespect of educational systems, human government and all aspects of ordering human life are, of course, variations on Aldous Huxley, George Orwell and so on. His extension of their visions into a general defense of anarchy is too broad to be taken seriously, and his own intellectualism makes his argument self-contradictory. In a way, *Kaspar* smells of excessive and repetitive thinking, yet it does have a rhythmic power and it does create a warm, lovable, innocent, Wozzeck-like victim in Kaspar. Its dramatic style is a combination of absurdism and German Expressionism, both of them now slightly dated but, in this case, still effective, and Handke's use of four extra Kaspars is a striking device. . . .

But *Kaspar* remains a play by a thinker rather than an artist, not to mention having an exceptionally weak second act. And, even still, it is remarkable and stimulating and, as theater, visually extraordinary. (p. 310)

> Martin Gottfried, in a review of "Kaspar," in Women's Wear Daily, *February 16, 1973. Reprinted in* New York Theatre Critics' Reviews, Vol. XXXIV, No. 8, Week of April 9, 1973, pp. 309-10.

MICHAEL WOOD

We have heard a good deal, from Thomas Mann as well as from John Barth and Harold Bloom, about the lateness of the modern artist, and no doubt the sensible response to such a proposition is to ask who is holding the watch. Who sets the time for these feasts or lessons or performances which are always ending just when our representatives arrive? But there is a form of lateness which is familiar to us all. It is possible, for example, to fall in love and find the language you need already in use, shabby and dog-eared from misapplication, and there is a celebrated passage in *Madame Bovary* where Flaubert, irritated by a character who doesn't understand that clichés may reflect the most passionate sincerity, allows himself the sort of complaint we normally see only in his letters: . . .

> As if the fullness of feelings did not sometimes spill out through the emptiest of metaphors, since no one, ever, can give the exact measure of his needs, or ideas, or sorrows, and since human speech is like a cracked cauldron on which we beat out tunes for dancing bears,

when we wish to attract the sympathy of the
stars. . . .

A great part of the gift of Peter Handke, a much-acclaimed
young Austrian novelist and playwright, lies in his sensitivity
to this situation. Yesterday's lyrics are today's advertisements,
and when the central character in Handke's novel *A Moment
of True Feeling* crosses the Pont Mirabeau in Paris, he recalls
the obligatory line from Apollinaire: *"Sous le pont Mirabeau
coule la Seine / Et nos amours / Faut-il qu'il m'en sou-
vienne. . . ."* But he is too late. A poster describing high-rise
apartment buildings is there before him, saying: "Seen from
the Pont Mirabeau, Paris is a poem." . . .

"We behave as if being alone were a problem," Handke says
in *Nonsense and Happiness*, a book of rambling meditative
poems. "Perhaps it's an *idée fixe.*" Perhaps it is the *idée fixe*
of a culture which has managed to package even alienation, to
turn it into the necessary accouterment of any educated, self-
respecting, disaffected middle-class life. . . .

He knows, of course, all about Flaubert's cracked cauldron.
His great successes—*A Sorrow Beyond Dreams, Short Letter,
Long Farewell,* both reprinted, along with the more programmatic and less satisfactory *Goalie's Anxiety at the Penalty Kick,*
in *Three by Peter Handke*—are the crisp and mournful tunes
he gets out of it. He knows that one can exploit a packaged
despair even as one complains about the packaging. . . .

But in spite of this knowledge and these successes, there is a
lot of flat and unreconstructed existentialist orthodoxy in Handke,
a whole world of threadbare thought which he is not attacking
but merely bathing in. Life is absurd, and we know this because
at certain moments its consolatory fictions of meaning splinter,
and senselessness is everywhere. (p. 22)

Gregor Keuschnig, in *A Moment of True Feeling,* has a bad
dream one night and stumbles excitedly through the two following days, feeling both violent and vulnerable, exposed to
life's inanity: "nothing made sense." "How steadfastly they
go through with it," he thinks of other people. And at another
point: "How human they all seemed in comparison with him."
His own life now appears to him as a complicated fraud. . . .

The name Gregor, like the name Joseph in *The Goalie's Anxiety
at the Penalty Kick,* is no doubt meant to recall Kafka, and we
may remember that Gregor Samsa, who woke up one morning
to find he had turned into a cockroach, had passed, like Gregor
Keuschnig, a night of "unquiet dreams." There are enough
mentions of nausea in *A Moment of True Feeling* to indicate
Handke's awareness of his other major predecessor in the exploration of this treacherous and alarming ground. Handke has
made Sartre's lonely protagonist a married man, with a child,
and a job at the Austrian embassy, and he has placed him in
1970's Paris; takes him to a press conference, has him give a
dinner party for an Austrian writer, where he cracks up, takes
off his clothes, and smears his face with stew.

But the sense of Sartre revisited seems more powerful than
Handke wants it to be. Kafka is alluded to, but Sartre is systematically echoed, and I wonder whether in fact Handke has
not read *La Nausée* lately, and is for that reason borrowing
from it so freely, with reckless and not very conscious abandon.
Or it may simply be that Sartre has covered this ground so
well that every excursion into it will look like an imitation.
The discovery that life doesn't make any sense, while not
exactly a piece of historical news, may still be an intense private
experience, and an experience of this kind appears in all of

Handke's works that I have read. He often motivates it by a
plot, gives it an objective cause or correlative—the loss of a
job, the death of a mother, a fear that your wife is out to kill
you, and even, in *A Moment of True Feeling,* a prehistory of
fits of terror—but the experience really seems prior to these
occasions, a form of anxiety or metaphysical unease simply
waiting for its chance to spring out into the world and devour
everything that looks like a meaning.

The trouble with this experience for a writer is that, authentic
or not in life, it has been worked over in literature, and not
only by Sartre; and this literature in turn has been raided by
the various agencies of our culture, so that it would not come
as a surprise to see references to Kafka or Sartre on posters
advertising the delights of Prague or Le Havre. Get away from
it all. Visit the scenes of two of modernity's most famous
losses of meaning. Play it again, Franz. . . . None of this diminishes anyone's actual, lived anxiety, of course, but it does
make the experience harder to write about.

There are intelligent and lucid passages in both *A Moment of
True Feeling* and *Nonsense and Happiness.* Gregor's breakdown is described as "a complicated fracture of the mind," a
medical metaphor for a spiritual disaster: you can break your
soul (Handke's word is *Seelenbruch*) as easily as you can break
a leg. In the poems flies die "obtrusively" and cats sniff in
mausoleums, activated, it seems, by a complementarity in the
words themselves ("Katz" and "Maus"). But the poems generally are pretty slack and meandering, and they tend, unfortunately, to rob the novel of some of the benefits of doubt.
Gregor seems less a character than a prolongation of the poems,
a man who is being indulged rather than examined. Nausea
here is a little too comfortable, and neither Handke nor his
protagonists seem to care very much how cracked the cauldron
is as they rattle out a handful of established existentialist tunes:
"I'd like to be a character in a novel"; "This face is not mine";
"Words don't mean a thing"; "Isn't this an ugly day?"; and
"How long has this been going on?"

Still, the cauldron is cracked, and apart from the infinitely
variable strategies of self-consciousness—all those plays and
poems and novels *about* cracked cauldrons which make up so
much of modern literature—there appear to be only three things
we can do with it. We can play very modest tunes, quiet and
careful numbers which the cracks in the cauldron can't really
spoil; we can play whatever we feel like playing and hope
something will survive the cacophony; and we can try to make
the cracks themselves sing in some way. Peter Handke exercises the first and the third of these options with great skill—
frequently in *Short Letter, Long Farewell,* consistently in *A
Sorrow Beyond Dreams.*

Handke's modest tunes are those of a patient, stylish observer
of the world. (p. 23)

Like Flaubert, Handke collects quotations ("People will always
eat," "They weren't my type") and italicizes clichés (*admirers, distance*). Unlike Flaubert, he does this out of affection
for his subject, as a means of approaching a life that will be
lost if you don't write about it (because it will simply be
forgotten), but may also be lost if you do write about it (because
you will dress it up in fine, self-observing phrases).

Cliché, frequently the writer's most recalcitrant enemy, is seen
as a form of memory, what Handke calls "the linguistic deposit
of man's social experience." It is important, of course, to avoid
fussiness or parody in the use of such language. "The essential
is to avoid mere quotations; even when the sentences look

quoted, they must never allow one to forget that they deal with someone who to my mind at least is distinct.'' To his mind; and to our minds. The individual shares a history with others, and can be remembered through this communion.

When Handke's mother [in *A Sorrow Beyond Dreams*], in post-war Berlin, becomes ''a city person, adequately described in the words: *tall, slim, dark-haired*,'' she has stepped into a stereotype, and of course she is all but imprisoned in it. A life of her own, adjectives of her own, would be better. But how many of us really rise to that, and how often? Handke shows us how to find the glitter of truth in dull-looking common-places, and his tall, slim, dark-haired mother is more alive to me than countless well-described figures in more ''original'' novels and biographies. She becomes an emanation of the Forties without ceasing to be a private, if scarcely visible, self.

It is late, then; and language regularly falls short of our needs. But we should be careful not to pretend that it is later than it is, and even the weariest language will point us back to the world if we know how to read it. Naïve and old-fashioned as the thought may seem, Handke's best writing appears when he has patently ''really experienced something'': the break-up of a marriage in *Short Letter, Long Farewell*, the death of his mother in *A Sorrow Beyond Dreams*. In these cases, a general metaphysical anxiety not only finds an objective correlative but is refined and specified by a demanding reality. I interpret this to mean not that Handke is sincere in these works and half-faking in the others, or that the others don't rest on experience at all, but that his more urgent and more localized experiences caused him to put a pressure on his language which he does not always apply. Language points to the world, and the world begs for language. If you have any talent you will get some sort of tune out of the cracked cauldron; but beyond that, the quality of the tunes must depend on the depth of your need for the music. (p. 24)

Michael Wood, ''Play It Again, Franz,'' in The New York Review of Books, *Vol. XXIV, No. 11, June 23, 1977, pp. 22-4.*

STANLEY KAUFFMANN

The wonderful young Austrian writer Peter Handke . . . was first published in this country in 1970. *Kaspar and Other Plays* went largely unnoticed at the time, but already much of what's in the book is widely held to be a permanent addition to dramatic literature. The succeeding books of Handke that appeared here were obviously by the same man and obviously different. His novel *The Goalie's Anxiety at the Penalty Kick* (1972) departed from the existentialist symbol of *Kaspar* for madness as modern metaphor. . . . His next novel, *Short Letter, Long Farewell* (1974), was about a young Austrian writer traveling in America—a metaphysical thriller conveyed, as so much young European art is, through the strophes of American pop culture. Two books of poems, *The Innerworld of the Outerworld of the Innerworld* (1974) and *Nonsense and Happiness* (1976), seemed like flowers picked along the way. Handke's meditation on his mother's suicide, *A Sorrow Beyond Dreams* (1974), must surely stand as one of the best European prose works since the war. . . .

[*A Moment of True Feeling*] is a short novel set in Paris. These facts are quintessential. All Handke's prose works have been relatively short: the very physical shapes of his books are statements of view about the function of writing today—intensity and compactness rather than a large, embracing world for the reader to sink into. And the Parisian setting means that the protagonist, an Austrian, is a stranger in a place with which he is nevertheless quite familiar. (p. 22)

Gregor Keuschnig is a press attaché at the Austrian embassy, married, with a four-year-old daughter. His routine is to get to his office by 7:00 A.M. for an early start in his work of scrutinizing the French press for references to Austria; to make a midday visit to his mistress, a widow with two children; then more work; then home. The day and a half that we spend with him are, as the title indicates, a peak in his life, but Keuschnig does not have the kind of sensibility for which routine could ever be level and snug. He *sees* his life.

The difference in this day and a half, along with the scale on which the difference is built, is indicated in the opening line: ''Who has ever dreamed that he has become a murderer and from then on has only been carrying on with his usual life for the sake of appearances?'' That dream—of murdering an old woman—is what alerts Keuschnig to a sense of crisis in his life. He has a number of other dreams in the book, including one of dancing with his mother. . . . The entire book is situated between dreaming and waking and is further complicated by the fact that through all his waking moments Keuschnig carries a dreaming self within him as he takes his buses and subways, sits at his desk, strolls, sleeps with his friend. This dreaming self doesn't in itself make Keuschnig unique—very few of us do not carry a secret fantast within us as we move through the day—but Handke's fiercely perceptive account of Keuschnig's *triple* state, dreams plus double waking life, gives the book a unique quality: not wooziness or vagueness, but extreme clarity. Every picture, every glance, every fantasizing reaction is cut in crystal.

During the course of the book Keuschnig does some extraordinary things. He copies a woman's telephone number written in chalk on the sidewalk, telephones her, and makes an appointment that he is just going to keep as the book ends. He has a quick, feverish affair with a girl in an office down the hall at the embassy to whom he has apparently never even spoken before. He behaves outrageously at a small dinner party at his home and, though she says nothing at the time, his wife, with whom he has not been close, leaves both him and the child the next day. All these matters are like surface eruptions of a lava flow started by that opening dream. But that is an incomplete statement: because the dream didn't come to a man innocent of preparations for that dream.

It is no Kafkaesque guilt from that dream that colors Keuschnig. Rather it's an increased conviction of mortality, of limitation, of hunger to know what he is doing, and why, every moment. . . . Throughout the book come stabs of new possibility, like fractures in a covering sky. (''Who said that the world has already been discovered?'') This longing for a realer life is, in a man like Keuschnig, not so much greed for more joy as it is a wish that the pain could at least be real pain instead of the irritation of trivial dissatisfactions.

Through much of the book Keuschnig is observed by a writer he knows, a fat man. This writer, never named, and his wife are the couple at dinner in Keuschnig's home when he behaves outrageously. . . . The writer commits the offense of understanding Keuschnig uncomfortably well, and Keuschnig defends himself by denying the truth of the other man's perceptions. This writer seems to be a device of Handke's to put a writer's consciousness right inside the perimeter of the book; and Handke makes him a man who has (he says) no joy in his own life, who lives by seeing ruthlessly. But that writer can also be taken figuratively, as part of Keuschnig that Handke has split off and made into another man for dialectic use.

This fat man is determined to "get" Keuschnig on paper. He keeps making notes; and Keuschnig protects himself by silence or misstatement. Before the writer leaves that night, he says airily: "Once I get the hang of it, I can make do with your gestures. But when your situation gets critical, you'll have to start talking."

Soon enough the situation does get critical, and though Keuschnig still doesn't do much talking, the writer gets what he wants. On the next afternoon, his wife having left that morning, Keuschnig takes his child to the park. He reads while the little girl plays. After a while he looks up. She has disappeared. (pp. 22-3)

Then comes an eight-page passage in which Keuschnig is on his way to the police.... Every detail in the city around him seems sharper than ever. He stops in a café. He feels a sexual thrill as a woman passes by. He walks right past a police call box.... It's a difficult and dangerous section. Handke is not worried that we may lose "sympathy" for Keuschnig; he wants to probe beneath the tropes of conventional response to reach the minutiae of contradictory reactions, paradoxes.

Then Keuschnig catches sight of the fat writer watching him. The writer shuts his notebook, says he has been following Keuschnig all day making observations, that the missing child is at his place with her mother, that he has no further need of Keuschnig....

The observer of Keuschnig—the other part of him?—has no further need of him. Keuschnig's first action now is to change his clothes: he stops in a shop and buys a new suit, new socks, and shoes. Then he moves toward his "telephone" date, with an unknown woman, a new possibility, a possible new being for himself....

But no theme is realized, no explicable point is made. In one sense, although I've tried to be accurate, I have done the book a disservice by sketching its story as a story, by suggesting that it builds to a crisis that leaves the protagonist changed. These things are there, I think, but they are not—theme included—what Handke wrote the book *for*. They do not relate to the risks he has taken....

In Handke's earlier novel *The Goalie's Anxiety,* he devised a fairly complex (for him) story of mental collapse as an armature for an internally seismographic texture. In *Short Letter* the story is somewhat less complex; the emphasis is even more on the texture of "experiences." Now Handke presses on with "the gradual removal of unnecessary fictions." In this latest novel the story is even less important: the texture—which means much more than style alone—becomes the book.

What Handke is moving toward, I think, moving toward stunningly and courageously, is the novel as poem. This is not the same as a poetic novel, which, for instance, *The Goalie's Anxiety* surely is. It is much more congruent to the prose poem, a term that Baudelaire devised but that has a history dating back a century and a half before that. In this new novel there is just enough narrative to convey the protagonist forward in his truly important agon: living from second to second amidst the prismatic blaze of sights and memory flashes and fancies that glitter continuously inside one's head and are metamorphosed, not lost, when one sleeps. It's the unflinching yet distilled rendition of that glitter—a process of poetry—that is Handke's growing concern. (p. 23)

To write a novel as a prose poem, we may infer from Handke, is to shift concern from traditional character portrayal and development, to dwell among the electric currents of the brain, to treasure everything sensory and imaginative on an almost unvaried plane of importance, and confront the mysteries of illogic.... [From] Handke's view, a novel with this texture and purpose presumably contributes to what he sees as "the progress of literature."

What lies ahead of this splendid, still young writer? It's particularly enticing, in his case more than in some others, that we cannot predict; and Handke himself, although he has already finished more work, cannot even want to predict. Certainly this new book proves further that, in power and vision and range, he is the most important new writer on the international scene since Beckett. Like Beckett, any falterings of faith he may feel in the act of writing will probably find their way into good writing. But that is ignominiously to cross our fingers. Handke is alive, having his life, writing in life; by now his writing is part of every reader's good fortune. (p. 24)

Stanley Kauffmann, "The Novel as Poem," in Saturday Review, *Vol. 4, No. 19, June 25, 1977, pp. 22-4.*

JOHN UPDIKE

[The essay excerpted below was originally published in The New Yorker, *September 26, 1977.]*

[Handke] is widely regarded as the best young writer, and by many as the best writer altogether, in his language; and there is no denying his willful intensity and knifelike clarity of evocation. He writes from an area beyond psychology, where feelings acquire the adamancy of randomly encountered, geologically analyzed pebbles.... [*A Moment of True Feeling* is] a kind of list of Keuschnig's incessant and usually unpleasant feelings.

Who is Gregor Keuschnig? He is a young employee of the Austrian Embassy in Paris.... He has a wife, Stefanie, a four-year-old daughter, Agnes, and a mistress, Beatrice, who has two children. He seems at best bored and at worst horrified by these intimates in the course of the two days that pass during *A Moment of True Feeling;* but perhaps he is not himself. The novel begins with a dream in which he murders an old woman.... Handke fervently pursues the volatile moods and hallucinatory sensations of this hero cut off from the reality of his own life. Keuschnig and his wife, presumably, have been estranged for some time.... His mistress and he, one suspects, have until now been happier.... The violence latent in such an erratically connected citizen of the quotidian yawns behind every quirky event and distended perception Keuschnig suffers; we are more relieved than surprised when, while entertaining an unnamed Austrian writer and his mistress, Keuschnig takes off his clothes, smears his face with stew, has a fistfight with his guest, and insults his wife by blurting out one of his day's two infidelities.

The next day dawns with a thunderstorm, and his wife is leaving him.... [The] peculiar crazy, sleepless staleness of our great domestic crises is here captured. Keuschnig spends the rest of his day babysitting with his daughter, in so desultory a style that he loses her in a playground.... Early in his two-day odyssey, he noted a telephone number chalked beneath the exclamation *"Oh la belle vie"* and, impulsively, phoned the number and made a date for the Café de la Paix; as *A Moment of True Feeling* ends, Keuschnig, his spirits somewhat revived, is striding, hands in pockets, loosely knotted necktie swinging, across the Place de l'Opéra to keep the blind date.

Should we rejoice? Just as a passerby, encountering Keuschnig, is "repelled by the chaos in his face," so we tend to smirk and turn away in the face of a novel so pitiless, of a hero so repulsive and overwrought. It is true, our lives, stripped of their padding of numbness and habit, do appear horrific, flickering, and absurd. . . . But, having survived such visions, to emerge again into the sunny daze of normal ongoing working, loving, and eating, one reads about them a bit as one reads about dreams and fevers. Dostoevski's Underground Man wrote over a century ago, "I swear, gentlemen, that to be too conscious is an illness—a real thoroughgoing illness." But compared with Keuschnig, the Underground Man is a jolly companion—a keen philosopher and jaunty editorialist. Also, Keuschnig seems not only overwrought but overfamiliar. Handke is the complete child of modernism; Kierkegaard's absurdity, Sartre's nausea were mother's milk to him. Like Kafka, he has a hero called Gregor who awakes monstrously metamorphosed; like Joyce, he has his hero wander a city street by street; like Robbe-Grillet, he sets down physical details with a flat precision that conveys a menacing emptiness. Also like Robbe-Grillet, he is an abundant theorizer, who has announced that "story" and "invention" have become superfluous, and who in a confessional memoir of his mother, *A Sorrow Beyond Dreams,* has described letting "every sentence carry me further away from the inner life of my characters, so as finally, in a liberated and serene holiday mood, to look at them from outside as isolated insects."

At his best, Handke is a kind of nature poet, a romantic whose exacerbated nerves cling like pained ivy to the landscape. . . . At his worst, Handke is a despiser of his characters, disdaining to give them coherent actions, on the theory that all human acts are essentially nonsensical; yet he asks us to follow Keuschnig—as a dogged parent follows a sulking child from room to room—and perhaps to share the holiday mood when, at the end, his tantrum exhausted, Keuschnig vows for himself "a more sustained yearning" and crosses the avenue to tryst with a stranger his disgust and terror have not yet contaminated. (pp. 442-46)

> *John Updike, "Northern Europeans: Discontent in Deutsch," in his* Hugging the Shore: Essays and Criticism, *1983. Reprint by Vintage Books, 1984, pp. 424-56.**

ANATOLE BROYARD

"He writes from an area beyond psychology, where feelings acquire the adamancy of randomly encountered, geologically analyzed pebbles." I read this quotation from John Updike's review of Peter Handke's last novel [see excerpt above] on the dust wrapper of *The Left-Handed Woman,* and I wondered whether this statement was intended as a compliment. If it is, it shows you what the avant-garde novel has arrived at.

It would mean that when we want to praise a book now, we say that its action is beyond understanding or motivation. . . .

If Mr. Updike's remarks are not to be taken as praise, then I agree with him and I am proud to be in his company. I think that, with admirable conciseness, he has identified what is most exasperating about Mr. Handke.

To put it another way, I think that Mr. Handke has an aversion to ordinary questions. You might say that he feels a brilliant impatience toward people. Because he cannot, or will not, accommodate himself to their slow processes, he accelerates them beyond psychology. . . .

Let me tell you about *The Left-Handed Woman.* Marianne is 30 years old, she has an 8-year-old son and a prosperous husband named Bruno, who is just returning from a successful business trip. Let's go out and have a wonderful dinner, Bruno says, and they do, in an elegant hotel. After dinner, Bruno is so happy with his wife and his life that he asks the waiter to reserve them a room because they want to sleep together immediately. The room is in a tower.

In the morning, as they're walking home through the park, Bruno turns a somersault, out of sheer high spirits. At this point, I made a mental note to the effect that he seemed to be a lively and appreciative husband. His wife, however, says to him that she feels he is going to leave her and she would prefer not to wait for this to happen. She tells him to go away immediately.

Now I've read books before and I have some idea what is going on here. Mr. Handke wants to geologically analyze the randomly encountered pebble of dependency, to take it beyond psychology and kick it around a bit. He wants to show us the adamancy of a determined woman. It is not an unreasonable idea. It even has a certain topical catchiness. But, as if in obedience to a "revolutionary" principle, he will not trouble himself to make his fiction persuasive. He refuses to enable us to suspend our disbelief and respond emotionally instead of "geologically." It is as if Mr. Handke finds it necessary to assert his independence of his characters' emotions and ours as well. He will not prostitute himself to human nature.

I think the difficulty begins with a kind of disillusionment, with the feeling that credibility has been discredited. Only a popular or pedestrian author would stoop to it. In any case, who cares why people do things? Nothing could be so boring as understanding someone. Just imagine the patience it requires, the fatiguing progression from cause to effect. As Marianne says, "Everything seems so banal with people around."

> *Anatole Broyard, "New Novel by Handke," in* The New York Times, *June 17, 1978, p. 19.*

ERNST PAWEL

Few would now dispute the authenticity of [Handke's] talent, though the results remain controversial, to say the least. Mr. Handke's plays and novels have been dismissed as trivial, denounced as boring, and hailed as manifestations of a budding genius comparable in scope to Beckett, Ionesco and Goethe. Such wildly divergent reactions only prove the obvious: tastes differ, and so does an artist's output, especially if he takes large risks. Moreover, they need not be mutually exclusive; entertainment value, while possibly related to a writer's cash worth, is no measure of his true significance. The best writers have their *longueurs* and arid stretches, and Mr. Handke is no exception. In some of the earlier work, form often won out over substance, and a youthful urge to *épater le bourgeois* had a way of obscuring genuine originality. But his most recent writings show a clear shift of emphasis from self-assertion to self-assurance, and his new novel [*The Left-Handed Woman*] is his best so far.

A novella, really, barely 88 pages long. But weight depends on specific gravity, and by fashioning his sentences with scrupulous regard for the limits of language, Mr. Handke articulates the ineffable that lies beyond. Evident throughout is the lingering influence of Wittgenstein, not only on the thought but on the very style itself, which often seems to echo the cadences of the *Tractatus*. Like his great compatriot, Mr. Handke rejects all metaphysics: "That which we cannot speak about must be consigned to silence." Yet in following Wittgenstein's injunction by focusing exclusively on hard-edged reality, Mr. Handke manages to evoke "that which we cannot speak about" far more eloquently than many an effusive quest for existential verities ten times the length of this slender volume....

The midlife crisis of the middle-class housewife is not in itself a promising theme, though it did inspire a few of the world's great novels. But Mr. Handke's heroine is neither a refurbished Madame Bovary nor a belatedly liberated suburbanite enlisting in sexual warfare. Instead, she is a sleeping beauty who, having slept with her prince charming long enough to have an 8-year-old child, slowly wakes up to the fact that the prince is really a frog and that the dream she lived is a nightmare. What she does with this unwanted but inescapable awareness growing in her like a tumor becomes, in Mr. Handke's almost clinical account of its symptoms, an upending of clichés, a questioning of received wisdom and, finally, an exploration of possibilities that the world around her not only rejects out of hand but classifies as madness. Instead of joining in the desperate flight from loneliness, she settles into it with a measure of contentment and watches spacious silence grow around her....

It is a haunting piece, in which language serves as the vehicle for thought.

> Ernst Pawel, *"Sleeping Beauty as a Housewife,"* in The New York Times Book Review, *June 18, 1978,* p. 10.

SUSAN WOOD

[There] is little doubt that Handke is a master at evoking the particular....

Since clarity and precision are qualities to be admired in a writer, why then does one not *like* [*The Left-Handed Woman*] better? Handke is, after all, the young Austrian writer who has been called "the most important new writer on the international scene since Beckett." ...

The answer perhaps lies in Handke's attitude toward his fiction, his disavowal of the necessity of invention, his desire, as he expressed it in his memoir *A Sorrow Beyond Dreams,* to let "every sentence carry me further away from the inner life of my characters, so as finally, in a liberated and serene holiday mood, to look at them from outside as isolated insects." Insects, unless one is a sci-fi horror buff, do not make very interesting subjects for fiction, and as Henry James once said, "The only obligation to which we may hold a novel ... is that it be interesting."

That observation no doubt sounds flippant, but something more serious is intended. It is, to put it simply, that a novel which ignores the inner lives of its characters has no life at all.

As befits Handke's theories of objectivity, *The Left-Handed Woman* is a short novel, really a novella.... Its protagonist is Marianne, usually referred to as "the woman," a young matron of 30.... When her husband, Bruno, the sales manager

in the office of a porcelain manufacturer, returns from a long business trip, she suddenly decides, without apparent motivation, that he will one day leave her for good. To protect herself against that desertion, she sends him away instead.... In the end, when all the characters are gathered at an impromptu party at Marianne's house, she can look into the mirror and say, "'You haven't given yourself away. And no one will ever humiliate you again.'" It is the fulfillment of her earlier resolve that "'I don't care what you people think. The more you have to say about me, the freer I will be of you.'"

It is all a little too pat. Handke has not only read Wittgenstein, apparently, but also Sartre, Kierkegaard, Robbe-Grillet. Life is absurd, one is always alone; even his precise rendering of physical detail, like Robbe-Grillet's, only serves to convey the world's emptiness. The absurdity of human existence is not a difficult proposition to argue in this existential world, but what makes Handke undeserving of comparison with a writer like Samuel Beckett is his lack of sympathy, indeed his callousness, toward his characters. For Beckett the failure to communicate not only defeats man, it reveals his common humanity; Hamm and Clov make us laugh, and when Hamm covers his face at the conclusion of *Endgame,* we weep—for him and for ourselves.

Great literature—whether the work of Beckett or Dickens or Faulkner—does not depend on a reduplication of external reality, but rather through invention—what the critic Albert Guerard has called its "illuminating distortion"—it heightens reality to throw light on the human capacity for endurance and suffering, extending our own capacity for feeling. In *The Left-Handed Woman,* there is nothing to feel—nothing to laugh about, nothing to weep for.

> Susan Wood, *"Under Handke's Microscope,"* in Book World—The Washington Post, *July 9, 1978, p. E5.*

MAUREEN HOWARD

Peter Handke's very short work *The Left-Handed Woman,* is as good as anything I've read in a long time. I'm inclined to think of his fiction as cinematic, but that's too easy. Film is a reference: camera techniques are constantly alluded to in his cuts, his lighting, his frames. In *Short Letter, Long Farewell,* Handke follows his characters (across a surrealistic America) with a style that has the accidental excitement of a hand-held camera. In *The Left-Handed Woman* he tracks them steadily in and out of a cool modern condominium until we can feel, in the rooms of that convenient rented place, the subtle changes of time and mood, and see the big plate glass window as an abstract black square. It's a relief when there is an exit into the town or neatly planned woods outside the apartment. We have entered a highly visual world in which as readers we become seemingly passive, in which the demands of language, of the few lines spoken by Handke's characters, become immensely important to us. (p. 439)

The Left-Handed Woman is a tale of modern perversity. Marianne's story is worth a dozen novelistic testimonials of women's flight to ordinary social and sexual freedom. She does not maneuver her husband out of the apartment to fulfill herself or to pay off old debts. Her rejection of love is deeply irrational and seems to spring from a need to control the world in the only way she sees possible—by denial, by setting up tests for herself that become a form of self-definition. Marianne starts working again at translating—jobs she gets from her old boss— but she works at home without any claims to creative pleasure, irritated by Stefan and his playmate, enclosed in the apartment, and there she constructs a dreary social life, ghastly drinking parties, while the child sleeps in his bedroom and the adults disport themselves joylessly like figures in an Antonioni movie.

In the walled-off world of this woman's mind, the spoken words of her son, her friend, the publisher begin to take on a significance that is larger than the usual conversational exchanges in fiction. . . . [All] the people who surround Marianne become more strident, playing unreasonably to her calmness, her silence, her wish not to participate, anxiously hoping to elicit a normal response. Each time she retreats from the assault into herself. So the husband rages and gets drunk and the friend, Franziska, overarticulates the theories dealt out in her women's support group; the publisher confesses his loneliness in melodramatic weeping, and so forth. It's a fine stroke on Handke's part—to let his characters lose their names and come to exist in the novel as the child, the chauffeur, the actor, as their real identities recede for Marianne.

The Left-Handed Woman is a novel about the unsaid. From Marianne's first excited notion, which she terms "an illumination" and in which she sees herself free and alone in the future, to the stark moment when she looks in the mirror and says—"You haven't given yourself away. And no one will ever humiliate you again"—she has kept her own counsel. What Handke has exposed in this beautiful novella is the terrible emptiness which lies at the center of behavior based on an aesthetic idea of freedom. The solitary pain and deranged loneliness which Marianne brings on herself betrays life, and that negative claim confessed to her own reflection—not to be humiliated—reveals the very thin line which exists between her instincts for self-destruction and self-preservation. (pp. 440-41)

> *Maureen Howard, in a review of "The Left-Handed Woman," in* The Yale Review, *Vol. LXVIII, No. 3, March, 1979, pp. 439-41.*

JEROME KLINKOWITZ AND JAMES KNOWLTON

[*In the essay excerpted below, the critics discuss several works by Handke, including three which had not yet been translated into English. The critics translate the titles of the three works as* Slow Journey Home, The Lesson of Sainte Victoire, *and* Children's Story. *These works were later translated into English and combined to form one book—*Slow Homecoming.]

Recent German literature has experienced a fundamental transformation from espoused goals of political enlightenment, predominant in the radical 1960s, to a recourse to inwardness and subjectivity—hence the intensified sensibility so apparent in the writing of the 1970s and early 1980s. (p. 76)

The alternative movements have softened their once universal demand for revolutionary action and have redirected their attention to more modestly specific goals, including feminism, environmental issues, and the antinuclear peace movement.

If alienation and commodification could not be overcome in the political arena—and this was the thrust of the largely documentary-style literature that dominated the 1960s—then they had to be resisted by a reemphasized subjectivity in groups and individuals dedicated to reexamining and renewing their contacts to self and nature in the quest for private transformation. The political struggle had failed, and rather than seek the reason for this failure in the prevailing order, many German intellectuals sought reasons in themselves, in self-perceived inade-

quacy. Thus, introspection as a form of self-doubt began to supplant militant political action; subjectivity gained ascendency over critical theory. Instead of following Marx's dictum that the goal of philosophy was not to comprehend the world but to change it, writers of the 1970s such as Peter Handke, Nicolas Born, Jürgen Theobaldy, Botho Strauss, and Peter Schneider turned their quests inward, attempting to stake out epistemological conditions of knowledge and perception untainted by established norms. (p. 77)

The literature of new subjectivity is intensely individualistic. It views the public sphere as a realm imbued with and dominated by forces beyond individual control—in short, as a world of unfreedom. Human existence has been stripped of its decisive aspect of subjectivity; that it, its primal self-identity as the knowing and creative subject of human history is repressed. Instead, through this absorption of self into a world of reified objects, people have become objects of alienated social and historical forces beyond their control. . . . If the public sphere has become impenetrable to rational and active cognition, and if even language, that vital mediator between subjective individuality and the outerworld, has been rendered suspect by its use as an instrument of political and economic manipulation, then there remains but one alternative: retreat into an innerworld to discover and actualize an authentic and purely individual "I." This new subjectivity then can set out on an intellectual journey to reconquer a world of objects untainted by preexistent systems of perception and to impose on these objects one's own individuality—to recreate them as purely concrete knowledge. This is the quest undertaken by many of the writers of the New Sensibility who, in refusing to affirm the existing order of things, invoke the subversive power of negativity residing in their art. In doing so, they attempt to construct visible antagonisms between individuals and the existing social order by reappropriating the world and displaying this newly created universe of fiction as personally secured knowledge imbued with subjectivity. The fiction of New Sensibility stands as a counterweight to the prevailing order; its steadfast refusal to affirm the world as it is militates as an impetus toward change. (p. 78)

From *The Goalie's Anxiety at the Penalty Kick* through *Short Letter, Long Farewell* and *A Sorrow Beyond Dreams* to *A Moment of True Feeling* and *The Left-Handed Woman,* Handke's fiction has emphasized the subjective and autobiographical aspects of narration even before they were in fashion. His characters are in a constant quest for identity with themselves and the world. (p. 80)

With the publication of *The Weight of the World* (1977   ), however, Handke at once radicalized and expanded new-subjectivity tendencies already present in his thought and writing. In this most unusual journal, encompassing the period of his life in Paris from November 1975 to March 1977, and dedicated to "those it concerns," writing becomes the process of self-reduction to an actively perceiving "I" that constitutes both itself and the outerworld by perceiving, recording, and thus preserving objects and events as pure knowledge imbued with subjectivity—and thus saved from the process of reification into the estranged network of hostile signification systems confronting individuals in the public sphere. But *The Weight of the World* also adds a new dimension to Handke's literature. For the first time, subjective perception and the literary representation of that perception is deemed insufficient as a process in itself. *The Weight of the World* thus signals a new period in Handke's writing, marked by his desire to go beyond subversion and deconstruction of preexisting systems toward constructing generally valid meaning.

Outerworld segments appropriated by consciousness must, to gain compelling force for others, be tied into a greater system of signification. This system, Handke now recognizes, is myth as a sense-giving link between individuals and a greater sociocultural whole. If there is to be meaning in people's lives, Handke's journal indicates, it must be created by the poet who can penetrate the "idiocy of language" (a phrase that Handke uses often) and create an exemplary new world containing the impetus to create new myths to replace the exhausted ones of Western culture and so relink alienated individuals with their roots in nature. Nature, myth, and history have thus become the themes of Handke's literature of the late 1970s and early 1980s. As a result, one of the first German-language authors to delve into himself in search of subjective authenticity demonstrates a potential exit from the introspective stance of the New Sensibility—the quest of the poet-redeemer, purified through the process of coming to self, for universally valid myth in nature and culture. . . . (pp. 80-1)

The Weight of the World represents Handke's most radical attempt to come to grips with the world as perception and with the reflection of this perceived world as language. As with *A Sorrow Beyond Dreams,* the author once again turns to family history to see whether his newly achieved fictional techniques can bear the test of life. But Handke avoids the traditional diary form in favor of a protocol-like registering of unsorted and purposeless perceptions, all arranged in generally brief entries consisting of sentences and fragments. Such a seemingly peculiar undertaking is in line with the positivistic method developed by the Vienna Circle philosophers Rudolf Carnap and Ludwig Wittgenstein, who insisted that scientific knowledge, to maintain its empirical base and thus remain verifiable, must be reducible to immediate sense perceptions. Wittgenstein and the Vienna Circle mistrusted the abstractions of modern intellectual contructs, and the implicit bias of positivism toward the minimal is an attempt to extract the truly scientific from the metaphysical underpinnings of knowledge. Handke's *Weight of the World* proceeds in a similar vein, attempting to liberate from the ideologically perverted body of language the substratum of truth that resides in raw perception, clothed only in minimal language form. Thus Handke chooses a nonsequential, noncausal diary as his vehicle, discarding the traditional form of a personal diary in favor of a deliberately unsystematic recording of unordered perceptions. Most writing of any sort presumes a framework in which perceptions are ordered by a central intelligence that guides the process of selection, sorting, and ultimate presentation. But this very process is the crux of the problem for Handke, for in it resides the danger that this world, instead of being perceived with absolute neutrality, will be filtered through a shaping consciousness and thus limited by ideology and misdirected by rhetoric.

Handke therefore sets himself the task of mechanically registering his sense perceptions in the form of diary entries with no intended connections. Each stands alone as an experiential monad naturally sealed off against the others. Hence, Handke's journal is not much of a find for biographers, for although some personal details work their way in, such as the death of a friend or a stay in the hospital, the only pattern is that of coincidence—no meanings are allowed to accumulate. (pp. 82-3)

The Weight of the World marks a turning point in Handke's writing, a change that becomes even more evident in his recent novels: the search for new forms of self-expression has led to a quest for myth as the core of meaning. Handke's early prose proceeded from a fundamental critique of language as a social institution linking the individual as knowing and perceiving subject with an estranged world of people and objects. The material world, Handke would have argued, is not accessible to knowledge. As part of a reflective system, language acquisition is an appropriation of the outerworld in symbolic form. Its objects, after all, cannot be seized physically and put within consciousness. But in a rapidly changing world these symbols, once established, become petrified; they continue to exist in a fixed form, even though the world they represent is in flux. Thus they provide an illusion of mastery—mastery of a world that no longer exists. Hence, language becomes an empty form, no longer able to represent and express. The break of this link to the outerworld makes that world look strangely unfocused and unknowable.

Handke's mature prose has its foundation in the consciousness of this widening break; its emotional core is the feeling of forlornness and estrangement. But instead of reverting to the language study of his earlier works, Handke now signals a retreat to a new subjectivity that leads to a critique of consciousness instead. It is here that the perceiving epistemological core, the "I," resides. Handke's version of the New Sensibility establishes the singularity of his consciousness. In this inchoate state he can proceed to reexperience and reconquer the object world as something concrete and coherent.

Handke's recent books are characterized by a powerful yearning for redemption, for a healing of the schism between "I" and the outerworld. *Slow Journey Home* (1979 . . .) [is] a book in style and concept quite unusual by the standards of the author's earlier prose. . . . (pp. 86-7)

[*Slow Journey Home*] is more readable than his early prose and is more accessible than any of his plays. It revels in a sense of pleasure from pure narration, with complexly subordinate constructions and minute detail. Its selection of vocabulary and narrative style betrays a refashioning of eighteenth- and nineteenth-century modes—we know that Goethe, Keller, and Stifter guided Handke's artistic development. These features in turn reveal a renewed interest in more simply human concerns for which nature is only the most apparent metaphor. *Slow Journey Home,* Handke has emphasized, represents the attempt to negate the fragmentary character of modern experience by creating harmony and beauty to serve as a counterweight to the existing world's banality. The novel, which he calls an "epic poem," is an "attempt to reach a world harmony and at the same time to reach a universality for myself as someone who writes. . . . I have the feeling that for centuries this has not been tried: To capture this harmony with language, and to pass it on contagiously." But beauty and harmony, once created, become hermetically enveloped entities that "come into conflict with the history of my ancestors, which is also in me." Unlike the hermetic self-apparency of his earlier work, Handke's recent writing has begun to emphasize "problems with home, with language, with family, with history, with nature." (pp. 90-1)

In his newest fiction, Handke seems more ready to accept the linguistic state of affairs, devoting his efforts toward more active work with other forms of perception and communication by which life proceeds. *The Lesson of Sainte Victoire* (1980 . . .) appears to be a book about Paul Cézanne, in particular the painter's later work; the Sainte Victoire of the title refers to a mountain range in Provence where Cézanne found his most challenging subjects, and it is Handke's metaphor for how, against the most severe aesthetic tests, life goes on. But a book like this is hard to classify. *The Lesson of Sainte Victoire* is not fiction, at least not in the traditional sense. Yet the term *nonfiction* would also be a misnomer, for Cézanne and his work serve only as a backdrop before which Handke's development as an artist in the late 1970s is sketched. (pp. 91-2)

Like *Slow Journey Home, Sainte Victoire* exemplifies Germany's New Sensibility; in this book Handke delves into himself and examines his subjective relationship to art and life. But here, as in the later *Children's Story,* his style assumes the biblical quality hinted at in his previous novel. Handke's prose is replete with antiquated words and phrases, with syntactical constructions straight from the last century. The book is nevertheless both a continuation and exegesis of *Slow Journey Home.* . . . This book, too, treats Handke's disturbed relationship to the outerworld and to potential new myths that might reinterpret our being in the world. Through Cézanne's art, Handke attempts to break out of the strictures of his individuality and to experience directly the world of objects, bypassing the customary mediation of language and conceptual analysis—just as Cézanne painted through his perceptual notions to capture once more a living sense of the real. (p. 92)

The book's concluding chapter, a word picture of the woods near Salzburg apparently unrelated to Handke's study of Cézanne, attempts to provide a natural description adequate to his newly found Cézanne-like comprehension of the individual's relationship with nature. The entire thrust of the chapter, including its tone and style, stand in stark contrast to the emotional soul-searching of the rest of the book. But it would be wrong to criticize this chapter, as some have done, as strangely incompatible with what precedes. *The Lesson of Sainte Victoire* is no more a book about Cézanne than it is a book about a French mountain range. Rather, it is the study of the writer's relationship as artist with the knowable world. Is the writer a seer, a creator and grantor of myth with near universal validity? Or is the kind of mystical experience Handke describes relegated to the private sphere, with little bearing on the cognitive facility of other people? Critics have pointed out that Handke has chosen Spinoza, the pantheistic philosopher of the seventeenth century who believed in the oneness of God and nature, as his mentor. Handke's visionary thought and elliptical style betray his preference for an earlier time, for an age when idealistic philosophy reigned supreme. Both *Slow Journey Home* and *The Lesson of Sainte Victoire* work to subvert the perniciously antihumanistic progress of science and scientific thought—geology plays an important role in both books—by proposing a synthesis of twentieth-century positivist thought with the idealism of a past era. (p. 94)

Children's Story (1981 . . .) continues Handke's line of development in the style and mood of the New Sensibility. In this book, the object of contemplation is neither the earth's forms nor works of art but Handke's own child. In this perhaps most autobiographical of Handke's books, the narrator (clearly Handke himself) tells the story of his relationship with his daughter from her birth to about age ten. But the book's purely autobiographical quality is somewhat obscured by the author's refusal to name his characters, himself and his daughter—they are simply called "the man" and "the child" or "the grownup" and "the growing child." As in *The Lesson of Sainte Victoire,* nevertheless, the degree of fiction is hard to determine, for Handke—in pursuit of myths—tells his story in the most general of terms, using a style at once biblical and ro-

mantic while introducing a new conceptual framework. It is a rare author who has the nerve to claim that he is "working on the secret of the world" . . . , as Handke does, or to add that "he knew the truth and was pervaded by the obligation to transmit this truth" . . . for "gradually it became a certainty that, for people like him, a different world history has always been valid." . . . (pp. 95-6)

Of course this world history is quite different from that which we find in history books: not a record of facts, but one of myth and its linkage to the human community—a history accessible only to the poet, the prophet, the seer; a history not of change but of constancy, of eternal laws with universal validity. Whereas in Handke's two previous books the forms of the earth and then the shapes and colors of Cézanne's art provided impetus to find and pursue the call of providence, now the child offers him insight into the eternal myth-giving laws of the universe. In one instance, the narrator is able to read the forms of world history "which appeared to him in the lines of the sleeping child." . . . In another, when he is observing his daughter in the garden, the narrator is overwhelmed by the moment's mythical quality: "Such moments should never pass or be forgotten. They demand perpetuality: musical strains, epic song." . . . (p. 96)

In a recent interview, Handke described the process that led him to write *Children's Story,* how he came to view children as symbols for "the law of the world" as he calls it. As if to underline the mythical content of his book, he stresses the formal parallel he constructed between Thucidides' history of the Peloponnesian War and his *Children's Story.* . . . Handke's interest in classical antiquity stems from his belief that history, especially the history of art, can provide him with the formal possibilities appropriate to his view of art and the world. And classical antiquity has managed to demonstrate the universality he envisions for his own art: "Thus *Children's Story* arose; it is a story of today and of all times." . . . In this manner, the obstacles of language are overcome, and fiction, stripped of its outdated and distracting conventions, can more directly serve human needs, not the least being its author's own.

The redemptive aspect of Handke's work, which was particularly apparent in *Slow Journey Home,* assumes its most compelling form in *Through the Villages* (1981 . . .), the fourth and final of Handke's homecoming works. *Through the Villages,* as a minimally dramatic play, continues the developmental line that Handke began in *The Weight of the World,* in which for the first time myth and its connections to history, art, nature, and human community were invoked. (p. 98)

Unlike his early plays, which in discarding traditional modes of theatrical representation and attempting to subvert the theater as an institution faithfully representing social reality create a world totally concrete and self-apparent, *Through the Villages* invokes the theater's historical tradition. It returns to the Greek stage in search of inspirational models that might provide a vehicle to portray universality of form and myth. (p. 99)

Handke, who in 1971 abandoned the stage as a literary arena, in 1981 returned to the theater not as a brash, young innovator but as a mature writer with a message of human redemption through art and nature. As such a message, *Through the Villages* is the culmination of the process—Handke's search for myth and form—initiated in *The Weight of the World* and intensively realized in *Slow Journey Home, The Lesson of Sainte Victoire,* and *Children's Story.* Whereas Handke's earlier drama reveled in its hermetic self-apparency, its sense of play, and its insistent refusal to bear a message, *Through the Villages* represents the attempt to give public expression to his new understanding of the human condition, to effect change in his audience. (p. 103)

Jerome Klinkowitz and James Knowlton, in their Peter Handke and the Postmodern Transformation: The Goalie's Journey Home, *University of Missouri Press, 1983, 133 p.*

WALTER GOODMAN

For fullest appreciation of this assemblage of opinions, descriptions, reflections and snatches of conversation, daydreams and nightmares, one would have to be as fascinated with the mind of Peter Handke as Peter Handke is. Yet given a bit of patience, a reader can find satisfaction [in *The Weight of the World*], passages that are striking on their own or for the opening they offer into a writer's mind.

Mr. Handke, the Austrian novelist, playwright and film maker, lived in Paris with his daughter between November 1975 and March 1977 and, in the manner of writers, he kept a notebook. . . .

In the months covered, Mr. Handke apparently suffered a mild heart attack, a sweet-and-sour love affair, the middle-age pains of having to supervise the growing-up pains of his daughter, and a chronic fear of death and of life: "I dreamed of my death last night; up until then I had been the hero of my book; after my death I was only the reader." . . .

The prevailing theme is Mr. Handke's separation from others, from the world, not least from himself—"New feeling of remoteness, unconnectedness, of *congealed* beside-myselfness." There is a self-conscious envy of exuberant life: "A beautiful, severe, statuesque, cold, enthusiastic woman, who walks bouncingly, and to make matters worse starts singing a revolutionary song. How I hate her!" Mr. Handke is offended by noises and odors and by most other signs of human existence. "Which is worse," he asks, "anxiety or people?"

The diarist does not seem to have permitted his reaction to Franz Kafka's diaries—"I find that his complaints and self-recriminations no longer interest me"—to temper his own complaints. The most startling line in this book is, "I laugh too much."

But just as one is beginning to wince at the whines, the writer comes through with a redemptive passage: "A beautiful girl with bare shoulders entered the Metro car; at first the other women seemed vexed—but then, as they looked at the girl and took a liking to her, they seemed to grow younger." . . .

Some entries are pretentious—"Rediscover the forgotten, anonymous language of all mankind, and it will shine in self-evidence (my task)"; some are perplexing—"Don't eat carrots—they kill your desire for anything else"; some are banal—"No luggage, nothing to carry; the joy of having your hands free: 'Just a toothbrush'"; some are striking—"At the sight of the switchblade, the thought that I could use it to defend myself if my own body assaulted me"; and some are brilliantly simple: "The sun shines on my writing hand and strengthens it." Now and then, an observation calls up an amen: "Hatred of people who bed their eyeglasses in their hair."

There are even a few very short short stories: "The girl's story: "'I followed a man into the Metro. From station to station I

felt more beautiful—when he finally spoke to me I was unapproachable; too beautiful.'"

This review seems to have turned into a sampler, which, like so many other things, will probably offend the author. He writes: "The most mindless of mortals: those who only leaf through books." But what is one to do with a book that demands, and repays, leafing?

Walter Goodman, in a review of "The Weight of the World," in The New York Times, *July 12, 1984, p. C21.*

RICHARD LOCKE

[Handke's *The Weight of the World*]—journals he kept in Paris from November 1975 through March 1977—is his most forthright attempt at autobiography. This might suggest a revelation of the man behind the mask (one thinks of Rilke, another literary German resident in Paris, and his *The Notebooks of Malte Laurids Brigge*). But these journals are hardly indiscreet. What is most interesting about them is Mr. Handke's attempt to create a minimalist collage that will function as a kind of photorealistic self-portrait. It's as if some glum and fanatical student of Wittgenstein were laboring to produce a work with the spiritual intensity of a Dürer.

The Weight of the World is a daily record of random thoughts and observations, many only two or three sentences long. There are almost no sustained narrative or essayistic passages, no portraits of other people, few literary or cultural thoughts that are more than passing references. Current events don't exist. . . . Unlike the notebooks of Henry James or Kafka, these are not full of plot outlines, trial runs, false starts or first drafts of stories, novels or plays. There are a few fragments of dreams but nothing suggesting an interest in psychoanalysis or Surrealism. People are referred to only by the letters of their first names: a few girl friends, a married couple, a former wife or mistress, one or two passing journalists but most of all his daughter, "A," who seems to be between 5 and 7 years old. She is the only person with whom Mr. Handke appears to have a close or continuous relationship. They live together; her mother is absent; we don't know why. . . .

The overwhelming majority of entries consists of snapshots of city street life and of a steady drone of unhappy self-absorption. Over and over again, we read that Mr. Handke is tense, panicky, hopeless, grieving, morose, dejected, lonely, painfully imprisoned in himself, forlorn, forsaken, yearning, bored. "Which is worse," he asks, "anxiety or people?" At times he feels contempt for or rage at other people. He refers to his volubility, persuasiveness and skill at social interaction, but it's hard to spot this from the entries. He is filled with a fear of death: "Purest, strongest feeling = consciousness of death." Only writing seems to calm him down: "Tense, unnerved, and close to madness before writing." "How necessary art is to me day after day, if I am not to wish some of the people I love best would die, or kill them with my indifference." "If I didn't write, life would slip away from me." . . .

At one point he wistfully speculates, "The myth of Narcissus: doesn't it seem possible that the long, inquiring contemplation of one's own mirror image (and, in an extended sense, of the things one has made) prepares and equips one for long, steady, penetrating contemplation of others?" No, not in this instance. Mr. Handke is drowning in Narcissus' pool. In his fear of ready-made linguistic systems and the prison of social life, he is reduced to counting the bars of his cell. At his best, he gives us a vivid, fleeting glimpse of a patch of sunlight and a pattern of leaves outside the window. Occasionally we hear sounds and voices coming from the next cell. His only escape seems to be his strong feeling for his daughter—though it too is often self-referential—and his writing.

The fragmentary form of these notebooks does not serve him well. Mr. Handke seems to need, indeed to thrive on, the defensive manipulation of experience, the conscious dream-work of artistic fabrication, as he did in *Short Letter, Long Farewell* and *A Sorrow Beyond Dreams,* which were dense, shapely and emotionally risky. Unlike the sketchbooks and novels of Max Frisch and recent stories and novels by Milan Kundera, Renata Adler, Donald Barthelme and Elizabeth Hardwick, which share a fascination with fragments of experience that can be shored against our ruins, Mr. Handke's notebooks—unlike his novel and memoir—feel like a dead end. We may never recover the high art and self-confidence of the Modernists, and the prestidigitation of Nabokov, Pynchon, García Márquez and Grass may seem grandiose to many contemporary writers. But as Mr. Handke would be one of the first to note, cultural nostalgia is often little more than enlightened self-pity. At his best, a strong writer like Mr. Handke can advance our self-knowledge.

> Richard Locke, ''Down and Out in Paris,'' in The New York Times Book Review, *July 22, 1984, p. 10.*

STANLEY KAUFFMANN

[*The Weight of the World*] is a combined journal and writer's notebook. First published in Austria in 1977, the book covers the period from November 1975 through March 1977 when Handke was living in Paris with his small daughter, referred to as A.... During this period, too, he published his novel, *A Moment of True Feeling,* which deals with an Austrian, employed by his embassy in Paris, who lives with his small daughter; and Handke also worked on his film, *The Left-Handed Woman* which, as novel, is set in Germany but which he shot in Paris. These works are adumbrated in *The Weight of the World.* (pp. 37-8)

Obviously such a book can't be read as an organic work, and a reader is not likely to pick up such a book without a previous interest in the author. But after granting those points, what do we expect from it?

One fact that makes a difference in expectation is the time when it appears.... Handke himself put this book forward; more, he worked over the English version with the exemplary Ralph Manheim and eliminated a total of ten pages from the German original. Because the author himself gives it to us and because of the book's material, the reader is inescapably reminded of Kafka's Hunger Artist, who said, ''I always wanted you to admire my fasting.'' But the Hunger Artist explains that he didn't choose to fast, he couldn't help it; and somewhat in the same manner, Handke is justified. His book is exposition, not exhibition.

Still, the only right criterion for a book of this sort, especially if the author himself presents it, is to expect every entry to be a gem: of illuminating privacy or artistic gestation or relevant experience. Of course this expectation is never wholly satisfied, but it seems fair. Handke, particularly in his earlier pages, presents too many rhinestones. Here are two of them, complete:

> A woman went by and my heart stood still
>
> Need for philosophy

(He puts no periods at the ends of entries.) Numerous other entries are equally dim; instead of ten pages, a total of something like a third of the book could have been beneficially dropped. But well over half of the entries are indeed gems—of varying depth and brilliance.

Many of the entries could be subsumed under headings. One such recurrent sort is the epiphanized commonplace, the very ordinary experience seen extraordinarily—a mode that readers will remember from Handke's novels: . . .

> I prepare myself for the hug, but also for the embarrassment after it
>
> Brief feeling of warmth during the day when I know that a rare film or a football game will be shown on television that evening (even when, as usual, I have no intention of tuning in) . . .

Another sort of entry, plentiful throughout, is the severe self-judgment:

> I'm not quick-tempered, that would be an attractive vice; I only lack self-control . . .
>
> (p. 38)

Many, many of the entries are about observing, learning from, his small daughter. (''A. said to me, 'You speak Italian the way I swim.''') In one aspect, the author is leading a double life: he is trying to scrap everything in his mind that survives just because it is traditional, yet he is nourished by his daughter in an ancient way. An irony results: the truth of what her life does for him only underscores his needs. Implicitly he would like to straighten out the world for her before she comes to understand what it and she lack.

One more theme must be noted—death. Handke's hospital stay underscores the theme, but it is not new for him; it has always been a counterpoint to his life....

For us, at our end of the translation-publication process, *The Weight of the World,* though warmly welcome, is an interim book, while we wait for work that has already been written, let alone what may come after it. Still, this book, lapses and all, is not to be discounted: it has its own wry, painful, lovely rewards. Yet when Handke's subsequent books appear, this one may seem to grow, as it fits into a progressing career. (p. 39)

> Stanley Kauffmann, ''Moments of True Feeling,'' in The New Republic, *Vol. 191, No. 10, September 3, 1984, pp. 37-9.*

RUTH BAUMGARTEN

Memory is not the purpose of [*The Weight of the World*] but the simultaneous penetration of a new reality and language: 'Refrain from opinions and keep observing until at last the gravitational pull of a life-feeling sets in.' . . . [The] mass of observations, overheard or imagined sentences and miniature sketches of emotions or perceptions accumulate into a peculiar space where reader and author meet impersonally and yet intimately. Handke's horror of false meanings and big names leads him to a reductionist form of writing in which his child, a sentence in a book, a noise or the briefest irritation or satisfaction all carry the same weight.

That words become as concrete as objects; that perception and expression should merge into 'the moment of language' where privacy opens into generality is the avowed aim of this 'reportage of consciousness'. Started as working notes for a mute play, it comes increasingly close to Handke's definition of literature as the discovery of 'localities that have not yet been claimed by meaning'. This immediacy is the 'weight of the world' which the title announces and the close encounter with another consciousness and its contagious lust for perceptions makes the book seductive.

And yet the neutral attentiveness which can turn a heartbeat into an *objet trouvé* ends at times in chilling reading. No narrative, no explanation smooth the impact of the occasionally recorded act of brutality or of the use of observation as a weapon. Instead, they stand up with the same right as any other emotion claiming their place as experience, no different really from the clumsy pride in being accosted by prostitutes and gradually liked a little better by dogs.

This reverence for the authentic, however raw or minute, with its vehement lack of trust in any narrative, paradoxically puts Handke's book squarely into a highly traditional conception of the writer and of literature which has the world articulate itself through the inner life of a writer. And, though Handke's undertaking looks, on the surface, more modest, his attempt to construct a sense of identity by formulating the identity of the world around him is unthinkable without the belief in the writer's direct rapport with the universe.

And yet his suspicion of any organised structure of meaning, be it history or a patrician ideal of harmony, inevitably rests on preconceptions and established areas of meaning. Handke hails suburbia as his ideal, using its lack of picturesqueness and drama as a foil against which he identifies, records and validates the sensations of everyday living. But this insistence on the unadorned plain and ordinary amounts to just as emphatic an endorsement of a narrative—the myth of the dignity of the ordinary—as all the media myths he denounces.

Handke assigns fiction simultaneously too much and too little weight: 'Attempts to pull myself out of the swamp—as though this swamp (and occasionally the world of miracles) were my actual habitat and as though there were nothing outside it but the deadly mechanics of opinions.' Sentences like this rely on a preconceived split between the outer world, totally devoured by trashy fictions, and a subjectivity which can penetrate to the fiction-free essence if it only isolates itself well enough. Handke's journal is the living proof of the fertility of this particular myth and despite the irritating complacency of such a monument to subjectivity, despite the occasional pretentiousness, he succeeds singularly in his central aim: fusing sensation and language into a living and yet analytic whole, he creates moments in which the mute finds a voice and in which a trembling leaf or the shadow on a ceiling bear witness to the integrity of perception and perceiver. (p. 30)

Ruth Baumgarten, "Bare Facts," in New Statesman,
Vol. 108, No: 2793, September 28, 1984, pp. 29-30.

STANISLAW BARANCZAK

"I am working on the secret of the world," declares the narrator of one of the three fictions—perhaps "three philosophical parables" would be a more adequate term—that make up Peter Handke's [*Slow Homecoming*]. The author, who made his first big splash in 1966 (at the age of 24) with the play *Offending the Audience,* has come a long way since that time. The distance between "offending the audience" and "working on the secret of the world" is a measure of both maturity and ambition. Indeed, the title of *Slow Homecoming,* with its many references to the journeys of the book's characters, could also serve as an apt description of Handke's own creative journey. It has been, in fact, a gradual return to the demanding tradition of the great Austrian novelists of our century, Robert Musil or Hermann Broch, whose work, for all its artistic novelty, was likewise spurred by an obsession with metaphysics.

In the book itself, the notion of "homecoming" acquires several different meanings. The first story, "The Long Way Around," introduces this concept through the creation of a fictional plot, which has perhaps the most to do with homecoming in its literal sense. The main character, Valentin Sorger, a geologist from Europe who is doing field work on the configurations of the earth near the Arctic Circle, is yet another modern incarnation of Odysseus. His Troy is an Alaskan village, where he immerses himself in the realm of natural objects. (p. 31)

Though he is initially more or less reconciled to his rootlessness, to his "constant whereverness," and even enjoys "the intoxication of being forever alone," Sorger begins to yearn for his Ithaca, which, for him, means not only a geographic return to Europe but also a social return to human community, a historical return to the continuity of time, and a semantic return to unrestricted communication with others. . . . [Having] abruptly decided to end his Northern adventure, he makes his "long way around" the globe, toward the Ithaca of his European home.

He makes stops in more and more crowded and modern places—first the West Coast, then Denver, finally New York City—and finds himself, through accidental encounters with friends and strangers, "back in the game of the world again." . . . At last, in a Manhattan coffee shop, he experiences a flash of mystical illumination, "a law-giving moment" in which he realizes the essence of both his uniqueness and his participation in the human world and the process of history. At this point, he is genuinely ready to return to "the world of names," to the sphere of man-made forms that make communication and belonging possible.

The authorial narrator, who presents Sorger's story in an apparently traditional third-person account (yet highly original in its combination of stylistic fragmentation and concision), becomes a first-person narrator-character in the book's next section, "The Lesson of Mont Sainte-Victoire." This is, to all intents and purposes, an autobiographical story about the conception of the idea of "The Long Way Around." At the same time, this is also another, nonfictional variation upon the same theme—the theme of the relationship between the metaphysical Law inherent in the world and the Form in which the human intellect tries to express the essence of this Law. . . . Just as in the preceding story, to enter "the world of names" means here to participate in human history and human community; to write means, in the most profound sense of the word, to love.

After the high-strung, at times almost mystical, tone of the book's first two parts, the third one, "Child Story," might seem anticlimactic. At first glance, it seems to be a quite realistic account of family troubles—the story of a father who virtually singlehandedly copes with all sorts of problems in bringing up his daughter during the first ten years of her life. Moreover, the relationship between this story and the previous two is not immediately clear. The main character, again presented in a third-person narrative, and called simply "the adult," apparently has little in common with either Sorger or the authorial narrator. Yet a closer look reveals a strong thematic thread that binds the three stories together and, despite all their differences, makes of them an artistic whole. What they share is, again, the motif of "homecoming," of finding the way to one's Ithaca by trying to discover the "universal law" of existence and to think out forms capable of communicating this discovery to others.

In Sorger's story, the metaphor for this problem is the image of a journey through geographic space and historical time, from Arctic primordiality to European modernity. In **"Child Story"** we find an analogous metaphor, only this time the journey is through the time of childhood, from the "oneness" of infancy to the complexity inherent in one's inevitable participation in society and history (even as a child, the girl is perceived, while abroad, as a *German* child, and thus becomes unknowingly an heir to a certain historic legacy). (pp. 31-2)

Peter Handke's book, brimming with existential questions and yet coolly precise . . . is one of those works of literature that tell as much about their authors as their characters. Like Flaubert, Handke has the right to say: Sorger (or "the adult") *c'est moi.* At the outset of the third story, the main character makes a significant decision—after the birth of his daughter he severs his ties with a certain political group, of which we know only that it was characterized by its collectivist spirit and utopian belief in the mechanisms of "history." In fact, the baby's birth becomes for the father "a pretext for turning his back on history."

This decision—the decision to see mankind's history as condensed in the living, breathing individual, instead of subordinating the individual to History meant as some abstract, anonymous force—is, I think, deeply symbolic, not only for Handke himself, but also (one hopes) for the generation of West European writers he represents. "Turning one's back on history" is not to be taken literally, of course; the heroes of all three stories, after all, accept the human heritage and choose to contribute to it rather than enclosing themselves within the walls of their individual selves. What Handke expresses by "turning one's back" is rather his contempt for, in his own words, "those non-beings who need history for their lives." As in a pocket mirror, the disillusionment of our age is reflected in this brief phrase. (pp. 32-3)

Stanislaw Baranczak, "Fault Lines," in The New Republic, *Vol. 192, No. 24, June 17, 1985, pp. 31-3.*

STEPHEN KOCH

Slow Homecoming contains two long essays (one on fatherhood, one on Cezanne) and one near-fiction, tracking a Handke stand-in's trip home, from Alaska, across America, to Germany. The "slow homecoming" in question is therefore a difficult, contested, intellectual and spiritual journey which it is impossible not to respect and honor.

And yet, and yet—I find it almost incredible that a man of such gifts can make such rich material so stupendously dull as Peter Handke does in this book. He had everything—just *look* at his subjects: art and ethics in post-war Europe; a new German's dream of peace; the terror generation. There are philosophy and home; parenthood and desolation. *Slow Homecoming* is about exile and America, about father-love and mother-

tongues; about landscape from the tundra to the South of France; about—not to skip the isms—solipsism, radicalism, modernism. In short, it presents a trayful of the prime hors d'oevres of life in our merry post-modern age.

How can such a selection fail? Well, Handke brings to each new luscious bit the same clotted, undramatic, entirely self-obsessed intelligence that spoiled the last. In each case, the thinking wearies even as it impresses. This book bores with a tedium so uncanny as to be almost interesting, numbing the mind almost exactly to the degree that curiosity is piqued. This sado-masochistic transformation of interest into ennui is echoed throughout by the prose itself, which the unresponding intellect vaguely senses growing more gorgeous and confident as it sinks deeper into unreadability. How, one asks (lips stiff with intellectual Novocaine) how can such intensity produce—this?

The answer lies in the solipsism that has been essential to Handke's artistic indentikit since day one. Handke has, in truth, only one subject, and it is not Cezanne. It is his own splendid self, or more precisely, his splendid self-absorption. Lesser issues merely test the staying power of this subject of subjects. True, he *worries* about his solipsism on almost every page, rather like the bore who keeps asking, "Am I boring you?" He abuses the tar-baby of his self-obsession endlessly. Nonetheless, that obsession is all that really interests him. Handke may slap and beat the tar-baby with self and other, ego and object, ecstasy and history. No matter. They all sink into the gloppy tar of Peter Handke, and there all interest, absurdly misfocused, dies. The tar-baby of the self may absorb everything, but as Uncle Remus pointed out, it don't *say* nothin'. . . .

Solipsism and dissociation have been, despite all their treachery, fonts for many a wonder in the arts of our time. These wonders have held an almost hypnotic power over that generation raised on academic modernism and the politics of the post-war world. It is inevitable, of course, that so isolating a source of energy will come in time to seem like an evil. It has come to seem so to Handke, and he rails against it here. Railing, however, does not help. The only way out is of course a surrender to community and culture; for the writer, it consists of some human vision of the reader—which for any writer, must be the unseen presence that is *the* Significant Other. The tar-baby of self-obsession is no substitute for this encounter. *Slow Homecoming* reveals it, instead, as the unconquerable simulacrum it is—just another tarry scarecrow on the wide road to dullness itself.

Stephen Koch, "The Obsessions of Peter Handke," in Book World—The Washington Post, *July 28, 1985, p. 6.*

MALCOLM BRADBURY

[*Slow Homecoming*] has a title that suggests it is about moving back toward the homely, familiar and real. It is a complex three-part reflection, heavily autobiographical, on the shapings and formings that consciousness uses in its attempts to understand and the relations of these with landscape—a tripartite quest in the direction of "home." . . .

Mr. Handke's work has come a long way, and as with other postmodern writers in a time when that movement seems half-exhausted with its own deconstructionist inquiry, it has moved far closer to a Romantic affirmation. Mr. Handke knows that affirmation in art can only be presented with a bleak rigorousness and that artists are allowed no more than a very slow homecoming. But he leaves us with an old problem of the art of modernity. Like William Carlos Williams, Ezra Pound and Hart Crane, he wants fragments to be more than ruins. Yet the direction of our most demanding and subtle art has been against certainty, its curious truth living more in its fragments and contingencies than in its affirmations of beauty, sublimity or oneness. Mr. Handke draws us more by the stubborn uneasiness of his quest than by the moments of full knowledge he seeks to summon into the imperfection of discourse and form. His touches of intolerance and rage, his self-portrait of the artist, leave us with curious, intractable doubts. What is clear, however, is that these are doubts that can only be induced by the work of a totally serious major artist.

> *Malcolm Bradbury, "A Moment of True Feeling,"*
> *in* The New York Times Book Review, *August 4,*
> *1985, p. 11.*

Barry Hannah

1942-

American novelist, short story writer, and scriptwriter.

Hannah's fiction, usually set in the contemporary South, is characterized by absurd humor, surrealistic violence, and unusual narrative twists. Because of his Southern background, Hannah is inevitably compared to William Faulkner for his use of the South as a microcosm for the universal human condition and to Eudora Welty and Flannery O'Connor for his creation of eccentric characters enmeshed in violence. Most critics, however, agree that Hannah has an original and distinctive comic voice.

Hannah's first novel, *Geronimo Rex* (1972), is a ribald initiation tale centering on Harry Monroe, a Louisiana youth in search of meaning whose personal traumas are set against the social upheaval in the South. Monroe reappears as a secondary character in *Nightwatchmen* (1973), a farcical murder mystery featuring a wealthy eccentric and an unconventional seventy-year-old detective. Both novels are permeated with black humor and violence.

Many of the twenty pieces in Hannah's first short story collection, *Airships* (1978), were originally published in *Esquire* magazine. They range in subject from the obsessive love of a homosexual soldier for a Confederate general during the Civil War to the horrors of a future American apocalypse. These stories evidence Hannah's experimentation with narrative, time, and place. Reviewing this work, Michael Wood stated: "When [the stories] work, as most of them do . . . , they follow, with careful sympathetic wit, the string of unlikely shocks and half-hearted enthusiasms that often make up a life." In his next novel, *Ray* (1980), Hannah details the hallucinatory recollections and musings of an alcoholic Alabama doctor who had served as a pilot in Vietnam and often daydreams about the Civil War era. Although Hannah's fragmented narrative has been praised for its lively humor, critics also note that he attempts to connect the past with the present to emphasize the tragedy of war.

The Tennis Handsome (1983) is a novel consisting of two seemingly unrelated stories reworked from *Airships*. In this work, the exploits of a handsome tennis player and his demented coach intertwine with the return of a Vietnam War veteran to his hometown. As in his previous works, Hannah's graphic violence is presented with comic energy and irreverence. In some of the short stories in his recent collection, *Captain Maximus* (1985), Hannah retreats somewhat from the manic style of his previous works in favor of a more subdued and less blackly humorous approach. For example, "Getting Ready" is a Hemingwayesque tale about a fisherman's attempt to land a big fish, and "Idaho" is a tribute to the late poet Richard Hugo. In a review of this work, George Stade commented: "Of the many American short-story writers who have recently won acclaim, Mr. Hannah is the most invigorating: he does not write in the prevailing style of scrupulous meanness, and the desperation of his characters is anything but quiet."

(See also *CLC*, Vol. 23; *Contemporary Authors*, Vols. 108, 110; and *Dictionary of Literary Biography*, Vol. 6.)

PUBLISHERS WEEKLY

[Hannah] is an original southern talent, and his latest oeuvre of black humor [*The Tennis Handsome*] is a trip on a ship of crazy fools—hilarious, twisted and wonderfully written. The tennis handsome in question is French Edward, a beautiful professional tennis player who becomes brain-damaged after trying to stop his coach, the weird Dr. Word, from jumping off a bridge. Dr. Word has been having an affair with French's mother, Olive, and getting away with it by posing as the town homosexual. Both Dr. Word and French go off the bridge, and French is fished out with only half his mind intact. . . . Where all this leads to is hard to say, as plot is not the novel's strong point. Neither is the entrance of Bobby Smith, a Vietnam vet who for several chapters acts as narrator. But Hannah's sheer inventiveness, jumpy, loony and manic, deflects the reader's attention from these lapses.

A review of "The Tennis Handsome," in Publishers Weekly, Vol. 223, No. 5, February 4, 1983, p. 363.

JACK BEATTY

[*The Tennis Handsome*] is a lax drifting cloud of a book, full of casual mayhem. There are suicides and strokes, eyes are gouged out and legs are broken. And this is only in the first thirty pages. Later on a man is shot with a crossbow, a woman is raped by a walrus, and an American soldier incinerates twenty V.C. with a fire gun. In the John Irving manner, these scenes are narrated without feeling; unplotted and unmotivated, they are like the violence in children's cartoons. The crime pages of *The New York Times* are more shocking, pack more emotional punch, and so are closer to literature than this TV writing. . . .

The novel involves the doings of a handsome, imbecile tennis player, his fond coach, his promiscuous mother, his doctor friend, and the obligatory Vietnam veteran, your stock symbol of rage and anomie. There is no plot, no unfolding logic of development, no growth of character. These people are simply stewed together in a lurid gumbo of inconsequence—unwholesome, flavorless, and indigestible.

> *Jack Beatty, in a review of "The Tennis Handsome," in* The New Republic, *Vol. 188, No. 15, April 18, 1983, p. 39.*

CHRISTOPHER LEHMANN-HAUPT

The appeal of Barry Hannah—whose previous books include *Geronimo Rex, Nightwatchmen, Airships* and *Ray*—is that he seems to have chewed up and swallowed the entire rhetorical tradition of the American South and then spit it back out in a rainbow of hilarity and nonsense. . . .

The trouble is that in *The Tennis Handsome* . . . the manic language palls eventually, and there is little in the way of credible characterization to bring us relief. Finally, the only living thing in *The Tennis Handsome* is the author's fierce determination to stun us with his zaniness. This works for a while, but it's simply not enough to sustain us for the length of a novel.

> *Christopher Lehmann-Haupt, in a review of "The Tennis Handsome," in* The New York Times, *April 18, 1983, p. C15.*

IVAN GOLD

In fashioning [*The Tennis Handsome*], Barry Hannah, a fine, frugal writer, has reached back to plunder his third, the highly regarded collection of stories called *Airships* (1978). He has made off not only with characters, themes and situations but with the bounty of the prose itself. Which is to say that the first two chapters of *The Tennis Handsome* are scarcely altered versions of what appeared to be unconnected stories in *Airships*, bearing the titles (in both places) of **"Return to Return"** and **"Midnight and I'm Not Famous Yet."** Some novelizing adhesive has been daubed on here and there, and beyond that the stories are worth repeating.

"Return to Return" follows the baroque adventures of the world class tennis player French Edward, so extraordinarily handsome that "Women anguished to conceive of his departure from a tournament," and the parallel bizarre doings of his unsavory companion and sometime caretaker, Baby Levaster, wag and self-defrocked M.D. **"Midnight and I'm Not Famous Yet,"** which was regarded on its initial publication in *Esquire* and subsequent appearance in *Airships* as one of the best short stories to come out of the Vietnam War, is a first-person account by Capt. Bob Smith—who hails, as do French and Baby, from the environs of Vicksburg, Miss.—of the capture by his

company of a North Vietnamese general, Li Dap, and Smith's unavoidable murder of this valuable prisoner almost immediately after. (p. 11)

[In *The Tennis Handsome*] French Edward is intermittently feebleminded, having almost drowned in an attempt either to save from suicide or speed the departure of Dr. Word, his former tennis coach. Word was jolted out of lifelong homosexuality some years earlier by the sight of French Edward's mother, Olive, whom he then seduced, clandestinely observed by French himself. A monster of vengefulness, Edward forces the aging Dr. Word to play tennis so far beyond his capacity that he has a stroke, which damages his vision and obliges him to speak thereafter at the top of his lungs.

This does not, however, diminish his enthusiasm for Olive, nor his admiration for French Edward's tennis skills: "The man was crazed with partisanship." French's faculties are temporarily restored when he is struck by lightning during a match. The bolt also brings with it a gift of partial second sight and the inclination to turn out verse, cloying doggerel that becomes scatological in time.

Meanwhile, Capt. Bob Smith has returned from the wars to become integrated into the story. He has an affair with his own aunt, who, before she runs off with a very Southern senator, is nearly raped by a walrus. Levaster, who had himself made merry with Olive in her mellower years ("a dreadfully beautiful old lady"), is dispatched with a crossbow by French Edward's wife. There is issue from a brief union Edward had with an oversexed polio victim. (pp. 11, 19)

Time flies. ("Some years passed and Levaster was forty.") Language is made to juggle with its snout, standing on its tail. I can hardly tell you how bizarre things really get or why the weirdness is usually satisfying. While *The Tennis Handsome* may not be his "best" book already assembled or yet to come, it's as good a place to start reading Barry Hannah as any. He is an original, or if names are to be dropped, Carson McCullers rewritten by Groucho Marx. (p. 19)

> *Ivan Gold, "Yoknapatawpha County of the Mind," in* The New York Times Book Review, *May 1, 1983, pp. 11, 19.*

CAROLYN CLAY

The Tennis Handsome is set on the largely asphalt court of post-Vietnam America, where senseless combat is the monotonous norm and love the lowest score. On the sidelines, like some Kerouac'd-out Bud Collins, sits Barry Hannah, taking notes (and possibly drugs) on the sex, violence, and religiosity of it all. His Christ, who survives both drowning and a close encounter with lightning, may be the first to wear tennis whites and a visor of thorns.

Hannah's sports reportage—centered on the seemingly endless career of ageless ace French Edward, "the happiest man on the court, and the prettiest," if a near-mental defective—displays an imagination as lush and befouled as the Mississippi delta that spawned him. His is the world according to some red-neck Garp: vicious and arbitrary in the bleachers; primeval grace where the gods in sneakers gambol, churning up the thrill of victory, the agony of defeat, without actual bloodshed. As a shell-shocked Vietnam survivor remarks from the stands, "It was wonderful and nobody was being killed." . . .

Alas, Hannah's hallucinogenic yarn is as relentless as his vision. The gonzo approach, in which he is well versed, may be best suited to short fiction. Even this brief novel, almost devoid of scenery and sentiment, becomes exhausting, its barbed whimsy ground to cuteness. Careering through a low-down America high on athletics and prurience, the book is full of brilliant notions; they just keep coming at you, like balls spewed by one of those practice machines. Only sex and sport seem to merit play-by-play coverage, and while the former is brutal, the latter is holy. "It's a *church*," Levaster thinks as he watches French stride onto a tennis court. "We are close to the godly meadows here."

Perhaps. But Hannah has no intention of stopping to smell the celestial flowers. It's slam, bam, thank you, ma'am, as image after potent image is lobbed over the fence. Hannah's talent, teetering ominously on America's cracked foundation, is undeniable, even frightening. But in the end it tumbles down on us—as he says of one of Levaster's dreams—"like the bricks of a hysterical mansion."

> Carolyn Clay, "Off the Court," in New York Magazine, Vol. 16, No. 20, May 16, 1983, p. 66.

CHRISTOPHER LEHMANN-HAUPT

In *Captain Maximus*. Barry Hannah seems to be calming down a little. . . .

His people seem ready for simpler resolutions than in his previous work. In "Getting Ready," Roger Laird, a big-time fisherman who had "never caught a significant fish," settles for a 15-pound sand shark because he "was tiring" and "his senses were shutting down." . . .

The result of this settling down (if that is what it can be called) is not always salutary. Some of the more extreme effects now seem strained and self-conscious, as if the new Barry Hannah felt he had to compete with the old one. Despite its many powerful passages, Mr. Hannah's film synopsis—which could be said to represent a stricter formal challenge than his spawling stories—remains a strikingly solipsistic exercise, difficult to get a handle on, let alone describe.

Still, there is more narrative movement in the pages of *Captain Maximus* then there was in either of Mr. Hannah's last two books, *Ray* and *The Tennis Handsome,* both of which exhausted themselves in their efforts to stun us with their apocalyptic despair. And Mr. Hannah's highly original prose is as vital as always, vital enough to lift us over the faults in the terrain.

> Christopher Lehmann-Haupt, in a review of "Captain Maximus," in The New York Times, April 29, 1985, p. C18.

TERRENCE RAFFERTY

The air of Barry Hannah's fiction is usually thick with the noise and smoke of gunplay, but in [*Captain Maximus*] only a single shot is fired and it's not a clean one—a double-barreled shotgun blast of whale dung, fired by a mean drifter on a Wind Surfer. This is a fully characteristic Hannah act, the sort of thing that might just as easily have been done by the students and crackers of *Geronimo Rex,* the Confederate soldiers and demon lovers of *Airships,* the mad doctors of *Ray* and *The Tennis Handsome,* those fabulously unconvincing characters who seem to reflect their creator's imagination simply by being wild, exuberant and proudly, aggressively full of it.

Captain Maximus, though . . . is too thin to be full of anything at all. Hannah may intend the shotgun episode which occurs in a story called "It Spoke of Exactly the Things," as a kind of self-parody, a way of announcing that he's got all the *Moby Dick* crap out of his system. After all, the obsessive fisherman of this book's opening story, "Getting Ready," finds peace of mind after landing a small gray sand shark (which he throws back into the water). And even Maximus, whose story ("Ride, Fly, Penetrate, Loiter") begins with his account of being stabbed in the eye with his own fish knife, isn't, finally, a very alarming figure—just a benign biker / writer / teacher who has visions in his dead eye and who says, near the end, "At forty, I am at a certain peace." Statements like that could be taken as justification for the relatively subdued style and even for the very smallness of the book, as if the narrowing of ambition and the drastic reduction of means were marks of maturity, the midcareer writer burning off the fat—a justification obvious enough for us to be suspicious of it. Hannah's new modesty is so insistent that it begins to reveal, in spite of itself, a cunning side; he's found a way to disguise the anxious, wiry frame of an assassin as the athletic trim of a boxer training for a comeback.

Consider "Idaho," probably the plainest seven pages of fiction Hannah has ever published, a kind of tribute to the poet Richard Hugo, who died shortly after Hannah met him at the University of Montana. "I read his 'Letter' poems and saw what could be done with honest sentiment," the writer says, and this story seems to be Hannah's demonstration of what he can "do with" his own. The voice *sounds* honest, personal, but the sentiment comes out all wrong—as it has to, conceived purely as material for use. . . .

If we feel uneasy at the conclusion of "Idaho," it's not because we've been blown away by its honesty, rocked by its self-revelatory force, but rather because we sense something furtive and crafty in it, another message, a coded, occult one that we were never meant to read: this "letter" story isn't really addressed to us, and it does not speak exactly of the things on Hannah's mind. "Idaho," for instance, is a strange title for a story about a Southerner in Montana who admits he never crossed the border into the other state, but only "bought an Idaho patch for my jacket and have ever since lied about seeing Idaho." What's unspoken is the name of Hemingway, who was in Ketchum when he put a shotgun to his head: does "Idaho" mean "Hemingway"? (Or "suicide"?) (p. 677)

Unspoken, too, is the question to which "I look down at my hand. [It's not a gun. It's only a pencil. I am not going anywhere.]" is the answer: it's "Hey Joe, where you goin' with that gun in your hand?" and it's the first line of Jimi Hendrix's first hit record. The reply in the Hendrix song is "I'm goin' down to shoot my old lady." Is this story not about a poet's natural death but about the narrator's veering back and forth between suicide and murder? Maybe it is and maybe it isn't. Once we discover that a writer's been burying little references, like land mines, beneath the surface of the story, we don't trust the terrain enough to see it whole, and anything is possible. Is it significant that Hannah, Hugo, Hemingway and Hendrix share an initial? If we played "Idaho" backward, at the wrong speed, and with the volume turned way up, would we hear a croaky voice telling us that someone's dead?

And "Idaho" is the best, most scrupulously crafted story in *Captain Maximus*. It's distressing to see Hannah's work become so cryptic and spare, as grudging of its revelations as his first novel, *Geronimo Rex,* was prodigal. This collection has the feel of those grim, creepy miscellanies that appear after an artist's death, like all the albums assembled from unearthed, marginal Hendrix material, full of vagrant riffs and aimless jams, fragments which serve only as eerie reminders of the stilled voice. A writer who represents himself in this way during his lifetime is either profoundly alienated from his own activity or simply exhausted—worn out from throwing too many punches in the early rounds.

Hannah has always been a jabbing, assaultive writer, the kind who wants to rip things open and see blood, and he's drawn to characters who embody that approach to experience: obsessive poets and musicians, careless doctors with quick needles and messy smocks, and warriors of every description (including cavalry officers, Indian chiefs, bomber pilots and athletes). The hero of *Geronimo Rex,* Harry Monroe, is, or imagines himself to be, most of those things in the course of the novel, and all of his roles are splendidly accommodated by the book's picaresque structure. Overstuffed with weirdness and careening from one slapstick skirmish to another, Harry Monroe's saga has an effortless and unselfconscious vitality: the pranks, the desperate wooing and even the stray bursts of gunfire are all just a young man's adventures, not a program for living, and even if the experiences themselves seem unfamiliar, a mite extreme, their youthful, giddy absurdity does not.

Most of the early stories collected in *Airships* have the same eccentric vivacity, but the shorter, more concentrated form makes the characters' individual quirks just a little more pointed: every oddball trait seems to carry a shade too much significance. And Hannah's language in these stories is different, too, with the kinds of jumps and distortions poets use when they want our attention, startling us with the unexpected word ("a crowd of the sorrowful and the inept had gathered") and clubbing us at the end of nearly every story—no matter how wispy its narrative, how random its details—with a blunt, decisive punch line ("I'm going to die from love," or "We were both crucified by the truth"). Even the most unassuming stories in *Airships* have a phrase or two that come at us out of nowhere, that mean to pierce us like the abrupt chords and keening isolated notes that break the surface of a Hendrix song, that mean, in their way, to wound us with the truth.

In *Airships,* as fine as much of it is, we can see something ominous happening to Barry Hannah, the beginnings of an almost mystical belief in his own easy manipulation of language—as if the exact combination of words and images will induce visions, like a prayer. This is a feeling that's probably more common in poets and musicians than in novelists—novels are too roomy, exploratory, approximate—and in the work he's published since *Airships,* Hannah is barely a novelist at all. *Ray,* the hallucinatory monologue of a Tuscaloosa doctor, is laid out in fragments of imagery and narrative and is completely successful in its own terms, but it's really no more than an intricate mosaic of phallic motifs—guns, swords, hypodermics, bombers, the thing itself. This short book is a kind of demented inspirational pamphlet, with doctor / pilot / poet Ray as its example of how to penetrate reality like a bright shaft of light: it's the esthetic of the short stories turned into an ethic. *Ray* pretty much embodies the complete system of Hannah's myths, honed and polished—and it's the sort of work that leaves a writer nowhere to go except farther inward, rearranging his private stock of images, elaborating them in different ways. For *The Tennis Handsome,* Hannah went right back to *Airships,* ripped out two unrelated stories and drew them out to novel length, adding a couple of new shoot-life-between-

the-eyes metaphors (tennis and lightning) to the ones he already had. *The Tennis Handsome* is as crazy as *Geronimo Rex,* but less reckless; this picaresque is straining to transcend itself, and it's a joyless, panicked book.

The new fiction in *Captain Maximus* is a sort of vacation from the desperate exertions of Hannah's previous work, but it's a solitary, meditative one, filled with the memories of old obsessions—a weekend of fishing in the big two-hearted river. He's not charging around with guns and sabers, or trying to attach himself to the whale's back with the cord of an electric guitar; he's just still, holding his line and waiting, hoarding his secrets. (pp. 677-78)

Barry Hannah is an immensely gifted writer, but he should cut out the voodoo and try speaking to us again in the expansive, outgoing novelist's voice of *Geronimo Rex.* With each book, he's becoming less and less like the appealing Southern hell raiser Harry Monroe and more and more like the edgy, darting Union Army spy in the *Airships* story **"Behold the Husband in His Perfect Agony,"** all his knowledge sealed inside as he glides quietly, vigilantly through the streets of Richmond—the spy who, in the end, whirls suddenly and kills what he most loves, fearing that it's betrayed him. (p. 679)

Terrence Rafferty, "Gunsmoke and Voodoo," *in* The Nation, *Vol. 240, No. 21, June 1, 1985, pp. 677-79.*

GEORGE STADE

[Hannah's fiction reads] as though written by a good ol' boy become self-conscious. His lead characters, most of whom (like Mr. Hannah) have erupted from the Deep South, are defiantly what they are, but they are not so sure they like it. . . . Mr. Hannah's protagonists, who usually narrate their own stories, tend to be randy, violent, hard drinkers, good haters and intermittently psychopathic, but they suffer from remorse and an outraged sense of style. They value grace under pressure, but lose their balance in thinking about it, in their fury at the moral pipsqueaks and "monsters of piety" around them. ("The only thing was to get drunk and fire at will.") Of the many American short-story writers who have recently won acclaim, Mr. Hannah is the most invigorating: he does not write in the prevailing style of scrupulous meanness, and the desperation of his characters is anything but quiet. . . .

[The] stories in *Captain Maximus* rush out to us, on the shock and thud of metaphor, the sentences abrupt, the silences between them full of menace. Two of the stories might have been written by a fiercer and more elliptical Hemingway. In **"Getting Ready"** a man loses nearly everything in a manic attempt to catch "a significant fish," but makes do with a sand shark. In **"Even Greenland"** a jet pilot cracks up—in both senses—over the way his best experiences are stolen from him by the formulations of other people. In two stories, **"I Am Shaking to Death"** and **"It Spoke of Exactly the Things,"** the narrators yolk themselves by violence to the "terrific women" they hope will redeem them—more fishermen and sand sharks. And in **"Fans"** four moral cripples gather in a bar before the big game in Oxford, Miss., to talk about a star defensive back, a born-again Christian, and, as it turns out, the vilest human botch you can imagine. The one failure is **"Idaho,"** in which the autobiographical currents flow sluggishly and too near the surface.

But even **"Idaho"** could only have been written by Mr. Hannah, who writes like no one else. **"Power and Light,"** the "idea for a film" that makes up the second half of this volume, is evidence that Mr. Hannah has more than one way of writing like no one else. The prose now is cool, distant, mostly without personal inflection. Instead of the usual collision of metaphors, there is now an interplay of sharp visual images. Instead of one discontinuous narrative (all Mr. Hannah's narratives are discontinuous), there is a succession of vignettes that in the mind intertwine, combine, separate and regroup in new combinations. Character and meaning are revealed strictly by what the players say and do, by their relations to the objects around them. There is no commenting narrator, no direct access to the players' minds. And the cast is an unusual one, for Mr. Hannah.

In the lead roles are five working women: a dispatcher, a doctor, a crane operator, a linewoman (all employed by City Lights, the Seattle power and light company) and a jet pilot. Their men are of the leeching or miching sort—an oafish son, a drugged-out brother, kinky or self-absorbed lovers. And there is an assortment of grotesques—a protofascist with a glorious white bulldog, an insane lounger ("casualty of a long, impossible lust") and a man who sends the women letters that may be either threats or mash notes. Cut by cut, the heart of a situation, a city even, is exposed. The scenes are visually sharp, but ambiguous in meaning, too complicated for summary. I don't know how seriously Mr. Hannah means **"Power and Light"** to be taken as an idea for a film but it seems to me more like an experiment in writing what he calls "camera philosophy." A full-length experiment of this sort from Mr. Hannah would be something very much worth having.

But then anything written by Mr. Hannah is well worth having.

> *George Stade, "Lives of Noisy Desperation," in* The New York Times Book Review, *June 9, 1985, p. 14.*

DORIS BETTS

In an interview he gave two books ago, Barry Hannah explained why his novel, *Ray,* had been cut from 400 pages to a short book in which short scenes "hit your mind and are gone." He wanted a "pageturner" not dependent on serial events and meant plot to be viewed in its many facets rather than accumulated in a sequence. Since then he has been using his cinematic techniques in writing movie scripts.

In *Captain Maximus,* seven stories and a narrated screen treatment, the same techniques remain skillfully at work, often more abbreviated than ever, though what hits the reader's mind is apt to become imbedded there. . . .

In Hannah reality is strange; stories are true; energy is all.

If his fiction makes you want to read more Hugo poetry and more Hannah fiction, it does so without ever nailing down the conclusions which would rob either's work of mystery. In **"Even Greenland,"** one of the most candid stories, two competing writers are flying an F-14 in trouble at 75,000 feet; the high flier who ejects leaves the other to die and thus "win," by carrying his last original metaphor into posterity. **"Getting Ready"** is about a fisherman who throws back the huge sand shark caught in the surf on an ordinary Zebco rod and reel and is himself transformed. . . .

"Power and Light," subtitled an "Idea for Film" presents 40 pages of quick camera cuts among a cast of characters in Seattle

("builder of ships"), Washington ("most electrified state of the United States"). Most are women; many have ties to City Lights, the electric company. A mysterious Eurasian is mailing anonymous prophecies, signed Sweed Truitt, to some of them, especially Polly Buck, a power linewoman. The links between lives, the speedy changes and revelations held together by an obviously good-natured affection for women, kept me turning pages even when the serial events flew out of the plot as the bulldog does in the end, "like a white small fat angel." It would be pointless to paraphrase plot/theme in a story which is read the way energy pulsates, which comes with pleasure into the mind in the form of its title, as power and light.

> *Doris Betts, "Barry Hannah: Where Energy Is All," in* Book World—The Washington Post, *June 23, 1985, p. 11.*

JAMES WOLCOTT

Captain Maximus doesn't have the sex or wild, automotive force of *Ray* and *The Tennis Handsome,* but this isn't necessarily a bad thing. *Ray* and *The Tennis Handsome* were so packed with wicked, fast improvisations that they wore themselves out trying to maintain their headlong drive. Nor does *Captain Maximus* have the juiced-up violence of *Airships,* where one notorious story ended with the narrator bashing in a woman's skull with a tombstone. There's no denying that compared to these books, *Captain Maximus* seems a bit sickly and sowhat. A thin book, it has a lot of loose flesh hanging from its bones. Frequently Hannah seems less interested in telling a tale than in embellishing a reputation as demon drinker and campus tongue:

> The university was a neo-Grecian dump with a good ball team. The only thing was to get drunk and fire at will. The chairman fired back with drinking and eating female students.

> Ah, those beauties sweet to me when I was down: Val, Ann, Rita Veranoff, a few others who can't be told because of their boyfriends.

Along with Val and Ann and Rita, we're furnished with the names of Hannah's best pals in **"Idaho,"** the novelist Tom McGuane and his wife Laurie. Here the affection really turns to candy. "Later, my nephew Taylor and I ate at the George Street Grocery with the McGuanes, who had their new baby Annie with them. Oh, it was wonderful. McGuane is a giant in heart and body, and where are you giants anymore?" Such a pat on the back may be a minor offense, though the tone here is awfully fawning. More grievously, Hannah ruins a fine, neat Hemingwayesque story, **"Getting Ready,"** by tacking on a freaky finish. **"Getting Ready"** is about a man who has never caught "a significant fish," and who after much welldescribed labor lands a shark. Hannah doesn't stop there, unfortunately. The story ends with a triumphant fisherman teetering around on stilts and yelling at rich people as they come off their sailing boats, "Fuck you! Fuck you!" Too often in *Captain Maximus* Hannah himself is up on stilts, trying to make a scene. (p. 33)

> *James Wolcott, "Southern Discomfort," in* The New York Review of Books, *Vol. XXXII, No. 11, June 27, 1985, pp. 33-4.**

Joseph Hansen

1923-

(Has also written under pseudonyms of James Colton, James Coulton, and Rose Brock) American novelist, short story writer, poet, critic, and editor.

A prolific author of crime and suspense fiction, Hansen is best known for his series of novels featuring homosexual insurance investigator David Brandstetter. In these books Hansen avoids the standard presentation of gays as either frivolous or guilt-ridden by portraying Brandstetter as tough and humorless and by depicting West Coast homosexual lifestyles without resorting to condescension or sensationalism. By focusing on homosexuals whose indiscretions or unstable relationships lead to conflict, Hansen comments on isolation and unhappiness as a part of gay existence. Newgate Callendar claims that Hansen "is of the Ross Macdonald school—unsentimental, clinical, with the world-weary *Weltschmerz* that is a Macdonald trademark." The novels in the Brandstetter series include *Fadeout* (1970), *Death Claims* (1973), *Troublemaker* (1975), *The Man Everybody Was Afraid Of* (1978), *Skinflick* (1979), *Gravedigger* (1982), and *Nightwork* (1984). The hero also makes several appearances in stories collected in a volume of short fiction, *Brandstetter & Others* (1984).

Hansen is also the author of several other books written under pseudonyms or his own name. *Longleaf* (1974), Hansen's best-known novel under the pseudonym Rose Brock, is a historical romance in which a southern woman attempts to regain the family fortune that was lost during the Civil War. *A Smile in His Lifetime* (1981), Hansen's first mainstream novel written under his own name, concerns a homosexual author whose sense of loneliness and isolation intensifies when his supportive wife leaves him. In *Backtrack* (1982), a book Terry Teachout termed a "short, pithy *Bildungsroman* disguised as a suspense novel," Hansen examines a young man's thoughts about his deceased father's latent homosexuality and its possible role in his death. Homosexuality is again a central theme in *Job's Year* (1983), a novel in which a gay actor faces middle age and mortality when he realizes that his sister is dying and his lover is leaving him. As Rob Schmieder stated, the book gives "the lie to the picture of the homosexual as a pleasure-seeker free from family responsibilities."

(See also *Contemporary Authors*, Vols. 29-32, rev. ed. and *Contemporary Authors New Revision Series*, Vol. 16.)

ALLEN J. HUBIN

I'm not sure that there would be much out of the ordinary about Joseph Hansen's *Fadeout* ... were it not for the fact that homosexuality—of the investigator-protagonist and several others in the cast—plays so frontal a role, but Mr. Hansen portrays that other world sharply and without condescension. Dave Brandstetter, mourning the loss of his lover of 25 years, reluctantly takes on another insurance case for his father's agency. The death—the questionable death—is that of Fox Olson, late

© Jerry Bauer

blooming and much beloved folk singer and radio entertainer in a California ranch town. . . . Brandstetter probes into a political situation that Olson's whimsical candidacy threatened, into his twisted family ties, into, more critically, the indiscretions of his gayer youth.

Allen J. Hubin, in a review of "Fadeout," in The New York Times Book Review, September 20, 1970, p. 48.

NEWGATE CALLENDAR

[Joseph Hansen's *Death Claims* is unusual] if only for the fact that its detective is a homosexual. . . . The hero [David Brandstetter] here is a claims investigator for an insurance company in the Los Angeles area. He is looking into a drowning. Accident? Suicide? Murder? His path takes him into various byways; and on top of that he has his own troubles to take care of.

Hansen is of the Ross Macdonald school—unsentimental, clinical, with the world-weary *Weltschmerz* that is a Macdonald trademark. His writing abounds in such dialogue as:

"You are. Tonight. When you get home."

"Home?" he said. "Where's that?"

But on the whole, Hansen avoids cliché, and he does manage to wrap the reader up in the emotional troubles of his hero without getting sloppy about it. And the crime elements are smoothly handled, building to a credible denouement.

> *Newgate Callendar, in a review of "Death Claims," in* The New York Times Book Review, *January 21, 1973, p. 26.*

O. L. BAILEY

[*Death Claims*] marks the return of David Brandstetter, the insurance investigator who happens to be a confirmed homosexual. Introduced in Hansen's innovative first novel, *Fadeout,* he is, interestingly, one of the genre's most appealing new detectives. In *Death Claims* a has-been screenwriter's demise finds Brandstetter on the Hollywood scene encountering . . . [characters] of all kinds. By the time he finally sorts out the sordid strands of several lives he has one thoroughly engrossed. Throughout, Brandstetter and his private life are handled with taste and without sensationalism—absolutely straight so to speak—leading the reader to insights he might otherwise miss. (p. 68)

> *O. L. Bailey, "On the Docket," in* Saturday Review, *Vol. 1, No. 2, February 3, 1973, pp. 67-9.**

ROGER BAKER

[*Fadeout* is, on] the face of it, a commonplace enough thriller. Insurance claims investigator Dave Brandstetter is unconvinced that Fox Olsen is actually dead. His car has been found battered in a storm flooded river, but not his body. So Brandstetter talks to the widow, the secretary and the daughter and uncovers a personal history which offers any amount of openings for suicide or murder. There are clues, surprises, revelations and we seem to be working through a fairly familiar detective story routine. And ultimately we are. When Brandstetter starts his investigation, Olsen is not dead at all; but he is murdered before very long and the murderer duly discovered with appropriate surprise on the part of the reader, one hopes.

But *Fadeout* has other claims to attention. For Dave Brandstetter, our middle-aged, tough, humourless hero is in fact homosexual. And so is Fox Olsen, middle-aged, married popular figure in his community. This is probably the first novel in which the homosexual has not been portrayed in stereotyped terms as either a frivolous fantasy-afflicted figure, or as someone ridden with guilt and driven to dire acts by the furtive quality of his existence. Brandstetter has been living with another man on a marriage basis for many years; but Rod has just died. Brandstetter's emotions, his memories of their life together and attitudes are presented, without apology, as perfectly equal and valid to those of a heterosexual man in the same position. . . .

The presentation of the homosexual as being a perfectly ordinary person is long overdue in fiction. The average gay novel has always been a matter of derision. . . . [Hansen's] information it seems is refreshingly truthful. It is possible to argue that Hansen has engineered the hero a little too glibly. That is, just as some homosexual writers simply make their female characters men or boys with a girl's name, so Hansen seems to have taken a stereotyped detective and transferred the heterosexual response to a homosexual one. Thus, just as your butch investigator is going to eye a nice pair of tits, so Brandstetter allows himself to linger over a hippy youth in a jockstrap

and to engage in rather too gentle conversations with a comely Japanese houseboy. And we have the full heterosexual double-standard bit at the end as well. . . . Still, these are minor cavils; Hansen's view is correct and I'm looking forward to his next Brandstetter book.

> *Roger Baker, in a review of "Fadeout," in* Books and Bookmen, *Vol. 18, No. 6, March, 1973, p. 81.*

LINDA MASEK

[In *Longleaf*] young Bird Thatcher travels to New Orleans in a search for true identity after her foster mother's death. She meets a host of villains who try everything from black magic to strangulation to keep Bird from learning that she is the heiress to a fortune of gold. Things work out for the best, however, when the girl's true love arrives in the nick of time to save her from the hands of the evildoers. The atmosphere adds to the suspense, and [Hansen, writing under the pseudonym] Brock, has done a clever job of plotting. For those readers who want a Gothic novel, this is more than adequate to fill the bill.

> *Linda Masek, in a review of "Longleaf," in* Library Journal, *Vol. 99, No. 10, May 15, 1974, p. 1406.*

MARGHANITA LASKI

Joseph Hansen writes West Coast crime with an insurance investigator as private eye, and has, to my mind, been overpraised because the hero and the ambiences are homosexual. But look at them in a heterosexual light (say, the scene between the hero and his manly, understanding father), and the cloying sentimentality and special pleading place [*Troublemaker*], as Hansen's other books, rather with the newer West-Coast minority-plea novels than with classical West Coast crime.

> *Marghanita Laski, "Crime and Intensity," in* The Listener, *Vol. 93, No. 2409, June 5, 1975, p. 748.**

JEAN WHITE

[David Brandstetter] is a homosexual, but author Joseph Hansen doesn't use that fact merely for cheap exploitation to come up with a new quirk on a sleuth. Through Brandstetter's own search for satisfactory relationships and a stable life-style, Hansen reflects the often unhappy, lonely moments of those who have chosen the "gay" life. In *Troublemaker,* Brandstetter investigates an apparently clear-cut case of the murder of one homosexual by another for money, but finds the motive cuts much deeper—into teenage sex encounters and the lives of both hidden and open homosexuals.

> *Jean White, in a review of "Troublemaker," in* Book World—The Washington Post, *September 21, 1975, p. 2.*

IAN HAMILTON

[In *The Man Everybody Was Afraid Of*] Hansen's gay sleuth continues to out-butch the opposition: this time a herd of bull-neck cops in a small West Coast town. The ridiculously all-powerful police chief has been slain and his bereaved colleagues close ranks when an insurance investigator from LA queries their instant arrest of a local gay activist leader. . . . Some of this is tedious, but Hansen's mostly witty dialogue and his gift for painstaking local colour do much to compensate for any creakings in the plot.

> Ian Hamilton, "Crime Ration," in The Observer, November 5, 1978, p. 30.*

MARGHANITA LASKI

The cumbersomely titled *The Man Everybody Was Afraid Of* is conventional better-grade West Coast [fiction] with the difference . . . [that] Dave Brandstetter is gay. This story, of the murder of a nasty small-town police chief, carries . . . a discreet torch for discreet homosexuality—but, no more than the heteros, can it resist the near-obligatory details of physical attachment. (p. 63)

> Marghanita Laski, "Dead of Winter," in The Listener, Vol. 101, No. 2593, January 11, 1979, pp. 62-3.*

JEAN M. WHITE

If Joseph Hansen were not an excellent craftsman and a mature writer with taste, *Skinflick* . . . might have deteriorated into an exploitative book, what with its nymphets, transvestites, religious vigilantes, teenagers on drugs and porno-filmmakers. But Hansen, one of the best practitioners of the California private-eye school, takes this sleazy scene and turns it into a tense tale with real human beings, humor and even some tender moments. . . .

In *Skinflick,* Gerald Dawson, a religious zealot who scourges porno book shops, is murdered. The police have the obvious suspect in the bookstore owner. But Brandstetter discovers that Dawson collected girlie magazines and shared a secret love nest with a teenage runaway; moreover, Dawson's partner dabbled in porno filmmaking and gave drug parties on his boat.

Hansen tends to allow the psychos to run away with the plot, but he still writes crisply with a lean, spare prose that echoes Hammett, Chandler and Macdonald.

> Jean M. White, "Extortionists and Exhibitionists," in Book World—The Washington Post, October 21, 1979, p. 16.*

NEWGATE CALLENDAR

[In *Skinflick*] Brandstetter now is on his own, a freelance insurance investigator with his own office. His father is dead, which means that he has come into money and a house. In the meantime, of course, he has a job to do. A religious crusader against pornography has been killed, and Brandstetter has been retained by the insurance company to look into the matter. A suspect is already in jail, but Brandstetter doesn't believe that the police have the right man. . . .

In addition to the murder, *Skinflick* concerns a missing teenage girl, and it also has something to say about the hypocrisy of righteous crusaders. As usual, the writing is objective. Mr. Hansen is not one for much preaching. There is a bit of a letdown in the last few pages, however, and there is also an unexpectedly cute last paragraph. Let's hope Mr. Hansen has got such writing out of his system, because otherwise the book is tough, unsentimental and fast-moving.

> Newgate Callendar, in a review of "Skinflick," in The New York Times Book Review, *November 4, 1979, p. 24.*

CHRISTOPHER SCHEMERING

[In] *A Smile in His Lifetime,* a "serious" change-of-pace novel, Hansen's [gay character] Whit Miller . . . has few moments of affability. The book begins promisingly: Whit is a middle-aged married writer who, with his wife's tacit approval and always-available hanky, keeps a few male lovers—all troublesome—on the side. When his new novel goes through the roof, his wife leaves him, explaining that he no longer needs her now that he's successful. . . .

The scenario, which had some tension and narrative drive, slows down to a maudlin trot then falls over into a melodramatic ditch. Whit moves from man to man, from scene to scene, drinking himself to the point where big bugs start crawling out of his typewriter. He is moved to thoughts of violence, is mugged twice, and is hospitalized. As the crying scenes multiply, the drama and dialogue ("I don't want to be beaten up again—not outside, not inside") seem to be lifted from an AFI tribute to Susan Hayward. This is regrettable since there are flashes of wry observation and humor between those interminable crying jags. But these passages are obscured by Hansen's tendency for literalness—for example, just as Whit's life falls apart, his beach house does likewise. And it is distressing to see a talented writer who has made a distinct effort to present a variety of gay men (Whit's lovers are ethnically and culturally balanced) fall back on a stock character like the hero's stereotypical castrating mama. . . . The moments of quality which drift through the novel are finally lost in a jeremiad of self-pity and obviousness.

> Christopher Schemering, in a review of "A Smile in His Lifetime," in Book World—The Washington Post, June 7, 1981, p. 6.

AVERY CORMAN

[*A Smile in His Lifetime*] deals with a bisexual man who drifts away from his wife toward homosexuality. This is not a book that is going to encourage many people to sign on for homosexuality. The emotional landscape is bleak, lonely; sex does not buy happiness, nor do fame and money.

The setting is Los Angeles in the late 1960's. Whit Miller, a writer struggling with his work and with his sexual impulses, turns to serial relationships with men, which are vividly described. "You're going to be all right now," his wife assures him when he achieves literary and commercial success with a book; but he is as helpless and emotionally isolated as before. He is savagely beaten in a homosexual cruising area; his public sends him get-well cards, which fill him with self-loathing. He is suicidal, but he chooses life instead and endures. (p. 14)

Joseph Hansen has chosen a tough, staccato style for this novel, and it works against much of the emotional material, making it appear melodramatic. The style is better matched to the action scenes, which are extremely well written. (pp. 14-15)

Ironically, despite the lean quality of the prose, the novel is weakened by the author's decision to tell us too much. There is a long section dealing with Whit Miller's obsession for a young man, Jaime, a not very interesting character who is surrounded by other not very interesting characters. The novel gets caught in the obsession. Then, as we are drawing to the end of the book, we are given the details of an early homosexual relationship of Miller's, which is late in the novel for this kind of exposition. These choices damage the narrative line, resulting in a novel more effective in its parts than as a whole.

Joseph Hansen wavers in his narrative, but his intentions are courageous, and he is always on the mark in confronting the feelings, even the darkest feelings, contained in his material. (p. 15)

> *Avery Corman, "Love and Hate," in* The New York Times Book Review, *June 28, 1981, pp. 14-15.**

TERRY TEACHOUT

After Lew Archer, what? The question, sad to say, is no longer academic, six years having passed since Ross Macdonald's last book, and aficionados of the hard-boiled crime novel with a touch of literary class are beginning to wonder when someone will come along to keep the line going. The smart money now is on Joseph Hansen, a Los Angeles writer who, in his 1970 mystery *Fadeout,* introduced a decidedly off-beat character: Dave Brandstetter, an insurance investigator specializing in "death claims." Though Brandstetter fits easily into the Spade-Marlowe-Archer mold—aging detective, sunny California, virtue at bay in a society full of rampant corruption—Hansen has a few fresh angles of his own that keep the Brandstetter novels from becoming just another exercise in déjà vu, like avoiding showy similes and opting for a cooler third-person narrative mode. As for Dave Brandstetter, there's also something different about him: he's gay. . . . If the very idea of a hard-boiled homosexual offends you, don't bother. If not, then Hansen has a new Dave Brandstetter novel out, an excellent missing-person caper called *Gravedigger* in which Dave barely escapes getting shot to pieces while searching for a bankrupt lawyer and his cult-crazy daughter. Though Hansen's work lacks the thoughtfulness and scope of the later Macdonald, there's no one more promising on the detective-story scene today, and *Gravedigger* is Hansen's best book yet. It's exciting to think what he'll be doing with the form in another five years—which is no reason to wait that long before checking him out. (pp. 645, 647)

> *Terry Teachout, in a review of "Gravedigger," in* National Review, *Vol. XXXIV, No. 10, May 28, 1982, pp. 645, 647.*

NEWGATE CALLENDAR

[In *Gravedigger*] a girl is missing, maybe dead, She had been a member of a desert cult in which there had been mass murder. A policy has been taken out on her. Is she dead? Brandstetter has to find out. Also missing is her father, a disbarred lawyer.

Brandstetter finds out more than he has counted on. And his private life enters into the story; his newest lover helps him with the case. Good plotting and realistic locales—as always in the Brandstetter books—keep *Gravedigger* at the high norm of the previous ones in the series. The ending is wild, yet through it all Brandstetter never loses his cool.

> *Newgate Callendar, in a review of "Gravedigger,"* The New York Times Book Review, *May 30, 1982, p. 15.*

TERRY TEACHOUT

Joseph Hansen's latest fictional effort [*Backtrack*] lies well outside the canon of his popular Dave Brandstetter mystery series: it is a short, pithy *Bildungsroman* disguised as a suspense novel about a California teenager's search for the killer of his father, a small-time homosexual actor. An accomplished poet, Hansen commands a sharp-eyed prose style so vividly observed as to recall Evelyn Waugh's admiring remark about P. G. Wodehouse—"One has to regard a man as a master who can produce on average three uniquely brilliant and entirely original similes to every page"—and *Backtrack,* like the Brandstetter novels, is enriched by the judicious artistic effects that Hansen obtains through the use of this striking style. . . . Equally effective is the author's flawless ear for dialogue, here enhanced by his use of a first-person narrator. There is a touch of sentiment and a loss of tension in the denouement of *Backtrack,* and a novel that is paced like a mystery naturally arouses expectations of a tauter ending than this one. Still, it is good to see this imaginative writer able to do satisfying work without recourse to the road-tested pleasures provided by Dave Brandstetter and his colorful friends.

> *Terry Teachout, in a review of "Backtrack," in* National Review, *Vol. XXXIV, No. 25, December 24, 1982, p. 1630.*

NEWGATE CALLENDAR

Joseph Hansen has had a near monopoly on the homosexual mystery story, thanks to his Dave Brandstetter series. . . . [In *Backtrack*] Mr. Hansen drops Brandstetter. But not the homosexual world of the West Coast.

Instead of Brandstetter, Mr. Hansen gives us an unusual hero—an 18-year-old boy who is waiting for a killer to come to him. The story alternates between Then and Now (in the author's terminology). In the flashbacks, the boy is seen trying to learn about the death of a father he never knew. The father had been a well-known actor who walked out on the family when the boy was a baby. . . .

The boy turns out to be extraordinarily bright, perhaps a genius. Yet, with all of his brightness, with all of his cynicism, he really is an innocent. Especially a sexual innocent. But in tracking down the mystery of his father's death, he learns a lot. With its gritty sex, *Backtrack* is a gamy book; yet Mr. Hansen does not pander. Furthermore, he has written a brilliant piece in which even flashbacks are handled convincingly. His characters are splendidly fleshed out. It is not a happy book, and it has a sad, bitter ending. But it is a book that commands respect.

> *Newgate Callendar, in a review of "Backtrack," in* The New York Times Book Review, *January 16, 1983, p. 26.*

ROB SCHMIEDER

[In *Job's Year*] Oliver Jewett, a moderately talented, moderately successful Hollywood actor, finds his quiet middle-age turned into a bitter series of losses: his sister is dying of leukemia, . . . and his lover Bill is leaving him. Bill's family, a pack of losers and cheats, is . . . [taking] his last chance to start a new life. The trials they inflict, and Jewett's devotion to his sister, give the lie to the picture of the homosexual as a pleasure-seeker free from family responsibilities. Sleuth writer

Hansen has grown since his last mainstream novel, *A Smile in His Lifetime.* He creates an affecting world in which homosexuals have past as well as present lives—something all too rare in gay fiction.

Rob Schmieder, in a review of "Job's Year," in Library Journal, *Vol. 108, No. 13, July, 1983, p. 1381.*

ANN MAUREEN GALLAGHER, I.H.M.

In a word, [*Job's Year*] is *excellent!*

Dividing it into twelve chapters, one for each month, Joseph Hansen skillfully takes the reader not only through the year, but through the life of the protagonist, Oliver Jewett. That the latter happens to be a homosexual in no way cheaply sensationalizes the novel, but, rather, is a means to stretch and deepen one's understanding. In other words, this is not "the sensitive handling of a timely topic." Hansen's development of the character of Oliver is more timeless than that; and the author's treatment of the lives which he presents is not only sensitive but deeply human.

Early on the reader is introduced to Jewett's crippled sister, Susan, who has become world famous for her tapestries and hangings. The relationship between Oliver and his sister, after enduring several years of disrepair, is restored and developed when Susan reveals to her brother that she is suffering from a terminal illness. . . .

[During] the course of "Job's year," . . . [Jewett] comes to grips with the fact that he has never achieved anything in his career that nearly matched his aspirations and that, indeed, he shouldn't have, since his ability has always been only meagre. Then, in an attempt to bring his life at last into the realm of the real, Oliver decides to buy and operate a bakery in his home town even though his friend, Bill, threatens to leave him because of the decision.

At the end, things seem to go to the dogs,—literally, though, rather than in essence. This is a rare book about a warm and generous person. As I mentioned earlier, it is excellent reading.

Ann Maureen Gallagher, I.H.M., in a review of "Job's Year," in Best Sellers, *Vol. 43, No. 8, November, 1983, p. 281.*

NEWGATE CALLENDAR

[*Nightwork*] is every bit as good as its predecessors. . . . [Insurance investigator] Brandstetter's homosexuality is presented as a way of life. From the beginning of the series, Mr. Hansen has avoided prurience, giving us the portrait of a smart, resourceful investigator whose private life is his own. In *Nightwork* Brandstetter still is with the handsome young black man who became his lover in a previous book and was shot up for his pains. He wants very much to help Brandstetter and does.

The case has to do with truck drivers who may or may not have been carrying contraband. People are frightened and will not talk. Brandstetter's investigation takes him to a desolate town controlled by warring youth gangs. He encounters a weird figure—an old, rich homosexual living as a recluse. The showdown takes place in the desert. All this is handled with sophistication and verbal elegance. Mr. Hansen is one of the best we have.

Newgate Callendar, in a review of "Nightwork," in The New York Times Book Review, *April 8, 1984, p. 18.*

KATHLEEN MAIO

Nightwork focuses on the death of an independent trucker whose fatal accident turns out to be the result of a carefully placed explosive. The vividly portrayed characters include frightened widows, an elderly reclusive transvestite, and teen-aged boys all too familiar with violence and death.

Hansen's brand of realism does not require him to tie up everything in a bright ribbon at book's end. Brandstetter stumbles upon the murderer's identity, but several equally criminal and tragic subplots are given no easy solution. This slim volume, while not one of Hansen's best, is still a very fine novel of suspense. And Dave Brandstetter remains a quietly heroic and very believable detective. (p. 54)

Kathleen Maio, "Murder in Print," in Wilson Library Bulletin, *Vol. 59, No. 1, September, 1984, pp. 54-5.**

KIRKUS REVIEWS

[*Brandstetter & Others* features five] longish-to-long stories by the author of the Dave Brandstetter mystery-novel series. **"The Anderson Boy,"** which also appeared in *The Best Mystery Stories of 1984* . . . , is an initially engaging, ultimately heavy-handed tale of a crime-haunted past—with psychosexual overtones. Similarly, **"The Tango Bear"** begins well—horse-rancher Hack Bohannon gives refuge to an injured runaway girl, who refuses to explain what she's running from—but ends in a farfetched tangle of spies and scientists. . . . But the longest piece here, **"Willow's Money,"** is an unfortunate soap-opera/melodrama centering on the intense lesbian relationship between youngish Willow (a disinherited heiress) and older, suicidal, Mabel, a would-be writer: the tortured plot-turns include Mabel's long-term coma, Willow's wealthy and idiotically ever-adoring suitor . . . and, finally, Willow's nobly-motivated pregnancy, which Mabel (emerging from coma) takes the wrong way. Lesser work, then, from a talented but erratic suspense-writer. (pp. 1069-70)

A review of "Brandstetter & Others," in Kirkus Reviews, *Vol. LII, No. 22, November 15, 1984, pp. 1069-70.*

PUBLISHERS WEEKLY

[The] five short stories [in *Brandstetter & Others*] are well-crafted tales of murder and twisted love that go down as easily as popcorn. In two briskly paced and tightly plotted yarns, **"Election Day"** and **"Surf,"** Hansen's insurance-investigator-turned-detective looks into a couple of insurance claims that spell death for a gay bartender and a would-be comeback singer. . . . In the weakest narrative of the collection, **"The Tango Bear,"** a young girl flees for her life but won't reveal who it is she fears. And finally, in **"Willow's Money,"** Hansen avoids mystery altogether as he develops an O. Henry-like romance with poignant irony.

A review of "Brandstetter & Others," in Publishers Weekly, *Vol. 226, No. 20, November 16, 1984, p. 55.*

William (Ruth) Harmon

1938-

American poet, critic, and editor.

Harmon's poetry is characterized by its energetic language and ironic wit. His first book, *Treasury Holiday* (1970), which begins with the line "I am the Gross National Product," is a Whitmanesque litany filled with details of contemporary American life. Harmon's succeeding volumes, *Legion: Civic Choruses* (1973), *The Intussusception of Miss Mary America* (1976), and *One Long Poem* (1982), are similarly patterned and also elaborate on personal concerns. The poems in these books display the influence of such poets as Allen Ginsberg and Wallace Stevens. While some critics fault Harmon's poetry for verbosity and pretentiousness, others praise its vitality and scope. In a review of *One Long Poem*, Peter Stitt calls Harmon "one of the most neglected contemporary American writers, a poet of astonishing intellect and verbal range, who does not neglect the warmer virtues of poetry." Harmon has also authored a literary study, *Time in Ezra Pound's Work* (1977).

(See also *Contemporary Authors*, Vols. 33-36, rev. ed. and *Contemporary Authors New Revision Series*, Vol. 14.)

THE ANTIOCH REVIEW

Imagine a poet who sounds like Walt Whitman and Allen Ginsberg tempered with the metaphysical wit and wild pedantry of James Joyce and you will come close to comprehending this poet, William Harmon, who begins his book [*Treasury Holiday*], a long poem that is the first part of a new American epic, with the invocation "I am the gross national product." Harmon's politics are humane and typically liberal . . . , and this may explain why he succeeds at identifying himself with America and *all* that nation is. Harmon accepts America's grossness . . . , but it is with an irony like that of his opening line, an irony that saves him from despair, that admits his connection with America's ugliness . . . and that allows him to admit, as in a lover's quarrel, that something holy is waiting to be salvaged. Harmon says "I count all things I witness I am a teller," and the poem's form is indeed that of a list, an incantation of persons, events, artifacts, places, times that sum up the triumph and tragedy of America and the world as well. In his fierce and witty way Harmon tells us the truth about America and helps us to account for it—the poem occurs in the first month of "the new fiscal year"—though what we do about the accounting is clearly up to us. Given the vision the poem presents, the need if not the way seems obvious.

> *A review of "Treasury Holiday," in* The Antioch Review, *Vol. XXX, Nos. 3 & 4, Fall, 1970 & Winter, 1971, p. 465.*

WILLIAM CUNNINGHAM

William Harmon's *Treasury Holiday* claims to be the 'Gross National Product' and to include 'all things all goods.' In a

word, it claims to be America. I am happy to see a bold, Horatian opening to an American poem. . .

One of the happiest features of the book is the elaborate verbal juggling act that takes place outside the murky areas of the psychological swamps—swamps probably exhausted temporarily by the Surrealists, Conrad, Joyce, Proust and exhumed by their third-generatoin imitators. Harmon is straight-forward (in a round-about way!) and joyfully Rabelaisian in finding, setting and then highlighting gems of new diction. His poetry also has that epic sense of heroic past and chagrined but not disenchanted present which allows the poems to provide a collision of forces that represents some of the best in the modern American literary consciousness.

If we do a bit of etymologizing (Harmon is fluid in this language), the title of the poem becomes a real key. The poems are a treasury and a holiday as well as a holy day. It is a Balzacian inventory, a Joycian thesaurus and a celebration. (p. 68)

I do have one quarrel with *Treasury Holiday* which I cannot completely resolve after close attention. The numerous lists of things which are all a part of America and the modern scene become boring. One occasionally feels the strain of reading want ads in the newspaper and the un-wanted ads all along our highways. I am sure that Harmon wants us to feel frustration, and that is certainly one of the purposes of the poems, but poetry should make us yea-sayers to all of the lines even when the grotesque is being described. Still the overall shape of the poem is intact and Harmon seems to be writing a kind of verbal mobile which the author-critic Butor calls the best symbol of America today. The mobile form of art is a real and profound commentary on America. Both are composed of many movable parts which have no accountable symmetry but seem to balance one another in every wind. There comes to mind the single word, adjust.

In any case where there is too much writing (I mean too many unprovocative words), there is also some brilliant zero degree writing. At times Harmon uses this elliptical prose style to an advantage that would do justice to any of the Europeans who are so adept at condensed writing. This is a technique which is broadcast in the work and cannot be treated in a short review, but it is one of the poet's hallmarks, and it requires a true talent to leave the reader with the impression that the author's intellectual, esthetic and moral equipment is not also zero degree. Few Americans have done this successfully. It has something to do with the politics of experience, literary and otherwise.

I have said that the poem is a celebration, and it ends with a serious if light-of-touch prayer which reminds one of Charles Ives leading his audience through the most curious mazes of musical syntax only to end a chamber piece or even a symphony with a variation of the simplest hymn. The celebration is one of a mind capable of semantic revels while writing a wake, and the poet wants us to realize this. Exactly four lines from the closing recessional he speaks of 'Finnegan's Final Fall' and mentions a 'Hellzapoppin' Götterdämmerung.' Just imagine reading a *Harvard Lampoon* issue of *Life Magazine* which gleefully pokes fun at the American scene, and then on the last page finding trimmed in mourning black the Kipling refrain 'Lest we forget.' (pp. 69-70)

> *William Cunningham, in a review of "Treasury Holiday," in* Carolina Quarterly, *Vol. XXIII, No. 1, Winter, 1971, pp. 68-70.*

THE VIRGINIA QUARTERLY REVIEW

Out of an amalgam composed of elements as various as the involved linguistic commerce of "Finnegan's Wake," the expansiveness and frustration of "Howl," the droll seriousness of "The Dream Songs," Harmon strikes a coin bearing a profile that, despite diverse influences, is unmistakably original. The visage [presented in *Treasury Holiday*] is clearly troubled by the Gross National Product and the fact that all is "subordinated quite to one gross & national product in terms of / the lordly Long Green / money the only mother / money the only poetry." The book . . . employs much cataloguing, some of which tends toward extravagance. Finally, however, one accepts the extravagance and random appropriations as part of Harmon's vision of America and the history that produced a GNP, which, the book concludes, "came from them / Him me you / O go down / On our / Knees / now."

> *A review of "Treasury Holiday," in* The Virginia Quarterly Review, *Vol. 47, No. 3 (Summer, 1971), p. cvi.*

ROBERT B. SHAW

[*Treasury Holiday*] is a poem in long, Whitman-like lines, described in a subtitle as "Thirty-four Fits for the Opening of Fiscal Year 1968." . . . The opening lines are a fair example of the whole:

> I am the Gross National Product
> absorb & including all things all goods Fab with Borax
> Kleenex Clorox Kotex Kodak & Ex-Lax
> I contain the spectacular car-crash death of the movie
>   star Jayne Mansfield
> & the quiet death of John Masefield the word star
>   equally
> the Baby Ruth no less than the Crab Nebula. . . .

As Dr. Johnson said of Ossian, "Sir, a man might write such stuff for ever, if he *abandoned* his mind to it." And this may in fact be Mr. Harmon's intention: the book jacket reports that he conceives of this volume as the opening section of a nine-part poem. In such unimaginative assaults on the modern corporate state the potentiality for boredom seems unlimited. As for the attacks on individuals, and especially the one directed at the late critic Morton D. Zable, I found them cheap and rather contemptible. (p. 343)

> *Robert B. Shaw, "The Long and the Short of It," in* Poetry, *Vol. CXIX, No. 6, March, 1972, pp. 342-55.**

ALICIA OSTRIKER

The literacy [evident in William Harmon's *Treasury Holiday*] absorbs and includes . . . plenty of Whitman; also Pound, Ginsberg, Eliot, Dylan Thomas, Carl Sandburg, poor Kit Smart, some imitation Widsithy Gross Old English, newspapers, comics and so on. Hero pursues action-packed and pun-filled episodes in his role of "teller" (of poems and money, natch), ringing up American dreams from John Coltrane to Nagasaki. Finishing o'erwearied, I am of two minds. Mind One: this is a spectacular and brilliant book, and how Harmon manages to sustain his manic vitality throughout his "Thirty-four Fits" I cannot imagine. Mind Two: energetic, yes, but it smells like a Graduate School and gives me an academic headache. Let's see what he does for encores. (pp. 466-68)

> *Alicia Ostriker, "Weapons and Words," in* Partisan Review, *Vol. XXXIX, No. 3, Summer, 1972, pp. 464-68.**

PAUL SMYTH

William Harmon's second book, *Legion: Civic Choruses*, is without a redeeming feature. It is swollen with prep-school humor, clumsy rhetorical devices, shrillness, a compulsive and indiscriminate cataloguing of thing and event, ghastly puns, crudely ironic literary allusions, a liberal measure of dead-end surreal metaphor, a wide repertoire of postures, and a creaking "structure" of parts, sub-parts, and sub-sub-parts—swollen, the book attempts to convey the consciousness which suffers awareness of the perversions, refuse, and failed ideals of Western Civilization. Further, it attempts to teach the all-suffering consciousness a sustaining ironic outlook: "what-the-hell". It never occurs to this writer to look beneath surfaces for meaning, or even to sweep up some of the debris in the midst of which he seems always to be standing. He continually implies that to speak of or for hope, or any possible small gain for men, is trivial, not at all contemporary, not at all the thing. Here ego, convinced that it is the cosmos, expands inexorably toward dispersion or collapse, and in the end the book does nothing more than to insist on the energies of self. Undeniably, it exists;

but there is little urgency in the one question it raises, which is, So what? (pp. 166-67)

Occasionally, a line or phrase gives pause ("but nothing new is as new as a new tennis ball"), but these relatively brilliant flashes fail to light the way out of the vast swamp of purposelessness through which the reader slogs, accompanied only by the undiminished clacking of Mr. Harmon's typewriter. And we are told, in a *Note*, that *Legion: Civic Choruses* is but part of a projected "long poem"—many, many volumes are threatened. This is pretentious and immature writing, and to say so is merely to play the part of the child in *The Emperor's New Clothes*. (pp. 167-68)

> *Paul Smyth, "Less Tit than Tat," in* Poetry, *Vol. CXXIII, No. 3, December, 1973, pp. 165-73.**

PAUL RAMSEY

In *Legion: Civic Choruses* [William Harmon] is against theology, religion, Washington, business, nuns, chastity, killing Viet Cong, the American Legion, the family, *Time*, Hallmark cards, football, doctors, philosophy. But if he is for, say, *U.S. News and World Report*, the commune, the Viet Cong, promiscuity, socialism, or other opposite numbers, it is a well-kept secret. (He may however be for baseball—see **"Four Men,"** a nice poem.) The method is any details about America in any order in elaborately scribbled satiric rhetoric. (p. 402)

He is always ingenious and sometimes, but too seldom, witty, funny, perceptive, or touching. As a universal American disrespecter, he is amateurish compared to Mencken. Mostly he rattles on, intelligence and verbal talent gone to waste. (pp. 402-03)

> *Paul Ramsey, in a review of "Legion: Civic Choruses," in* The Sewanee Review, *Vol. LXXXII, No. 2, Spring, 1974, pp. 402-03.*

CHOICE

[Anyone who expects from *Time in Ezra Pound's Work* a] careful, comprehensive, illuminating textual analysis will be disappointed. Harmon's ambiguously titled book is a brief but discursive work on several aspects of Pound: the concept of *paideuma*, the continuity of personality, the contemporaneity of culture, Pound's sources, his methods of translation, his changing aesthetics, his "accuracy." The titular promise is fulfilled only in the fourth chapter and part of the fifth (out of five). Even there, more emphasis and space are given to Pound's theories of time and to a gathering of some of his statements concerning time than to a study of his authorial handling of time and the results. Too slight to be a good introduction, too general to be useful to the specialist or the advanced student, too selective to be of much use to the general reader or the lower-level undergraduate, it is another artifact of the Pound industry aimed, presumably, at enthusiasts. (pp. 228-29)

> *A review of "Time in Ezra Pound's Work," in* Choice, *Vol. 15, No. 2, April, 1978, pp. 228-29.*

WILLIAM CLARKSON

Just after his celebrated definition of the image as presenting "an intellectual and emotional complex in an instant of time," Ezra Pound wrote that such a complex could give a "sense of sudden liberation; that sense of freedom from time limits and space limits." . . . For Harmon "poetry is not a time art or a space art; it is a complex process that takes place (and takes time, as well) in a rich continuum of physical and psychological dimensions." Whatever success a poet may have had in achieving a "transcendent timelessness," his achievement proceeded out of a struggle in and with time. Pound's struggle is the focus of Mr. Harmon's book [*Time in Ezra Pound's Work*].

Not surprisingly the struggle is marked by frustration. The opening chapters deal with Pound's early writing on culture (through about 1920) and his later writing in the same vein (through World War II). In each case he describes a "pattern of optimism and disappointment," a struggle for timeless ideas reduced to timebound action. (pp. c-ci)

[The] chapters devoted to Pound's prose left me disappointed at times. Of *Jefferson and/or Mussolini* Harmon says, "a book so confused defies description by any terms." Yet he describes the book so firmly and exposes its weakness with such assurance that one expects much from his proposed defense of the equally perplexing *Guide to Kulchur*. Unhappily his demonstration is too slight either to convert the opposition or to inform the adherent. And I object to the critic's charge that the famous principles of imagism ("direct treatment," "no word that does not contribute," "rhythm . . . of the musical phrase") are "vague" and "too weak to have much value." By confusing the circumstances of their first publication (they appeared with the supplementary "Don'ts by an Imagiste") and by ignoring their cultural background (the idea of the *mot juste*, for example), Mr. Harmon takes them out of context and, to my mind, trivializes them unfairly. When in chapter 4 the critic deals with the shorter poems, however, he is persuasive. . . . The commentary is perceptive and helpful though all too brief.

Turning to the *Cantos* in his last chapter, Mr. Harmon begins by conceding the harshest criticism Pound's opposition has put forward: "the form of the whole seems to be incomprehensible"; the poem is clearly long but "everything else about it remains unclear"; "no literary work is more obscure or difficult"; and it is "moral peculiarity that, much more than the verbal or formal irregularity, makes the poem difficult." But Mr. Harmon proceeds determinedly to defend the work as a faithful and vivid record of the poet's struggle in time. "A ragbag *The Cantos* may be; but it seems to me that these rags in this bag make up a more respectable aesthetic act of the human will than almost any other work of this century." The demonstration which follows may still fail to convert the opposition, but there is much to inform the poem's adherents. The discussion of the *Cantos* shows how the time struggle is evident at every level, from the broadest considerations of form to the slightest tics of the poet's speech. We are brought a long way toward understanding both the personal and the poetic complexities of Pound's attempt to beat time. (pp. ci-cii)

> *William Clarkson, "Beating Time," in* The Sewanee Review, *Vol. LXXXVI, No. 3, Summer, 1978, pp. c-cii.*

KIRKUS REVIEWS

[Harmon] is an underappreciated poet, abundant proof of which comes [in *One Long Poem*]—a book that mixes high and low as elegantly and steadily as a good bartender making a *pousse-café*. Harmon can be very funny, as in **"The Lilies of the Field Know Which Side Their Bread Is Buttered On."** He can craftily foam up vernacular mixtures. . . . And he has a gift for acid parody, as in a poem called **"Stevens."** . . . But, in addition,

Harmon is a poet of sneakily effective progressions (the superb **"Where Scars Come From"**) as well as a first-rate, Zukofskian musician: "Shifting hinges sing dry numbers / Until the winds die down and sleep awhile / Without gnashing or rapid eye movement." Or: "Again the time and blood consuming sun crosses its corner / With a web of new born light / And there the last stars literally starve." When you put literary panache, wit, and lovely sound together, a voice is irresistible. Harmon's here, is exactly that.

A review of "One Long Poem," in Kirkus Reviews, *Vol. L, No. 18, September 15, 1982, p. 1099.*

DAVID KIRBY

[*One Long Poem*] is not one long poem . . . ; it is a group of short poems, most of which are highly dysphonic. Lines choke on adjectives (" . . . they are wings of occidental hardwood fastened to lead beams by means of mortal nails") or stutter alliteratively (" . . . pointblank pingpong nipples / a pink that peaks up pink by pink . . ."). These poems sound as if they had been written for the classroom: one can almost hear a teacher asking for the significance of "the notorious dormitory of hierodules and screwballs."

David Kirby, in a review of "One Long Poem," in Library Journal, *Vol. 107, No. 18, October 15, 1982, p. 1991.*

PETER STITT

The love of words, of arabesque verbal structures, is everywhere evident in William Harmon's *One Long Poem*. . . . What is most striking about this book, both at first glance and ultimately, is its dazzling surface display of formal and linguistic pyrotechnics. Looking just beneath that façade, however, we quickly see that it is a feeling book as well, and offers a good deal of human warmth, knowledge of human frailty, human sympathy.

What makes many of these poems so successful in both areas is Harmon's ability to create a speaking persona who can awe-strike us with his words, but whom we like nonetheless, one with whom we can easily identify, suffer, and celebrate. Which is what we meet in the opening stanza of **"Zubby Sutra,"** subtitled "Introduction to a Farewell to Religionswissenschaft":

> You know, reading the Bhagavadgita at bedtime can
>   have its drawbacks;
> last night, for instance, falling asleep in that ebbing free
>   fall in
> wandering mazes of direct or indirect objects lost, I
>   floated undulant
> in a kind of zero gravity free-wheeling, wondering why
>   I should wonder
> about Gods so much, inasmuch as I seem such a
>   radically secular, casual
> character, ascetic of the concrete, kickrock, cardinal in
>   the college of
> middleclass suburban bureaucratic skepticism, monk
>   among two-headed
> ice-cream cones, partiflavored, anchorless anchorite
>   whose one deep

> eventful cave of commitment remains in libidinous
>   perpetuity the
> luminous numinous phenomenon of the human female
>   bombshell bosom
> (cartoon barbell boobs with pointblank pingpong nipples
> a pink that peaks up pink by pink to dots of virgin
>   burgundy).

The imaginative freedom of this passage, as of the entire poem, is remarkable, offering pleasure on several levels and instruction.

Zubby is a cat, and the poem, among its other virtues, is also a sidewise parody of Ginsberg. There is a good deal of this sort of thing in these poems, reminding us that Harmon is a real post-modernist poet, not just historically but in method. Among other things, this means he inhabits the ironic mode identified by Northrop Frye, and so we are not surprised by sly parodies also of Hopkins . . . and Stevens. . . . (pp. 432-33)

It is easy to predict when Harmon is going to be good or bad. The book contains several short poems, less than half a page, which rely entirely upon the verbal tricks, seeming even to eschew meaning, much more that human warmth so prevalent in the longer poems. He seems to need space to develop the voice of his speaking character, which is all important. This reservation aside, William Harmon is surely one of the most neglected contemporary American writers, a poet of astonishing intellect and verbal range, who does not neglect the warmer virtues of poetry. He is in addition a critic of piercing insight and prose style, as interesting when he is wrong as when he is right: a writer to catch up with and pay close attention to. (p. 433)

Peter Stitt, "'Words, Book Words, What Are You?'" in The Georgia Review, *Vol. XXXVII, No. 2, Summer, 1983, pp. 428-38.**

WILLIAM H. PRITCHARD

One Long Poem is [William Harmon's] title for a book of short poems, and in a sense it's not mistitled, since the individual poems don't have any inevitability about their limits—one mixes up the titles and it doesn't much matter. What happens is, at least in my perusal of the volume, that Mr. Harmon soon becomes infectious as a companion. . . . Who else would write a poem with a hero named **"Succotash"**? Or come up with memorable formulations like **"The Lilies of the Field Know Which Side Their Bread Is Buttered On"**? Not for nothing did William Harmon edit the *Oxford Book of American Light Verse;* he does capable pastiches of Stevens, Auden, Berryman, and once in a while permits himself a mainly non-joky reflection, as in **"Interoffice Memorandum to James Seay."** He doesn't touch the heart, but his poems are tonic, the personality in them irrepressible. (pp. 232-33)

William H. Pritchard, in a review of "One Long Poem," in Poetry, *Vol. CXLIII, No. 4, January, 1984, pp. 232-33.*

Andrew Holleran

1943?-

(Pseudonym of unidentified author) American novelist and critic.

Holleran's first novel, *Dancer from the Dance* (1978), elicited much favorable critical attention. This loosely autobiographical work candidly examines gay life in New York City through the experiences of Malone, its young homosexual protagonist. *Dancer from the Dance* chronicles Malone's search for emotional security and love within the hedonistic furor of the homosexual community. Critics praised Holleran for his accurate recreation of the gay subculture while avoiding stereotypes and clichés.

Nights in Aruba (1983), Holleran's second novel, is described by the author as "the dreary reality of a gay man's dealing with his family." Abandoning the fast-paced and glamorous setting of the first novel, *Nights in Aruba* is the story of a middle-aged man's struggle to come to terms with his homosexuality, his conflicts with his Catholic upbringing, and his problems in relating to his aging parents. James E. Prevet considered this work "less a novel than a meditation on the aloneness of the human being and his demeaning descent into oblivion."

PAUL ROBINSON

Dancer from the Dance is a homosexual novel, and who wants to read homosexual novels? Homosexuals, naturally. But I can't imagine anyone—anyone who has read a novel, that is—not enjoying this book, which is beautifully written, single-minded and at once evocative and hilarious. It is also a novel of some political consequence. If I am not mistaken, it marks an important shift in the homosexual community's self-image, a kind of coming of age, in which concerns of political expediency have been set aside for the sake of art. Some might be inclined to call the book premature or disloyal, and they have good cause, because in one respect it plays right into the hands of reactionaries: it acknowledges a politically damaging fact about homosexual life, namely that it is narcissistic. But here that fact achieves the pathos of a great historical mistake, without which humanity might be happier but almost certainly poorer. *Dancer from the Dance,* one might say, is a post-liberation document. It lacks political shrewdness—it tells the truth.

If I were not afraid of scaring off readers I would say that it is a novel of ideas, in the tradition of *The Magic Mountain*. Through its two principal characters—an outrageous middle-aged queen named Sutherland and a handsome ingenue, Malone—it examines the proposition that homosexual life substitutes beauty for happiness. The author's preoccupation with this idea has led to an occasional weakening of the characters themselves. I found this especially true of Malone, the repressed young man who, under Sutherland's tutelage (Sutherland is a kind of Settembrini, but with the values of Oscar Wilde), is transformed, as he puts it himself, into a "profes-

sional faggot." Innocence and jadedness coexist in Malone right to the very end, and one experiences less a development of character than the simple superimposition of one personality on another. Yet even when Holleran's creations seem incredible, they nonetheless tell a truth, reveal a tendency, represent an ideal (or unideal) type. Their self-consciousness, vanity, and sheer physicality . . . are, according to enlightened opinion, fabrications of the enemy, or, to the extent they exist, the pathology of an oppressed class. Homosexuals, we know, are really just like everybody else, or would be, if only they were left alone. Holleran's novel is a brilliant rebuttal of this liberal trivialization. Here homosexuals have a style and tragedy of their own, which make them infinitely more interesting and valuable than those bland creatures who differ from their fellow men only in their sexual preference. The novel celebrates homosexual narcissism—that love of one's own body that is the obvious corollary to the love of one's own sex. (p. 33)

[*Dancer from the Dance*] is a first novel, and it sometimes shows signs of less than perfect control. There are repetitions that a good editor would have banished; the narrative voice is inconsistent . . . ; and the narrator himself is too much in the story not to be more fully developed. Holleran tries to correct this last defect by beginning and ending the novel with a series of letters between the author (who closely resembles Sutherland) and a friend, Paul, who might be described as Malone liberated from New York City. The letters themselves are wonderful, but they don't really solve the structural difficulty in the body of the novel. One could also complain that the literary references in the text—to St. Augustine, Keats, or, as in the title, to Yeats—give all too transparent evidence of the novel's determination to be intellectually serious. Not that they are inappropriate, but a more experienced writer would have integrated these references into the text in order to avoid any suggestion of pretentiousness.

These are minor faults. Much more important are the author's surefootedness in describing a particular culture, his moral and esthetic poise, and his uncanny ability to combine emotional abandon and high comedy. He has captured with wonderful accuracy a possibility of the human condition that homosexuals have explored most profoundly: "Beauty—that oddest, most irrational of careers." What the Jews have done for the life of the mind, the French for food, and the Protestants for capitalism, homosexuals have done for the body. In Andrew Holleran they have found a worthy memorialist. (pp. 33-4)

Paul Robinson, in a review of "Dancer from the Dance," in The New Republic, Vol. 179, No. 14, September 30, 1978, pp. 33-4.

FRANK KELLY

[*Dancer from the Dance*] is a brave and beautiful novel. Brave because it is a gay novel which does not settle for the popular cliches of character, plot, and theme of that sub-genre. Beautiful because it meticulously recreates in prose of considerable grace and power the sensuous yet ephemeral world of New York discomania.

The principals are Malone, a beautiful young man, and Sutherland, his eccentric friend, as seen through the eyes of one of the many dancers whose orbits often intersected theirs. Its central theme is Malone's obsessive search for love while exhausting himself with sex, and the glimmering trail of light which he leaves behind in the lives of the men he meets. The novel's narrator is often amusingly aware of the difficulty of the task he has set for himself. "I do not know whether to use as a quote to open my novel a line of Nietzsche or the Shirelles." Nor is he always completely successful in avoiding a rather awkward alternation between camp and bathos. But most of the time his art wins through. . . .

At a time when it seems the greatest accolade which can be paid to a novel is that it is "soon to be a major motion picture," it is a joy to discover a writer who commands not only plot but style. It is unlikely that Mr. Holleran will realize Malone's great fear: "He did not wish to be the man to whom nothing was ever to happen."

> *Frank Kelly, in a review of "Dancer from the Dance,"
> in* Best Sellers, *Vol. 38, No. 10, January, 1979, p.
> 299.*

JOHN LAHR

"New York is a tropical city," observes the narrator of Andrew Holleran's superb novel about homosexual life, *Dancer From the Dance*. And erotic heat percolates through these pages. Men burn for love; the metaphor for their obsession is dancing. . . .

Here men dance with rags of ethyl chloride stuffed in their mouths to keep ecstasy from evaporating. As in all festivals, this orgy of energy holds the hope of renewal. While the characters go through these sad rituals, they know that, as for Dionysus, a career of pleasure exacts a violent price.

A meditation on ecstasy, *Dancer From the Dance* is constructed as a memoir of one very special member of this world: Malone, a paradigm of the romantic ideal. Handsome, generous, endowed with wonder at the subterranean world he has chosen, Malone gives up his passion for success to pursue passion itself. It's a testament to Mr. Holleran's narrative skill that he can make Malone's shift from the straight world so compelling. Chaste for so long, Malone finally gives into desire and becomes its prisoner. (p. 15)

Malone becomes a circuit queen, but an aura of innocence not odium surrounds him. His delirium becomes a kind of saintliness; he gives love to the ugly as well as the beautiful. The money he earns from impersonating so many sexual fantasies uptown is doled out to panhandlers. . . . The novel treats Malone as a legend—a mercurial and strangely moral figure—and builds the characterization shrewdly. He is remembered, chronicled, debated: a mystery that remains deliciously unsolved.

The Virgil who leads Malone through this inferno is an outrageous transvestite called Sutherland. Where Malone is beautiful, Sutherland is wise. Malone is the personification of love; and Sutherland, a leper in the gay world, is beyond the hope of love. He has his real triumph in talk. Whether Mr. Holleran is reporting or inventing Sutherland doesn't much matter. He's a hilarious camp. And as we get to know this wonderful character, we see how his frivolity is a rebellion against the meaningless he finds around him. When a Puerto Rican pulls a gun in a movie house and threatens to shoot randomly into the crowd, Sutherland's voice pipes up: "Shoot *me*, darling. I'm

on so much speed that the only thing that could possibly bring me down is to have you blow my head off. This *is* the source of the trouble anyway, isn't it? We think too much! Blow my head off, darling." In this style of laughter is a seriousness that much of the straight world is afraid to hear, that registers a lack of faith in both the peace it seeks and the pleasure it finds. (pp. 15, 39)

> *John Lahr, "Camp Tales," in* The New York Times
> Book Review, *January 14, 1979, pp. 15, 39-40.**

VALENTINE CUNNINGHAM

What's important about *Dancer from the Dance* is that it's neither overwhelmed by Huxley's horror over homosexuals (remember *Eyeless in Gaza*'s repelled glimpse of Beppo Bowles in the eternal urinal at Marble Arch?) nor wholly given up to Genet's excitements over outlawry and blasphemy.

To be sure, some of the novel's efforts fail to come off. Its religious touch, its own talk of beatific visions and the like, lacks Genet's force, because Genet knows exactly which church, which commandments he's inverting and hence precisely what blasphemous frisson he's after, whereas America's traditional religious liberalism offers too unpronounced an opposition and too vague a religious thrill to its subverters. And though Holleran's affection for writing in purple patches gives up some telling disco-land scenes, vivid catalogues of wardrobe-contents, a stupendous final party, and some moving *nostalgie* of the 'that summer' variety, his prose can too much labour its changeless city, its prisoners of love, its 'If Helen Keller can get through life, we certainly can' attitudinising. Still, *Dancer from the Dance* is extremely memorable. It may be that the attempt to do a Scott Fitzgerald on gay America, to rewrite *The Great Gatsby* with recessive Malone as the mysterious 'figure on which everything rested. The central beautiful symbol' of our dancing years, pongs a little of the Creative Writing course recently undertaken. But Andrew Holleran is a new novelist of whom we'll hear much more.

> *Valentine Cunningham, "In the Wry," in* New
> Statesman, *Vol. 98, No. 2524, August 3, 1979, p.
> 171.**

JOHN BROSNAHAN

Holleran's [*Nights in Aruba*] could almost be a sequel to his *Dancer from the Dance*. . . . With the manic gay ambience of that earlier work now muted, the current book's homosexual narrator begins to deal with the nagging loneliness that confronts him as he approaches middle age. His parents are getting old, and his observation of their declining years dredges up memories and problems from the past. For him, true love and now even sex still prove illusive, but an almost fatalistic sense of new opportunity seems to offer a balance if not a stability for his future. Holleran sometimes makes a bit too much of his character's pained lyricism, but the psychological portrait remains effective and even touching. . . .

> *John Brosnahan, in a review of "Nights in Aruba,"
> in* Booklist, *Vol. 79, No. 19, June 1, 1983, p. 1246.*

EDITH MILTON

Andrew Holleran has been widely—and perhaps unfairly—admired as a homosexual writer since his first book was published, five years ago.

Dancer From the Dance, a book of spirited elegance and energy, was written in part in an epistolary mode, an oddly eighteenth-century vehicle for its unequivocally contemporary content. *Nights in Aruba,* Holleran's second novel, is also filled with literary echoes—evocations of a bygone decorum, of libertines weary of license, of the interweaving of lust and death. And, like *Dancer From the Dance,* it deals with a universal sorrow; though its characters are homosexuals and its ambience is the homosexual world of Lower East Side New York, it is much more about life's transience than about the particular sexual bias from which that transience is illuminated.

The obsessive amorous awareness, the nights of the bars and baths, dancing and high-camp slang, though they begin as the liberation of deep needs and feelings, become, in time, a wearyingly artificial sexual ritual, distractions to keep the mind away from the encroaching realities of time and decay. "I am about to grow old, my friend. The sin for which there is no forgiveness," says Mr. Friel, once a professor of American history, whose academic career was sabotaged by sexual bigotry. . . . And the narrator, Paul, who has lived in the city so long he thinks any nature more natural than Central Park needs a landscape architect, also feels weary as he makes forays onto Second Avenue, looking for yet another lover but aware that he has lost "the youthful heart which had made such moments radiant a decade earlier."

The balance in Paul's life to this increasingly empty eroticism is his bond to his parents, particularly his beautiful, emotionally grasping mother, whom he loves but cannot talk to. And the beginning and ending of the book describe the dark night of Paul's soul, shuttling between the city and the small dull town in northern Florida to which his parents have retired, the two voids of which his world is made.

Commuting between voids is, in fact, the general human condition in *Nights in Aruba,* which suggests its characters' lives, their jobs, seductions, social involvements, are often comic and always empty. Though their relationships are reflected in witty conversations, any possibility inherent in them is lost in the darkness of the narrator's viewpoint. . . .

Brought up a Catholic, like most of the men who are not quite his friends but who form both his sexual and social milieu, . . . [Paul] has lost his faith, and his religion has become merely another ritual without meaning in a world filled with them. Losing faith seems to inspire him to no particular guilt, and it is the result rather than the cause of the same essential passivity, the same cringing from commitment, that leaves him unable to confide his homosexuality to his mother, whom he loves, or to give himself to the man who briefly, but unrestrainedly, loves him.

Nights in Aruba describes a general modern malaise, though homosexuality gives it a sharp and particular focus. And if I have made the novel sound bleak, let me correct that impression at once: Andrew Holleran is, to begin with, very funny. And, to go on with, he gives his characters moments of extraordinary grace: for instance, the aging children, whose lives are hidden, discussing with their parents, whose lives are over, the developments in the day's soap operas, establishing communication while avoiding real life. In a world in which artifice has largely replaced reality, watching television together has become an act of love, and when Mr. Friel suggests that Christ's plaintive question of his disciples "Could you not watch an hour with me?" has new implications for the contemporary world, neither he nor Holleran is being entirely sardonic.

There is, in fact, a comic beauty in Holleran's despair, a suppleness in his writing, which allows him with marvelous effect to begin a thought with Allen Tate's definition of civilization as an agreement to ignore the abyss and end it with a bowl of Sealtest Heavenly Hash. That is despair very stylishly got up, and *Nights in Aruba* succeeds wonderfully at being at the same time a deeply serious revelation and very lively, very satisfying company.

> Edith Milton, "Laughing into the Abyss,' in New
> York *Magazine, Vol. 16, No. 30, August 1, 1983,*
> *p. 56.*

JAMES E. PREVET

Nights in Aruba is less a novel than a meditation on the aloneness of the human being and his demeaning descent into oblivion. . . .

As a novel, *Nights in Aruba* has its shortcomings. There is more reflection than drama, and the philosophic and personal conflicts the book raises are unresolved. The writing however, is lyrical and lucid. Andrew Holleran's eye for detail is unfailing: everything is recognizable. Many readers may find much in the novel startlingly foreign, even sordid, but they will also find a touching articulation of the soul's confrontation with the sadness of the world.

> James E. Prevet, in a review of "Nights in Aruba,"
> in Best Sellers, Vol. 43, No. 6, September, 1983, p.
> 204.

CAROLINE SEEBOHM

Nights in Aruba is in some ways a continuation of the theme described in Mr. Holleran's *Dancer from the Dance,* in that the hero is a white, middle-class homosexual struggling to find a place in contemporary America.

But whereas *Dancer* was written in a white-hot style, full of electrifying dialogue and a dizzying sequence of scenes of homosexual life in New York, *Nights in Aruba* is a slow, reflective novel about a homosexual's relationship with his family—in this case an unfulfilled Catholic mother and an austere businessman father who retire from the Caribbean island of Aruba to a mangy settlement in Jasper, Fla., where they measure out their lives with TV Guide. The son, after an Eastern education, confronts his sexual predilections in the army and from then on lives a double life—one in a cockroach-infested walk-up on Manhattan's Lower East Side, where he roams the parks and homosexual baths in search of sex and love, and the other in Jasper, where he visits his parents on an increasingly extended basis, spending months or longer, filial, celibate and unrevealed, until driven back to the erotic life he craves in New York.

One senses that this novel, like *Dancer,* is deeply autobiographical. . . . But *Aruba* lacks both the intensity and the flashing wit of the earlier book. Mr. Holleran seems to have become sobered by the difficulties of his own past, and *Aruba* reflects this burden. (pp. 14, 30)

This is not to say that there aren't any brilliant passages and observations in *Aruba,* as one would expect from the author of *Dancer.* I liked Mister Friel, a character reminiscent of those in the first novel, who on one occasion says, in relation to so many people's refusal to talk about their parents, "You'd think most people in New York were hatched from an egg." Mr.

Holleran's powers of physical description have not dimmed, although his accounts of his protagonist's trips to Florida become repetitive and dreary. . . . And one grows impatient with the extended interior monologues, even during the peep-hole views of homosexual promiscuity. Mr. Holleran grants his hero's only loving relationship about 10 pages before it is found wanting and summarily destroyed. After so many chapters of his romantic mooning, the failure merely makes one lose sympathy with the fellow.

Nevertheless, Mr. Holleran is an authentic writer, and maybe now that his personal baggage has been so thoroughly plundered, he can travel lighter. (p. 30)

> *Caroline Seebohm, "Husbands, Lovers and Parents," in* The New York Times Book Review, *September 25, 1983, pp. 14, 30.**

John (Winslow) Irving

1942-

American novelist, short story writer, and essayist.

A leading contemporary American novelist, Irving is best known for *The World According to Garp* (1978), a critically acclaimed best-selling novel which was later adapted for film. An admirer of Charles Dickens and other novelists of the nineteenth century, Irving is an outspoken advocate of reestablishing plot as a central concern of the novel and is dedicated to the morality and accessibility of art. Irving's fiction, while not difficult to read, is structurally complex and reveals itself on several levels. Among his recurring themes are the value of family, the inexorability of fate, the helplessness that often accompanies misfortune, and the relationship between art and life. In his narratives Irving espouses what Michael Priestley has called a "truth through exaggeration" approach to writing. By exaggerating reality, Irving attempts to enhance human experience, thereby dramatizing its essence. His unsettling method of combining humor with violence and tragedy is another of his predominant stylistic techniques. Much of the controversy surrounding Irving's work centers on his graphic depiction of violence. Some critics find these incidents sensational and gratuitous, while others argue that they are necessary to underscore the irony of his novels. Despite his portrayal of bizarre and morbid events, Irving's fiction has a life-affirming quality evident in the resiliency of his characters.

In his first novel, *Setting Free the Bears* (1969), Irving combines the horrors of war with a youth's troubled journey into manhood. He introduces many of the themes and motifs that are developed in his later works: Vienna, bears, violence, the nature of freedom, the power of fate, and the necessity of remembering the horrors of the past. At the heart of the novel is a young Austrian student's journal which interweaves the story of his family's struggle to survive the atrocities of World War II with an account of his plan to avenge their oppression by freeing the animals in the Vienna Zoo. *The Water-Method Man* (1972) is an intricately structured story of spiritual and personal confusion concentrating on the failed life of Fred "Bogus" Trumper, a blundering but likable person in search of a more meaningful existence. With the help of a diary he is keeping and an Old Low Norse epic poem he is translating, Trumper begins to make sense out of his life so that, at the novel's conclusion, he is at peace with himself and his world. In this work Irving extends his earlier themes to include marriage and fidelity, the vulnerability of children, and the role of art in understanding life. *The 158-Pound Marriage* (1974) is a corrosive tale about freedom and responsibility in which two married couples agree to swap mates. The characters inhabit a grotesque, black-comic world where no moral or spiritual values remain to stabilize their lives.

Irving's next book, *The World According to Garp*, is widely regarded as his finest work. This complex novel develops and extends the themes and motifs he explored in his earlier fiction. Despite its multiple thematic threads, however, the book is essentially a comic and compassionate coming-of-age novel about a man, his family, his friends, and his vision of the world. Gabriel Miller stated that "*The World According to Garp* is at once a personal masterpiece, an important contem-

© Joyce Ravid

porary artifact, a clear explication of Irving's moral and aesthetic vision, and a certification of his talent. It signals the arrival of a writer in full command of his abilities, entering upon the mature phase of his career." *The Hotel New Hampshire* (1981) departs from Irving's previous fictional methods. While sharing some of the themes and superficial aspects of his other works, this novel has been described as a kind of contemporary fairy tale. More symbolic in character and setting than his earlier books, *The Hotel New Hampshire* is on the surface a humorous story about family, children, and growing up. This novel was adapted for film.

Irving's recent novel, *The Cider House Rules* (1985), is his most overtly moralistic work. Here Irving examines the function of rules in society, fatherly love, and abortion. The story revolves around the relationship between Dr. Wilbur Larch, an illegal abortionist and director of St. Cloud's orphanage, and Homer Wells, an orphan whom Larch has prepared to succeed him. Homer, however, disagrees with Larch's position on the morality of abortions and harbors other aspirations than becoming a doctor. As in *The Hotel New Hampshire*, Irving's characters may be seen as emblematic figures representing different dimensions of the thematic dilemmas. Benjamin DeMott stated, "*The Cider House Rules* manages, despite the odds, to speak as though the tragedy of a country blinding itself to the history of its own moral progress mattered. . . . At its best, this novel is an example, now rare, of the courage of imaginative ardor.''

(See also *CLC,* Vols. 13, 23; *Contemporary Authors,* Vols. 25-28, rev. ed.; *Dictionary of Literary Biography,* Vol. 6; and *Dictionary of Literary Biography Yearbook: 1982.*)

JANE BOWERS HILL

John Irving is mad. There can be no doubt that . . . [he] is not satisfied with the literary world *Time* magazine labels him a leader of. . . . [Exactly] what is it that Irving, dissatisfied with response to his first three novels (too little public approval despite high critical praise), can complain about, having set out with *Garp* admittedly and, one presumes, *The Hotel New Hampshire* to write books that the general public would embrace, having tried and succeeded at being genuinely admired and accepted and made rich—what is it that this man has a right to be angry about?

If one carefully reads Irving's novels and criticism, and his post-*Garp* interviews, if one studies the thoughtful comments he makes about his concept of fiction in general and the novelist's job in particular, I think it is quite clear that throughout his professional life Irving has, to use one of his most common metaphors, wrestled with the problem of the fiction writer during an age when the very validity of this genre itself has been challenged. This lifelong struggle, as well as the more recently developed anger, come to full flower in Irving's 1979 essay **"Kurt Vonnegut and His Critics: The Aesthetics of Accessibility."** This essay makes these points: that critics have too often misread and too easily dismissed both Vonnegut's fiction and his world view precisely because Vonnegut is a popular, accessible writer; that too many contemporary writers of fiction are too busy fiddling with an elephant's left ear to notice that the elephant is standing on a baby (a metaphor Irving borrows from John Gardner); that critics, professors, and an audience primarily composed of second-year graduate students may, in fact, gravitate toward writers more difficult and obscure than Vonnegut not because their work is inherently more valuable but because their work provides more time-consuming and job-producing activities for critics, professors, and second-year graduate students; that Vonnegut's insistence, in the tradition of Shakespeare and Dickens, that art and entertainment are natural allies rather than enemies should be recognized as a strength rather than attacked as a weakness; and that what Vonnegut writes might appropriately be labelled "responsible soap opera," a label that is, for Irving, high praise. (p. 38)

Historically, of course, the novel has been the accessible genre, the one born to serve the needs of a rising middle class. It was, by definition, intended for popularity. In his book, *The Early American Novel,* Henri Petter discusses what has been a catch-22 for American novelists, in particular, since the earliest days of the form in this country. Because the birth of the novel and the birth of this country are chronologically coincidental, the first American novelists attempted the almost impossible task of writing books that depended for their popularity upon responses and expectations of a not necessarily well-educated reading public, one without even the solidifying quality of a national character. Thus, the novelist was, from the beginning, faced with a choice: did he write to these expectations, whatever they might be, however faulty they might

prove, and thus write books that would be read, or did he disregard these perhaps questionable expectations and fail by writing books that no one would read? Petter chronicles the decision of our earliest novelists to follow the public's expectations, a decision that led to novels often so bad that modern readers cannot get through them. . . . But Petter also sees another approach to the novelist's dilemma, one that developed fairly quickly once Americans began to write novels. He says that the best and cleverest of our early writers (Brackenridge, Brown, Washington Irving, even some of their precursors whose names are less familiar) gradually learned to use the form dictated by public expectation and thus insure an audience while they simultaneously began to expand the form, slowly and often rather clumsily bringing the American novel closer to what we might label art.

Not all novelists, however, sought to deviate from the publicly defined standards; thus, from its very beginning American fiction has been a house divided into what I will label high art and low. For purposes of quick definition, I will say that most often high art novels have fewer readers, low art novels receive less or no critical praise. In *The American Novel and Its Tradition,* Richard Chase addresses the problem of this split, first by dismissing, perhaps too easily, a 1915 Van Wyck Brooks essay which proposes that the future livelihood of the novel as a genre could best be served by a healing, a reconciliation of what Brooks calls the highbrow and lowbrow approaches. Such reconciliation would produce, according to Brooks, the most desirable course of all, the middlebrow. Chase says that such a solution, despite its "charm," would be inappropriate because it denies polarities that do exist and because it produces literature that is "generally dull and mediocre." Howells is Chase's middlebrow and, therefore, inferior novelist; his "best" writers fall into the highbrow category. James, for example, or the lowbrow, Twain, Dreiser, Norris, for instance—or into a third category Chase labels highbrow/lowbrow, a group that includes Melville, Faulkner, and Hemingway. Chase doesn't explain, but one must assume that a highbrow/lowbrow uses techniques of both schools in a purified form that preserves their integrity, while the inferior middlebrow writer somehow distills the techniques he uses so that they lose the artistic integrity that produces a "great" novel. . . . Chase does allow that this problem with middlebrow fiction is an American problem, one not shared by the British, whose fiction represents a great middlebrow tradition best represented, perhaps, by Dickens.

And Dickens is perhaps the novelist most like John Irving, the one Irving most admires. . . . The middlebrow, sprawling, often sentimental novels Dickens writes are not the kind of novel critics tend to praise these days; it is a strange model for a young writer coming to professional maturity in the sixties and seventies to take in order to build a reputation as a "serious" novelist. . . . I think one reason Irving is so angry is that the critical world that awarded him a serious reputation on the basis of his first three novels, now calls his movement to works more overtly Dickensian in form, style, and treatment foolish or mistaken, while he sees it as courageous. . . . (pp. 39-41)

So, Irving writes three novels, then sets out to write a novel in the manner of Dickens, one that the public would idolize in much the way they idolized, say, *A Christmas Carol.* . . . Leslie Fiedler says that Irving's transition from the man who wrote **Setting Free the Bears, The Water-Method Man,** and **The 158-Pound Marriage** to the man who wrote *Garp* is an extraordinary example of a writer consciously deciding to move from high art to low, or as Fiedler perhaps more accurately labels the split, from minority writer to majority writer. Can we say then that Irving took a risk, gained popularity, lost some of his critical stature, and began to whine? Can we say that all this defense of Vonnegut and Dickens is really defense of an overly-sensitive Irving, that his aesthetic theory is really not so much a theory as it is self-indulgence, not so much a rational effort to deal with serious questions about the nature of art as it is the easiest way to live with a self one doubts?

If we do say those things, however true they may seem, I think we too easily dismiss the important role a writer like Irving and theories such as his can play in keeping the novel alive for people, not just for critics. In *What Was Literature?* Fiedler discusses the death of the novel as an ultimate medium. He sees the high art, or minority, novel as destined for transformation into professorial notes and chalkboard diagrams and the low art, or majority, novel as created with full intention or hope of immediate translation into film. Thus, for Fiedler, the novel has already been relegated to the position of way-station, a mere pause between writer and translator, that is teacher/director. Irving's fiction stubbornly sets out to breathe new life into the genre without actually acknowledging such a death. Thus, Irving's aesthetics are not merely author as spoiled whiner, but, more importantly, author as a sort of literary lifeguard.

His methods in his own work point the way for what Irving sees as the solution to the problem of the "new" fiction, that is, the self-reflexive novel most often considered the high art novel today, the novel frequently about the novel's death that may with purpose and intention cause the very death it reflects. From his second novel, *The Water-Method Man,* through *The Hotel New Hampshire,* Irving builds into each book a character or characters who stand aghast at the new fiction. . . . (pp. 41-2)

None of [Irving's] fictional characters finds an adequate solution to the questions they raise about fiction. But Irving does, a solution that brings us back to Vonnegut's responsible soap opera. Even more clearly than does Vonnegut, Irving writes just such soap opera. . . . In a postcard to his editor, the late Henry Robbins of Dutton, upon the completion of *Garp,* Irving says that book has "all the *ingredients* [Hill's italics] of an X-rated soap opera." I emphasize the word "ingredients" because this statement is frequently misquoted or confused with one made by Garp's fictional editor, John Wolf, who said Garp's *Bensenhaver "is* an X-rated soap opera," Irving providing his own italics for Wolf's "is." The difference in those two statements is the key to the difference in what those who criticize Irving most vociferously really dislike about his work and what Irving is trying to do, which is to *use* soap opera, with all its ingredients. In other words, Irving employs the sub-genre that best embodies the popular mindset of our time, uses soap opera, as his earliest American predecessors used the grossly sentimental, exaggerated form their public imposed upon them, to expand the boundaries of the novel to life size again, to combat the contemporary novel's anorexic tendencies. Such use of a widely accepted world view puts Irving into a tradition at least as old as Dante, whose simplicity, universality, and perpetual quality of being easy to read T. S. Eliot attributes to use of allegorical method, which was the common, the popular, way of looking at the universe in Dante's time. (pp. 42-3)

At the same time Irving embraces older, nineteenth-century ideas of the novel . . . and responsibly exploits the popularity of soap opera, he slips into his books, from first to last, the classic elements of modernism as defined by Monroe K. Spears: temporal, aesthetic, metaphysical, and rhetorical discontinuities. He teaches an old public (that is, a public which has, by and large, ignored new fiction) many of the tricks of that fiction. I won't enumerate specific examples, but I will note that in moving from *Setting Free the Bears* through the three middle books to *The Hotel New Hampshire,* Irving seems to be moving further from overtly including the modernist techniques and questions to more subtly acknowledging their place in the world view. . . . Irving's interest in the role of the writer and his craft in society, as revealed in his fiction, his criticism, and his interviews, has remained strong, as strong as that of any of the writers more critically celebrated as writers of fiction about fiction. (p. 43)

Like Vonnegut, Irving is concerned not with the elephant's left-ear hairs, but with the baby the elephant stands on, us, the world. Like Vonnegut, he wants to open that concern up to as many of us as he can, as skillfully as he can. He also, like Vonnegut, wants to entertain us. It is not my purpose to evaluate the quality of his five novels here, although, obviously, I think them very fine. It is instead my purpose to suggest that his aesthetic theory, his technique, his purpose for writing are life-affirming, that they are less concerned with ethics (Gardner's theory) or aesthetics (the theories of new fiction) than with what Fiedler calls, by way of Longinus, ecstatics; that is, Irving wants to write novels which transcend all rhetorical rules in order to dissolve the normal limits of flesh and spirit. (p. 44)

> *Jane Bowers Hill, "John Irving's Aesthetics of Accessibility: Setting Free the Novel," in* The South Carolina Review, *Vol. 16, No. 1, Fall, 1983, pp. 38-44.*

CHRISTOPHER LEHMANN-HAUPT

The rules referred to in the title of John Irving's new novel [*The Cider House Rules*] are the rules that are posted by the light switch in the cider house of Ocean View apple orchard on the coast of Maine where about half the action of Mr. Irving's story is set. "Please don't operate the grinder or the press if you've been drinking," one of them typically reads.

But these rules are more or less ignored. An altogether different set is followed by the migrant workers who stay in the cider house. . . .

Similarly, two sets of rules vie with one another at the locale where the rest of Mr. Irving's novel is set. The law of early 20th-century America says that doctors mustn't commit abortions. But at St. Cloud's orphanage, which is inland from Ocean View and is a different sort of orchard, Dr. Wilbur Larch follows his own rules. "No one," he believes, "should ever make a woman have a baby she didn't want to have." . . .

The point—which is driven home with the sledgehammer effect that John Irving usually uses—is that there are always multiple sets of rules for a given society. Heroism lies in discovering the right ones, whether they are posted on the wall or carved with scalpels, and committing yourself to follow them no matter what. As Dr. Larch writes to Homer Wells—his surrogate son and unwilling heir apparent—"How can you allow yourself a choice in the matter when there are so many women who haven't the freedom to make the choice themselves?" And, "How can you feel free to choose not to help people who are not free to get other help?"

Actually, this is a sharper point than Mr. Irving has made in any of his previous five novels, the most recent and famous of which have been *The World According to Garp* (1978) and *The Hotel New Hampshire* (1981). His novels have tended to sprawl both in tone and focus, but in *The Cider House Rules* he has positively streamlined his form.

There are other refinements as well. There are no bears, no bodybuilding obsessions, no visits to Vienna and not a single successful rape, at least not of any immediate member of the cast of characters. . . .

Even Mr. Irving's excesses seem a little less excessive. It's true that the novel is full of the mixture of comedy and violence that by now has become almost the author's trademark. An excessively outdoorsy couple goes swimming in some rapids and gets swept away and killed by a log drive. A lobsterman who loves to tinker blows himself and his lobster pound to pieces while building a homemade torpedo. (Parts of the lobsters land near an ice-cream stand hundreds of yards away, prompting one wise guy to ask if the proprietor is working on a new flavor.) A large and angry woman named Melony goes around wrecking buildings and beating up any men who try to molest her.

The novel is also full of Mr. Irving's special brand of cuteness. The family of a man dying of Alzheimer's Disease (they've always thought him a drunk) can't remember the word Alzheimer's and so refers to it as Al's Hammer disease. An interfering trustee of the St. Cloud's orphanage wants to accuse Dr. Larch of being "a nonpracticing homosexual." . . .

And yet the familiar elements of the macabre, the violent and the cute all seem more controlled and pointed, more dedicated to the end of advancing Mr. Irving's story toward a definite and coherent resolution. The same can be said of the author's penchant for sentimentality, for aphoristic statements and for locker-room humor. It is as if he had made up his mind to stop pretending to be anything but a realist writing a morality tale, and to devote all his strengths and weaknesses to that particular end. . . .

The Cider House Rules has greater force and integrity than either of its two immediate predecessors. It's funny and absorbing, and it makes clever use of the plot's seeming predictability.

> *Christopher Lehmann-Haupt, in a review of "The Cider House Rules," in* The New York Times, *May 20, 1985, p. C20.*

BENJAMIN DeMOTT

By turns witty, tenderhearted, fervent and scarifying, *The Cider House Rules* is, for me, John Irving's first truly valuable book. The storytelling is straightforward—not the case with his huge commercial success, *The World According to Garp*. . . . The theme is in firm focus—not the case with *The Hotel New Hampshire*. . . . The novelist's often-deplored weakness for the cute and trendy, although still evident, is here less troubling.

Far more important, *The Cider House Rules* has a public dimension—could, indeed, play a significantly assuasive role in an American social conflict that is now dangerously exacerbated. The book is, to be sure, a novel (the author's sixth), not a tract; it follows several human lives from youth to maturity, gripping our attention as chronicle rather than argument.

But it is also a book about abortion, and the knowledge and sympathy directing Mr. Irving's exploration of the issue are exceptional. Pertinent history, the specifics of surgical procedure, the irrecusable sorrow of guilt and humiliation, the needs and rights of children—their weight is palpable in these pages. Responsive to the ideals and passions that drive both parties—pro-life, pro-choice—the author does not tease himself with delusions that a sunny negotiated accord waits just down the road. There is no maddeningly abstract prattle about the possibility of determining, "scientifically," the precise moment at which "the fetus becomes human." But Mr. Irving draws readers close, in the space of his imagination, to an understanding of essential links, commonalities—even unities—between factions now seething with hatred for each other. (p. 1)

The time frame extends from the first through the sixth decades of the 20th century (we stop well short of the 1973 Supreme Court decision in Roe v. Wade that legalized abortion). There are two heroes: the book's first half is dominated by Dr. Wilbur Larch, a celibate physician who directs an orphanage, delivers babies and performs abortions illegally ("when he was asked and when it was safe"). The second half belongs to the orphaned, "unadoptable" Homer Wells, whom Larch loves as a spiritual son and schools informally as a gynecological surgeon. The setting is Maine, or rather the two Maines, dark and light. Larch's orphanage, St. Cloud's, is located in a dank, stripped, far northern river town founded as a logging camp and plunged into decline when a paper company moves downstream. Wells spends his 20's and 30's on a seaside farm where Atlantic breezes clean the air and apple and lobster harvests alike confirm the rightness of hope.

Wars, elections, public personages obtrude intermittently. . . . There is wry scrutiny of several cultural innovations relevant to the book's subject, including drive-in theaters. There are striking successes in evoking, unsentimentally, the imaginative lives of the poor. . . . And there are a half-dozen or more love stories. (pp. 1, 25)

But the novel's core is the developing conflict between Larch and Wells, spiritual father and son, concerning the unlawful termination of pregnancies. Through a series of complicated schemes—Mr. Irving, the inventive, clever-zany wit is in clear sight here—Larch not only trains the orphaned lad as surgeon, but arranges an alternative identity for him as a licensed physician. . . . The goal is to insure that, after Larch is gone, help will still be available to poor women facing unwanted pregnancies. But it emerges that the cliché-ridden pro-life statements sardonically fabricated for Wells are not at total variance with his views. Repelled by the surgical procedures of abortion, persuaded that "the fetus has a soul," Wells pulls back from the place prepared for him, and a contest of wills ensues. . . .

Viewed in literary terms, *The Cider House Rules* is hardly without defect. Its young hero and several lesser characters lack presence and independent vitality. The accounts of diseases, treatments and operations are impressively detailed—Mr. Irving acknowledges debts to his grandfather, an obstetrician and author of technical manuals, and to Dr. Richard Selzer, a surgeon and essayist—but improbabilities abound in the narrative. And there are other difficulties, none negligible. Often the tone wavers; the graphic mode gives way to ghoulishness or bawdy. And surely no other writer of literary reputation is as absurdly certain as Mr. Irving that the repetition of the words "tears" and "kisses" unfailingly summons emotion.

No one aware of the present literary climate, however, blames failures to sustain poised thematic seriousness solely on individual novelists. It is one thing to counsel an author choosing Mr. Irving's themes to aim for the nobility, solemnity and heartbreakingly perfect restraint of, say, a masterwork like Rodin's "Mother With a Dying Child." It is another to explain how these qualities are to be achieved in an age ill at ease with the notion that art can have a subject, an age half-persuaded, in fact, that no subjects exist except language, the death of feeling or the artist's proud (or nervous) separation from society. For whole chapters at a time *The Cider House Rules* manages, despite the odds, to speak as though the tragedy of a country blinding itself to the history of its own moral progress mattered, and as though a writer's work has to do not with exterminating pity and anger but with animating them. At its best, this novel is an example, now rare, of the courage of imaginative ardor. (p. 25)

> Benjamin DeMott, "Guilt and Compassion," in The New York Times Book Review, May 26, 1985, pp. 1, 25.

WALTER CLEMONS

Behind its elaborate gingerbread trim, [*The Cider House Rules*] is an old-fangled doctor saga of the kind that A. J. Cronin and Lloyd C. Douglas provided for the popular audience of 50 years ago. Dr. Wilbur Larch, founder of an orphanage in rural Maine in the early years of this century, is a dedicated obstetrician who is dubbed Saint Larch by a smitten nurse who serves him. . . .

Irving's twist is that Dr. Larch is also a pioneering abortionist, devoted to saving women from butchery by back-street practitioners. . . .

Dr. Larch's orphanage is populated by children as cute as the chorus of "Annie." The doctor's favorite, Homer Wells, is groomed to become his successor. But when asked to dissect a fetus, Homer parts ways with his mentor. . . . Homer asks not to assist any further. Talented though he is, he decides he doesn't even want to become a doctor. So far, so good. A dramatic conflict is set up.

Then the story moseys off into soap operetta. When a golden engaged couple shows up for an abortion, Homer falls in love with the pregnant Candy and becomes the best friend of her fiancé, Wally, a rich apple grower. While Wally is away in World War II, Homer gets Candy pregnant. They adjourn to Dr. Larch's orphanage for the birth and then pass off their son—named Angel, I'm sorry to say—as an orphan adopted by Homer. When Wally comes back from the war crippled, Candy feels obliged to marry him. For the next 15 years Wally and Candy, Homer and Angel Live a Lie, until a friend from orphanage days drops in and instantly recognizes, as nobody else has, that Angel is a dead ringer for Homer. Will Candy tell Wally the truth? Will Homer tell Angel? Will Homer have a change of heart and return to the orphanage to take over from Dr. Larch? Is the Pope Catholic?

If this plot summary sounds ramshackle, that's the way the book proceeds. The sound of hammering is heard throughout as Irving tries to build an ark that will float. . . .

[*The Cider House Rules*] is a slog. John Irving is charmed by Dickens, and he adopts a jocular tone, derived from his master, in which characters are repeatedly identified by their full names— "He was nothing (Homer Wells) if not of use." This authorial tic, intended as rollicking, has the unintended effect of making us feel we never know his characters well. They have no inner life. Irving simply pastes a few traits on them and busily shoves them around. . . .

The Cider House Rules is far from a total waste of time. Irving has studied up on apple-growing (this is interesting) and early 20th-century obstetrics (this is gruesome). When Dr. Larch tries to sew up the damaged uterus of a woman suffering from scurvy, "his stitches simply pulled through the tissue, which he noticed was the texture of a soft cheese—imagine trying to put stitches in Muenster!" Irving has been praised by feminists. Am I entirely wrong in finding his gynecological details pruriently sadistic?

His sentimentality is even harder to stomach. Homer saying "I love you" to Dr. Larch and then discovering he's addressed a cadaver by mistake; lonely Dr. Larch kissing his orphans good night after Homer's departure ("How he wished he had kissed Homer more, when he had the chance!"); the orphans conducting a little ceremony of farewell for one of their number who has been adopted; Homer having a cheery heart-to-heart pep talk with his adolescent son about masturbation—the sugar content in these scenes may be hazardous to your teeth.

When *The Cider House Rules* has lazed along through the first half of this century, it's kind of a surprise to find a page devoted to the televised McCarthy hearings, for we haven't heretofore been treated to much information about the actual world outside Dr. Larch's orphanage and Wally Covington's apple farm. Most of the novel is cozily confined to fantasy land. Stock characters with stock gestures appear and disappear. When they reappear after an absence, one has to leaf back to rediscover who they are. Fuzzy Stone? Was he the orphan with the runny nose? No, that's Curly Day. One never feels that this was a story that imperatively had to be told, except that Irving had a $1.3 million book contract to fulfill.

> Walter Clemons, "Dr. Larch's Odd Orphanage," in Newsweek, Vol. CV, No. 21, May 27, 1985, p. 80.

PAUL GRAY

The Cider House Rules is essentially about abortions and women's right to have them.

It is impossible to miss Irving's message, but his method of conveying it is ingenious in the extreme. . . .

Irving's mastery of plot and pacing has never been more engagingly on display. Yet the restrictions imposed by these skills are also evident. In the world according to Irving, characters are the passive victims of life. They are either children or childlike, dependent on forces beyond their control. They "wait and see" (an ongoing refrain in this novel), wondering, like Homer and Dr. Larch, "What is going to happen to me?" What literally happens to them, of course, is the tricks, sometimes macabre, visited upon them by their creator.

Although Irving admires and emulates the expansive methods of Victorian fiction, he is, after all, a product of this century and all of its horrors. He cannot, like Dickens, honestly trick out a story with coincidences that will allow good people to triumph; the best Irving can offer is a tale that concludes with a few survivors who are not entirely maimed or deranged by what they have been through. Irving's plot absolves his people; it is so punishing that they are innocent by comparison. If abortion can ease their suffering, then the abortionist must be heroic. That is one way of looking at life; *The Cider House Rules* errs only in suggesting that it is the only way.

Paul Gray, " 'An Orphan or an Abortion'," *in* Time, *Vol. 125, No. 22, June 3, 1985, p. 81.*

MARGARET WALTERS

John Irving has always been intrigued by the parallels between the novelist and the doctor. His writer-hero in *The World According to Garp* likened himself to 'a doctor, who sees only terminal cases.' In this dark, exuberantly comic novel [*The Cider House Rules*], Dr. Larch discovers the uses of fiction. He invents histories for his orphans which turn out more convincing, as well as happier, than real life....

It's hard to pin Irving down. On one level, the novel is making a thoughtful and timely case for legal abortion; it's also a serious and sometimes moving study of fatherly love. But it takes a cast-iron stomach to get through the novel's obsessive obstetrical detail about D and Cs and autopsies and difficult deliveries. Cadavers and dead foetuses litter the pages, and Irving writes about them (footnoting his sources to assure us that he's got his surgical procedures down correctly) with an almost adolescent relish, a black and bloody humour, and more than a touch of sadism.

His enormous story-teller's energy seems to pull him in too many directions. He switches within a page or so from video horror to the sweet dry naturalism of a Norman Rockwell painting, from grotesque comedy to a kind of folksy sentimentality. *The Cider House Rules,* like the rest of Irving's fiction, is often disconcerting, but always exciting and provoking.

Margaret Walters, "The Saintly Abortionist," *in* The Observer, *June 23, 1985, p. 22.**

ROGER LEWIS

The Cider House Rules is a thick brick of a book. It deserves to be thrown back through John Irving's window. A black comedy about abortion is not funny, not because abortion can't be made funny but because Irving isn't a comedian. Homer Wells is a Holy Fool (like Garp) who, in being winsome, is tiresome. Dr. Wilbur Larch, abortionist, is the tenth carbon of a Dickens grotesque (*David Copperfield* is quoted passim to little effect)....

A ghoulish idea, conveyed with a misfired levity.

Roger Lewis, "Larger than Life," *in* New Statesman, *Vol. 109, No. 2832, June 28, 1985, p. 29.**

ANTHONY BURGESS

I picked up *The Cider House Rules* in some fear of occasionally being nauseated for my own good. This, thank God or Mr. Irving, did not happen. We can be morally depressed by the main theme, which is the terrible truth that some children are born unwanted or, being unwanted, are not permitted to be born, but the depression is balanced by our knowledge that there are people like the hero, Dr. Wilbur Larch, a saint of obstetrics, as ready to bring the unwanted into the world as to abort them. The setting is the St. Cloud's orphanage in the state of Maine, and readers may wonder what this has to do with the title, or the other way round.

There is another locale nearby, a commercial apple orchard where cider is pressed, and the seasonal workers there have to follow rules about smoking in bed and so on. I think the point of the title is that there have to be rules for everything and that apples can be metaphors for human souls as well as for human sin, which sprang out of the eating of an apple (Adam and Eve broke the rules of the first cider house). This gloss may be too naive. Umberto Eco, commenting recently on his novel *The Name of the Rose,* said that titles ought to mislead (*The Three Musketeers* is about a man who becomes the fourth musketeer), so that the author shall not seem at the outset to be imposing his own interpretation on what should be a machine for generating a multitude of interpretations. But he refers to a kind of novel that is raw material for deconstructionists. *The Cider House Rules* is not like that at all; it is in the plain, realistic tradition. The trouble is that it is a little too plain for nearly six hundred pages: we long for tougher intellectual or aesthetic engagement than Mr. Irving is ready to give us. His characters are just not interesting enough. (p. 99)

There always has to be a strong subjective element in literary criticism, even more so in that hurried and debased branch of it called reviewing. If I do not like this book, it is because it seems to me to lack art. An artist would have thought of compression, not the wind-filled prolongation that makes for the best seller.... It also lacks qualities that I think desirable in fiction—wit, irony, even good, honest, knockabout humor. The only remotely memorable piece of intended humor is a dirty limerick about the Duchess of Kent, which I, as an Englishman, would have to find unfunny even if it were not. The characters, with the exception of the doctor, who is too closely identified with his function to be interestingly complex, are mostly animated pasteboard. Homer, whose speech is chiefly limited to "Right" (it might as well have been "Garp"), the brutal Melony, the war casualty Wally and his wife, just do not generate enough drama to sustain the substance of a book as long as this.

Henry James, in a letter to the young Hugh Walpole, who had as much art as Mr. Irving and became quite as successful, said something worth pondering: ...

> ... There is nothing so deplorable as a work of art with a *leak* in its interest; and there is no such leak of interest as through commonness of form.

Mr. Irving may comfort himself in the face of James's lofty aesthetic by reflecting that James never wrote a best seller. Or, if he wishes, excuse himself by saying that the subject of discharged dead fetuses has found an exact stylistic analogue. (pp. 99-100)

Anthony Burgess, "A Novel of Obstetrics," *in* The Atlantic Monthly, *Vol. 256, No. 1, July, 1985, pp. 98-100.*

ROBERT M. ADAMS

John Irving's *The Cider House Rules* is a fine example of the kind of novel that brought linear plots and their cutout characters into disrepute in the first place. It has an intricate plot in the old sense of an intrigue, as well as several subplots, all of which it pursues with relentless disregard for elementary probability and complete indifference to the mental or emotional life of its actors....

The Cider House Rules gets its title from a set of typed rules posted annually in the cider house of the apple farm for the guidance of the picking crew who come every fall. Though simple and sensible, the rules are not much observed, partly because the apple pickers are almost all illiterate, partly because the crew boss has his own rules, which he enforces with a well-used knife. The cider-house rules are thus dead letters; and by elevating them into his title, Irving surely wants to suggest that most rules can and should be treated as dead letters. That surely is the triumphant tale of Homer Wells, who gets the use of Candace without any of the responsibilities, gets eased into medical practice without the need of formal training for it, and solves his moral dilemmas over abortion without the necessity of thinking about them.

The weight of Irving's plot combined with the thinness of his characters puts a heavy burden on the author's prose, which combines Dickensian jocularity with Dickensian sentimentality. He is better at dealing with processes—scraping a uterus, crushing a load of apples, fixing machinery, fighting—than at conveying the feelings of people. Irving is quoted as saying he wanted to write a "Victorian" novel; it would be an exercise in the ridiculous to compare the moral weight of *The Cider House Rules* with that of, say, Trollope's *Orley Farm*. (p. 20)

Robert M. Adams, "The Story Isn't Over," in The New York Review of Books, *Vol. XXXII, No. 12, July 18, 1985, pp. 20-3.**

George S(imon) Kaufman

1889-1961

American dramatist, scriptwriter, journalist, and critic.

An important dramatist who collaborated on more than forty plays during his long career, Kaufman is best known for the sharp, scathing wit which informs most of his works. He satirized such diverse subjects as politics, the entertainment industry, and pretentious values of the middle class by using put-downs and comic one-liners. The musical comedy *Of Thee I Sing* (1931), written in collaboration with Morrie Ryskind, was the first musical to be awarded the Pulitzer Prize for drama, and his direction of Abe Burrows's *Guys and Dolls* earned him the Antoinette Perry (Tony) Award in 1951. In addition to his work for the stage, Kaufman contributed to several film scripts, including the Marx Brothers comedy *A Night at the Opera* (1935). Although critics have faulted his plays for shallow characterization and for failing to address some of the complex social problems of his time, Kaufman's works are often revived by both professional and amateur theatrical groups.

While working as a drama reporter and critic for *The New York Herald Tribune* and *The New York Times* during the 1920s, Kaufman began to collaborate on plays with Marc Connelly. They were members of a literary and theatrical group known as the Algonquin Round Table. Such writers as Alexander Woollcott, Dorothy Parker, and Robert Benchley, along with Kaufman and Connelly, held weekly meetings at the Algonquin Hotel, refining the sharp verbal repartee that greatly influenced American popular culture in the 1920s and 1930s. Kaufman and Connelly's first play, *Dulcy* (1921), was a commercial and critical success. The play revolves around a scatterbrained heroine whose unorthodox attempts to entertain her houseguests result in ludicrous situations. *Merton of the Movies* (1922) clearly displays Kaufman's disdain for Hollywood in its story of an incompetent yet successful young filmmaker. Kaufman wrote one of his most ambitious plays, *Beggar on Horseback,* with Connelly in 1924. Based on the experimental drama *Hans Sonnenstössers Höllenfahrt* by Paul Apel, *Beggar on Horseback* centers on a young composer torn between artistic integrity and the financial security he could obtain by marrying into his girlfriend's wealthy family. During a dream sequence the protagonist becomes enraged at his fiancée's family and murders them. They come back to life to testify against him, and he is ultimately sentenced to work at an "Art Factory" that forces him to produce only trite, commercial work. Critics found the play highly innovative in its use of exaggeration and surrealism.

After the Kaufman-Connelly partnership ended in 1924, Kaufman wrote *The Butter and Egg Man* (1925), which ridicules Broadway in its story of a naive midwesterner who attempts to produce a play. This work was poorly received, and Kaufman never again wrote without a collaborator. With Ring Lardner he wrote the musical farce *June Moon* (1929), and he collaborated with Alexander Woollcott on the plays *The Channell Road* (1929) and *The Dark Tower* (1933), which are bleak in tone and considered ill-suited to Kaufman's comic talents. Kaufman also wrote a number of musical comedies with Morrie Ryskind. Their most popular and critically acclaimed work was the political satire *Of Thee I Sing*. The play, set during the

Depression, lampoons the American electoral system by featuring zany politicians vying for the presidency. Carl Carmer called *Of Thee I Sing* "the first of a new genus of satires with music—comedies of manners designed to laugh out of existence the silly practices of modern life." Edna Ferber was another of Kaufman's collaborators. In this partnership, Kaufman's cutting humor often served as a foil for Ferber's sentimental and melodramatic style. Theater and society people are recurring subjects in their work: *The Royal Family* (1927) is a thinly disguised portrait of the famous Barrymore family, and *Dinner at Eight* (1932) resembles Kaufman's previous plays in its story of a society matron whose well-planned itinerary for visiting British nobility results in a comedy of errors.

Kaufman's most enduring and accomplished plays were written with Moss Hart. *Once in a Lifetime* (1930), their first collaboration, introduces the multiplicity of characters and outrageous incidents that became a hallmark of their work. *You Can't Take It with You* (1936) concerns the eccentric Sycamore family and their friends, whose assorted activities include ballet, candymaking, manufacturing fireworks, playwriting, and painting. The contrast between the mad confusion of the Sycamore household and the staid behavior of a visiting family provides much of the play's humor; the determined individualism of the Sycamores is portrayed as the more fulfilling lifestyle. Kaufman received his second Pulitzer Prize for this play, and it remains one of his most popular works. Kaufman and Hart also cowrote *The Man Who Came to Dinner* (1939), which many critics consider their finest work. The play's protagonist, based on Alexander Woollcott, is an unpleasant, sophisticated man whose barbed wit is aimed at the conservatism of his middle-class hosts. While the plot is simple and the characterizations slight, the play demonstrates Kaufman's mastery of rapid-paced dialogue and searing wisecracks.

Among Kaufman's most successful plays of the 1940s and 1950s are *The Late George Apley* (1944), written with John P. Marquand, and *The Solid Gold Cadillac* (1953), with Howard Teichman. One of Kaufman's last original productions, *Silk Stockings* (1955), coauthored with Leueen MacGrath and Abe Burrows, was widely acclaimed. Primarily a musical adaptation of the film *Ninotchka*, the play had a respectable run on Broadway. Despite these well-received plays, critics generally concede that Kaufman's work during this period did not match the achievement of his earlier plays. Kaufman himself sometimes doubted the value of his work, yet the continuing interest in and revivals of his plays testify to their endurance. As Moss Hart commented: ''[Kaufman] completely underestimated the contribution he made to the theater of his time. Yet no history of that can be written without George S. Kaufman, and his influence on it, looming large and clear.''

(See also *Contemporary Authors,* Vol. 108, Vols. 93-96 [obituary] and *Dictionary of Literary Biography,* Vol. 7.)

CARL CARMER

[The essay from which this excerpt is taken was originally published in Theatre Arts, *October 1932.]*

Playwrights generally approach their work from one of two angles. Either they have something to say in play form and they hope that audiences will receive it, or they have studied the playgoers' taste and "give the public what it wants." Of the group that would gauge popular desire no American dramatist has been more successful than George Kaufman. (p. 159)

[*Dulcy,* Kaufman's first play written in collaboration with Marc Connelly in 1921] seemed to demonstrate the superiority of the two-mind theory. To the long series of collaborations which began with this play Connelly brought human sentiment to complement Kaufman's accuracy of observation, a poetic fancy to balance the sense of the ludicrous. . . . [Through] this play the elastic formula was established which Kaufman has been able to use with success again and again, a method based on the humor that is to be found in accurate reporting of the conversation of commonplace characters. The formula involves the selection of a main character, an easily recognizable type, lovable as a rule but utterly lacking in common sense, a protagonist at whom the audience may laugh with the jolly feeling of superiority and tolerance. The unpleasant complications which confront the character as a result of his stupidity are completely overcome at the end of the play with a magnificent stroke of luck, frequently occasioned by this very thick-headedness. (p. 160)

It was not merely in its main character that *Dulcy* became a model on which other plays could be patterned. The playwrights realized that if the laughable qualities of their satiric portrait were to be fully appreciated by a Broadway audience,

they must be pointed out and accentuated. In the part of William Parker, Dulcy's brother, they made an interpreter who should help the playgoers to an appreciation of the play's humor, one who indicated his complete understanding of the foolishness going on and who, though frequently exasperated by it, found it amusing. (pp. 160-61)

Dulcy found so warm a welcome on Broadway that its authors immediately cast about for other subject matter on which to exercise their talents. Kaufman must have supplied a large share of the background and color in the ensuing comedy, *To the Ladies,* out of his experiences as a traveling representative and in a politician's office, for the play lampooned those unimaginative mixers of business and society, the Rotarian business men in their more inspired moments at the banquet table. It contained all the selective truth that sometimes emerges from accurate observation and literal reporting, but American audiences in 1922 were either Rotarians themselves or still looking on Rotarianism as a movement in the advance of civilization, and they considered the play more impudent than funny.

Perhaps realizing then that if they were to make money out of the business of writing an American *comédie humaine* they had better attack native society in smaller segments, the coworkers turned their attention to Hollywood and the motion pictures. In Harry Leon Wilson's story [of the same title], *Merton of the Movies,* they found a character ready-made to fit into their formula. The pathetic country-boy who had romantic yearnings to be a movie star, who talked the sentimental patter of the movie magazines and who, by acting a part seriously, became famous as a burlesquing genius, was perfectly suited to be the main character in the pattern. The wise, hard-boiled little extra who elects to stand between him and the cruelty of the world is a feminine counterpart of Bill Parker—the interpreter for the audience. The other characters in the cinema world are painted broadly and in much the same caricaturing manner as the minor roles in *Dulcy*. Performances were crowded and the authors realized, from two successful ventures out of three, that they had a reasonably sure method of making a popular play, one to which they could revert at any time (and did once more before they parted company, with a too slight play called *The Deep Tangled Wildwood*). Ambitiously they went on to more experimental and less certain productions. (pp. 161-62)

[Kaufman's last collaboration with Connelly, *The Beggar on Horseback*], combined the best qualities in both dramatists. The pathos and imagination, the poetry and understanding, which Connelly was to show later in *The Wisdom Tooth* and *Green Pastures* were foreshadowed in this fantasy out of the American scene. All the penetrating observation of dialogue, the knowledge of character, the sense of the humorously incongruous, which have made Kaufman an important figure on the stage found expression here as well. Although many of their favorite characters peopled the play, the rich business man, his silly wife, their silly daughter, the nice, sensible, comradely girl, their well-tried method had been discarded for one less artifical and more imaginative and literary. From a suggestion which Winthrop Ames found for them in a German play, Paul Apel's *Hans Sonnenstoesser's Holenfahrt*, they built a play that has become a landmark in the history of modern American Drama. The pitful barrenness of big business had been attacked before with the weapons of cruel realism, but never had it been dealt such a blow as by this dream-play with its impressionistic sort of fancy. The hideous nightmare of bad taste, conceit and subservience to wealth visited by the god of trade upon his worshippers had been recognized for its true self. Two young commercialists of the theatre had suddenly turned poetic and had found the change profitable.

Kaufman again turned from his usual methods when he joined forces with Edna Ferber. *Minick,* while not a strong play, emphasized the complementary qualities of talents which, united, became a powerful alloy. The play served as an excellent trial flight for the two dramatists who were soon to produce that modern classic, *The Royal Family.* The fable of the latter is significant, the progressive realization by three generations of an actor-family that the stage is the most powerful influence in their lives. While the parallel between the characters and the members of a well-known American family group is obvious, the basis is one of general appeal, and the piece would be quite as effective if it provided no opportunity for identifications. *The Royal Family* contains less of the material that the public has come to recognize as characteristic of Kaufman than any play on which he has worked. His characters in many cases in the past had been so general as to be, in a literary sense, composite photographs made from the lives of typical people. The very subject of this comedy required individualization. Only the speeches of the rich suitors of the mother and daughter are echoings of the talk of their kind. Probably due to Miss Ferber's skill as a narrator, this is the most workmanlike of the dramas to which her collaborator has devoted his abilities. It moves forward briskly and efficiently, never stopping for the effective speech merely because it is effective as a speech—a weakness sometimes noticeable elsewhere in Kaufman's work. The wisecrack is supplanted by shrewdly thought-out dialogue in character, the bludgeonings of satiric burlesque by the keen wit of comedy. The over-sentimental emotionalism into which the story might easily have been led, however, is avoided through a sureness of treatment and a businesslike theatricality which is attributable, with a fair degree of certainty, to the more experienced dramatist. *The Royal Family* remains, a few years after its original production, a thoroughly enjoyable not-dated play, more than can be said of much other work for which Kaufman has been at least partially responsible. (pp. 163-65)

The last two years have seen two crowning productions, one in each of the fields to which Kaufman has devoted himself, which prove him a hard worker at refining and developing his talents. *Once in a Lifetime* would seem to be the ultimate goal of the old formula begun with *Dulcy.* It is the essence of Broadway theatricality, the wisecracking comedy at the top of its bent. As an exposé of the insanity of Hollywood it had those who have been there explaining that things identical or quite as impossible really happen there constantly. With an almost incredibly stupid young vaudeville actor—a "dead-pan" comedian—as its main character, with a charming and experienced young lady who sees life about her in its true perspective and remarks on it with bitter wisdom, with an unassuming author (first played by Kaufman himself) to help her make clear to the audience what a mad, hopelessly topsy-turvy world the talking cinema has created, with many of the silly beings that America's fourth biggest industry nurtures providing local color, it is a hilarious satire on the grotesquerie that may exist wherever values are ignorantly determined. The play is a complete justification of its author's method—at least as far as entertainment and box-office receipts are concerned. It brings the realization with it that, given equally rich material, Kaufman could fashion a hit out of it as readily as a tailor makes a suit. His imitators have already had a few unsuccessful

tries at the most obvious current subject, the world of the radio. He may yet turn to that and show them how to succeed.

The committee on the Pulitzer Prize [for] drama for 1932 defended its choice against those who claimed that a musical comedy was not eligible by declaring that the winning piece was a play. Their argument has strong support, for it is easy to find in *Of Thee I Sing* much of the technique that Kaufman has put into comedies without music. The silly, well-meaning central character is this time Alexander Throttlebottom, candidate for vice-president. Written for a more sophisticated and intelligent audience than his previous formula-comedies, the work contains no interpreter to point the satire with caustic comment. But the act-of-providence climax—the birth of twins which saves the President from impeachment—is reminiscent of all the other unforeseen events which have provided the Kaufman comedies with happy endings. (pp. 165-66)

All of the play does not keep to the high level of its best passages. Frequently the characters, echoes of American mediocrity, are not as keenly observed as in previous plays; their humor is too obvious, too superficial, too slapstick. Too often the satire is directed at political idiosyncrasies which others have ridiculed for years—mellow oratory, honeyed hypocrisy, trickery, and the insignificance of the vice-president. Indeed, the last joke is hammered home so many times that only a performance of genius saves it from being dulled. Aided, however, by George Gershwin's music and Ira Gershwin's lyrics which give audiences the impression that at last they have something native that is close to Gilbert and Sullivan, *Of Thee I Sing* deserves the encomiums which hail it as America's most sophisticated and intelligent musical comedy, the first of a new genus of satires with music—comedies of manners designed to laugh out of existence the silly practices of modern life.

So long and consistent a record as that of George Kaufman in the modern theatre ought to provide some logical basis on which a prophecy as to his future might rest. If a reckoning may be taken now it would seem to point to a few simple conclusions: that a playwright who has always written with the ticket-buying public in mind and has pleased that public is not likely to change his method; that a playwright who, through over a decade of steady production, has displayed a limited number of talents will, in all probability, not add to them; that a playwright who has been able to develop the powers in his possession through over ten years of hard work to the point where they are largely responsible for two of the most popular successes of recent times will continue to develop those powers; that a playwright with so thorough a knowledge of the theatre, a dramatist who is also a successful director, should be treasured by those who look for a theatre renaissance.

Kaufman has found two forms in which he is skillful. He seems to be satisfied with the number. They have brought him material rewards and literary recognition, though he has never sought the latter. No living American is more adept than he at spanking the silly vagaries of his contemporaries. Scholars may feel that his rod of correction is too much of a slapstick to allow of his endeavors being dignified by the term, comedy of manners, but their purpose is very evidently the same that Congreve claimed. Modern America continues to provide exactly the sort of material that he can use most effectively. The pattern which he first used in *Dulcy* is still in the mode. . . . Whether his undertakings this season be type-satires or musical comedies, it is likely that one of our native and popular institutions will suddenly find itself shorn of its assumed dignity and quite involuntarily wearing the motley. (pp. 167-68)

Carl Carmer, "George Kaufman: Playmaker to Broadway," in Theatre Arts Anthology: A Record and a Prophecy, *edited by Rosamond Gilder & others, Theatre Arts Books, 1950, pp. 159-68.*

DESMOND MacCARTHY

[Written in collaboration with Edna Ferber, *Dinner at Eight*] is an exceptionally animated performance: violent, unintermitted animation—that is the outcome and the aim of this ingenious mixture of ingredients [excitement, satire and speed], each of which is pungent enough to flavour for some palates the whole play. I can well imagine one playgoer declaring afterwards that *Dinner at Eight* is excruciatingly funny, and another, that it is excruciatingly painful. The fact is *Dinner at Eight* is both; it is extremely amusing *and* thoroughly remorseless; which of these aspects will predominate in your own retrospect depends upon whether you happen to be tender or tough; but while you are in the theatre, in either case, you will be swept along by its vivacious velocity.

One important point at which the transatlantic stage differs from ours is *tempo;* their pace is double ours. . . . Now, an English audience was once content to ruminate receptively while the playwright was preparing his situations. It used to be for connoisseurs even an added pleasure to be able to observe him at it, digging with deliberation the dry trench down which the water was eventually to flow. In the well-made three-act drama the whole of the first act, and often the greater part of the second, was devoted to this steady trenching. But the modern, and especially the American-modern, temperament hates preparation and adores—surprise. (p. 41)

One of the tests I apply to plays, before recommending or cursing them, is the degree to which I have lost self-consciousness myself in the theatre. If I have been so riveted that I ceased to know that I was a human-being sitting between others, then, whatever on reflection I may think of its *value,* that performance goes straight into my category of good entertainments. The play and actors have passed the great, elementary, fundamental test. . . . [With *Dinner at Eight*] from the rise to the fall of each curtain, and even during the short "blacking-out" intervals between the four scenes of which each act is composed, the performers succeeded in turning me into a mere characterless percipient attentive only to them. But, and this also is criticism of the play, I did not spend the act-intervals (though I was eager enough to get back to my seat to see what was coming) in that delicious state of gently-heaving emotion and astonished clarity of mind that fine drama produces. I did not wander about the lobby hoping to Heaven no one would speak to me; on the contrary, click, I was back again in myself, ready to talk about anything and wondering, not about the play, but if I was thirsty enough to enjoy a glass of beer and when I could get my hair cut. Well, if the reader thinks me a reliable thermometer, after those two statements he ought to know for himself where to place, roughly, *Dinner at Eight* as a play and, for certain, that it was exceedingly well acted. "But what was it like? Shall *I* enjoy it?" These, too, are questions, whatever reader asks them, it is my business to try to answer.

Well, it was like Peter Arno's *Parade* come to life, with an undertow of tragedy pulling through it. Does the *New Yorker* amuse you? Do you enjoy the bite of its humour, its gay toughness, its amoral and anti-social social satire? . . . [If] you have recognised in modern American satire of Americans—

yes, through the very heyday of "bunk" and "bally-hoo" and of a snatch-as-snatch-can society—the survival of a civilised, intellectual standard as cruel and incorruptible as that of Forain and Lautrec in Paris of the 'eighties—then, you will thoroughly enjoy this play. (pp. 41-2)

Desmond MacCarthy, "Excitement, Satire, Speed," in The New Statesman & Nation, *n.s. Vol. V, No. 99, January 14, 1933, pp. 41-2.*

GRENVILLE VERNON

To say that *Merrily We Roll Along* is a really important play, or that it marks a step forward in the American drama, would be to say too much, but it does mark a step forward in the career of George S. Kaufman, this time in collaboration with Moss Hart. And what happens to Mr. Kaufman is certainly not without interest to the American drama. Mr. Kaufman is now the most adroit technician writing for the American theatre, and he has occasionally given proof that he might be far more than that; that he is interested not only in pulling rabbits out of a hat, but also in sentiments, characters and ideas. It is because of this that his latest collaboration assumes an interest beyond the mere fact that it is superb theatre.

The story he has taken is not an original one, despite the fact that he has chosen to tell it in a most original fashion. It concerns the moral and artistic disintegration of a playwright, the first act taking place on his fortieth birthday, and the last eighteen years previously at the moment when he appears as valedictorian of his class. This method of approach, in deliberate reversal of the usual time element, is undoubtedly a vital element in making the old themes seem new, but it is not the only one nor the most important. It is in the depiction of the character of the playwright that the real importance of the play becomes evident, for Richard Niles is etched in lines at once sure and subtle. The ability to create living men and women is the touchstone marking the true dramatist in contradistinction to the playsmith, and in Richard Niles the authors of *Merrily We Roll Along* have given to the theatre a vital living figure, a figure who makes those in previous Kaufman plays seem inconsequential. The other characters, admirable as they are for the purposes of the play, are rather more in the conventional theatrical tradition, and once or twice, as in the case of the woman novelist, their psychology seems forced into a strait-jacket for purposes of dramatic effect. But the figure of Niles is powerful, pitiful and unforgettable.

In the opening scene we see Niles, the worldly success and the spiritual failure; the writer of meretricious plays, already engaged in a new affair with his latest leading woman, and tired of his actress wife. In the following scenes we see how this wife had been responsible for his downfall, the cause of his divorce and the rotting of his artistic ideals; and so we move up step by step backward through the years, each scene showing him nearer to the man he should have been, until he stands in the pulpit of his college chapel, young, ardent, hopeful, closing his plea for fidelity to ideals with the words of Polonius:

> "This above all: to thine own self be true,
> And it must follow as the night the day,
> Thou canst not then be false to any man."

This from the man whom we have seen in the opening scene false to everything—to his friends, to both his wives, to his artistic integrity. It is a picture as poignant as it is tragic, the irony heightened by the manner of its presentation, each scene being prepared as it were in reverse by the scene which comes before. In its evocation of spiritual tragedy the play is admirable, and it is indeed a pity that at times the authors should have found it necessary to put lines into the lips of the characters which are offensive to taste and unnecessary artistically. . . .

Let us be thankful that, despite its occasional lapses from good taste, **Merrily We Roll Along** does not, like so much in the modern theatre, play ducks and drakes with the moral code. And it is none the less interesting because it does not.

> *Grenville Vernon, in a review of "Merrily We Roll Along," in* Commonweal, *Vol. XX, No. 25, October 19, 1934, p. 589.*

JOSEPH WOOD KRUTCH

It is unfair, of course, but anyone as good as George S. Kaufman must pay the penalty for not being a great deal better. He has paid it before and he will have to pay it again in connection with **Stage Door** . . . , which he has written in conjunction with Edna Ferber. Since the penalty generally includes an extremely profitable run, it is perhaps not too severe, and yet Mr. Kaufman must have heard "It's enormously amusing but—" too often not to entertain very melancholy convictions on the subject of human ingratitude. The scene is a boarding-house for aspiring young actresses somewhere in the fifties, and all of the play's very good best is strictly topical in nature. Underneath is a sentimental story and a familiar sentimental moral— that the real actor would rather starve in the theater than live in luxury anywhere else, even in Hollywood—but what really counts is the succession of what would have been called in the seventeenth century "the humours of a boarding-house."

It is true that even these may not be strictly new. One could easily guess beforehand that one was going to meet the girl who could play anything if she was given a chance, the girl who thinks that men are dreadful, and the girl who goes wrong in mink. But Mr. Kaufman and Miss Ferber have hit them off with such crisp, amusing strokes that they seem quite fresh, and the whole thing moves with such perfect ease in such a perfectly calculated tempo that one is carried irresistibly forward on a ripple of laughter. All the gags, whether expressed in words or embodied in "business," are as smart as a night club which won't open till tomorrow and as quotable as what the *New Yorker* will say next week. . . . "It's tremendously amusing but—."

The real reason that it is impossible to enjoy one of Mr. Kaufman's shows without feeling a certain undercurrent of resentment is, I think, that the lines are not only much better than the play itself but also actually upon a much higher level of intelligence. At its best his wit is pretty nearly everything which wit ought to be. It is smart and sophisticated and crisp; it is also based upon shrewd insight and a keen sense of sham even in its most modish embodiments. Why is it that the plays themselves must be fundamentally incompatible with the spirit of their dialogue, that they must be based upon hokum of the very sort which the man who writes them was born to expose? How merry he himself could make with the thesis he is preaching and with the more sentimental of the scenes through which he develops it! Or could he? Perhaps, after all, the answer is that his intelligence and his power of criticism exhaust themselves in a phrase, that the part of him which speaks in epigrams cannot make any whole of itself. (p. 557)

> *Joseph Wood Krutch, "Too Good Not to Be Better," in* The Nation, *Vol. 143, No. 19, November 7, 1936, pp. 557-58.**

JOHN MASON BROWN

[*The essay from which this excerpt is taken was originally published in* The New York Evening Post, *December 15 & 19, 1936.*]

In a world in which the sanity usually associated with sunshine is sadly overvalued, **You Can't Take It With You** is something to be prized. It is moonstruck, almost from beginning to end. It is blessed with all the happiest lunacies Moss Hart and George S. Kaufman have been able to contribute to it. The Sycamore family is the most gloriously mad group of contented eccentrics the modern theatre has yet had the good fortune to shadow. Its various members comprise a whole nest of Mad Hatters. They are daffy mortals, as lovable as they are laughable. Their whims are endless. So, too, for that matter, is the fun they provide, except when Cupid is foolish enough to force his way into the family circle.

The Sycamores, bless them, live uptown in New York. They are, however, not nearly so far removed from Wall Street as they are from the rent-day worries to which most of us are heir. Grandfather Vanderhof . . . has for some years now refused, on very sensible grounds, to pay his income tax. More than that, though he still has some money, he has long ago retired from business in order to seek happiness in attending commencements, visiting zoos, and collecting snakes and stamps. All the members of his demented household have hobbies of their own and practice the gospel of relaxation which he preaches. His daughter, Mrs. Sycamore . . . , has abandoned painting, to which she temporarily returns, for playwriting because eight years ago a typewriter was delivered by mistake to the Sycamore bedlam. (pp. 177-78)

The quiet lunacy of the family is established by . . . Grandfather Vanderhof, [who] is as lovably gentle as he is unworldly. . . . Old though he is, he is happy because he has been able to remain a child of impulse in a sternly coercive world. He is more than strange. His strangeness is the measure of his wisdom and the point of his philosophy. His is a serenity and a goodness which make it possible for him, when saying "grace," to speak directly to his Creator with a reverent simplicity such as has not been equaled hereabouts since *The Green Pastures* and such as should be the property of all bishops and archbishops in a Panglossian universe. (p. 179)

[Mrs. Sycamore's] head may be light, but her heart is filled with the same kindness which floods Grandfather Vanderhof's. She, too, sets about the business of being flighty and foolish with a blessed unconsciousness of how laughable she succeeds in being. So, also, does . . . her amiable husband. And so, for that matter, do the rest of the agreeably demented Sycamores.

It is only when workaday reason invades the Sycamore home; when dull normalcy makes its appearance; when an orthodox Cupid bursts into this inspired bedlam, that **You Can't Take It With You** suffers. The Sycamores . . . are too fortunate in their nonsense ever to be disturbed by something as illogical as ordinary common sense. (pp. 179-80)

> *John Mason Brown, "The Sensible Insanities of 'You Can't Take It with You'," in his* Two on the Aisle: Ten Years of the American Theatre in Performance, *W. W. Norton & Company, Inc., 1938, pp. 177-80.*

JOHN MASON BROWN

[*The essay from which this excerpt is taken was originally published in* The New York Evening Post, *November 3, 1937.*]

[*I'd Rather Be Right*] is gay, witty, topical, and audacious—the kind of irreverent satire which could be written and seen only in these much-abused United States. (p. 286)

Let no one be deceived into thinking *I'd Rather Be Right* is a Tory Feast at which the President is drawn and quartered for the delectation of a Bankers' Convention. Mr. Roosevelt would undoubtedly enjoy it himself. Nor would he have to take laughing gas to do so. It is an unsparing script. The lyrics are no more merciful. The authors have gone to work with their gloves off. But what they have administered is a series of slaps which for the most part are so good-natured that their ultimate destination seems to be the back.

The President in *I'd Rather Be Right* is from beginning to end a likable man. He may have lost his way. He may be spending a lot of money. He may be thinking of ways to increase taxes. His Cabinet members may not, with two or three exceptions, play important roles. Nonetheless, he is a lovable fellow who is trying hard. In particular, he is trying to find some way of balancing the budget so that Peggy and Phil, two young lovers he has met during a walk through Central Park, can get married.

Mr. Kaufman and the Zwei Herzen—Moss and Lorenz—get many unsparing and uproarious things said. They have their laughs at the fireside chats, at the Federal Theatre, at the Wagner act, at Mr. Farley, and Secretaries Perkins and Morgenthau. They even get in some thrusts at Mr. Landon and the Supreme Court (though they have dealt far more freshly and effectively with the justices in the past). However telling, timely, or side-splitting their gibes may be, they have the additional virtue of being amiable. Their very amiability and extravagance are in almost every instance the guarantee of the remarkable good taste of the whole proceedings. (pp. 286-87)

My one regret is that the President himself could not find time to visit *I'd Rather Be Right* and sit in a box, and smile his famous smile, and laugh uproariously into a newsreel camera wired for sound at every gibe, at every thrust, at every good-natured impertinence in the script. The picture of Mr. Roosevelt in a box laughing at Mr. Roosevelt on the stage would be as fine an advertisement for the virtues of democracy as could anywhere be found. I doubt if the film would get by the authorities in Berlin, Rome, or Moscow. Hitler, Mussolini, and Stalin would not understand it or would fear it because their people might. They would be as terrificd by its implications as they would be overjoyed to learn *I'd Rather Be Right* had been tampered with by the Government in any way. Tokio would be wary in showing such a film. In England it would be seen and its hopeful implications understood, even if it might perplex Britain's Lord Chamberlain. But to those of us who saw it, and to citizens in democracies everywhere, it would mean a lot.

Even without such a newsreel, the mere fact *I'd Rather Be Right* can be produced and run its course unchallenged should prove encouraging. It should indicate certain of the blessings which are ours and which we frequently tend to overlook. It should swell our pride in the freedom we enjoy and in the gift for laughter which must be counted among our national assets. The more good-humored liberties Mr. Kaufman's and Mr. Hart's musical satire takes, the more liberty its mere performance bespeaks. Regardless of how pointed its criticism may be, the very lack of mercy it is allowed to show should persuade us that even now all's better along the Potomac than some people like to think. (pp. 288-89)

John Mason Brown, "The Gridiron Club and 'I'd Rather Be Right'," in his Two on the Aisle: Ten Years of the American Theatre in Performance, *W. W. Norton & Company, Inc., 1938, pp. 286-89.*

HEYWOOD BROUN

During the state election in New York last year there was a whispering campaign against Governor Herbert Lehman and his running mate Charles Poletti. The slogan which was passed around by word of mouth and printed on surreptitious leaflets was "Vote the American way." When a play under that title [*The American Way*] was announced, I anticipated that it would be a ringing answer to all the implications of prejudice contained in the phrase. It is an answer, but to my ear it does not ring. The mark of caution is all over the big spectacle which George S. Kaufman and Moss Hart have written. . . .

The reviews have been enthusiastic. In fact in certain quarters the praise has been so warm that I think the playwrights really should go into a period of self-examination to decide whether they have actually preached a candid and courageous sermon on the subject of patriotism. Hundred-percent patriots are traditionally and justly, I believe, suspected of too much protestation. And a work of art designed to inspire both Liberty Leaguers and liberals may well cover too much territory for coherence.

It seems to me that there should be a definite point of view in any play which is frankly designed as propaganda. Merely to say, "I am against all 'isms'," constitutes a negation rather than a rousing affirmation. Patriotism itself is an "ism." . . .

I doubt if any fine play should be all things to all men. And as far as I can see, the authors in this case have wrapped themselves so deep in the folds of the flag that their own political philosophy is hidden entirely from sight by the wrapper. Patriotism can be the first refuge of a dramatist bereft of an idea. . . .

Since *The American Way* undertakes to give us an outline of the American scene from the days of McKinley down into the New Deal, I think it should take a position on such modern problems as labor, anti-Semitism, the New Deal, democracy and fascism. I did not catch any reference whatsoever to anti-Semitism. The problem of labor is dismissed with a scene in which the employees of a furniture factory speak of their boss as a good guy who pays time and a half for overtime and furnishes free beer. The sight of the happy toilers scrambling back to the factory upon the suggestion of free beer is hardly one which will inspire many trade-unionists to get up on their hind legs and turn cartwheels.

As far as fascism goes, the authors have dealt with it, but somewhat gingerly. . . .

In the case of the attitude toward Roosevelt and the New Deal I think it is even more necessary that the playwrights should be asked to make up their minds and declare their side. There is an exciting scene picturing a run on a small-town bank. A playwright, of course, has a right to dramatic license, but I think history is harshly dealt with when the suggestion is advanced that the collapse of America's financial structure in the last days of Hoover was caused wholly by mass hysteria. . . .

Following the crash of the banks the audience in the next scene hears the voice of Roosevelt while the curtain is still down. The passage is possibly from the first inaugural. If so, the authors have spotted unfairly and undramatically a speech which is likely to stand in American history as the most influential oration ever delivered in this country. The first-night audience did not know whether to laugh or applaud because they were in doubt as to whether or not the dramatists intended to be satirical. It would seem to me as if that were the intent, for after a sentence about the money-changers having been driven from the temple the curtain rose to reveal a group of WPA workers leaning on shovels. That was a big belly laugh for the mink and ermine trade. Still I don't think it would have been more humorous if the same supers had been used to picture a breadline.

Mr. Kaufman once coined the superb pun, "One man's Mede is another man's Persian." The same can be said of brands of patriotism. *The American Way,* to my mind, is a pageant which confuses patriotism with Hearsting the flag.

> Heywood Broun, *"Muffled Musketry,"* in The New Republic, *Vol. LXXXXVIII, No. 1262, February 8, 1939, p. 14.*

GRENVILLE VERNON

To demand that a show planned to fill the spaces of one of the world's hugest theatres should have any subtlety of expression or should answer any world-shaking question would be idiotic, and yet the latter at least is precisely what one of our popular columnists, Mr. Heywood Broun, has asserted George S. Kaufman and Moss Hart should have done in *The American Way* [see excerpt above]. What Mr. Kaufman and Mr. Hart have done, and it is not small triumph that they have been able to do it, is to concoct a panorama of American life from the days of McKinley to the present time which has weight, variety and color enough to fill the Center Theatre with delighted audiences. *The American Way* tells the story of a German immigrant who rises to wealth and respect in his community, loses his son in the war, and his fortune later in attempting to support the bank of the man who had befriended him, is killed at a Nazi meeting, and finally is buried amid the tears of his townspeople. It tells the story very simply and perhaps naively, but it tells it with a wealth of sympathy, and in the early scenes with nostalgic longing. The ideal of *The American Way* is the ideal of the America of Lincoln. . . . It is a sentimental America certainly, an America that never could completely exist except in the ideals of its lovers, but enough of it did exist and still exists to make us willing to live for it and if need be die for it. The response of the great audiences which have greeted it has proved that it is an ideal far more vital than Mr. Broun perhaps might wish, an ideal which is still ours and which the example of Germany and Russia has certainly strengthened in our hearts. . . .

The American Way, if not an epoch-making work, is one so heart-warming that it must be seen.

> Grenville Vernon, *in a review of "The American Way," in* Commonweal, *Vol. XXIX, No. 16, February 10, 1939, p. 441.*

JOSEPH WOOD KRUTCH

There is no doubt about the fact that *The Man Who Came to Dinner* . . . is one of the best and funniest of the farces which Mr. Kaufman has written with either Mr. Hart or any of the other numerous collaborators with whom he has worked. In a very general way it belongs in the category of *The Royal Family* and *You Can't Take It with You,* though it is technically smoother than either, and doubtless owes part of its effectiveness to the steadily accelerating tempo and the mounting complications which ensue as one character after another is introduced to keep the pot a-boiling. And yet, sound as the workmanship is, it is still, I think, not entirely clear just why the enthusiasm of an audience is quite so unreserved, unanimous, and unqualified as it actually is, just why the plays of Mr. Kaufman and Mr. Hart should be treated as absolutely *sui generis* and find audiences whose applause is not so much a judgment as the confirmation of a foregone conclusion. Perhaps the fact that they are so treated helps to give the authors an air of confidence, helps them to be what it is already taken for granted that they are. Perhaps Mr. Kaufman and Mr. Hart are made funnier by being thought funny, just as a beautiful woman is said to be made more beautiful by the knowledge that she is loved. But that probably does not prevent other comic writers from asking themselves what the unloved are said to ask: "What's he got that I haven't?"

The answer is as difficult in the second case as it is in the first, but part of it probably is that Mr. Kaufman and Mr. Hart have a certain power of suggesting that they are very much in the know, that to laugh with them is to laugh in the most up-to-date company, and that, contrariwise, to fail to see the point in this satiric thrust or that is simply to confess that one does not know one's way about the metropolis. *The Man Who Came to Dinner* has, that is to say, something of the warm, cosy malice of a gossip column. Of course the man in question, a man who came unwilling and stayed for weeks because he broke a hip on the doorstep, is not really Alexander Woollcott; Alexander Woollcott does not wear a beard as this man does. But were it not for this essential incongruity, that intimate inner circle—strictly limited to forty or fifty million persons—which shares the carefully guarded secret of the Town Crier's habits, tastes, and mannerisms might suspect that this sentimental egotist with a serpent's tongue was intended as a far from flattering portrait. Even as it is, one may speculate wickedly upon the question whether or not the British jack-of-all-theatrical-trades was intended to bear some resemblance to Noel Coward, and when a much-discussed character—a practical joker from Hollywood most mysteriously known as "Banjo"—finally appears, one may nudge one's companion and say, "That's probably Harpo Marx. 'Harpo' and 'Banjo.' Get it?" The play does, to be sure, poke fun at just the sort of celebrity worship to which it appeals, and on Christmas morning the gifts received by the man who came to dinner include, among others, little remembrances from Shirley Temple, William Lyon Phelps, and Admiral Byrd. But though you may laugh as you will, neither you nor I really know so many people whom any autograph hunter would prize.

Perhaps I am merely being perverse, for my laughter was as loud and as long as that of the audience about me. Perhaps Mr. Kaufman is only an Aristides who has been called "the funny" once too often. But I do not think that it is merely that. *The Man Who Came to Dinner* is too bright, too hard, and too competent. It is funny without being gay, and it leaves no pleasant chuckles behind. I do not mean merely that it is cynical, though, except for a few inevitable and incongruous passages of sentiment, it is as loveless as tinkling cymbals. I do mean that there is no ebullience even of cynicism, no real joyousness, in it. Laughable it certainly is; merry it certainly is not. And the best of comedies are somehow merry. (pp. 474-75)

Joseph Wood Krutch, "What Nothing Succeeds Like,"
in The Nation, *Vol. 149, No. 18, October 28, 1939,
pp. 474-75.**

JOSEPH WOOD KRUTCH

[The essay from which this excerpt is taken was originally published in 1939.]

[One of Mr. Kaufman's distinctive] qualities is the result of an almost unrivaled instinct for dramatic construction of a sort which is seldom if ever really subtle or original but is always precisely right at the moment. No one can keep a play more continuously moving or more unerringly place a laugh precisely at the point where it is most needed, and this gift has made him the nearly infallible expert whose deft "doctoring" of a script or equally deft staging can be relied upon to save any potentially popular play which seems just about to miss fire. His other outstanding quality is a kind of knowingness which makes him admired and feared in any gathering of those whose pride it is "to be on the inside."

Mr. Kaufman went from a newspaper office into the theater; he is perfectly at ease when dealing with foibles of actors or men about town and his best characters are those who belong in the lower depths of "show business" or the related worlds of night club and cabaret. Whatever knowledge he may have of history or literature—and it is probably considerable—he is careful to conceal. He would die of shame if anyone were to call him "cultured" and he would be as unlikely to quote Shakespeare as Walter Pater would have been to talk cockney. But if his characters know nothing outside their own world, if they never read a book or have never so much as heard of a play earlier than *Within the Law* they know their world thoroughly. One may rest assured that the argot they speak is the argot, not of yesterday, but of today, and that if they refer familiarly to the bar of a certain hotel that is the hotel which their kind really frequent at the moment. . . . His particular field is the "wisecrack" and if there is no better—if indeed, there is no other—name for the special sort of scornful observation or flippant repartee to which some unknown genius gave that name it still awaits exhaustive definition.

The wisecrack has, of course, certain things in common with more literary forms of wit. It is cynical, it is knowing, it is elliptical, and it is, very often, ironic—a sort of shorthand reference to facts or attitudes calculated to abash or annihilate the victim who stands convicted of a sentimental disregard for what every intelligent person knows. But the wisecrack is also all these things in a special way. In the first place its knowingness is of the kind previously described, a knowingness which is based wholly upon the moment and which, if it is actually part of the wisdom of the ages, is completely unaware of the fact. In the second place the wisecrack, instead of striving as the epigram does toward a perfection of elegance and polish in language, deliberately exploits the grotesque vocabulary and the syntactical vagaries of the sort of person into whose mouth it is commonly put. Many of Mr. Kaufman's wisecracks could be transferred without change from one of his characters to another quite as readily as the witticisms of Congreve or Oscar Wilde could be similarly taken from one character and given to another. But that is not because the wisecracks have no style. It is merely because his plays are as inevitably peopled with unlettered wits as those of Congreve and Wilde are inevitably peopled with mocking exquisites. (pp. 140-43)

Nothing is more typical or more revealing than the reply attributed to Mr. Kaufman himself when he was asked why, instead of such popular entertainments as he was accustomed to compose, he did not try his hand at genuine and consistent satire. "Satire," he said, "is what closes Saturday night." Mr. Kaufman has said much funnier things but none that more perfectly illustrates the nature of the wisecrack and at the same time reveals his own self-imposed limitations. In the first place the remark is shorter by almost two-thirds than "The drama's laws the drama's patrons give, and we who live to please must please to live." In the second place, while it says just as much, it says it not only in terms whose reference is to the moment alone, but also in the idiom of those who close shows on Saturday night. The "is what," the deliberate choice of definition in the form which Teachers College designates as midway between the moronic definition by iteration and the intellectual definition in terms of essential qualities, is masterly. It puts the remark on exactly the level where Mr. Kaufman wants it. He is answering in character. (p. 144)

[Mr. Kaufman] has remained essentially the "columnist" he was during his early newspaper career—one, that is to say, whose chief business it is to make brief random comments upon a thousand things. Members of that profession are not required to develop a philosophy or to have anything independent to say. They are supposed to sparkle a dozen times a day, not to throw the steady light of sustained criticism upon either society or life as a whole, and it is an exception when one is found who has developed a consistent point of view. Certainly Mr. Kaufman, for all his brilliance, has not. He has said a hundred witty things; yet it would be difficult after seeing all his plays, more than a score in number, to say that they tend in any one direction. One knows what Mr. Lardner or Mr. Behrman stands for. The quality in each case is almost as unmistakable as that of Eugene O'Neill. But in the case of Mr. Kaufman one cannot be sure of anything—except that one will be amused.

Shrewd flights of wit and shrewd touches of character are not enough to make a play. It has to be held together by a plot and the plot must tend somewhere. But Mr. Kaufman, being primarily a wit, does not know how to make a plot or even, probably, in just what direction he would want it to tend even if he could concoct it. A wisecrack is usually what is known in the language of our generation as "a good comeback" and a good comeback is something which not only arises out of the moment but is intended only for the moment. It may imply, perhaps, a philosophy in solution but it does not necessarily imply a consistently formulated attitude and it is quite compatible with a complete inability to expand any further the criticism which it suggests. Mr. Kaufman must therefore borrow his plots and he borrows them from the sources nearest at hand. He gives his play a conventionally sentimental ending because that is the way those plots have usually ended before and also, perhaps, because he has never explored his own mind thoroughly enough to know what sort of ending would actually be consistent with the tone which the dialogue consistently maintains.

At least once he apparently wanted to be taken with complete seriousness and in *Merrily We Roll Along* collaborated on a play treating a story perennially tempting to very popular writers who are almost but not quite content with their popular acclaim—the story, that is to say, of the promising talent which loses its way in the midst of worldly success. It was told backwards, the first scene exhibiting the hero at a gathering of drunken wastrels, the last showing him delivering a valedictory address full of high ideals at his own college commencement; but the violent novelty of the device was not sufficient to compensate for the banality of the tale and the play was not the hit that its authors' works usually are. Moreover, it suggests that if he is ever to rise above his own level it will not be by adopting themes radically different from those which he has already treated with a large measure of success, but by inventing a fable really consistent with the spirit of the wisecracks which enliven it; one, that is to say, which is not only timely but caustic and tough-minded as well.

All but one of Oscar Wilde's comedies exhibit in exaggerated form what is essentially the defect of Mr. Kaufman's plays. They are sprinkled with epigrams in every one of which the wit gives to the fatuous moral of the play as a whole the lie direct. But Wilde did not rise above his own habitual level by returning to the style of *Vera*. He rose above it by inventing, for once, the scheme of *The Importance of Being Earnest* in which action and moral alike are as reckless and perverse as the dialogue can manage to be. Mr. Kaufman happens to be as skillful as Wilde was clumsy in handling a conventional plot. He is also a man whose wit is as racy as the wit of Wilde was precious and literary. But he has the same difficulty in imagining a story inspired throughout with the spirit of the talkers who act it. He puts his whole wit into a jest and then, as often as not, plants that jest in the midst of a play upon the fundamental naïveté of which only he could make the appropriate comment.

When judged as a whole Mr. Kaufman's work is seen to hesitate between pure farce on the one hand and, on the other, topical satire of the sort which made such early plays as *Dulcy, To the Ladies,* and *Beggar on Horseback* a part of the post-War revolt against current ideals and sentiments. Even at his most purposeful, however, his references are always exclusively to the local and temporary; he never pretends to go below the surface of manners, and on the whole his later tendency has been to turn either in the direction of sentimental melodrama or mere farce rather than in the direction of a more deep-cutting satire. (pp. 148-51)

> *Joseph Wood Krutch, "Comedy," in his* The American Drama Since 1918: An Informal History, *revised edition, George Braziller, Inc., 1957, pp. 134-225.**

WOLCOTT GIBBS

Although nearly everything in the world is wrong with *The Land Is Bright,* . . . it still manages to be an almost continuously interesting show. Roughly, I should say that in spirit and execution it resembles one of those articles in the Hearst Sunday magazine section which make a study of the turbulent affairs of bygone Vanderbilts, Goulds, and other pillars of society. Like these pieces, the play constructed by Edna Ferber and George Kaufman is marked by a strangely innocent and excitable point of view, contains practically every cliché in the language, bursts with melodramatic and implausible action, and offers an enormous cast of characters, all much larger than life but none in any sense lifelike. It is a gaudy simplification of the behavior of the American plutocrat, and like all popularizations of difficult (and preferably scandalous) subjects it has its appeal for the best of us.

In the space available here, it is hard to tell you much about a plot that traces the history of four generations of the Kincaid family. . . . It is much too meaty for synopsis, but the theme, briefly, is the progress of the Kincaids from the wicked vitality of the founder, a robber baron, through a period of luxury and decay, characterized chiefly by a series of misalliances with harlots and decadent nobleman of the comic-strip variety, and up at last to the spiritual rebirth of the third and fourth generations, rather arbitrarily brought on by the present emergency.

While even the most attentive spectator is apt to have a pretty hard time keeping track of all the intricate relationships in the cast, especially in view of the fact that everybody ages violently during the intermissions, *The Land Is Bright* is a very satisfactory prescription for a lively and simple-minded evening in the theatre. It is only a pity that it turned out to be little more than a parody of the play Miss Ferber and Mr. Kaufman must have had in mind when they started to write it. (pp. 36, 38)

> *Wolcott Gibbs, "Well, Yes and No," in* The New Yorker, *Vol. XVII, No. 39, November 8, 1941, pp. 36, 38.*

LEWIS NICHOLS

John P. Marquand and George S. Kaufman have fashioned one of the fall's cheerful and amiable evenings. *The Late George Apley,* it is called, and it is a liberalized, or perhaps Broadwayized, version of the Pulitzer Prize novel [of the same title] which a few years ago sent Bostonians to looking reflectively in their mirrors. . . .

[The play] is a little uneven, like the lives of the Apleys themselves. As in *Life With Father,* not a great deal happens. There is an incident about the election of a new president of the Bird Watchers, and that about Cousin Hattie's burial in the wrong part of the Apley plot. What story there is beyond these scattered reports of events elsewhere concerns the efforts of the two children to marry away from Beacon Hill. The first act is excellent, but some parts of the last two lag a bit, and when the late George is not about they lag even more. Unlike the book, the play shows Apley telling his son of his own early love affair, a scene which is not the evening's best.

Since the Messrs. Marquand and Kaufman presumably think alike about all things, it is impossible—and, of course, quite unnecessary—to tell where one stops and the other begins. Both have at least read *The Late George Apley,* and the general mood of Boston of 1912, as seen through the proper eyes, is still there. But something has been added, also. In a discussion of Freud is this one, more Broadway than Luisburg Square: "Sex largely governs the lives of people—in other parts of the country." And this, during a discussion of the Apley family dentist, who is "so old he can't see the cavities"—"No, but he is very good if you find your own." Times Square still has some tricks.

> *Lewis Nichols, in a review of "The Late George Apley," in* The New York Times, *November 22, 1944, p. 26.*

RUSSELL W. LEMBKE

It is time that we took another look at the thirty-four plays written in the years between 1920 and 1946 which bear the name of George S. Kaufman as author or collaborator. They have been smugly passed over by drama critics; but as social history alone, as vivid pictures of the life, particularly the city life, of the times, they do not deserve such treatment. There is an economy, a consciously painstaking selectivity, in the technique of writing which is not only good but which can be identified as Mr. Kaufman's own. (p. 341)

A survey of the Kaufman plays will reveal that they present American social history with vividness, economy, and thematic significance—qualities which are present to such a degree that the lack of critical appreciation is difficult to understand. At least the critics who seem to stress the importance of social consciousness might have been expected to recognize values as important as these.

It is remarkable, in view of the fact that he is known as a "topical" playwright of the "popular" and transient sort, that not one of Kaufman's plays in the 1920-1930 period caters to the craving for minor excitements of the time beyond his representation of fast tempo. What are alleged to be Kaufman's "thousand random comments" include few of those minor American fads and excesses of the decade set forth in Frederick Lewis Allen's *Only Yesterday* or the Lynd's *Middletown*, such as: Mah Jong, Coué, drinking, marathon dancing, flag-pole sitting, bootlegging, and racketeering. The fabulous crossword puzzle craze, the Florida land boom, and Lindbergh are only mentioned by Kaufman characters as very incidental to the main dialogue. Kaufman concentrates rather upon satirizing the business-success creed, including the advertising business, speculation, and big deals; the hero racket; and the influence of the business and social scheme upon art. This is not mere topicality; it goes far deeper than that.

Note how vividly Kaufman presents his picture, how expertly he pierces certain core problems of the 1920-1930 decade. Examine the thousand things that Americans were doing as illustrated by their fads and notice how these derive or gain impetus from the fundamental scheme of living at the time. There was a wider participation in business and public life, a development of organized entertainment for more people; and an increased dissemination of information through the newspapers, the movies, and then the radio; and, as a consequence, an emphasis upon the celebrity—the famous "personality." These are the things with which Kaufman dealt; they are the basis for hero and celebrity worship, fads, marathons, fast living, and the like.

Dulcy (with Connelly, 1921), the first Kaufman play, is remarkable, considering the hectic age in which it was written, for including so few purely topical references of a minor sort. The craving for excitement and for the sensational which marked the 1920's is not used by Kaufman and Connelly to bolster dramatic action; rather, the authors have managed to catch the mood of the times with respect to the particular by transient bits strategically and economically chosen to emphasize the general application. (pp. 341-42)

Other plays of the period between 1920 and 1930 reflect, as does *Dulcy,* core attitudes and essential problems of the time; but it is *The Beggar on Horseback* (with Connelly) of 1924 which gives us the clearest focus upon middle-class family life in America, the ways of the socially elite whose mode of life is aped by others, and the effects upon these groups of our industrial system. The protagonist, Neil McRae, is an artist who escapes from materialistic domination, the only Kaufman hero to dominate his surroundings. Neil McRae lives in a democracy where he and his fellow protagonists have at least a

freedom of choice—to conform or to temporize with actuality, to dominate or to outdo disorder, or to improve their state. The whole of a Kaufman play, whatever the choice of the characters, reflects a geniality which looks toward the ideal logical order of things. This is true of his plays in the fretful twenties even more than in the later plays which look back upon our history.

The Butter and Egg Man (1925) makes good fun of the economics of the theatre and indirectly comments upon American business at the time when flourished the gospel according to Bruce Barton and Red Grange, Henry Ford and Graham McNamee, the Kiwanis Clubs and Coolidge prosperity. There followed further comments along the same line illustrated by the Marx Brothers' antics in *Cocoanuts* (with Berlin, 1926) and *Animal Crackers* (with Ryskind, 1928,) and by *The Good Fellow* (with Menkiewicz, 1926,) a gibe at fraternal-order high jinx.

June Moon (with Lardner, 1929) is the last Kaufman play of the decade. There was political cynicism in 1929, but the country still sang the songs that Rudy Vallee crooned and prayed for a Big Bull Market. . . . Kaufman and Lardner pointed maliciously at our June and moon rhymes while at the same time they allowed their moronic hero (just one of us) to have his fool's success.

The years of the next decade, the 1930's, were much more seriously lived in America. Prosperity was gone; there were fewer fads and more fears. . . . In general, there was a unifying interest in politics. Kaufman carried over to the thirties his interest in the arts and in business and social life, but turned more to comment on politics and patriotism. Again he chose what constituted the core interest of the time.

I'd Rather Be Right (with Hart, 1937,) one of these later plays, has more transient references than any other of the Kaufman works. Predominantly they are references to particular people in the news of the day. The topical bits of most Kaufman plays, however, simply serve to set the scene and are few and easily understood. *Of Thee I Sing* (with Ryskind, 1931) becomes no more specific even in its satire on the handling of unfinished business in the U.S. Senate than to have a Senator recall a bill first brought up in 1804 and again in 1852 to provide a pension for Paul Revere's horse, Jenny. The Senator suggests a moment of silent tribute when he learns that Jenny is dead. Here is a good comic reference which serves all the purposes of specific critical satire and retains a wealth of generalized significance.

There were other Kaufman plays or musicals of the 1930-1940 decade concerned at least in part with politics. This was the era of depression, followed by Roosevelt and the New Deal. In this decade, too, came *Once in a Lifetime* (with Hart, 1930,) the superb attack on Hollywood "art" and super-promotion told with unrivaled expertness in terms of the wisecrack and all the gaudy grotesqueries of the American faddist; true the hey-day of Coué, Mah Jong, Bananas, and the crossword puzzle was past, but miniature golf, Huey Long, and talking pictures had come along by 1930, when Kaufman and Hart made this powerful comment upon our fads as they intruded into art and all aspects of the social scheme. Similarly, *You Can't Take It With You* (with Hart, 1936,) *The Man Who Came to Dinner* (with Hart, 1939,) and *George Washington Slept Here* (with Hart, 1940) are fine comic treatments of our cultural idiosyncrasies. (pp. 342-43)

Kaufman's vivid and economical method of handling historical materials is demonstrated most clearly in the later, more definitely historical, plays. In these plays Kaufman was concerned chiefly with the time since 1900 during which each of four decades was marked, respectively, by ruthlessness but by an increasing social consciousness; by an interest in business and sentiment; by cynicism; and, finally, by patriotism and a growing concern over public issues.

With *Merrily We Roll Along* (1934) Kaufman and Hart turned toward the type of production which was to be carried further in *The Fabulous Invalid* (with Hart, 1938,) *The American Way* (with Hart, 1939,) and *The Land Is Bright* (with Ferber, 1941). These plays depend for their effect upon a certain display of scenic richness and upon a theatrical treatment of the substance of American history. (p. 344)

The theatrical display in these historical plays is in no sense extraneous to the expressive purpose of the playwrights; it results in a striking fulfillment of that purpose in each case. *The Land Is Bright* presents the raw materials of life, the evils of corruption, violent climaxes, and overdrawn details of setting and vocal attributes; it projects our confused, coarse, often vulgar, generally physical approach to national and world problems. We are shown a distinctive picture of the rough and coarse nineties; the slickness and slyness, the jazz and the imitation of Europe in the twenties; and the stock-taking attempt at a return to essential democracy, the more human yet foreboding quality of the forties.

Kaufman has always been primarily interested in the man who is ostensibly a success, showing at the same time how others ape the ways of the financially successful. In *Merrily We Roll Along,* playwright Richard Niles' two wives, Althea and Helen, are products of materialism at two levels of society, and thus are symbols of the sort of environment under attack. We are concerned with their effect upon him in the same way that we are concerned with the effect of other discordant elements in the environment.

The climax of this play comes in Act III when the purposive will of the playwright is completely beaten by the opposition of Helen, the first wife, and her father and mother—the Murneys. Richard stands motionless, alone and defeated at the end of Scene 1; the power of the contrast with the noisy intensity of previous high points is typical of the way in which many Kaufman plays achieve a climactic moment, typical of Kaufman's contrast of the noise and disorder of the times with the need for spiritual sensitivity. Compare the scene in *The Land Is Bright* in which a member of the Kincaid clan, just freed from a concentration camp, totters slowly and silently across the stage. All of the significance of the play is gathered together vividly and economically in such moments of silent pain in the midst of bedlam. Both of these plays reveal a greater cynicism than before. The years of both, 1934 and 1940, were serious times; in 1934 economic recovery was lagging badly, and in 1940 England was fighting for her life. Perhaps, too, Kaufman felt more justification for cynicism with respect to the past and its relation to the present. (pp. 344-45)

Important themes accent Kaufman's pertinent comment upon living interests—themes which by implication reveal the ideal world. There is no grandiloquent presentation, but through the pictures of dissonance come thematic variations upon matters of great interest which may serve to clarify focus: the spiritual vs. the physical, the destruction of platitudes, the value of even the smallest esthetic phase in experience and art, the value of free expression.

In *Dulcy* the bromide is ribbed, and "success" is revealed as often a thing of mad men. In *The Beggar on Horseback* the artist discovers that his cell door was unlocked all the time; he was always really free to do as he pleased, and in this case he does escape the restrictions of materialism. *The Butter and Egg Man* symbolizes in the one word "sweetheart" all the sham of the promotion business. (pp. 345-46)

Perhaps Kaufman's strongest theme is the conflict of the spiritual vs. the physical. What better dramatic juxtaposition could be devised than the fist fight between the campaigning followers of Bryan and McKinley and the final killing by a fascist-minded gang in *The American Way*? The rough-and-tumble, even vicious, methods of business and politics seem natural, but the people are stunned when Martin Gunther is beaten to death by a mob. The physical approach of the American to his problems when taken to the ridiculous extreme of fascism is exposed again in *The Land Is Bright*.

Here in the Kaufman plays is social history presented with vividness, economy, and significance. The most obvious of all the errant nonsense contained in the defamation of the Kaufman plays is the contention that his social criticism is vitiated by a conventional story. That satire is only strengthened when Dulcy's husband successfully achieves his business merger. The success creed continues its insane hold and Dulcy continues her bromidic ways—certainly this satire is the strongest kind of comment; moreover, we in a democracy have the right to make fools of ourselves if we wish. (p. 346)

Every conventional story which Kaufman offers is set within a satirical pattern which reveals the conventional in its true light. The method is that of direct but genial ridicule; it is exaggeration. [In *You Can't Take It With You*] Penny writes plays because eight years ago a typewriter was delivered to the Vanderhof home by mistake. When a Saroyan character writes a book and each book consists of one word, such as "tree" or "brother"—the word whose meaning he has learned in an ecstatic moment, that method consists of understatement. The critic may prefer one method over another; but Kaufman has also made his choice and has done excellently by it.

Kaufman has reiterated the fact that our history reveals revolutionary effects resulting from scientific and economic changes, that our thinking and our artistic sensibility and freedom have not kept pace with these changes, and that we must, nonetheless, for the sake of our own sanity, maintain a genial attitude toward the present which seeks values wherever we may find them. Mr. Kaufman, himself, might scoff at this as too grandiloquent a conclusion, but I find that there is more than a passing pleasure to be gained from his work, that there is demonstrated more than a financially profitable energy and ingenuity. (pp. 346-47)

> *Russell W. Lembke, "The George S. Kaufman Plays as Social History," in* The Quarterly Journal of Speech, *Vol. XXXIII, No. 3, October, 1947, pp. 341-47.*

WOLCOTT GIBBS

[In *The Small Hours*, written in collaboration with Leueen MacGrath, the] idea seems to be that most of us lead lives of secret terror and loneliness, and consequently have a desperate need for understanding. This is undoubtedly a valid point, but the authors have cluttered it up with so many bizarre characters, such as a boy whose latent homosexuality drives him to smoking marijuana; so much scenery (there are twenty-six scenes, which shift with dizzying speed); and so much stylish but unlikely conversation that the total effect comes dangerously close to absurdity. The plot, ruthlessly compressed, focusses on the wife of a New York publisher, who, apparently as the result of having been born and brought up in Milwaukee, has almost no social manner and so suffers intensely among what she describes as her husband's "circle of fascinating friends." Her condition is aggravated by the fact that her husband, who also came from Milwaukee but has somehow outgrown it, takes a mistress, in the shape of a female writer even more appalling than most; that her daughter contracts an unhappy marriage; that her son is the drug addict mentioned above; and that she is helplessly intimidated by her butler's air of chilly superiority. All these circumstances combine to bring on a nervous breakdown, and she takes to her bed, under the hysterical impression that she can't walk. Eventually, she is cured by the realization that all the other members of her family are even worse off than she is and need her help. It is not for me to say that Mr. Kaufman and Miss MacGrath are unfamiliar with metropolitan literary society, but I can't help feeling that in this instance they have achieved nothing but a wild caricature of it, the manners, conversation, and general behavior portrayed by them somehow suggesting the conception of upper-middle-class American life apt to be held by a British novelist who has never got around to crossing the Atlantic. Now and then, there are traces of Mr. Kaufman's former wit and felicity, and sometimes a scene seems true and touching, but for the most part the play struck me as vacant and synthetic, substituting a profusion of picturesque types . . . , and an extraordinary range of locale for any real thought or emotion. (pp. 66, 68)

> *Wolcott Gibbs, "The Mighty Fall," in* The New Yorker, *Vol. XXVII, No. 2, February 24, 1951, pp. 66, 68.**

WOLCOTT GIBBS

As I have sometimes observed, there is no form of composition more difficult and potentially more embarrassing to the author than fantasy, and this point was amply demonstrated in *Fancy Meeting You Again,* the joint work of George S. Kaufman and his wife, Leueen MacGrath. . . . The plot had something to do with a young woman . . . , who had been pursuing a man for some five thousand years, through several incarnations. At the opening of the play, she was a sculptress in New York, whose work was a rather fetching combination of the primitive and the modern, though not especially admired by the other members of the cast. She was, at that time, in the process of being married to a young businessman of standard and wholesome design, but in the middle of this ceremony shadowy memories of the past and the long chase made her decide that she couldn't go through with it. After a drunk scene with her low-comedy secretary, in which some of the aspects of immortality were discussed, the true object of her affections turned up, this time in the form of an art critic and archeologist, who not only expressed a poor opinion of her work but also, as he had been through the centuries, was prepared to offer her anything but honorable matrimony.

Except for what I took to be a happy ending, this scene is essentially a summary of the play, since the ones that followed, including flashbacks to a Neanderthal cave and a disorderly house in ancient Rome, did little but present the same characters—variously disguised, of course—saying just about the same things. Conscious, perhaps, that their product was somewhat lacking in substance and variety, Mr. Kaufman and Miss

MacGrath inserted a few subordinate characters, such as a club lady, who also appeared as the operator of the bordello; a pale and mysterious stranger, who represented the voice of doom or eternity or some such and whose function it was to inform the heroine that she could expect no more lives; a judge, who had almost no rational connection with the proceedings; a maid, who had even less; a couple of Nubian slaves, who showed up in the last act as deliverymen, or what are known as "sight gags;" and a handsome white poodle, who entertained me, I'm afraid, more than anybody else on the stage. There were also a good many topical references to people, ranging from Nick Kenny to President Truman. None of these added attractions, however, were quite enough to save *Fancy Meeting You Again* from a certain air of desperate and not particularly inspired invention. (pp. 54-5)

> *Wolcott Gibbs, "The Butcherbird," in* The New Yorker, *Vol. XXVII, No. 50, January 26, 1952, pp. 53-5.**

WALTER F. KERR

[*The Solid Gold Cadillac* is] a fairy-tale about a Cinderella who waddles . . . , a Prince Charming who is having considerable difficulty with his setting-up exercises . . . , and Four Ugly Corporation Directors who would like to give both Cinderella and the Prince the heave-ho from the company in which they own stock.

This information is relayed to us by the voice of Fred Allen, story-teller extraordinary, and Mr. Allen is at great pains to keep the suspense rolling from blackout to blackout. At one point when things are darkest for our loved ones, Mr. Allen assures us that the play will, after all, end happily. If it doesn't he adds, each member of the audience will be given a refund. There is, he adds further, a fine fat chance of that.

I don't think you're going to want a refund. But we'd better get the facts straight, right off. George S. Kaufman and Howard Teichmann haven't written what you're likely to call a play. It's more like a series of revue sketches, with most of the dancing left out. Call it a musical comedy without the music, if you like. You're bound to notice, too, that it ambles along without anything very probable on its mind, that the mythical plot twists are neither so inventive nor so funny as the casual asides, that there are wan moments right alongside some wonderful ones.

But—for this reviewer at least—*The Solid Gold Cadillac* has its own special delights. . . .

[The] most interesting thing about *The Solid Gold Cadillac* is the sudden reappearance of satire on the Broadway stage. It must be a good many years now since anyone has devoted an entire evening to straight kidding; perhaps the last such samples were presented by Mr. Kaufman himself in the thirties. The author is, in fact, reworking some of his old gimmicks—notably the business of incorporating motion picture lampoons of the latest news broadcasts. But why shouldn't Mr. Kaufman borrow from himself? The thrusts are still juicily funny.

It would be misleading to suggest that *The Solid Gold Cadillac* had the sturdiness, the structural hilarity, or the sting of the author's best-remembered parodies. But it's good for a hatful of chuckles.

> *Walter F. Kerr, "Gold Leaf, Anyway," in* New York Herald Tribune, *November 6, 1953.*

RICHARD WATTS, JR.

Out of *Ninotchka,* a celebrated motion picture that kidded the Russians amusingly and provided the incomparable Greta Garbo with one of her most notable roles, some talented theater people have made an entertaining musical comedy called *Silk Stockings.* . . . Here following a tumultuous road tour and apparently quite a bit of intramural battling, it turned out to be a vigorous, tuneful and often hilariously satirical show, which gives every sign of being a hit and, in most part, deserves to be.

On a few occasions, particularly in the second act, the book tends to grow a little serious about Soviet dogmatism and tyranny, as if slightly fearful of its general good nature. Chiefly, though, it keeps its anti-Muscovite lampooning remarkably on a pleasant level of humorous amiability, and I think it is all the more effective because of its lack of spluttering indignation. Some of its thrusts are pointed and telling, especially because *Silk Stockings* keeps its temper. It would be cheering to think an anti-American show in Moscow could be so unhysterical.

Indeed, the new musical comedy doesn't hesitate to glance in the direction of a few local targets, too. It manages to find time to laugh at Hollywood movie stars and the antics of our filmmakers abroad, and it even reveals a considerable courage in taking for its American hero, the man who combats the totalitarians and wins the serious-minded Russian girl over to democratic gaiety and freedom, a Hollywood actors' agent. Here is a vulnerable national type for mockery, if ever I heard of one. The second act, by the way, does fall off somewhat.

This libretto, which, unless my memory has faltered more than usual, has been pretty freely adapted from Melchior Lengyel's film scenario, is the work of George S. Kaufman, Leueen MacGrath and Abe Burrows, all three of whom are notable for their sense of intelligent humor. The fun in *Silk Stockings,* which is often witty and pungently pertinent, is more the result of dialogue than situation. The plot, you may recall, has to do with three nitwit commissars who are sent to Paris to watch a Russian composer, and the girl who is sent to watch them. . . .

Silk Stockings doesn't always live up to its best moments but it is good, tuneful fun.

Richard Watts, Jr., "Kidding the Muscovites to Music," in New York Post, *February 25, 1955. Reprinted in* New York Theatre Critics' Reviews, *Vol. XVI, No. 6, Week of February 28, 1955, p. 357.*

Alfred Kazin

1915-

American critic, autobiographer, essayist, and editor.

Best known for his study of twentieth-century American literature, *On Native Grounds* (1942), Kazin is highly regarded as an influential critic for his ability to analyze a literary work in conjunction with the author's heritage and the prevailing social climate. Unlike the New Critics, whose interpretive methods consist of detailed textual analyses and close attention to form, Kazin insists that literature and writers be understood in relation to their culture. Some critics fault Kazin's approach to literature for its deemphasis of formal analysis and abstract theory. However, Leo Marx defends Kazin's methods, in particular the manner in which he "saturates himself in a writer's work, distills the ideas and emotions it evokes, describes them to us concisely, and then asks, 'What have I gained?'" Kazin's principal concern in his criticism is to involve the reader in a literary work.

On Native Grounds outlines the beginnings of social realism in American literature. Kazin correlates its rise with the enormous political and technological developments of the early 1900s, yet he also maintains that most writers felt estranged from their environment during this period. His examinations of such authors as Theodore Dreiser and James T. Farrell in relation to their social milieus were highly praised. Kazin continued to explore the relationship between literature and society in the collections *The Inmost Leaf* (1955), *Contemporaries* (1962), *Bright Book of Life* (1973), and *An American Procession* (1984).

Kazin is also well regarded for his autobiographical works and memoirs. In *A Walker in the City* (1951), he recounts his youth in the Brownsville section of Brooklyn during the Depression. *Starting Out in the Thirties* (1965) chronicles his early years as a critic and includes sketches of prominent writers he met during those years. In *New York Jew* (1978), Kazin narrates his experiences from 1942 through the late 1970s. Critics generally praise his colorful and often poignant accounts of his life and the people and events that influenced him, and some suggest that these works are representative of Kazin's role as a critic, which, in his words, is to examine literature "against the background of man's striving."

(See also *CLC*, Vol. 34; *Contemporary Authors*, Vols. 1-4, rev. ed.; and *Contemporary Authors New Revision Series*, Vol. 1.)

© Jerry Bauer

HOWARD MUMFORD JONES

[The absence of interest in literary history is] amazing because the central problem . . . has been the extent to which literature influences, or is influenced by, society. On the extreme left this influence is felt to exist, to be central, and to be demonstrable. On the extreme right it is denied, and the work of literature exists in a sort of Crocean vacuum as an exercise in sensibility. In between there are all sorts of theories. One would suppose that writers might turn dispassionately to examine the relevant historical evidence (of which there is a great abundance), but they have not done so. It is a slow process, this sifting of historical evidence, and it is much more fun to dogmatize. Mr. Kazin, however, in *On Native Grounds,* has tried to sift evidence and to refrain from dogma. He has tried, in other words, to write literary history.

I am not sure I know what literary history is, but I suppose its practitioner tries to answer four questions. First, do the leading, representative, or influential books of a period fall into any sort of pattern that makes sense at once to the historian and to the modern reader? Second, what are the social forces, the public issues, the general intellectual controversies that have shaped the literary trends of the epoch? Third, what are the drives, conscious or unconscious, rational or irrational, revealed in the biography of the author or in his writing that have helped to shape his work? And lastly, what is the probable human importance of his work either as an esthetic experience still having vitality or as a philosophic expression of human values?

These are, at any rate, important questions, and these are the questions which Mr. Kazin tries to answer about the prose literature of the last half century. By and large he has done a better job than anybody else. The organization of his book is at once chronological and thematic, a dual arrangement that permits him to discuss a work which is merely representative or documentary when that illumines a decade, and also to discuss a work which, he thinks, still illumines us.

He has omitted the drama and poetry, so that in the opinion of some he has omitted consulting two of the most sensitive barometers of our spiritual life, but there is no use asking for a different sort of book. He is sensitive, sympathetic, and informed. He has, so far as I can see, no theory to prove except the theory that literature ought to mean something to mankind. Too many writers talk as if men exist for books.

There are, to be sure, weaknesses. The last decade is too close for perspective, and I do not here comprehend the proportioning of his space. His discussion of Marxian criticism is out of all relation to his own estimate of its importance; and he is betrayed here and there—in his discussion of Ludwig Lewisohn or of Irving Babitt—into unwonted repetitiousness. There are a good many social influences upon books and book-making he has ignored. He says nothing about the relation of creative writing to the magazine or to the vulgarization of the magazine; and though he hints at Hollywood, he says little about the profound effect of the moving picture. He does nothing with publishing history—with the courage of publishers who defied monopoly and the censor. He ignores the equally profound and sometimes deleterious effect of the Book-of-the-Month Club on publishing. Like too many other literary historians he has ignored the whole business of getting into print, the publicity racket, and much else. (pp. 5-6)

Nevertheless no one, I think, has been more deft in setting the social scene for the appearance of literature in the successive stages of literary development; and no one has more economically marshalled his writers upon that stage. Equally admirable is the flexibility of temperament which enables Mr. Kazin to enter sympathetically into the inner life of so many writers so diverse. One has pleasure in the intelligence of his judgments, even if one occasionally wishes to disclaim them.

His style is always competent and occasionally distinguished; and though sometimes the adjectives flow a little freely, one is seldom at a loss as to what he means. In sum, Mr. Kazin, if he does not answer all my four questions, strives to answer them—knows, indeed, that they need answering, and tries to put the reader in the way of drawing conclusions of his own. I do not remember any literary history recently to appear that is more judicious or more sensitive or less inclined to take sides. Perhaps the appearance of *On Native Grounds* marks the recrudescence of an intelligent treatment of literary history *qua* history rather than as arsenal for controversial forays. (p. 6)

Howard Mumford Jones, "Literary History and Literary Plenty," in The Saturday Review of Literature, *Vol. XXV, No. 44, October 31, 1942, pp. 5-6.*

PETER MONRO JACK

"Never before," writes Mr. Kazin, thinking of the number of books about America, "did a nation seem so hungry for news of itself." *On Native Grounds* is a news report, a majority report, of the interpretation of American life through its novels and critical essays. In the Parrington tradition of social realism, and to be considered alongside DeVoto, Cowley, Geismar and others who are vigorously protecting the health of American letters, Mr. Kazin adds a personal and sometimes unpredictable brilliance of opinion. He already has made his name as one of

the best reviewers of novels in the country through his ability to analyze the nature of a book, to recognize its natural distinction, and express its sense and style rapidly and expertly. He is astonishingly well read. At the age of 27, as other reporters will be pointing out, he has apparently read every important book in American literature and every other book written about them. This decision and industry he has used in writing [*On Native Grounds*], probably the most inclusive documentation of modern literature in America. . . .

As a critic of critics Mr. Kazin is the most adroit of writers. When Van Wyck Brooks wrote sentimental and despairing lamentations about the present generation Mr. Kazin simply pins him down by his own words. He does the same for Waldo Frank and Ludwig Lewisohn, Babbitt, and More, Mencken and Krutch. The point that Mr. Kazin makes is that Brooks does not help writers by his attack: there is nothing they can learn from him. In a sort of prophetic vein Mr. Kazin declares himself: that no value can be lost in our civilization even in a time of war. There will be "differences among men and the explorations of the human imagination"—these, he hopes, will continue in literature as much as they actually do in life, and no form of censorship or critical interference should prevent this "literature of nationhood." There is a certain independence in this criticism. If it were more so, if its options were as resolute as its knowledge is sound, Mr. Kazin's book would take its place as a junior and modern Parrington. In point of fact, no one has covered as completely and penetratingly the literature of our time.

Peter Monro Jack, "The Literature of Our Time—An Interpretation," in The New York Times Book Review, *November 22, 1942, p. 8.*

GRANVILLE HICKS

If [*On Native Grounds*] limits itself to fiction, criticism, and some works of philosophy, economics, and journalism, and if it suffers by the omission of poetry and drama, it does embrace the entire modern period, from the later Howells to the latest Steinbeck. By thus taking into its province the three generations whose works constitute American prose literature of this century, it exhibits such continuity as this literature has as well as its abrupt discontinuities. In this age, as has often enough been pointed out, one generation has come quickly after another, usually with foot raised for a contemptuous kick, and when one of these generations is considered by itself, as in Beach's *American Fiction, 1920-1940* or Geismar's *Writers in Crisis,* the effect is to exaggerate the isolation. Mr. Kazin knows that each generation has belligerently set itself apart from its predecessors, and he makes all that needs to be made of the absence of a sustaining tradition, but his book permits one to see the framework within which the sudden changes have taken place.

The book is divided into three parts: "The Search for Reality (1890-1917)," "The Great Liberation (1918-1929)," and "The Literature of Crisis (1930-1940)." Mr. Kazin is twenty-seven and his age, though in most ways irrelevant, does influence his attitude towards his three groups. The writers of the first generation are, obviously, a long distance away from him; they are writers he has "worked up," read only, or chiefly, for research purposes, and he maintains toward most of them a slightly disinterested curiosity, occasionally touched by surprise. On Howells—for whom he has so marked and so sound a feeling that I hope he will do the full-length study he has talked of doing—he is illuminating, but about the younger writers of the '90's and the early part of the century he says mostly what has been said before, though he often says it well and sometimes, as in the paragraphs on Stephen Crane, brilliantly. Apart from the discussion of Howells, the most interesting section is the chapter on Edith Wharton and Theodore Dreiser, in which Kazin seems to be trying to say something new about both writers and not quite succeeding.

The second generation he approaches with more freshness and vigor. These are the writers whose reputations were still shining brightly when he reached, no doubt precociously, the age of serious reading. He witnessed the sudden decline of those reputations, but he merely witnessed it, taking no part in the critical battles that it involved. . . . As for his general feeling for the mood of the '20's, it is wholly sound, giving his comments a great superiority to the bizarre distortions of Maxwell Geismar's first and last chapters.

Good as Part II is, however, one senses in its concluding chapter, as in the whole of Part III, a sharp quickening of the author's critical pulse. Here at last he is talking about the books he grew up with, read as they came from the press, argued about with his friends. Here is the warmest feeling, and here are some of the finest insights. Nothing better, I think, has been written about Scott Fitzgerald or James T. Farrell, nor has anyone commented more wisely on the quality of the lost generation's disillusionment or described more eloquently the fierce, vengeful brutality of recent naturalism. On the other novelists of the '30's—Dos Passos, Hemingway, Steinbeck, Faulkner, and Wolfe—he seems to me somewhat less impressive, but there is not one of these novelists about whom he has not something new and discriminating to say.

Here, then, is a book that considers in detail as many as fifty writers of the twentieth century. With almost startling intensity Kazin has given himself to scores and scores of novels and books of criticism, relentlessly demanding of himself the fullest response of which he is capable. And rarely has he come away from them without some penetrating thrust of the imagination. This is the least that can be said of *On Native Grounds.* (pp. 22-3)

What, then, are the bases on which *On Native Grounds* is written? One of them, I think, is quite clearly a determination not to do certain things. "It may be sufficient to say here," Kazin writes in his preface, "that I have never been able to understand why the study of literature in relation to society should be divorced from a full devotion to what literature is in itself, or why those who seek to analyze literary texts should cut off the act of writing from its irreducible sources in the life of men." This is well said, and even though Kazin in his Chapter XIV may exaggerate the "twin fanaticisms," he has been wholly right in seeking to avoid these opposing dangers. Yet the mere avoidance of error is far from "positive affirmation."

Then there is what Kazin calls "the greatest single fact about our modern American writing," by which he means "our writers' absorption in every last detail of their American world together with their deep and subtle alienation from it." On this theme he has good things to say, especially in the section on Thomas Wolfe, but in a last chapter, in the course of which he talks about the journalistic exploration of America—the W.P.A. guidebooks, the photographic studies, the books of travel, and so forth—he seems to overlook the more obvious explanations of the new interest in the American scene of the present and past, while striving for a subtlety that in the end becomes mere confusion.

The real organizing principle of the book is a faith—and I would call it a blind faith—in the importance of literature. I call it blind because it seems to me that Mr. Kazin does not know why he feels so intensely about books and their authors. His emotion is so vague, so diffuse, so out of proportion to his sensibility—which is nevertheless very real—that there is a painful contrast between what he says and the way he says it. The evidence is in the style, as [in] two passages—one the conclusion of the section on Dreiser, the other the conclusion of the section on Robert Herrick. . . . (pp. 25-6)

There are many such passages, passages that mean nothing at all or at any rate considerably less than Mr. Kazin must have thought they meant. They are not the product of wilful obscurity, the kind of pretentiousness with which some writers conceal their emptiness, for Kazin is always honest. They are the result of a violent emotion that has no clearly defined object. Kazin is seeking not to impress the reader but to express himself. His failure not merely to say what he wants to say but in some cases to say anything at all comes because he has nothing to say that is commensurate with what he feels.

I ought to acknowledge before I go further that I am one of the critics with whom Mr. Kazin quarrels, that he refers to *The Great Tradition* as "not so much a bad book as a book of monumental naïveté," and that he calls me "a profoundly earnest but essentially unimaginative scholar" and "a little Calvin of the left." I don't particularly like those phrases, but my objections would not be worth recording if I did not feel that the entire section on Marxism is inadequate. Mr. Kazin has, I feel, a rather special animosity toward Marxism, an animosity that makes him see only one aspect of the rise of revolutionary sentiment in the '30's—its narrowness and bitterness. Here—and, as a matter of fact, in the whole chapter called "Criticism at the Poles"—the critic is fighting battles of his own, and I think he is less sure of himself than he tries to pretend. (p. 27)

Yet in much of what he says about Marxism—and, for that matter, about my work as a Marxist—he is right. It is true, for instance, that the vast generalizations and terrible impatience of Marxism acted like strong drink on the converts of the '30's. It is true, also, that the economic and philosophic generalizations of Marx and Engels, even insofar as they were sound, were so remote from literary experience that we Marxist critics could function only by improvising a whole new apparatus of cultural analysis. . . . If we had contented ourselves with writing studies in social change, we might have made in the long run a contribution to criticism, and we would have little now for which to apologize. But the strong drink was acting upon us, and, especially in the early stages of our intoxication, we attempted tasks for which we were unprepared. Though there was considerably more sense than Mr. Kazin admits—he obviously has not looked for it—there was a good deal of foolishness written in *The New Masses* and other left-wing periodicals. There was also a good deal of stupid sectarianism, but this, far more often than Mr. Kazin admits, was the sectarianism of strong feeling rather than the sectarianism of the party line. Against this latter sectarianism most of us struggled, and the cause for regret is not that we succumbed, as Mr. Kazin would have it, but that we spent so much energy in resistance, and were so often distracted by irrelevant conflicts.

And whatever the justice of certain rebukes, it remains true that he misses the whole spirit of the left-wing movement in the '30's. He can see only the anger, the fear, and the partisanship. They were there, but so also were compassion and hope. If Mr. Kazin had studied more carefully the changes of tone in the novels of Dos Passos, Farrell, Steinbeck, and Hemingway, instead of treating the work of each author as a static whole, he would have perceived how, at that moment when they could believe, they were lifted up. I know that what lifted them seems now—to them and to most of us—to have been an illusion, but is is a phenomenon not to be overlooked by the historian of literature that, as they felt themselves moving, not alone but with others, toward a society cleansed of foulness and disease, the most sensitive and acute of our novelists seemed to be freed of their own sicknesses. This is what a critic might look at, not the failures of the lame little men who hobbled along on dogmas. (pp. 27-9)

I wish [Kazin] had looked more resolutely at the whole problem of the writer's behavior in a diseased civilization. He seems to have been so horrified by the extravagances and follies of the left-wing movement in the '30's that he is unwilling to discuss directly the question of the writer and politics. Although I have said much on that subject that I would not repeat now, I was never foolish enough to suggest that there is a necessary connection between political beliefs and literary merit. But, whatever may be true of this writer or that, I doubt that the majority of writers are likely to be nonpolitical in times like these. If there are authors who can quietly and successfully go about their work while the world crumbles around them, that is the thing for them to do, but most writing men and women cannot deny their responsibilities to their fellow human beings without some vital loss to themselves. I believe that our writers would be stronger and better if they had today what some of them thought they had five or ten years ago—unity between themselves and their readers based on faith in and action for a social organization less viciously defective than ours. Even if they were only camp followers—as a decade ago Dos Passos wisely defined their role—they might lose the sense of frustration and helplessness that is so apparent in their work today. I am not saying that writers ought to go out and found a political party, but merely that Mr. Kazin as a critic might have lifted his nose for a moment out of his books. (p. 30)

Granville Hicks, "The Ground Alfred Kazin Stands On," in The Antioch Review, *Vol. III, No. 1, March, 1943, pp. 21-31.*

IRWIN EDMAN

Nearly ten years ago Alfred Kazin wrote an eloquent and imaginative book on American literature entitled **On Native Grounds**. He has now written [**A Walker in the City**], a book on his own native grounds, the Brownsville section of Brooklyn, where he grew up in the midst of the poverty of an immigrant Jewish community. To everyone on those streets, especially to a sensitive child, everything outside Brownsville was "Beyond." Beyond lay Manhattan, the middle-class Jewish section, the Negro slum a few blocks away, and the Italian district a mile off—and all America, and the Russia and Poland his parents talked about with a bittersweet remembrance.

Kazin has written a tender and a true book, sensuously alive sometimes to the aching point and emotionally intense to the degree of passionate pain. Memory is said to be the mother of

the muses and memory is the origin of the extraordinary evocation which constitutes the dominant quality of this book. . . .

Using as a thread walks remembered from childhood and walks taken to Brownsville Revisited, Kazin recaptures the place as he knew it in the late twenties and in the early days of the depression. . . .

One could write American life in terms of autobiographies: "Life on the Mississippi," for instance, with Mark Twain's young, remembered, dusty, dreaming afternoons along the fabulous river; Henry Adams, who on the first page of his story says his name marked him as definitely as if as if it had been Israel Cohen. Alfred Kazin seems to have felt himself less marked and more attached—to a community and to a communion with all the immigrant families, all poor, all Jewish, and mostly Socialist, of his time and his place.

There is certainly no recent autobiographer with so exact and lyric a memory. Kazin does not sentimentalize: "the smell of the leak in the men's room in the subway station at Rockaway Avenue" is mentioned on the first page. Yet before the reader has finished these 176 pages, he has come to see with sympathetic vision the whole texture, color and sound of life in this tenement realm which is revealed as tapestried, as dazzling, as full of lush and varied richness as an Arabian bazaar. His chapter on Sabbath Eve (Friday evening) in the kitchen of his family's home is a triumph of imaginative recall: one enters the brightly burnished flat, tastes the savory foods, heeds the cozy and exciting conversation, experiences the sense of oneness with Judaism, with socialism, with all mankind. . . .

There is a good deal that Kazin leaves half implicit, reflections which the reader may make for himself. Indeed, the best in this book (and a large part of it is the best) is the evocation itself and the intimations suggested. The fact is that Kazin's prose becomes a little too glibly generalized and overblown when he makes moral points too expressly. Yet the moral implications are there. One of them is the complex quality of rootedness and unrootedness in the lives of so many Americans. In the child Alfred Kazin, this is manifest by his awareness of two backgrounds—the one of his neighborhood colored by the past of his parents and their European origins, and another of the America to which he pledged allegiance in the public school salute to the flag (an America which was symbolized by Theodore Roosevelt, the hero of San Juan Hill). . . .

What Kazin has written is more than a celebration of a place. It is the delineation of the search by a very young American Jew (intensely aware of his Jewish bonds and his American "apartness") for a specifically American heritage. He finds it vicariously in the brownstone, gas-lighted, horse-car era he had never known. This book is the record, too, of the awakening of this young Jew, this young American, to a world not only beyond Brownsville but beyond provincialism of any kind, of his initiation into the worlds of music and literature and art. It tells movingly the part that the Brooklyn Museum and the branch library played in this awakening and, among less likely educational instruments, the light on a tenement wall in an autumn dusk. The greater part is classic in its simplicity, proportion and directness, and a small classic in its total effect.

Irwin Edman, "Urban Landscape, with Figures," in The New York Times Book Review, *October 28, 1951, p. 1.*

CLEANTH BROOKS

The essays in this bright and readable collection [**The Inmost Leaf**] range in date from 1941 to the present. . . . In subject matter they range from Thoreau to Fitzgerald and Faulkner, from Flaubert and Gorky to E. E. Cummings. Along with such critical essays and reviews, Alfred Kazin has also reprinted his introduction to *The Portable Blake* and excerpts from the journal that he kept in Italy during the year 1947.

Mr. Kazin takes criticism seriously enough to have bestowed some thought upon the kinds that are possible and the kinds that are desirable. . . . He prefers to focus upon the author rather than the work. He would not be distressed at the impeachment that his own judgments have their bias. His concern more often than not is with relating the work under discussion "to our living."

Such a definition of the critic's function throws considerable light upon the merits and the limitations of Kazin's book. This formula focuses attention upon the reader, whose fullness of life the critic means to foster. But it also raises a question—a question that Mr. Kazin's casual and generously uncritical phrase, "to our living," tends to conceal. *Our* living is whose living? I am tempted to answer: not that of universal man, nor even that of the average American, but more precisely that of the urban Easterner, a white collar worker or a member of one of the professions, a liberal, who probably reads The New Yorker, who almost certainly voted for Truman, and who, as a good naturalist and secularist, hopes to salvage from the collapse of religion and from the disappointments of the revolutionists a generous but scientific humanism. Those of us who only partially or uncomfortably fit this formula will find that Mr. Kazin often does not tell us what a particular work can mean to *our* living.

Mr. Kazin's stance does, however, account for certain features of his criticism. In the first place it accounts for the fact that his writing can be as bright and easy as it is. More than most critics, he can "see" his audience and thus avoid the ponderousness and obscurity that attaches to so much of the criticism written by men who are going blind or who are in conscious reaction against the audience to which they address themselves, or who try to engage some of the problems Mr. Kazin can ignore or dismiss.

Mr. Kazin of course pays a price for his easiness. To me, many of his generalizations seem overconfident; many of his statements, mere half-truths. Mr. Kazin remarks of one American writer that "his work is as full of loose opinions as a columnist's" and some of Kazin's own pages sprawl with loose opinions. . . .

Kazin seems to me at his ablest as a critic in his remarks upon the recent and growing tendency to reduce all serious literature to myth. In the chapter on "Melville as Scripture" Kazin points out that the "myth critic" is "farthest from the true spirit of criticism," for such a critic makes "the fewest discriminations between good work and bad." The great weakness of the myth approach in criticism, as he justly remarks, is that "by showing man everywhere to be the same, it reduces history to an illustration." He is equally acute in diagnosing the attraction that myth exerts upon the liberal mind: "It presents so many gods, one need not believe in any one." Mr. Kazin refuses so easy a way out. In dealing with the general problems of our culture and with literary documents, he insists upon making discriminations, maintaining "the true spirit of criticism."

> *Cleanth Brooks, "A Critic of Art, Life and Criticism," in* The New York Times Book Review, *November 6, 1955, p. 40.*

LEO MARX

[*The Inmost Leaf*] is no mere hodge-podge miscellany. In fact it has greater thematic coherence than most unitary works. Not that I think Kazin has been calculating the effect all this time. Rather, the book seems to have grown from a deep inward need. The title is from Melville, who compared his own development to the unfolding of a flower from outer to inmost leaf.

The unity of *The Inmost Leaf* is especially striking in view of the fact that it is about thirty-odd writers widely separated in time and space. Kazin ranges from William Blake, who was born in 1757, to Simone Weil, who was born in 1915. He writes about Dostoevski, Thoreau, Kafka, Joyce and Proust—to indicate all the nationalities represented. Yet somehow these people all come to seem astonishingly alike. They are more alike, in fact, than the members of any single literary generation that appears in *On Native Grounds*. This is not to say that Kazin fails to tell us what is special about each writer. His forte is the precise elucidation of his reading. With the stab of a perfect phrase he often recovers for us the way we felt on first reading a particular writer. On the other hand, Kazin's reasons for selecting his subjects, his literary values, his very method all result in molding these writers to a pattern.

To begin with, his criticism is subjective. "Impressionistic" might be the word, but for the slap-dash arbitrariness it can suggest. Kazin is a rigorous and conscientious critic. He is not much interested in "placing" one writer in relation to others. Nor does he go in for formal analysis. (Though he proves, in his brilliant essay on Blake, that he too can dismantle a poem.) His criticism is essentially utilitarian. He saturates himself in a writer's work, distills the ideas and emotions it evokes, describes them to us concisely, and then asks, "What have I gained?" His chief test is the power of art to change the world—that is, to change the way the world strikes Alfred Kazin. Of course this sort of criticism is only useful to those who share important attitudes with the critics.

If it sounds simple, by the way, just try it. Kazin writes criticism that is art. The experience he conveys, his reading, is much more complicated than the experience conveyed in the ordinary well-tailored novel. And it has more to do with our lives. That is one reason we sometimes read critics rather than writers nowadays—if the distinction means much. What is most appealing about Kazin is his passionate devotion to the relevance of literature. Relevance? Relevance to what?

The answer, surely, is not what it would have been in 1942. Granted that the two books are different in purpose, the change in Kazin is unmistakable. He wrote *On Native Grounds* to show, among other things, that modern American literature came out of a crucial period and was "molded in its struggles." It seems unlikely that he would say so today. He is no longer much interested in the relations between writing and social struggle. *The Inmost Leaf* is about the painful but necessary inwardness of the great artist. All of Kazin's current heroes are alienated people. A writer's excellence reflects his capacity to reach the inmost self, and that means avoiding the corrupting influences of society. . . . To understand [Kazin's] development one should read his autobiographical meditation, *A Walker in the City* (1951). There he tells how, in a very real sense, he was saved by literature. What literature is relevant to, then, is individual salvation, nothing less nothing more.

If Kazin were to reduce this vision of art to an argument (the idea would repel him), it would go something like this. All great works bear the mark of a unique man. In the presence of forces aiming to stifle uniqueness, the artist's best defense is withdrawal. Accordingly, the dominant theme of modern literature is the exploration and affirmation of the self. Given our incapacity for faith, our "mob age" (bitter and revealing phrase), the artist inevitably suffers hideous loneliness. To survive he cherishes his anguish. If this is existentialism, Kazin's writing is free of all modish allusions to that cult. He seems to have arrived at this position his own way. Sometimes, in the severity of his moral judgments, the skepticism with which he regards all motives, the unfailing gravity of his tone, he sounds most like a bearded Hebrew prophet. Against all social science, all humanitarian pathos, all determinism he insists on the individual's absolute responsibility. The final meaning of modern literature is that each must save himself.

Kazin has come a long way since 1942. The balance that distinguished *On Native Grounds* has given way to something close to a religion of art. In 1942 Kazin thought that society often hurt independent men; but then he also seemed to allow that it fulfilled indispensable human needs. In *The Inmost Leaf*, however, society is almost wholly evil, the great writer unfailingly heroic. One has only to compare Kazin's treatment of Faulkner in the two books to observe the change. (pp. 18-19)

At the center of his thought is the doctrine that all value, all meaning stems from the inviolate suffering self. It is one thing to celebrate individual identity as a counterpoise to conformity; it is another to make it the pivot of all one's ideas. For it omits so much of life, hence of art. It omits all that the race creates in its anonymous, collective existence. All but a very few lives, by this token, are meaningless. The joys and satisfactions of shared experience mean nothing. And it is difficult to know what Kazin now would say of the world's great artists who have gloried, not in their own sick, lonely souls, but in men's capacity for delight in one another. What about Homer or Chaucer or Shakespeare? They do not reveal the inmost leaves. For that matter, what about Kazin's hero, Melville, who suffered at the hands of the community, to be sure, but like many of the other great moderns, continued to affirm that man without community is nothing?

The superb intelligence we meet in *The Inmost Leaf* is, in the most rewarding sense, disquieting. Through it we can feel the pressure of devotion and despair. Only passionate devotion to art, along with despair of society, could provoke so intense a piety of individual consciousness. It may be true that American optimism has waned since Hiroshima, but few Americans know anything like Kazin's bleak outlook. If he seems to cherish the idea of neurotic withdrawal, it is because for him the alternative is not a fancied healthy community but annihilation—annihilation, if not of the race in a physical sense, then of the few original minds it might churn up—which amounts to the same thing. *The Inmost Leaf* will dismay those who believe that our best hope is to keep alive the Apollonian image of man. No such vision is possible in Kazin's world of art. It is too grim and exclusive and dark. (p. 19)

> Leo Marx, "Kazin and the Religion of Art," in The New Republic, *Vol. 133, No. 22, November 28, 1955, pp. 18-19.*

ALBERT J. GUERARD

[The] essays and reviews [in *Contemporaries*] reveals a diversity of interests rare in this age of literary specialists. Who else (except Edmund Wilson, of course) could move with such

assurance from the American past of Thoreau's Journal to the world of Sholom Aleichem, from the Civil War to Auschwitz and Buchenwald, from Russia to Israel, from Dreiser to Salinger, from Freud to President Kennedy and his intellectual entourage? (p. 6)

To an extraordinary degree one feels the same mind and sensibility at work in these diverse essays. There is an unremittent moral seriousness, an undeviating common-sense compelled to reject not only the antics of the beatniks but even the pessimism of Robert Penn Warren. There is a scorn for the trivial, whimsical and eccentric except where these accompany a raw love of life. Kazin's is (except in the stunning *Moby Dick* essay) a calm mind that scorns flashiness, and that declines to take risks. It offers no radically original argument, makes no startling judgments or revaluations or discoveries—and not once in its five hundred pages advances the claims of an unknown or underrated writer. It is not seriously interested in technical criticism or in the mysteries of creation, and has little use for questions of unconscious symbolic content.

What we have instead is an Arnoldian sanity, a centrality of moral intelligence that refuses to accept catastrophe and that turns away from pessimism. The world, Kazin insists, . . . is not yet at an end, and is a world the writer must love rather than scorn or withdraw from. The most personal note in Kazin's writing is what I can only call a spiritual attitude to things, to places and substances, to life's "beautiful and inexpressible materiality." Man on this earth, man in society rather than man in solitary converse with himself—these, he argues, are the great concerns of literature.

There is courage as well as strength in a clinging to this unpretentious sanity and unfashionable moral seriousness. The commitment does involve, in the literary critic as such, certain limitations. One is that Kazin shows a marked preference for the kind of social realism few serious novelists seem capable of writing any more. He overrates Dreiser and even Marquand, though he repudiates John O'Hara plausibly and with insight. . . . Not unexpectedly Kazin dislikes the finely-wrought art novel, and considers even Wright Morris—Morris with his fine American "materiality"—too "literary."

Another limitation is an utter and humorless lack of sympathy for the grotesque, for the deviant fantasy, for the highly personal nightmare of hallucinatory vision, even for the element of playfulness in art. These are tolerated or overlooked in Melville and Dostoevsky, or in such "living classics" as Bellow and Henry Miller. But other mildly eccentric writers fare badly indeed. (pp. 6, 18)

To me at least these are limitations, though they may not seem such to others. But they are limitations in the equipment of a major critic, who consolidates with this volume his high place in American letters. (p. 18)

> Albert J. Guerard, "This World Is One the Writer Must Not Scorn but Love," in The New York Times Book Review, *April 22, 1962, pp. 6, 18.*

WILLIAM BARRETT

Alfred Kazin is distinguished by great versatility and energy of mind, and in *Contemporaries* . . . he has given us an important and lively book that ranges over almost the whole field of modern letters. The contemporaries he starts with are not writers now living, but our own American classics—Melville, Thoreau, Emerson—because these authors are still a living part of the modern mind. Coming closer to the present, he gives us notable essays on Faulkner, J. D. Salinger, John O'Hara, Saul Bellow, and a great many others; there is some highly perceptive and interesting travel reportage on Russia, Israel, and Puerto Rico. . . . (pp. 125-26)

This extraordinary range is no casual accident, but the deliberate project of a mind passionately enmeshed in the life of its time. Much in this time is troubling to Mr. Kazin. By temperament his own deepest leanings are those of traditional humanism, and many modern works seem to be at war with such values. But as a critic he has great generosity of spirit—not to be confused with softness, for he can come down like a pile driver on a writer, like John O'Hara, whom he dislikes—and he can expend himself generously on writers whose values are not his own. To my mind, it is just this fine tension between a lively sense of tradition and an acute feeling of modernity that forms the unity of Mr. Kazin's critical vision and makes this book so distinguished a contribution to current criticism. (p. 126)

*William Barrett, in a review of "Contemporaries,"
in* The Atlantic Monthly, *Vol. 209, No. 5, May,
1962, pp. 125-26.*

JOSEPH HELLER

To read Alfred Kazin's collection of essays, *Contemporaries,* is to come away with the impression of a man who hates literature and loathes his life's work. . . .

Kazin's chief weakness as a critic of modern literature is his unwillingness to enjoy it. To write intelligently about authors of the past is largely a matter of scholarship, and Kazin's erudition is enormous; to write intelligently about one's own contemporaries, however, involves the additional factor of *taste,* and in the field of modern fiction he often seems naïve and obtuse. He can speculate plausibly in different parts of the book about the dimensions of fiction and the functions of criticism, but he is incapable of applying his own principles consistently to the specific works he elects to review. . . .

For the most part, he appears too timid to damn and too stingy to applaud. Even with books and authors he obviously admires, he is incapable of giving praise without nullifying it almost immediately; sometimes he seems to praise *in order* to derogate, setting up comparisons only to prove them invalid. Like the Lord, Mr. Kazin giveth and Mr. Kazin taketh away. And frequently his (Mr. Kazin's) objections are expressed in sentences that are almost unintelligible or plainly absurd. (p. 23)

In many of Kazin's utterances, there is a suggestion of a kind of narcissistic arrogance that holds opinions are important because he has them, that things are so because he says they are so, and that he, as a critic, is of more interest than his subjects. . . . When Mr. Kazin writes on these levels, he is not criticizing but carping, and to campaign in this fashion so persistently against so many of his contemporaries is not to be discriminating but querulous. His prose may be better than Eisenhower's, and almost as good as *Life*'s, but his basic attitude toward current American fiction is hardly more enlightened. It is, in fact, identical: the attitude that books are not good because they are not the books he wants them to be, and that authors are deficient when they do not write their novels precisely the way he would like their novels to be written. (pp. 24, 26)

And, of course, Kazin fudges a bit on his own past as a critic. The name of Faulkner seldom appears in this volume without some accompanying tribute to the immensity of his talent, and *Light in August* is treated as "a great novel." But Kazin did not think nearly so well of Faulkner in 1942 when he published his *On Native Grounds* (he described Faulkner's "failure" as a novelist) and had almost nothing complimentary to say about this same novel. . . . Either it was *Light in August* and other pre-1942 novels by Faulkner that have improved since then, or Kazin's taste. If he is right about Faulkner now, he was wrong about him then; and if he was wrong about *Faulkner* then, then he ought at least to keep in mind that he might be wrong about *anyone* now!

There is naked envy in his passages on Salinger and something close to hatred in his treatment of Norman Mailer, and the target of his resentment in both cases does not seem to be these authors themselves, or even their work, but the large measure of fame both have won. . . .

In this way does he belittle the reputations of two men who labor more successfully to create an interest in serious contemporary literature than he does to destroy it. The pity is that Kazin does have so much knowledge and that his information, when he presents it with some degree of objective clarity, is more often appropriate than not. (p. 26)

*Joseph Heller, "Too Timid to Damn, Too Stingy to
Applaud," in* The New Republic, *Vol. 147, Nos. 4
& 5, July 30, 1962, pp. 23-4, 26.*

HILTON KRAMER

Alfred Kazin's *Starting Out in the Thirties* . . . though chronologically a successor to *A Walker in the City,* is a different sort of book. The latter, dealing with the author's childhood and youth in Brooklyn, was a pure distillation of experience—poetic, vivid, deeply moving, attaining at times to a Proustian luminousness which secured its subject against the corruptions of both the politics that had often turned similar material into a bludgeon and the sentimentality that was already, in the early '50s, turning it into a commodity. About *A Walker in the City* there was a lyricism, an emotional resonance, which seemed to find for every one of the author's abundant (sometimes overabundant) feelings an exact and memorable image. In writing that memoir of his youth in Brownsville, Kazin produced an unforgettable chapter in the moral history of his generation.

Starting Out in the Thirties has nothing of the completeness, and only intermittently the lyric élan, of the earlier book. It sets itself a harsher subject: the author's involvement in the literary and intellectual ferment of the '30s. Inevitably, then, it is a book that oscillates—sometimes wildly, sometimes painfully, and always with a moral fervor that moves easily from ecstasy to despair—between the most naked personal avowals and the political pressures that lay ready, even more in that decade than in our own, to consume a writer's personal identity and place it at the service of "history." If the childhood and youth of *A Walker in the City* were the natural materials of the lyric mode, the concerns of *Starting Out in the Thirties*—manhood, the realization of a literary vocation, and the self's entry into history—ought to have been the material of a chronicle on the order of those novels of the last century which trace the course of the provincial protagonist's vindication in the big world. Yet like most writers of our time who have essayed subjects of that scale, Kazin gives us not the full story but a fragment—a sketch in lieu of the large canvas the material as well as the author's gifts call for.

As a sketch, it is beautifully rendered and deeply affecting. From that first hot summer afternoon of 1934 in the opening pages, when we see Kazin at the age of 19 barging into the office of John Chamberlain, then the radical daily book critic of the New York *Times,* to protest the easy assumptions about "youth" with which Chamberlain was regaling his readers, until the closing paragraphs of the brief epilogue, dated 1945, when the narrator sits stupefied in a newsreel theater in Piccadilly watching the first films of Belsen, one cannot help being carried along by the pitch of excitement and wonder which the author confers on the experience of that period. Kazin's racy, headlong style is equally good at dealing with books and people, and his fragmentary narrative is strongest where he shows both responding with all their energies to the accelerating catastrophies of the prewar years.

Kazin was well placed to observe the writers as well as the exacerbated politics of that decade, and he did so with a curious mixture of detachment and commitment. Brought up as a "Socialist" in more or less the same manner that he was brought up a Jew, through family ties and sentimental association as much as through outright conviction, he seems never to have been a real ideologue: "'Socialism' was a way of life, since everyone else I knew in New York was a Socialist, more or less; but I was remarkably detached from it intellectually, and spent my days reading Blake and Lawrence and Whitman."

This easy intellectual alliance between radical politics and his passion for what Kazin calls "the rebels of literature, the great wrestlers-with-God," became the basis of his literary vocation. For his rash encounter with John Chamberlain marked the beginning of his career as a writer. Astonished that Chamberlain would even receive him, Kazin talked the afternoon away and left with an introduction to Malcolm Cowley, then the influential literary editor of the *New Republic.* (p. 23)

It is from that vantage point, as a fledgling contributor to the *New Republic* and the Sunday papers who went home every night to the family circle in Brownsville, where "everyone" was a Socialist and a Jew and poor, that Kazin records his impressions of the literary-political world of the Depression. There was wonderful, affectionate glimpses of James T. Farrell and William Saroyan in the days of their first fame, glowing accounts of Clifford Odets' plays and Orson Welles' magnetic performances, and evocative descriptions of what it felt like to read certain books—*Man's Fate, Fontamara*—at a time when the morning headlines reverberated with the very phrases and images on the page.

But the most vivid of the portraits Kazin sketches here is undoubtedly that of the late Otis Ferguson, Cowley's extraordinary assistant on the *New Republic* and in some respects a prophet of things to come. . . . Responsive as he was to the energy and freedom of Ferguson's style, respectful as he still is of the man himself, Kazin defines very sharply the quality that separated Ferguson from a literary sensibility like his own—the quality that made Ferguson something of a cult in his lifetime and something of a legend ever since. . . . (pp. 23-4)

Curiously, though, with the exception of Ferguson, it is not the writers around the *New Republic* who come through most dramatically in *Starting Out in the Thirties,* but rather the intellectuals in the circle of V. F. Calverton and the *Modern Monthly* and, at the close of the book, the disaffected radicals of the *Partisan Review.* . . .

Kazin obviously felt closer to the anti-Stalinist intellectuals of the *Modern Monthly* and *Partisan Review*—Calverton and Max Eastman and Sidney Hook, Bert Wolfe and Mary McCarthy and Philip Rahv—for whom politics and ideology were matters of more intense polemic and debate. "After 1935," he writes, "the Communists rode to new influence on the United Front, and hated no one so much as intellectuals like Hook, Eastman and Calverton who still preserved revolutionary ideas in the form of honest personal judgments." Yet, whether Kazin is being affectionate or harsh in his own judgments—the accounts of Wolfe and Rahv are sympathetic, though hardly starry-eyed, whereas the acid portrait of Mary McCarthy will act as a balm on the sensibilities of anyone who has watched, appalled, at the preposterous success of that cold and malevolent talent—one feels his uneasiness as the prospect of the intellectuals taking over from the writers and artists looms more and more clearly. Discussing the *Partisan Review* group of 1940, Kazin writes: "The ability to analyze a friend, a trend, a shift in the politico-personal balance of power, was for them the greatest possible sign of intellectual power. Creative imagination they unconsciously disdained as simple-minded—except if it came from the Continent, and thus could serve as an analogy to their kind of intelligence. This boundless belief in criticism was actually their passport to the postwar world. . . . The intellectuals who had failed at revolution were to succeed as intellectual arbiters."

That, in a way, has proven to be the real, unforseen heritage of the '30s as Kazin recounts them: the uneasy but emphatic triumph of the intellectuals, the displacement of poetry and the imagination by ideologies of power and the kind of criticism that serves as their forum. It is that displacement in the hierarchy of literary values—that, and the prophecy implicit in Otis Ferguson's frenetic war on high culture—which most directly connects the events described in Kazin's pages with the dilemmas of the present moment. It is to Kazin's credit, I think, that while he is himself clearly of this change, he just as clearly stands apart from it. Whatever ideological scars he may bear, his literary sensibility has, if anything, deepened in the face of this essentially anti-literary age. Short and incomplete as *Starting Out in the Thirties* is, it is nonetheless an act of faith in the literary mind, an attempt to restore the rights of imagination in recapturing the shape of a past buried under ideological debris. (p. 24)

> *Hilton Kramer, "The Age of the Intellectuals," in* The New Leader, *Vol. XLVIII, No. 19, September 27, 1965, pp. 23-4.*

LEO MARX

To my mind [*Starting Out in the Thirties*] is most rewarding when read as a kind of intellectual history—impressionistic to be sure—of that anomalous era when the literary and political *avant-gardes* briefly joined forces. No one, I think, has so vividly conveyed what it felt like to be a radical in those days. Today one often hears people refer to the 30's as a time of oppressive anxiety, and it is true that the objective situation was fearful. Yet the mood of the radical intellectuals was positive, even ebullient, and Kazin brilliantly recaptures that élan. Wherever he went, he says of one of the headier moments, he felt the moral contagion of a single idea; there seemed to be no division between his effort at personal liberation and the apparent effort of humanity to deliver itself. What the intellectuals then had, and what some of them are rediscovering in the civil-rights movement, is clarity of purpose. They were alive with an idea that carried them out of themselves, that made them feel they were being carried by universal strivings. It was what they had, in Hemingway's phrase, instead of God. (p. 121)

As history, *Starting Out in the Thirties* is least satisfactory in conveying the serious ideological issues debated in the period. Perhaps because of his own suspicion of abstract thought, Kazin was untroubled by many of the questions that agitated intellectuals. We get no sense, accordingly, of the efforts of left-wing literary people to reconcile their political values with the seemingly contradictory ethos of the brilliant modernist writers (Yeats, Joyce, Lawrence, Pound, Eliot, *et al*) whom they recognized as the true stylistic radicals of the age. Nor was Kazin seriously involved in the endless debate about revolutionary Communism. Of course he is perfectly clear about his rejection of Stalinism, but he seems never to have confronted the more profound, theoretical, and not so casily rejected rationale for the authoritarianism of the Left. One of the truly distinctive features of the 30's is that for a few years some Americans did treat the ideas of Communists as intellectually respectable. Kazin knows this, to be sure, but since he himself had remarkably little interest in such matters, he gives us almost no sense of that odd circumstance. The fact is that Kazin's "socialism" never does acquire substance. At the end of the book it is the same cloudy moral idea it was at the beginning, and confirms his description of himself as an exclusively *literary* radical, "indifferent to economics, suspicious of organization, planning, Marxist solemnity and intellectual system-building."

When read as a moral fable, *Starting Out in the Thirties* proves to be a remarkably sustained attack upon all abstract thought. Virtually every incident in the book, whether it occurs in Kazin's private life or in the world of public events, is made to reveal the evil inherent in the unfleshed idea. Sometimes, as in the deft account of Otis Ferguson's supper with the family, the results are comic. Under the impression that Ferguson will find the Jewish cuisine exotic, young Kazin drags him to Brooklyn on a hot Friday night in August and then realizes, too late, what his guest is suffering, sitting there in the heat, under the harsh light, being stuffed with cabbage and meatballs by his mother while his father slurps soup and his cousin Sophie stares in silence. Afterward Ferguson makes the point: "'What in the hell,'" he asks, "'was so exotic about that?'" And sometimes, as in the dreadful story of Kazin's mother's unmarried cousin Sophie, the results are tragic. After years of brooding loneliness, she and the family have become so obsessed with her need for a husband, so desperate, that she goes off with a virtual stranger. When he deserts her, she goes mad—destroyed, we are made to feel, by the idea of marriage in the abstract.

Again and again we are shown the danger of thinking ideologically, programmatically, calculatingly, or even, for that matter, deliberately. The point is that the idea becomes dangerous or anti-life, as D. H. Lawrence would say, as soon as it is removed from a specific, historic, sensual context. This deep distrust of abstraction and corresponding reverence for the specific, tangible, physical experience has of course been a cardinal principle of the modernist movement in literature. There its salutary influence (at least until recently) would be hard to deny. It is the basis, in fact, of Kazin's own literary method, and of much that is praiseworthy in this book. But when the principle of tangibility is taken out of a literary context and extended to all modes of thought, when it is made the key to all value, it not only loses its cogency but it can easily

become the basis for an oppressively self-enclosed view of reality. Perhaps that explains why, at the end of this uniquely valuable book, Kazin does not salvage from the story of the 30's a redeeming idea or, indeed, any idea not rooted in his own immediate experience. (p. 122)

Leo Marx, "A Literary Radical," in Commentary, *Vol. 40, No. 6, December, 1965, pp. 118, 120-23.*

V. S. PRITCHETT

In [*Bright Book of Life,* a] study of the American novel from Hemingway to Mailer, Alfred Kazin is a critic with whom the foreigner can see eye to eye. He understands that novels are novels and will stand or fall by the way they are done. He believes in "the patience and depth of fiction itself"; it is not journalism. It brings no news:

"The world is a world, dumb as nature, not a novel. The world as our common experience is one that only the journalist feels entirely able to set down. It is a confidence that those who stick to fiction do not feel, for the 'world' is not an experience in common, still less is it a concept on which we all agree. It is not even as close as we think." . . .

Kazin has his obscure passages when he telescopes his ideas, but he is, for the most part, clear and graceful. His book is useful to the foreign reader for he has read everything worth reading from Hemingway onwards, but it is more than a work of reference. If one tests him on Faulkner, Carson McCullers, Ellison, Nathanael West, Baldwin, Mailer, O'Hara, Flannery O'Connor and Nabokov—to take names at random—he goes for the essence of his novelists, major and minor, rather than for the social or metaphysical conundrums surrounding them. He is a catholic and discursive commentator who makes excellent asides. He knows where his argument is going as the novel leaves the confidence of the Hemingway period for the brilliant assertions that have marked the disintegration of forms we are now getting used to. . . .

After these masters, we move on to that extraordinary outburst and rapid turnover of American talent that has followed in every decade since. American novelists usually complain that they are isolated; but if this is so it has had the advantage of making every man his own prophet. Every voice acquires a personal urgency which will be eclipsed only when someone more urgent appears—urgency being connected with the changes in the canon of "the American experience." (I do not notice that European novelists are much concerned with the corresponding "European experience" as an inciting myth: obviously criticism that looks to such a canon will have a dramatic but chauvinist effect.)

But the American novel has excelled in regional outbursts, like the Southern; or racial ones like the Jewish or the black, which flash upon the screen with all the force of the newly released. In the last two categories there is a strong element of "making it"; in the former there is, or was, that older if colonial spirit of having "endured it."

As he passes from writer to writer in his long list Kazin sticks as well as he can to the way the thing is done: in the long run this is what matters. So he gets on with the definitions of talents that may be major or minor, but certainly have had their moment. (p. 3)

Where I find Kazin's utterances most thoughtful are in the later pages where he spends some time on two aberrations of the

American novel: what he calls the fact novel: e.g., *In Cold Blood* and the novel as journalism. His argument goes like this: the novel of the camera, the tape-recorder, the strictly factual document was intended to replace fiction and to be superior to it as contemporary history; but in achieving this it makes our participation in the story narrow and helpless. . . . (pp. 3, 30)

Kazin's book comes to no conclusions. It ends a pleasant examination of Nabokov, with a sentence: "He has saved *us* from being always at the mercy of the age." I do not see why we should not be grateful for that respite, whatever may happen to the novel in the future. Like "the world," the Age also is as dumb as nature. (p. 30)

> *V. S. Pritchett, in a review of "Bright Book of Life," in* The New York Times Book Review, *May 20, 1973, pp. 3, 30.*

CHARLES NICOL

Attempting an all-inclusive look at important American fiction from the Thirties to the present, Alfred Kazin necessarily leaves out as much as he puts in, and his chapters seem dubious attempts to organize his sure opinions about certain authors into larger views about literary trends. [*Bright Book of Life*] should have been restricted to those authors on whom Kazin could expand indefinitely in his aphoristic, mildly rhetorical but extremely attractive style. Where he is best he is eternally quotable, sewing up the heart of his author with stitch after perfect stitch.

Unfortunately however, Kazin apparently thought of this book as an objective history of recent fiction, as though such a thing were possible to write. His opinions rarely surprise—one has the feeling that he is suppressing his personal enthusiasms, deliberately calculating the number of pages due each author according to contemporary standards and awarding no more, no less. . . . One wonders if this critic has the courage of his convictions. There are of course no literary "discoveries" here.

So in general Kazin is both safe and sound. His only major errors are the large part he assigns Norman Mailer and the way he organizes his authors into chapters. We have division by gender, race, and region in the chapters on writers who are women, Jews, and Southerners. We do not have chapters on black authors, writers from California, Catholics, homosexuals, etc., although all these would be equally possible. We have distinction by subject in the chapter on war novels, and distinction by viewpoint in the chapter on "Absurdity as a Contemporary Style." In this ungainly and pointless division of contemporary writing into horses, tables, and anything that flies, Kazin gives extended discussions of Norman Mailer in three different chapters, while Kurt Vonnegut comes under the heading of war novels and both William Styron and James Baldwin are grouped under the nonfiction novel. You figure it out.

Kazin's other real critical error is to assume that a dominant author's voice is the major indication of a successful fiction. Thus he admires Susan Sontag's writing for the worst possible reason, because "we do not experience a novel; we experience her readiness to see what she can think of next." Thus Norman Mailer's "fantasies and ideas broke into the texture of every fiction he now wrote—and one remembered these books" apparently "not because these books communicated themselves as novels, but because they didn't." It is clumsy sleight of hand rather than brilliant paradox to admit something has failed and then label it a success. (pp. 851-52)

After beginning with a nice essay on Hemingway, this study ends with a nice summary of Nabokov. One wonders occasionally if Kazin is partially misled even here, since Nabokov should be admired for the total control of his art and instead we hear that "he is the one twentieth-century master novelist whose mind and heart we know best—whose every personal opinion we know better than we have ever known Joyce and Proust." This totally misses the point.

But Kazin has his own point to make, one certainly worth discussing. He began the book by noting that "Hemingway attempted that absolute identification of life with literature, in the name of precision of feeling, that was the hallmark of the moderns." And he ends with a similar and equally sound observation: "So, with Nabokov, we come back to something that everyone else has doubted: the indissolubility of life with fiction." The point is true enough, and marks both these writers as great. But Kazin is wrong to assume that an entire book of criticism should separate them, wrong to assume that an entire epoch separates them. After all, fellow historians of literature, Hemingway and Nabokov were born in the same year. (p. 852)

> *Charles Nicol, "Survey, Not History," in* National Review, *Vol. XXV, No. 31, August 3, 1973, pp. 851-52.*

GEORGE H. DOUGLAS

The death of Edmund Wilson in 1972 was a grievous blow to the field of literary criticism in our country. No doubt the blow was strongly felt by the educated public for a number of reasons, but mostly perhaps because Wilson was preeminently a critic of American literature and American life, and critics who have committed themselves deeply and passionately to our own national experience have always been few in number. . . . For the generation of writers who came to maturity in the years just before the first World War—writers like Wilson, Brooks, and Vernon L. Parrington—America was not so much a subject as it was an obsession, an obsession sometimes joyous, sometimes painful, but always nagging, irresistible, and relentless.

None of that generation is still alive, but a few of the next generation, somehow cut of the same cloth, are still writing; and a few of these have persistently practiced historical criticism in the grand manner. One such is Alfred Kazin, whose critical writings on American literature have always been well received by the public, although perhaps he has not built for himself quite the enviable reputation of an Edmund Wilson. He is one of the last of an apparently dying breed that continues to be a creative force in our literature—a happy reminder of the golden age of historical criticism.

In speaking of Kazin as part of a unique tradition of men of letters who devoted themselves to American literature and American culture, it might be well to begin by recalling that Kazin grew up in a different day and a different environment than did the writers of the first American awakening. Like Wilson and Brooks, Kazin was a product of the progressive era, and, like them, he is strongly identified today with the liberal thirties. On the other hand, Kazin had no strong personal roots in the older America. His spiritual life began with the century of his birth: he is a child of twentieth-century urban life and his genius is bound up with that life. His imagination does not hark back, as does that of Edmund Wilson, to the old republican America; his inspiration was not nurtured in the open spaces of upstate New York where Wilson's Tory fore-bearers struck out for freedom, but rather it grew directly in the tumultuous conditions of the new America, and it was the new America that gave him his powerful perspective on the old, not vice versa, as with Edmund Wilson.

Still, the most important fact about Kazin as a critic is that his work is more closely allied to the earlier discoverers of Amer-ica—the Brookses, Bournes, Santayanas, Wilsons—than to the sociological critics of the thirties. True, he "started out in the thirties," and we identify him somehow with the younger writ-ers of that time, but still the thirties did not exactly form Kazin the way they did Granville Hicks, or Calverton, or the writers of the *Partisan Review*. These writers believed themselves to be in rebellion against an America that had grown stale and flat, in which social inequalities festered like a wound, obli-terating all that had gone before, even the American traditions in literature, Kazin, unlike so many of his contemporaries, was determined to saturate himself in America before passing judg-ment on it, and while he grew up tied to the usual ideologies of the thirties, they did not really do a great deal to shape him. (pp. 203-04)

On Native Grounds is a remarkable achievement in American criticism because it is an ambitious rereading and reinterpreting of twentieth-century American prose. To realize his objective, Kazin had to cut through a complex web of many critical platitudes that had been spun out by the various intellectual traditions of the twentieth century. His aim was to return to the writers themselves, to find out which ones had gained a hold on our imagination, and why, and to determine which ones had penetrated to the heart of contemporary American experience.

In using the expression "back to the writers," Kazin was quite naturally attempting to evoke a different meaning than that intended by the "New Critics," who also used the same ex-pression. Kazin's aim was to combine the best of aesthetic criticism with the best of historical criticism. (pp. 211-12)

Kazin's goal in *On Native Grounds* was to bring the full force of his sensibility to bear on works of twentieth-century Amer-ican literature, works which must all be seen as inextricably bound up with the experience of our native soil and our time. In Kazin's view so much of American literature has been mis-read, either because it was delivered to us by critics who were attached to the older genteel traditions of the nineteenth century and who could only see the vulgarity and immorality of the new literature, or by critics of the progressive or reform era who praised the modern writers (Dreiser, let us say) but for the wrong reasons, or finally by the formalistic critics who just pretended that writers like Dreiser did not exist, even though it was obvious that those who pretended that Dreiser did not exist were simply not alive to the American literary present.

Perhaps Kazin's writings on Dreiser serve as an excellent tes-timony to his stature as a critic. For it was chiefly Kazin who opened up to us the kind of understanding we have of Dreiser today and paved the way for the critical literature we have had on Dreiser in the last twenty years. While Kazin has continued to write on Dreiser throughout his career, his chapter on Dreiser in *On Native Grounds* is an excellent representation of his achievement as a critic of American literature. (p. 212)

Kazin's distinction as a critic has always been due to his deep commitment to our American writers and to the precise con-ditions of life that pounded them into existence. His subject matter is the world of writing as it actually confronts us as a historical people in a given historical period. Unlike the critics who followed the high road of aesthetic criticism and for whom writers like Dreiser are best forgotten, Kazin was always care-ful to insist and to demonstrate that if you want to find the juices that flow in our literature you must not limit yourself to the favored masters but must pay close attention to those writers who are important because they speak to Americans as a people. American literature is an intimate and highly personal litera-ture, and to grasp it in all of its intimate and highly personal dimensions, we must seek to find it not in the aesthetician's study but at the transfusion point between art and the life of our own time.

Since the publication of *On Native Grounds*, although he has published a number of excellent volumes of literary criticism, Kazin has not produced another large work of historical crit-icism. In a sense, this is to be regretted, especially since he has concerned himself from time to time with earlier American literary figures and might well have embarked on a larger historical project, bringing some of these figures into focus as a part of a continuing process. On the other hand, it is not at all strange that he has not done so. Kazin's allegiance has always been, and continues to be, to twentieth-century Amer-ican experience. In his more recent collection of essays, *Con-temporaries*, we find him devoting himself once again to How-ells, Dreiser, Sinclair Lewis, Gertrude Stein, Faulkner, and other writers he had already dealt with in *On Native Grounds*. In addition to this he has given us perceptive pieces on Amer-ican writers who have come to the fore since World War II: Salinger, Mailer, Baldwin, Roth, Capote, and many others. And nobody would consider it a falling off of Kazin's pro-ductivity that he has not tried to marshal these figures into a large historical panorama. The truth is that Kazin has consis-tently followed his own highest ideals of criticism. He has continued to believe that the critic's duty is to bring his imag-ination and intelligence into play in an effort to understand the central problems of his own time, and accordingly he has been involved not only with our best literature but with our folk arts, our intellectual life, our morals, our life style.

Like Edmund Wilson, Kazin is best characterized as both a literary critic and a general critic. And refusing to believe from the first that a rigid boundary between these two forms is either possible or desirable, Kazin has continued to be a strong force in our intellectual life. He has been, or so it would appear, increasingly disturbed by the texture of American life in the years since the war, and his writing has taken on a moral cast, sometimes a kind of peevishness. In the process he may have lost some of his former sprightliness and some of his youthful powers of forceful expression. But he continues to be an im-portant and valuable critic. He has continued to believe that criticism should be serious and concerned, that it should not descend to the Sunday supplement style of reviewing where every cultural artifact is put on the same plane as every other and where nothing really "matters." But he has done this while retaining his belief that the critic must speak to the public, that fundamentally he must be a writer, and that his main tool must continue to be the imagination. And above all he has continued to insist that the critic's main concern is the living presence of the writing of his own day. (pp. 215-16)

*George H. Douglas, "Alfred Kazin: American Critic,"
in* The Colorado Quarterly, *Vol. 23, No. 2, Autumn,
1974, pp. 203-16.*

MORDECAI RICHLER

Only the title goes against the grain. It's touchy, defiant. *New York Jew* would seem to be the invention of a man who descends on a room full of strangers not anticipating delight but personal insults, whereas Alfred Kazin, a lifelong partisan of literary excellence, should look forward to argument, yes, but argument informed by honest appreciation. Even gratitude, that rarest of virtues in the literary world. A world wherein, as Thurber once put it, nobody sits at anybody else's feet unless he's been knocked there. Mr. Kazin's views are not only deeply felt, they matter.

Mr. Kazin'a latest memoir, which I take to be a companion volume to *Starting Out in the Thirties* and the splendid *A Walker in the City,* a book I still cherish, should give pleasure to anybody interested in the literary history of our times. It should give pleasure, but also make the reader wonder at what self-serving rascals most of our literary heroes are. *New York Jew* is filled with illuminating anecdotes about the great and the near-great, scrabbling over one another in these turbulent pages, clamoring for attention, each one shouting me, me, me! It's a front-line dispatch from an intelligent if somewhat bruised survivor of literary and marital wars, charged with appetite and high purpose, but not above administering an accurate little jab as often as a passing salute. (p. 1)

New York Jew can be read as a lively account of a spiritual voyage, begun in 1942, when Mr. Kazin was 27, already an editor of The New Republic and author of *On Native Grounds,* but still too naïve to understand the sexual meaning of Stark Young's clownish winks and leers. Until one day at lunch, after Max Lerner had denounced everything he found politically vile about the South, Young leaned across the table and, in his richest plantation voice, said dreamily, ''Hasn't Max the most beautiful eyes?'' (p. 38)

Mr. Kazin's tangled personal affairs, stormy marriages, mistresses, are not overlooked. Occasionally his treatments of these personal details are understandably reticent, even sketchy; other times, also understandably, they suffer from his critic's penchant to imbue everything with significance. . . .

Mr. Kazin writes that Trilling once protested he was ''too Jewish,''too full of his lower-class experience, which seems to me, as it must to Mr. Kazin, an affront. To be sure, however, there are times when Mr. Kazin does appear a little too operatically Jewish, thrusting it on totally disinterested strangers, but just as surely it is out of the richness of that background and his American experience that he has hammered out such a compelling, vibrant literary memoir of our times. I finished *New York Jew* with a sense of delight and a certain exhaustion. Exhaustion only at being subjected to the demands of so many contending egos. I'm grateful to have read about the great and the near-great first hand, from such a lively primary source, an impassioned witness, but I'm equally glad I do not have to endure most of them in my living room. (p. 39)

Mordecai Richler, ''Literary Ids and Egos,'' in The New York Times Book Review, *May 7, 1978, pp. 1, 38-9.*

ROBERT TOWERS

As autobiographical writing *New York Jew* achieves neither the lyric intensity of *A Walker in the City* nor the stereoptical focus and the shapeliness of *Starting Out in the Thirties.* Its greater length and the time span covered (1942 to the present) work against such qualities. In the new book the impulses of the autobiographer, the memoirist, and the social commentator seem to clash, to jostle each other for position instead of providing a mutually enriching counterpoint. Perhaps a really successful autobiography of a certain length needs, as much as does a novel of comparable size, the propulsive force of a sustained narrative to carry the reader along. Or, failing that, it requires the unifying imprint of an artfully ''realized'' sensibility (as in Rousseau's *Confessions*) or else—paradoxically—the subordination of the self to some great movement or system or unfolding idea (*The Confessions of St. Augustine, The Education of Henry Adams*). Too often in *New York Jew* Kazin gives the impression of halting the action in order to resume his roll call of the Famous People I Have Met (Henry Luce, T.S. Eliot, Bernard Berenson, etc.); after appending a few paragraphs of description and character analysis, he takes up where he left off. One misses the integration of portrait and narration which he achieved in *Starting Out in the Thirties.*

The writing, too, seems to move in sudden bursts and remissions. Some of Kazin's most consciously ''brilliant'' effects—his description of the perpetual freak show of upper Broadway . . . or his desolating account of his father's illness and death in a Coney Island hospital and old-age home—seem not merely the heightening of an always fluent style but rather the assumption of a voice quite other than the one that prevails elsewhere in the book. . . .

Kazin regularly presents himself as the free-lance, independently minded critic at odds with the pedagogues and stylish critics entrenched in academia—especially those who in the late Sixties whored after the radicalized young or celebrated their ''performing'' selves. He writes bitterly about the English Department at Amherst which effectively isolated him during his several unhappy years of residence there. It is therefore strange, given his anti-institutional bias, that he fails even to mention that he spent *ten years* as a Distinguished Professor of English at Stony Brook. One would like to know more about this particular professor's running fight with the professoriat. One would like to know more, too, about his attitude toward his own literary career. After the heady section on the publication of *On Native Grounds* he says little about his ambitions and goals—an odd omission in an autobiography. Does he feel that he has achieved them? (p. 33)

The old themes of Jewish identity and of being an outsider surface repeatedly throughout the book. From 1943 on, Kazin's consciousness of the Holocaust becomes ''the nightmare that would bring everything else into question, that will haunt me to my last breath.'' . . . It is this awareness that after the war impelled him to visit a transient camp for Jewish DPs outside Salzburg, to fly to Belsen for the twenty-fifth anniversary of its liberation, and to relate how his third wife Beth ''spoiled'' a smart dinner party when two Indian diplomats explained that the Holocaust had never occurred.

These sections of *New York Jew* are impassioned and moving. Less psychologically persuasive—to me at least—is Kazin's attempt to relate the Holocaust to his private life and especially to his position as an outsider. The distinction between Jewish identity and personal idiosyncrasy or behavior becomes blurred. Kazin brings the Holocaust right into his West Side apartment and links it to the fear of annihilation—of the ''dismemberment and torture of the Jewish family''—which, he says, underlay the fierce quarrels of his third marriage. While the Holocaust could certainly intensify and lend its imagery of horror to such a fear, one may suspect that the fear itself had its roots—for these two American-born Jews—in early familial experiences that predated the extermination camps and had no necessary connection with being Jewish. He writes as if their public fighting, which provoked a ''sly laugh'' from the Amherst faculty, were somehow distinctively Jewish, as if such behavior were not also to be found, with certain variations of style, in Irish Catholic taverns or at Cheever-ish cocktail parties populated by Westchester Wasps. (pp. 33-4)

There is much intelligent commentary throughout *New York Jew*—on English manners and class divisions at the end of the war, on the whiff of power that so intoxicated intellectuals during the Kennedy era, on the student rebellion of the late Sixties—but the book, I think, will be most valued for its literary portraits, of which Edmund Wilson's is only the most elaborate. The memoirist ultimately triumphs over the auto-biographer and the social historian. Kazin can be unkind—openly in the case of Diana Trilling, who snubbed him during his one and only visit to the Trillings' apartment, more subtly with regard to what he saw as the achievements and evasions of her husband. But his most memorable evocations are of the people whom he really knew (as opposed to the Famous Names he occasionally met), people whom (like Wilson) he could love as well as dissect, to whom he could respond with affection, exasperation, and respect.

A number of his portraits—especially those of Delmore Schwartz, Isaac Rosenfeld, Paul Goodman, and Hannah Arendt—are much like the reviews he has written of books that have deeply engaged his attention. To them he brings the powers of observation and analysis, the eye for psychologically significant detail, the semi-novelistic sense of milieu that have made him such a consistently effective reviewer and critic of fiction over the past thirty years. Whatever its deficiencies as a self-portrait, *New York Jew* is an unfailingly interesting book, a book that will assume a conspicuous place in the documentation of the literary life of our times. (p. 34)

> *Robert Towers, "Tales of Manhattan," in* The New York Review of Books, *Vol. XXV, No. 8, May 18, 1978, pp. 32-4.*

ROGER SALE

[*The essay from which this excerpt is taken was published in a slightly different form in* The New York Review of Books, *March 21, 1974.*]

Yes, the bright book of life indeed, not just the novel, as Lawrence said, but the American novel of the last thirty years, as Alfred Kazin now says [in *Bright Book of Life*]. It has all the necessary qualities of a great form gaining and sustaining its energy in an historical period, like the Elizabethan drama or the eighteenth-century satire in couplets: it is distinct, it has produced some great works, it has proven sufficiently powerful and attractive that many minor writers have been given a voice they might otherwise not have had. (p. 157)

The sad shock is that . . . [Kazin's] book is terribly disappointing, not dull, but enervating, self-defeating. It's hard to say just why without seeming merely to outline the book one would have written oneself, but the effort must be made.

There are two obvious ways to put together a book such as the one Kazin wants to write, and had Kazin refused either of the two he could have justified himself easily enough, but instead he has refused both. The first way is like Lawrence's in his book on American literature: sustain all opinions and differ-

ences in authors by means of a vision of the country and its history. Kazin refuses this, on grounds of temperament or prudence, and with the sure knowledge that most people who try to do it Lawrence's way end up with what in academic circles is called an ''idea'' but what is really a gimmick, a way of sacrificing authors for the sake of scheme. The second way is to look only at those authors about whom one has strong feelings, and really go at them with all the intensity and freshness one can muster. This is the way, say, of Leavis's *The Great Tradition*, or of Kenner's books on modern authors. Kazin refuses this, too, presumably because he wants to avoid the appearance of making contemporary fiction into his sandbox of favorites.

Having made these choices, however, for whatever good reasons, Kazin seems not to have seen what an odd book would be the result. Here are . . . Faulkner, Taylor, McCullers, O'Connor, Percy, Mailer, Jones, Heller, Vonnegut, Cozzens, O'Hara, Cheever, Salinger, Pynchon, Malamud, Roth, Porter, Sontag, Plath, Lurie, Oates, Didion, Capote, Baldwin, Ellison, Burroughs, Barthelme. I want to offer some comment later about that list, but certainly it is not one that can be faulted on grounds of crankiness or parochialism; the only obvious omissions are Hawkes and Barth. But thirty authors in a book of three hundred pages, about each of whom one tries to say the most important things, means in effect that it is authors that are treated, not books, and authors treated rather summarily at that.

It is one thing for Kazin to assume we have read all these books, another to assume we all agree on what is in them, and that Kazin need not describe, or evoke, or *lean* on the books. There are precious few quotations here—and unfortunately they are set off in tiny italics so as to resemble the words on tombstones—and that has the effect of making Kazin *only* a summarizer, only a writer of capsule sentences. It's as though quarrels, worries, doubts, quirks, preferences about contemporary fiction were all behind us, as though literature were not something that always must be looked at freshly.

Furthermore, because of this encapsulating habit and the lack of any unifying web or tissue, a chapter called ''The Absurd as a Contemporary Style,'' to take one example, begins with Ellison and goes on to ''black humor'' and its usual accompaniments, but by the time we get to Barthelme (''We have been cut off by the words hanging over our heads; our poor little word-riddled souls are distributed all over the landscape'') and Pynchon (''The key to Pynchon's brilliantly dizzying narratives is the force of some hypothesis that is authentic to him but undisclosable to us'') we have totally lost Ellison. I tried to construct that last sentence to indicate the kind of effect that is achieved; here is a subject, and everything is seemingly in place, but the conveyor belt quality of its sense of place prevents anything from staying in the mind after it has been dropped from immediate attention.

What is asked to serve as construction here, as connecting tissue, are the all too obviously arranged chapters: ''The Secret of the South,'' ''The Decline of War,'' ''Professional Observers,'' ''The Earthly City of the Jews,'' ''Cassandras.'' Though Kazin intends nothing of the sort it is almost an insult to his writers to put them in such slots, so that we know the moment we are done with Bellow and Malamud we are soon to be on to Roth and Mailer; finish Cozzens and can O'Hara, Salinger, and Updike be far behind? It might have worked better had Kazin really taken these categories as anything other than conveniences, had he sought to come up with something new about Southern or Jewish or absurdist or WASP fiction. But he doesn't because he isn't interested in the categories so much as in the authors, with being good about them. Except, to come back to that, they don't have time enough to breathe and be themselves as they are hustled along down the conveyor belt. (pp. 158-60)

At one point Kazin offers us the accurate statement that "novels seem more expendable these days than ever, but *novelist* is still any writer's notion of original talent." Here he is accounting for Capote's strange desire to call *In Cold Blood* a novel, and the situation he describes is, however true, deplorable, as he well knows. Yet if he is not going to treat the novels he most admires with any more care than he has done in *Bright Book of Life* then it's no wonder that people of less intelligence and with less interest in fiction are going to end up chattering away about novelists whose works they have read only casually and partially.

That such a thoughtful and scrupulous critic can be accused of such oversights as these seems odd, I know, and I wish I knew how to account for it. My only suggestion is that we might return to Kazin's original choices for subjects and note the almost antiseptic absence of quirks in it. At one point he offers us two pages about William Eastlake's *The Bamboo Bed*, at another two on Jane Bowles's *Two Serious Ladies*, and those are the only places where he looks, however cursorily, at writers who wouldn't necessarily be on one's list of those one had to discuss if one meant to give a complete account of contemporary fiction.

The point is not that Kazin has only read books he had to read, and the point certainly is not that he somehow hasn't read enough. It is, rather, that contemporary American fiction is for him already a *received* subject, something he has lived with for so long, perhaps, that he cannot work with it except in his thoughtful, summarizing way. If he seems to have no enthusiasms of his own among the countless other writers he might have allowed to intrude into his company, he seems to have lost or mislaid his enthusiasm for *The Victim, Seize the Day, The Assistant,* and other books about which he wants to say they are their author's "best" or "most brilliant" and have done.

Could it be that this is what happens to someone who makes contemporary literature into his main subject of interest? That he teaches and writes and lectures about it so much that he finds it difficult to get back into that frame of mind in which he originally read because it was a novel and he was a man alive? If so, then it is a powerful argument indeed against letting "contemporary literature" be a subject to teach or be the subject of wise retrospective lead essays in journals. The last thing one needs in dealing with any literature, but especially our own living literature in its own most vital parts, is grayness, and I'm afraid that for all its intelligence and its author's care *Bright Book of Life* is a gray book. (pp. 161-62)

Roger Sale, "Alfred Kazin," in his On Not Being Good Enough: Writings of a Working Critic, *Oxford University Press, 1979, pp. 157-62.*

ROBERT ALTER

[The essay from which this excerpt is taken was originally published in a slightly different form in Commentary, *June, 1978.]*

At the beginning of *New York Jew* Kazin flatly asserts, "The Jews are my unconscious." If one were to construe "unconscious" rigorously, the statement would be nonsense, but it works, suggestively and revealingly, as a metaphor. To the Manhattan sophisticate, moving through the glitter of New York, in touch, as he tells us, with the pulsating centers of power that are the chief fascination of the great city, the Jews represent a primal realm of struggle for bare survival, a constant condition of raw vulnerability, perhaps a closeness to the instinctual, to what is opaque and intractable and scary or awesome about human existence. The Jews, in other words, become the substance of a personal myth, which may be viable as a "fable of identity" (to borrow Northrop Frye's phrase), but which as a writer's perspective seems more appropriate to the poet, who is led by the nature of his medium to link the here-and-now with the eternal and the archetypal, than to the critic, who deals with the observable realities embodied in text, culture, and history. Indeed, Kazin himself is at his best in his acute treatment of observable realities, perhaps more strikingly in *New York Jew* than in anything else he has written. After the recollection in tranquility of the emotions of childhood that constituted *A Walker in the City,* he undertook in both subsequent volumes of his trilogy two discrete roles, that of the autobiographer and that of the memoirist. He is, I would contend, an uneven autobiographer but a gifted, even brilliant, memoirist. (p. 200)

The problem I find with Kazin as an autobiographer is that the self-revelation is so intermittent and at times so teasingly elliptical. The manikin of the virtuous boy in the first volume of the trilogy seems to have been succeeded at many points in the two subsequent volumes by the manikin of a virtuous man, the recorder of experience making himself only occasionally an object of real self-scrutiny. When we are given, then, brief glimpses into the intimate life of the writer—like the breakup of his first two marriages, the fluctuations of his relationship with his present wife—they seem a little out of place, sometimes almost embarrassing, and are generally vouchsafed with a vagueness or schematic quality that makes them less than convincing. Kazin, it seems to me, either should have been much more unsparing in reporting these aspects of his life or (as I am more inclined to think) should have excluded them entirely as irrelevant to the story of the growth of the critic's mind in the pungent atmosphere of the New York intellectual world. There are, to be sure, some notable exceptions to the rule I have proposed. In *New York Jew,* one might mention in particular the moving autobiographical accounts of the deaths of the writer's parents, which are handled with candor, passionate intensity, and delicacy of feeling. By and large, however, the last two volumes of the trilogy convey at best a fragmentary sense of an evolving self; more often, we find ourselves in the presence of an unquestioned self, secure in its wisdom and virtue, scrutinizing the world around it.

That, of course, is the stance of the memoirist, whose task is to tell not his own story but the story of his times as he has witnessed them. This does not mean that the memoirist is an "objective" observer. On the contrary, the sharpness of his version of important people and public events depends on his having been engaged in what he observes, on his seeing the human immediacy of his subjects through the vivifying air of his own sympathies and antagonisms as a narrator intimately involved with the materials of his narration. Kazin's concise, deftly written accounts of the tenor of intellectual life during the Marxist thirties, the deradicalized postwar era, and the haywire sixties are lucid, persuasive, and eminently sane. Readers who look too hard at the autobiographer himself may be a little put off by what could be construed as an edge of complacency about his own unflagging reasonableness through the follies of three decades; but viewed as a memoirist, recording his times from the vantage point of his own opinions and values, he can hardly be faulted. In any case, the most brilliant writing in *New York Jew* (there are already a few intimations of it in *Starting Out in the Thirties*) is not in generalizations about the age but in the individual portraits of writers Kazin has known.

His prose is never more alive than when he is doing these character studies, as he manages to attend simultaneously to the visual details of portraiture, to the psychology of his subjects, and to the themes and strategies of their work. (pp. 201-02)

The most interesting of his mixed portraits, and also the most extended, is his treatment of Lionel Trilling, who clearly has been important to him, as a model, a competitor, and an intellectual eminence who never altogether accepted him. We have already seen how Kazin contrasts his own personal style, social allegiance, and Jewish affiliation with Trilling's. He traces his wariness about Trilling to their first meeting in the *New Republic* office in the early forties. The younger man sensed an "immense and even cavernous subtlety" in the author of the study of Matthew Arnold that he had admired. If the physical description of Trilling in *New York Jew* reflects a certain personal edginess, it nevertheless captures something essential about Trilling's presence. . . . In the pages that follow, and again later in the book, there is a good deal of open polemic with the elusiveness of Trilling's political positions, his subtle role in the process of deradicalizing American intellectuals, and with what Kazin construes as the oddly Victorian notion of "culture" which he claims displaced abrasive earthly realities in Trilling's work. "No one," Kazin notes in one of his epigrams, "could have been more discerning, and less involved." One could object that he misperceives certain basic aspects of Trilling's critical enterprise, and that he insists too harshly on Trilling's supposed self-importance, but even in his antagonism he never allows himself to forget his rival's extraordinary fineness of mind, or how Trilling set new high standards in using the critical essay as a dramatization of the fluctuating life of the mind. . . . (p. 203)

I have deliberately invoked the language of rivalry because the one pervasive element of the New York intellectual world that Kazin reflects most sharply is its unrelenting competitiveness. His was the first full-grown generation of American-born sons of the Jewish immigrants from Eastern Europe. From the Lower East Side, Brooklyn, and the Bronx, from as far away as Chicago's South Side, they congregated during the thirties and forties in Greenwich Village, midtown publishing offices, and the academic centers of Manhattan, each impelled by a formidable sense of his own high destiny in literary life, each guided by a calculating wariness about the necessary means for achieving that destiny. Paul Goodman, unabashedly proclaiming himself in conversation the best poet, playwright, and literary theorist around, exerted a "power over people" that

"visibly enlarged him in the moment of contact." (As Kazin goes on to elaborate this metaphor, he clearly intends a sexual innuendo.) The young Saul Bellow exhibited a sense of superiority that was less the quasi-erotic reflex of a need for self-assertion, more firmly anchored in an absolute faith in his own large talent. . . . (pp. 203-04)

Among the offspring of an immigrant group a single-minded intentness on getting ahead in the world is a familiar enough phenomenon in many spheres of endeavor. What is noteworthy about these newcomers to the centers of American literary power is the extraordinary confidence in their own future that so many of them evinced. If great men, as Freud observed, start out in life with an enormous fund of unqualified mother love, one might speculate that the powerful Jewish mother, notorious for her smothering affection, might have played a far more constructive role than is generally allowed, and that the Jewish father of immigrant background, usually thought of as a weak and ineffectual figure, may have actually provided in many instances a strong model for an assertive male role.

Be that as it may, the essentially competitive nature of this whole intellectual milieu of the thirties and forties in which the sons of the Yiddish-speaking immigrants began their careers had ambiguous effects. It obviously impelled writers to great efforts of achievement, but I think it also sometimes directed energies that should have been channeled into intellectual work toward mere self-promotion and the nervous maneuvers of warring personalities and cliques. This did not necessarily mean that people wrote less than they should have but rather that what they wrote was too narrowly, too self-consciously devised as an incessant demonstration—as with Paul Goodman and, beginning a decade later, Norman Mailer—that they were first in the field.

Kazin made his initial ascent on a surer road, concentrating with scholarly patience on the variety and complexity of his large subject, obtaining the authority he wanted through the mastery of the subject. Yet in his case, too, there is a poignancy about the imponderable consequences of ambition pursued and consummated. He would remain an alert commentator and a skillful writer, but he has not since been able to summon up the resources of sustained will that produced his first precocious achievement. In that first book, he made himself intellectually one with the American cultural tradition, and through the deserved success of the book, he made himself socially one with the New York literary elite. But both these ends having been accomplished, it seems as though he had lost the motive for finding a great new subject that would require an architectonic effort of the critical imagination. What chiefly remained for him was a lesser role, though one he would forcefully enact, to become the chronicler of life among the intellectuals, whose world he had so swiftly conquered. (pp. 204-05)

Robert Alter, "The Education of Alfred Kazin," in his Motives for Fiction, *Cambridge, Mass.: Harvard University Press, 1984, pp. 190-205.*

Camara Laye

1928-1980

Guinean novelist, autobiographer, and short story writer.

Laye's work is considered an important contribution to West African literature and appeals to an international audience. Infused with spirituality and the vibrance of traditional African culture, his books also confront such modern dilemmas as alienation and the search for identity. Laye was exiled from his home country in 1965 because of his opposition to its government, and he lived in Senegal until his death. Much of his writing chronicles the plight of the exile and the problems of adapting to change and cultural dislocation. Adele King observed that Laye's work "belongs within the tradition of classic world literature, describing a personal and cultural dilemma in accents that speak to all mankind."

After receiving a French education in Guinea, Laye went to Paris to complete his studies. While living in France he produced his first work, *L'enfant noir* (1953; *The Dark Child*), an autobiography of his early life in the village of Kouroussa. Laye's account of his childhood is characterized by its affectionate portrayal of traditional African life. Some reviewers faulted Laye for ignoring the realities of colonial rule and idealizing the past, but others praised his depiction of the beauty and autonomy of African culture. Laye's next book, *Le regard du roi* (1954; *The Radiance of the King*), is widely considered his finest work. Reversing the conventional idea of a black person in an alien culture, *The Radiance of the King* centers on a white man alone in an African village; he must adapt to his surroundings if he is to survive. The mysticism and spiritual presence of nature central to the African tradition figures strongly in the novel, as in all of Laye's work. Abiola Irele commented: "[Laye's] preoccupation with the possibilities of a deep spiritual experience which the African world seemed to him to offer constitutes the unifying point of view of all his work . . . [and] finds its supreme expression in *Le Regard du Roi*."

Like *The Dark Child,* its sequel, *Dramouss* (1966; *A Dream of Africa*), mirrors the events of Laye's life. After spending six years in Paris, the protagonist of this work returns to Guinea and finds it changed from the country he remembers. A product of Laye's disillusionment with his country's post-independence political situation, the book constitutes a harsh indictment of the Guinean government and led to Laye's exile. Though valued by some critics as a record of a turbulent historical period, most consider *A Dream of Africa* Laye's least effective work, claiming that political urgency overshadows structural and literary concerns. Laye's last book, *Le maître de la parole: Kouma lafôlô kouma* (1978; *The Guardian of the Word*), is more universally praised. For the basis of this work Laye visited the African storyteller Babou Condé and recorded his story of Soundiata, the legendary leader of the Mali empire. Transcribing spoken history into written language, Laye assumed the role of mediator between the ancient oral tradition of Africa and the modern audience. He drew praise not only for preserving and celebrating a fragment of African culture, but also for bringing to it his own creative force. Martin Tucker observed that "although Laye's last work is filled with surrealistic shades and European psychological insight, it is invigorated by the traditional African vision of the spiritual and historic."

Laye's recurrent depiction of this vision has placed him at the center of African literature.

(See also *CLC,* Vol. 4 and *Contemporary Authors,* Vols. 85-88, Vols. 97-100 [obituary].)

ABIOLA IRELE

Shortly after the publication in 1954 of Camara Laye's autobiography, *l'Enfant Noir (The African Child)* [published in the United States as *The Dark Child*], a review signed by a certain Alexandre Biyidi appeared in the journal *Présence Africaine* in which Laye's work was attacked and its author taken to task for turning his attention away from the exactions committed by the French under the colonial system and escaping into a world of African innocence. To Biyidi (none other than Mongo Beti, writing under his real name and at that time, the very beginning of his career, as a novelist of the colonial situation), Laye's book appeared as a futile diversion from the necessary political and social role of the African writer in the historical context of colonialism.

The irony was that, far from being an endorsement of colonial rule, with its specific French justification as a "civilising mission", Laye's book was in fact a form of denial of the assumptions and explicit ideological outgrowth of the French colonial enterprise. For against the idea of a primitive order of life in traditional African society by which the coloniser sought to justify his presence, Laye's autobiography presented an image of a coherence and dignity which went with social arrangements and human intercourse in the self-contained African universe of his childhood. Investing that image with a warmth that gave his book a special appeal as a literary work, Laye also gave it an ideological implication as an ardent defence of his African antecedents against European denigration. For if Laye's book cannot be construed as an explicit anticolonial statement, its whole meaning tended towards the same end, so that its position in the development of a modern Africa expression gives it a historical value of the first importance from both a literary and ideological point of view. (p. 617)

[The] whole bent of Laye's stylistic effort—even with its lapses, understandable in a first work—is specifically the evocation of a particular atmosphere with which his imagination has endowed the life and society he experienced as a child. And it is through this evocation that we are able to participate with our emotions, rather than with our heads, in the quality of life he recreates. Laye's purpose in his autobiography is thus at the opposite pole to that of Maxim Gorky or Ezekiel Mphahlele, for example, whose explicit intention is to present the hard and even sordid conditions under which they did their apprenticeship of life.

It has often been remarked that the dominant feeling in *The African Child* is the pervasive nostalgia determined by its theme, but this element of Laye's autobiography has no real meaning unless taken in its close association with his sense of profound attachment to the world of his African childhood and to its values, a sense which the book evinces so distinctly and with such convincing charm. The human significance of the book resides in its record of the process of development of an individual personality within the living context of a social and cultural environment which defines ultimately a moral and spiritual universe.

It is in this respect that *The African Child* points to the matter and spirit of the two novels that follow. Laye's three imaginative works are in fact organised around his historical personality and express through this organisation his individual understanding of the world as conditioned by his early experience. His preoccupation with the possibilities of a deep spiritual experience which the African world seemed to him to offer constitutes the unifying point of view of all his work, which finds its supreme expression in *Le Regard du Roi (The Radiance of the King)*.

As Wilfred Cartey has suggested (in his study. *Whispers from a continent*) Clarence, the white hero of this novel, can be taken as a reversed image of the African Child of the autobiography, the embodiment of Laye himself in his spititual self at the end of the process it describes. The adventure of Clarence becomes in this light the return movement of Laye's alienated consciousness towards an original "realm of infancy.". . . . The wider meaning of Laye's symbolic novel is of course clear—the journey motif immediately calls attention to the archetypal dimension of Clarence's adventure and experience. But if the significance of the novel at this level is large enough not to be missed, it remains clear that its theme is rigorously particularised, related directly to the historical situation in which Laye's

imagination is operating. The allegorical reference is thus not to some abstract universal of human consciousness, but rooted in the historical and racial dialectic of the colonial relationship. In other words, the novel prolongs the theme of the autobiography and accomplishes in a symbolic register its implication; for Laye, it is as much a question of projecting a visionary ideal of African spirituality as making a statement upon man's eternal quest for fulfilment and illumination.

The impressive achievement of *The Radiance of the King* has raised two problems which it is necessary to consider for its proper appreciation. The first concerns the extent of Laye's indebtedness to Kafka in the novel. The mazes and labyrinths, the enigmatic characters and the atmosphere of moral oppressiveness that marks the human situations at many points in the novel can certainly be ascribed to the influence of Kafka. But to fasten upon these details is to disregard the important fact that the symbolic scheme of the novel and its very spirit owe nothing to Kafka, but issue directly out of an indigenous African tradition of symbolic narrative. (pp. 617-18)

The other problem concerns the rumour that has been growing in scope and volume and tending to cast doubts on Laye's authorship of the novel, as indeed of *The African Child*. . . . [The] literary argument is based on the fact of a subsequent disappointing performance which is employed to cast doubts on an earlier achievement. In the case of Laye, the feebleness of *Dramouss (A Dream of Africa)* is taken as an indication of his fundamental incapacity to produce a *tour de force* of the order and quality of *The Radiance of the King*. The weakness of this argument lies in the well-proven fact that even the greatest writers have been known to produce work of indifferent quality in their "nodding moments". It was the same Conrad, for instance, who wrote masterpieces like *Nostromo* and *The Secret Agent* who went on to write the feeble melodrama of *Chance*.

What is more, any sensitive reader ought to be able to discern the remarkable continuity of Laye's style in all his writing . . . : a style distinguished by its naive-like pattern of repetitions. . . .

It is true that *A Dream of Africa* must be counted largely a failure, yet it is bound to the earlier works in the sense that it carries forward Laye's preoccupation into the post-colonial situation. Laye's imagination is clearly not a political one, of the order of Ngugi's, for example; in its immediate social and political reference, the last novel does not manifest an intelligence of the realities of contemporary Africa comprehensive enough to sustain a statement as compelling, in its own terms, as that of the preceding novel. Nonetheless, it represents an effort to situate the historical evolution of the continent in the perspective of the spiritual ideal elaborated in *The Radiance of the King*. To that extent, it is the same imagination at work in both novels, an imagination attuned to the spiritual, and bent towards an exploration of the deep recesses of the human mind in its responses to the elemental, to the whole compass of human experience and possibility.

And it is especially in Laye's effort to derive a live sense of this dimension of human life and consciousness from his understanding of and feeling for the spiritual potential of our ancestral culture that, I believe, the value of his achievement will be seen to reside. (p. 618)

Abiola Irele, "Camara Laye: An Imagination Attuned to the Spiritual," in West Africa, *No. 3272, April 7, 1980, pp. 617-18.*

ERIC SELLIN

The publication of *Le maître de la Parole: Kouma lafôlô kouma* . . . was something of a literary event, for the book appeared after a twelve-year silence on Laye's part, a silence which critics—unaware of the personal problems and serious illness which had plagued Laye during the preceding decennium—had come to feel indicated that Laye was "washed up" as a writer.

Laye's first book, *L'enfant noir*, a reminiscence of his childhood and youth in Guinea, appeared in 1953 and won him . . . instant acclaim and lasting respect as a limpid stylist. The following year saw the publication of *Le regard du roi*, whose clever reversals, dreamlike evocations, surreal effects and implementation in prose of techniques proper to film (well before Robbe-Grillet, Jean-Pierre Attal and others made these techniques commonplace) have caused some admirers to deem it the finest African novel.

Readers had to wait twelve years for the publication of Laye's third book, *Dramouss* (1966), a hastily written autobiographical account of the author's return to Guinea and the virtual sequel to *L'enfant noir*. *Dramouss* is weak compared to the first two books: there is little effort displayed in building a narrative structure, and the dialogue is stilted, while portions of the description are flat and lifeless. . . .

[After the publication of *Dramouss* there] ensued another silence, punctuated by reports of a novel in progress on the theme of exile. As the years passed and Laye's silence grew deafening, critics—summarily dismissing *Dramouss* as an underachievement—said that Laye had been a flash in the pan (admitting, at least, that the productivity of 1953-54 had been brilliant) and were skeptical when the novelist mentioned that he was involved in research on the materials of African oral history.

The appearance of *Le maître de la Parole* will, no doubt, meet with some cavils on the part of those who somehow felt Laye owed us a great masterpiece built, as it were, on the magnificent promise of *L'enfant noir* and *Le regard du roi;* but it is a testimony to Laye's courage that he was able to bring out any book at all. (p. 392)

As to the notion that Laye had turned to historical materials because he lacked the creative energy to construct an original novel as projected, we may return to the 1966 preface to *Dramouss* in which Laye actually recommends that the African writer turn, before it is too late, to his oral history and in which he underscores the urgency that young African poets and novelists draw their inspiration from "les vérités historiques de nos civilisations particulières, et dans les réalités africaines." . . .

In choosing to recount the story of the childhood, young manhood and ascension to power of the legendary ruler of the ancient Mali empire—Sundiata Keita—Laye, though acting only as a "modeste transcripteur et traducteur," selected a character and a geographical area that could not help but elicit his sympathy.

The story of *Le maître de la Parole* is that of Diata, son of Sogolon Condé, hence Sogolon-Diata, which was shortened to Sundiata (Soundiata). A cripple most of his childhood, Sundiata walked through determination and because it was destined. Prophecies of his great future alarmed Fatoumata, Sogolon's rival wife, for Fatoumata had political aspirations for her own son. When Fatoumata's son did become *mansa*, or king, of the city of Niani, they banished Sogolon and her children as a precaution against the fulfillment of the prophecies of Sundiata's leadership.

After years of exile under the protection of neighboring kings to the north—during which period Niani fell under the dominion of the cruel tyrant Sumanguru (Soumaoro)—Sundiata grew into a strong and gallant warrior. He secured against invaders the area of his foster king . . . and appeared destined to inherit his throne. In Niani, meanwhile, Sumanguru had taken his nephew's wife, with the result that the nephew turned on him with a significant portion of the army. Sumanguru sacked Niani. The elders decided that the only person who could save them was Sundiata. . . .

With the assistance of his half-sister, who had seduced Sumanguru into revealing the taboo against his powerful totem (Sumanguru was only vulnerable to the spur of a white cock), Sundiata was able to defeat the opposing army and kill Sumanguru. Sundiata assumed the throne in Niani, swore his officers to fealty as vassals and reigned till his death over a vast empire covering what is today Guinea, Senegal and Mali.

The tale as told by Laye contains the basic historical facts, but it also conveys the traditional bardic embellishments and the heroic exaggerations characteristic of epic tales from any culture. (p. 393)

Laye chose not to dwell on Sundiata's great imperial years but rather on the years of exile and quest which preceded his ascension to power. Once Sundiata has succeeded in gaining control of his home city, Laye devotes a scant eight pages to the rest of Sundiata's life. To stress, in this manner, the years of deprivation and wandering is not inappropriate, for all Laye's works underline, in one way or another, the themes of exile and the quest for identity or fulfillment. In a sense, *Le maître de la Parole* is the transferal of Laye's private story to the broader base of historical saga and collective heritage: we have here, then, a universalization of the theme of exile and its elevation to the status of myth.

In Laye's other works the moment of resolution is left more or less in abeyance. In *L'enfant noir* it is a sad and bewildered young man who takes off from Dakar for Paris. In *Le regard du roi* the final radiant embrace in which the Frenchman Clarence undergoes some sort of sublimation is subject to half a dozen reasonable interpretations but, in any case, occupies only the last few lines of the novel, whose pages are preponderantly devoted to the process of humiliation, loss of identity and the quest for whatever elusive thing it is that the final illuminating moment entails.

A short story, **"Les yeux de la statue,"** published in *Présence Africaine* in 1957, is an interesting converse of *Le regard du roi*, the pessimistic verso or, possibly, an alternate ending to the brilliant upbeat finale of the novel. In the short story a young woman on a vague quest finds herself in a ruined town overgrown with creepers. There is a statue with strange eyes lying in the foliage. The woman loses her orientation, the creepers rise like the tide until they overpower her, and, in the final moment of the story, the statue, which has risen on the swell of creepers and has fixed its eyes upon her, either strikes her on the forehead or is involved in some way in her transformation, perhaps into a statue. . . .

Finally, in *Dramouss* the protagonist comes home to Guinea only to find that his vision of a new independent Africa has turned to a nightmare and that he must depart again without having seen an end to his exile. His usually omniscient father promises him that when he next returns, "the time will have come" and things will be different; but when he does return after some years, nothing has changed. The longed-for fulfillment is indefinitely deferred.

Le maître de la Parole is based on an account by the griot Babou Condé, whom Laye visited and recorded on tape in 1963. Laye learned, among other things, that among the Malinke of his region there are four categories or periods *(Paroles): kouma lafôlô kouma,* the story of the first Word, or the story of Sundiata; *kouma koro,* the ancient Word, or the story of men before our time; *kouma korotola,* the aging Word, or the genealogy of the different tribes of the area; and *kouma,* the Word, or the story of Samory (1830-1900) and of our own times. In light of this information, both the meaning and the structural implications of the book's subtitle *Kouma lafôlô kouma* are clear, and we see in which sense the word *Parole* is intended in the title.

It would appear that Laye made some use of chronicles other than that taped from Babou Condé, and it seems, to me at least, that he imparted some personal touches to the text here and there. But that he was basically the transcriber of historical accounts, as he averred, seems clear. . . .

In speaking of the griot's recitation, Laye states that it always contains two truths: that carefully constructed one designed to amuse his listeners, which is peripheral; and that other, more profound truth which is the historic truth. In retelling this particular story, regardless of the degree to which he relied on existing material, Laye injected into it a third truth, that of his psychic identity with Sundiata, who managed to overcome personal handicap and long years of adversity and exile to fulfill his call to greatness. . . . (p. 394)

> Eric Sellin, "Trial by Exile: Camara Laye and Sundiata Keita," in World Literature Today, Vol. 54, No. 3, Summer, 1980, pp. 392-95.

GERALD MOORE

There is sometimes a danger in thinking of writers too rigidly in terms of their generation, and the work of Camara Laye should remind us of it. Born only a few years before fiercely anti-colonial writers like Mongo Beti or David Diop, and a year later than Sembène Ousmane, his early writing seems to inhabit an entirely different world. In Diop's poetry, for instance, the menace and cruelty of Europe are never absent, oppression seems to enclose his writing on every side, making his talent spring like a tiger. Both Mongo Beti and Sembène Ousmane, even in their treatment of rural themes, write of an Africa profoundly degenerated by the experience of colonialism, and by the years of encroaching slavery and conquest which preceded it. . . . Likewise, from their earliest writing, Beti and Sembène see Africa as having lost, irretrievably lost, its traditional values and historical innocence. It is not mere decolonization which can reverse the processes of degeneration begun over a century ago; African societies, in their view, cry out for revolutionary change; a change which will sweep away the vestiges of feudalism and traditional inequality as completely as those of colonialism and dependence.

In Laye's work, the colonial theme hardly obtrudes at all. The Africa he recollects and recreates had still its own authentic vision of the world, its integrity, its total system of values. These things vanished, not a century, but a mere generation ago. Many of them died, it seems, with the author's own father and his contemporaries. Can all these writers be speaking of the same Africa, the same historical experience? The answer is: not quite. Although it is legitimate to generalize to some extent about African indigenous cultures, or about the nature and impact of colonial rule, it remains true that Africa is the world's second largest continent, and that the same influences, even if everywhere felt, are not felt with the same intensity. Above all, what Wole Soyinka has recently called the African's 'self-awareness', the ability to experience and interpret the world for himself, did not suffer the same blows in, say, Yorubaland, Upper Guinea, the Dogon country of Mali or the Lo-Dagaa country of Northern Ghana, as they suffered in the mines and slums of Johannesburg, the rubber plantations of King Leopold's Congo, or the 'White Highlands' of Kenya. These differences in the quality and intensity of deprivation persisted, not only a generation ago, but into our own day. They help as much to explain certain aspects of Soyinka's own writing as they help to explain Camara Laye or *The Myth of the Bagre* or *The Mwindo Epic.* And they make the charge so often levelled against Laye, that he ignores the colonial impact, appear in some degree irrelevant. For to insist, as Laye does, that a certain kind of African authenticity has survived the colonial whirlwind, and will perhaps survive the whirlwinds that follow in its wake, is to make a much stronger apprehension of self than to be wholly absorbed in castigations of 'the Other'. Such castigations allow the Other to appear as the most important factor in one's experience.

Camara Laye was born in the ancient city of Kouroussa, which stands on the head waters of the Niger in the great plain of Upper Guinea. This part of the Western Sudan has known historical civilizations for a thousand years. Though conquered and administered by France, a city like Kouroussa was complex and self-sufficient enough to go very much on its own immemorial way. Its people, if we are to judge by Laye's writing, were not constantly obsessed with the alien presence of Europe in their midst, but were far more occupied with their own concerns of hunting, trade and craft. Above all, the city itself was not, like so many cities of Africa, the product of colonial settlement.

To make the contrast yet stronger, Laye's father was the town's leading goldsmith and blacksmith, a figure universally respected both for his skill and for his magical powers, as smiths so often were throughout West Africa. Growing up in such an environment, Laye was able to know intimately a life which was still intact, though beginning to disappear; a life which was not essentially changed from that of the empires of the Mansa Musa or Sundiata which had ruled these riverine cities six or seven hundred years earlier. Yet Camara Laye was born in 1924.

This vanishing world, so rich in dignity and human values, has been recorded by Camara Laye in an autobiography which will live as long as men are interested in Africa. . . . [*L'Enfant Noir*] is a unique book in many ways, written with a singular and gentle sincerity, yet with very conscious artistic skill. Laye does not proclaim his negritude or announce the coming dawn; he records what his childhood was, what was the quality and the depth of the life from which he sprang. (pp. 85-7)

Does Laye idealize the old life in . . . [*L'Enfant Noir*]? Perhaps, for his mood is frankly nostalgic and will naturally select the high spots of the past. Yet there is great authenticity about [his descriptions]. . . . The warmth of comradeship and shared labour, the simple joy of harvest, the sparkling blue weather of the dry season, these were real enough. No doubt some of the reapers got drunk and beat their wives, some of the children died, victims of superstition and dirt. But there is a curious inconsistency about the sort of chauvinistic criticism which, whilst asserting in the abstract the virtues of African civilization, can read . . . [this book] and ask indignantly: 'where are the horrors of colonialism?' The genuine writer is not a marionette; he dances to a music of his own, and not to one dictated by others. The vision of *L'Enfant Noir* is integral and only the crassest imagination can fail to register that integrity. (pp. 88-9)

Laye's second book, the symbolical novel *Le Regard du Roi (The Radiance of the King),* appeared only a year after his autobiography. . . . It has many of the qualities we should expect from the author of *L'Enfant Noir;* the same simple but beautifully modulated prose, the same compassion, the same sense of mystery investing ordinary things. But it displays also some entirely new aspects of his art. Nothing in his first book has prepared us for this gift of sustained unportentous symbolism, this daring alternation of narrative speed and exploratory slowness, or the racy, cryptic humour of much of the dialogue. (p. 90)

The publisher's blurb announces confidently that this book is an allegory of 'man's search for God'. . . . Quite as much as a search for God, Clarence's pilgrimage seems to be a search for *identification*. He becomes more and more like his human companions, plunging far deeper into sensuality than they only in order to purge away his separation and superiority. (p. 96)

Some interpreters have suggested that Clarence is not so much a white man as a 'been-to', an African whose soul has been whitened by over-exposure to European influence and values. Such a person is, in fact, often referred to as a 'white man' among his own people, whether ironically or in admiration. This interpretation cannot be dismissed: it should rather be considered as evidence of the mulitivalence of a work of art; but it certainly is not necessary to regard Clarence as anything but what he is described as—a white man entirely strange and new to Africa. (pp. 96-7)

The art of symbolical fiction depends upon the interest and variety maintained on the immediate level of perception. The mind should not be continually aware of 'pregnant significances' as it reads, but should be fully entertained and absorbed by the story itself. The search for parallel or inner meanings should come later. This means that the surface narrative and dialogue may be largely naturalistic and even sprightly in tone, though the events and conversations described may be bizarre enough. A heavy, portentous style, drugged with its own significance and continually drawing attention to its own profundity must be abjured above all. In *The Radiance of the King,* Laye has avoided these dangers. He has written a book which we can read with enjoyment, amusement and keen absorption, but which occupies the mind in such a way that new perceptions keep rising to its surface when the reading is over. (p. 97)

[*Dramouss*] is undoubtedly a disappointment after the level of achievement in his first two works, but although uneven and marred by too much authorial intrusion, it also contains some of the most intense and searching pages to be found in recent African writing. The weakness of the book stems mainly from Laye's failure to make up his mind whether to write a memoir or a novel; the early pages read like the former and the final pages, like the latter. The use of an authorial *persona* called Fatoman arouses expectations of a work of fiction, but the account of Laye's first return to Guinea in the late 1950s is not sufficiently distanced or transmuted to achieve the status of fiction. (pp. 97-8)

The broken structure of the book is the expression of a personality which Laye himself describes as divided:

> My being . . . was the sum of two intimate selves: the first, closer to my sense of life, fashioned by my traditional existence of animism slightly tinted with Islam, enriched by French culture, was in conflict with the second, who, for love of his native soil, would betray his own thinking by coming to live in the heart of this regime.

In *Dramouss,* Laye has not found the overall structure which can contain and transcend this conflict. But his use of vision to express it is no sudden aberration; it is deeply consistent both with the whole tradition of the Malinke and of his own writing. (pp. 102-03)

Gerald Moore, "The Aesthetic Vision," in his Twelve African Writers, *Indiana University Press, 1980, pp. 84-103.*

ADELE KING

L'Enfant noir might be compared to such novels as James Joyce's *Portrait of the Artist as a Young Man,* and Marcel Proust's *A la Recherche du temps perdu,* in which the author's reminiscences have been given an artistic form. In the process the personal becomes universalised and representative of widely shared forms of experience. Thus Joyce's novel is a portrait of *the* artist as a young man, not simply memories of his own youth. Laye's book is about the modern African child. (p. 17)

A major subject of the book is the traditional culture of Laye's childhood and what it means to him. New, European-influenced historical pressures, however, lead him away from his family and society. His life can be said to be representative of many Africans who find it necessary to go to the city and eventually to Europe for further education. To find his place in the modern technological world, the African risks losing contact with his family, village and tribal traditions. African writing in English and French often deals with cultural conflicts or protests against the process of estrangement from traditional life. Unlike many writers, Laye handles this subject with nostalgia; something important has been lost, but the loss is a necessary part of modern life.

Another major theme in the story, not especially African, is the loss of childhood innocence, the necessity of growing up and moving beyond the security of one's family. Related to this theme is a more religious one, the need to follow one's destiny, or maybe the path that God has ordained. Thus the book deals with life in a traditional society, the problems of young Africans at a particular moment of history, and the universal themes of growing up and fulfilling one's destiny. It is in the blend of these various elements that the artistry of *L'Enfant noir* is to be found. (pp. 17-18)

[It] is a carefully controlled story . . . presented with economy and restraint. The mother is both an individual dramatically portrayed and a symbol of Africa, continent of warmth, mystery and love. The setting is presented vividly, but without strong emphasis. . . . Effects of contrast are achieved subtly, without explicit statement, through the juxtaposition of events

. . . . [Language] and tone reflect the child's widening awareness of the world. Each chapter is clearly constructed, rising to an emotional climax usually followed by a statement of the narrator's sense of loss. His nostalgic tone, however, is balanced by an awareness of the inevitability of change. The theme of regret for the lost African past is treated not with self-pity or political polemics, but with restraint. A particular moment in Laye's life and in the history of Africa has been transformed into a minor classic, in which the autobiographical form has been raised to the level of art. (pp. 36-7)

[*Le Regard du roi*] is a bizarre, often comic story of a misplaced white man [Clarence] in archetypal Africa, and is narrated from the point of view of this white man. It embodies, however, the same essential themes as *L'Enfant noir:* cultural conflict and the quest for salvation. (p. 38)

Le Regard du roi may be seen as a story about a man's attempt to find meaning in an ambiguous world in which his accepted values have been undermined, in which the behaviour of other people is often incomprehensible and in which perceptions are always fluctuating. (p. 40)

The culture of Aziana [the African village where Clarence lives] is based on closeness to the physical world, on emotion rather than reason, on chance rather than rights. It is a culture opposed to the rationalistic, mechanistic society of modern Europe. Clarence's main aim initially is mere survival. . . . [Eventually] he changes and his idea of what he is seeking also changes. He loses the need to assert his individuality and his rights; he becomes part of a community and attuned to the physical world surrounding him. His experience might be seen as the correction of European rationality by African sensuality and reliance upon emotions and dreams. The novel suggests that life in such a traditional society may be closer to the fundamental truths of human nature.

Clarence's adaptation to Aziana may therefore be considered as an illustration of some of the themes of the Negritude movement. According to [L.S. Senghor], the black soul is sensitive to 'the apparently imperceptible rhythms of the world'; the black man 'cannot imagine objects as essentially different from man . . . all of Nature is animated by a human presence'. Black culture is based upon emotion rather than reason. African religion is dominated by love. 'Morality consists in not breaking the communion of the living, the dead, the spirits and God.' The community is of primary value and the individual develops best within communal organisations: 'the need for fraternal communion is more profoundly human than that of retiring within one's self'. *Le Regard du roi* reflects this view of African culture, a culture which Laye assumes, as does Senghor, to be common to black Africa.

There is a sense, however, in which *Le Regard du roi* can be read as a gentle parody of Negritude. Because the Africa that Clarence discovers doesn't appear to be on the map or in the twentieth century, it seems an ideal for which one might yearn, but not a political or cultural entity to be found in the modern world. Just as in *L'Enfant noir* Laye realises that the world he is describing is already past . . . , so in *Le Regard du roi* he paints an ideal for which he might feel nostalgia but which he does not suggest can be recovered. He knows he is not portraying a real Africa and seems to be mocking the concern of the Negritude movement to define an essential African culture as if it did still exist. (pp. 42-3)

As in *L'Enfant noir,* Laye has universalised his story. Beyond being an image of the confrontation of European and African cultures, the novel deals with the theme of any man trying to adjust to a strange society, of every man's homelessness in the world. Clarence is not only a European in a strange land, he is the average man in a world where faults can be committed inadvertently, where nature will often appear cruel, where sensuality will frequently overwhelm common sense. Making this ordinary European a symbol for Everyman is a way of countering 'black racism', a way of showing that the essential human experiences go beyond colour. The story then transcends the realm of human culture to become a tale of man's search for God. Laye has brought to his work his African world view and his personal religious mysticism, but expressed his vision in a work that has universal resonances. (p. 47)

[*Dramouss*] is the story of the development of the African child [introduced in *L'Enfant noir*] (now called Fatoman) when he goes to France, as he learns to blend two cultures—traditional Malinké and French—and tries to find the best of the two worlds to which he is now attached. It is also the story of his disillusionment when he realises that neither of these two cultures has a place in his native land after its independence, and that he cannot find the role for which he thought he had prepared himself. Like the narrator of *L'Enfant noir,* the hero of *Dramouss,* who tells his story in the first-person, is a type, representing the Guinean intellectual of Laye's generation. . . . (p. 63)

Fatoman as an individual is less important than the community. The story of his life is interwoven with the larger story of the problems of Guinea just before and after its independence, and with reminders of its traditional culture. *Dramouss* is rather a portrait of Guinea than a portrait of a person. Its themes include the demagogy of a developing political system that is moving towards a one-party state, the weakening of the ties with France, and the decline of traditional artistic culture. It is also a portrait of Laye's generation of European-educated Guineans and the problems confronting them as they seek to understand how their homeland has changed.

The story of Fatoman's life since he left Guinea to study in France is told in long chapters, interspersed with other kinds of material; at the centre of the novel there is a folk tale told to Fatoman and his family by a traditional griot. The narrative is episodic: Fatoman's return to pre-independence Guinea after six years in France, and his marriage to Mimic (the Marie of *L'Enfant noir*); a restless night when he thinks back on his life in Paris; a visit to his family home in Kouroussa where he hears the griot's tale, talks to his father in his workshop and attends a political meeting; another restless night during which he has a strange dream, prophetic of his country's future. After a break in the narrative representing a passage of several years, there is an epilogue recounting Fatoman's return to settle in Guinea after independence, when he finds that many of the worst fears expressed by his father or foreseen in his dream have become realities. Essentially, therefore, action in the present is followed by reminiscence or by dreams of the future. Laye deliberately destroys the autobiographical linearity. The broken chronological sequence reflects Fatoman's uncertainty as to how his life is developing. The pattern is present, past, present, future, with an epilogue in which the foreseen future has become the present. (pp.63-4)

Laye's purpose in *Dramouss* is not to recreate a life story, but to explain, through a mosaic of different situations narrated in varying manners, why the conflict—between his desire to live in his native land and his love of both Malinké and French culture—has arisen. Fatoman is a representative type, embodying a problem that Laye himself was facing: a problem that has little to do with personalities, but rather with fundamental moral and political issues. (p. 74)

Dramouss is addressed to . . . the European-educated African who expected that from his own tensions and sufferings would be born a new culture, remaining true to its traditional roots while combining the best of Africa and Europe. The present disillusionment of such hope and the prophecy that the dream of Africa may yet be realised are the basic themes of the novel. Laye sees his role of artist as entailing an analysis of present failings and preserving hope for the future. (p. 80)

The religious theme in *Dramouss*, which goes beyond Fatoman's personal problems and even beyond the dilemma of Guinea, shows Laye's profound conviction that in spite of our tribulations God is watching over us and we must try to follow his way. It is essentially the same quest for salvation as in *Le Regard du roi*, posed here on the level of a people rather than of an individual. . . .

Dramouss is, however, less successful as a novel than Laye's earlier work. . . . Characterisation is wooden, dialogue is often rather stilted. Fatoman is primarily a spokesman for the author's opinions and uncertainties concerning the role of the educated elite, the problems of independence and the future of the country; he is not a well-rounded fictional character. (p. 81)

In *L'Enfant noir* Laye found a simple, classic structure, and a way of creating an artistic distance between his experience and the novel through a narrator who looks back on his childhood. In *Dramouss,* Laye changes the names of himself and his wife, simplifies the events in his life—omitting, for instance, any reference to the fact that he had written and published two successful novels while in France—and fragments the chronology of the narrative. Since the emotional wounds he experienced in returning to Guinea were still open, he cannot, however, adopt the detached tone he used in *L'Enfant noir.* (p. 82)

[Nevertheless, the] stylised political allegory, the blending of various kinds of narratives to show the transitional era in which one culture was breaking down when no viable alternative had been established, the evocation of a nightmare tyranny and of an eventual divine salvation, all give *Dramouss* value as an expression of the tensions of Laye and his generation; value which, in the final analysis, outweighs its formal weaknesses as a novel. (p. 83)

[*Le Maître de la parole*] is the story of Soundiata, the thirteenth-century Manding leader who united a number of small kingdoms to form the Empire of Mali, one of the great political dynasties of Africa. It is the history of Camara Laye's own people: Soundiata's capital, Niani, was close to the site of Kouroussa; one of the warrior kings who supported him was Tabon Wanna Fran Camara, from whom Laye claimed descent. The book is a literary transcription of the history of Soundiata told by a Malinké griot, Babou Condé, whom Laye recorded in 1963 in Upper Guinea. Babou Condé, who was at least eighty years old when Laye interviewed him, was a griot of considerable renown. He told Laye the oral tradition he had learned from his own family, which traces its line back to the thirteenth century when an ancestor was the griot of Soundiata's nephew. (p. 86)

Laye speaks of the oral tradition preserved by the griots as essentially artistic; its significance is less as historical document than as aesthetic preservation of the essential values of traditional culture. . . . (p. 89)

In writing *Le Maître de la parole,* Camara Laye attempts to fulfil the role of the griot in a modern context and for a modern audience. The griot uses traditional material. The basic historical and legendary material of the narrative in *Le Maître de la parole* has been written before, in various renditions in English and French. Laye, however, uses it for his own purposes. By conveying a picture of the essential facts of the moral and social life of his people, he wishes to show the relevance of the legend to modern life and also to amuse his contemporary audience with an entertaining tale. (p. 90)

Before beginning the tale, Laye includes several introductory chapters in which he discusses some of his favourite themes. The material world is not all important; spiritual forces direct our destiny and can be approached by those with mystical insight. Such insight is more readily available to those close to the natural world; thus, in general, to Africans. A knowledge of the past is essential to help modern African countries define themselves. . . . The problem, as he defines it, is that an assimilationist colonial policy, coupled with a lack of historical documentation on the precolonial era, has left Africans with little knowledge of this past.

Laye's view of traditional Malinké civilisation is that it was only slightly influenced by Islam, that it reached its apex in the fourteenth century in the Mali empire, and that it has since remained static. This means that the history of the Manding people is largely internal; its civilisation rose and fell independent of outside influences; it was already in decline before European colonisation started. Laye has claimed that *Le Maître de la parole* is the most authentically African of his books because it all takes place before the colonial era. He cites, however, among the reasons for the decline of Manding civilisation, the Moroccan invasion and the slave trade. It is the present that will show if this traditional culture can again develop vitality. For Laye such a renaissance means both studying the past and being open to benefits to be gained from other cultures. As usual in his work, respect for tradition goes hand in hand with welcoming the best of foreign culture. (pp. 90-1)

Laye also uses the narrative of Soundiata to attack, rather indirectly, the present regime in Guinea. Soumaoro's dictatorship is based on terror and the destruction of his opponents. The destiny of Soundiata, who came to power with the aid of many rulers oppressed by Soumaoro, was to 'incarnate the collective consciousness of the exasperated peoples of the savannah, to make of it a white-hot fire of revolt against the tyrant.'. . . *Le Maître de la parole* concludes: 'May the example of Soundiata and his people guide us as we walk on the slow and difficult path of the evolution of Africa,' . . . thus expressing the hope that a new Soundiata will arise, probably a slight hope to Camara Laye by 1978. (p. 91)

Laye is thus working in a fashion similar to the griot's, stressing moral truths and showing their contemporary relevance. Like the griot he occasionally intervenes in the story (as well as in the notes and introduction) to make observations. He defends, for instance, the role played by women in Malinké society, as he did in *L'Enfant noir.* He speaks of the value of liberty, only recognised when it is lost, and castigates the use of torture—allusions to contemporary Guinea. He makes Soundiata think of how he is different from the Arab traders he meets, defends monotheism, and even comments that the most beautiful woman is always one with whom a man has never spent a night—a curiously modern commentary in a medieval epic. Like the griot, Laye occasionally refers to his own personal experience.

Le Maître de la parole uses techniques common to traditional oral tales. There are praise songs in Malinké (followed by translations into French), and recitations, genealogies and celebrations of heroes, which are undoubtedly close to Babou Condé's own words. There is also a basic story mode, told in the author's words; after the introductory chapters, Laye does not claim that the form of the tale is directly attributable to Babou Condé. Laye aims at simplicity. He called *Le Maître de la parole* an 'exercice de style', an attempt to make an ancient legend seem real to the reader, and comprehensible even to children. If he explains customs for his European reader (divination systems, proof of virginity at marriage rituals, Malinké musical instruments), he is more specifically aiming, as in *Dramouss,* at African readers. The simplified dialogues and action are perhaps explicable in terms of the goal of reaching an audience less sophisticated in the techniques of modern fiction.

The style of *Le Maître de la parole* is appropriate to an epic; it includes frequent repetitions, and more images and metaphors than in Laye's previous work. . . . While the use of images based on the local environment may in some cases be attributable to Babou Condé, Laye is seeking a style appropriate to the epic story: 'The children nestled in the branches of the trees like clusters of grasshoppers' . . . ; 'the ground into which it sank as if into a ripe papaya.' . . . Sometimes, however, the comparisons seem modern, anachronistic: 'she became as burning, as feverish as a body attacked by malaria.' . . .

Laye does, however, make significant changes in the traditional epic, changes influenced by the role of the artist in contemporary Africa and which reflect his own previous work. *Le Maître de la parole* is in may ways a logical continuation of his novels. If it represents a departure from the contemporary world of *L'Enfant noir* and *Dramouss,* it is similar in setting to the feudal African kingdom described in *Le Regard du roi.* *Le Maître de la parole* also stresses many of the themes of his earlier work: the importance of the sacred, the mystery of the world, best approached by those attuned to nature and able to read its signs; the quest to understand and follow God's will; the need to be part of a community and to be humble in the service of that community; the need to undergo an arduous initiation into adult responsibilities. (pp. 92-3)

Laye has turned the narrative into something closer to the novel form. He often portrays [scenes] . . . in a realistic fashion; he describes the social organisation of the Niani community, without the idealisation of village life found in *L'Enfant noir*. He builds up longer episodes than those found in other versions of the narrative: the hunters' search for the buffalo, Sogolon's wedding, Soundiata's birth, his first steps at the age of ten, the game of Wori, and Nâna Triban's discovery of Soumaoro's vulnerability. In each of these scenes there is extended dialogue and detailed description of the thoughts of the characters, often presented as a kind of interior monologue. As the story is legendary and filled with miraculous events, the result is a tension between the subject-matter and the method of narration. *Le Maître de la parole* is an interesting, but sometimes disconcerting amalgam of epic events and supernatural occurrences—with no attempt to give them rational explanations—combined with a realistic fictional technique and psychological analysis more common to the European novel. (p. 94)

Le Maître de la parole is less intense in tone than Laye's earlier work. Its aims are perhaps too mixed. Although including historical notes and a word list of Malinké, it is not a scholarly study of Manding culture. As a transcription of a traditional tale, it is perhaps too modern and literary. As a novel within the European tradition, the narrative contains too many long genealogies, secondary characters and interventions in the plot. It is perhaps impossible to combine successfully all the *genres* that Laye was attempting within one work. *Le Maître de la parole*, however, fulfils an essential aim in recalling the relevance of traditional moral values for the present. By writing a story which the contemporary African reader, accustomed to modern fiction, can find entertaining, Laye was continuing, in a new fashion, the work of the griots, and contributing to the search for an African fictional form. (p. 96)

When we look for a psychological unity in Laye's work we may find it in an extreme attachment to his mother-land. In *L'Enfant noir,* published six years after he left Guinea, Laye wrote: 'it was a terrible parting! I do not like to think of it. I can still hear my mother wailing. It was as if I was being torn apart.' Although he says that he worked out his anxiety about leaving Upper Guinea by describing his departure, it is probable that this traumatic event has provided the emotional charge behind all his work. (p. 124)

Whether or not *L'Enfant noir* is better than *Le Regard du roi,* the same experience of feeling uprooted from a childhood paradise, of feeling alienated in a foreign culture, directly expressed in *L'Enfant noir,* is transposed in the fiction of *Le Regard du roi,* and explains the emotional trauma of *Dramouss,* written when it was apparent that no return was possible and that exile was inevitable. This trauma is even apparent in *Le Maître de la parole.* Soundiata's exile often suggests a parallel to Laye's own; the triumphal return to Niani, described in other versions of the legend, is omitted.

Laye's life was in many ways an illustration of a moment in cultural history. He was representative of a kind of experience that is unlikely to recur at present. For him the normal problems of growing up were combined with the shock of a radical change in culture, a shock which—in the world of the transistor radio even in the poorest villages of West Africa—can never again be so powerful. Laye gave this experience perhaps its purest literary expression. In spite of the modesty of his background, in spite of the many obstacles to his desire to write, he managed to produce work of great interest at a moment when West African literature was in its infancy.

African literature in European languages had a remarkable development in the years just before and after independence, a flowering that many critics have predicted will not continue. It was a moment when the tensions of traditional and modern cultures produced a heightened sensibility and when the definition of self seemed also to be the definition of the tribe, the country, or even Africa itself. The poetic and the social functions of literature could be united to a degree seldom possible in modern western civilisation. Camara Laye is one of the seminal figures in this development. If his work never reaches the heights of the masters on whom he modelled himself—Flaubert, Kafka—it belongs within the tradition of classic world literature, describing a personal and cultural dilemma in accents that speak to all mankind. (pp. 124-25)

> *Adele King, in her* The Writings of Camara Laye,
> *Heinemann Educational Books Ltd., 1980, 144 p.*

MARTIN TUCKER

[Camara Laye] achieved world recognition for *The Dark Child,* a memoir of his childhood in Kouroussa, and *The Radiance of the King,* a surreal novel in which a white beggar wanders in search of a black king who will liberate him by the radiant smile that smites all sickness in a troubled soul. Laye's second work is allegorical, Kafkaesque and African in a unique way; it is a powerful and disturbing exploration of exile, quest and reconciliation with a power greater than logic or reason.

Although Laye's first book is often regarded as the perfect example of negritude—a work that illuminates the essence of African identity—he did not believe in the separatism the negritude movement spawned. His ideal was a unity of culture, just as the hero of his last work united the many kingdoms of the Upper Niger into the Mali empire.

Laye describes *The Guardian of the Word* as a "translation" of the legend "Kouma Lafolo Kouma," which he heard sung by the famed griot Babu Condé. The legend tells the history of the "great Sundiata, the son of the buffalo-panther and of the lion," who became the first Emperor of Mali and ruled from 1230 to 1255. In his rendering, Laye assumes the voice of a griot, who is the historian of his tribe as well as a performer and storyteller. In adopting this guise, Laye is adhering to a profound convention, for the traditionalist African writer did not claim individual authorship but considered himself a "keeper" of sacred words available to all. . . .

Some writers can criticize their society only indirectly—through legend. Laye had inveighed against the policies of [Guinean President] Sékou Touré in an autobiographical manuscript, *L'Exil,* but he could not publish it while his wife remained in a Guinean jail. . . . A careful reading of Laye's Sundiata epic, however, reveals that again he was hurling charges at his old adversary.

Laye's tale has dimensions beyond its relationship to specific history; he was attempting a revitalization of his work by returning to the basic resource of any literature—the springs of its traditions. Still, his intent was not to preserve tradition; he was interested in nourishment and enrichment of contemporary life. Thus, although Laye's last work is filled with surrealist shades and European psychological insight, it is invigorated by the traditional African vision of the spiritual and historic. Camara Laye is saying that myth creates kinship among us all.

> *Martin Tucker, "Son of the Buffalo-Panther," in* The New York Times Book Review, *June 24, 1984, p. 24.*

ALAN CHEUSE

The Guardian of the Word is an epic on the scale of the *Chanson de Roland* or *El Cid,* one of those books that transmit from one generation to the next elemental visions on which society is founded—on the laws and customs and manners by which it remains stable. It presents an etiological version of the founding of the 13th-Century Malian empire, or one that shows us why events occurred as they did, not just that they took place. And it opens with all of the breadth and color of our own culture's finest myths.

> There were once two hunters, the elder called Moke Mussa, the younger Moke Dantuman. A sudden anger seized them. 'What!' they cried. 'A buffalo can prevent a whole people from living in peace. . . .'

And off they go on a quest that matches in passion and intensity some of the best epics we know. Moreover, the good griot tells his tale—from the point of origin to the laying out of the laws for pacified Mali territory at the end—in a style that gives us great light, color, emblem, action. Here, for an example, is the way the narrator offers up the end of the hunt for the mythic buffalo:

> They cut off the golden tail . . . and started on their way back. As evening began to fall, it got cooler, the air became lighter and moister: It was a sudden freshness after the stupefying heat of mid-day, made all the fresher by the dew clinging to the tall grasses through which their path went winding on . . . Night suddenly fell, but the moon was full; its milky, ghostly radiance illumined everything, and tenderly caressed the leaves of trees. . . .

The milky, ghostly radiance of such passages illuminates these pages, and where magic does not obtain (or the creation of rituals for initiation into adulthood, marriage and politics), we can be caught up in a presentation of physical love that passes far beyond the (artificial) boundaries established in the epics of our own Judeo-Christian (predominantly puritanical) culture. Eros presides in this empire of the senses with an intensity that Western poetry has known rather infrequently.

> *Alan Cheuse, "Empire of the Senses in Africa," in* Los Angeles Times Book Review, *September 2, 1984, p. 6.*

Claude Lévi-Strauss

1908-

Belgian-born French anthropologist, theorist, and essayist.

Considered the founding father of structuralism, Lévi-Strauss is one of France's foremost intellectuals and is internationally recognized as having greatly affected post-World War II Western thought. His seminal studies in structural anthropology draw upon the theories of such varied disciplines as linguistics, sociology, philosophy, psychology, and mathematics and have given rise to the term "Science of Man." Taking an essentially scientific approach to the study of cultural patterns, Lévi-Strauss seeks to expose the structures underlying human thought and reveal their universality. Described as the study of the system of systems or the relation of relations, structuralism is an elusive term that has generated much discussion and critical debate over its various precepts and the exact nature of the term itself. In her book *The Age of Structuralism,* Edith Kurzweil describes structuralism as "the systematic attempt to uncover deep universal mental structures as these manifest themselves in kinship and larger social structures, in literature, philosophy, and mathematics, and in the unconscious psychological patterns that motivate human behavior." Although many critics claim that as a scientific method structuralism ultimately fails, Lévi-Strauss's contributions to the social sciences and to the evolution of human thought are regarded as among the most significant of the twentieth century.

Lévi-Strauss studied philosophy and law at the Sorbonne in Paris, from which he graduated in 1932, but shortly thereafter his interest in fundamentals led him to pursue a career in anthropology, which he believed bridged the gap between philosophy and science. In 1935 he went to Brazil to fill a position as Professor of Sociology at the University of São Paulo, which enabled him to make several journeys to the Brazilian interior to study the culture and behavior of primitive tribes. These studies form the basis of much of his subsequent work. In 1939 Lévi-Strauss returned to France to serve in the armed forces, but in 1940 he departed for New York City. There he taught at the New School for Social Research and came under the influence of the prominent linguist Roman Jakobson. Jakobson was largely responsible for introducing Lévi-Strauss to the formal methods of structural linguistics which, when applied to cultural phenomena, constitute the theoretical base of structural anthropology. In 1947 Lévi-Strauss returned to Paris to continue his studies and to teach sociology and anthropology. He has received many honors and awards abroad and in his home country, among the most prestigious of which was his election in 1973 to the Académie Française.

Lévi-Strauss has published numerous essays in scholarly journals as well as many books. Of his early essays, "L'analyse structurale en linguistique et en anthropologie" (1945; "Structural Analysis in Linguistics and in Anthropology") is among his most notable. Introducing the model which all of Lévi-Strauss's later works expand upon and develop, the article addresses the relationship of structural linguistics to cultural codes and human behavior. His first major book, *Les structures élémentaires de la parenté* (1949; *Elementary Structures of Kinship*), applies this model to a study of kinship and marriage rites in primitive tribes. In this work, Lévi-Strauss views in-

tertribal marriage as a system of economic and ritual exchange similar to the linguistic exchange of words.

Of Lévi-Strauss's works published in the 1950s, *Race et histoire* (1952; *Race and History*), *Tristes tropiques* (1955; *A World on the Wane*), and *Anthropologie structurale* (1958; *Structural Anthropology*) have received the most attention. Lévi-Strauss's view of history, partially propounded in *Race and History,* has been challenged, particularly by Marxist critics, for its lack of political emphasis, and debate frequently centers on the political and historical differences between the theories of Lévi-Strauss and those of social philosophers Karl Marx and Jean-Paul Sartre. *A World on the Wane* exemplifies the diversity of Lévi-Strauss's concerns. Based on his early field work in Brazil, this book is a spiritual and philosophical as well as anthropological account of a modern traveler amongst tribal communities. Susan Sontag considers *A World on the Wane* "one of the great books of our century," and Edith Kurzweil noted that "the book not only made [Lévi-Strauss] famous but paved the way for his *Structural Anthropology,"* which collects seventeen essays written since the 1940s.

Le totémisme aujourd'hui (1962; *Totemism*), *La pensée sauvage* (1962; *The Savage Mind*), and the four volumes of his opus *Mythologiques—Le cru et le cuit* (1964; *The Raw and the Cooked*), *Du miel aux cendres* (1967; *From Honey to Ashes*),

L'origine des manières de tables (1968; *The Origin of Table Manners*), and *L'homme nu* (1971; *The Naked Man*)—collectively represent Lévi-Strauss's predominant concern with myth and his efforts to demonstrate the connections between primitive and civilized humans. These works contain extensive analyses of North and South American Indian myths and present Lévi-Strauss's notion that all modes of thought, both conscious and unconscious, can be structured according to binary oppositions.

Although few of Lévi-Strauss's studies are specifically concerned with literary works—the most notable exception being his analysis, written in collaboration with Roman Jakobson, of Charles Baudelaire's poem "Les chats"—his structuralist precepts have been adopted by many literary theorists, and structuralism as an approach to literature dominated literary criticism in the 1960s and 1970s. In recent years structuralism has given way to poststructuralism and deconstructionism, but the influence of Lévi-Strauss's ideas is still clearly visible. George Steiner notes: "The bearing of [the work of Lévi-Strauss] on the notion of culture, on our understanding of language and mental process, on our interpretation of history is so direct and novel that an awareness of Lévi-Strauss's thought is a part of current literacy."

(See also *Contemporary Authors*, Vols. 1-4, rev. ed. and *Contemporary Authors New Revision Series*, Vol. 6.)

SUSAN SONTAG

[*The essay from which the following excerpt is taken originally appeared in a slightly different form in* The New York Review of Books, *November 28, 1963.*]

Most serious thought in our time struggles with the feeling of homelessness. The felt unreliability of human experience brought about by the inhuman acceleration of historical change has led every sensitive modern mind to the recording of some kind of nausea, of intellectual vertigo. And the only way to cure this spiritual nausea seems to be, at least initially, to exacerbate it. Modern thought is pledged to a kind of applied Hegelianism: seeking its Self in its Other. Europe seeks itself in the exotic—in Asia, in the Middle East, among pre-literate peoples, in a mythic America; a fatigued rationality seeks itself in the impersonal energies of sexual ecstasy or drugs; consciousness seeks its meaning in unconsciousness; humanistic problems seek their oblivion in scientific "value neutrality" and quantification. The "other" is experienced as a harsh purification of "self." But at the same time the "self" is busily colonizing all strange domains of experience. Modern sensibility moves between two seemingly contradictory but actually related impulses: surrender to the exotic, the strange, the other; and the domestication of the exotic, chiefly through science.

Although philosophers have contributed to the statement and understanding of this intellectual homelessness—and, in my opinion, only those modern philosophers who do so have an urgent claim on our interest—it is mainly poets, novelists, a few painters who have *lived* this tortured spiritual impulse, in willed derangement and in self-imposed exile and in compulsive travel. But there are other professions whose conditions of life have been made to bear witness to this vertiginous modern attraction to the alien. Conrad in his fiction, and T. E. Lawrence, Saint-Exupéry, Montherlant among others in their lives as well as their writing, created the métier of the adventurer as a spiritual vocation. Thirty-five years ago, Malraux chose the profession of the archaeologist, and went to Asia. And, more recently, Claude Lévi-Strauss has invented the profession of the anthropologist as a total occupation, one involving a spiritual commitment like that of the creative artist or the adventurer or the psychoanalyst. (pp. 69-70)

So far, Lévi-Strauss is hardly known in this country. A collection of previously scattered essays on the methods and concepts of anthropology, brought out in 1958 and entitled *Anthropologie Structurale,* and his *Le Totémisme Aujourd'hui* (1962) have been translated in the last year. Still to appear are another collection of essays, more philosophical in character, entitled *La Pensée Sauvage* (1962); a book published by UNESCO in 1952 called *Race et Histoire;* and the brilliant work on the kinship systems of primitives, *Les Structures Élémentaires de la Parenté* (1949). Some of these writings presuppose more familiarity with anthropological literature and with the concepts of linguistics, sociology, and psychology than the ordinary cultivated reader has. But it would be a great pity if Lévi-Strauss' work, when it is all translated, were to find no more than a specialist audience in this country. For Lévi-Strauss has assembled, from the vantage point of anthropology, one of the few interesting and possible intellectual positions—in the most general sense of that phrase. And one of his books is a masterpiece. I mean the incomparable *Tristes Tropiques,* a book that became a best-seller when published in France in 1955, but when translated into English and brought out here in 1961 was shamefully ignored. *Tristes Tropiques* is one of the great books of our century. It is rigorous, subtle, and bold in thought. It is beautifully written. And, like all great books, it bears an absolutely personal stamp; it speaks with a human voice. (pp. 70-1)

[The] greatness of *Tristes Tropiques* lies not simply in [the] sensitive reportage [of his field research in Brazil], but in the way Lévi-Strauss *uses* his experience—to reflect on the nature of landscape, on the meaning of physical hardship, on the city in the Old World and the New, on the idea of travel, on sunsets, on modernity, on the connection between literacy and power. The key to the book is Chapter Six, "How I Became an Anthropologist," where Lévi-Strauss finds in the history of his own choice a case study of the unique spiritual hazards to which the anthropologist subjects himself. *Tristes Tropiques* is an intensely personal book. Like Montaigne's *Essays* and Freud's *Interpretation of Dreams,* it is an intellectual autobiography, an exemplary personal history in which a whole view of the human situation, an entire sensibility, is elaborated.

The profoundly intelligent sympathy which informs *Tristes Tropiques* makes other memoirs about life among pre-literate peoples seem ill-at-ease, defensive, provincial. Yet sympathy is modulated throughout by a hard-won impassivity. In her autobiography Simone de Beauvoir recalls Lévi-Strauss as a young philosophy student-teacher expounding "in his detached voice, and with a deadpan expression . . . the folly of the passions." Not for nothing is *Tristes Tropiques* prefaced by a motto from Lucretius' *De Rerum Natura.* Lévi-Strauss' aim is very much like that of Lucretius, the Graecophile Roman who urged the study of the natural sciences as a mode of ethical psychotherapy. The aim of Lucretius was not independent scientific knowledge, but the reduction of emotional anxiety. Lucretius saw man as torn between the pleasure of sex and the pain of emotional loss, tormented by superstitions inspired by religion, haunted by the fear of bodily decay and death. He recommended scientific knowledge, which teaches intelligent detachment, equanimity. Scientific knowledge is, for Lucretius, a mode of psychological gracefulness. It is a way of learning to let go.

Lévi-Strauss sees man with a Lucretian pessimism, and a Lucretian feeling for knowledge as both consolation and necessary disenchantment. But for him the demon is history—not the body or the appetites. The past, with its mysteriously harmonious structures, is broken and crumbling before our eyes. Hence, the tropics are *tristes*. There were nearly twenty thousand of the naked, indigent, nomadic, handsome Nambikwaras in 1915, when they were first visited by white missionaries; when Lévi-Strauss arrived in 1938 there were no more than two thousand of them; today they are miserable, ugly, syphilitic, and almost extinct. Hopefully, anthropology brings a reduction of historical anxiety. It is interesting that Lévi-Strauss describes himself as an ardent student of Marx since the age, of seventeen ("Rarely do I tackle a problem in sociology or ethnology without having first set my mind in motion by reperusal of a page or two from the *18th Brumaire of Louis Bonaparte* or the *Critique of Political Economy*") and that many of Lévi-Strauss' students are reported to be former Marxists, come as it were to lay their piety at the altar of the past since it cannot be offered to the future. (pp. 72-3)

It is strange to think of these ex-Marxists—philosophical optimists if ever such have existed—submitting to the melancholy spectacle of the crumbling prehistoric past. They have moved not only from optimism to pessimism, but from certainty to systematic doubt. For, according to Lévi-Strauss, research in the field, "where every ethnological career begins, is the mother and nursemaid of doubt, the philosophical attitude par excellence." In Lévi-Strauss' program for the practicing anthropologist in *Structural Anthropology,* the Cartesian method of doubt is installed as a permanent agnosticism. "This 'anthropological doubt' consists not merely in knowing that one knows nothing but in resolutely exposing what one knows, even one's own ignorance, to the insults and denials inflicted on one's dearest ideas and habits by those ideas and habits which may contradict them to the highest degree."

To be an anthropologist is thus to adopt a very ingenious stance vis-à-vis one's own doubts, one's own intellectual uncertainties. Lévi-Strauss makes it clear that for him this is an eminently *philosophical* stance. At the same time, anthropology reconciles a number of divergent personal claims. It is one of the rare intellectual vocations which do not demand a sacrifice of one's manhood. Courage, love of adventure, and physical hardiness—as well as brains—are called upon. It also offers a solution to that distressing by-product of intelligence, alienation. Anthropology conquers the estranging function of the intellect by institutionalizing it. For the anthropologist, the world is professionally divided into "home" and "out there," the domestic and the exotic, the urban academic world and the tropics. The anthropologist is not simply a neutral observer. He is a man in control of, and even consciously exploiting, his own intellectual alienation. A *technique de dépaysement,* Lévi-Strauss calls his profession in *Structural Anthropology.* He takes for granted the philistine formulas of modern scientific "value neutrality." What he does is to offer an exquisite, aristocratic version of this neutrality. The anthropologist in the field becomes the very model of the 20th century consciousness: a "critic at home" but a "conformist elsewhere." Lévi-Strauss acknowledges that this paradoxical spiritual state makes it impossible for the anthropologist to be a citizen. The an-

thropologist, so far as his own country is concerned, is sterilized politically. He cannot seek power, he can only be a critical dissenting voice. Lévi-Strauss himself, although in the most generic and very French way a man of the Left (he signed the famous Manifesto of the 121, which recommended civil disobedience in France in protest against the Algerian War) is by French standards an apolitical man. Anthropology, in Lévi-Strauss' conception, is a technique of political disengagement; and the anthropologist's vocation requires the assumption of a profound detachment. "Never can he feel himself 'at home' anywhere; he will always be, psychologically speaking, an amputee." (pp. 73-4)

[Always] anthropology has struggled with an intense, fascinated *repulsion* towards its subject. The horror of the primitive (naïvely expressed by Frazer and Lévy-Bruhl) is never far from the anthropologist's consciousness. Lévi-Strauss marks the furthest reach of the conquering of the aversion. The anthropologist in the manner of Lévi-Strauss is a new breed altogether. He is not, like recent generations of American anthropologists, simply a modest data-collecting "observer." Nor does he have any axe—Christian, rationalist, Freudian, or otherwise—to grind. Essentially he is engaged in saving his own soul, by a curious and ambitious act of intellectual catharsis. (p. 75)

[Anthropology], for Lévi-Strauss, is an intensely personal kind of intellectual discipline, like psychoanalysis. A spell in the field is the exact equivalent of the training analysis undergone by candidate psychoanalysts. The purpose of field work, Lévi-Strauss writes, is to "create that psychological revolution which marks the decisive turning point in the training of the anthropologist." And no written tests, but only the judgment of "experienced members of the profession" who have undergone the same psychological ordeal, can determine "if and when" a candidate anthropologist "has, as a result of field work, accomplished that inner revolution that will really make him into a new man."

However, it must be emphasized that this literary-sounding conception of the anthropologist's calling—the twice-born spiritual adventure, pledged to a systematic *déracinement*—is complemented in most of Lévi-Strauss' writings by an insistence on the most unliterary techniques of analysis and research. His important essay on myth in *Structural Anthropology* outlines a technique for analyzing and recording the elements of myths so that these can be processed by a computer. European contributions to what in America are called the "social sciences" are in exceedingly low repute in this country, for their insufficient empirical documentation, for their "humanist" weakness for covert culture criticism, for their refusal to embrace the techniques of quantification as an essential tool of research. Lévi-Strauss' essays in *Structural Anthropology* certainly escape these strictures. Indeed, far from disdaining the American fondness for precise quantitative measurement of traditional problems, Lévi-Strauss finds it not sophisticated or methodologically rigorous enough. (pp. 75-6)

Thus the man who submits himself to the exotic to confirm his own inner alienation as an urban intellectual ends by aiming to vanquish his subject by translating it into a purely formal code. The ambivalence toward the exotic, the primitive, is not overcome after all, but only given a complex restatement. The anthropologist, as a man, is engaged in saving his own soul. But he is also committed to recording and understanding his subject by a very high-powered mode of formal analysis—what Lévi-Strauss calls "structural" anthropology—which obliterates all traces of his personal experience and truly effaces the human features of his subject, a given primitive society. (p. 77)

Lévi-Strauss' favorite metaphor or model for analyzing primitive institutions and beliefs is a language. And the analogy between anthropology and linguistics is the leading theme of the essays in **Structural Anthropology.** All behavior, according to Lévi-Strauss, is a language, a vocabulary and grammar of order; anthropology proves nothing about human nature except the need for order itself. There is no universal truth about the relations between, say, religion and social structure. There are only models showing the variability of one in relation to the other. (p. 78)

The demonic character which history and the notion of historical consciousness has for Lévi-Strauss is best exposed in his brilliant and savage attack on Sartre, the last chapter of **La Pensée Sauvage.** I am not persuaded by Lévi-Strauss' arguments against Sartre. But I should say that he is, since the death of Merleau-Ponty, the most interesting and challenging critic of Sartrean existentialism and phenomenology.

Sartre, not only in his ideas but in his entire sensibility, is the antithesis of Lévi-Strauss. With his philosophical and political dogmatisms, his inexhaustible ingenuity and complexity, Sartre always has the manners (which are often bad manners) of the enthusiast. It is entirely apt that the writer who has aroused Sartre's greatest enthusiasm is Jean Genet, a baroque and didactic and insolent writer whose ego effaces all objective narrative; whose characters are stages in a masturbatory revel; who is the master of games and artifices, of a rich, overrich style stuffed with metaphors and conceits. But there is another tradition in French thought and sensibility—the cult of aloofness, *l'esprit géometrique.* This tradition is represented, among the new novelists, by Nathalie Sarraute, Alain Robbe-Grillet, and Michel Butor, so different from Genet in their search for an infinite precision, their narrow dehydrated subject-matter and cool microscopic styles, and, among film-makers, by Alain Resnais. The formula for this tradition—in which I would locate Lévi-Strauss, as I would put Sartre with Genet—is the mixture of pathos and coldness.

Like the formalists of the "new novel" and film, Lévi-Strauss' emphasis on "structure," his extreme formalism and intellectual agnosticism, are played off against an immense but thoroughly subdued pathos. Sometimes the result is a masterpiece like **Tristes Tropiques.** The very title is an understatement. The tropics are not merely sad. They are in agony. The horror of the rape, the final and irrevocable destruction of pre-literate peoples taking place throughout the world today—which is the true subject of Lévi-Strauss' book—is told at a certain distance, the distance of a personal experience of fifteen years ago, and with a sureness of feeling and fact that allows the readers' emotions more rather than less freedom. But in the rest of his books, the lucid and anguished observer has been taken in hand, purged, by the severity of theory.

Exactly in the same spirit as Robbe-Grillet disavows the traditional empirical content of the novel (psychology, social observation), Lévi-Strauss applies the methods of "structural analysis" to traditional materials of empirical anthropology. Customs, rites, myths, and taboo are a language. As in language, where the sounds which make up words are, taken in themselves, meaningless, so the parts of a custom or a rite or a myth (according to Lévi-Strauss) are meaningless in themselves. When analyzing the Oedipus myth, he insists that the parts of the myth (the lost child, the old man at the crossroad,

the marriage with the mother, the blinding, etc.) mean nothing. Only when put together in the total context do the parts have a meaning—the meaning that a logical model has. This degree of intellectual agnosticism is surely extraordinary. And one does not have to espouse a Freudian or a sociological interpretation of the elements of myth to contest it.

Any serious critique of Lévi-Strauss, however, must deal with the fact that, ultimately, his extreme formalism is a moral choice, and (more surprisingly) a vision of social perfection. Radically anti-historicist, he refuses to differentiate between "primitive" and "historical" societies. Primitives have a history; but it is unknown to us. And historical consciousness (which they do not have), he argues in the attack on Sartre, is not a privileged mode of consciousness. There are only what he revealingly calls "hot" and "cold" societies. The hot societies are the modern ones, driven by the demons of historical progress. The cold societies are the primitive ones, static, crystalline, harmonious. Utopia, for Lévi-Strauss, would be a great lowering of the historical temperature. In his inaugural lecture at the Collège de France, Lévi-Strauss outlined a post-Marxist vision of freedom in which man would finally be freed from the obligation to progress, and from "the age-old curse which forced it to enslave men in order to make progress possible." Then:

> history would henceforth be quite alone, and society, placed outside and above history, would once again be able to assume that regular and quasi-crystalline structure which, the best-preserved primitive societies teach us, is not contradictory to humanity. It is in this admittedly Utopian view that social anthropology would find its highest justification, since the forms of life and thought which it studies would no longer be of mere historic and comparative interest. They would correspond to a permanent possibility of man, over which social anthropology would have a mission to stand watch, especially in man's darkest hours.

The anthropologist is thus not only the mourner of the cold world of the primitives, but its custodian as well. Lamenting among the shadows, struggling to distinguish the archaic from the pseudo-archaic, he acts out a heroic, diligent, and complex modern pessimism. (pp. 79-81)

Susan Sontag, "The Anthropologist as Hero," in her Against Interpretation and Other Essays, *Farrar, Straus and Giroux, 1966, pp. 69-81.*

GEORGE STEINER

A page of Lévi-Strauss is unmistakable (the two opening sentences of **Tristes tropiques** have passed into the mythology of the French language). The prose of Lévi-Strauss is a very special instrument, and one which many are trying to imitate. It has an austere, dry detachment, at times reminiscent of La Bruyère and Gide. It uses a careful alternance of long sentences, usually organized in ascending rhythm, and of abrupt Latinate phrases. While seeming to observe the conventions of neutral, learned presentation, it allows for brusque personal interventions and asides. Momentarily, Lévi-Strauss appears to be taking the reader into his confidence, *derrière les coulisses,* making him accomplice to some deep, subtle merriment at the expense of the subject or of other men's pretensions in it. Then he withdraws behind a barrier of technical analysis and erudition so exacting that it excludes all but the initiate.

But through his aloof rhetoric, with its tricks of irony and occasional bursts of lyric élan, Lévi-Strauss has achieved a fascinating, sharp-etched individuality. Rejecting the Sartrian view of ordered, dialectical history as yet another myth, as merely another conventional or arbitrary grouping of reality, Lévi-Strauss adds: *"Cette perspective n'a rien d'alarmant pour une pensée que n'angoisse nulle transcendance, fût-ce sous forme larvée."* The sentence is characteristic in several ways: by its mannered Pascalian concision and syntax; by the implicit identification which Lévi-Strauss makes between his own person and the "abstract concretion" of *une pensée;* but principally by its note of stoic condescension. It is that note, the cool inward and downward look, the arrogance of disenchanted insight, which fascinates Lévi-Strauss's disciples and opponents. As the young once sought to mime the nervous passion of Malraux, so they now seek to imitate the *hauteur* and gnomic voice of the Professor of Social Anthropology at the Collège de France. (pp. 239-40)

Only the comparative anthropologist and ethnographer are equipped to pass judgment on the solutions which Lévi-Strauss puts forward to complex problems of kinship and totemism, of cultural diffusion and "primitive" psychology. The technical literature which has grown up around the work of Lévi-Strauss is already large. But the bearing of that work on the notion of culture, on our understanding of language and mental process, on our interpretation of history is so direct and novel that an awareness of Lévi-Strauss's thought is a part of current literacy. "Like Freud," remarks Raphaël Pividal, "Claude Lévi-Strauss, while solving special questions, has opened a new road to the science of man."

That road begins with the classic achievement in sociology and social anthropology of Durkheim, Hertz, and Mauss. In the latter's "Essay on Certain Primitive Forms of Classification" (1901-2) we see outlined important aspects of the study of taxonomy and "concrete logic" in *La Pensée sauvage.* As he makes clear in his own "Introduction à l'oeuvre de Marcel Mauss," it is to Mauss's way of thinking about kinship and language, and above all to Mauss's *Essai sur le don* of 1924, that Lévi-Strauss owes certain assumptions and methodologies which inform his entire work. It is in this essay that Mauss puts forward the proposition that kinship relations, relations of economic and ceremonial exchange, and linguistic relations are fundamentally of the same order.

Beginning with his paper on structural analysis in linguistics and in anthropology . . . and his first full-scale treatise, *Les Structures élémentaires de la parenté* in 1949, Lévi-Strauss has made this conjecture of essential identity the core of his method and world-view. Examining a specific problem of kinship nomenclature and marital taboos, Lévi-Strauss argues that the evidence can only be sorted out if the women exchanged in marriage are regarded as a *message,* allowing two social groups to communicate with each other and to establish a vital economy of rational experience. Beginning with the particular instance, Lévi-Strauss has elaborated the view that all cultural phenomena are a language. Hence the structure of human thought and the complex totality of social relations can be studied best by adopting the methodology and discoveries of modern linguistics. What political economy is to the Marxist concept of history (the circumstantial, technical basis underlying an essentially metaphysical and teleological argument), the work of

Saussure, Jakobson, M. Halle, and the modern school of structural linguistics is to Lévi-Strauss.

As summarized in the chapters on "Language and Kinship" in the *Anthropologie structurale,* Lévi-Strauss's image of culture can be expressed, quite literally, as a syntax. Through our understanding of this syntax particular rites, processes of biological and economic exchange, myths and classifications as they are set forth in native speech may be analyzed into "phonemes" of human behavior. This analysis will disclose the true interrelations of otherwise disparate or even contradictory elements, for like structural linguistics Lévi-Strauss's anthropology regards as axiomatic the belief that each element of social and psychological life has meaning only in relation to the underlying system. If we lack knowledge of that system, the particular signs, however graphic, will remain mute.

Speaking to the Conference of Anthropologists and Linguists held at the University of Indiana in 1952, Lévi-Strauss evoked the ideal of a future "science of man and of the human spirit" in which both disciplines would merge. Since then he has gone farther, and it is hardly an exaggeration to say that he regards all culture as a code of significant communication and all social processes as a grammar. According to Lévi-Strauss, only this approach can deal adequately with the question asked in each of his major works: how do we distinguish between nature and culture, how does man conceive of his identity in respect of the natural world and of the social group? (pp. 240-42)

Increasingly, the thought of Lévi-Strauss can be understood as part of that revaluation of the nature of language and symbolism whose antecedents may be traced to Vico and Leibniz, but whose most radical effects have been modern. No less than Wittgenstein's *Tractatus, La Pensée sauvage* and *Le Cru et le cuit* infer that man's place in reality is a matter of syntax, of the ordering of propositions. No less than Jung, Lévi-Strauss's studies of magic and myth, of totemism and *logique concrète,* affirm that symbolic representations, legends, image-patterns, are means of storing and conceptualizing knowledge, that mental processes are collective because they reproduce fundamental structural identities. (p. 243)

Since *Tristes tropiques* (1955), if not before, Lévi-Strauss has done little to mask the general philosophic and sociological implications of his technical pursuits. He knows that he is arguing a general theory of history and society, that his specific analyses of tribal customs or linguistic habits carry an exponential factor. Of late, as if by some instinct of inevitable rivalry, he has challenged Sartre and the relevance of the existentialist dialectic. This may, in part, reflect the circumstances of contemporary French intellectual life. More pervasive has been Lévi-Strauss's concern to delimit his own thought from that of the two principal architects of rational mythology, Marx and Freud. His work is in frequent self-conscious dialogue with theirs. (p. 244)

In the *Anthropologie structurale,* Lévi-Strauss cites Marx's well-known remark that the value of gold as repository and medium of wealth is not only a material phenomenon, but that it also has symbolic sources as "solidified light brought up from the nether world," and that Indo-Germanic etymology reveals the links between precious metals and the symbolism of colors. "Thus," says Lévi-Strauss, "it is Marx himself who would have us perceive and define the symbolic systems which simultaneously underlie language and man's relations to the world." But he goes on to suggest, and this is the crux, that Marxism itself is only a partial case of a more general theory of economic and linguistic information and exchange-relations. This theory will be the framework of a truly rational and comprehensive sociology of man. Not surprisingly, the Marxists have challenged the "totalitarian" claims of Lévi-Strauss's "science of man" and have attacked its irrationalist, "antihistorical" aspects (the general issues are carefully set out in Lucien Sebag's *Marxisme et Structuralisme*).

In *Tristes tropiques,* Lévi-Strauss relates Marxism to the two other main impulses in his own intellectual development and conception of ethnography: geology and psychoanalysis. All three pose the same primary question: "that of the relation between the experienced and the rational (*le sensible et le rationnel*), and the aim pursued is identical: a kind of superrationalism seeking to integrate the former with the latter without sacrificing any of its properties." Which may be a very abstract way of saying that Marxism, geology, and psychoanalysis are aetiologies, attempts to trace the conditions of society, of physical environment, and of human consciousness, to their hidden source. Social relations, terrain, and collective imaginings or linguistic forms are, in turn, the primary coordinates of Lévi-Strauss's *étude de l'homme.*

As Lévi-Strauss advances more deeply into his own theory of symbolism and mental life, the Freudian analogues grow more obtrusive and, probably, irritating. Hence the sporadic but acute critique of psychoanalysis throughout the *Anthropologie structurale,* the argument that Freudian therapy, particularly in its American setting, does not lead to a treatment of neurotic disturbance but to "a reorganization of the universe of the patient in terms of psychoanalytic interpretations." Hence also, one may suppose, Lévi-Strauss's determination to appropriate the Oedipus motif to a much larger context than that put forward by Freud. In Lévi-Strauss's ethnic-linguistic decoding of the legend, and of its many analogues among the North American Indians, the primary meaning points to the immense intellectual and psychological problem faced by a society which professes to believe in the autochthonous creation of man when it has to deal with the recognition of the bisexual nature of human generation. The Oedipus motif does not embody individual neurosis, but a collective attempt to regroup reality in response to fresh and perplexing insights. Again, as in the case of Marxism, the Freudian theory of consciousness emerges as a valuable, but essentially specialized and preliminary chapter in a larger anthropology.

How does *Le Cru et le cuit* fit into this powerful construct? It is a detailed, highly technical analysis of certain motifs in the mythology of the Indians of the Amazon, more exactly, in the creation myths of the Bororo and Ge peoples. The first volume is the start of a projected series and deals with one sub-topic of the larger binary unit: nature/culture. This sub-topic is the discrimination between raw and cooked foods as reflected in Indian myths and practices. Starting with one Bororo "keymyth," Lévi-Strauss analyses significant elements in 187 Amazonian legends and folk-tales; by means of complex geographical, linguistic, and topical matrices, he shows that these myths are ultimately interrelated or congruent. The argument leads to the proposition that the discovery of cooking has profoundly altered man's conception of the relationship between heaven and earth.

Before the mastering of fire, man placed meat on a stone to be warmed by the rays of the sun. This habit brought heaven and earth, man and the sun into intimate juxtaposition. The discovery of cooking literally set back the sphere of the gods and of the sun from the habitat of man. It also separated man

from the great world of animals who eat their food raw. It is thus an immensely important step in the metaphysical, ecological, psychic severance of the genus *Homo sapiens* from his cosmic and organic surroundings. That severance (there are definite echoes from Freud's *Beyond the Pleasure Principle* and *Civilization and its Discontents*) leads to the differentiation and strenuous confrontation between the natural and cultural stages of human development.

But the design of the book reaches beyond even this large theme. To what Lévi-Strauss defines as the "primary code" of human language and the "secondary code" of myths, *Le Cru et le cuit* aims to add "a tertiary code, designed to ensure that myths can be reciprocally translated. This is why it would not be erroneous to regard this book itself as a myth: in some manner, the myth of mythology." (pp. 245-47)

Lévi-Strauss is seeking a science of mythology, a grammar of symbolic constructs and associations allowing the anthropologist to relate different myths as the structural linguist relates phonemes and language systems. Once the code of myths is deciphered and is seen to have its own logic and translatability, its own grid of values and interchangeable significants, the anthropologist will have a tool of great power with which to attack problems of human ecology, of ethnic and linguistic groupings, of cultural diffusion. Above all, he may gain insight into mental processes and strata of consciousness which preserve indices (the fossils or radioactive elements of the palaeontologist and geologist) of the supreme event in man's history—the transition from a primarily instinctual, perhaps pre-linguistic condition to the life of consciousness and individualized self-awareness. This, and the flowering of human genius and "concrete logic" during the neolithic era are, for Lévi-Strauss, realities of history far more important than the brief adjunct of turmoil and political cannibalism of the past 3000 years. (p. 247)

Philosophically and methodologically, Lévi-Strauss's approach is rigorously deterministic. If there is law in the world of the physical sciences, then there is one in that of mental processes and language. In the *Anthropologie structurale,* Lévi-Strauss presages a time when individual thought and conduct will be seen as momentary modes or enactments "of those universal laws which are the substance of the human unconscious" (*des lois universelles en quoi consiste l'activité inconsciente de l'esprit*). Similarly, *Le Cru et le cuit* concludes with the suggestion of a simultaneous, reciprocal interaction between the genesis of myths in the human mind and the creation by these myths of a world-image already pre-determined (one might say "programmed") by the specific structure of human mentality. If human life is, basically, a highly developed form of cybernetics, the nature of the information processed, of the feedback and of the code, will depend on the particular psychosomatic construct of the mental unit. . . .

Once more, the substance and empirical solidity of Lévi-Strauss's case can be judged only by the qualified anthropologist (is he right about this or that aspect of Bororo life and language?). But the general implications are wide-ranging. This is particularly true of the first thirty pages of *Le Cru et le cuit,* entitled "Ouverture." They constitute the richest, most difficult piece of writing Lévi-Strauss has produced so far. It is not easy to think of any text as tightly meshed, as bristling with suggestion and fine intricacy of argument since the *Tractatus.* (p. 248)

Some of the difficulty seems gratuitous. There is hardly a proposition in these opening pages which is not qualified or illustrated by reference to mathematics, histology, optics, or molecular chemistry. Often a single simile conjoins several allusions to different scientific concepts. Looked at closely, however, a good many of the scientific notions invoked are elementary or vaguely pretentious. How much mathematics does Lévi-Strauss really know or need to know? But this constant use of mathematical and scientific notations points to a much larger and more urgent motif. In "Ouverture" Lévi-Strauss is articulating a radical distrust of language. A theme which has been latent in much of his work now comes to the fore: set against the pure syntax and tautological efficiencies of mathematics, of symbolic logic, and of scientific formulas, traditional discourse is no longer a predominant or wholly satisfactory medium. By universalizing structural linguistics, Lévi-Strauss is, in fact, diminishing the unique genius and central authority of common speech. As storehouses and conveyors (the vacuum tube and the electronic impulse) of felt life and human conjecture, myths embrace words but go beyond them toward a more supple, inventive, universal syntax.

Yet even they fall short of the "supreme mystery among the sciences of man" which is music. That arresting formula concludes a dazzling rhetorical flight in which Lévi-Strauss contends that "to think mythologically" is to think musically. Wagner has proved the quintessential kinship of myth and musical statement. Among all languages, only music "unites the contrary attributes of being both intelligible and untranslatable." It is, moreover, intelligible to all—a fact which makes "the creator of music a being similar to the gods."

In consequence, *Le Cru et le cuit* is given the formal structure of a piece of music: overture, theme and variations, sonata, fugue, three-part invention, rustic symphony in three movements. The conceit is not new: one finds it in Baudelaire's theory of "correspondance" (to which Lévi-Strauss implicitly refers), in Mallarmé, and in Broch's *Death of Virgil,* a novel divided in analogy with the changes of mood and rhythm in a string quartet. Lévi-Strauss does little, moreover, to enforce the musical mimesis. It remains a rather labored *jeu d'esprit.* But the underlying concept has a deep fascination. The idea that music and myth are akin, that they build shapes of being more universal, more numinous than speech, haunts the Western imagination. It is incarnate, as Elizabeth Sewell has shown, in the figure of Orpheus. He is myth himself and master of life through his power to create harmony amid the inertness of primal silence or the ferocity of discord (the fierce beasts pause and listen). . . . In its celebration of music and mathematics, in its proud obscurity and claim to be itself a myth unfolding, a song of the mind, *Le Cru et le cuit* is, in the literal sense, an Orphic book. (pp. 249-50)

Le Cru et le cuit is work in progress, and it would be fatuous to pass any general judgment on the complex ensemble of Lévi-Strauss's achievement to this date. That it is one of the most original and intellectually exciting of the present age seems undeniable. No one seriously interested in language or literature, in sociology or psychology, can ignore it. At the same time, this newest book exhibits to a disturbing degree characteristics latent in Lévi-Strauss's work, certainly since the early 1950's. It is prolix, often arbitrary, and maddeningly precious (a technical discussion of the relations between Amazonian myths and the zodiac is entitled *"L'Astronomie bien tempérée"*). The argument is decked out with an apparatus of pseudomathematical notations which appears to carry more weight and relevance than it actually does. At times, the hard astringent scruple of Lévi-Strauss's best style yields to an odd,

post-romantic lyricism. . . . It is as if the prophet were pausing to draw his mantle close. . . .

Perhaps this is both the genius and the danger of the enterprise. It is not, primarily, as anthropology or ethnography that this fascinating body of work may come to be judged and valued, but as extended poetic metaphor. Like so much in Marx and Freud, the achievement of Lévi-Strauss may endure, to use a term from *La Pensée sauvage,* as part of "the mythology of our time." It is too early to tell; *Le Cru et le cuit* ends with a catalogue of myths, not with a coda. (p. 250)

George Steiner, "Orpheus with His Myths: Claude Lévi-Strauss," in his Language and Silence: Essays on Language, Literature, and the Inhuman, *Atheneum Publishers, 1967, pp. 239-50.*

EUGENIO DONATO

[*The essay from which the following excerpt is taken was originally presented in a slightly different form at the symposium entitled "The Languages of Criticism and the Sciences of Man" during the week of October 18-21, 1966, at Johns Hopkins University.*]

The works of Lévi-Strauss and Lacan have taken the place of the works of Sartre and Merleau-Ponty, and it is toward them that marginal disciplines, such as literary criticism, are turning in search of a methodological guide; in the same way as, a few years ago, they turned toward phenomenology and existentialism. (p. 89)

We may today be able to proceed without Sartre and Merleau-Ponty, yet without them I believe it would be impossible to understand the general acceptance that structuralism has had. Indeed, in spite of the divergences that may exist between, for instance, the anthropological theories of a Lévi-Strauss and the Freudian readings of a Lacan, one of the few undisputed points of agreement between them would be their common denunciation of the notion of subject that had dominated phenomenological thought in general, and the works of Sartre and Merleau-Ponty in particular. (pp. 89-90)

Lévi-Strauss's statement in *Tristes tropiques,* dismissing phenomenology and existentialism, provides us with one of the most lucid explanations for such an avowed hostility to the notion of subject:

Phenomenology I found unacceptable, in so far as it postulated a continuity between experience and reality. That the latter enveloped and explained the former I was quite willing to agree, but I had learnt from my three mistresses [Freud, Marx, Geology] that there is no continuity in the passage between the two and that to reach reality we must first repudiate experience, even though we may later reintegrate it in an objective synthesis in which sentimentality plays no part. As for the trend of thought which was to find fulfilment in existentialism, it seemed to me to be the exact opposite of true thought, by reason of its indulgent attitude towards the illusions of subjectivity. To promote private preoccupations to the rank of philosophical problems is dangerous, and may end in a kind of shop-girl's philosophy—excusable as an element in teaching procedure, but perilous in the extreme if it leads the philosopher to turn his back on his mission. That mission [which he holds only until science is strong enough to take over from philosophy] is to understand Being in relation to itself, and not in relation to one-self. Phenomenology and existentialism did not abolish metaphysics: they merely introduced new ways of finding alibis for metaphysics.

The end of Lévi-Strauss's statement concerning the abolishment of metaphysics gives us implicitly the philosophical tenor that anthropology, psychoanalysis, and linguistics have, since their scientific project is seen as the only alternative to a specific philosophical tradition and the only way of providing a radical critique of it. (p. 90)

In 1945 Lévi-Strauss in an article entitled **"L'Analyse structurale en linguistique et en anthropologie"** advocated the use of models taken from structural phonetics to the description of the human phenomenon and in that particular case to kinship systems. This article contained in a nutshell the great developments of the elementary structure of kinships and delineated the main lines of a system that was to develop in a linear fashion from *Les Structures élémentaires de la parenté* to *Le Cru et le cuit*. The problem he faced was twofold for it implied on the one hand the Saussurian distinction between signifier and signified and on the other hand the more explicit reference to phonetics. The simultaneous translation of these linguistic categories to a non-linguistic domain cannot but raise some methodological problems.

The phonetical dimension of language exists at a different level from the one in which words are apprehended as distinct units to which Saussure's analysis applies. The two orders, even if hierarchically subordinated, are discontinuous and the laws that govern each one of them are quite different.

An isolated phoneme by its very nature cannot exist in a relationship of sign. From that point of view it does not fall within the division of signifier and signified, but is only a consequence of its corresponding to a certain *découpage* of the former. Could the same be said of a kinship term? The question is rhetorical. To apply to the study of kinship systems patterns derived from structural phonetics—and we must keep in mind that when Lévi-Strauss in his early works speaks of linguistics his reference is usually to the works of Jakobson in particular and to those of the school of Prague in general—implies two distinct operations which have rather different consequences. Once a kinship term is *reduced* to the status of a phoneme then one may go and search for rules of combination which remain constant in different systems and thus arrive at certain laws which could be said to be *similar* to those that prevail in phonetics. At this level the relationship of the linguist's enterprise and that of the ethnologist is purely analogical. However, as we suggested, this analogy is based on the first operation—namely, that which reduces the status of the kinship term to that of a phoneme—the status of which is more ambiguous and the consequences more radical.

The importance of the linguistic theory and of Saussure's treatment of the linguistic sign was that they permitted the introduction of the notion of discontinuity, which Lévi-Strauss claims to be essential for the rational understanding of any given phenomena. The value of Saussure's division of the linguistic sign into signifier and signified lies, I believe, within the unbridgeable gap that exists between the two orders. (pp. 92-3)

If we were to look for a brief moment at, say, [Lévi-Strauss's] treatment of kinship systems, in spite of his own vehement

statements there is nothing in them that is quite similar to a signifier or a signified, and his treatment is not a simple, mechanical application of a linguistic model. What we do find, however, is his distinguishing within his subject matter two distinct orders. One in which his object of study is apprehended as its own end, governed by its own laws constituting it a system, and the other order, namely, that through which an individual enters, perceives, and understands the system. The two are discontinuous and the anthropologist's task is to study the former and to discard the latter. The distinction between the two orders becomes even more apparent if one turns to problems of primitive classification, ritual, or myth, and it is in part this latter development which underscores the fact that what we are witnessing in a work such as that of Lévi-Strauss is not a simple application of a linguistic model but the use of Saussure's formula as what one may call, for want of a better term, an epistemological operator. It is the possibility of maintaining the discontinuity between the order of the signifier and the order of the signified that permits Lévi-Strauss to avoid dealing with the problem of an individual subject and makes for the extreme rigor of his work. Others are not so fortunate. Strangely enough, it is language that does not lend itself to such an absolute separation between the two orders. It is, of course, true that the Saussurian distinction permitted the methodological success of structural phonetics; yet we cannot be completely sure that even the phonetic level of language can be understood independently from all semantic considerations. Even if this were so, it is far from exhausting the linguistic phenomenon. The relationship that the order of the signifier maintains to the order of the signified, of words to their semantic content, or more simply stated, of words to things, is a paradoxical one, for it is a relationship that has to be defined simultaneously by two propositions which are contradictory: the word *is* the thing; the word is identical to that which it represents, and the space between the two is continuous. Yet, words are different from things, words do not merely represent things; the two orders are discontinuous, their relationship is one of difference. It is difficult to think of a better statement of this paradox than Mallarmé's famous phrase, rose "absente de tous bouquets." And as some critics, such as Barthes, have pointed out, it is this very paradox which constitutes in a way the essence of literature, since language is always communication, yet at the same time, in as much as it states its linguistic nature, it cannot but denounce its instrumental nature. Literature would be, and a poet such as Mallarmé would tend to confirm this, difference denouncing identity. (pp. 93-4)

It should be possible to see, for literature, both the necessity and the dilemma of an enterprise such as that of Derrida, in as much as language in its being is difference, yet it cannot escape the tyranny of the linguistic sign; that is to say, identity and presence. It has the constant and interminable task of demystifying itself, but it can only do so from a position which it can never occupy. Grammatology, as the science of a language from which presence is banished, is a project which can never be accomplished yet one which has to be stated, since it is only from that virtual position of a future perfect that one can denounce the inevitable residue of metaphysical presence that language carries within itself. The nature of Derrida's enterprise shows how the literary act is at the same time always new and necessary yet inessential and derivative, since it is always parasitically dependent on a previous position.

Derrida's enterprise also reveals within our modern context the impossibility of drawing an essential line between literature and criticism. Literature can only be a denunciation of literature and is not therefore different in essence from criticism. Criticism, in as much as it is a denunciation of literature, is, itself, nothing but literature. Henceforth the distinction between the two types of discourse is blurred, and instead what we have is language and the single problematic it imposes, namely, that of interpretation. Something no doubt which we should have known since Nietzsche and Freud, but which we are barely beginning to understand. (pp. 95-6)

It is by the name we give others that in the last analysis we identify ourselves, and at this juncture it is difficult not to mention the name of Freud, who was the first one to see that interpretation was not normative but, at best, that it uncovers a number of phantasms which are themselves already interpretations. The analytical dialogue between two subjects, through the establishment of those elusive relations which are transference and countertransference, is open ended. If analysis is interminable, if it never uncovers a founding origin, it is perhaps because analysis has carried to its extreme conclusion the implacable logic of interpretation. After Freud we must all come to recognize that, to use a formula coined by Jean Wahl, "Nous sommes tous malades d'interpretation."

To return to our original statement of Lévi-Strauss, his reproach to phenomenology stemmed in part from postponing forever the project of a science and, in the last analysis, making it perhaps impossible. Science with respect to interpretation might be only a Pascalian *divertissement*. Yet the possibility of its existence is well worth considering, if only to give us a brief breathing space from the heavy demands of interpretation. As Foucault has shown in his *Les Mots et les choses,* analysis and interpretation are only two valid approaches to language. These two modes co-exist yet are fundamentally opposed to each other. If interpretation plays on the gap resulting from the interjection of the subject, analysis requires the elimination of that subject as a necessary prerequisite to the study of the formal properties which condition the unfolding of any particular type of discourse. More specifically for literature, as Barthes has eloquently argued, a science of literature hinges upon the possibility of being able to treat literary works as myth. The word myth may here be understood with the precise meaning that Lévi-Strauss gives it, namely, a type of discourse from which the subject of the enunciation has been eliminated. Whether such a science of literature will ever be possible remains to be seen.

I should like to finish by mentioning the paradox offered to us by such works as *Le Cru et le cuit* of Lévi-Strauss. Successful literary works seem to have the property either of indicting the ideology which provoked them in the first place, or else of achieving what would seem ideologically impossible; and to me a work such as *Le Cru et le cuit* falls into the latter category. It offers itself as an analytical study of South American myths and the material lends itself to the scientific treatment that Lévi-Strauss imposes upon it. The author succeeds by a set of transformations in showing the unity of the particular discourse constituted by South American myths. So well does he describe the laws of the grammar that govern them that it is not inconceivable for a reader to write himself what would qualify as a South American myth. Yet as Lévi-Strauss points out, his treatment of those myths is nothing but another version of those myths. It is as if through the language that he lends them the myths interpret themselves. I believe that it is impossible in a work such as *Le Cru et le cuit* to separate myth and literature, science and interpretation, and analysis and criticism, and I believe that it is in the attempt to understand such works that the future of literary criticism lies. (pp. 96-7)

Eugenio Donato, "The Two Languages of Criticism," in The Languages of Criticism and the Sciences of Man: The Structuralist Controversy, *edited by Richard Macksey and Eugenio Donato, The Johns Hopkins University Press, 1970, pp. 89-97.*

JAMES A. BOON

'Neologics' is one man's name for a portion of Lévi-Strauss' game—namely, Theodore A. Cheney's in 'The Power of Irrelevant Thinking.' . . . Cheney's Neologics has to do with the preverbal thought of our forefathers in which 'any particular experience was stored as a memory of what it sounded like, what it smelled like, how old it was, what season it happened, how hairy it was, how soft, how hard, etc.' Derived from the supposition that man still cross-files on 'sensory barbs,' the doctrine is as simple as it is total:

> Neological theory holds that there is an inter-relatedness about the world which means that almost anything may turn out to be relevant to something else, if looked at in a different light. . . .

As might be expected, this doctrine fathers a method. When confronted with a traditionally logical impasse, Operational Neologics advocates judgment suspension, silence and soliloquy, distraction, and irrelevance: one 'uses peripheral reading, environmental scanning, analogies, metaphorical play and accidents in the hope that at least one will turn out to be relevant.' . . . The relevance of the above ideas . . . to Lévi-Strauss is clear, in light of one lesson implicit in all his works: 'One understands the thought of savages neither by mere introspection nor by mere observation, but by attempting to think as they think and with their material.' . . . And that Neological, preverbal, sensory-barb cross-filing is exactly the means of organizing that Lévi-Strauss finds in preliterate *bricoleurs,* that . . . [can be] found in Mallarmé, and that was evidenced in [Baudelaire's] 'Les Chats.' (pp. (pp. 209-10)

Not only is Lévi-Strauss stimulated by myth, poetry, and virtually all cultural productions to reason 'irrelevantly,' he induces us to do likewise: 'Faced with the challenge of a new point of view one is suddenly able to see the familiar in quite a different way and to understand something which was previously invisible.' . . . Furthermore, this non-Academic outlook—absolutely contrary to 'linear' *raison*—typifies the whole 'structuralist movement.' . . . Perhaps France's ingrained Academic and encyclopedic traditions of *raison* and *bon sens* afford a solid foundation for negative reactions such as Symbolism and structuralism (but then stifle their *'fleuraison'*?). Be that as it may, this common interest in 'preposterous classifications' is partly responsible for the fact that many different sorts of current scholars in France have received the label 'structuralist'.

In addition to recognizing that his own methods are inspired by mythic logic, Lévi-Strauss praises previous thinkers who had similar inclinations. For example, Bergson and Rousseau seem to have penetrated 'the psychological foundations of exotic institutions . . . by a process of internalization, i.e., by trying on themselves modes of thought taken from elsewhere or simply imagined.' . . . Neologics! Thus, while certain periods or groups may tend more toward Symbolist-structuralist patterns of conceptualization, the latter are always potential: '. . . every human mind is a locus of virtual experience where what goes on in the minds of men, however remote they may be, can be investigated.' . . . (pp. 210-11)

[One can see throughout both Symbolism and structuralism] how the self is 'made manifest in "experience"' and how character is constituted more by language than the facts of experience. . . . From any idealist viewpoint this language-experience exists in and of the subject; for scholars with structuralist tendencies 'the subject is an activity, not a thing. . . . The subject produces itself by reflecting on itself, but when it is engaged on some other object it has no being apart from the activity of being so engaged.' . . . The ultimate denial of any possibility for a science of the subject stems from the feeling that 'the subject cannot be the object of science because it is its subject.' . . . Yet, once the self is equated with processes of conceptualizing experience, there is still an open range of idealist attitudes that can be assumed. Both Symbolists and myth-makers ground 'reality'-as-conceived in the structure of the transformations (correspondences) among systems in orders arranged analogously. If the transformations are regarded as *fixed* and permanently embedded in the person of the creator (to which the world of experience is subordinated), what results is the narcissism such as that set forth in novelist Maurice Barrès' early work *Le Culte du Moi.* It is a somewhat different case when Lehmann speaks of the Symbolists' 'vulgar solipsism': 'At that level "idealism" meant simply the inalienable right to look on the world in whatever way one pleased; or to invent worlds on an equal with the "common sense world".' . . . From this vantage point any tendencies to consider, for example, Baudelaire's systems of correspondences fixed and 'natural' appear solipsistic. In the eyes of sympathizers Baudelaire would escape this charge through his assumption of a different realm which transcends the forest of symbols suggesting it. Both of these strains of idealism (narcissism and solipsism) would fall into Robert Champigny's first definition of Symbolism in which there is 'a symbolic usage of language in which the first signified is material and the second signified is spritual.' . . . (pp. 213-14)

The binary opposition of the distinctive feature of these first two idealisms generates a second variety: idealisms of *non-fixed* systems of analogies. Mallarmé's arbitrarily, but consistently, constructed codes of symbols demonstrate this variety, as do the analogously structured native myths—whether consciously (analytically?) or not—from the analyzer's viewpoint. (Analogies are always fixed from a viewpoint within the poemcode or myth-code—i.e. from a non-comparative viewpoint.) Champigny distinguishes this kind from the others by pointing out the absence of any hierarchical aspect:

> Finally let us suppose that the relation between the signifieds be rendered symmetrical. One will thus have texts which are more or less clearly polysemic, wherein the themes will not each constitute an autonomous domain of meaning but will inform themselves one to the other in order to compose the global meaning. . . .
>
> (p. 214)

If one then takes this rejection of an assumed hierarchy in any particular set of transformable systems and applies it to all systems—language especially—with equal enthusiasm, the resulting brand of 'idealism' is what has been deemed, among other things, the 'new humanism.' Take for example, Ernst Cassirer:

A 'humanistic philosophy of culture' is needed . . . to do justice to man and his freedom. The whole gamut of cultural phenomena bears witness to man's 'will to formations.' 'What man achieves is the objectification, the intuition of himself, in and through the theoretical, aesthetic, and ethical form which he gives to his existence. This is exhibited even in the very first promptings of human speech and it is unfolded and developed in rich and many-sided forms in poetry, in the fine arts, in religious consciousness, in philosophical concepts.' . . .

Thus, if one remains skeptical over Lévi-Strauss' efforts to be moving toward a demonstration of final structures of the human *esprit,* he could still greet his work as this sort of humanism. Far from brandishing a bland solipsism, Lévi-Strauss in light of cross-cultural evidence determines to make of human productions Symbolist poems and of the producers poets, himself not excluded. (p. 215)

Lévi-Strauss amasses evidence that what we are calling a Symbolist mode of encoding the *other* is universal in systems of meaning. And the general moral feeling that results is somewhat as follows: while we may never confront the other directly (substantively) in communicable terms, nevertheless, thanks to the human 'texts' that abound (which are, of course, always distorted by any subject collecting them), we at least have the fraternal comfort of knowing *they* are 'out there' translating; and we can too. Through his portrayal of this anthropological moral stance, through his taking possession 'of that untamed [*sauvage*] region of himself, unincorporated in his own culture, through which he communicates with other cultures,' . . . Lévi-Strauss has come to influence French intellectual life in general. For the suggestion that the stark relativity of cross-cultural experience eventually fulfills the individual by disaggregating his cultural self-centeredness complements a general thread of French moral thought. This notion of the individual as a potential locus of inter-communication in turn reflects a notion of life itself:

> Just as with discourse things, signs, and persons intertwine themselves in a single continuous fabric whose internal logic we unravel; so it is with life. . . .

The striking feature of Lévi-Strauss' anthropology is that this Symbolist conception of existence does not justify withdrawing from the world, but engaging in the world, the experience of which engendered the conception in the first place. And Lévi-Strauss comes to bear on his age:

> Faced with the two temptations of condemning things which are offensive to him emotionally or of denying differences which are beyond his intellectual grasp, modern man has launched out on countless lines of philosophical and sociological speculation in a vain attempt to achieve a compromise between these two contradictory poles, and to account for the diversity of cultures while seeking, at the same time, to eradicate what still shocks and offends him in that diversity. . . .

It is against the above background that his structural approach to cultural phenomena has been accorded in France the rank of an '-ism.' (pp. 216-17)

James A. Boon, "Interpretations and Conclusion," in his From Symbolism to Structuralism: Lévi-Strauss in a Literary Tradition, *Basil Blackwell, 1972, pp. 209-31.**

EDMUND LEACH

[Scholars] who call themselves social anthropologists are of two kinds. The prototype of the first was Sir James Frazer (1854-1941), author of *The Golden Bough*. He was a man of monumental learning who had no first-hand acquaintance with the lives of the primitive peoples about whom he wrote. He hoped to discover fundamental truths about the nature of human psychology by comparing the details of human culture on a world wide scale. The prototype of the second was Bronislaw Malinowski (1884-1942), born in Poland but naturalized an Englishman, who spent most of his academic life analyzing the results of research which he himself had personally conducted over a period of four years in a single small village in far off Melanesia. His aim was to show how this exotic community "functioned" as a social system and how its individual members passed through their lives from the cradle to the grave. He was more interested in the differences between human cultures than in their over-all similarity.

Most of those who at present call themselves social anthropologists in either Britain or the United States claim to be "functionalists"; broadly speaking they are anthropologists in the style and tradition of Malinowski. In contrast, Claude Lévi-Strauss is a social anthropologist in the tradition though not in the style of Frazer. His ultimate concern is to establish facts which are true about "the human mind" rather than about the organization of any particular society or class of societies. The difference is fundamental. (pp. 1-2)

From the very start [Lévi-Strauss] has been a straight scholar-intellectual. Apart from some engaging photographs of naked Amazonian ladies tucked in at the end of *Tristes Tropiques* (1955), he has refrained from popularizing gimmicks of the kind which led Malinowski to entitle one of his Trobriand monographs *The Sexual Life of Savages*. By Malinowski standards Lévi-Strauss' field research is of only moderate quality. The outstanding characteristic of his writing, whether in French or in English, is that it is difficult to understand; his sociological theories combine baffling complexity with overwhelming erudition. Some readers even suspect that they are being treated to a confidence trick. Even now, despite his immense prestige, the critics among his professional colleagues still greatly outnumber his disciples. Yet his academic importance is unquestioned. Lévi-Strauss is admired not so much for the novelty of his ideas as for the bold originality with which he seeks to apply them. He has suggested new ways of looking at familiar facts; it is the method that is interesting rather than the practical consequences of the use to which it has been put. (pp. 2-3)

Lévi-Strauss' quest is to establish facts which are universally true of the "human mind" (*esprit humain*). What is universally true must be natural, but this is paradoxical because he starts out with the assumption that what distinguishes the human being from the man-animal is the distinction between culture and nature—i.e., that the humanity of man is that which is non-natural. Again and again in Lévi-Strauss' writings we keep coming back to this point: the problem is not merely "in what way is culture (as an attribute of humanity) distinguishable from nature (as an attribute of man)?" but also "in what way is the culture of *Homo sapiens* inseparable from the nature of humanity?"

Lévi-Strauss takes over from Freud the idea that it is meaningful to talk about human beings' having an Unconscious as well as a Consciousness; and, for Lévi-Strauss as for Freud, the unconscious Id is natural, the conscious Ego is cultural. When Lévi-Strauss tries to reach into the "human mind" he is grasping at the structural aspects of the Unconscious. But Lévi-Strauss' approach is through linguistics rather than through psychology. The linguistic model which Lévi-Strauss employs is now largely out of date. Present-day theoreticians in the field of structural linguistics have come to recognize that the deep-level process of pattern generation and pattern recognition that is entailed by the human capacity to attach complex semantic significance to speech utterances must depend on mechanisms of much greater complexity than is suggested by the digital computer model which underlies the Jakobson-Lévi-Strauss theories. . . . I am ready to concede that the structures which [Lévi-Strauss] displays are products of an unconscious mental process, but I can see no reason to believe that they are human universals. Bereft of Lévi-Strauss' resourceful special pleading they appear to be local, functionally determined attributes of particular individuals or of particular cultural groups. . . . However, as Yvan Simonis has observed, although Lévi-Strauss originally set out to display the structure of the "human mind," he has ended up by telling us something about the structure of aesthetic perception. (pp. 125-27)

[Myth] and music (and dreaming) have certain elements in common; they are, says Lévi-Strauss, "machines for the suppression of time" . . . ; the last movement of a symphony is presupposed by its beginning just as the end of a myth is already implicit where it began. The repetitions and thematic variations of a musical score produce responses in the listener which depend in some way on his physiological rhythms; and, in like measure (asserts Lévi-Strauss), the repetitions and thematic variations of myth play upon physiological characters of the human brain to produce emotional as well as purely intellectual effects. (p. 129)

The massive volumes of *Mythologiques* [published in the United States as *Mythologies: An Introduction to a Science of Mythology*] are designed to exhibit the logical mechanisms and concealed ambiguities which evoke these emotional responses, and the thesis is that when we really get down to the roots of the matter the interdependence of logical structure and emotional response is much the same everywhere—for the nature of man is everywhere the same.

Of course, there must be a sense in which Lévi-Strauss is right, and yet reductionism of this degree of comprehensiveness seems to defeat its own ends. When, in the early days of psychoanalysis, the orthodox Freudians asserted as dogma the universality of the Oedipus complex, the Oedipus complex as such became devoid of all analytical value. *All* evidence, no matter how contradictory it might appear, was forced into the predetermined mold. And the same kind of thing seems to be happening to Lévi-Strauss. His writings display an increasing tendency to assert *as dogma* that his discoveries relate to facts which are *universal* characteristics of the unconscious process of human thought. At first this was simply a matter of generalizing from his primary schema of binary oppositions and mediating middle terms (which is little more than the Hegelian triad of thesis, antithesis, synthesis), but lately the whole system seems to have developed into a self-fulfilling prophecy which is incapable of test because, by definition, it cannot be disproved. (pp. 130-31)

The genuinely valuable part of Lévi-Strauss' contribution, in my view, is not the formalistic search for binary oppositions and their multiple permutations and combinations but rather the truly poetic range of associations which he brings to bear in the course of his analysis: in Lévi-Strauss' hands complexity becomes revealing instead of confusing. (pp. 131-32)

Edmund Leach, in his Claude Lévi-Strauss, *revised edition, The Viking Press, 1974, 146 p.*

RENÉ GIRARD

[*The essay from which the following excerpt is taken was originally published under the title "Differentiation and Undifferentiation in Levi-Strauss and Current Critical Theory" in* Contemporary Literature, *Summer 1976.*]

The conclusion of Claude Lévi-Strauss's *L'Homme nu,* entitled "Finale," asserts that myth embodies a principle of differentiation identical with language and thought. Ritual, on the other hand, tries to retrieve an *undifferentiated immediacy*. It tries to undo the work of language. Fortunately, Lévi-Strauss adds, this perverse undertaking will never succeed. The "undifferentiated" of ritual can only be made up of objects already differentiated by language and artificially pieced together.

Unlike "immediacy," about which I will speak later, the notion of "undifferentiated" certainly corresponds to part of what goes on in rituals all over the world: promiscuous sexual encounters, the overturning of hierarchies, the supposed metamorphosis of the participants into each other or into monstrous beings, etc. One cannot agree, however, that rituals are committed to this "undifferentiated" once and for all. All great traditional interpretations, notably the Hindu and the Chinese, attribute to ritual the end that Lévi-Strauss would reserve to myth alone: differentiation.

Before structuralism, no anthropologist had expressed a different view. Lévi-Strauss would reply that in all the examples that seem to verify my objection, language has been reintroduced and a secondary effect of differentiation has occurred, alien to ritual as such. Yet, there are innumerable instances of ritual differentiation visibly independent from the words that may or may not accompany them. In all *rites de passage,* for instance, the temporary loss of identity, or whatever ordeal the postulant may undergo, fits very well the undifferentiated conception of Lévi-Strauss but only in a first phase that, rather than being an end in itself, is a means, paradoxical no doubt but constantly reasserted, toward the ultimate goal of ritual. This goal is obviously (re)differentiation, because it consists in a new and stable status, a well-defined identity.

The same is true of sacrifice, singled out in *La Pensée sauvage* for a preliminary skirmish against ritual. Frequently, the victim must be carved along rigorously defined lines that correspond to the structural subdivisions of the community. Each piece goes to its own subdivision. Here again, the first phase belongs to the undifferentiated that culminates in the immolation where it turns into its opposite. The communion aspect of sacrifice coincides not with the undifferentiated, which is invariably conflictual, but with the end result, which is the regeneration of differences.

If ritual is no less committed to differentiation than myth, the converse is true: myth is no less involved with the undiffer-

entiated than ritual. . . . [It] is the same involvement; it occurs in the same manner and probably for the same reasons. The undifferentiated presents itself as preliminary to (re)differentiation and often as its prerequisite. The original chaos of the Greeks, the *tohu wa bohu* of Genesis, Noah's flood, the ten plagues of Egypt, and the companions of Ulysses turned into swine by Circe are all examples of mythical undifferentiation.

In order to achieve this undifferentiation, myths, as well as rituals, resort to make-believe. They, too, piece back together entities that, "in reality," are already distinguished by language. Monsters are nothing else. We have a typical variation of this in a myth analyzed in *Le Cru et le cuit.* At the beginning, according to Lévi-Strauss's reading of that myth, living creatures were so numerous and so compressed that they could not yet be distinguished. Later on, one single component is removed and the compactness of the mass is reduced. Interstices appear that make the necessary distinctions possible. Lévi-Strauss has a diagram showing that the space provided by the removal of even a small fragment can be distributed along a continuous line in such a way as to produce a number of separate segments, with no change in the total length of the figure. This myth and others are read by Lévi-Strauss not as differentiated solely, as any text would be, but as differentiation displaying itself. Myth is not simply structured, it is structuralist. It is not a mere product of symbolic thought, it is the process of symbolization made visible as process.

Lévi-Strauss also says that myths are able to think each other as myths. The formula has been most successful but its real meaning is not explained. It cannot mean only that many variations of the same myth are found. In nature, many varieties of the same species are found, many varieties of ants, for instance, but we would not say that these different ants think each other. In order for myths to think each other, it is necessary that each myth, up to a point, think itself as myth. And myths appear to think themselves because they provide the mirror in which they reflect their own process. Since the process is one of pure differentiation, the only appropriate mirror is the undifferentiated. This mirror is identical with the "primordial stuff" the myths are supposed to carve up. It is the presence in myths of the undifferentiated that allows Lévi-Strauss to say that they "think each other as myths."

In myth as well as in ritual, this undifferentiated can only be a *representation*. There is no difference and yet myth and ritual are treated quite differently by Lévi-Strauss. Ritual is severely rebuked for entertaining artificial representations of something language cannot really express. In myth, the same representations are praised, at least implicitly, since we would not even know without them that the myth intends to distinguish certain objects. We must have that first moment when these objects are supposed to be stuck together. In reality the undifferentiated plays the same role everywhere. Is it reasonable to describe the incentive for plunging a postulant into the undifferentiated waters of baptism as "a nostalgia for the immediate"? The postulant will not stay in there forever; he will drown only symbolically in order to reach the shore of a new differentiation.

The facts contradicting Lévi-Strauss are so massive that he cannot disregard them entirely. The combination of the undifferentiated plus differentiation is so commonplace that Lévi-Strauss grudgingly acknowledges its presence but he views it as no less unnatural and perverse than ritual. He explains it by the existence of bastardized myths that are primarily the account of some ritual. They should not influence the theoretical perception of the problem. The truth of the matter is that Lévi-Strauss is going to tortuous extremes of scholasticism to defend his assimilation of myth with differentiation and of ritual with the undifferentiated, but it cannot be done. The two are always present together and their juxtaposition produces the standard profile of both myth and ritual. This profile has been identified and described in various languages and terminologies since time immemorial. To recognize this is to recognize a structural fact of life that Lévi-Strauss has always implicitly denied in his analyses and that he denies explicitly in the "Finale" of his *Mythologiques*. (pp. 155-57)

There are no anthropological reasons to cast myth as the hero and ritual as the villain in a drama of human intelligence. The reverse formula has already been tied, at least up to a point, with equally unsatisfactory results. The reasons for this anthropological supreme court are not anthropological. A major one, of course, is the structuralist commitment to the so-called "model" or "pilot" science of linguistics. Ritual uses language extensively but not exclusively like myth. This really leaves no choice. Since Lévi-Strauss is almost as eager to castigate religion as to extol language, he can assimilate the non-verbal means of ritual to the hard core of religious behavior and kill two ideological birds with the same stone.

There is still another bird from whose back Lévi-Strauss likes to pluck a few feathers once in a while, and it is philosophy. This third *bête noire* is also assimilated to ritual. The definition of ritual as "a nostalgia for the immediate" has a curiously philosophical ring for an anthropologist. One of the reasons could be that it is also Lévi-Strauss's definition of philosophy.

When we read such phrases as "l'immédiateté du vécu," we are inevitably reminded of the philosopher who dominated the French scene during the formative years of Lévi-Strauss: Henri Bergson. If we keep Bergson in mind as we read the "Finale," we cannot fail to discover many more Bergsonian expressions, and they are far from limited to those things Lévi-Strauss detests and assimilates to philosophy and ritual. His references to the structural principle he espouses are also couched in phrases borrowed from that philosopher, such as "discontinuité," "découpage," "schématisme de la pensée," etc. Lévi-Strauss is convinced there is not an ounce of philosophy in him, especially Bergsonian philosophy. We can readily understand the cause of that belief. He and Bergson are literally poles apart. The two poles, however, are those of Bergson's metaphysics. If you turn these poles around, you understand better why the undifferentiated and differentiation mean so much to Lévi-Strauss, why he hates to find them in conjunction. Everything Bergson embraces Lévi-Strauss rejects; everything Bergson rejects Lévi-Strauss embraces. (pp. 157-58)

The similarities between Bergson and Lévi-Strauss are more than an amusing paradox; they reach down to the core of structuralism. The fact that Bergson privileges one pole of the metaphysical dualism and Lévi-Strauss the other makes little difference. The important thing is that, in each case, both reality and the mind have been replaced by a metaphysical principle. These two principles appear closely interrelated but are really independent. Reality's being assimilated to a pure undifferentiation does not suggest in what manner it should be carved. It provides no guidelines to the differentiating principle that operates in the void. Any mode of differentiation is as good or as bad as any other.

When Lévi-Strauss becomes aware of the metaphysical substitutions I have just detected, he attributes them to mythology itself, he views them as a brilliant intuition of mythical thought and the end result is the same. (pp. 159-60)

Following the lead of [Emile Durkheim], Lévi-Strauss shows that much that formerly appeared senseless in primitive cultures really makes sense. The sense is made through binary networks of symbolic conjunctions and disjunctions that can be methodically mapped out. If there is a "manifest destiny" of structuralism, it is to extend as far as possible the area of meaningfulness in the structural sense. In *Le Totémisme aujourd'hui*, Lévi-Strauss reaches the conclusion that the whole problem of totemic institutions is not only wrongly labeled but unreal. The illusion that the so-called totemic cultures do not think like us and need to be set apart rests entirely on ethnocentric fallacies. . . . (pp. 161-62)

Lévi-Strauss speaks of his surprise when he found that Bergson had anticipated his own elegant dissolution of the totemic problem. Such a coincidence, Lévi-Strauss speculates, must come from the very primitiveness of the philosopher's thinking, from an emotional empathy that puts this creature of instinct directly in touch with *la pensée sauvage*. The same intuition can only reappear at the end of the intellectual tunnel, fully articulate this time, in the cold scientific glare of structuralism.

We might have anticipated this miraculous agreement. Focusing as he does upon "la continuité du vécu," Bergson shows little interest in the various ways in which this continuity can be broken. If you bring to his attention something like totemic institutions, he will immediately realize that they are as far from his cherished immediacy as Socratic dialectics or medieval scholasticism. All modes of articulate thought allow this immediacy to slip from their grasp. Bergson will be inclined, therefore, to lump totemism with all the other modes as, of course, Lévi-Strauss also does.

Let us see, now, what happens with an investigator who is not Bergsonian in any form, not even in reverse. As a critic of the ethnocentric fallacy and an initiator of structuralism, Durkheim is especially appropriate. In some respects, his view of totemic names as "emblems" is even more destructive of the problem than that of Lévi-Strauss. At no point, however, does he substitute a metaphysical undifferentiated for the perception of the real world. As a consequence he finds himself asking concrete questions about the so-called undifferentiated. What can it be? What may have caused it? (p. 162)

Because he does not confuse the undifferentiated and differentiation with the two poles of a Bergsonian metaphysics, Durkheim *must* ask himself why primitive thought can have at the same time so many monsters and so many distinctions that are sound. . . . His position avoids both the extreme of the so-called primitive mentality and the other extreme represented by structuralism and its various offspring. Durkheim's position may look at first like a timid compromise between two valorous knights-errant of anthropology who fearlessly radicalize the problematic. In reality, Durkheim's perspective is the only one from which the problem of culture, or the problem of language, or, if you prefer, the problem of symbolic thought, becomes concrete.

Durkheim speaks of an *extremely powerful cause* that must make reality accessible to man and at the same time partly transfigures it; he suggests the same origin for primitive religion and for symbolic thought itself, a volcanic origin that makes reality appear both under aspects that belong to it and under aspects that do not belong to it. This view of the problem may well be the most precious legacy of Durkheim that later developments have obscured and pushed aside.

Lévi-Strauss perceives that the origin of symbolic thought is a legitimate theoretical question. He denies, however, that this question can be concretely investigated. As a proof of this, he mentions the failure of those who tried, the Freud of *Totem and Taboo* and Durkheim himself, who were unable, in the hypotheses they formulated, to divest themselves of the cultural rules and symbolicity for which they were trying to account. These failures are real but they do not mean the undertaking is meaningless. There is a lot to learn, anyway, both from Durkheim's idea of a collective *effervescence* and from Freud's idea of a primordial murder, even if neither idea is an acceptable solution of the problem.

In my view, the achievements of Lévi-Strauss himself make more meaningful a new attempt at solving the same problem. His specific contribution, I believe, lies in these two categories of differentiation and undifferentiation that he has developed but that he cannot fully utilize because he turns them into metaphysical absolutes. (pp. 162-63)

> René Girard, "*Differentiation and Reciprocity in Lévi-Strauss and Contemporary Theory,*" in his "To Double Business Bound": Essays on Literature, Mimesis, and Anthropology, *The Johns Hopkins University Press, 1978, pp. 155-77.*

EDITH KURZWEIL

[In examining the theories of Claude Lévi-Strauss], the following must be kept in mind. First, Lévi-Strauss' attempt to systematize myths—that is, the telling of all myths in every version in relation to its culture—is an ongoing task which is never complete. The basic premise of Lévi-Strauss' approach is contrary to most American systems theories, which tend to deal with observable data and to ignore unconscious structures of mind. Second, the French use of the term "scientific" is not linked to empirical proof in the same way as its American equivalent is. Third, French writers traditionally have brought personal experiences to their interpretations of history. Together, these intellectual habits have generated a highly allusive form of discourse which allows for many divergent interpretations of Lévi-Strauss' original theories.

Lévi-Strauss . . . frequently transforms speculative ideas into facts and past reflections into current assumptions. He justifies the mixing of personal experience with intellectual interpretation by claiming geology, psychoanalysis, and Marxism for his "three mistresses." For example, because Lévi-Strauss the boy had noted how plants grow in different soils, or how residues of different epochs merge within the complex involutions of rocks, Lévi-Strauss the anthropologist speculated that all perceptions are permeated with past experiences, and "continue to exist in the living diversity of a moment . . . commingling space and time." If we too can accept the notion that "unlike the history of the historians, history as the geologist and the psychoanalyst sees it is intended to body forth in time—rather in the manner of a *tableau vivant*—certain fundamental properties of the physical and psychical universe," then we can agree with Lévi-Strauss that history, when recollected, becomes part of the present. This ahistorical (or synchronic) perspective was, of course, unpalatable to the Marxists, especially because Lévi-Strauss thought that "Marxism proceeds in the same way as geology and psychoanalysis. . . . All three show that understanding consists in the reduction of one type

of reality to another; that true reality is never the most obvious of realities . . . because the problem is always due to the relation . . . between reason and sense-perception."

Lévi-Strauss also had a fourth mistress, music, whose influence is evident in *The Raw and the Cooked.* Although he appears to have later deemphasized this influence, he did incorporate the three-dimensional quality of music in his method, by insisting that the many versions of tribal myths could be read like a musical score. *The Raw and the Cooked* and the "Finale" of *L'homme nu* . . . are organized around musical themes.

Once introduced to structural linguistics by Jakobson, Lévi-Strauss began to look at Saussure's study of language as a self-sufficient system that postulates a dynamic relationship between the components of every linguistic sign, that is between language system (*langue*) and individual speech (*parole*), and between sound image (*signifier*) and concept (*signified*). Upon this basic dualism, Lévi-Strauss superimposed Jakobson's model of phonemic analysis, which, in structural linguistics, attempts to prove that the structure of any language always follows a certain binary path of parallel constructions. (pp. 14-15)

Because Lévi-Strauss was intrigued by the way that languages as well as myths of different cultures resembled each other and appeared to be structured in a similar fashion, he attempted to show that they actually are constituted in the same way. At the same time, he had to account for the fact that events belonging to the distant past are told and retold in the present and therefore seem to move back and forth in time. He also had to distinguish *la langue* and *la parole* by the different time dimension of each (synchronic and diachronic). To account for the shifts in time, he added a third dimension—a dimension which required another unit of analysis. He called this new analytical tool the "gross constituent unit," defining it as a meaningful combination of two or more words in a sentence. This constituent unit, which can be a sentence or a part of a sentence, is probably the most controversial component of his theory, because it allegedly overcomes limitations of time to mediate between the past, the present, and the future. Jakobson had postulated binary oppositions between consonants and vowels and between contradictory relationships (e.g., the emotive versus the conative dimension of the speech event) as the basis of his own structural linguistics. Thus, in order to "overcome the inability to connect two kinds of relationships," Lévi-Strauss assumes that in myth, just as in language, contradictory relationships can be perceived as identical as long as they are self-contradictory in a similar way. When applying this method to social phenomena, Lévi-Strauss could not search in the customary manner for the "true" version of a myth; he had instead to analyze every existing version of every myth. First, he had to break down each myth into short sentences and to catalog them; each of these short sentences (constituent units) could produce a functional meaning only when it was combined with other such units into "bundles of relations" that would account for the two-dimensional time-referent, revertible and nonrevertible time, and would constitute the primary elements of most myths. He then proceeded to unravel a myth as if it were an orchestra score, to read it in three-dimensional fashion. . . . (pp. 17-18)

But Lévi-Strauss always stressed that analysis of a myth goes beyond the analysis of its terminology or contents; he focused on discovering the relations which unite all mythologies. These relations became the ultimate objects of his structural analysis. According to Lévi-Strauss, the meaningful and unifying structures of mythology surface through the analysis of myths in the way that unconscious thought emerges into consciousness through psychoanalysis. Hence, the unveiling of the structures becomes a kind of cultural psychoanalysis. At the same time, Lévi-Strauss continually asserted that by discovering the structural "laws" of myth, he would ultimately transform fairy tales into science. Thus, the success of the structuralist enterprise promised to allow for the apotheosis, on a primitive, unconscious level, of everyone's childhood fantasies. (pp. 19-20)

Lévi-Strauss' reading of Freud leans toward the philosophical rather than the clinical. The Oedipus complex, which, as we know, occupies a central position in Freudian theory, emerges as one of Lévi-Strauss' universal structures; and he relied on it to supply at least partial credence to the argument for structuralism. Lévi-Strauss also adapted others of Freud's ideas—defense mechanisms, repression, reaction formation, substitution, and blocking—in order to explain transformations of structures from logical to irrational and from conscious to unconscious thought. But where Freud asked his patients to free-associate in order to uncover traumatic events in their individual pasts, Lévi-Strauss listened to natives retell the traumatic memories of their tribe in well-known myths. (p. 20)

[Whereas] Freud used the symbolic systems of dreams to reconstruct individual history, the structuralist's ambition is to decipher the symbolic systems of myth in order to reconstruct cultural history. To justify this aim, Lévi-Strauss used Freud's fleeting allusion to the "two traumas"—personal and universal myth. In *The Future of an Illusion* Freud states that "a human child cannot successfully complete its development to the civilized stage without passing through a phase of neurosis [the individual's neurotic myth] . . . which is later overcome spontaneously [or through psychoanalysis]. . . . In just the same way, one might assume, humanity as a whole, in its development through the ages, fell into states analogous to the neuroses . . . precipitating processes resembling repression. The residue of these repressionlike processes, which took place in antiquity, has long clung on to civilization. . . . Religion would thus be the universal obsessional neurosis of humanity." (pp. 20-1)

Lévi-Strauss was also inspired by the Freudian psychoanalyst Jacques Lacan, who, in turn, acknowledged how various notions of structural anthropology had enriched his psychoanalysis. The common concern of the two men with unconscious structures—the former with tribal myth and the latter with individual thought—led a few of their followers to cooperate for a brief period. They attempted by using computers to establish the connection between the "constituent units" of myth and the "constituent units" of analysands' dreams. Inevitably, the task failed. Had it succeeded, the emergence of Lévi-Strauss' structures would have proven the scientific claims of structuralism; and the use of computer technology would have furnished it with scientific credentials. As it turned out, Lévi-Strauss' interpretation of Freud seems more literary than scientific. (p. 21)

Sartre was one of the first to attack Lévi-Strauss. To Sartre, who denied the existence of an unconscious, Lévi-Strauss' unconscious mental structures were unthinkable. He also considered Lévi-Strauss' complex method of free association as a methodological tautology which demonstrated the truth of an idea simply by showing its connection to other ideas. Finally, and not least, Sartre attacked from a Marxist position. . . . Sartre was bound to dismiss Lévi-Strauss' rather simplistic interpretation of Marx and the meaning of history, as well as Lévi-Strauss' neglect of individual existence. (pp. 21-2)

Like Marx, Lévi-Strauss assumes that economic production arises from human needs; but whereas Marx argued that culture is conditioned by the economic structure of society, Lévi-Strauss adds the notion that culture emerges from universal unconscious structures. (p. 22)

Although Lévi-Strauss' dialectic "springs directly from the customs and the philosophy of the group . . . [from] whom the individual learns his lesson . . . [from] his belief in guardian spirits . . ." and from the fact that "society as a whole teaches its members that their only hope of salvation, within the established social order, lies in an absurd and despairing attempt to get free from that order," he never touches on Marx's conclusions about the polarization of the classes, the inevitability of revolution, or the withering away of the state. (pp. 22-3)

Lévi-Strauss and Sartre differ in their approach to history. Lévi-Strauss interprets the oral traditions of primitive societies in an ahistorical fashion. For him, history is reconstituted each time a myth is retold or the past is recollected. History, rather than being a series of "objective" events tied to a specific era, exists within an interplay of mental structures that takes place at a specific "moment." By having the past become part of the present, Lévi-Strauss' theory discounts traditional theories of progress or evolution. [Edmund Leach] explains Lévi-Strauss' system well, when he suggests that data stored in human memories can be compared to a very complicated computer that sorts out information according to an "adjustable program."

Whereas Kant, for example, approaches experience in terms of basic *Anschauungen* (kinds of intuition about space, time, and causation) which do not extend to what is behind the phenomena, Lévi-Strauss assumes an as yet unknown structural order which "directs" all social variables. It is an unconscious order, similar to Durkheim's collective unconscious, which appears to be—at least until its final unveiling—some sort of planned disorder. Durkheim, however, postulated "two beings in man: an individual being which has its foundation in the organism, . . . and a social being which represents . . . society." Lévi-Strauss extends this notion to include humanity—on the level of deep, unveiled structures.

Sartre, for whom consciousness is linked to personal action, neither recognizes Lévi-Strauss' type of order nor the destiny it implies. He objected to Lévi-Strauss' approach to the study of man on existential grounds. In Sartre's view, structuralism is remote from human existence and even denies its fundamental condition—that is, freedom. Consequently, structuralism presents a distorted and even morally suspect concept of this existence. (pp. 23-4)

Sartre was only one of Lévi-Strauss' critics. Lefebvre attacked structural anthropology for confusing the search for unconscious structures of myth with certain invariable natural laws which govern humanity; and he accused him of avoiding politics. Lévi-Strauss had not engaged in any of the controversies that divided the French during the Algerian war; he had been occupied by the search for the structures that would prove the validity of his method. This circumstance led Lefebvre to denigrate structuralism as politically effete, a "fetishism of knowledge, baptised 'epistemology,' which sacrifices the division of labor on the intellectual level, and which protects the division of knowledge under a mantle of encyclopaedism."

Still, the nonpolitical nature of structuralism had appealed to more conservative thinkers such as Ricoeur, whose hermeneutics were increasingly linked to structural linguistics. Ricoeur, however, attacks Lévi-Strauss' linguistic base. He objected to a linguistic "system which is not established at the level of the speaker's consciousness but at a lower level . . . and to the consequences from this epistemological model which directly affect the presuppositions of existentialism," because they called his own hermeneutics (his philosophy of will, of personal choice over good and evil) into question. According to Ricoeur, Lévi-Strauss' theory only "considers the closed system of discrete [linguistic] units which compose a language; [this] no longer suffices when one approaches discourse in act," for it leaves out questions of morals and ethics.

Though Lévi-Strauss' claims to science were never really established, his theory of the elusive, unconscious structures did lead to the creation of various new subjects of inquiry such as the relationships between the structures of all signs in language, their function within messages, and their rapport with other sign systems, such as music, gestures, body language. (pp. 24-5)

Lévi-Strauss' structuralism promised not only a new theory of nature and culture, but political and ideological unity as well. Its fusion of radical thought with political conservatism appealed to liberal reformists and to Marxist "minimalists," to all those who did not want to take "hard" political positions. Nevertheless, the social and economic upheaval that occurred in France during May and June of 1968 brought hard political realities to the forefront and quickly shunted structuralism to the sidelines. Unquestionably, the events of this brief period played a large role in prompting Lévi-Strauss to return to his earlier concern with philosophy and kinship structures.

But in the final pages of *L'homme nu,* after disposing of all the "pseudo-structuralists," he again reaffirms a belief in his own theory, suggesting that we apply "real" structural techniques to all of culture. He proposes what might be called a "superstructuralist" work-hypothesis for structuralism itself, which leads him to locate the four "major families"—mathematics, natural languages (these subsume the sciences), music, and myths—on opposite poles of two intersecting axes. This first appears to be a systematic procedure but soon turns out to be a convoluted exercise of transpositions, transformations, and oppositions along and between the "scientific" axis (mathematics and language) and the "sensual" one (music and myth). And when, for the sake of his argument and for symmetry, he states that "myth had to die for its form to depart like the soul leaving the body, in order to demand from music a means of reincarnation," or when he talks of the meetings of molecules of sound or image and those of sense as a "sort of copulation," then it is clear that he has soared into metaphysics—or bad poetry. Nevertheless, the scientific posturing, with oppositions, axes, and four-cornered analyses, is oddly reminiscent of the Parsonian four-cornered framework. Lévi-Strauss has apparently incorporated the network of "mini-structuralisms" into a "macro-structuralism."

Lévi-Strauss never seemed to realize that his questions were generally more scientific than his answers. For he sidesteps the whole question of science and myth when he talks about the ultimate and fundamental opposition of structuralism as represented in Hamlet's dilemma, which he finds to be at the bottom of everything. He says that Hamlet has no choice between being and nonbeing: he is eternally caught and forced to swing between ever-new contradictions until he dies. Thus life and death, Lévi-Strauss concludes, are both the fundamental and the ultimate opposition of structuralism. This is, of course, pure metaphysics. Inevitably, Lévi-Strauss was attacked for this conclusion to his *Mythologies*—a conclusion

that appeared to belie the scientific pretensions. For this final structuralist message seemed to carry religious overtones. Clearly, Lévi-Strauss had come a long way. Perhaps not only the challenges to his theory, but his own disillusionments as well, made him retreat to a more narrow anthropology.

But even if structuralism as a "grand theory" failed, one cannot deny the impetus it gave to the French intellectual community. Nor can one question its author's genius and his intellectual versatility. Though his structuralism's complex dialectic at times seemed to rely too much upon Lévi-Strauss' free association of ideas, its failure as an all-inclusive theory should neither obscure its influence in other fields, particularly in anthropology, nor diminish Lévi-Strauss' stature. Nor can we forget that this theoretical invention did accommodate underlying political ends, insofar as the shifting focus from existentialism to structuralism (with all the diversionary discussions) was part of the intellectual climate that produced a more realistic appraisal of the Communist reality and of Marxism. Hence, Lévi-Strauss unconsciously supplied the French Left with an honorable means of reevaluating both Marxism and existentialism. Inevitably, his grand theory was bound to collapse. (pp. 28-9)

> Edith Kurzweil, *"The Father of Structuralism," in her* The Age of Structuralism: Lévi-Strauss to Foucault, *Columbia University Press, 1980, pp. 13-34.*

INO ROSSI

[The] whole of Lévi-Strauss' approach is based on the assumption that there exist isomorphic relations between the biological, psychological, and cultural level of reality. "The assertion that the most parsimonious explanation comes closest to the truth rests, in the final analysis, upon the identity postulated between the laws of the universe and those of the human mind." . . . In various places, although at times incidentally, Lévi-Strauss has discussed his conception of the relation between nature and culture, the nature of brain and the nature and origin of culture. In the 1960 inaugural lecture at the College of France he stated that "culture was at once the natural result and the social mode of apprehension" of "the structure and functioning of the brain." . . . In turn "culture created the intersubjective milieu indispensable for the occurrence of transformations, both anatomical and physiological." . . . Culture is based on the way mind structures biological and natural reality: "The transition from nature to culture is determined by man's ability to think of biological relationships as systems of oppositions." . . . Whereas "the natural state recognizes only indivision and appropriation, and their chance admixture," the dialectic activity of mind "ineluctably give(s) rise to the world of reciprocity, as the synthesis of two contradictory characteristics inherent in the natural order. The rules of kinship and marriage are not made necessary by the social state. They are the social state itself, reshaping biological relationships and natural sentiments, forcing them into structures implying them as well as others, and compelling them to rise above their original characteristics." . . . This does not mean that culture is an heterogeneous order, an order based on principles of organization different from the natural ones. On the contrary the natural and cultural orders are bound to be isomorphic because the human mind has the same laws of physical reality, and the structuring activity of mind is what gives origin to culture: "the laws of thought—primitive or civilized—are the same as those which are expressed in physical reality and in social reality, which is itself only one of its aspects." . . . In 1969 Lévi-Strauss drew an explicit corollary out of the premises he had laid down in 1947: "Ultimately we shall perhaps discover that the interrelationship between nature and culture does not favour culture to the extent of being hierarchically superimposed in nature and irreducible to it. Rather, it takes the form of a synthetic duplication of mechanisms already in existence but which the animal kingdom shows only in disjointed form and dispersed variously among its members—a duplication, moreover, permitted by the emergence of certain cerebral structures which themselves belong to nature." . . . Seen in this context, a famous passage from *The Raw and the Cooked* which has puzzled many commentators becomes clear: "Myths signify the mind that evolves them by making use of the world of which it is itself a part. Thus, there is a simultaneous production of myths by the mind and a production, by the myths, of an image of the world which is already inherent in the structure of mind." . . . Lévi-Strauss' isomorphic conception of nature and culture also clarifies his statement that structural analysis is based on the postulate that a rationality is immanent within the universe even before the advent of consciousness—that is, before man becomes aware of its existence. Were this not the case we could never understand cultural data through our cognitive apparatus. Lévi-Strauss forcefully expresses this point by stating that within the universe there exists an "objectified" thought which functions rationally even before man becomes aware of its existence.

Precisely because of the isomorphic hypothesis Lévi-Strauss can claim that structuralism offers an epistemological model which is superior to the ones previously offered by anthropologists for at least two reasons. (1) First, structuralist anthropologists discover the unity and coherence behind cultural phenomena by studying the relationships among phenomena rather than the phenomena themselves, which are more complex and difficult to penetrate than their reciprocal relationships. (2) Secondly, structuralists reintegrate man with nature because they study man objectively, as if man were nature, by putting aside subjective consciousness and intentionality. In Lévi-Strauss' opinion, the "subject" has for too long a time attracted all the attention of social scientists and has prevented serious scientific progress. . . .

There are some social scientists who are interested in the notion of deep symbolic codes but not in what they call "metaphysical" notions such as human mind or unconscious. In a sense, the question of the human mind is of secondary importance in relationship to the notion of the structuring principles of cultures and of the mathematical nature of those principles. Lévi-Strauss himself has opened the way to a cybernetic, rather than a strictly intellectualist, conception of the origin of culture. "In the last analysis, if customs of neighboring people manifest relations of symmetry, we do not have to search for a cause in some mysterious law of nature or mind. This geometric perfection synthesizes at the present more or less conscious and innumerable efforts, accumulated throughout history all to the same end; to reach a threshold most profitable to human societies, where a just equilibrium among their unity and their diversity takes place." . . . Moreover, in his 1965 Huxley lecture, Lévi-Strauss stated that he "had invoked rather hastily the unconscious processes of the human mind" to explain kinship systems which "far from being the recent outcome of unconscious processes, now appear to me as true discoveries, the legacy of an age-old wisdom for which more evidence can be found elsewhere." . . . "The question may be raised as to whether the superiority in functional yield, which most societies attribute to cross-relationships over parallel ones, far from

being the outcome of unconscious processes, does not stem from a mature and well balanced reflection." . . .

[The] essential premises of structuralism are the following: (1) The isomorphic nature of mind and reality; (2) The structural nature of data and mind; (3) Mathematical properties of the deep structures of nature and mind. . . . These three assumptions are at the foundation of the structural approach, which has introduced the following methodological principles in social sciences: (1) The observable and conscious levels of phenomena are useful only as a starting point to inquire about their constitutive principles; (2) The task of the structuralist is to discover the logical principles of classification which organize and underlie cultural reality; (3) Structuralists should aim at formulating the mathematical laws of the organization and combination of these principles. It is precisely this cybernetic and mathematical thrust of structuralism that the empiricist detractors have often not attended to or have misunderstood. . . . (pp. 18-20)

> *Ino Rossi, "On the Assumptions of Structural Analysis: Revisiting Its Linguistic and Epistemological Premises," in* The Logic of Culture: Advances in Structural Theory and Methods, *edited by Ino Rossi, J. F. Bergin Publishers, Inc., 1982, pp. 3-22.*

DAVID PACE

[There are] many facets of Lévi-Strauss. . . . [One can see] him in the guise of the artisan of knowledge, the strict practitioner of the art of his guild. But . . . [there is also] Lévi-Strauss the romantic traveler, the loner cut off from his society and its values, the man who finds his solace in nature or in the contemplation of the 'primitive' or the traditional European peasant. There [is] . . . also Lévi-Strauss the philosophe, the man with an opinion ready on every topic from abstract art to the youth culture, and Lévi-Strauss the narrow social scientist, who spun out esoteric and demanding theories about the most technical aspects of his field of specialization. And . . . [he can be seen] both as an idealist, who eloquently pleaded the case of the vanishing peoples of this planet, and as an opportunist, who knew how to manipulate the socio-intellectual system around him. . . .

I have no desire to break open this kaleidoscope of ever-shifting images in order to reveal a single characterological structure, socio-economic configuration, or niche in the history of ideas. (p. 185)

Yet, one problem remains: the estimation of the position which Lévi-Strauss—or, more precisely, this set of Lévi-Strausses—occupies in the intellectual history of the second half of the twentieth century. . . .

In very general terms it is not difficult to give a meaning to Lévi-Strauss's speculations on history, values, and Western culture. He is clearly one of the great prophets of the decentered post-colonial universe in which we now find ourselves. He has explored the meaning of a world in which time is not an arrow, in which the values of the West are not eternal verities, and in which learning the wisdom of other societies has become a necessity.

But such a general classification of Lévi-Strauss as a philosopher of the post-colonial world is not sufficient. This category is too large and too vague to do justice to his thought. . . . (p. 186)

The problem [of focussing upon the work of Lévi-Strauss and examining its contributions to our world-view] must be divided into two different questions: first, what is the political significance of Lévi-Strauss's work and, secondly, what is his contribution to the moral and ethical debates of his epoch? (pp. 186-87)

[The] first question is difficult to answer because Lévi-Strauss has been rather unwilling to express his own political beliefs openly. His political stance has been marked by a decided disinclination to take clear political stances. The significance of this a-politicism can be seen in rather striking terms through a bit of counter-factual intellectual history. It is possible to imagine that Lévi-Strauss's career might have taken a very different turn. He might have chosen to openly enter the growing post-colonial re-evaluation of world history, and it might have been Lévi-Strauss in the late 1950s, and not Schumacher in the late 1960s, who became the great proponent of the belief that 'small is beautiful.' This possibility is particularly intriguing, since Lévi-Strauss had focussed on debunking the myth of cultural evolution and had laid the foundations for a non-evolutionary philosophy of history. This absolutely crucial dimension was lacking in the cultural critiques of many of the other opponents of Western superiority and could have given a coherence to this line of thought that has been generally missing.

But Lévi-Strauss did not follow this path. He chose, instead, to hide his light beneath a bushel. He has made no real effort to disseminate his ideas of cultural progress to a large popular audience or to translate them into any political movement. On the contrary, he has taken every opportunity to deny the importance of his own speculations on these topics and to focus attention upon his technical achievements in structural anthropology. (p. 187)

But, despite this decision to remain aloof from politics, there is a definite political content to his writings. Regardless of his claims or intentions, his ideas have tended to support certain positions on the French ideological spectrum and to weaken others. (p. 188)

Like many of his predecessors, [Lévi-Strauss's] thought cut across the categories of left and right in a rather confusing fashion. While his rejection of Western values seems to connect him with a more radical tradition, his concern with maintaining the traditions of the past suggests a much more conservative political heritage. His concern for diversity shows definite links with the thought of Montesquieu, and his reaction to the worldwide monoculture he discovered in his travels in the Americas is in many ways parallel to that of Tocqueville, who a century earlier expressed his own concern with an earlier form of American monoculture. But . . . an even closer parallel may be demonstrated between his views and those of Durkheim. The corporatism of the latter may be seen as the counterpart to Lévi-Strauss's obsession with inter-societal diversity. And Durkheim's doubts about the increasing anomie within France may be related to Lévi-Strauss's fear of the monoculture.

Thus, it is possible that Lévi-Strauss's ideology of primitivism represents a projection onto the stage of world history of a set of problems which had long obsessed French political thinkers. The resistance of the French to large-scale industrial organization and their ambivalence towards the ideals of the great Revolution may have found yet another reincarnation in Lévi-Strauss, whose ultimate ideal is not the noble savage, but rather the traditional peasant, living in a slowly evolving harmony with nature.

But Lévi-Strauss was unwilling to advocate openly even this ideal. It remained implicit—projected onto the peoples of the New World or hidden within the sense of loss which marks his writings. Nowhere did he provide a clear basis for political action. There is only remorse at the passing of some ill-defined state of grace.

This failure to carry through the implications of his own thought carries us back to the issue . . . [of] Lévi-Strauss's definition of the intellectual as artisan. By implication this analogy would seem to indicate that political or ethical views should play no greater role in the work of intellectuals than they do in that of artisans. But Lévi-Strauss's own career demonstrates the problems implicit in such a bifurcated role. In the first place, it seems to be impossible for anyone, or at least anyone who is not working on an extremely narrow and insignificant topic, to avoid the intermingling of personal concerns and professional production. Moreover, the desire to avoid the implications of one's own ideas may lead to a weakening of those ideas. Lévi-Strauss has avoided the political and moral consequences of his own work by constantly backtracking, denying its value, hiding his philosophical and political speculations within technical passages where they really do not fit, and substituting the modern 'table talk' of the recorded interview for the balanced and well-argued essay.

It might, in fact, be argued that Lévi-Strauss's image of the intellectual artisan has, ironically, made his thought more subject to his own personal whims and prejudices. Because of the secondary role which he accorded to the political aspects of his thought, he was never forced to deal with the contradictions between the implications of his speculations and the political positions he was taking. Moreover, he was able to dismiss or totally ignore criticisms, which might have provided him with the basis for highly useful modifications in his world-view.

All in all, it would seem that his professional self-image has done him a disservice. The ideas which he has put forth in his non-technical writings are significant and deserve a better presentation than he has allowed. And his structuralist writings have not been aided by the manner in which they have become the covert receptacle of his personal concerns. (pp. 195-96)

Throughout, Lévi-Strauss had failed to respond to the demand, which Sartre expressed so eloquently in both his life and his work, that the intellectual justify his or her existence and the resources which society has invested in it. Lévi-Strauss's analogy with the artisan has one important flaw; the artisan produces goods and services which are in demand from the society as a whole, whereas the intellectual, as conceived by Lévi-Strauss, is pursuing projects that are defined, legitimized, and consumed completely within the guild of knowledge itself. It is, in fact, largely by violating his own rules of conduct that Lévi-Strauss has continued to produce a service which is of relevance to a large number of his contemporaries.

This problem might have disappeared had Lévi-Strauss maintained the link between science and progress, which has traditionally served to legitimize scientific research. But, instead, he explicitly separated the two, advocating science-for-science's sake while denying the possibility of progress. Therefore, ironically, it may be argued that Sartre's image of the 'engagé' intellectual actually is a less idealistic response to the problems of the intellectual in modern society than Lévi-Strauss's concept of the artisan of knowledge.

Thus, in the broader perspective of contemporary intellectual history Lévi-Strauss may be seen as father of a political impulse, which he himself has attempted to abort. His self-defined social role has prevented him from championing his own ideas, and when it appeared that this role might be threatened, he immediately began to distance himself from all of the more radical implications of his own ideas.

But, if Lévi-Strauss's political thought can be characterized as self-limiting, can the same be said about the ethical stance implicit in his writings? Here we find ourselves faced with the second question. . . . Has Lévi-Strauss enunciated an important statement on the moral dilemmas of our age or is he simply a social scientist, who has moralized on occasion?

The Buddhist references in his writings provide a way to begin to approach this question. His concern with Buddhism seems to be integrally connected with his denial of the value of material progress, his concern with harmony with nature, and his rejection of Western humanism. (pp. 197-98)

Octavio Paz and Ivan Strenski have presented convincing demonstrations of the formal similarities between Buddhism and Lévi-Strauss's writings. Strenski, in particular, has placed him in the context of a broader twentieth century interest in this Eastern philosophy and religion, and it seems undeniable that both his structuralist theory and his comments on value and history have clear affinities with Buddhist perspectives. . . .

[Nevertheless], Buddhism, perhaps even more than Marxism, is fundamentally a philosophy of praxis. The point is not to understand the world, but rather to do away with it. And there is not a hint of a Buddhist praxis in Lévi-Strauss's work; he never loosens his attachment to a 'world on the wane.' He holds to his loss, as if it were his most valuable possession, and he never even suggests any formal practice, such as meditation, which might have aided him in freeing himself from attachment to suffering. (p. 198)

Lévi-Strauss has criticized Western values and preached a kind of intercultural relativism. But he has almost never actually affirmed any ethical stand. . . . He has denied the universality of norms in his writings on history and value while in his structuralist theory he has insisted that it is absolutely necessary for each society to have such norms. The conflict might have been resolved had Lévi-Strauss attempted to affirm some set of values within his own society or even the possibility of the affirmation of value within a relativistic context. But he has avoided serious discussion of this problem. Except for a rather vague insistence that we have an absolute responsibility to protect endangered species, he has left us without any ethical rudder whatsoever.

Thus, there is something fundamentally nihilistic about Lévi-Strauss's world-view. He accepts the Buddhist critique of value, but he avoids all reference to the Buddha's four-fold path to salvation. There is neither a serious effort to protect the things which he sees as threatened nor an attempt to abandon his attachment to them. He himself has described his own position as a 'serene pessimism' and there is clearly something to this characterization. But, there is also an element of Nietzchean 'ressentiment' in his orientation towards the world. His work is marked, not by the affirmation of what is good, but rather by the rejection of what is evil. . . .

[Lévi-Strauss's] entire world-view may be viewed as a lamentation for a world which is disappearing *and which he has done virtually nothing to preserve.*

This lamentation seems to have been connected with the two great emotions which dominated Lévi-Strauss's writings: anger and loss. The first found expression in his frequent attacks on Western civilization. It is, of course, not necessarily a sign of displaced anger to criticize one's own society. But a close reading of many of Lévi-Strauss's diatribes leaves little doubt that there was a great deal of very personal rage behind these sweeping characterizations of Western civilization. (pp. 198-99)

Alongside this anger there is a continual sense of loss. The locus of sadness is quite obviously not in the tropics, but rather in Lévi-Strauss himself. He approached the disappearing cultures of the Mato Grosso in exactly the same terms that he experienced the paintings of Vernet, the landscapes of four continents, the world of the Sorbonne, the University of São Paulo, or the students of 1968. The world was always disappointing to Lévi-Strauss. Value always rested in the distance.

This tendency to remain obsessed with a loss, which he never seems to have the slightest inclination to prevent or forestall, suggests, once again, that there may have been an element of projection in Lévi-Strauss's concern with the disappearance of cultural diversity. It is as if the disappearance of the 'primitive' is a symbol of some other great loss, which Lévi-Strauss has never admitted, as if he has spoken *through* and not *about* 'primitive' societies. (pp. 200-01)

[It] would seem clear that Lévi-Strauss has not addressed this loss in its own language, that he has not acknowledged its existence in terms of its social, familial, or psychological roots. Instead, he has focussed upon another loss, the loss of the 'primitive,' which serves to represent a greater pain and a different anger. Since the deeper nature of his pain was not acknowledged, it was impossible for Lévi-Strauss to resolve his dilemma. He was left in the position of Nietzschean 'ressentiment.' Unable to project into the future because he had not accepted some element of the past, he has remained fixated on an immovable object.

This fixation led him to some very significant insights, for as Nietzsche noted ressentiment lies at the heart of some of our greatest thought. He has succeeded in breaking out of a concept of World History, which was no longer relevant to our experience. He preached the message of cultural contact and openness to new experiences. In his structuralist theory he provided new ways to translate the wisdom of other peoples into a language we can understand. And, as he himself indicated, he does seem to have achieved some degree of serenity over the years, through his cosmic pessimism.

But there remained a self-imposed limit on Lévi-Strauss's thought, which kept him locked up within an endless discourse about the failure of Western civilization. He could never introduce a language of the self—his own self—into his work. To be sure, there is the illusion of reflexivity in *Tristes Tropiques*. But, despite the comments of the earlier reviewers of the work, there is no indication that Lévi-Strauss ever fully dealt with his own position within the schema of the world he had constructed. He constructed a self-questioning persona, but he never developed a sociology of his own knowledge, a psychology of his own passions, or an anthropology of his own academic culture.

Lévi-Strauss could never really turn back upon himself because from the beginning of his thought he had rejected the possibility of introspection. For him introspection was always illusory. Having characterized the approach identified with existentialism as a shallow 'shop-girl's metaphysics' the only route to self-knowledge was through an encounter with another society. But, since Lévi-Strauss never adequately analyzed what he brought to this encounter with the anthropological 'Other,' he had no basis upon which to divide experience from projection or his theories from his own interests. (pp. 202-03)

In the process of avoiding his own desires, fears, and interests, he has tended to minimize this aspect of the human experience. He has remained locked up in a world of abstract structures and mental schemas, in which the needs and desires, fears and horrors of human experience—'civilized' and 'primitive'—had no place. This is nowhere more obvious than in Lévi-Strauss's ruminations on Buddhism. For him Buddhism is an intellectual system, a means of explaining our experience without resorting to unnecessary metaphysical assumptions, and, to a limited extent, a method of ordering society. But there is no image of the absolute horror of human existence or of the Compassionate One, the man who postponed nirvana in order to end the sufferings of others.

There is, in fact, increasingly little compassion expressed in Lévi-Strauss's writings. The sympathy for concrete individuals which overflowed in his early descriptions of the Nambikwara was slowly replaced by rather formulaic statements of the need to protect 'primitive' peoples from Western expansion. These appeals were increasingly abstract and colorless and seemed to be based more and more upon his desire to maintain preserves for anthropological field-workers rather than upon a real concern for the tragedy of those individuals whose cultures were disintegrating.

And yet, even in his isolation and detachment, there are great lessons to be learned. For, if Lévi-Strauss has not offered us a clear new direction in the confusion of our post-colonial world, he has taught us much about false directions, the blind alleys which our humanistic tradition presents to us. He has not taught us to love, but he has given a new meaning to the word tolerance. And his very distance from action gives us a bit more perspective on those activities with which we fill up our lives.

All of these themes are stated nowhere more clearly than in the last paragraph of *Tristes Tropiques,* where Lévi-Strauss distilled that wisdom which is his to give:

> Just as the individual is not alone in the group and each society is not alone among the others, man is not alone in the universe. When the rainbow of human cultures will have finally collapsed into the void created by our frenzy, so long as we are still alive and the world still exists, this tenuous arch, which connects us to the unattainable will remain, demonstrating a path which is the opposite of our slavery and

which even if it is not pursued, provides man with the single grace he knows how to gain: to stop his progress, to restrain the impulses which compel him to fill one after the other the open fissures in the wall of necessity, finishing his work at the same time he closes his prison; this grace which each society covets, whatever its beliefs, its political regime, or its level of civilization, and to which each society attaches its leisure, its pleasure, its repose, and its liberty, consists of the good fortune, vital for life, of *detaching oneself* and—adieu to savages! adieu to voyages!—during the brief intervals in which our species can endure to interrupt its hive-like activity, to seize the essence of what it was and continues to be on this side of thought and the far side of society: in the contemplation of a mineral more beautiful than all of our works; in the perfume, more learned than our books, which is inhaled in the hollow of a lily; or in the wink, heavy with patience, serenity, and reciprocal forgiveness which an involuntary agreement sometimes permits us to exchange with a cat.

There is no more touching passage in the entire corpus of Lévi-Strauss. It expresses an expansiveness of identification, an openness to the non-human universe, and a deep and abiding tolerance for difference which may long serve to counter the hubris of our species. In an age in which no culture is protected from its fellows by insurmountable geographical barriers and when nature itself is no longer secure from the assaults of man, this is a message which must be heard.

And, yet, the spirit of ressentiment has shaped every word of this paragraph. Its wisdom was purchased at the cost of abandoning value and forsaking action—even the Buddhist action of non-action. Only by distancing himself from the values of his own group and by denying himself real human communion could he gain such a perspective. If this were linked to a compassionate practise, as it is in Buddhism, it might offer a real alternative to Western humanism. But without a praxis it threatens to become a path to nihilism. For behind the pantheistic affirmations of this passage, there lie the hidden negations which have structured Lévi-Strauss's being-in-the-world: the retreat into abstraction, the rejection of the frenzy of human passions, the desire for detachment from the patterns of social interaction, and the deep need to flee the world of other humans and to find beauty in a rock and forgiveness from a cat. (pp. 204-06)

David Pace, in his Claude Lévi-Strauss: The Bearer of Ashes, *Routledge & Kegan Paul, 1983, 262 p.*

Peter (Ambrose Cyprian) Luke

1919-

English dramatist, scriptwriter, novelist, short story writer, autobiographer, editor, and director.

Luke is best known for his play *Hadrian VII* (1969), which he adapted from the underground classic novel *Hadrian the Seventh* by Frederick William Rolfe, also known as Baron Corvo. The novel, which is generally interpreted as an autobiographical fantasy, portrays Rolfe's alter ego, George Arthur Rose, who is denied entry into the priesthood but through extraordinary circumstances finds himself elected pope. Luke dispenses with the character of Rose and centers on the personality of Rolfe, whose eccentric behavior in his papal duties results in much of the play's humor. By having the same actor portray both Rolfe and Hadrian, Luke underscores the element of fantasy in the novel.

Luke is also the author of the play *Bloomsbury* (1974), in which he depicts members of the well-known London literary circle of the 1920s and 1930s. The action of this play derives from the thoughts of Virginia Woolf, who acts as narrator. Luke's other literary endeavors include two volumes of memoirs, *Sisyphus and Reilly: An Autobiography* (1972) and *The Mad Pomegranate and the Praying Mantis: An Andalusian Adventure* (1985), the novel *The Other Side of the Hill* (1984), and *Collected Short Stories* (1979). Luke has also written, directed, and produced several films for British television.

(See also *Contemporary Authors*, Vols. 81-84 and *Dictionary of Literary Biography*, Vol. 13.)

Photograph by Anne James

***THE TIMES*, LONDON**

The job of a new officer suddenly assigned a seasoned body of men to command would seem, judging by Mr. Peter Luke's [television] play **"Roll on Bloomin' Death"** . . . to be much like that of a new teacher faced with a difficult fifth remove.

Unfortunately Lieutenant Babington, straight out from England to take over a platoon somewhere in Europe in the winter of 1944, seems to have failed his practicals where discipline is concerned. Although admittedly he has to deal with an extravagant number of crises in his first day, he has difficulty even with the basic things such as stopping troublemakers from talking back at him, dismissing the transparent excuses of backsliders, and detailing enough men for a fighting patrol when (unsurprisingly) no one is willing to volunteer. . . .

Lieutenant Babington is a special case, too humane for his own good in a world where decisiveness at all costs is the rule and there is seldom time for his brand of scruple. Equally evidently, he is going to establish himself before long in the eyes of his men. In these stories the end is predictable; it is only the subtlety with which it is achieved that varies.

Mr. Luke gained over most others to treat the subject by refusing to oversimplify—we see the process of mutual understanding between officer and men just beginning (as a result of a minor feat of heroism on the officer's part) rather than being concluded in one improbable flash of insight. The accent throughout is on the interaction of complex individuals rather than on black and white contrasts of good-bad, brave-cowardly and officer-men.

"New Officer Makes His Mark," in The Times, *London, November 6, 1961, p. 14.*

CLIVE BARNES

[*Hadrian VII*] has been based by Peter Luke upon the novel *Hadrian the Seventh* and other works by the curious turn-of-the-century English writer Fr. Rolfe, who occasionally called himself Baron Corvo.

The novel is an autobiographical fantasy, and has been an underground classic for years. It tells how George Arthur Rose, an unsuccessful candidate for the priesthood, is visited by bishops one day and belatedly summoned to Holy Orders, his years of indignity washed away.

Moreover, he is sent to Rome as a companion-secretary to the Cardinal-Archbishop of Pimlico and the Bishop of Caerleon. Here the Papal Conclave is sitting to select a new Pope. After many deadlocked sessions, the choice finally falls upon Rose, who is thus transported from layman to prelate in a few short weeks, the first English Pope in modern history.

As Pope, the newcomer is unconventional and, even more, unworldly. He proposes selling the Vatican treasures to ease the poverty in the world, and sees priests more as men of calling than men of destiny. Rolfe was always at pains to point out that he loved the Catholic religion and the church but detested Catholics. His comments here are sharply to the point.

Mr. Luke has taken the novel and also, very reasonably, taken a few liberties in the adaptation. First we see Rolfe himself, in his dingy lodgings, beset by debts and invaded by bailiffs. The story of Hadrian is his own fantasy, and the hero now is no longer George Arthur Rose, but Rolfe himself. . . .

Mr. Luke's ingenuity has a touch of genius about it. By beginning and ending with Rolfe himself, he provides the play with a nicely coherent form, and the melodramatic ending of the novel can be included but cut down to size in its relationship to the play's complete pattern. The best of the writing remains Rolfe's, and Mr. Luke has been to pains to keep as much as possible of some of the dialogues and confrontations that are among the special minor delights of early 20th-century English literature. . . .

To an extent—yes, even to a large extent—the original Rolfe had a style and manner that the play cannot catch. The perfect details of the papal election must be lost, for Rolfe went to pains not only to describe actual historical figures in the Vatican but also to offer in superb political depth a view of Vatican politics that even now is sweet in its comprehension. Yet the play does have the mystery of the original, the sight of a modern, wish-fulfilling Pope, smoking on the throne and mocking the very conventions in which he totally believed, and most of all, the atmosphere of the original.

> Clive Barnes, "'Hadrian VII', English Pope," in The New York Times, *January 9, 1969, p. 22.*

MARTIN GOTTFRIED

It's kind of spooky to see a play in London, be terribly moved by it, and then find the New York production strangely wan. This is what happened with Peter Luke's **Hadrian The Seventh** . . . , and I'm not exactly sure why. Possible explanations: The script was changed (it wasn't); or the cast was changed (somewhat), but the play or the overall acting isn't quite as good (that's so); or the production has been changed (some truth in that); or the play isn't the kind to see twice (I'm sure of that).

Still, **Hadrian The Seventh** is a frightfully personal look into the soul of a human being, embarrassing like *Long Day's Journey Into Night* for its brutal revelation of another man's blood. I have yet to see its like for the sheer stripping of defenses to indecently reveal the most protected, most vulnerable parts of a human being.

You wouldn't think any playwright capable of exposing so naked a truth and in fact it is not Luke's writing that has done it. Frederick Rolfe was a real person and he did it himself in his strange novel, *Hadrian The Seventh* (from which this play is drawn, at many times verbatim). Rolfe was a clever, educated, charming antagonistic man and a paranoiac. Obsessed with the Catholic Church and determined to be a priest, his emotional problems prevent it. . . . He was to die with his frustration intact, having realized his dream of priesthood only in this novel, which sets its painful tone at the very start—"In

mind he was tired, worn out by years of hope deferred, of loneliness, of unrewarded toil."

Luke has used a most unimaginative device to put this novel into a theatre—ironically enough, an unnecessary device. The play begins in Rolfe's shabby room, where he is persecuted by his landlady, bill collectors, and an anti-Catholic who holds a bewildering grudge against him. Between these brief, tormenting visits, he sits with his crucifix and ikons, and decides to write *Hadrian The Seventh*. Suddenly there is a knock at the door and a Cardinal-Archbishop is there to offer him a priesthood, along with an apology for past offenses. In a flash Rolfe takes his orders, is whisked to Rome to assist the English delegation in the election of a new Pope and is himself named to the Papacy.

Calling himself "Hadrian The Seventh" (the only previous English Pope was Hadrian The Fourth), he becomes a marvelously civilized, delightful Pope whose reforms anticipate and go beyond those of John. He is also disconcertingly down to earth (hitching himself up to the throne, cigarette in hand) and off-hand in his dealings with Vatican protocol.

But these are the dreams come true of a paranoiac, and along with such dreams are the nightmares. A paranoiac thinks that both his hopes and his fears will somehow come true, and Rolfe's mad fantasy of being named Pope is no more bizarre than his fantasies of being conspired against and done in. Which is exactly what happens.

That is just where the play should have ended. Instead, Mr. Luke insists on giving us a thoroughly unnecessary explanation (it was all the writing of a novel) that demeans the soul-spilling that went before. That we have been witnessing hallucination has been brutally obvious. In fact, a good deal of the play's power is just in our knowing that without being told. . . .

Robert Fletcher's physical production is intentionally bare, to contrast the shabbiness of Rolfe's real life with the gorgeous robes and trappings of Roman Catholic ritual. In this it supports the play's secondary intent, which is to compare the Roman Catholic religion with the official Church and with Catholics as individuals.

But the play is too absorbed with its character to shed much light on this, and the influence of Rolfe's novel is too powerfully egocentric to allow it. In any case, and despite all these criticisms, I suspect that your first viewing of **Hadrian The Seventh** will approximate mine. You should see it because it is an especially sensitive and moving dissection of a man very much like all men. Luckily, our frights and deliria are more under control but there, in the hapless extreme, are we.

> Martin Gottfried, in a review of "Hadrian the Seventh," in Women's Wear Daily, *January 9, 1969. Reprinted in* New York Theatre Critics' Reviews, *Vol. XXX, No. 1, week of January 13, 1969, p. 393.*

WALTER KERR

Hadrian VII, finally arrived here after its tremendous success in London, is exciting in one respect and thoroughly flattening in another. What the evening offers us, overall, is the spectacle of an extraordinary character . . . thrashing about in a play that can never hope to live up to him.

The character is, of course, Frederick Rolfe, alias Baron Corvo, that late 19th-century fantasist, failed painter and schoolteacher, who wrote an ornate and wistfully semi-autobiographical novel in which a reject for the Roman Catholic priesthood was suddenly and most profitably elected pope. In the novel Rolfe daydreamed himself onto the throne of Rome under another name. In adapting the daydream to the stage, dramatist Peter Luke has simply skipped such nonsense and given us Rolfe plain, Rolfe perverse, Rolfe in person at all times. It is Rolfe who slaps his leather-patched elbows for warmth as he paces a shabby room planning the story he will write and Rolfe who sits in the chair of Peter exhaling cigarette smoke between anathemas. (p. 1)

Unfortunately, what is genuinely arresting about the evening is seriously undermined, sometimes made dull and finally made foolish, by its dramatic structure. Mr. Luke seems to bring no more than a journeyman's hand to patching scenes together. The first act survives on promise alone: almost nothing is happening, but we stick it out in hope and trust. The second wobbles awkwardly between effective outbursts from a white-cassocked [Rolfe] and unbelievably gauche accountings of a plot that is being hatched in London to blackmail him. The language throughout pretends to pithiness but is actually overstuffed and imprecise. Rolfe describes himself near curtain-fall as a man "who made the frantic and fatuous mistake of living before his time." The alliteration sounds pretty. But do the words "frantic and fatuous" actually *mean* anything in the context?

At the last, though, we have got to excuse Mr. Luke and turn once more to Mr. Rolfe, the real Mr. Rolfe. There was probably no getting around the sillinesses he thought would pass for a story. The weakness of the creative imagination from which *Hadrian VII* is spun becomes most obvious in two key sequences close to, or precisely at, the climax of the evening.

The pope is forced to clear himself, before a gathering of cardinals, of charges which have appeared in a Belfast newspaper. He has refused to pay blackmail, the secrets of his early life are coming out. The cardinals are horrified by the newspaper revelations; the sense of urgency at the confrontation in the Vatican is great; the pope must summon up all of his courage and all of his silken skill to contend with the situation. But there is no situation. When the charges are read, they are nothing at all: a few unpaid debts, the loss of a job. We have been imagining tremendous disclosures; everyone on stage behaves as if the disclosures were in fact tremendous; a man nearly breaks over them. And they are insipid which means that the scene must be.

Not long after, the blackmailers—a former landlady and an Irish bigot out of some Boucicault melodrama—appear at the Vatican for an ultimate test of strength. We can accept the fantasy of their being there, more or less; the ground rules for the evening are to a degree fantastic. But in return for our acceptance we ask that the scene have narrative substance. Alas, the substance is less than thin; it is patently preposterous. The Irish editor-bigot is proposing that the pope, an Englishman, pay £40,000 in damages for the crime against England of having agreed to be pope. ("Think of an Englishman sinking so low!" is the way the thread of thought runs.) We are not only asked, now, to take seriously what is scarcely more than a low comedy gambit, we are expected to accept it as a resolution of the entire action: the Irishman, denied his money, shoots the pope on the spot. After this, it is difficult for his body to be carried away with any solemnity, though the effort is made.

Rolfe's qualities were both rare and unstable. What is rare about them comes through in the intensity and complexity of

[Alec] McCowen's performance, and in the perceptiveness that foresaw a religious crisis in the making. What is unstable about them, unhappily, crops up in the plotting, in the master plan and foundation on which everything else must stand. An actor survives; but the flooring is constantly, and sometimes tediously, being sucked away from beneath his feet. (pp. 1, 22)

Walter Kerr, "The Actor Is Inspired . . .," in The New York Times, Section II, January 19, 1969, pp. 1, 22.

HAROLD CLURMAN

A prominent London producer's habitual word of praise is "clever." I am never able to tell whether it is an example of English understatement or indicates a reservation. *Hadrian VII*, Peter Luke's dramatization of Baron Corvo's novel . . . , is a clever play. By this I mean that it possesses more cunning than content, more adroitness than substance. Its skill consists in flattering its audience with a comfortable feeling that what it is seeing is intellectually sharp, humanly perceptive, artistically polished, while in truth it is mostly hokum that employs a great many devices of the middle-class theatre ever since there was one. (p. 124)

The play's message suggests that religion is to be respected even by those who profess none, and that the truly devout are not to be identified with the often shady machinations of the clerical bureaucracy. This "lesson" is one that everybody can noncommittedly approve. It is here couched in well-rounded quips besides being animated by a villainous Irish-Protestant bigot as the antagonist, a shrewdly genial Italian prelate to add local color in splendid cardinal red . . . and well-phrased invectives hurled at the myrmidons of the Church. All of this is softened by touches of sentiment on behalf of the humble, the modestly pure in heart, before whom the acidulous Rolfe himself melts to kindness. Every scene is composed of a disguised stereotype.

Though less strenuously stylish, the play is written after a fashion which reminds me of the literary self-congratulation in *The Lion in Winter*. *Hadrian VII* may therefore be set down as engaging, entertaining or whatever other encomium conveys an emollient without injurious ingredient. For purposes of publicity, one may go so far as to declare it "one of the best plays of the season," for on Broadway at the moment there is only *The Great White Hope* and *The Man in the Glass Booth* to set beside it. In itself the play is what the French characterize as *le faux bon*—the fake good, the "sophisticated." (pp. 124-25)

Harold Clurman, in a review of "Hadrian VII," in The Nation, Vol. 208, No. 4, January 27, 1969, pp. 124-25.

GERALD WEALES

At the end of Peter Luke's *Hadrian VII*, just before we return to the shabby room of Fr. William Rolfe, the young priest (called, too cunningly, George Arthur Rose, Rolfe's name for the hero of [his book] *Hadrian VII*; Luke, mixing undisguised biography with Rolfian fantasy, calls his hero Rolfe) sums up the play's central character as the body of the murdered pope is carried past in state. The summation is an open bid for understanding for a complicated man, one whose defensive outer shell is cover for a fearful yearning for human contact. The speech ends with the last lines of Rolfe's novel, "Pray for the repose of His soul. He was so tired." Those words, however, are a benediction for Rolfe's George Arthur Rose, who expected to find pleasure in "Really nothing—except to flee and be at rest." A man who thought himself incapable of love, one whom the wounds of rejection made wary, Rolfe's Hadrian could act in love and friendship, but always doubling on his tracks, covering each act with papal aloofness or a satirical line, the token of the invective that he used more directly on other occasions.

Luke's Hadrian is something else again, a sentimental hero, the old curmudgeon with the heart of gold, closer in tone to C. Aubrey Smith being softened by Freddie Bartholomew in *Little Lord Fauntleroy* than to Rolfe's Hadrian. I am surprised that Luke passed up Rolfe's scene in the garden between Hadrian and the boy Prince of Naples. Other sentimental moments are there, too, too bald now without the insistent self-love and self-irony with which Rolfe hedged every scene, too skeletal, too bluntly doing a job. Most of the material is borrowed directly from the book (the best lines certainly are), but the scenes are shifted around to form a conventional self-discovery play. The penniless writer, long denied the priesthood that was rightfully his, is made pope at the end of Act I. This is the put-down act, Rolfe getting his own back from the hierarchy who failed him, but his wit, his playfulness (imagine Rolfe's hero singing a variety-hall song!), his nervous concern that the room be as neat as possible for the visiting clerics are all signs that his talk of "revenge" is not to be taken seriously. This man is just waiting to be pried open by love and the second act gives the prying scene (pope to novice, Hadrian to an image of his own youth, father to son), replete with saccharine gesture (he almost places his hand on the head of the kneeling young man), followed by the results: the folksy old-servant scene, the confession of his pain, the reconciliation with Cardinal Ragna, the decision to give away the Church's wealth. Then, the final schmaltz irony, his murder by the vindictive Protestant fanatic, the man who has been hounding him all his life, and his dying forgiveness of the man and the dead.

Rolfe, as a writer, did not hesitate to dip into melodrama or sentimentality if it suited his purposes (although I suspect he imagined he was writing high drama or out of pure sensitivity), so it may be a bit unfair to blame Luke for the softness of the scenes in the play. Yet he is responsible for making explicit what is implicit in Rolfe, cutting away the protective settings, removing the ambivalent undertones. Luke's Ragna scene is built on a few lines of Rolfe's and, out of the malicious pleasure of Rolfe's Hadrian, Luke's pope is forced to play a comic friendly-enemy scene as phoney as Flagg and Quirt. The homosexuality that underlays Hadrian's visit to his old college is absent from the so-that's-love scene with the novice. It is in the scene with the serving woman, however, that the distance between Luke and Rolfe can be seen most clearly. The same kindly, gossipy, tiresome old dear visits the pope in both scenes, acknowledges the gift that makes her independent, offers the unwanted pickled delicacy that she thinks Hadrian loves. In the play, the pope accepts the onions, opens the jar, eats one painfully, forces one on the young priest who grimaces becomingly, and then, the visitor gone, speaks to the audience: "I know, I'm a hypocrite." In the novel, it is not onions, but pickled samphire (a form of glasswort, which gets its name from *Saint Pierre,* thus Saint Peter's herb and the kind of arcane joke Rolfe liked) and Hadrian buries the jar, unopened, in the Vatican garden. (pp. 588-89)

Hadrian VII was never the masterpiece the Corvoquesters thought it was, but it is a distinctive and idiosyncratic work. The best

of it is lost in the play version and, for me, what Luke . . . [has] substituted is both empty and tiresome. (p. 589)

Gerald Weales, "Black Smoke for 'Hadrian VII'," in Commonweal, *Vol. LXXXIX, No. 18, February 7, 1969, pp. 588-89.*

D. M. BURJORJEE

As an ardent Corvinist I looked forward to the reviews of the two American presentations of *Hadrian VII.* I hoped for some penetrating assessments of Peter Luke's attempt to integrate for theatre the biography of Frederick Rolfe, one of the most bizarre outsiders of the *fin-de-siecle* literary period, with Rolfe's novel about his equally remarkable creation, a twentieth-century English pope, whose Christian socialism is redolent of Henry MacKenzie's nineteenth century *Man of Feeling.*

I was disappointed on both occasions, for most of them refrained, I suppose, from being too "academic." . . . Nowhere amidst the somewhat-dilletante phrases of the reviews did I encounter a really serious dramaturgical examination of Rolfe's paranoia, which is difficult to exaggerate, which conditioned his life and his art, and which constitutes the *action* of the play.

I wish that the critics had said more about the dramatic considerations of Rolfe's paranoia. Indeed this is the central problem of the play, for very few in the audience could be aware of its actual extent and intensity. They need to know much more about Rolfe-Hadrian than they could possibly learn in two hours. (pp. 68, 70)

Rolfe was, at the very least, a highly-gifted individual—a first-rate photographer, an accomplished musician, a competent painter, a pains-taking translator, and a writer of splendidly-purple prose—and he desired fervently, in rather eccentric and arrogant ways (which involved him in the quarrels he delighted in) to place his talents at the disposal of the Church. His books reflect an unhappy genius which required, for its fulfillment, the unstinting patronage of magnificos of the order of the Borgias. His life . . . reveals not only the "loner," the alienated man, but a man whose sentiments were precursors, in many respects, of similar feelings on the part of an increasing number of people in our own time with regard to the Establishment and its cohorts.

The decision of Rolfe's creation, Hadrian, (in *Hadrian the Seventh*) to distribute the wealth of the Vatican to the poor—not at all taken kindly by the Curia and others—is, I think, that kind of sentiment that is seriously entertained by many today. Besides, the point that has been missed by the critics, and which cannot in short space be adequately made by the playwright, is that in his own life Rolfe was constantly striking nonconformist attitudes and acting in unconventional ways which made him an intellectual and social pariah. (p. 70)

Richard Coe, who . . . reviewed *Hadrian VII,* applauded the play as "a character study in comic terms." Nevertheless, in another article, he quotes Hume Cronyn's rather illuminating remark on the manner in which, as Hadrian, he delivers the lines on the distribution of the Church's wealth to the poor: "I play the scene very seriously because this is truly the essense of William (sic) Rolfe's dreams. For all his irritating egoism, he is an idealist." The idealism is conceded, but the paranoia is reduced to an "irritating egoism," and this is my complaint. In *Hadrian VII* the more universal tragic possibilities of its real-life character have been abrogated for lesser comic expressions. One might concede that paranoia, while not particularly amusing to the paranoid, can be claimed by the Comic Muse. Yet, it seems to me, that the humour in such arrogations could, especially in Rolfe's case, successfully provide the contrapuntal element for an intensely tragic-comic treatment of the plight of the maverick in the social condition.

Peter Luke's play is remarkable, perhaps original, for I know of no other like it which actually dramatizes the artist at his work. In addition, the identification of the artist with his creation is not affected by mere juxtaposition, but by the subtlest refinement of an old device—the play within the play—which dramatically integrates the identities of Rolfe and Hadrian. But this success is achieved at some cost, for the implications of the resolution, aesthetically and dramatically speaking, are weak, if not unacceptable. In the Rolfe-Hadrian nexus the martyrdom of his alter-ego inevitably endows Rolfe with an unwarranted halo and, in so doing, reduces the public tragedy of the papal assassination to a merely pathetic *deus ex machina*. This, it seems to me, does such serious damage that the play descends below its higher comic reaches, and I am tempted with Dryden to comment, "'Whip-stitch, kiss my arse,' / Promised a play and dwindled to a farce?" On the one hand, the black comedy of the real-life truth in Rolfe's case is so much more powerful, and on the other it is the compelling tragedy of a man who, after his many frustrations turned to an appalling viciousness, terminated only by his solitary death. This tragedy is rooted in Rolfe's own psyche, but the play virtually ignores the role of social forces, of secular and religious organizations, in his destruction.

It is unlikely that Fr. Rolfe (so his visiting-cards were printed) would have become a saint, but the brutal fact is that the Establishment would not take the risk of giving him his chance. If it knew, it absolved itself from caring about his "paranoia," just as it neither knows nor cares about an increasing number of people like him in our time. Even the motivation of the assassin in *Hadrian VII* is ironically significant to us in these terms. All the craftsmanship and wit in Peter Luke's play could have been directed to such a consideration. He could have given us serious, rather than serio-comic, theatre in a dramatic comment, with "style"—replete with his (and Rolfe's) bon mots, epigrams, and sardonic humour—which is singularly lacking in the often-inelegant didactic of the contemporary stage. (p. 71)

D. M. Burjorjee, in a review of "Hadrian VII," in
Players Magazine, *Vol. 46, No. 2, December, 1970
& January, 1971, pp. 68-71.*

THE TIMES, LONDON

[Peter Luke's *Sisyphus and Reilly*] is a diverting series of autobiographical remembrances of things past—a cosmopolitan childhood, Eton, followed by a disastrous early marriage, and war with the Rifle Brigade, ending up as Major, acting Lieutenant Colonel, with MC. Peacetime brought another wife, children, an uninspiring job in the wine trade, parting from wife, children and job, and taking to writing TV plays under the terrifying aegis of Sydney Newman, and on the dramatization of *Hadrian VII,* the jackpot of success, which hung around, unperformed, for six years. Some old scores are wittily settled: some people will probably never speak to him again. In his dreams, the author has always been able to fly by exerting a strong enough effort of will, and this beautifully written book really takes off.

A review of "Sisyphus and Reilly," in The Times,
London, *July 13, 1972, p. 10.*

SANDY WILSON

Peter Luke's *Bloomsbury* is one of the most ambitious new plays to open in London since the same author's *Hadrian The Seventh* began its triumphant career . . . six years ago, and it would be nice to be able to report that it is likely to achieve an equal success. As it is, one must, I think, regard it, not as a failure, but as a very commendable attempt—an attempt, that is, to transfer to the stage, in the space of less than three hours, a complete literary, aesthetic and social era as it was lived by the collection of self-regarding writers, painters and other artists who were christened the Bloomsbury Group.

In fact we never visit Bloomsbury itself at all, not even, if I may make so bold, a room therein. The action, which covers the years from 1914 to 1932, passes mainly between Lytton Strachey's country cottage and the home of Lady Ottoline Morrell at Garsington Manor, with interludes at a Military Draft Board and Buckingham Palace, and is presented as taking place, one presumes, in the somewhat disordered mind of Virginia Woolf. Moreover the story centres almost entirely on Lytton Strachey and his curious ménage à trois which comprised himself, Dora Carrington and Ralph Partridge, whom they both loved. It commences with Carrington's rejection of the tempestuous painter, Mark Gertler, in favour of an asexual liaison with Strachey, and ends with her suicide shortly after Strachey's death. The pivotal episodes are Strachey's dismissal by the Tribunal, during World War One, after Partridge's powerful defence of his pacifism, the publication of his most successful book, *Eminent Victorians,* and his last illness and death. Around these Mr Luke has constructed not so much a play as a kind of revue, a Bloomsbury Follies, if you wish, through which the bizarre and slightly ridiculous members of the group cavort in a series of sexual and aesthetic encounters, and to which Virginia Woolf . . . acts as a daemonic compère. It is a perfectly valid conception and, when it works, it works very well; but it tends to leave one at the end with a slight feeling of indigestion and a suspicion that much of the depth and significance of the events we have witnessed has been sacrificed for the sake of a jolly Evening in the Theatre—an aim not necessarily to be despised at the present time. (pp. 40-1)

Sandy Wilson, in a review of "Bloomsbury," in Plays
and Players, *Vol. 21, No. 11, August, 1974, pp. 40-1.*

JOHN SIMON

Peter Luke, the author of the overrated *Hadrian VII,* came up with a new "literary" play, *Bloomsbury.* . . . This unviable contraption gave the impression that the entire Bloomsbury circle consisted of a half-dozen persons, all of them hurtling into caricature. A further disaster was centering the play on the love-hate between Virginia Woolf and Lytton Strachey without ever allowing them to occupy the stage simultaneously. Woolf and Strachey were even, briefly and absurdly, engaged to marry, yet Luke never juxtaposes them. What with sparse scenery and inept slide projections . . . , Bloomsbury became an underpopulated literary limbo, a British *No Exit,* in which the same handful of ghosts kept nastily nuzzling one another. Paltry ending for an eccentric but dazzling chapter of English cultural history!

John Simon, "London Diary, VII . . . and Out," in New York *Magazine*, Vol. 7, No. 38, September 23, 1974, p. 67.

J. W. LAMBERT

The loose-knit group of literary persons who took their inspiration from the Cambridge of the beginning of the century and generally known, if known at all, as Bloomsbury don't seem an obvious subject for wide popular appreciation, although their erratic sexual and emotional lives, developed in escape from intense Victorian family pressures, may have been thought to have some interest for those even now innocent enough to be amused—and when I attended, not on the first night, Peter Luke's **Bloomsbury,** the audience . . . undeniably sprang to life whenever a joke about homosexuality was, so to speak, broached, and became quite animated with amusement when three Bloomsbury figures, one woman and two men, were seen, albeit inertly, in bed together; they appeared understandably unmoved by the periodic appearances of . . . Virginia Woolf, a narrator gradually trapped, like her original, in her own hysteria. Save for one feature, the play is a shoddy piece of work to have come from the author of **Hadrian VII.** One doesn't, for example, expect a dramatist to stick to unvarnished fact but why when the writer Lytton Strachey, describing his experiences before a conscientious objectors' tribunal, says that he was treated with courtesy and consideration, does Mr. Luke make the members of the tribunal into a trio of grumpy buffoons? For easy laughs, I suppose—but how dimly vulgar thus to substitute a tired stereotype for a surprise, for all the world as if it were Robert Morley writing (and it would have been an effective surprise to be shown people of that kind, at that date, behaving so humanely). At any rate Mr. Luke has made something interesting out of Strachey. . . . [The character of Strachey] almost justified wasting an evening on the rough and ready cartoons of his associates, who bear little resemblance to their originals and generate no dramatic interest on their own account.

J. W. Lambert, in a review of "Bloomsbury," in Drama, *No. 114, Autumn, 1974, p. 48.*

PHILIPPA TOOMEY

The author of **Hadrian the Seventh** and the autobiography **Sisyphus and Reilly** for his first novel [**The Other Side of the Hill**]

has chosen the Peninsular War and the romantic marriage of Harry Smith and his Spanish wife, Juanita. Mr Luke has done all his research, knows the county well (he lives in Spain) but it keeps intruding into the dialogue, which is pretty stiff. . . . Not quite a novel, not quite a history.

Philippa Toomey, "George Smiley at the Court of Queen Bess," in The Times, *London, August 23, 1984, p. 9.**

SARAH JANE EVANS

When **Hadrian VII** opened . . . to rapturous acclaim, its author was down to his last pesetas in southern Spain and wondering where on earth he and his family were to live. Peter Luke had gone to Andalusia to make a film about Federico Garcia Lorca and stayed on. The sale of the film rights of **Hadrian VII** came providentially, enabling him to buy and convert a house in the country outside Alora in the mountains above Malaga, and there they stayed for ten years, returning to Ireland in 1977.

Peter Luke follows in an honourable tradition of those who have gone from Britain to settle in Spain, and have written of their experiences. [**The Mad Pomegranate and the Praying Mantis: An Andalusian Adventure**] differs in his interesting thesis that the Andalusians are very like the Irish, and he illustrates his case with anecdotes and life histories of the country folk he knew. He fulfils his aim to 'show something of the customs of the people of a small enclave in southern Spain' pretty well, avoiding the excesses of sentimentality and condescension to the 'natives' so common in books of this type. He has also tried—and succeeded—to keep out the autobiographical element, which makes a welcome change. He is less successful in attempting a comparison between his life as a farmer and that portrayed by Virgil in the *Georgics*. Nor will his endorsement of the suggestion that the International Brigade were in part attracted to Spain by the sun, or that Franco wasn't really so bad, receive universal approval. But these are minor quibbles. His picture rings true, and I look forward to his writing a similar work on Cadiz, to which he one day hopes to return.

Sarah Jane Evans, in a review of "The Mad Pomegranate and the Praying Mantis: An Andalusian Adventure," in British Book News, *April, 1985, p. 254.*

Kamala Markandaya

1924-

(Pseudonym of Kamala Purnaiya Taylor) Indian-born English novelist.

Markandaya is praised for her vivid recreation of life in India's villages and cities and for her examination of contemporary social issues. In her works she often focuses on the clash between traditional Indian lifestyles and the challenges of modernization. These conflicts are frequently intensified by cultural differences between her Indian and English characters. Among Markandaya's best-known works are *Nectar in a Sieve* (1954), her first novel, and *The Golden Honeycomb* (1977), both of which won critical and popular acclaim.

Nectar in a Sieve centers on an Indian woman who witnesses many hardships during the course of her life. Set in an Indian village, the novel explores the effects of nature on its inhabitants and the problems that ensue when a manufacturing plant is built nearby. In her second novel, *Some Inner Fury* (1955), Markandaya depicts the tensions that arise when a young Brahmin woman falls in love with a visiting Englishman. *A Silence of Desire* (1960), her next novel, centers on conflicts between old and new Indian customs in a story of a woman who prefers to have her illnesses treated by a faith healer rather than by a doctor.

Conflicts between Eastern and Western cultures are further developed in several of Markandaya's later works. *Possession* (1963) concerns a talented young Indian artist who is dominated by an English woman. Critics note that the relationship between the two characters is reflective of Anglo-Indian relations. *The Nowhere Man* (1972) depicts the effects of widespread racism following World War II on an aged Indian man living in a London suburb. In *Shalimar* (1982), a Western corporation constructs a luxurious resort in an isolated fishing village, altering the traditional lifestyle of the villagers.

The Golden Honeycomb is a historical novel in which Markandaya focuses on life in India from the late nineteenth century to the beginning of World War I. Critics particularly admired Markandaya's blend of the exotic and the realistic in her depiction of the social problems of this era. Charles R. Larson considers *The Golden Honeycomb* "the major novel of [Markandaya's] literary career."

(See also *CLC*, Vol. 8 and *Contemporary Authors*, Vols. 77-80.)

DONALD BARR

The basis of eloquence is knowledge, and *Nectar in a Sieve* has a wonderful, quiet authority over our sympathies because Kamala Markandaya is manifestly an authority on village life in India. Because of what she knows, she has been able to write a story without reticence or excess. . . . But that makes the imaginative achievement of this novel all the more extraordinary.

Photograph by Gilbert A. Jain

For this is not autobiography. . . . Rukmani, the I of her novel, is an aged peasant woman who recollects, in the last tranquility before the burning ghat, how she was married—beneath her, the villagers said, for she was the daughter of their headman— to the tenant-farmer Nathan; how with this proud and kindly man she knew the passionate simplicities, and pain; how they lived at the mercy of nature, and nature, as they knew, had no mercy; how the tannery came, and devoured their livelihood and their family peace, their gentle son and at length their land itself; how their daughter became a prostitute, and they temple-beggars; how Nathan died and Rukmani returned to the village.

All this is developed from the emotional universals, one may say, for everything that is of final importance in life can happen in a village; and yet, Indian social distances being what they are, for Miss Markandaya to write of them as she has done here, neither as documentary nor as drama pasted on documentary background, must have taken a great act of imagination.

Moreover, she has written them in English, a language instinct with alien assumptions about life. And she has made Rukmani intelligible to our alien minds, in which a philosophy of accepted helplessness goes only with breast-beating or willed sacrifice. Nothing is so easy to abuse as literary authority. With her material Miss Markandaya might have made that popular commodity, the art-peasant, the orphic lout. She might have become a dealer in wisdom of the East. She might have fed us on that highly sophisticated confection, the utterly stark style.

Instead, she opens in a prose transformed by love, moves through the iron moods of famine and oppression to a modest triumph of the spirit over objective hopelessness.

> *Donald Barr, "To a Modest Triumph," in* The New York Times Book Review, *March 15, 1955, p. 4.*

RUMER GODDEN

[*Nectar in a Sieve*] might be called the minor of the major novel I have always hoped would one day be written of India, by an Indian.

India's life is in her villages; they are her heart, they are her calm, and *Nectar in a Sieve* is written from that heart. It is the story of Rukmani, one of the millions of peasant women of India; at twelve years old she is married and her husband, Nathan, a tenant farmer, brings her home to a mud hut thatched, small, set near a paddy field. Across the doorway is a garland of mango leaves, symbol of happiness.

It all seems auspicious, but for the Indian peasant everything depends on rain and rice. One year there is a storm and the crops are washed away, another year the rains fall and there is famine; two sons die, the daughter sells herself. . . .

I do not know why Kamala Markandaya chose to use a quotation from a Western poet as a title, nor why she thought it fitted her book. "Work without hope draws nectar in a sieve," says the poem, but this is not a novel about hope, or the lack of it; it is a novel about faith and love, especially love; when hope is gone and faith seems useless, love remains. . . .

[It] is, as I have said, minor, but it has something better than power, the truth of distilled experience; it is disconnected, sometimes a little bald, but that makes it seem even more like life, and it is minor in the musical sense as well, sad, muted and haunting. Its little glints evoke a real India: the paddy fields, the green of the young rice, kingfishers, the sandalwood paste on the wicked Kunthi's hips, the champak flowers, the grinding of chilis, the trotting bullocks, the sun, the dust, the bells and the drums, the gods and goddesses, the gnawing hunger, and always the rice, the rain and the rice.

> *Rumer Godden, "Faith and Love in a Village in India," in* New York Herald Tribune Book Review, *May 15, 1955, p. 3.*

WILLIAM DUNLEA

Kamala Markandaya has written her saga of a peasant family of modern India [*Nectar in a Sieve*] in an English fresh and limpid, only slightly ornate in stylization. (p. 500)

Although the rice-growers of this story are not the worst off—and are admirable for their innate courage before all the trials that afflict them—nature is both their livelihood and their enemy. It is theirs but to work in hope and fear, then wait and pray. But still, in their humble pride, Rukmani, her husband Nathan, their daughter and countless sons know something of peace and quiet satisfaction until a tannery goes up not far from their little hut and paddy: nature takes her pound of flesh, but so does man.

Without the intrusion of the tannery the writer would merely be saying that the simple, sweet, and painful experiences of everyday are sacred in their constant but unique reality; or, with so many of our own novelists, that life is an enigmatic ritual of inevitable accidents. Here the arrival of the tannery introduces a new note: industrial progress, which can at once improve and degrade the lot of those who toil. Nevertheless, the book could not maintain its balanced presentation without eschewing ambitious polemic, and historical exactitudes lie in shadow. . . .

Miss Markandaya views numerous human types found in every society with a shrewdness we are accustomed to as "Western;" and yet she can jolt us into a realization that the color bar is double-edged. By assuming the impersonal "I" (that of Rukmani in retrospect), and its intimate objectivity, she does manage to make the Indian peasant's attitude patterns more vital to us without sacrificing their remoteness.

Yet there remains a problem of approach, with the impersonal "I" subtly wrong, so that it becomes the measure equally of the individual beauties and strengths and of the limited scope of the book as a unit. If in various respects *Nectar in a Sieve* were not a striking first novel, this could go as academic; it would be put aside appropriately as a warming experience. The good peasant mother reads and writes but differs in no other discernible fashion from other good but inarticulate peasant mothers, save that she is "writing" this book. It is a too complaisant, if never ingratiating "I" that precludes any direct association on the reader's part, a stream of consciousness missing psychological depth and proportion.

Nectar in a Sieve is true without being revealing, promising not remarkable. Still, for all its hybrid qualities, it need not be consigned to a literary limbo; its literary success might not be clear-cut, yet in its pre-eminently sentimental vein it could become a classic. The author shows skilful artlessness in persuasion of the sentiments; she renders no opinions, but conveys the eloquence of resignation. While we feel for her people—who pray to God and "the gods" in the same breath—and not with them, the pity she enlists is more honest than if she had designed her tableaux for that growing number who think even wisdom should be exotic. (p. 501)

> *William Dunlea, "Tale of India," in* Commonweal, *Vol. LXII, No. 20, August 19, 1955, pp. 500-01.*

H. M. CHAMPNESS

In *Some Inner Fury* Miss Kamala Markandaya has achieved the curious feat of writing a book about war-time India without once mentioning Japan, but given the circumstances of Southern India, this is less odd than it may seem. She is admirable on her chosen but restricted ground. Mirabhai, her heroine, belongs to a rich, cultivated and more or less orthodox Hindu family; her brother, Kitsamy, returns from Oxford to join the ICS and brings a young Englishman with him as a guest; an idealistic but sensuous love affair develops . . . ; there are progressives in the background, including a revolutionary adopted brother who is far from non-violent. All this is excellent; the small points of shame and etiquette, the social collisions immortalised by E. M. Forster at picnic and collar-stud level, not to mention the firm Hindu domesticity from which they grow, emerge with pointed clarity; this is the chosen ground which Indian novelists acutely, vivaciously and somewhat repetitively cover. They seem less happy outside; the violence and tragedy in which this novel culminates are unconvincing, though their thinness by no means ruins the book. Mr. Forster has often praised the Indian use of English; Miss Markandaya shows a crisply exotic elegance in which even a cliché can acquire an unfamiliar pungency.

*H. M. Champness, in a review of "Some Inner Fury,"
in* The Spectator, *Vol. 195, No. 6646, November 11,
1955, p. 629.*

RUMER GODDEN

When—as does not often happen—a writer, a real writer, is born in a first novel, her critics look forward to her second with eagerness, interest and, if they are versed in the ways of writers, with trepidation and sympathy as well, for this is the novel on which the newcomer will cut her teeth, almost invariably a painful process.

Kamala Markandaya showed her quality last year with *Nectar in a Sieve;* now comes her second book, *Some Inner Fury.* She is an Indian writer and her scene is India again, not the India of the peasant but that complicated, entangled India of politics, of the strange hybrid society of Englishmen living in India, of Westernized Indians living spiritually in England. It is the story of the clash of that society with the common people under the pressure of war—it culminates in 1942—of the people's struggle for freedom, and is told, in the first person, through the love of Mirabai, only daughter of rich and orthodox Hindu parents, for the young Englishman Richard.

It is a grand theme, well conceived, but Miss Markandaya's talent is not yet equal to the writing of it; she has chosen to use, perhaps unconsciously, the extraordinarily difficult technique of the flash-forward which, with her, ends in the book being so loaded with portents that the reader is never left free to enjoy the guileless charm of some of the writing.

The story is at times incoherent; even this reader, who experienced those years of bitter feeling, violence and bloodshed in India, had difficulty in knowing what was happening. Things are hinted at, not told. . . . Every word of the book is true, but it gives a feeling of untruth because, with its lack of plain statement, it suffers from over-statement as well. Miss Markandaya should contrast her court scene with Forster's in *A Passage to India*; it should be a salutary lesson.

Only a lesson, I hope, for she is a writer in whom I believe; in fact there could be a complaint that this review criticizes not *Some Inner Fury* but the writer. Well, she transcends her book. She should be watched.

*Rumer Godden, "A Talented Indian Writer's Tale of
a Strife-Torn Land," in* New York Herald Tribune
Book Review, *March 11, 1956, p. 4.*

EDWIN KENNEBECK

Miss Markandaya's characters [in *Some Inner Fury*] are typical without being types. Similarly, some of her scenes can "represent" East versus West, or personal affection versus national feeling, without blurring the colors they have on their own terms. Her style, basically bare and simple, now and then flowers quite naturally into a small arabesque of description or even of "philosophizing." (p. 669)

Of the three overlapping patterns in her novel—the girl's life with her family, her love affair with the young British official, and the story of the anti-British demonstration—the first seems to have had Miss Markandaya's most loving care. With her admirable ability to write adroitly with feeling, she draws a warm picture of the girl's family—the practical and compassionate mother; the father, a stern man of complete integrity; the brother, just back from England and comfortably at home in two worlds; the intense and single-minded foster brother; and the lovely young girl herself. They are beautifully rendered in their environment—a genteel, well-to-do Hindu household. . . .

Manners, traditions, the landscape and the very furniture, and a small group of sensitive, intelligent people, so deftly and affectionately created as separate living souls—they form harmonies and tensions enough for a story. But midway in the novel Miss Markandaya's heroine is persuaded to leave her home to live and work as a journalist in a large city. She breaks from her parents in the most abrupt and seemingly unfeeling manner. In the growing story of organized nationalist rebellion, the domestic manners and provincial flavor are superseded by political opinions and physical danger. The personal intensity of the novel's first part recurs only in some passages about the girl's affair with the Englishman. Alas for these lives that the new India should have to invade and shatter them so cruelly. Alas too, that, in telling of it, the novel—though it continues readable, professional, even moving, virtues we now expect from Miss Markandaya—should lose much of that flavor.

Edwin Kennebeck, "Of New India," in Commonweal, *Vol. LXIII, No. 26, March 30, 1956, pp. 669-70.*

ANTHONY ARAU

[In *Some Inner Fury,* Markandaya] gives further evidence of her ability to write fiction of dignity and sensitivity. Using as an entering wedge a gentle love affair between a young Englishman and an Indian girl of aristocratic background, she explores the possibility of Anglo-Indian understanding among the young, well-educated, well-intentioned, and relatively unembittered classes of either side. Her outlook is hardly optimistic. For what at first appears to be understanding takes on an aura of uneasiness under stress, and then, as tension develops, shifts into bewildered anxiety, and, finally, as violence erupts between the races, disintegrates into bitterness and recrimination. Her point seems to be that individuals from either culture, despite their enlightened status, are after all products of inescapable and mutually exclusive heritages; in other words, there may, at best, be cordiality but, as crisis reveals, hardly profound and shock-resistant understanding. An ironic sidelight is Miss Markandaya's implied belief that it is not, really, a matter of East and West not understanding each other, but rather a matter of West being somehow incapable of understanding the deeper East. Her heroine seems to say, "I knew, after all, that it would not work out, but he . . .''

Nonetheless, this is a close to first-rate performance. Here, violence is not merely atmosphere but an essential element, used deftly to provoke and illuminate subtle changes in the situation and to throw personalities and relationships into sharp relief. Although not all the characters in *Some Inner Fury* are developed as adequately as they might have been, all are credible, and even Govind, the fanatic half-brother, can be accepted with genuine sympathy since we understand something of the unenviable lot that has helped to twist him. The chief criticism that must be made of Miss Markandaya's work is that it is formidably stiff, nearly Victorian in its style. This may be a reflection of self-consciousness, common to early novels, or it may, which is more likely, be traceable to the 19th Century models that the author seems to have drawn upon. In any event, *Some Inner Fury* is an impressive second novel, and leaves one waiting with agreeable anticipation for a third. (p. 20)

Anthony Arau, "Some Proper Studies," in The New Republic, *Vol. 135, No. 4, July 23, 1956, pp. 20-1.**

PAUL PICKREL

The main characters in *A Silence of Desire* are a middle-class Indian couple with three children. They have been married for fifteen years agreeably enough; the husband is a clerk in a government office. Then he discovers that his wife is often away from home on unexplained business; she is disposing of the few family treasures and keeps the picture of a strange man in a trunk. Under the influence of his office colleagues who have advanced ideas about sexual intrigue derived from Western (American) movies, and for lack of any other explanation, he is forced to conclude that she is having an affair. Finally he stays away from work to follow her, and he discovers that she is going to a faith healer to be cured of an illness.

The man is half-Westernized; he does not want his wife to fool around with such primitive sorcery; he wants her to go to the hospital. But she knows that her mother and sister died in the hospital, possibly of similar illnesses, and anyway she belongs to the old India, where mind was more important than body. She feels better when she goes to the faith healer and that is enough for her.

Many novels have been written about the meeting of East and West, including one that I regard as a wonderful book, E. M. Forster's *A Passage to India.* Miss Markandaya is not a novelist of Forster's subtlety or richness, but I doubt that anyone has ever written a more moving or human or beautifully true story about what the conflict of cultures can mean for two humble people than *A Silence of Desire.* Both the husband and wife are so exquisitely right by their own standards; all they are trying to do is to find a place to live, a room for their love, space to work out their problems, between the two views of life that are dividing them. (pp. 98-9)

Paul Pickrel, in a review of "A Silence of Desire," in Harper's Magazine, *Vol. 221, No. 1323, August, 1960, pp. 98-9.*

ROSANNE ARCHER

A Silence of Desire is the story of a middle-aged clerk whose placid life becomes tormented as he begins to suspect his wife of infidelity. She has indeed turned from him, but in fear: she has turned to a faith-healer, whose influence threatens to swallow up their home, their relationship, and the welfare of their children. As his life comes slowly apart at the seams, as one after another of the tiny fragments which made up the happiness of an ordinary family slip away, Nandekar becomes terribly aware of each piece which went unnoticed in the mosaic of days and years. Each fragment of life becomes magnified and isolated under the glaring light of disintegration, and, confused and helpless, he struggles against the drift.

Delicately, with intense, humane insight, Miss Markandaya explores this family whose members are losing all that made their lives meaningful, and she raises profoundly human issues. . . .

But this is not a philosophical novel, nor a literary scalpel which uses a situation to expose the author's premises. It is rather a moving and sensitive story which implies questions always remaining to be repeated, like a gallant counterpoint to Thoreau's theme: Most men live lives of quiet desperation.

Several excellent novels written in English by Indian authors seem to share with *A Silence of Desire* the quality of human truth seen in a clear bright light and commonplaces refreshed as realities. Perhaps because Indian English is so often the fluent language of people for whom it is not a mother tongue, it has taken on an admirable directness and clarity which can be heard even in ordinary speech. In the hands of a skilled writer like Kamala Markandaya, Indo-Anglian acquires a sharpness of precise and telling detail which reminds one of the wonderful Indian miniatures, so brilliant, so colorful and so clear.

With deftness and precision, Miss Markandaya has given us a vivid picture of Indian town life and of an ordinary Indian civil servant who reflects, in a particularly Indian situation, the universal qualities of men and women caught unawares by trouble. It is a beautiful book.

Rosanne Archer, "Vivid Picture of Indian Town and Family Life," in New York Herald Tribune Book Review, *August 7, 1960, p. 5.*

ROBERT PAYNE

[Miss Markandaya] knows exactly how to produce the effects she desires in a prose that is remarkably agile and completely her own. She could, I suspect, write about anything; she has an almost frightening skill. In *Possession* Miss Markandaya has chosen to describe the life of an Indian shepherd boy who has a great gift for painting, and who is suddenly transplanted to England, where he receives the acclaim due his talent, and then founders because he has no roots in the country of his adoption.

It is a good theme, and might conceivably have been an important one, but England keeps getting in the way. Kamala Markandaya writes best about India; her England is chic Belgravia accurately observed, but oddly jaundiced and disheveled at five o'clock in the morning after an all-night party. One wonders why she goes to such lengths to stick the pin so accurately into the entrails of the butterfly.

The boy Valmiki is a brilliant invention, and so is Ellie, the frail, gawky refugee from a concentration camp who wanders miserably into his life and becomes his model and his mistress. I am not so sure about Lady Caroline, the rich, beautiful, and complaisant Englishwoman, who takes the boy under her wing and parades him like a monkey on a stick through fashionable London. Fiction is littered with Lady Carolines. This one is a tougher chicken than most, and much more demanding.

It is a testimony to the author's power that we come to believe all the boy's liaisons, and sympathize with him and like him, in spite of the giddy presence of Lady Caroline. He fills the canvas. The trouble is that he has to bear the weight of the story almost alone, and he has not quite the strength for it.

So there it is—not a great novel, nor even a particularly good one, but one that has a quality of writing and a keenness of perception that demand respect. It suggests other books of far greater scope that the author could write if she ever set her mind to it.

Robert Payne, "The Homesick Shepherd," in Saturday Review, Vol. XLVI, No. 21, May 25, 1963, p. 34.

MARGARET PARTON

Theoretically, *Possession* should be a good book. First of all, because Kamala Markandaya in her three previous novels has demonstrated a brilliance and depth outstanding even among India's current crop of highly talented novelists. And secondly, because the Pygmalion theme is always interesting.

In this case, the Pygmalion is Lady Caroline Bell and her Galatea is a young South Indian goatherd. Lady Caroline, a wealthy, international-set divorcee, meets Valmiki in the course of a toddy-hunting village expedition, discovers that he has enormous artistic ability and whisks him off to London. All this is accomplished with the reluctant aid of Suya, the narrator, an Indian woman writer with a British education and an acid tongue....

But alas, this seems to be the one disappointing book which perhaps should be permitted to every good writer. There is something sour about it—even bitter, in a way uncharacteristic of Miss Markandaya (just as the clumsy writing is also uncharacteristic). Because the author has used the first person narrative we never really get into the minds of Lady Caroline or Valmiki; failing to understand them, we dislike them. And lastly, if Miss Markandaya intends this story of possession to be analogous to the relationship of Britain and India, she fails completely on the ground of superficiality.

Margaret Parton, "A Pair about India," in Books, June 9, 1963, p. 10.*

JOSEPH HITREC

The regional patterns of India are so diverse that it is almost an axiom for an Indian writer to stay faithful to his own milieu while hoping that his story will have an appeal beyond geography and ethnic divisions. Kamala Markandaya, a South Indian writer who uses the medium of English, has done this, most successfully, in a series of novels dealing with timeless human problems in the villages and hamlets of her native region—notably in *Some Inner Fury* and *Silence of Desire*. Now, with *Possession,* she has broken from the mold. The result is a taut reminder of another axiom, that talent and artistry have primacy over setting, even in the case of tradition-bound India.

Although her story begins and ends in South India, its central problem has very little to do with the Indian canvas per se. The theme is the possessive urge of human beings in their relations to each other, and she explores this on a level of consciousness higher than in her previous books....

In concept and treatment, *Possession* departs so strikingly from the usual conventions of the Indian novel that at times Miss Markandaya sounds more English than Indian. Her story is sparse and beautifully controlled from beginning to end. There is a ring of truth in the way she arranges her confrontations, and her viewpoint is neither fuzzy nor sentimental. While *Possession* is not meant to enlarge our understanding of Indian folkways, it places the author firmly and solidly at the head of her country's storytellers.

Joseph Hitrec, "How the Possessor Was Possessed," in The New York Times Book Review, June 23, 1963, p. 28.

ORVILLE PRESCOTT

One of the great functions of fiction, perhaps its greatest, is to particularize and dramatize, to make specific, personal and moving general conditions of life and general truths about character. For instance, the terrible poverty of India is only an abstract fact to most Americans. Figures about it in the newspapers are only statistics, horrifying but soon forgotten. But anyone who has read Kamala Markandaya's *Nectar In A Sieve* has vicariously suffered a harrowing experience. He has been deeply immersed in the poverty of an Indian village. Anyone who reads Miss Markandaya's new novel, *A Handful Of Rice,* will feel himself equally intimately acquainted with the poverty of Indian city life. He will also know the satisfaction of having read a psychologically astute and thoroughly readable book. This, of course, is only to be expected. Miss Markandaya is probably the finest living Indian novelist writing in English.

This is the story of Ravi, who fled from the desperate misery of his native village to seek his fortune in a big city very like Madras. When we first meet Ravi he is a drunken vagrant and petty criminal fleeing from a policeman he has bitten. Ten years later when Miss Markandaya ends her story Ravi is an embittered, desperate, furiously unhappy tailor wavering between respectable misery and crime.... But Ravi's conscience, his decent upbringing and his love for his wife and children kept him at various last moments on the right side of the law. Ravi's struggle to survive is the principal theme of *A Handful of Rice.*

And Ravi and his family, brilliantly characterized though they are, are not just individuals. They are symbolical representatives of millions of others—millions who endure life always on the brink of starvation because there are so many of them, so few jobs, such crippling handicaps of family obligation and traditional custom. *A Handful Of Rice* is an education in the social and economic woes of India.

Ravi is no hero. His weaknesses and follies are many. But no one not genuinely heroic could have withstood the various pressures, strains, worries and humiliations of Ravi's life....

Living always on the edge of destitution, pitifully subject to the whims of customers, harassed by feuds and clashing personalities, helpless when illness or disaster of any kind struck, Ravi and his in-laws were still better off than many of their neighbors. Reading *A Handful Of Rice* is by no means as dreary as its subject matter may suggest. Miss Markandaya writes with narrative power, with flashes of somewhat grim humor and with deep compassion. When Ravi is cruel to his wife he does not suddenly become a cruel man. He is only a partly broken man. Ravi could not endure his disappointments, frustrations and fears without outbursts of psychological explosion. Could many others do better or as well? Miss Markandaya does not ask this question, but it is implicit in her deftly written and engrossing story.

Orville Prescott, "Life among the Woes of India," in The New York Times, August 9, 1966, p. 35.

ARTHUR LALL

Kamala Markandaya's writing, in [*A Handful Of Rice*], is deft and often beautiful. As she traces the course of some 10 years or so in the life of a young villager named Ravi, who comes to a city somewhere in South India—intimations of Madras appear in the writing—she creates and holds before the reader moments of arresting sensitivity. One occurs when Ravi becomes really aware of Nalini, the girl he goes on to marry, and of "the wholesome quality he discerns in her, a kind of vulnerable purity that he wanted to enclose and guard, feeling himself cleansed and enriched by it." . . .

Some of the most powerful contrasts are provided by Ravi's encounters with Damodar, another young adventurer in the city, who climbs to the top by bootlegging, theft and worse. Ravi, who never really "makes good," admires Damodar— of course with tinges of revulsion—as a counterpoint to the grinding poverty in the household of his in-laws.

The novel focuses on the life and ill-fortunes of Ravi. But there are other excellent portraits of lesser characters: Apu, the tailor whose house Ravi breaks into at the beginning of the book and who becomes successively the young hero's employer and fa-ther-in-law; the master-tailor's loud and lusty wife, Jayamma, who thinks it quite natural that her son-in-law should sleep with her, in circumstances that safeguard her reputation; and of course Nalini, Ravi's beautiful, traditional wife—obedient, long-suffering, who receives with equanimity her husband's love and blows.

As a novel, as a story with a plot, the book has weaknesses. Much of it is descriptive of life in the little house of Apu and Jayamma, which also shelters their daughters, their husbands, and other relatives. For this reader, there is not enough move-ment—though there are disturbances enough!—in this house-hold. There is little drama in the events, and less artistic inev-itability. There is also a certain abstraction about the setting. Perhaps this simplifies the inevitable strangeness of India for the non-Indian reader. For his Indian counterpart, the result is thinness of texture.

> Arthur Lall, "*Ravi and Damodar,*" *in* The New York Times Book Review, *November 11, 1966, p. 55.*

KENNETH GRAHAM

The Coffer Dams is for two-thirds of its length a fine corrective to mysticism: complex and delicate in language, knowledge-ably devoted to objects and men at work—catching birds in the jungle or wielding a power crane. A dam is being built in the highlands of South India by a consortium of English and Indians, with foreseeable complications—racial, sexual, cli-matic and technical. To my surprise, the patently schematic nature of the characterisation caused me little worry. Clinton, the head of the project, is the harsh western pragmatist, the archetypal dam- and empire-builder. His wife, all sympathy and openness, communes with the local tribesmen and sleeps with the tribesman-engineer at the dam—another western Woman Who Rode Away. And there are other assorted types, from Memsahib to embittered Nationalist, who thicken out the dense interplay of attitudes to life, and compensate for the lack of internal characterisation by all the interest and play of a trial scene or a debate. Tension mounts as the deadline of the mon-soon approaches, and then the whole book is swept away in the symbolic deluge that ensues. Quite suddenly, unforgivably, the style completely changes: syntax becomes distorted, dia-logue as stiffly mannered as narrative. Engineering passes into phantasmagoria, the ithyphallic gods of India are at work, an old chief becomes a mage, and a good novel dissolves into an inane Walpurgisnacht.

> Kenneth Graham, "*Wind and Shadow,*" *in* The Lis-tener, *Vol. LXXXI, No. 2094, May 15, 1969, p. 636.**

LINDA HESS

[*The Coffer Dams*] is supposed to be a grand-scale novel of the new India: hulking cranes in the jungle, stiff white ribs rising to curb a mighty river, TNT exploding in the faces of tribesmen, a monsoon-crazed *memsahib* who won't believe the Empire has fallen, British bosses who don't believe it either but go through the motions of respect, Indian engineers who despise their continued dependence on the former masters, and the juggernaut of technology hurtling on, more powerful and inevitable now than jungle or monsoon.

But the men are stick figures, and the morals are handed out on trays like airline lunches. . . .

It is in descriptive phrases and passages that the author is at her best, noting how a restive audience cringed like "oyster flesh under lemon juice," or how Helen caught a glimpse of the attractive Bashiam "and something in her shifted, very slightly like a few grains in a sand hill whose movement in-definably alters the whole structure." There is a subtly erotic scene where she and Bashiam accompany a bird-catcher to the thick of the forest before dawn to watch him capture live, with net and lime and reedflute, the mynas, finches, cuckoos, bul-buls, and other breeds that proliferate in the jungle. . . .

Miss Markandaya seems to write best about what she values most: organic things, earth and flesh. The rest of the novel— industrial drama, intercultural confrontation, socio-economic dislocation—flows by leaving hardly a mark; water over the dam.

> Linda Hess, in a review of "*The Coffer Dams,*" in Saturday Review, *Vol. LII, No. 24, June 14, 1969, p. 35.*

MARTIN LEVIN

Mrs. Markandaya's novel [*The Nowhere Man*] is an unrelenting anatomy of alienation and racial polarity. (p. 24)

Mrs. Markandaya is an elegant stylist who translates bigotry into a chain of arresting images. Over and over again she reinforces the sense of being passed over, turned down, pa-tronized. In colonial India Srinivas' livelihood is taken away when the British decimate the family timber forest for a military road. In London he gradually wilts, although toward the close of his life he is succored by a saintly English divorcee who keeps him company till the end.

The powerful though static atmosphere of intolerance would be more affecting were it not adulterated with a surfeit of more primary troubles. Srinivas contracts leprosy. His wife dies of tuberculosis. One son rejects his family, the other is blown up driving an ambulance in wartime London. In the thick of such indiscriminate agony, social acceptance diminishes in priority. (pp. 24-5)

> Martin Levin, in a review of "*The Nowhere Man,*" in The New York Times Book Review, *January 14, 1973, pp. 24-5.*

RONALD BRYDEN

[Srinivas, the protagonist of *The Nowhere Man,*] an elderly Indian trader in spices, has lived in South London since the Twenties, benefiting from his neighbours' English indifference and decency sufficiently to raise his sons as brown Englishmen and to feel at home. But the post-war immigrant influx suddenly turns him into a statistic, local Powellites daub hang-the-wogs graffiti opposite his door and, almost as a psychosomatic expression of his shock, he contracts leprosy.

That sounds excessive, and some of the efforts to enter the racialists' consciousness founder in baffled luridness. But mostly the novel is restrained, distinguished and sad, remembering affectionately the England which found foreigners odd but acceptable, where Indian and native could share a bomb-shelter in the Blitz. The immigrant view of it has seldom been explored better: to Srinivas, Brahmin and vegetarian, Christmas means a hideous silence in farm-yards over the land, but he forgives his neighbours' innocence and lights a Christmas tree in his window. When he has to recognise their change as the plague which convulsed Hitler's Germany, the effect is not of reproach but of distressed love.

> *Ronald Bryden, "Kinship," in* The Listener, *Vol. 89, No. 2298, April 12, 1973, p. 489.**

JOHN SPURLING

I did not warm to *Two Virgins* by Kamala Markandaya until about halfway through. Primitive village communities are not perhaps in themselves less interesting than advanced urban ones, but they are certainly not more so. This Indian Ambridge is not improved by Kamala Markandaya's *faux naïf* style, all short sentences and proper names repeated instead of pronouns. Things liven up eventually with the arrival of a film producer and the seduction of one of the virgins, but the best part of the book is set in the city, where the offended family goes to confront the villain. The rapid deterioration of relationships and identities is sympathetically conveyed; you enter the story at last and feel the sweat, discomfort and sadness of characters who impressed you as boring in their better days.

> *John Spurling, "Precious Stone," in* New Statesman, *Vol. 87, No. 2252, May 17, 1974, p. 703.**

ROBERTA RUBENSTEIN

It is not often that a novel satisfies one's aesthetic, emotional, and intellectual yearnings so richly, through such a simply told and authentic story as one finds in *Two Virgins*, by Kamala Markandaya. What might have been merely a vivid picture of life in a traditional post-Gandhi Indian village is given its imaginative power by being told through the eyes of a young girl, Saroja, whose education—sexual and otherwise—frames the larger issues of the novel. From the beginning, the reader is drawn into immediate participation in the details of daily existence in Saroja's village.... (p. 225)

However, the novel is more than a finely realized moving tableau of life in the village; part of its theme is the archetypal one of the journey from innocence to experience, involving not only Saroja, but also her older sister, Lalitha. A natural beauty, spoiled and favored by her parents, Lalitha is the counterfoil to Saroja's innocence. The most obvious contrast between the lives of the two daughters, and the incipient seed which grows into their very different fates, is the difference in their educations. While Saroja attends a traditional Hindu village school, Lalitha is indulged by being sent to a Western one run by Miss Mendoza, an Indian convert to Christianity.

There, Lalitha learns the gentle arts of deception and appearances, as well as dissatisfaction with and contempt for her family's simple life—*sans* refrigerator and other mechanical "necessities" of Western culture. It is ironic that a major subject at Miss Mendoza's school is "moral science"—since Lalitha's moral decline begins with Miss Mendoza's introduction of a filmmaker to the village. Cinema becomes a suggestive symbol for the world of appearances which quickly seduces Lalitha.

While Lalitha becomes critical of the traditional ways, Saroja develops a critical consciousness of another kind: she learns to keep her own counsel, to discriminate among the hidden meanings in gestures, tones of voice, and words not spoken. From her position as the over-looked younger daughter, she develops an acute sensitivity to the emotional undercurrents of her family's relationships. For example, she senses a certain attraction between her mother, Amma, and the Sikh hawker who buys her (Saroja) off with a free toy. "Saroja could see if the hawker's hand strayed ever so little it would touch her [mother]." Amma "wanted to know, Isn't there anything else you can find to do? and she sighed, said children are such a tie, forever under your feet, using her second tone, which was resigned, the first one intended for Saroja had been exasperated and shrill." (pp. 225-26)

These and other episodes are part of Markandaya's acute insight into the mind of a young girl as well as the politics of family life. One might say that she creates an almost Jamesian world (though certainly without his rarification)—pitting the worlds of innocence and sophistication, of purity and corruption, against each other. (p. 226)

The consolidation of the novel's movement is in the theme implied by the title *Two Virgins*—for, among other things, the story traces the sexual education and initiation of both daughters. Soroja's natural curiosity about her world includes questions about her own body, about the taboo subjects of childbirth, birth control, intercourse, and death—intimations of which her sensitive eyes and ears pick up.... Her knowledge grows out of close observation of the daily events of village life—from piecing together innuendoes and bits of information from her sister, her school friends, the sweet-maker Chingleput, and the milkman's wife. Lalitha's education, on the other hand, comes in a more dramatic way. From the beginning, the older girl's vanity and flirtatiousness reveal a highly sensual nature, as well as a disposition to believe that the glamourous world she imagines outside the village (shaped largely by Miss Mendoza's suggestions) is a far better one. These qualities of her personality are brought together when the filmmaker, Mr. Gupta, comes to make a documentary of "real life" in a "typical" Indian village—an occasion which Markandaya presents with marvelous irony. Given a naiveté far more self-destructive than Saroja's because it is so easily seduced by appearances, Lalitha follows her illusions by running away to the city to become a film star.

The contrast between city and village—a theme which runs through Markandaya's fiction from her first novel, *Nectar in a Sieve,* to this most recent one—is most effectively drawn in the sections which follow. The reader, like Saroja and her family, learns through inference that Lalitha's experience in the city—the details of which are embroidered for her family's sake—is more than she can handle. After an extended absence and a few cryptic communications, she returns to the village, broken, bereft of both her psychic and physical innocence. With her, the family makes a pilgrimage of sorts to retrace the steps of her fall to the filmmaker, Gupta, and to demand recompense from him for their daughter's pregnancy. Saroja, accompanying her parents and sister to the city, takes a parallel journey into experience which follows Lalitha's at a safe distance. For, very imperceptibly in the forward movement of the story, Saroja has grown from childhood to the stage of budding sexuality; Gupta's assistant, Devraj, prompts in her the first stirrings of passion like those which overwhelmed her sister—but just enough for Saroja to recognize and resist them. (pp. 227-28)

What makes the archetypal theme of initiation so fresh in this novel is Markandaya's unfailing eye for detail—both physical and psychological—as well as the suggestive power of her writing. More than the charting of the alternative ways of confronting what is referred to in the novel as "society," but understood as a knowledge of good and evil, the novel puts forth a living and utterly real microcosm—socially, politically, economically complex. The issue of sexuality alone, rendered through the growth of awareness in the two girls, also brings with it a feminist's survey of the position of women in India today—from Aunt Alemelu's pronouncement that "women were born to suffer," to Lalitha's misguided observation that "you have to be quick," to Saroja's recognition that "women had no boltholes. There was no escape for them, they had to stand where they were and take it." Saroja learns about the forms of sexual tyranny which know neither age nor class.

Markandaya also weaves through the narrative a sense of political consciousness, filtered through Appa's forward-looking if ineffectual pronouncements, and his recollections of the influence of Gandhi and the injustices suffered under British rule. (pp. 228-29)

However, the most remarkable quality of *Two Virgins* is its tone. Throughout, one finds a gentle, compassionate irony—sometimes manifested through humor, other times through understatement. Saroja is a perfect vehicle for both qualities; not a single note rings false. (p. 229)

> *Roberta Rubenstein, in a review of "Two Virgins,"*
> *in* World Literature Written in English, *Vol. 13, No.*
> *2, November, 1974, pp. 225-30.*

APARNA JACK

Tully, the principal character in [*Pleasure City* (published in the United States as *Shalimar*)] has antecedents in Kamala Markandaya's work. These men were basically decent Englishmen, who understood the feelings of the natives and thought of India during the Raj as an occupied country. Tully has shrugged off the mantle of Empire worn by both his grandfathers, but occasionally finds himself tripping over its discarded folds. . . .

The change in Tully is wrought by Rikki, an orphaned fisherboy, who sees in Tully someone who 'could advance a horizon or a dream'. Their friendship grows against the background of the building of Shalimar [a luxury resort]. Rikki is not obsequious by nature and he speaks English. Tully has recognisable white, liberal tendencies and is viewed with some mistrust by Shalimaris like Mrs Contractor and his English superior, a survivor from colonial times. Do Tully's imperial connections make him think of India as a home from home, or is he going native, and drinking tea with the labourers? Such responses do seem dated, but their power is demonstrated in a discussion of Forster's infamous incident in the Marabar Caves. Rikki overhears the debate and questions Tully; they find themselves racially aligned. Rikki thinks that either Miss Quested was raped or she wasn't—there can be no confusion—whereas Tully enters more into the Forsterian spirit and says that what matters is Miss Quested's conviction that she was violated.

But the relevance of these responses to the past is difficult to assess. The links between the two brands of imperialism experienced by Forster and Tully are established, but comparisons cannot be too far pursued. What Shalimar seems to destroy in the fishing village is communal suffering. When the catch is bad, the fishing families starve, when it is good they eat and forget the bad times. Only the village headman hankers after the old ways. Rikki's adoptive mother, on the other hand, is grateful for the electric light and the leftovers which Rikki brings home from Shalimar. Rikki, too, lists his gains—a quartz watch, green frog flippers, a radio cassette.

What, therefore, does the fishing village lose? The answer, presumably, lies in matters of broken tradition, divided families and soaring land prices—but all this is left unsaid. The author neglects to go into it, much as she neglects to describe the great Shalimar project, which is completed with what some would see as rather un-Indian speed, efficiency and unobtrusive bureaucracy. Whatever the background, its workings must occasionally be apparent if it is to have any impact.

Tully imagines that Rikki will return to the life of a fisherman, to a oneness with the landscape and the sea. He sees the incongruity of Rikki making meringues and learning how to serve drinks. Yet no sense of irony is apparent in the fisherman's family sharing a spoonful of caviar, though it is Tully's perceptions the writer endorses in the novel. Rikki has no desire to relinquish his perks as a waiter and life-saver at Shalimar. Rikki's 'soul was taken hostage' quotes Tully, and recognises his part in it.

Shalimar is identified with materialism in a somewhat specious opposition to the old values of the fishing village—which so eagerly embraces materialism when it gets the chance. . . . [The] contrasts of the novel display a stereotyped romanticism about people who live a breadline existence. Tully, we may be perfectly certain, did not have to suffer the disadvantages of such an existence.

> *Aparna Jack, "Pale Hands," in* The Spectator, *Vol.*
> *249, No. 8045, September 18, 1982, p. 24.*

JUDY ASTOR

[*Pleasure City*] is a thoroughly nice book. There is no evil in it, and not much sin, original or otherwise. By that I do not mean it is dull; Kamala Markandaya's story about the impact on a little Indian fishing village when a huge new luxury hotel and leisure complex begins to be built next door has enough gentle charm to sustain one to the end. Or very nearly. It is a confrontation between the primitive and the sophisticated and also between East and West; and if the issues are a little bit fudged, and the characters a little bit romanticised, Miss Markandaya still has a shrewd way of placing them and a good ear for dialogue. (p. 24)

> *Judy Astor, "Nice and Nasty," in* The Listener, *Vol.*
> *108, No. 2779, September 23, 1982, pp. 23-4.**

ELIZABETH CLARIDGE

Indian hosts take Western visitors on a picnic at some caves. An upsetting and ambiguous incident disrupts the adventure. The episode is of no great importance to the narrative of Kamala Markandaya's new novel [*Pleasure City*]: its function is symbolic. In reminding the reader so explicitly of Forster's *A Passage to India,* she implies that her book may be seen as coda to his, the story of his story's aftermath. Where he dissects British and Indian attitudes in the last phase of the Raj, she traces their residue in independent India.

Her *mise en scène* is simple in outline, rich in significance. Onto a lyrical stretch of Indian coastline, 'unaware, dreamy, with a slight air of being shelled out of time', descends the Atlas International Development Corporation to build Shalimar, a resort for rich tourists. There is nothing vulgar about Shalimar, nothing overtly discordant with the landscape, just unobtrusive elegance and luxury with an attendant-guest ratio of nine to one. (pp. 107-08)

Kamala Markandaya is too delicate a quarryer of truths, too much a connoisseur of paradox, to label Shalimar simply as imposition on innocent India, an imperialist venture in contemporary guise. Imposition on innocence there is, in the encroachment, physical and psychological, on the local fishing settlement. The pleasure city seduces, corrupts, sews envy, undermines old fidelities. Yet there is collusion of a kind, too, as there is in the larger issue. A-political AIDCORP, which builds almost anything for anyone anywhere with dazzling virtuosity, builds Shalimar by Indian invitation, with Indian management as well as labour. There is much-needed foreign exchange in it for India, and there is prestige, proof of modernity, competence, sophistication. Kamala Markandaya is interested in something more subtle than symptoms of latter-day imperialism. Her concern is the extent to which Shalimar is a consequence of, a reaction to, the old imperialism. She elaborates the theme: effects, outcrops, vestiges of the Raj persist, modulating the evolving relationship of India and the West as they do the responses of individual Indians and Westerners.

Another kind of writer, Paul Theroux or William Boyd for example, would extract from this theme material for comedy or satire or farce. Kamala Markandaya's tone is a shade solemn, is a little lacking in edge, a tendency noticeable in the work of other Indian women writers. Nevertheless, she is capable of discomfiting observations. A peripheral character in her story, Mrs. Adeline Lovat from New Jersey, writes novels about India which are admired everywhere, except in India. Diligent as she is with note-book and tape-recorder, she finds this puzzling. A glance over her shoulder as she bumps about in a bullock-cart *en route* for the picnic offers illumination: '*Emerald oases,* she noted, *women like parakeets in red and green saris bent double in the paddies . . . the noble carriage of these smiling peasants . . .* went down on her pad, and would later confirm every image in her readers' minds of a happy, laughing, backward race'.

That such enlivening flashes of scorn are rare is the obverse of a cardinal virtue. She unfolds her story with remarkable lack of censure and dogmatism where both could be expected. Forster's characterizations in *A Passage to India* are sharp in every sense. While he reserves contempt for Anglo-Indian foibles, he is often mocking about Indian ones. His is an unmistakably English voice speaking of India. Kamala Markandaya is more benign and, for the most part, as charitable towards her Western characters as she is towards her Indian ones. Apart from occasional Indian inflexions in her prose, a sense of words omitted

and sentences truncated, her voice is not detectably partisan. In her own way, which is indeed different from Forster's, she is no less perceptive than he for being more generous. She has a considerable gift for 'working through to the silent syllabary of another'. (pp. 108-09)

It was brave, and perhaps foolhardy, to invite direct comparison with Forster, and only a consciously literary writer would introduce such a device. Measuring her book against his one can see particularly clearly that it is too much a novel of ideas, too little a novel which generates its own life. The narrative lacks development and tension, the characterization shows signs of being imposed. Against this must be set the subtlety, intelligence, and interest of the ideas, and descriptive passages of haunting beauty. They make *Pleasure City,* another view of staying on, a rewarding book. (p. 109)

Elizabeth Claridge, "Aftermath," in London Magazine, *Vol. 22, No. 7, October, 1982, pp. 107-09.*

DEAN FLOWER

In a style by turns cryptic and simple, slow-moving and abrupt, [*Shalimar*] tells the story of a friendship between an Indian youth named Rikki and a middle-aged peripatetic British businessman named Toby Tully. Rikki is a fisherman's son, orphaned, an instinctive swimmer, at one with the sea from infancy; but he takes to books—to Bible stories and the English language—almost as readily, under the guidance of a Christian missionary couple, the Bridies. Soon Tully takes their place in Rikki's life, and becomes his access to the interesting Western world. Tully represents AIDCORPS, an anonymous "multinational consortium" which is building an elaborate resort-hotel complex of the sort found in Cancun or Maui nowadays, this one an hour or so from Culcutta and to be called Shalimar. Tully arrives to see that everything runs smoothly. Descendent of merchants and consuls who once ruled India, Tully takes up residence in an old mansion named Avalon, a "dream castle" built by one of his imperious ancestors. So history repeats itself; Tully restores the old place even while the new complex goes up—a hotel "out of the Hilton mold," stainless steel kitchens, cabañas and pool, and many new jobs for the simple folk of a fishing village. Instead of a story about how ugly imperialist empire-builders destroy a beautiful native way of life, or for that matter how the mysterious East defeats the know-it-all Western way of life, Markandaya's story eludes politics and categories.

Tully is a quiet man, subtle enough to be both thrilled and puzzled by Rikki's friendship, and thoughtful about their ways of communication. Rikki veers from generous impulsive gestures to injured pride, and from odd spasms of shyness to unself-conscious candor. He also learns to mix drinks, ride a surfboard, and teach old ladies how to swim. That he is drawn away from his step-family by becoming a lifeguard and a waiter at Shalimar is not after all the problem: social change affects them all, and Rikki seems better equipped to deal with it than most. Oddly, there is almost no suspense at all, and perhaps only one climax. Instead Markandaya prefers many small episodes of amusing and revealing anti-climax. (pp. 305-06)

With infinite patience and tact the novel shows how the Anglo-Indian world has reversed itself. Avalon has not after all been restored for Tully or his likes, nor finally will Shalimar belong to its makers. The landscape itself exerts its own insistent authority, its seductive lure and threat. A Hindu-Brahmin by birth, Markandaya knows the ways of time and fate. "Subtle country, my boy," says Tully at the end. "The minx knows . . . what she's given, and how to give back, in exact proportion." We leave this rueful British observer with his final reflection on India's adroitness: "He could not for his life have sorted the aloes from the honey." Nothing is italicized in this novel, and it is very hard to take anything out of the subtly-meandering narrative stream without its losing color and value. Markandaya is a crafty and wonderful writer, unlike anyone else. (p. 307)

> *Dean Flower, in a review of "Shalimar," in* The Hudson Review, *Vol. XXXVII, No. 2, Summer, 1984, pp. 305-07.*

Stanley Middleton

1919-

English novelist and scriptwriter.

A prolific author, Middleton writes provincial novels set in the English Midlands where he has lived most of his life. His characters are ordinary, middle-class people, and his accurate and detailed descriptions of their homes, meals, and clothes convey a distinct sense of realism. His authorial voice is subtle, which allows an objective presentation of character and a text free of didacticism and sentimentality. Critics consistently praise Middleton's understated style and his perceptive insights into human relationships. In 1974 Middleton was named cowinner of the Booker McConnell Prize for his novel *Holiday*.

Middleton's work is generally serious in tone, displaying little humor as his characters struggle with dissolving relationships or other personal crises. Societal pressures often hinder communication between couples, as in *Two's Company* (1964), where an affair between a rebellious, middle-class young man and an uneducated, lower-class woman is grim and eventually destructive. Death is another recurrent motif in his work. In *The Golden Evening* (1968), the death of a woman leads to the maturation of her adolescent son and daughter and forces her husband to begin life anew, and in *Ends and Means* (1977), characters threaten to commit suicide in order to force love and attention from others. In other works, infidelity causes upheaval in the lives of Middleton's protagonists. For example, in *The Other Side* (1980), a man betrays his wife, and in *Valley of Decision* (1985), a woman betrays her husband. Each work records the hurt and resentment that result from extramarital affairs, with the first novel taking a slightly unconventional approach by focusing on the couple's attempt to rebuild their marriage after the affair has ended.

Despite Middleton's consistently subdued tone and the similarity of his character types and settings, critics often comment on the engaging quality of his work. As Mary Hope states: "[Middleton] takes the most unlikely, restrained material and weaves the deftest web of moral dilemma and emotional power."

(See also *CLC*, Vol. 7; *Contemporary Authors*, Vols. 25-28, rev. ed.; and *Dictionary of Literary Biography*, Vol. 14.)

D.A.N. JONES

Two's Company is a grim little story of inter-class sex in Nottingham. Stanley Middleton, a serious novelist, leaves moralising to the reader, who won't find it easy. The hero, David, comes from a car-owning household which feels superior to the working class: his parents know something about accents and careers, how to get into grammar school and university, how to deal with the authorities. But their son leaves college without a degree and adopts the unplanned life-style of the majority—a dead-end job, leisure the only concern. He takes to his bed an unusually dense factory-girl and treats her with mindless brutality. But he still can't escape his class status. He has to use it to save the girl from the magistrates; his parents get at her and improve her accent. When he coldly punches her face, his landlord (instead of knocking the little swine down as one can't help childishly hoping) merely says, 'You of *all* people, Mr Berresford.' There is much truth in this story but it seems incomplete; perhaps it needs actors and camerawork. It's hard to tell whether David knows what he's doing. His thoughts are indicated with a subtle, allusive eloquence which might be his own or the author's. Certainly David doesn't talk that way. Maybe he has no one to talk to; he, or the author, has chosen his working-class companions with a strong bias towards stupidity and violence. The local accent, which obsesses Notts novelists, is used not descriptively but as a symbol of unintelligence.

D.A.N. Jones, "Papal Bull," in New Statesman, Vol. LXV, No. 1683, June 14, 1963, p. 910.*

IAN JEFFERIES

Terms of Reference concerns eight Midlanders—a young married couple, their parents and two friends—and examines the reactions of the peripheral players to the marital ups and downs of the young pair. The idea is a good one, but one returns to the book after the first reading not because it was effective but to try and discover why it was not. The answer lies in the people portrayed: they are oversimplified; they are also unnaturally (and unnecessarily, since Stanley Middleton intersperses a witty commentary) dull. They speak of each other in denigratory terms that turn out to be justified, and one loses interest in the pedantic professor, the spoiled son, the aggressive tycoon, and their awful wives. Success would require different people, and a longer book, but not a new author. Stanley Middleton's qualities shine through.

Ian Jefferies, "Midlanders," in New Statesman, *Vol. 72, No. 1846, July 29, 1966, p. 174.**

STANLEY REYNOLDS

Stanley Middleton is a novelist who has shunned the exotic climes, even swinging London, to hoe the long artistic row of the Midlands; and not even the Midlands of salty dialect and sweaty miners, but the quiet suburbs of the lower middle class. In his last novel, **Terms of Reference,** he dealt with sex in the semis; now with **The Golden Evening** Middleton shows us death in the suburbs. The novel opens with the family going to visit the mother, who is in hospital dying of cancer, and ends with the mother dead and the family home from the funeral switching on the telly. . . .

We have seen a young teenage daughter trying to cope with sex and first love; a young son engaged to a glamorous and rich widow trying to balance his happiness with his mother's pain and his father's sorrow; and we have had the father forced into a Lear-like posture with only a back garden to play the role in. Now the book ends with them all silent around the television. One is reminded of Chekhov's dictum about drama being a family seated at the dinner table quietly eating while their whole world falls about them. Middleton is able to take the unassuming middle class, the material of jokes and send-ups, and turn it into tragedy.

Stanley Reynolds, "Bit of a Legend," in New Statesman, *Vol. 76, No. 1952, August 9, 1968, p. 177.**

JAMES PRICE

Daniel Cleaver, the hero of . . . [**Wages of Virtue**], is brought up in lower-middle-class Nottingham during the Thirties. From his forthright anticlerical mother he inherits articulateness and the gift, or curse, of taking a position and sticking to it. From his carpenter father he inherits a love of music. In the Reverend A. Dennison Pearl he observes faith in action. He grows up, learns how to kiss girls, somehow avoids being bedded by older women, gets a job as an office boy at two pounds a week. War comes, and Dan appears before a tribunal for conscientious objectors. . . .

Dan's moral growth is observed, as one expects, without flourishes and calmly, without agonising over the pains of adolescence. . . . Mr Middleton is so close to his hero that parts of the book read like straight autobiography. On the other hand he's never so close as not to be fair to the other characters, who frequently see more and feel more than Dan does. The justness of this author/character relationship is the rock on which the novel is built.

It's fatally easy to make a Stanley Middleton novel appear deadly dull, which it never is. The small stuff of life, the claims of family, the ordinary but decisive choices, the individual's sense of his own past and future: these are the substance, and how awful it sounds to say so. More awful still if one says—which I believe to be the truth—that among our active novelists

he is one of those in that small circle closest to the central tradition in English fiction. He is too humane and too modest a writer, perhaps, ever to produce anything one would care to call a masterpiece; but as book succeeds book, in a style ever more simple and lucid, he patiently maps out his world. **Wages of Virtue** is his ninth novel, and it gripped me to the end. (p. 739)

James Price, "A Serious Person," in New Statesman, *Vol. 77, No. 1993, May 23, 1969, pp. 739-40.**

NORMAN SHRAPNEL

The architect hero of **Apple of the Eye** is busy designing a new church, and in his spare time he beds a schoolmistress young enough to be his daughter and gets involved in affairs with his ex-mistress and also his ex-wife.

This would surely be satire if satire still existed, but no such thing. This is people, behaving with that air of normality Mr Middleton always uncannily preserves through his highest stylistic flights. He has an irritatingly jerky way of assembling his novel, but though one's belief is often suspended it is brought bouncing down to earth again by these heavier-than-air, essentially believable characters. There are no pretensions, no high-charged sensitivity, except in the language. Nor is there any willingness to hurt. This amoral hero behaves with a kind of adept clumsiness, like a child systematically breaking its toys.

Norman Shrapnel, "Refugees from Domesticity," in Manchester Guardian Weekly, *March 12, 1970, p. 18.**

CAMPBELL BLACK

[**Brazen Prison** is] a subdued, conscientious, well-made work. . . . [We] are in the closely-observed environment of a North Midlands town with a small cast of characters: Charles Stead, a novelist and television personality, who abandons Hampstead for an ascetic life in his home territory, where he may work on his epic novel; his wife, Esther, who at first urges him to work on his book and then, deprived of what she knew best in London, begins to doubt that he has any talent anyway. Stead is an extraordinary, dehydrated character who has all the charisma of a bad schoolmaster, but who is touched just the same by a nagging remembrance of things past: the woman, Iris, who took his virginity many years before, and the girl, Barbara, who might be his daughter. Stead shifts back and forth between the present and the past, as well as the imagined past he is trying to create in his novel. But he isn't sufficiently involved in the things around him for the centre to hold and slowly everything disintegrates—including the meaningful novel.

Part of Stanley Middleton's achievement here is that most difficult of things—the portrait of a novelist at work. He doesn't bore the reader with the trivial details of the novel-in-progress—the blunt pencils and the persons from Porlock, the dead details of creation. Instead we are shown, sometimes with surprising cynicism, how an ache in the writer's shoulder can result in him considering the death of a central character; the doubts, the self-questioning, the ultimate fear that nothing one is writing has any validity. **Brazen Prison** has been conceived and executed on a small scale, but it is written with style and considerable perception.

Campbell Black, "Total Recall," in New Statesman, Vol. 81, No. 2094, May 7, 1971, p. 642.*

ROSALIND WADE

If in these days anyone can regard seventy as elderly, it will still be admitted that a man who has reached the age of four score and ten is not an intriguing subject for a novel. Stanley Middleton has chosen a man of this age as the central character for his new novel, **Cold Gradations**. The opening is not easy. Too many conflicting and unrelated strands of interest seem to trail across the consciousness of the widower-schoolmaster, James Mansfield, who is attempting after a severe illness to make something positive out of his solitary existence. The chemistry of his deteriorating body dictates that he would be better left alone, undisturbed by conflict with other people. Yet loneliness compels him to pay more than transitory attention to the various members of his family. This muted theme gradually builds up into an expression of sanity and sound sense. The go-getter son who ironically dies before his father—the socialite daughter-in-law whose ambitions contribute to the sterile quality of her marriage, the gauche grand-daughter who descends upon her grand-father only when no better prospect offers—these, together with a sub-plot concerning neighbours who suffer the misfortune of a retarded child, provide a subtler commentary on human behaviour than is often provided by noisier judgments. (pp. 46-7)

Rosalind Wade, in a review of "Cold Gradations," in Contemporary Review, *Vol. 221, No. 1278, July, 1972, pp. 46-7.*

ROBERT NYE

Stanley Middleton is . . . [a] writer who should be much better known. **A Man Made of Smoke,** set like all his books in a Midlands town, concerns itself minutely with small but crucial moments in the life of a retired army sergeant who finds himself in charge of a factory. Mr Middleton's prose is not poetical, but it is in an unobtrusive way poetic. He is a moralist, a patient sifter of the debris of contemporary culture, and previous comparisons of his work with that of George Eliot are not far wide of the mark.

John Riley, the "man of smoke" who gives the book its title, must be one of his most compassionately created characters to date—but even the word "compassion" belies the seriousness of Mr Middleton's intent. There is a sadness and an irony at work here which make the novel read like one of Hardy's best "satires of circumstance."

Robert Nye, "Embarrassment of Riches," in The Guardian Weekly, *Vol. 108, No. 24, June 9, 1973, p. 24.**

JULIAN BARNES

Mr Middleton is a cautious and courteous writer, a shopkeeper among novelists. He lays out his characters neatly, plumping them up for display so that they fall into perspective. He promises fair dealing, an honest attention to detail, and regular rotation of stock even after 15 previous novels. . . . **Still Waters** craftily explores the dynamics of two middle-class, middle-income, middlebrow Midlands families who become entangled; the Lindsays (Victorian detached, private means, musical soirées) and the Bournes (terraced, unrelaxed). Neatly graded and observed, especially in matters of who tells what to whom, their world is one of fretting about old age, heart attacks, and the kids' A levels, and submitting good-heartedly to the toad work. John Lindsay, humane *père de famille,* ends the novel impotently shaking a fence-post while a funfair pounds out, racked by his inability to control even his own life. It's Larkinland really, though with less panache to the gloom.

Julian Barnes, "Role Me Over," in New Statesman, *Vol. 92, No. 2373, September 10, 1976, p. 348.**

JOHN MELLORS

[There] are some very disturbed characters in **Ends and Means:** one kills herself and another tries. The protagonist is 48-year-old Eric Chamberlain, who has made 'a small pile' out of writing thrillers and has retired from schoolteaching to live in his native Nottinghamshire and be a full-time author and reviewer. . . . The plot hinges on the family's survival through adultery (Eric's), a nervous breakdown and attempted suicide (the son's) and a successful suicide (Eric's mistress and the wife of his best friend). Eric himself sums up what the book is really about: 'Tragedy's flung into the faces of people no more or less ordinary than we are.' . . .

Depressingly bleak as this may sound, **Ends and Means** is, in fact, a bracing, invigorating book, largely due to the quality of the writing. Metaphors and images are freshly fashioned. . . . Trivial happenings are described as carefully as more significant events: a lorry moves 'at a clanking waddle'. Indeed, it is only in the more intense moments of love and passion that the style falters into the predictable.

John Mellors, "Anon Events," in The Listener, *Vol. 98, No. 2528, September 29, 1977, p. 410.**

JEREMY TREGLOWN

If the differences between Stanley Middleton's novels were not as subtly well-defined as those between his characters, **Two Brothers** would be in danger of the kind of repetition he must sometimes fear. The novelist in **Ends and Means** certainly had this worry, his most recent fiction seeming to him 'a patchwork job, its faults hidden by a sharpness of realistic detail, a worthless return to an exhausted vein'. There's no patchwork in **Two Brothers,** except insofar as the structure consists of a working together of the main narrative with recollected earlier incidents, slowly and unchronologically piecing together the protagonists' lives: Frank, a successful poet who makes a living as a schoolteacher; his old girlfriend and later mistress Kathleen; and his brother, her husband Jack, an aggressively successful Nottinghamshire businessman. And although the 'vein' is familiar—the sheer emotional attrition between people's unrevealing ordinariness—it's by no means exhausted.

The novel's centre of interest is the shifting balance of sympathy between the cautious, sensitive Frank and Jack, initially seen as a fat philanderer, a grossly complacent sexual thug. It becomes increasingly clear that Frank's poetry lives on the capital of his brother's experiences, and as the novel proceeds Kathleen's marriage to the man of action, rather than to the contemplative who first proposed to her, comes to make surprisingly optimistic sense.

The scales are in the end perhaps too heavily loaded on Jack's side . . . and it's a pity—though, in the given structure, inevitable—that the switch mostly occurs after Frank's death two-thirds of the way through, which has reduced the story's momentum. There are times in this latter part of the book—so much of it taken up with unexpected discoveries about Frank's and Jack's past—when Middleton's writing seems unusually washy. I'm not sure how much of this to attribute to his generally successful use of style-change as a device for characterisation. It's arguably appropriate, for example, that the educated southerner Kathleen, in a moment of deep middle-aged, middle-class gloom, should be seen through a cloud of sub-Eliotic clichés of inanition; but clichés they remain. . . . Elsewhere there's happily less room for doubt, and Middleton movingly succeeds in showing hopeless, commonplace suffering being almost arbitrarily assuaged, without losing his distinctive, unsentimental view of individual isolation. (p. 479)

Middleton has no monopoly of fiction about bourgeois adultery, though the comparisons this week's publications provide—by no means feeble in themselves—help gauge his depth of sympathy and the unostentatious alertness of his style. (pp. 479-80)

> *Jeremy Treglown, "On the Side," in* New Statesman, *Vol. 96, No. 2482, October 13, 1978, pp. 479-80.**

JOHN NAUGHTON

The life which concerns Stanley Middleton is that of the middle classes in a Midlands town—territory he has traversed before with distinction. This time [in *Two Brothers*] he focuses on two brothers, Francis and Jack Weldon. The former is a widowed schoolteacher and poet of national renown, the latter a lecherous and prosperous local businessman, married to the woman his brother once loved. . . . Everyone involved in the story wants more out of the situation than they are getting; yet all are afraid to ask for what they want, or even to acknowledge the extent of their needs. Very middle-class, in fact.

In the course of time, two events—a death and a sudden drama—disturb this relatively tranquil pool. Nothing changes outwardly as a result of these events, yet for the survivors everything is changed. They grow closer together, become—temporarily, at least—a group, and are able to face even the possibility of love. It all might be represented, I suppose, as just another example of a half-alienated family closing ranks in the face of shared adversity. But I think that Mr Middleton's book is rather more than that—being essentially a parable about how death looms larger than anything else, making our habitual rivalries and inhibitions temporarily seem infinitesimal by comparison. Parable or not, *Two Brothers* is a fine novel, beautifully done. (p. 865)

> *John Naughton, "Going Downhill," in* The Listener, *Vol. 100, No. 2591, December 21, 1978, pp. 864-65.**

JOHN LUCAS

At the end of *Two Brothers,* Stanley Middleton's last novel, Kathleen Weldon, betrayed wife, stands in the dark of her house, looking over Nottingham, and thinks of the people she knows and loves, all of them busy with their own affairs. 'She pressed her cheek to the cold pane. She stood alone, stood for the solitary'. It's a modest, defiant stoicism that Middleton catches there. It doesn't amount to a full look at the worst, but it has its own integrity. . . . It's a distinctively modern awareness, one most usually associated with Frost, who captures it wrily, uneasily, comically, in poem after poem.

In A Strange Land is frosty and Frostian. Its central character, James Murren, is a man who stands very much alone. But in his case it isn't so much a matter of self-knowledge or pained acceptance as of indifference. Murren is a brilliant musician, who finds himself with a teaching job in a Midland city. He's soon in demand with local musical societies and equally with local women. Murren may sound reminiscent of the hero of that early, very fine Middleton novel, *Harris's Requiem.* But there's a crucial difference. Harris felt himself to belong to his community, to the locality. Murren doesn't give a damn for either. He's in a strange land, waiting for the call from London. (By the end of the novel it's come.) If he stands for the solitary it's because he prefers it that way. When he gives piano lessons to a bored, unhappy housewife, and she throws herself at him sexually, he takes what she offers, but without concern or curiosity. . . .

Murren is a cold man. Middleton is good on that, good also on his relationship with the selfish Jessica, one that founders just because they're so incurious about each other, apart from when they are in bed. . . .

The problem Middleton faces . . . is to convince us that anyone would care for or about this iced-over, ruthlessly selfish man. And I don't think he entirely solves it. . . .

Murren is the more or less passive observer, who watches 'the hail of occurrence clobber life out / To a shape no one sees.' Others are clobbered, especially Walter Payne. Jessica's father, a retired bank-manager, husband to a vitreous-hard headmistress wife who undergoes a frightening crack-up, Payne is one of Middleton's finest inventions. Prim, ordinary, not very good with words (Murren begins by despising him), Payne nevertheless finds himself committed to the sufferings of others, trying, helplessly, to assuage Jessica's grief over her dead fiancé, to bolster his wife's suddenly shattered confidence, to help a family of Poles, who themselves are in a strange land, the father dying of cancer, the mother scarcely able to speak English, the daughter mis-married to a Scottish miner. Middleton doesn't soften any of this. There's an appalling and appalled bleak truthfulness about the way he shows us the indignities that all these people go through. . . . It's familiar Middleton territory, of course; but it's rarely been better explored.

> *John Lucas, "I'm Sorry," in* New Statesman, *Vol. 98, No. 2536, October 26, 1979, p. 640.*

CHRISTOPHER WORDSWORTH

Stanley Middleton's gloomy tensions and the dogged idiosyncracies and compressions of his style can inflict a kind of Chinese torture. Samples of this from *In A Strange Land* include "no-pulse," "his do-nothing," "the wild posse in his head pillaged him," "pithered," "soul-fen," "he occupied a large black armchair and himself with The Times," "'You and this woman aren't,' he slowed up, 'attributing this miracle to our,' he coughed, 'appearance then?'"

But this is a patient craftsman who does not plant us in these drab pubs and solid sitting rooms among pent thoughts and the aspirations and antagonisms of provincial life with the sole purpose of observing dead ends. From a sombre beginning with a drowned corpse via menopausal quarrels and broken or jagged affairs in shapes as a study in isolation and aimlessness and since the only predicament that moves one is that of the dying Polish patrician saddled with a lumpish Midlander for son-in-law, that seems the only dignified link with the title. At some point difficult to define and after one had thought that the art which conceals art had also very nearly buried it, the talented young musician marooned in this wilderness is alive with needs and purpose to elucidate the inner significance of the title.

Christopher Wordsworth, "Searing Face of War," in Manchester Guardian Weekly, *November 4, 1979, p. 22.**

JUDY COOKE

In *The Other Side* Stanley Middleton takes a stock situation—marital infidelity—and turns it on its head, inviting us to consider the other side of the question and the coin. The story is only a little way into the first chapter when the central character, Elizabeth, learns that her husband has a mistress and intends to leave home; 15 pages forward and he has changed his mind, decided to stay for the sake of their daughter. These two events are more often found at the conclusion of a novel; it is intriguing to see what might lie beyond the point of resolution. How high a price will be required of the man for such a sudden, total act of betrayal? Will the woman ever be able to trust him again?

These are shock waves which must have rocked many a marriage; it is Middleton's strength as a novelist to give them their due, tracing the initial disturbance through every last ripple of resentment. He is an exact and compassionate recorder, probing deep, suggesting that it is easier to forgive than to be forgiven. His characters reveal themselves through dialogue: the hardest thing to write, some say, the easiest thing to read. (p. 24)

Judy Cooke, "Black Mass," in New Statesman, *Vol. 100, No. 2592, November 21, 1980, pp. 22-4.**

ALAN BROWNJOHN

[Somewhere in *The Other Side*] a writer implies that there can be no genuine interest in thrillers because the issues they raise are unimportant. In some twenty novels Middleton has been demonstrating constantly that the important issues are indeed to be found elsewhere, in more ordinary places; and it seems superfluous to do much more than celebrate this palpable and underrated truth when he produces another book as good as most of those that have gone before. Yet the bare bones of the plot of *The Other Side* seem so unlikely to produce the absorbing performance he gives us that it may be worth the risk of labouring the point to state it once more. David Watson tells his wife that he is going to leave her and set up home with a mistress. Three days later, almost before Elizabeth has absorbed the shock and worked out the implications, "This Gill Paige business is off." The rest of the novel is concerned with the business of adjusting to the changed situation created by the chance that David might have gone. . . . (pp. 90-1)

The most that happens apart from one (natural) death is that the pattern of relationships between these people shifts, just a little, as their mutual knowledge increases; and the last scene suggests a mending and reconciliation. . . . Yet somehow Middleton manages to convey that almost everything of importance that could happen to people has somehow happened to the Watsons and the Paiges in these few months. They have reached some sort of abyss, and drawn back, for reasons they do not fully understand; and the return is the hardest thing of all to deal with. . . . Middleton assumes the limitless interest of the small eddies and concealed patterns of ordinary living; and among current novelists he is almost unique in his ability to transcribe them. In *The Other Side,* as in *Cold Gradations,* or *Holiday,* or *In a Strange Land,* it is an enlightenment and a pleasure to watch him deftly exposing that "something hidden from us" which decides and shapes human destinies. (p. 91)

Alan Brownjohn, "Breaking the Rules," in Encounter, *Vol. LVI, No. 5, May, 1981, pp. 86-91.**

ADRIAN POOLE

There is a point in Stanley Middleton's *Blind Understanding* at which a man does not eat a dry biscuit. Listening to the sound of the nine o'clock television news from the distance of his kitchen, a 70-year-old retired solicitor remarks his immunity to the sad record of violent death, industrial disorder and foreign famine in worlds elsewhere. 'Such did not touch him nearly; he could be disgruntled without adventitious help. He decided against eating a dry biscuit.' By such minute and precise notations . . . is this rich and dense account of a life rendered. As John Bainbridge sifts through his rag-bag of memories, we close in on the events and people and things that have nearly touched him nearly: the death of a young subaltern in the war, an adulterous affair with his sister-in-law and with many others, a painting, an unsuccessfully defended murderer—but usually, death. He is a man who has devoted himself to shrinking feeling to the point where the renunciation of a dry biscuit can signal a tiny, disgruntled triumph of the will.

Middleton's title, drawn from Fitzgerald's *Rubaiyat,* is cunningly oracular. The relation between seeing and understanding is left nicely unresolved by a phrase in which 'blind' may suggest either the loss of the means to understanding or the grace of an understanding that decides its own means. Bainbridge is not a man to let understanding have its own way: he will interpret his life to his own satisfaction. He is shrewdly alert to his own and others' weaknesses, and exempt from vanity and self-pity. He doesn't imagine that he or they have much to give, that promises are worth making or grieving over when broken. Death has been memorably frequent in his life, and birth rare.

One of the few gifts he remembers making is associated with the birth of his sister-in-law's only child, whom he may or may not have fathered. It is a painting of a naked woman, praying at a bedside, 'dragging up, curling the mattress out and back with stretched arms in her frenzy'. It is a strange gift for a prospective mother, but in its oblique and enigmatic way it is as near as Bainbridge ever gets to confiding a feeling. The painting he offers his sister-in-law marks the end of their adultery, but it also seems to prophesy the despairing prayers of a bereaved mother over an empty bed. The boy will die at the age of four. . . .

At his mother's funeral, Bainbridge's wife weeps discreetly, in relief. That compound, of grief and discretion and relief, seems to be at the centre of this distinguished and beautifully written novel. It begins with a friend's funeral, at which Bainbridge chooses to be more exasperated by the raucous voice of the priest than moved by the words that it speaks: 'I am the resurrection and the life . . .' At another point in the novel, his wife, the daughter of a bishop, is moved by the image of the condemned men in a prison chapel to recall a favourite text of her father's: 'And the word of the Lord was precious in those days; there was no open vision.' No open vision, but blind understanding. At the close, his wife and her sister interpret Bainbridge's surprising but unimportunate desire to visit Hungary and its 'unpronounceable names' as his cryptic way of talking about dying. He is angry at being understood—he is not used to being surprised. But just before they separate for the night, his wife calls him 'husband' for the first time in their marriage, and takes hold of both his hands. He is right to remind the women, tetchily and jokily, that he and they are not dead yet. (p. 18)

> *Adrian Poole, "Fiction and Failure," in* London Review of Books, *April 15 to May 5, 1982, pp. 18-19.**

JOHN MELLORS

Blind Understanding is Stanley Middleton at his best. John Bainbridge, 70, recalls episodes in his life as wartime soldier, prosperous solicitor, husband, father—and seducer of his sister-in-law when his pregnant wife could not give him all the sex he wanted. Middleton is the least extravagant of writers, but he has a pungent wit and a command of sharp, telling imagery. All is delivered with a truly Tacitean compression. . . .

Middleton's tone is so low-key, his attitude so gruffly matter-of-fact, that sudden disclosures of adultery or incest or violent death are all the more shocking. Not that one is unbelieving. The corroborative detail makes everything real: his sister-in-law's knickers, which Bainbridge 'eased down her legs, dropped to the carpet, were grass-green'. Bainbridge's father-in-law, a bishop, had preached in a 'dry way, without emphasis or hyperbole, as if the truths he expounded spoke for themselves, needed no rhetorical devices'. That is a good description of the way Middleton writes—but never preaches.

> *John Mellors, "Secret Lives," in* The Listener, *Vol. 107, No. 2760, May 13, 1982, p. 27.**

D.A.N. JONES

With Stanley Middleton we must expect to be confined to a city in the English Midlands. A firm hand at the reins prevents his readers and himself from galloping away from this tranquil place. *Entry into Jerusalem* is about an admired landscape painter; just before he moves to London and the flashy world of international metropolitan art-and-journalism. The title is allegorical and so is the name of the painter, John Worth. The title is also the name of Worth's controversial new picture, in which he depicts Jesus with a skinhead haircut, standing on the pillion of a motorbike, congratulating himself like a football hero, while the fans rip off branches from ornamental cherry trees.

The vulgar perversity of this idea, skilfully carried out by a famously chaste and discreet landscape painter, would undoubtedly attract the collectors and the media. . . . Worth's picture would be easy meat for Sunday supplements and television culture shows. *Anyone* could proffer an opinion.

This deftly-told story starts with Worth listening to advice about his career from Turnbull, a rather patronising but admiring old friend, a teacher who has taken a new young wife, rather a temptation for Worth. Turnbull has in his time been a local hero. Worth admires him as a schoolmaster and he finds that even . . . [his girlfriend's] disagreeable old father has revered him as a rugby player. But Turnbull withers while Worth blossoms—soon to be overblown and run to seed. Stanley Mid-

dleton is good at suggesting the future. 'Worth remembered this day when almost two years later he sold his parents' house and moved, against his oath, to London. He could have kept the old bricks and mortar, but he refused to be sentimental.' Worth, the reader feels sure, is making an entry into temptation, not into triumph. (p. 18)

> *D.A.N. Jones, "Beltzi's Beaux," in* London Review of Books, *March 3 to March 17, 1983, pp. 18-19.**

ROSALIND WADE

Stanley Middleton is a strangely disturbing and paradoxical writer. As a former joint winner of the Booker prize for fiction, he has long been acclaimed for his laconic, highly idiosyncratic style and interesting exposure of seemingly tedious people. In his new novel, *Entry into Jerusalem,* we are once again confronted with a gallery of mediocre men and women living out their lives amid hideous decor, consuming unpalatable meals. The central character, John Worth, is an artist *manqué* and content to remain so, until he is prodded towards greatness by a perceptive dealer, abandoning his usual pallid style to produce a sensational portrait of Christ entering Jersualem. With this unexpected and barely credible twist, Stanley Middleton is not running entirely true to form. As the drab group moves from one uninspiring conversation to the next, it is tempting to speculate on the result if Stanley Middleton decided to harness his considerable powers to describe attractive, interesting people. As it is, the reader is obliged to stay with him as he is, or chooses to be. The scene in which the ailing father of John Worth's mistress crouches over an inadequate fire, coughing repulsively, and dominating the lives of those around him is vintage Middleton and as always, surprising as this may seem in view of its subject matter, provides compulsive reading.

> *Rosalind Wade, in a review of "Entry into Jerusalem," in* Contemporary Review, *Vol. 242, No. 1407, April, 1983, p. 215.*

ANTHONY THWAITE

John Richardson, at the centre of Stanley Middleton's *The Daysman,* is headmaster of a large, successful comprehensive school; and he himself is successful enough to be sought after by publishers, editors, radio and television producers, as a man of opinions and experience. As what his wife calls 'an agent for good,' he is constantly put in the position of being the go-between, catalyst, fixer: not only coping with the distressed married lives of his staff, a boy caught cheating in an A-level exam, a fatal accident on a school trip, but having demands made well beyond Penrose Comprehensive—everything from a distraught man whose primary school has burnt down to a neurotic woman whose daughter commits suicide and whose husband expects Richardson to send him reports abroad about the state of things. . . .

Stanley Middleton is adept at loading his characters with moral chains and then seeing how (or whether) they extricate themselves, and in *The Daysman* he has excelled himself. He also likes the curious densities and the shaded gradations of the everyday, so that against a certain plonking earnestness (sometimes reminiscent of C. P. Snow) he is often capable of playing the inexplicable and the ungovernable, disturbing irrational elements that lie just under the banal events.

> *Anthony Thwaite, "Dickensian Underworld," in* The Observer, *February 19, 1984, p. 25.**

HARRIET WAUGH

Stanley Middleton's immersion in the unexceptional humdrum lives of ordinary middle-class English folk is celebrated in *The Daysman* through the evocation of a comprehensive school headmaster called John Richardson. As in most of his other novels, there are few surprises and no scandals, but then Stanley Middleton is unusually adept at showing ordinary people leading unexciting lives without being in the least bit boring about it. (p. 24)

It is one of Stanley Middleton's virtues—or anyway idiosyncrasies—that, as a writer, his authorial voice is so gentle as to be almost indiscernible. Readers are left to decide for themselves, as they might about fresh acquaintances in real life, whether they like his characters and find them estimable, amusing, dreary or what have you. Most writers highlight drama whether it is emotional, social or political. Stanley Middleton approaches drama as a snail might. He crawls close, antennae extended, and then at the barest touch quickly withdraws. This, he seems to say, is what real life is about. Desperation does exist . . . but it does not seriously concern the reader any more than it does his main characters. Only the ugliness manifested by desperation causes John Richardson unease.

Although Mr Middleton's characters owe everything to his unstated skill, they seem to exist in their own right as well. When readers close the book, they known that John, Joanna and their three children, Margot, Virginia and Fay, are still going about their usual activities while being annoying, annoyed, grumpy and happy. Like the silent social group they come from, these people continue on and on. (p. 25)

> *Harriet Waugh, "The Snail's Antennae," in* The Spectator, *Vol. 252, No. 8124, March 24, 1984, pp. 24-5.*

ANTHONY THWAITE

About a third of the way through Stanley Middleton's *Valley of Decision,* one of his main characters, David, sees with surprise the sudden dusty demolition of a factory which, only a year before, he'd noticed with his wife was full of 'ordered bustle,' fronted by a line of smart administrators' cars and, inside, well-dressed young women mincing round with folders.

Middleton is too undemonstrative a writer to underline how this is both an image of the apparent collapse of David's own marriage and of present-day England. But the wan poetry of its figurativeness is characteristic of Middleton's neutral-tinted vision. His is a world in which sudden change happens, but almost without being noticed until afterwards; in which people, though known intimately, are often 'vaguely waving from parallel lines.'

At the same time, Middleton's people are 'decent'—that slightly old-fashioned English term of approbation for which there are no proper synonyms. They can't behave badly without knowing it and regretting it. Mary, David's wife, behaves badly. A highly gifted amateur singer, she gets the chance after a year of marriage to take up a temporary semi-professional engagement in America, which may lead to even higher things. David, a schoolmaster, is also a talented amateur, a cellist, and is keen for Mary to take that chance. Away from him, her head turned by success and strangers, she has a brief disorienting affair with a formidable opera director. For a time she's determined not to return, but can't bring herself to tell David.

The movement, the strains, up to, through, and away from this episode in what had seemed a happy marriage, is the substance of the story. Parents, friends, colleagues, fellow musicians, make varyingly 'decent' gestures of sympathy and understanding. Personal fulfilment, professionalism, have to contend with everyday demands.

Increasingly, Middleton's command of the ordinary has become extraordinary, in laconic descriptions, and in unflinchingly facing moral imperatives which are always bedded in real, even humdrum, circumstances. And in . . . [*Valley of Decision*] the rigours and solaces of making music are cleverly (but uninsistently) counterpointed with the human relationships that accompany them.

> *Anthony Thwaite, "Point Counter-Point," in* The Observer, *February 10, 1985, p. 26.* *

MARY HOPE

Watching Arthur Schnitzler's *Lonely Road* the other week, it occurred to me once again that the portrayal of extreme intelligence in action is one of the most mysterious, difficult and inexplicable gifts of the great actor; and that, conversely, the sleight of hand involved in giving tongue to the inarticulate is one of the great challenges and tests for a writer. It is a hurdle which sorts out the men from the boys and at which many a long-distance runner before and since Sillitoe has disastrously stumbled. Not so Stanley Middleton who, in *Valley of Decision,* takes the most unlikely, restrained material and weaves the deftest web of moral dilemma and emotional power. . . .

Stanley Middleton does not put a foot wrong, from the exact detail of David's home life (cocoa and electric blankets, essays to be marked, Midlands public parks, dripping, sodden and unkind) to the slightly *nouveau riche* cultural scene he skirts, or the ordered, unexciting, unexceptionable but sensitive relationship with his parents and the edgy one with Mary's, the minute class distinctions painstakingly pinpointed. The tiny actions which, in some lives, take the place of words . . . are as exact as the awkwardness in handling the telephone, which is not only true of a certain generation, but also a metaphor for the circumspection of their communication. It is all exact, riveting, a drama which gains from the power of understatement. A wonderful book. (p. 31.)

> *Mary Hope, "The Gift of Tongues," in* The Spectator, *Vol. 254, No. 8176, March 23, 1985, pp. 31-2.* *

John (Treadwell) Nichols

1940-

American novelist, nonfiction writer, and essayist.

Nichols is an author of tragicomic novels about ordinary people thrust into emotional or social conflicts. He is probably best known for his novel *The Sterile Cuckoo* (1965) and for his series of novels which examine the destructive effects of modernization upon ethnic communities in New Mexico. While Nichols's early fiction deals humorously but compassionately with the emotional plight of the individual in the modern age, his later novels about New Mexico reveal a strong commitment to historical, cultural, and social justice. John McLellan outlined the major qualities of Nichols's prose when he praised his "virtuoso style, the profusion of strange but believable characters, the skill with which small incidents are developed and the curious blend of humor and pathos, which are often found fighting for supremacy in a single phrase."

Nichols's first novel, *The Sterile Cuckoo,* achieved considerable critical and popular acclaim. The book concerns the humorous yet poignant college experiences of Pookie Adams, a bright but disturbed girl who seeks to regain her lost childhood through a love affair with the novel's young narrator, Jerry Payne. Payne, however, unsure of his own identity and needs, rejects her as he fumbles toward maturity, and Pookie's future is uncertain at the book's conclusion. This novel was later adapted for film. Nichols's second novel, *The Wizard of Loneliness* (1966), also focuses on themes of childhood loss, love, and maturity. This book relates the story of a stubborn young boy who gradually comes to realize his need for others while living with his grandparents after the death of his mother and during the wartime absence of his father. Though critics noted Nichols's characteristic narrative strengths, the novel was faulted for falling short of its ambitions.

Nichols's novels about New Mexico are informed by the author's deep sense of culture and heritage. He stated, "I am strongly committed, in my life and my work, to bringing about changes in the nature of our society which I believe absolutely necessary to the well-being of us all." Nichols's commitment deepened after he moved to the southwestern United States in the early 1970s. His New Mexico trilogy, comprising the novels *The Milagro Beanfield War* (1974), *The Magic Journey* (1978), and *The Nirvana Blues* (1981), traces forty years of conflict between the rural residents of a traditional Chicano and Pueblo community and the land developers representing white, middle-class suburbanites seeking escape from the urban environment. At their most comic, Nichols's nonplussed protagonists assume mythic stature as they temporarily overcome the forces threatening cultural extinction; at their most tragic, these characters become symbols of futility and hopelessness, ultimately surrendering to what Nichols called "the pizza-fying of America." Critics generally praised the trilogy, and Norbert Blei called it "one of the most significant contributions to American literature in some time."

In addition to using New Mexico as a setting for his novels, Nichols has produced two works of nonfiction about the area: *If Mountains Die: A New Mexico Memoir* (1979) and *The Last Beautiful Days of Autumn* (1982). In these books, which com-

bine photographs, autobiographical reminiscences, and philosophy, Nichols compassionately examines the rapidly vanishing terrain, history, and culture of his adopted state.

(See also *Contemporary Authors,* Vols. 9-12, rev. ed.; *Contemporary Authors New Revision Series,* Vol. 6; *Contemporary Authors Autobiography Series,* Vol. 2; and *Dictionary of Literary Biography Yearbook: 1982.*)

THOMAS CURLEY

[*The Sterile Cuckoo*] is about Pookie Adams, who wrote a poem in which she identified herself as a sterile cuckoo. Pookie Adams is a crazy mixed up kid, but she's not the sort of bird that would hatch her eggs in anyone else's nest.

It would be easy to go on in this manner, putting Mr. Nichols's first novel down by making light of it. Easy because this is a book by a 24-year-old writer about a college love affair; easier, still, because the boy and girl are white and well-to-do [and] the love affair is straight—no drugs and no perversions. . . . And easiest of all because, at first glance, *The Sterile Cuckoo* seems to do little more than update *This Side of Paradise.* The center of interest has shifted from the boy to the girl; Mr. Nichols, unlike Fitzgerald, avoids any casual generalizations on Western Culture as well as any suggestion of religious belief or unbelief; and the sex, though still adolescent, is more explicit.

Yet such an exercise, besides being self-righteously "mature," would be only another example of the arrogant blindness of critics. Mr. Nichols set out to write a love story and nothing more; he succeeded, and nothing more.

His art is impressive. The first sentence reads: "Several years ago, during the spring semester of my junior year in college, as an alternative to either deserting or marrying a girl, I signed a suicide pact with her." The significance of the statement is not felt until we come to the suicide pact and realize that the statement was false. Jerry Payne did not sign the pact as an alternative to either marrying or deserting Pookie Adams; he signed it as an easy way to leave her. The suicide pact is not fulfilled, and Pookie leaves Jerry and school as well—only to send him a suicide note a year later, which he never bothers to verify.

The author's use of his narrator is fairly subtle for a first novelist. It is through Jerry that we come to believe in the genuineness of Pookie's emotions; it is through him that we discover his own phoniness. Pookie is in love. She wants to get married and have children, one at least. Jerry is "in love" but he doesn't want to get married and certainly doesn't want children; he wants to pass his oral examination in biology. . . .

"Phoniness" may be too harsh a term for Jerry, but it is provoked by the extraordinary sympathy for Pookie that Mr. Nichols elicits from the reader. At first only a plain little girl who is something of a "character," she talks her way into your affections, rather like a frisky puppy who insists on your attention. After all the talk, she begins to suffer, and that does it, suffering being the one evidence of life that contemporary cant allows. And as she suffers, Jerry Payne freezes up. And that's it, the end of the affair.

There may be a moral to be drawn here, even some sociological significance of use to student counselors, but beneath it all is the love story and the character of Pookie Adams. It was worth doing, and it was done well.

> *Thomas Curley, "The Growing Pains of Pookie Adams," in* The New York Times Book Review, *January 17, 1965, p. 46.*

CHARLES SHAPIRO

[Most modern] academy romps are set in the first-person singular, the "I" being supposedly masculine, lubricious, and determined to be honest about himself and his playmates. These "I"s are in a state of perpetual self-analysis. Consider Jerry Payne (get the clever last name?), who is the wailing chronicler of John Nichols's *The Sterile Cuckoo,* possibly the feeblest pop college novel to date. . . . Jerry's adventures with a sad, semiwhimsical co-ed, Pookie Adams, form the core of the book. "Why I didn't flunk out of school between Winter Carnival and spring vacation of my sophomore year I'll never know. Because as a scholar during that time, I was dead. As a lover, however, I had just been born: my heart bloomed into a most rare and irrational flower." Jerry's heart's desire is regarded by their peers as a wild child, but this isn't really and truly so, for she has an eye for beauty. . . .

Pookie also has an eye on *the important things in life.* "That's what kids are, Jerry—all heart. Big round blueberry hearts. The trouble is—the older you get, the more you grow away from your heart. . . ." But all is not high philosophy between these two students. "Rather than argue, I kissed the top of her head, her forehead, the tip of her nose, and one ear . . . and, on my inspiration, we mixed up a batch of Purple Jesuses in a gallon mayonnaise jar and went to the college graveyard to have a party."

Nichols has a tin ear, at least when that ear is turned in the direction of college girls. . . .

> *Charles Shapiro, "Classrooms Are for Sleeping," in* Saturday Review, *Vol. XLVIII, No. 5, January 30, 1965, p. 26.**

ALBERT GOLDMAN

[Though *The Sterile Cuckoo* might seem embarrassingly] square at first sight for its evocation, through half-amused, half-boastful reminiscence, of frat-house drinking revels, redolent of Dartmouth Winter Carnival—at second glance, Nichols' book takes on a deeper dimension. With astuteness and unfailing intuition, the young author has placed at the heart of his college recollections an absolutely unique yet broadly representative character named Pookie Adams. A comedienne, who has adopted the new humor as her personal life style, Pookie is the type of today's funny little old college girl.

The essential Pookie is engagingly depicted at the long overdue consummation of her first "affair." Having reeled in the narrator from miles below the surface of sexual maturity . . . , she is faced with the problem of easing him off the hook. . . . [They] have found their bower of bliss in a tacky motel, as cold as a cabin in the Klondike. To help the boy, who is numb with anxiety, alternately freezing and sweating on the brink of his first complete sexual experience, Pookie starts to work the room like a stand-up comic. Her fist a make-believe mike, she does an on-the-spot broadcast from The Kozy Kabins, conjuring away with laughter the lumpy bed, the embarrassment of the visits to the john, the getting undressed "bit." And after urging her lover to peel off her sweater and skirt, and maneuver the inevitably troublesome brassiere fastener, she offers him his long-desired sight of the promised land, turning around and around like a mechanical doll in her glasses and her loafers, keeping up a stream of self-disparaging wisecracks.

Although Pookie often appears a fragile, childlike moppet encased in a gauzy pink cocoon of Disneyland fantasy . . . , her actions and daydreams suggest pathological hatred. Actually, at 18, she is a veteran neurotic with a classic case history. Cut off from her classmates by a bad heart, remote from her parents for whom she has no respect, Pookie spent her childhood concocting fantasies of revenge, acted out with frogs, spiders and other little creatures. Unconsciously associating "real feeling" with violence, she is compelled to destroy things with ruthless vigor, starting with herself. From one end of the book to the other, she is injured in a series of "accidents" that seem to pursue her with malignant fatality. . . . Hurtling off the train to give her boy friend the hug she has been rehearsing for weeks, she knocks him to the ground in a fall that splits his skull. Some of the fantasies into which she escapes are masked by deliberate nonsense, but there is no mistaking the meaning of her favorite daydream: "to walk into a very crowded station some day with a machine gun and let everybody have it. . . ." Spunky as her efforts are to exorcise fear with farce, their ultimate effect is to make her a "sterile cuckoo," cut off from life by the comic persona she originally adopted to protect her deeply damaged personality. Pookie Adams is an emblem of the extreme precariousness of the comic adjustment as a means of survival, and the utter insufficiency, indeed severely thwarting effect, of this strategy the minute we reach for the genuine intimacy of friendship or marriage.

Granting that people have always used humor to dispel tension, to conceal embarrassment and to win sympathetic attention, still it seems clear that the intensity, ubiquity and automatism of humor in contemporary American life goes far beyond anything known from history. As sick comedy has established itself as our accustomed way of seeing things, every man has become his own sick comic, with the result that whatever was not ridiculous in our world is now being made so by this uncontrollable mental tic. What an ironic and devastating criticism is implied by this single fact—that in ducking behind the comic mask, we actually believe we are boldly facing reality. (pp. 143-44)

> *Albert Goldman, "The Comic Prison," in* The Nation, *Vol. 200, No. 6, February 8, 1965, pp. 142-44.**

WILLIAM BARRETT

[*The Sterile Cuckoo*] is Mr. Nichols' first novel, and he is clearly a comic writer with a natural and original gift. College life might seem to be exhausted by this time as story material, but Mr. Nichols has managed to bring it to fresh life again in all its crazy fun and undercurrents of sadness.

The star who steals the show in *The Sterile Cuckoo* is Pookie Adams, a girl of wild and whirling words but determined will, who has marked down the narrator-hero, Jerry Payne, as hers from the moment she laid eyes on him out West. When Jerry and Pookie turn up as students at two nearby Eastern colleges, the stage is set for their romance. The love affair does indeed blossom, and intensely; but sadly it collapses from its own intensity and Pookie's unpredictability.

Much of their romance has to do with the problem of getting to bed together, and Mr. Nichols is very explicit about the sexual episodes, though strangely enough his account is funny and candid enough to be pure rather than prurient. Still, there is something a little frightening about the younger generation that goes about the business of acquiring experience with the grim seriousness of an educational program.

Indeed, if Mr. Nichols is an accurate reporter . . . , his book is quite a document on the new generation of collegians. Among other things, these young people have now evolved a line of patter quite new to us oldsters. Part of it is a watering down of old hipster and jive talk, but it has also become heavily interlarded with phrases from television commercials, violently and often hilariously torn out of context. This generation has obviously grown up spending a great deal of time looking at that tube. They haven't entirely believed in what they have seen, which seems to make them all the more determined to go out and discover things for themselves. (pp. 193-94)

> *William Barrett, in a review of "The Sterile Cuckoo," in* The Atlantic Monthly, *Vol. 215, No. 3, March, 1965, pp. 193-94.*

ALAN PRYCE-JONES

[In *The Sterile Cuckoo* Nichols] kept the scale small, he husbanded his resources. [In *The Wizard of Loneliness*] he has tried something much more ambitious: a fresco, radiating out from a single family, depicting a small Vermont town towards the close of World War II. On Mr. Nichols' canvas everybody is grouped round one small boy. Wendall Oler is rising eleven. His father is away at the war; his mother has died; he is dispatched to his grandparents in Stebbinsville, much against his will.

What Wendall needs is love, though he does not understand this. Outwardly he is a rough and crafty kid, like a million others. He finds himself bossed by his grandmother, cherished by an inefficient and lovable grandfather, perplexed by an aunt and chivvied by an uncle. . . .

Mr. Nichols' gifts remain. He has quick sympathies, a camera eye, a good ear (most of the time) for dialogue. But he cannot yet manage a crowded scene. The tone of his book is unexpectedly, even sentimentally, old-fashioned. The golden-hearted, crusty grandmother, the darling old ass of a grandfather, the poetic small boy and his dreams, come out of some such book as *Anne of Green Gables,* even if Stebbinsville has been updated to the mid-twentieth century, with its extra perplexities and vexations.

Perhaps he has written too fast. It looks as though he writes "tenant" when he means "tenet." He certainly writes of someone being "consummated by fatigue." His descriptions of events beyond his obvious range are often perfunctory and his awareness of mature emotions is sketchy in the extreme.

More importantly, however, he has not rested on his laurels. This is a much more ambitious book than *The Sterile Cuckoo,* even if it is a less satisfying one. Though the architecture of the whole is weak, it has felicities to offer. And Wendall himself is entirely credible, so that the final resolution of his problems seems just as well as appropriate. Next time, please, put the mix, less sugar, into a slightly hotter oven.

> *Alan Pryce-Jones, "Ambitious Novel, but Weak," in* New York Hearld Tribune, *February 24, 1966, p. 21.*

GRANVILLE HICKS

[John Nichols] published his first novel, *The Sterile Cuckoo,* a year or so ago. I picked it up, as I pick up many books, and, as doesn't often happen, was moved to read it through. *The Sterile Cuckoo* seemed to me the best of many novels I have recently read about sex and the younger generation. For one thing, it presented a heroine who was both attractive and credible and for the most part unstereotyped. For another, I was impressed by the skill with which the author let the narrator expose himself as a heel.

Nichols's second novel, *The Wizard of Loneliness* . . . , is the story of the transformation of a ten-year-old boy, Wendall Oler. With his mother dead, with his father in the Marines (the time is 1944), Wendall is sent to live with his grandparents in Vermont. When he arrives, Wendall is a difficult child, contrary, malicious, precocious, skilled in discomforting his elders. In the course of a year he learns to play games, to stand up and fight, to say his prayers, to love his grandfather, and, in short, to be and to behave like a normal American boy.

If the summary suggests that the novel is a little bit on the corny side, I'm afraid it's fair enough. There are other themes besides the metamorphosis of Wendall.... But the story of Wendall is central, and, alas, it is not convincing. It is difficult to believe in him as a bad boy and impossible to accept him as a good one.

The Sterile Cuckoo was no masterpiece, but it was fresh and honest, and, though there were juvenile touches, I felt in it an essential maturity. I wonder how *The Wizard of Loneliness* happens to be so inferior. Some of the elements seem to be so close to slickness and so appealing to the tender-minded that one might suspect Nichols of trying to fabricate a best-seller, but I somehow doubt it. Surely everyone is entitled to at least one mistake. (pp. 29-30)

> Granville Hicks, "Labor Leader's Lost Love," in Saturday Review, Vol. XLIX, No. 9, February 26, 1966, pp. 29-30.*

THOMAS J. FLEMING

One of the important images in [*The Wizard of Loneliness*] is a huge Harley-Davidson motorcycle. Early in the story, it takes the self-styled wizard of loneliness, a precocious 11-year-old named Wendall Oler, on a wonderful whizzing ride to a secret lake in the mountains. Later, it goes completely out of control, throws its rider a country mile and winds up a smashed and sputtering wreck. Pretty much the same thing happens to the story-line of this ambitious novel. For the first hundred pages, author John Nichols seems to be soaring on a unique blend of humor and sadness toward a new dimension in American fiction. Then he goes haywire.

As in his first novel, *The Sterile Cuckoo,* this young writer creates instant attention with some startling characters. But where the earlier book was concerned only with a doomed and offbeat college love affair, Mr. Nichols has now taken on a tribe. Wendall, the alienated young wizard, spends the last year of World War II with his grandparents in a small town in Vermont. We meet old Doc Oler, who talks amusing nonsense about "detmoles in the rondo-sketiaptic dispeller," his nagging wife Cornelia, his war-widowed daughter Sibyl, his morose 4-F son John, handyman Bernie Aja and a host of small-town characters....

In this bustling company, Wendall's loneliness slowly melts. But his deliquescence seems to loosen Mr. Nichols's grip on his story.... Mr. Nichols is unable to control [the] mélange of insights and problems. Consequently, the novel ravels away in a string of scenes, some brilliant, many repetitious. A dazzling ability to invent dream images, particularly for Wendall, verges close to a padding device. Finally comes the certain sign of lost control. Mr. Nichols starts to *tell* us what he is driving at.

[The town's erstwhile athletic hero], Duffy Kahler, he announces, is "a kind of guilt running through the state"—a statement he has nowhere attempted to support artistically.... Next he loses control of Wendall, and in the book's climactic (and badly coincidental) scene, when Doc Oler runs over Duffy Kahler, Wendall thinks what no 11-year-old, even one who reads Hemingway, ever thought—"because of his heart he was one of the most mortal and vulnerable beings in the universe." And then, as if one final heave stood the author on his head, his grip on his style goes, too. Wendall sees in adult eyes "a feeling of crippledness."

Mr. Nichols has remarkable insight into life's crazy blend of comedy and tragedy. For dozens of pages at a stretch *The Wizard of Loneliness* is pure pleasure to read. It is too bad the author did not hang on for another rewrite. He might have made that big bold machine he built in his first 100 pages go all the way.

> Thomas J. Fleming, "The Sorrows of Wendall," in The New York Times Book Review, *March 6, 1966,* p. 52.

RICHARD A. BLESSING

Nichols has produced, I think, an important contribution to the popular literature of the '60s.

The Sterile Cuckoo surely qualifies as a piece of popular culture by the crudest and simplest of definitions.... [It] has been and is being taught in some colleges and it enjoys a good deal of cultist favor with the sort of college student who likes *Goodbye Columbus* or *A Separate Peace;* it has been published in England, translated into Dutch, German, Italian and Japanese. Nichols' *Cuckoo* may not rival *Gone With the Wind* in popularity, but the saga of Pookie Adams has become widely known.

Perhaps the value of great literature, good old "high culture," if you will, depends upon its ability to "tell the truth," as Lionel Trilling once wrote that *Huckleberry Finn* tells the truth. But the value of a work of "popular culture" seems to lie more in its ability to *reflect* the truth about the tribe, the generation, the folk, who respond to it. The popular novel, comic strip or film *may* be as false as a general's "light at the end of the tunnel," but we can learn much that is true about the tribe by studying the falsehoods that it chooses to honor with popularity. Thus, in a study of popular culture, we must spend as much time watching the audience as we spend examining the work. So it is with *The Sterile Cuckoo.* Nichols tells the truth mainly, with a slew of "stretchers," but *The Sterile Cuckoo*'s real value lies in what it reveals about the culture that esteems it.

It seems clear that those who like the book (and the movie) do so primarily because they are taken in by Pookie Adams. She runs away with the book (whether Nichols wishes her to or not).... Those who favorably review the book invariably seem to be half in love with its heroine. (pp. 124-25)

Now I think Pookie is a monster, yet I must confess to being a bit in love with her myself. She is, after all, less the original product of Nichols' teeming imagination than she is a caricature, and not a very gross one at that, of the girls we used to date ten years ago.... They wrote bad poetry and were obsessed with their childhoods and were very very sensitive and swore a lot because of it. Like Pookie, they fought a constant battle to become as little children and we valued them according to their innocence in the midst of our immensely corrupt and fallen selves. Nichols' ear is not so tinny as is sometimes supposed. Such girls were quite capable of echoing Pookie's "The sun is shining, and everywhere there are drifts of powdered gold as high as mountains." It is now time, perhaps past time, to jilt Pookie (and the qualities she represents) and so save ourselves. (pp. 125-26)

[Pookie's] cute name is our first clue. Pookie Adams—(Winnie-ther) Pookie, child of Adam. Both names suggest the innocence of childhood, though "Adams" has also the darker overtones of the terrible Fall and, consequently, of our immense human capacity for depravity.... But the horned half is concealed in the ambiguities of "Adams," and when Jerry Payne tries to imagine that mind, he fails. "I suppose I thought of something like spun glass or pink cotton candy . . . the distant slow beat, the child heart." . . . Though he is wrong, it is the cotton candy that draws him in, and, I suspect, that catches us all by the sweet tooth. It is the *imagined* child-mind that we remember and revere, the mind of a Pookie that we half-perceive and half-create.

Critics of both the novel and the movie have scoffed at its lack of "realism," comparing its characters with the students from 1965 (the date of publication) until the present. *Cuckoo*'s students, we are told, have no social awareness; they live in an ivory towered world of football games and houseparties and fraternity initiations. A more discerning reading will show that the nightmare of violence in the atomic age is so pervasive in *The Sterile Cuckoo* that there is scarcely a page on which it is not present. . . . Let me suggest that Pookie and her friends are as aware of the horror of modern life as are their more recent counterparts at Columbia or Berkeley, but that their response to that horror is different, is more grotesque because the horror is more real and more grotesque to them. (pp. 126-27)

The games people play in Cuckooland are "horror shows," and some of them are called "bomb the submarine" and "nigger pile-up." Their songs are "Transfusion" and the "Hitler, He Only Had One Ball" song. They picnic in cemeteries, dismiss the political situation "by deciding to hydrogenically blow up Africa, Russia, China, Viet Nam, and South America" . . . and then they immediately switch to telling moron jokes. . . . The terrors of war appear as metaphors again and again: bombs, rifles, firing squads, submarines, machine guns, parachutes, mad scientists who experiment on human beings and, finally, the mushroom cloud of an atomic explosion. The ivory tower turns out to be a wing of a castle of horrors. . . . (pp. 127-28)

Pookie's search for "peace," for escape from horror (particularly the horror of time and change) has occupied her for most of the book. The knowledge that "Peaceful doesn't exist any more," that her imagined worlds *never* existed, is the knowledge of the serpent. As soon as Pookie bites into *that* wormy apple, she is no longer the girl with whom Payne (and the rest of us) fell in love. Like "Grandmother Adams," she is a deposed Queen, a fallen Queen of Children, and we, like Payne, sense that she is "dying" but know that we ourselves are "too sick to help her, that's for certain." . . . (p. 128)

[Pookie's "dying"] is the death of a lie, the death of the fictive possibility of inviolable innocence. Pookie has believed in the possibility of triumph over time and change; and she has been obsessed with death . . . , with stasis, with her childhood. The obsessions are closely related and all are manifestations of that understandable (yet monstrously destructive) desire to preserve all things against flux, against mutability.

For Pookie, death is at once desirable as a cure for the motion that is life and horrible as the ultimate and unavoidable reality. She is both fascinated and repulsed by it. She solves her dilemma in the simplest way. Rather than die herself, she becomes "quite a prolific little killer." In the course of the novel, she does away with sixty or seventy frogs, a spider-friend, a batch of fireflies and a crow. She approaches a sexual encounter with the serio-comic warning "you're a dead pigeon," and one of her dreams is to walk into a crowded railroad station with a machine gun and let everybody have it. Pookie is hard on her lovers, a kind of female black widow, in fact. . . . Pookie

is quite right when she announces, "I'm a tommy-gun in disguise." . . .

One might say that Pookie only kills the ones she loves and that she kills in order to preserve. The frogs she does in are given names, eulogized and preserved in memory. The friendly spider she squashes is preserved by an enchanted circle drawn with her finger around his "little yellow mess." The dead crow is recorded "for posterity" with a Brownie bought especially for that purpose, and as Pookie runs to claim her kill she shouts, "Don't forget the camera!" . . . Motion is the enemy, and Pookie tries to defeat it on every front.

Pookie's happiest moment comes when, still living to appreciate it, she can combine the thought of death with the physical fact of stasis. . . . [One] of her good moments takes place in New York City while she rides the merry-go-round, a ride which Jerry derisively declines as being "fun for kids." The merry-go-round, with its eternal music, the horses always and never moving, always returning to the place from which they start and always fixed in attitudes of flight, is a kind of museum in which the memory of childhood may be preserved. During her ride, Pookie becomes "for a short time the Queen of the children," but the ride must end and she returns to Jerry and the week-end begins to grind on toward disaster. (pp. 128-30)

If Pookie's good moments are those in which there is no apparent motion (or those in which she seems to move in slow motion), her worst experiences are those involving change. She hates train rides . . . , departures of all kinds, commencements. After her high school graduation, Pookie returns to the womb of her room where she locks herself in and spends three hours "pulling the ring in her teddy bear's head." When bear baiting fails, she immerses herself in the Tadpole Pond of her childhood (which she finds shrunken) and returns to the house "feeling a little better." And, when her romance shatters like the teddy bear's mechanical heart, she longs to go back—not just to school, but further still. . . . Presumably she returns to her old, sealed-up room, to the shrunken Pond. (p. 130)

It may seem paradoxical that a victim of ingrown innocence like Pookie should initiate Jerry Payne into the world of sexual manhood. However, sex with Pookie is much like pre-lapsarian sex—it is not, perhaps, done well, but it is remarkable that it is done at all. . . . Her sex appeal is described adequately when Payne refuses to kiss her on their first "date." "If you were good-looking or stacked or something, I would . . . But who wants to kiss something that looks like a Korean orphan? I feel sorry for you, I want to give you some bread." . . . The final proof of the innocence of her sexuality comes while Payne is undressing her for his big moment. "I can remember Grandpa Adams doing this," Pookie says,

> getting me into a snowsuit and making sure that everything was tight and snug, my mittens clipped firmly to my cuffs and all, then, when I came inside all wet he unzipped me. He was very careful and always "Lift your chinny-chin-chin" so my skin wouldn't get pinched. . . .

That Payne manages to lose his virginity after the speech is the most remarkable sexual feat that I know of in literature, its only rival being James Bond's performance in a steam room.

And, of course, Pookie is the *sterile* cuckoo. Though they use nothing but rhythm, she never conceives and their relationship remains free of adult responsibility and guilt. Her "conception" takes place only in the womb of the mind, and the offspring is "A green and gold Pookimum Jerriensis with one hundred legs." . . . In short, sexuality in Cuckooland seems as much a fantasy as cows with eleven stomachs. It is simply another kind of game, not much different from nocturnal football or cemetery parties. (pp. 131-32)

Richard A. Blessing, "For Pookie, with Love and Good Riddance: John Nichols' 'The Sterile Cuckoo'," in Journal of Popular Culture, *Vol. 7, No. 1, Summer, 1973, pp. 124-35.*

FREDERICK BUSCH

[In *The Milagro Beanfield War,* Nichols] opens out his purview and ambitions, moving away from the sentimental narrowness of *The Sterile Cuckoo* and *The Wizard of Loneliness,* facing big issues—social justice, the American class system—but failing to rise to his material. Joe Mondragón reclaims his ancestral land, refuses to be a downtrodden New Mexican peasant, steps on the financial and psychic toes of big government and avaricious developers, and the Milagro beanfield he decides one day to irrigate with forbidden water becomes a little battlefield. The novel is not Joe's story, or that of anyone else, really, though it jumps with characters, situations, events. The novel is Nichols's story, and he dominates every page, every moment, with his wit. He does not let the characters act or move but that he steps in and *says.* The book is so full of his saying, that little else gets done.

Nichols's attempt to make his love for an area and his social concern coincide with his often celebrated sense of humor is doomed by his own always visible hand. It takes 24 pages of small print for the novel's situation to get going because Nichols must first tell the story of Amaranto Cordova, a sometimes-funny set piece, which is not there because Cordova is essential to the design of the novel, but because he amuses Nichols and Nichols needs to spin a tale. He does so constantly, everyone in the book does. But the fabulation doesn't work here as it does in, say, Eurdora Welty's epic of tale-spinning, *Losing Battles.* Miss Welty's subject is story itself; Nichols's appears to be his own wit.

But if the characters were hypnotically made, and if the prose were compelling, such objections would easily be overridden. They aren't. The characters, first of all, are stereotypes: Bloom, the Jewish liberal lawyer living among "the people"; Ruby, the robust sexy widow; Montana, the clean-cut secret agent. They don't exist in and of themselves, and they don't act because of inner necessity. Neither does Joe, the novel's prime mover. They seem instead to act for the sake of yet another amusing tale told by a decent, charming fellow-drinker during an afternoon in a quiet bar.

As for the prose, it is either so slack as to be hastily composed, or so intentionally folksy as to be patronizing to the folk. (pp. 53-4)

Now, early in the novel, Nichols says "Joe Mondragón's beanfield was another story which might also one day grow to the proportions of myth." So it is possible that the interminable telling of tales, and the loose prose, are Nichols's effort to make a myth of and for the common man. I don't think that the common man speaks and acts in clichés only; I don't think he so consistently fails to transform his actions and speech into something marvelous. I wonder if there *is* a common man. Nichols's insistence of turning the potentially magical into the stereotyped, cardboard cutout comes across not as the large-

heartedness he obviously intended—his descriptions of love-making are often gentle, funny, transcendent—but as an act of literary colonialism, an acquisition of images by the writer for the sake of his own sensibility. A writer's characters deserve more consideration than he does. (p. 54)

Frederick Busch, in a review of "The Milagro Beanfield War," in The New York Times Book Review, *October 27, 1974, pp. 53-4.*

LARRY L. KING

The Milagro Beanfield War is John Nichols' third novel. Otherwise, what is it? Is it a social commentary on the rise of the downtrodden Chicano? Or a modern day Western tale, pitting the little ranchers against the big land owners and their villainously mustachioed banker friends? Is it a morality play set in northern New Mexico? Or an allegory harking to the escalations of the Vietnam misadventure? Or is it, as the publisher's blurb claims, a "wildly comic" novel?

Perhaps it is bits and pieces of all of these. But mainly it is a big, gassy, convoluted book that adds up to a disappointment—one somehow failing to equal the sum of its many parts. John Nichols provides some of the fun and sadness found in his earlier works, *The Sterile Cuckoo* and *The Wizard of Loneliness*. But where those books seemed controlled and taut, *Beanfield War* sprawls and rambles at the expense of getting on with the story.

Milagro, N.M., is a scurvy old town. . . . Its natives and their ancestors were simple bean growers, but modernity has overwhelmed the town. Now it is in the economic clutches of one Ladd Devin The Third . . . , [who] is assisted in his despoilings by real-estate sharks, developers of dude ranches, and corrupt politicians whose water compacts preclude irrigation rations to the peons.

Enter an improbable hero, one Joe Mondragon "small and ferocious," a handyman and sometime migratory worker when he isn't in jail for fighting, drinking, or cursing the cops. Frustrated and angry, he one day illegally taps an irrigation ditch to begin cultivating beans in an old abandoned beanfield once owned by his late father. The beanfield becomes a symbol to the fed-up Mexican locals, who at once think Mondragon crazy and cheer his one-man revolution.

As the beanfield grows, so does the community's resentment. Eventually there are sneak attacks by rowdy imports against the locals, then retaliations. "We will be like the Vietnamese," says one Chicano. At this point, one looks forward to what shapes up as a major beanfield war—to a clear confrontation of Good vs. Evil.

But, somehow, it never comes off. Though Nichols provides a victory for Mondragon's ragged army, it is not convincing. I had the notion that by the end of the book, John Nichols was as anxious to finish it as I was.

Larry L. King, "Few Shots in a 'Beanfield War'," in The National Observer, *November 16, 1974, p. 27.*

MOTLEY DEAKIN

Like Frank Norris' *The Octopus* and John Steinbeck's *The Grapes of Wrath*, *The Milagro Beanfield War* has a basis in actual events, in this instance the struggle in the 1960's and

'70's by Hispano-Americans in northern New Mexico to restore ancestral land grants taken from them by the Anglos. There are vital similarities among these novels: the importance of the land both as a means of sustenance and as a condition for establishing a social community, the deterministic power of economic interests to erode and destroy that community and misuse that land, the sense that life is a confused, often desperate struggle that is made bearable by the capacity of those who live it to snatch moments of happiness and to hold on to a dream that something better is possible.

In Mr. Nichols' novel land is important, but the most precious natural substance is water. He who controls water controls life; to realize this fact is to recognize a basic reality of the West. . . . In the real West water is a constant of a given quanity that the inhabitants have had to learn to conserve and use. Thus Mr. Nichols can attach great actual and symbolic significance to his hero's assertion of his traditional water rights. (p. 249)

This aspect of the novel establishes for it a basic seriousness that helps give stability to a presentation that is episodic, constantly shifting and, like the American humor of the frontier West, may begin with a common reality, but gradually distorts that reality until the reader is left contemplating an absurdity that is both outrageous and amusing. If this is the situation in which these characters must exist, they are compensated by the gifts of endurance, of an intuitive sense of the appropriate action, an ability to make do with what they have, an affinity for the environment in which they live. . . . The hope is that they too will not just endure, they will prevail.

I have the impression that in *The Milagro Beanfield War* John Nichols has found himself as an author. It bodes well for his future. (p. 250)

> *Motley Deakin, in a review of "The Milagro Beanfield War," in* Western American Literature, *Vol. X, No. 3, November, 1975, pp. 249-50.*

JONATHAN YARDLEY

My hunch is that [*The Magic Journey*] is going to be the next college-bookstore cult novel. Certainly it has all the ingredients: It is long (*very* long); it touches on just about all the traumatic events of recent history, the 60's in particular; it pits the good-guy Mexicans and Indians against the bad-guy Anglo exploiters; its politics are safely and certifiably Love Generation; it has enough characters to populate a small town, as indeed they do; it has joyful sex, tear-inducing violence and an unhappy climax softened by a morally uplifting denouement.

This probably makes it sound a lot worse than it really is. The tale of how progress comes to the little Southwestern settlement of Chamisaville—transforming it into the "playground of the Land of Enchantment" and displacing its true owners in the name of profit—is consistently diverting and occasionally amusing. It takes a long time for John Nichols to bring his main character, the beautiful and vibrant April Delaney, into focus, but once he gets her there, things pick up steam.

The first chapter, which is quite fine and gave me excessively high hopes for the 500 pages to follow, has an appealingly zany, W.C. Fields tone. . . . But Mr. Nichols gets more and more solemn as he pits the "Anglo Axis" against the noble lawyer Virgil Leyba and his downtrodden followers. You can agree with just about everything Mr. Nichols says, as I do, and still get mighty weary of all that preaching.

There is a good deal of fantasy in *The Magic Journey*—ghosts coming and going, inexplicable excitement occurring—and in that respect, as in some others, Mr. Nichols shows himself to be heavily under the influence of Gabriel García Márquez. But this is no *One Hundred Years of Solitude*. It is nice, friendly and fun, and it has about as much depth as *Tommy* or *Jesus Christ, Superstar*. (p. 15)

> *Jonathan Yardley, "Looking Backwards," in* The New York Times Book Review, *April 16, 1978, pp. 15, 36.**

JEFFREY BURKE

The same sort of players and political conflicts that John Nichols found success with in his previous book, *The Milagro Beanfield War*, take the stage in [*The Magic Journey*], his fourth novel. While the rest of the country enters the Depression, the Southwestern town of Chamisaville prospers. An industrious con man bedazzles the town's Pueblo farmers with his garish version of the American dream, and soon speculators, developers, politicians—the usual crowd of cashers-in—have weaned the locals away from a land-based economy to the almighty greenback and introduced them to the marvels of installment plans, menial labor, and debt. By the time the older Pueblo get around to actively protesting, they've lost their children, their culture, their farms to the maw of red-blooded, white-skinned capitalism. . . .

The Magic Journey is a plausible history of exploitation, lush with eccentric characters, with myths, legends, ghosts, and revealing shards from the past four decades, all carried by a Dickensian narrative exuberance. But the novel is a little too much of a muchness in light of its sober message. Unlike *The Milagro Beanfield War*, in which humor and absurdity prevailed, this work asks to be taken seriously, suggests justifiably and angrily that the Pueblo's loss is America's as well. Yet Nichols's creative energy runs so often to comic invention, to caricature instead of character, to spates of bathos and discursive high jinks, that he entertains far more than he instructs, to use the classic formula; the imbalance makes for ambivalence.

> *Jeffrey Burke, in a review of "The Magic Journey," in* Harper's, *Vol. 257, No. 1539, August, 1978, p. 89.*

KIRKUS REVIEWS

Nichols, novelist . . . and New Mexico activist, salutes "Andres Martinez, Bernabe Chavez, Pacomio Mondragon" and others native to Taos Valley [in *If Mountains Die*]. And that's the rub: Nichols' brief for the close-knit life his Chicano neighbors are losing, for their "subsistence, marginal culture" undermined by middle-class Anglo development, is ill-served by [William] Davis' stunning full-color photographs—which not only slight the human investment Nichols upholds, but indeed make the landscape "picture-postcard beautiful" (irrelevant, in Nichols' view) and can only encourage the exploitation he decries. It's not unlike reading about welfare mothers alongside the luxury ads in *The New Yorker*—all the more so because Nichols comes across as sincerely committed to the *acequias* (irrigation ditches) he helps maintain. . . . Nichols had childhood roots of his own on Long Island, a factor in his identification with the Chicanos; he had been bowled over by the crazy mix of experience on a teenage visit West; and, as a refugee from the N.Y. anti-war maelstrom, he'd grown crankily comfortable with the adobe house he bought in 1969 for $14,500. . . . that's now worth $50,000 to $60,000. Seeing the Chicanos outmaneuvered and outpriced, he has harsh words for the hippies whose lifestyles affronted the locals and triggered a diversionary class war (on the eve, Nichols believes, of genuine social change) as well as for the whole gaudy, money-grabbing glut. "Newcomers will wonder where the magic went," he writes—which makes the pictures look all the more like a preview of Lost New Mexico. (pp. 562-63)

> *A review of "If Mountains Die," in* Kirkus Reviews, *Vol. XLVII, No. 9, May 1, 1979, pp. 562-63.*

DORIS GRUMBACH

The novelist John Nichols, who wrote *The Sterile Cuckoo,* settled in Taos, N.M., eight years ago. A few years later he met the photographer William Davis, and together they have assembled a handsome book [*If Mountains Die*] that records in words and . . . photographs their great love of the landscape, the mountains, river, mesa, forest and desert that make up the Taos Valley of Northern New Mexico.

But this is not simply a picture book. Mr. Nichols has written a vivid account of how he lives, what he does, what the land in all its changing splendor means to him, and how his future is tied to his neighbors' struggles against irresponsible transients, against a proposed dam, against the incursions of building, overpopulation and traffic. . . . This is a moving, entertaining and beautiful book.

> *Doris Grumbach, in a review of "If Mountains Die," in* The New York Times Book Review, *June 10, 1979, p. 18.*

JOEL SWERDLOW

[With *A Ghost in the Music*] Nichols has dropped the fantasy, polished the eye-popping phrases ("glossy lipstick that glistened like nitroglycerine"), and returned to his roots with a skinny sarcastic heroine remarkably similar to Pookie Adams of *Cuckoo* fame.

A Ghost in the Music doesn't so much have a plot as a tightly coiled spring getting pressed tighter and tighter. New Yorker Marcel Thompson has been called to the wilds of New Mexico by his vagabond father, Bart. . . . Bart plans to parachute into the wild Rio Grande gorge. Jagged rocks have already ripped apart a test dummy. It's just part of filming a B-movie, but chances are Bart will die.

The son's assignment is to hold the hand of Lorraine, his father's pregnant, hillbilly, café-singer girlfriend. Like her predecessor Pookie, Lorraine is more than able to hold her own in a man's world. But times have changed. Unsure whether she's had three or four abortions, Lorraine considers herself a prude.

Although the absence of action may dissatisfy many readers, Nichols is in good company—Jerzy Kosinski and William Saroyan immediately come to mind—in writing a novel with no plot. *A Ghost in the Music* is simply a Boswellian account of prejump and postjump days. . . . Nichols emphasizes that the very moment for which his book exists—the parachute jump—is not even dramatic. . . .

Everything comes down to the jump, with everyone properly in place—Bart the center of attention, Marcel and Lorraine waiting to applaud him or to sweep up the pieces. They all know the stunt will be violent, irreversible and unnecessary, yet they wallow in an existential malaise bred by boredom. Bart must jump because it is the "one thing that has made him special." Lorraine threatens to abort his child and run away if he survives. Like Bart, she could simply choose a more positive option, but she, too, is unable "to change the inevitably bitched nature of things in general."

With no strong story to serve as a distraction, Nichols provides painful insights into people whose concept of affection is to keep talking on the telephone after the other party hangs up. Even conversations about life and death radiate gracelessness. . . .

All of this suggests *A Ghost in the Music* will die once Bart jumps. It doesn't, however, because Nichols' finale makes the Bart-Marcel relationship speak for fathers and sons loving each other everywhere. Throughout, Marcel has been trying to understand his father, to comprehend why he imposes suffering on those he loves. Bart always keeps him at a distance, revealing in a moment of weakness, for example, that what he really misses most in life is "to experience once again what it felt like to believe in Santa Claus."

Only after the jump does Marcel realize that life's truly worthy problems cannot be anticipated. He is left at peace with his own emotions, at the same time numbed by the same desire he had before the jump, a need to "cast a net around my father and pluck him from his own life, setting him down tenderly on a foreign shore where he might begin again. . . ."

Nichols may still write another best seller. But he'll never do a better job of capturing how it feels to love someone who doesn't stay around to be loved.

> *Joel Swerdlow, "Fathers and Sons on the Brink," in* Book World—The Washington Post, *September 9, 1979, p. 6.*

AL BAROZZI

In his earlier novels, John Nichols has been able to hold the reader's interest and carry a weak plot by providing one or two interesting characters and sensitive insights into them. In [*A Ghost in the Music*], however, Nichols' talents have failed him, and the final product is shamelessly uninspired. . . .

A Ghost in the Music is Bart Darling's biography. The fatal flaw is that Bart Darling is not worth the attention. A totally unsympathetic character, in no way did he come alive and produce any emotion in this reader. His bravura world of motion picture stunts is vapid and the "movie people" sharing his home are not even sketched. They are merely flashed before us as a parade of types.

At one time years ago it was thought that Nichols had some ability to produce "genuine" dialogue. This ability has surely left him in this book where the dialogue is purely and solidly obscene. Never in popular fiction have I encountered such foul language. His ignorance of the English language, moreover, is as monotonous as his profanity.

The book has nothing to offer: no plot, no characters, no style, no elevating ideas.

Al Barozzi, in a review of "A Ghost in the Music," in Best Sellers, Vol. 39, No. 8, November, 1979, p. 283.

LOIS BRAGG

John Nichols's latest offering [*The Nirvana Blues*] has been announced as the final volume of his New Mexico trilogy. It is only to be hoped that this is so. It is not that Nichols writes poorly—he doesn't—but that he says so little at such great length. . . . *The Nirvana Blues* is the story of four days in the life of Joe Miniver, ex-Madison-Avenue-ite and Chamisaville garbageman. It opens with the arrival of a tea box full of pure cocaine, which when sold will enable Joe to buy 1.7 acres from The Last Chicano in Chamisaville. Thus, the bright but naive Joe plunges himself into a world of sex, drugs, and violence, tempered by a good measure of WASP guilt. Adventure follows adventure at a reckless pace. If the situation is a cliché . . . , well, then, Nichols drives it into the ground until it really is funny. If the situation is novel—while lamenting the nonexistence of fireflies at Chamisaville's altitude, Joe has one fly directly into his mouth—Nichols drops it slyly on the reader and moves quickly on. His sense of humor is hard to resist, as are his frequent throw-away allusions to everyone from Shakespeare to Janis Joplin.

Joe Miniver is a communist who wants to own land, an agnostic who talks to angels, a loving husband and father who treats his family abominably. Most readers will recognize the absurd victim of these ambiguities as the Taos version of Everyman. How then account for the author's lack of interest in these larger issues, his complacent acceptance of conventional liberal politics and morality, both vintage 1968? *The Nirvana Blues* is a funny, entertaining book which should appeal to white, middle-class undergraduates. The thinking reader will find it much ado about nothing.

Lois Bragg, in a review of "The Nirvana Blues," in Best Sellers, Vol. 41, No. 6, September, 1981, p. 209.

PUBLISHERS WEEKLY

[*The Last Beautiful Days of Autumn*] is pretty much a standard run-of-the-wilderness book, with many fine descriptions of the country around Taos and some of the more engaging characters Nichols has encountered in his peregrinations there. Also included are vignettes of life on eastern Long Island, where Nichols grew up. There is, however, a lot of the Hemingway-esque poseur in the author, with great white angler stalking the wily trout and making love with the blood of a dead bird on his hands. . . . Best are the sections contrasting the New Mexico country as it was and as it will be, with "The Dukes of Hazzard" replacing Spanish and Indian legends and development houses crowding out adobe huts.

A review of "The Last Beautiful Days of Autumn," in Publishers Weekly, Vol. 221, No. 24, June 11, 1982, p. 54.

LYNN Z. BLOOM

The Nirvana Blues, the final novel in John Nichols's New Mexico trilogy, is the third act of a modern morality play. . . . [The previous books] explore the conflicts between the longtime Hispanic residents living in harmony with the peaceful, natural, beautiful New Mexican terrain and the Anglo agribusinessmen and land developers whose "hundred innovative lethal programs" will destroy both the land and the indigenous culture.

By the beginning of *The Nirvana Blues* this destruction is almost complete, and Chamisaville has become the province of the "spaced out, sex-crazed Great White Wounded Middle Class." The Chicanos have been bought out; even the longtime holdout, Eloy Irribarren, 83, must sell his 1.7 irrigated acres to pay horrendous debts. He chooses as the purchaser the novel's anti-hero, Joe Miniver, a Manhattan advertising transplant and for three years a Chamisaville garbageman. Joe has "dreams of being a caretaker with a soul," preserving for his wife, Heidi, and their two children, this "precious land, their Future, their shot at a Real Start, their commitment to a Time, to a Place, and to a Way of Life."

However, with characteristic lack of scruple, foresight, or insight, Joe has chosen an immoral means to accomplish these moral ends. He expects to sell five pounds of uncut cocaine to make the $60,000 needed to buy the land. Yet, as the morality plays unfailingly point out, corrupt means not only produce destruction, but compound the evil. In a comic-ironic vein, most of the novel explores the ramifications of Joe's corrupt decision, as he plunges ever more deeply into the degradations of sex and violence. (pp. 372-73)

Every time Joe goes home to try to make amends, things get worse. Conversations, civilly begun, degenerate into strings of obscenities and often end in physical battles. The machinations of getting instant, illicit riches corrupt Joe's human relationships absolutely, as he suspects his wife and partners of double-crossing him, and they engage in other forms of betrayal, including threats on his life. He in turn betrays them all.

Yet this increasingly barren landscape is populated by a comical cast of candidates for Fellini's *Satyricon*, including Nick Danger, a sinister shyster toting a secret suitcase of inflatable pornographic dolls; and Rimpoche, the omnipresent dog who collapses "in a sort of Uriah heap."

Nichols's cautionary tale makes us yearn for heroes, saviors of the land, preservers of stability, natural beauty, integrity of human relationships. But only Eloy Irribarren responds, and his aged shoulders are too frail to bear this burden, as we head full-tilt toward the once golden land, now paved over and strewn with the "transient, unrealized tatters of our dreams." (p. 373)

Lynn Z. Bloom, in a review of "The Nirvana Blues," in Western American Literature, Vol. XVII, No. 4, Winter, 1983, pp. 372-73.

DONN RAWLINGS

The Last Beautiful Days of Autumn is a companion piece to John Nichols's 1979 volume, *If Mountains Die*. Both subvert the coffee-table genre, giving us sex and politics in the guise of pleasant photographic mementos of the Taos valley. . . . The essays accompanying the photos explore Nichols's efforts to bring his own history to terms with that of the valley, the locale of his notable trilogy of novels *The Milagro Beanfield War*, *The Magic Journey*, and *The Nirvana Blues*. The essays describe his attempt not only to hold to a political vision, but also to celebrate in exuberant love and living the ground that could sustain the vision. (p. 54)

Paranoia is the only imaginative stance that could begin to measure the forces which—with seeming inevitability, and often abetted by our best intentions—are rapidly turning New Mexico's upper Rio Grande valley into another sprawling Aspen or Lake Tahoe—with better food and a readier supply of kitchen help and motel maids, no doubt, but with its rich diversity of life and integrity of environment diminished to an attractive legend sold in local bookstores. (pp. 54-5)

Nichols tries to look at the valley whole, to see the comedy and pain of its descent into flamboyant money-grubbing kitsch: the vision has a fine Marxist bite. It is also easy to criticize on its own grounds. Despite denials, Nichols broadly sentimentalizes the remnant Hispanic farmers. . . . No matter. Whatever feudal grimness a more searching economic analysis might find in the Rio Grande's early history, no country or people deserves the trashing that has proceeded from the later land grant swindles to the latest condo scheme.

And more to the point (while not discounting his gutsy politics), aren't those big, goofy, messy emotions Nichols's peculiar disarming talent? As the title would suggest, *The Last Beautiful Days of Autumn* is shaped by such emotions. Loving the autumn poignancy, musing over the aging and death of friends and relatives, aware of his own (tachycardic and asthmatic) mortality, thinking always of the threatened death of the valley, Nichols finds an antidote to despair in Walter Lowenfels's line: "not to know and love the tragedy of your own life is not to know the joy of being here at all." The joy of being here is the durable rationale for persisting against all odds. Nichols indulges his joy in rambling, often hilarious affirmations: wild, self-rejuvenating fishing trips into the Rio Grande gorge (the best writing in this book); wood-gathering jaunts in the conventional Taoseno style—axle-bending pickup loads, blowouts; love trysts in aspen glades; absurd contests with his decaying athletic friends. He imagines withdrawing to his newly purchased quarter section on Carson Mesa (aware of the ironies, having joined the land speculators), dreams of sexual adventures heightened by consciousness of death—dancing bones, a jaunty *calavera*, provide the accompaniment to his lovemaking.

The danger in all of this is that every gesture becomes theatrical, if not ideological. . . . Where is the steady, unselfconscious life on the land? Nichols is aware of the problem, worries a lot about being a writer with an outside income, and bemoans the paradoxes of his art: "at the same instant I also kill the thing I venerate." . . . Still, Nichols opts for wonder and celebration, and, in the balance, one can be glad that he does. Who can argue with a man who so insistently includes his faults in his act of devotion? As in the final words of the book: "Life as it should be, darlin'. Purple prose and all." (pp. 55-6)

Donn Rawlings, in a review of "The Last Beautiful Days of Autumn," in Western American Literature, *Vol. XVIII, No. 1, Spring, 1983, pp. 54-6.*

JOHN E. LOFTIS

In *The Milagro Beanfield War,* the best, I think, of the three novels in his New Mexico Trilogy, Nichols draws upon possibilities inherent in the genre to write a social novel different from most socially oriented American novels. The central conflict in this novel is between two cultures, two ways of life, two views of reality: the Anglo and the Chicano. Rather than focus on a single protagonist, a "hero," he develops a collective central figure: the real protagonist of *The Milagro Bean-*

field War is the Chicano community of the town of Milagro. In creating this protagonist, Nichols not only examines particular social changes but also offers, implicitly, a theory about the nature and processes of such social change. (p. 201)

Early reviews of *Milagro* praised it for its entertainment value, but only one, by Frederick Busch [see excerpt above], took it seriously as a novel. In his review, Busch makes several astute observations, but because of the ways in which he applies these observations to the novel, he condemns it for what seem to me wrong reasons. First, he observes that "The novel is not Joe's story, or that of anyone else.". . . He is right, of course, but this only becomes a flaw in the novel if one assumes that every novel (as most in fact do) must have a single individual at its center. Second, he points out that many of the central characters are stereotypes, and about this he is partly right. He continues by complaining that "they don't exist in and of themselves, and they don't act because of inner necessity.". . . If by "inner necessity" Busch means that we should be able to analyze characters' motivations according to some system of individual psychology, he is probably right; but the novel provides us with a context that suggests another, collective psychological model that does accurately account for characters' actions. (pp. 201-02)

We generally expect a novel to have an individual protagonist, and Joe Mondragón seems at first to be that protagonist. As we begin to recognize the social intent of the novel, we anticipate his being like Yossarian in *Catch 22* or Tom Joad in *The Grapes of Wrath,* the character who comes to embody the values central to the novel and who thus becomes the measure of the absurd or corrupt society around him. Joe is not this protagonist. Irrigating the west-side beanfield that belonged to his father triggers the central conflict of the novel, but Joe does not remain the principal figure or the leader in that conflict. He never intends to raise the issues or create the class and race conflict that ensues. Ironically, Joe does not have *any* conscious political intent when he irrigates the field: "one day Joe suddenly decided to irrigate the little field in front of his dead parents' decaying west-side home . . . and grow himself some beans. It was that simple.". . .

The effect of his action, however, is dramatically political. Ladd Devine's empire in the Miracle Valley depends on control of water, and Joe's action threatens that empire: immediately and urgently it threatens Devine's practical power to control water on the west side of Milagro, water that he owns by law and that he must control to proceed with development of his year-round resort. On a broader scale, it serves as a reminder of Devine's past manipulations and raises anew the squalid history of Anglo manipulation of land and water in the Southwest. Thus those in power, from Ladd Devine to the Governor, fear the beginning of an organized Chicano revolution, while many Chicano residents of Milagro hope and believe that Joe is emerging as the leader of such a revolution. Both sides, Anglo and Chicano, are wrong about Joe. (p. 202)

No individual, including Joe, controls events or leads a revolution in *Milagro;* the Chicano "movement," in as much as it is a movement, is unorganized and spontaneous. Several individuals believe that they understand what is happening and that some other individual is in control. Amarante Córdova, for example, incorrectly believes that Joe is the leader and that he irrigated the field because "God had ordered him to start the Revolution without any further delay." . . . Benny Maestas sums up their history of organized action when he says, "United we flounder, divided we flounder.". . . But even with the lack of organization, there is power and direction in the actions of the community in spite of itself.

If the motivation of Joe and the other Chicano characters seems vague or random to us, the motivation of the Anglo community, in contrast, is clear and recognizable. The Anglo establishment assumes that it is dealing with an organized revolution because organization and rationality are the modes by which it operates. Individual and corporate greed, methodically implemented, characterizes the Anglo community. Ladd Devine's first response to the potential trouble Joe initiates is systematically to contact his local cronies; when word reaches the capital, the Governor assembles his advisers; they then dispatch undercover policeman Kyril Montana to Milagro to try to subvert this Chicano "movement" before it gets out of hand. . . . Kyril Montana exemplifies the faceless, ruthless, manipulative Anglo establishment that knows what it wants and (it thinks) how to get it. This conscious organization pitted against an unconscious, collective will generates the chaos that becomes the comedy of the novel. And the victory of the Chicano community in this novel, temporary though it may be, results from the misjudgment of the Anglo establishment: its rationality and order cannot overcome, or even comprehend, the apparent irrationality and spontaneity of individual actions motivated by collective ideas and feelings.

Here then is the title conflict of *The Milagro Beanfield War:* the irrational, unorganized, superstitious Chicano community is at war with the rational, organized, manipulative Anglo community. Wars, after all, are fought between social groups, not individuals, and Nichols chooses not to focus on an individual protagonist whose personality, values, and consciousness usually provide coherence and continuity to a novel. Instead, he creates and develops an identity for his Chicano community and allows that community to function as protagonist. To accomplish this, Nichols employs a variety of strategies: he permits individuals to intensify their conflicts with individuals on the "enemy" side, making clear that such heightened tensions are widespread and a direct result of the larger beanfield conflict; he creates episodes in which existing subunits from the two sides can come into conflict in situations apparently unrelated to the beanfield war; and he manipulates accidents and coincidences to bring groups from the two sides into conflict. (pp. 203-04)

Individuals in *Milargo* create conflict, but they do not create political and social change. The community as a whole, however, does create that change: the major conflicts of the novel are directed by the collective will of the Chicano community. . . . Joe consistently disclaims leadership, yet his action precipitates collective resistance to Ladd Devine and his planned Indian Creek Dam and the Conservancy District it needs for support. And not only is there no individual leader, but the collective will of the Chicano community manifests itself in spite of internal conflicts: the members of the Chicano community fight as much with each other as with their Anglo "enemies." In fact, the central act of violence that leads to the climax of the novel is Joe's shooting of Seferino Pacheco and his marauding pig, the pig for invading his beanfield, and Pacheco, who retaliates for the shooting of the pig, in self-defense. Only when Joe is arrested does the Chicano community finally show solidarity by spontaneously rallying at the state police headquarters and securing his release. (p. 207)

The Chicano community is the protagonist of Nichols' novel and the vehicle for his central theme; he develops his characters so that they define the society of which they are a part. Once

we see that the protagonist of *Milagro* is the Chicano community, the function of the "set pieces" on Cleofes Apodaca in the prologue and of Amarante Córdova in the opening chapter becomes clear: each is a symbolic representation of the community protagonist, Cloefes Apodaca of the culture historically, and Amarante Córdova of this particular community in Milagro at the time of the action of the novel. In the prologue especially, Nichols is careful to establish the kinds of motivation and action typical of the Chicano community: "Milagro was a town whose citizens had a penchant not only for going crazy, but also for precipitating miracles.". . . The history of Cleofes Apodaca, like that of Joe Mondragón, begins with an apparently crazy event, an irrational and potentially self-destructive act, and ends with a miracle, an unpredictable, even unexplainable, good result.

Cleofes, a nineteenth-century sheepherder, was the town outcast, the very symbol of bad luck. Not only had he punched the Bishop who confirmed him, he grew up violating every taboo of the community. . . . He assumed magical qualities for his neighbors: he possessed "El Ojo," the evil eye, and he transformed himself into a black mongrel who at night killed frogs along the irrigation ditches. When his own dog, Pendejo, disappeared, Cleofes neglected himself and his other animals to search for his pet. . . . (pp. 209-10)

Cleofes' actions, on the one hand, are clearly crazy, irrational, and absurd: fanatic attachment to a dog that leads him to destroy his livelihood, his health, and ultimately his life. . . . These same actions, on the other hand, are superhuman and miraculous. The same devotion to his dog that seems crazy is also admirable: love for another creature that is so totally selfless, so willing to sacrifice, so oblivious to other concerns, so impossible to divert from its purpose is analogous to the highest forms of Christian love. Cleofes is a self-destructing paradox, both pitiable and admirable. As he is to his little society, so the Chicano community is historically to its larger social context. Cleofes insanely but admirably destroys himself in his singleminded pursuit of his own idiosyncratic goals, and the society around him watches curiously and tries to turn a buck on the show. In the same way, the Chicano culture "crazily" follows its old ways, and its individual members pursue their own individual forms of madness, while the dominant Anglo culture watches and profits by its disintegration.

This seems to be Nichols' long range view of Chicano society in America, a view confirmed by the subsequent novels in his New Mexico Trilogy. By the end of *The Nirvana Blues,* the old man Elroy Irribarren, called the Last Chicano, has been killed by the Anglo establishment while preparing to irrigate the land that has been his all his life. But in *Milagro* things are not yet so bad, and the portrait of Amarante Córdova modifies and qualifies this bleak prediction. Amarante symbolizes the status of Chicano culture at the time of the action of *Milagro,* and while he shares many characteristics with Cleofes Apodaca, he also differs from him in some significant ways. Like Cleofes, Amarante is victimized by his physical and social environments: he had always "lived in the shadow of his own death." . . . Unlike Cleofes, however, Amarante does not self-destruct, even at age 93. Amarante's son Jorge, on his third trip home to visit his perpetually dying father, observes that Amarante "had reached some kind of nadir ten or twelve years ago and now he was growing backward, aiming toward middle age, maybe youth." If Cleofes symbolizes the mad, self-destructive nature of Chicano society, Amarante Córdova symbolizes the simultaneous possibility of its vitality in spite of the suffering it endures. Amarante will die, of course, and the possibility, the imminence of his death is always before us; but he does not die during this novel. Instead, he is one of the Chicanos who actively participate in the conflict, singlehandedly at one point driving a bulldozer across the desert and dumping it into the Rio Grande canyon. The unorganized revolution, however, is like Amarante's renewed youth: it is a bright and energetic interlude in a grim drama. The "set pieces" on Amarante Córdova and Cleofes Apodaca, then, are crucial to the design of the novel: [Cleofes] prepares us for Amarante, and together they prepare us for the many other crazy and miraculous characters. . . . (pp. 210-11)

The prologue and part one of the novel serve essentially to introduce the protagonist, the Chicano community, and the antagonist, the Anglo establishment, by introducing the individuals who make up these communities . . . Just as we are interested in a protagonist with some psychological complexity because he or she is at the center of the major conflict of a novel, so we are interested in the psychological and social complexity of the Chicano community (as presented through its parts, the individual characters who make it up) because it is at the center of the conflict in *Milagro*. The characters, then, need no more complexity, independence, and inner life than their role as parts of that community requires.

By the end of the novel, little has changed and yet a great deal has changed. The Indian Creek Dam has been defeated, but only temporarily . . . The Chicano community has come together in spite of itself, without a leader, without a hero to encourage and organize it; its victory is minor and temporary, as Nichols makes clear in his subsequent novels.

The two cultures, Chicano and Anglo, and the values they represent are the protagonist and antagonist in *The Milagro Beanfield War;* they are forces too powerful to be controlled, too intertwined to be separated into clearly defined and formulated principles, and too random and haphazard in events to be represented by any one character. Nichols' concerns as novelist are primarily social, and he has created an unusual kind of protagonist, and thus novel, to give artistic form to these concerns. Without denying or debasing the individuality of character that enlivens and informs the novel, Nichols has reshaped the genre. . . . The flexibility and vitality—the very "novelty"—of the novel lie at least partly in its ability to nourish and revitalize itself from its own historical sources. *The Milagro Beanfield War* taps those sources to reemphasize and reshape the social as well as the individual nature of the novel. (pp. 211-13)

John E. Loftis, "Community as Protagonist in John Nichols' 'The Milagro Beanfield War'," in Rocky Mountain Review of Language and Literature, *Vol. 38, No. 4, 1984, pp. 201-13.*

Heberto Padilla

1932-

Cuban poet, novelist, and translator.

Padilla is an important Cuban writer who now lives in the United States. Though not by nature a commentator on political concerns, his conflict with the Cuban government during the late 1960s and early 1970s has had a profound effect on his career. An early supporter of his country's 1959 revolution, Padilla grew disillusioned with Fidel Castro's regime. He was jailed after criticism of the government was detected in his poetry, and his subsequent humiliating "confession" caused a furor in the international literary community. Critics have noted in Padilla's work a desire to exclude the public sphere and focus on a private world where love, memory, and unrestrained thought are allowed to prosper.

Padilla produced a volume of poetry when he was only sixteen years old, but his first work to attract critical attention was *El justo tiempo humano* (1962). This book contains verse which, though written in a spare poetic style, reveals the influence of the English Romantic poets who continue to interest Padilla. *Fuera del juego* (1968), though not directly critical of the Cuban government, describes in tones of anger and disillusionment the hardships of living in a regimented society. The book won a major Cuban literary prize but was harshly condemned in *Verde olivo,* the publication of the Cuban army. In 1971 Padilla was imprisoned and shortly thereafter made a public statement denouncing his own work and accusing several other writers, including his wife, of anti-government sentiment. Padilla spent the rest of the 1970s translating the works of English Romantic poets and published none of his own poetry. In 1980 he was allowed to leave Cuba, and he settled in the United States.

Legacies: Selected Poems (1982) collects poems Padilla wrote during his period of silence and also includes several verses from the 1960s and 1980s. Because the poems are not dated, some critics contend that the reader is unable to form any sense of chronology or context. Several reviewers speculated that this disorder is intentional and stems from Padilla's desire that his work be viewed apart from political considerations. The poetry in *Legacies* covers a wide range of topics, including childhood, love, friendship, and historical and literary figures. Like his earlier work, these poems are unadorned and direct yet reflect a romantic sensibility.

Padilla's novel *En mi jardín pastan los héroes* (1982; *Heroes Are Grazing in My Garden*) centers on two main characters: Gregorio, a writer struggling with alcoholism, apathy, and constraints on his work, and Julio, whose job as a translator for his repressive government has left him disillusioned. Michael Wood characterizes the book as "a novel of disappointment and creeping fear, of the hardening of revolutionary fervor into dogma, and of the pollution of private lives by politics."

© Jerry Bauer

LEWIS HYDE

[In] the last twenty years, Heberto Padilla's literary career has passed through almost every possible permutation of the modern conjunction of art and politics, and it is tempting to settle on a single such permutation as the entry into his poetry.

Born in Cuba fifty years ago, Padilla, who spent some of his youth in the United States, has been both the child of Third World colonial capitalism and its expatriate. His return to Cuba after Fidel Castro came to power made him a revolutionary; he worked first as a cultural editor at the daily *Revolución* and then as a correspondent for the Cuban news agency in London and in Moscow.

Padilla slowly became the gadfly of the revolution, writing with growing skepticism of modern socialism and its theorists. In 1968 he was the focus of a literary scandal when an international jury awarded him Cuba's annual poetry prize only to have the government try to block the award. In 1971 Padilla was jailed, briefly, and then humiliated into a public confession of his "errors." He spent a decade in isolation and last year was either forced or went voluntarily into exile, depending on who you talk to.

This history is so varied, and it plays such an important role in the poems, that the absence of any critical framing or chronology is one of the [few faults of *Legacies*]. A poem telling us that "the best ground for a man to be on is his own ground, his garden, his own house," may read a little differently depending on whether it was written in 1951 in New York, 1961 in Havana, 1971 in jail or 1981 in New Jersey, where Padilla is settled at the moment. And the poem **"Between March and April is the cruelest month"** makes more sense if we know that Padilla was imprisoned between March 20 and April 25, 1971.

But I should temper this complaint somewhat. Padilla had a hand in assembling this collection, and it must be his hope that the poems will not be read only as messages from the situations of their writing. The soldier thugs who appear in **"Between March and April"** are not that different, really, from the "inspector of heresies" who appears in a poem from the late 1950s. Interrogators are interrogators, whether they are Batista's or the C.I.A.'s or Castro's.

One of Padilla's "obsessive themes" (as he calls them) is a complaint about our modern ideologies of history. In a brief sketch called **"The traveling companion,"** a young woman reading her manual of Marx and Lenin looks out the window of a train and exclaims that she sees history going by; Padilla looks out and sees "roads and barbed wire / and beasts / male and female. . . ." An aphoristic quatrain warns

> Don't you forget it, poet.
> In whatever place or time
> you make, or suffer, History,
> some dangerous poem is always
>   stalking you.
>
> (**"According to the old bards"**)

This may not fit very well into a history-will-absolve-me kind of revolutionary society, but it is not a defense of individualism, either. It's a defense of the imagination. History teaches that history cannot teach everything.

There is a word that keeps appearing in these poems: *clave*. *Clave* usually means a code or the key to a code, but in the context of Padilla's work it comes to mean something closer to gnosis, or spiritual insight. Thus in the complicated and evocative poem **"The childhood of William Blake,"** a voice chastises Blake as a child: "You've a bad tongue. You steal / from the larder. / Your face is dirty. / You're always making riddles [*claves*], / etchings / engravings." Blake's poems themselves are the *claves* he has left us, "symbols, / your gifts / shining in the wilderness."

The word *decifrar*—to decipher—recurs alongside *clave*. The poet stands "at the door of a butcher shop / open-mouthed deciphering signs," for example. The two words denote the complementary tasks of the poet: to decode the real and to leave behind the work, the "keys," by which we may do the same.

Throughout this book, however, we find Padilla dubious about such undertakings in the twentieth century: "Impossible . . . to compose a poem at this late stage of civilization. . . . / Impossible . . . to find . . . / a window with no radar, / a pine table with no maps, no calculations." Our environment is now so rationalized and politicized as to be inhospitable to the part of our being that creates a work of art. (p. 87)

In a short essay in *The New York Times* last September, Padilla wrote: "During the last 20 years, I lived in a world made up of ideas painted in black and white." It is the work of the imagination to resolve the opposites, to find those secondary shades that are neither black nor white, to be a seamstress to the real. Some third thing must lie between "individualist" and "revolutionary." The imagination resolves conflict not through that old dialectic of Hegel but through the even older one of Ovid: metamorphosis. I do not mean to say that polar opposites have no place in the world, but when everything *must* be cast in such terms, then there is no true debate, and certainly no art.

This is sad stuff, really. Poetry is not impossible in this century, as these poems testify, but in Padilla we have, I think, a poet who has not been able to mine the richest veins of his sensibility because of the situation of his birth. He is temperamentally closer to W. H. Auden or Antonio Machado than, say, to Nicolás Guillén or Ernesto Cardenal. Left alone in London or Mexico City for the last twenty years, he might have given us a different group of poems—more poems on childhood, on sexual love, on the voices of the past, on landscape and spirit, and, yes, on politics, but political poems less busy adjusting their voices so as to slip between the slogans, black and white.

Long ago Padilla told a friend, "The last thing I want to be is the Rebel Poet in a socialist society." But that is what he became. And now? Now we have the first American selection of his work. His publisher is to be congratulated for bringing it out. But we could have had most of this book ten years ago. We have it now because we are going to make Padilla the Ex-Rebel Poet in a capitalist society. . . . My hope is that we don't do this to him, that we leave him alone so that in five or ten years we will see another book, one with a touch more of the Blakean prophetic voice and a touch less wry irony. . . . (pp. 87-8)

Lewis Hyde, "Deciphering Codes," in The Nation, *Vol. 234, No. 3, January 23, 1982, pp. 87-8.*

GERRY CLARK

Long recognized as one of the great Spanish speaking poets, Heberto Padilla is still virtually unknown in the U.S. . . .

Legacies is an overview of Padilla's poetry. There is no clue of the dates of the works, but the reader can trace the development not only of Padilla's poetry, but also of his social and political awareness.

His early themes are personal and simple, dealing with love, dreams, and relationships (like the lovely, but unusual **"To Belkis, when she paints"**). Gradually, Padilla becomes more strident in his political opinion, writing poems of frank protest (**"Don Gustano"**). Some of his best work, however, deals with poetry and poets: **"Only among walkers," "Relief,"** and **"According to the old bards."** . . .

Whatever the theme, Padilla's writing is always rythmic and forceful, and the images are crystal-clear. It is the sheer melodiousness of the poems, however, that is their strongest asset; the flow and ebb of the lines is unforced and perfectly metered, bringing each poem to a natural and satisfying conclusion. Poems this splendid, even after translation, are certainly of the highest order.

Gerry Clark, in a review of "Legacies: Selected Poems," in Best Sellers, *Vol. 42, No. 2, May, 1982, p. 69.*

ORLANDO ROSSARDI

The Cuban poet Heberto Padilla's *En Mi Jardín Pastan Los Héroes (Heroes Graze in My Garden)* is a novelized account of events the author lived through in his homeland. The slice of life told in the novel, which a character named Gregorio Suárez is writing in Moscow and Havana—intermingling the two locations—alternates with the experiences of his antagonist Julio, like Gregorio an alter ego of the author's. Both travel the same road of adventures and misadventures, which culminates at the novel's end with an almost allegorical hand-to-hand struggle. Herein identities mix and merge, Julio calling himself Marx and Gregorio invoking the name of Engels.

The novel's plot is simple, and the characters are ordinary people caught up in circumstances in which the individual who wishes to rebel is besieged, overpowered, and totally destroyed. The "Prologue of a Novel," anticipating the work that follows, serves to clarify the experience the novel then narrates in equally simple language, making no concessiones to the latest fashions in fiction.

> *Orlando Rossardi, in a review of "En mi jardín pastan los héroes," in* Américas, *Vol. 34, No. 3, May-June, 1982, p. 64.*

ELIZABETH MACKLIN

Heberto Padilla has been generous with passion—his poems are a roué's tumblers, up to the brim—but he's been stingy in at least one respect: he has done us the disservice of not dating the poems in *Legacies*. True, he has intimated that he wishes this first bilingual book-length collection would not be received politically here in the United States; and it could be this that has led him to take these poems, which span so many, and such contradictory, years, and shuffle them out of chronological order, leaving no clues. (p. 125)

[Shuffle] these poems as he might, arrange them and rearrange them—at random, even—it doesn't seem possible that Padilla will be able to get his wish. This is a peculiarly political time he is living in, and although he makes his home in this country now, until March of 1980 he did live in his native Cuba. And then, too, there are the specific poems he has written.

One can see how he might think such a wish possible, though. The poems in *Legacies* are so clear and compelling that perhaps he is still inside them. His subject matter is not political—except perhaps by default. Padilla's great ability is to put pure emotion into words, lines, stanzas, building a frame for an impression that shocks with immediacy: he feels = you feel. In this, he's somewhat akin to the English Romantics, whom he's translated, and whom he adores: he knows the value of the disguises a poet finds for his own reality; his view of the world, like theirs, seems so painful and chancy and beyond the pale that it gets chalked up to heaven or omniscience, and comes back down masked as a Vision. The greater the need to hide, the more exotically forceful the Vision, or image. But something is different.

While the Romantics were deep inside their time and place (one thinks especially of Shelley, or of the Blake who wandered observant near the "charter'd Thames"), and refined the oppressively heavy ore of their strip/mined surroundings, Padilla digs and scrapes at another seam. His immediate time and place bend around him, serve to reflect him. He doesn't really seem to touch them. His emotion is personal, quite private. He digs at his own heart in isolation. (pp. 126-27)

It would probably be most accurate to say that his poems *in their inception* are not political—they are conceived, as it were, in a private house, and become political only when they hit the outer air. Whatever it is he is hiding in there, it is evident that he is hiding *something*. And since the outer air is revolutionary . . . , what happens once the poem enters the public sphere is politically determined.

Heberto Padilla was born in 1932, in Pinar del Rio, Cuba. His first book of poems was published when he was sixteen. In 1959, at the time of the overthrow of Fulgencio Batista, he had been living in New York, working for Berlitz as a teacher and translator; when the July 26th movement took power, he was given the post of New York correspondent for Prensa Latina, the Cuban press agency, and he stayed on in the city a few months longer, until he was called home to work on Carlos Franqui's new paper, *Revolución*.

Over the years, Padilla had work in his trade, or work that took him travelling. He was a correspondent (for both Prensa Latina and *Revolución*) in the Soviet Union. He helped to found the Cuban Writers and Artists Union, and acted as the director of its literature section, and worked on the editorial board of its publication, *Unión*. He was head of the cultural-import enterprise Cubartimpex, bringing foreign books to Cuban readers. He represented the Ministry of Foreign Trade in Scandinavian countries and in the Soviet Union. Meanwhile, he was writing: early on, the literary supplement *Lunes de Revolución* published parts of a novel; Casa de las Americas awarded an honorable mention to his book of poetry *El justo tiempo humano (Just, Human Time)*; other poems turned up in anthologies.

1968 and 1971 were bad years for Padilla. Ever since the Revolution, of course, Cuba had been adjusting—tightening and loosening belts; tightening and loosening ties with the Soviet Union; engaging in the kind of broken-field running that comes with pushing for, then controlling, sweeping social change and is highly bewildering to peripheral souls. . . . In retrospect, the 1968 incident in Padilla's career actually began the year before and had all the earmarks of a squabble among literati—or, rather, would have had, if one of the pseudonymous high-strung later participants had not been writing in *Verde Olivo*, the publication of the Cuban Army. (And the Army was, if not the midwife of the revolution, at least its attentive godparent.) This, therefore, lent a pulse-taking tinge to the bickering. In 1967, to counterbalance the gala publication of *Pasión de Urbino*, a novel by Cuban writer Lisandro Otero, Padilla had written a defense of another novel, *Vista del amanecer en el trópico (Daybreak, Viewed in the Tropics*, later revised into *Three Trapped Tigers*, which had taken Spain's highly regarded Biblioteca Breve prize in 1965, beating out Otero's work, which had also been entered that year. Complication: the prize-winning novel's author, Guillermo Cabrera Infante, also Cuban, had been living abroad for some time (though in silence, as far as politics went), and it was rumored that he would not be returning home. When, in midsummer, 1968, in a written interview that ran in the Buenos Aires paper *Primera Plana*, Cabrera finally came out, repudiating the Revolution in stinging terms . . . , pulses, so to speak, raced still faster. It was just a few months later that Padilla's new book of poems, *Fuera del juego*, was chosen to win the Julian del Casal poetry prize of the Writers and Artists Union. The poems themselves were highly critical of the revolution—astonishingly so, for someone who worked in government. There was a short, breath-holding pause. Government relations with "cultural workers" had tightened and loosened with the rest of the social fabric since 1959. In general, artists and writers had been given their head, though there had been questions concerning foreign films in the early Sixties. Then again, this particular juxtaposition of factors had never arisen before.

Verde Olivo came on the scene, with a critique of Padilla so stinging that it could (but for its heavy-handedness) have rivalled Cabrera. Padilla ended up working at the University of Havana, no longer in government. The Writers and Artists Union, sizing up the situation, objected to what had been done under its aegis, and objected strongly: 1968 would be the last year the Union appointed any foreign judges to weigh the entries for the Julian del Casal.

Nevertheless, *Fuera del juego* was published in due course, with a prefatory supporting statement by the judges and a prefatory disclaimer by the Union—all of which, along with the poems themselves, amounted to an electrical fire in the intellectual circuit box, the first episode of *el caso Padilla,* the Padilla Affair: lightbulbs flashing and bursting all the way down the line.

The second, 1971, episode, which could have been subtitled "Everyone Pushes His Luck," was a deepening of the same theme, and it was played out in dead earnest. Taking off, one assumes, from the title of the 1968 *Verde Olivo* polemic, *"Las provocaciones de Padilla,"* Padilla called a new group of poems *Provocations;* he read from them before the Writers and Artists Union and was jailed, from March 20th until April 27th. On the evening of his release, he spoke before the Union again, having apparently been asked to make a statement of self-criticism and of criticism of other writers, among them his wife. His talk was exhaustive, personal, rambling, and humiliating (reading the twenty-seven closely spaced pages of transcript is painful), and its repetitions and reassurances reveal a very, very tired man.

From 1971 until 1980, Padilla worked at translations: Shelley, Blake, Coleridge, Burns. Nothing of his own could be published in Cuba. He wrote a novel, *En mi jardín los heroes* (*Heroes Graze in My Garden*). And he wrote many of the poems that appear in *Legacies.* When the opportunity came to leave Cuba, he left, bringing with him to the U.S. twenty-one years condensed like a millefiori paperweight. Most of these years appear somewhere in *Legacies.*

All that specific time left a series of changes in Padilla's vocabulary. Little by little, new words were added—accumulating just as steadily as the events that piled up within the Cuban Revolution itself: the Bay of Pigs, say, and, layered on it, the continuing blockade; the texture of Castro's lukewarm support for the 1968 Soviet invasion of Czechoslovakia; on that, the failed million-ton sugar harvest of 1970. These events are not in this book, of course. Padilla's poems are only his own, the words arising from his more or less unconscious response to his surroundings.

One never knows the nuances of any given revolution, the first small impacts on the day-to-day. At first, it seems it might be any other change: a new President, a shift in attitude, a slight alteration in the air. Platforms and promises are easily broken, it's hard to tell beforehand; intent is what you bet on, at higher or lower odds. Padilla came home into a kind of euphoria: Batista had been no bargain, the constraints had been great. He slipped into daily life. Work was clothed in a different language, but it was not, perhaps, so different from that of New York. And he was in Cuba, which in all his poems appears as light, warmth, soil, green. There is a sense of surprise in

the poems before *Fuera del juego,* of something unforeseen coming into view—approximating—and then sinking in: "**The Childhood of William Blake**" is one of these poems, and "**Odalisque.**" In both, the feeling isn't named yet, it's only a feeling. These poems are not political. Of the woman in "**Odalisque**" Padilla says, "She empties herself / just as your chest does / but you never heard her breathe." Something closing in, taking you over, sweeping you maybe off your feet, maybe away completely. . . . Padilla regards the post-Batista changes: the wind tugging at the Coca-Cola signs; the Canada Dry courtesy clocks, "stopped / at the old time." (pp. 127-31)

"**In love's place,**" one of the more ambiguous poems in *Fuera del juego,* is another approximation. A man and a woman are making love. "Always, over your shoulder, I see the world," he says. "It gives off sparks in storms." Through fifteen lines, the eye focuses and refocuses: near, far. One wonders if the world has become wider, or if it is simply infringing, intruding into "the place where your shoulders / turn cooler, more fragile." He focuses again, away from the act of love:

> Always, over your shoulder
> (something that now we can never avoid),
> there is a list of missing persons,
> a village destroyed,
> a child trembling.

These things infringe. Reading the poems in *Legacies,* one comes to see in Padilla a deeply apolitical man, a man who wants merely to be left alone. . . . The progression of his language as he searches for a satisfactory solitude—welcoming a few friends, or his wife, on condition—is of great interest. For in these years the society still seeks to draw him in, as it becomes more wholly politicized—as everything, more and more, is political. Things keep intruding, and his response takes on newer and newer forms.

In Budapest, in autumn,

> while the old waiter covered us
> with wool shawls
> and kind words, untranslatable, long
> like organ music
> that crosses summer

a friend intrudes, telling the poet, "Try to be admired / as someone who lives wisely, / sworn enemy of pride, / of misanthropy, of deceiving virtue / and of all mistaken or supernatural gush." This poem, "**A sidewalk cafe: Budapest, autumn,**" from *El hombre junto al mar,* reads like a follow-up to the poems in a section of *Fuera del juego* called "**The birch tree of iron,**" which covered Padilla's impressions of Russia. Intrusion there was a harsher thing, to Padilla's mind, but it could still seem distanced, set in neutral scenery. In "**Song of the Spasskaya Tower,**" the language of blows is sampled: executions, a guard, the "outcast court," terror—but the tower that contains these indications is made of wind. (pp. 131-32)

It is when he arrives home that the uncertainty inherent in revolutionary change hits him personally, and he sees it changing his own life. There is the discrepancy between what one remembers from childhood and what exists now, but, more important, there is the contrast between what one wants—what one had dreamed of—and what one gets, especially if one is Padilla and has Padilla's desires and the country is Cuba. The images of this personal vision are biting, black humor, violent. (p. 133)

The categories of Marxism (History, particularly), bitterly twisted, and the language of Stalinist blows are emotionally accurate for Padilla, well before their time; to consider whether they are strictly true or not would seem to him beside the point. The point, for him, is that the Revolution is, elevator-like, stopped two or three floors below him, freighting and unloading what the people down *there* need; the doors aren't opening for him, and there are some things he'd like to have. **"Advice to a Lady"** (from *Fuera del juego*) specifies one request. It is a striking, violent poem, intertwining political words with sexual demands. Its focus is a woman with a "spinster face," her shades lowered, telephone wires cut. "You won't be able to erase reality," he tells her at first. Then, "Dare. Open the windows wide." He turns her into a she-cat, transfigures her. "The fence is low," he goes on, urging, "easy to jump over, / and in those lodgings students live." The poem ends with a punchline coda:

> Take a scholar to bed.
> Let your thighs enact the struggle of contraries.
> Let your tongue be more cunning than all dialectics.
> Come out on top in this class struggle.

There are other requests: if not such release, at least a shelter zone. (p. 134)

[In **"Nuclear Umbrella"** Padilla states] the dilemma: "The world no longer has any shelter zones." But there he is—having done nothing, yet under suspicion, threatened, tapping his foot for an eternity—a Cuban. Although "Cuba" has equalled "light," "air," "warmth," "green" in his dictionary, he now accepts the verdict, and the language, of . . . the other half of the shelterless world. (p. 135)

One feels that Padilla's departure [from Cuba] gathered itself over time, little by little acquiring the words appropriate to his sense of constraint. In **"Advice to a Lady,"** as in **"A Question for the Frankfurt School,"** or **"Traveling Companion"**—all defiant poems of disillusionment—he recodes words, names, images to fit his emotional-poetic context; they don't mean to him what they mean elsewhere. It was for this type of Babel that he was imprisoned and exhausted. **"Between March and April is the Cruelest Month"** is the title of the confirmation: it was as he'd thought. There could be no further communication, and, isolated, he gave up hoping, and entered into himself with a will.

In 1977, Padilla wrote **"The Last Thoughts of Sir Walter Raleigh in the Tower of London."** Six years had passed since his own imprisonment, and the poem reads in Spanish as an interior history. . . . In **"Sir Walter Raleigh"** there is a before and an after, two diametrically opposed states of mind. Padilla goes inside them both, and charts them, the exploratory and vivid map of passions and losses. "Yesterday" is the axis on which the poem turns. Until then, he says, he could move; he vibrated at the center of life, he says; every word shredded the word that went before—"tree or light or street or sea or sky"—confirming the elements he moved through. . . . But until yesterday he had moved blindly—blindly but without knowing that he was blind.

Until yesterday he did not realize that it would truly be necessary to leave Cuba. Without leaving the Tower of London, he shows us his future in the U.S.:

> beggars and kings inevitably fasting,
> under bridges,
> dressed up like doormen,

> sporting multicolored rags,
> fornicating with beasts, or masturbating—
> but free . . .

And he shows us the old dream: Sir Walter Raleigh speaks it in the first person, and italicized. *I can see El Dorado, I can still see it.* But what was missing—and he asks, "Must there always be something *imprescindible*, something one can't do without, something essential?"—what was missing was the "wide sky of the Southern Cross,"

> and—even more painful—
> great distances
> prairies   the expanse of the Americas
> where I could see the atoms of the wind. . . .

It is gone as quickly as it came: a dream of wide, sweeping, high fulfillment, grasped like a marriage of self to the world—now brought down to earth, and ended in divorce. "A plan," he says—you can almost see the arms hanging loose at his sides, after a final shrug. Or, rather, he adds, a dream that took on the shape of a nightmare. Given the circumstances—Sir Walter Raleigh looks out from his cell—all this place can hold for him now is the iron ash of the metallic protest of the trapped bird tarred and drying on the riverbank outside the Tower.

He cries out in italics, *I am not deceiving myself, you unbelievers.* That place existed, he says, and that fountain; he envisioned it when he was young—that is to say, when he was delirious: a mixture of stubbornness and hope. The next line says: "Perhaps this tower sweats blood." And the poem ends:

> People hide in or find comfort in metaphors.
> For me, they are no more than stones under the rain.
> Only things shine on their own;
> men need jesters or mirrors.

You've been carried through, carried inside Padilla's metaphor, and you see and feel his stone-cold logic, and the pain running from it. But still there is a murmur from far outside him: a current of doubt. And you wonder what [his wife] Belkis, for one, would say—speaking as a mirror. (pp. 137-39)

> Elizabeth Macklin, "Paperweight," *in* Parnassus:
> Poetry in Review, *Vol. 10, No. 1, Spring-Summer,*
> *1982, pp. 125-39.*

J. M. COHEN

Padilla's first volume—if we omit a small collection he published at the age of sixteen—reveals in its title *El justo tiempo humano* (*The Right Moment for Humanity*) the poet's optimism in 1962. It is scantily represented in [*Legacies: Selected Poems*]. The poetry is spare but romantic. For Padilla's predominant influences have been Blake, Wordsworth, and Byron, and those Russian poets who were strongly influenced by English romanticism. The outstanding sequence of this first Padilla volume is **"The Childhood of William Blake,"** a series of ten reflections on incidents in Blake's life and on his art, projected forward from imagined forebodings in his childhood. From these brief poems Blake emerges as a poet and engraver, as a wanderer in the London streets, and as the prophet not only of industrialism and its horrors, but also of the new Jerusalem. . . . [In **"The Childhood of William Blake"**] Padilla voices his fear that terror will eventually overcome the new Jerusalem that seemed to be coming to birth in Cuba. This sequence is a social poem, but one of great depth and perspicacity. *El justo* *tiempo humano,* however, contains many buoyant poems whose exclusion from *Legacies* I regret.

Padilla's next volume, *Fuera del juego* (*Sent Off the Field*), which was completed by 1968, proclaimed his fear much more loudly. It contained several poems of the quality of the William Blake series, among them a group written in Russia, where he had worked as a foreign correspondent, and others critical of regimented societies, though none that referred directly to Cuba. Indeed several of them celebrate the poet's delight in love and nature, in language that recalls the early Pasternak of *My Sister, Life.* . . .

The book *Fuera del juego* was closely analyzed for the Cuban authorities by a pseudonymous "detector of heresies," who shredded every poem for possible counterrevolutionary meanings. His criticism was published in *Verde olivo,* the organ of the Cuban army. . . . The poet was imprisoned, humiliated, silenced, in the tenth year of the new "age of justice" that he had welcomed. (p. 32)

The prevailing mood of *Fuera del juego* is one of anger and disillusion reinforced by the romantic feeling that in the new society there is no place for the poet. He is rejected, indeed "sent off the field." But still Padilla was not attacking the revolution itself. There was good reason, however, for the bureaucrats' objections to the book, more than I saw at the time as a liberal used to judging poetry by poetic standards. Most of the poems in *Fuera del juego* are brilliant with a barbed economy and originality of phrase. . . .

Between the controversy over the prize and his arrest Padilla continued to write satirical poems, which he sent to his friends abroad. In their wit and conciseness they recall some of Blake's attacks on his favorite enemies. . . .

After Padilla's release and "confession," only a few poems were sent abroad, and these few were published in this journal. But a number written in the ten years before he was allowed to emigrate are printed without dates in *Legacies* and interspersed with poems from his two published books. This disorder is unscholarly and deplorable. The reviewer can, however, attempt to divide them according to theme, and so isolate Padilla's preoccupations during his years of silence.

There are first those pieces, like the title poem **"Legacies,"** devoted to the theme of childhood and ancestry. In these Padilla seems to demolish the time sequence and see himself as the contemporary of his grandparents who first landed in Cuba. His second and related concern is also with history, particularly with those characters in the past with whom he can identify himself in his present situation. There is Pico della Mirandola, master of all knowledge who yet did not foresee his own fate; and the Spanish poet Quevedo, who identifies himself with all poets of every age since Homer, and Sir Walter Raleigh, imprisoned in the Tower of London and isolated by his own thoughts from an outward beauty that he can now no longer recall. These poems, while somewhat reminiscent of Auden's on Edward Lear and Rimbaud, are, however, less objective and detached. Each of Padilla's models reflects some aspect of himself. . . .

Third, there is a group of poems addressed to his wife Belkis, herself a fine poet, which turn on the theme of passion, and of the impossibility of shutting out the world in mutual delight. These poems evince not only joy in marriage but an enhanced pain at the omnipresence of a hostile and unpitying world. And last, there is the remarkable poem to his friend and fellow poet

Pablo Armando Fernández, now silent though tolerated by Cuban regime. This is the one poem in the book that reaches out toward the metaphysical, a quality so far absent from Padilla's poetry. For he entrusts to Pablo Armando, a theosophist "who can argue with death on its own terms," the duty of interpreting and defending him after his death—a condition that he, Heberto Padilla, cannot now understand:

> for there is no magic that is denied
>   to your hand
> and all our tongues learned from
>   yours.
> If after my death anyone should
>   want it,
> only you could unlock me for
>   them,
> key by key.

This poem, more than all the rest, points to new directions open to Padilla in the future. (p. 33)

[As] I have already said, the poems [in *Legacies*] are printed in a regrettable disorder. There is nothing to tell the reader, for instance, that **"The Childhood of William Blake"** was written many years before the poem addressed to Pablo Armando Fernández, his friend and fellow poet. Further, some very good poems from Padilla's first volume which voice his initial enthusiasm for the revolution are unaccountably omitted. I do not think, from my knowledge of the poet, that he has any Audenesque wish to edit his past. Yet *El justo tiempo humano* is here reduced to two or three poems.

On the subject of the translations I am in even greater difficulty. These are, in many cases, too literal to be poetic. Though Padilla's statements may appear at first sight straightforward, they are often in fact highly ambiguous, in the manner of the Spanish seventeenth century. In many of the poems when Padilla refers to his ancestors, with whom he often feels himself to be a contemporary, he is referring not merely to his grandfathers who came to Cuba from Spain, but to those Spanish poets to whom he feels akin. Indeed, one of the best poems of the present collection is dedicated to that master of black irony, Francisco Gómez de Quevedo, who saw the walls of his country falling apart. (pp. 33-4)

Padilla's poetry is deceptively simple at first sight, far more complex on a second reading. Those who follow the Spanish on the left-hand page of *Legacies* will appreciate layers of meaning that do not emerge on the right. They will conclude, I think, that Padilla is one of the most important poets of the last quarter of a century.

He is a poet who has lived through that dawn in which for a while it was exciting to be alive, but who, in rejecting inflated hopes, has not sunk into disillusion and bitterness or crabbed conservatism, but continues to accept and interpret new experiences. Moreover, having spent his formative years in the United States and some time also in London and Moscow, he unites elements of the English and Russian traditions. Indeed he spent some of his years of isolation in Cuba translating the English romantic poets, especially Blake. Thus he is that rare creature, an international poet, capable of making his native Spanish move to new rhythms. (p. 34)

With whom may Padilla be compared? I think of the best of Voznesensky, of the Lowell of *Life Studies,* and the poems of Seamus Heaney.

"This man," the poet and communist editor Roberto Fernández Retamar said to me during the controversy over the prize, "wants to be our Pasternak." This was said in malice, and showed a narrow view of Pasternak. But whether Padilla intended to take such a part or not, it belongs to the past. The later poems of *Legacies* show him to be moving into a phase in which defensive action is over. Padilla is now reasserting the claim Blake made for poetry as a prophetic art. (p. 35)

> J. M. Cohen, "Prophet," in The New York Review of Books, *Vol. XXX, No. 11, June 30, 1983, pp. 32-5.*

TOM GRANAHAN

Mr. Padilla is primarily a poet, and this novel [*Heroes Are Grazing in My Garden*] is multi-layered like a good poem. The bitter story of Gregorio, an alcoholic writer, and Julio, a frustrated, disenchanted government translator, is largely allegorical, an impressionistic web of fantasy, dreams, and reality. It is a novel of ideas more than character and plot, rewarding the reader who looks beyond the rather stagnant surface to the possibilities of the book's central metaphor.

Disillusionment, frustration, and a sense of betrayal permeate the lives of Gregorio and Julio, where the sole refuge of the individual is fantasy and dreams. Each struggles against the enervating effect of lost purpose and identity. In the end, however, even the dream betrays.

There is a dour message here, addressed, I think, not to Castro's state, but to those individuals who have become so much livestock in any corral of repression, whether it is self-imposed or state-imposed. (pp. 329-30)

> Tom Granahan, in a review of "Heroes Are Grazing in My Garden," in Best Sellers, *Vol. 44, No. 9, December, 1984, pp. 329-30.*

MICHAEL WOOD

"History, old Marx," Heberto Padilla wrote in a poem published . . . in 1971, "is not enough." He is still right, but history obviously didn't take kindly to the remark. Padilla was imprisoned by Castro as a dissident and forced to recant. He spent nine years under virtual house arrest, and was allowed to leave Cuba in 1980. His case became a signpost for many foreign supporters of the revolution, an instance of how very little dissent the regime was prepared to tolerate. Padilla, a distinguished poet and translator, doesn't say when he wrote his novel *Heroes Are Grazing in My Garden,* but a version of it seems to have been part of the brief against him in 1971. It is a novel of disappointment and creeping fear, of the hardening of revolutionary fervor into dogma, and of the pollution of private lives by politics. . . .

In an afterword to his novel Padilla speaks of the imperfection of "books written under socialism"—as distinct, he must mean, from books written by socialists living in Paris, *pace* Mitterrand. The books of Cuba, or of the Eastern bloc, Padilla suggests, are necessarily desperate or neurotic. They "require an impossible reading by an impossible reader, since no reader will have the kind of knowledge required for their understanding." The argument is not entirely clear to me, but Padilla seems to say that we must overpraise or overdisparage or overexcuse writers like himself or Solzhenitsyn or Kundera or Pasternak, whom he mentions: we can't look at them straight.

This is probably right, but I don't see why we shouldn't try to look at them straight, and the whole line of thought sounds like a premature apology. If there are no readers, why is the book being published, and who are we?

The plot, or rather the unresolvable central situation, of the novel concerns two men in Havana: Gregorio, an alcoholic novelist trying (not very hard) to reform, hampered by his sloth and despair, and by the energetic help of his wife, who reconstructs his lapses and errors like a "furious archeologist, throwing up to him his own shameful skeleton, his ugly prehistory"; and Julio, a translator who cannot find an outlet for his diffuse and murmuring resistance to what is happening to Cuba. Julio argues with his brother-in-law, learns he is being followed, and finally has some sort of breakdown in which he sees the heroes of the title, "heroes of all sizes and ages—heroes suddenly as puzzled as clumsy, frightened children, heroes who moved like lancers to the sound of fife and flute," chewing the grass he has been meaning to cut for days.

> They grazed—on all fours they cut the greenery with their teeth . . . they brandished their useless weapons, which would never again destroy. Children would come later, or a council of old men, under the clean vines returned to their original innocence, purged of history. He wanted this deluge to swallow everything—acts, speeches and apothegms, philosophers and enchanters, prophets and kings and secretaries-general and bishops of all churches.

It is a telling vision, an impossible peace, and it answers an earlier dream of Julio's, in which he meets Castro and can't voice his complaints. Castro blows out a huge puff of smoke from his cigar and asks, "And what would you do if you were Prime Minister? I'll give you one minute to answer. What would you do in my place?" He waits. Julio's "intelligent, sick, old weight of objections" is no use to him now, and he answers, "Exactly what you do, Fidel." The novel ends with Gregorio and Julio, who at times seem like figments of each other's imagination, getting drunk and going swimming, incoherently sharing their helplessness.

Julio has other problems, since he bullies his mistress cruelly, and can't bear the thought of whatever sexual experience she may have had before she met him. In spite of Padilla's remarks about political tensions creeping into everything, it's really hard to see what the revolution has to do with this, or with Gregorio's drinking and baffled daydreaming. Much of this novel clusters around the ideas of getting old and getting lost; around the amount of battering and patching up a human relationship will stand; around the distaste some Cubans feel for their steamy tropics, their longing for the clean, cold winters of the north.

It must have been the unhappiness of the book that irritated the authorities, since the revolution has prohibited gloom and despair. It is a brave work in this sense, a statement of the right to sadness, which is as important as any other right. That said, and without putting in any kind of plea for positive heroes, I must admit I find Gregorio and Julio a pair of old whiners, so deeply dipped in self-pity that they tend to brush away all continuing sympathy and sustained interest. Kafka's Joseph K., whose miserable end is evoked in the novel, is an eager extrovert by comparison. (p. 34)

> Michael Wood, "Ah, the Fredonna Tree," in The New York Review of Books, *Vol. XXXII, No. 12, July 18, 1985, pp. 33-6.**

Robert Pinsky

1940-

American poet, critic, and editor.

Pinsky is respected for his carefully crafted, usually discursive poems which evoke a wide scope of subjects in a style that blends imagery and abstraction. He is particularly praised for creating expansive narratives which are thematically diverse and intellectually stimulating yet are also clear in presentation and optimistic in tone. Charles Molesworth notes: "Pinsky's poetry does not involve a total rejection of the imagistic poetry heralded by Pound and Williams, nor does it require a return to Augustan decorum. What it does instead is use the past, both the near and distant past, as a way of making the present resound."

Pinsky's first volume of verse, *Sadness and Happiness* (1975), contains both long and short poems but is particularly noted for the 17-page poem "Essay on Psychiatrists." Containing a variety of literary and cultural references, this poem typifies Pinsky's use of the discursive form. Similarly, the verse in *An Explanation of America* (1979) forms a long, unified work in which the poet, addressing his daughter, attempts to describe his country's past so that she may use this knowledge to realize the promise of the future. The title poem of *History of My Heart* (1984) is an extended narrative that draws on Pinsky's experiences as a child, adolescent, and adult in a lyrical evocation of memory and desire. Reviewers of *History of My Heart* lauded Pinsky for his ability to confront his past while avoiding sentimentality.

Pinsky's penchant for the long, meditative poem and his attention to morality have led some critics to compare his poetry with the work of several eighteenth- and nineteenth-century English poets. This alliance is also evident in Pinsky's critical work, in which he espouses his belief in the importance of the tradition established by his poetic forebears. *Landor's Poetry* (1968) is a study of the nineteenth-century Romantic poet Walter Savage Landor, and *The Situation of Poetry* (1976) analyzes the role and significance of literary tradition in modern poetry. These works have earned Pinsky critical acclaim for his intelligent appraisals and knowledge of his subjects.

(See also *CLC*, Vols. 9, 19; *Contemporary Authors*, Vols. 29-32, rev. ed.; and *Dictionary of Literary Biography Yearbook: 1982*.)

ELIZABETH FRANK

The core of Robert Pinsky's third book of poems is the long title piece, "History of My Heart." Pinsky has written long poems from the beginning and established himself as a poet in the discursive mode with serious moral purposes. "The poem, new or old," he has written in his admirable book of criticism, *The Situation of Poetry*, "should be able to help us, if only to help us by delivering the relief that something has been understood, or even seen, well."

© Thomas Victor 1986

Pinsky has used himself as a subject before, notably in his first long poem, "Sadness and Happiness," but in *History of My Heart* he is more directly autobiographical, more centered in self. Yet his focus is still less on his own spiritual innards than on the etiology of desire. (pp. 421, 423)

Pinsky mixes warm and often funny autobiographical anecdotes with long comfortable passages of commentary, so that it is always astonishing and unexpected when he makes wild, almost allegorical leaps into another realm of imagination. Remembering a prized flashlight received . . . [one] Christmas, he envisions the heart not yet awakened to desire as "a titular, / Insane king who stares emptily at his counselors" and follows with the grotesque figure of the brain "settling / Into the morning *Chronicle*, humming to itself, / Like a fat person eating M&Ms in the bathtub." It's a mixture of Poe's "The Haunted Palace" and an R. Crumb cartoon.

In *The Situation of Poetry*, Pinsky took a stand against what he saw as the contemporary fashion of poetic nominalism (more loosely, surrealism), and his sense that there is an impervious, bullying reality out there, defying the poet to make something out of it, has never been stronger. Nevertheless, Pinsky is taking greater risks with imagery, allowing it to assume a new supremacy over the explanatory mode. In "The Figured Wheel," the bizarre juggernaut of the title rolls unstoppably over the world, gathering all times, places, persons, mythologies, religions and literatures into its gorgeous hangings and inscriptions, which add up to nothing less than the human race's whole inheritance of metaphor. In the course of finding "The exact forms of the ordinary," particularly the "unfabulous" American urban ordinary, Pinsky imagines ironic-marvelous *tableaux vivants,* filled with grim enchantment. . . .

What's especially interesting is the way Pinsky refrains from embedding his figures and fables in obligatory explanation. His voice is still engagingly talky, still confiding, anecdotal, funny, sober and reflective—the voice of a storyteller and, occasionally, a teacher—but it seems to pause more often, to see more deeply into the strangeness of things, and to be less concerned about continuity, connection and closure. (p. 423)

> Elizabeth Frank, "The Middle of the Journey," in *The Nation, Vol. 238, No. 13, April 7, 1984, pp. 421, 423-24.**

R. W. FLINT

Robert Pinsky is one of a number of poets for whom story telling has become steadily more desirable. Even during the apocalyptic 1960's, poetic narrative had its stout underground defenders. But the growing skepticism with which the once talismanic word "confessional" is regarded today is indication enough of a wider return to sanity. Confession as a literary expedient really belongs to practical religion and secular therapy.

Mr. Pinsky's *History of My Heart,* its title notwithstanding, is a considerable advance over his earlier *An Explanation of America* in the direction of concocting stories that stand on their own—independent of gimmicks like trying to explain "America" to a teen-age daughter or contrasting a suave translation from Horace with nervously subtle commentary. He was never a showoff; his leanings toward virtuosity have always been under admirable control. Now his manifold talents have become better servants of memory. *History of My Heart* includes fine portraits of his parents and boyhood neighbors, Fats Waller warming the Christmas crowd at Macy's, holocaust victims and the inspired derelicts beautifully summoned up in the poem "The New Saddhus":

> And not young men, but the respectable Kurd, Celt, Marxist
> And Rotarian, chanting and shuffling in place a little now
> Like their own pimply, reformed-addict children, as they put aside
>
> The garb, gear, manners and bottomless desires of their completed
> Responsibilities; they are a shambles of a comic drill-team
> But holy, holy—holy, becoming their own animate worshipful
>
> Soon all but genderless flesh, a cooked sanctified recklessness—
> O the old marks of elastic, leather, metal razors, callousing tools,
> Pack straps and belts, fading from their embarrassed bodies!

Mr. Pinsky has a rare gift for portraits of this kind, for action, character and atmosphere clearly and buoyantly proportioned.

"The New Saddhus" reminds one more of Saul Bellow or Philip Roth than of any of his contemporaries in poetry.

> R. W. Flint, "Feeding the Hunger for Stories," in The New York Times Book Review, *April 8, 1984, p. 14.**

MARY KINZIE

The contemporary poem tends to be spoken by a great Shadow-I, one of whose problems, whatever else may occur in the poem, is that he must worry-out and worry-through the way he sounds. This worrying of the style in and through which the voice progresses is, however, more a necessity of personality than of intellect—and even at that rate more compelling for technical reasons than psychological ones (although one should not discount the almost theurgic superstition with which contemporary writers set out to tamper with words). On the other hand, unlike many a nineteenth-century writer, surer of his relation to literary convention, the Shadow-I must invent a language that sounds at once indebted to other speakers *in general* (hence the blurred or shadow quality) and thoroughly orthogonal to the norm, with a snap eccentric to himself (hence the function of the retrograde ego in the enterprise). In this way the contemporary writer is almost compelled to work against himself. . . .

[The] Shadow-I who speaks the poem may risk or even induce clumsiness, fragmentation of thought as well as expression, and straitened provisionality of outcome. These hobblings warrant the genuineness of the problem (the problem of finding simultaneously a self, a theme, and a language) as they testify to the sincerity of the one who so ruefully and, it may be, misguidedly, tries to cope. If the Shadow-I stumbles or temporizes or breaks off, it is because these acts are the preconditions for the kind of breakthrough in which the world and the ego merge into one interpretive terrain. Distractions of consciousness presumably diagnose the uneven rhythms and sudden adjustments of external matter and objective fate to laws of their own. His very weakness is his armor as the error-ridden, incomplete, uncertain verbal hero forays out into a chaos of possibilities, a paradise of imperfections. (p. 38)

In his excellent reflections on contemporary verse in *The Situation of Poetry* (1976), poet-critic Robert Pinsky makes an attractive argument for the virtues of prose in poetry. . . . [He embraces] the "prose freedom and prose inclusiveness" of the modernist tradition. The modernist poets he has in mind are T. S. Eliot, William Carlos Williams, and Wallace Stevens:

> I have in mind a range of passages in which the dull plains of description or the exactions of the "image" are not abandoned, but transcended: the poet claims the right to make an interesting remark or to speak of profundities, with all of the liberty given to the newspaper editorial, a conversation, a philosopher, or any speaker whatever.

That is a wide range of idiom, from the undefined conversation to the highly delimited address of a philosopher—so wide that one might doubt the reach of the covering term. But modernism's democratic spirit makes little of the distinction between compressed and dilated forms. That all these prose possibilities could be part of one aesthetic mentality is anything but evident—until one supplies (as Robert Pinsky persistently does) the post-Romantic desire for transcendence over the contingent world. More simply, the Shadow-I is permitted to do whatever is necessary to work its way out of the muddle.

There is one poet who has been more successful than most at muddling through. Perhaps the scrappiest burrower, most ingenious mingler of idioms, and most elusive generally of the poets to inherit the glass cape of modernism is the shadowy John Ashbery. I may be mistaken in believing that Robert Pinsky is haunted by Ashbery; there is no mistaking that he is haunted by one of Ashbery's ghosts, Wallace Stevens. But then, it is ennobling to be drawn by Stevens's hypnotic and sacramental meditations on being, especially at a sufficient remove that one is always involved in one of those special gaps of time and sensibility of which Nabokov writes: "It is a question of focal adjustment, of a certain distance that the inner eye thrills to surmount, and a certain contrast that the mind perceives with a gasp of perverse delight." It is just such a thrilling curtailment of scale between himself and Stevens, while maintaining the categorical interval between them, which Robert Pinsky explores.... Although more particulate and realistic than Stevens, ... [passages] from Pinsky's volume personify, metaphysical-ize, indeed rhapsodize very much as Wallace Stevens does.... The end to which the metaphysical tends in Stevens is a definition of true being as it embraces self, weather, and (odd as this may seem) the seismic tremors of world event. Not merely the sum of impressions, the being derived from world is rather an "organic centre of responses, / Naked of hindrance, a thousand crystals." ... [This] being is [elsewhere] described as the exact "poverty" of one's true element, as what one believes in. "What / One believes is what matters." Even if one were removed to an extreme world where circumstance becomes alien and belief impossible, say to the moon, or (by implication) to a world at war ..., one could still return at night, scourged of idea, "naked of any illusion," and be taken back into the truth:

> returning from the moon, if one breathed
> The cold evening, without any scent or the shade
> Of any woman, watched the thinnest light
> And the most distant, single color, about to change,
> And naked of any illusion, in poverty,
> In the exactest poverty, if then
> One breathed the cold evening, the deepest inhalation
> Would come from that return to the subtle centre....

(**"Extracts from Addresses to the Academy of Fine Ideas"** ...)

Between [Pinsky] and the Stevens of penetration and convergence there is a huge intellectual and temperamental difference. But one need only read the closing lines of **"History of My Heart"** to hear the broad rhetorical bond. The heart

> Yearning further into giving itself into the air, breath
> Strained into song emptying the golden bell it comes
>   from,
> The pure source poured altogether out and away.

Both passages express imaginative energy in somatic terms; even emotion-freshened affirmations like love and belief are brought into prominence with the action of breathing, as though Wallace Stevens could take in his deep and subtle knowledge with the very air, and as if Robert Pinsky could pour out his love by exhaling his musical celebration of it.

But the end to which the metaphysical serves in the younger poet's verse is un-Stevensian; he is not out to find the imaginative center in its own terms but to explore memories on the one hand, lush and devious artifice on the other. Through this latter trait, he brings us back to John Ashbery, who dominates

his own blend of surrealism and parody with steely control and magisterial beauty.... But the surfaces of his control are actually unreliable indicators of order and connectedness. The younger poet resembles him in devices of great verbal beauty that are several layers of nuance removed from coherent denotation, while elusively suggesting links to life and thought.... [In comparing Ashbery's "Fragment" and Pinsky's **"History of My Heart,"** it is apparent that the] two poets have in common a drift toward auditory aspiration ... placed against the clear dentals. Correlative with these auditory patterns is the faint tension between an imagery of release, efflorescence, disappearance, and airy dissolution on the one hand, and on the other the few weak counters that might have tied these floatings down (the promise of crashing and piercing—of real anecdote and locale).... [The] movement of consciousness is "out and away" from us toward a vaporous distance where shapes are formulated against the sky and summer is a band of children. A further support for the manifold dissolvings is the use of abstractions that sound almost like particulars. In Pinsky these are *the air, a music, the heart itself, the idea of the giving of desire, the notes of wanting, the golden bell, the source,* and in Ashbery, *these ages, the distance, the welcoming, iron bells, the method of thought, a rhythm, this motion toward.* Furthermore, in at least two of these "abstract particulars," a double ambiguity is imbedded: Pinsky treats the gold bell of song and Ashbery the iron bells of welcoming as both real and analogical, the emotion suggested by each metaphor at once pressing toward embodied fact, and merely hovering over its ornamental status.

After a time this lexicon and these idioms come to look wispy and translucent, at least in Ashbery's work. W. H. Auden in his introduction to *Some Trees* (Yale, 1956), reflected on the temptation to manufacture oddities "as if the subjectively sacred were necessarily and on all occasions odd." Pinsky also warns against "the horrible ease with which a stylish rhetoric can lead poetry unconsciously to abandon life itself." Thus, whatever impulse there is in his own poems toward an Ashberian suspension of realia is balanced against a confessional urge, which he sometimes indulges with the happily ironic aplomb of Frank O'Hara, as when he recalls dancing with a girl in the back room of her parents shop (what could be more reassuringly concrete?), with a pleased erection at the thought, *"She likes me, / She likes it,"* made happy "To see eyes 'melting' so I could think *This is it, / They're melting!"* Here, the speaker's solipsism is comic; elsewhere, it is angular and unwieldy. To correct the proclivity of his melodious and stylish rhetoric to become merely derivative and literary, he sacrificially intrudes into the fabric of his poems, himself, "Robert Pinsky," whose father prescribed hearing aids and eye glasses for Mr. Monk and Mrs. Rose Vogel; whose school principal was Mr. Ringleven, whose bus driver was Ray; whose mother had a little printer's stamp made of his name; whose name figures as one item over which the great wheel of destiny and generation indifferently rolls. The wheel, "hung with devices," rolls "unrelentingly" over everything, including

> A cow plodding through car traffic on a street in Iasi,
> And over the haunts of Robert Pinsky's mother and
>   father
> And wife and children and his sweet self
> Which he hereby unwillingly and inexpertly gives up,
>   because it is
>
> There, figured and pre-figured in the nothing-
>   transfiguring wheel....

The effect of these maddeningly ingenuous moments of vanity is similar to the ego-centered unmaskings in a fairy tale. This writing is of course anything but "inexpert," but at the same time the sensibility here is alien to the surrender of selfhood which the "sweet self" of "Robert Pinsky" is nominally unmasked to accomplish.

Unlike Ashbery, who avoids the equation of using all styles, even the confidential, indirectly and unsentimentally, Pinsky stitches his personal story to his literary rhetoric with frankly visible seams. In **"The Living"** . . . we see passing at length in ragged order before us a quasi-medieval rabble of the drugged and afflicted lords of life (with whom the Shadow-I counts himself. Like Ashbery, and correlative with the theme of consciousness turned inward on its own movements, he is wont to view from a seven-league perspective the movements of pageants, triumphs, corteges, hordes, and armies, just as he is pleased to imagine the Golden Hind anchored off New Jersey and the pomp of empire progressing down Rockwell Street). All of a sudden, in a completely scoured and modern idiom, we hear that a woman right next to the speaker falls down and has a seizure. All the speaker can think of is that he is "acting the part / Of a stranger helping," that he is hypocritical in his charity and must appear so to the other pedestrians, that not only they but *she* is critically scrutinizing his maladroit and embarrassed person "As if I had made her fall." To extricate himself from this mildly paranoid interlude, the Shadow-I plunges into a truly Jamesian spate of evasions, projecting his paranoias upon the ailing woman, who looks at him as if he were not a stranger

> but a son, lover, lord
> And master who had thus humiliated her,
>
> And now, tucking the blanket around her,
> Hypocritical automaton, pretended
> To urge—as if without complicity or shame
>
> Or least sense of betrayal—the old embrace
> Of this impenetrable haze, this prolonged
> But not infinite surfeit of glory.

Impenetrable haze indeed, however gorgeous. It is impossible to tell whether the "surfeit of glory" is her gaze, his gaze, their looking at each other, his discomfort, hers, the complete tableau with onlookers—or, finally, whether the surfeit is "this prolonged but not infinite" triadic swatch of verse before us, which, with these words, concludes.

A peculiar similarity links the seized woman in **"The Living"** with the ostensible focus of the title poem, the poet's mother (an appealing figure, despite the brevity of her appearances). Both women fall; but events are swiftly transformed by the stranger/son into sidelights on his own peformance. Indeed the effective context for the closing triads of **"History of My Heart"** is the assertion, "My poor mother fell . . . she got better. But I was lost in music." The protagonist plays the saxophone to which—or rather, to his yearning and absorbed playing of which—Robert Pinsky plays tribute in an idiom reminiscent of Eudora Welty's in "Powerhouse":

> Over the years, she got better. But I was lost in music
> . . . .
> Sometimes, playing in a bar or at a high school dance,
>   I felt
> My heart following after a capacious form,
> Sexual and abstract, in the thunk, thrum,

> Thrum, come-wallow and then a little screen
> Of quicker notes goosing to a higher fifth, winging
> To clang-whomp of a major seventh: listen to *me*
>
> Listen to *me*, the heart says in reprise until sometimes
> In the course of giving itself it flows out of itself
> All the way across the air, in a music piercing
>
> As the kids at the beach calling from the water *Look,*
> *Look at me*, to their mothers . . .

The reader will recognize the passage that has been progressively unveiled from its Stevensian close back through its Ashberian penultimate lines to the original vehicle that now makes those other authorial echoes less commanding, the use of their idioms less relevant. For this is the child/boy/youth at once ruthless in putting himself before those who love him, and desperately anxious to be noticed and liked. As proficient, urbane, and clever as the poet is, as good at undercutting rhetoric both ridiculous and sublime (in one poem, for example, he counters the smug reality of topics like dentistry and tuition with the admitted fustian of phrases like "finite piercing restlessness of men"), the poet is also discovering how graceless the insistent ego can be, and how difficult it is to lyricize emotion the critic in him would be the first to call self-protective and prosaic.

Preparing to tour a concentration camp near Krakow, Poland, he remembers what he coyly designates "a sleep-time game," a weirdly nasty movie fantasy of violent revenge. In this game, he is invisible and savors the growth of his lethal designs, until he slays while thinking "kill kill kill kill," like a comic-strip tough or movie villain. He dispatches the man who holds the cyanide pellets for the gas chambers, then beats to death "the pet collie of the Commandant's children / And in the end flushes everything with a vague flood / Of fire and blood as I drift on toward sleep." The sensibility is callow and cruel, uncritically; the Shadow-I moves from sheepish candor to the musty rhetoric of blood and flood uncritically too. Even the further escalation in formality fails either to sweeten the sour taste, or to make logical or psychological sense. This movement merely occurs, because it can: the Shadow-I carefully bumbles a religious invocation: "And so, / O discredited Lord of Hosts, your servant gapes / Obediently to swallow various doings of us," trying "to take in what won't be turned from in despair." This poem could be explained, I suppose, as a madrigal of mixed voices on the subject of the banality of gross and systematic evil, a banality which implies horror as well, as if a yawn were always on the point of turning into a scream. But the poem is not a convincing argument for such a subtle theme; the idiomatic gymnastics are so very agile that the work veers off into highjinks and conceit. Suffice it to say that these interruptions of the train of thought about the death camps are not the only kinds of prosaic freedom that might be pursued in their regard. Nor is their arbitrariness controlled by the fiction of the Shadow-I, who perhaps as a rule invites digression too early in the poems' evolution. (pp. 39-41)

Mary Kinzie, "Idiom and Error," in The American Poetry Review, *Vol. 13, No. 5, September-October, 1984, pp. 38-47.**

B. F. DICK

[The title poem of ***History of My Heart***] may well become a classic, although, like most attempts to mingle memory with desire and lyric with narrative, it does not so much terminate in a climactic idea or image as merely end—and too soon. Yet it is an achingly vulnerable reminiscence, evoking, as only a poet can, the half-formed thoughts of adolescence and the intensity of emotion known only to the young. Pinsky has written the poem from a dual vision: a poet with the soul of a boy looking back at a boy with the soul of a poet.

Yet there are poems in the collection expressing emotions peculiar to adults, especially **"The Unseen,"** in which Pinsky relives a visit to a death camp as if his memories had been memorialized on film. Rather than raise an angry fist to heaven, the poet in an epiphanic moment sees the agony that took place there as part of a broader canvas of suffering which even includes Christ's. **"The Unseen"** is one of the most original responses to the Holocaust ever written, but it is not the only reason for reading *History of My Heart.* Anyone who can remember ever being young or who can accept the demands and the responsibilities of memory should welcome it.

> B. F. Dick, in a review of "History of My Heart,"
> in World Literature Today, Vol. 58, No. 4, Autumn,
> 1984, p. 609.

CHARLES MOLESWORTH

[Robert Pinsky] stands out by virtue of his emotional rightness. Now such an attribute may be more stigmatizing in a cynical age than being called traditional. I mean by emotional rightness that balance of feeling and intelligence that is often hard-won but never agonized in its display. We live in an age, to put it mildly, that doesn't care much for tact. Emotional rightness is nearly a synonym for tact, but it adds to tact a sense of urgency, a willingness to break rules and transgress boundaries when necessary. . . . Pinsky has increasingly become a moral poet, that rarest of modern types, not by being a scourge or a satirist, but by returning to questions and matters of right and wrong, truth and error, and seeking to prove—more in the sense of test than vindication—his feelings about such matters. This is not to say (here comes a disclaimer) that his work has none of our contemporary concerns, such as fascination with popular culture, an obsessive interest in certain mythic topics, and a penchant for psychoanalytic assumptions about human behaviour. Pinsky draws on such concerns and more, but he manages to be personal without being confessional, sophisticated without being glib, and knowledgeable without being world-weary or cutely playful.

Reading Pinsky offers positive delights as well as negative ones, however. His poetic language has many of the best features of good prose, as its connections and complexities flow from a straight-forward approach to his subjects. His subjects, especially in his latest book, *History of My Heart,* are chosen with an eye to both scale and variety. He can write about a visit to a concentration camp, his New Jersey childhood, Fats Waller, or an apocalyptic vision, all with deft control. As for his critical skills, his book on Walter Savage Landor might be taken as a model of how to approach a neglected, less-than-major figure and show his accomplishments and pertinence to a new generation of readers. His book on contemporary poetry [*The Situation of Poetry*] was the first to offer intelligent scruples about those dominant verse conventions that had become rigidified by the middle of the nineteen-seventies. . . . All in all, a decent claim could be made for Pinsky being the most accomplished poet-critic in America under the age of fifty. . . . I want especially to argue that Pinsky's strength derives from his use of both irony and compassion in a way that these two

attitudes, normally seen as opposites, are called into a test of one another. It is through this test that Pinsky gets at the emotional rightness that is his main focus and creates the artistic complexity that is his achievement. Taking the long view, we can say that such a test and a poet's willingness to submit to it are not the result exclusively of either an experimental or traditional cast of mind or temperament. But it is Pinsky's traditionalism, especially his use of multiple cultural and historical dimensions, that I think best accounts for the special quality of his work.

Pinsky's first book of poetry, *Sadness and Happiness,* often anchored its title subjects in an abiding sense of weather and atmospherics. The atmosphere remains one of the more traditional ways to image forth the congruence of inner and outer sensations. Weather is a trope where the pathetic fallacy is likely to overwhelm the poet, however, and "angry clouds" and "peaceful dawns" can soon do his thinking and his feeling for him. . . . Pinsky, ever aware of how the rhetorical can become merely formulaic, works both with and against the weather as a way of representing the emotional truth [as he demonstrates in **"Ceremony for Any Beginning"**]:

> Therefore when you marry or build
> Pray to be untrue to the plain
> Dominance of your own weather, how it keeps
>
> Going even in the woods when not
> A soul is there, and how it implies
> Always that separate, cold
> Splendidness, uncouth and unkind—. . .

Here the language possesses a sort of decorous, Augustan control, reminiscent of Richard Wilbur and other "academic" poets of the post-war period. But the poem argues *against* decorum, at least in the sense that it warns the impersonal addressee to mistrust any compliant, automatic equation between self and world. . . . Relying on metaphors of atmosphere and weather threatens to reduce experience to a deterministic sense of the natural order. For Pinsky, the human will can be too coldly accepting of its place in the world, acting as just another force . . . among the myriad forces that sustain the physical universe. "One's life is one's enemy," the poet announces, invoking an almost Yeatsian, defiant note of self-dramatization and self-definition through antithetical struggle. If it's true, as one poem claims, that "the unseasonable soul holds forth," it is also true that "what happens / Takes over, and what you were goes away." The dialectic of self and world, of identity and experience, is an on-going one in which neither term can be counted on to define total victory or our highest value. As another poem in the book says, speaking of the "hours which one / Had better use," the passing moments come bearing "Their burden of a promise but a promise / Limited." Here we have another turn of irony's screw that late modernism makes possible: knowing how freedom and necessity intersect, how promises and burdens make each other felt, we can learn to live with the "ordinary unhappiness" that might be our only true destiny.

Obviously a world in which promise can be burdensome is an ironic world, and potentially a bitter one as well. But if the promises are limited then so is the burden. Pinsky's **"Poem About People"** confronts the "hideous, sudden stare of self," and tries to adjust to a Sartrean awareness of the hell of the other's need, "unlovable" and lizard-like in its reptilian urgency. This poem ends with an image of "the dark wind crossing / The wide spaces between us," and the neurosis and bigotry and urban anomie, all the psychopathologies of everyday life, engulf us and yet link us with their windy, unenlightened chill. We are close to a gloom that matches that of the Tory satirists (Dr. Johnson's notion that there is more on earth to endure than to enjoy). But if we see this gloom as essentially that of post-Romantic irony—the Keatsian cry that "but to think is to be full of sorrow" stripped of its promise of Keatsian sensual bliss—then not only will we be more historically accurate, we will see Pinsky's way out as well.

The "ordinary unhappiness" of which Freud spoke emerges in Pinsky's work as the centering goal and condition of the poet's struggle to balance irony and compassion. This struggle comes to a peak in the **"Essay on Psychiatrists."** Rife with wit and social observation, the poem features a persona whose bemusement borders on the naive and yet whose analytic sophistication almost outstrips his subject. . . . The voices of Pinsky's early personae often appear to have come to terms with a late-modernist despair, a despair that purchases and approves its own special brand of sanity. But though sane adjustment to such threats as enthusiasm, demonic concern, or even lyric rapture (now excused in post-Freudian awareness as neurotic displacements of the self's unlovable need), is hard won, this adjustment is only part of Pinsky's view of our emotional life.

The **"Essay on Psychiatrists"** reaches an apogee of wit and thoughtful balance when it uses Euripides' *Bacchae* as a gloss on the psychiatric profession. In Pinsky's subtle reading of the classical drama we can see both Pentheus and Dionysus as the model of psychiatric concern and method. This double vision illustrates how Pinsky balances his irony and his compassion. Pentheus stands as the man of affections, the compassionate but mistrusting doctor who "raises his voice in the name of dignity." Dionysus, on the other hand, is the ironist, one who turns to grim humor, "With his soft ways picking along lightly / With a calm smile." Obviously Pinsky imagines that healing, especially healing our own natures, requires both perspectives, and furthermore he realizes Pentheus' compassion is threatened by his panic in the face of disorder, while Dionysus' irony can quickly become "bland arrogance." We might take this reading of Pentheus and Dionysus as a show of Pinsky's Augustan perspectival balance and decorum, or as a wry commentary on psychiatry's frequent desire to have it both ways when explaining character and motivation. And we are also cautioned about psychiatrists near the end of the poem that "we must not / Complain both that they are inhuman and too human." Finally we realize that Pinsky's view of psychiatrists is nearly completely congruent with his view of all people, and what we have been reading is less a sociological dissertation than an updated "Essay on Man."

Pinsky's ability to use a classical text and his own gloss on it as the center of an extended poetic argument sets him apart from the great majority of his peers. (In *An Explanation of America* he uses Shakespeare's "The Winter's Tale" in much the same Augustan manner, and also uses an equally complex persona.) Such ability itself determines the special nature of Pinsky's enviable artistic achievement, as he faces language with a richly layered awareness of our inescapably linguistic condition. Language is for Pinsky both the sign and the scene of our sadness and happiness, our burden and our promise, a wealth of "terms of all kind mellow with time, growing / Arbitrary and rich." Again, our souls' weathers must be resisted or we can blindly accept as natural that which is arbitrary—in other words we must be prepared to be ironic about our own desires. But we also have to accept the rich wisdom

of common sense, so often embodied in tag-lines, *loci classici*, axioms, or "old sayings," for often compassion recognizes in such ordinary language the extraordinary pressures of being human. In an epoch when experimentalism and unsubstantiated metaphoric license, often justifying itself as surrealism, form a large part of contemporary poetry's idiom, Pinsky may appear unduly conservative in his verbal invention. But I think Pinsky's poetic gifts are devoted to a just separation of the truly public and rhetorical from the glibly easy and formulaic uses of words. Put bluntly, I think Pinsky sees language as he sees people, both ironically and compassionately. This dual attitude to language involves Pinsky in a related struggle, namely the vexed question of whether any logical or verbal act can preserve the truth of our everydayness. (pp. 2-6)

One of the forms the argument over language has taken in the modern era is the argument between imagistic poetry and discursive poetry. In his critical study, **The Situation of Poetry**, Pinsky joins this argument largely on the side of discursive poetry. By explicating Keats's "Ode To A Nightingale"as a poem struggling both against and for the desire to capture the immediacy of sensation and experience, Pinsky re-affirms the essentially abstract, conventional, and discursive nature of language itself. Poetry, especially the post-Romantic poetry dominated by the contemporary styles of imagistically dense presentation, proceeds vainly when it seeks to escape completely the discursive qualities inherent in language. Rather than recapitulate all of Pinsky's argument, it helps to focus the issue by looking briefly at one of its counter-responses, an essay by Jonathan Holden, from *Field* magazine, called "The Attack on the Image." Holden defends imagistic poetry enthusiastically and, though he grudgingly grants that Pinsky is in part persuasive, he finally says that arguments for discursiveness are arbitrary, limited, and limiting to the sensibility needed to appreciate a kind of poetry that can be "tremendously sophisticated and successful." Such polemical arguments—and this one has been a lightning rod for polemic in contemporary poetry for twenty years or so—can easily be dismissed as elaborate justifications of personal taste or shunned as extreme versions of simple truths that should be seen pluralistically or kept in balanced harmony.

In fact, such arguments often conceal fundamentally divergent assumptions, and it's to Pinsky's credit that he makes his assumptions about language as clear as possible. But obviously these assumptions in turn involve a complex set of beliefs and ideas about experience, the self, emotional structures, and even moral attitudes. (p. 6)

Pinsky's poetry does not involve a total rejection of the imagistic poetry heralded by Pound and Williams, nor does it require a return to Augustan decorum. What it does instead is use the past, both the near and distant past, as a way of making the present resound. This requires not using the past to judge or censure the present, or vice versa, but to use both cultural dimensions as a commentary on each other. As he put it in **Landor's Poetry**, his study of that poet who was both classical and romantic:

> Landor's procedure is to revitalize, through profound energies of understanding and a cleanly exactitude of style, an already established situation or observation. Stylistic perfection . . . demonstrates the degree to which the chosen commonplace has been comprehended, and the skill of thought so demonstrated is personal and original.

One of the most persistent biases of modernism is the stricture against commentary and explanation. So not only in his criticism, but in the very title of his second book of poems, *An Explanation of America,* Pinsky sets himself against the grain of certain received ideas. Yet this second book invites comparison with other modernist long poems, such as Williams's *Paterson* and Olson's *Maximus Poems,* in its use of both everyday and historical materials in the matrix of a quasi-epic scale. But if Williams and Olson are the imagist and objectivist models we see distantly behind Pinsky's *Explanation* there is also the discursive, philosophical accent of Stevens, especially the *Notes Toward A Supreme Fiction.* These, however, are distant models, echoed in the subject matter of the poem and in the titles of its divisions ("**Its Many Fragments,**" "**Its Great Emptiness,**" etc.). Close to the poem's surface and texture (and closer to its moral vision) is the model of Horace's familiar epistles (one of which, Book I, xvi, the poem translates, glosses, and incorporates in a daringly inventive perspective by incongruity.) The poetry is basically that of the middle style, in blank verse, subtle enough to incorporate diverse areas of experience, from rioting urban black youths to Jefferson's epitaph, yet integrated enough by a consistent tone of what we might call patient but genuine puzzlement, so that a rational attitude is neither despaired of nor insisted upon.

Two other structural principles animate and control the poem's explorations. Pinsky addresses the poem to his daughter, or rather his "idea" of his daughter. This enables the poem to modulate its familiar approach with more weighty attitudes. He speaks both through and to the daughter, weaving explanation with apology, instruction, conjecture, even a confessional excursus from time to time. Rather than weight the poem with sodden self-consciousness, this weaving of stances matches the diversity of material and also creates a sense of authority based not on absolute certainty but rather on an earned and skeptical reverence. He labors to get it right, to make sense, and the effort is seldom strained or postured. The other structuring device is to use and yet question certain standard topics about America, such as its love of speed and space, its conscience haunted by the recurrent moral obtuseness and civic inefficiency of electoral democracy, and so forth. This gives the poem a thematic variety that again answers to the wealth of the subject, and allows the poet to incorporate various kinds of knowledge, mythic, historical, philosophical, anthropological, common-sensical, into his "explanation." (pp. 8-9)

In his third and latest book of poetry, *History of My Heart,* Pinsky leaves the epistolary style and epic subject of *An Explanation of America* to return to the scale of the intimate lyric. In doing so he gives vent to an attitude that is in part confessional, but he never relinquishes the moral and public tones of the previous book. This mix of private and public stands apart from the work of most contemporary poets, and does so in part by reversing certain obvious and hidden features of American poetry. First, Pinsky willingly makes clear his wanting to connect the large patterns of fate with his homebound destinies. There are several poems here ("**The Street,**" "**Song of Reasons,**" "**The Figured Wheel,**" chief among them) that juxtapose large historical or even cosmic figurations against Pinsky's personal feelings and memories. Many poets, of course, invoke or hint at larger patterns of significance, but do so glancingly or only with protective irony. On the other hand, what Pinsky conceals or at least underplays is the tendency of the lyric to fondle its own metaphoric energies, to become intoxicated with its own tropes. (This is especially true in American surrealist poetry.) Pinsky does sometimes make his trope quite obvious,

as in "**The Figured Wheel,**" but just as often his comparisons, analogies, inversions, and closures exhibit an understatedness that can make some of the lyrics seem off-hand, almost apologetic. (pp. 11-12)

I don't mean to suggest that all of Pinsky's poems are judiciously measured through a grid of perfectly balanced irony and compassion. Indeed, at least two of the poems in *History* that are most memorable, "**Song of Reasons,**" and "**The Unseen,**" face considerable challenges of tonal balance. The first of these . . . begins with two perspectives that look at first to be totally abstruse, a change of key in the song "Come Back to Sorrento" and the right of a certain French noble family, the Levis-Mirepoix, to ride their horses in Notre Dame. The theme of the poem is how any "history or purpose arcane" that is used to explain odd facts or relations in the world manages to be both "businesslike as a dog / That trots down the street" and as phantasmagoric as "the animal shapes that sing at the gates of sleep" in our childhood. The song of reasons is just that: a lyric finesse of the rational, a way of charming and disarming the ineradicable inexplicable facticity of events and the way they express human nature. The Levis-Mirepoix have their extraordinary privilege because they "killed heretics in Languedoc seven centuries ago," and yet "they are somehow Jewish" and claim "collateral descent" from the Virgin Mary. It is a reason, and it isn't a reason. The girl in the poem (apparently Pinsky's daughter) loves the part of the daily newspaper called "The Question Man," that column of man-in-the-street responses to such inane questions as "Your Worst Vacation?" or "Your Favorite Ethnic Group?" Again, people have reasons for such heart-felt responses, and the reasons even have a history—every heart has a history as well as reasons it knows and knows not of—but the "**Song of Reasons**" can not offer any reason why all this should be so. Pinsky's irony appreciates the bizarre humor of claiming descent from the Virgin Mary, and his compassion appreciates the way the child's favorite newspaper feature steadies her world: "The exact forms of the ordinary . . . show / An indomitable charm to her." But the aesthetic charm of the poem, its ability or luck in finding a fact such as that of the Levis-Mirepoix on which to build its wry playfulness, means it cannot give or challenge any final explanation. In one sense this is only fair, as the lyric mode is not charged with providing philosophical certainty or rigorous logic. Finally, I think, the affection of the speaker for the child saves the poem, for it is here that the lyric impulse is truest. The poem is like a nursery rhyme we sing a child to sleep by, covering up the narrative or logical holes with false totality and sweet song ("and down will come baby, cradle and all"). (pp. 13-14)

But there is another poem in the book whose rhetorical authority is even more challenged: "**The Unseen**". The obvious point must be made at the start that no poem about concentration camps can be without flaw. Just to attempt the subject, especially in a short lyric of over fifty lines, shows moral courage or artistic aplomb beyond the ordinary. Luckily for us, Pinsky has both. So when I question the poem I do so only on the highest level. Briefly my point is this: the stance at the end of the poem is accusatory, not towards the Nazis only and obviously, but toward the Godhead, the "Lord of Hosts." But can such an accusation stand? Ordinarily such accusatory rhetoric is the privilege (if that's the right word) of mystics and rationalists. The "regular believer" cannot claim the depth of experience or the alternative ontological grounds by which to challenge the deity. (That Pinsky speaks as a Jew to a deity imaged in Christian terms alters this argument only slightly, I think.) If I'm right in this, then Pinsky's speaker (to use that old-fashioned literary convention) must base his rhetorical authority on being a rationalist (he clearly is no mystic in the poem), and not a regular believer. But the compassion of the closing lines is not a rationalist's compassion; it's that of a believer. Thus Pinsky must somehow combine the ironic scepticism of a rationalist and the compassionate acceptance of a believer. To my mind he doesn't fully succeed, though that he nearly does so is enough to make the poem gripping and memorable. (p. 14)

The title poem of *History of My Heart* is over seven pages long, and its scale is even longer in a way. Superficially the poem is autobiographical and might be compared to those works by Henry Adams or Stendhal that speak of education as it applies to sensibility and awareness. The education of Robert Pinsky is an education into and through desire. The record of the education has several traditional motifs: the loving mother, the bestowing of the name, the first scene of arousal, the typology of gifts, and the finding of a vocation (in this case playing the saxophone) that allows the young artist to achieve maturity. It's a song of reasons in that it tells us how and why Robert Pinsky came to feel the way he does, and it resembles "**The Street**" in that it relates the topography of his childhood to larger patterns of destiny. It also has the obsessive probing of *An Explanation of America,* and the turns and quick shifts in perspective of "**Essay on Psychiatrists.**" In many ways, it's the definitive Pinsky poem.

Perhaps the best way to get at the central drama of the poem, and by extension the entire volume, is to reflect on two master terms, history and nature. (What follows draws erratically on Adorno's essay, "The Idea of Natural History," in a recent issue of *Telos,* and Susan Buck-Morss's explication of it in *The Origins of the Negative Dialectic.*) The standard meanings of the two terms allot to "nature" an unchanging, quasi-divine, eternal fixity, and to "history" a sense of change, flux, and even chaos. But in our personal lives, in the histories of our hearts, we can see where the two terms begin to overlap and even change into one another. What seems "natural" to us is often "second nature," the result of a long history of emotional patterning and appetitive habit. And the flow of our dailiness, our constant change and growth, can be felt as the bedrock of our identity—we are (only) as we come to be. (p. 15)

The history of one's heart, then, is the story of how we developed our "second nature," taking as given and natural that which is accidental and contingent. Such a naturalizing of what would otherwise be a shapeless congeries of events must determine our sense of emotional rightness. Now, somewhat surprisingly, Pinsky's poem begins with an incident that occurred before he was born, a visit by Fats Waller to Macy's department store on Thirty-Fourth Street one Christmas. Pinsky's mother worked in the Toys section of the store and so was able to see (and obviously begin the process of naturalizing) Waller's immensely entertaining show ("as he improvised on an expensive, tinkly / Piano the size of a lady's jewel box or a wedding cake.") This incident became for Pinsky the emblem and type of desire. For him desire needs a setting, a sense of "amazing good-luck," and reciprocity, the "mutual arousal of suddenly feeling / Desired." The poem is loaded with other incidents that explore these requisites of desire, rendering them both strange and familiar, giving us a history in the form of nature, and a nature shaped by history. (p. 16)

The poem ends with a complex and suggestive passage that echoes some of the spirit of Whitman's "Out of the Cradle"

and Wordsworth's *Prelude*. By this I mean it deals with the mystery of individuation, especially in terms of that rich awareness of connection-and-separation that marks the growth of ourselves as individual egos. The passage weaves around certain fairy-tale motifs of the foundling (and the changeling) as well as a kind of pantheistic yearning. . . . The saxophone playing [described in the seventh tercet] becomes a mediation of irony and compassion, as the young man truly gives himself over to the playing and at the same time sees himself as a performer, as someone asking for attention and affection. This joining of display and submission, ego-centeredness and altruism, feels like second nature to us, but it is in fact the working out of several life-historical patterns of expectation, need, and assertion. In the grimness of "**The Unseen**" Pinsky remembered a Biblical phrase: "I am poured out like water," and there the phrase had connotations of loss and waste and unrecoverability. But in "**History**" the image of pouring out takes on a different tonal cast, for here we sense the gesture of emptying is a gesture of both self-less love and personal fulfillment. These are the final lines of the poem:

Sometimes, playing in a bar or at a high school dance,
  I felt
My heart following after a capacious form,
Sexual and abstract, in the thunk, thrum,

Thrum, come-wallow and then a little screen
Of quicker notes goosing to a fifth higher, winging
To clang-whomp of a major seventh: listen to *me*

Listen to *me,* the heart says in reprise until sometimes
In the course of giving itself it flows out of itself
All the way across the air, in a music piercing

As the kids at the beach calling from the water *Look,*
Look at me, to their mothers, but out of itself, into
The listener the way feeling pretty or full of erotic
  revery

Makes the one who feels seem beautiful to the beholder
Witnessing the idea of the giving of desire—nothing
  more wanted
Than the little singing notes of wanting—the heart

Yearning further into giving itself into the air, breath
Strained into song emptying the golden bell it comes
  from,
The pure source poured altogether out and away.

"The giving of desire" is a phrase that stands as a cap-stone to Pinsky's work so far, for it catches up the paradoxical network of irony and compassion that takes place when a "beholder" witnesses a moment of completely passionate ecstacy, when there is "Nothing more wanted." Also, without pushing things too far, I think we can see here the sense of possessing nature—"the pure source" in all its ongoing fullness—now joined with a particular unfolding of events—that description of the musical passage, with its "thunk, thrum, / Thrum, comewallow" capturing the essence of sequentiality.

We can read *Sadness and Happiness* as a book of emotional meteorology, and *An Explanation of America* as a book of imaginative geography. This leaves us, then, to read *History of My Heart* as a book of psychological economy. The economics of desire, what is given or taken, what is lost, what gets stored and what spent, is Pinsky's thematic center in all his books—this is why he is such a profound traditionalist; he keeps track of how and what is passed on—but especially in his latest volume such questions of economy dominate. Pinsky has laid bare his heart, often complete with a "fumbling drama," and shown us that it has stored in it the light of day and the dark of night. But the great strength of his poetry is that he also shows us how the night turns into day, and how the light was set in its firmament. (pp. 17-18)

Charles Molesworth, "Proving Irony by Compassion: The Poetry of Robert Pinsky," in The Hollins Critic, *Vol. XXI, No. 5, December, 1984, pp. 1-18.*

STEPHEN COREY

The rhythms of Robert Pinsky's work are characterized by a graceful sheen and ease that some readers have taken as an indication of a moral naïveté or indifference or even flippancy; he has been thought too decorous, too much the aesthete, for our difficult age. But his caring and wisdom run deep, and the quiet tones of his poems only lay a delicate skin over the abyss he has seen too well. Apparently, he finds the lullings and liftings of music to be among the only stays sufficiently strong for our bleak confusions: "The world, random, / Is so real, it is as if our own / Good or bad luck were here only / As a kind of filler, holding together / Just that much of the adjacent / Splendor and terror."

One way to bend the luck, to try to steer the random for a moment, is by making memory work hard enough—driving it down to the specific places and names in our histories. Sometimes the drive leads to terror, as in **"The Unseen"** [in *History of My Heart*], a poem about visiting the "monument" of a concentration camp. While there, Pinsky recalls that he has daydreamed about achieving a Learlike vengeance upon the Nazis by roaming the camps invisibly: "At first I savor my mastery / Slowly by creating small phantom diversions, / Then kill kill kill kill, a detailed and strangely / Passionless inward movie."

Other times, terror softens to profound sadness, as in **"The Questions"**: with a sympathy reminiscent of Philip Levine's in *The Names of the Lost*, Pinsky returns to the stream of adults who moved through his childhood in his father's office: "I want for them not to have died in awful pain, friendless. / Though many of the living are starving, I still pray for these, / Dead, mostly anonymous (but Mr. Monk, Mrs. Rose Vogel) / And barely remembered: that they had a little extra, something / For pleasure, a good meal, a book. . . ."

And for Pinsky, there are even times when splendor wins out— really wins, except for that tinge of sadness whose emergence from all things is the only certainty we have. In the long title poem, Pinsky offers a believable hope and innocence almost extinct in serious American poetry of this century. Across some two hundred lines, he confronts and defeats constant threats of sentimentality as he explores the minutiae of autobiography, searching for what can only be called a theory of desire. Early in **"History of My Heart,"** Pinsky says that "happiness needs a setting," and nearly all of the poem is devoted to providing this—from his mother's early stories of life before his birth, on up through his own memories of infancy, childhood, and adolescence. (p. 213)

Stephen Corey, in a review of "History of My Heart," in The Georgia Review, *Vol. XXXIX, No. 1, Spring, 1985, pp. 213-14.*

David (Robert) Plante

1940-

American novelist, short story writer, memoirist, and translator.

An experimental fiction writer, Plante is praised for the understated effects of his lean, elegant prose and complex characterizations. By evoking a broad range of nuance through subtle manipulation of brief, pertinent incidents, Plante comments on fragile human relationships and such themes as love, death, and solitude. His characters often exist in intellectual and emotional isolation; they are detached from society and seek individual fulfillment, identity, and meaning. While some critics contend that Plante's deliberately vague and ambiguous prose sometimes blurs the focus of his stories, many reviewers assert that this quality is what gives his fiction its impact.

Plante lives in Great Britain and gained prominence there with the publication of his first five novels. These works are derivative in influence yet experimental in technique. Although the books are realistic in detail, Plante rejects narrative tendencies of the traditional novel in favor of nonchronological structures, unspecified settings, and ambiguous resolutions. Characters are often unnamed or referred to only by their first names. In Plante's first novel, *The Ghost of Henry James* (1970), five American siblings drift through Europe in search of their spiritual roots, each becoming involved with someone who poses a threat to the stability of their family circle. In *Slides* (1971), a novel comprising sixty-seven short episodes, five young Americans seek individual forms of isolation when forced into close, claustrophobic contact with one another. In *Relatives* (1974), a bisexual man named Val and his sister develop an intimate, platonic relationship after Val's wife disappears. Plante again focuses on the character Val in *The Darkness of the Body* (1974). In this novel, Val discovers a sexual attraction developing between himself and a married couple he meets during a cruise between two unidentified countries. Plante's most experimental novel, *Figures in Bright Air* (1976), is the story of a love affair between the novel's narrator and a younger boy. Conceived as an attempt, according to Plante, "to create something that reverberates, as music does," the work employs a stream-of-consciousness technique reminiscent of the French *nouveau roman,* or antinovel.

Plante first received significant critical attention in the United States with his Francoeur novels, a series of loosely autobiographical works which examine the life and family of a character named Daniel Francoeur. Critics noted a more direct approach in these works, though Plante does not view the series as a departure from his previous concerns. In *The Family* (1978), Plante examines the troubled lives of the Francoeurs, a working-class family of French-Canadian descent living in an immigrant district of Rhode Island. The novel celebrates family ties, focusing on Daniel's Roman Catholic upbringing and his prayers for domestic peace. His need to escape family responsibilities, to become a "foreigner," becomes intense in *The Country* (1981), in which Daniel, now middle-aged, faces the death of one parent and the mourning of the other. *The Woods* (1982), chronologically the second book in the series, concerns what Jack Beatty called "the adolescent dread of selfhood and its loneliness." Now a college student nearing graduation in

the 1950s, Daniel is metaphorically "in the woods," facing combined pressures regarding work, heterosexuality, and military service. Don Shewey maintained that Plante's novel *The Foreigner* (1984) is a possible addition to the Francoeur series, and the book's unnamed protagonist resembles Daniel in several ways. This character is a young college student from Rhode Island who travels to France to absorb a new, foreign culture. However, he feels out of place in France and goes to Spain, where he becomes involved with a black American woman and her lover, a violent American expatriate. Together they pursue revolutionary, criminal, and sexual obsessions. Harriett Gilbert praised the novel as "a superb account of late adolescent dislocation; progressively, something more disquieting and ruthless."

Difficult Women: A Portrait of Three (1983), Plante's first nonfiction work, contains sketches and reflections of his experiences with novelist Jean Rhys, feminist Germaine Greer, and Sonia Orwell, wife of the late British author George Orwell. The book was widely faulted for its unflattering portraits of its subjects. Jaimy Gordon summed up the critical consensus by commenting: "Plante's decision to omit background seems glaringly ungallant with Rhys and Orwell, who are literally, and bitterly, at the ends of their lives during this period, and who deserve some evocation of their former selves to place beside their twisted remnants, as a corrective, or even as a token of respect.''

(See also *CLC*, Vols. 7, 23; *Contemporary Authors*, Vols. 37-40, rev. ed.; *Contemporary Authors New Revision Series*, Vol. 12; and *Dictionary of Literary Biography Yearbook: 1983*.)

JONATHAN YARDLEY

David Plante is a tremendously gifted and accomplished writer, and a most appealing one as well, but at this point in his chronicling of the history of the Francoeur family he has put the loyalty of his readers to the acid test. *The Woods* is the third novel about the Francoeurs, a working-class French-Canadian family in Rhode Island, and specifically about Daniel Francoeur, one of the more transparently autobiographical figures in contemporary American fiction. Like its predecessors in the Francoeur story, *The Family* and *The Country*, *The Woods* is elegantly written and thick with emotional resonance; but it is so often so self-absorbed that the reader, whose interest in Daniel's late-adolescent rites of passage is perhaps less intense than the author's, is likely to find his mind wandering elsewhere.

On Plante's behalf, it needs to be said that a central subject of *The Woods* is late-adolescent self-absorption; to dismiss the novel as merely narcissistic would be to misunderstand what Plante, whether successfully or not, is attempting to do. At this time in his young life, Daniel Francoeur is a student at a college near Boston. The novel opens there, then flashes back to a previous summer when, vacationing at his family's lakeside house, Daniel is both literally and figuratively in ''the woods''—a period when he confronts his psychological isolation from the world and when he attempts to reach an understanding of the possibilities and limitations that life offers him.

Plante has a very clear appreciation of the complexities of the late-adolescent mind. His depiction of its fiercely contradictory timidity and arrogance is subtle and sensitive. *The Woods* conveys a rare understanding of the tension between the young person's belief that on the one hand ''you can have everything'' and, on the other, his fear of the constricting obligations that lie in wait for him: military service, work, marriage, fatherhood, indebtedness, domestic routine. For Daniel, nearing maturity in the late 1950s, the Army looms as symbol of all that he fears and hates. . . .

[Daniel's body is] a storehouse of longings, some of them vague and some of them quite specific but all of them passionate in the way that only adolescent longings can be. All of them boil down to the question that haunts every young person: ''What do I want?'' In particular the longing is sexual, though Daniel is uncomfortable identifying it as such, and it becomes focused on his summertime neighbor, Lillian Cooper. She is somewhat older than he—how much older Plante does not, for whatever reason, make clear—and possessed of her own supply of misgivings and yearnings. But she understands Daniel in ways that he himself does not. She tells him: ''I want you to come out of your dark woods,'' and: ''What I object to is that you always seem to be alone in your woods, doing nothing.'' Though she does not want to be drawn into ''the woods'' with him, eventually she responds to her own ''longing, longing,

not for him or what he could give her, but for everything, and nothing she knew,'' and offers him the comfort that they both need.

This central section of the novel—novella is really the more accurate word for it—is noteworthy for its sustained sexual tension and for its fine descriptive prose. . . .

Plante is an exceptionally deliberate, careful, economical writer. His prose is as notable, and laudable, for what he leaves out as what he puts in; there is no waste here, no fat. Yet when it comes to the explication of his characters' emotions, Plante's desire to be clear and precise leads him into difficulty. He is not content to show us how they are feeling; he insists on telling us. He gives them thoughts that people simply do not think: ''He lowered his face to kiss a breast and as he did he wondered, with the great spacious wonder of why this should occur to him, what made of the body a soul.'' . . .

Plante has made the mistake of intellectualizing what is not, in point of fact, an intellectual or rational process: an adolescent's struggle to come to terms with a world considerably more ambiguous than he is capable, at this point, of understanding. Not merely does Daniel Francoeur spend too much time feeling sorry for himself, but he does so in thoughts and language that are quite implausible for one of his inexperience and immaturity. There's plenty of lovely writing in *The Woods*, and that is reason enough to read it; but most readers are likely to tire of Daniel's humorless brooding, to wish that Plante himself would leave the woods of self-absorption and get back to the business of examining the world around him.

> *Jonathan Yardley, ''Lost in the Thickets of Adolescence,'' in* Book World—The Washington Post, *August 8, 1982, p. 3.*

EDITH MILTON

Daniel Francoeur, who was also the protagonist of David Plante's other recent novels, *The Family* and *The Country*, is again his autobiographical alter ego, and the setting of *The Woods* is again the French-Canadian working-class milieu of Rhode Island into which David Plante was born. But in *The Woods*, unlike the earlier novels, Mr. Plante is not interested in the sociology of Daniel's world nor in the psychology of the people he shares it with; he explores instead the boundary between Daniel's ruthlessly insignificant everyday existence and the vast landscape of his inner apathy, examining through Daniel's eyes the proposition that matter and spirit are irreversibly divided from each other and that both are irrevocably alien to him.

The book opens in the spring of Daniel's freshman year at Boston College. . . .

It is tempting to see the three short interrelated sections that make up *The Woods* as . . . arranged almost syllogistically. They are studies in irreconcilable contrasts, between mind and matter, body and soul. Whether he is walking through Boston or picnicking in the Rhode Island woods, Daniel perceives only the parts and pieces of things; his imagination is filled with lists of components that he can never quite add up to any whole. He tends to get lost, metaphorically and literally; he sees objects—lampposts, apples, human beings—framed in empty space, a sort of visual manifestation of a cosmic void. Particularly, of course, people elude him. In the first section Daniel and his roommate, Charlie, whom he loves, speak to the air between them, confined in their individual isolations. . . .

The second section, which takes place during the summer between Daniel's freshman and sophomore years, moves to a pastoral landscape as Daniel, on holiday at his parents' lakeside cottage, is reluctantly wooed from his apathy by Lillian, a somewhat older woman who conducts her courtship by boat. The progress of their encounters is by far the most cogent section of the novel. In a setting in which drinking tea is a major event, seduction takes on the stature of myth. There is a suggestion here of Morgan le Fay and other island enchantresses who lure their passive victims into pagan illusions of freedom and sensuality, only to reject them again into a world even colder and emptier than it was before their encounter. (p. 11)

The prose style of *The Woods* is flat and naturalistic, but the sensibility of this second section seems almost gothic. The landscape, tinged with magic, hides dreamlike dangers; Daniel's difficult journey through the underbrush to Lillian's cottage seems weighted with allegory, a journey to Chapel Perilous. Still, Daniel's mind, as he wavers between a yearning to lose himself in some restful vastness and an absolute terror of sinking into oblivion, seems evenly balanced between mysticism and numbness. Reflecting this, the novel is alternately dominated by Daniel's intense, metaphor-laden mood and the more homey details of his everyday self-absorption. He sits naked before a mirror and draws the reflection of his body to educate himself in its reality, but, caught in a vortex of self-inspection, he ends up drawing "a body drawing a body." It is an image that one can take, I think, as representing David Plante's creative method and limitations as much as Daniel's. At times the author seems almost as reticent about coming to grips with his novel's emotional center as its hero is.

But despite the tight focus on self-absorption, *The Woods* seems to me a book of considerable moral power. Throughout, Daniel has recurrent visions of himself as a soldier forced "to march with his unit until he didn't have a body of his own." War to him stands for whatever is "outside him and his control, something he would have to, because he had no choice, give in to." This surrender to the void, which he sometimes longs for and sometimes dreads, becomes palpable in the novel's third section through Daniel's older brother Albert, a Marine Corps major who is paying Daniel's way through college. For Albert war is everything and everything is war. (pp. 11, 21)

Albert, devoured by war, has disappeared into a state of rage in which God's will is synonymous with battle and duty merely the obverse side of loathing. Albert is a poignant, even admirable character, but he lives in despair so lethal and so unconscious that by comparison Daniel's self-obsession, moral ambivalence and emotional paralysis no longer seem like the foibles of adolescence but celebrations of integrity. His reticence and honesty as he tries to reconcile his pacifist convictions with his affection for his war-loving brother are gestures of heroic grace.

The Woods is a very short and a very dense novel. And it has its faults. It could be accused of lacking resolution, of being elliptical to the point of being obscure, of indulging a hero so passive that next to him Oblomov would look like an activist. But it is also a brilliantly original work, intense, illuminating and compelling. Eccentric enough to be beyond the pale of most critical judgment, its virtues certainly are worth considerably more than its faults. (p. 21)

Edith Milton, "Exploring Love," in The New York Times Book Review, *August 15, 1982, pp. 11, 21.*

MICHAEL GORRA

"There is another Russia"—so runs the epigraph, from Maxim Gorki, with which David Plante starts *The Family*, the first of his three novels about the Francoeurs, a family of French-Canadian origin now living in Providence. The epigraph pits Plante's vision of New England against the ways in which the region has been seen by other writers. . . . If one thinks of the region's literature, one remembers James's novels about comfortable, prosperous Protestants, or Hawthorne's half-brooding, half-whimsical tales, or perhaps Frost's poems. . . . Yet much of New England, as Plante's novels remind us, has little to do with that past. Much of it is Catholic, much of it is urban and ethnic and far from prosperous. And in the 1950s, at the time *The Family* takes place, many people in New England still lived in immigrant neighborhoods centered around the church, where the children grew up bilingual and played in the streets or on front stoops.

The Family begins in 1952 when Daniel, the trilogy's protagonist, is twelve, and follows the Francoeurs' tempestuous life until he leaves home for college. The family lives on the edge of a French-Canadian parish surrounded by Irish, Italian, and Polish parishes. Neighbors are identified and characterized by their ethnic origin; and for the Francoeurs' seven sons, French remains the language of intimacy and prayers. (p. 34)

Daniel wants above all to escape from the density of his family life, from sharing a bed with his brother Julien in a house full of their parents' quarrels. "'They were so mismatched, our mother and father, so utterly,'" Richard, the eldest son, says in *The Country*. Jim, the father, is so sternly demanding of himself that ". . . he never asked himself if he was all right. He did what he thought he had to do," no matter what the cost to himself or others. . . . And Reena, whose natural gaiety has been stifled by the claustrophobia of her tiny home and her solitary position in a family of men, dwells aloud on her shortcomings as a wife and mother, trembling always on the edge of a breakdown.

But that summation of the Francoeurs' marriage is reductive, does no justice to the book's great strength—the complexity and subtlety of Plante's characterization of the tensions that connect individuals within a family. That complexity, however, is related to the book's main problem—the fact that *The Family* is at first confusing. A character's sudden flares of anger seem random, unpredictable, and unexplained. Why is Reena a bit of a guiltmonger? Why is Jim so inflexible? Who's to blame? Plante reduces narrative commentary to a minimum; actions aren't set in a context that could justify them.

Nevertheless, the characters grow familiar over time. It's as if one watched and listened to a family sitting in its living room, night after night, but were told nothing about the family except their names. At first their behavior would be confusing. But as one watched and listened, one would see actions repeated, bits of the past discussed. A pattern would emerge, and what first appeared to be isolated incidents would be revealed as part of a consistent whole. So it is with *The Family;* this passive method of narration allows Plante great flexibility, keeping him from the simplification that explanation requires, and from easy answers, just as the Church keeps Reena and Jim from the easy answer of divorce.

Plante wrote *The Family* in the third person; in *The Country,* he switches to Daniel's first-person account of three visits to his parents in the late 1970s, the last of them to attend his father's funeral. Daniel is now a writer, living in London, but he tells us nothing of his life there. Instead he concentrates on his parents' old age. Their minds wander, and their sons must work hard to keep them talking and busy. . . . But Reena and Jim are no longer angry. They're confused, miserable, and afraid, yet have also fought through time to a difficult tenderness and self-knowledge that they lacked before.

The Francoeurs' neighborhood has also changed. Daniel tells his father that he wants to take a walk through the parish. But Jim says, "'The parish? The parish doesn't exist anymore.'" It has slipped away, as has Daniel's French. Yet though Daniel now finds the world in which he grew up strange and somehow crude, it remains a part of him that, at his father's wake, he can't help but accept. . . . (pp. 34-5)

The world of the Francoeur novels is an impersonal world with an impersonal Catholic God; it makes sense only if one believes that a realm of principles and truths exists beyond it. Yet this world is also possessed of a stark and painful beauty, like bare trees in a New England winter whose shapes are seen cleanly and truly without the confusing elaboration of leaves. Plante's style matches that world. At first, like those trees, it seems monotonous, an unrelieved terseness of expression. But as one reads, one begins to see variations, begins to understand that Daniel's voice is both richly sensual and beautifully spare, a voice filled with the poetry of detail presented with absolute simplicity of diction.

The Woods, Plante's new novel about the Francoeur family, charts Daniel's initial moves toward freedom, his attempt to escape from the world into which he was born. The book's action is set shortly after the conclusion of *The Family,* and it is once more told in the third person. Part of the book takes place in Boston, where Daniel is at college; the rest happens at the house on a Rhode Island lake that his older brothers have bought for their parents. The Francoeurs are temporarily at peace; at least they aren't fighting openly. And rather than concentrating on Daniel's relationship with his family, *The Woods* deals instead with his growing awareness of the outside world into which he feels the need to escape. But where to go? For much of the novel Daniel is "in the woods," lost and confused, brooding on the relation of the self to the body, on the questions of self and sexual identity. The novel hints, with delicate understatement, at the lure of homosexuality. Daniel does have an affair with a girl named Lillian Cooper, whose family has a house on the same lake. But it is unsatisfactory, and leaves him wanting—wanting something unknown except insofar as it includes escape from the entire set of conventional expectations for a young man in the late 1950s: the need to go into the Army, get a job, get married, father children.

The book's language is as tightly controlled as that of its predecessors, but conveys an intense, even sexual awareness of the physical world, an awareness not just of bodies but of streets and lakes and small islands overrun with poison ivy and wild blueberries. *The Woods* captures the way an eighteen-year-old boy, educated in the importance of the spirit, opens up before the cacophany of the physical. All this seems a quite conventional portrait of the artist as a young man. But it is not. One knows that Daniel becomes a writer only because of information provided about his later life in *The Country.* Plante doesn't once mention art or the desire to create; the result is

a more generalized, and more valuable, portrait of adolescent confusion. . . .

The Woods is an interlude between *The Family* and *The Country.* Each novel can be read on its own, although inevitably they enrich one another. Read singly, *The Country* is perhaps the most satisfactory of the three, and *The Woods* perhaps the slightest. Taken together, they form a whole that I believe to be one of the finest achievements by an American novelist in the last decade. Plante roots his trilogy in the local, in a conscious and necessarily narrow range of place, character, experience. But that narrow range, like Hawthorne's or Frost's, is deceptive, a reminder that good regional literature is first of all good literature. (p. 35)

Michael Gorra, "The Other New England," in Boston Review, *Vol. VII, No. 6, December, 1982, pp. 34-5.*

ROBERT TOWERS

A literary typologist would probably want to classify the Novel of the Sensitive Youth as a minor subdivision of the *Bildungsroman*—less ambitious, less philosophical, and much shorter. Though perennial, it probably reached its heyday in the 1940s and 1950s when a spate of such works appeared in this country—small, carefully wrought novels about teen-age boys or young men standing hesitantly on the threshold of adult life, full of inchoate yearnings, often troubled about their sexual identity. . . . David Plante's *The Woods* provides evidence that the genre still lives, its tremulous sensitivity intact.

Though it is the third in the series of novels dealing with the Francoeurs, a working-class family of French Canadians settled in Providence, Rhode Island, *The Woods* is second in chronology, taking place in 1957-1958. . . . [It is] the shortest and most fragile [book of the three novels]. Once again the protagonist is the next to youngest of the seven Francoeur sons, Daniel, who, when the book opens, is completing his freshman year at a Catholic institution easily identifiable as Boston College. . . .

What partly redeems this almost plotless little novel from preciosity is the way in which Plante manages to surround almost every object and every inconsequential event with a kind of luminescent space, like a halo. By following Daniel's attention as it moves very slowly from one thing to the next, he produces an effect of hallucinatory realism, in which each detail seems to exist in its own right, to have a quasi-mystical "thingness" about it, quite apart from whatever significance it may or may not have in the larger picture. . . .

After the much more full-blooded treatment of the Francoeur family in the earlier parts of the trilogy, *The Woods* comes as a disappointment. Plante is a powerful writer when he wants to be, capable of locking the reader in the mute, chest-crushing hug of inarticulate family love, of creating scenes of raw anguish as brothers strive and their parents grow old, crack, die, or helplessly survive. His ability to render the physical world is never less than impressive. But in *The Woods* Daniel is too numbed a character to engage our sympathies, and the events narrated are too brief, too fragmentary, to provide the thematic weightiness that the author apparently intends them to have. (p. 38)

Robert Towers, "American Graffiti," in The New York Review of Books, *Vol. XXIX, No. 20, December 16, 1982, pp. 38-40.**

JAMES WOLCOTT

Soft as acorns drop the novels of David Plante, a young writer with a tremulous regard for the leafy things of life. (p. 54)

The mood of David Plante's novels is wan and autumnal, so it comes as small wonder that although they have been handsomely regarded by (among others) Frank Kermode and Philip Roth, they haven't caught on with the book-buying public, which prefers its family sagas laced with blood and semen, in the John Irving manner. Instead, David Plante has become one of those writers whom critics love to stroke for being a master of "craft"—a writer's writer who, like Wright Morris or M.F.K. Fisher, seems destined to be chronically underappreciated. But it's lonely being a critics' pet, a writer wants to hear more than a caressing echo after the release of a new book, and as if to break out of this fur-lined trap David Plante has now brought out a racy, chatty, celebrity-cruising memoir, *Difficult Women,* an account of rough and tender dealings with Jean Rhys, Sonia Orwell, and Germaine Greer. No acorn, this book; it lands with the thud of a cannonball.

In the novels, Plante (through his alter ego) comes across as a citified John-Boy Walton—the good son who returns home to help his troubled folks. . . . [In] *Difficult Women* he emerges not as a caring son with furrowed brow but as a beleaguered male escort. . . . (pp. 54-5)

Plante baby-sits the novelist Jean Rhys, who is portrayed as a dotty old souse with tear-streaked makeup and irascible manners; squires George Orwell's widow, Sonia, through the dusty corners of Italy, where she boozes morosely and complains about the backwardness, the filth; and accompanies the feminist writer Germaine Greer on a trip to Santa Fe, where Plante tinkles into a snowbank and Germs calls out, "Can I watch?" Each of these women proves to be an unholy handful, and every now and then Plante stretches across the bed and, contemplating the ceiling, sends up a few puffs of idle self-chastisement. He tells himself that he's trod upon their corns somehow, somewhere. (p. 55)

[Surely] Jean Rhys, Sonia Orwell, and Germaine Greer were pretty formidable customers long before David Plante and his qualms swam into view. *He* didn't make them difficult, any more than Lillian Ross made a boastful blowhard out of Ernest Hemingway—he simply happened to be on the scene when booze and bad nerves helped set these women disagreeably off. The real question is why David Plante insinuated himself into the confidence of Rhys and Company only to do an about-face and give them an exasperated, catty trashing. He describes Jean Rhys being stuck in a toilet with sopping knickers, has Germaine Greer going on about the wonders of "nigger cock" and traipsing about in the altogether ("She grabbed the fat round her waist and squeezed it into a roll"), and portrays Sonia Orwell as a pathetic, name-dropping witch. And he doesn't balance his crass disclosures with any sort of fine discriminations about their lives and work—we learn nothing, *nothing,* of Sonia Orwell's relationship with her husband, or of the hard-won wonders of Jean Rhys's novels; and from these pages no clue is given as to how imposingly brilliant Germaine Greer can be when she sets aside her randy kinks and rises to the full scolding height of her rhetoric. . . . Instead, Plante simply attaches himself to their notoriety, with attentive suckers. And he reveals himself to be a classic wet. Even after Sonia Orwell has withered him with a blast of scorn at a party, Plante notes, "I made myself write Sonia a thank-you note." Swallowing his resentment and biding his time, David Plante is now able to write kiss-off notes. The sour comedy of *Difficult Women*

is that he's carrying on as if he were delivering valentines—celebrating with a sigh these women's rugged virtues.

The book's title is a tip-off to Plante's furtive designs. After all, anyone who's made even the most casual whirl through the literary world knows that it's crawling with difficult *men*—macho frights and sly smoothies who seem to have wormed their way out of the footnotes to Pope's *Dunciad.* Why single out the women and subtitle the book "a memoir of three," as if there were ranks of fuming harpies trailing behind the trio he's chosen to write about? The truth is that *Difficult Women* does dirt to women and not just difficult women but women, period. Women are messy creatures in this book, dominatrices with wattles, wrinkles, flab, sloppy habits, and moods that easily roll off the tracks. . . . I find it difficult to believe that Plante would categorize men with such scrutiny, right down to their chipped cuticles. . . . Only with women would Plante feel confident enough to dare such trivializing, such moony doting.

What is the source of David Plante's kick against women? That's the true enigma resting at the bottom of these muddy waters. . . . [In] *Difficult Women,* Plante is dealing with real people (two dead, one living), and one wants him to come clean with his motives, particularly his psychosexual motives. To put it starkly, *Difficult Women* is a book that seems to keep peeping out of the closet.

Evasion-wise, David Plante does some pretty fancy dancing in these pages. . . . [On one] occasion, Plante tries to keep a fire going, and Greer takes command: "'You're doing it like a fucking fairy. Let me do it.' 'Like a what?' I asked.'' Perhaps Plante should turn up the volume on his hearing aid, for it's clear that Greer is assuming (rightly or wrongly) that Plante is homosexual. Plante's sexual leanings are his own concern, but it does seem something less than forthright to go through a book pretending not to pick up on what others are saying—particularly since he doesn't hesitate to nail down details of the sex lives of his difficult women. The frankness of his approach demands that he be frank with himself, and with us, but instead he vapors off into confusion, vague sentiment, and platitudes. . . . [Perhaps] Plante sees Greer and the other difficult women as demanding mommy surrogates, and is acting out some intimate Oedipal struggle. But whatever the cause, *Difficult Women* reminds one of those conversations overheard in movie or theater lobbies in which devotees give some Great Lady (a diva, perhaps) a suave bitching. The only difference is that their malice is out in the open with bells on, while Plante is hiding his in velvet gloves. He's playing pensive and sincere, wanting still to be thought of as the good son. (pp. 55-6)

Difficult Women, in its lack of tact and discretion, serves to unmask the reticence in Plante's novels and reveal it to be an actorish stance. . . . In dishing Jean Rhys, Sonia Orwell, and Germaine Greer in *Difficult Women,* David Plante has not only nudged his lance into the sickly creature that was once chivalry but he's done violence to his own respectable name. He's dished himself. (p. 56)

James Wolcott, "The Sensitive Plante," in Harper's, *Vol. 266, No. 1592, January, 1983, pp. 54-6.*

VIVIAN GORNICK

David Plante has known, with varying degrees of closeness, Jean Rhys, Sonia Orwell and Germaine Greer. *Difficult Women* is a series of memoirs of the three, linked together by Mr.

Plante's idea that his own complicated motives in devoting himself to these friendships is part of the story he has to tell. The idea, however, is a suggestion, not an intrusion. Mr. Plante is too good a writer to lose his balance or his subject: the spectacular exaggerations of will and character the three women embody. . . .

[The Memoir of Jean Rhys] is a remarkable achievement. Rhys was in her 80's when Mr. Plante met her: a tiny woman hunched over with arthritis, drunk by lunchtime, wearing flowered dresses, brim hats and makeup applied with a shaking hand. Determinedly infantile (and made even more so by years of enforced solitude and obscurity), Rhys was literally carried about by people who knew enough to revere the famous forgotten novelist locked up inside the helpless old lady. Mr. Plante readily became the last of these people. He visited Rhys daily at her London hotel, talked with her, drank with her and set out to help her write her autobiography. He also moved her from bed to bath to chair and, in the most notorious incident in the memoir, rescued her when she fell into the toilet.

But Mr. Plante never forgot who Jean Rhys really was and what made her valuable, so that while he captures neatly the shabby dishevelment of the narcissistic girl-woman fallen into confused old age, he also achieves full recognition for the writer whose eloquence and maturity are endlessly redeeming. (p. 9)

Although Mr. Plante tells us often enough of his worldly ambition, and that his own emotional avarice makes him anxious (Why am I here? he asks continually. What do I *really* want from her?), inevitably we are disarmed by his openness. But with Sonia Orwell one is inclined to agree with rather than indulge the self-accusation.

Sonia Brownell married George Orwell a few months before his death and became the heir to Orwell's literary estate. Out of this circumstance she made a profession. A minor literary salon-keeper . . . , Sonia Orwell was a compulsive manipulator of literary and intellectual people, intensely invested in therapy-like intimacies with writers and painters. She emerges in this memoir a cold, angry, restless woman, murderously defensive, a dinner party drunk, possessed of no redeeming gifts of mind or spirit. . . .

With Germaine Greer, however, not only are we back on solid ground, all the strands of psychological insinuation are pulled together (we *know* what Mr. Plante is doing here) and brought into vivid relief through a realized portrait of the largest figure of all.

Germaine Greer is the most wonderfully exaggerated difficult woman anyone might ever want to know. A cross between Margaret Sanger and Brendan Behan, the celebrated feminist speaker and writer seems all crude appetite and missionary-like responsibility. A large, blowsy woman, not beautiful in the parts but spectacular in the sum, Greer eats, drinks and lusts after men with a heartiness that feeds her compulsive sociability. . . .

Greer herself, though, is anything but helpless. Educated to live in the world, she knows—really knows—how to build a house, fix a car, plant a garden, drive tirelessly, cook brilliantly. And everyone around her knows that she knows. . . .

Greer commands the room wherever she is. Repeatedly she takes the conversation by main force and delivers a passionate speech on whatever is currently on her mind—female circumcision in Africa, practices of abortion and contraception around the world, whatever. She is able to do this because no one in the room cares about what they care about as much as she cares about what she cares about. The intensity of her engagement is the source of her power; it is self-generating and to a large degree self-feeding; she does not really need any of the people who are listening to her, she only needs people to listen. . . .

That Mr. Plante admires and loves "the person she was" is not in question. Tough, singleminded, unbelievably appropriating, Germaine Greer emerges at the last as warm, funny, generous and very intelligent; a demanding and altogether worthwhile presence.

Mr. Plante's relationship with Greer is the most extensive of the three—he is her guest in Italy, they visit each other in London, travel together in the American southwest—and it is with her that his internal carryings-on about what he, an open homosexual, is doing with these strong-minded women is most fully articulated. . . . They all gave him "something," promised him "something" that made him cleave to them. With Germaine Greer the mysterious something is out in the open. In her company he shivers with excitement, imagines her taking him into her capacious body, loves falling asleep feeling safe and happy because Germaine is in the next room, watches her in her bath in Italy as a child peeking through the half-open door might watch guess who.

Difficult Women is the result of a psychological fixation that illustrates delightfully what might be called adaptive neurosis. Mr. Plante's preoccuation with the meaning of his attachment to Rhys, Orwell and Greer neither distorts his subject nor pushes his prose out of shape; it only indicates the source of his engagement and reveals his wholly admirable ability to convert necessity into virtue by bringing these extremely interesting women to brilliant, mythic life. His special intensity leads us to something of larger importance as well. . . .

Difficult Women is moving, intelligent and very much of its time. (p. 21)

> *Vivian Gornick, "Complicated Friendships," in* The New York Times Book Review, *January 16, 1983, pp. 9, 21.*

JAIMY GORDON

[In *Difficult Women*, Plante recounts] the progress of his relations with novelist Jean Rhys; Sonia Brownell Orwell, widow of George; and feminist writer Germaine Greer, during the years from about 1975 to 1980. It is an oddly conceived and sometimes annoying book, rather preciously spare where it might be ample, and ill-advised, I think, in the sites the author chooses for candor. But even as a failure, *Difficult Women* makes interesting reading, especially if you can supply to these women the context of past lives and accomplishments that Plante prefers to omit.

For instance, an admirer of Jean Rhys's fiction (and I am one, though Plante confesses more ambivalence) will find a nightmarish logic in the opening views of Rhys in *Difficult Women:* the fatalistic demimondaine of the novels has come, in an old age, to the only end I could imagine for her, dying as she lived in a shabby hotel, in the London that she hated, surrounded by old people, and hard up, owing to the vigilance of the management, for sweet vermouth. She is paranoid and tawdry under her wide-brimmed hat, abusive, weepy, self-pitying, and drunk as often as she can get hold of the stuff. . . .

Sonia Orwell, self-appointed custodian of Rhys's dotage, has introduced Plante to Rhys, but Orwell is by now performing her own grim parody of once lively traits that the end of a life so often enacts. . . . The young woman who, according to Malcolm Muggeridge, "represented everything [Orwell] has always longed for . . . beautiful, and in a generous, luxuriant way: gifted socially, the familiar of writers and painters," appears in *Difficult Women* as a ferocious middle-aged snob, radiating tension and unhappiness in every direction, drinking three bottles of wine at a sitting, prone to sudden attacks on the friends and protégés (especially Plante) she invites to dinner, and given to compulsively reiterating, "How ridiculous! How ridiculous!" It is through Orwell that Plante becomes current in London literary circles; nevertheless she barks at him at one soireé, "What do you know about writing?"

Plante's peregrinations with Germaine Greer . . . are more amusing; here the air is heavy with sexual portent, although we know (and so, I think, does Greer) after a page or two that it will come to nothing. These scenes, and Plante's deadpan views of Greer striding around gigantically, speaking a hundred languages and managing everything expertly, . . . lend a comedy not wholly intentional to Plante's melancholic ruminations on the ineradicable distance between them.

The focus Plante chooses for *Difficult Women* is decidedly narrow, fixed on dimly glowing beads of realization that travel upon one gracile thread: the relationship of each of the difficult women to Plante himself. Plante gathers these in, and compares them. That is the meaning of his book. Over and over, stanching his wounds, he asks himself what he is doing with these troublous *grande signioras*. And he answers himself: He wants to have the secrets of Jean, because she is the same Jean Rhys who once sat in a Paris cafe with Ford Madox Ford. He wants to draw closer to Sonia "because she, who commanded a place in the world, was justified in her darkness, and justified mine." He hopes with Germaine to be "taken into the private world of a public woman." And yet, what has made them public women does not interest Plante, for the purposes of this book. Rather, from each woman—because she has a public—he tries to extract, in disparate views, scenes, conversations, something private, something for himself alone. Not sex, mind you, but intimacy, confidence. And he is always baffled, for what makes them not only public, but also difficult, women is a tendency to monumental episodes of irritability, especially towards Plante. . . .

Thus Plante suffers, for he devoutly covets their approval: "They could justify me in my body and soul," he says. If *Difficult Women* has an ethos, this sentence expresses it; whether the reader will believe it or not is another question. In effect, we are asked to understand that some profound redemptive hope is foremost in his attraction to these towering females whom he neither desires sexually nor even, in any ordinary sense, likes; we are also asked to forget that by mere association with them he gains prestige on the worldly plane. . . . But after I am finished sneering at the artless candor of a writer whose application for a sort of sainthood requires us to see a trio of celebrated women as Furies on the wing, I have to admire him for daring to express it in print. Really. He must, I am convinced, believe it himself.

Studied as it was, Plante's decision to omit background seems glaringly ungallant with Rhys and Orwell, who are literally, and bitterly, at the ends of their lives during this period, and who deserve some evocation of their former selves to place beside their twisted remnants, as a corrective, or even as a

token of respect. Why does Plante deny them this? Perhaps, in a sense, he is simply continuing to do what he has done before. For his Francoeur novels, Plante received warm praise from critics, above all for their brooding, shadowy but visually exact style. . . . The effect of [*The Family, The Country,* and *The Woods*] is often that of moody black-and-white photography, low-lit except for certain small areas, and peopled by grotesques. That the nervous, even squeamish quality of Plante's attention to corporeal detail tends to create grotesques is a trait of his novels that was not much commented on, perhaps because no one minded if he made grotesques of a set of dying but otherwise undistinguished parents.

But Plante has not outgrown that style for these memoirs. In this book, too, Plante makes nothing really attractive but trees, gardens, and skies. No Edmund Wilson has stepped in to work the clay, for the purpose of writing about famous women. No more as a memoirist than as a novelist does Plante rise to the broad vantage of omniscient narrator, or social historian, or worldly biographer. He is satisfied, always, to peer out the tiny window of a private, delicate, hoarded sensibility. When he peers this way upon three difficult women, they too become grotesques, minatory figures in flesh, word and gesture, fountains of curses as often as balm.

I doubt Plante realizes how very like malice the unflattering portraiture is, especially coupled with his incessant appraisal of each woman's position in the world. I, little I, am here among these brilliant women, he seems to say. He has no intent to exploit, only to serve, to soothe, to understand. If he can't help noticing a roll of fat, . . . it is because he possesses the startled eyes of an ingenu, a half-grown youth with charming manners who looks and looks but never pretends to know too much. Plante maintains a presumption of his own simplicity that he must hope will disarm his detractors. And though I was not disarmed, I was not downright offended until he revealed his belief that this tender, costive, secluded sensibility is the literary sensibility. . . . [When] Sonia Orwell rails at Plante because he doesn't *think,* he readily admits it, then adds blandly that, as a writer, he doesn't trust thinking. Try telling that to a writer like George Orwell, late husband of Sonia. How ridiculous!

There are bad books that are certain to be read, either because their subject matter arouses curiosity, or because they fail in an interesting way. *Difficult Women* qualifies in both categories. It is the sort of failure as a book that tempts clinical analysis, so that reviewers have plunged in upon it with pious frowns but feverish glints in their eyes, like medical researchers who discover a new pathogen and set to it with something strangely like welcome. . . .

One thing that does not occur to Plante in these pages is that his tender sensibility alone might provoke outbursts in women of more assertive temperament. He becomes a sort of asexual *cavaliere-servente* to three accomplished heterosexual women who have, to say the least, been around. He offers himself as confidant, commiserator, solicitous escort; but from the point of view of a certain kind of woman in a certain brittle humor, he might also appear passive, opinionless, quietistic, too humidly soulful and a sexual deadend. Likewise a certain kind of reader, far from sympathizing with his childlike quest for approval from these devouring-mother-surrogates, will want to leap over the small figure of Plante to join the camp of the edgy but queen-sized women on the other side. I must admit I did.

Jaimy Gordon, in a review of "Difficult Women: A Memoir of Three," in The American Book Review, *Vol. 5, No. 6, September-October, 1983, p. 11.*

ANATOLE BROYARD

In *Difficult Women,* his last book, David Plante wrote about Jean Rhys, Sonia Orwell and Germaine Greer because he was interested in the way they had set themselves against the world. Their lives were quarrels with their culture, and he eavesdropped on them as a child might listen to his mother quarreling with his father in the hope of discovering what adult life was really like.

In *The Foreigner,* his new novel, Mr. Plante goes further in this direction. His anonymous 19-year-old narrator is not satisfied to contend with his culture: He wants to free himself from it altogether. To be a foreigner is his ambition, to enter into a kind of otherness that would be impossible as a citizen of his own country. . . .

His narrator goes to Europe to disinherit himself of his history. He is not an expatriate, someone who lives abroad in order to find himself. What he seems to want to do is lose himself and find someone else to be. It's a radical ambition, as well as a teasing idea for a novel. And *The Foreigner* opens so brilliantly that we begin to believe that Mr. Plante can bring it off.

His great risk in going abroad, the narrator observes, is that he may become "a phony." He may end by affecting what he can't feel or experience. This is a risk for Mr. Plante too, for phoniness is always lying in wait for novelists who pursue originality: And as it turns out, he doesn't entirely escape from phoniness.

The first 65 pages of *The Foreigner* are very good. On the ship to France in 1959, the narrator eats brains for the first time, a fine, multilayered image of his quest. He meets Angela, a young black woman who hates America and says, "I've got to have everything strange." Angela is already estranging herself from her native language. She speaks "as though she were carefully eliminating slang, or even idiom, from her talk."

In Paris, the narrator is almost paralyzed by the foreignness of France. . . .

Like many Americans on their first trip abroad, the narrator is pierced by what might be called a nostalgia for the permanent. "If they made me feel joy," he says, "objects made me feel, too, that they were the visible points of some great, invisible suffering, as though they had survived a devastation, a great war, in which everything but these objects had been destroyed. Deeper than joy, I had a pity for them as if they were all that was left of life in a death camp—false teeth and hanks of hair and shoes and purses." He says "I loved these objects with an American love."

The Foreigner begins to deteriorate when the narrator leaves Paris for Barcelona. Mr. Plante seems to have exhausted his powers of observation, or perhaps the narrator has, for Barcelona is only a rumor of a city. A shoeshine boy provides the best image in this part of the book. Snatching off the narrator's shoes before he can stop him, the boy nails thick rubber soles on them, so that the wearer is insulated from contact with Barcelona and made clumsy in his movements.

Angela, the black woman who has to have everything strange, inducts the narrator into the criminal underworld of Barcelona. Far from being strange, it is dull and monotonous, mostly a matter of waiting around in bars and transporting illegal packages. Crime comes across here as a kind of empty frenzy arising out of nothingness and anomie. . . .

Mr. Plante's style has been described as minimalist prose, and this kind of terseness works only when the content is high. Toward the end of the book, when nothing much is happening, his stinginess with words seems like a double parsimony in their rather self-conscious diligence, his sentences are like ants crawling on a windowpane.

Mr. Plante seems puzzled by his own project and allows his story to decompress and drift away. As far as one can tell, the narrator never finds an alternate or foreign self. And perhaps this is the message of the book: that there is no other, just one to a customer.

Anatole Broyard, in a review of "The Foreigner," in The New York Times, *September 12, 1984, p. C20.*

HARRIETT GILBERT

A quote from Hemingway opens the book—'In Spain you could not tell about anything'—but David Plante's *The Foreigner* is still more flavoured by Henry James than Ernesto. Its sentences may be short and sharp, its paragraphs know when to stop, but its hero-narrator would have made the bullfighter spit. A 19-year-old American on a year's 'study program' in Europe, he handles machismo as though it were a stranger's jockstrap: when it falls into his lap in the shape of Vincent, a crazy, criminal, US ex-pat. who 'came to look' at the Spanish Civil War and never turned back to the States, he can only stare at it with fascinated horror—a condition which shifts, as the novel progresses, to horrified fascination. . . .

Having crossed the Atlantic by steamer (during which crossing he first meets Angela: black, mysterious and, it transpires, Vincent's lover and partner in crime), our hero sets out on whatever the passive form of a 'rampage' might be. He smuggles something (he doesn't ask what) through French customs; he agrees to deliver a sealed letter to Spain; he participates in an abortive robbery (or is it? again, he doesn't ask)—all without personal commitment. The consummation of his sexual arousal by Angela/Vincent/Angela-and-Vincent is achieved with the same kind of chilling, obsessive uninvolvement. It's a strange, uneven, unsettling book: initially, a superb account of late adolescent dislocation; progressively, something more disquieting and ruthless. If, besides the Hemingway and James, there's a strong tang of Paul Bowles's thrillers, Plante has added an astringent impassivity of his own.

Harriett Gilbert, "States of Desire," in New Statesman, *Vol. 108, No. 2799, November 9, 1984, p. 32.**

DON SHEWEY

David Plante's ninth novel [*The Foreigner*] is a continuation of his trilogy—*The Family, The Woods, The Country*—reissued in paperback last year as *The Francoeur Novels.* . . . In *The Woods,* the slim midsection of the trilogy, [Daniel Francoeur] begins college in Boston and has his first sexual experience aside from masturbating over muscle magazines. *The Foreigner* picks up the story from there; though the first-person narrator is never named, he's clearly Daniel Francoeur (whose biography closely resembles Plante's).

The Foreigner takes place during the summer of 1959, as Daniel begins what is ostensibly his junior year abroad. Shipbound for France, he befriends a black American named Angela who is on her way back to a dismal love affair in Barcelona. After a few boring, distinctly unromantic weeks in Paris, Daniel decides to join her in Spain, where he, too, falls inexplicably under the spell of her sexy but charmless boyfriend, a small-time crook named Vincent. He surrenders his savings to Vincent and trails him and Angela like a mascot, even standing at the foot of the bed while they make love when Vincent orders him to do so. (pp. 47, 49)

Plante practices a peculiarly blank kind of storytelling—a literature of ignorance. In his novels as well as in *Difficult Women*, a memoir . . . , the narrator is a helplessly passive guy who sees all and understands nothing. The dialogue is oddly stiff and unnatural, functional but purposely dead, without personality. The details he picks out are plain, even obsessively banal, and his descriptions of people almost entirely avoid psychological observation to focus on their hand and foot movements, as if they were stick figures. Statements like ''He stepped back'' or ''He touched his throat'' occur frequently. . . .

There's an excuse for this rudimentary prose, and it works about half the time. Plante wants to conjure a large and complex world from small, simple incidents—to give what's unspoken the same weight as what's said, because he is haunted by the turbulent reality, or mystery, that exists beneath the placid surface of everyday life. Although it's never discussed, Daniel's real quest in Europe is for the secret of masculinity. He has fled from the standards of his stubborn, stoical father and his oldest brother, Albert, the Marine Corps officer and spiritual head of the household, hoping that being in Europe will convey upon him all the masculine attributes represented by Hemingway-the-glamorous-expatriate: worldly knowledge, manly action, heterosexuality.

What a Victorian idea, but the twist is that Plante's protagonist fails utterly. In Paris he doesn't know what to do, where to go, or even what to eat. He fumbles sexual opportunities not just because he fears his own homosexuality but out of a weird Catholic body-shame. His lucidity about his own ignorance becomes a fascinating kind of antiheroism: Plante captures the dreadful, all-too-commonplace feeling that your life is controlled less by what you know than by what you don't.

His triumph, however, is also his downfall. When too much is left unsaid, the writing gets pretentious, like those unbearable French films where people say and do the most mundane things and you're supposed to think that what's really happening to them is something large and inexpressible and sad if not tragic. . . . [The] characters in *The Foreigner* remain ciphers. I could never tell exactly what Angela or Vincent looked or sounded like, or why Daniel found them attractive.

It's intriguing to watch Plante develop his technique of observation-without-interpretation (he did it best in *Difficult Women*). His scientific approach to emotion and his struggle to avoid clichés link him variously to Gertrude Stein, Alain Robbe-Grillet, Jean Rhys, Joan Didion. And it's exciting when he succeeds in making the unsaid felt; the sweaty-palm terror he creates out of nothing in that final train ride through Spain reminded me of the paranoid all-night drive through Ireland that was the best part of Renata Adler's *Pitch Dark*. What's frustrating is that too often in *The Foreigner* Plante gropes for an elusive truth and misses. (p. 49)

Don Shewey, ''Foreign Bodies,'' in The Village Voice, *Vol. XXIX, No. 47, November 20, 1984, pp. 47, 49.*

FRANCIS KING

David Plante's last book, *Difficult Women,* had a rough ride. No one could object to the quality of the writing or to the uncanny manner in which, as one's eyes moved over a page, one seemed to hear the voice of Jean Rhys, Sonia Orwell or Germaine Greer actually talking from behind one's shoulder. Yet the hostility was widespread. 'Bad taste' was the phrase most often used; but I think that what really disturbed both reviewers and readers was something more subtle. Few people who knew these three women could, hand on heart, dissent from Plante's judgments of them; but there was something eerie about the passivity and pliancy with which he had submitted himself to their wills and whims, while at the same time remaining so watchful and so critical. Jean Rhys's importunate egotism and Sonia Orwell's ferocious unreasonableness had often driven the kindest and mildest of people to exasperation and even fury. It was precisely because Plante's narrative never betrayed either of these two emotions—precisely because he never said 'Oh, for God's sake, Jean, think of someone else for a change!' or 'Oh, do shut up, Sonia!'—that the word 'creepy' was used of the book in at least one review.

The same passivity and pliancy characterise the narrator, never named, of Plante's fascinating, tantalising, demanding new novel *The Foreigner*. Plante always writes best when he is closest to his own experience, and I should guess that there is a strong element of autobiography in this account of how a French-Canadian boy, financed by a doting older brother, leaves Providence, Rhode Island, to submit himself to what is, in effect, his spiritual rape by Europe. Hemingway has set him the example—'He was what I wanted to be, but would have to risk everything to become: a foreigner.' . . .

What he feels towards other people—the black American girl, an Englishwoman trying to make a living as a cabaret artiste in Barcelona, his Spanish landlady in Paris—is, with one notable exception, never revealed, much less analysed. The exception is his declaration at one point in the narrative that he has fallen in love with Vincent, a mentally disturbed, possibly criminal American, who has lived in Spain since the Civil War. . . .

Constantly the boy is described as touching himself, smelling the odours of his own body and looking at his reflection. It is as though he were under an unrelenting compulsion to establish not merely who he is but whether he exists at all. Vincent is also constantly touching himself, at one point even violently pinching his body all over, at another 'palpating a nipple'. Having exchanged his isolation as a Frenchman in America for no less desolate isolation as an American in France and Spain, Plante's 'foreigner' exhibits the voracious *voyeurisme* of a starved urchin pressing his nose against the plate-glass of an expensive restaurant. The climax of this *voyeurisme* comes when, watching Angela and Vincent make love, he achieves a spontaneous orgasm.

This book employs many of the devices—clandestine letters and parcels to be delivered, guns to be concealed, rendezvous to be kept—of the modern thriller; but this is a thriller without solution, even without explanations, so that when, on the last page, the unheroic hero arrives in Almeria with his letter, we never learn what it contains or to whom he delivers it. What we have here is the fictional equivalent of one of those Pinter plays—*The Homecoming* is the obvious example—in which a fog of criminality and sexual passion thickens and thickens, never to be dispersed. The narrator constantly seems to be saying 'Do with me what you will', the book no less constantly to be saying 'Make of me what you will'.

In extremely short sentences, with little use of simile or metaphor, Plante writes with an airy clarity in which the most familiar things—a walk along a street, a wait on a railway platform, a meal in a restaurant—become as new and strange for the reader as they are for the narrator. It is in this creation of a 'foreign' world, peopled by 'foreigners', within the humdrum world already known to us, that the success of an elusive but always absorbing novel must chiefly be sought.

> *Francis King, "Pliant Plante," in* The Spectator, *Vol. 253, No. 8159, November 24, 1984, p. 29.**

ROSALIND WADE

David Plante is a writer who makes a virtue of straying as far as possible from the orthodox views of places and people. In *The Foreigner* the settings are Paris and Barcelona, with glimpses of Valencia and Alcazar. The novel is about a young French Canadian whose obsession is to explore Europe during a break in his studies. Paris seems to be the place to aim for and he seeks lodgings at an address casually handed to him on the voyage by a beautiful black girl named Angela. Here he endures discomfort and general privation, partly through his own inability to make proper arrangements. 'Madame' is not unkind and often offers him snacks and coffee, but for most of the time he wanders around the capital, exhausted, hungry and ill until she gives him his marching orders. He obeys her instructions to go to Barcelona, where Hemingway's memorable phrase 'in Spain you could not tell about anything' proves to be only too true. By coincidence he meets Angela, his companion on the sea-crossing. She allows him to tag along with her in an existence as disorderly and inconsequential as his own.

Presently, they contact Vincent, an American who remembers the Spanish civil war and still seems affected by it. This rootless, impecunious person makes mysterious telephone calls, frequents seedy clubs and cafes and indulges in uninhibited sex-play with Angela which the young man attends as an unwilling *voyeur*. Not surprisingly, he passes the days and nights in a state of mild shock. . . . He arrives on the final stage of his tour as confused as when he set out, aware that soon he will be returning to his homeland for the start of his first university term, enriched, it would be anticipated, by his bizarre experiences. The factually-minded reader may be tempted to enquire as to the precise nature of Angela's and Vincent's activities and to wish to tie up the loose ends of the narrative. There would be no advantage in doing so. *The Foreigner* lingers in the memory as a supreme intellectual and emotional experience unhampered by probabilities. Any traveller who has strayed from the fashionable end of the Rambla and the main Paris boulevards will be reminded of sounds and sights so vividly described as to become actual.

> *Rosalind Wade, in a review of "The Foreigner," in* Contemporary Review, *Vol. 246, No. 1428, January, 1985, p. 47.*

Stephen Poliakoff

1952-

English dramatist and scriptwriter.

A prolific dramatist who writes principally for London's "Fringe" and studio theaters, Poliakoff focuses on such issues as class warfare, urban alienation, and the breakdown of society. While his plays often contain touches of cynical wit, their undertones are serious. Poliakoff imparts a strong sense of dramatic tension and impending doom to his plays; the majority of his works feature young protagonists who are driven by an aimless sense of frustration or disillusionment. Alienated by contemporary society, they frequently resort to self-abuse and violence in confronting their urban existence. Poliakoff stated: "I'm writing about what's happening now, about people searching for beliefs in what is no longer a religious country, and about how individuals of charisma and power can polarize things. . . . I'm not an anarchist but I'm reflecting the uncertainty of our time."

In many of his early dramas Poliakoff studies the conflict between social classes, usually portraying the upper class in an undesirable light. Oleg Kerensky noted that "Poliakoff was fascinated by the fascist strand in everyone, especially the young and ambitious." In *The Carnation Gang* (1973), tension arises between two financially secure brothers and the lower-class youths to whom they sell drugs. In *Clever Soldiers* (1974), Poliakoff explores the effects of societal and military pressures on his young protagonists. Set at Oxford University in the first act and in the trenches of World War I in the second, the play presents a disturbing view of class conflicts and the ways in which violence and power take the form of both self-abuse and abuse of others. In *Heroes* (1975), Poliakoff depicts two men of different classes who join a fascist party, and *Strawberry Fields* (1977) chronicles the activities of two right-wing revolutionaries as they wander the British countryside collecting funds for munitions needed to fulfill their vague, nihilistic plans for social anarchy. The dramas *Shout across the River* (1978) and *Favourite Nights* (1981) further develop Poliakoff's concern with violence, alienation, and tensions between youths and society.

Poliakoff's disaffection with urban life often leads him to examine the superficial aspects of popular culture, with particular emphasis on the commercial music industry. In the satirical one-act play *Hitting Town* (1975), a rebellious young man has a sexual encounter with his sister, then tells about it on a radio phone-in program, attempting to shock and anger the program's host and audience. The host, however, is revealed in the companion play *City Sugar* (1975) to be similarly cynical and manipulative. Barely masking his contempt for commercial rock music and his fans, he turns a radio contest into a scene of humiliation and psychological abuse. In *American Days* (1979) and *The Summer Party* (1980), Poliakoff again explores the ways in which power-hungry individuals manipulate popular culture to their own advantage.

While many critics consider Poliakoff's statements shallow or simplistically pessimistic, he is often commended for his ability to create tension through the ominous characters and situations in his plays. In his recent work, *Breaking the Silence* (1984),

Poliakoff departs from his customary British urban settings to depict a Russian aristocrat in conflict with political authorities after the 1917 Russian Revolution. Michael Coveney noted: "Much of Poliakoff's distinctiveness comes from . . . [the] collision in his work between an exotic European consciousness and the objectively observed evidence and detritus of fall-out in a consumer society." Poliakoff has also written several screenplays for television and film.

(See also *Contemporary Authors,* Vol. 106 and *Dictionary of Literary Biography,* Vol. 13.)

HAROLD HOBSON

On strictly social grounds *The Carnation Gang* is to be regarded with cautious misgivings. There is no reason at all why plays should not be written on any subject whatever: but the manner of writing them can be the cause of social evil. I do not say that such evil will result from *The Carnation Gang,* and drugs, given the place they occupy in the world today, are a permissible reference point for drama. But the specific methods of drug-taking, both oral and by injection, are here so prolongedly shown, and their consequences so partially and incompletely revealed, as to make me uneasy. Nevertheless, *The Carnation Gang* is a very good play; its story is well conceived; and its ending is not in the least what it seems to be.

The Carnation Gang is not essentially about drugs at all; it is about the relationship of two brothers, the elegance of whose manner matches the taste of their surroundings, who happen profitably and in a very civilised way to sell drugs to a small but wealthy and educated clientele. One of them, Daniel . . . is himself susceptible both to drugs and to women; his brother Alec . . . is susceptible to neither. He is in fact incapable of emotion, just like Anouilh's Becket: beneath the smooth surface of his relaxed appearance he is vaguely conscious, as Becket was, that this is a lack in him. If he has feelings at all, these are experienced through the feelings of his brother, under whose slightly decadent surface tension is easily perceptible.

Now it is evident that Daniel's smooth facade could be quickly cracked, so that it is in a condition of dangerously vulnerable equilibrium that the couple live. The play shows us how this equilibrium is destroyed, and then (here lies its theatrical skill) how that equilibrium is restored by what seems at first glance to be a further and final destruction. We are in a realm of dubious morality; but also in a realm of Paradise, lived in, Paradise lost, and Paradise regained.

> Harold Hobson, "A Remarkable Performance," in The Sunday Times, *London, September 29, 1974, p. 38.*

BENEDICT NIGHTINGALE

On the evidence of *Clever Soldiers*, Stephen Poliakoff is a young man of great promise and some spleen. His play begins with the humiliation of a fag in a public-school locker-room, ends in the Flanders mud and, in between, has scarcely a line that is not a jibe or an exchange that is not a squabble. The characters spit tacks and, during a typically tetchy picnic, actually start chewing razor blades, presumably to sharpen the edges with their knife-grinder tongues. The main character [Teddy] . . . rages at pre-1914 Oxford for its 'grey, scabby, complacent face', leads his friends in a rousing chorus of 'wake up', directed at the dreaming spires, then stomps off to war and ends by haranguing the soldiers under his callow command for daring to submit to his orders. One reason for his anger is . . . that he himself cannot resist exploiting the power he knows he should not have. It is worth saying, and energetically said. But there were times when I thought Mr Poliakoff's interpretation of the phrase 'dramatic conflict' absurdly literal, and other times when I wished his heart would get back under his sleeve and take a rest.

> Benedict Nightingale, "Magidome," in New Statesman, *Vol. 88, No. 2280, November 29, 1974, p. 798.**

HAROLD HOBSON

[*Clever Soldiers*], taken in conjunction with Mr Poliakoff's *The Carnation Gang,* . . . marks the entry into British drama of a writer of outstanding potentialities.

In *The Arrest* . . . Jean Anouilh absorbs one layer of time into another. Mr Poliakoff does something similar with ideas and emotions, inextricably mingling 1914 with 1974. There was a time when reformers looked forward to the day when the ad-

vantages of the few should be available to the many; to the day when everybody, to put the matter metaphorically, would be able to read Ancient Greek. . . .

[But the] progressive opening up of intellectual treasures has led to the belief, in many quarters, that this treasure is only dross.

This is the basis of Mr Poliakoff's *Clever Soldiers*. His setting in the first act is Oxford in the summer term of 1914: in the second, the trenches. Mr Poliakoff is as sensitive to the breathtaking beauty of Oxford as Matthew Arnold was: Balliol and Oriel Street and Christ Church Hall are names that make divine music in his imagination.

There are some of us who regard Oxford as the first of universities. Paradoxically Mr Poliakoff himself may not be wholly opposed to this view. . . . Nonetheless it is his argument that Oxford, and all that it represents, and Cambridge, and other universities represent, must be destroyed. This is a proposition that revolts me. But Mr Poliakoff does not write to express my convictions, but his own: and he expresses them well. If he is an an enemy of the good, he is a good enemy.

He follows the fortunes of two young men, Teddy . . . [and Arnold], from their public school to Oxford and the Great War; and, in a manner basically naturalistic, but which makes free with transitions of time and place, and evidently regarding his characters as symbolic of the upper class, he studies the breakdown of their nerve, in the one case gradual, in the other sudden, sharp and intensely dramatic. To all outward appearance, to the very end, Arnold is the perfect public school officer, impeccably correct, entirely without fear. His behaviour under fire betrays none of the ravages within, and the moment is indeed dramatic when, with no warning, in fact with his usual coolness and self-command, he shoots himself through the mouth.

Teddy is more closely studied. He is influenced by the quizzical, amused hatred of his tutor for what Oxford represents: he is upset by the attentions of an aesthetic undergraduate. . . . Teddy's breakdown is seen in the hysterical bravado with which he risks other men's lives as well as his own. But it is perhaps a weakness in the play that we are given no suggestion of what it is in Oxford that has provoked Teddy's decline. The nearest we get to it is a rather Bacchanalian evening with the Bullingdon Club. Mr Poliakoff makes no attack upon the studies of the place, and does not even try to imply that the world would be better if it had never heard of Plato. Nevertheless, Mr Poliakoff's passion against the convictions on which universities are founded is real. It is a felt emotion, not a manufactured one. As far as the theatre is concerned, that is the important thing.

> Harold Hobson, "Playwright of Promise," in The Sunday Times, *London, December 8, 1974, p. 37d.*

RANDALL CRAIG

'Skin-erupty' was D. H. Lawrence's word for Strindberg. The living playwright who most deserves the description is probably Stephen Poliakoff, who not only looks like becoming as prodigiously prolific as the tormented Swede but projects a comparable high-voltage edginess. . . . *City Sugar*, his new full-length play, . . . is his best yet. A companion piece to *Hitting Town* . . . , it is less frantic, more controlled, more resonant, subtler and deeper in its characterization. There is no mention of the incestuous brother and sister, but the action is again set in Leicester, and Nicola Davies, who was the waitress in the Wimpy Bar, reappears as a supermarket salesgirl . . . , while the local radio disc jockey, Leonard Brazil, who was only an amplified voice in **Hitting Town,** now features as the main character. . . . (p. 74)

An ex-schoolmaster, Leonard Brazil is now expert at pumping unstimulating trash into the young minds he is no longer trying to educate, despising himself for being so good at his new job but unable to resist the lure of a lucrative offer from a commercial radio company in London. He also feels more contempt than compassion for the audience that laps up the footling wisecracks he energetically churns out. . . .

Stephen Poliakoff very neatly focuses the man's ambivalences in two relationships. . . . One is with Rex . . . his studio assistant, who not only gawps at him adoringly but imitates him shrewdly, grooming himself to follow on in the same job. The other is with Nicola Davies, whose flat young voice appeals to him when she rings in. He knows that she represents the median type of the girls who listen to him; he also feels sexually attracted, as Rex guesses. . . . Stephen Poliakoff cleverly delays the confrontation between them. We cut between the studio, the supermarket and the bed-sitter, where she stuffs almost everything she owns into a life-sized doll, a floppy statue of a pop-star, which she makes to enter a competition devised by the disc jockey for his listeners.

The results are rigged so that she is one of the finalists, and the anti-climacteric confrontation in the studio is excellent—well written, well staged, well acted. They are disappointed in each other, unable to communicate, unwilling even to try. In one outburst of hysteria she flings a plastic cup of milk to the floor, and in the middle of the live transmission—a quiz competition with one other finalist . . .—she tries to walk out of the studio, but mostly the tension is kept under the surface until he manipulates both girls into humiliating races around the control panel in a game of swapping chairs. Afterwards, when he reverts to his schoolmaster persona, trying to exert power through patronizing advice, she defends herself with sulky silence. . . . [The] scenes of non-relationship between the two girls, like the scenes between the two men, make extremely effective statements about loneliness. (pp. 74-5)

> *Randall Craig, in a review of "City Sugar" and "Hitting Town," in* Drama, *No. 119, Winter, 1975, pp. 74-5.*

JONATHAN HAMMOND

[*Clever Soldiers* shows that] Stephen Poliakoff clearly has much to offer. His characterisations and sense of dramatic structure are neat, his dialogue often extremely literate and witty. It is just that someone using the form of a play in an attempt to free himself from the hang-ups imposed by his public school and Oxford background does not automatically create an interesting and moving work of art. . . . (pp. 31-2).

I am being a little unfair as I happened to hear Poliakoff talking very intelligently and articulately about his play on the radio the night before I saw it. So I know that he intended the central situation and location of *Clever Soldiers*, Oxford University in 1914 and during the First World War, to be a metaphor for the Oxford of today, where Poliakoff himself has recently been a student. The author's not very original or illuminating thesis is that Oxford today serves the same function as it did 60 years ago, that of turning out new recruits for the ruling class, to

take their rightful places as captains of industry, politics, commerce, literature and whatever else.

But the interest lies, of course, in how he does it. We first see Teddy . . . in the changing room at his public school with Arnold . . . on the eve of their both going up to university. At Oxford, Teddy comes into contact with Harold, an aesthete . . . and also his tutor David . . . , a talented semi-alcoholic from a relatively humble background. . . . David and Harold are emotionally crippled by their surroundings, in different ways; Harold because he is trapped by the university's superficial glamour and, as a recognised 'character', is part of that glamour, David because he has clearly expended most of his energy getting to Oxford in the first place and so has none left with which to fight its all-pervading values. Teddy, on the other hand, initially preserves an air of detachment toward the place and what it signifies. He meets Sarah . . . and falls in love with her.

Comes the second act and the First World War. Teddy and Arnold both enlist. David and Harold are left at the university, David because he is medically unfit, Harold because he is a coward. Through his adventures in the trenches and his contacts with working-class lads . . . , he slowly comes to realise that he is inescapably part of his class and what it represents.

There is one superb scene near the end of the first act, which brilliantly conveys in a concise dramatic image the sense of futility engendered in sensitive upper-class people by a place like Oxford. Indeed, it is almost worthy of Chekhov. On a picnic by the river, Sarah starts to chew a razor-blade, followed by Teddy, to the fascination and horror of their companions and the audience. . . .

But who, in the end, cares about an upper-class boy trying to escape from his background? (p. 32)

> *Jonathan Hammond, in a review of "Clever Soldiers," in* Plays and Players, *Vol. 22, No. 5, February, 1975, pp. 31-2.*

RANDALL CRAIG

Now that Howard Brenton is 32, while David Hare and Christopher Hampton are both approaching 30, who is the leading flower amongst the next crop of playwrights? . . . [One] has no hesitation about awarding the silver cup to Stephen Poliakoff, who goes on improving steadily.

Hitting Town may have been written a little too quickly. The consummation of the incestuous relationship between the university student and his elder sister is less electrifying than the build-up to it, and Stephen Poliakoff seems so confident that the flow of good theatrical ideas will continue in full spate, that he doesn't always bother to develop them fully. **Hitting Town** therefore isn't as good a play as he could probably have made it, but it's never boring, often extremely funny and often deeply unsettling. The uneasy flow of nervous energy puts goose-pimples on the skin of the dialogue and we sit there, rather in the way we watched *Who's Afraid of Virginia Woolf?*, grateful to be embarrassed, and embarrassed to be entertained.

It was a very good idea to involve a third party, a waitress and would-be singer, in the goings-on of the evening: the brother-sister relationship would otherwise have been too unbalanced by giving so much of the ingrown destructive initiative to Ralph. He is a much more credible, much more deeply thought out character than Teddy in *Clever Soldiers*. . . . [Yet] Poliakoff is still identifying so violently with his self-destroying heroes that the other characters are relatively bloodless. . . .

A Wimpy Bar sequence is particularly effective, with Ralph, impatient at not being served, messily squeezing a do-it-yourself dish out of the rubber ketchup bottles. There is a skin-prickling moment with a handful of dead beetles and an amusing sequence involving the bland voice of a disc-jockey on a commercial radio phone-in. He reacts with Puritanical intolerance, sharpened to please his listeners, when Ralph rings in provocatively pretending to be a much younger boy who is sleeping with his sister.

> *Randall Craig, in a review of "Hitting Town," in* Drama, *Summer, 1975, p. 71.*

BENEDICT NIGHTINGALE

[*Heroes* is] about the pressures that provoke two young men to join a fascist party. One is an upper-crust dandy . . . , the other a growling prole . . . , both awkwardly allied against a world where you can rarely find a day's work, the day's work hardly buys a cream bun, and the cream buns are stale. . . . I must say, I found this latter-day Pilgrim's Progress a bit culinary in its emphases. But I was less worried than my colleagues by the vagueness of Mr Poliakoff's setting. They gave me the feeling that, because he's substituted 'the city' for 'London' or 'Leicester', he's written a bad play; if he'd made these trifling insertions, it would have magically become good. Actually, the idiom of the characters persuaded me from the start that I was watching the first dramatic attempt to identify Britain with Weimar: a connection that seems less fanciful with every spasm of the sinking pound.

This is the third Poliakoff I've seen, and already he's a distinctive voice: edgy, nervous, a bit callow. His people always seem to be spoiling for a fight, whether with society, their acquaintances, or themselves. . . . It is a peculiar world, maybe a perverse one; but it is out of peculiarity and perversity that interesting playwrights emerge. (pp. 62-3).

> *Benedict Nightingale, "Necessary Evil," in* New Statesman, *Vol. 90, No. 2312, July 11, 1975, pp. 62-3.**

JONATHAN HAMMOND

Stephen Poliakoff's *Heroes* was deceptive in its form. It appeared to draw ambitious parallels between Weimar Germany of the '20s and hyper-inflation-torn Britain of the '70s, even to the rather heavy-handed extent of giving the three main characters the Germanic names of Julius, Rainer and Albert. Julius . . . is a young aesthete and artist, dressed in a white suit and carnation, surprised in his flat at the outset of the play by Rainer . . . , a working-class man on the dole. . . .

The play explores their uneasy relationship, as the locale shifts back and forth between the flat, a vaguely decadent café where the ageing upper-class Albert . . . laments the glories of the past; and the streets where Communists and Fascists are marching against each other. Mutual hostility between Julius and Rainer develops into a recognition of their interdependence, both sociological and psychological.

Stripped of its fashionable trappings—'fashionable' because comparison of the '70s with the '30s, while apt in many ways, is the latest modish cliché among middle-class intellectuals—*Heroes* has essentially the same theme as *The Carnation Gang* and *Clever Soldiers* among the author's other works. This is the middle class's guilt at its relative comfort and affluence depending in the final analysis on the sweat and guts of the working class. The public school dope pushers in *The Carnation Gang* and the *angst*-ridden public school and Oxford-educated hero of *Clever Soldiers* find their counterpart in Julius in this play. Likewise, the street urchins of the first play and the socially underprivileged tutor of the second have their various qualities merged in Rainer, a sardonically intelligent illiterate. . . . Poliakoff can certainly ring the imaginative changes on his central obsession and hang-up as a dramatist very skilfully; but, until he has succeeded in objectifying his background and advancing out of his apparent neurosis, it is difficult to see how he can develop further.

> *Jonathan Hammond, in a review of "Heroes," in* Plays and Players, *Vol. 22, No. 12, September, 1975, p. 32*

RANDALL CRAIG

Stephen Poliakoff's ironically titled *Heroes* may not be his best play, but it is deeply unsettling and not easy to forget. The structure is unsatisfactory, the basic argument schematic, the central relationship unconvincing and the ending patently contrived. It is impossible to believe that these two 'heroes' would become friends or that they would end up astride a motor-cycle which will take them to the Fascist headquarters, where they will commit themselves to the Party. Nevertheless, . . . *Heroes* offers a series of glimpses—which would be less worrying if they seemed less plausible—into what Britain could be like in the not very distant future if inflation is not controlled and if democracy is eroded. . . . [It is] apocalyptic images that the play sharply projects. The dandyish young Julius [is] pleasurably abed late in the morning when the scruffy, disgruntled prole, Rainer, bursts through the door, threatening to take possession of the room and rummaging through the drawers, ignoring Julius's polite protests. He has never worked except as a dilettante artist, so what right does he have to his possessions? It shouldn't have been necessary to make him wear a white suit and a carnation, but the production, like the writing, was best at the moments of dangling on the edge of violence. Sometimes violence is self-inflicted, as when Julius removes the bulb from the lamp to pep himself up with electric shocks. . . . Sometimes it is the off-stage violence of a stormy communist demonstration. . . . There was an excitedly hysterical sequence of stone-throwing to smash a police searchlight during a night scene (reminiscent of the one in *Hitting Town*) and another good scene of hysteria when Julius almost goes berserk with a pair of cymbals. It is not the self-plagiarism that worries me, but one important question in Stephen Poliakoff's future as a playwright will be whether he can ride his hysteria, which is like a superb stallion. It could easily kick him to death.

He spends very little time on relationships and a great deal on evoking the mood of a particular city at a particular time. I use this word deliberately because he was criticized irrelevantly for refusing to specify place and time. In fact he told us all we needed to know about where and when. The parallel between Weimar in 1925 and any big British city in 1980 would have been less effective if he hadn't generalized to the extent that he did, which didn't prevent him from evoking strong impressions of the difficulty of getting work, the seething discontent, . . . the desperation of children taking to prostitution and armed violence. All this was well done, but the plot depends too heavily on a developing relationship between two characters who aren't so much characters as externalizations of the aristocrat and the prole inside Stephen Poliakoff's tormented mind. (pp. 70-1)

Randall Craig, in a review of "Heroes," in Drama, *Autumn, 1975, pp. 70-1.*

JONATHAN HAMMOND

Having criticised Poliakoff quite severely in the past, it's a pleasure to report that *City Sugar* . . . , a companion piece to *Hitting Town* . . . , is by far his best play to date. For the first time, he has managed to relate his personal obsessions and guilt about class to an objective reality. *City Sugar* centres around Leonard Brazil . . . , a DJ on a local radio station in Leicester, with a superb line in patter—sharply and idiomatically written by the author—only partly concealing an utter contempt for his working-class listeners. An ex-teacher who loathes himself but enjoys his work in a masochistic kind of way, Brazil is a complicated character at odds with most of the people around him. . . . (p. 26)

But his chief antagonist in the play is Nicola Davies . . . , a young girl who works in a Leicester supermarket and who listens to Brazil's show to break the monotony of her existence at work. After taking part in a phone-in, she enters a competition for which the prize is a few days in London with a yobbish pop group. She gets to the last stage and appears on Brazil's programme, along with another girl. There she is put through a nauseating and exploitative routine of question-and-answer, with a rigged ending. Nicola realises that she has been set up as a media victim; and the climax of the play comes when Leonard, in an offhand way, attempts to excuse his behaviour and performance to her while she sullenly answers in mono-syllables. (pp. 26-7)

The play is a savage indictment of the way in which modern capitalism exploits a section of the working-class by conning them into accepting 'pop culture', a shabby, third-rate set of values, represented by Leonard's highly glossed trash. It combines deep feeling, acute observation and a harsh wit and irony in about equal measure. . . . (p. 27)

Jonathan Hammond, in a review of "City Sugar," in Plays and Players, *Vol. 23, No. 3, December, 1975, pp. 26-7.*

MICHAEL COVENEY

[*City Sugar* is] Poliakoff's bristling evocation of Competition Week on Radio Leicester, a show compèred and distorted by a disillusioned and cowardly deejay on the verge of defecting to London notoriety. The elements and trappings of the play, which all stem from Poliakoff's beautifully wry response to the subcultural detritus piling up around us, make this an event with unique appeal for a [wide audience]. . . .

Leonard Brazil is an inspirational idea for a character: flip, competent, self-denigrating, he is attracted to the waifish tones of a phone-in customer who, unusually, is grudging with the respect he both needs and abhors. So Nicola Davies reaches the final of the competition, having stuffed a home-made effigy of one of the awful Yellowjacks with half her bedroom. She withers disgustedly before Len's glutinous shrine, while Len uses her disappointment and pretence to indifference as an excuse for self-examination. Raw self-criticism, tough analysis, might have made for an even stronger play; for the studio

kerfuffle boils down to no more than Len harking back (who doesn't?) to the good old days of the Sixties as he moves on to London with a barely articulated contempt for the kids who main-line with the pap he shoots at them down the radio waves.

The play both uses and criticises the popular radio phenomenon, yet never without a fundamental affection for the entire process whose lulling, corrosive result drifts along the wallpaper. The dimension is ingeniously created with an extreme, yet realistic snatch of life at the other end: Nicola and her restless, block-headed friend, Susan, work in a draughty corner of a huge store where Leonard Brazil arrives as a piped and muzzy background to humdrum jobs and mounting irritability.

Michael Coveney, in a review of "City Sugar," in Plays and Players, *Vol. 23, No. 7, April, 1976, p. 41.*

JOHN COLEBY

Stephen Poliakoff, a professional playwright for seven years is but twenty-three. He has a good ear for the ways people speak which he uses to make convincing, if impersonal, dramatic statements. His plays are strengthened by his unusual combination of talent, technique and sheer shortness of time on this planet. He has been taken up by many . . . ; he is now about to take off. *Hitting Town* and *City Sugar* are companion pieces in that Nicola Davies, a young female person, and Leonard Brazil, a disc jockey, appear in both. In *Hitting Town* they are peripheral in different ways to the night of love of young Ralph and his older sister Clare; the confrontation of 'LB' as a pop cannon and Nicola as its fodder is at the heart or at least the guts, of *City Sugar.* . . . But in *Hitting Town* the impersonality is strong and although one can visualize Ralph and Clare, clear outlines enclose insubstantial masses. The plot is slight; the only event, the incest, takes place off stage and its effect on the participants is not particularized. The play seems to need more of either characterization or plot than there is in the text, although it has been lively and moving in performance. It is the popular theatre of common problems seen in terms of stereotypes against familiar backgrounds.

John Coleby, in a review of "Hitting Town" and "City Sugar," in Drama, *No. 122, Autumn, 1976, p. 78.*

MICHAEL COVENEY

In Poliakoff's play [*Strawberry Fields*] strawberry blonde Charlotte remembers Kentish fruit fields as a way of negotiating the grim, grey present. She is a fanatic serpent masquerading as an English rose and is prepared ruthlessly to shoot her venom into a national body soft with nostalgia and dripping with lethargy. Travelling north along the motorway, she and her colleague in the English People's Party pick up, reluctantly, a hitch-hiking teacher, Nick, who remains unimpressed by their vague vision of apocalyptic holocaust. . . .

Stephen Poliakoff has already established himself as the chief dramatic spokesman for a young generation windswept in the tunnels of cheerless modern architecture and immunised against life-involvement by the incessant background muzak of canned sound, tannoyed instructions and ventilation buzz. In *Hitting Town* we saw tentative, malformed incestuous instincts explored in the sordid limbo of a Wimpy Bar; in *City Sugar,* the humiliation of a phone-in customer by her disc jockey hero was placed in memorable relief by an interlude in a faceless, neon-lit supermarket where the sound waves lapped irritatingly around the comparatively heedless workers. Aimlessness and frustration are conditions you feel the playwright knows well. What can he *do?* Well, so far he has written a series of imaginative, poetic, small-scale plays that have focused his voice as a theatre writer of considerable talent. Unfortunately, and by accident, I heard Poliakoff mumbling away on a radio programme about how things went suddenly dead about ten years ago. A media person jabbered on about how brilliant his play was, but nobody asked young Poliakoff why he felt like he did. . . . (p. 26)

Whatever Poliakoff's political persuasion . . . , you would get no positive clues from *Strawberry Fields.* Some critics have dismissed the play on the grounds of being no more than absurd speculation, but that is unfair. Surely a playwright is entitled to deliver his judgement of the political and social climate he inhabits without shouts of "What About Analysis" from the critics. . . . The complaints centred chiefly around the fact that the teacher offers no serious counter-argument to the paranoid dribblings of Charlotte and her fellow-traveller Kev. But debate is never remotely in Poliakoff's air. On the whole, he fantasises; but the play does at least remind you of the size of the racist poll in the recent by-elections at Walsall and Stetchford. And, on a different tack, has not Thatcher recently avowed that the student vote could win the next election for the Tories?

All that, however, is left as a subject for private meditation. The revolt of Charlotte and Kev is primarily aesthetic. Filth everywhere. The play . . . moves atmospherically from one eerie location to another along the road north. In the first scene, Kev gets excited about a dirty straw. He has a disease of the retina and is going blind. Before then he wants to see every movie ever made and clean up the countryside. . . . But Kev's motives are strangely confused. . . . [He] emerges as a fidgety maniac liable to accelerate into frightening over-drive when asked to project the details of a horror film from his memory onto a dilapidated wall. The 'question of England' he raises is not half as compelling as the question of his own sanity.

That would, for some, summarise the chief flaw in the play. But I keep remembering the eeriness of the nightmare world so pungently evoked in play and production. . . . (pp. 26-7)

At Doncaster, Kev and Nick are trying to extract something to drink from the hot-dog stall when a young policeman accosts the group. [When he demands] to search Charlotte's handbag, she takes out a gun and shoots him dead. Interval. In Act Two, Nick, now an accomplice in crime, moves into a higher gear of nervous apprehension. . . . Kev, on the other hand, is busily concocting his very own home movie, *Bonnie and Clyde*-style. . . . He is a nutter without a cause, except for the naïve hogwash about 'disappointment' and environmental pollution. Charlotte, on the other hand, could be dangerous. She predicts civil war within two years and tells Nick that she carries a gun as protection against the armed leftist groups roaming the land. When Kev realises that the massed patrol cars do not in fact lie waiting on the other side of the hill, he runs whoopingly away. Nick tries once more, pained and no longer amused that Charlotte might believe all she says. She takes out her gun and shoots him. She walks off to continue her journey.

Poliakoff's dialogue has real muscle and much style. Few words are wasted. The play impresses most as a sort of Pinteresque fantasy with thriller overtones. . . . It will be interesting to see where Poliakoff goes from here. . . . (p. 27)

*Michael Coveney, in a review of "Strawberry Fields,"
in* Plays and Players, *Vol. 24, No. 9, June, 1977,
pp. 26-7.*

OLEG KERENSKY

[*Granny* was the second play Poliakoff wrote] but the first to be given public performances, organized by the 16-year-old author. . . . It seemed to show the influence of Pinter and Orton; Poliakoff himself describes it as 'a heterosexual equivalent of Hampton's *When Did You Last See My Mother?*'. It at once demonstrated his strong dramatic sense and command of vivid and often humorous dialogue. At that time he was naturally interested in the bizarre and often aggressive behaviour of teen-agers. The plot concerns two teenage couples who are supposed to be giving the last performance of a satirical revue in a Salvation Army hall. Their leader persuades them to stay at home instead, keeping the audience in the hall waiting indefinitely. He also tricks a pathetic German housekeeper into thinking that her boy-friend has arrived to visit her, and a man who has been Granny's devoted companion for thirty years into thinking that she has died. This study of sadism and mental sickness provides a foretaste of Poliakoff's next plays; so does the comparatively weak development of the plot, and the failure to provide a strong conclusion. (p. 247)

The first play of [Poliakoff's] to be professionally staged in London was *Pretty Boy*. . . . A mood reminiscent of Pinter's *The Caretaker* is established straightaway with the arrival of William and Benny in a deserted but posh-looking apartment. William is old and untidy, Benny is around 20. They are re-occupying the home where Benny was brought up, and where William evidently helped to bring him up. Benny is aggressive and ruthless, William is epileptic and has strange phobias. . . . [William, Benny and others] set out to shake and shock the inhabitants of the rich district around them, smashing windows, removing parking meters and plotting to wreck a literary party, only to find it has been cancelled because of the death of the hostess. All their activities turn out to be equally futile and unsatisfying, but there is constant suspense about their plans and their moods, generating considerable theatrical excitement. . . . The play ends inconclusively, with everyone gone except a very disturbed Benny, being nursed and encouraged to think of a new life by his girl. (pp. 247-48)

[*The Carnation Gang,* which] got very good notices, again combines suspense with teenage violence and excitement, and again leaves its dramatic situations unresolved. But the characterizations are stronger than in *Pretty Boy* and the air of menace is better sustained. Alec and Daniel are twin brothers, in their mid-twenties (modelled on the Kray Brothers, inspired by Howard Barker's *Alpha Alpha?*) who share a fairly smart flat, making their living by selling dope to a select circle of clients. . . . Alec and Daniel know how to cope with life, and in particular with their drug trade, while the [teenage drug users] can only turn to abuse and violence when they are thwarted, a contrast caused by class and educational differences. This contrast is made explicit towards the end of the play. (p. 248)

The drug-taking scenes in *The Carnation Gang* are so realistic and compelling that many people took the play as a plea for greater tolerance or as an attack on the drug culture. But rather it shows how intelligent, well-educated, rich people can easily find safe, if illegal, outlets for their instincts and aggressions, while the poorer and less educated fail to do so. The moral is similar to that constantly being pressed by Hare, Brenton and

Barker. Like their plays, *The Carnation Gang* succeeds mainly as entertaining and gripping theatre, rather than as any sort of tract. It comes to no real conclusion.

Class and educational inequalities and their effects on people's ability to cope with their lives, are recurring themes in Poliakoff's plays. So is the threat to comfortable existence posed by outside people or events. In *Clever Soldiers,* Poliakoff went back in time to a period outside his personal experience, the First World War. Again a safe, peaceful way of life is threatened, this time at Oxford University. The conflict is between officers and gentlemen on the one hand, and soldiers and a working-class don on the other. . . . [Reviewed] by most of the critics, *Clever Soldiers* divided opinions. It impressed a number of important critics and theatre people, some of whom found the trench scenes as convincing as those in *Journey's End.* But others complained that Poliakoff did not succeed in capturing the feeling of the First World War. Once again the play was theatrical and gripping; once again too, the message was less clear. (p. 250)

[*Heroes*] was less enthusiastically received [than *Clever Soldiers*], mainly because it took place in some nameless city, which sometimes seemed to be in present-day Britain and sometimes in pre-Hitler Germany. The irony is that this very uncertainty, much condemned by the critics, only occurred because Poliakoff listened to the critics who complained that *Clever Soldiers* betrayed ignorance of the First World War. He had originally written *Heroes* while still a student; then he had called it *Berlin Days* and it was unequivocally about the appeal of fascism to young Germans. Poliakoff was fascinated by the fascist strand in everyone, especially the young and ambitious. . . . At first it was Poliakoff's intention to revive [*Berlin Days*] in something close to its original form; he rewrote it, preserving its German setting, and it was accepted by the Royal Court in that form. Then, Poliakoff says, 'I got frightened by half the critics saying I couldn't write about a period before I was born, and I should stick to what I know about, and so I rewrote again. I broke a cardinal rule which you can't break, in England anyway, that a play must be set in a specific place. I decided to link present-day Britain with early fascist Berlin, so that the play could be then, could be now. . . . And then most of the critics attacked me for it.'

Perhaps *Heroes* was ahead of its time. If it had been produced a year later its picture of rapid inflation, rising unemployment, extremist political agitation and gratuitous violence might have seemed more obviously relevant to Britain and there could have been less argument about how far it related to pre-Nazi Germany. . . . Despite its vagueness about place and time, *Heroes* conveys a strong sense of doom and of political, economic and moral collapse. It contains some of Poliakoff's best dialogue, stylized and ambiguous, and several of his favourite themes and characters are brought together.

Once again, a comfortable bourgeois existence is threatened by a rough outsider and by feelings of guilt. Julius, a would-be artist living on an allowance from his mother, wakes up one morning in his lodgings to find Rainer, a total stranger, claiming the room as his own. Rainer, a strong working-class figure, attacks Julius for not doing any real work. Eventually, however, he leaves, only to follow Julius to a café and to join the conversation between Julius and Albert, an older man who has evidently known better days and whom Julius now partly supports. During the course of the play, Julius moves from his close relationship with Albert to a fascination and involvement with Rainer. Albert represents the past (he helped to bring

Julius up), and Julius eventually 'dismisses' him, explaining that he still hopes for the future. He goes off with Rainer on a stolen motor-bike to join the fascists and 'clean-up' the country. (pp. 255-56)

The relationship between Julius and Albert recalls Benny and William in *Pretty Boy,* the precocious children who demand cigarettes and go out on the streets looking for punch-ups remind us of the teenagers in *Carnation Gang* and the diatribe against synthetic cream and general slovenliness in the café anticipates the café scenes in *Hitting Town* and *Strawberry Fields.*

Hitting Town and *City Sugar* are companion plays, with two characters in common. . . . Both are set in a small provincial city, not anonymous as in *Heroes* but named as Leicester. *Hitting Town* is only a one-act play. Ralph, a practical joker, has come from Birmingham to visit his sister Clare. He takes her out on the town, setting out to shock her and everyone else, and eventually goes to bed with her. Just as drugs struck many people as the main theme of *Carnation Gang,* so incest dominated a lot of the publicity aroused by *Hitting Town,* but the play is mainly about the emptiness of urban life and how some people deliberately flout conventions to relieve their boredom. (p. 257)

Leonard Brazil, the disc jockey, and Nicola Davies, the idle waitress in the café—very minor characters in *Hitting Town*—are the protagonists of *City Sugar.* This two-act play [became] . . . Poliakoff's first work to reach the West End [theatre district]. (pp. 257-58)

Brazil, a former schoolmaster, is intended to be portrayed as a cynical DJ shamelessly exploiting his audience on Radio Leicester and aiming for a transfer to Capital Radio in London. He gets intrigued by Nicola Davies's voice on a phone-in, and fixes her to be one of the finalists in a big publicity-stunt 'Competition of the Century', in which the prize is a visit to London with a pop group. The other principal characters are Rex, Brazil's ambitious young technical assistant, and Susan, who works with Nicola in a supermarket. The play is partly a very amusing satire on commercial radio and audience participation shows, partly an exposure of the empty lives shared by the clever but disillusioned DJ and the stupid but naïve shop assistants who are exploited by his commercial stunts. (p. 258)

[*Strawberry Fields*] is similar to *Heroes* but much more directly related to present-day Britain. Some of Poliakoff's regular themes recur—for example the criticism of dirt and poor quality in cheap eating-places. The play includes predictions of civil war and warnings of the dangers of right-wing extremism. The action takes place during an exceptionally hot summer. . . . This period is seen as the end of an era and as the threshold of something disturbing and dangerous. A respectable middle-class girl and a strange male companion who claims to be going blind are driving around the motorways distributing literature against pollution, immigration and Communism. They want to keep Britain 'pure', and in the process they are collecting arms in preparation for violent conflict. . . . They claim that violence is needed to protect the country against violence and defend their killings as no worse than the 'murders' regularly committed on the roads by motorists. *Strawberry Fields* seems like a logical extension of the gloom about Britain shown in Poliakoff's earlier work.

But Poliakoff does not see his plays as pessimistic, though he does see a great deal wrong with our society and is as yet quite uncertain how it can be remedied. Left-wing in his sympathies, he is very different, politically, from writers like David Hare, Howard Brenton and Howard Barker. 'I'm not in any way a Marxist—I hardly would be considering that my father's family fled from the Soviet Union—and I don't think there will be a violent revolution. I think quite a lot of political drama is very remote from anything the audience can identify with. I'm concerned with individuals reacting to the pressures on them—authority, the environment, that sort of thing—rather than with political theories or themes. I'm writing about what's happening now, about people searching for beliefs in what is no longer a religious country, and about how individuals of charisma and power can polarize things. I start with a general atmosphere and feeling, and with one or two central characters, and the plays develop from there. There's an anarchic streak, a high energy level, a frenetic feel. I'm not an anarchist but I'm reflecting the uncertainty of our time. . . .' (pp. 260-61)

> *Oleg Kerensky, "Stephen Poliakoff," in his* The New British Drama: Fourteen Playwrights Since Osborne and Pinter, *1977. Reprint by Taplinger Publishing Company, 1979, pp. 245-64.*

EDITH OLIVER

Try as I may, I cannot accept the two plays—I cannot, that is, believe the characters or the lines they speak—by the young British dramatist Stephen Poliakoff. Both *Strawberry Fields* and *City Sugar* . . . deal in part with low-class types, so that comparisons with early Harold Pinter and Joe Orton and David Mamet (and Eudora Welty and V. S. Pritchett) are inescapable, and, without pronouncing any final judgment on Mr. Poliakoff, the comparisons do him no good. Time after time, he seems to be slumming or working at second hand. *Strawberry Fields* . . . is about a wellborn young woman and a lowborn young man, both of them right-wing radicals with horrendous opinions about race and other matters, who journey around England collecting money for arms and ammunition, and who are joined, against their wishes, by a schoolmaster with a more decent outlook. . . .

City Sugar is a slight improvement, much of it consisting of the on-the-air spiel and an off-the-air monologue—full of the usual self-hatred, bitterness, and cruelty—of a disc jockey at a radio station in Leicester. In order to attract listeners, he sets up a foolish contest, and a girl fan of his who works at the frozen-food counter of a supermarket becomes a finalist. Willfully, during a quiz at the studio, he does her out of the prize. (p. 54)

> *Edith Oliver, in a review of "City Sugar" and "Strawberry Fields," in* The New Yorker, *Vol. LIV, No. 18, June 19, 1978, p. 54.*

CATHARINE HUGHES

On the basis of his double American debut, Poliakoff is a dramatist to be reckoned with, though one who still has quite a few problems to deal with before he fully realizes his potential. . . .

Leonard Brazil [of *City Sugar*] is a popular disc jockey, ironic, frustrated, sarcastic, ingratiating. He has an assistant named Rex, who is gunning for his job and takes advantage of every opportunity to get his own voice on the air. Fully aware of what is going on, Leonard regularly informs his audience that Rex is very fat (which he is not) and puts him down at every turn (threatening to fire him just about as often).

Leonard is, in a sense, living in the past, hating the present, at the very least in terms of its music, which he loathes. He seems to have at least equal scorn for his young listeners and their lack of taste—and, perhaps, also for himself.

But Len Brazil is very successful. One of the big London stations is dangling an offer before him and, in his final week in Leicester, he launches a contest for his listeners. . . .

Nicola, whose voice Brazil has picked out during a phone call, is one of two finalists and is invited to the studio, where the D.J.'s sadism and irrational behavior go into full operation. He insults and taunts the two girls, asking them to respond to ridiculous questions. Nicola's response is apathy: She has begun to realize just a bit of what is going on. The other girl, Jane, wins.

The program over, Len goes off by himself to decide whether to take the London offer—to make his final sell-out. That he will is foreordained; in his bitterness and self-scorn, he cannot do otherwise.

Poliakoff . . . tells his tale of futility with scathing wit and just the right touch of poignance. He overextends it just a bit and perhaps drops just one or two cataclysmic symbols too many, but *City Sugar* is easily one of the more interesting new plays of the season.

Strawberry Fields . . . is not as good, though certainly not without its interest.

Two young representatives of the radical right (yes, right) meet in a cafe on the outskirts of London, then head north in their van with a supply of leaflets propagating the clandestine organization to which they belong. They are also scheduled to pick up funds.

Kevin . . . is going blind, a leftover from the London heyday of the 1960's who is now merely disillusioned with what has become of the country: the decline and fall of Britain, the influx of the blacks and coloureds, the alteration of the culture.

Charlotte . . . is more upper class, cooler, a somewhat snobbish take-over type. But she, too, laments what has been lost, decries pollution and the advent of multilane motorways, with the simultaneous destruction of the English countryside.

Against their wishes, they take on a hitchhiker, a young teacher who, at least initially, is amused by them, but eventually comes to realize they are dangerous. Yet he remains with them, even after Charlotte gratuitously shoots a policeman at the end of the first act. He is attracted to Charlotte, but also sees a need to convince them of the folly of their ideas and to abort their dangerous journey. He winds up their prisoner.

By the time they reach a Northumberland hillside, the police have started to close in. They are, Kevin mentions, on the site of some of the encounters of the Wars of the Roses. In this new civil war, they will be the first heroes. The conclusion is violent.

For those who remember the Beatles' song from which Poliakoff takes his title, "Strawberry Fields," this will be almost a memory play, a lament for things past, a cry of pain over what they became; "Living is easy with eyes closed," the lyrics went. "Misunderstanding all you see."

Strawberry Fields is not, unfortunately, as good as its subject matter invites it to be. Though it reveals characters of interest, it does not probe them in quite sufficient depth. Though it has "plot" and dramatic incident in abundance, it is poorly constructed. And it is far too melodramatic for its own good. . . .

But Poliakoff is only 25. The disappointment of both these plays aside, they bode well for the future.

Catharine Hughes, "Two by Poliakoff," in America, *Vol. 138, No. 24, June 24, 1978, p. 506.*

FRANK MARCUS

Stephen Poliakoff, moralist and visionary, continues to express his obsessive concern with the quality of contemporary urban life in *Shout Across the River*. As the title indicates, he has chosen the jungle of South London as his locale; Leicester—hitherto his favourite black spot—has won a reprieve.

He opens with a scene in a headmaster's study. . . . [Mrs Forsythe]—a timid, blundering victim of agoraphobia—is being read a litany of her 15-year-old daughter's crimes. These include every imaginable offence. The girl is suspended from school, and the wretched mother promises to take her in hand.

It is a foredoomed attempt. The girl . . . totally dominates her mother. Moreover, she undermines her frail identity by ruthlessly revealing her hoard of trading stamps, old magazines, and mementoes of the husband who deserted her. Having reduced the mother to nothing, the girl proceeds to take her in hand by putting her through a course of 'lessons'. These involve a pilgrimage to places which make Dante's Inferno appear wholesome in comparison. Who says that launderettes, rooftop cafes and discos fulfil harmless and useful functions? They give Poliakoff—like Marchbanks in 'Candida'—a touch of the poetic horrors. . . .

Nevertheless, the daughter's therapy succeeds. In the end, an exchange of personalities is effected. Mrs Forsythe has regained some confidence, but the girl, exhausted after a week's voluntary fast, awaits removal to an approved school. The play is written in cryptic prose. The characters are victims, made monstrous by their environment. Poliakoff extends sympathy to all except the representative of authority. . . .

The style might be best described as uneasy naturalism: it never takes flight into fantasy. No attempt is made to create varieties of mood and atmosphere.

At the age of 25, Stephen Poliakoff is strategically well placed to invent as his main characters a girl of 15 and a woman of 35. He is more successful with the girl. . . .

Shout Across the River is a passionate *cri de coeur* that leaves us deeply troubled. No hope, and certainly no political panacea, is offered. There is something heroic in the playwright's attempt to swim against the currents. We ignore Poliakoff's shouts at our peril.

Frank Marcus, in a review of "Shout Across the River," in Plays and Players, *Vol. 26, No. 2, November, 1978, p. 29.*

COLIN LUDLOW

Stephen Poliakoff is concerned once again with the situation of young people in the contemporary world. Unlike his previous plays that have explored this theme though, *American Days* is not set amid the sterile squalor of supermarkets, Wimpy bars and motorway service stations, but in the plush luxury of an international record company's London office. . . .

Into this unlikely setting are thrust three teenagers: Tallulah, a punk from Birmingham, Gary, a cheeky and intelligent youth from Isleworth, and Lorraine, a very young and emaciated girl from Sheffield. They have all been spotted by a talent scout and summoned to appear before a top-ranking executive called Sherman, who will decide whether any of them are to be given recording contracts. . . .

Under his control, their auditions turn out not to be an opportunity to perform and display their musical talents, but a bizarre ritual of random questions and requests. Poliakoff has an acute perception of the anarchic disorder of the human mind, and he uses that here to delightful effect. Sherman flits wildly from one idea to the next, lining the teenagers up against the wall, giving them name badges, making Tallulah take her boots off and put them in the fridge because they distract him. . . . The proceedings repeatedly border on the realms of fantasy, but they possess a persuasive fascination and are frequently very funny. . . .

Though the play progresses in an apparently haphazard fashion, it is held together and given dramatic tension by the fact that Gary, Tallulah and Lorraine are effectively participating throughout in a form of competition. Underlying all that takes place is the question of which, if any, of them will be signed up. The idea of a ridiculous and degrading competition for young people run by an older man is one that Poliakoff used previously in *City Sugar*. The significant difference here is the youngsters' much greater reluctance to play along. Though all three unquestionably wish to be taken on, they are not simply prepared to do as they are told. Gary constantly objects to Sherman's more inane requests, and refuses point blank to use any material other than his own, even if that means losing the chance of a contract. In the end, it is he who walks out on Sherman, not Sherman on him. Similarly, when Lorraine is told she is not wanted, she does not meekly depart, but with steely determination sticks around until she eventually persuades Sherman to give her a try-out in the recording studio. Her persistence proves triumphant when finally Sherman not only offers her a contract, but also misses his plane as a result of waiting to hear her perform.

American Days is not a play about punk, but the rebelliousness and self-assertion of punk provide its necessary context, and seem clearly to have influenced Poliakoff when writing it. The play identifies a changed attitude among teenagers, a new-found defiance and energy on which Sherman remarks, and which Gary and Lorraine embody. This energy makes *American Days* far more positive than most of Poliakoff's earlier work, but Poliakoff declines to over-value it and indulge in facile optimism. His characters still live in a world beyond their control in which they must struggle to survive. Lorraine's gritty stubbornness is shown to derive from an almost desperate anxiety to escape from what she sees as a dead-end situation. She has no illusions about stardom or lasting success. She simply wants to make enough money to get away, probably to America, and live a life that offers her some future and hope. Her strength lies in the clear appreciation she has of her own situation, and it is this to which Sherman responds. For in his own way he is also desperate—obsessed by the endless and unstinting change of the business in which he works. His manic activity and movement from city to city are finally revealed as a frantic attempt to keep up. . . .

In the second act, Poliakoff introduces Murray, one of Sherman's earliest discoveries, into the action. He is a grotesque anachronism—fat, long-haired and dressed like a cowboy. In many ways he is an unsatisfactory character, since his physical grossness makes it impossible to take him seriously and really believe that he was ever a star. This reduces his impact, but his presence still serves as an invaluable reminder of the relentlessly changing world in which he and all the other characters live. Unable, or unwilling to adapt to it, he cuts a sad and sorry figure, left stranded by the remorseless destiny of modern life.

The play presents a rich and provocative vision of our times, and is written, for the most part, with taut economy.

> Colin Ludlow, in a review of "American Days," in Plays and Players, Vol. 26, No. 10, July, 1979, p. 23.

JOHN PETER

[*The Summer Party*] is set in the VIP enclosure of a vast and unbelievably expensive pop concert organised by a sleek and unbelievably rich young man who frets about the late arrival of his stars and mutters nervous instructions into his walkie-talkie. He also frets about the unexpected presence of the county's Chief Constable who seems to be there out of unexplained curiosity.

Actually, he's there because he's part of Poliakoff's Message. This is, roughly, that if we're a tribe, then pop-stars and policemen are our totems: we love them and hate them and expect magic from them. There is a theme there, yes; but it comes over as trivial twaddle, a long way from tough plays like *City Sugar* and *Hitting Town;* instead of raw slices of life Poliakoff is serving up heavy slices of half-baked pudding. Theatres . . . have done excellent work to encourage new talent which is what they should do; but as I staggered out at the end I wondered whether they wouldn't sometimes serve a successful young writer better by telling him to go away and put his new play in a shredding machine.

For when I say that the strain is beginning to show in Poliakoff I mean in form as well as content. The writing is both flat and flatulent, and the dialogue contains every theatrical cliché from "I don't really think you believe in anything" . . . to "You could be home secretary one day."

How can actors utter such lines with conviction? The answer is, with great difficulty.

> John Peter, "The Playwright Who Needs to Take a Break," in The Sunday Times, London, March 16, 1980, p. 41.

NED CHAILLET

There is nothing in [*The Summer Party*] to suggest that [Poliakoff] has ever listened to anything since [he wrote *City Sugar*], with the possible exception of inner voices and the tapping of typewriter keys.

Yet he is still sending out his messages like some boyish Joan of Arc signalling from his private flames or a horror-stricken Peter Pan with new doubts about perpetual childhood. In *The Summer Party* he builds an elaborate parable about a miraculous policeman and just manages to make it clear that his charismatic chief constable is meant to charm everyone with his unorthodox manner; everyone, that is, except a typist who sees through his benign manner and recognizes his fascistic hunger for absolute power.

Rather like a rabbit trying to pull a magician from his hat, Mr Poliakoff gets all the details of reality wrong. As if he had read about rock stars and heard that they perform at open-air festivals he has placed the action in an idyllic backstage glen on such an occasion. . . .

I might scoff at Mr Poliakoff's fantasy that fans would idly endure the time from dusk until dawn without entertainment and be only mildly restless. I could chortle at his invention of a pre-pubescent poltergeist act meant to enthrall the thousands. . . . But I can only wonder at his assumption that the chief constable could exist in a uniform that has not got the arms tied behind the back. Instead he would have us believe that the crowds cheer him when he offers only the beauty of the sunrise for their £8 tickets.

> Ned Chaillet, "A Lack of Reality," in The Times, London, March 17, 1980, p. 7.

STEVE GRANT

[Poliakoff's] most memorable creations are scenes of urban disintegration and adolescent claustrophobia. *Hitting Town* (1975), a sophisticated study of a brother and sister on the town in concrete jungle land, is not only intriguing for its incestuous overtones but for its splendidly vibrant images of modern consumerist convenience-orientated society *in extremis:* in a Wimpy bar a tomato ketchup container is cut open to reveal revolting contents. . . . (p. 141)

Poliakoff is particularly adept at illustrating the elemental nature of youthful disquiet, its potential for nihilism and morbidity. . . . In *City Sugar* (1975), a Leicester DJ, who alternates between self-disgust at the failure of his sixties' idealism and contempt for his audience, confronts a hostile but rather emotionless shop assistant, Nicola, after a bizarre radio contest, part of which has involved the building of dolls in the shape of a pop artist. Nicola and her friend fill the doll with frozen food and in another exchange the friend, Susan, describes in typically gory detail the soggy contents of a fused refrigerator. As in other of his plays, *City Sugar,* though wittily and intelligently written, presents a fascinating balance of inarticulate and articulate forces: the snappy DJ Leonard Brazil and the sullen, recalcitrant teenager, Nicola.

Poliakoff remains an intriguing figure in contemporary theatre, not least because he has shown a marked and increasingly uncommon interest in characterization for its own sake: in *Shout Across the River,* the creation of Mrs Forsythe, a mother in early middle age with an enveloping terror of social intercourse and a problem teenage daughter with whom she strikes up a bizarre and passionate relationship, is marvellously sensitive. (pp. 141-42)

> Steve Grant, "Voicing the Protest: The New Writers," in Dreams and Deconstructions: Alternative Theatre in Britain, edited by Sandy Craig, Amber Lane Press Limited, 1980, pp. 116-44.*

VARIETY

[*American Days* is] a harsh dissection of crassness and exploitation in the recording business. British playwright Stephen Poliakoff . . . continues to impress as a writer with substantive vision.

American Days is about three rock singers summoned to the London office of a big record company for an audition. Their judge is a coolly manipulative producer who's supposed to be a crackerjack talent spotter, although he admits having little personal interest in music.

Poliakoff is a specialist in the creation of alienated working class characters, and his three hungry punk rockers are sharply drawn. He's less successful with the shallowly cynical record biz nabob, who too often sounds like a pop sociology article come to life.

The play makes intriguing points about the commercial expropriation of artistic impulses, and the Americanization of British culture. . . .

The author views corporate showbiz with undisguised contempt, and in the end sacrifices plausibility for dramatic effect, when one of the three singers is signed to a two-year contract on the basis of a two-minute song audition. This is not a play to be staged at a record industry convention.

Like many young British playwrights, Poliakoff writes from a firm leftwing socio/political viewpoint, and his plays have passion and bite. So far, however, and *American Days* is no exception, they lose strength toward the finish and end on arbitrary and unconvincing notes. But the author has the talent to become a major theatre figure.

> *Humm., in a review of "American Days," in* Variety, *January 7, 1981, p. 66.*

JOHN SIMON

[Stephen Poliakoff] is a kind of second-generation Angry Young Man. Whereas the dramaturgical generation before his was wrathful at the old bourgeois establishment, Poliakoff and his contemporaries have unleashed their ire at the disestablishmentarians who have taken over the controls. In *American Days,* Poliakoff's subject is the rock-music empire, more precisely an international record company whose London office is run by a young executive of the new kind: spaced-out yet shrewd; seemingly absentminded and self-absorbed, yet playing a vicious power game with his staff and the kids who come to audition. . . . His name is Don Sherman, and he seems to have imbibed Pinter with his mother's milk.

Sherman domineers by understated indirection, confounds with casually tossed-off cruelties. . . . His intimidated, servile sidekick, Ian, is sweaty of palm and collar, and oozes accommodation. When abused beyond endurance, he strikes back with the self-righteous deviousness of the subaltern. Sherman makes or pulverizes stars: We hear him destroy one slipping career with one brief, merciless phone conversation. The three young rockers whom Ian has rounded up for auditions are cowed by Sherman and try to defend themselves, each in his own way. The self-styled Tallulah, an aspiring punker, wraps herself more tightly in the cloak of kookiness, and remains all but imperturbable. . . .

Gary—a rangy, ducktailed, earringed, chrome-studded protest singer—tries to assert his superiority with swagger, sarcasm, and minor disobedience, such as refusing to wear the laminated nameplate Sherman insists he needs to remember a postulant's name, yet holding the plate up on demand. (p. 39)

The third candidate is Lorraine, a typical English street kid, at once mousy and aggressive, defensive and insolent, and ominously taciturn. Somewhat predictably, she proves the most sinister of the three. Also on hand is a former pop star, Murray, now going to fat and to seed. This character does not quite

live up to his vaguely threatening possibilities; indeed, Poliakoff's plotting is not nearly so good as his dialogue and atmosphere. There is some repetitiousness as well as inconsistency here (notably concerning Lorraine's musical performing), and even the key image of Sherman, the killer by telephone, himself dancing attendance on the telephone voice of his master from America, is not fully developed.

But the texture of *American Days* is absorbing. The very coldness of the company listening room . . . , the deracinated Sherman, swelled up with sadism and self-pity, and not really giving a damn about any aspect of his work except power; the ubiquitous jockeyings of the six for ascendancy that drive one of them to reject a perfectly good chance—all this affords a sobering view of that rock world presumed to be the hot core of our youth culture, but in truth all ice.

Even if the play is finally a little less than the sum of its parts, those parts are mostly good. (p. 40)

> *John Simon, "Alice in Blunderland," in* New York Magazine, *Vol. 14, No. 3, January 19, 1981, pp. 38-40.**

BENEDICT NIGHTINGALE

[Poliakoff makes us] look afresh at the everyday tat of our civilisation and recognise the extreme weirdness of it all. A plastic tomato, the sort you find in cheesy cafes, suddenly seems to belong in a folk museum, the sort you find on the edge of Indian reservations in the US. And Poliakoff tacitly, and sometimes not so tacitly, presses his inquiry further: isn't it perilous to the soul to live too close to such constructs?

A revolving high-rise restaurant, plush public furniture nailed to the floor, multicoloured cocktails, a rubber plant turned yellowish by hastily disposed-of alcohol, constant muzak: much that obviously fascinates Poliakoff the anthropologist is invoked or shown in *Favourite Nights* itself. The play starts in a singularly charmless hotel foyer, but its geographic centre is what, on bad days, seems to me the spiritual centre of our culture. It's set in a casino, complete with roulette and blackjack tables, mushroom-faced croupiers, cameras perpetually scanning the punters, even a phone-cord long enough to stretch across the stage from paybox to fruit machine. To the Golden Wheel, as it's called, comes Catherine, with her adoring younger sister and the Austrian businessman for whom she's both language teacher and professional escort; and for a time it seems as if the play is to involve another of Poliakoff's pet subjects—resistance, resilence, the tiny and usually ineffective gestures of defiance people make from the cracks in the concrete. The rules of the place are designed to suppress all spontaneity and warmth. The staff may not hobnob with the clientele; the clientele's manner must be strictly robotic. And yet here's Catherine's sister whooping and banging about with impunity. . . . (p. 24)

There's life within the urban machine; and yet, of course, the machine has successfully stunted that life. As the evening progresses, it becomes clear that Catherine is actually a regular, an addict, maybe even a gambloholic. Poliakoff is over-deliberate when he tries to explain her psychology, and doesn't coalesce all his play's ingredients quite successfully; but, thanks to passages that could have come only from his offbeat pen, . . . Catherine does credibly exist and perhaps even mean something beyond herself. She's the academic high-flyer of the family, the victim of parental expectations which, frustrated by her own and the world's insufficiencies, have made her destructive to herself and others. Life for her now consists of indulging sad Poliakoffian pleasures, and principally of playing power-games with passing men and whatever gods rule the gaming tables. Her innards are turning to red plastic chips.

Evolution means adapting to environment, and if your environment is a Golden Wheel, an Alphaville, or maybe even a Barbican, evolution can mean erosion or worse. (p. 25)

Benedict Nightingale, "In Alphaville," in *New Statesman*, Vol. 102, No. 2642, November 6, 1981, pp. 24-5.

BRYAN APPLEYARD

There has been something grimly predictable about the publicity generated by Stephen Poliakoff. "Royal Court play by 19-year-old", it begins, moving on to "Playwright prodigy", to be followed inexorably by "Stephen Poliakoff is irritated with being labelled the Boy Wonder of the theatre."

After 13 years of that where exactly is Poliakoff?...

To Poliakoff his headlong and prolific progress—writing plays such as *City Sugar*, television such as *Caught on a Train* and films such as *Runners*—is unamazing....

Poliakoff is not one to be pinned down.

But at the centre of all his work lies the conviction that people should not be categorized, that we should not be crushed into thinking in straight lines.

[Poliakoff's drama *Breaking the Silence*] is about the precarious process of the release of human creativity and energy and it is based on the experiences in immediately post-revolutionary Russia of Poliakoff's paternal grandfather and his family. But it is *not* . . .—repeat *NOT* a family memoir.

"The biographical events are a small part of the urge to write the play. I don't want the audience wondering what's true and what isn't. It's just that when you take something that's quite close to you you have to reboil it to make it into a universal fiction."

Poliakoff's grandfather was an extravagant nineteenth-century figure who persisted in his haut-bourgeois ways after the revolution. And, incredibly, he was indulged, given a sinecure and told to get on with it. The reason was that the authorities knew he was genuinely close to coming up with an invention of worldwide significance....

Poliakoff's own—rather reluctantly described—analysis of his *oeuvre* involves two strands: his "urban canyon" plays set in the postwar desolation of Britain's cities and his "European" plays. *Breaking the Silence* goes back to the Russian roots of the latter category and the story was told to him when a teenager by his grandmother.

The use of that brief, creative era in Russia before Stalinism intervened is also significant for Poliakoff's work because of its contrast with the usual cultural background of his drama. In *Breaking the Silence* the environment is vibrant, alive and dangerous, but at least it offers the opportunity for human contradictions and ambiguities to be embraced and simulated.

In his "urban canyon" plays his characters find themselves in a wasteland in which all their energies are absorbed by the simple effort of remaining human.

"The people in the urban plays are not zombies, they are not turning into urban vegetables. They fight back, they have an imaginative life that makes them human. That is, if anything, an over-optimistic view. Certainly I've never thought of myself as a pessimistic writer. It is a pessimistic view of the culture—obviously in Thatcher's England . . ."....

His first interest is character so he works specifically against the style of Brechtian alienation, aiming rather for total involvement: "My plays are designed to work on people's imaginations."

But what, I wonder, is all the energy for? What do his plays do? "Do?" he looks startled.... "What do they do? I don't know. You set out to involve, entertain, to move people, I suppose, make them look at the world differently. If you achieve just one tiny bit of that . . ."

Brian Appleyard, "The New Land for a Restless Writer," in The Times, *London, November 3, 1984, p. 6.*

MICHAEL COVENEY

Adventure, fantasy, the whole idea of 'getting out', inform the plays and films of Stephen Poliakoff . . . , [who] has produced a body of work of strong consistency and much flavour.... (p. 9)

All [of his plays], in one way or another, involve the upheaval and excitement of travel and escape. In his last play, *Breaking the Silence*, . . . Poliakoff turned for the first time to his own Russian Jewish family background. In a wonderfully imaginative design gesture, he places his forbears in an Imperial railway carriage to which, after the Revolution of 1917, they have been consigned by the Commissar of Labour.

Nikolai (based on Poliakoff's great grandfather) is a dandified Russian aristocrat secretly on the verge of marrying sound to pictures on film. He has been appointed, however, telephone examiner on the Northern railway, and the play develops as a preparation to emigration against a background of mounting political and private tensions. In a central episode of considerable power, Nikolai's turncoat son Sasha destroys the newly arrived secret consignment of lenses and appliances.

Much of Poliakoff's distinctiveness comes from this collision in his work between an exotic European consciousness and the objectively observed evidence and detritus of fall-out in a consumer society. His characters are very often psychologically unconvincing; what happens to them, the *sensuality* of their fate, is never less than gripping. They exist in stories that are told chronologically, with a minimum of narrative tricks—no flashback ever, and though the mode of expression is rarely dripping with wit, Poliakoff's dramatic speech is, as John Spurling once remarked, never dull and always energetic.

The plays of the early 1970s—*Pretty Boy, Berlin Days, The Carnation Gang, Clever Soldiers* and *Heroes*—attracted critical approval partly, one felt, because of their lack of aggressive political oratory. The latter three were all about young confused adolescents.... [The] appeal of the real world as opposed to academic security was something Poliakoff experienced by moving from Westminster to Cambridge and then leaving without taking his degree. In *The Carnation Gang* this jejune sense of conflict was powerfully stated in a vicious confrontation between dope-peddling upper-class twins and a group of working class teenagers.

The real break-through came in 1975. *Hitting Town* and *City Sugar,* companion pieces of inner city disaffection located in Leicester in the neon-lit limbo of desolate cafés and super-markets, created an enormous impact. (pp. 9, 11)

[Poliakoff] won the Standard Promising New Playwright award for 1976 and was appointed the National Theatre's first resident writer. The general critical climate since then has suggested that Poliakoff has gone off the boil. I feel there have been unfortunate productions of his work—Peter James's production of *Favourite Nights* (1981) . . . [for example] was a disastrously inert affair. . . .

What sometimes happens is that the imaginative properties of the work are harder to pin down in performance than they are to appreciate on the page. Thus *Favourite Nights* sounds terrific, classic Poliakoff territory, charting a strange and listless journey through the soulless world of West End gambling casinos, coloured cocktails and rattling roulette tables. The element of *mysteriousness,* though, did not convince, and the David Hare-like central character of Catherine did not survive the lack of psychological penetration in her creation.

Either side of this play, though, there are three outstanding theatre pieces—*Strawberry Fields* (1977), *Shout Across the River* (1978, Poliakoff's own favourite) and *The Summer Party* (1980); and three remarkable, evocative films—*Caught on a Train* (1980), *Soft Targets* (1982) and *Runners* [1983], all of which expand upon the physical obsessions of the stage plays and all of which have attracted actors and directors of the highest calibre. (p. 11)

[In *Strawberry Fields*] Kev is going blind. He has a disease of the retina but he is determined to see every movie ever made and to clean up the countryside. The play itself belongs to the road movie genre, the headlong rush to catastrophe punctuated with pungently sensual interludes in the sun-lounge of a motorway stop-off, the chill emptiness of a site at Doncaster where an abandoned hot-dog stall stands outside a disused cinema, the rumbling motorway verges and the searching dazzle of headlights. (pp. 11-12)

The atmospheric menace does not always come off on the stage. But in *Strawberry Fields,* the question of England was interestingly balanced against the question of Kev's sanity. . . . *Strawberry Fields* was Poliakoff's first thriller, his first suspense drama. Confused notions of fame, a recurring theme, are bound up in the fates of Charlotte and Kev, and one of the great achievements of the play is its conveying of Charlotte's

manipulative supremacy over Kev and her brutalising, finally murderous, impact on the quivering teacher.

In *Shout Across the River* Poliakoff offers his most despairing and concentrated view of a brutalised urban existence in the family trio of mother, daughter and son. Kids can only acknowledge each other through mugging and casual sex—the girl, according to her school report, is permanently splashed in semen. There are scenes in a discothèque, on a bleak ice-cream terrace, in a hospital bed where brother and sister are locked together in something vaguely reminiscent of affection. . . .

This gripping, muscular play derived its tension from its *denial* of movement, and sheer frustration of the characters imprisoned in their urban misery. . . . Poliakoff created a similarly inert situation in [*The Summer Party*]. . . . Although one tetchily disappointed critic suggested that Poliakoff should pack it all in and set down his quill for a few years, the play was in my view underestimated. It contained a riveting distillation of the rock concert experience and, in the figure of Kramer the constable, one of Poliakoff's finest adventures in character portrayal. . . .

[Poliakoff's films] *Soft Targets* and *Runners* deal . . . in pursuit: the first introduces a Russian journalist into a distorting world of high society social events and Whitehall officials. There are some beautifully handled set-pieces—the remains of a party in the dawn light, a wedding in Sussex. Alex the journalist is himself the quarry who turns hunter when he loses the enigmatically attractive Celia after a car crash. He finds her working as a waitress, just as the distraught father in *Runners* finds his daughter, after a much more extended search, distributing car hire leaflets. In both pieces, there is an aching spiritual gap at the heart of the structure: the actual *nature* of Alex's and Celia's relationship is no more articulated or explained than is Rachel's disappearance from home after *her* road accident.

But the films work as atmospheric confections, as poetic responses to social dilemmas. It is now a far cry from the stark simplicity of *Hitting Town,* but the individual voice of the dramatist is still discernible in its hallucinatory loud-hailer tone, raking across the scenes of urban and spiritual desolation, the waste land of a dangerous and seductive society lacerating and worrying itself to an inevitable and apocalyptic demise. (p. 12)

Michael Coveney, "Strange and Listless Journeys,"
in Drama, No. 156, Spring, 1985, pp. 9, 11-12.

Jonathan Reynolds

1942-

American dramatist and scriptwriter.

Reynolds is an author of witty, madcap farce and satire whose literary forebears include Broadway dramatists Ben Hecht and George S. Kaufman. Reynolds's plays, which make use of black humor, one-liners, and improbable plots and situations, are characterized by what Jesse Kornbluth called "mean-spirited dialogue and a disrespect for naturalism." By placing his protagonists in familiar settings which grow increasingly chaotic and uncontrollable, Reynolds comments on inane aspects of American obsessions and institutions.

Reynolds made his debut as a dramatist with the off-Broadway production of two one-act plays, *Rubbers* (1975) and *Yanks 3 Detroit 0 Top of the Seventh* (1975). The first is a satire in which the men of the New York state legislature react with outrage to a liberal woman's proposal for a bill requiring that contraceptives be clearly displayed and priced in stores. In the second play, described by Jack Kroll as "a Walter Mitty fantasy in reverse," an aging baseball star in the midst of pitching a no-hit game slowly loses control while contemplating his mid-life crisis. In *Geniuses* (1982), Reynolds's first farce to reach Broadway, a costly African war epic is filmed in the Philippines under circumstances similar to those surrounding Francis Ford Coppola's production of *Apocalypse Now*. As the picture lags behind schedule, a typhoon forces four self-obsessed, creative people together. The production's last days evolve into a hilarious spoof on such aspects of filmmaking as sexism and the conflict between commercial greed and artistic statement. In his recent play, *Fighting International Fat* (1985), Reynolds addresses America's narcissistic compulsion to be thin and satirizes the roles of sex, food, and television in contemporary society.

Critical response to Reynolds's plays has been mixed. While some reviewers consider his jokes predictable and find his characters to be caricatures, others praise his ability to direct the diverse elements of farce toward a meaningful statement. Reynolds is also the author of several scripts for film and television.

(See also *CLC*, Vol. 6 and *Contemporary Authors*, Vols. 65-68.)

Martha Swope Associates/Susan Cook

sent-minded bitterness by the scriptwriter. The resemblance of the bearded makeup man to Ernest Hemingway becomes a springboard for more of those "Papa" jokes, which grow increasingly offensive with the years, and the actress is a walking parody of the kind of California chatter ("I feel good about myself") that has been parodied so often before. Hers is the traditional but always enjoyable role—the Judy Holliday role—of the beautiful, dumb broad who outsmarts everybody else in the end. Why and how she does it must be kept secret, but the scene . . . is a gem.

The plot, such as it is, is concerned largely with the strain of sexual attraction between actress and writer that runs beneath all the guff. . . . Mr. Reynolds' *Yanks 3 Detroit 0 Top of the Seventh,* in 1975, showed him to be a true, original humorist and a born playwright, and that makes *Geniuses* all the more disappointing. (pp. 102, 104)

> Edith Oliver, "On Location," *in* The New Yorker, Vol. LVIII, No. 14, May 24, 1982, pp. 102, 104.*

EDITH OLIVER

[*Geniuses*] is a very trying exercise in facetiousness that somehow pulls itself together in the third act. . . . The action takes place in a small village in the Philippines, where a movie that, as described, resembles *Apocalypse Now* is being shot, and where its scriptwriter, art director, makeup man, and an actress . . . are trapped for four days during a typhoon. They while away the time with some of the most tiresome talk imaginable—monologues that sound like recycled comedy routines, on such dog-eared subjects as Los Angeles versus New York, the Actors Studio, and West Coast psychotherapy in all its manifold guises, most of this stuff being poured out with ab-

VARIETY

Imagine *Boy Meets Girl* crossbred with *Rain* and brought up to date and you'll have some idea of *Geniuses,* a blisteringly funny satire by Jonathan Reynolds about Hollywood lunacy. . . .

Not many years ago a comedy like *Geniuses* would have been produced on Broadway with name performers and would have earned a solid run. Since almost nobody will produce a new play directly for Broadway now, enterprising nonprofit theatres . . . occasionally fall heir to skillfully written, fully developed works of high professional merit, as distinct from the interesting but technically gauche plays that make up most nonprofit schedules.

Geniuses is a fullblown surprise, a finely crafted piece of satirical yockery, with fully dimensioned characters, funny dialog, an intriguing plot and meaningful thematic underpinnings. It's in the dormant Broadway satirical farce tradition of Kaufman and Hart, Hecht and MacArthur and the Spewacks. It may not be on the same plane of accomplishment as those antecedents and obvious influences, but it still warrants comparison.

Geniuses unfolds against the backdrop of a Hollywood African war epic being filmed in the Philippines, a setting presumably inspired by *Apocalypse Now*. (The fictitious film is titled *Parabola of Death*). The characters include a panicked screenwriter who's under pressure to devise an ending for the film, a voluptuous starlet a la Billie Dawn, a cynical veteran film makeup expert, an emotionally unbalanced art director and the gleamingly self-confident young director.

When a typhoon shuts down production and confines all the characters except the director to their jungle motel, cabin fever accelerates their professional tensions and there's an outpouring of frustration, most of it in the form of hilarious exchanges about the film business, Los Angeles lifestyles, tropical food and sexual politics. Reynolds has a talent for daffy but accurate character jokes, and his darts are tipped with acid.

The farcical tone is put aside at the end of the second act when the brooding art director becomes unhinged and beats up the sexy actress. Her revenge makes up most of the third act, and it's a brilliantly sustained comic scene. The only noteworthy fault is an unexpected and unconvincing ending in which the screenwriter steps out of character. . . .

Playwrights of Reynolds' comic talent are all too rare in today's theatre, and if Dustin Hoffman, Morgan Fairchild and Edward Asner could be recruited for a Broadway production, *Geniuses* could run for years. As it is, it cries out for a commercial moveover to another off-Broadway house, has definite feature film potential and should be a perennial earner in nonprofit theatre and stock.

> *Humm., in a review of "Geniuses," in* Variety, *May 26, 1982, p. 80.*

WALTER KERR

[*Geniuses*] is, roughly speaking, a satirical comedy about moviemaking. I use the phrase "roughly speaking" advisedly, because Mr. Reynolds's play eventually begins to speak—and to behave—very roughly indeed, especially for a piece that first presents itself as lightminded parody. Furthermore, the kind of moviemaking that is getting its head kicked in here has nothing to do with Hollywood sound stages or the West Coast's old-fashioned ways. It has to do with the much newer fashion of going halfway around the world . . . to make portentously titled spectacles . . . about suitably catastrophic events . . .

complete with helicopters, typhoons that tear down half the scenery and directors with three names. . . .

If *Geniuses* is describing a radical change in the way millions of dollars can be wasted to no great purpose, it is also taking note—sometimes very funny note—of the qualities of mind possessed by the creative folk who make such smashing bloopers. We have, of course, been entertained by satirical stage thrusts at the great enemy, Film, before. We've had good caricatures and bad, artful nose-thumbing and labored gouging. But virtually all of the theater's lampoons of film have, until now, had one thing in common. They have presented the people who make films as idiots. Nice idiots, perhaps. Likeable idiots, at least half the time. Monsters, occasionally. But whatever they've been, they've been dummies, misfits, incompetents all—whether they were amiable or not. *Geniuses* switches that completely around.

Each of its luckless lunatics possesses a considerable intelligence, native or acquired. Even when the harassed scriptwriter, interrupted in his chores by a colleague given to random philosophizing, lifts his head to utter a lofty "I think we are in the presence of a profound chowderhead," we know from the phrasing and from the choice of epithet that we are in an updated milieu with a gamy ambiance all its own. There are no real chowderheads here, in these flimsily run-up shacks with thatched roofs, there is something far, far stranger. . . .

[There's] an eerie streak of intelligence in the act of ripping a sheet of paper from a typewriter. The screenwriter has rolled paper in, typed a few lines, ripped the paper out and torn it up. He's done it a second time, typed a bit, ripped and crumpled. He has then put in the third empty sheet, stared at it for one second, and torn it out and destroyed it without sullying its virgin blankness. Up to a point that's a gag, and we laugh. But we laugh beyond the gag, we laugh more than a mere gag would have warranted, because we understand what has happened. The writer wasn't being simply capricious. The instant he put that sheet into the machine he saw the words that were going to go onto it, and they were hogwash. He was only being reasonable.

As I say, one way or another these makers of the dream have brains and have been known to use them—down to and including the blond centerfold girl who's being paid a great deal of money to do a naked 30-second walkthrough, in which case, what's the new target? Intelligence is. The intelligence they actually possess, the intelligence that's being put to such unintelligent use, the intelligence that's being wasted just as all the money is being wasted, the intelligence that's been dislocated and hurts like a wrenched elbow or a bad knee.

These people are bright enough to know when they're using a cliché, to know that they *can* be ridiculed, to know how to catch the dart that's going to be flung at them and heave it back before it's drawn any blood. They know where they're vulnerable. They can make the joke first. And they *can't* stop the tidal wave of stupidity that they themselves have set in motion and that is overwhelming them right now.

This is obviously a complex and difficult thing for a satirist to set up. Get it right and you will have comedy on the double; the comedy of the gaffe, and the comedy of the good mind that made it. Playwright Reynolds doesn't always get it right. He takes rather too long to get his story line rolling, letting most of the company sit around idly while screenwriter and sexpot establish themselves by trading insults; the inactivity seems even odder when you consider that the typhoon is due to strike any minute. . . . The comic level wavers every now and then. But sometimes it's not so much wavering as it is deferring to a new and interestingly offbeat tone that's coming along, underground. (p. 3)

Walter Kerr, " 'Geniuses' Is Winning Satire," in The New York Times, *May 30, 1982, pp. 3, 24.*

JOHN SIMON

[The characters in *Geniuses*] are in equal measure geniuses and maniacs, which is what makes them so amusing, endearing, scary, and related to us. The scene is a village hut 200 miles north of Manila and considerably closer to nowhere, a locale that stands in for Angola, about which the boy-wonder movie director Milo McGee McGarr is shooting a multi-million-dollar war epic, *Parabola of Death.* . . .

What we get is a thoroughly funny farce about Hollywood away from home, when it tends to behave even worse; about the sensitive but absurd writer, Jocko Pyle, whose highbrow East Coast values are in acrimonious conflict with those of the West Coast Eldorado, off which he is trying to make some bittersweet bucks; about the broader clash of East and West, as the movielanders confront and all but founder on the chaotic but cunning ways of the Filipinos . . . ; about the power plays in the realms of fame, wealth, and sex that sap the churning out of this lagging superproduction.

Lagging indeed, because Jocko tears up sheets of manuscript as fast as he can type them, and sometimes, in despair, even before he has typed them. Lagging also because in a particularly costly battle sequence none of the Philippine army helicopters was in frame, the appropriate palms (the greedy, not the leafy, kind) having been left ungreased. And about to lag even more because a typhoon is bent on destroying the sets built by the irascible and sadistic Eugene Winter—a typhoon that also threatens Eugene himself, Jocko, Winston, the ace makeup man Bart Keely . . . , and Skye Bullene, the blond sexpot, former *Playboy* playmate, current McGarr bedmate, soon to be a 30-second nude walk-on in this major movie. All of them are sardined, or piranhaed, together in this hazardous, typhoon-battered hut, into which the odd, peremptory radio message from Milo in his private helicopter penetrates to spread further disarray. Milo himself doesn't alight till Act III, but then with enough ominous *désinvolture* to put a basilisk on his guard.

Reynolds has wrought a highly civilized satire that stays almost consistently in high gear, even while its freewheeling ways manage to roll over and flatten everything from est and its likes to the prose style of Papa Hemingway. But it also has more serious implications as it chronicles the rise to power of Skye Bullene from sexy blonde, cultureless and cultist ("If it's been worshiped, I've done it!"), to impending movie mogul, or examines the wising up of Jocko Pyle, from sarcastically compulsive truth-teller to (at least partial) accepter of the world as it is and of cookies as they crumble you. Sometimes, as at the end of Act II, the play becomes a bit too straightforwardly grave for its devious levity, but comic disorder is soon enough restored.

There are moments of letdown: New York-versus-Los Angeles jokes, for example, have a way of sounding tired even when they are freshly and adroitly minted. . . . Yet all is forgiven when such rollicking characters as Skye take over, or Bart, the wizard of many-hued bruises and wounds, who measures the

artistry of a film in the number of gashes, slashes, and gory demises. (p. 92)

"We are in hell!" is the last line of one of Jocko's endless attempts at an ending, after which the hapless scenarist reads out: "Dissolve to the Holocaust. THE END." In *Geniuses,* we too are in a hell of predatory proximities, mitigated however by peals of parabolic laughter; no cure, but the loveliest of palliatives. (p. 93)

John Simon, "Footnotes to the Apocalypse," in New York *Magazine, Vol. 15, No. 22, May 31, 1982, pp. 92-4.**

ROBERT BRUSTEIN

If anything as amorphous as American drama can be said to have a shape, it is possible to detect a pattern in the new plays of the 1980s; at least, a number of their authors share similar values, characteristics, and backgrounds. . . . What unites them is a wry, jaded, urban sensibility, and a fascination with their own college-educated, over-psychoanalyzed, media-saturated generation. The dexterity with which they perform sociological CAT-scans suggests that they are also the children of Jules Feiffer and Garry Trudeau, though they have yet to show the interest of their mentors in moral or political issues.

The school of playwrights I am describing includes, among others, Christopher Durang (*Beyond Therapy*), Wendy Wasserstein (*Uncommon Women and Others*), Ted Talley (*Coming Attractions*), James Lapine (*Table Settings*), and Debbie Eisenberg (*Pastorale*), all of them writing in a cogent, amusing, often acid style. To this list we can now add the name of Jonathan Reynolds, whose new play, *Geniuses,* is on its way to another theater after a successful debut. . . . [Based on circumstances surrounding *Apocalypse Now*], the plague-ridden movie [*Parabola of Death*] is being shot in a small village in the Philippines; when the play begins it is clear why it is so far over budget. The screenwriter is demolishing his typewriter because he can't think up an ending, the art director is shooting crippled water buffalo, the Playboy bunny has dysentery, the makeup man is wrestling with the delusion that he is Ernest Hemingway, and the set is being battered by a typhoon.

These are the ingredients of farce, and for the first two acts Reynolds displays the manipulative skills of a literate farceur—Ben Hecht with an honors degree in English. The play seems like a rewrite of *Twentieth Century,* its subject being the capricious rule of imperial "genius" directors—today invested with the means to create their own nations, even their own wars. What this playwright tells us is that the contemporary American film world is significant not as an arm of culture, but rather as an extension of venture capitalism, possibly even an alternative form of government. For Reynolds's bankable prodigy, Milo McGee McGarr, "the deal is the only exciting thing about making a movie—five points, ten cases of Guinness, my own chopper." In short, the prime dividend of films is *making* money—not having it or spending it: "There is nothing as creative or romantic as business in America."

Reynolds regards this with a detached air, alternately awed and amused by the monster he has uncovered. He is equally neutral toward Milo's cowering, typhoon-locked underlings—particularly Jocko, the screenwriter—as they scurry about trying to hold onto their jobs, their Stolichnaya, and the half-exposed buttocks of Skye, the Playboy bunny with whom they share their wicker quarters. Skye's tempting *pulkes* motivate the only action in the play. A quintessential West Coast loony, having gone through EST, actualization, and primal screaming before being converted to "wattage therapy," she has a passion for her place of origin exceeded only by Jocko's contempt for it ("I don't hate L.A. where the smog creeps in on little rat's feet"). Their arguments over the relative merits of the two coasts form the basis for a witty, if somewhat loquacious, sexual debate. But the plot grows darker when Skye is badly beaten by the sadistic art director whose advances she has spurned.

Although Skye's colorfully bruised face is hugely admired by the makeup man (he is always looking for fresh inspiration), it is potentially dangerous to Milo when that worthy finally makes his appearance late in the play. He needs his art director; she wants to imprison him for life. The impasse is broken with a deal. In return for a huge sum of money (tax-free), a part in Milo's next picture, the privilege of pummeling the art director's private parts, and the possibility of becoming the next president of Paramount, she agrees to return to her beloved Pismo Beach—and Jocko, abandoning the picture before he is fired from it, agrees to meet her there for three glorious days of sex and wattage therapy.

With its frenetic pace and rough masculine banter, *Geniuses* never quite decides whether it wants to be social satire or commercial farce, the movie of *M*A*S*H** or its incarnation as a television series. . . . [The] ambiguity of attitude plunges the play into a moral vacuum—an uncertainty of tone so typical of the playwrights of the 1980s, so reflective of their confused, unanchored world. (pp. 23-4)

> Robert Brustein, "The Shape of the New," in The New Republic, *Vol. 187, No. 2, July 12, 1982, pp. 23-4.**

RICHARD GILMAN

Geniuses has received a number of enthusiastic notices, but I find myself unable to climb on the bandwagon. Jonathan Reynolds's spoof of Hollywood movie makers has moments of wit and a degree of raw energy, but for the most part it struck me as possessing the comic force of a TV sitcom. The problem with satires of the movie industry is, of course, the obviousness of the target, and *Geniuses* does nothing to overcome this handicap. Clichés pounce upon clichés; stock situations are treated with stock comedic means; familiar foolishness meets with familiar put-downs.

The play's specific objects of satire are Francis Ford Coppola and the making of *Apocalypse Now*. . . . There is a good deal of contempt expressed for the host country—"the worst country in the world," someone calls it—which makes for an impression of smart-alecky sophistication. My identification with the proceedings was severely hampered by lines like, "Should I pack these typewriter ribbons or leave them for the natives to eat?"

While not always so obnoxious, Reynolds's humor almost never rises above one-liners. . . . A melancholy thought came to me as I left the theater: the minds and souls of the people who set out today to satirize the denizens of Hollywood or California or Madison Avenue are, with a few exceptions, precisely the same as those of their targets. That wasn't true of Jonathan Swift or, closer to home and to the subject, Nathanael West. (pp. 154-55)

> Richard Gilman, in a review of "Geniuses," *in* The Nation, *Vol. 235, No. 5, August 21-28, 1982, pp. 154-55.**

JOHN SIMON

In *Fighting International Fat,* Jonathan Reynolds, the gifted author of *Geniuses, Rubbers,* and other funny works, set himself two overwhelming handicaps. First, he wrote a one-joke play. It concerns the efforts of Roz Gambol, the founder of Fighting International Fat, an organization using unconventional methods for reducing, to get a few of her ex-fatties on Shep Bradley Diedricksen's immensely popular TV show. In this she is hampered by the unruliness of her flock, the jadedness and egoism of Shep (even seducing him yields only middling receptivity), and the unexpected appearance of a powerful and unscrupulous rival, D. Raleigh Bell, a former behemoth turned svelte and gorgeous through surgery: 38 operations both cosmetic and intestinal. Raleigh, who also has political ambitions, tempts Roz's faithful with a board groaning under a profusion of goodies and countless calories, prearranged surgery for all, and the freedom thereafter to gorge themselves, what with plastic, hermetically sealed entrails. She even steals Shep from Roz, catering to some of his kinkier appetites—sexual, not gustatory.

Roz and Raleigh, a good and an evil angel locked in combat for human bodies, not souls, is a basically funny but single-joke idea. It can never get very far from eating, despite detours into sex, politics, Canadians, Phil Donahue . . . , and some other "serious" subjects Reynolds injects into all that ingestion. But there is, unavoidably, a surfeit of food jokes, and somewhere between *ab ovo* and *usque ad mala,* the auditorium threatens to become a vomitorium.

The second handicap Reynolds imposed on himself is a play without characters, only caricatures, so as to allow absurdity to reign supreme. But even these sundry walking eccentricities or dementednesses are not developed to a sufficiently involving degree of zaniness to elicit that second-degree empathy reserved for successful farce. For a moment, the French Canadian F.I.F. member, Jacques LaFace, does take off into true farcical vitality with a redolent tirade of self-loathing . . . , but no other passage has the same density.

[*Fighting International Fat*] is a bright idea that goes nowhere and has no real passengers: a Grumman bus stuffed with grotesque dummies. There are not a few funny lines . . . , but there is no barrage of steady wit and not enough of that comic choreography, that bombarding with sight gags, the nerves and muscles of farce. Sure, the author was after bigger things than mere farce—social, even political satire—but these aquiline aspirations cannot make it on passerine wings. Still, *Fighting International Fat* is by no means a total failure; call it a Pyrrhic defeat. (p. 76)

> John Simon, "Nice Tries," *in* New York Magazine, *Vol. 18, No. 24, June 17, 1985, pp. 76-8.**

EDITH OLIVER

[*Fighting International Fat*] is an attempt at satire (target: evangelism, a plum ripe for the picking) which doesn't work, partly because Mr. Reynolds lets his comic ideas run away with him—not that there are enough of them to sustain the play's two acts in any case. International Fat Fighters, a group under the leadership of one Rosalind Gambol, is dedicated to losing weight by "obsessional self-denial;" when the play opens, the members are rehearsing their confessional material, much of it as disgusting and lurid as possible, for a television talk show whose m.c. is about to audition them. The m.c., Shep, is unimpressed by the candidates but more than impressed by Rosalind. The immediate sexual interlude that follows is very funny, and he changes his mind. Changes it for a few minutes, that is—until the entrance of the slim and beautiful D. Raleigh Bell . . . , formerly a Rosalind Gambol disciple but now an equally dedicated advocate of weight loss by surgery, who is determined to win away Miss Gambol's acolytes. The dramatist outdoes himself in his description of the thirty-some operations Miss Bell underwent to remove unwanted tissue from her person. Another, far flakier sexual interlude follows with the eager Shep. The two weight-loss experts proselytize the disciples, who move first one way, then the other. And that's all there is. Nevertheless, in spite of Mr. Reynolds' skimpy material and his self-indulgence—he never brings his script into focus or allows his points to register—there is true originality here, and humor, too. Much of the humor is in the weight-losers, my favorite of them being a peculiar Canadian loner, the only man in the bunch. . . .

> *Edith Oliver, in a review of "Fighting International Fat," in* The New Yorker, *Vol. LXI, No. 17, June 17, 1985, p. 118.*

EILEEN BLUMENTHAL

The energy that otherwise reasonable people put into their feeding habits, and the amount of punishment that we inflict on ourselves, obviously has to do with more than appetite or even vanity. Jonathan Reynolds's cartoony parody, *Fighting International Fat*, attacks obsessions with food and "looks-ism" as abdications of self-responsibility, as attempts at neurotic self-control—but always as forms of total narcissism. . . .

If Reynolds's themes are not exactly new, his gloss on them is sharp. And he has some neat plot twists at the end. Still, while a would-be madcap comedy need not exactly follow logic, these characters' behavior is *too* random. Roz prompts her auditionees to tell Shep the most grotesquely humiliating true confessions; then she criticizes him for expecting people to bare their pasts for him. One former fattie insists on telling Shep how she and Roz were lovers, saying he needs to know this and is too dense to figure it out himself; having sparked his interest, she immediately says that he's nuts if he thinks she'll say that on the air.

More important, while claiming to criticize TV trivializations, Reynolds constructs his play like a dopey TV sitcom. His auditionees are a smorgasbord of clichés—bad-tempered old lady, rich Jew, Midwestern wimp. Much of the humor is on the order of Mrs. Rapkin using Yiddish words. There is a wonderful nationalistically defensive tirade by a Canadian disciple of IFF, but it has virtually nothing to do with the themes of this work, and could have been patched in from another play.

Partaking of values he claims to criticize is not a new problem for Reynolds. His *Geniuses,* supposedly exposing lust for violence and power, wound up on the verge of celebrating it, showing the alternative as victimization, which is even less attractive. *International Fat* also shares *Geniuses*'s ugliness of spirit, presenting a world filled only with people who are unbalanced, self-obsessed, and often downright deranged.

> *Eileen Blumenthal, "Cellulite Comedy," in* The Village Voice, *Vol. XXX, No. 25, June 18, 1985, p. 110.*

Ntozake Shange
1948-

(Born Paulette Williams) American dramatist, novelist, poet, and essayist.

Shange is best known for her innovative play *for colored girls who have considered suicide / when the rainbow is enuf* (1975). In this, as in much of her work, Shange draws upon her personal experiences as a black woman to passionately express her concerns with racial, political, and feminist issues. She reveals her characters through loosely structured sketches that illuminate their dilemmas without providing formal characterization. Shange's keen ear for black American idioms, as recreated in the rhythms and nuances of the language of her characters, informs her work with vitality and authenticity. Doris Grumbach observed that Shange "is a mistress of the color, shape and ringing, accurate imagery of [her characters'] thought and their speech."

Shange's first play, *for colored girls who have considered suicide / when the rainbow is enuf*, was originally produced off-Broadway. This "choreopoem," as Shange described it, is a cycle of poems combined with music and dance. Shange explores the sufferings and joys of seven black American women and rejoices in their ability to share and overcome their sorrows. Shange was faulted for her unsympathetic treatment of black men, who are depicted as obstacles to the social and spiritual freedom of black women. However, most critics viewed the play as an affirmation of a people's will to survive. Toni Cade Bambara stated that Shange "celebrates the capacity to master pain and betrayals with wit, sister-sharing, reckless daring, and flight and forgetfulness if necessary. She celebrates most of all women's loyalties to women."

Shange's numerous other plays include *Spell #7* (1979) and her adaptation of Bertolt Brecht's *Mother Courage and Her Children* (1980). *Spell #7* is set in an after-hours bar peopled by a group of black theatrical performers. Through poetic vignettes blended with song and dance, Shange explores her characters' feelings on being black in America. *Spell #7* is structurally and thematically similar to *for colored girls who have considered suicide / when the rainbow is enuf,* but it relies more on such conventional elements as dialogue and plot development. Like much of her work, Shange's adaptation of *Mother Courage and Her Children* met with mixed reviews. Shange moves the play's setting from seventeenth-century Europe to the post-Civil War United States, and she portrays Mother Courage as a black woman selling her wares during the battles between United States Cavalry units and American Indians.

In her volumes of poetry, *nappy edges* (1978) and *A Daughter's Geography* (1983), Shange also explores racial, sexual, feminist, and political themes. Critics consistently praise her skillful and surprising use of language as well as her powerfully expressive poetic voice.

In 1977 Shange published *Sassafrass: A Novella,* which was later expanded into her first novel, *Sassafrass, Cypress & Indigo* (1982). In this work Shange focuses on three sisters and their mother living in Charleston, South Carolina. Shange combines lyrical language with a rich evocation of various cultural

Photograph by Val Wilmer

milieus in depicting her characters' struggles for self-fulfillment in an often hostile society. Shange's second novel, *Betsey Brown* (1985), is a semiautobiographical work set in St. Louis during the late 1950s, when that city began to integrate its schools. Betsey is a thirteen-year-old black girl who enjoys a comfortable home life. When she is bused to an integrated school across town, she becomes aware of differences between blacks and whites. Shange is concerned with Betsey's reconciliation of her cultural heritage and her new environment. In reviewing this work Nancy Willard stated: "Despite the problems it confronts, [*Betsey Brown*] is a healing book and a loving celebration of the differences that make us human."

(See also *CLC,* Vols. 8, 25; *Contemporary Authors,* Vols. 85-88; and *Dictionary of Literary Biography,* Vol. 38.)

DORIS GRUMBACH

"Colored" Hilda Effanie has three daughters with husband Alfred: [the title characters of *Sassafrass, Cypress & Indigo*]. They live in Charleston, South Carolina. Indigo is a mad little "girl-child," just turned 12 and silent except with her dolls to whom she talks and who talk to her. She has too much "South in her"; she believes in the magic of her beloved Aunt Haydee the midwife; she thinks her dolls are alive and talking to her as she talks to them; briefly she becomes a member of a motorcycle gang. Her older sister Sassafras is, like her mother, a skilled artisan in weaving and making hangings, a free spirit who gravitates to the West Coast, forms a faithful alliance with a n'er-do-well lover Mitch and becomes a deeply believing member of the spiritual New World Collective. And Cypress, a trained dancer, goes to New York, loves both men and women, experiences black, exciting, violent New York City, and dreams of black women's liberation, for herself, her mother, her ancestors.

Shange is the author of the successful play, *for colored girls who have considered suicide when the rainbow is enuf* (1975), a moving work full of choral poetry and genuine evocation of feminine black experience. In 1978 she published a volume of poetry, with some prose, called *nappy edges,* a book dedicated to the same three sisters whose names form the title of this her first novel. The play and the poetry might have prepared us for the beauty and force of *Sassafrass, Cypress & Indigo.* Shange is primarily a poet, with a blood-red sympathy for and love of her people, their folk as well as their sophisticated ways, their innocent, loving goodness as much as their lack of immunity to powerful evil. She is a mistress of the color, shape and ringing, accurate imagery of their thought and their speech.

But her voice in this novel is entirely her own, an original, spare and primary-colored sound that will remind readers of Jean Toomer's *Cane*. (p.1)

Shange is a unique lyric singer whose voice is very seldom high-pitched or raucous; always it is modulated into a poetic, orchestrated sound that is not so much characteristic of fiction as it is the vocal quality of poetry. Into her narrative potpourri she tosses all the graphic elements of southern black life: wonderful recipes (or so they seem to me, a noncook), spells and potions (how to rid oneself of the scent of evil), prescriptions (how to care for open wounds when they hurt), letters (from Mama to her beloved but straying and erring daughters, full of calm reason and uncritical love, always advising accommodation to the hostility and blindness of the white world). Mama says to the picture of her dead husband at the end: "You know, Al, I did the best I could, but I don't think they want what we wanted." They are once again together at home: Sassafras to bear Mitch's child; Indigo, taking the dead Aunt Haydee's place, to deliver the child; Cypress to massage her birthing sister. And of course, Mama is there.

Shange's gift lies in her ability to convey the texture both of simple and of sophisticated life, in a kind of shorthand laced with uncannily appropriate imagery. (pp. 1-2)

Whatever Shange turns her hand to she does well, even to potions and recipes. A white reader feels the exhilarating shock of discovery at being permitted entry into this world she couldn't have known; a black reader must experience a most satisfying shock of recognition at encountering Shange's poetic-real world. (p. 2)

> Doris Grumbach, "*Ntozake Shange's Trio*," in *Book World—The Washington Post, August 22, 1982, pp. 1-2.*

SUSAN SLOCUM HINERFELD

[*Sassafrass, Cypress & Indigo* is] made of written spoken words, colloquial in both dialogue and narrative. Shange has a play-

wright's ear. The spoken word is her manna, and her dialogue is wondrous, but her narrative is sometimes faltering and foolish.

This is a crowded novel, filled with people and their sound, their slang: the provincial speech patterns of Carolinians who are mostly black and poor, the trade talk of black musicians, the assertive statements of black lesbians, the patter of true believers, the jargon of art and ballet, the patois of illiterates; the varied and mixed tongues of people caught between idioms, between styles, between cultures and classes. Shange's special genius is that voices arise from the babble: individual, eccentric and true. . . .

Of all voices in this book, Hilda Effania's is sweetest, most consistent, most clearly motivated. What she wants is her daughters' happiness. What she offers is love and good sense. What she says reflects precisely who she is: a black woman rooted in Charleston, but a black woman with a trade, with dealings in business, with responsibilities; a woman who consults only herself and the spirit of her husband to reach her decisions; a woman of feeling and discipline.

Hilda Effania sounds sometimes homely, sometimes worldly, sometimes old-fashioned. At times she makes herself sound surer than she is. But she always sounds purely herself. . . .

Shange meets the problem of setting down dialect head-on: ". . . Who's that ya got witcha?," ". . . I haveta grow up, my dolls don't haveta." Her "and" is an ampersand: "You & me," in a curious and complex substitution: The ampersand, a written symbol, somehow looks less formal and more speech-like than the literal form "and." (In another game of conversion, Cypress embroiders choreographic notations, and Sassafrass, canny for once, says ". . . If the white folks knew you were doin' this, they'd steal all of it and put it in a museum!") . . .

What Shange has to say can't, it seems, be contained in old baggage: The narrative breaks for recipes, for announcements and invitations, for a dream of Cypress' and for Sassafrass' poetry, for Indigo's formulas, for excruciating recitals of Cypress' reactions to dance, to art. . . .

What's unsettling about this book is a lack of synchrony of its parts—and the fact that the lack of synchrony may only reflect the black experience in America.

> Susan Slocum Hinerfeld, "*A Poet's Crowded Colloquial Novel of Black and Poor Carolinian Women,*" in *Los Angeles Times Book Review, August 22, 1982, p. 2.*

SUSAN ISAACS

Ntozake Shange's first novel [*Sassafrass, Cypress and Indigo*] reads like the product of a collaboration among a gifted poet, a trendy revolutionary and a social director at a California resort. Sassafrass, Cypress and Indigo, the three sisters of the title, are introduced as young girls, and the reader is charmed by them as well as by the gracefulness of the introduction. Miss Shange's language is rich and economical and the three characters are compelling both as individuals and as personifications of black culture and the feminist spirit. But as their world begins to widen, the writing starts to deteriorate. When the sisters leave the protection of their mother—the best-drawn character in the book—they drift into relationships so banal they seem no more substantial than mist over a redwood hot tub.

Sassafrass, Cypress and Indigo are the children of a Charleston, S.C., weaver, Hilda Effania; she is an adoring, no-nonsense, ambitious mother who wants only to see her children fulfilled, as long as their fulfillment occurs in a comfortably upper-middle-class setting. (p. 12)

Her daughters, however, are not drawn to church suppers and Thursday night bridge games. Comfortable conventionality is not for them. Nor apparently is it for Miss Shange. . . . *Sassafrass, Cypress and Indigo* is no simple expository work of fiction about a group of young women seeking their places in society. Although her subject is a familiar one, not unlike that of novelists from Jane Austen to Mary McCarthy to Rona Jaffe, Miss Shange does not move her characters along a plotted line past standard cultural landmarks. Instead she combines narrative with italicized passages of poetry, magical incantations, dreams, recipes, letters and theatrical criticism in what seems to be nothing less than an attempt to capture the essence and the glory of black culture.

She sometimes succeeds. A few lines of poetry say more about Cypress' decision to abandon classical ballet for an Afro-American dance group than pages of prose: ". . . / challenge the contradiction of perfected pirouette with the sly knowin of hips that do-right / stretch till all the stars n sands of all our lands abandoned / mingle in the wet heat / sweat & grow warm / must be she the original aboriginal dancin girl." (pp. 12-13)

But sometimes the writing is startlingly superficial. Sassafrass, a weaver like her mother, falls in love with Mitch, a tenor-saxophone player who is also an ex-convict and ex-junkie. The evocation of her joy, however, would not have been credible even in Haight-Ashbury in 1967: "Sassafrass was so full of love she couldn't call anybody anything without bringing good vibes from a whole lot of spirits to everything she touched." Nor can the reader comprehend Sassafrass' devotion, for Mitch is a cad and a bully. (p. 13)

Indigo, the youngest daughter, is a spinner of spells, both a magician and musician so sensitive her fiddle can capture a person's individual pitch, play it, even elaborate on it. It's an intriguing idea, but it fails because although the author tries to present Indigo as a wise innocent, a mystical power, a joyous embodiment of the black spirit, the rhetoric of her musings is earthbound radical-feminist, predictable and silly. . . . (pp. 13, 16)

And if Indigo's black magic is real, if she can banish her mother's overbearing white employer by conjuring up a wind to blow the woman out the door, how can she and her people—a people with such potent magic—tolerate the evils the author catalogues so movingly? . . . If the magic is metaphor, or Indigo's fantasy, or the author's evocation of African or black American folklore, it is not presented with enough clarity. The reader remains mildly fond of Indigo—people who talk to dolls can be enchanting—but is nonetheless befuddled about her role in the novel.

The reader with a knowledge of African and black American history and arts will probably get more from this novel than the reader who lacks it, for Miss Shange's work is rich in references to these cultures. But the author seems to go a step further. In a poem about dance, she implies that whites will not understand black art: ". . . / it's how we remember what cannot be said / that's why the white folks say it aint got no

form / what was the form of slavery / what was the form of jim crow / & how wd they know . . ."

When Ntozake Shange's art is accessible it can be good. Her Christmas morning at Hilda Effania's is a triumph of warmth and intelligence, and the episode in which Sassafrass responds to a trio of black male chauvinists is a dramatic marvel. Like Hilda and Sassafrass, Miss Shange sometimes loses a thread and makes a mess. When she's weaving well, however, her fiction is very fine indeed. (p. 16)

Susan Isaacs, "Three Sisters," in The New York Times Book Review, *September 12, 1982, pp. 12-13, 16.*

ESTHER COHEN

Sassafrass, Cypress & Indigo is more like a pastiche, a collage of elements taken from a highly textured existence, than it is a novel. In fact, the strong sense the book gives is that the reader is not reading but seeing pictures, hearing voices, watching an unusual narrative presentation.

While the imagery is indeed potent, and much of the language is compelling, the narrative problems are great. In a way, it's as though Shange is asking us to see what the lives of those black women look like onstage, but not to participate vicariously in the lives: We don't become emotionally involved with the women because they are shown more as exotic bits and pieces than evolving, real people. She makes it possible for us to see them, but not to understand. Her writing is not explanatory: She doesn't tell us why Sassafrass, for instance, insists on staying with Mitch even though he is destructive, why she is compelled suddenly to lead a spiritual life, why she spends her life weaving. Nor does she explain why Cypress moves from women to men.

In separate stretches, in paragraphs here and there, Shange's writing overtakes any objections, and the power of her language is enough. Overall, though, the novel doesn't hold together. Even so, many of the fragments make the book worth reading.

Esther Cohen, "Three Sisters," in The Progressive, *Vol. 47, No. 1, January, 1983, p. 56.*

CHOICE

[Shange, in *A Daughter's Geography,* has] written a series of hard-hitting poems that show her daughter both the internal and external (Nicaragua, Haiti, Atlanta) geography that are her heritage. Many of the poems are fueled by Shange's anger, as in **"About Atlanta."** She writes of various kinds of men—macho, the flasher, obscene phone caller—with the same anger. But when she writes in the section titled **"From Okra to Greens / A Different Kinda Love Story"** she calls up images of her childhood and of black history to throw light on the present and some of the anger disappears. These poems would read well aloud: they have strong rhythms.

A review of "A Daughter's Geography," in Choice, *Vol. 21, No. 5, January, 1984, p. 708.*

HOLLY PRADO

Getting close to many poems in [*A Daughter's Geography*] is distinctly uncomfortable. Her strength is tension. Sometimes the tension is resolved—a breath of relief at the end of a poem.

But sometimes we're left with Shange's fear of being unseen as a black and as a woman; her fear for all blacks, for children. "We need a god who bleeds now / whose wounds are not the end of everything": a plea for vitality rather than invisibility. These poems have been performed. Their jazzy, oral quality must be great aloud. On the page, repetitions can dull, and images, as in the delightfully quirky "okra and greens" poems, can fuzz. Still, Shange has the heated energy of the subjects she struggles with. It's worth getting into the fire.

> *Holly Prado, in a review of "A Daughter's Geography," in* Los Angeles Times Book Review, *January 8, 1984, p. 9.*

KIRKUS REVIEWS

[*See No Evil: Prefaces, Essays & Accounts, 1976-1983* is a collection of very] slight credos and jottings.... Most substantial and eloquent is a brief essay on the lack of distinctive voices among black writers, in comparison to black musicians.... Elsewhere, Shange reprints the *for colored girls* preface, rails against white-audience racism, and recalls her experience in adapting Brecht's *Mother Courage* for Joseph Papp's Public Theater—moving the action to post-Civil War America. ("i now have no further need to experience intimately the thought processes of a great white dead writer....") There are reprises of her radical/feminist/black-separatist esthetics and—written in a more conventional style—uncritical reviews of black dance performances. Plus: political notes, in verse and shorthand prose, from Texas and Nicaragua—mostly simplistic, radical/sentimental, but with a few echoing lines. ("Everyone in Nicaragua can name at least one dead poet.") Disappointingly thin and repetitious work from a genuine talent, then, with only a few glimmers that show development rather than reiteration.

> *A review of "See No Evil: Prefaces, Essays, and Accounts 1976-1983," in* Kirkus Reviews, *Vol. LII, No. 5, March 1, 1984, p. 252.*

PUBLISHERS WEEKLY

Playwright Shange takes the title of [*See No Evil: Prefaces, Essays & Accounts, 1976-1983*] from her dedication to numerous goddesses, witches and her daughter: "We shall see no evil / We shall strangle it." This statement sets the tone for these strident writings.... Throughout, Shange is concerned with the interconnections among the various arts. Although the volume is slim, it takes some time to slog through Shange's writings.... Additionally, while one senses a powerful person behind the passionate issues discussed, Shange's language—for all its wrenching—remains flat and irritating rather than innovative and affecting.

> *A review of "See No Evil: Prefaces, Essays & Accounts, 1976-1983," in* Publishers Weekly, *Vol. 225, No. 11, March 16, 1984, p. 81.*

KARL KELLER

There are a couple of valuable ideas in this collection of brief writings by Ntozake Shange [*See No Evil: Prefaces, Essays and Accounts*]—a few program notes, fits and starts of ethnic aesthetics, catalogue of black performers and black performances and some poetry about Latin America—that redeem the book.

One, taken from Frantz Fanon, is called "combat breathing." Shange says that everything she has ever written and everything she hopes to write is an attempt to take in the country as a whole, a race as a whole, the daily pulsations of a whole people through the act of breathing itself—that is, through performances involving dance, mime, song, anything kinetic and alive, any body art. In "combat breathing," there is a war on old forms of art but no occupation of territory; there are individuals acting out the forms of their daily lives and yet no independence of persons.

As artist, one takes the energies of a people—in Shange's case, mainly the energies of black women—as a natural artistic form. On the stage, whether "smitten by my own language" in performed poetry or in dance with "the ethnicity of my thighs & backside" or improvising one's everyday body motions, her objective with "combat breathing" is to "clarify our lives—& the lives of our mothers, daughters & grandmothers—as women." Kinesis gives legitimacy to her vision. Body movement is art; body movement is politics....

Anything visceral is naturally art to her, for it comes from a black woman's body, it emerges from the daily lives of a people, it displaces dead European forms in theater and poetry, and it gains acceptance of "black personal reality."...

Another valuable Shange idea is in the form of a plea. She feels that as a black female performer / playwright / poet, she has wanted "to attack deform n maim the language that i waz taught to hate myself in. I have to take it apart to the bone." This she feels can be done if writing can come close to what has made black music such a successful art form if audiences will accept a new visceral black theater and poetry with the same ear they have accepted black music. "You cd imagine us like music & makes us yrs." We give the musicians more space to run with, she claims, more personal legitimacy than we give writers." If you take us as seriously as you take a saxophone, maybe we'll have decades of poems you'll never forget."...

Yet Shange does not go far in exploring these two good ideas. She is too brief, too scattered, too piecemeal. If she means it when she says, "Our lives depend on this," then let us hear far more of the anger, the ideas, the music.

> *Karl Keller, "A Performing Playwright / Poet Who Records the Pulse of a People," in* Los Angeles Times Book Review, *July 29, 1984, p. 4.*

NANCY WILLARD

Growing up isn't easy for the 13-year old heroine of Ntozake Shange's second novel, *Betsey Brown:* "Gosh, she wished her mother understood there was so much in the world to feel and see." Miss Shange writes, "A girl had to get out of the house and into the thick of life, the heat of it, not knowing what all one could do with whoever you happened to be." Betsey happens to be a black girl coming of age in St. Louis in 1959, the year that city began to integrate its schools. The thick and the heat of life are the very fabric of this novel, which revolves around an eccentric and marvelous black family. Betsey's father, Greer, is a doctor. He wakes the children with conga drums in the morning and quizzes them on black history. His wife, Jane, a social worker, is trying to raise four of her own children and one of her sister's, run the household, and sort out her own identity—"be who she was when Greer first courted her, a lady of intellect, mystery and surprises." While the parents make love in the morning, the grandmother frets about the children. "Four chirren and God only knew how many more. Please, Lord, no more. Thy Bounty is Mightily Received."

Miss Shange's descriptions of life in the large, rambling house brilliantly evoke children's longings for secrecy. . . . To Betsey, growing up means giving up her secret perch in the tree where she listens "for her city to sing to her so she could respond." The children help each other, fight each other, dream, tie shoes, set fires, fall in love and ask questions. "Why did she have to take three different buses to learn the same things with white children that she'd been learning with colored children?" Betsey wonders. "Why didn't the white children come to her school? . . . Why did the Negroes have to do everything the hard way? Why weren't they good enough already?"

Does this book have some kind of ax to grind? Thank heaven, no, though Miss Shange's characters confront plenty of problems and sometimes flee them. . . .

Miss Shange is a superb storyteller who keeps her eye on what brings her characters together rather than what separates them: courage and love, innocence and the loss of it, home and homelessness. Miss Shange understands backyards, houses, schools and churches. *Betsey Brown* rejoices in—but never sentimentalizes—those places on earth where you are accepted, where you are comfortable with yourself. . . .

Leaving home for an integrated school brings the differences between black and white into sharp focus for all the children. "They weren't nearly as bad as I thought they'd be," says Betsey. "But they're not like us. . . . They don't talk the same. It's almost like going to another country." And yet, despite the problems it confronts, this is a healing book and a loving celebration of the differences that make us human. As one character puts it, "You are different and it's not the color of your skin, either." . . .

More straightforward and less idiosyncratic than Miss Shange's first novel, *Sassafrass, Cypress & Indigo, Betsey Brown* creates a place that is both new and familiar, where both black and white readers will feel at home. The characters are so finely drawn they can be recognized by their speech alone. Readers of Miss Shange's poetry already know that she has an extraordinary ear for the spoken word.

> *Nancy Willard, "Life Abounding in St. Louis," in The New York Times Book Review, May 12, 1985, p. 12.*

SUSAN SCHINDEHETTE

It would be wrong and unfair to describe Ntozake Shange's new work [*Betsey Brown*] as a bad novel, for it has some wonderful trappings: lively characters, colorful dialogue, and a sense of time and place that ensnare a reader.

Betsey Brown has lyricism and personality, and Shange certainly knows how to use words. (p. 74)

But through the book, which tells the story of an adolescent black girl in 1957 St. Louis, there is no glue to bind these elements into a flowing whole. Finally, toward the end of the book, the reason becomes clear: this isn't really a novel after all. It is dramatist Shange's latest play.

There are some hints that this might be a play masquerading as a novel. The jacket notes describe the author as a "distinguished playwright" and teacher of drama at the University of Houston, and there is also mention made that *Betsey Brown* is slated for production at Joseph Papp's New York Public Theatre next year.

But the real giveaway is the book's style: It is more an episodic mood piece, a sequence of scenes, than it is a traditional novel with climax and denouement.

Shange's work has merit, but it will be better when its language is performed, its words spoken out loud—when it makes its way into the theater and is called by its right name. (p. 75)

> *Susan Schindehette, in a review of "Betsey Brown," in Saturday Review, Vol. 11, No. 3, May-June, 1985, pp. 74-5.*

CAROLYN WEAVER

Shange has a nice way of evoking the physical textures of her story [in *Betsey Brown*]—the solidity and mystery of the Browns' old house, the vitality of a run-down urban neighborhood, a madam-cum-hairdresser's morning dishabille, her wig askew and breasts tumbling out of her robe. Shange's dialogue is often sharp, funny, and salty. She is working relatively neglected fictional territory here, and this lends *Betsey Brown* a freshness that the exhausted genre novel of growing up can use.

But although the material for a novel is here, it is present only in collapsed form. Shange does not dramatize her situations and characters so much as explain them to us. Some conflicts are resolved as patly as in a half-hour television drama; others are half-sketched and abandoned.

Betsey Brown, like a reminiscing friend, asks to be taken on faith. Although egocentricity and telescoped epiphanies are accepted in a friend, in a novel we expect more structure and discipline—in short, more art.

> *Carolyn Weaver, in a review of "Betsey Brown," in Mother Jones, Vol. X, No. V, June, 1985, p. 58.*

Thomas W(illiam) Shapcott

1935-

Australian poet, novelist, editor, librettist, and critic.

A leading Australian poet, Shapcott is noted for the vigorous musicality of his verse and for his masterful handling of both traditional and experimental prosody. The subject matter of Shapcott's poetry is varied and progressive, encompassing personal, social, urban, mythological, religious, and historical themes. Among the concerns of Shapcott's verse are the contrast between the poet's inner perceptions and the external world, the unalterable nature of time and existence, and the artist's search for self-definition. While he is often considered a regional poet, Shapcott sees himself "rather as one man rediscovering himself through others."

Shapcott began writing poetry in the 1950s, influenced by such poets as Dylan Thomas and T. S. Eliot. His first collection, *Time on Fire* (1961), presents his reflections on love and marriage, urban life, and the destruction of nature in his native Queensland. The poems in *The Mankind Thing* (1964) convey a greater sense of resignation and an acceptance of nature's ironic balances. *A Taste of Salt Water: Poems* (1967) is a diverse collection of social meditations, containing sonnets, elegies, religious verse, and experimental poems on mythological themes. Several sections of *Inwards to the Sun* (1969) also center on mythology. In "Minotaur," for example, Shapcott contemplates the notion that all human beings are by nature half-man, half-beast. In *Fingers at Air: Experimental Poems 1969* (1969), Shapcott departs from his customary style to experiment with "visual" or "kinetic" poetry, arranging the words on the page to form overlapping visual patterns. *Begin with Walking* (1972) also features several experimental pieces in which Shapcott ponders his feelings of anonymity while visiting San Francisco. Related verse, composed during a trip to New York City, is collected in *Seventh Avenue Poems* (1976). One of Shapcott's best-known works is *Shabbytown Calendar* (1976). This collection consists of what he terms "fugues," or poems which build to a symphonic climax. *Welcome!* (1983) features poems on European history as it relates to the Australian present.

In his first novel, *The Birthday Gift* (1983), Shapcott explores the dualistic natures of a pair of twins growing up in Queensland. Juxtaposing their childhood experiences with events from early adulthood, Shapcott balances one twin's artistic endeavors with the dull, middle-class life of the other. In the historical novel *The White Stag of Exile* (1984), Shapcott traces the tempestuous life of Károly Pulszky, a wealthy Hungarian eccentric who exiled himself to Australia after his attempts to establish a museum of fine art in Budapest resulted in scandal and dishonor. Shapcott has also written an art monograph, *Focus on Charles Blackman* (1967), and the libretto for a musical play, *The Seven Deadly Sins* (1970).

(See also *Contemporary Authors,* Vols. 69-72.)

Courtesy of Australian Information Service

DAVID MOODY

[It has to be said that on the basis of *Time on Fire* Shapcott does not appear] to be developing towards a full mastery of his mind in art.

The cause of this . . . seems to be that he is not able to comprehend the whole of his experience in his imagination. . . . [The quality of art cannot be separated] from the quality of the comprehension.

Mr. Shapcott's best passages are those in which his finely attentive response to the natural scene develops inwardly: the pressure of the scene and the pressure of his own preoccupations fuse in a meaningful vision, as in the first two . . . [stanzas] from **"The Lake in Winter."** But . . . the vision and the verse lapse when he attempts to attend explicitly to the human situation. Since this is broadly characteristic of the volume as a whole, I am led to suggest that certain forms of his experience, and especially those that matter to him most, are not available to his imagination as material for art.

> The intellect of man is forced to choose
> Perfection of the life, or of the work.

I am left with the impression that Mr. Shapcott is more drawn to the former than the latter—and why not? The choice is better or worse either way only according to what a man can make of it. But, if my impression is just, he should not then give way to the temptation, as he does seem to in the inferior later sections "Metropolis" and "A Journey in Love," to fake poetic equivalents for emotions which have rather sought their satisfaction in another form. The tendency in these later sections to willed writing, to a reliance upon the mere forms of verse and to imitation or pastiche, is in sad contrast to the promise of the first section: the art has become a substitute for the experience, and it is thereby falsified. I should add that if I seem to come down more severely on Mr. Shapcott than on the poetical versifiers, that is a measure of the extent to which I felt encouraged to take him more seriously. (pp. 503, 505)

> David Moody, in a review of "Time on Fire," in Meanjin, Vol. XX, No. 4, December 1961, pp. 503, 505.

S. E. LEE

[In some ways Mr Shapcott has a highly] characteristic voice . . . and an authentically poetic one at that. With a fine feeling for language and the kind of mind that images its ideas in concrete unforced figures drawn from common experience, Mr Shapcott's poetry [in *The Mankind Thing*] conveys a sense of warm human, companionable enthusiasm and goodwill—of innocence almost. Many of the poems move easily and spontaneously, especially the personal ones. Here the "innocence almost"; one feels occasionally, with the love poems, for example, rather like an intruder overhearing confidential declarations not intended for the public ear. But in the more mature poems—the more knowing and socially-involved ones—the feeling though intense is under firmer control. Thus there is a sense of tension that is missing from more personal lyrics. In some of these poems—the ones that seek to make significant comments about modern society through the retelling of ancient legends—Mr Shapcott gets fairly close to the impersonal voice of an objective narrator. . . . (pp. 135-36)

But Mr Shapcott is at his best, I feel, in the middle ground, in the poems where the poet's own fresh personality comes clearly through. . . . (p. 136)

> S. E. Lee, "Six Voices of Australian Poetry," in Southerly, Vol. 25, No. 2, 1965, pp. 131-37.*

ROBERT WARD

[A Taste of Salt Water] displays a mature and intelligent poetic talent. The book is divided into five sections, and these contain, in order, sonnets and lyrics, a New Testament sequence, poems with various urban themes, elegies celebrating the deaths of people and things, and a very polished poem entitled "Macquarie as Father", which deals with the birth of a son to that Governor. The thoughts, ideas, and attitudes the poems express are always interesting and clearly put, and overall the book is a positive accomplishment.

Mr. Shapcott is a poet who rarely needs consciously to create effects. His language is simple and candid, and the images, colours and textures it contains are always developed naturally and carefully controlled. He can surprise one by saying "Let me sing: / even the buzz of flies defines the spring", which looks slight on this page, but which neatly rounds off its sonnet. . . .

The New Testament poems are made of . . . colder stuff. . . . The religious poems make no positive points, and nor do they seem devotional exercises. They are more colourings of the history or, if you like, the myths.

So the poetry unfolds, intelligently organized, technically accomplished, tasteful, sometimes emotive, most times sinuous yet clear-headed. The book displays all the virtues of the professional mid-century Australian poet, and, let it be said, the one vice: a simple lack of passionate intensity.

> Robert Ward, in a review of "A Taste of Salt Water," in Australian Book Review, Vol. 6, No. 12, October, 1967, p. 197.

JAMES TULIP

To read Tom Shapcott's poems, or, better still, to hear him reading them is to be listening to a new and representative voice in Australian poetry today. More than any other poet he is pushing ahead with a devaluation of the currency in poetry, exploring how close to prose he can go without losing the "whatever it is" that is a poem, and, generally, locating new levels of awareness and experience, new subject matters and characters; and all without losing a steadiness and suppleness that is characteristic of his writing. He is immensely open before a poem, he travels lightly, and he always captures a clarity of statement that still carries with it a certain abrasiveness. He seems to enjoy a kind of provinciality; it helps him set off his philosophizing mind. . . . [In "Home Paddock," environment] is the primary thing, and man *is* how he responds to environment; yet in a supple, probing, quiet-toned response man can learn to be free within his environment. These seem to be principles within Shapcott's poetry.

A Taste of Salt Water offers us a series of adroit, sensitive ventures into a variety of subjects. There is no fixation on a particular local environment even though the presence of an Ipswich-Brisbane world is recognizable in many ways; to feel it in the people Shapcott writes about is to acknowledge its strength for him. Beyond this there are large sections of the book given over to a religious sequence, modern redactions of ancient myth, a new kind of historical poem on Lachlan Macquarie, and, strongest of all in my view, poems dealing with closely observed personal relations among his family, friends and acquaintances. At all of these points Shapcott is keeping open a number of valuable options for poetry today.

His particular strength, however, is that his verse has character. This is somewhat hard to define since I do not feel it as dramatic character or even as positive character. It is more a tone, an honesty, a registering of personal engagement with the facts of normal living. In its most active form, it comes close to a satiric character; and yet there is always an overlay of sympathy to it. (pp. 71-2)

At this point, however, there is also room for an objection to Shapcott's method. Oddly enough, [some of Shapcott's poems] . . . strike the reader as humourless. The sympathy is being directed in one way only; it does not include the poet as well. It reminds one almost of charity. This is, in my view, a fault since the poet is capturing life as a dramatic process, a flux, and yet not including his own awareness in this same process. It is a fault, also, because it explains a general and troublesome quality in Shapcott's work as a whole; his lightness of tone often becomes a mildness of tone, and his attitudes soft and self-indulgent. One often wishes that his verse would sparkle more; as it is, it tends to be melancholic. The poetry does not accept responsibility for its own meanings; they tend to be imputed from some outside source that is not being rendered.

This is a point worth hammering. Shapcott, of all Australian poets now writing and in this volume in particular, comes closest to the *Life Studies* achievement of the American Robert Lowell, and it is precisely on this point of how the poet renders his own identity in a poem that Lowell has made his break-through in modern writing. The self-objectification that Lowell is capable of in humour and anguish and anger allows the reader full access to the whole world of the poem. It is the freedoms both of and after the confessional state that are not yet available to Shapcott. (p. 73)

> *James Tulip, in a review of "A Taste of Salt Water,"*
> *in* Southerly, *Vol. 28, No. 1, 1968, pp. 71-3.*

S. E. LEE

Thomas Shapcott's *Fingers at Air* comprises five sequences "frankly experimental in technique and attitude". Here Mr Shapcott tries his hand at the faddish "new" concrete or kinetic poetry, whose words, to quote a [*Times Literary Supplement*] pundit "must intersect, overlap, make patterns, change letter by letter, or make their effect by repetition".... [The] poet feels that traditional syntactical and grammatical conventions shackle the creative spirit.... (p. 309)

Thus the attempt to convey such poetic impulses as "meditative introspection", "sensuous delight" and "increasing awareness poised between anguish and celebration" (to quote the jacket notes) in verses that depend for their total meaning on visual patterns, on juxtaposition of unconnected words and phrases, on repetitions of all three, so that a cumulative impression is built up. Without the hindrance of syntax "ordering" his responses the reader is supposed to feel and sense for himself—be involved in a concrete sensory experience. (pp. 309-10)

Take the first sequence **"Dance Dance"**. It runs I think for 12 pages ... and employs a recurring line design that one commonly observes on old-fashioned tiled floors, where a central diamond shape is fitted into four square tiles with their inside corners mitred off. The spaces inside and outside the diamond are gradually filled with cryptic words and chunks of sentences taken out of context until at the end we have a cluttered page that looks anything but "meditative" to my untutored gaze.

I fear that this poem will fail to move most readers to the "meditative introspection" the poet talks about simply because like me they lack the necessary reading skills, which a Mr Mike Weaver of the "International Kinetic Poetry Fund" has spelled out. The reader, he says, must be conscious

> ... of a sequence in which the verbal elements are implemented and organized by the rhythm of the turning pages; by a rhythm that rises vertically up over the edge of the page to fall into the trough of the horizontal spread of the next page. Outside this intense sense of movement the poem does not exist.

Admitting freely that I understand neither Mr Weaver's prose nor Mr Shapcott's poetry—and thereby possibly disqualifying myself as critic—I still feel that a gifted natural poet is being diverted from his true medium, the traditional lyric, personally adapted and developed. I invoke [T. S. Eliot's Introduction to Ezra Pound's *Selected Poems*] and commend his distinction between the "true innovators" (those who *develop* technique)

and players of poetic "sports" (those who exhibit "spurious originality" or "inventiveness"). The latter "sport" as Eliot said, "is contrary to life. The poem which is absolutely original is absolutely bad; it is in the bad sense 'subjective' with no relation to the world to which it appeals." ... (p. 310)

> *S. E. Lee, "Confessional and Experimental Verse,"*
> *in* Southerly, *Vol. 30, No. 4, 1970, pp. 306-11.**

PETER WARD

I think one could say that Shapcott's main concern [in *Inwards to the Sun*] is the interpretation and delineation of the more emotive side of human and personal relationships. Many of his poems ... do not appear to work on a first reading (some of them don't on subsequent attempts) because the base material is either too personal or really only to be appreciated by those who are capable of riding the same waves of oceanic feeling, related as they often are to garden chores or rock ferns.

The best verse in the volume occurs in longer, more ambitious pieces like **"Portrait of Captain Logan"**, who was a martinet commandant of the Morton Bay Penal Settlement. In this poem something outside the immediate range of experience is being examined, and the result is an effectively drawn picture of cruelty and "flint-eyed" Victorian authoritarianism.

In the five-poem sequence **"Minotaur"** [Shapcott] is again concerned with brutality and passion but here the range is greater: we are all in a sense Minotaur, half man, half beast.... (p. 128)

> *Peter Ward, "Springs Eternal," in* Australian Book
> Review, *Vol. 9, No. 5, March, 1970, pp. 127-28.**

JAMES TULIP

It is interesting to see how different readers have come to like different poems in Tom Shapcott's *Inwards to the Sun*. What one person will like, another will dislike. This suggests not only that Shapcott has a range and variety in his work but that his several emphases are tending towards a state of excluding one another as well. What has held them together is a moot point. But it may be that given the fragmentation of his method in the experimental *Fingers at Air,* Shapcott's old synthesis of tone and stance which were generally consistent throughout the 1960s is being broken up to prepare for some new style of approach in the 1970s. Whatever the outcome is, we have to acknowledge at this point the intense activity that lies behind Shapcott's place in Australian writing today, an activity that ... is felt in the urgent forays that his verse has been making on quite opposed aspects of reality.

Some readers like in particular Shapcott's **"Ceremony for Cedar, in an Old House"** sequence from *Inwards to the Sun*.... The poem ... moves out into a sensuous conservatism, now historical and dramatic, now local and intimate, and not easy to place. It is as though a William Carlos Williams' subject were being done with a Wallace Stevens' feeling. Yet it has the low critical pitch and tone, which is Shapcott's characteristic idiom, and the underpinning of prose from which his feelings and imagination have projected themselves into the fulsome life they offer here. This makes the poem Shapcott's own, and a striking disclosure of his self-possession in the world of his home, family and local history.

Other readers admire Shapcott's **"Minotaur"** sonnets. Here through the metaphor of myth a state of personal existence is enacted, cruel and tender by turn as the poem drives towards an understanding (a self-understanding, too) of the beast who possesses a world as a maze and whose identity matters more than all the experiences that men draw from his fate and fortune. There is no denying the aptness and power to Shapcott's intelligence in meeting the challenge of this subject, but I find the same intelligence working in the more personal way of **"Ceremony for Cedar"** in other poems. . . . (pp. 72-3)

[The phrase] "inwards to the sun" is a notion of inverse romanticism. It signals a retreat from the search for (or dream of) some ideal or absolute Object *out there;* it inclines towards the human, perceiving Subject, the poet's own innerness, as its authority, and is activated most keenly when the poet is enabled to recognize and give value to a world which his Self is committed to exhausting and transcending. Poetically, this move works best when the poem stays within the ethos of the object that is being exhausted, and **"Ceremony for Cedar"** illustrates this condition well. But I do not think that Shapcott generally has come to terms with the deeply conservative instincts that are released in this new stance of his. The sense of "clambering" towards this inner sun, of forcing the issue of his subjectivity, aptly describes several of his more recent moves as a poet and public figure on the cultural scene. (p. 73)

> *James Tulip, in a review of "Inwards to the Sun,"*
> in Southerly, *Vol. 31, No. 1, 1971, pp. 72-3.*

CARL HARRISON-FORD

It would be difficult to imagine a poet whose publishing history was as misleading as that of Thomas W. Shapcott. . . . [Fairly recently] L. J. Clancy was able to write of Shapcott as the author of two collections of verse displaying more potential than achievement and moving from assertion into a more graceful note of introspection. Since then he has published five more selections of verse, a prose study of Charles Blackman, two anthologies and a libretto. (p. 300)

Shapcott's chronology would suggest that he began as a rather formal poet and only freed his verse gradually. This has never been the case. It is, rather, a reflection on the comparative editorial conservatism of the 1950s and early 1960s. While some embarrassingly naïve sonnets were published, a good deal of freer and, in some instances, markedly superior verse remained unpublished. Those critics who reviewed *Fingers at Air* with frank lack of comprehension would have had no idea that the volume related to personal experiments of anything up to fifteen years earlier.

This knowledge in some ways mitigates the many serious faults lurking in Shapcott's first collection, *Time on Fire* (1961). That volume won the Grace Levin Prize but was marred by a stressed, assertive sense of supposed wonder. The country boy of those poems, living in a sordid city and a Neutral Bay boarding-house in particular, launched himself into cliché and disillusionment. Even the enthusiasm for nature is slowly undermined as it is seen as being trampled by urban experience. Such an attitude eventually undermines Shapcott's painterly, observational sense without in any way amplifying it. The city is so awful, the bush itself warns against it.

In **"Virgin Forest, Southern New South Wales"**, Shapcott's first published poem (1956), he asserts more than he can himself believe. . . . Beyond the assertion is an intellectual and emotional void. Yet in **"Kirsten"**, written in 1954 and published last year, Shapcott had been clearly attempting a more

tangible, sensuous apprehension of leaf- and word-truths: and the fragments of **"April Fool's Day."** . . . The Fool's sequence of 1954, as with **"Kirsten"** pays some attention to jazz phrasing and is not unlike the poetry of LeRoi Jones. . . . Shapcott's sequence is marked by repetition, sharp fractured lines and partly through the mention and invocation of song and nursery rhyme titles, a rather fragmented sense of melody.

For all its obvious faults, there is a vitality here that was to be knocked out of much of *Time on Fire* and be replaced with **"A Journey in Love"** or the rhetorical questioning of **"The Sleeping Trees"**: 'will it resolve to wakening or to death?'

By the time his second book appeared—*The Mankind Thing* (1964)—Shapcott himself would have realized that were trees to sleep they still could not cope with teleology. This is revealed most clearly in the fine sequence, **"Two and a Half Acres"**. The surest sign that the bush is natural and largely unspoilt lies in its inability to issue dire warnings against the city; that job is the rustic poet's own intrusion.

But the themes are still those of personal reflection. As well as the introduction of dimension through introspection the poems also employ the defensive-cum-urbane wisdom that is most easily expressed in terms of irony. It is at this stage, rather than in the emoting poems, that the poet becomes visible as a man with particular attitudes as well as themes. In the Christ poem in the **"Twelve Bagatelles"** the three kings make their journey

> and full of awe
> they grovelled deep.
> The child himself stayed fast asleep.

The only previous attempts at such succinct comment were in **"Woman in the Bar"** and **"La Glutton, in Suburb"** from the previous collection. . . . (p. 301)

In **"Twelve Bagatelles"** and **"Two and a Half Acres"** Shapcott gains control of his styles and is able to maintain the [poems]. . . . The rhetoric is in the service of the poet. In **"Two and a Half Acres"** his fourteen poems avoid the T. S. Eliot "Preludes" style, an influence that had been in danger of becoming his stock-in-trade. The magpie is not described as black and white but 'white and black and white' as the eye takes it in. The natural cycles of nature foster an awareness of form and of variety within it that obviously relates to his aims in poetry. Shapcott sums this up succinctly yet unobtrusively:

> My fingers catch
> at bark, twig, seed. There's no captivity
> to hold them in. The act escapes from me.
> Matter is form to hold such mystery. . . .

> (pp. 301-02)

Such a dual concern has emerged as one of Shapcott's major themes. Rather than recording the life of a poet or writing poems of the life of a humble man, he has become more interested in the partly self-referent aspects of his life-in-art. As the poems, as sheer verbal constructs, are there as part of the poet's personal life and experience he feels constrained to discuss them. Though the poem about poetry is seen by many critics as being invalid or an instance of later-day aestheticism, his example proves how fruitful such an issue may prove. (p. 302)

[*A Taste of Saltwater*'s] pivotal sequence remains **"The City of Acknowledgement'**. Other groupings reflected an unsure talent. The **"Aubades"** and **"Madrigals"** attempted a tone he could not maintain and, even where most successful, he could not sustain their images. **"Autumn Madrigal"** developed a tone of whimsical comic verse . . . and the poem could not hold. In **"A Whipbird Straps the Light Awake"** the title and opening line remained stranded and inorganic.

"The City of Acknowledgement", however, is superior in scope and reflective dimensions. A series of fourteen Christ poems moving from Nativity to Easter, they adopt two of the most enduring myths of Western poetry—the city and the life of Christ. The ironic treatment of the life of Christ is so germane to Shapcott's vision it seems incorrect to label it irony. The twisted and the face-about are taken as though for granted, in Christ's life and our own:

> The cross is raised up, one among many.
> Acknowledgement is not easy in our city.
> Acknowledgement is never easy in our city.

The ramifications of this last line, an extension of the two-line chorus of the Easter poem, are crucial. Civilization and the city are seen as destructive but not inhuman monsters. If Shapcott's early poetry of the city was filled with a righteous revulsion, the ironic detachment of the later sequence involves the poet as well and the despairing 'never' of the last line seems highly personal. That there are many crosses is, perhaps, the cross Shapcott himself has to bear. But the cross symbol also carries the implication of salvation. The struggle for value informs value, and may both justify and preserve it. The poem moves between the presumption of identification with, and the stupidity of ignoring, the pervasive Christ myth. The city is more than a convenient symbol of society. As with the poets from Virgil through Milton, W. C. Williams and Charles Olson the city is a central social unit but completely beyond the familial gathering. (p. 303)

Such a position seems to be constantly risky, staring at both the vacuous and the introverted opaque. Further, there is a chance of falling into some trap of belief that the present, any present, is something of a cultural peak. Identity is constantly incipient but the essential humility of such a position is in danger of being aggrandized. The libretto of [Shapcott's musical play] **The Seven Deadly Sins** takes issue with such a danger. Apollo claims 'I am the God behind your eyes' and Morality replies:

> I am God enough before your eyes
> enacting what your vision needs to raise
> as Throne, as Power, and as Judge. . . .

On the page the libretto makes a rather heavy-handed poem. But at a considerably less cosmic level its concerns run through most of Shapcott's mature verse. This is not surprising as the poet's stance is open without being naïve, using the poem as a forum for his struggle with identity rather than as a bulletin of progress reports and conclusions. (p. 304)

The first of the highly experimental poems [in **Fingers at Air**] **"Dance, Dance"** was originally given the apter title "The Dance of Form". It begins in a diamond box on a quartered right-hand page. . . . The following right-hand pages have variations on this and are faced by statements that seem raw material for the more complex word arrangements. These statements justify the "I to I" or "I to object and object back to me" theme that emerges from the poet's felt relationship with the natural world of weather and seasons. The last page, left-hand, reads: "singing". The sequence, and those that amplify it, suggest that dialogue's sources have transcended themselves

and that, in examining the dialectic of personal assertion, song in its essence, its *idea,* is achieved. Subsequent poems run down a right-hand margin or struggle with the box of form until the paradox of such freedom requires formal and formed expression: "and all the syntax squeezes me again in cages." (p. 305)

Fingers at Air is a stimulating, sometimes unsuccessful, attempt to push the *issues* of poetry to that area which is usually considered the domain of content, even by those critics who sensibly see the content/form dichotomy as unreal. Poetry is a human endeavour and a fine subject for poems but it has seldom been treated, in itself, so openly by a local poet. As suggested earlier, however, these concerns have saved an impressionable Shapcott from a fall into mindless imitation or a good deal of occasional verse. Given an open view of the range of poetry, such meta-critical work is scarcely less therapeutic or frank than that of the US "confessionals". . . .

The many poems published since **Fingers at Air** suggest that those naked experiments proved fruitful. The privately produced **Interim Report** (1972) includes many of those poems and displays a style that is new and characteristic. Where the earlier poems seem diverse though the product of one talent, there is a stronger indication of unity in the more recent poems. In part, this relates to **Fingers at Air**'s **"Dance, Dance"** sequence and its spoken resolution of **"Singing"**. The subsequent poems seem musical but make small attempt to be lyrical in any sing-song way. . . .

For all the strengths of his verse, it would seem that Shapcott's development has suffered from a lack of a strong poetic debate and critical flurry. Responsive to influence and criticism, he has had to write in what he tends to see as a less than vital culture. He moved between highly experimental and highly formal poems and in each instance seemed to fall short of a personal style. In **Fingers at Air** there was a somewhat desperate attempt to go it alone, and that book's legacy has been a harsh style but his own. (p. 306)

Carl Harrison-Ford, "The Dance of Form: The Poetry of Thomas W. Shapcott," in Meanjin, Vol. 31, No. 3, September, 1972, pp. 300-07.

JAMES TULIP

Thomas W. Shapcott's **Begin with Walking** is [a solid volume]. . . . It has four sections which describe the range of his interests and experience: exercises in verse with literary, musical and general aesthetic forms; reflective or dramatic monologues based in Australian history; personal and social experience; and a recent American visit. There is really too much for the reader to absorb. Especially since it seems now to be Shapcott's forte to go for strong lines and an undifferentiated tone.

What is striking in **Begin with Walking** is the contrast between the Brisbane and the San Francisco poems. Shapcott has a rational point to make about getting down to ground level in Australian writing. But he forces his passiveness upon the reader. Abroad, Shapcott was obviously caught by surprise at the punch which the big American cities can carry, and luckily his poetry rose to the occasion. Humour, bewilderment and detailed reporting fall into place in a new idiom for Shapcott. . . . The whole fourth section of Shapcott's book is evidence of the images he has brought home to develop. His poetry has taken a lively leap forward.

James Tulip, in a review of "Begin with Walking," in Southerly, Vol. 33, No. 2, June, 1973, p. 239.

CHRISTOPHER POLLNITZ

At their best Shapcott's *Seventh Avenue Poems* approach the transparency of a Japanese prose-and-haiku travelogue. At their worst they dwindle to toyings with found speech. The portentous one-word lines signal more poetic desperation than illumination. (p. 468)

[However, Shapcott's *Shabbytown Calendar,* an] intricate and mature volume, . . . traces all twelve months, allotting three poems to each. Two poems deal with persons, places, flora and weathers loosely appropriate to the season, the third is a "fugue" dedicated to the month. Human death breaks with the natural cycle; so **"In memory of Francis Webb"** is an odd poem out in the monthly pattern. The elegy hints at a fragmentary quality in Webb's achievement, yet claims that all poetry, and each poem, can be only a fractured glimpse at greater patterns. (p. 469)

Shapcott envies Webb his spiritual struggle and faith, and fears his own lapsing in arid scepticism. He does not deny moments of vision, but when the miracle descends, when rain falls from the barren thunder of **"Storm Weather"**, the cloudburst is too great, too multiple for his eye. His reality has moments of hallucination

> The blotched sunlight is a brilliant insect
> sucking the moist out of us

but settles into a more mundane, accommodating domesticity. Unlike Webb's, his explorer "did not perish in the desert": he is a botanist, Cunningham, who left his mark in the botanical name of the Hoop Pine, brought indoors by the children for Christmas trees. The very attempt to construct a past, to hold converse with his botanist-explorer, is for Shapcott an act of faith: "we make a continuing dialogue with ghosts—. . . compelled, as Marx saw, to conjure spirits". The overriding concern of the *Calendar* is with time, with ways of mummifying, recapturing, regenerating, transcending or being reconciled to time. In place of Yeats's or Webb's mysticisms Shapcott offers a reverence for the mysteries inside of time:

> Nothing is promised
> but we have been given
> ash and fragrance
> and a changed way of remembering.

As statement these lines have clarity and a certain nobility, but as formal verse they lack intrinsic or extrinsic ordering, any reason for their having been stated in just this form. Shapcott's free verse often seems this friable. A handful of poems of sympathy, **"April Fugue"**, **"Autumn"** and outstandingly **"Town Edge"**, have an intensity that supplies their law from within. They have an intrinsic law, in saying which one expresses a critical ignorance of how they work, gratitude for the fact they do, and a desire not to meddle further. But the few interior poems stand out starkly among the many in which the poet eschews bardic accoutrement or confessional nakedness. In his monthly fugues, however, Shapcott has made a significant technical breakthrough. The fugues repeat, with minor variations, simple phrases that pass through changing auras of concept, emotion and scene. Each phrase recombines and grows in suggestive range until, as the fugue draws to its summation, it bursts upon us, simple and charged with grandeur. . . . Since motifs from a single fugue are picked up and developed

throughout the *Calendar,* the final effect is as symphonic as fugal. Shapcott may have found a hint for this formal innovation in . . . contemporary American poetry. . . . But the importance of his discovery and achievement in these fugues is for contemporary Australian poetry, in providing a model which others might profitably pursue. (pp. 469-70)

Christopher Pollnitz, "Exuberance and Recklings," in Southerly, Vol. 36, No. 4, December, 1976, pp. 464-70.*

KEVIN HART

[Shapcott], at times, tends to wander in a metrical wasteland. *Shabbytown Calendar* is flawed by a number of inconsequential sketches of the townspeople. . . . But to dwell on this aspect of the book is to ignore its achievement. *Shabbytown Calendar* is memorable for its longer more meditative poems such as **"June Fugue"**, **"October Fugue"**, **"Old Master"**, and **"The Spectrum Dream"**. . . . The poems do not stand up well to quotation in an article such as this. Their effect is cumulative and, at the end of the book's hefty 104 pages, I was left with the impression of a strong imaginative mind meditating on central human concerns. *Shabbytown Calendar* must be seen as a flawed but persuasive attempt at a verse-novel. Its main problem is . . . that the general tone struck is too low to allow Shapcott to reach for the high points required to justify the collection's length.

Shapcott is an energetic presence on the Australian scene and a great deal of his energy is directed towards the public recognition of the American poets. His work as an editor of several anthologies is responsible for bringing new alternatives to light but, I want to suggest, underneath his search for and patronage of experimentation there lies a firm but affable "traditionalist." Perhaps it is an awareness in himself of what the apostles of the New Poetry would call conservatism that makes him so energetic in his continual support of serious but sadly misdirected talents such as Garrie Hutchinson's. Shapcott sees value in both sides and can write well in both "styles." But what distinguishes a poem by (say) Garrie Hutchinson from one by A. D. Hope is not merely style but a fundamental difference in what makes a poem. It is this lack of a lasting commitment to any one perception that prevents Shapcott from assuming his rightful place as a poet of major importance. The Americans have not helped him. . . . One can—must—learn from the Americans, but no advance will be made in continually jumping between Scylla and Charybdis. (pp. 79-80)

Kevin Hart, in a review of "Shabbytown Calendar," in Southern Review, Vol. X, No. 1, March, 1977, pp. 79-80.

THOMAS SHAPCOTT [INTERVIEW WITH JIM DAVIDSON]

[*The interview from which this excerpt is taken was conducted on October 30, 1978.*]

[Davidson]: *To what extent do you regard yourself as a regional writer?*

[Shapcott]: I've never consciously thought of myself as a regional poet. It's true that, particularly in the early years of my writing, the regional data of my experience were in the foreground—they were what was largely available to me. I've also had a certain consciousness of landscape since the beginning, because one lives in a landscape, one moves in and around it, and that can be a townscape, a cityscape, or a suburbscape. That is as valid a part of the resources one draws upon as any other. And in my poetry it could be traced from the early poems about hawks and things like that right through to later poems like **"Miss Nora Kerrin Writes to Her Betrothed"**, which is essentially about an Anglo-Indian transplanted to Australia, who has to face the question of responding to the strangeness of the countryside, which then becomes internalised and somehow transfigured. So, in other words, I see myself, basically, as someone concerned with exploring a sort of metaphysic rather than a physic.

Clearly that's so, because a recurrent theme in your poems is a concern with time, and not merely in images. The early historical poems are in a sense exploring all the implications of a particular moment, such as Governor Macquarie going back to Sydney to become a father. (pp. 56-7)

Time is an essential element. There's a tremendous number of poems written in the present tense, because I've been concerned with getting a feeling of what I might call energy into the poem. That has to do with time, and re-making it or re-thinking it. The Governor Macquarie poem very early, and in a sense quite unconsciously, was trying to show that experience is a thing of immediate surprise and perception, outside the formal chronology of time. In other words it's the nowness of the event, it's not the historical perspective that interests me.

And it's used as a vantage point, so that the emphasis in **Shabbytown Calendar** *falls as much on the calendar as on Shabbytown.*

Yes indeed, and it's quite central. The construction of **Shabbytown Calendar** is such that it has an accelerative movement: I mean, the first two sections are four months, the third section three months, and the last section is one month. (p. 57)

One of the things one is very conscious of . . . in your work, is a recurrent image of mirrors—and a sense of discomfort about them. I wondered whether this doesn't perhaps reflect the split level on which you've had to operate more than most Australian poets—being an accountant by day in a small country town, and a poet by night or afternoon or whatever?

I'd never picked that thing up, self-consciously. But yes, there is obviously an intense and uncomfortable dislocation. In other words, I lived a completely schizoid existence, until the beginning of this year. Which has been a major decision on my part, very far reaching. 'Tom comes out' sort of thing.

That's interesting, because the other images which occur very strongly are those of cages or windows, juxtaposed with nature. There's a fascinating poem at the end of that **"Laughs in the Open Tombs"** *sequence, where the character is on the inside, alive and yet entombed, while the insects representing nature are on the outside, dying in their attempts to penetrate the glass barrier. That's the strongest statement, but there are echoes of it all through the verse which, combined with the mirror pre-occupation, makes one feel that there's a very interesting, if oblique, statement regarding identity and related problems.*

You tell me most interesting things about myself . . . (laughter). (pp. 60-1)

[The] overall impression one gets from your poetry is that it does reflect the fact that you've felt a loner, and that there's a kind of rawness of place and a rawness of time present there together. And I wondered about the degree to which you see

a great deal of your poetry as being an attempt to work through this predicament, to create a myth and a way of coping, as it were. Those unmediated qualities of rawness place all of us in Australia at an extremity to some degree, and in Queensland even more so; which could be particularly oppressive if you'd been cocooned in a very comfortable middle class world while knowing its innate frailty. Would you like to comment on that?

That sense of working from a position of being both comfortable and at an extremity I think is very important. I mean, I can't complain that I haven't lived in material comfort, haven't had a reasonable placidity of outward appearance. But of course inside there's not only that sense of absolute void which we all have to face, but also the social unviability of much of the life, not only my own but those all around me in the whole town. One of my very early poems is called **"Sleeping Trees"**: it's premised on the fragility of our European existence in this continent, and is about how the towns that we've built could be replaced almost overnight by new sapling forests (by other cultures). That sort of thing has been pervasive. The myth poems, as you might call them, (the historical poems) really do trace a progression in growth in my personal terms—and apprehension about them—starting with that early one about Macquarie as father in which the birthing experience, becoming a father, is an attempt to break down time dimensions into a sort of core of nowness. That was followed by the Logan poem, which is much more savage, angry at this particular person, but also an attempt to create very much a sense of Brisbane. I mean, that world of Moreton Bay is still what one feels about Moreton Bay. That was followed by a sequence called **"Ceremony for Cedar"**, which tried to reconcile or incorporate a personal domestic framework within that outer world for which I used the image of cedar. There are only two basic images in Australia that have immediate resonance for people as soon as you say the name, and that's cedar as in cedar timber, or Ned Kelly. Bring them into a conversation and people immediately react or spark in some way. Of the two cedar is the stranger one, and it seems to me much less brought to the forefront. . . . What is it that lies within this particular softwood timber? Once you look at the history of cedar-cutting in Australia, of course, it opens up the most frightening world. Rape, exploitation, fine craftsmanship—that poem was deeply about what seemed to me one of the basic myth areas, 'myth area' because the word has a resonance that goes beyond itself. Our unconscious history. From there I moved on to **"Miss Nora Kerrin"**, coming to terms with the natural environment, but dropping out of society, as it were, (into a sort of madness, or at least remoteness) in the process. In Queensland there is always the raw tropic feel of humidity to make a mock of the outward appearances. I may examine the hypocrisies and thin veneer of our culture, but I am really seeking the point of identification. Those aspects of our living that are, to use one of my once favourite words, celebratory. (pp. 67-8)

*Jim Davidson and Thomas Shapcott, in an interview,
in* Meanjin, *Vol. 38, No. 1, April, 1979, pp. 56-68.*

BRUCE GUERNSEY

Shapcott's **Selected Poems** documents one poet's search for a voice. The first half or so of the book is, frankly, a bore. Its language is prosaic, Shapcott speaks as persona, not person, and the poems lack commitment. But the later sections, especially the 1971-1976 years, are another matter. We have an "I" who both speaks and sees. . . . Interestingly, some of the best poems in this later work have American settings. It's as if Shapcott, an Australian, had been searching among British models early in his career but found the American language, its diction and syntax, a more vigorous way of speaking.

> *Bruce Guernsey, in a review of "Selected Poems,"* in Library Journal, *Vol. 104, No. 14, August, 1979, p. 1570.*

LAURENCE S. FALLIS

[Shapcott begins his] *Selected Poems* [with] an extended portrait of a brutal commandant of one of the Australian penal settlements. . . . We can see here the qualities for which Shapcott [is known]. . . . First, there is the mastery of complex forms. The poet is equally at home with the sonnet, the ballad and the open structures of contemporary poetics. Next, Shapcott's verse is informed by an intense musicality. This can be seen in the titles of a number of his poems—**"Traditional Songs," "Piano Pieces," "A Motet for Tomas Luis de Victoria," "January Fugue"**—as well as in the contrapuntal structure of the works themselves. Finally, in his narratives as well as his lyrics, Shapcott demonstrates the rare ability not only to catalogue the significant details of daily life but to turn those details into the very stuff of poetry itself.

The image of the unfortunate Captain Logan set upon by . . . carnivorous ants will stay with you long after a hundred lesser talents have taken their turn at center stage.

> *Laurence S. Fallis, in a review of "Selected Poems,"* in World Literature Today, *Vol. 53, No. 4, Autumn, 1979, p. 743.*

JAMES TULIP

[Shapcott's first novel] *The Birthday Gift* takes incidents from the lives of a pair of twins, Ben and Benno, and intermingles events from a Queensland childhood with events from early adulthood. The 1940s are juxtaposed with the 1950s. Experiences in Ipswich stand side by side with experiences in Sydney and Italy. It is as if formal structuring has become a solution for authorial absence. The book points to a search for identity and meaning in the criss-cross of two lives that are so alike and yet so unalike. It does not come up with an answer.

Shapcott strikingly focusses on the modern—especially Australian—obsession with dualities of characters. Ben is the would-be and future artist; Benno is the "ocker". Paradoxically, it is the "ocker" whom Shapcott brings to life in his novel. It is as if he is too nice, too indulgent to the hopes and aspirations of the artist in himself to objectify him. The *alter ego* of Benno gives him something to resist and bite into. *The Birthday Gift* lacks fictional freedom; it is one step removed from being a journal, an autobiography, a confession. It does, however, have that quality which has won Shapcott so much respect for being a central reflecting intelligence of his generation.

> *James Tulip, "Poets and Their Novels," in* Southerly, *Vol. 43, No. 1, March, 1983, pp. 113-18.**

ANNETTE V. JANES

There is varied and interesting background of Australian family life and customs [in *The Birthday Gift*], but some of the idioms will send readers scrambling for interpretation. The book is written in rich and sensitive prose; yet, it seems to be a series of sketches awkwardly strung together rather than a novel. The story shifts forwards and backwards in jagged time fragments, making it difficult to follow.

> *Annette V. Janes, in a review of "The Birthday Gift,"* in Library Journal, *Vol. 108, No. 21, December 1, 1983, p. 2263.*

MANLY JOHNSON

The first poem of [Shapcott's *Welcome!*] arises from his interest in the exuberant fantasy life of children. **"The Eel Teller,"** in its first of two twelve-line stanzas, purveys the beloved tall tale of the eel that wouldn't be killed; the second stanza features the nutritional animism that still flourishes in adult imagination. The observant eye of Shapcott the novelist would dominate **"Exorcising Ghosts and Ancestors"** were it not for the speculations, also novelistic, about the relationship of family to ancestral lands.

The genealogical devotion to the past of Europe, prominent in several of these poems, might appear to indicate in Shapcott's thinking that kind of Old Country nostalgia that worked for a time against the development of an indigenous culture in Australia. Even the poems here with European settings, however, have a distinctly Australian orientation. And **"Conrad Martins in 1850"** speaks of how "our pride is humbled" by Aboriginal technological accomplishments, though Shapcott gives this acknowledgment a characteristically complex twist by adding, "we are desperate to have them gone." . . .

Shapcott's formal range is wide. **"Make the Old Man Sing"** is a sequence, mostly sonnets of considerable experimentation in end- and internal rhyme. *"The Joyner Act:* **A Queensland Text"** consists of a page of flowing fourteeners, and **"Old Man's Fugue"** is a series of seventy irregular, off-rhyme couplets in ten parts (decades, perhaps).

Out of this variety of modes and concerns, the collection ends with a powerful expressionist statement, **"His First Real Snow,"** which brings into a relationship images of banknotes, trees, a hand, snow and blood in an effect that is cryptic, unsettling as a challenge and finally convincing about the integrity of the commitment to life and imagination embodied by these poems. This last one ends with the double-edged word "Welcome." Readers of Shapcott's latest volume will agree, I feel sure, that it is unambiguously welcome.

> *Manly Johnson, in a review of "Welcome!" in* World Literature Today, *Vol. 58, No. 3, Summer, 1984, p. 471.*

JONATHAN KEATES

The art which conceals art is scarcely the most important consideration in *White Stag of Exile*. Novelists writing in English have now begun investigating the apparently limitless possibilities of Austria-Hungary before World War I. *Ach*, but the background she is so rich! . . .

Thomas Shapcott almost hits it off, so much so that if we choose to ignore its bursts of literary portentousness, *White Stag of Exile* may emerge as one of the most arresting novels of recent months. His protagonist is the dancer Nijinsky's weirdly megalomaniac Hungarian father-in-law Karoly 'Charlie' Pulszky, whose dream was to create a museum of fine arts worthy of *fin-de-siècle* Budapest. Charlie's downfall is brought about through the blurring of vision with insanity, hastened by the scandal of a liaison with the cocotte Cléo de Mérode, who passes herself off as a countess and acts as intermediary in the purchase of a spurious Sebastiano del Piombo at a Milanese auction.

This, and the details of Charlie's self-imposed exile to Australia . . . , offer splendid material for treatment *à la Schindler's Ark* with the narrative filtered through a sheaf of letters, official documents, newspaper reports, police records and fragments of memoir. Some of this is ferociously convincing, the more so since Shapcott bases his understanding of period and atmosphere on an intuitive appreciation rather than on the mere ploddings of research. It is only when Charlie, albeit unhinged, starts growing delphic about things like art and pain and timelessness that our good faith begins to crack a little. Sympathy in the end rests less with this prosing imbecile than with the patient throng of onlookers and admirers surrounding him in his harrowing collapse, yet even here, as the novel ironically suggests, his overwhelming charm has continued triumphant.

> *Jonathan Keates, "What's Become of Waldo?" in*
> The Observer, *July 29, 1984, p. 20.**

ROGER MANVELL

[*White Stag of Exile*] is an absorbing combination of fact and fiction. The author, a distinguished Australian man of letters, became fascinated by the unkept grave of an Hungarian, Károly Pulszky, which he discovered near his home in Brisbane. Aided by foundation grants, he researched the facts . . . of how this brilliant man, who became the centre of controversy, political and artistic, in Hungary, came to exile himself in Australia and, in a state of poverty, shoot himself in 1899 while only in his mid forties. 'Charlie' Pulszky was from a cosmopolitan family, his father well known in Hungarian society, arts and politics. . . . Pulszky obtained generous government grants to establish a National Gallery in Budapest, but his extravagant way of life, his incessant travelling, his total unaccountability in purchasing works of art led to political scandal, charges of embezzlement, alleged insanity, and such disgrace for himself and his family that he chose exile and finally suicide. This extraordinary story is reconstructed by Thomas Shapcott, . . . substantially relying on invention to portray the complex, obsessive, over-emotional natures of Pulszky and his wife, revealing them through fictional self-portrayals, correspondence, and even occasional poetry. The structure is non-chronological, oblique, the story seen through the minds and emotions of Pulszky and his family and gradually moving inwards to the climax of Pulszky's disgrace and exile. The book is a notable combination of research and invention.

> *Roger Manvell, in a review of "White Stag of Exile,"*
> in British Book News, *December, 1984, p. 750.*

Isaac Bashevis Singer

1904-

(Has also written under pseudonym of Isaac Warshofsky) Polish-born American short story writer, novelist, author of books for children, memoirist, dramatist, journalist, and translator.

Singer is widely considered the foremost contemporary Yiddish writer. Although he has lived in the United States since 1935, Singer writes almost exclusively in Yiddish, and his works are frequently set in the Polish-Jewish villages, or *shtetls,* of his heritage. In 1978 he was awarded the Nobel Prize in Literature for his ''impassioned narrative art which, with roots in the Polish-Jewish cultural traditions, brings universal conditions to life.'' Highly praised as a consummate storyteller, Singer explores the individual's search for faith and guidance in a world that makes belief difficult.

Many critics claim that Singer's short fiction is his best work. Alexandra Johnson writes that his short stories ''compress intricate dramas into a few single pages.'' Singer's characters, many of whom arc torn between their faith in God and earthly temptations, are often tormented by demons, ghosts, *dybbuks,* and other evil forces. In a review of *Collected Stories of Isaac Bashevis Singer* (1982), Michael Levin noted that Singer depicts man as ''defenceless, unprotected and, worse still, unable to protect himself before powerful, callous or malevolent forces.'' The protagonist of the well-known title story from *Gimpel the Fool and Other Stories* (1957) typifies one reaction to this worldly situation: Gimpel is a ''divine fool'' whose innocent naiveté provides humor but also conveys a simple goodness that combats evil. Singer has published many collections of short stories, among them *The Spinoza of Market Street* (1961), *Short Friday and Other Stories* (1964), *Passions and Other Stories* (1975), and *Old Love* (1979). Although they are sometimes faulted for repetition, Singer's stories are generally viewed as evidence of his exceptional storytelling skills. Irving Howe noted that Singer ''plays the same tune over and over again'' but added that ''if Singer moves along predictable lines, they are clearly his own, and no one can accomplish his kind of story so well as he.''

In his novels Singer tends toward a realistic, straightforward style, especially in his three epic novels chronicling a Jewish family history from the 1800s until the onslaught of Nazi Germany. *The Family Moskat* (1950), *The Manor* (1967), and *The Estate* (1969) are detailed narratives written in the expansive mode of nineteenth-century fiction. They are praised for their vivid evocation of Old World cultural and religious traditions. As effective as these works are in delineating the lives of ordinary families, critics generally agree that Singer's novellas, including *Satan in Goray* (1935) and *The Slave* (1962), are superior to his full-length novels. *Satan in Goray* depicts the Eastern European Jews' acceptance of the false messiah, Sabbatai- Zevi, after the Cossacks' raids in 1648 and 1649. *The Slave* incorporates several stories from the Old Testament, including that of Joseph's bondage in Egypt.

Singer has said that he creates his fiction out of personal experience. Many critics contend that *Shosha* (1978) is a novelized version of his memoir *A Young Man in Search of Love* (1978). Shosha is one of Singer's innocents who symbolizes

© Nancy Crampton

a return to the uncomplicated world of childhood, while the narrator, who succumbs to material pleasures, represents the moral disintegration of modern life. The moralistic tone of Singer's work is again evident in his novel *The Penitent* (1984), a long monologue which relates the odyssey of Joseph Shapiro as he travels in search of a pure way of life. More didactic than most of Singer's work, this novel has been faulted for lacking the ironic perspective and multidimensional depth of his earlier works.

Other popular works by Singer include his stories for children. *A Day of Pleasure: Stories of a Boy Growing Up in Warsaw* (1969) won the National Book Award for children's literature. Singer has also written several volumes of memoirs, among them *In My Father's Court* (1966), which relates his early experiences and intellectual development against the backdrop of his father's rabbinical court. *A Little Boy in Search of God: Mysticism in a Personal Light* (1976) and *A Young Man in Search of Love* continue Singer's quest for understanding the nature of God and His creations.

(See also *CLC,* Vols. 1, 3, 6, 9, 11, 15, 23; *Children's Literature Review,* Vol. 1; *Contemporary Authors,* Vols. 1-4, rev. ed.; *Contemporary Authors New Revision Series,* Vol. 1; *Something about the Author,* Vols. 3, 27; and *Dictionary of Literary Biography,* Vols. 6, 28.)

CYNTHIA OZICK

On one flank Singer is a trickster, a prankster, a Loki, a Puck. His themes are lust, greed, pride, obsession, misfortune, unreason, the oceanic surprises of the mind's underside, the fiery caldron of the self, the assaults of time and place. His stories offer no "epiphanies" and no pious resolutions; no linguistic circumscriptions or Hemingwayesque self-deprivations. Their plenitudes chiefly serve undefended curiosity, the gossip's lure of what comes next. Singer's stories have plots that unravel not because they are "old-fashioned"—they are mostly originals and have few recognizable modes other than their own—but because they contain the whole human world of affliction, error, quagmire, pain, calamity, catastrophe, woe. Things happen; life is an ambush, a snare; one's fate can never be predicted. His driven mercurial processions of predicaments and transmogrifications are limitless, often stupendous. There are whole fistfuls of masterpieces in this one volume: a cornucopia of invention.

Because he cracks open decorum to find lust, because he peers through convention into the pit of fear, Singer has in the past been condemned by other Yiddish writers outraged by his seemingly pagan matter, his superstitious villagers, his daring leaps into gnostic furies. The moral grain of Jewish feeling that irradiates the mainstream aspirations of Yiddish literature has always been a kind of organic extension of Talmudic ethical ideals: family devotion, community probity, *derekh erets*— self-respect and respect for others—the stringent expectations of high public civility and indefatigable integrity, the dream of messianic betterment. In Singer, much of this seems absent or overlooked or simply mocked; it is as if he has willed the crashing down of traditional Jewish sanity and sensibility. As a result, in Yiddish literary circles he is sometimes viewed as—it is the title of one of [the stories in *The Collected Stories of Isaac Bashevis Singer*]—"**The Betrayer of Israel.**"

In fact, he betrays nothing and no one, least of all Jewish idealism. That is the meaning of his imps and demons: that human character, left to itself, is drawn to cleanliness of heart; that human motivation, on its own, is attracted to clarity and valor. Here is Singer's other flank, and it is the broader one. The goblin cunning leads straight to this; Singer is a moralist. He tells us that it is natural to be good, and unholy to go astray. It is only when Lilith creeps in, or Samael, or Ketev Mriri, or the sons of Asmodeus, that evil and impurity are kindled. It is the inhuman, the antihuman, forces that are to blame for harms and sorrows. Surely these imps must be believed in; they may have the telltale feet of geese, like Satan their sire, but their difficult, shaming, lubricious urges are terrestrially familiar. Yet however lamentably known they are, Singer's demons are intruders, invaders, no true or welcome part of ourselves. They are "psychology"; and history; and terror; above all, obsessive will. If he believes in them, so, unwillingly but genuinely, do we.

And to understand Singer's imps is to correct another misapprehension: that he is the recorder of a lost world, the preserver of a vanished sociology. Singer is an artist and transcendent inventor, not a curator. His tales—though dense with the dailiness of a God-covenanted culture, its folkways, its rounded sufficiency, especially the rich intensities of the yeshiva and its bottomless studies—are in no way documents. The Jewish townlets that truly were are only seeds for his febrile conflagrations. . . . Though every doorstep might be described, and every feature of a head catalogued (and Singer's portraits are brilliantly particularized), parables and fables are no more tied to real places and faces than Aesop's beasts are beasts.

This is not to say that Singer's stories do not mourn those murdered Jewish townlets of Poland, every single one of which, with nearly every inhabitant, was destroyed by the lords and drones of the Nazi Gehenna. This volume includes a masterly memorial to that destruction, the brokenhearted testimony of "**The Last Demon.**" . . . (pp. 14-15)

[The author's] tenderness for ordinary folk, their superstitions, their folly, their plainness, their lapses, is a classical thread of Yiddish fiction, as well as the tree trunk of Singer's own Hasidic legacy—love and reverence for the down-to-earth. "**The Little Shoemakers**" bountifully celebrates the Fifth Commandment with leather and awl; the hero of "**Gimpel the Fool,**" a humble baker, is endlessly duped and stubbornly drenched in permanent grace; the beautiful story "**Short Friday**" ennobles a childless old couple who, despite privation and barrenness, turn their unscholarly piety into comeliness and virtue. . . . Through a freakish accident—snow covers their little house, and they are asphyxiated—the loving pair ascend in death together to Paradise. When the demons are stilled, human yearning aspires toward goodness and joy. (p. 15)

In Singer the demons are rarely stilled, and the luminous serenity of "**Short Friday**" is an anomaly. Otherwise pride furiously rules, and wild-hearted imps dispose of human destiny. In "**The Unseen,**" a prosperous and decent husband runs off with a lusty maidservant at the urging of a demon; he ends in destitution, a hidden beggar tended by his remarried wife. . . . Elsewhere, excessive intellectual passion destroys genius. An accomplished young woman is instructed by a demon to go to the priest, convert, and abandon her community; the demon assumes the voice of the girl's grandmother, herself the child of a Sabbatean. . . . Character and motive are turned inside out at the bidding of imps who shove, snarl, seduce, bribe, cajole. Allure ends in rot; lure becomes punishment.

This phantasmagorical universe of ordeal and mutation and shock is, finally, as intimately persuasive as logic itself. There is no fantasy in it. It is the true world we know, where we have come to expect anguish as the consequence of our own inspirations, where we crash up against the very circumstance from which we had always imagined we were exempt. In this true world, suffering is endemic and few are forgiven. Yet it may be that for Singer the concrete presence of the unholy attests the hovering redemptive holy, whose incandescence can scatter demons. . . .

Not all the stories in this collection emerge from that true world, however. The eerie authority of "**The Cabalist of East Broadway**" is a gripping exception, but in general the narratives set in the American environment are, by contrast, too thin. Even when intentionally spare—as in the marvelous "**Vanvild Kava,**" with its glorious opening: "If a Nobel Prize existed for writing little, Vanvild Kava would have gotten it"—the European settings have a way of turning luxuriantly, thickly coherent. Presumably some of these American locales were undertaken in a period when the fertile seed of the townlets had begun to be exhausted; or else it is the fault of America itself, lacking the centripetal density and identity of a yeshiva society, the idea of community as an emanation of God's gaze. Or perhaps it is because many of these American stories center on Singer as writer and celebrity, or on someone like him. It is as if the predicaments that fly into his hands nowadays arrive because he is himself the centripetal force, the controlling imp. And an imp, to have efficacy, as Singer's genius has shown, must be a kind of dybbuk, moving in powerfully from outside; whereas the American narratives are mainly inside jobs, about the unusual "encounters" a famous writer meets up with. (p. 16)

[Unfortunately, Singer's translators] cannot reach the deep mine and wine of Singer's mother tongue, thronged (so it was once explained to me by a Tel Aviv poet accomplished in Hebrew, Yiddish and English) with that unrenderable Hebrew erudition and burnished complexity of which we readers in English have not an inkling, and are permanently deprived. Deprived? Perhaps. *The Collected Stories,* when all is said and done, is an American master's "Book of Creation." (p. 17)

> Cynthia Ozick, *"Fistfuls of Masterpieces," in* The New York Times Book Review, *March 21, 1982, pp. 1, 14-17.*

GABRIELE ANNAN

The stories [in *The Collected Stories of Isaac Bashevis Singer*] fall into three main categories, all mixed up together: Galician stories, set either in the early decades of the century or in a past which seems medieval or legendary, but actually cannot stretch back more than two hundred years; transitional stories with an autobiographical element, set in Warsaw or the West; and later stories about survivors of the Holocaust, still 'lost in America' after forty or fifty years. . . .

The Galician tales are presented with a deliberately naive directness, which may be derived from early 19th-century anthologies of Hassidic tales, but to a Western ear sounds like the Brothers Grimm: 'In the town of Lashnik, not far from Lublin, there lived a man and his wife.' Singer's Galicia is as far from modern Europe as Carlo Levi's Lucania, but instead of an anthropological approach you get an Expressionist dream landscape: the sky is lurid with a weird and possibly apocalyptic light, like the sky in a Chagall painting; nature throbs with pantheistic energies, and ghosts and demons wander about. The Jews, though, mostly stay indoors in their dilapidated, insanitary and fire-prone houses. The place is a feminist's nightmare. The highest calling is to study the Scriptures, an economically unsound occupation reserved to men. Marriages are arranged for girls in their mid-teens, but if given a choice by exceptionally indulgent parents they will pick the weedy, unappetising scholar rather than the stalwart carter, cobbler or carpenter: so they have to be breadwinners as well as housekeepers. . . .

With obvious approval, Singer introduces bluestockings who learn Hebrew and read the Scriptures; one of them even becomes a transvestite in order to study at the *yeshiva.* This leads to complications that vaguely resemble the plot of *Twelfth Night,* but end more messily. Singer's attitude towards women is ambivalent: the bluestocking rebels turn into patient Griseldas on marriage, and he seems to approve of that too. Meekness in women appears to turn him on (and so does its opposite, a sort of demonic gypsy sexuality). He is a very sexy writer. Compared to, say, Ian McEwen or Martin Amis he is not very outspoken: there is something prurient about the way he closes the bedroom door on his couples, a sort of blindfold voyeurism.

No doubt this springs from and reflects the claustrophobic puritanism of the society he writes about, a society, one cannot help feeling, which is only partly based on reality and is partly the exaggerated creation of Singer's love-hatred for his antecedents. It is a society in which everyone over-reacts: the most trivial occurrence or rumour produces screams, wails, fits. And having created this hysterical world, Singer over-reacts to it with disgust, on the one hand, and, on the other, with an overintensity of admiration and longing. . . .

[His Galician Jews] believe in the transmigration of souls from animals to humans and back again. Metempsychosis is only one among their many weird and occult superstitions. Demonic possession is common, especially among innocent young girls. This is one of Singer's favourite themes. Possession focuses the fear of sex and the fear of heterodoxy in closed puritan societies, whether in 17th-century New England or Eastern Europe. Several stories are told in the first person by demons. Since Singer never allows himself to intrude into his narratives ('genuine literature,' the Author's Note says, 'tolerates commentary by others,' but 'it should never try to explain itself'), the demons are a useful device: they rejoice when the characters go wrong and despond when they behave well—the reader knows what he is supposed to think.

In the story **"The Destruction of Kreshev"**, Satan himself is the narrator. He converts a pious young student called Shloimele to the heresy of Sabbatai Svevi, a false Jewish messiah of the 17th century who perverted the Hassidic doctrine of 'the descent in behalf of the ascent'—i.e. that contact with evil is necessary for a full apprehension of God. Some of his followers believed—not unlike members of the Russian Chlysty sect— that only the most abject sinner can fully experience God's mercy: 'Sin is cleansing'; 'an excess of degradation meant sanctity.' Singer's novel about the Sabbatai Svevi movement, *Satan in Goray,* enabled him to paint a whole Jewish Walpurgis night full of lecherous demons and naked witches. **"Kreshev"** is on a smaller scale, but strong, horripilous stuff all the same. With a lot of quotation from the Cabbala Shloimele persuades his innocent and loving young wife to fornicate with her father's coachman while he looks on. Eventually all three are publicly disgraced, the wife commits suicide, and the town where they live is destroyed by fire. Shloimele himself becomes impotent quite early on: impotence as a punishment for perverting sex is another regular subject. Sex as such is good, so long as it is spontaneous. Then it is an expression of man's longing for God; it can even be a mystical union with Him: 'our genitals are actually the expression of the human soul, defiant of lechery, the most ardent defenders of true love.' (This is from *Lost in America:* it does not infringe the embargo on authorial comment in fiction.) (p. 17)

The old man to whom being a Jew is a full-time occupation is the hero of **"Grandfather and Grandson"**. The title looks like a deliberate echo of Turgenev's *Fathers and Sons:* the grandson rejects Judaism, becomes a socialist, and is shot during a riot. The old man forgives the apostate and prays for him: 'His intentions were good. He wanted to help the poor.' This story forms a transition between the *shtetl* stories and those set between the outbreak of the First World War and the aftermath of the Second. They are written in a more conversational style and there is also more conversation in them. The Jews have left the *shtetl* and are fighting literary feuds in the Warsaw cafés. They drink, they telephone; sometimes they even dance to a victrola. The young are scattered in attics and studios all over the town, writing, painting from the nude, and sleeping together, constantly changing partners, or else not changing them but allowing them to accumulate. There is much sexual athleticism: 'Those who have to do with women must boast.' The older generation contains an inordinate number of sad, disoriented eccentrics; many of the young seem literally crazed—with sex, certainly, but ultimately because the problem of living with 'the kind of secular Jewishness that defies all definition' is too much for them. The most hectic of all these hectic stories describes a *ménage à trois* between a man and two beautiful, witch-like, hysterical sisters who have survived both the German and the Russian invasions of Poland. Like Shloimele, the man becomes impotent, and he finally bolts when an apparition in their Paris apartment tries to castrate him. . . . (pp. 17-18)

In the last group of stories Singer takes his preoccupation with the paranormal with him to the States. The occult there has been institutionalised: there are mediums, séances, spiritualist magazines, weekend conferences on parapsychology. All this gives him an opportunity to exercise his underexploited gift for Jewish black humour. . . .

The European Jews in the States dabble in occultism because even after forty or fifty years they are still 'lost in America', no matter whether they half-starve on a daily visit to the take-away somewhere on the Upper West Side or cosset themselves in a sea-view apartment on Miami Beach. Crazier than ever, they are now lonelier than ever too. Physically they are falling apart: their false teeth don't fit, hair sprouts on their noses, their legs are feeble, their bladders out of control; cancer and heart attacks lurk. Worst of all, not being full-time Jews any more, their occupation's gone, and their orientation in the world with it. Instead, they have become a metaphor for humanity.

> Along with the atom, the personality of *Homo sapiens* has been splitting. When it comes to technology, the brain still functions, but in everything else degeneration has begun. They are all insane. . . . This metropolis has all the symptoms of a mind gone berserk.

New York is largely a Jewish metropolis, of course, and it is surely not without significance that in the recent *Levitation,* a sequence of 'five fictions', Cynthia Ozick's Jewish heroine, Ruth Puttermesser, works for the New York Administration. She is a generation younger than the youngest of Singer's characters, but still rootless: 'Poor Puttermesser has found herself without a past. Her mother was born in the din of Madison Street. . . . Her father is nearly a Yankee.' So Puttermesser invents an ancestor by updating her Orthodox great-uncle Zindel, who died four years before she was born, and convincing herself that she learnt Hebrew at his knee. You could say that Singer owes some of his immense popularity in the States to the fact that he can be Uncle Zindel to every American Jew.

Still, they are not uncritical. In the story **"The Cafeteria"** the cafeterianiks come up to the author-narrator's table and reproach him 'for all kinds of literary errors: I contradicted myself, went too far in descriptions of sex, described Jews in such a way that anti-semites could use it for propaganda.' To take the last criticism first: it strikes one that the life-style and ethos of Singer's Galician Jews—and his own mixture of admiration and abhorrence—uncannily illustrate Nietzsche's account of Pauline Christianity, which, according to him, was based on the values of the oppressed Jews of the Diaspora. . . . 'The principle of *Love,*' he says, 'derives from the small Jewish community: the soul that glows here under the ashes of humility and poverty is a more passionate soul.' According to Nietzsche, Christianity discovered from the Diaspora Jews 'that the most miserable life can be made rich and immeasurably precious by raising the temperature.' On the basis of observations such as these Nietzsche has been accused of fuelling anti-semitism. To

level the same accusation against Singer (with his chronically raised temperature) is naive. Besides, it is asking him to be bland, to eliminate the tension that makes his work both disturbing and meaningful.

Leaving aside the second reproach—too sexy—we come to the most serious one: 'that I contradicted myself.' In his Author's Note Singer denies that he has a message: 'The zeal for messages has made many writers forget that storytelling is the raison d'être of artistic prose.' But Singer's tone tends to be vatic. His reader feels there must be a message; and in a sense to write in Yiddish in New York in the 1980s in itself conveys some kind of message. The trouble is that Singer does not so much contradict himself as jumble everything up in a mystic brew which he stirs like some slightly suspect sorcerer. You really have to keep your eye on his fingers to see what goes into the pot. The basic stock is Hassidism, a mystical religion which aims at the apprehension of God, on the one hand, through contemplation and asceticism, and, on the other, through spontaneity, joy and even sex—and which therefore appears to contradict itself about the kind of life-style the believer should adopt. Hassidism contains many elements from the Cabbala, the esoteric Medieval teachings of Judaism; and the Cabbala, in its turn, was much influenced by Sufism, Neoplatonism and various Christian doctrines. It also dealt with such recondite subjects as cosmology, numerology, demonology, and magic. Into this heterogeneous mixture Singer throws a little Spinoza, some Quantum Theory, a measure of Dostoevskyan Weltanschauung, psychology (Jungian, Freudian and Gestalt, at a guess), findings from parapsychological research, and much else besides.

The mixture sometimes turns out too strong. With ideas, Singer is perhaps only a sorcerer's apprentice, after all, and lets them get the better of him. With words he is a fully qualified magician. His descriptions of landscapes and townscapes are visionary, hallucinating. He may be over-emotional, but he never overwrites in the sense of using two words where one will do. 'My valise would not close and I had bound it with many shoelaces which I had purchased from a blind beggar'; 'Eiserman, the dentist who had translated Shakespeare's sonnets into Yiddish, told me that he had offered to make Yabloner a set of false teeth, but Yabloner had said to him, "There is only one step from false teeth to a false brain."' Three people and something of their backgrounds emerge from these two sentences, and something of Singer's charm, which may or may not be one's cup of magic potion. The trouble is he is such a gripping narrator that one may swallow the stuff whether one likes it or not. (p. 18)

Gabriele Annan, "Uncle Zindel," in London Review of Books, *September 2 to September 15, 1982, pp. 17-18.*

FRANK TUOHY

There is one story in Isaac Bashevis Singer's [*Collected Stories*] which I'd choose as a test-case, a sort of *pons asinorum* in the progress to appreciating his work. **"Short Friday"** is one of his best-known stories; it belongs with that half of his work which deals with the vanished life of the Polish ghetto, and the legends and mysteries surrounding the traditional faith of the Jews.

"Short Friday" has something of the quality of a parable or a fairy tale. Shmul-Leibele is a poor tailor, devout and sweet-natured, but bad at his craft and unprepossessing in appearance.

His wife Shoshe compensates for these deficiencies: she is beautiful—Singer's stories tend to be populated by ugly little men and beautiful women—a wonderful housekeeper and a better tailor than her husband. The couple's childlessness is probably his fault rather than hers. They are happy and contented in their piety and benevolence. On the shortest Friday of the year they perform the pre-Sabbath rituals, they eat the frugal but delicious food that Shoshe has prepared. Later, while winter snow piles up outside, they sleep. Once they wake and, Shoshe being ritually clean, they make love. They wake again and talk to each other, but discover that they are in their graves: the fumes of the stove have killed them.

"**Short Friday**" loses everything in the retelling, which indicates that it is much more than an anecdote. In its power to move, it reminded me of Tolstoy's legend of the three hermits: in extreme old age, these holy men are taught the Lord's Prayer for the first time by a visiting bishop. They soon forget it and the bishop sees them following him for him to remind them, walking across the water behind his boat. A fairy tale can suspend disbelief, risk sentimentality and win through.

"**Short Friday**" has larger reverberations, of course. What happens to the tailor and his wife is a symbol for the disappearance of a whole world in the gas-chambers of Maidanek and Auschwitz. In invoking the supernatural, it reveals a linking factor in Singer's work. The dybbuks and devils of stories like "**The Gentleman from Cracow**" are linked with the crazy spiritualists and students of the Cabbala in New York.

There seems every reason for approaching Singer's work with trepidation. He describes a world from which the *goyim* are almost entirely excluded, and his choice of Yiddish as a literary language must distance him from modern Israel. A few of his stories ... belong entirely to our world: "**The Bus**" is an excellent example. But how far is it our world? Only two Anglo-Saxons appear in these forty-seven stories. They are called John Parker and Rose Beecham—awkward dull names provided by a writer whose attention is elsewhere.

Singer's stories, whatever their setting, are full to the brim with their subjects. It is only later that one realizes how much his career constitutes a slap in the face for American self-esteem. He has not bought any of the myths associated with immigration (only one story "**The Little Shoemakers**" veers towards sentimentality in this respect). He has left it to others, the Leon Urises and their like, to cash in on the holocaust. New York, equally, is Purgatory or Gehenna. Even for the mouse, Huldah, in the wonderful story "**The Letter Writer**", the world is a place of horror: 'In relation to them, all people are Nazis; for the animals it is an eternal Treblinka. And yet man demands compassion from heaven'.

Various translators have contributed to the Englishing of Singer's stories. Some of the later ones, however, have no attribution, and perhaps he is now out on his own. There are some oddities.... (pp. 124-25)

Singer and his aides, attempting to be timeless, have been forced back to the sort of translator's jargon we can only too easily recognize: words like wag, simpleton, mollycoddle, greenhorn, prankster, unused in ordinary speech.... One can see why Singer needed his own language in order to bear witness to his own world, now irretrievably lost, and must be grateful that his stories are here to tell us of it. (p. 125)

Frank Tuohy, "Reverberations," in London Magazine, *Vol. 22, Nos. 9-10, December, 1982-January, 1983, pp. 124-25.*

ANATOLE BROYARD

[Though *The Penitent*] is presented as a novel it reads more like a series of thou shalt nots. It is less a novel than a long complaint against what the author calls modern Western culture.

The Penitent opens with the timeworn as-told-to device. In a preamble, Mr. Singer describes his meeting with the narrator of the book during a visit to Israel in 1969. At the end of the book, in an Author's Note, he ambiguously agrees and disagrees with the narrator. The general effect is of Mr. Singer delivering himself of an exasperated attack through the agency of a puppetlike character.

As a novel, *The Penitent* is rather perfunctory and undramatic. Joseph Shapiro, the penitent of the title, describes his life in a summarizing fashion, interspersed with harangues against lechery, greed and man's inhumanity to man. At one point, Shapiro says to his imaginary listener, who never enlivens the narrative, "I know what you want to say: 'Tell the story, don't preach,'" But he does preach. In fact, there's more preaching in the book than anything else....

What price purity? The reader may ask himself at the end of this grumpy and unconvincing book. There is not much evidence here of the lovable fantasist or lighthearted storyteller who won the Nobel Prize. Rather, Mr. Singer sounds like a neglected grandfather complaining to two or three generations of his children.

It's remotely possible that Shapiro is meant to be taken ironically, and his accusations as hyperbolical half-truths. Irony, in the form of social or metaphysical complaint, has become something of a tradition, almost a responsibility, in the modern novel. Yet, because it is all surface, *The Penitent* hardly encourages such a reading. It seems, rather, to be a case in which the author's moral indignation overwhelms both his irony and his sense of craft.

Anatole Broyard, in a review of "The Penitent," in The New York Times, *September 22, 1983, p. C22.*

HAROLD BLOOM

The Penitent is a translation of a short novel called *Der Baal Tshuve* in Yiddish. Perhaps this title should have been translated as "The Master of Turning," which would have been more literal and also a proper tribute to its distinguished author, who is a master of metamorphoses. But perhaps this book, first published in 1974, ought not to have been translated at all. It is a very unpleasant work, without any redeeming esthetic merit or humane quality. Singer's best book ... was his *Collected Stories*, published last year. *The Penitent*, a failed attempt at a Swiftian diatribe against the contemporary world, is his worst book, and yet it does expose limitations that are not Singer's alone, and so it sadly defines much that is uneasy and probably insoluble in the dilemmas of Jewish culture at this time.

Singer's strength in *The Collected Stories* is in a rare exuberance of narrative invention, rather than in the creation of character, but *The Penitent* has almost no story and invests itself in the character of its monologuist, Joseph Shapiro.... Shapiro is the master of penitence, having returned to orthodoxy after an archetypal Jewish wandering, from Poland in 1939 through Stalin's wartime Russia on to America, success in real estate, failure in marriage, disaster in a love affair, despair over all fashionable ideologies, and subsequent flight to vegetarianism and to Meab Shearim, the neighborhood of extreme orthodoxy in Jerusalem.

Unfortunately, the reader can develop no interest in Shapiro because the author develops none. Shapiro is only a voice: negative, intense, apprehensive, fascinated by lust yet filled with revulsion toward it. The voice is indistinguishable from Singer's own, and there is no way to read this book except as Singer's tirade. A tirade is in itself a perfectly respectable literary form.... Singer is to be faulted not for his chosen genre but for his execution; his jeremiad has no surprises, no wit and little variety. Nevertheless, it does have force, though this force is hardly its own. It is a force internalized by many among us, Jew and gentile alike, and can be called the Moral Majoritarian hovering in each of us, however enlightened we pride ourselves on being.

Here is a typical passage from Shapiro's diatribes: "There's no such thing as morality without religion. If you don't serve one idol, you serve another. Of all the lies in the world, humanism is the biggest. Humanism doesn't serve one idol but all the idols. They were all humanists: Mussolini, Hitler, Stalin." The last of those sentences crosses over from extravagance into nonsense but is consonant with everything else asserted by Singer/Shapiro. Merely to list some of the moral reflections to which we are treated may suggest that this book is an involuntary satire upon itself. Denounced throughout are: all women except those who are Orthodox Jewish; all "Jewish Reds" (rather widely defined); liberalism; the American judicial system; American newspapers; "acclaim of stupid books, dirty plays and films"; professors of history. To list more would be redundant. Sometimes, the uncanny effect is that Singer seems to be parodying some of Saul Bellow's minor characters. (p. 3)

Before one decides that Singer has simply become a Biblical literalist, one might remember that orthodox Judaism is now less a Biblical faith than it is the continuation of the particular interpretations that the rabbis have placed upon the Bible. Singer's spokesman, Shapiro, fitly prefers those interpretations to Scripture itself; "Lately, I have come to understand why pious Jews never believed, and still don't believe, in studying too much Scripture. The horror stories in the Scriptures somehow didn't befit the spirit of the Diaspora Jew. Rabbi Isaac Luria and Baal Shem Tov are closer and more understandable to him than Joshua, the son of Nun, and King David. Joshua and King David had to be justified and defended, but Rabbi Isaac Luria and Baal Shem Tov needed no defense whatsoever.... I'm not talking against the Scriptures, God forbid. The Scriptures are holy. But Jewishness has developed. All things start out raw, and ripen with time. When the apple is green, it doesn't have the same sweet taste as when it is ripe. The basement of a house is not as elegant as a drawing room."

Does "Jewishness" here mean Judaism? Singer's "Jewishness" can hardly be questioned, but is that the only aim of his spokesman's drive, of his repentant turning to become as Jewish a character as Singer is a Jewish writer? Isaac Luria, the 16th-century founder of a modern Kabbalah, and the Baal Shem Tov, 18th-century founder of Hasidism, are certainly the principal sages of the mystical and ecstatic strains in modern Jewish piety. But if one thinks of the Singer who wrote the major and famous stories, then even Luria and the Baal Shem Tov seem too normative and orthodox, too tame for the ethos of Singer's fictive world.

The Singer who matters most seems to be the complement to the late Gershom Scholem's massive studies in Jewish mysticism, messianic apostasy and Gnostic demonology. Against the Singer of those extraordinary tales, we perhaps now must set the strident moralizer of *The Penitent*. Ironically, Singer executes a very personal turn upon the patterns of messianic apostasy as charted by Scholem. The most remarkable of these messianic apostates was Sabbatai Zevi, who in the 17th century eventually converted to Mohammedanism. It is as though Singer is a Sabbatai Zevi who becomes not a Moslem but an orthodox bigot. Singer's most characteristic attributes as a writer—his sexual obsessions and demonic impulses—are thus reabsorbed into the most atavistic strains in contemporary Jewry.

Among the principal targets of Singer/Shapiro's diatribes one would expect to find psychoanalysis. Though there are some passing and glancing animadversions throughout, Singer shies away from a direct confrontation with Freud's critique of all religions, Judaism included. The doubly repressive force—of Singer's deliberate forgetfulness of both Freud and his own most intense impulses—becomes at once the rhetorical strength and the conceptual weakness of this book. The only amusing moment in *The Penitent* occurs on the flight to Israel, when Joseph Shapiro postpones his new life long enough to be frustrated by the difficulties of making love on a jetliner:

"It's hard to sin physically on an airplane. Passengers kept going to and from the rest rooms, the stewardesses weren't sleeping, the lights weren't completely extinguished, only dimmed. I felt some passion for this female, but I also felt revulsion. It's odd, but although modern woman is always ready to commit all kinds of abominations, nevertheless she girds herself in such a thorough fashion that it's a struggle to get at her. The desire to appear slim is even stronger than the urge to sin. We fumbled around this way for many minutes."

Roused by what Freud would have called the "incitement premiums" of confined jet-space and well-girded woman, the unfortunate Shapiro is inspired to the very heights of his great argument on behalf of religious morality. Here the old Singer indeed breaks through, and for once the book's humor is not involuntary. But the new Singer then interposes himself, and the unintended hilarity returns:

"Suddenly a man walked by me. He wore a rabbinical hat, had a wide blond beard, long earlocks, and the front of his coat was open to display a ritual garment with fringes.... I realized at that moment that without earlocks and a ritual garment one cannot be a real Jew. A soldier who serves an emperor has to have a uniform, and this also applies to a soldier who serves the Almighty. Had I worn such an outfit that night, I wouldn't have been exposed to those temptations." (pp. 3, 26)

How has Singer come down to this? I do not think that we have here only another episode in the decline and fall of practically everybody. Singer, like the somewhat subtler though equally pungent Cynthia Ozick, is representative of what might be called Jewish literary neo-orthodoxy. This attitude condemns as anti-Judaism or idolatry every acknowledged rupture or felt discontinuity that exists between the tradition and contemporary Jewish intellectuals.

Yet it is the illumination of the ambivalences and the ambiguition of such rupture that may have made Freud and Kafka, somewhat unwillingly, the authentic representatives of Jewish culture in and for our time. Miss Ozick has praised Singer as a moralist who "tells us that it is natural to be good, and unholy to go astray" [see excerpt above]. Perhaps that praise is merited by *The Penitent*. Had Singer written often thus, he would indeed be remembered as a master of neo-orthodoxy, but hardly as a master of the intricate turnings of stories. (p. 27)

Harold Bloom, "Isaac Bashevis Singer's Jeremiad," in The New York Times Book Review, *September 25, 1983, pp. 3, 26-7.*

BRINA CAPLAN

An urgent stranger accosts Isaac Bashevis Singer and tells him a story that becomes, in turn, the story Singer is telling us. Singer has used this device as an entrance into narrative more than once, although never in a novel. *The Penitent* begins in 1969 in Old Jerusalem during Singer's first visit to the recently recaptured Wailing Wall. He regards the crowd wryly: residents and European Hasidim, Israeli soldiers, professional beggars, the schmoozers and the prayerful. "The Almighty," he observes, "conducted business here on a twenty-four-hour basis."

Such irony is pure Singer—especially the autobiographer of *In My Father's Court, A Little Boy in Search of God* and *A Young Man in Search of Love*. In writing about his own life, Singer has led us to expect a detached view both of human beings, who persist in contradictory or self-interested or impiously destructive behavior, and of their Creator, who persists in working out the details of an incomprehensible but plainly unwieldy divine plan. What is astonishing about *The Penitent* is the abrupt loss of this perspective. Approached at the Wailing Wall by Joseph Shapiro, formerly an American businessman and now a born-again Hasid, Singer becomes a listener, in effect turning over the narrative to his central character. Once Shapiro takes over, puzzlement about God's plan narrows into certitude, skepticism gives way to dogma, and irony toward erring mankind sours into loathing. Shapiro's message is absolute: "The slightest compromise that you make with the pagan culture of our time is a gesture toward evil, a nod to a world of murder, idolatry, and adultery." Only "Talmud Jews," who live in the ritually exacting manner of their grandfathers, will avoid complicity in "a civilization that is a slaughterhouse and brothel."

Like the Ancient Mariner, Shapiro has a story to tell of alienation and fortunate escape. "Penitent" in Hebrew is *baal tshuve,* "one who returns." Shapiro has reached home—that is, the spare purity of Orthodox Judaism—but only after years adrift on the sea of modernity. (p. 497)

Having disengaged from [his life of material prosperity and spiritual degradation] . . . , Shapiro must find a way of living that is conducive to decency. He becomes a vegetarian. He sets out for the Holy Land.

His search in Israel amounts to a programmatic review of the moral possibilities of modern Judaism. He looks into city life in Tel Aviv and into the rural world of the kibbutz. He samples intellectualism, politics and commerce. Everywhere he finds the same disrespect for the Ten Commandments, the same promiscuity and pursuit of pleasure that drove him from America. Modern Jews have mistaken materialism for joy and power for morality. (p. 498)

Shapiro remains beleaguered until a turning in the streets of Jerusalem brings him to a community of Orthodox believers whose strictured way of life prevents adultery, thievery, murder and deception. He settles among them and marries again, saved not by chance or luck but by God's delivering hand. "Coin-cidence," as the old rabbi, his future father-in-law, reminds him, "is not a kosher word."

Nor is albatross a kosher dish, but much of what Shapiro serves up has the flavor of that symbolic bird. Indeed, reversing the Ancient Mariner's conclusion, "He prayeth best, who loveth best," produces the dictum Shapiro has come to deliver: Those love best who pray best, that is to say, a traditionally observant life must precede goodness. Maybe so. It is hard to judge from the account Shapiro offers us, since it contains so little that is loving. No generous or mutual relationships are dramatized in *The Penitent*. Shapiro's is the only voice we hear, his perspective the only point of view. And from that perspective, neither affection nor respect nor empathy mediate the abrasive differences between contemporary men and women.

Differences, he warns us, are dangerous outside a closed community of belief that holds individuals in right relation to one another—sexual differences in particular. Without traditional restraint, women become abusive and cruel. . . . [His ex-wife and former mistress, he reports,] "had often accused me of lacking respect for women. But what was there to respect about them?" The only answer to that question is a question: How can there be anything to respect about the women of *The Penitent* when they are never realized as characters but remain merely the symbols of Shapiro's desire and loathing? The worst of them are albatrosses hung about his neck until faith removes them; the best are shadows, adumbrations of Orthodox virtue. (pp. 498-99)

Do you detect misogyny in Shapiro's inability to know the women in his life? Your mistake, he insists; on the contrary, he is a defender of women's intrinsic worth:

> When the evil spirit . . . tried to prove to me that the whole female gender is wanton and vicious, I thought of my mother and grandmother. Everything that the Devil, who played the role of an anti-feminist now, said about women had no connection whatsoever to these old-fashioned women. They didn't enslave our grandfathers but helped them to earn a living. They were everything at once: wives, breadwinners, mothers. . . . They were saints, and they didn't have to brood about orgasms.

Actually, the reasoning here may be less misogynous than narcissistic. Shapiro would have us believe that women are to blame for the unwanted feelings he experiences in their presence. All goes well as long as those saints and grandmothers behave so as to hide thoughts of sexuality, anger and conflict from male awareness. When women have desires of their own, however, men become "enslaved" by demands and urges beyond toleration. No wonder Shapiro fastens onto his audience with the bony grip and baleful eye of an Ancient Mariner. He has quite a discovery to reveal: women implant thoughts and feelings in men. Of course, power of this sort had better be leashed by a traditional code of behavior.

Usually, Singer's field of view is wide enough to allow for competing values, for irony and wonder. The mystery of *The Penitent* is why he has reduced its range to the few simplicities Shapiro can appreciate. (pp. 499-500)

Brina Caplan, "The Path of the Self-Righteous," in The Nation, *Vol. 237, No. 16, November 19, 1983, pp. 497-500.**

SARAH BLACHER COHEN

Isaac Bashevis Singer was awarded the Nobel Prize for his "impassioned narrative art" with roots in the Eastern European Yiddish cultural tradition, but his plays differ in important and interesting ways from those representative of that tradition. The plays of Avrom Goldfadn combined melodrama and music to dramatize stirring Biblical events and inspirational stories from Jewish history. Those of Jacob Gordin sought to elevate the Yiddish language and enlighten the Jewish masses with their realism and moralizing. Sholem Asch made the theater his soapbox and wrote social protest plays denouncing the ills of the Jewish community. Singer's plays, however, veer off in their own direction. At the age of sixty-eight, he created his own special brand of Jewish folk drama, while retaining many of the conventions of the standard form. Through deceptively simple writing, he has artfully fashioned a naive world, where wonder and superstition prevail over skepticism and reason. The structure of his plays is also uncomplicated; a leisurely beginning, an accelerated middle, and a startling end recur in the customary two acts, each with many short scenes. The plots are simple; each has a central action in which improbable events occur suddenly and swiftly. Most of the protagonists are distraught females in the grip of powerful obsessions who act recklessly and defiantly. Their language is of a feverish intensity, but the dialogue of the minor characters resembles the cute prattling of children or the cryptic utterances of old crones.

Singer's plays, however, depart from the traditional folk drama in one crucial way. "The folk play centered thematically on the response of the characters to the land on which they lived. Close to the soil, their identities and destinies were shaped by a force they sensed moving in the earth." The Jews Singer writes about were excluded from having vital connections with the land; they did not experience the hardship of its sterility or the joy of its fertility. Nor, for that matter, were they permitted to survive at all in their landless ghettos. Deprived of the sustaining theme of folk drama, Singer mobilizes greater forces of his imagination to invent an alternate theme and related setting for his folk plays. He pretends the Holocaust did not exist and writes about these Jews as they live in his memory and imagination. Believing that "literature must have an address, that it just cannot be in a vacuum," Singer constructs his version of the *shtetl* and converts it into an appropriate backdrop for his resurrected Jews to act out their parts. In place of the idyllic or malevolent land of the typical folk drama, he creates idyllic or malevolent *shtetls* to shape the destiny of his characters. Just as the land became more symbol than fact, so Singer's *shtetl*, stripped of historical verisimilitude, is more a stylized creation of his imagination than a realistically specified place. In this alternately charming and grotesque realm of his fancy, the world is finally "but lure and appearance, a locale between heaven and hell, the shadow of larger possibilities." And the quaint Jewish folk, the temporary inhabitants of this insubstantial sphere, are intent not on cultivating a piece of land but on purifying their souls. The greatest deterrent to their doing so is the temptation of illicit sexuality, either adultery or homosexuality. Though they yield to temptation, the primary evil lies not in their forbidden indulgence in the carnal but in their surrender to the secular hedonism which the carnal represents. Their struggle on earth and in the world beyond is to forsake this hedonism and embrace the austere life of piety. The spiritual territory recedes before them, but still they journey toward it.

At their best, Singer's dramas are authentic expressions of a folk culture whose speech, emotions and thought he intimately knows. They are also products of his idiosyncratic imagination, which freely consorts with the improper and the farfetched. But Singer's plays have not emerged full-blown from his head as plays. They are adaptations of his short stories made with the assistance of literary collaborators and theatrical advisers. (pp. 197-98)

Singer's first boyhood association with the theater was as a place of evil. From a sermon his rabbi father preached, he learned that "the wicked sit day and night in the theater, eat pork and sin with loose women." Many years later, therefore, *The Mirror*, the first play Singer adapted from his similarly titled short story, concerned the seduction of a loose woman by a demon. In **"The Mirror,"** one of several demon-infested stories Singer wrote for a projected volume, *Memoirs of the Spirit of Evil*, the first-person demon narrator performs different functions than he does in Singer's play. As a witty teller of the tale, who seems more like a puckish wedding jester than a grim fiend, he causes us to take a lighthearted view of Zirel, the beautiful but bored *shtetl* woman who succumbs to temptation. By emphasizing his maverick origins and wily stratagems to ensnare her more than her anguish at being ensnared, he distances us from her plight. He takes the sting out of evil by showing its charming irresistibility and infects us with his cavalier attitude toward it. Because he is the demonic master of ceremonies, he determines the pace and length of the story. . . . The English translation of the story, with its rapid narration of events and snatches of dialogue at only the most crucial junctures, is only eleven pages long. Little is revealed about Zirel's life before the demon's arrival, what actually prompted her capitulation, or the full extent of her remorse in Sodom. The story's larger questions are left unanswered. "Is there a God? Is he all merciful? Will Zirel ever find salvation? Or is creation a snake primeval crawling with evil?" . . . The demon pleads ignorance. Since he is a "minor devil" who is unlikely to get promoted, he is deprived of a larger omniscience.

Singer expands our understanding of Zirel's plight and the philosophical issues connected with it in the two-act play he wrote for the Yale Repertory Theater in 1973. He leaves behind the demon's limited point of view and focuses on Zirel's behavior before, during, and after her fall. Zirel is another of Singer's educated women, who, denied access to the study of sacred writings, has no function in the *shtetl*'s male-dominated world of traditional Judaism. Nor is she blessed with children to absorb her energies and give her status as a worthy Jewish wife. At the play's beginning, Singer treats her dilemma more whimsically than tragically. Unlike the angry heroines in Singer's stories, Zirel does not grievously lament her fate and castigate a patriarchal society for its gross injustice. Rather she acts like a wayward fairy-tale creature who resorts to subversive means to obtain compensating pleasures. She stealthily reads erotic supernatural tales and, like the wicked stepmother in "Snow White and the Seven Dwarfs," continually gazes at her mirror to confirm she is the fairest of them all. Zirel is not totally to blame for her profane reading and idle vanity since in the play, unlike the story, her cabalist husband, Shloime, is so engrossed in his messianism that he wears his breeches to bed to be ready for the Messiah's coming. Zirel, for her part, is so sexually frustrated that she can only jest at her own expense: "All I have is a marriage contract. He's either praying, studying, or just murmuring." . . . Indeed a measure of the first act's humor concerns the burlesqued clash of values between the puritanical husband and the sensual wife, which for Singer symbolizes the irreconcilable conflict between religious asceticism and carnal delight. The more extreme each character's behavior becomes, that is, the more each renounces the body for the soul and the soul for the body, the more desperately comic Zirel and Shloime become.

Since Zirel cannot wait for Shloime's love in the world to come, she practices self-love in this world. In Singer's value system, worship of self replacing worship of God is a sign of demonic possession. Drawing upon the Jewish folk tradition, Singer, therefore, has the mirror become the devil's hiding place. The demon in the mirror distorts reality and points up the void at the heart of existence. . . . At the same time the demon-inhabited mirror becomes a magnifying glass that expands Zirel's imagination. It contributes to her erroneous sense of a double identity: the dutiful wife and the wild harlot. Projecting an illusion of a titillating worldly realm, the mirror also offers her an escape from provincial Krashnik, the stultifying Polish village she lives in. . . . Above all, the mirror confuses Zirel's aesthetic and ethical judgment. She finds the ugly demon beautiful and infinitely preferable to a pious Jew, for she would rather have "one measure of debauchery than ten of modesty." (pp. 198-200)

The first act of *The Mirror* belongs to the morally flawed but humorously quaint world of Krashnik. Its characters, resembling the stock figures of Plautine comedy and the commedia dell'arte, are the familiar types of Singer's folk parables: the rascally servant, the religiously fanatic husband, the sexually spurned wife, the demon lover, and the specious sorcerer. The situations are sparse and sketchily developed. The seduction scene, which is the focal point, is economically and wittily drawn, but the exorcism is but a hackneyed version of the one in Ansky's *Dybbuk.* The dialogue in the remainder of the play is, for the most part, original. The demon, whose power resides in words, has the most arresting lines, by turns lyrical, antic, and exotic. Reb Yoetz is a master of Singer's folk aphorisms, a blend of the ribald and the religious, cast in the rural idiom. Zirel's language has verve when she is the comic ironist ridiculing her unconsummated marriage. The minor characters, however, could be directly imported from *Fiddler on the Roof,* for they speak in the same Yiddishized primer language of predictable simpletons.

The second act is anything but predictable. Just as Zirel takes a leap of faith, or more appropriately faithlessness, to follow her demon Hurmizah to the *sitra achra,* the other side of the mirror, so Singer takes an imaginative leap by depicting the supernatural realm beyond the mirror, the surreal world of Sodom, his equivalent of Hell. While Singer's Hell contains the requisite amount of tortures and perversions, it is more a caricature of both Hell and earth. The only sin in Sodom is not to sin. Desiring "all good things now," the demons, like contemporary Americans, are constantly rushing to indulge in as many pleasures as possible. (pp. 200-01)

Zirel soon realizes that she has been lured to Sodom under false pretenses. She is not to have her lust sated by the demons, but is to arouse their lust. Sodom, she ruefully discovers, is not the delightful haven of the damned. Its desperate hedonism proves ultimately as confining as her life in Krashnik. At this point, the play's allegorical implications are obvious. It is impossible for the person with a rarefied imagination to survive in a tedious ritual-bound society or in its obverse equivalent: a compulsorily exciting, aimless existence. It is far more satisfying to remain inside the mirror, the realm of possibility, removed from the fixed position of either sphere. Singer, however, advances a more religious interpretation of the play. *The Mirror,* he claims, is about "a person who cannot be happy

with God and cannot be happy with the Devil. God—the way the Jews understand God—is too boring, too dogmatic, too stagnant. So Zirel thought the Devil—let's call it the secular life—would be good. But the play shows that the secular life is also full of dogmas, also full of silly duties, also full of checks, not of assets—and a lot of cruelty in addition."

For Singer, the way back from Hell is impossible. . . . Subscribing to the doctrine of the irreversibility of sinful actions, Singer consigns Zirel to the interior of the mirror, his form of limbo, where she suffers for her own misdeeds and assumes the guilt of all former Zirels. She thus joins the ranks of the penitents in Singer's novels who immure themselves to painfully work out their own and the world's salvation.

Singer's idea of having a person who cannot live with either the religious or the worldly remain within a mirror is ingenious. However, in Act Two it takes Singer too long to get Zirel into her mirror. A good deal of extraneous happenings impede the resolution of the principal action: The orgiastic dance numbers are too excessive and lengthy; a gratuitous civil war breaks out between Sodom and Gomorrah; a precipitous love affair occurs between Zirel and a sodomite Reb Yoetz. But above all, the cryptic philosophizing most retards the pace. Moreover, all these distractions prevent Singer from fully developing Zirel's character. Devoid of the vitality she had in the first act, she is not as convincing as the pathetic object of demonic torture and mental anguish. The vibrant folk character of the first act becomes an enervated figure of allegory. Singer's circumscribed world of Krashnik thus proves more interesting than the orgiastic revels of Sodom and the solemn truths from the mirror's interior.

In *Teibele and Her Demon,* Singer's most recent play, which he, with collaborator Eve Friedman, adapted from his short story by the same name, there is no danger of getting lost in *The Mirror's* phantasmagorical netherworld or being detained in its murky realm of abstraction. The setting in *Teibele and Her Demon* is the palpable world of Frampol, Poland, in the 1880s, which, like Krashnik, is another of Singer's self-contained *shtetls* ruled by its own set of orthodox laws and unorthodox superstitions. Frampol, like Krashnik, is untouched by the shifting trends of secular thought or of the convolutions of history. The only current events that interest these villages are the moral rise and decline of their inhabitants and the swift administration of just rewards and punishments.

Since a deserted Jewish wife and her demon lover are the central characters of both *The Mirror* and *Teibele and Her Demon,* it would seem Singer is as much obsessed with depicting this incongruous couple as they are obsessed with each other. But the couples are not identical. Though the male lovers are both named Hurmizah and both employ the same lurid, exotic language in their seductions, the one in *The Mirror* is an actual demon but an impotent one. . . . Hurmizah in *Teibele* is an ordinary mortal, the lackluster teacher's helper, Alchonon, who masquerades as a very potent demon much devoted to Teibele. Indeed, in the original short story Alchonon as demon risks his life for Teibele, dying of pneumonia from his winter visits to her. His true identity and self-sacrifice are never revealed even at his funeral which Teibele by chance attends.

Obviously, Singer and Friedman did not feel that the death of a selfless male would be the most compelling subject for their play. Following the advice of Poe, one of Singer's favorite authors, they dramatized instead the death of a beautiful woman. Before Teibele's death, however, they involve her in a very lively bedroom farce.... In the first act, six wry elliptical scenes reveal the origin and intensity of Teibele's and Alchonon's sexual craziness. The convoluted rising action produces the hilarity of preposterous gullibility and farfetched deception. It captures the antic hypocrisy of daily respectability and nightly licentiousness. The dialogue conveys the inflated lyricism of new-found love and the deflating bawdy language of unabandoned mating. The characters are endearing folktale types, but their unlikely union makes for improbable transformations. Every Wednesday and Saturday night, the bedraggled Alchonon ceases being the village *schlemiel* and disguises himself as the demon Hurmizah, the genital superman who overwhelms Teibele with his sexual prowess and his sensual cabalistic lore. She, in turn, leaves off being the pious Jewish wife to become the uninhibited lover of her demon, though his breath smells of garlic and his nose sniffles in winter.

Sex, as in Singer's short stories, immediately becomes a leveler, removing distinctions between class, body, and mind. It also becomes an anesthesia numbing those in its power to any of its injurious effects. Teibele especially is so caught up in her passions that she sees nothing wrong with the affair. Alchonon, however, grows to dislike the relationship.

In a comic reversal of the typical male-female conflict, he resents being viewed as a sexual object and wants to be valued for his mind as well as his body. He objects to playing a role, to pretending to be someone he is not. He wants Teibele to cherish him as a mortal not a demon. He, therefore, resorts to further deceit by having Teibele's absent husband declared legally dead and in his guise as Hurmizah orders her to marry Alchonon, the man he actually is. By refusing to remain a supernatural creature and settle for a supernatural love, Alchonon transforms the play from a light-hearted romantic comedy to a serious drama with tragic overtones. For in Singer's moral universe, once an individual commits a falsehood and does not confess it, he is compelled to practice more and more damaging forms of deception until the accumulated weight of his subterfuge crushes him and those he implicates.

While Alchonon painfully complicates his life by relinquishing fantasy for reality, Teibele in Act Two suffers from clinging to fantasy and not accepting reality. Enthralled by the fiery raptures of her demon lover, she cannot tolerate the lukewarm connubial pleasures of her prosaic husband. Her nocturnal transports of joy with Hurmizah degenerate into daily marital strife with Alchonon just because her faulty imagination cannot discern that they are the same person. Teibele is thus Singer's embodiment of the perennially dissatisfied mortal who craves magic over the mundane, the exotic over the ordinary. For her these qualities are mutually exclusive categories which she cannot envision existing in the same individual. (pp. 201-03)

Teibele's failure to recognize Alchonon's dual identity has been criticized not only as a flaw in her character, but as a flaw in the play itself. Since Alchonon's appearance and language are not significantly altered between his demonic and human state, the question arises: how could she not be aware of the tricks played on her? Walter Kerr claims that our credulity, if not hers, has been taxed, that the play's "compounded sleight-of-hand," its "improvised twists and turns" defy the "bothersome laws of human logic." But what Kerr overlooks is that *Teibele and Her Demon* is not meant to be either a realistic problem play or a convincing psychological case study. It is another of Singer's erotic fables with its own idiosyncratic logic, its intentionally obvious mistaken identities, its outrageous improbabilities. As a fable, it adopts the childlike view

that anything can happen in the world of adults and does not offer elaborate explanations for these happenings. It simply presents the implausible as plausible and asks us, in the name of make-believe, to accept the conversion. (pp. 203-04)

Largely relying on Singer's familiar brand of stylized realism, [*Teibele and Her Demon*] is most innovative in the kind of love story it tells. The erotic is not merely trivial foreplay for a moralistic climax as in *The Mirror*. Nor is its magic dispelled by weighty philosophizing. In *Teibele* the erotic becomes the primary focus where it is accorded the highest reverence and the most intricate development.... Through the first half of the play, the couple's love is ... more divine than demonic, more soaring in mystical heights than plummeting into naturalistic depths. But no matter how uplifting ecstatic consummations are, they are not long-lasting so that in the remainder of the play their love becomes more human than divine. Its lack of fulfillment, however, proves just as moving as their earlier requited love. (p. 204)

When the spotlight is on the two principals caught up in the turbulent course of their love, *Teibele and Her Demon* is an absorbing play. But when Singer and Friedman introduce subsidiary characters whose only function is to provide exposition or tone down the eroticism with irrelevant levity, the results are disappointing.... The same holds true for the adapters' inclusion of quaint bits of Jewish ritual: a partial exorcism, a few lines of a *Purimshpil*, an abbreviated wedding ceremony. When these are an integral part of the play, reinforcing characterization and theme, they greatly enhance the work. But many of these ethnic scraps of local color serve only as kosher-style forms of parochialism to satisfy the commercial taste for things Jewish. Some of the dialogue is also the source of artificial Jewish seasoning. When the secondary characters imitate Catskill comedians straining for laughs, they are both anachronistic and cloying. Fortunately, the mercurial wit and poetic eloquence of Teibele and her demon drown out these voices.

This is not to suggest that Singer is incapable of creating authentically funny ethnic stereotypes who, in their own right, assume center stage. In *Shlemiel the First*, a play I have worked on with Isaac Bashevis Singer, the entire town is populated with dwarfed intellects whose sole excuse for being is to amuse. The amusement we devise for them makes no pretense at profundity. It consists of adolescent ruses, moronic credulity, domestic slapstick. The scantily developed characters suffer mounting escalations of confusion, but their humor of verbal retrieval enables them to make light of their mishaps. Their dialogue is filled with risible nonsequiturs, foolish aphorisms, and silly travesties of Talmudic logic.

In many ways *Shlemiel the First* burlesques the serious concerns of Singer's spiritual dramas. The questioning of values, the sexual misdeeds, the *shtetl* puritanism, and the misapprehensions of reality so earnestly discussed in *Teibele* and *The Mirror* are drolly treated in *Shlemiel the First*, which more resembles the classic numbskull tale than Singer's philosophical fantasies. The play, like the numbskull tale in which "misunderstanding results in inappropriate and absurd actions," deals with the compounded misunderstanding of Shlemiel, the docile town fool who agrees to spread the wisdom of Gronam Ox, the self-proclaimed sage of Chelm. Ox's wisdom consists of such gastronomic idiocy as: "The Tree of knowledge ... was a Blintze Tree" ... and "Cain killed Abel because he thought blood was borscht" ..., yet the addlepated Shlemiel, inspired by these truths, volunteers to go to the ends of the earth to convey this knowledge.

Fortunately, Shlemiel does not travel far, since the local vagabond, Chaim Rascal, tricks him into believing that he is heading toward the world when he is actually returning to Chelm. Thus upon his arrival home, Shlemiel mistakenly thinks he has discovered Chelm Two and convinces everyone, including his dubious wife, that he is a visitor from another Chelm. (pp. 205-06)

What follows is a ludicrous imitation of *Teibele and Her Demon,* whereby the power of illusion transforms the same man into a sexually more appealing one so that he ends up cuckolding himself. Mr. and Mrs. Shlemiel, like Singer's marriage violators, are guilt-ridden over what they believe is an adulterous union and are convinced they will be punished in Hell. However, in *Shlemiel the First,* they undergo a mock penance and are granted a mock salvation. Chaim Rascal, not the Angel of Death, confesses his deception and frees them of their delusion. Gronam Ox, the caricature of the merciful rabbi, pardons them for their unintentional sins and reunites them in lawful marriage. The final wisdom he dispenses is not another of his ridiculous pronouncements but a well-worn truth which serves as the real wisdom of this numbskull tale: while waiting for Paradise, "enjoy life" in this world. (p. 206)

Of Singer's strictly adult plays, the most mature and substantial of them is *Yentl,* which absorbed viewers primarily because it deals with problems of identity confronting Jewish women in the late-nineteenth-century Polish *shtetls,* problems that have not been resolved in our own century. In *The Mirror* and *Teibele and Her Demon,* the heroines' craving for otherworldly sensuality suppresses any desire they have for intellectual fulfillment in this world. In *Yentl,* however, the heroine's love for Torah vies forcefully with her love for a man. Her yearning for mental and spiritual liberation is strongly at odds with her need for physical and emotional union. Singer's play explores the religious context that gives rise to Yentl's conflict, subtly analyzes the complex dimensions of it, and compassionately depicts the painful consequences of the need to choose one alternative. (pp. 206-07)

Yentl is complex enough to warrant a modern psychological interpretation as well as a traditionally religious one. According to Singer, one of the principal reasons he wrote the drama was to show that "the human soul is full of contradictions." Just as a thief steals a prayer shawl to worship the Lord, "so Yentl breaks the law in order to be able to study the law." Yentl errs by trespassing in the male's learned domain, and by dressing in men's clothes to do so, she also damages her own God-given femininity. She is contravening the Torah's prohibition against men and women switching apparel, for "when the body dresses in strange garments the soul will be perplexed." . . . Appropriate clothing, according to this view, prescribes correct behavior and preserves rightful identity, or as Singer states, "clothes guard a person just as words do." By donning alien apparel and being possessed by it, Yentl assumes an alien sexuality and acts in unpredictably illicit ways. What starts out as a pragmatic disguise for the purest of motives ends up as a major transgression in which Yentl perverts her own desires and harmfully deceives those closest to her. Her male disguise as Anshel prevents her from consummating her natural love for her study partner, Avigdor, and leads her into an unnatural marriage with Hadass, to reclaim her for Avigdor. What results is a sinful homosexual union, since it blurs the "distinctions between the sexes," distinctions that traditional Judaism be-

lieves are as important as those between the weekday and the Sabbath, the Gentile and the Jew. Moreover, the union is sinful because it not only thwarts Hadass's personal need for maternity, but it makes impossible the Biblical injunction: "Be fruitful and multiply." Thus Singer implies that if the world were made up of only Yentls who devoted their lives to being Torah scholars, there would be no Jews born to study the Torah. To stress the need for perpetuating the Jewish people, he ends the play with the lawful heterosexual marriage of Hadass and Avigdor and the birth of their son, Anshel. There is no room for Yentl the Yeshiva student in this society whose survival depends upon reproducing itself. She must depart as a male to attend another seminary where as a female, Singer leads us to believe, she will secretly atone for her sacrilegious study of sacred texts. But there is a final reason Singer, the traditionalist, must rout Yentl from the community: she is not dependent on a man to define her identity and, therefore, does not provide a model for man's dependence on God. Viewing herself the accomplished rival of any man, she encourages man to view himself the accomplished rival of God.

However, Singer, the modernist, sees some worth in Yentl's depravity. Because she possesses the "divine androgyny of the soul" . . . , she is able to combine the strength of both sexes in her pursuit of wisdom. Her intellectual understanding of the Torah and Talmud is augmented by her enriched powers of perception. Her spiritual involvement with these holy writings is enhanced by her added religious fervor. Similarly, her ability to love both Hadass and Avigdor in ways which please each is due to her special sensitivity. Her decision to leave both of them is a reflection of her high degree of altruism. Though Heaven may have made a mistake in giving Yentl "the soul of a man" . . . and creating her a woman, the mistake has its compensations. Thus for Singer *Yentl* has a "kind of cabalistic meaning" in that sins can serve to "lift up the soul."

The blending of the traditional and the modern pertains not only to *Yentl*'s thematic concerns, but to many other features of the play. Of all of Singer's dramas, *Yentl* contains the most resemblances to the traditional Yiddish theater. They both include ingenious female disguise to enrich characterization and heighten romantic complications. Molly Picon, in a Yiddish drama by her husband, played a mischievous Yeshiva boy named Yankl, and in the Yiddish film, *Yidl mitn Fidel,* she masqueraded as a young male fiddler temporarily prevented from marrying the man she loves. However, Molly Picon's comedies emphasized the farcical not the psychological, the musical not the meditative. Jewish rituals, on the other hand, serve the same function in *Yentl* as they did in the Yiddish theater. They are not only colorful spectacles in their own right, but they lend Jewish authenticity to the works. Their cultural and religious import convey ready-made profundity to commonplace scenes. The emotions they evoke increase the audience's involvement with the dramatic action and intensify their identification with the characters. Unlike Singer's other plays, *Yentl* has compelling full-length rituals performed in the original Hebrew and quaint *shtetl* customs celebrated exactly as they were in the past. The only difference is that Singer and Napolin have taken certain liberties with them. The *Kaddish* for Yentl's father is the familiar prayer for the dead, but it is made even more moving by Yentl's forbidden recital of it. The wedding ceremony is the legitimate orthodox one, but it consecrates the illegitimate union of two women. Consequently, the bride's premarital rite of purification, while correct in form, does not have kosher results. Conversely, the wedding jester's chastisement of the bride and groom for their former sins is not just the standard speech, but it is unwittingly appropriate. Aside from these ironic variations, Singer and Napolin tried to make *Yentl*'s orthodox world as genuine as possible. The actors had an orthodox rabbi to advise them; they "visited several Boro Park Hasidic communities; they went to Jewish weddings; the women went to a real *Mikvah* [ritual bath]; and Tovah and her understudy both passed as boys and got into a Yeshiva to observe." The resulting duplication of this world is so accurate that *Yentl,* of all of Singer's plays, is most steeped in the kind of literal realism prevalent in the Yiddish theater. Yet Singer occasionally yielded to the temptation of modernizing this world. Here he parts company with the more puritanical Yiddish theater, for he introduces such shockingly implausible *shtetl* behavior as male and female frontal nudity, latent pederasty, and gratuitous transvestitism.

The structure of *Yentl* is also not in keeping with strict realism. Its two acts consist of a series of essential and nonessential short scenes that are not always cohesively linked to each other. The first act is split between a dramatized feminist polemic and a subtle parody of it, while the second act is more symbolic and tragic. Disguise and the unmasking of disguise constitute the rising and falling action, but there is no clear-cut resolution. The play ends with no successful explanation of "the mystery of appearances, the deceptions of the heart." . . . (pp. 208-10)

The dramatic mode of *Yentl* is equally unrealistic. It is a mixture of the presentational and the representational. Yentl and Avigdor are both characters within the play and outside commentators on it. They frequently interrupt a scene to give the audience necessary background information and important narrative transitions. Their animated preview of what is to come gives the play added excitement, just as their confidential soliloquies and asides make for a greater sense of intimacy. Some have claimed, however, that their chatty intrusions give the play an unnecessary rambling quality and an undramatic linear development. But I would argue that their engaging anecdotal skills help retain the charming folktale quality of the play which is, after all, the most winning feature of Singer's drama.

Isaac Bashevis Singer considers himself a novice at playwriting. "Playwriting is the most difficult art," he says, "the greatest challenge to a writer. A great play should be from the beginning written as a play. But since there are very few great plays, and many people who want to go to the theater, it becomes the custom to make from a story a play. So, I, too, try my hand at it." Clearly, Singer's most deft and original hand is that of a storyteller. As a dramatist he does not always have full artistic control of his hand which sometimes lacks agility through inexperience and is sometimes pushed in the wrong direction by the commercial demands of the theater. Yet given American audiences' hunger for plays of authentic Jewish content, Singer's folk dramas, with their substantial roots in the life and spirit of Eastern European Jewry, more than satisfy this hunger. Like Yiddish theater, Singer's plays are an entertaining substitute religion that revives the dead past and evokes communal solidarity in the present. (p. 210)

Sarah Blacher Cohen, "The Jewish Folk Drama of Isaac Bashevis Singer," in From Hester Street to Hollywood: The Jewish-American Stage and Screen, *edited by Sarah Blacher Cohen, Indiana University Press, 1983, pp. 197-212.*

Studs Terkel

1912-

(Born Louis Terkel) American nonfiction writer, biographer, memoirist, journalist, critic, and dramatist.

Terkel is the author of several best-selling oral histories which consist primarily of interviews with average American people. Using a tape recorder, Terkel elicits and occasionally guides his respondents' thoughts on specific social or historical topics. He then edits the tapes to make sure that "the person is retained, the essence of the man, with nothing of me in it." Although critics have expressed various reservations about his methods and results, most consider Terkel's personal approach to be a valuable contribution to social research.

Through his experiences as an interviewer for several Chicago radio and television stations, Terkel developed a rapport with people of diverse backgrounds and occupations. His experience as a jazz and folk music critic informs his first book, *Giants of Jazz* (1957), a collection of biographies of celebrated jazz performers written for young adults. Terkel's love of Chicago and its people prompted his first oral history, *Division Street: America* (1967). The book's title is a metaphor for the economic and social divisions characteristic of contemporary American cities. Despite the varied attitudes, opinions, and lifestyles of his subjects in this work, Terkel notes that they commonly complain of loneliness, aimlessness, and frustration. In *Hard Times: An Oral History of the Great Depression* (1970), Terkel records the reminiscences of Americans who lived during that era and also includes opinions about the Depression from the youth of later decades. Terkel focuses on how American attitudes toward work have changed since World War II in *Working: People Talk about What They Do All Day and How They Feel about What They Do* (1974). While many people complain of the monotonous and impersonal nature of their work, some workers seem to take pride in performing ordinary or mundane tasks well. *American Dreams: Lost and Found* (1980) explores national attitudes toward success and fulfillment. Robert Sherrill considers the work a "dark-hued book of frustrations and disillusionment," but also a "stirringly hopeful book."

Terkel received a Pulitzer Prize for *"The Good War": An Oral History of World War II* (1984). This work concerns the responses of Americans and Europeans to an era of international crisis and renewal. Terkel's respondents alternately express repulsion for a period of great misery and nostalgia for a time of national unity and moral certainty. In addition to his oral histories, Terkel has also written a drama, *Amazing Grace* (1967), and a volume of autobiographical reminiscences, *Talking to Myself: A Memoir of My Times* (1977).

(See also *Contemporary Authors*, Vols. 57-60 and *Contemporary Authors New Revision Series*, Vol. 18.)

LEARNED T. BULMAN

No one man invented jazz, but the twelve musicians portrayed . . . [in *Giants of Jazz*] have advanced and refined it to points

never imagined when King Oliver and, later, Louis Armstrong were blowing the blues in New Orleans.

This is not a book for the knowledgeable jazz fan; there is little here that he does not already know. For the neophyte, though, this is a fine introduction to the work of such titans as Fats Waller, Benny Goodman and Bix Beiderbecke. It will go a long way toward explaining their dedication to that work—and, in fact, to explaining what makes them tick. That Mr. Terkel . . . loves his subject is evident in the writing—it's the kind that makes you want to hear the records of each of these musicians as you read of his life. (pp. 20, 24)

Learned T. Bulman, "They Took It to the Top," in The New York Times Book Review, *November 17, 1957, pp. 20, 24.*

MARTIN E. MARTY

"Although there is a Division Street in Chicago, the title of this book [*Division Street: America*] is metaphorical." The America of the title is no less metaphorical. Reduced to microcosm, it refers to nothing more than Chicago and 72 of its people. In the hands of interviewer-author Terkel, however, it takes on macrocosmic dimensions and serves—I know this sounds pretentious—as a comment on The Human Condition.

But the subjects of this book do keep their feet on the ground in Chicago, and their setting helps explains them. In which Chicago? There are two, if we accept the intuitive distinction of the late Isaac Rosenfeld. One is a skinny strip of lake-oriented civilization, where the universities, museums, art and commercial centers strive to civilize the city. . . . Beyond the Gold Coast and the Magnificent Mile, urged Rosenfeld, "proceed out on . . . Division Street, where the hog butcher lives . . . Stashu-plain West Division Street with the blond-brutal, crew-cut hair." (p. 1)

Studs Terkel needs both Chicagos. His world would collapse without the gross sequences of blocks, because Terkel . . . is one of the few people permitted to commute spiritually between the two Chicagos, one of the few who cares to understand both. The political fat cats dominate from lake-Chicago and exploit the Division streets. Not Terkel. Tape-recorder slung from his shoulder, he visits with people and with apparent artlessness retells what they have told him is on their minds. When they do not get around to his chosen subjects he stops playing Socrates and [urges them on]. . . .

Most written products of tape-recorded sessions turn out to be non-books. Not so in Terkel's hands. He asks and edits and writes with care. I can think of few books since Harry Mayhew's century-old *London Labour and the London Poor* which give the sense of closeness to nameless people that *Division Street: America* does. Negro scrubwoman Lucy Jefferson (Terkel gives his people names) puts it best: "There's such a thing as a feeling tone. One is friendly and one is hostile. And if you don't have this, baby, you've had it. You're dead." Terkel has feeling tone. He can live.

Critics of poll-takers and social analysts claim that even American primitives are by now sophisticated enough to provide misleading answers to anticipated questions. Thus, since prejudice is "out," one can express pro-toleration feelings while disguising actual personal hatreds. Not when Terkel probes. Here again he is a stage mother, bringing up subjects for unpredictable answers. The specter of race hatred shadows the lives of most of his urbanites. Ideological racism is rare: these people have to survive, and ideology is deadly. But just as rare are sunny liberal comments on human goodness as a basis for race relations. In order to live on Division Street, citizens have to learn to half-disbelieve in everything—in neighbors and selves and God. That's it: half-disbelief. Overcommitted people get wounded, especially by the nice people.

Survival depends on one's relationship to clout. . . . [Chicagoans] think of clout less provincially as a universal idiom for the fundamental fact of life. If you don't have this, baby, you've had it. You're dead. Few of Terkel's friends have clout, so they sidle up to those who promise to parcel it out. Or they die. . . .

Few sound the way urbanites in "the secular city" are supposed to sound. The swingers may live along the lake shore, but Division Street represents a superstitious and semi-sacral city. After stage mother Terkel pushes God forward, people go on at length about the clout that God and Church possess. Their values were largely shaped before the Vatican Council, so religion is largely a matter of sociological predestination, routine, and petty legalism. But "it isn't any big deal any more." . . .

Terkel, the last of the old humanists or the first of the new, cannot disguise his feeling tone. (p. 2)

Martin E. Marty, "Chicago: The Divided City," in Book Week—World Journal Tribune, *January 15, 1967, pp. 1-2.*

HERBERT MITGANG

Nobody in *Division Street: America* would make the invitation list for a Truman Capote masked ball. They are not Beautiful People or People Who Can Do You Some Good. Studs Terkel . . . created his book from tape-recorded talks with seventy people—landladies, cops, Golden Glovers, senior citizens, homeowners and homemakers, schoolteachers, salesmen, Negroes and other minorities, socialites, and members of the John Birch Society. Out of all this comes an interior sociological study, not necessarily valid and universal for the types covered but effective in conveying the mumbled malaise that haunts many Americans at the two-thirds-of-a-century mark.

All the interviews, running from one to seven pages each, are with Chicagoans, including those who arrived from other parts of the country because this city was somehow their place of dreams. So these are, to begin with, regional people living in a Nelson Algren Gehenna. . . .

Selection being the essential element of taped talks, the author's personal vision of his city comes across clearly. Despite the vitality that runs through the book the loudest sounds are of loneliness, aimlessness, unhappiness. (p. 36)

[After reading these spoken impressions] a question arises in the reader's mind. Is the note of despair caused by exterior events such as Vietnam or by personal experiences such as prejudice? The author of *Division Street: America* does not himself offer the answer.

"This book is in no way intended as a survey," Mr. Terkel explains. "Nor is it an attempt to spell out conclusions, joyful or joyless, about Chicago or any other American city. It is neither the believer's Good News nor the doubter's bad report. It is simply the adventures of one man, equipped with a tape recorder and badgered by the imp of curiosity, making unaccustomed rounds for a year, trying to search out the thoughts of non-celebrated people—thoughts concerning themselves, past and present, the city, the society, the world."

And therein lies the nagging doubt about a book derived, for the most part, from recorded talks. When a machine stands between interviewer and subject, artistry suffers; memorable reportage must be one author's own distillation and interpretation. In addition, a mosaic book has too many bits and pieces visible—unless it is a rare work of art, like Dos Passos's *U.S.A.* The medium should not intrude on the message, least of all in books. *Division Street: America* is excellent research in search of a book. *Chicago: City on the Make*, by Nelson Algren, remains the classic study of that city and its people. (p. 37)

Herbert Mitgang, "Squalls in the Windy City," in Saturday Review, *Vol. L, No. 4, January 28, 1967, pp. 36-7.*

RICHARD STERN

Is *Division Street* more than a pile of good human apples? Is it, in other words, a real book? . . . A book like this has little to do with build-up, careful collision, *scenes-à-faire,* brilliant climaxes, a coherence whose every line reveals a single mind. It is, though, a carefully arranged collection of selected and well-edited materials. The old, the middle-aged, the young, rich, poor, Negro, Mexican, Wasp. . . .—all pour out their witness to the workings of the city, the death of neighborhoods, the threat and promise of machinery, the war, the mayor, God, buying and selling, delivering, conning, dropping out, rescuing.

Without dominating opinion into coherence, Terkel exhibits a great spectrum of distinctions. If no Chaucer, he is at least a good Harry Bailey. Social scientists will be able to organize this book's materials in numerous ways; thus, though a book itself, it is, in addition, a source for more familiar sorts of books.

The book is a treasury, not a ledger, and the treasury is of articulate human energy engaged with concrete experience. No matter where Terkel's people stand on the scale of usefulness, narcissism, triumph, defeat or despair, if they have expressive power, they triumph here. (p. 377)

> *Richard Stern, "Farming the Tundra," in* The Nation, *Vol. 204, No. 12, March 20, 1967, pp. 376-78.*

RICHARD RHODES

Hard times. Roger, a 14-year-old Appalachian boy, living in Chicago: "See, I never heard that word 'depression' before. They would all just say hard times to me. It still is." In a worthy sequel to *Division Street: America* . . . [*Hard Times: An Oral History of the Great Depression*] offers up the Great Depression in the words of more than 160 Americans, most of them survivors, a few of them young people like Roger in counterpoint. The effect is constant surprise. Surprise not only at the extent of the experience that most people called "hard times," but the extraordinary depths of the memories Mr. Terkel evokes. With few exceptions, his most articulate spokesmen are not the wealthy and the educated but the working people who felt the Depression most personally. They are natural novelists.

Peggy Terry, a Southern white living in Chicago: "This may sound impossible, but if there's one thing that started me thinking, it was President Roosevelt's cuff links. I read in the paper how many pairs of cuff links he had. It told that some of them were rubies and precious stones—these were his cuff links. And I'll never forget. I was setting on an old tire out in the front yard and we were poor and hungry. . . . And I was wondering why it is that one man could have all those cuff links when we couldn't even have enough to eat." (p. 1)

Epiphanies: *Hard Times* is full of them.

Other facts emerge. That many who lost jobs in those days felt personally guilty, ashamed, frustrated, defeated. That it occurred to few that they might riot or loot despite the obvious provocations. That those who profited by the Depression generally refuse to admit that it happened, possibly from a different kind of guilt: Jerome Zerbe, society photographer, "the thirties was a glamorous, glittering moment.". . .

The technology of oral history requires an interviewer skillful enough to make people forget the wheeling machine in front of them. Mr. Terkel, a radio broadcaster in Chicago, has this skill to a remarkable degree. Guilty people do not easily share with a stranger the memories of their shame. Mr. Terkel draws them out, guilt, irony, humor and pain intact. The result is a sort of Domesday Book, St. Peter's ledger, with each citizen's moral strength, or lack of it, laid out on the page for you to weigh and judge. . . .

Confronted with so immense a variety of people, you find yourself at last suspending judgment: These are people; we are this various, this pungent, this tough. And these qualities of variety and strength range so wide a spectrum in *Hard Times* that it puts fiction—most fiction—to shame. Perhaps we retreat to fiction for its simplicity. *Hard Times* contains vast amounts of factual history, the Roosevelt Administration, labor movements, farm movements, cultural changes, riots and mobs, the beginnings of the war in Europe, without ever directly mentioning them. It does not need to: they exist in the racial memory, facts clothed in individual flesh. (p. 35)

> *Richard Rhodes, in a review of "Hard Times: An Oral History of the Great Depression," in* The New York Times Book Review, *April 19, 1970, pp. 1, 35.*

SAUL MALOFF

"Hard times," of course, is an ancient and honorable expression; it is also the title of one of Dickens' least-read novels, and the title refers to a terrible decade in English history. There is no way of telling whether Studs Terkel had the Dickens novel somewhere in his mind when he put together his *Hard Times: An Oral History of the Great Depression* . . . ; but the two decades abound in interesting parallels. . . .

[Studs Terkel] set out with his tape recorder to interview the survivors [of the Depression]; his aim was to gather up a kind of folk-say, and his method, accordingly, seems to have been no more grand than to get his subjects remembering and talking, himself occasionally interpolating a question to jog or steer memory. Not quite as free-wheeling as that: Terkel attempts a loose, easy, casual demography, placing his characters along an occupational/regional/typological spectrum. But this purpose remained far more general than, say, that of the more rigorous, systematic Oscar Lewis or Eliot Lebow: to evoke from the collective memory, from the sound of America speaking, some sense of the way we lived then. . . . Apart from the intrinsic significance of such works, all of them require finally to be judged as art.

Art does not happen by the accident of random and copious speech. *Hard Times* is not art; it isn't really "oral history." Despite laborious editing, the book seems stitched together; and it would have benefited greatly from still closer editing. Much in it is slack—mere drift; in its present form the book is an anthology of uneven quality. Perhaps, as in the romantic view of folk-art, a great and ancient tradition of *speech*, of folk-saying, as in pre-literate cultures, must provide the enabling source; whatever the case, either it is not true that if you hang around the county courthouse or village store long enough, you'll find hordes of untutored poets and golden-tongued tale-tellers; or Terkel didn't hang around long enough; or they were all dead by then, buried beside the still waters of the Spoon River. Terkel did find some, however; and veins in others; and the best passages strung together are pure gold. (p. 319)

[A] man asks, "What the hell's this all about?" The trouble was something called The System; or, more devastatingly (the theme appears again and again), the trouble lay in oneself: some inner fault brought down the misery. And if the flaw was inner, the rate and despair could flow in no other direction. ". . . it was your own fault," a man says. "You took it and kept quiet. A kind of shame about your own personal failure. I was wondering what the hell it was all about." The "dominant thing," another says, "was this helpless despair and submission. There was anger and rebellion among a few but, by and large, that quiet desperation and submission."

So far the speakers have been white; even when they have been more or less destitute for generations—dirt farmers, tenants, sharecroppers—they have still been white. "*Great* Depression," an elderly Negro laughs. "I made out during that . . . *Great* Depression. Worked as a teamster for a lumber yard. Forty cents an hour. Monday we'd have a little work. They'd say come back Friday. There wasn't no need to look for another job. The few people working, most all of them were white. So I had another little hustle. I used to play pool pretty good." "The Negro was born in depression," he says. "It didn't mean too much to him, The Great American Depression, as you call it. There was no such thing. The best he could be is a janitor or a porter or a shoeshine boy. It only became official when it hit the white man." (p. 320)

Notoriously, there is a grave risk that, having survived a great (or even a small) historic (or personal) occasion, Terkel's people cannot help but sentimentalize and melodramatize their past; but all risks notwithstanding, I am convinced by the evidence that between then and now something vital went out of the national spirit—a humanly catastrophic loss of feeling, of human resonance, of whatever it is that attracts us to some people and not others, some places and not others, indeed some historical periods and not others, or, for that matter, some works of art and not others. The theme beats insistently: then we were human; now we are something less than that. We are thing-ridden half to death; the salt has lost its savor—though in this book, of course, you won't find such posh and trendy words as alienation, estrangement, anomie, dehumanization. . . . "Everything was important," a woman recalls. "If one man died, it was like a headline. Life was more important . . . that this *one* man died . . . Now we hear traffic tolls, we hear Vietnam . . . life is just so, it's not precious now." "Life was important," a man says. "Life was significant." "All in all, a painful time, but a glorious time," another remembers. (pp. 320-21)

> Saul Maloff, "Life and Hard Times," in Commonweal, Vol. XCII, No. 13, June 26, 1970, pp. 319-21.

MARCUS CUNLIFFE

Oral history means getting people to reminisce into a tape recorder. In itself that sounds dubious—partly for the incidental reason that 'oral', one of our new four-letter words, suggests the fake candour of a sex-manual. Historians have other reservations about the technique. People's memories are usually inaccurate, as well as self-regarding. Even if they could recollect the truth, most people don't really want to tell it, or at least not if this entails exposing their own failures. And then there is the problem of the interviewer: he may prompt and prod the person being interviewed to suit his own particular purposes. If he also goes on to edit the tapes and publish them, he has the power to shape the material—in other words to distort that which may already be distorted.

So what can we expect from [*Hard Times*], a collection of reminiscences of the Great Depression in the United States? Can Americans still faithfully recall the atmosphere of a generation ago? . . . With Mr Terkel's book, a few of these questions do raise themselves now and then. As with his previous collection of recorded remarks about Chicago, *Division Street: America,* his method of organisation is idiosyncratically loose.

He doesn't explain how and why he came to pick his subjects, or why some are fully identified and others not.

Even so, . . . [*Hard Times*] is an extraordinary book. As with *Division Street,* it is apparent that Studs Terkel has a marvellous knack of finding people—the authentically nice, the authentically horrible, and the mass who lie in between. He has picked them up from all over, and it is obvious that his amiable, nonjudging, burly yet self-effacing approach arouses the urge to talk. He is the sympathetic stranger in a bar or on a train, to whom you unburden yourself. Here are innumerable life-stories, some only a paragraph, some stretching to several pages. Of course they are not invariably 'reliable': certain people are probably liars, or at any rate anxious to present the best side of themselves. . . . Often you feel not that you are reading a recorded message, but that you are eavesdropping, or reading people's diaries. Since we are all, by an instinct at once prurient and healthy, Peeping Toms, this book meets our profound urge to lip-read the motions of the man who is opening and shutting his mouth behind the glass of a telephone kiosk, or of the party sitting at the other end of the restaurant. Their very banalities are precious. We yearn for the sudden felicities of the vernacular, but also for the verity of language that may be actually ill-used. Fortunately there are plenty of felicities in the American ordinary speech—so much so that this documentary exactness is a quality we prize in American fiction. It was, for example, beautifully caught in Saroyan's early and, alas, unrepeated masterpiece, *The Daring Young Man on the Flying Trapeze,* which caught much of the truth of the Depression years. To the short stories in Saroyan's book, and the magnificent effort at identification with the Southern poor in James Agee's *Let Us Now Praise Famous Men,* we can now add the infolded voices of *Hard Times*.

Most of the Americans who talked to Mr Terkel prove to have remarkably vivid memories. The Depression was the equivalent of Britain's two world wars, in leaving scars that never quite heal. But that needs to be restated. There are astonishing non-scars, people immune from or even benefited by the disaster. One of the valuable reminders in this collection is that life is capricious. Some—entertainers, slick admen, those in the oldest professions—did quite well out of the American slump. . . . Looking back on it all, the old are amazed by their own docility. Their children too, also interviewed by Mr Terkel, clearly believe that the parents were a spineless lot. Indeed, the gulf between the generations is pathetically emphasised. The young, it must be said, usually sound ignorant and querulous in these extracts. But there is one final and terrible sequence in which a 19-year-old explains why his father would not let him take a trip on a raft down the Mississippi. Each is right and each is wrong, immured in his time-cubicle: 'You know, his ship's come in. He doesn't want to see our raft go out.' (pp. 377-78)

> Marcus Cunliffe, "Taped Traumas," in New Statesman, Vol. 80, No. 2062, September 25, 1970, pp. 377-78.

MARSHALL BERMAN

One of the most poignant and powerful of American dreams is the dream signified by the expression "Popular Front." These words are ordinarily held to denote a political and cultural policy adopted by international Communism from 1934 to 1946: a policy of de-emphasizing struggles for revolution, and striving instead to unite liberal and democratic forces within each country in the face of the dangers of Fascism. At the end of World War II, in accord with shifting needs and interests, Communist policies were abruptly and drastically changed. But, in America at least, the Popular Front policy had liberated immense imaginative energies that no party directive could kill. It had articulated a vision of a genuinely democratic community—perhaps the first such vision in American history. . . .

[Terkel has spent most of his life] investigating the lives of the "common," "ordinary" people who fill our land, trying to make their stories seen and heard, in the hope of showing the people how much we all have in common "deep down," and bringing us together to work to change a social system that strains and drains us all. He should be seen as part of a whole generation of great documentary film-makers (Pare Lorentz) and photographers (Dorothea Lange, Walker Evans, Helen Levitt) and folklorists (B. A. Botkin, John and Alan Lomax) who were inspired by the Popular Front ideal, and whose work we are only just beginning to understand as an organic whole. (p. 1)

[Through his histories and his recent book *Working,* Terkel has] revived one of the favorite literary forms of the Front period, what I will call the We-The-People-Talk book. This is a book, usually put together by an author who has traveled up and down the country, in which a variety of people—of every age, class, race, creed, etc.—tell their life stories and "speak for themselves." Titles like Benjamin Appel's *The People Talk* and Nathan Asch's *The Road: In Search of America* should convey the idea. Some of the most famous and best writers of the age—Sherwood Anderson, James Agee, Erskine Caldwell, Edmund Wilson—worked in this vein. *Division Street,* appearing amidst the turmoil of 1967, was like a breath of fresh air. It was full of decent, warm, generous, sympathetic folks. Yet after a while it felt rather too much like the air of 1939: though Terkel's people are "socially conscious" and legitimately angry—at business, government, "the big boys"—the book keeps entirely on the sunny side of their psyches. Any dark, murky, irrational feelings that might complicate fraternity and solidarity are left out. A little while after putting down the book it is hard to remember who is who. Just as in the Popular Front models of the genre, people tend to be reduced to ingredients in "the people."

Terkel's next book, *Hard Times: An Oral History of the Great Depression* (1970), tried to explore people's memories of the Depression years. Although full of vivid and moving stories, it seemed to lack focus. It suggested important questions about the ways biographical and historical memory transforms human experience, but it did nothing to even try to resolve them. Nevertheless, it showed Terkel's perspective getting deeper and more complex.

In his new book, *Working,* Terkel returns, as his subtitle [*People Talk About What They Do All Day and How They Feel About What They Do*] suggests, to the classic format of the We-The-People-Talk book. He could have taken his epigraph from Earl Robinson and John Latouche's archetypal Popular Front composition, "Ballad for Americans." This passage . . . at once describes the scope and conveys something of the spirit of Terkel's project: "I'm everybody who's nobody and the nobody who's everybody. . . . I am . . . AMERICA."

And yet, if Terkel gets closer than ever to the Popular Front vision in this book, he also diverges from it more radically than ever—or else, maybe, carries the vision to new heights and depths. For the first time in Terkel's work, his people are present in all the full radiance and frightfulness of their individuality. He is confronting all the explosive psychic realities that the Front generation did not care—or could not bear—to see.

Terkel has chosen a subject that is particularly timely. The disturbances at Lordstown, the H.E.W. "Work in America" report, the increasing intensity of bitterness expressed by workers in every occupation—blue and white collar, unskilled and executive alike—should be enough to convince readers that Americans have come to perceive work as a central problem, maybe *the* central problem, in the 1970's. Terkel provides an enormous amount of exciting material indispensable for any full understanding of this problem. He uses the discussion of work to get at so much of what is deepest and most intimate in so many people's lives, to understand work as Freud understood it, as the individual's firmest connection with reality. He has learned, as it were, to listen with the third ear. His book should be a best seller, and it deserves to be. . . .

One of the most persistent themes among Terkel's people, young and old, high and low on the social scale, is the ways in which people's attitudes toward their work have changed. Older workers complain that younger ones lack what Veblen called the "instinct of workmanship," a desire to do their job well. On the other hand—this usually comes out in second thoughts or free associations—they feel a grudging but intense admiration for young people's willingness to stand up both to arbitrary power and to work that may, after all, be meaningless. (p. 2)

It is striking to see how self-conscious so many of these people have become, how they have learned to ask intricate and sophisticated and tough questions about their work—both about its organization and patterns of authority, and about its ultimate "meaning." This "existential" question, which not long ago was supposed to be of interest only to pampered middle-class students, turns out to be crucial to a great many workers, of all ages, with little education and less ideology but plenty of passion and intelligence. A young proofreader speaks of trouble in his shop: the workers, particularly the young ones, have begun to ask why things are organized in a particular way; the boss, who has never been asked such questions, feels threatened, panics, overreacts. And yet, "Nobody refused to do anything, but we want to know why." This may turn out to be the most significant long-term legacy of the sixties: a generation of workers who are determined to know why.

And yet some of the most humanly attractive people in the book have consciousness that would rate as irremediably "low." What are we to say of the pride that Alfred Pommier, a 49-year-old black parking lot attendant, takes in his job? . . . He tells his story, in a rap full of bluesy double entendre: "In my younger days I used to be a wizard, I could really roll. I could spin a car with one hand and never miss a hole. . . . I could drive any car like a baby, like a woman change her baby's diaper. . . . I was so good, I make that swing with one hand, never need two." . . .

[By political standards, people like Alfred] are drowning in "false consciousness." They don't even know they're being exploited! And yet, they are the salt of the earth. Oblivious to politics, living as if they were outside history, they have been able to pour meaning and beauty into social niches and activities that appear to be barren and empty. Their sort of creativity can generate self-deceptions, can (in Rousseau's phrase) teach them to love their own slavery. And yet, without their capacity to create meaning, the human race would be lost. We must wrestle with contradictions like these, and there is no end in sight.

Sometimes this can be demoralizing. One of the difficulties with this book is that Terkel loads us down with so much exciting and problematical material, but himself does hardly anything to help us assimilate and integrate it all. There are individual sections, small clusters, that stick together very well—interviews with three auto workers in the same shop near the beginning, a section on "Fathers and Sons" at the end—but little coherence in between. He is like some sort of magician or genie, bringing an incredible abundance of marvelous beings before our eyes, yet as soon as we reach out to grasp at any one, he whisks it away from us and replaces it with another and another, in dizzying and exhausting succession. It may sound ungrateful to complain of a superabundance of exciting material. This is not exactly the problem. What the book needs is a more active intelligence, giving some sort of structure and coherence to the marvelous material.

Nevertheless, although the specificities of Terkel's vision are uncertain, its over-all form and direction are clear. It is the great American dream of a Popular Front revived—a new Front that will be more honest and genuine, and hopefully more solid and enduring than the old. Where the old Front was based on false simplicities, mindless pieties, contentment with easy answers—or with no questions asked—maybe the people can be drawn together today by their common questioning and impiety. . . .

Terkel has given the mural a new coat of paint and added a new dimension, the dimension of psychic inwardness and depth. At a moment when the American people—all of us—are faced with a complex of unprecedented crises, it may turn out to be more real than ever before. (p. 3)

> Marshall Berman, "Everybody Who's Nobody and the Nobody Who's Everybody," in The New York Times Book Review, March 24, 1974, pp. 1-3.

ROBERT BOYD

Mr. Terkel's greatest asset as a writer may be that—strictly speaking—he isn't one. He is a broadcaster, equipped with a tape recorder and a wonderful sensitivity for the nuances of the spoken language. With these, and with honesty and sympathy, he probes the collective American mind, surprising us again and again by our callousness and our intelligence, our sophistication and our stupidity. . . . In *Working,* subtitled *What People Do All Day and How They Feel About What They Do,* [Mr. Terkel] trains his tape machine on the frustrations and gratifications of people who are trying to earn a living and at the same time hang on to their sense of individual worth. The results are in several respects monumental.

In the first place, *Working* is a big book. . . . Included among the 130 subjects are people from every conceivable occupational area, from every socioeconomic group, from every major American ethnic group. There are some immediately recognizable names: the actor Rip Torn, the film critic Pauline Kael. . . . Then there are the names nobody knows, the people who have no public faces, like the washroom attendant Louis Hayward ("I don't go around saying I'm a washroom attendant . . . I always wanted to be a writer. Most people like to say how rich or rewarding their jobs are. I can't say that"). . . . Between the poles of celebrity and anonymity there are others, car salesmen, mail carriers, bank tellers and factory hands, whose feelings about their jobs tell us some encouraging things about the way things are going in America—and some profoundly disturbing things as well.

What they tell us, good and bad, is monumental in the sense that it is both a celebration of the American (or Protestant) work ethic and a testimony of its demise. Not that the people Mr. Terkel interviews don't want to work, or that they have lost all interest in craftsmanship; the problem is that the economic and technological aspects of our society make it all but impossible for them to hang onto their ideals. . . . In our technocracy, the functioning of each worker is isolated and depersonalized, and the product of his work may well be both invisible and unacknowledged. The results are tension, frustration, paranoia. Work is translated into war, the employee versus the company. "Funny thing is," says the auto worker Phil Stallings, "I don't mind working at body construction. To a great degree I enjoy it. I love using my hands." But, he goes on, "How can I feel pride in a job where I call a foreman's attention to a mistake, a bad piece of equipment, and he'll ignore it. Pretty soon you get the idea they don't care. You keep doing this and finally you're titled a trouble maker." This paradox—the employee's desire to do his job well, frustrated by the corporate bureaucracy—is a recurrent theme in *Working,* not only among assembly-line hands but among white-collar workers and middle-level executives as well. Another recurrent theme is isolation and distrust. (p. 443)

The news isn't all bad, of course. Beyond the despair of the uneducated, trapped in menial jobs, and beyond the plastic happiness of the salesmen and models, there is the sincere satisfaction, the fulfillment, found in working by men like . . . fireman Tom Patrick, whose words close the book: "I worked in a bank. You know, it's just paper. Nine to five and it's shit. You're lookin' at numbers. But I can look back and say, 'I helped put out a fire. I helped save somebody.' It shows something I did on this earth."

Studs Terkel says that *Working* is concerned with the "search for daily meaning as well as daily bread, for recognition as well as cash. To be remembered was the wish, spoken and unspoken, of the heroes and heroines of this book." The book itself is a significant contribution to our society. It does not proffer solutions; rather, it helps us to see ourselves more clearly and thus to define more clearly the problems we face. It derives its considerable power from the information it contains rather than from the style in which it is written—Mr. Terkel, unlike some so-called New Journalists, considers his subject more important than his ego. In the long run, that attitude seems likely to guarantee that he will be remembered, and recognized, not only for his talent as a reporter but for his humanity as well. (p. 444)

> Robert Boyd, "Materials for a Nation," in The Nation, Vol. 218, No. 14, April 6, 1974, pp. 443-44.

BERNARD A. WEISBERGER

[Terkel's] brilliant tape-recorded interview techniques (or perhaps lack of techniques), which produced moving testaments of city life in *Division Street: America,* and of the Depression in *Hard Times,* have [in *Working*] created another first-class documentary-in-print.

It is a pleasure to join the hallelujah chorus. The talk in *Working* is good talk—earthy, passionate, honest, sometimes tender, sometimes crisp, juicy as reality, seasoned with experience. It is tempting to say that people are naturally interesting talkers, but that would be untrue to our memories of boredom past and ungenerous to Terkel's skill. God knows how many subjects he sifted, and how many dull passages he spared us with the tape-scissors. Whether he has given us a lot or a little of his material, however, it is a rich remnant. He has a formidable gift for evoking and recognizing articulateness in a variety of people and coaxing it from private shelters.

Having said so much, I would like to add that I think many reviewers missed the book's true intent and savor. Mostly they took it as a brief in support of the thesis that work, today, is dehumanizing, alienating, uncreative, undignified, routine. They cite a threnodic note that runs through many of the interviews. . . . [Workers recurrently] complain to Terkel that they feel like tools, like barkers in a carnival of huckstering, like victims, like nullities. All are aware of how limited an imprint they make upon things, of how little self some jobs can leave, of how expertly our society praises work and yet puts down those whose physical work is hardest and most basic.

Yet I do not see that as the book's sole focus. *Working* would not be worth much attention if it told us only that work was hard and unrewarding for the most part. We have all known that for a long time. "In the sweat of thy brow shalt thou earn bread" was a curse; Paradise, by contrast, was idleness. There have been no golden ages of happy peasants and workers outside of political fairy tales.

But *Working* is more than an anthology of disaffection. Surprisingly, it shows that many of the "respondents," as a social scientist would call them, like their jobs, and find in them the purposes and satisfactions which they require for wholeness. Perhaps they are in a minority. Perhaps their work simply answers neurotic cravings in them. But they are very much present in the book.

Moreover, a close reading of the text shows that even the malcontents are not simply unhappy with their jobs. What they are painfully handling, for our ears, is the texture of their whole existence. . . .

What bursts on us is that the subject is not work, but life. The job is the core around which the book's narrators marshal their feelings about themselves and their universe. And Terkel is, in fact, an anthropologist, taking field notes on the meaning, for our culture, of the ritual of the job—the ritual which takes half our waking hours, two-thirds of the days each year, for nearly three-quarters of our lifetimes. . . .

It is interesting that Terkel's kind of book has actually been done by at least one professional anthropologist, the late Oscar Lewis. By going among poor Mexican and Puerto Rican people with humaneness and honesty (he did not call them "respondents," I am sure), he induced them to talk freely, and embodied their lives in such insight-rich volumes as *Five Families, La Vida* and *The Children of Sanchez.* Terkel seems to be doing the same for selected Americans.

I am not sure, of course, that a trained sociologist or anthropologist would accept the comparison. He would probably miss, in *Working,* the signs of a method—a roadmap of inquiry, pinpointing questions, justifying the selection of subjects, screening the usable from the "merely" interesting. And he might well be justified, for what scholars do for a living is to devise inquiries, and then arrange the materials and evidence of life in ways that may yield replies. An historian, too, for example, might find the outpourings of previously voiceless people like those in *Working* (or in *Hard Times,* which in some quarters was described as informal; oral history) a marvelous mine of material about our age. But when it came time to refine

it, and to extract hard, safe, argued-from-the-facts general statements from it, he would have no easy time.

Nonetheless, the raw material of life, even when immune to "critical analysis," is neither to be despised nor ignored. There is plenty of random wisdom and pleasure in *Working.* In fact, a reviewer who read it as part of his job might say that it provided one of those happy times when work and enjoyment were nicely fused.

Bernard A. Weisberger, "Another Day Older and Deeper in Debt. . . ," in Book World—The Washington Post, *May 5, 1974, p. 1.*

ROSS THOMAS

For years now Terkel has been asking people questions, often impertinent ones, which he firmly believes are the best kind, and in his autobiographical *Talking to Myself,* he tells something of what he has learned and discovered, not only about others, but also about himself. Much of it is interesting, some of it is fascinating, and almost none of it is dull.

Apparently, if you grew up in Chicago's 42nd Ward, as Terkel did, you soon acquired a rather seasoned view of politics and of those who follow that often gamey calling. You also gained a perspective which permitted very few personal heroes, almost none of whom ever got elected to public office. And if you were lucky, as Terkel was, there were a lot of dirty old men around who kept thrusting little blue books into your hands that cost a nickel and were written by such as Eugene V. Debs, Clarence Darrow, Thomas Paine, Bob Ingersoll, and Voltaire. Or as Terkel says, "That bunch." . . .

Had it not been for such early influences, Terkel speculates that he might have grown up to be a Daniel Patrick Moynihan, or a Henry Kissinger, or a respected contributor to Commentary, of which fate he seems to feel there is none worse.

Instead, Terkel grew up to be a sometime actor, an occasional operatic spear carrier, a disk jockey, a tireless supporter of doomed causes, and a skilled interviewer of people. All kinds of people.

Terkel writes in a rather pleasantly rumpled style, which is no doubt harder to achieve than it seems. Along the way one learns that he has a law degree from the University of Chicago, although he never practiced; that his given name is Louis; that he is devoted to both opera and jazz, and that he probably has seen virtually every motion picture ever produced and remembers them all clearly.

Some of Terkel's most interesting passages deal with his interviews abroad with persons like Ivy Compton-Burnett, Fellini, Alan Paton, and Bertrand Russell. But as he interviews them, his thoughts keep turning home—back to Chicago . . .— and his reflective comparisons provide much of the book's considerable charm. . . .

Terkel comes through in his book as the epitome of the interested bystander who somehow invariably gets caught up in the events of his own time, a bemused man perhaps, and one who, like those he interviews, would be interesting to know.

Ross Thomas, "Now You're Really Talking Terkel," in Book World—The Washington Post, *April 24, 1977, p. E1.*

GIL MULLER

Goethe went to the core of autobiographical writing when he observed that "man knows himself only as he knows the world, and becomes aware of the world only in himself, and of himself only in it." *Talking to Myself* is rare, compelling and perhaps great, because it adheres to this principle. Terkel refuses to dwell on the simple "facts" of his life, or to rely on the confessional mode. His mother emerges momentarily in the delightful sequences on their days at the Wells Grand Hotel; his brother Ben is a lightly sketched figure leading him into and out of adolescent scrapes; and his wife steps out of the Montgomery March to confuse his taping ploys. Yet these private figures are kept at the periphery; the author's preoccupation is with his relationship to the much larger world.

The work at first seems haphazard. Tone and style suggest a loose, whimsical, anecdotal rendition of the autobiographical urge. Further reading, however, reveals a complex tapestry that resembles the associative patterns of conversation, moving over characters and events without strict attention to chronology. At the same time, the deep structure imitates improvisational jazz—among the many kinds of music that have informed Terkel's approach. He plays here a series of musical riffs placed upon a skeletal frame—his own life. Merely one of the numerous soloists creating and performing, he waits (as he once explained his interviewing technique) for the phrase that explodes. . . .

Yes, Terkel knows about suffering humanity. Yet what he discovers in the pain, oppression and even failure (we must remember that *Hard Times* and *Working* are books about failure) of individual and collective lives is an affirmative note— "a sense of mortal community," as James Cameron, a gifted British journalist Terkel introduces as his mirror image, puts it. . . .

Like Cameron, Terkel "has been around." He has left his Kilroy's mark on Chicago's wards, Montgomery's streets, South Africa's mines, exploring persistently "the fragile possibility against the brutal fact." Indeed, many brutal facts are recorded in *Talking to Myself,* especially where they involve abuses of power and wealth. The FBI, Mayor Daley, Jack Kennedy and his "small brother," the media elite, Kissinger—none are among Terkel's favorite drinking companions. Still, he is gentle with them, laconic, almost gracious in satirizing without savaging, in never losing his sense of *caritas.*

Charitable as Terkel is, he is also a charmer, a trifle crafty. He can get what he wants out of people, good and bad. Shaking his sickly Sony, shuffling like Chaplin into dangerous turf, this innocent abroad constantly changes colors, moving as easily with gangsters, corrupt officials, racists, and mandarins of society as he does with people he admires and loves. (p. 19)

Large sections of *Talking to Myself* are devoted to the men and women who have very special seats at Studs' Place. Fellini, Vittorio DeSica . . . , A. S. Neill, Nelson Algren, Billie Holliday, Mahalia Jackson, and Big Bill Broonzy are some of the stars who share space with the scores of ordinary persons the author loves. . . .

Haunted by the beauty of people and the drama of their existence, . . . [Terkel] understands, as he noted of Danielo Dolci, that life is a work of art. So the words he uses to describe his friend Cameron could apply equally to him: The author has the heart of the innocent, the eye of the experienced, the style of the master. One gets the feeling that he also has much more

to tell us about his friends and himself. I hope he keeps talking to himself. (p. 20)

Gil Muller, "Playing Back a Life," in The New Leader, *Vol. LX, No. 15, July 18, 1977, pp. 19-20.*

ROBERT SHERRILL

American Dreams: Lost and Found, the best of [Mr. Terkel's "oral history"] series, is a continuation of what, in *Division Street,* Mr. Terkel called "simply the adventure of one man equipped with a tape-recorder and badgered by the imp of curiosity . . . trying to search out the thoughts of noncelebrated people (with a few 'newsworthy' exceptions)—thoughts concerning themselves, past and present, the city, the society, the world."

This time Mr. Terkel spent three years . . . traveling around the country with his tape recorder and speaking with more than 300 people. The 100 he considered the best are here. (p. 1)

Why Mr. Terkel calls the compilation *American Dreams* beats me. Very few of these people seem to be driven by dreams, by inflated expectations. There aren't many Leo Blooms here, romping around a fountain and shouting "I want everything I ever saw in the movies," as that character did in the movie *The Producers.* A better title would be *American Awakenings.* The outstanding quality of most of the people Mr. Terkel sticks his mike in front of (though there are a few introspective whiners) is a gutsy and cheerful willingness to wrestle with reality.

On the whole, they are much saucier, more outspoken, than the people we met in *Division Street,* doubtless reflecting the changing mood of the country in the last 20 years. "Something's happening, as yet unrecorded on the social seismograph," Mr. Terkel writes. "There are signs, unmistakable, of an astonishing increase in the airing of grievances: of private wrongs and public rights. . . . In unexpected quarters, those, hitherto quiescent, are finding voice."

It would seem so. Many of these 100 Americans tell us how they discovered that "the system is rigged," as one of the interviewees, Cleveland's ex-mayor Dennis Kucinich, expressed it.

American Dreams is a dark-hued book of frustrations and disillusionment, but it also is a stirringly hopeful book because most of the people who talk to us here are as scrappy as Mehitabel the cat. By sheer gall they've managed to wrest something from the system and they're not through yet. The spirit of rebellion goes right down to such plain folks as Joe Begley, 60, a general-store proprietor in Kentucky, who's willing to get violent, if necessary, to stop such things as strip mining. . . .

Some of the most exciting memories are of those moments when people first came truly alive, ready to fight back. Hartman Turnbow, 75, grandson of a slave, who lives in the meanest section of Mississippi, remembers going down to the courthouse in 1963 with a group of blacks to register to vote. The sheriff stepped forward and shouted menacingly, "All right, now, who'll be the first?" Mr. Turnbow recalls: "Twenty of us, lookin' one at the other. I said to myself: These niggers fixin' to run. So I just stepped out of line and I say: 'Me, I'll be the first.'" . . .

It's fascinating, too, to see that ordinary people are finally getting wise to how the Bourbons, the old-style segregationists with clout, have used the race issue to stay in power. C. P.

Ellis, the former exalted cyclops of the Durham, N.C., Ku Klux Klan, is now the regional business manager of the International Union of Operating Engineers. He grew up dirt poor. The harder he worked, the worse things seemed to get. . . .

[When Ellis] became head of the Klan, the town's leaders secretly urged him on. But they wouldn't speak to him publicly. When they saw him coming, they would cross the street.

"I began to think, somethin' wrong here. Most of 'em are merchants or maybe an attorney, an insurance agent, people like that. As long as they kept low-income whites and low-income blacks fightin', they're gonna maintain control. I began to get that feeling after I was ignored in public. I thought: You're not gonna use me any more. That's when I began to do some real serious thinkin'."

When he started to organize unions, "I began to see far deeper. I began to see people again bein' used. Blacks against whites. I say this without any hesitancy: management is vicious. There's two things they want to keep: all the money and all the say-so. They don't want these poor workin' folks to have none of that. . . . I tell people there's a tremendous possibility in this country to stop . . . the fights between people. People say: 'That's an impossible dream. You sound like Martin Luther King.' An ex-Klansman who sounds like Martin Luther King. (Laughs) I don't think it's an impossible dream. It's happened in my life. . . ." (p. 32)

Studs Terkel's *American Dreams* offers us an apple on every one of these pages. (p. 33)

Robert Sherrill, "Looking at America," in The New York Times Book Review, September 14, 1980, pp. 1, 32-3.

MICHAEL GARVEY

"Out there," says Mr. Terkel, lies "a reservoir of untapped power and new astonishments." The assertion is difficult to dispute, and the television producers of the program "Speak Up America" are probably making even more money from it than will Mr. Terkel with his latest volume [*American Dreams*]. What perplexes me is that 470 pages of typeface can so easily transmogrify this reservoir into one of this year's least interesting mudpuddles. Americans are a pretty diverse and fascinating bunch of folks, all right, but surely they deserve better coverage than this.

"In this book are a hundred American voices, captured by hunch, circumstance, and a rough idea." *Very* rough, it seems; you can almost see the old cigar stub puffin' above the swirling miles of tape while this indefatigable democrat lets the *folks* talk. None 'o that sissified stuff like structure here, Pal. Go talk to them briefcase totin' bureaucrats for *that* stuff. This is America, Buddy. Listen to the common dreams or else beat it. (p. 5)

[Around] this fragile tentpole of an excuse for hasty assemblage, Terkel hangs a hundred texts of a hundred tape recordings of a hundred Americans. You get a Big Surprise on page one. Miss America '73 possesses more wit than a Barbie Doll. That *is* astonishing, but after that you have 99 dreams and 464 pages to go, and that's some pretty inpenetrable Whitmanesque terrain. A few ambitious capitalists waxing poetic . . . ; a few funky Kentucky philosophers (Joe Begley observes that "life is short as it is"); a nostalgic radical or two, with a deeply religious man like John Howard Griffin thrown in. And that's

about it, folks, but this is a democracy, after all. That means rough edges and a faith in whatever anybody has to say.

But that doesn't make for much of a read.

If you are genuinely astonished by the fact that gas-station attendants, bankers, and housewives are generous, mean, intelligent, imaginative, courageous and cowardly, you will find this book intriguing. (On the other hand, you'd be emotionally overwhelmed by a supermarket tour.) If not, you may be reassured to find that a writer of Mr. Terkel's stature confirms your suspicion that people are really something. . . . [In this light] Mr. Terkel's vision seems less than urgent. (pp. 5-6)

Michael Garvey, in a review of "American Dreams: Lost and Found," in The Critic, February, 1981, pp. 5-6.

JONATHAN YARDLEY

Studs Terkel has put the title of his oral history of the Second World War [*"The Good War": An Oral History of World War II*] in quotation marks because he understands that there is a double edge to it. On the one hand the war was "good" in the sense that an Allied victory was morally and politically necessary. . . . Yet on the other hand no war can really be called "good," and the current tendency to romanticize World War II is, in the words of a California woman, pure delusion:

"The good war? That infuriates me. Yeah, the idea of World War II being called a good war is a horrible thing. I think of all the atrocities. I think of a madman who had all this power. I think of the destruction of the Jews, the misery, the horrendous suffering in the concentration camps. In 1971, I visited Dachau. . . . [But it] doesn't take a visit to make you realize the extent of human misery."

This dichotomous view of the war as both necessary and evil, and of the experiences of its participants as both exhilarating and debilitating, is the dominant theme of *"The Good War."* It is the only responsible view to take, recognizing as it does both the imperatives of history and the sufferings of the people who live through it, but perhaps inescapably it gives the book an oddly inconsistent tone. The stories of agony and deprivation in combat and the concentration camps are mixed, often incongruously, with nostalgic yearnings for the good old days when America was, or so we like to imagine that it was, more united and less corrupted by wealth than it is today. The incongruity, though, is not Terkel's fault; it is an accurate reflection of a terrible war's ambiguous legacy.

As in Terkel's previous oral histories, *"The Good War"* is a clangorous but carefully orchestrated jumble of voices. The speakers are the prominent and the unknown, the wealthy and the poor, the articulate and the awkward, but all of them have been induced to talk with great clarity about a period that was, for many of them, the time of their lives. "Looking back on the war," one of them says, "in spite of the really bad times, it was certainly the most exciting experience of my life. As a character in *Terry and the Pirates* once put it so eloquently, 'We shot the last act in the first reel.' As I see it, at that young age, we hit the climax. Everything after that is anticlimactic."

This man, as it happens, fought in the brutal combat in the Ardennes; was captured by the Germans and sent on a forced march through the snow after being stripped of his boots; crammed into a POW railroad car on a train that was mistakenly attacked by RAF airplanes; [and subjected to numerous injuries]. . . . (p. 3)

That someone could survive so prolonged a series of terrible experiences not merely in good humor but with the feeling that it was the "most exciting" period of his life may seem incomprehensible to today's reader, yet it is a recurring theme in Terkel's history. In part, no doubt, this can be explained by the timing of the war; coming as it did after a decade of Depression, it gave purpose and prosperity to a nation that had been short on both. In larger part, though, it is explained by the general conviction—utterly foreign to Americans whose only wartime memories are of Korea and Vietnam—that what we were doing was right: "To see fascism defeated, nothing better could have happened to a human being. You felt you were doing something worthwhile. You felt you were an actor in a tremendous drama that was unfolding. It was the most important moment in my life. I always felt very lucky to have been part of it."

Almost every American with whom Terkel spoke doubtless would agree with that sentiment, yet there is also in these voices a rueful acknowledgement that the war did not turn out to be quite the blessing they anticipated while they fought it. For one thing, it did not turn out, any more than World War I did, to be the war to end all wars. . . . For another, as a retired admiral observes, it made us a militaristic nation. . . . Or, as a former New Dealer puts it:

"The most single important legacy of the war is what Eisenhower warned us about in his farewell speech: the military-industrial complex. In the past, there were business representatives in Washington, but now they *are* Washington. And with the military buildup beyond all our imaginations, we have a new fusion of power. It has become a permanent feature of American life."

This is true, and most lamentably so, yet the observation would be more convincing were it balanced against the recollections and opinions of someone who came through the war persuaded of the necessity of a massive military-industrial establishment. The chief shortcoming of *"The Good War"* is that the viewpoints expressed in it (with many of which, for what little it matters, I strongly agree) seem largely to be Terkel's own. As maestro of the performance he is obviously entitled to choose the players and let them sing the tunes he likes, but the result is a book that, however fascinating, does not give the whole story. (pp. 3, 9)

This isn't nitpicking; the skewed viewpoint of *"The Good War"* undermines its claims to being an inclusive oral history of the war. But that having been said, let it be noted that as usual Terkel proves himself to be the best listener around; no one brings out the deepest thoughts and recollections of other people so sensitively as he does, and no one edits them more skillfully than he does. *"The Good War"* may be only part of the story, but it's still a wonderful story. (p. 9)

> *Jonathan Yardley, "World War Two: The Best Years of Their Lives," in* Book World—The Washington Post, *September 30, 1984, pp. 3, 9.*

LOUDON WAINWRIGHT

Ten, 20, 30 years from now the best witnesses to World War II will be largely gone. But Presidents honoring them will surely have access to a copy of Studs Terkel's most recent exercise in memory harvesting, *"The Good War."* It is hard to see how any reader now or then can fail to benefit from its 600 pages. For Mr. Terkel, who in six books over the past 15 years has turned oral history into a popular literary form, has captured an especially broad and impressive chorus of voices on his tape recorder this time. The result, whatever its limitations, is a portrait of a national experience drawn in the words of the men and women who lived it. . . .

Here also, in a kind of counterpoint, are the voices of a number of non-Americans, among them a Russian war hero and novelist who lost most of his family and friends ("The bullet that killed us today goes into the death of centuries and generations, killing life which didn't come to exist yet") and a British woman who read Cinderella to her children during the blitz ("You'd hear the bomb drop so many hundred yards that way. . . . You'd think, My God, the next one's going to be a direct hit. But you'd continue to read. . . . And you'd think, My God, I can't stand it"). . . .

This sort of thing is tremendously compelling, somehow dramatic and intimate at the same time, as if one has stumbled on private accounts in letters long locked in attic trunks. Poignant ironies surface here and there. One former medic who had won a Silver Star for rescuing wounded men under fire in the Philippines had a son who refused to be drafted during the Vietnam War decades later. Killing was against his principles, the young man said, and he was sent to prison for three years. "What he did took more guts than what I did," his father tells Mr. Terkel. "These big heroes grab him, put 'im in handcuffs right away, like a criminal. . . . It's like takin' a flower and cuttin' it and just throwin' it in the corner."

There are shortcomings in the book. Inherent in all oral history, however persuasive the personal accounts that go into it, is a certain vagueness and imprecision, for it is based on memory—which sometimes acquires hindsight—and is shaped inevitably by feelings. We often recall only what we want or need to recall, and we can be surprised later by our own distortions of the past. . . . *"The Good War"* sometimes leaves one with the feeling that he should be reading some other book at the same time, not necessarily for the correction of errors but so that the events reported by Mr. Terkel's people may be located more exactly in time, place and context. Mr. Terkel's comments are spare and admirably self-effacing (he was a sergeant in the Air Force) but a reader attempting to follow the details of some accounts . . . finds himself lost in a welter of names, places and facts.

It is inevitable that a book of this size would have some dull stretches. Occasionally the voices have a sameness and one sometimes feels that Mr. Terkel has never interviewed a man he didn't like. Now and then in *"The Good War"* . . . Mr. Terkel uses the reflections of several people who are better known than most of his subjects. This is in apparent defiance of a Terkel maxim outlined some years ago to a reporter, Mary Kerner. "The so-called ordinary people," Mr. Terkel said then, "are far more interesting than celebrities, because for the first time they're talking about themselves." . . .

Still, Mr. Terkel's book gives the American experience in World War II great immediacy. Reading it, I felt a renewed connection with that slice of my own past and a surprisingly powerful kinship with the voices from it. How much the book will appeal to younger people who do not have their own recollections of the period is impossible to say. But it certainly offers them sharp and unlaundered glimpses of a generation and a conflict they've grown up seeing romanticized in late night television movies. The reasons for our being in World War II were far clearer than those for being in Vietnam, and the national enthusiasm for it was much greater. But the realities of life and death and human behavior were just as raw—and on a bigger scale. In terms of plain human interest, Mr. Terkel may well have put together the most vivid collection of World War II sketches ever gathered between covers. (p. 7)

Loudon Wainwright, "'I Can Remember Every Hour'," in The New York Times Book Review, *October 7, 1984, pp. 7, 9.*

BARRY GEWEN

Ask the average person to describe what historians do, and you are likely to be told they collect facts about the past. Historians know better. In one of the best descriptions of their craft, the small, tightly argued volume *What Is History?,* the late E. H. Carr explained why the common-sense notion is wrong. Facts by themselves tell us very little worth knowing, for everything that has ever happened is a "fact"—from the date Columbus discovered America to the time I caught the subway yesterday morning. Anyone who does history has to select which facts to present, and that inevitably presupposes an aim other than simple accuracy, namely interpretation. (p. 12)

Studs Terkel, who over the last several years has published a number of remarkably successful collections of interviews built around common themes, possesses a layman's false notion of history. He obviously believes facts do speak for themselves, that if enough people are given the opportunity to talk openly about some Major Event, the bits and pieces of their personal experiences will add up to a coherent picture. I suspect he also feels that such a picture will be more accurate than the narratives of conventional historians because it is unmediated, free of interposed interpretations. *"The Good War": An Oral History of World War Two* . . . is Terkel's second attempt to re-create our recent past through memories; the first was his 1970 book, *Hard Times: An Oral History of the Great Depression.* Both are hodgepodges, shapeless blobs, and *"The Good War"* is more of a blob than its predecessor.

Neither is in any true sense history, but at least *Hard Times* had something of a point. By juxtaposing the painful recollections of those who lived through the slump with complacent comments from the post-'30s generation . . . , Terkel revealed the distressing lack of continuity in American life, raising the fear that we might have to suffer another economic calamity in this century because we had failed to learn from the first one. He hints at a similar purpose in his Introduction to *"The Good War":* "It appears that the disremembrance of World War Two is as disturbingly profound as the forgettery of the Great Depression." Yet the lesson we are to take away from this new work is not at all clear—that war is bad? that some wars are not so bad? that unintended benefits arise from wars, as well as unexpected evils? Even the title, with those ambiguous, distancing quotation marks, leaves a reader up in the air. Despite more than 100 reminiscences from a wide range of speakers, . . . there is nothing here to sink one's teeth into. Reading this book is like chewing water.

Terkel might have profited from looking at Carr's remarks on the deceptiveness of original sources: "No document can tell us more than what the author of the document thought—what he thought had happened, what he thought ought to happen or would happen, or perhaps only what he wanted others to think he thought, or even only what he himself thought he thought."

Terkel's witnesses are relating events that occurred 40 or more years ago, and there is no way of knowing when they are exaggerating, embellishing, dramatizing, or simply lying. The book is relatively free of the kind of chest-pounding normally associated with fish or war stories, though one man says he escaped from seven different German prison camps. The problem is that everything is presented uncritically, on its own terms. When a veteran claims he remembers "every hour, every minute," Terkel apparently expects us to take this at face value.

Most unreliable of all are those occasions when the speakers attempt to move beyond their immediate experience. According to one man, the U.S. military command in Europe tried to spare the lives of the infantry by relying on artillery and tanks as much as possible. Another declares that the Japanese, unlike the Germans, were particularly savage in combat. Both statements might be accurate, or neither. A reader won't know from either account, or from anything else in the book—although if he looks carefully enough through these pages, he will learn why he won't. In a commentary, the writer Garson Kanin, who helped film the D-Day invasion for the Office of Strategic Services (OSS), explains the limitations of eyewitness reports on war: "The curious thing we discovered was that men involved in the actual battle itself knew less about it than the people at headquarters who were seeing the film shots." . . . (pp. 12-13)

In Terkel's *American Dreams: Lost and Found* and *Working: People Talk About What They Do All Day and How They Feel About What They Do,* the blur between what individuals thought was happening and what really was going on did not interfere; it was opinions that Terkel was after. In *"The Good War,"* however, the truth is often crucial. One of the most affecting stories in the book is undermined because we aren't given all the facts.

John Smitherman was a sailor stationed near two atomic bomb tests in 1946. Following each explosion, he sailed to ground zero, in one case climbing aboard a target craft to put out fires and check test animals. Smitherman reports that he and his crewmates drank the water from the area, swam and washed in it. About a month later, he discovered burns on his feet and legs, and from then on experienced increasing trouble.

At the time Terkel interviewed him, he had already had both legs amputated, was being urged to have a hideously swollen arm removed as well, and was suffering from terminal cancer. An unsophisticated and ingenuously patriotic man, Smitherman was convinced that his problems were related to the bomb blasts. Nevertheless, the Veterans Administration turned down his disability claim six times, saying that the radiation exposure was insufficient to have caused the illnesses. As the crippled Smitherman tells his tale, we are initially outraged at what appears to be either bureaucratic callousness or a government cover-up. Then reason pulls us back because we realize we are not getting the total picture here, neither the VA's side nor data on the fate of the other crewmen. In the end, when Terkel tells us Smitherman died in 1983, all we can feel is frustration. . . .

Terkel is at his best in presenting not the essence of the period but its odd particulars—the off-beat, the unique, the unseemly. . . .

But for sheer eccentricity, nothing can top the experience of Hans Massaquoi, an editor of *Ebony Magazine.* The son of a black-African father and German mother, he grew up in Hamburg during the '20s, eager to be an enthusiastic Nazi and a member of the Hitler Youth. . . . He could not understand why he was always being turned down; he even rooted for Max Schmeling to knock out Joe Louis. Reflecting on this bizarre comedy of errors, Massaquoi says the one thing that saved him from Auschwitz was the fact that the only racial inferiors the government was rounding up in Hamburg were Jews. Massaquoi could always fill out official forms honestly because they asked about religion, never race. No one thought to look for blacks in Nazi Germany.

Such stories are the raisins in this porridge, and picking one's way through *"The Good War"* is probably the best approach to reading it. There are captivating tales collected here, some so remarkable that for a few diverting moments we do not demand the complete truth. We ignore the lack of connecting tissue that would give the book pace and direction. We cease to ask Terkel, ''what is that to us?'' (p. 13)

Barry Gewen, ''Facts Are Not Enough,'' in The New Leader, *Vol. LXVII, No. 20, November 12, 1984, pp. 12-13.*

J(ohn) R(onald) R(euel) Tolkien

1892-1973

South African-born English novelist, short story writer, poet, editor, critic, nonfiction writer, and scholar.

A leading philologist of his day, Tolkien was an Oxford University professor who, along with Oxford colleagues C. S. Lewis and Charles Williams, helped revive the medieval romance and the fairy tale. Tolkien is best known for his epic fantasy/romance trilogy of novels, *The Lord of the Rings* (1954-56). *The Lord of the Rings*, which is set in an enchanted land called Middle-earth, focuses on a timeless cosmic struggle between the forces of good and evil, embodied in such magical beings as wizards, elves, humanlike trees, sorcerers, trolls, and hobbits, the small, furry-footed creatures with human qualities that Tolkien introduced in his first novel set in Middle-earth, *The Hobbit; or, There and Back Again* (1937). Beneath the charming, adventurous surface story of Middle-earth lies a sense of quiet anguish for a vanishing past and a precarious future. Tolkien gained a reputation during the 1960s as a cult figure among youths disillusioned with war and the technological age; his continuing popularity evidences his ability to evoke the oppressive realities of modern life while drawing audiences into a fantasy world. Many critics contend that the success of Tolkien's trilogy has made possible the contemporary revival of "sword and sorcery" literature.

A devout Roman Catholic throughout his life, Tolkien began creating his own languages and mythologies at an early age and later wrote Christian-inspired stories and poems to provide them with a narrative framework. Tolkien's ideas came to fruition at Oxford when, together with Lewis and Williams, he helped establish a literary society called The Inklings, and Lewis convinced Tolkien to publish *The Hobbit*. Based on bedtime stories Tolkien had created for his children, *The Hobbit* concerns the reluctant efforts of a hobbit to recover a magic treasure stolen by a dragon. During the course of his mission, the hobbit discovers a ring of power capable of making its bearer disappear which is sought by the wizard Sauron, Lord of Darkness. The effort of the hobbits to destroy the ring in order to deny Sauron unlimited power is the focal point of *The Lord of the Rings* trilogy, consisting of the novels *The Fellowship of the Ring* (1954), *The Two Towers* (1955), and *The Return of the King* (1956). In these books Tolkien rejects such traditional heroic attributes as strength and size, stressing instead the capacity of even the meekest creatures to prevail against evil. Since the ring corrupts its bearer in direct proportion to his heroic stature, the most virtuous champion of good is incapable of resisting its seductive power. Despite Tolkien's belief in the worth of the smallest creature, the trilogy ends on a note of uncertainty. When the ring is destroyed, Middle-earth's magical beauty and creatures will slowly fade as a new age begins in which humans become dominant.

The initial critical reception to *The Lord of the Rings* varied. While some reviewers expressed dissatisfaction with the story's great length and one-dimensional characters, the majority enjoyed Tolkien's enchanting descriptions and lively sense of adventure. Religious, Freudian, allegorical, and political interpretations of the trilogy soon appeared, but Tolkien generally rejected such explications. He maintained that *The Lord of the*

Rings was conceived with "no allegorical intentions. . . , moral, religious, or political," but he also denied that the trilogy is a work of escapism: "Middle-earth is not an imaginary world. . . . The theatre of my tale is this earth, the one in which we now live." Tolkien contended that his story was "*fundamentally linguistic* in inspiration," a "religious and Catholic work" whose religious aspects were "absorbed into the story and symbolism." Tolkien concluded, "The stories were made . . . to provide a world for the languages rather than the reverse."

Throughout his career Tolkien composed histories, genealogies, maps, glossaries, poems, and songs to supplement his vision of Middle-earth. Among the many works published during his lifetime were a volume of poems, *The Adventures of Tom Bombadil and Other Verses from the Red Book* (1962), and a fantasy novel, *Smith of Wootton Major* (1967). Though many of his stories about Middle-earth remained incomplete at the time of Tolkien's death, his son, Christopher, rescued the manuscripts from his father's collections, edited them, and published them under his father's name. Tolkien began one of these works, *The Silmarillion* (1977), while a soldier in the trenches during World War I. *The Silmarillion* takes place before the time of *The Hobbit* and, in a heroic manner which recalls the Christian myths of Creation and the Fall, tells the tale of the first age of Holy Ones and their offspring. *Unfinished Tales of Numenor and Middle-earth* (1980) is a similar collection of incomplete stories and fragments written during World War I. *The Book of Lost Tales, Part I* (1984) and *The Book of Lost Tales, Part II* (1984) deal respectively with the beginnings of Middle-earth and the point at which humans enter the saga. In addition to these posthumous works, Christopher Tolkien also collected his father's correspondence to friends, family, and colleagues in *The Letters of J.R.R. Tolkien* (1981).

Tolkien's career as a professor of English literature spanned nearly forty years. Though he published only two major studies during his career, *A Middle English Vocabulary* (1922) and *Chaucer as a Philologist* (1949), Tolkien's careful examinations of problems and issues encountered in Old and Middle English literature continue to be read and discussed. Reorganized lecture notes of the 1930s and 1940s on the ancient poem "Exodus," collected in *The Old English "Exodus": Text, Translation and Commentary* (1981), display Tolkien's insights into this problematic work. *The Monsters and the Critics, and Other Essays* (1983) includes lectures and writings on such works as *Beowulf* and *Sir Gawain and the Green Knight.* Lectures on the heroes of *Beowulf* and the Old English poem "The Fight at Finnesburg" were reconstructed as *Finn and Hengest: The Fragment and the Episode* (1983).

(See also *CLC,* Vols. 1, 2, 3, 8, 12; *Contemporary Authors,* Vols. 17-18, Vols. 45-48 [obituary]; *Contemporary Authors Permanent Series,* Vol. 2; *Something about the Author,* Vols. 2, 24, 32; and *Dictionary of Literary Biography,* Vol. 15.)

BRIAN SIBLEY

Strictly speaking, [stories in *Unfinished Tales of Numenor and Middle-Earth*] are not all 'Tales', since the book includes several pieces of purely descriptive writing and lengthy genealogies. Everything, however, is 'unfinished'; although unfinished in different senses of the word. Some passages, such as **"Of Tuor and his Coming to Gondolin"**, literally lack an ending; which, despite the grandeur of Tolkien's prose and the proliferation of editorial notes, makes for frustrating reading. Other pieces are more or less complete, but largely unpolished, and still others are little more than scraps held together by Christopher Tolkien's commentaries.

Unfinished Tales clearly shows the extent to which Tolkien revelled in his game of Middle-earth—annotating many of his drafts with comments which draw attention to, and justify, discrepancies between these and other texts—but the book also demands that its readers should possess an equal passion for the game.

It is, I suspect, only the later fragments that will prove of real interest to those readers who know and admire *The Lord of the Rings,* but who are this side of slavish adulation. These pieces include accounts of the Palantíri (the Seeing Stones), the Drúedain (the Wild Folk of Haleth who make only a fleeting appearance in the history of the War), and the Istari (the order of wizards which numbered Gandalf, Saruman, Radagast and two lesser-known 'Blue Wizards').

Altogether less satisfying is **"The Quest of Erebor"**, an episode originally intended to form part of the tidying-up-the-loose-ends chapters of *The Lord of the Rings,* in which Gandalf attempts to correlate that book with *The Hobbit.* 'Bilbo,' he explains, 'did not know all that went on,' as a consequence of

which he overlooked such important matters as the rise of Sauron. Poor Tolkien! How he must have wished he'd known what he later knew *before* he wrote **The Hobbit**! Now, of course, we have **Unfinished Tales,** and can fit most of the puzzle's hitherto missing pieces into place.

Unfinished Tales is not another Tolkien classic. It is an expensive, 500-page postscript that adds little to its author's reputation or to the appreciation of his other work; but which also, mercifully, takes nothing from them. (pp. 443-44)

> Brian Sibley, "History for Hobbits," *in* The Listener, *Vol. 104, No. 2681, October 2, 1980, pp. 443-44.*

FREDERICK BUECHNER

[It] was out of homesickness as much as anything that I opened **Unfinished Tales** hoping for some return of the old enchantment, and hence my disappointment. Enchantment returns only very rarely if at all, nor does Christopher Tolkien, the author's son and editor, pretend otherwise. "Much in the book will be found unrewarding by readers of **The Lord of the Rings**," he says in his introduction. (p. 15)

Some of [the pieces] are fragmentary narratives or sketches of narrative written not with the extraordinary immediacy and concern for human and sensuous detail of the trilogy but in the sonorous and archaistic cadences of **The Silmarillion.** **"Of Tuor and His Coming to Gondolin"** and **"The Tale of the Children of Hurin"** are the longest of these, the former written by Tolkien on sick leave from the army in 1917, in crowded army huts, filled with the noise of gramophones, when one imagines that even the fateful battling of dark Morgoth and his villainous Orcs against the combined chivalry of men and elves must have seemed a fair haven from the shabbier horror of the trenches. . . .

There are moments of high adventure . . . , but they are seen as if from a great distance of time and space and recounted with epic stateliness. The earthiness of earth and the stoniness of stone, the homeliness of hobbits and dwarves who grow weary, cantankerous, hungry, and smoke their pipes to ward off despair—all this is as missing here as it is in *The Silmarillion* and with it is missing the uncanny sense that Tolkien at his fabulist's best can convey of participating in the events of a world as real if not realer than our own.

In **"The Quest of Erebor,"** Gandalf, the great wizard, reappears to explain in some detail many things that happened before his visit to Bilbo and the subsequent "Unexpected Party" of *The Fellowship of the Ring,* but there is again the sinking sense of something vital missing in it, a kind of summarizing flatness and sketchiness about it which makes one feel that Tolkien was right in cutting it out of the trilogy "to lighten the boat," as he put it in a letter to his son.

"The History of Galadriel and Celeborn" is not really a tale at all but an essay more or less on Tolkien's narrative technique, incorporating fragmentary quotations from virtually all his unpublished materials on the history of the Second Age in Middle-earth. Inconsistencies are allowed to stand on purpose . . . and such interest as the piece has derives from the view it gives of the author's changing conceptions and from the wistful question it raises as to what he might have made of so many intricate narrative threads if he had lived to weave them into a seamless whole.

There are as well other generalized and discursive essays with little or no element of story to them on such subjects as the seven Seeing Stones known as the *palantíri,* the military organization of the Riders of Rohan, and the dynastic records of the Kings of Númenor from the founding of the City of Armenelos to the Downfall. Christopher Tolkien has also redrawn on a larger scale, and with new features and names, the map of Middle-earth that accompanies *The Lord of the Rings* and reproduced the only map of Númenor that his father ever made.

Unfinished Tales is, in short, a production less of Tolkien himself than of the Tolkien industry—a book for the specialist, the scholar of Middle-earth, the addict, who will doubtless revel in the wealth of lore that it provides. For the rest of us, I'm afraid, it cannot be more than a dim echo of glories past, a scattering of crumbs left over from a great and unforgettable feast. (p. 20)

> *Frederick Buechner, "For Devotees of Middle-Earth," in* The New York Times Book Review, *November 16, 1980, pp. 15, 20.*

JESSICA YATES

Unfinished Tales is easy to describe and hard to assess. It is an anthology of the best unpublished stories and essays from Tolkien's Middle-Earth mythos. Two stories are longer versions of hero-tales we have already read in *The Silmarillion,* of Tuor and his kinsman Túrin. Another is a romance new to the reader, **"Aldarion and Erendis,"** a tale of Númenor. The rest of the book consists of background material to *The Lord of the Rings,* and will be most enjoyed by [fans of that trilogy], even those who found *The Silmarillion* hard going. There are essays on Galadriel, Celeborn the Wild Men, the Wizards and the palantíri. There are also extra episodes written late in Tolkien's life to tie up loose ends in [the trilogy]. . . .

On first reading, even Tolkien's admirers will be frustrated by the fact that the most promising fresh material, the epic of Tuor and romance of Erendis, is unfinished. The fan will enjoy the supplementary material to *The Lord of the Rings* and wish in vain for more. No one who is not a Tolkien fan should attempt to read this book. And yet Tolkien's severest critics must admit from the evidence it gives of Tolkien's composing habits—his drafts, his revisions, and the way his pen would run away with him to turn a summary into a full-blown narrative—that Tolkien was a gifted, compulsive tale-teller. The Tolkien Phenomenon—the way Tolkien synthesized northwestern mythology into his epic of Middle-Earth, . . . while making many enemies among literary critics—still awaits objective analysis.

> *Jessica Yates, in a review of "Unfinished Tales of Numenor and Middle-Earth," in* British Book News, *January, 1981, p. 57.*

NAOMI LEWIS

[*The Letters of J.R.R. Tolkien* is a volume] of some importance to Tolkien-readers, and with areas of interest for others. Not every writer is also a letter-writer. Tolkien was; he turned to paper easily and obsessively: on likes, dislikes, ideas, beliefs, and always on work in progress. . . .

Because of all this material the book doesn't aim to be complete. But Humphrey Carpenter is a selector and editor to be trusted; his choice, monitored by Tolkien's son and centring

on the course and problems of Tolkien's books, is, I would guess, as apt as any could be within its bounds.

Somewhere in these pages Tolkien wryly observes that the chief biographical fact of his life was the completing of *Lord of the Rings. The Hobbit,* published in 1937, an oddity in a don's life, did well, and a sequel was required. This sequel, he soon tells Stanley Unwin, 'is getting quite out of hand. It progresses towards quite unforeseen goals. . . . It is held up by war, by work, by domestic problems, by the need to earn extra money by marking papers ('the examination treadmill'), by its own difficulties. In 1950 he reports to Unwin that he has produced 'a monster: an immensely long, complex, rather bitter and very terrifying romance, quite unfit for children (if fit for anybody): and it is not really a sequel to *The Hobbit* but to *The Silmarillion.* The two must be published together'.

Yes, *The Silmarillion*—this was the book of his heart, the one that he really desired to see in print. All through the letters, from the earliest pages, runs its great unwieldy trail. (It never was truly finished.) . . . To Tolkien, it was essential as a prelude to *Lord of the Rings.* . . .

Here, as always, Tolkien the letter-writer is Tolkien the human: he wins you, loses you, wins you back, the whole course of the way. Rightly he is furious when in July 1938 a German publisher, negotiating for *The Hobbit,* requests a statement that he is of 'aryan' origin. He drafts two irate letters for Unwin's choice. A cheer for Tolkien. . . .

Dip again into the letters. About Charles Williams he writes: 'We enjoyed talking (mostly in jest) but we had nothing to say to one another at deeper or higher levels . . . I had read or heard a great deal of his work, but found it wholly alien, and sometimes very distasteful. I remained entirely unmoved. Lewis was bowled over.' A point here to Tolkien, I would say. (On Dorothy Sayers he is even less polite.) Yet he is quite bowled over himself by the flamboyant Roy Campbell, accepting whole (among other Campbellisms) his total approval of Franco. Lewis would have none of this. A point to C.S.L.

There are other irreconcilables. Tolkien idolised his mother; many of his valued correspondents were intelligent women. Yet his stated views on the nature and role of women could belong to another century. . . . Yet when he says that his writing has no intended didactic allegory, that he doesn't like the genre, he is speaking the truth. You can read all through *Lord of the Rings* without learning that its author was a devout Roman Catholic. . . .

In a letter written to his son, just after his wife's death, Tolkien refers to 'things that records do not record: the dreadful sufferings of our childhoods, from which we rescued one another, but could not wholly heal the wounds that later often proved disabling.' Yet little can be learnt here of his strange early life, his mother's death, the guardianship of a dominating priest, the forbidden courtship and other chances behind his marriage: all were in the past when the letters begin.

Again, for all the many references to C. S. Lewis, they do not bring out the character and real importance of their vexed and battling friendship. Even so, these pages call to life a good, troubled, fallible, touchy, kindly, likeable man, modest, not complex, but possessed and sustained by a quite extraordinary gift. Chance had ordered most of his views and creeds—even his religion was an emotional legacy from his dying convert mother. But his gift, with its roots in language, was inborn.

Naomi Lewis, "Myth in the Making," in The Observer, *August 23, 1981, p. 23.*

A. N. WILSON

J.R.R. Tolkien's genius was all of a piece. In his academic career and in his personal life and in his art, he was the same man. . . . Eminent scholars are, more often than not, bored with their subjects. And there is often so complete a division between the 'writing persona' and the 'real self' of an author that the task of biography becomes necessarily offensive. None of this applies to Tolkien. That is what gives his mythologies their power. Plenty of people have disliked them, or been jealous of their commercial success; but no one, with justice, could ever have thought them whimsical or posing. They sprang naturally out of his apprehension of the real world, as we can now perceive by reading this remarkable selection of letters [*The Letters of J.R.R. Tolkien*]. . . .

In many obvious senses [Tolkien] was not at home in the modern, materialist world. . . . [Not] merely did he feel displaced in 'this polluted country of which a growing proportion of the inhabitants are maniacs'. In the human body itself, he felt a stranger. After an unpleasant session with a doctor in old age he wrote to his son, 'We (or at least I) know far too little about the complicated machine we inhabit'.

With good Augustinian, not to say Platonic, precedent, Tolkien's sense of the present world's futility, folly and unreality stemmed from his lively faith in a world beyond: and this other world was, primarily, the Heaven of conventional Catholicism. So, to his son Christopher, posted to South Africa during the war, he can write, 'Remember your guardian angel. . . . God is . . . behind us, supporting, nourishing us (as being creatures). The bright point of power where that life-line, that spiritual umbilical cord touches: there is our Angel, facing two ways, to God behind us in the direction we cannot see, and to us'. . . .

When, years later, this umbilical cord was loosed and his correspondent lost a sense of this other world, it was an enormous grief to Tolkien: 'When I think of my mother's death . . . , I find it very hard and bitter when my children stray away from the Church'. In the same letter he writes, '*in hac urbe lux solemnis* has seemed to me steadily truc'.

Yet its truth was best apprehended, in his distinctive imagination, when transformed into story and mythology. His love of language suggested much of the myth's substance. In the case of the 'ents', for example, the majestic walking trees of his story, 'as usually with me they grew rather out of their name than the other way about. I always felt that something ought to be done about the peculiar Anglo-Saxon word *ent* for a "giant" or a mighty person of long ago—to whom all old works are ascribed'. He was not content to leave the ents as they appear on the page of *Beowulf*, shadowy, unknown figures of an almost forgotten past. A natural story-teller, Tolkien invested them with shapes, voices and habits of his own creation. Many of his fellow-mediaevalists have found *The Lord of the Rings* perpetually irritating for this reason. Any student of Anglo-Saxon knows that an ent is not a walking tree: it is some sort of giant, perhaps a nickname for the Romans. But in the imaginations of the millions, in their Gandalf T-shirts, the ent has taken leave of its Anglo-Saxon origins and become something other. . . .

The objectors fail to recognise the wholeness of Tolkien's imaginative sweep. . . . [The tales] are an expression of his whole experience of life. This is what the *Letters* make so fascinatingly clear. At the beginning, in an undergraduate letter to his future wife, he reports that he has 'done some touches to my nonsense fairy language'; but the importance of this invented grammar had not yet dawned on him; he can still apologise for it as 'such a mad hobby'. . . . [By] the late 1930s, when Tolkien had returned to Oxford as Rawlinson and Bosworth Professor, all the strands of his life had become enmeshed in their inevitable pattern: the love of philology; the sense of the Church as the one city in which *lux solemnis* shines on in a dark world; the zest for story-telling; the poignant and increasingly strong sense that 'Men are essentially mortal and must not try to become "immortal" in the Flesh'. Thus the divisions between his imagined world and the world of all of us grow shadowy. 'I am historically minded', he protests to one correspondent, 'Middle Earth is not an imaginary world . . . The theatre of my tale is this earth, the one in which we now live'. This is not whimsy. The letters reveal innumerable glimpses of how it was, in his own life, literally true. (p. 17)

These letters, then, are primarily interesting because they reveal more of the mind which created *Lord of the Rings*. There are extended epistles to admirers or publishers, giving commentary on the great tale and answering points of difficulty with donnish precision. (pp. 17-18)

But it must be stressed that these are very good letters in themselves, quite apart from their relevance to hobbit-lore. There are good gossipy vignettes of Oxford: C. S. Lewis downing three pints of beer before lunch and insisting that he was 'going short for Lent'. . . . There are letters which reveal Tolkien as a wise counsellor, a kind friend, an admirable father. The best, and most moving, are those written to his son Christopher during the war, sent out with installments of *Lord of the Rings* as the tale grew. In perhaps the most impressive of all, he recounts a sermon by Father Douglas Carter on the raising of Jairus's daughter. The sermon moved Tolkien so much because it captured what he called the *eucatastrophe* of that story: 'the sudden happy turn in a story which pierces you with a joy that brings tears'. (p. 18)

A.N. Wilson, "Beyond the Misty Mountains," in The Spectator, *Vol. 247, No. 7992, September 12, 1981, pp. 17-18.*

ROGER SALE

Tolkien was always nervous about Tolkien fans:

"An enquirer asked what [*The Lord of the Rings*] was all about, and whether it was an 'allegory.' And I said it was an effort to create a situation in which a common greeting would be *elen sila lúmenn' omentielmo*, and that the phrase long antedated the book. I never heard any more."

The elvish greeting is "A star shines on our meeting," but Tolkien seldom felt such stars shone when he confronted a reader. He loved not hearing any more.

If Tolkien had persisted in such responses, he would have written many fewer letters and [*The Letters of J.R.R. Tolkien*] might never have appeared. . . .

Because of its huge success *The Lord of the Rings* drew him into being a public figure, into explaining. Sometimes he responded to letters with dogged and thorough politeness, sometimes with tense irritation, sometimes with open exasperation. But always he explained. He was a philologist, so he explained words. He was a mythologizer, so he explained his myths. But I wish he had bought a stack of postcards instead and had written *elen sila lúmenn' omentielmo* and his initials on each one.

Alas, he lacked such ironies. As a result he provided, in his letters, much fodder for a class of people he thought should not exist, "scholars" pursuing tenure and advanced degrees. Mere lovers of Tolkien will find little in his explaining. Those who "need" the last half of this volume are those who are altogether too eager to take the word for the deed, the explanation for the thing explained, the theology for the myth. One wishes they could have been denied such shortcuts.

The rest of us, though, are not entirely shut out here, mostly because of the letters to Christopher Tolkien when he was stationed in South Africa during the war. Christopher, along with Lewis, constituted Tolkien's instinctively admiring audience in the year when *The Silmarillion* took shape. . . . These letters give us, as the later ones to fans cannot, glimpses of domestic life, offhand opinions, and many signs that this shy private man could be openly loving and affectionate to his children. More than that, the fact that these letters were being written itself prodded Tolkien into getting on with *The Lord of the Rings* at a time when the press of wartime and duties could have allowed him the procrastination he often practiced.

He was writing what became the heart of the work, the second half of *The Two Towers*. Foolishly, Tolkien always loved *The Silmarillion*, but he knew the trilogy was better, and knew that Frodo, Sam, and Smeagol were the best of the trilogy:

"For myself I was prob. most moved by Sam's disquisition on the seamless web of story, and by the scene when Frodo goes to sleep on his breast, and the tragedy of Gollum who at that moment came within a hair of repentance—but for one rough word from Sam."

Thinking of himself, always, as "sub-creator" rather than original, Tolkien was free to be moved by what he wrote. . . .

The greater teller of stories did not want to be one. He was going public in *The Lord of the Rings*. Better the vanished past.

Which means we are faced with miracle, or with terribly lucky accident. The elfish languages, with their private pleasures, were what Tolkien wanted. He loved *The Silmarillion* but could not get it published as such, and so its partially told and dreary myths became, in effect, the "untold stories" that lie behind *The Lord of the Rings*. They clutter it up. The poems, almost everyone agrees, are bad. But their presence inspired Tolkien somehow, as he was telling Frodo's story, which had to be told or there'd be no story. Without them, no Ring.

Roger Sale, "Lore of the Rings," in Book World—
The Washington Post, October 18, 1981, p. 11.

D.J.R. BRUCKNER

[In *The Letters of J.R.R. Tolkien*] Tolkien's biographer, Humphrey Carpenter, and his son Christopher Tolkien have gathered 374 letters written over 60 years by the creator of all those elves, hobbits, orcs, ents, dragons, magicians and spooks. There are letters to his fiancée in 1914, later letters of advice to his children, a few about his scholarly work; but most are about his popular books—letters to publishers, friends, fans, critics.

For the serious students of the tales this is a trove worthy of protection by one of his dragons. (How that man loved dragons!

His first story, written at age 7, was of a dragon. Dragons lurk about in these letters everywhere.) Here is Tolkien discussing sources, the development of his ideas, the meanings of incidents, the origins of words. Letters to his son while writing *The Lord of the Rings,* long letters to a man he wanted to publish it, others to the proofreader in the company that finally did publish it could be printed as a textual introduction to the book. (p. 7)

Excited to rare but real anger by a column written by Harvey Breit in the New York Times Book Review in 1955 (Breit had quoted a fragment of a Tolkien description of his work in a way that he felt ended up misrepresenting him), [Tolkien] wrote to his American publishers that his work "is all of a piece, and *fundamentally linguistic* in inspiration. . . . The invention of languages is the foundation. The 'stories' were made rather to provide a world for the languages than the reverse. To me a name comes first and the story follows." (pp. 7, 26)

In this volume a letter to W. H. Auden, who was about to make a BBC broadcast about him, gives a clear chronological account of how his immensely various literary interests fit together. To Christopher Bretherton he wrote what is really an interior history of his reading and imagination. Two of the most revealing insights occur in a 1953 letter to Robert Murray, a Jesuit priest:

"*The Lord of the Rings* is of course a fundamentally religious and Catholic work; unconsciously so at first, but consciously in the revision. That is why I have not put in, or have cut out practically all references to anything like 'religion,' to cults or practices, in the imaginary world. For the religious element is absorbed into the story and symbolism." Farther on: "Certainly I have not been nourished by English literature. . . . I was brought up in the Classics, and first discovered the sensation of literary pleasure in Homer. Also, being a philologist, [I get] a large part of any aesthetic pleasure that I am capable of from the *form* of words (and especially from the *fresh* association of word-form with word-sense)." Add to that his lifetime work on the old northern European languages and their sagas, and you have almost the entire foundation of his work.

In these letters we find him explaining that Middle Earth—the location of his stories—is merely our own round ball, but before human history. For some incidents he cited general sources in old legends. To a lady who asked about Smaug, the dragon, he wrote that the name is the past tense of an Old High German verb meaning "to vent" and confessed it was "a low philological jest."

Many wrote him that they were haunted by half-remembered thoughts when they saw names of his characters. Naturally; the names are echoes of the very roots of our languages. In a 1958 letter to Father Murray, Tolkien gives a glimpse into the workings of his mind: ". . . in an historical enquiry we are obliged to deal simultaneously with two variables each in motions that are independent fundamentally, even when affecting one another 'accidentally': the meanings and associations of meaning are one, and the word-forms another, and their changes are independent. . . . We do not know the 'original' meaning of any word, still less the meaning of its basic element . . . there is always a lost past."

He then outlines his intuitive process of tracing, fixing, defining a word according to a complex system of variable rules, the mastery of which depends as much on art as on learning. Of course, that is what he did professionally all his life. His mind moved certainly and swiftly through the lost histories of words, and countless times his surmises would later be proved right. That mental agility tells a great deal about his rare technical skill in constructing his complex "fairy tales and romances."

Tolkien's assertion that his stories are Catholic explains many of the reactions to them, some of which surprised him. While he was writing **The Lord of the Rings** he could tell his son that the hobbit hero "Frodo is not so interesting, because he has to be highminded and has (as it were) a vocation." But at a crucial point in the **Rings** Frodo's willpower fails. So we find Tolkien writing later to many correspondents that there is a difference between evil and weakness and getting into long discussions of morality. It is striking that both the questions and his responses use language right out of an old-fashioned Roman catechism. He had touched a nerve unwittingly, and the letters he writes sound like a lawyer arguing for the defense.

Sometimes he just got fed up with the stupidity of his correspondents and told them they took his stories too seriously. (p. 26)

His compassion had its limits. He wrote to John Masefield, the Poet Laureate, acidly informing him that Geoffrey Chaucer was *not* the first English poet. He would rap the knuckles of Auden or C. S. Lewis when they were being dull. And he was obviously dismayed by proposals to adapt **The Lord of the Rings** for other media. One letter is contemptuous of the BBC for its inept attempt to convey his tales to its listeners, and another is absolutely vitriolic in a schoolmasterly way about a "treatment" a film company proposed to him for a movie version of the Rings. (pp. 26, 28)

Tolkien began writing **The Lord of the Rings** near the start of World War II. The war-years letters are filled with apprehension about mankind's addiction to the use of force. . . . The noise in the popular mind worried him more; propaganda and the decay of values signified by harsh or stupefying language appalled him. . . . Anyone wielding power was dangerous. "If we could get back to personal names, it would do a lot of good. . . . If people were in the habit of referring to 'King George's council, Winston and his gang,' it would go a long way to clearing thought, and reducing the frightful landslide into Theyocracy."

Writing from his study about war to a son who was in the war produced its own self-deprecating humor, but "I imagine a fish out of water is the only fish to have an inkling of water," he said. In 1945 he wrote that "the first War of the Machines seems to be drawing to its final inconclusive chapter—leaving, alas, everyone the poorer, many bereaved or maimed and millions dead, and only one thing triumphant: the Machines. . . . What's their next move?" In the mythical battles in **The Lord of the Rings** there is a sense of dread, of an evil more threatening than the worst war among political equals. No wonder.

If there is melancholy anywhere in this correspondence it is in Tolkien's dealings with academic friends, notably C. S. Lewis and Charles Williams. He hints in some letters at the kind of corrosive gossip the Oxford dons would use in their bewildered failure to understand how a man they had to honor for his learning could be so popular. That hurt him because he needed friendship more than anything in life, although he was, as he admits in one letter, no good judge of men's characters. So he was close for a time to Lewis and Williams and realized only in later years that he never really understood Lewis and did not have a very high opinion of Williams's abilities or ideas.

A few of the letters to and about Lewis are really painful to read. . . .

Tolkien was a strange, complicated, quiet, difficult and humble man. There is a great deal of him in these letters. (p. 28)

> *D.J.R. Bruckner, in a review of "The Letters of J.R.R. Tolkien," in* The New York Times Book Review, *November 15, 1981, pp. 7, 26, 28.*

KATHARYN F. CRABBE

The Silmarillion, Tolkien's posthumously published account of the First Age of the world, is the densest, the most difficult, and for the general reader the least attractive of all his works. As a backdrop to **The Lord of the Rings** and **The Hobbit, The Silmarillion** is perhaps the most essential of Tolkien's works; at the same time it is the least able to stand alone as a unified vision. Although individual tales from this chronicle of the earliest age of Middle-earth may be exquisite, or majestic, or horrifying, **The Silmarillion** as a whole has neither unity of tone nor unity of style. In addition, the number of characters is simply staggering. So while **The Silmarillion** is Tolkien's most ambitious project, it is in many ways his most flawed performance. (p. 112)

Like the poem *Beowulf,* which Tolkien studied and loved, **The Silmarillion** is not really a narrative in the sense that it tells a story in a straightforward and sequential manner. Instead, the collection of tales with its cross-references, modifications, and contradictions is presented as a mythology which, having come from divers hands and divers places, cannot be expected to achieve any great degree of inner consistency. The pose of the narrator, then, as a translator or as an editor obviates criticism of the lack of unity in the work.

To say, however, that **The Silmarillion** lacks narrative unity is not to say that it lacks structure. Indeed, the work is highly structured, taking the form of a triptych, a three-paneled picture often used as an altarpiece. This structure seems to have been part of Tolkien's own plan for the work, for Christopher Tolkien notes in the Foreword that the first and third panels "are included according to my father's explicit intention."

The large central section, the *Quenta Silmarillion,* or "History of the Silmarils," is flanked on one side by the story of the creation in the *Ainulindalë* and the *Valaquenta,* and on the other by the story of the decline of the elves and the rise of men in the *Akallabêth* and *Of the Rings of Power and the Third Age.* As in an actual triptych, the central panel is the largest and carries the most meaning, but the two side panels provide a context for the central panel, give a perspective on it, and direct the eye toward it. . . . Thus by placement of the parts and by proportion, **The Silmarillion** is an account of the history of the elves of Middle-earth. It is, at the same time, a symbolic representation of the fall of man because it is in the nature of myths to link gods, demigods, and men.

In **The Silmarillion** the two most important influences in Tolkien's life came into direct opposition: his religion and his love for the ancient and heroic north. On the one hand, his philologist's mind told him that the mythology of the ancient Britons must be similar in most ways to other northern mythologies. On the other hand, as much as he loved those mythologies, and as much as he celebrated the heroes of the unbendable will, he was a Christian and thus could not rid his mind utterly of the notion that this life is but a prelude to another. **The Silmarillion** thus reflects a mythology that combines the values of the unconquerable will with the certainty that whatever the outcome of the temporal battle between good and evil, the last battle is yet to come. (pp. 113-15)

The first panel of the triptych, which depicts the creation of the universe, begins with the assumption of a single, ruling, creative force: "There was Eru, the One, who in Arda is called Ilúvatar." In describing Eru and the creation, Tolkien uses the familiar notion of a world that is built to music and is, therefore, ideally "harmonious." He is quick to establish a tone which aspires to the heroic through the use of unusual words (Arda, Ilúvatar).... The combination of heroic tone and religious connotation identifies *The Silmarillion* as mythic. It also helps Tolkien to establish the ultimately hopeful nature of his work. Even in the first panel, as he raises the specter of the long trials that will comprise the central portion of the work, Tolkien evokes the splendor and the glory of the first conception of the world by the Ainur.... Tolkien immediately asserts without equivocation an eschatological vision of harmony: There will be an end to this world, and after that end perfection will once more be attained. But until that time, the music will be less than perfect. The vision of harmony after the end is one that Tolkien attributed to early Christians in Briton, and one that stands in dramatic contrast to the stark hopelessness of the more ancient northern mythologies. Thus, though he has created a mythology for England in *The Silmarillion,* he was providing it from the beginning with a Christian element. (pp. 115-16)

Like the *Ainulindalë,* the *Valaquenta* is at once foreboding and hopeful. As a narrative it is remarkably weak, for it simply focuses on each of the Valar in turn, describing their powers and their responsibilities.... It is a catalogue of characters, not a story. But though the *Valaquenta* tells no story, it heightens the sense of impending disaster at the same time as it encourages the careful reader to look ahead with hope. The sense of foreboding grows by virtue of the organization of the *Valaquenta.* Evil, introduced under the heading "Of the Enemies," is given the position of power: Morgoth and Sauron are introduced last, so that the section closes with an evocation of the darkness, suffering, and treachery they will visit upon Middle-earth. (p. 117)

As the overall structure of *The Silmarillion* is architecturally tidy, so is that of the central panel. The *Quenta Silmarillion* has twenty-four books; elves dominate the whole but are the exclusive subjects of the first half (men do not even appear until chapter 12). In the second half the *Quenta Silmarillion* develops the connection between elves and men and depicts the ultimate combining of the blood of the two kindreds in the greatest hero of the First Age, Eärendil the Mariner.

The *Quenta Silmarillion* is therefore not only the history of the Silmarils, but of the elves as well. (p. 118)

Although the title of *The Silmarillion* suggests that the fate of the jewels draws the unnamed narrator to the tales of the elves, such does not actually seem to be the case, for many of the episodes have little direct connection with the jewels. Rather, the Silmarils are primarily important as the means by which elves and men become estranged from the Valar and thus from the One. The tales are unified not so much by the jewels as by the theme of the struggle against Morgoth, that personification of malice, greed, and destruction that is the evil side of the heroic life.... Thematically, *The Silmarillion* is first concerned with the undying, yet hopeless, struggle of man against evil and the inevitable decline of the children of the earth.

As long as the Eldar are content to accept the gifts of the Valar and Ilúvatar, they are innocent and protected. But in Fëanor comes the kind of knowledge that contributes both to the rise and to the decline of man. On the one hand, it makes men more nearly the equal of those beings they call gods; on the other, by destroying their innocence, it cuts them off from the protection they enjoyed in the unified world of the golden age. Fëanor's original name, *Curufinwë,* contains the root *skill* (curu); *Fëanor* itself means *spirit of fire.* From skill and spirit Fëanor brings to the Eldar, among other gifts, the letters "which the Eldar used ever after." Thus Fëanor, as *spirit of fire* is a culture hero like Prometheus. And as was true of Prometheus, his gift to his race is double-natured: It is an *ipso facto* blessing, but it is also the cause of great misery.... Fëanor's knowledge, like that of Prometheus, is gained at the cost of the happiness and peace of mind of the whole race.

Fëanor's rebellion and his transgression of the assumed law of Arda, obedience to one's betters, is an elvish fall from grace, analogous to the fall of Adam and Eve in the garden of Eden. When, like Adam and Eve, elves must leave the garden, a messenger appears at the very edge of the guarded realm to deliver "the Doom of the Noldor": "Tears unnumbered ye shall shed; and the Valar will fence Valinor against you, and shut you out, so that not even the echo of your lamentation shall pass over the mountains." (pp. 119-21)

Because of the pride and disobedience of the elves as symbolized in Fëanor, the world of the *Quenta Silmarillion* is a vale of tears.... [The] heroes of elves and men suffer physically and spiritually under the formidable assault of evil on Middle-earth. The recurrence of the torture of heroes in *The Silmarillion* points out the hopelessness of their earthly lives. (p. 121)

[Yet, for] all the suffering it recounts, the *Quenta Silmarillion* concludes with hope. After twenty-three chapters chronicling the failure of heroes to transcend the doom of the Noldor, the twenty-fourth, "Of the Voyage of Eärendil and the War of Wrath," tells of the forgiveness of the Valar and the return of divine mercy and pity to Middle-earth. Here Eärendil is a hero in the most mythic and the most religious sense: He is someone who saves us. In doing so, he not only secures the pardon of the Valar, he also succeeds in returning the elves to the west. Further, Morgoth is banished into the Void. Yet the world cannot be remade and the seeds of evil are still fertile even though Morgoth himself is destroyed. (p. 122)

The most important theme of the *Quenta Silmarillion* is the decline of mankind. The second most important is the union of opposites. As the tone is both foreboding and hopeful, as Eärendil is both man and elf, The Two Trees of Valinor also combine opposites. The Two Trees, the sources of the light of the Silmarils, are born from the green mound called Ezellohar, called forth by the song of Yavanna and the tears of Nienna. Yavanna is the giver of fruits, the lover of all things that grow. Nienna is the mourner: She mourns for the marring of the world by Morgoth and for those who wait in the halls of Mandos, i.e., those who are dead. From the moment of origin, then, the Two Trees and the light they literally shed on the ground of Valinor is made up of generation and decay, of growth and decline, of birth and death. (p. 123)

[The] Silmarils, like Christ, serve as a symbolic link between the spiritual and physical worlds, the realm of the Valar and the world of men and elves. Determined and self-sacrificing as he is, Eärendil cannot find the straight road to the west, the spiritual world, until he receives a Silmaril to light the way. It is the symbol of grace that allows men and elves to transcend the bounds of the mundane world. When the first Silmaril reaches its rest, bound to the brow of Eärendil, disposition of the two remaining Silmarils indicates the approaching equilibrium in *The Silmarillion. . . .* Fëanor's sons steal the gems only to find that they cannot bear to hold them. (pp. 124-25)

The third panel of the triptych, the *Akallabêth* or "Downfall of Númenor" and "Of the Rings of Power," provides a coda to the central panel, a recapitulation of the theme performed by different principals. Like the elves, the men of the three faithful houses are given a land of their own with every promise of a blissful life. But, like the elves, they come under the shadow—this time in the person of Sauron. The freedom, or *free-doom,* of the men of Númenor is reflected in the physical location of Númenor itself; it rises out of the sea between Middle-earth and Valinor, symbolizing their position midway between the totally spiritual and the totally physical. As was the case with both Morgoth and Fëanor, the desire to approach the godlike drives men toward evil. (pp. 125-26)

Like the two books that deal with the coming of the elves into the world, the books that tell of their parting are at once hopeful and filled with foreboding. The departure of the elves from Middle-earth is continually alluded to and used to evoke a state of loss. Without the presence of the elves, men are deprived of "good counsel and wise lore" and fall into the "Darkness." The beauty of elvish voices and elvish arts is withdrawn from the world, as is the memory of a time without evil. In the Third Age, the image of what the world of the elves was is preserved only by the power of the elven rings. . . . When the destruction of the Ruling Ring ends the power of the three rings of the elves, the last traces of the Noldor pass out of the world.

At the same time, the destruction of the Ruling Ring achieves the final overthrow of Sauron. The greatest servant of evil is vanquished, and his final destruction marks a moment of rebirth as spring comes again to the earth. (pp. 126-27)

As the narrative quality of *The Silmarillion* resembles that of *Beowulf,* so does the strategy of the poet. Tolkien has created in *The Silmarillion* the illusion of surveying a past that reaches back to a long history of sorrow, one noble and fraught with great significance. The recurrent allusions to lost tales . . . serve to create a sense of a past that must have been truly heroic and noble to have given rise to so many heroic tales. The recurrent references to source poems also create the sense that the author is working in the context of a widely known and well-accepted body of literature—a living mythology. However, *The Silmarillion* as we have it is not the mythology itself, but a heroic, elegiac poem based on it. The poet's wide acquaintance with and knowledge of this heroic past allows him to see in the recurrent joyous creation and sorrowful destruction something of permanent value. He tells again the oldest of mythic tales, the unending struggle of good against evil; he depicts again the oldest of human tragedies, the inevitable death and destruction of man and all his works; and he balances the two possible responses to the inevitable end—the pagan and the Christian.

The pagan or pre-Christian eschatological view, as Tolkien explained in his essay on *Beowulf,* is based on "the creed of unyielding." In the northern mythologies, at least, the heroic assumption was that the destruction of man and his creations was inevitable. The creed of unyielding, then, holds that chaos will eventually triumph and that, for that reason, human life can be made meaningful only by opposing chaos with all one's

strength and will until death inevitably comes. The heroic life may end, but the heroic will is indomitable. (pp. 129-30)

The concept of heroism in *The Silmarillion* is far more diffuse and ironic than in Tolkien's earlier works. In contrast with *The Lord of the Rings,* which provided heroes at every level of mimesis and at every level of society, *The Silmarillion* seems to lack even one unifying champion. Tolkien felt the lack of a single hero and at one time proposed to provide the needed continuity by framing the tales with a sea-farer to whom all the stories could be told. However, the sea-farer never materialized, and the continuity that does exist comes from the enemies, Morgoth and Sauron, rather than from the legions of elves and men who oppose or resist them. *The Silmarillion* shares this feature with another great collection of myths, the Bible, in which a succession of heroes of men all come to stand for one man who, in turn, stands for all men. This, then, is the key to the heroism of *The Silmarillion:* The heroes of the Valar, of the elves, and of men are all aspects of one man whose significance is universal, whose struggle is unending, and whose earthly fate is never in doubt. (p. 131)

The highest and only undefeated power of *The Silmarillion* is Eru, the one, also called Ilúvatar. It is he who creates the Valar and from whose thought they create Arda, "the Realm." It is also he who creates elves and men, and who decrees that the Valar are to be "chiefs" rather than "gods" to them. It is he alone who knows the fate of the world after the end of all the ages. Finally, it is he who knows and understands how the great design is unified, how everything has its origin in himself and contributes to his own greater glory.

In this conception of the One, Tolkien has clearly created a source of good like the Christian god and one which embodies the same paradoxes. For example, he is the source of all creation and yet is not responsible for the presence of evil. He knows what will occur (that is, he sees the whole "design") but he does not will it. . . . He is, in short, all powerful and all knowing, but also incomprehensible, and because he represents a heroism we cannot understand, much less hope to emulate, Ilúvatar is no more the hero of *The Silmarillion* than Jehovah is the hero of the Old Testament. For heroism as it is commonly understood, we must look to the lesser orders of beings.

Next in power below Ilúvatar are the Valar who, inspired by the thought of the One, create Arda. In them we see the first outlines of a comprehensible heroism in *The Silmarillion,* for the Valar are the first in Arda to oppose evil in the form of Morgoth. The heroism of the Valar is rooted in their determination to realize the visions that come to them from the One. Although they know that after the first assault on Arda by Morgoth they cannot achieve the perfection of the original vision, they persevere in their attempts to bring the world they have imagined into being. In doing so, they are creative, obedient to the will of Eru, and loving toward their fellow creatures. (pp. 131-32)

The relationship between the Valar and Ilúvatar is fundamentally Christian in nature because, although the Valar love the world they create and their creations for the world, they also understand that beyond the realm of the earthly is the realm of Ilúvatar, and that even the marring of Arda accrues to the glory of the One. To the elves, however, the world is a darker place than it seems to the Valar. Their characteristic attitude toward the world is more nearly pagan, marked by an unwavering will and a strict adherence to the law of loyalty to the lord that is the core of the heroic pagan code. . . .

Among the elves, the greatest protagonists are Fëanor, maker of the Silmarils, and Turgon, Lord of Gondolin. However, the tragedy of the elves is that, thanks to the oath of Fëanor and the ensuing doom of the Noldor, they have only heroes whose actions bring catastrophic results. Allegiance to the code of the will can not bring victory; it can only bring, at best, glorious defeat. (p. 134)

Fëanor shares with the Valar a desire to create, and as he is "... the most subtle in mind and most skilled in hand" of all the elves, he is so nearly godlike that his creations are nearly divine in their beauty. Unlike the Valar, however, Fëanor fails to respect the necessary freedom of all creations, including his own, and he fails to recognize or to accept responsibility for his fellow creatures. For example, the oath by which he binds his sons and followers to him effectively destroys the free will he should strive to enhance. In his desire to control others rather than to help them to be more fully themselves, he fails to be merciful or protective, or to discharge the responsibility of a leader. (p. 135)

Turgon, the second great hero of the Noldor, is one who swore Fëanor's oath and defied the Valar with him. Betrayed by Fëanor and left to brave the ice fields of the Helcaraxë, he turns away from the oath-keepers and, at the urging of Ulmo, Lord of Waters, builds a hidden city. The city of Gondolin . . . becomes the last refuge of the Noldor in Middle-earth, a city of bliss, beauty, and wisdom. But from the moment Turgon fails to repudiate the oath and his own will and make himself subject to the will of the Valar, the fall of Gondolin is foretold. That is, it too is part of the doom of the Noldor. The fall of the city is brought about by the same heroic flaw that drives Fëanor to his death: the overweening pride of the creator in his own creation. (pp. 135-36)

Among the race of men, heroes suffer less because they transgress the rules of obedience and responsibility than because they are victims of a world that fails to reward action with justice. For men, the world visits evil on the just and unjust alike. And as men are frailer, shorter-lived, and more limited in understanding than elves, they are even more susceptible to the evil of the world and less able to believe that a greater power loves and protects them than the elves. (p. 136)

Among the most celebrated creations of *The Silmarillion* are the texts of the tales that make up the work itself. Here, as in *The Lord of the Rings*, Tolkien creates a narrator who is styled as the translator and editor of old texts. His knowledge of Elvish mythology is wide and deep, and his delight in the Elvish languages is apparent in the attention he gives them in his appendices and glossaries.

Tolkien's fascination with languages is, by now, no surprise. What is surprising in this work is the difficulty that fascination creates for the reader. Of *The Lord of the Rings* one could say without hesitation that the language themes were beautifully integrated with other thematic concerns; in fact in that work the themes and the language are perfectly suited to one another. However, the success of Tolkien's uses of language in *The Silmarillion* is questionable. It can be argued, as Jane Nitzsche has done, that Tolkien's fascination with languages has made *The Silmarillion* nearly unreadable. . . . However, having acknowledged the limits of Tolkien's use of the language theme in *The Silmarillion,* one may go on to appreciate even a minor achievement. This "plethora of names" is not simply the self-

indulgence of an aging writer; instead it is a major part of one of the most important themes of the work, the centrality of the creative impulse to human experience.

Thematically, the naming and renaming that is so prominent in these tales is a constant allusion to the principle that to use language, particularly to name, is to create. Impatience with *The Silmarillion* is often a result of expecting it to be something it is not: a well-plotted adventure story, say, like *The Hobbit* or *The Lord of the Rings.* But *The Silmarillion* is not basically a narrative; it backtracks, modifies, contradicts, and reconsiders far too often to be trying to tell a single story. Rather, its purpose is to tell *stories* and, in doing so, to evoke a feeling for a time, a culture, and a set of values. The issue is not what becomes of Fëanor, or even of Eärendil, but what becomes of people (good and bad) when pride and envy and blind fear conflict with humility and self-sacrifice. (pp. 140-41)

The Silmarillion, then, is the story of a world that is too dangerous and unforgiving to be comic; it is also the story of a world that is far too capricious, far too capable of rewarding even the good with ashes, to be really tragic. Instead, Tolkien here portrays a world that is ironic: Danger is everywhere, villains may be banished but not vanquished, the longed-for apple is rotten at the core. The inhabitants of this world live lives in which conventional notions of relations between actions and rewards are exploded. They live lives in which the odds against good winning over evil are almost absurdly high. However, caught in this trap between high odds and bad bets, Tolkien's heroes do the most heroic thing ironic heroes can do: They endure. (pp. 143-44)

> *Katharyn F. Crabbe, in her* J.R.R. Tolkien, *Frederick Ungar Publishing Co., 1981, 192 p.*

EDWARD B. IRVING, JR.

If Tolkien had not become so renowned as author of the classic *Lord of the Rings,* we can be certain that . . . [*The Old English "Exodus": Text, Translation and Commentary*], now ably reconstructed from his lecture notes of the thirties and forties by Joan Turville-Petre, would never have seen the light. As an edition it is obviously incomplete, lacking a glossary and any extensive discussion of palaeography, sources, and language. In the time since he began work on it nearly fifty years ago, two full editions of the poem and many articles on it have appeared. Consequently we can hardly be surprised to find much of his commentary old-fashioned. A number of the problems with which he struggled have since been solved, though a disturbingly large number have not.

But there is much we can gain from reading this text, though it may not be what we ordinarily derive from an edition. The confrontation between a learned and imaginative scholar-poet and one of the most infuriatingly difficult poems in Old English strikes some exciting sparks and teaches us something about each combatant. Tolkien was a fine critic, one who sensed the sporadic brilliance of *Exodus* and who also dared to make strongly evaluative judgments, to say one passage succeeds and another fails. Yet, like other students of the poem, he was often simply balked in his appreciation by its obscurities, lacunas, and general oddness. His frustration took the form of anger at the scribe and resulted in a number of high-handed emendations. (p. 538)

Tolkien's deep suspicion of the scribe's competence led him to describe the word *beohata* . . . amusingly as a "scribal falsehood'' . . . , to grumble at the scribe's "tiresome omissions'' . . . , and elsewhere to complain often of the confusion added to a text already "crabbed, dark, and antiquated''. . . . It also led him, with much less justification, to adopt some drastic rearrangements of lines in the text . . . and to suggest a number of unnecessary emendations. Some of these are merely the setting right of unorthodox spellings or incorrect case-endings (he admitted to wanting a tidy and readable text for students), but others are easy solutions to hard problems and thus not good editorial practice. To take instances from one part of the poem: *fela meoringa . . .* has long bothered editors, but Tolkien's change to *felamodigra* is too extreme; *hergas on helle heofon pider becom . . .* is certainly mysterious but probably authentic for this peculiar poet, and not to be strongarmed into *hergas onheldon heof pider becom. . . .* Often Tolkien asserts roundly that a tenable reading is ''nonsense'' (a favorite word) and goes on to rewrite the poem more to his own taste. All editors do a little of this, but Tolkien goes well over the permissible quota of revisions. No doubt if his work had been finally prepared for publication he would have rethought many of these changes. (pp. 538-39)

Tolkien shows himself quite aware (as a Roman Catholic would be likely to be) of the symbolic or typological dimension of *Exodus . . .* and the poem's probable relationship to the liturgy for Holy Saturday. . . , but unfortunately he made almost no use of patristic glosses or commentaries, or enough use of parts of the Bible other than the book of Exodus. He states flatly that the poet was far from bothering about the meaning of Hebrew names . . . , but in fact a fair number of the puzzles he grappled with have been explained in recent years by research of just this kind. Most of the explainers have erred in their turn by virtually ignoring the native-Germanic dimension of the poem that Tolkien saw so clearly with his deep knowledge of Old Norse literature. While we can be sure now, for instance, that the imagery of sail and tent comes from traditional Christian symbolism (including Hebrew etymologies), it may be salutary to have Tolkien remind us of the "old sea-language'' . . . of the Anglo-Saxons that is here effectively bonded to Mediterranean material. To what extent he might have revised his total view of the poem in the light of recent findings we will never know. . . .

Anglo-Saxonists will be glad to have this partial edition available. If it necessarily falls short of the thoroughness and completeness we demand in a published edition, it is, as Joan Turville-Petre points out, a remarkable memorial to Tolkien's way of lecturing and teaching. (p. 539)

> *Edward B. Irving, Jr., in a review of "The Old English 'Exodus': Text, Translation and Commentary," in* Speculum, *Vol. 58, No. 2, April, 1983, pp. 538-39.*

HUMPHREY CARPENTER

Christopher Tolkien's foreword [to *The Monsters and the Critics and Other Essays*] makes it clear that they aren't really essays at all—with one exception they were all delivered as lectures—and they aren't precisely 'academic' either, as they were mostly addressed to non-specialist audiences. They certainly deal with subjects at the very centre of Tolkien's academic interests, but they do so in a rhetorical, ear-catching manner, making a small number of points and making them over and over again. . . . Moreover, all but two of the pieces in *The Monsters and the Critics* have already been published, some of them several times

over. So the book isn't going to change anyone's view of Tolkien. But it gives us a chance to assess, or at least try to describe, his mind and imagination as they operate in this rather hybrid 'semi-academic' context.

In fact I doubt if anyone coming to this book straight from *The Lord of the Rings,* or at least its appendices, would find themselves in very strange territory. The collection opens with "*Beowulf: the Monsters and the Critics*", Tolkien's celebrated defence of the great Anglo-Saxon poem against generations of critics who had valued it as a mine of history or folklore, but had little opinion of it as literature. The lecture was delivered to the British Academy in 1936 just as Tolkien was finishing *The Hobbit,* and really he might be talking about his own story. . . . (pp. 25-6)

In fact you could say that *The Hobbit* is partly a narrative commentary on *Beowulf,* and that Tolkien's *Beowulf* lecture also looks forward to some of the themes of *The Lord of the Rings,* and so on and so on, until the professor and the storyteller become quite indistinguishable. Indeed the lecture itself, like most of those in this collection, is a kind of story. You simply can't detach yourself from it to question its pronouncements; it is oracular rather than academic. As Auden once said of Tolkien reciting *Beowulf* itself, the voice is the voice of Gandalf.

In just the same way, Tolkien's lecture on *Sir Gawain and the Green Knight . . .* is a pronouncement on *The Lord of the Rings*. The central passage discusses Gawain's confession to a priest before he goes out to face probable death at the hands of the Green Knight. Gawain says nothing in his confession about the fact that the lady of the castle, who has been trying to seduce him, has given him a magic girdle which she promises will save his neck. A previous editor of the poem, Sir Israel Gollancz, decided that this meant Gawain was not making a proper confession at all—though the poet didn't realise it. Tolkien dismisses this as nonsense, and goes on to argue that Gawain's lightness of heart afterwards shows that it must have been a true confession. 'A light heart is certainly not the mood induced by a bad confession,' he observes, and he should know, since as a deeply committed Catholic he had plenty of experience of the psychological effect of absolution.

The Monsters and the Critics, then, is largely about J.R.R.T. himself. If the essays in the book look faintly dusty now as pieces of academic or semi-academic work, they are certainly fresh enough as bits of intellectual autobiography. Hardened Tolkien addicts will want to buy the book for one essay in particular—"**A Secret Vice**", in which he explains the history of his hobby of inventing languages. (p. 26)

> *Humphrey Carpenter, "Tolkien's Secret Vice," in* The Spectator, *Vol. 250, No. 8074, April 9, 1983, pp. 25-6.*

IAN HISLOP

Tolkien, son of Tolkien, has put together a collection of his father's essays, which were mostly delivered as lectures, and given them the title [*The Monsters and the Critics and Other Essays*]. . . .

Like many other undergraduates, I first encountered [Tolkien's lecture "*Beowulf: The Monsters and the Critics*"] in the Upper Reading Room of the Bodleian in Oxford, a place noted for the sort of sterile research that Tolkien describes elsewhere. His criticism then and now seems like a breath of fresh air, removing the dusty pedantry that covers this Anglo-Saxon poem. He pours witty scorn on the literary archaeologists, men who dig for Icelandic History, Primary Sources, Archetypes, anything but read the poem as a whole. How the modern critics must hate this essay and how one regrets that Tolkien is no longer available to attack the new critical bores of our generation. His brilliant evocation of the Nordic World Picture is unrivalled: the Gods and Heroes valiant in inevitable defeat by the Monsters of Time and Death, vainly contesting the outer darkness in small circles of light. It is not hard to see the genesis of his creative work in his critical work.

A previously unpublished essay on "Sir Gawayne and the Green Knight" continues the thread of the Beowulf piece. Tolkien again attacks those who would murder to dissect, the critics who concentrate on the sources of this 'Greater fairy-story' rather than deal with it as a living poem. His own theory on Gawayne is that the poet uses the folk-tale elements to place the hero in a position where he must make a complex moral choice: between the code of Chivalry and the demands of Religion. He can thus conclude that 'The Land of Faerie is under Heaven'. This essay is as illuminating on Tolkien as it is on Gawayne Poet.

"On Fairy Stories" continues in similar vein and widens the scope from Beowulf and Sir Gawayne, his academic specialities, to fairy-stories generally. Once again he warns off the anthropologists, who wish only to categorise similarities in archetypal terms, and stresses diversity. . . . The Professor then begins what is basically a defence of Faerie, dismissing "erroneous sentiment about children" and arguing that the stories are for adults too. His definition of a fairy-story is not limited to ornamental Shakespearean creatures but includes heroes, Kings, Dragons (of course), sorcery, elves, trolls and all. . . . The essay goes on to talk of the rewards of Fantasy but refuses to accept the label of escapism. Tolkien argues that the modern technological age is no measure of realism and you can feel the conviction as the British Leyland works at Cowley crept menacingly towards his city of spires and gargoyles. He ends with the ultimate justification for the fairy-story, the conclusion that the Incarnation and the Resurrection is the greatest fairy-story of all. . . .

These three essays go some way to justifying Christopher Tolkien's claim that the essays are a unity. Their accessibility to non-academics go some way to justifying the new collection. The rest unfortunately do not. . . . The Valedictory Address on leaving as Professor is largely concerned with the intricacies of the Oxford English Syllabus. Only Tolkien's final quotation (on leaving) of 'The Wanderer' and 'The Seafarer' with a poem of his own, **"The Lament for Galadriel"**, is interesting in showing the imaginative continuity of Old English and Elvish.

This leads into the last essay, **"A Secret Vice"**, which explains Tolkien's invention of a language of his own. (This was delivered well before **The Hobbit** appeared and shows it to be a lifelong vice.) . . . The linguistic invention, the fruits of the philology are dry on their own. Though Tolkien argued that Lang. and Lit. must not be separated, it is the literary criticism that is interesting here *not* the linguistics. Equally in the creative work it is the mythology that is compelling not the Elvish language. I read **Lord of the Rings** in six days but skipped the verse. It would have been a more worthwhile collection if the non-specialist did not have to skip three of the essays.

Ian Hislop, in a review of "The Monsters and the Critics and Other Essays," in Books and Bookmen, *No. 333, June, 1983, p. 34.*

G. L. BROOKS

Both in his academic and his creative work [Tolkien] combined philological erudition with poetic imagination. Those who complained that there was little academic work, though it was first-rate in quality, had to be content with the belief that much of it was never published but embodied in lectures given to his students in Oxford. That belief is now confirmed with . . . [*Finn and Hengest: The Fragment and the Episode*, a study of] two fifth-century heroes in northern Europe of whom our knowledge is obtained from the Old English poem *Beowulf* and a desperately difficult fragment generally known as *The Fight at Finnesburg*. The study is now edited from Tolkien's lecture notes by Professor Alan Bliss, whose study *The Metre of Beowulf* was published in 1958. . . . Most of Tolkien's notes were written more than fifty years ago—and fifty years is a long time in scholarship—but they have been brought up to date by Professor Bliss's skilful and unobtrusive editing. He has added footnotes in square brackets which supplement, and occasionally contradict, Tolkien's statements. Most of the subjects discussed are matters on which one cannot be certain, but Tolkien, though sometimes hard-hitting, never overstates his case. . . . The book is indispensable for all advanced students of Old English, but it is not easy reading, and admirers of *The Lord of the Rings* who, in the words of the blurb, turn to it 'to see how Tolkien handled a story which he did not invent' will be disappointed.

G. L. Brooks, in a review of "Finn and Hengest: The Fragment and the Episode," in British Book News, *July, 1983, p. 455.*

D. C. BAKER

Any work of Tolkien's is to be appreciated and studied thoughtfully. No exception is his commentary and translation of the Old English *Exodus* [*The Old English "Exodus": Text, Translation, and Commentary*], and we are grateful to Oxford and to Joan Turville-Petre for making these lecture-room materials available. . . . For lecture-room materials they are. Lesser mortals, in their preparation for lecturing undergraduate students, do not prepare themselves in this way; they do not edit the texts on which they are to expound; they do not provide a commentary exhaustive in its learning together with original criticisms and suggestions. These are the work of a master, a master of all he surveyed. As Joan Turville-Petre notes in her introduction, her bringing these materials to public attention is not a labor of piety or of archeology; she believes that Tolkien's unpublished materials of forty-five years ago have utility today to students of *Exodus* and of Old English. She is clearly right. . . . [Had] he lived to be a hundred I do not think [Tolkien] would ever have published the material himself. They were, after all, only the materials of teaching. And, ironically, Tolkien was by normal standards not a good teacher. He muttered, thought aloud to himself, and made no effort to be popular. And yet it was as a teacher that he had his greatest effect, for he published little as things are reckoned today. To this man all students of Old and Middle English owe an enormous debt. (pp. 59-60)

D. C. Baker, in a review of "The Old English 'Exodus': Text, Translation, and Commentary," in English Language Notes, *Vol. XXI, No. 3, March, 1984, pp. 59-60.*

IAN HISLOP

The Book of Lost Tales: Part One is the first title in a series called The History of Middle-Earth which publishes for the first time unseen segments of the vast Tolkien Mythology. It is a process [editor Christopher Tolkien] began with *The Silmarillion* and in fact there is a certain amount of overlap there with *The Book of Lost Tales,* since these were begun and then left incomplete very early in Tolkien's career. He spent much of his life reshaping and elaborating these myths which appear only as glimpses in the more accessible *Hobbit* and *Lord of the Rings.* . . .

[The book] is interesting undoubtedly, but it is not magic and it is somehow unsatisfying. Epic poetry uses digression in the form of story-telling or song to create an impression of depth and richness. The *Beowulf* admirer was well aware of this when he wrote his own epic *Lord of the Rings,* but when the digressions become the core of a book they fail to stand in their own right. . . .

This reviewer does not mind sentences like: "As lief and liever would we have the untrammeled world" and quite enjoys being told continually to "Know then", or "Behold". Yet the mythology without the narrative structure of the Hobbit's Quest and the Elvish Lore without the earthy balance of Bilbo or Frodo is unsatisfying. (p. 33)

The Tales themselves are concerned with the very beginning of Middle-Earth. Iluvatar, the supreme being creates the Ainur, one of whom rebels and seduces others to do the same. This evil one then wreaks havoc on Iluvatar's next creation the Elves. *Paradise Lost* cannot have been very far from the young Tolkien's mind when he wrote this series of creation myths and Eden parallels. . . . Both *Beowulf* and Keats' *Fall of Hyperion* spring to mind in reading. The Elves and Gnomes bring the story closer to the time of Tolkien's better known creations and we must await the next volume for more.

I enjoyed the exercise in allegorical mythology and the exuberance of the linguistic invention, but the tales remain a footnote or at most a backdrop to Tolkien's literary achievement rather than a continuation of that achievement. In this form, there is a sense of indulgence in the work of both father and son, and this book remains one for Tolkien 'believers' rather than just admirers. (pp. 33-4)

> *Ian Hislop, in a review of "The Book of Lost Tales,"*
> *in* Books and Bookmen, *No. 343, April, 1984, pp. 33-4.*

BARBARA TRITEL

[In *The Book of Lost Tales: Part One*] Christopher Tolkien shows himself to be his father's son, delving into the question of Elvish genealogies with the ardor of a Talmudic scholar. In commentaries that are often longer than the texts, he gives the reader histories of each character's name as it evolved in the course of Tolkien's revisions, along with variations and etymologies of words in the two made-up languages, wretched but relevant poems dredged up from the author's youth and speculations about why one version of a tale was rejected in favor of another. Tolkien devotees will no doubt rejoice, but for the uninitiated reader who is not thoroughly familiar with the other works, the commentaries may prove a bit arcane.

But much of the imaginative source material for the creations of the *Lord of the Rings* can be recognized in these tales, and so can the evolution of Tolkien's style. The engaging but somewhat "antiqued" diction of *The Lord of the Rings* was preceded by an often stilted pseudoheroic style in *The Lost Tales.* The many compound nouns, phrases strung loosely together and mid-paragraph temporal shifts give the impression that the myths were translated from Old English by a literal-minded translator.

But it is for his invention that Tolkien is best loved, and his creative powers are already in evidence in the earliest writing. In one of these tales, **"The Theft of Melko,"** the myth of the Fall of mankind is reworked with a deliciously evil cast of characters. There is a spider called Gwerlum the Black, clearly a predecessor for that favorite among Tolkien's nasty characters, the lisping ring-keeper Gollum. Gwerlum lives by sucking light and "spinning a clinging gossamer of gloom that catches in its mesh stars and moons and all bright things that sail the airs."

> *Barbara Tritel, "Language and Prehistory of the Elves," in* The New York Times Book Review, *May 27, 1984, p. 7.*

PAUL M. LLOYD

Tolkien evidently began to jot [down the stories in *The Book of Lost Tales, Part I*] when he was in his early twenties, at first while he was in the army during World War I. He often wrote them in pencil, which naturally has blurred and deteriorated with age, although in some cases he later erased the original text and then wrote a revised version of the same story in ink. Since he wrote in bound notebooks, he sometimes ran out of space and had to put parts of one story on pages in the middle of other stories. This practice has created intricate problems for the editor, often as complicated as the tracing of the stemmae of medieval manuscripts. . . .

Some of the notebooks indeed contain only preliminary drafts of future stories and in some cases there are only notes on later stories and comments on the languages of the myths. Nor did Tolkien write them in the order in which the events are supposed to have occurred, although the editor finally decided that the only way he could appropriately present them to the reader was in the order of the sequence of the narrative of the tales taken as a whole. Thus this volume contains the "tales of Valinor" and two further volumes will contain the tales culminating in the fall of Gondolin, and the lays of Beleriand. Tolkien's conception of his work evolved continually throughout his life so that some of the names and words of his invented languages were later changed, and the events recounted do not all correspond to their later forms.

Christopher Tolkien has done his best in the introduction and in the commentaries and notes on each story to assist the reader in tracing the evolution of Tolkien's thought and his conception of the whole history of Middle Earth. Thus inevitably much of this text will be of interest mostly to those who wish to follow in great detail that evolution. Still, even those who are not dyed-in-the-wool Tolkien specialists may be intrigued to see how the primitive conception of the mythology differed from its later forms. We find, for instance, references to Gnomes, who later vanished with that name (they apparently became a branch of the elves), the Valar referred to as "gods," and a great many other things that were later reshaped. Many lovers of *The Lord of the Rings* may find that there is a good deal more here than they care to know, and yet I am sure that I am not alone in feeling glad to have available now so much that casts light on how Tolkien's mind continued for so many years to rework and reshape the marvelous world of his created mythology.

Paul M. Lloyd, "Rich Lode for Tolkien Scholars," in Fantasy Review, Vol. 7, No. 5, June, 1984, p. 32.

PUBLISHERS WEEKLY

Recalling at once the engrossing, cryptic tales of the Welsh *Mabinogion* and dry medieval historical chronicles, [*The Book of Lost Tales: Part II*] is an academic exercise sealed up in a mannered pseudo-archaic style. Only the vast popularity of Tolkien's later work has made possible this ongoing series of posthumous publications.... [Outside] the Tolkien industry, the work will share the fate of its predecessors, *The Silmarillion* and *Unfinished Tales.* That is, it will be bought by readers seeking more of the joy and excitement of the Hobbit stories. But only the most persistent will actually manage to read through this one.

A review of "The Book of Lost Tales: Part II," in Publishers Weekly, Vol. 226, No. 15, October 12, 1984, p. 41.

JESSICA YATES

J.R.R. Tolkien began to write *The Book of Lost Tales* in 1916-17, as his first attempt on 'a mythology for England'. He felt that the English people, as opposed to the Greeks or the Celts for example, had no 'body of . . . connected legend' of their own. All we had was *Beowulf* (imported from Denmark) and our native fairy stories. So partly with the sense of mission and partly as an escape from the horrors of the First World War, he wrote a series of tales about the creation of the world and the coming of the Elves, of evil Melko and the wars of Elves and Men against him.... [*The Book of Lost Tales: Part II*] deals with the conflict between Elves and Men, especially those of Tinuviel, Turambar, the Fall of Gondolin, and Eärendil....

Although this Part 2 is more interesting in terms of story content than the first part, it is still written in the archaic style of William Morris that Tolkien was to refine years later. There is no hint of the events of *The Lord of the Rings,* which, after years of gestation, and the composition of *The Hobbit* in the 1930s, was developed as the new conclusion to the old mythology. Whereas the *Lost Tales,* echoing Tolkien's feelings at the time of the First World War, lays the blame for conflict in our world upon Melko as an evil spirit working through Men; *The Lord of the Rings,* written during the Second World War, presents a stark conflict between Good and Evil.

The Tales will be appreciated by those who have read *The Silmarillion* and wish to examine how Tolkien improved his story and style from their original form, and how eventually *The Lord of the Rings* came to stand independently with only a few hints from the early mythology. With that epic, in fact, Tolkien achieved some of his early purpose: the creation of a body of legend that English people would take semi-seriously. He had more success with the lay reader than with his academic colleagues, and was not a little shocked by the ensuing 'cult'.

Jessica Yates, in a review of "The Book of Lost Tales: Part II," in British Book News, December, 1984, p. 751.

E. CHRISTIAN KOPFF

To give us a taste of what [Tolkien's] philology was, Christopher Tolkien has edited seven of his father's lectures [in *The Monsters and The Critics and Other Essays*]. Significance for understanding the *Rings* is one criterion for inclusion, and so we see the essay on "A Secret Vice," "On Fairy-Stories," and even "English and Welsh," since Welsh was used as a model for some of the names in the *Rings.* Even the title essay, "Beowulf: The Monsters and the Critics," may have been included because in it Tolkien explains how a Christian writer could create a powerful picture of a world before the knowledge of Christ. The Hobbit-lover notices that the lecture was delivered before the British Academy in 1936 and published the next year, the same that saw the publication of *The Hobbit.* (p. 6)

It is scarcely too much to say that this one essay changed forever the study of a major work in the canon of English literature, that it established *Beowulf* as a major literary work, whereas before it had been treated as little more than "a philological curiosity." . . . In 1936 Tolkien found that "*Beowulf* has been used as a quarry of fact and fancy far more assiduously than it has been studied as a work of art."

["*Beowulf*: The Monsters and the Critics"] is far more than the literary Pharisaism than the last sentence suggests. In fact, it touches on most of the poem's problems, from the putative influence of Latin epic to its vision of the German heroic ideal and the mind, at once Christian and elegiac, that created it. To call *Beowulf* studies since 1936 a series of footnotes to Tolkien would be unjust, and yet how often even the most original work ends up reflecting or rejecting Tolkien's apodictic insights. For example, *Beowulf: The Poem and Its Tradition* by . . . John D. Niles is a thorough and thought-provoking study, with chapters on areas that scarcely existed in 1936; but with all his originality and critical insight, Niles's understanding of the poem is often a confirmation of Tolkien's (or a slight modification). (pp. 6-7)

Tolkien never saw himself as a literary critic. His "Valedictory Address" is quite clear about his scholarly origins in the "language" or philological side of the split Oxford English faculty. To that extent, the essays in *The Monsters and the Critics* are misleading about Tolkien's scholarship and teaching. More representative are two recent volumes, his text, commentary, and translation of *The Old English Exodus* . . . and *Finn and Hengest: The Fragment and the Episode.* . . . In the latter, Tolkien takes a brief and fragmentary tale sung by a bard in *Beowulf* and a fragment of a separate version of the same story that survives on a single manuscript page and tries to reconstruct the history that lies behind the two sources. For Tolkien, not surprisingly, it is the story of the fall of a great, prehistoric people and the birth of a new age. The Jutes fall with the death of their young prince, but Hengest rises from the tragedy to lead the German people into Celtic Britain and found Anglo-Saxon England. We are moved at the scope and sympathy of the reconstruction even while acknowledging that too little survives for certainty and that some aspects of the argument are forced or unlikely.

Tolkien's philology reminds us of what he said about two great epics: "The real resemblance of the *Aeneid* and *Beowulf* lies in the constant presence of a sense of many-storied antiquity." It is a trait both works share with *The Lord of the Rings.* With *Beowulf* too much is lost for a secure reconstruction of its mythological or historical backdrop. Much more can be done for the *Aeneid* and a great deal for the *Rings.* Behind its hints of ages and great races almost vanished from memory in the fading past lay a detailed history of that past, composed, of course, by Tolkien himself. (p. 7)

Say not the labour naught availeth. Without the pedantry and sometimes misconceived ingenuity that we find in his lectures on the Old English *Exodus* and the Finn Fragment, Tolkien could not have given us *Beowulf* alive and renewed. Similarly *The Lost Tales* and *The Silmarillion* gave to *The Lord of the Rings* its depth of concreteness in language and history. We laymen, on the other hand, may rest satisfied with knowing some half-dozen Old English poems besides *Beowulf*. We soon tire of the complicated narrative and high-falutin language used on the stories that lie behind the *Rings* and long for the company of Frodo and Sam Gamgee. . . . We thought that we wanted a "sense of many-storied antiquity," and discover that we were rejoicing in the mystery of fragments of stories to which our own imagination had contributed much of the tragedy and excitement. When the gaps are all filled in, the excitement has disappeared along with the mystery.

In his clever essay **"On Fairy-Stories,"** Tolkien defended the aesthetic—and Christian—rightness of the eucatastrophic closure, the Happy Ending. Herein may lie the true difference between philologist and literary critic. The literary critic is a perpetual optimist. He sees a work attacked or misunderstood, waves his magic pen, and *voilà*, all is light. . . . The philologist lives in the tragic world of the partially lost or broken. He knows the 18th-century fire that ate away just that page of *Beowulf* that explains why the dragon attacks after so many ages of rest. . . . Tolkien, who had worked in his youth on the *Oxford English Dictionary*, knew that once upon a time *grammar* and *glamour* were the same word and devoted his life as pedant and poet, not to making us know that as a fact, but to feel it as a reality, the lively, moving reality that once existed before our broken and desiccated present. (pp. 7-8)

> *E. Christian Kopff, "Inventing Lost Worlds," in* Chronicles of Culture, *Vol. 9, No. 4, April, 1985, pp. 6-8.*

Herman Wouk

1915-

American novelist, dramatist, nonfiction writer, and script-writer.

Wouk first gained prominence with his Pulitzer Prize-winning novel *The Caine Mutiny* (1951) and has since written several bestselling novels, including *The Winds of War* (1971) and *War and Remembrance* (1978). His fiction is characterized by a direct narrative style in which the protagonists describe the events they experience. Wouk's novels uphold such traditional values as respect for religion, belief in honor and valor, patriotism, and deference toward authority and order. Wouk rejects modernist devices in favor of traditional storytelling, and several of his novels recall the narrative techniques of other authors. His first novel, *Aurora Dawn* (1946), a satire on the advertising industry, is reminiscent of Henry Fielding's novel *Tom Jones*; *The City Boy* (1948) and *Marjorie Morningstar* (1955), both initiation novels about Jewish youths, echo Sinclair Lewis, Mark Twain, and Booth Tarkington; and *The Winds of War* and *War and Remembrance* were compared to Upton Sinclair's Lanny Budd stories.

In *The Caine Mutiny*, Wouk draws on his own naval experiences to detail life aboard a minesweeper during World War II. The mutiny, which ensues after the ship's chief officer, Captain Queeg, instigates a number of dangerous incidents, results in the trial and acquittal of Lieutenant Maryk, the crew member who was persuaded by the others to relieve Queeg of his command. The extremities and dangers of Queeg's abnormal behavior are dramatized at great length throughout the novel. However, in the last section of the book, which takes place at the crew's post-trial celebration, the defense attorney condemns Maryk as being morally guilty for challenging Queeg's authority. Some critics faulted this abrupt reversal and asserted that it destroys the credibility of the previous material and the continuity of the book. *The Caine Mutiny* was adapted for the stage as *The Caine Mutiny Court-Martial* in 1953 and for film in 1954.

The Winds of War and its companion volume, *War and Remembrance*, have been praised for their extensive detail and historical accuracy. The protagonist of both books, naval Captain Victor "Pug" Henry, serves as a dramatic link to major historical figures and events of World War II and represents the strong, conservative hero characteristic of Wouk's work. Both novels examine the effects of the war on an average American family, but a second focus, developed more extensively in *War and Remembrance,* presents the war from the Nazi perspective. In this work, Henry, now an admiral, translates the memoirs of a fictitious German general involved in the rise of the Third Reich. Wouk's depiction of the Nazi military mind prompted high praise for its realism, as did his accounts of the great naval battles of World War II. Paul Fussell noted: "The quality of the military reasoning . . . is impressive, and so is Wouk's scholarship . . . in contemporary history." Wouk wrote the original teleplay of "The Winds of War," which was broadcast on American network television in 1983.

Wouk's recent novel, *Inside, Outside* (1985), in which he explores the Jewish-American experience, is a fictional memoir

by Israel David Goodkind, whom many critics view as Wouk's alter ego. This work addresses the conflict between religious tradition and cultural assimilation and is set mainly in the post-Watergate era, although by tracing Goodkind's heritage it also touches on earlier historical events. James Michener noted: "*Inside, Outside* offers some hearty laughs, much valuable instruction about the Jewish religion and a nostalgic reminiscence of the 1930s." Wouk has also written a nonfiction work, *This Is My God* (1959), about Orthodox Judaism and its cultural customs.

(See also *CLC*, Vols. 1, 9; *Contemporary Authors,* Vols. 5-8, rev. ed.; *Contemporary Authors New Revision Series,* Vol. 6; and *Dictionary of Literary Biography Yearbook: 1982.*)

SPENCER KLAW

In *Aurora Dawn*, Herman Wouk has applied the technique of *Tom Jones* to the subject matter of *The Hucksters.* The result is a delightfully fresh and funny satire on radio advertising that never descends to mere burlesque and is all the more effective because the author—a former radio writer—refrains from grinding any personal axes.

Mr. Wouk has modeled his first novel on the eighteenth-century mock-heroic chronicle. In one of his many charming digressions into the fields of literature, science, philosophy and comparative religion, he grabs the reader by the lapel and explains the nature of such a work. It is, he says, "a literary form in which the hero may be a madman, a thief, a scoundrel, a scamp, a coxcomb, a busybody, in fact anything but a hero in the received sense of the word.". . .

Mr. Wouk has put to excellent use the manner of his eighteenth-century masters in satire. It is a manner which enables him to display his characters with affectionate tolerance and good-humored detachment. It even permits him to make fun of the whole narrative apparatus of the novel, including his own assumed role of disinterested chronicler and discursive moralist.

It would be unfair, however, to attribute his success solely to his employment of what is, after all, no more than a very clever trick. Actually his skill as a humorist is quite as evident when he is speaking through the mouths of his characters as when he is discoursing with mock gravity on such topics as the studied sloppiness of a debutante's sweater or the Ptolemaic celestial hypothesis.

The most thoroughly satisfactory of his characters is Father Stanfield, Mr. Wouk's true hero. This shrewd and pious man is shown to best advantage, perhaps, when "the reader, by a magic older and blander than that of the X-ray, is permitted a glimpse" into his soul. . . .

In a brief preface Mr. Wouk explains that he started work on *Aurora Dawn* to "relieve the tedium of military service at sea" while he was on a destroyer in the South Pacific. It might be advisable for his publishers to send him off to sea again in the hope he will be bored into writing another novel. Since the over-all effect of his first book is achieved in part by its novelty, one hopes he will not be tempted to give a mere repeat performance. But a writer of Mr. Wouk's extraordinary comic and satiric gifts is not likely to fall into any such trap.

> Spencer Klaw, *"A Delightfully Fresh and Funny Satire,"* in New York Herald Tribune Weekly Book Review, *April 20, 1947, p. 3.*

RICHARD B. GEHMAN

Mr. Wouk's first book, *Aurora Dawn,* was a skilfully-devised farce of radio advertising, written in the manner of Fielding; it was the dreadful sort of long-winded, enervating "humor" that one could expect from a Max Shulman. . . .

In *The City Boy,* Mr. Wouk, no longer Fielding, now seems to be a sort of composite of Booth Tarkington and Sinclair Lewis, more the former than the latter, and combining the worst features, in style and in thought, of both. Again, he is not writing parody; this time he is deliberately using others' materials, and imitating them. In all of Herbie Bookbinder's adventures, joys, and sorrows—his infatuation with his teacher, his grand passion for little Lucile Glass, his first dinner in a restaurant with his father and the latter's business associates, his rise from summer-camp joke-butt to hero, his theft of money from his father to achieve this—there is not one incident that has not been done before, and with more success, by the two writers mentioned above. . . .

By announcing that his tale "will seem to reflect a measure of truth," Mr. Wouk must be trying to tell us that human nature does not change; that human situations vary almost not at all; that the same things which happen to fat little Herbie Bookbinder could happen to anybody, anywhere in America. It's true enough that they could (let's acknowledge that for the purposes of this piece, anyhow), but since they have been done before in fiction, since we recognize them so readily, there doesn't seem to be much point in working them again in the same way. Switching the locale from the backyards of Indiana to the apartment-hives of The Bronx and a Berkshire summer camp does not necessarily alter the basic situations.

There is another point, perhaps even more important. Tarkington was writing of a boyhood in an age of innocence—the late nineteenth and early twentieth centuries. . . . A great deal occurred . . . between the boyhoods of Baxter and of Bookbinder; and while we cannot expect boys in fiction to have any exaggerated sense of their own time, we at least can expect it of their creators. That Herbie's attitudes, actions, and store of information are little different from those of Penrod would indicate either that Mr. Wouk has progressed no further than Mr. Tarkington, or that he has fallen prey, willingly, to certain concepts which have no meaning, these days, save to characters in B-movies and hack fiction: everything and everybody is either good or evil, nothing changes (O sweet youth), everything comes out all right in the end. Since Mr. Wouk must certainly be more aware, if only because he is alive in an age when communication is swifter and easier, we must assume that, for the purposes of his book, he has swallowed this gagging dose without questioning it. This makes the circle complete and makes his novel a total failure.

The novel, but not necessarily Mr. Wouk. Perhaps I have been inordinately severe with him. After all, this is only his second book. For the reasons stated above, both must be considered as exercises. Mr. Wouk does have a fine eye for living detail, a good ear, and, despite a tendency to become coyly platitudinous in the manner of Sinclair Lewis, he apparently has enormous sympathy for his fellow beings. Perhaps some day he will write like Herman Wouk.

> Richard B. Gehman, *"Bronx Penrod,"* in The Saturday Review of Literature, *Vol. XXXI, No. 34, August 21, 1948, p. 10.*

NORA MAGID

The moral [of *Marjorie Morningstar*] is: if one's destiny is suburbia, there is no point in seeking to "be an actress" rather than "a fat dull housewife with a big engagement ring." The moral is also that a man who has written an interesting book from a masculine point of view (*The Caine Mutiny*) shouldn't push his luck too far by trying to reverse the procedure. At one point in her life, Marjorie Morgenstern finds that she is "very bored with the problems of being a girl." Herman Wouk's problem is plainly that he has never been one, and he cannot quite manage to tell a girl's story from a girl's point of view. *Marjorie Morningstar* is soap opera with psychological and sociological props. . . .

The story is told in the third person. Mr. Wouk tries to see it all obliquely from her perspective, and the effort proves too much. . . . [Mr. Wouk] thinks that girls in their teens wear rouge before they wear lipstick, walk arm-in-arm, call one another dear and darling and baby, punctuate their sentences with gee and gosh and gad, think exclusively in hyperbole.

The men are as unbelievable as the ladies. Noel, the Greek God, who is dedicated to dissolution is nothing if not articulate; he regularly announces his own motivation—his crippled arm, his Oedipus complex, his early seduction by an older woman, his anger at and attraction to what constitutes being Jewish. Set up in opposition to him is Mike Eden, the other man, whose grandfather has technically freed him by changing the family name of Einstein, but Mike carries his burden of guilt and he atones by smuggling Jews out of Germany—the only political note in a book notable for omission since it takes place in the '39's. . . .

The environment Wouk creates is vivid and enormously complex. It touches on economic mobility—the moves from the Bronx to the Upper West Side to the suburbs, the compromises at Hunter between the Jewish and the Christian sororities for political control, and the relationship of City College to Ivy League students; the conflicts between the older, immigrant generation—sweet, squashed, and loving—and the younger, growing up in a world that includes Freud and pork and the Unitarian Church; the flight from and to Jewishness.

The fascinating cultural scene is, however, backdrop to the banal love story.

> *Nora Magid, "The Girl Who Went Back Home," in* The New Republic, *Vol. 133, No. 10, September 5, 1955, p. 20.*

FREDERIC I. CARPENTER

Herman Wouk's first novel—a pleasant little satire on the advertising business—initiated a brilliantly successful literary career.

Wouk's first novel is interesting both in its own right, and for the light it throws on the later career of the author of *The Caine Mutiny*. It suggests answers to some of the puzzling questions which have been asked about him—Is he a "one-book" man, or are all his novels and plays good? Is he merely a successful entertainer, or may he be considered a major novelist? Is his sense of values clear or confused? (p. 1)

Wouk named his first novel *Aurora Dawn*, intending the tautology of the title to suggest that American advertising is often silly. For "Aurora Dawn" is the name of a soap company which uses the picture of the naked goddess Aurora as its trademark. The plot follows the hero, Andrew Reale, in his devious efforts to promote the sales of soap and to win the hand of his boss' daughter. But the story ends surprisingly with Andrew's marriage to the beautiful but virtuous model who has posed for the picture of Aurora (and who, of course, has loved him devotedly all the time). Thus the plot describes a kind of American "success story" in reverse: the hero's dream of marrying the boss' daughter fails, and therefore he lives happily ever after. It is a very pleasant and neatly moral fable.

But the style and technique of this first novel are more interesting than the plot, and suggest Wouk's later literary intentions. Although the story describes the hectic life of contemporary New York, the style is mock-heroic and self-conscious, recalling an eighteenth century *Joseph Andrews*, rather than a twentieth century *The Great Gatsby*. The name of the hero, Andrew Reale, implies a moral allegory in which the "realist's" schemes lead only to defeat. . . . Meanwhile the author, speaking in asides to the reader, repeatedly asserts that he will never resort to such dubious modern techniques as the stream-of-consciousness or the Freudian analysis, but will tell his tale in a straightforward manner, using only the words spoken by the characters. (*The Caine Mutiny* and *Marjorie Morningstar* use these same traditional techniques of allegorical implication and conversational realism to develop their plots.) (pp. 1-2)

Wouk quickly followed the minor success of *Aurora Dawn* (1947) with another minor success: *The City Boy* (1948). In this second novel the rather bookish humor of the first gave way to a joyously realistic humor, as the author narrated the adventures and misadventures of young Herbert Bookbinder of the Bronx. The late Joseph Henry Jackson greeted this as a "modern Tom Sawyer"; and sometimes the comedy is as hilarious and the gusto as great as Mark Twain's. . . . As a whole, the novel succeeds in doing for the modern city something of what *Tom Sawyer* did for the country of a century ago.

But *The City Boy* falls far short of the greatness of *Tom Sawyer* for two reasons. Whereas Tom's adventures had involved him in a genuine conflict of loyalties between the good Aunt Polly and the disreputable Huck Finn, Herbie Bookbinder never doubts that father knows best. Therefore, the deep excitement of the adventures of Tom Sawyer makes the boyish pranks of Herbie seem pale and unimportant. And whereas Tom's vague yearning for Becky Thatcher furnished a humorous contrast to the serious masculine business of boyhood, the love of Herbie for Lucille Glass seems exaggeratedly romantic. *The City Boy* is often high-spirited and hilarious, but sometimes becomes moralistic and sentimental.

Next Wouk turned to the theatre, and *The Traitor* was produced on Broadway in March 1949. The play was successful on the stage and was quickly published; but it remains probably his weakest effort. However, both its success and its weakness are significant. It tells of an idealistic scientist who tries to betray the secret of the bomb to Russia, because he believes that war will then become too terrible to be contemplated. Written before the Klaus Fuchs case, it prophesied its actual psychology, and achieved success on the wave of public reaction to this and to the Hiss case. But it remains melodramatic: the scientist suddenly becomes convinced of the error of his ways, turns the communist spies over to the F.B.I., and dies heroically in a cops and robbers ending. Meanwhile the professor of philosophy, whose liberal ideas have been responsible for leading the scientist astray, quickly decides to sign the loyalty questionnaire which he has been fighting. The success of the play was topical, and its melodramatic weakness lies in its failure to provide sufficient psychological motivation and explanation (other than the mood of the times) for the sudden switch of the idealistic scientist and the liberal philosopher. Seen in perspective, *The Traitor* becomes a practice effort at treating the larger problem soon to be embodied in *The Caine Mutiny*.

In 1951 Wouk published his most successful novel. And beyond any question *The Caine Mutiny* is also his best novel. (pp. 2-3)

The Caine Mutiny is a straightforward, realistic novel, in the tradition of W. D. Howells and Sinclair Lewis. Following the literary credo outlined in Wouk's first book, it rejects the whole modernist tradition from Joyce to Faulkner, which emphasizes ambiguity, the stream of consciousness, distortion of the time sequence, verbal violence, and similar devices. In complete contrast to that other most successful novel of the Second World War, *The Naked and the Dead*, it tells its story from A to Z, relying only on character, incident, and the cumulative effect of simple but significant detail. Inevitably, this very simplicity and directness, attractive to the popular reader, has tended to repel the more sophisticated critic. But judged by its own realistic standards, the novel is very good indeed. (p. 3)

[As] its title implies, **The Caine Mutiny** is not simply a realistic novel about the Second World War. It is rather a novel about the problem of war in general; or, more specifically, about the conflict of individual liberty with totalitarian authority in time of war. It is a philosophic novel in that it focuses sharply on this problem, although articulating it only through the words and actions of its characters. The problem is the same as that of Melville's *Billy Budd*—indeed, Tom Keefer [Captain of the *U.S.S. Caine*] calls attention to this parallel. Without ever putting the question explicitly, it asks whether civil rights of individuals must always be abrogated in time of war—whether the "mutinous" Billy Budds must always be condemned to death.

The tremendous popularity of **The Caine Mutiny,** as book, as play, and as motion picture, is due in some measure to its challenging treatment of this fundamental American problem.—Is the American dream of individual liberty, embodied in the Declaration of Independence and in the Bill of Rights, an illusion which the modern world at war makes impossible? Even in the peaceful nineteenth century, Melville had denied the dream of individual liberty, because "the world's peaces are but truces," and had condemned his Billy Budd to death, even though Billy had been conscripted against his will and had intended no "mutiny." *The Caine Mutiny* now alters the conditions somewhat, contrasting an unjust Captain Queeg with a just Captain Vere. But the mutineers of the *Caine* would also be condemned except for Queeg's neurotic self-incrimination. In time of war, martial law must prevail, even though the captain be cruel and incompetent. (p. 4)

The novel gains force by focusing on this fundamental problem. Moreover, it gains realistic conviction by describing the problem through the eyes of Willie Keith, who first appears as an irresponsible young romantic, grows gradually into a more responsible officer, but is seduced by Tom Keefer into "mutiny," then enjoys a kind of conversion through the agency of lawyer Barney Greenwald, and ends as a responsible adult fit to become "the last captain of the *Caine*." But a weakness in the novel appears, I think, in its insufficient psychological preparation for Willie's conversion to the necessity of absolute authority, with its denial of individual judgment. As he had failed to do in **The Traitor,** Wouk here fails clearly to motivate his hero's sudden abandonment of his earlier convictions, and seems even to suggest that all of Willie's early ideas were false. Many readers have found it difficult to accept the paradoxical assertion of Greenwald that Captain Queeg, by simple virtue of the authority vested in him, might really be made the hero of the tale.

But the play, **The Caine Mutiny Court-Martial,** by focusing exclusively on the final trial and by changing the point of view from that of idealistic Willie Keith to that of disillusioned Barney Greenwald, achieved greater unity and greater conviction. The confused beliefs of the immature idealist gave place to the clear-eyed disillusion of the mature lawyer: not only must military authority prevail in time of war, but even in time of peace the military activity of the Queegs may be more important than the legal activity of the Greenwalds, because cold wars always exist, and shooting wars must be prepared for. The defendants of **The Caine Mutiny Court-Martial** are acquitted legally but not morally. Greenwald has defended them, but only because he found out that "the wrong man was

on trial." Tom Keefer, the irresponsible romantic, was the true "author" of the *Caine* mutiny and the true villain of the story.

Wouk's latest novel, **Marjorie Morningstar,** continues his indictment of the irresponsible romantic. Now Noel Airman takes the place of Tom Keefer, and young Marjorie Morningstar takes the place of young Willie Keith. The setting shifts to New York City in time of peace, and the plot shifts from war to love; marital discipline no longer prevails, and the heroine is free to choose her own life. Like Willie Keith, she also dreams romantically of glory in a brave new world. Like Willie, she is seduced by the glamour of a sophisticated intellectual. Like Willie, she is abandoned in time of trial. Like Willie, she learns wisdom from an intensely disillusioned Jewish intellectual, Mike Eden. Like Willie, she finally confronts her former idol, faces him down in a battle of wills, and becomes at last captain of her own soul.

I have emphasized this thematic parallel between **The Caine Mutiny** and **Marjorie Morningstar** because it suggests the central problem of Wouk's writing. But the obvious artificiality of this outline may, by contrast, suggest the relative excellence of these novels as creations of realistic fiction. These characters live; these scenes must actually have happened. Noel Airman is as different from Tom Keefer and as uniquely an individual as can be imagined, except for his basic outlook on life. And the richly human scenes of Marjorie's Jewish family life are just as different from the scenes of life on board the *Caine*. Moreover, both sets of scenes are unlike anything else in fiction: they have the freshness of flavor, the originality of conception that only a born novelist can achieve. There is nothing phony, nothing slick about Wouk's fictional realism.

But there remains something artificial. Although **Marjorie Morningstar** creates characters more living and scenes more vivid than **Aurora Dawn** or **The City Boy,** the author remains a moralist. The pattern sometimes intrudes. The title again underlines the allegorical intention, and where **Aurora Dawn** had forestalled criticism by remaining frankly allegorical, the very vividness of the realism of **Marjorie Morningstar** emphasizes the presence of the pattern. If an author creates living characters, he must not seem to manipulate them. (pp. 4-5)

Much of the interest of these novels comes from their treatment of basic American problems. Much of their excellence comes from the vivid characters they create to explore these problems. But much of their weakness comes from the black and white answers which they suggest. For, although Wouk protests that he takes no sides and plays no favorites, all his readers have disagreed. Tom Keefer is a heel, and Noel Airman is a heel; but Barney Greenwald is a hero, and Mike Eden is a hero. Always romantic rebellion is bad, but clear-eyed disillusion is good, and salvation is achieved by renouncing the foolish dreams of youth.

The trouble is that, neither in fact nor in fiction, is all rebellion bad or all the dreams of youth foolish. And even when foolish, the romantic impulses of youth are usually not so much renounced as transmuted into the mature activities of middle age. But in **Marjorie Morningstar** this continuity between youthful dream and mature reality is absolutely denied. Marjorie abandons her stage name, renounces her romantic lover, and marries a man the exact antithesis of her former lover and one whom she had formerly ignored. She becomes a different person.

In the final chapter . . . an early friend comes to visit Marjorie, now Mrs. Milton Schwarz. The two talk of old times until the friend realizes that Marjorie has convinced herself that she never really had admired Noel Airman at all. "She's rewritten history in her mind," he exclaims. And later he adds: "She is dull, dull as she can be. . . . You couldn't write a play about her that would run a week, or a novel that would sell a thousand copies. There's no angle." Critics have called this ironic, yet it is literally true. Mrs. Marjorie Schwarz is as dull as she can be, and Wouk has not written a novel about her. He has written an interesting novel about Marjorie Morningstar, but then has killed his romantic heroine off, leaving a zombie to tell us how foolish she really was.

Author Tom Keefer of the fictional *U.S.S. Caine* published no more novels after the famous court-martial; yet, I think, he still lives on in Herman Wouk's subconscious mind as a kind of alter ego, and he may have helped write Wouk's romantic scenes. For these describe romantic heroes and heroines with much sympathy; but the conscious author always intervenes to chastise these heroes, and usually converts them to respectable goodness. There is a persistent but disguised moralism in all Wouk's fiction.

The Caine Mutiny remains the best of Wouk's novels because it is the least moralistic. (p. 6)

Frederic I. Carpenter, "Herman Wouk and the Wisdom of Disillusion," in English Journal, *Vol. XLV, No. 1, January, 1956, pp. 1-6, 32.*

WILL HERBERG

[With *This Is My God*] Herman Wouk has written the "intelligent woman's guide to orthodox Judaism," and it will do for intelligent men as well. It is, in the first place, a genuinely felt confession of faith. . . . But the book is also a clearly written layman's manual of what Mr. Wouk takes to be the essentials of the Jewish religion. The combination is a happy one: the confessional element gives life to the exposition of doctrine and practice, and the exposition provides content for the confession of faith. Even those who do not agree with Mr. Wouk's presentation and emphasis at all points will be grateful for what he has done to make orthodox Judaism intelligible to large numbers of Americans, Jewish and non-Jewish alike, whose cultural presuppositions are so remote from those of the ancient Jewish faith. . . .

The merits of this book—a work of popular theology by one of the best known of American novelists—are many and real. It is, at least so far as I can judge, substantially sound as a statement of orthodox Judaism, whatever differences there may be on points of selection, emphasis and interpretation. It is written smoothly and ingratiatingly, obviously for the mass reader, but it makes no concession on essentials for the sake of popularity, and it is poles apart from all the familiar "peace of mind" literature of the day. . . . And above all, the book is written with real seriousness, with a personal religious earnestness that is most impressive.

Yet, to this reader at least, Mr. Wouk's presentation of Judaism reveals difficulties over and above any secondary criticism that may be made of text, notes or bibliography. To put it plainly, Mr. Wouk's presentation of Judaism seems to me to be too relaxed, too externalistic and too partisan to be fully satisfactory.

Authentic religion, as I understand it, is a profound, often agonizing venture of the spirit, not a pleasant, relaxing activity that fits in well with the pattern of gracious living in modern suburbia. Whether he intends to or not, Mr. Wouk gives the impression that being a Jew is lots of fun; the true pathos of Jewish existence is better given, I suggest, in the age-old Jewish plaint, which Mr. Wouk must surely have heard from his grandfather, the rabbi, to whom the book is dedicated: "It's hard to be a Jew!"

Connected with this point of criticism is the second—that of externalism. Mr. Wouk devotes very little space to the inwardness of Jewish faith, whether of commitment or belief; he is mostly preoccupied with the externals of observance and behavior. Admittedly, these externals are important manifestations of the Jew's faith, but they are not that faith itself. Such externalism did little harm to the traditional Jew, who had appropriated the inner commitment without need of articulating it; but it can be very confusing today when it is precisely the inner commitment that is at stake. This failure to focus the attention of the reader upon the inner reality of faith appears to me to be the most serious shortcoming of the book. . . .

These criticisms are important, I think; but they should not be allowed to obscure the real value of the book, which survives them all. Anyone who wants to know what orthodox Judaism means to an informed and intelligent orthodox Jew, who is at the same time thoroughly American in outlook and culture, will do well to study this work.

Will Herberg, "Confession of Faith," in The New York Times Book Review, *September 27, 1959, p. 50.*

DAVID DEMPSEY

Based on the life and milieu of a successful American novelist, *Youngblood Hawke,* deals primarily with the love of money, the burning desire to get rich. It is an honest work, destined for great popularity: this author's narrative talent, whatever it lacks in literary grace, is a formidable one. If nothing else, it takes us back to the tradition of Sinclair Lewis—who, in fact, could have written this novel himself.

Here are vivid American types, raised to the third power yet somehow breathing the breath of their creator rather than the breath of life. Here is dialogue hair-tuned to just the right wave length for each character. Here are plot and subplot; and as cap sheaf on the shock, here is the urgent theme that has so often haunted the American success story—the wasting of power that tragically becomes the price of great achievement. . . .

[Youngblood Hawke's first book] is not a very good novel, but it gets talked about, and it has a certain rough power that stamps its author as a comer. . . . Hawke is immediately sought after by rival publishers, Hollywood producers, movie actresses, reprinters, theatrical folk, movie agents and minor pimps and practitioners of the smart money. Wouk's handling of these types is a stunning and merciless approach to a world he obviously knows well, and admires not at all. What is remarkable about these people is their prescience: they can *smell* money before it is made, and Hawke is soon embroiled in half a dozen schemes to make him rich. (p. 1)

A giant of a man with an inexhaustible supply of energy and a compulsion to write at least fourteen manuscript pages a night, Hawke is loosely modeled on the late Thomas Wolfe. But the shade of Mark Twain is present too, as he fights off an increasingly numerous and clamoring mob of creditors. (Like Twain, Hawke at one point makes the mistake of setting up his own publishing house.) He has discovered that being a successful writer virtually compels one to become a business man, while to succeed in business (or even to fail) risks the destruction of the artist.

In either case, the real venture capital, the genius of his art, is lost. Hawke soon finds himself grinding out novels to support the ill-advised schemes which were to give him the leisure to write his ambitious *American Comedy*. In the end, he is a victim of those two ancient and yet ironically modern villains, the tax collector and the money lender. "As wealth increases, so do its devourers," Wouk aptly quotes at one point.

If Hawke is part Wolfe and part Twain, he also seems at times to speak for his creator. There is a strong resemblance here between the type of novels Hawke turns out and those that (since the publication of *The Caine Mutiny*) have made Herman Wouk the most successful fiction writer, commercially speaking, of his generation. . . . Hawke, speaking to his real love, Jeanne Green, admits: "I'm nowhere for symbolism or poetry or the despair-of-civilization business. That side of the street has to be worked by other hands—but for the plain tale told by the daylight of Cervantes, without fancy figureskating, I think *Boone County* (another Hawke novel) will stand for awhile, maybe."

This curiously defensive note is struck again and again in *Youngblood Hawke,* and one can only agree that the book invites the sort of criticism its author has anticipated. We have not read very far before we find we are dealing with the mechanics of a writer's life rather than the interior forces that drive him; that the man who is being gulled is strangely insensitive to what is happening. Much the best characters in the story are the corrupters, just as the best scenes are those that do least to elucidate the central problem of Hawke's career—which is why he is vulnerable to the pursuit of that which means so little to his happiness.

If the pursuit itself tends to become tedious, we are nevertheless repeatedly caught up by Mr. Wouk's telling insights into the exploitative world which drags the writer to his defeat. Pretentious novelists, shifty literary critics, vainglorious actors, scheming women, the wheeler-dealers of finance—the author picks over their bones like a man eating spare ribs at a picnic. The difficulty is, we are all too aware that this is a picnic, and not a night at the opera; that the method here, setting its own limits, risks little beyond the story it serves, and that a superb craftsman has yet to make the final leap into his art. (pp. 1, 38)

> David Dempsey, "It Didn't Pay to Strike It Rich," in The New York Times Book Review, May 20, 1962, pp. 1, 38.

THOMAS BRENNAN

Don't Stop the Carnival deals with a New York sophisticate, Norman Paperman, who after a heart attack, despairs of his urban treadmill existence and sets out to build a new life in the Caribbean. Armed only with his experience as a Broadway publicity agent, he buys and attempts to manage an island hotel. As you can imagine, once we learn this, what follows is about as predictable as a vintage "I Love Lucy" television script.

The plumbing, the local help, the insects, the "quaint" customs of another culture all add up to a good case of cultural shock for Norman. Now cultural shock can be a very serious matter (maybe even material for a novel), but it also has its humorous side; and the humorous seems to be what Mr. Wouk

was aiming for in this book. But we do not laugh. We hardly even smile. Why?

The main reason seems to be that the author is panning for laughs in a stream that has already been badly overworked. . . . Evidently Mr. Wouk thought something more remained to be squeezed out. But the noticeable strain of his efforts to come up with original situations attests to his misjudgment.

It is obvious that this is Mr. Wouk's first major attempt at humor . . . , for he badly miscalculates the sophistication of his readers. The humor is of the situation variety which is available on television any night of the week. (pp. 85-6)

As the story line moves from situation to resolution to the next situation to the next resolution, one comes to the insulting conclusion that Mr. Wouk is in constant fear that his audience will not get the "bit." Consequently, he laboriously emphasizes every contributing detail to every minor crisis so that his punch lines are telegraphed long before he puts them into words. A constant repetition of this habit drives the reader to skimming in order to create surprises for himself. But even while skimming, the book's faults are difficult to overlook.

Curiously enough, amidst all this foolishness, Mr. Wouk manages to create some eminently dull but nevertheless believable characters. His hero, Norman, is easy enough to identify with at the beginning of the story. But after we see the author put him into some extremely implausible situations and watch him react in a highly uncharacteristic manner he begins to look like a buffoon. And the story doesn't call for a buffoon.

Iris, the alcoholic ex-movie star who is mistress to the island's Negro governor, has real potential as a vehicle with which the author might have explored the relatively untouched realm of biracial love. And Wouk does make a half-hearted pass at such an exploration. But to inject any sort of profundity into a novel that is geared for belly-laughs is a very precarious business; and in the end, the author seems to realize this. When the affair reaches a pregnant impasse it is merely eliminated by way of a meaningless accident and the reader is left empty-handed.

Other characters in the book are also painstakingly created and woven into the story, seemingly with the intent of bringing them all together for some marvelous denouement. (Say, maybe this is a novel!) But no, the action abruptly ends like Mr. Wouk got tired or had to make a deadline.

All of these pointless goings-on are put down in Mr. Wouk's very readable non-style which neither clouds nor enhances what he has to say. But in this book he has nothing to say. (p. 86)

> Thomas Brennan, "Ho, Hum, Herman!" in The Critic, Vol. 24, No. 1, August-September, 1965, pp. 85-6.

L. J. DAVIS

Like *The Winds of War,* its predecessor and companion volume, Herman Wouk's *War and Remembrance* is one of those whacking big popular novels that manages to achieve a measure of genuine significance without once impinging on the precincts of art, quality, or enduring merit; if it were something else—and if it were only a little less skillfully done—it would be ridiculous. It is a simplistic yet ambitious book, implausibly plotted, weakly characterized, and at the same time strangely effective, a historical novel of the very recent past written by an involved and committed contemporary.

Doubtless with an eye to both its obvious weaknesses and undeniable strengths, Wouk chooses to call it a romance. The description is as good as any and better than most despite the rather obvious questions that are begged by the title and the theme, inviting a comparison with Tolstoy that is at once spurious and moot. . . .

As before, the central character is Captain Victor "Pug" Henry, USN, an all but incredibly peripatetic figure who, with his progeny, his in-laws, and his girlfriend, contrives to be virtually everywhere of importance during the course of World War II, a sort of Lanny Budd in gold braid. *The Winds of War* ended with his timely arrival at Pearl Harbor on December 7, 1941, and the sequel takes it from there, moving him like a Monopoly marker to Midway, Guadalcanal, the White House, the Russian Front, the Tehran Conference, the battle of Leyte Gulf, and the White House again. As if this weren't enough, the circle of his acquaintance includes Roosevelt, Harry Hopkins, Stalin, Admirals King, Nimitz, Sprague, and Halsey, the Prime Minister of Iran, Eisenhower, and Harry Truman, all of whom appear to believe that he is a sterling fellow. (p. 1)

There is something of Maddox Ford's Captain Tietjens in Wouk's Captain Henry—a good man caught between the upper and nether millstones of a global catastrophe and a disintegrating family—but there is not nearly enough. The personal affairs of Wouk's hero are more reminiscent of the sentimental movies of the period than of the accidents of flesh and soul; like everyone else in the book, although not as much as some, he is a type rather than a person. *War and Remembrance* is less a novel than a fictionalized layman's history of the war, and an extremely good one at that. Henry and the others are, in effect, tabulae rasae—naive observers who go everywhere and do everything and witness every horror and to whom everything has to be explained, surrogates for the reader rather than captains of their fate. On that level, they work very well indeed. When it comes to the events and monstrosities of history, Wouk's powers of description are considerable.

Which is, of course, to beg another question: Do we need *another* layman's history of World War II, even a superior one? Battle and concentration camps have a way of making some eyes light up with glee and others to take on a faint but unmistakable glaze, but that is precisely the point at issue here; very often they are the same pair of eyes. Popular history is usually read selectively and written in such a way that it is possible for the enthusiastic amateur to have grand fun with, say, Nazi haberdashery and the Battle off Samar while ignoring the somewhat more disturbing implications of Manila and Theresienstadt. It is precisely this sportive view of combat that Wouk, to his great credit, will not truckle to, and therein lies the book's one great value that makes up for all the rest. Unlike all too many romantics, he is aware that great wars are also great crimes, and World War II was the greatest of all. It was the good guys against the bad guys, and the good guys won. They had to. We are in danger of forgetting that. (p. 6)

> *L. J. Davis, "The Battle Hymn of Herman Wouk,"*
> in Book World—The Washington Post, *October 8,*
> *1978, pp. 1, 6.*

PAUL FUSSELL

The whole two-volume work [*The Winds of War* and *War and Remembrance*] constitutes a very good popular history of the Second World War and the Holocaust in the guise of a very bad novel. Actually Wouk is only dubiously a novelist, pre-sumably enticed to that genre by the emoluments now attaching to it and its residuals. He is really something else, and when he functions as something else his work is often interesting and occasionally admirable.

But when he is merely novelizing he is embarrassing. The characters and plot of *War and Remembrance* are purely early 1950s Metro-Goldwyn-Mayer. . . .

The character of Victor Henry, the Lanny Budd of these proceedings, abundantly indicates what's wrong with *War and Remembrance* as fiction. He is not to be believed. As Madeline tells her brother Byron, "You and I have an incredible father." Too true. With his "awkward smile" and habit of being always right, he charms the world's leaders, who never tire of complimenting him. "You have insight, Pug," Roosevelt tells him, "and a knack for putting things clearly." He is a master of every subject—not just naval and military strategy and engineering, but wine and food, tanks, atomic fission, the history of philosophy, international politics, art history, and the history of Europe since 1870. He speaks languages and reads "Shakespeare" and "the Bible." He drinks but doesn't get drunk. His bravery is legendary. His personal mail is likely to include chatty letters on "creamy" White House stationery. He is gifted at literary composition, and he translates and edits like a scholar. He is one of those rare creatures whose obtuse superiority makes him "popular" instead of hated. . . . Powerful fantasy seems to be at work in Wouk's creation of Pug, and unkind readers may suspect autobiographical projection. Although Pug is actually a prig for all seasons, Wouk imagines that the reader will admire him without reservation. Pug's world is equally unreal. . . .

One stylistic symptom of Wouk's primitive conception of character and his rationalist view of the world is Elegant Variation. Thus Pug is "the naval officer," W. Somerset Maugham (who makes a brief guest appearance) "the British novelist," Stalin "the Communist dictator," Hitler "the Austrian adventurer," and FDR "the masterful old cripple" residing in "the executive mansion." Without typecasting everybody and everything Wouk would be lost in a world more complicated than he and his readers can tolerate. Unable to conceive an original character or to equip anyone with feelings above the commonplace, he must resort to wholly external classifications. His people are devoid of inner life. Their professional identity is their whole reality and they are entirely what they seem: stick-figures whose only function is to take their places in Wouk's retrograde middle-class allegory of success.

Although Wouk imputes sadism and unreason to the Nazis, he has eliminated the irrational from the behavior of the Allies, with the result that the war fought by the Henrys, unlike Heller's war, or Vonnegut's or Pynchon's, lacks the crucial dimension of the lunatic, the cruel, and the self-destructive. . . . A mere 20 years after the heroic sacrifices Wouk celebrates, infantrymen were fragging their officers. From *War and Remembrance* it would be impossible to guess why. (p. 32)

But there's another part, never satisfactorily joined to the MGM part, written by what I take to be more authentic Wouk, the learned descriptive and analytic essayist, and it is surprisingly fine. Much of it consists of powerfully imagined strategic theory and military history from the pen of the fictive German general Armin von Roon, whose book *Land, Sea and Air Operations of World War II*, written while its author is imprisoned for war crimes, is translated by Victor Henry, who annotates the text and sets the author straight on numerous points. The quality of the military reasoning in this document . . . is impressive, and so is Wouk's scholarship (that really is the correct word) in contemporary history. Impressive too is the strategic and tactical understanding in Wouk's accounts of naval battles like Midway and Leyte Gulf. Indeed, in his narration of Leyte Gulf he seems to recognize how much more interested he is in the history of naval operations than in the behavior of One Man's Family, whom he forgets for pages while he goes on, admirably, in the role of naval historian. As a historian of naval warfare Wouk is as good as Samuel Eliot Morison, while as an analytic narrator of land battles, particularly Soviet here, he invites comparison with someone like B. H. Liddell Hart. If the idea of "the novel" had not been his fatal Cleopatra, he could have distinguished himself as a contemporary historian. As it is, his failure to achieve a masterpiece can be seen as a generic miscarriage.

When he turns from people to significant public environments and "things," Wouk is also wonderful. . . . Wouk does even the inside of the cattle cars superbly: give him an environment of any kind—the Kremlin, Hitler's Wolfsschanze in the East Prussian forest, the president's private quarters in the White House, a gas chamber posing as a mass showerbath, the flag-plot room on a battleship, an atomic pile, the interior of a submarine or a bomber—and he renders it persuasively. There's hardly a contemporary writer so good at depicting locales authentically, places as varied as Honolulu, Bern, Lisbon, Leningrad, Columbia University, and London. They are perfect. I find it also to Wouk's credit that he is serious about the Second World War and conceives that interpreting it is the most pressing modern intellectual and moral problem. I respect the elegiac impulse that prompts him to interrupt his narrative of the Battle of Midway to display on three pages the names of the actual dead naval aviators from *Yorktown, Enterprise,* and *Hornet.* It is only with living people that he fails.

He has wanted to register the facts of the Holocaust so that they will never be forgotten. It is sad that the vulgarity of his romance of the Henrys compromises this admirable end, and by proximity demeans his skillful historiography. (p. 33)

> *Paul Fussell, in a review of "War and Remembrance," in* The New Republic, *Vol. 179, No. 16, October 14, 1978, pp. 32-3.*

PEARL K. BELL

[*War and Remembrance*] chronicles the wartime fortunes of the imaginary and actual persons who appeared in *The Winds of War* . . . and many, many more. In the foreword to *War and Remembrance,* Wouk calls that earlier volume a prologue . . . to his main tale, which is nevertheless self-contained. And in characteristically didactic tones he tells us that "I have put this theme (the end of war) in the colors and motion of the fiction art, so that 'he who runs may read,' and remember what happened in the worst world catastrophe."

The odd biblical phrase raises uncomfortable questions. How well and how much do we remember a story made for "he who runs"? Wouk makes no bones about the reader he aims to please, and this places *War and Remembrance* unequivocally in the bin of good-bad books—an undemanding vividness and ease take precedence at all times over any daunting complexities of thought, craft, or human behavior. This was particularly true of *The Winds of War,* which, for all its heft and soap-opera crudities, I could not, as the saying goes, put down. Unfortunately this obsessive magic is largely absent from *War*

and Remembrance. . . . [For one thing], the model navy family we first encountered in the "prologue" seven years ago is essentially so cinematic and stereotyped that the characters, subjected to a relentless dose of domestic familiarity, have become acutely tedious.

But the main reason Wouk's imaginary persons now seem so preposterous and irritating is that the backdrop for their crises of love and war is the harrowing reality of history between 1941 and 1945. Juxtaposed against Wouk's masterly recreations of the Pacific naval battles of Midway and Leyte Gulf; his angry account of American bureaucratic callousness, high and low, toward Jewish refugees from Hitler; his knowledgeable descriptions of Theresienstadt and Auschwitz—the fictional creatures playing out his romance seem not merely trivial but offensively so. (pp. 70-1)

Wouk's large design, of course, is to dramatize both the nobility and the horror of World War II by means of the tragic experiences endured by one ordinary, typical American family. Yet there is hardly a genuinely ordinary person among them, from the plastic perfection of Victor Henry to his conveniently Jewish daughter-in-law, who brings the fate of the European Jews into the Henry family circle. When her submarine officer husband is sent to the Pacific, Natalie Jastrow Henry finds herself trapped in Italy with her uncle, Aaron Jastrow, a bestselling historian. . . . Once the United States and Italy are officially at war, Aaron and Natalie, who by now has an infant son her husband has never seen, are interned as enemy aliens. Desperate, they run from one false haven to another in Italy and France until the Nazis spring the final trap and they are imprisoned first in Theresienstadt, and then in Auschwitz, where Aaron dies in the gas chamber. Natalie and her child survive and are reunited with young Byron Henry to the strains of *"Rozhinkes mit Mandlen."*

Invariably, the sentimentality that blights his fictional episodes is absent from Wouk's straightforward use of the historical record, and it is very much to his credit that he does not reduce the Nazi destruction of the Jews to the mawkish platitudes of Gerald Green's *Holocaust.* Particularly in his account of the so-called Great Beautification in Theresienstadt, the supposedly privileged camp for *Prominente,* he writes with bitter and moving restraint. (p. 71)

Wouk is far less assured in dealing with Roosevelt's refugee policy of inaction. Committed as he is to historical facts, Wouk can scarcely overlook Roosevelt's disgraceful silence and procrastination, particularly his failure to act on the Wagner-Rogers Bill, which could have prevented the slaughter of thousands of Jewish children by admitting them into the United States. But Wouk, like his stalwart creature of fantasy, Victor Henry, cannot shake off his affection for Roosevelt. . . . Despite his faith in documents and records, Wouk cannot bring himself to acknowledge the full shame of Roosevelt's failure to deal with the refugee problem.

The reason for Wouk's generosity toward FDR is clear: in unabashed dissent from the mainstream of American novelists today, for whom the only credible hero is the anti-hero, he remains an unembarrassed believer in such "discredited" forms of commitment as valor, gallantry, leadership, patriotism. Such unfashionable convictions will predictably strike many reviewers of *War and Remembrance* as at best naive, at worst absurdly out of touch with the Catch-22 lunacy of all war, including the war against Hitler. It is precisely to confute such facile and ahistorical cynicism that Wouk devotes so large and sober a part of his novel to the Final Solution and the ideological poison that overwhelmed the German people during Hitler's twelve years of power. In an ingenious device, Wouk interrupts his romance and naval battles at intervals with excerpts from a military history of the war written in prison by the imaginary German general Armin von Roon, which Victor Henry translates and edits after his retirement from the navy. In this brilliant simulation of the Nazi military mind, Wouk includes an unforgettable image of Hitler in the last weeks of the war snarling and raging, uncontrollably flatulent, cackling maniacally at the execution films of the generals who failed in their plot, blaming everyone for Germany's defeat but himself.

But the most powerfully rendered episodes in *War and Remembrance* are not the portraits of historical individuals but the meticulously documented accounts of the great navy victories at Midway and Leyte Gulf. Even when he is simply ticking off the different kinds of vessels engaged in a single huge operation, Wouk's proud voice swells into a hallelujah chorus. (pp. 71-2)

Herman Wouk dedicated *The Winds of War* to his sons with the somber Hebrew injunction *zachor*—remember. It is impossible to deny the dignity and decency that inform Wouk's sense of this moral obligation, which sustained his prodigious effort of research and writing between 1962 and 1978. Yet *War and Remembrance* still cannot by any valid standard be judged a successfully realized work of literature. What is bad about this often very good bad book is not Wouk's passionate conviction that the defeat of Nazi Germany and its Japanese ally was the just cause of the war, but the sad evidence that he cannot free his imagination from the stale and debilitating conventions of popular fiction. The factual accuracy that Wouk guarantees his readers is admirable in a work of history, but does it also enrich the imaginative human life in a work of fiction? I very much doubt it, since with all the good will, moral passion, and finicky adherence to the facts displayed in Herman Wouk's epic of the war, the drama enacted by his navy family never rises above the sentimental level of best-selling romance. (p. 72)

> *Pearl K. Bell, "Good-Bad and Bad-Bad," in* Commentary, *Vol. 66, No. 6, December, 1978, pp. 70-3.**

KIRKUS REVIEWS

[In *Inside, Outside*] Israel David Goodkind, 58 in 1973, Zionist lawyer and quintessential "American Jew," recalls his growing-up years (1920-1941) in loving, leisurely, anecdotal detail—with a few digressions into his present-day feelings about the inside/outside Jewish-American identity. In fact, Wouk gives his fictional alter-ego plenty of 1973 matters to brood on: Goodkind is a recently appointed Special Assistant (for cultural/Jewish matters) to Watergate-enmired Pres. Nixon—a crook, perhaps, but the Jews' best White House friend "since Truman"; Goodkind's daughter, once leftishly anti-Israel, is about to undergo a Zionist/*Roots* awakening during the Yom Kippur War; his aged mother falls ill during a trip to Israel; and Goodkind himself plays a small role in the War, as a go-between for Nixon and Golda Meir. Fortunately, however, these rather preachy concerns get very little emphasis here. Instead, Goodkind gives most of the space to his affectionate memoirs, a "lighthearted gambol" that stresses Wouk's comic/satiric gifts—even as it leans hard on the familiar theme of Jewish tradition vs. assimilation. . . . [Even] those Jewish readers more in sympathy with Roth than Wouk will find solid

chunks of entertainment here—while older, more conservative Jewish readers will be both entranced and fortified. . . . (pp. 112-13)

> *A review of "Inside, Outside," in* Kirkus Reviews, *Vol. LIII, No. 3, February 1, 1985, pp. 112-13.*

JAMES MICHENER

Herman Wouk has frequently proved his standing as one of America's premier storytellers. In novels, plays, motion pictures and most recently a television series, he has captivated audiences, drawing on two main wellsprings—a rich Jewish heritage and an interest in history.

In this ambitious novel [*Inside, Outside*] he charts the spiritual and social adventures of Israel David Goodkind, Yisroelke to his intimates, I. David to President Nixon, who in the fading days of his doomed second Administration brings him into the White House to provide input on the Jewish and moral angles. Before reaching this exalted position, Goodkind has been a student at Columbia University, the author of a varsity musical, a dramatics director at a summer camp, a highly paid gag writer for radio, a law student and a successful New York lawyer specializing in corporate taxes.

Goodkind has two personalities—he is a devout Orthodox Jew in the midst of a large and wild New York family whose origins go back to Minsk, and he is a wisecracking wordsmith whose reflections on his family and the people he works with are rich and compelling. He is thus an insider religiously and an outsider in his relations with the workaday world. *Inside, Outside* is an interesting and amusing account of his efforts to keep these two lives in balance.

To a fellow writer, the way Mr. Wouk tells his story is significant. The novel has a multitude of chapters, some only three or four pages long and none overextended. These brief takes could be radio or televison skits, for they are compact, beautifully focused and often hilarious. (p. 1)

I like them, sparely used, and find Mr. Wouk's well done and suitable to his purposes, as in this example: "In any case, I will now tell you what really happened at Aunt Faiga's wedding."

Two other matters of style should be noted. First, Mr. Wouk uses a great many Hebrew and Yiddish words, always defining them, and through them conveys a fine sense of New York life. Readers who immerse themselves in this novel will learn much about Judaism. Second—and this will cause some eyebrows to lift—Mr. Wouk uses an all-out, freewheeling scatological vocabulary. . . . This is a far cry from the austere purity of *The Caine Mutiny* and illustrates just how much the American novel has changed in four decades. Yet Mr. Wouk is also the man who wrote the supremely devout *This Is My God,* explaining Judaism to the gentile world. Perhaps he is reminding us here that not all highly religious people are highly proper. In any case, he convinces us that this is the way his characters speak. (pp. 1, 42)

Inside, Outside leaps about in both space and time, moving from Washington to Minsk to New York to Israel and back to Washington and from the early 1900's (and the story of Goodkind's parents and family) through the 30's and down to the 70's, when Mr. Nixon is on his way out. Readers will find pleasure in trying to identify many of the major characters, who seem to be carefully drawn portraits of real people. I am not sufficiently familiar with the gag-writing profession or Hollywood to nail down people from those fields, but when Mr. Wouk gives us a major American novelist who is a wow with women, repeatedly married, burdened with alimony payments and the master of a scabrous vocabulary, one can hardly miss. . . .

It is not clear whether Goodkind ever resolves his dilemma, but at the end of the novel he confides: "The kaddish song has ended. So has my book. It is a kaddish for my father, of course, from start to finish; but in counterpoint it is also a torch song of the thirties, a sentimental Big Band number." Readers may be surprised at this statement, because much of the novel is carried on the back of Goodkind's typhoon of a mother. Perhaps he felt she needed no song of mourning.

In any case, *Inside, Outside* offers some hearty laughs, much valuable instruction about the Jewish religion and a nostalgic reminiscence of the 1930's. (p. 42)

> *James Michener, "Mr. Goodkind Goes to Washington," in* The New York Times Book Review, *March 3, 1985, pp. 1, 42.*

MARVIN HOFFMAN

When I was a graduate student at Harvard in the early '60s my mother approached me tentatively with a question. Her natural style was hardly tentative, so I knew that she must have been mulling over something *important*. "Marvin," she asked, "you think maybe you'll work for the President some day?"

Now that may seem a bizarre leap of illogic to the 1985 mind. In 1961, however, the equation was clear: Harvard = Arthur M. Schlesinger Jr. = John F. Kennedy. Even if JFK had remained on the scene longer, it is not likely that I would have given my mother any *nachas* on this score. But obliging child that he is, I. David Goodkind, the hero of Herman Wouk's latest saga, *Inside, Outside,* satisfies a dream of immigrant Jewish mothers for their sons second only to doctoring: He caps a lucrative legal career by becoming an adviser in the Nixon White House.

Never mind that he is working for the "wrong" President, or that he has so little to do he spends long uninterrupted hours in his office writing this novel in the first person. The important fact is that Israel David Goodkind has moved from Outside to Inside, a position permitting him to lecture the President on the joys of Talmud study. . . .

These encounters between the successful son and the wielder of international power frame the book, beginning and end, reflecting Wouk's relentless theme. Although he struggles to give his Inside-Outside construct a variety of psychological and social meanings (the bully versus the bullied, the initiated and the virgin), the Second Generation American Jew is his central subject. He focuses on the "marginal men" uneasily straddling two worlds—that of their immigrant parents, eternal outsiders, and of their American children, who move comfortably in a milieu they rightly or wrongly feel part of, alienation having given way to a cheerful and unselfconscious pragmatism. (p. 7)

The Second Generation has fueled, participated in and borne witness to a dizzying, bewildering ascent that occurred so rapidly, writers like Wouk act virtually as anthropologists. They gratify certain nostalgic impulses possessed by readers of their own age, and provide exotic information for younger people eager to find some content to fill out the uncomfortably empty shell of their Jewish identity. Goodkind comments that "Jews buy about half the hard-cover books in America." They are clearly this volume's intended audience. Yet Wouk knows he must nonetheless explain what a *shofar* is and spell out the laws of *kashrut* when Goodkind agonizingly thinks of violating them.

No less than in *This Is My God,* Wouk's popular compendium of Jewish law and practice, we are being educated here about Judaism, except this time we are also being entertained by a wily, experienced popular novelist. A lot of us who are serious readers do not often allow ourselves the indulgence of bathing in the warm chicken soup of works like *Inside, Outside.* You float effortlessly in it, buoyed by the schmaltz, and only later become aware of the somewhat unclean feeling that clings to you. I will exit from this risky metaphor, though, to admit that most of the novel is fun to read; many of the chapters are cleverly crafted short vaudeville routines.

Wouk's literary models are Outsiders, Sholem Aleichem and Mendele Mocher Sforim, not Insiders like D. H. Lawrence and Henry Miller. Even his style in much of the book imitates the tragicomic tone of the Yiddish writers, particularly their device of directly addressing the audience with tag lines that introduce and conclude the chapters: "Now for my father's departure from Minsk," or "Okay, short visit to the home of my Bay Ridge uncle, the Haskalist. . . ." These parallel Sholem Aleichem's "Go be a prophet and guess what a tragedy would hit us," or "All right. I'm coming back to my brother Elye's ink."

Finally, the conflict of the Inside-Outside theme is embodied in the joke of the novel's closing line, "Call me Israel." This at once affirms Jewishness by its insistence on the Outside name, and acknowledges the power of the Inside by providing us with a literary reference we all recognize that is a part of the general culture.

Saul Bellow, Roth (both Philip and Henry), Bernard Malamud, and many other novelists may have treated this material in more complex and serious ways. Wouk, however, speaks to a much larger audience and is the only voice of an eroding heritage likely to reach it. His message may be thin but it is positive: For this generation, Out is In. (p. 8)

> *Marvin Hoffman, "A Generation between Two Worlds," in* The New Leader, *Vol. LXVIII, No. 6, April 22, 1985, pp. 7-8.*

Marguerite Yourcenar

1903-

(Born Marguerite de Crayencour) Belgian-born American novelist, poet, essayist, critic, short story writer, dramatist, and translator.

In 1981 Yourcenar became the first woman to be elected to the prestigious Académie Française in its three hundred-plus years of existence. Her appointment, which created a sensation in the French literary world, was even more remarkable because she was born in Belgium and has lived much of her life in the United States. Despite the fact that she writes in French, neither her lifestyle nor her work is concerned with contemporary French society. Yourcenar deals primarily with the European past, and the high quality of her historical research lends an academic tone to her work. Displaying a vast knowledge of philosophy, history, and myth, Yourcenar uses her writing to link past with present and provide a deeper understanding of the human condition. Jean d'Ormesson commented: "The most striking aspect of [Yourcenar's] work is her use of specific historical situations to express the universal condition of man."

Yourcenar's reputation rests primarily with *Mémoires d'Hadrien* (1951; *Memoirs of Hadrian*), which is considered a masterpiece of historical fiction. The novel revolves around the great Roman emperor Hadrian who, as he nears death, recounts his life to the young Marcus Aurelius. Physical and intellectual needs unite in Hadrian, for he demands the sensual pleasures of life while also reflecting upon the essence of love and the reasons for his existence. He emerges as a powerful and complex individual, and Yourcenar was acclaimed for creating an insightful and credible portrait of this ancient Roman leader. As is characteristic of Yourcenar's work, the fully documented historical detail provides a backdrop for an exploration of social relationships.

At the time of her election to the Académie Française, only three of Yourcenar's works had been translated into English: *Memoirs of Hadrian; Le coup de grâce* (1939; *Coup de Grâce*), which is set in Eastern Europe at the time of the Russian Revolution and focuses on the unrequited love of a young woman for a soldier; and *L'oeuvre au noir* (1968; *The Abyss*), which concerns a sixteenth-century physician and alchemist and the conflict he encounters between the dogmatic beliefs of the Church and his own intellectual questions. Since her election, many of Yourcenar's earlier works have also become available in English, providing insight into her development as a writer. The sexual tension pervading much of her literature is evident in Yourcenar's first fictional work, *Alexis; ou, Le traite du vain combat* (1929; *Alexis*), in which the protagonist leaves his wife to engage in a love affair with another man. The novel *Denier du rêve* (1934; *A Coin in Nine Hands*) exemplifies her overriding concern for the human condition. In this work, the political impact of a plot to assassinate Mussolini is secondary to the lives, hopes, and dreams of her characters as each comes into possession of the same gold coin. Yourcenar's fascination with ancient Greek and Roman culture is displayed in the metaphorical prose poems of *Feux* (1936; *Fires*), which depict the passions of historical figures and fictional characters from these eras, and her knowledge of Far Eastern culture is reflected in the short stories collected in

© Lütfi Özkök

Nouvelles orientales (1938; *Oriental Tales*). Yourcenar has also written plays, scholarly essays, and criticism, and she has translated the work of such authors as Henry James, Virginia Woolf, and C. P. Cavafy.

(See also *CLC*, Vol. 19 and *Contemporary Authors*, Vols. 69-72.)

GEORGE STEINER

There were sovereign shades present at Marguerite Yourcenar's solemn induction into the French Academy, on January 22nd of this year. Mme. de Staël, first lady of European letters, had been banished not only from all official honors but from France itself by Napoleon, who deemed her a liberal busybody and virago. George Sand had, at times, worn men's clothes but had not succeeded in breaking the bounds that a woman's condition imposed even on genius. Colette had been recognized as one of the virtuoso craftsmen of her century, as an artist quintessentially French, in the mundane lyrical vein of Watteau and of La Fontaine. The Academy remained closed to her....

Yet now, after three hundred and forty-six celibate years, the Académie Française was welcoming into its august precincts a woman born in Belgium, and one who had only very recently, and with urgent view to the occasion, reacquired her French nationality after decades spent in virtual isolation on an island off the Maine coast. (p. 104)

The titles to renown of Mme. Yourcenar . . . rest squarely on one work: **Memoirs of Hadrian** (1951). Almost at once, this fictive autobiography was hailed as a classic. Written in a marmoreal yet introspective prose, it probes the ambiguous relations of supreme imperial power and private *tristesse*. The Emperor Hadrian is both a stoic and passionate, vulnerable lover. He is a memorialist whose incisive style and wary tolerance belong to a Roman, to a pagan world at the edge of its long twilight. Hadrian's view of the golden boy whom he loves, of the subtle treasons and coarsenings of sensibility around and within himself, on the other hand, comes after Proust. The entire composition is exquisitely poised.

Rereading it, one compares it, inevitably, with its two manifest precursors: Walter Pater's *Marius the Epicurean* (a work whose subterranean afterlife is far more active than literary historians have observed) and *I, Claudius,* of Robert Graves. Such recall is not altogether to Yourcenar's advantage. A good deal of the polish of the **Memoirs of Hadrian** is already in Pater, but Pater's philosophical intelligence is of a more unsettling order. And there is in Graves's reconstruction a robustness, a narrative pulse, that the Hadrian book's muted self-scrutiny does not really match. Nonetheless, it retains an undoubted distinction and may one day be heard as having struck a crucial note in the postwar mood of the West. (pp. 104-05)

Mme. Yourcenar is fascinated by minerals, rare metals, and the fantasies of medieval and Renaissance alchemists. She sees in the firelit darkness of the alchemist's den, in the perilous heresies of his occult speculations a manifold symbol of art and the artist. He, too, is a marginal being, a maker whose talents for creation, out of dross, out of apparent nothingness, dangerously mime and therefore challenge the creative primacy of nature and the Deity. Like Jung, whose metaphors of the collective unconscious, whose teachings on *imago* and *anima,* have clearly influenced her, Yourcenar locates in alchemy the underlying paradigm and hidden poetry of modern science. In their teasing, surrealist purity and "craziness," the paradoxes of Zeno, the pre-Socratic philosopher, continue to busy modern logic. Zeno is the name Mme. Yourcenar gives to the alchemist-physician who is at the center of **The Abyss** (1968). . . . The evocations of the novelist's native Flanders, between Middle Ages and Renaissance, are skillful. The narrative is shapely. But this is not major work.

The reservation applies even more strongly to Mme. Yourcenar's other publications. These include novellas, essays, a sizable but textually amateurish and fitfully translated anthology of classical Greek verse, a recent, faintly bizarre monograph on Yukio Mishima, the late Japanese master of violence and pose. It is on **Hadrian** that the case rests. It is in his eminent glow that the new Academician took her historic seat.

Only the resonance of this occasion will explain the translation and publication now of **Feux,** a brief set of cameos written in 1935. **Fires** . . . belongs emphatically to a spell of "neoclassical modernity" in French literature. It looks to the antique parables of André Gide, it aims at offsetting the ironic allegories on ancient myths in the plays of Giraudoux, it echoes Valéry's Hellenistic poetry and, above all, the fashionable, even par-

odistic treatments of Oedipus, Electra, Orpheus by Cocteau. Anthropology and Freudian psychoanalysis had given to Greek mythology a new spice. Broken by the First World War, aware of the coming of a second, France saw itself as a source and sanctuary of Attic values soon to be prey to the barbarians. Abroad, T. S. Eliot was invoking the Aeschylean Furies, and Eugene O'Neill the House of Atreus. Maurice Druon, a fellow-Academician, recalls that there was at the time hardly a young playwright, novelist, or essayist not at work on some version of the Antigone theme. Steeped in Pindar, already acquainted, one would guess, with the melancholy postclassicism of Cavafy and other modern Greek lyricists, Marguerite Yourcenar, then thirty-two, set down her variants on Achilles and Phaedra, on Antigone and Sappho. The dedication "To Hermes" is, of itself, a period piece.

There are everywhere in the little garland touches of nineteen-thirties montage: tanks roll through Antigone's Thebes; helmets are like hair dryers (pure Cocteau, this). Pregnant maxims and lapidary aphorisms are incised on every mannered page. Boy and woman "hated each other like lovers." It is God's great boon that "He saved me from happiness." "Slanders had ripened under the sun of Hate." Eyes are "farsighted in sorrow." Phaedra "gets drunk on the impossible, the heady basis of all mixtures of misfortunes." In French, with its Latinity and rhetoric of cadenced abstractions, such tags are more or less acceptable. But they do not wear well, especially in translation. Mme. Yourcenar's preface alludes dismissively to the "purely biographical residues" that deeper analysis might reveal in this little book. There is in fact no need to probe. What present life remains in this miniature springs from certain summonses to Eros. Phaedo recounts Socrates' last caress: "His slightly trembling hands were wandering on the nape of my neck as though in a valley alive with spring: guessing that eternity is only a series of instants, each one unique, he felt the silky blond form of eternal life flee under his fingers." "Sappho's dresses hang like women who have killed themselves," and "she hears cymbals clashing as though fever hit them in her heart." But such vivacities are only occasional amid the honeyed flow of a scholastic display.

Is there some wild and hidden opus in Mme. Yourcenar's sea-battered cottage? Or will she now expend her prestige on the sort of bland, sibylline interviews and pronouncements that have appeared since her election? It would, surely, be a pity if the Académie Française had chosen too academically. (pp. 105-06)

George Steiner, "Ladies' Day," in The New Yorker, *Vol. LVII, No. 26, August 17, 1981, pp. 104-06.*

JAMES BOATWRIGHT

The jacket illustration for **Fires** is a reproduction of "The Avenging Angel" from the Villa of Mysteries at Pompeii, and it is a wonderful introduction to this collection of nine prose poems, "a sequence of lyrical prose pieces connected by a notion of love," in the words of the author's preface. The angel, poised before blood- or flame-red walls, is a half-naked winged woman, her right hand grasping a rod raised to lash her . . . what? Victims? Suppliants? In this case the author herself, for **Fires** is a book born out of pain. Marguerite Yourcenar describes it as the "product of a love crisis," and her characters are the mythical or real people who have suffered a similar fate: Phaedra, Achilles, Patroclus, Antigone, Lena (concubine of Aristogiton), Mary Magdalene, Phaedo, Clytemnestra, and Sappho, characters who "serve the poet as props through time."

These stories . . . are interspersed with "unrelated *pensées* that were at first notes for a private diary." Having appeared in French in 1936, and only now in English, they are retellings of more or less familiar narratives, pulled out of their antique frames to "modernize the past": [for example], Sappho is a trapeze acrobat, traveling from circus to circus in Europe between the 20th-century wars, accompanied by or in pursuit of the lovely but unfaithful girl, Attys. . . .

The stories are variations on the theme of absolute love, its terrible price and transcendent rewards, whatever its form. . . .

Readers familiar with Hadrian's grave and limpid voice in *Memoirs of Hadrian,* Yourcenar's beautiful meditation on history and her best-known work, or the complex but conventional narrative voices of *The Abyss* and *Coup de Grâce,* her other novels available in English, will be surprised by the language and style of *Fires.* Aphoristic, paradoxical, rife with startling and often far-fetched similes and metaphors, these poems and the excesses of their style are convincingly defended by their author as "a legitimate effort to portray the full complexity and passion of an emotion."

Of the narratives of passion in *Fires* "Phaedo, or the Dance" is to my mind the most moving and the most successful, and it is the one that best prepares us for both *Memoirs of Hadrian* and *The Abyss.* From Diogenes Laertius' remarks on the adolescence of Phaedo—his beauty, the destruction in war of his family, his enslavement and degradation as a prostitute in a bordello, his salvation through Alcibiades' intervention—Yourcenar builds a monologue on the making of a philosopher, the disciple whose long hair Socrates caresses moments before he drinks the hemlock. . . . (p. 8)

Like the poet, lover, and noble prince Hadrian and the invented Renaissance physician and alchemist Zeno of *The Abyss,* Socrates is the greatest kind of hero, the hero of Knowledge and Wisdom, and as they do, he approaches those absolutes through his passion for the beloved, thereby uniting body and soul. . . .

In the preface to *Fires* (written in 1975) Yourcenar expresses . . . [this sentiment]:

"What seems obvious is that this notion of mad, sometimes scandalous love that is nevertheless permeated by a sort of mystical power could only survive if it is associated with whatever belief in transcendence, even if only within a human being."

The survival of this notion of love in Yourcenar's work, its unwavering persistence, is surely one of the truths Yourcenar alludes to in the conclusion to her preface to *Fires,* when she says that "certain passages in *Fires* seem to me to contain truths glimpsed early on that needed a whole lifetime to be rediscovered and authenticated." (p. 12)

> James Boatwright, *"The Disease and Vocation of Love," in* Book World—The Washington Post, *September 6, 1981, pp. 8, 12.*

STEPHEN KOCH

The 20th century has witnessed the emergence of a potent—and, I think, possibly even new—literary form, which we might dub, informally, the unwritten novel. The unwritten novel is a book, however polished, that seems a compilation of frag-

ments. A typical example looks like a salad of autobiography, notebook ecstasies, diaristic confessions, prose poems, epigrams, meditations, shafts of critical discourse. Yet these scattered works are not mere pastiches. They *do* have a unity; but theirs is the coherence of a unifying refusal, an energizing denial. These books insist—on every page—that they are *not* novels. They refuse to be novels. Yet through their fragmented alternatives, we still can glimpse the novels they refuse to be—tales otherwise untellable, masked and revealed—for reasons ranging from discretion to despair to a certain visionary breathlessness. An early example is Rilke's *The Notebooks of Malte Laurids Brigge.* Others are Colette's *The Pure and the Impure,* Cyril Connolly's soon to be republished *The Unquiet Grave,* and the last four published books of Roland Barthes. To this company we now must add . . . Marguerite Yourcenar's *Fires.*

Fires was written in 1935, when Marguerite Yourcenar was 32, "the product" (as she confides in a recent, backward-glancing preface) "of a love crisis." In the classic fashion of the unwritten novel, parts consist of pages from a love journal, aphorisms addressed to "you" provoked by this hectic and plainly unhappy liaison. Interspersed with these *cris de coeur* are nine highly wrought prose poems—or call them poetic tales—short, brilliant, contorted retellings of myths, from Phaedra to Achilles—probably called forth by the real-life passion.

Readers of *The Abyss* and the Yourcenar masterpiece, *The Memoirs of Hadrian,* know she combines high novelistic gifts with those of a good scholar. In *Fires* private sexual obsession sweeps the figures of myth into weird but masterly flights of the polymath's fancy: Mary Magdalene (the sole Christian in *Fires*) sinks into prostitution after an unconsummated marriage to a scornful, puritanic, impotent John the Baptist; hiding among the daughters of Lycomedes, Achilles forgets his disguise as a maiden and embraces Patroclus, only to be spurned as a slut; Antigone hangs herself *with* her husband Haemon, from the same noose: their dual deadweight swings as a "pendulum" that "rewinds the machinery of the stars." (p. 12)

Fires reflects the influence of three of Mme. Yourcenar's literary elders: It sometimes echoes the prose of Cocteau. . . ; it reacts against the *Parisian Athens* of Giraudoux; and it is under the spell of Valéry, who presides over the—to me—most splendid passage in the book, the soliloquy given to Phaedo, Socrates's pupil. In the preface she speaks of—and maybe patronizes a bit?—the dodges, confessions and dazzling flights of *Fires* as a "masked ball."

Fine. But what precisely is the "novel"—unwritten—that is both masked and unmasked in *Fires,* the story that is *almost* being told? The gnomic notebooks and myths conceal and reveal much. In fragments like those half-formed images that obsess the novelist's imagination in the earliest phase of a novel, we glimpse settings: "Cosmopolitan silhouettes in Constantinople bars," circa 1935. Morning walks in an Athens graveyard. Rumors of the Spanish Civil War. (pp. 12, 20)

Meanwhile, the jottings from the diary suggest a trajectory for the veiled love affair. The entries in Mme. Youcenar's love diary may be fragmentary, but they are fragments that follow a definite path: the plain path from love to rejection. In contrast to her feverish, mythic dreams, Mme. Yourcenar's aphorisms are simple talk about the feelings that come and go, from love's first excitement to its end. I assume Marguerite Yourcenar's diary was kept while the real love affair ran its course, but I suspect the more elaborate prose poems were composed after the affair's bitter ending. In the last one, Mme. Yourcenar spins an elaborate fantasy about Sappho's suicide. The legend is that the poet, rejected by some handsome sailor, flung herself from a cliff. In the Yourcenar version, the poet's fall miraculously does not kill her. She survives. On the book's final page, the love diary repeats this theme: "One can only raise happiness on a foundation of despair. I think I will be able to start building."

The unwritten novel among the fantasies and aphorisms of *Fires* is a classic tale. (p. 20)

> Stephen Koch, "Flights of a Polymath's Fancy," in The New York Times Book Review, *October 4, 1981, pp. 12, 20.*

BETTINA L. KNAPP

Les yeux ouverts [published in the United States as **With Open Eyes**], more like an inner monologue or a conversation than an interview, allows the reader to experience the fascinating world of Yourcenar's intellect and psyche. Matthieu Galey's questions are willfully succinct, each a catalyst encouraging Yourcenar to reveal her private thoughts, the mysteries which live inchoate in her novels, essays, dramas and poems. Yourcenar lives on an island off the east coast of the United States seven months out of the year. Her house is modest and comfortable, filled with books and objects, each infused with a personality of its own. Her world is lived in isolation and silence—in nature—interrupted only now and then by the sound of birds above, squirrels or other animals. In this bare exterior world, Yourcenar the artist creates her own magic, lives out the rituals of her religion which she transcribes in her writings. Her "Celtic eye" peers out into the world, which is universal in breadth and in scope. Hers is the mythic sphere which she encapsulates in her novels and essays and which encouraged her to study Chinese, Japanese and Hindu mysticism: she wrote *Préface à la Gita-Gavinda* (1958), among other philosophical works. . . .

Yourcenar traces her thoughts in this remarkable interview: from their inception, in the concrete world of childhood, to their complex ramifications in the abstract domain of the adult. Always she proceeds with "open eyes," relating her feelings and beliefs openly, forthrightly to the reader. Her Flemish childhood was in itself unique: her mother having died of puerperal fever, Yourcenar was brought up exclusively by her father. In fact, she never even saw a picture of her mother until she was thirty-five years old. Her childhood was solitary, cut off from other family members. She learned to love nature early in life; it responded to some need within her. . . . As a child, Yourcenar tells us, she had "mystical intuitions," and her religious instinct (religion in the true sense of the word, *religio* meaning "linking back") helped her gain access to an "invisible" or rather "interior" realm.

To reveal the details of Yourcenar's life experience might diminish the excitement the reader would experience in reading it himself, listening to her elegant way of depicting her fascinating world, replete with shadows and undertones yet majestic in its classical sense of beauty. *Les yeux ouverts*, like an exquisitely woven tapestry, allows us to follow its pattern, coloration, linear arrangement, each aspect of a rich and fulfilled existence spent in the timeless and dimensionless realm of the mind and the senses.

> Bettina L. Knapp, in a review of "Les yeux ouverts: Entretiens avec Matthieu Galey," in World Literature Today, *Vol. 56, No. 2, Spring, 1982, p. 303.*

JOSEPH EPSTEIN

Marguerite Yourcenar treats her novels rather as W. H. Auden did his poems: revising and reworking and even remaking them over the decades. In between work on her novels she has done a number of translations: of Virginia Woolf, of Henry James, of Cavafy, of Negro spirituals, of ancient Greek poets. She is clearly a writer who is interested in what she is interested in—which is to say, not a writer chiefly interested in doing what is best for her career. Consequences follow from this. As a result of the long delays between the publication of Mme. Yourcenar's books, and then of the often even lengthier delays between their appearance in French and in English, her English-reading audience has been deprived of anything even faintly resembling a clear sense of her development as a writer and any feeling whatsoever of the excitement of fresh work from her. A new Bellow, a new Naipaul, a new Solzhenitsyn, the works of such novelists create a stir, an air of intellectual anticipation. Yet there are not—or rather seem not to be—any new Yourcenars.

As if this were not enough, there is the additionally awkward fact that Marguerite Yourcenar's two most substantial novels—*Memoirs of Hadrian* and *The Abyss*—are, technically, of the genre contemptuously known as historical novels. When most people think of historical novels they think of books like *Gone With the Wind*, of costume balls done in prose. (*War and Peace* is, technically, a historical novel, but let that pass). Between Marguerite Yourcenar and Margaret Mitchell there is more than a vast artistic distance; on purely scholarly grounds alone the work of the former has been admired by historians of the ancient and medieval world. Yet another difficulty with historical novels is that people tend to think of them as not speaking to contemporary issues, questions, problems. Increasingly, the new Bellows, Naipauls, Solzhenitsyns do speak to these issues, questions, problems. Marguerite Yourcenar's novels, it must be said, do not. . . . (p. 61)

Marguerite Yourcenar, who is a writer interested in traditions, legends, memories of old days, is also an aristocratic writer. Someone once observed of her that she is the only novelist living today whose characters do not go about with one question uppermost in their minds: "Why am I not happier?" When a character in a Yourcenar novel is preoccupied with that question, he is rather to be pitied.

One of the marks of the the aristocratic novelist is that he writes chiefly about superior people, and in such a way that the identifying factor is almost nil. In a Yourcenar novel one does not "relate to" the characters. To be sure one does get caught up in her stories, but the pleasures she offers are not those provided by narrative alone. They are also the pleasures of style, and Mme. Yourcenar's style is aphoristic and philosophical. Hers is a style well suited for freshly formulating old and new experience. It is also imbued with the intellecutal quality known as gravity. She is serious about serious things—and that, nowadays, is not everybody's notion of how novelists ought to conduct their business.

If Marguerite Yourcenar can be said to resemble any 20th-century writer in her general tone, it is André Malraux. Like Malraux, she is especially good at the abstract expression of passion. Like Malraux, too, her heroes are men of action given to reflection, but reflection of a pitiless kind. (p. 62)

[Yourcenar's interests as a novelist] most distinctly do not lie in politics. A character in her novel *A Coin in Nine Hands* remarks that at La Scala, when they need to simulate crowd noises, they get performers to sing the highly sonorous word *rubarbara* in rounds from the wings. He then says, as Mme. Yourcenar herself might, "Well, politics, whether of the Left or the Right, it's *rubarara* for me, my boy." She is even less, this writer who is the first female member of the French Academy, interested in the condition of women, or indeed in any contemporary condition. Some novelists pull us more deeply into our own time; she pulls us away from it—or rather above it. Marguerite Yourcenar's subject is human destiny. It was the only serious subject for the Greeks, whom she so much admires. It has always been the great subject of the novel, and always will be, even though few writers in our day have been able to find the means to take it on, let alone so directly as Marguerite Yourcenar has done.

"I have encouraged experimentation with the thought and methods of the past, a learned archaism which might recapture lost intentions and lost techniques." So says the Emperor Hadrian in Mme. Yourcenar's *Memoirs of Hadrian;* so might the novel's author say in explanation of her own excursions into the past as a form of literary experimentation. Yet who better to discuss questions of human destiny than a Roman emperor, a man for whom the satisfaction of all worldly desires can be arranged without difficulty? And who better among Roman emperors than Hadrian (76-138 C.E.), successor to Trajan, precursor to the Antonines, a competent amateur in mathematics, literature, and painting, a dabbler in magic and astrology, a lover of Athens and Greece, a man of wide personal culture?

Memoirs of Hadrian purports to be an account of the Roman emperor's life as he presents it, in his waning days, to the young Marcus Aurelius. In it Hadrian recounts to Marcus the experiences of his twenty-year reign and the years that preceded it, of his travels outward from Rome, of his attempts to penetrate beneath the conventional ideas of his time. In these memoirs Hadrian attempts to extract, for the young Marcus but also for himself, such wisdom as his years have taught him. The novel's outlook is worldly; its tone philosophical; its feeling completely Roman. The book is a triumph of historical ventriloquism; it is impossible to read it and not think that, had Hadrian left memoirs, this is how they would have read. Next to *Memoirs of Hadrian*, Robert Graves's *I, Claudius* reads like a *Classic Comic*.

Now to bring off such a book requires not only artistry and scholarship but intelligence of a very high order. Intelligence is not much spoken of in connection with novelists—except to say that this or that writer is a novelist of ideas—but it looms larger than most people with literary interests are ready to allow. In fiction it is difficult—perhaps impossible—to create a character more intelligent than oneself, though this doesn't stop novelists from trying (or prevent them from failing). When in his novels the late Henry Miller used to divagate on the subject of Indian philosophy only the sheerest intellectual rube did not know that Miller was out of his water. When John Updike has a character in one of his novels talk about theology, one's mind generally takes a walk around the block.

This is not Marguerite Yourcenar's problem. If she has a problem as a novelist, it is that the quality of talk in her novels is so superior that it overwhelms the element of story, which in her longer novels, counts for a good deal less than setting and celebration (although, it must be added, she is extremely good at constructing chronicles of careers). Something similar occurs in the recent novel of Saul Bellow, the most thoughtful of American novelists, whose plots have come increasingly to matter less than the quality of his own observations. Not that Marguerite Yourcenar is quite so essayistic in her novels as Bellow has become in his, but it does often seem that, in recent fiction, plot contracts to accommodate the expansion of mind.

Plot does not figure prominently in *Memoirs of Hadrian*. The dying emperor's reflections are everything. These reflections are pitched at exactly the right—the Roman—level of generality. (p. 63)

It is on the divine nature of things, on the fundamental mysteries of love, food, the body, sleep, the soul, death, that Hadrian's thoughts linger in this novel.... Mme. Yourcenar offers the spectacle of a dying emperor, scarcely able to enjoy the simplest pleasures, craving death, taking the measure of the world around him as only a man who soon will have no stake in it can, yet even with death staring him full in the face not utterly devoid of qualified hope.... (pp. 63-4)

Passage after passage in *Memoirs of Hadrian* has ... [a] marmoreal quality; and reading this remarkable book about a 2nd-century Roman emperor by a 20th-century Belgian woman one recalls ... [a] sentence Marguerite Yourcenar has lent to the pen of Hadrian: "A man who reads, reflects, or plans belongs to his species rather than to his sex; in his best moments he rises above the human."

If *Memoirs of Hadrian* seems carved in marble, *The Abyss,* a novel set in 16th-century Europe, a Europe with one foot in the Renaissance and the other more firmly planted in the Middle Ages, seems the work of brush on canvas. Bosch and Breughel, as Mme. Yourcenar has averred, supply the background for portions of this book....

Zeno, the protagonist of *The Abyss,* is forever hastening his step. Born in 1509 in Flanders, the illegitimate son of an Italian aristocrat and a mother who becomes an Anabaptist, the young Zeno is a lover of freedom, a love which soon takes an intellectual turn. He studies botany and engineering, astrology and alchemy, earning his living as a physician and living, detached from society, as a philosopher. Zeno is in quest of the truth, while the Inquisition, more patiently but no less relentlessly, is in quest of him.

Zeno is the pure type of the scientist-philosopher: a man who takes nothing on faith and of whom an ecclesiastic who befriends him says that he has "too little faith to be a heretic." Faithless though he is, he is nonetheless filled with wonder for the simplest objects, not least the wall of flesh covering the human machine, which is the subject of Zeno's unending study as a physician....

Much as he has striven for freedom himself, Zeno knows he is not finally free. "For no one is free so long as he has desires, wants, or fears, or even, perhaps, so long as he lives." The abyss, Zeno is aware, "was both beyond the celestial sphere and within the human skull." Are we in the end, he wonders, any more sentient than the rabbits given to him one day by a peasant woman and which he looses in the fields? (p. 64)

A spectacle of rabbits—lascivious, voracious, timid yet playing with danger—is what Mme. Yourcenar offers in *A Coin in Nine Hands*. No Hadrians, no Zeno, no great men or women move through this novel. (pp. 64-5)

Montaigne supplies the novel's epigraph: "The right way to prize one's life is to abandon it for a dream." And it is true that in this book everyone is a dreamer of one sort or another. Some dream of love, some of revolution, some of a life of quiet dignity, some of the mastery of art, and some—might these be the greatest dreamers?—that they have grasped reality. In an afterword, Mme. Yourcenar writes that one of the reasons this slender novel "seemed worthy to be published again is that, in its day, it was one of the first French novels (maybe the very first) to confront the hollow reality behind the bloated façade of Fascism. . . ." Yet today this seems rather beside the point. The tragedies of the lives of the characters, however, do not.

"Destiny is lighthearted," begins an aphorism in Marguerite Yourcenar's book *Fires,* and in the pages of *A Coin in Nine Hands* one sees destinies worked out with a lighthearted arbitrariness: cancer for this one, an appetite for revenge for that one; good looks here, poverty of soul there; the belief on one man's part that no faith is worth dying for and the corresponding belief on one woman's part that without a faith worth dying for life is not worth living; an artist who has lived for art and in the bargain perhaps missed out on life. . . .

Intricate moral questions are usually not at the center of Marguerite Yourcenar's work. Human destiny, its meaning and even more its mysteries, are. She has a clearer sense than anyone now writing of the tragedy yet also the hope inherent in human lives. The great experiment, as her alchemist Zeno says, always begins anew. The effect of reading her novels is to be reminded of the difficulty of life and of its heroic possibilities—hardly a thing that contemporary literature does best, if at all. Most of us are undone by life. Ours is but to do, then die. Marguerite Yourcenar's novels make us question why. This is what major writers have always done. This is why she is among their number. (p. 65)

Joseph Epstein, "Read Marguerite Yourcenar!" in Commentary, Vol. 74, No. 2, August, 1982, pp. 60-5.

ANNE TYLER

[*A Coin in Nine Hands*] was written in 1934, some twenty years before *Memoirs of Hadrian,* and was considerably revised by the author in 1959. In an afterword to the later version, she explains that the revision was intended "to create a more complete, hence more particularized presentation of certain episodes, to allow a more penetrating psychological development, to simplify and clarify, and if possible, to enrich and add depth to the text." It is not, therefore, a matter of mere editing, and readers of French who can compare the two versions will probably learn something valuable about how a writer's skills may be refined with the years. (p. 42)

The coin of the title is a ten-lire piece that travels in a near circle around an anti-Fascist plot to assassinate Mussolini. Paolo Farina, abandoned by his young wife Angiola, gives the coin to a prostitute, Lina Chiari. Lina buys a lipstick from Giulio Lovisi, who in turn buys candles from Rosalia di Credo; and Rosalia pays Marcella Ardeati to fetch her some live embers. It is Marcella who is plotting to assassinate the Dictator. First, though, she passes the coin to her estranged husband, Dr. Sarte, as token payment for his gun. Dr. Sarte buys flowers for a woman he meets in a sleazy encounter at a movie theater. The flower-seller, Mother Dida, gives the coin to a "beggar"—actually Clement Roux, an artist, who tosses it into a fountain. It is finally retrieved by Oreste Marinunzi, who drinks himself into oblivion while waiting for his fourth child to be born.

These characters are not so ill-assorted as they may seem. First, they are linked by small coincidences, in ways that they them-

selves seldom realize. Rosalia the candle-seller, for instance, is actually the sister of that Angiola who abandoned her husband. And it's Angiola whom Dr. Sarte encounters at the movie theater. Giulio Lovisi, purveyor of lipsticks, is father-in-law to Carlo Stevo, the anti-Fascist who is Marcella's comrade-in-arms and the source of her political inspiration. And it's another comrade-in-arms who chances to help the aging artist home that night. Human beings, we're shown, are more closely connected than they know. Their muddled paths cross and recross, eddying around the central events of history.

Second, the characters are linked by the pathos, if not the outright tragedy, of their lives. They endure faithlessness, thanklessness, unhappy marriages, or old age. Lina Chiari is dying of cancer with no one to tell about it. Mother Dida is cursed with greed. Even Dr. Sarte, rich and successful, is disgusted by the stupidity of his life. Every person in this book is abjectly lonely.

But before you avert your eyes from so much misery, take another look. *A Coin in Nine Hands* is saved from grimness by the tone of its narrative voice, which is as pure and unadorned as that of a folktale. Events are stated so directly that—as in a folktale—they appear to be purposeful. The reader never doubts that there's a point to it all; and where there's a point, there's hope. (pp. 42-3)

Clement Roux, in a long and wonderful passage, muses upon the meaning of his life: "Two years of love; a child with a little white collar in the paintings of 1905, who now sells cars; another child who died. . . ." A young revolutionary, considering the would-be assassin Marcella Ardeati, tells himself, "Accept even this sensual incompatibility: she was closer to you than any woman ever will be, but you couldn't stand the oily, spicy smell of her hair. . . ." This same young revolutionary is astonished to recover a memory of escaping as a child from his native country; what he remembers is not the danger and discomfort that worried his elders, but the river islands submerged by spring floods, the cuckoos calling from opposite banks. Like Rome itself—a hauntingly beautiful and mysterious presence in this novel—those little islands endure.

Small human moments, then, set up a subtle tension against larger political moments. Each of these characters leads an intensely private life in which the Dictator is only a figure at the fringes—a force, but not an explicitly felt force. Mussolini is never named, in fact, but is often referred to as Caesar, as if he were playing a stage role filled by endlessly replaceable actors. . . . He is clearly powerful—he's the center pole of the plot—but in another sense, he has no real importance whatsoever. Far more important is Paolo Farina looking all about him, like a man who's just stumbled, to see who's noticed his wife's defection; or Lina Chiari carrying her new doctor's name in her purse like a saint's medal; or Rosalia de Credo's worshipful love of her sister Angiola who has never given her a thought. . . . [Yourcenar's] novel takes an emphatic, anti-Fascist political stance. But what lingers after the end of *A Coin in Nine Hands* is the shadowiness and puppetlike vagueness of the Dictator, and the compelling specificity of the so-called "common" people revolving all around him. (p. 43)

Anne Tyler, "Death to the Dictator," in The New Republic, Vol. 188, Nos. 1 & 2, January 10 & 17, 1983, pp. 42-3.

JOHN WEIGHTMAN

When I was young, long before the introduction of decimal coinage into Great Britain, English schoolchildren were regularly given as a subject for composition "The Adventures of a Shilling," a theme that was supposed to allow them to describe any series of experiences, arbitrarily linked by the passing of the humble folk-coin from one person to another. It may seem surprising that Marguerite Yourcenar, the reigning *grande dame* of French literature, . . . should have had recourse to such an elementary device to bind together the episodes in her third novel [*A Coin in Nine Hands*]. . . . But there it is: The original title, **Denier du Rêve,** refers to a 10-lira silver piece that changes hands several times during the space of a few hours or days in Rome around 1933 or 1934. The French expression *"le denier du rêve"* implies, it is true, an idea that is missing from the English version: In each instance the coin buys an escape from reality into dreams or illusion, but the escape itself is false or momentary, since each individual action is negated by death or by the imminence of death. (p. 10)

As Miss Yourcenar tells us in a postscript, she wrote the first version of the text in 1934, presumably as a result of her direct experience of Italy, and revised and extended it in 1959. It underwent therefore the same slow process of elaboration as her two famous novels [*Memoirs of Hadrian* and *The Abyss*]. One expects this work, then, to have the same interest and density; the blurb, indeed, assures us that it is "one of Yourcenar's major works . . . a novel of heroism . . . a meditation on love . . . a profound examination of political evil."

I regret to say that it seems to me to be none of these things but instead a disjointed and curiously artificial work, breathing a facile pathos. The failure is due partly, perhaps, to the mechanical nature of the linking device, which is emphasized by a welter of coincidences: for example the *amant de coeur* of the prostitute is also, for reasons that remain unexplained, the close friend of the middle-class woman who tries to shoot Mussolini. But the main reason, I suspect, is that contemporary society cannot be dealt with in the same half symbolic, sublimely distanced way as an imagined historical context. Miss Yourcenar's elaborately self-conscious style, always redolent of Virgilian *lacrimae rerum,* clothed her view of Ancient Rome and of Renaissance Europe with an acceptable poetic solemnity. Besides, in the two famous novels she was dealing directly with great themes: imperial authority in its heyday and the tension between alchemy and Christian belief. The temporary bombastic triumph of Mussolini is not of the same order, and in any case Miss Yourcenar does not put it at the center of her book or relate her various characters to it organically. It is just one incidental element among others, leading to a succession of human defeats, as if life were inevitably a series of failed dreams. This view of existence may well be true, but it needs to be expressed in a different, more realistic tone if it is to carry conviction for the modern world.

The text is full of phrases that seem to overreach themselves and that cannot be blamed on the deficiencies of the translator, since the author collaborated with her: "Using his cleverness as a bow, this sly peasant played on his misfortune as on a cello"; "like sorcerers who sell their souls to obtain power over things, this dotard had traded his mind for his own universe." . . . This is surely not good writing but "fine writing" in the pejorative sense—words used complacently and cloying to inflate banal or uncertain perceptions. (pp. 10, 29)

> John Weightman, "Adventures of a 10-Lira Piece,"
> *in* The New York Times Book Review, *January 30,*
> *1983, pp. 10, 29.*

RICHARD HOWARD

[*Alexis*], Yourcenar's first fiction, written when she was 24, affords proof, in an uneven translation, of remarkable talents which have subsequently ripened into grandeur through a long life, a patient career. "The Treatise of Vain Struggle," as it is subtitled in the French edition, concerns a young man's attempt to achieve self-awareness, and thereby self-acceptance, and thereby self-fulfillment. His discovery of sexual tastes which Alexis, an impoverished central European of noble stock, regards as unacceptably fixed on "beauty," decisively thwarts this 19th-century life, in which marriage and paternity fail to mend matters, and only art—musical composition, as it somewhat vaguely turns out—succeeds in releasing Alexis from his bad faith. The book is in the form of a confession, a long letter to the wife he is "abandoning," and it concludes on a devastated note of triumph: "With the utmost humility, I ask you now to forgive me, not for leaving you, but for having stayed so long."

Choosing for what she calls her "portrait of a voice" the tonality of the classical French moralists, the young author secured for herself, as ventriloquist, the possibility of a unity of tone exceptional in a beginner, and also the possibility of an aphoristic glitter which certainly compensates for meagerness of incident. (p. 3)

In a fierce little preface . . . , Yourcenar denies the influence of Gide's "great books" but acknowledges certain filiations with the author of *Corydon* and indeed devises formal parallels with the speaker of *The Immoralist,* whose confession antedates that of Alexis by some 25 years. Like Michel as he wrenches himself away from his wife Marceline in that celebrated breviary of estrangement . . . , Alexis prompts his reader, even prompts his creator, to wonder about *his* wife Monique's response. "But for now," Yourcenar reports in her preface, "I have abandoned that project. Nothing is more secret than a woman's existence."

Uninterrupted, then, by any conflicting utterance—in the best Gidean manner—Alexis tells his own story with the mild fluency of the 18th-century *maximistes.* Thereby he cuts down the blood-supply to the brain and instead maximizes, in another sense, the more general application of this cautionary tale. Given the stipulations of her chosen vocabulary and of the period taste to which she was appealing, Yourcenar could not use the word *homosexual,* or any of the rest of that technical vocabulary for "aberrations of the senses," as she observes they were called at the time: invert, pederast, pervert, uranist. And there is, for the reader, a certain mystification in all this "vain struggle" without any vivid apprehension of what Alexis eventually surrenders *to.* Dostoevski would not leave us, as the French say, on our hunger, in the fashion of La Bruyère.

Even so, granting a specifically *pallid* tonality, much transformed in her later works of course, I should claim for this first tale of Yourcenar's a certain precision and an authentic power in her hero's admissions which derive from just the degree of ironic detachment so handsomely administered. She cites, helpfully, the influence of Rilke's *Notebooks of Malte Laurids Brigge* (1910), and indeed the recurrence of devices normally thought to be "poetic" is a pervasive character of this (and all subsequent) Yourcenar fictions. The alternation of narrative and aphorism is a much-honored procedure here, and if we recall that *aphorism* is, etymologically, a wisdom broken, and that narrative is the ongoing, healing impulse of language to put things together, we observe how nicely this first brief *récit* fulfills the requirements of Yourcenar's imaginative genius, critical and lyric in close array. (pp. 3, 5)

Richard Howard, "Yourcenar's Immoralist," *in* Book World—The Washington Post, *September 2, 1984, pp. 3, 5.*

WALLACE FOWLIE

For the past 40 years, [Miss Yourcenar] has made her home on the island off the Maine coast that she insists on calling by the name Champlain gave it—I'lle des Monts-Déserts. There she wrote *Memoirs of Hadrian,* published in the 1950's in both French and English, after having learned from earlier writings how to project a story into the past. It is a recent past in her first novel, *Alexis* (1929), a distant past in *Fires,* published in France in 1936 and translated into English in 1981—prose poems about such figures as Phaedra and Mary Magdalene.

To move from the most recent work of Miss Yourcenar, published in the 1970's—the two still untranslated volumes of autobiography, *Le Labyrinthe du Monde* (in which she implies that the Minotaur is our subconscious)—to *Alexis* is to journey back in time through half a century. In its classical style of the *récit* and in the reticence surrounding its theme, it seems to belong in another age. When I read *Alexis* in French a few years ago, I was reminded of André Gide's short fictions, notably *The Immoralist,* but today . . . I think not of possible precursors but of this work's uniqueness, of the voice of Alexis, whose name was taken from Virgil's *Second Eclogue.*

The entire book is a letter written by Alexis to his young wife, Monique, after two years of marriage and the birth of their son, Daniel. It is a farewell letter, part confession of his inability to love her as he would wish and part testimonial to her goodness, to the quiet sympathy she had always expressed. The confession is several things simultaneously. It is, first, a faintly sketched case history of Alexis in which he hopes to explain, rather than justify, his abnegation, his departure. His meeting with Monique, the brief courtship, the marriage and the birth of Daniel are episodes in a novel, in a very condensed form of narrative. But the personal problem that obsesses Alexis and that he mutes in his confession is that of the sexual freedom to which he aspires and that he cannot find, and believes he should not find, within his marriage.

When this novel was written, its theme was still new and still looked on with disfavor. Miss Yourcenar explains in a preface that, contrary to her habit, she made no changes in the text when preparing a new edition in 1963. . . . This drama of Alexis and Monique, told by Alexis, is not dated. It is about the problem of pleasure found outside love, of pleasure separated from all the other emotions in a man's life. The serious writer is endlessly concerned with the enigmas of life, for which he may offer only partial explanations. In referring to other French women not honored as she was, Marguerite Yourcenar acknowledges this succession: Mme. de Sévigné, Mme. de Stael, George Sand and Colette. All four wrote about the problems of daily life. More poignantly than the others, she has often, as in *Alexis,* contended with the quasi-impossibility of explaining some of those difficulties.

The theme of chance in a man's life, such as that of Alexis, which Marguerite Yourcenar calls *amor fati* in her prefaces and autobiographical writings, is her major preoccupation. She has lived many years on a "desert" island close to the Canadian border, in a small world that has adopted her as friend and neighbor, in a remoteness that has been useful for her meditations and her work. Her life in Maine has not been unlike

Descartes's life in Amsterdam, one possibly explained by fate, by chance.

I find a remarkable unity in her *oeuvre,* from the confession of Alexis to the monologue of Hadrian to *Le Labyrinthe du Monde.* It has something to do with the unity of the human race as it faces the experience of suffering.

Wallace Fowlie, "Husband's Confession," *in* The New York Times Book Review, *September 16, 1984, p. 21.*

JOHN GROSS

Marguerite Yourcenar is best known in the English-speaking world as a novelist, above all as the author of *Memoirs of Hadrian.* The seven essays gathered in *The Dark Brain of Piranesi* make it clear that she is also an outstanding critic. They are forceful, deeply pondered, the record of a full imaginative response. But to stress their creative quality does not imply that they are capricious or loosely impressionistic. On the contrary, they proceed point by point, with notable lucidity; most of them could serve as introductions to the works they discuss.

At least one of them, the essay on the Greek poet Constantine Cavafy, was explicitly designed as such an introduction. Originally written as a preface to Miss Yourcenar's volume of translations from Cavafy, it sorts out his themes and divides his work into a number of readily grasped categories. But it does so with a compelling eloquence, and with wit, too. . . .

In order to bring a writer's qualities into sharper focus, she quite often resorts to an analogy with the visual arts. One Cavafy poem suggests an Ingres drawing, another a Mantegna, just as elsewhere the "cold perspicacity" of the Roman historian Suetonius calls to mind the realism of Holbein. In lesser hands, this kind of comparison could easily degenerate into a trick. But here, the parallels come naturally, with the same sureness of touch that she reveals in her discussion of Piranesi, where she moves into reverse and uses works of literature to illumine art—invoking Voltaire and Swift, borrowing her title from Victor Hugo, showing what Coleridge and De Quincey made of the Italian artist's work and what they distorted for their own Romantic purposes.

"The Dark Brain of Piranesi" is an essay that matches the somber poetry of its subject. It is equally persuasive whether it is defining the dreamlike qualities of Piranesi's prison drawings or relating them to his engravings of the antiquities of Rome (one series dominated by the concept of Space, the other by that of Time), and it includes some memorable observations on his visual effects—how he succeeds in convincing us, for instance, that the cavernous prison hall in which we find ourselves "is hermetically sealed, even on the face of the cube we never see because it is behind us." . . .

The subjects of the other essays in the book range from the lives of the later Roman emperors, as chronicled by the shadowy authors of the *Historia Augusta,* to the novels of Thomas Mann. Mann is placed in a double tradition, part hermetic and part humanistic, to which many modern German writers have belonged, but he is admired for being closer to Goethe than his mystically inclined contemporaries, nearer the humanistic end of the spectrum.

Miss Yourcenar finds less to esteem in the *Historia Augusta.* The men who compiled the greater part of it (somewhere between the middle of the second century and the end of the fourth century) are dismissed as hacks—not surprisingly, the biography of Hadrian is singled out for particular complaint. And yet the book fascinates her. A "dreadful odor of humanity" rises from its pages, and she extracts an ominous lesson for our own time from its account of Rome's decline.

A similar vein of pessimism runs through her conversations with the French literary critic Matthieu Galey, which took place over a number of years at her home on Mount Desert Island, off the coast of Maine, and which have now been translated under the title **With Open Eyes**. Sometimes you feel that the gloom is overdone, or too facile, but no doubt she would retort that such a reaction is complacent. At any rate, her views are all of a piece—those of a liberal and a humanitarian who believes that "the social problem is more important than the political problem," and whose deepest public concerns tend to be cultural and ecological.

It is not for such matters that most readers are likely to turn to these interviews, however, but for the light they throw on the author's personality and on her writing. And here they will not be disappointed.

By current standards, Miss Yourcenar is reticent about her private life, and she is more preoccupied with long perspectives than with the fashions of the hour. Even so, we learn a great deal about her, from the fact that she first read Racine's *Phèdre* when she was 8 years old to her feelings about her pen name. . . .

But the gossipy detail is less important than the feeling of being brought into contact with a quite exceptional woman—someone who can be flinty and intimidating when serious issues are at stake, but who also goes a long way toward embodying her own ideal of "intelligent sympathy."

> John Gross, in a review of "The Dark Brain of Piranesi and Other Essays" and "With Open Eyes: Conversations with Matthieu Galey," in The New York Times, December 27, 1984, p. C19.

HUGH LLOYD-JONES

The first essay [in **The Dark Brain of Piranesi and Other Essays**] is about the *Historia Augusta,* a collection of lives of Roman emperors of the second and third centuries, purporting to have been written by six different authors early in the fourth century, but very likely written by a single writer some 50 years after that. It is trivial, superficial and unreliable to a degree, and Miss Yourcenar knows this; but she pleads that it "makes overwhelming reading"; "no book," she says, "ever reflected so well . . . the history of the moment." The *Historia Augusta* is certainly amusing reading, and it supplies many anecdotes historians disdain but which the writers of historical novels like to make play with; it reflects not the judgment of the man in the street, but the lack of judgment of the third-rate rhetorician. Miss Yourcenar's kind words about it remind me of a book about the Greek poet Pindar she published in her youth; it tells one little of his works, but gives an imaginary picture of his life, about which we know virtually nothing.

Even the early book on Pindar is enjoyable, because Miss Yourcenar writes an ornamental and mellifluous French prose, studded with the literary allusions which come so easily to such a cultivated writer. She is not a historian, and it would be unfair to judge her by a historian's standard; her purpose is to create an imaginative picture of the past, of whose connection with the present and the future she is constantly aware. Read in the original, her elaborate prose gives pleasure, though less

pleasure than it would give if the somewhat solemnly sententious meditation were sometimes spiced with wit or irony.

Her second essay is about the Huguenot poet Agrippa d'Aubigné, who fought in the wars of religion and died in exile in Geneva in 1630. The work of his that most interests Miss Yourcenar is *Les Tragiques,* whose macabre accounts of the afflictions of persecuted Protestants will remind English-speaking readers of Foxe's *Book of Martyrs.* This interest links the second with the fourth essay, the one that gives the book its name. Miss Yourcenar gives a full and interesting account of Piranesi, the best thing in the book. The work of his which means most to her is the *Carceri,* that terrifying series of fanciful representations of prisons, which as she remarks seems like an anticipation of the French Revolution. . . .

In "**Ah, Mon Beau Château . . .**" Miss Yourcenar describes the successive owners and inmates of Chenonceaux, the most delightful of the châteaux of the Loire. She is concerned not simply to sketch their history, but to imagine their sensations and emotions. The elegant but icy Diane de Poitiers; Louise de Lorraine, the pathetic widow of Henri III; the 30-year-old Rousseau who stayed at Chenonceaux as tutor to the sons of one of its owners—are all portrayed, and George Sand and Flaubert make brief appearances as visitors. The fifth essay deals with the Swedish novelist Selma Lagerlof, in whom Miss Yourcenar seems rightly to see an affinity to herself.

An essay on Cavafy originated as an introduction to a translation of his poems, and is indeed a valuable introduction to his work. Miss Yourcenar draws attention to the deliberate dryness and spareness of his verse, observes that for him the images of the past exist on the same plane with those of the present in Alexandria, and remarks that he likes to focus on a particular moment or a particular situation in history, usually not the history of the classical age but that of the Hellenistic or the Byzantine period. She has an ear for the note of resignation that pervades his work; while in his private imaginings the poet might seem to be a pagan, a hedonist, an addict of forbidden pleasures, in ordinary life he accepts the inevitable triumph of hostile forces and shows no sympathy with the apostate emperor Julian or the despairing pagan poet Paliadas. The theme of homosexuality recurs often in Miss Yourcenar's own work; perhaps Cavafy's attitude toward it, of which she says little, is in some way similar to her own. . . .

[In the essay on Thomas Mann] Miss Yourcenar is not quite at home in the world of German culture, and she shows little interest in Mann's literary origins and affinities. She offers an external description of Mann's works and of its symbolism, saying much about the Joseph novels and little about *Felix Krull.* Her description would be better if she were less interested in the occult and more in Mann's Nietzschean heritage. Still, it is interesting to see how such a very German author appears in sympathetic French, or rather Belgian-French eyes.

> Hugh Lloyd-Jones, "How the Past Might Feel," in The New York Times Book Review, February 24, 1985, p. 16.

EDMUND WHITE

Marguerite Yourcenar's **Oriental Tales**, . . . [in comparison to *The Tale of Patrick Merla*], has a higher finish, a franker delight in turns of phrase, many of them ravishing. If Merla draws the tribe around the campfire, Yourcenar spins a yarn before the fireplace. Indeed, several of her stories begin with someone talking to another. Andrey stops into Old Stevan's shop and tells him of the death of Marko; "Tell me another story, old friend," Philip Mild entreats at the beginning of another tale.

In a third, a French engineer tells a tale to a Greek archeologist and an Egyptian pasha aboard a ship moored off a Balkan coast. If these framing devices have an old-fashioned, 19th-century realism about them, they are there merely to lend credibility to the passionate, always extraordinary anecdotes that follow. For instance, a heroic Serb named Marko attempts to escape death by feigning the insensibility of a drowned man. He gives no sign of life when nails are driven into his hands and feet nor when burning coals are laid on his chest, but when a lovely dancing girl swirls above him, he's forced to smile. (pp. 4-5)

Magic, a commonplace in Merla's stories, also appears in Yourcenar's, as in her **"How Wang-Fo Was Saved."** The Chinese Emperor, whose life has been spoiled because reality has never lived up to the beauty of Wang-Fo's paintings, condemns the artist to death. But before the execution is carried out, the painter is ordered to complete an unfinished sketch from his youth. So great is Wang-Fo's skill that the scene of a skiff on a lake becomes real and the artist and his disciple are able to row away to safety in the imaginary ship—a mysterious parable of the power of art to destroy some people and to save others.

Yourcenar's **"Milk of Death,"** the tale of a woman who, though buried alive inside a wall, is still able, even after her death, to breastfeed her infant through a chink between two stones, reminds us of Merla's tales, where family love is always the purest and strongest bond between people. By contrast, her **"Aphrodissia, the Widow"** is remote from Merla's world. Whereas he never writes of blind sexual passion, this emotion, joined to a pagan and ecstatic apprehension of physical beauty, is Yourcenar's forte. **Memoirs of Hadrian** is the locus classicus of this tendency, but even here, in **"The Man Who Loved the Nereids,"** we read, "Just as there is no love without a dazzling of the heart, there is no true voluptuousness without the startling wonder of beauty." The wonder of beauty, as the Chinese Emperor knew, can exact its price. A man becomes so enamored of the Nereids that he loses his senses and turns into a holy fool; Aphrodissia is so sick with love for the violent, handsome Kostis (who has murdered her husband) that she ends up plunging, dazed with grief and love, into an abyss. Similarly, in another story the head of the goddess Kali is mistakenly joined to the body of a prostitute. Driven by lust, this new half-divine creature embraces and kills everyone she encounters—the reverse of Merla's serene mergers of the human with the divine.

Whereas Merla acknowledges evil but redeems it through repentance, grace and wisdom, Yourcenar (who despite the title, **Oriental Tales,** is immersed in Greek paganism) celebrates passion—exalting, debasing passion—and explores its tragic glamour. (p. 5)

> *Edmund White, "The Way of the Storyteller," in* Book World—The Washington Post, *September 22, 1985, pp. 4-5.**

STEPHEN KOCH

Marguerite Yourcenar is one of the great scholar-artists. Her masterpiece, **The Memoirs of Hadrian,** . . . has riches for anyone interested in history, humanism or the psychology of power. But Miss Yourcenar's range is much wider than the classical scholarship of that book suggests. In **Oriental Tales,** first published in 1938, revised in 1982, and now translated for the first time, she ransacks many cultures—those of the Balkans in the Middle Ages, medieval Japan, Taoism, Hinduism—for the folklore that feeds the book's bewitched and esoteric stories of magic, dream, death, sex and transformation. Here is the scholar as Scheherazade.

Miss Yourcenar is a figure whose standing with the public has never quite matched her literary stature. . . .

Perhaps the [public] neglect was inevitable. Miss Yourcenar is a contemplative, interested only in a few unitary and unifying truths that necessarily require seclusion and long thought. Unlike her mentor André Gide, with whom she shares much, she has no talent for playing the public figure. Her politics are profound rather than inflamed. As a meditation on humanism and power, **The Memoirs of Hadrian** was surely written partly in response to the Hitlerian horror. Yet its angle on totalitarianism is very oblique. . . .

Miss Yourcenar has described herself as an artist "with one foot in scholarship, the other in magic arts." The magic has never been more evident than in **Oriental Tales.** They are filled with giants and demons and amazing transformations. Yet in some, the Balkan legends for instance, there is a link to modernity. The immemorial legends of passion and struggle are recounted to a group of travelers sailing the Adriatic. We see the steamer on the glassy sea, the beetling cliffs over the water, the rocky harbor towns with their small cafes and flapping awnings. The year is 1935. The world is about to change, forever. The threat of death is in the air.

"How Wang-Fo Was Saved" is based on a Taoist fable from ancient China. An emperor condemns a famous artist to death on the ground that he is so exquisitely skilled that his pictures make reality seem dull. Granted leave to make one last picture, Wang-Fo paints a sea, and the waters rise up and sweep him to safety. This tale is one of the few that are not erotic; most are heatedly erotic, marked in this case by a heterosexual passion, not the homosexual eroticism that runs like a pale covered flame through much of Miss Yourcenar's work. . . .

The stories are wonderful. . . . [Each] of them seems a small window opened, magically, on some quite real but lost world. For Miss Yourcenar, scholarship is the entryway to the imagination, and, like all her work, these borrowed stories are simultaneously efforts at reconstruction and new creation—a distinction that, in any case, I feel Miss Yourcenar would find suspect. At once immemorial and new, they show us the fabulist as mythographer and sage.

> *Stephen Koch, "Scholar as Scheherazade," in* The New York Times Book Review, *September 22, 1985, p. 42.*

MAVIS GALLANT

The long career of Marguerite Yourcenar . . . stands among a litter of flashier reputations as testimony to the substance and clarity of the French language and the purpose and meaning of a writer's life. In an age of slops, she writes the firm, accurate, expressive French that used to be expected in work taken seriously. Critics speak of language carved, etched, chiseled, engraved: simply, a plain and elegant style, the reflection of a strong and original literary intellect. . . .

It is a way of writing remote from everyday French discourse, which has become increasingly diffuse, imprecise, and dependent on clichés; some teachers say that outside the traditional *lycées,* with their selected student body, her work can scarcely be grasped or imparted. At the same time, almost any literate Parisian would be likely to recognize Mme. Yourcenar in the street, and regard her with respect and affection: more people have watched the television interviews in which she speaks her mind about the conservation of nature, or the decline of black culture, or the myths of family life, or other writers (as the French expression puts it, she can show a hard tooth) than have read *Memoirs of Hadrian,* her best known and most widely translated book. National reverence for authors does not necessarily encircle knowledge of their work.

Her mind, her manner, the quirks and prejudices that enliven her conclusive opinions, the sense of caste that lends her fiction its stern framework, her respect for usages and precedents, belong to a vanished France. She seems to have come straight out of the seventeenth century, with few stops on the way. Nicolas Poussin is her contemporary, for drama and serenity and a classically ordered world; so is Racine, for form, for unity of vision, for the laws of hierarchy and the penalty for breaking them. To read her books . . . is like moving along a marble corridor in the wake of an imperturbable guide. The temperature varies between cool and freezing. The lighting is dramatic and uneven. Only the calm and dispassionate approach never changes.

What are we told? How the body betrays us. Why we destroy faith and one another. That we can produce art and remain petty. What we can and cannot have entirely. Jealousy, but not envy, is allowed free entry. Reciprocated love is never mentioned and probably does not exist. The high plateau of existence, the relatively few years when our decisions are driven by belief in happiness or an overwhelming sense of purpose are observed, finally, to be "useless chaos." By the time Mme. Yourcenar reached this prospect, the view from old age, her fiction was written. Luckily: that useless chaos is what fiction is about.

The limpid pessimism of the voice speaks from a French tradition of right-wing literature, but even the most pernickety French mania for classification cannot hold her to that side of the line. Her life has been a reflective alliance with the rejected and put-upon, and she never misses a chance in an interview to overhaul racists and bigots of every stripe. (p. 19)

[Mme. Yourcenar] has no faith in experiments. She has rebuked the poets René Char and Yves Bonnefoy, hardly striplings, for taking liberties with form—an authoritative censure that prompted one critic to say he would trade all her Alexandrines for a line by Char. Her expedients are deliberately formal and artificial, from the epistolary novel to the outright cultural pastiche of *Oriental Tales. Hadrian* consists of a 295-page letter from the emperor to his heir, Marcus Aurelius. The eponymous narrator of *Alexis* leaves a letter for his sleeping wife, explaining why he is deserting her and their infant son for a life of homosexual freedom. In *Coup de Grâce,* Erick, the narrator, tells his life's story to a group of people in a railway station. *A Coin in Nine Hands* uses the trumped-up cinematic design of lives briefly linked by some casual token—in this case, a coin slipped from stranger to stranger in a handful of change. Inevitably, one thinks of Arthur Schnitzler and *Reigen,* but the *ronde* set in motion by Mme. Yourcenar is political and moral. The nineteenth century launched its hypocrisy and syphilis on the roundabout. By the 1930s, as this cool and dark story has it, sickness, sex, solitude, hatred, and terror move round the hub of the police state, to the tune of its contagious thuggery. Any human tie, even the most fleeting and fragile, brings nothing but bad, black luck.

At its worst and lowest, luck has to be viewed without a blink. To love eyes closed is to love blindly, Mme. Yourcenar writes in *Fires,* a collection of prose poems about a failure of her own. "Let us try, if we can, to enter into death with open eyes," is the last sentence of *Hadrian.* Marcella, the terrorist gunned down by Mussolini's police in *A Coin in Nine Hands,* stares with open eyes "into the void which is now her whole future." Mme. Yourcenar, who makes a dazzling whole of all religions, would appear to believe wholly in none. Wrenched out of the heart of her work, with the possibility of love, is any hope of redemption. An advantage gained from her early Catholic training, she tells [Matthieu Galey in *With Open Eyes*] . . . , is that it made her gentle. Gentleness is the last quality one would ascribe to her books, where violence and cruelty are played out against a world that seems immobile, like a painting, or a stage set. The theatrical quality is so strong that one often has the sensation of watching a curtain rise, revealing frozen, Poussin-like figures caught at a moment of incipient horror. When they move, it can only be into mortal danger. A prisoner opens his veins, and calculates his chances of dying before his blood runs under the cell door. A prostitute takes her breast cancer to a doctor for a verdict she already knows. A captured partisan, preparing to be shot by a man she was once in love with, starts to unbutton her tunic, in an instinctive feminine gesture of acceptance. Every shot is missed, just as every act is incomplete: the executioner shoots away half her face, and has to administer the *coup de grâce.*

The subject is not cruelty, but heresy—political, erotic, religious—and her characters are aristocrats, whatever their natural origin, their penchant for the losing side. They are immune to guilt, which makes them strangers to a convention of fiction we take for granted. They choose their sexual acquaintances—one can hardly say lovers, given the circumstances—but do not care to be chosen. They do not cringe, or dissemble, or wait with petit-bourgeois fatalism for the blow to fall. They are seldom hard-up for money, except by high-minded election, though their metaphysical gnawings can seem as acute as hunger cramps. Their neuroses are so stable and complete that they encourage rather than cripple decisions and action. They make devastating choices, taking short-term pleasure over lasting devotion, solitude over emotional dependency, death over disappointment. (pp. 20, 22)

Homosexuality, postulated as a condition of heresy, thus of moral aristocracy, is rarely named. Zeno calls himself a sodomite and a sorcerer, with the observation that it does not mean what "the herd" imagines, but *Abyss* was published in the late Sixties, a period exempt from caution. Earlier books mention tendencies and inclinations: obviously, contempt for the herd is no protection, if we set aside the Emperor Hadrian, who does not have to account to his wife for his private arrangements. . . . The plaintive and somewhat sappy Alexis informs his wife that he has found beauty, and leaves it to her to work out his meaning. This exasperating sidestepping has to be seen in its time, when a miasma of Beauty was expected to hang over the evocation of sex, and male homosexuality, in particular, was considered a criminal offense, or a flamboyant form of insanity, or a habit to be cured by the right girl and a vegetarian diet. A story about women might not have had the same resonance, or required the same amount of tact and circumspection. In Colette's Claudine novels, published a generation earlier, Claudine's husband cannot take a female rival seriously, just as Willy professed to be amused rather than outraged by Colette's feminine affairs. (p. 22)

Mme. Yourcenar has said that one cannot write about women because their lives are filled with secrets. The visible and open aspect of women's lives must surely be the least appealing, if we are to take as just the dismal ranks of scolds, harpies, frigid spouses, sluts, slatterns, humorless fanatics, and avaricious know-nothings who people her work, and who seem to have been created for no other reason than to drive any sane man into close male company. Alexis deserts a wife pallid of mind and character, wanly religious, and so ignorant—she never reads a newspaper—that he cannot be sure if she knows he is a celebrated concert pianist; such a ninny, in short, that the reader can only cheer him on.

Zeno, wondering why he ever bothered to sleep with a woman, decides it was "base conformity to custom." Even in heterosexual men, women arouse no more interest than an occasional need, grudgingly satisfied, followed by boredom and disgust. Henry Maximilian [a character in *The Abyss*] reflects that he will quit his life with the relief he has always felt on leaving a mistress. Alessandro, a doctor, in *A Coin in Nine Hands,* after provoking an anonymous exchange of masturbation with a woman in a darkened cinema is simply "grateful to be able to despise all women in her."

Alessandro seems to sum up the spite and the bitterness of the camouflaged homosexual, though it is not clear even after several readings if this is Mme. Yourcenar's intention. He may be meant as a representation of what men turn into after the hopelessness of trying to live with women. As it happens, his wife has left him. Her grounds for complaint are that he is young, good-looking, intelligent, prominent in his profession, well-to-do, and married her for love. The marriage strikes her as a criminal attachment, "which it was, since those passionate years had sidetracked her from her true vocation; that is, from tragic reality." Reality means the anti-Fascist conspiracy, and a political comrade to whom she feels bound "by common hatred rather than love," and her wild, solitary attempt to assassinate Mussolini.

There is more to it than singleness of purpose: "Wealth, success, pleasure, happiness itself provoked in her a horror analogous to that felt by the Christian for the flesh." We are in François Mauriac country, but without the familiar signposts: Marcella is an atheist martyr; there can be no deliverance, no reclamation. Women, like the coin, transmit death, the void, until they set the final example by dying. They are harbingers of the creeping glacier. Common hatred creates a rot more poisonous than the commonplace debacle of love. The end of the marble corridor is a wall of ice. (pp. 22, 24)

Mavis Gallant, "Limpid Pessimist," in The New York Review of Books, *Vol. XXXII, No. 19, December 5, 1985, pp. 19-20, 22, 24.*

Appendix

The following is a listing of all sources used in Volume 38 of *Contemporary Literary Criticism*. Included in this list are all copyright and reprint rights and acknowledgments for those essays for which permission was obtained. Every effort has been made to trace copyright, but if omissions have been made, please let us know.

THE EXCERPTS IN CLC, VOLUME 38, WERE REPRINTED FROM THE FOLLOWING PERIODICALS:

Africa Report, v. 13, May, 1968. Copyright © 1968 by the African-American Institute. Published by permission of Transaction, Inc.

African Literature Today, n. 1, 1968. Reprinted by permission.

America, v. 138, June 24, 1978 for "Two by Poliakoff" by Catharine Hughes. © 1978. All rights reserved. Reprinted with permission of the author./ v. 108, March 9, 1963; v. 109, November 9, 1963; v. 132, May 10, 1975; v. 135, August 7, 1976. © 1963, 1975, 1976. All rights reserved. All reprinted with permission of America Press, Inc., 106 West 56th Street, New York, NY 10019.

The American Book Review, v. 4, March-April, 1982; v. 5, September-October, 1983; v. 6, May-June, 1984; v. 7, November-December, 1984. © 1982, 1983, 1984 by *The American Book Review.* All reprinted by permission.

The American Poetry Review, v. 9, March-April, 1980 for "'Different Fleshes': The Poetry of Albert Goldbarth" by Michael King; v. 13, September-October, 1984 for "Idiom and Error" by Mary Kinzie. Copyright © 1980, 1984 by World Poetry, Inc. Both reprinted by permission of the respective authors.

The American Scholar, v. 35, Summer, 1966. Copyright © 1966 by the United Chapters of Phi Beta Kappa. Reprinted by permission of the publishers.

Américas, v. 34, May-June, 1982. Reprinted by permission from *Américas,* a bimonthly magazine published by the Organization of American States in English and Spanish.

Analog Science Fiction/Science Fact, v. CI, January 5, 1981 for a review of "Wild Seed" by Tom Easton. © 1981 by Davis Publications, Inc. Reprinted by permission of the author.

Another Chicago Magazine, n. 15, 1984 for a review of "I Brake for Delmore Schwartz" by Robin Hemley. Reprinted by permission of the author.

The Antioch Review, v. XXX, Fall, 1970 & Winter, 1971. Copyright © 1971 by the Antioch Review Inc. Reprinted by permission of the Editors./ v. III, March, 1943. Copyright © 1943, renewed 1970, by the Antioch Review Inc. Reprinted by permission of the Editors.

Aspect, n. 72 & 73, 1979 for "Twenty-Seven Statements I Could Make about Richard Grayson" by Susan Lloyd McGarry. Reprinted by permission of the author.

THE EXCERPTS IN CLC, VOLUME 38, WERE REPRINTED FROM THE FOLLOWING BOOKS:

Alter, Robert. From *Motives for Fiction*. Cambridge, Mass.: Harvard University Press, 1984. Copyright © 1984 by Robert Alter. All rights reserved. Excerpted by permission of the publishers.

Boon, James A. *From Symbolism to Structuralism: Lévi-Strauss in a Literary Tradition*. Harper & Row, 1972. Copyright © 1972 by James A. Boon. All rights reserved. Reprinted by permission of Harper & Row, Publishers, Inc.

Brotherston, Gordon. From *The Emergence of the Latin American Novel*. Cambridge University Press, 1977. © Cambridge University Press 1977. Reprinted by permission.

Cohen, Sarah Blacher. From ''The Jewish Folk Drama of Isaac Bashevis Singer,'' in *From Hester Street to Hollywood: The Jewish-American Stage and Screen*. Edited by Sarah Blacher Cohen. Indiana University Press, 1983. Copyright © 1983 by Indiana University Press. All rights reserved. Reprinted by permission.

Crabbe, Katharyn F. From *J.R.R. Tolkien*. Ungar, 1981. Copyright © 1981 by Frederick Ungar Publishing Co., Inc. Reprinted by permission.

Dodd, Wayne. From ''Back to the Snowy Fields,'' in *Robert Bly: ''When Sleepers Awake.''* Edited by Joyce Peseroff. The University of Michigan Press, 1984. Copyright © by The University of Michigan 1984. All rights reserved. Reprinted by permission.

Donato, Eugenio. From ''The Two Languages of Criticism,'' in *The Languages of Criticism and the Sciences of Man: The Structuralist Controversy*. Edited by Richard Macksey and Eugenio Donato. The Johns Hopkins University Press, 1970. Copyright © by The Johns Hopkins Press. All rights reserved. Reprinted by permission.

Girard, René. From ''Differentiation and Undifferentiation in Lévi-Strauss and Current Critical Theory,'' in *Directions for Criticism: Structuralism and Its Alternatives*. The University of Wisconsin Press, 1977. Copyright © 1976, 1977 The Board of Regents of the University of Wisconsin System. All rights reserved. Reprinted by permission.

Grant, Steve. From ''Voicing the Protest: The New Writers,'' in *Dreams and Deconstructions: Alternative Theatre in Britain*. Edited by Sandy Craig. Amber Lane Press Limited, 1980. Copyright © Amber Lane Press Limited, 1980. All rights reserved. Reprinted by permission.

Gray, Richard. From *The Literature of Memory: Modern Writers of the American South*. The Johns Hopkins University Press, 1977. Copyright © 1977 by Richard Gray. All rights reserved. Reprinted by permission.

Guicharnaud, Jacques, with June Beckelman. From *Modern French Theatre: From Giraudoux to Beckett*. Yale University Press, 1961. © 1961 by Yale University Press, Inc. All rights reserved. Reprinted by permission.

Kazin, Alfred. From *Bright Book of Life: American Novelists and Storytellers from Hemingway to Mailer*. Little, Brown, 1973. Copyright © 1971, 1973 by Alfred Kazin. All rights reserved. Reprinted by permission of Little, Brown and Company, in association with The Atlantic Monthly Press.

Kerensky, Oleg. From *The New British Drama: Fourteen Playwrights Since Osborne and Pinter*. Taplinger, 1979. Copyright © 1977 by Oleg Kerensky. All rights reserved. Published and reprinted by permission of Taplinger Publishing Co., Inc., NY. In Canada by the author.

King, Adele. From *The Writings of Camara Laye*. Heinemann Educational Books Ltd., 1980. © Adele King 1980. Reprinted by permission of Heinemann Educational Books Ltd.

Klinkowitz, Jerome and James Knowlton. From *Peter Handke and the Postmodern Transformation: The Goalie's Journey Home*. University of Missouri Press, 1983. Copyright © 1983 by the Curators of the University of Missouri. All rights reserved. Reprinted by permission of the University of Missouri Press.

Krutch, Joseph Wood. From *The American Drama Since 1918: An Informal History*. Random House, Inc., 1939.

Kurzweil, Edith. From *The Age of Structuralism: Lévi-Strauss to Foucault*. Columbia University Press, 1980. Copyright © 1980 Columbia University Press. All rights reserved. Reprinted by permission of the publisher.

Leach, Edmund. From *Claude Lévi-Strauss*. Revised edition. The Viking Press, 1974. Copyright © 1970, 1974 by Edmund Leach. All rights reserved. Reprinted by permission of Viking Penguin, Inc.

Moore, Gerald. From *Twelve African Writers*. Indiana University Press, 1980, Hutchinson, 1980. Copyright © 1980 by Gerald Moore. All rights reserved. Reprinted by permission of Indiana University Press. In Canada by Hutchinson Publishing Group Limited.

Nelson, Howard. From *Robert Bly: An Introduction to the Poetry*. Columbia University Press, 1984. Copyright © 1984 Columbia University Press. All rights reserved. Reprinted by permission of the publisher.

Orr, Gregory. From "The Need for Poetics: Some Thoughts on Robert Bly," in *Of Solitude and Silence: Writings on Robert Bly*. Edited by Richard Jones and Kate Daniels. Beacon Press, 1981. Copyright © 1981 by *Poetry East*. All rights reserved. Reprinted by permission of Beacon Press.

Ozick, Cynthia. From *Art & Ardor*. Knopf, 1983. Copyright © 1973 by Cynthia Ozick. All rights reserved. Reprinted by permission of Alfred A. Knopf, Inc.

Pace, David. From *Claude Lévi-Strauss: The Bearer of Ashes*. Routledge & Kegan Paul, 1983. Copyright © David Pace 1983. Reprinted by permission of Routledge & Kegan Paul PLC.

Priestley, J. B. From an introduction to *The Lost Steps*. By Alejo Carpentier, translated by Harriet de Onís. Knopf, 1967. Copyright © 1967 by Alfred A. Knopf, Inc. All rights reserved. Reprinted by permission of the publisher.

Pronko, Leonard Cabell. From *Avant-Garde: The Experimental Theater in France*. University of California Press, 1962. Copyright © 1962 by The Regents of the University of California. Reprinted by permission of the University of California Press.

Roscoe, Adrian A. From *Mother Is Gold: A Study in West African Literature*. Cambridge at the University Press, 1971. © Cambridge University Press 1971. Reprinted by permission.

Rossi, Ino. From "On the Assumptions of Structural Analysis: Revisiting Its Linguistic and Epistemological Premises," in *The Logic of Culture: Advances in Structural Theory and Methods*. Edited by Ino Rossi. Bergin, 1982. Copyright © 1982 by J. F. Bergin Publishers, Inc. All rights reserved. Reprinted by permission.

Schwartz, Ronald. From *Nomads, Exiles, & Emigres: The Rebirth of the Latin American Narrative, 1960-80*. The Scarecrow Press, Inc., 1980. Copyright © 1980 by Ronald Schwartz. Reprinted by permission.

Sontag, Susan. From *Against Interpretation and Other Essays*. Farrar, Straus and Giroux, 1966. Copyright © 1963 by Susan Sontag. All rights reserved. Reprinted by permission of Farrar, Straus and Giroux, Inc.

Souza, Raymond D. From *Major Cuban Novelists: Innovation and Tradition*. University of Missouri Press, 1976. Copyright © 1976 by the Curators of the University of Missouri. All rights reserved. Reprinted by permission of the University of Missouri Press.

Steiner, George. From "Orpheus with His Myths: Claude Lévi-Strauss," in *Language and Silence: Essays on Language, Literature, and the Inhuman*. By George Steiner. Atheneum, 1967. Copyright © 1967 George Steiner. All rights reserved. Reprinted with the permission of Atheneum Publishers, Inc.

Theroux, Paul. From "Six Poets: Dennis Brutus, Leurie Peters, Okugbule Nwanodi, George Awoonori-Williams, John Pepper Clark, Christopher Ikigbo," in *Introduction to African Literature: An Anthology of Critical Writing from "Black Orpheus."* Edited by Ulli Beier. Northwestern University Press, 1967. © Ulli Beier and Mbari, 1967. Reprinted by permission of Northwestern University Press, Evanston, IL. In Canada by Paul Theroux.

Toloudis, Constantin. From *Jacques Audiberti*. Twayne, 1980. Copyright 1980 by Twayne Publishers. All rights reserved. Reprinted with the permission of Twayne Publishers, a division of G. K. Hall & Co., Boston.

Updike, John. From "Northern Europeans: Discontent in Deutsch," in *Hugging the Shore: Essays and Criticism*. By John Updike. Knopf, 1983. Copyright © 1977 by John Updike. All rights reserved. Reprinted by permission of Alfred A. Knopf, Inc.

Wellwarth, George. From *The Theater of Protest and Paradox: Developments in the Avant-Garde Drama*. New York University Press, 1964. Copyright © 1964 by New York University. Reprinted by permission of New York University Press.

Zavatsky, Bill. From "Talking Back: A Response to Robert Bly," in *Of Solitude and Silence: Writings on Robert Bly*. Edited by Richard Jones and Kate Daniels. Beacon Press, 1981. Copyright © 1981 by *Poetry East*. All rights reserved. Reprinted by permission of Beacon Press.

Cumulative Index to Authors

This index lists all author entries in the Gale Literary Criticism Series and includes cross-references to other Gale sources. References in the index are identified as follows:

Author Index

Author Index

Author Index

Author Index

Author Index

Author Index

Author Index

Author Index

Author Index

Author Index

Cumulative Index to Critics

Critic Index

Critic Index

Critic Index

Critic Index

Critic Index

Critic Index

Critic Index

Critic Index

Critic Index

Critic Index

Critic Index

Critic Index

Critic Index

Critic Index

Critic Index

Critic Index

Critic Index

Critic Index

Critic Index

Critic Index

Critic Index

Critic Index

Critic Index

Critic Index

Critic Index

Critic Index

Critic Index

Critic Index

Critic Index

Critic Index

Critic Index

Critic Index

Critic Index

Critic Index

Critic Index

Critic Index

Critic Index

Critic Index